50¢

THE PHANTOM'S
ULTIMATE VIDEO GUIDE

THE
PHANTOM'S
ULTIMATE
VIDEO
GUIDE

By
The PHANTOM OF THE MOVIES

A DELL TRADE PAPERBACK

A DELL TRADE PAPERBACK
Published by
Dell Publishing
a division of
Bantam Doubleday Dell Publishing Group, Inc.
666 Fifth Avenue
New York, New York 10103

ISBN: 0-440-50212-8

Printed in the United States of America
Published simultaneously in Canada

November 1989

10 9 8 7 6 5 4 3 2 1

RRC

ACKNOWLEDGMENTS

A TIP OF THE PHANTOM HOOD GOES TO

Carol Aimetti, Billy and Joyce Altman, George Arthur, Richard Bakalyan (Early Phantom Role Model), Frank and Cheryl Balisteri, Peter Clark, Bob Condor, "Deep Sprocket," Tim Ferrante, David Franklin, Drew Friedman, Roy Frumkes, John Gallagher, Ira H. Gallen, Anthony Gardner, Bruce Goldstein, Alex Gordon, Guidance Ro-Man (spiritual support), Valerie Haller, Frank Henenlotter, Mary Hickey, Candace Hilligoss, Jerry Kantor, Joe Kane (Official Phantom Biographer), Bela Lugosi, (vherever you are), Bruce Lynn, Jay Maeder, "Mondo Mike" Maimone, Jon Marder, Mike McKay, Kate McMahon, Colin Medlock, Carl Morano, Nancy Naglin, J. Peter Orr, Pax the Clicker (emotional support), John Schnall, Nancy Stillman, Jeff Strate, The Thing in the Closet, Susan Toepfer, Tony Timpone, Ken and Bert Weiner, Edy Williams (for the generous invitation), Wade Williams, Ed Wood, Jr. (an inspiration to us all), Yossarian, John Zacherle, the entire Daily News *gang, and all the Phantom's relatives, friends, phans, the Phantomess, and the hardest-working editors in the pub biz, Jody Rein and Jeanne Cavelos.*

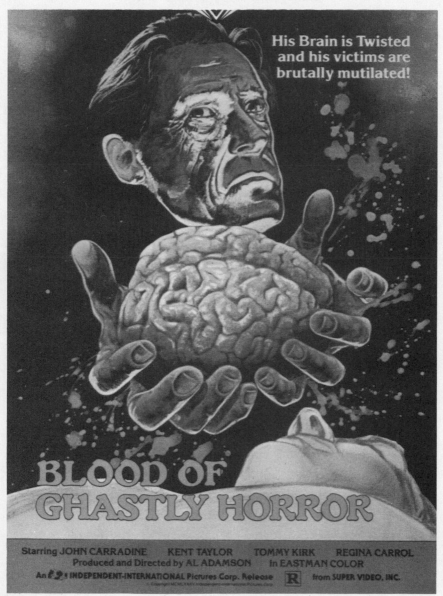

CONTENTS

ORIGINS OF THE PHANTOM

Born in a Gotham bijou not so very long ago in a galaxy practically right around the corner, the Phantom of the Movies happily misspent his youth haunting flea pits and picture palaces from the boroughs to the Deuce in search of offbeat film fare. Since 1984, he has served as the B-movie and video critic for the New York *Daily News.* The Phantom currently resides with his better half, the Phantomess, in darkest Manhattan, where he continues to haunt local theaters and video stores.

PHANTOM FOREWORD
CONFESSIONS OF A B-FILM FIEND, OR GROWING UP OBSESSED

During the Phantom's deformative years, there were no fewer than nine—count 'em—*nine* bijous within stealthing distance of his home. While he frequented all nine, it was at the legendary Savoy Theater—a sprawling triple-feature flea pit nestled deep in the wilds of Jamaica, New York—that your young Phantom received the bulk of his remedial B-flick education, occasionally at the expense of the more standard brand of enlightenment being offered at the local high school.

Home mostly to dozing winos, rambunctious kids, and budget-conscious retirees, the Savoy charged 75 cents for roughly five hours' worth of classic oldies, '50s and '60s B's and an incredible array of genre and sleaze obscurities, from *The Brain Eaters* to *Nudist Camp Confidential* (Savoy management *never* checked IDs) to Vic (*The Creeping Terror*) Savage's ultra-rare *The Streetfighter*. In addition to these eclectic triple-headers, a typical Savoy program also included trailers for the following week's attractions (since the theater changed shows three times a week, that translated into nine previews), a cartoon, *and* the ubiquitous boring short.

It remains one of the Phantom's greatest regrets that he never met the creative cinephile who booked that bijou's bizarre bills. He still vividly recalls catching Sam Fuller's *Shock Corridor*, paired with the Audie Murphy western *Seven Ways from Sundown* and the immortal *Brain That Wouldn't Die* on one bill; a revival of *Public Enemy* and *Little Caesar*, fleshed out by AIP's *The Screaming Skull* on another— and that's not to mention the plethora of William (*The Tingler*) Castle gimmick flicks that found their way there with bracing regularity. The Savoy's powers-that-were obviously went well above and considerably beyond the call not only in booking but in promoting (illustrated coming-attractions handbills were available in the spacious, if decrepit, lobby) what was essentially a derelict itch with terminally sticky floors, whole rows of damaged or missing seats, and an antiquated Voice of the Theater sound system.

Alas, the once-mighty Savoy—which, in the 1970s, briefly degenerated into an X-rated grindhouse before permanently darkening its once gloriously overcrowded marquee—has long since been reduced to a rubble-strewn lot with nary a trace of its erstwhile existence. A return visit to the Phantom's former nabe revealed that of the eight other theaters only one lonely, since-twinned bijou survives. Three— including the grandiose Valencia—have been converted into churches of various denominations; a department store, a parking lot, a medical office, and a rifle range (!) have claimed the rest.

Such was the sorry state of affairs that existed for nearly a decade, not only on the Phantom's onetime turf but clear across the nation. A number of oft-cited factors contributed to the decline of the once-flourishing neighborhood double-feature palaces. Television accounted for the first wave of casualties back in the '50s and early '60s. The ongoing Multiplex Menace, represented by those multiscreen fast-flick franchises that have sprung up in virtually every American mall and shopping center, eliminated most of the rest. By the mid-1970s, genre-starved fans were left with little more than late-night TV as their main source of B-movie viewing.

Luckily, video has ridden to our collective rescue. When we re-checked in 1988, our old nabe had sprouted more video stores than we would care to count. Not the same as the glory days of the neighborhood bijou, to be sure, but an enormous improvement over the vast wasteland of the postbijou, prevideo 1970s.

Not only have low-cost VCRs filled the vacuum left by the vanished nabes and drive-ins of yore, they come equipped with a powerful built-in advantage that even those great bijous gone by couldn't offer: Today's video viewer can be his or her own creative programmer, with a far wider range of viewing choices than any theatrical exhibitor has ever enjoyed.

There are among us those celluloid elitists who hold that video distorts movies to the point of ruination. True enough—picture resolution and scope are both reduced. And without letterboxing—a technique found more commonly on laser discs than on videocassettes that restores a film's original proportions by masking the top and bottom of the image—Cinemascope and other wide-screen processes lose their once-grandiose horizontal sweep.

Valid criticisms all, but hardly new phenomena: these are the same conditions under which home viewers have been watching movies on television for over forty years now. Far worse, TV prints are routinely edited, often outright butchered, to fit into prearranged time slots. And until the advent of public broadcasting, pay cable, and pay-per-view systems, it was virtually impossible to see a televised movie free of mood-killing commercial interruptions.

Video, on the other hand, has emancipated the home viewer from these cathode constraints. Some labels are not above trimming original film prints, but this practice remains far more common to television than to the vid industry. (E.g., Terry Gilliam's *Brazil*, intact on video, was mercilessly mutilated for its network TV premiere.) And though commercials have begun appearing on selected cassettes (an admittedly scurvy trend), we at least have the option of fast-forwarding past them.

With video we can also rewind and rewatch favorite scenes; freeze-frame interesting images; study a sequence in slow motion; and otherwise control our own viewing destiny. True, the old bijou ambience is missing. But even the average living room is more atmospheric than the typical prefab multiplex shoebox screening rooms that pass for bijous today.

Video places viewers firmly in control, allowing us access to a wealth of movie material that was, until recently, the private province of privileged film collectors. It's the Phantom's aim to help you, the home viewer, not only to relive fond movie memories but to explore previously unsampled, often hard-to-find film fare in the privacy of your own home theaters.

MONDO VIDEO

"Watch *what* you want, *when* you want."

That's the video credo, and one the Phantom fully supports. Too often, however, the *when* is easier to arrange than the *what*. Most neighborhood video stores—chains and independents alike—tend to be chronically understocked. Worse, they increasingly rely on multiple copies of the same new mainstream or A releases to fill their shelves (*depth of copy*, in vid-biz jargon; *breadth of copy* refers to the number of *different* titles an outlet carries).

The newer B or genre movies that turn up frequently do so—shortly after a token or nonexistent theatrical release—sans advance reviews and often with minimal or misleading advertising, leaving all but the most dedicated followers of B-movie fashions at a loss as to the tapes' quality or even content. As for vintage classics, foreign films, interesting obscurities, worthy direct-to-home-vid indies, and even well-known titles released on major labels just a few years back, these are frequently frustratingly impossible to locate via normal channels.

That's where the Phantom—and this volume—come in. While B movies are our business, they're not our *only* business. In addition to separating the gems from the junk among new genre releases, we've devoted much time and energy to seeking out sources for hard-to-find videos of *all* stripes.

Since initiating our "Mondo Video" column in the New York *Daily News* in 1986 as the video companion to our "Phantom of the Movies" B-film column, we've been deluged with letters from readers looking for more than can be found at the corner cassette store. While some requests *do* prove unobtainable from any quarter, many more are, in fact, out there—sometimes sequestered in the deepest recesses of Vidland's most remote sectors.

Taking his cue and direction from his readers' voluminous feedback, the Phantom embarked on a quest that has led, bit by bit, to the discovery of dozens of independent video-specialty companies and mail-order outfits offering everything from rare serials to forgotten fright flicks to vintage foreign films and other fare deemed incapable of competing with the new, big-bucks-backed studio releases for vidstore shelf space. Through the *News*, we began spreading the good word to an audience that many major video labels and retailers have virtually ignored. We've collected and expanded our findings in *The Phantom's Ultimate Video Guide.* Our capsule review chapters, supplemental Video Shopping List, extensive Videorama source guide, and Video Directory at the back of the book have all been designed to help you find your fave films on tape and let you know what else is out there. But first, a few important pointers for the novice vid-hunter.

LABEL-HOPPING

Since the video biz is yet a young and fluctuating one, not every tape may be available from the expected label or source. For example, some of the larger home-vid labels have been licensing previously rental-oriented tapes to smaller "sell-through" companies, who repackage the cassettes at affordable prices (often under $10). A prime example is RCA/Columbia's arrangement with Goodtimes Home Video, which was permitted to pick up such excellent RCA/Columbia genre titles as *Earth vs. the Flying Saucers* and *Curse of the Demon*. Even as the Goodtimes sell-through editions appear in supermarket and convenience-store racks, many video outlets continue to carry the original (and visually superior) RCA/Columbia editions as rental items. Likewise, Media Home Entertainment has a similar arrangement with the sell-through-oriented Video Treasures label, also resulting in separate cassette editions of the same films.

LIFE IN THE SLOW LANE

Recording speed is a major factor that affects both quality and price. The chief drawback with most smaller sell-through companies—Goodtimes, Video Treasures, Star Classics, et al.—is that, unlike the larger rental-oriented labels, they usually tape at the LP (middle) speed. This results in reduced visual quality. Said companies claim that the money saved on videotape is what enables them to offer the cassettes so inexpensively. On the other hand, the superior RCA/Columbia *Curse of the Demon*—which retains the old Columbia Pictures logo on its prints (important to some collectors)—will set you back a hefty $70 or so, a price too steep for most casual fans, *even if* they can find one for sale.

Many major labels have reduced their prices on slightly older titles in various promotional packages (e.g., Warner's "Video Hit Parade," CBS/Fox's "Action Collection")—a genuine boon to casual collectors who are assured of receiving a quality tape recorded at SP (fast speed) at sell-through prices (under $30). Lately, however, a few major labels, most notably Nelson (formerly Embassy) and International Video Entertainment (IVE), have also begun issuing their price-reduced videos on slower-speed tapes. It should be imperative that labels at least *specify*, somewhere on the video box, the recording speed used. Goodtimes' *Curse of the Demon* volunteers that vital info, but most do not.

The only other way to ascertain what tape speed has been employed is to check the T number on the cassette itself. A "T-45" for a ninety-minute film means it's been recorded at middle speed (LP); a "T-30" designates slowest speed (EP). Usually, the consumer is privy to that info only *after* a tape's been purchased or rented and removed from the box (and even then the "T" number is not always given). In addition to guaranteeing poorer visual clarity, slow-speed tapes can, with repeated playings, reportedly damage the heads of certain VCRs.

SECOND TIME AROUND

Some videos change labels when their original licensing agreements lapse. Smaller, B-oriented companies sometimes outbid the original copyright holders for reissue rights after the initial (generally seven-year) copyright agreements have terminated. Thus, Magnum Entertainment picked up the rights to the excellent cult chiller *The Wicker Man* from Media Home Entertainment. What had been a relatively minor title in the new-release-slanted Media catalog became a major—and hence more aggressively marketed—title for Magnum. Ditto for Unicorn Home Video, when it secured the rights to Jamaa Fanaka's jolting prison classic *Penitentiary* from Wizard Video. Cannon Video and Amvest are likewise reissuing lapsed titles. If anything, this trend should make the transferred titles in question even *more* visible at local stores—even if, in a few scattered cases, the original label info no longer applies.

VANISHING VIDS

In isolated instances, legit copyright holders may surface to reclaim films that were previously believed to have been in the public domain—i.e., unprotected by copyright laws due to their age or to a technicality of one kind or another. (See the *Night of the Living Dead* review for a flagrant example of the latter.) Even in that worst-case scenario, the determined videophile can—by consulting our thorough Videorama listings (replete with phone numbers and addresses)—at least begin at the original source and learn who the present owner and/or distributor might be. And many *officially* discontinued or withdrawn tapes—i.e., those no longer issued by their original labels (or by anyone else)—*are* still carried by the larger video-rarity specialists, such as Chicago's Facets Video, Philadelphia's Movies Unlimited, and New York's Evergreen Video. These and other sources often have copies of scarce titles (including dozens that have been withdrawn by CBS/Fox Video and Walt Disney Home Video many of which are being reissued at sell-through prices by MGM/UA and Touchstone, respectively) for sale and/or mail-order rental. In short, frustrated video seekers no longer have to accept their local vid-store's "no" for a definitive answer.

PUBLIC DOMAIN

Certified public-domain titles (see above) routinely appear on several different labels simultaneously, with varying prices and visual quality. Wherever possible, we've listed the label or source offering the best-available quality, while indicating that other outfits also carry the film.

   Other, "gray area" movies may also turn up on more than one label. The camp classic *Blood Freak*, for example, is available on the Regal Video label as *Blood Freak* and under the Simitar banner as the pluralized *Blood Freaks*. Donald Jackson's *Demon Lover* is available via United Home Video under that title, but in a version shortened by an entire reel; Regal carries the complete film, under the title *Devil Master*. Wherever possible, we've attempted to clear up any confusion due to alternative titles and/or sources that surround many of the more obscure genre tapes covered here. In those cases where companies (e.g., New Star, Nelson) have purchased defunct companies' (Cinema Group, Embassy, respectively) video inventories without issuing new editions of those tapes, we list the videos' original labels, since those are the tapes still in stock at vidstores.

PLANET OF THE TAPES

Spatial limitations keep us from covering the entire catalog of the perhaps thirty thousand or so feature films that exist—somewhere—on cassette. But nearly all the specialty companies listed in our Videorama section have catalogs available either for the asking or for a modest fee. We encourage you to contact them and continue your own video explorations beyond the borders of this book. To keep current with the constantly mutating cassette scene, or to pose any questions not answered in this volume, we invite you to send all video comments and queries to Mondo Video, Phantom of the Movies, New York *Daily News*, 220 East 42nd Street, New York, NY 10017.

For the record, we can guarantee that, except for the Phantomess's guest *Robot Monster* review, every word in this volume (some show up more than once) has been written by the Phantom's own spectral hand. (While we readily admit that our views are as slanted and subjective as any other reviewer's—if not, indeed, more so—we just as readily confess that we usually happen to agree with them.) It's long been our belief that a single voice can be more valuable than a consortium of disparate critics. Once readers get a sense of how a single reviewer's mind works (or malfunctions, as the case may be), the better able they'll be to gauge their own probable reaction to an individual video.

Since this is essentially a one-Phantom enterprise, we're also ready to accept the blame for the occasional errors that are bound to surface in a volume this massive and detailed. We hope you'll find the goodness in your human hearts to forgive the Phantom any such factual faux pas.

WHAT YOU SEE, WHAT YOU GET

We've arranged the videos listed in *The Phantom's Ultimate Video Guide* according to genre, beginning with "Action" and ending with our Trailer Tape chapter. For our rated reviews (see Ratings Key), we've chosen from among the latest (good and bad alike), greatest, and weirdest tapes that fall within the broad, admittedly subjective category of Phantom films and that are currently available in vidstores or via mail-order specialists. To keep this volume at a publishable length, we've omitted many genre offerings that we deem insufferably lame or even merely mediocre. Many other movies we'd *love* to cover have been omitted simply by virtue of the fact that they're not yet available on video—*the* single essential criterion for inclusion in this book.

Since this *is* a video guide rather than a traditional film reference work, we often cover more than one title within a given video entry or review. For example, our *Wild One* capsule critique expands to list virtually all the biker movies, regardless of individual quality, presently out on cassette and not covered in separate reviews. This enables celluloid-cycle buffs to binge out to their hearts' (and eyes') content. Similar lists center on certain popular genre personalities (e.g., Sybil Danning) and directors (Russ Meyer). The aim here is to inform as well as to critique and to arm videophiles with as much vital consumer info as possible. Those looking to obtain an individual title can refer to our Video Shopping List and/or the Video Listings Index for instant access to the name of the company that's issued the video and/or the specialty outfit that's likely to carry it. Addresses, phone numbers, and in many cases, ordering info appear in our extensive Videorama section at book's end.

The Phantom also breaks from the traditional review-guide format by incorporating a number of sidebars, including profiles and mini-interviews with the folks who make the movies we want to see— from John Waters and Wes Craven to George A. Romero and Stuart Gordon—and genre personalities like up-and-coming Scream Screen Queen Linnea Quigley—who've consented to share their thoughts with yours truly. Other pointed digressions include the Phantom's memories of the 1987 Cannes Film Fest, a history of Godzilla's checkered career, and other items included, well, just for the hell of it.

But enough of the Phantom's preliminary palaver. It's time to cut to the chase, or at least go to the videotapes. . . .

The Phantom and Phantomess select the evening's video entertainment in the privacy of their secret Gotham HQ.

CREDITS

Video titles are followed by year of theatrical release—or, in the case of direct-to-home-videocassettes, video release—followed by the Phantom's rating (see below), director's name, three or more prominent cast members, running time, video company and/or video source where the tape may be obtained. We've also done our best to specify when the same film is available on more than one video label (whether in slightly or drastically different versions). In the case of public-domain (PD) films, many of which are carried by several separate suppliers, we list either the sole or the most reliable supplier of a particular PD tape. We've also, when possible, included alternate titles for those films that have been retitled for video release, that appear on cassette under more than one title, or that have had more than one title during their theatrical releases.

RATINGS KEY

◆◆◆◆	Couldn't be better
◆◆◆◇	Excellent
◆◆◆	Good
◆◆◇	Not bad; worth watching
◆◆	Mediocre; worthwhile for fans of a particular thesp, director, or genre
◆◇	Poor, but may have points of interest
◆	Just plain bad
◇	Even worse than that
0◆	The pits
NA	Not available on video at this time
NR	Not rated. Applied to videos geared to special-interest audiences (e.g., cliffhanger fans, shockumentary buffs) and those genre titles included strictly FYI.
FYI	For your information

Note: All rated films are judged on the basis of their entertainment value, which is not always related to their "artistic" merit.

THE PHANTOM'S ULTIMATE VIDEO GUIDE

A IS FOR ACTION
(& ADVENTURE)

"When I want your opinion, I'll beat it out of you!"

Chuck Norris
Code of Silence

According to a 1988 Video Software Dealers of America report, the action category ranks as American video stores' single most popular category (outside of new releases), accounting for some 15 percent of all cassette rentals. It's also a category that offers a surfeit of titles that—beyond those A-level flicks starring Stallone, Schwarzenegger, Eastwood, and their ilk—are bound to bemuse the casual browser. The following represents the Phantom's roundup of the major, minor, and downright obscure actioners, recently released (many of them directly) to the home-vid market, as well as those older action/ adventure winners, weirdos, and curios now available on cassette. We've tried to encompass all action persuasions here, from bygone biker flicks to martial arts epics to chicks-in-chains romps to the best of the '70s "blaxploitation" ventures.

1

Where we lack the space to describe a film, we at least offer its video availability. If you don't find your fave listed as a separate entry, we suggest you consult our Video Listings Index at book's end for the page where the flick's video status is given. Likewise, if you don't see an individual review for any Golden Age adventure classic you may be looking for, chances are you'll find it mentioned, along with its video releasing company, in our Video Shopping List supplement, also located in the back of the book.

The Abduction (1975) ♦♦
D: Joseph Zito. Leif Erickson, Dorothy Malone, Judith-Marie Bergan. 100 minutes. (Media)

The definitive drive-in edition of the Patty Hearst kidnapping is a generally inept though determinedly lurid outing, of interest mainly as a companion piece to Paul Schrader's version *Patty Hearst*—the one Patty herself endorses.

Above the Law (1988) ♦♦♦
D: Andrew Davis. Steven Seagal, Pam Grier, Henry Silva, Sharon Stone, Ron Dean, Daniel Faraldo, Thalmus Rasulala. 99 minutes. (Warner)

Real-life martial arts master Seagal (pronounced "Sea-*gal*") makes an impressive debut as karate-trained Chicago cop Nico Toscani. Our at-times overly complicated story line finds the former CIA employee uncovering a Company plot to import controlled substances from Central America with the help of prominent Windy City hoods. Seagal scores high marks in both the swift *mano-

a-mano and the blazing-gunplay departments, as well as exhibiting more-than-adequate acting ability. The always-welcome Grier is at once solid and foxy as Sea*gal*'s soon-to-retire partner, while veteran screen villain Silva gives his venomous all as sadistic slimeball Zagon. The narrative, co-hatched by Sea*gal* (who also produced), has its fair share of holes, but action fans won't be disappointed by this nonstop caper, which also incorporates a cautionary anti-CIA message.

Across 110th Street (1972) ♦♦◊
D: Barry Shear. Anthony Quinn, Yaphet Kotto, Anthony Franciosa. 102 minutes. (Key)

Educated cop Kotto and old-liner Quinn square off in a violent, actionful, but unusually bleak Harlem-set caper about a gang of amateurs' disastrous plan to rip off the mob. Antonio Fargas turns in top work as one of the hapless would-be hoods. The video's been officially withdrawn but is still in stock at many vidstores.

Action Jackson (1988) ◆◇
D: Craig R. Baxley. Carl Weathers, Craig T. Nelson, Vanity, Sharon Stone, Bill Duke, Robert Davi, Sonny Landham. 95 minutes. (Lorimar)

If little else, *Action Jackson* at least offers viewers a crash course in How To Make a Bad Joel (*Commando*) Silver Movie. Take one muscle-bound maverick hero (Weathers as legendary Detroit dick Jericho "Action" Jackson), mix with a megalomaniacal villain (evil auto magnate Nelson) perpetrating an elaborate, psychopathic power grab, add a ditzy ethnic bimbo who becomes the hero's unwitting partner (Vanity, as a singing junkie/whore), dose liberally with loud shoot-outs, car crashes, and explosions, and—voila!—you have another brain-dead *Commando* clone. There are a *few* bright spots here: Carl (Apollo Creed) Weathers does what he can with the title role; the opening action sequence and auto-plant montage are well executed; and it's always a treat to hear Vanity croon "Undress Me" while staring directly into the lens. But when *Action Jackson* loses it—about three reels in—it does so with such crushing finality that the rest of the flick is sheer torture to endure.

Aguirre: The Wrath of God (1972) ◆◆◆
D: Werner Herzog. Klaus Kinski, Ruy Guerra, Del Negro. 94 minutes. (New Star)

Frequent fright-film thesp Kinski shines as a power-crazed sixteenth-century conquistador leading a contingent of Pizarro's men through the perilous Amazon jungles in a delusional quest for the legendary Seven Cities of Gold. Herzog's hallucinatory lensing and a haunting Peruvian flute score have helped make this offbeat adventure parable an enduring cult fave.

Al Capone (1959) ◆◆◇ **B&W**
D: Richard Wilson. Rod Steiger, Fay Spain, James Gregory. 104 minutes. (Key)

Steiger chews cigars and scenery with equal aplomb in a solid if unsurprising chronicle of erstwhile Chicago crime king Capone's oft-documented rise and fall.

American Justice (1986) ◆◆◇
D: Gary Grillo. Jameson Parker, Jack Lucarelli, Gerald McRaney, Wilford Brimley, Jeannie Wilson, Dennis A. Pratt. 96 minutes. (Lightning)

Those *Simon & Simon* boys (Parker, Lucarelli) of prime-time prominence produced and toplined in this semi-socially conscious B actioner. Lucarelli plays a troubled ex-cop who visits former partner Parker, now an Arizona trooper on the Mexican border beat, and chances to witness the cold-blooded desert murder—by Parker's sadistic co-worker Wheeler (McRaney)—of a young illegal-alien girl. When the chief trooper's (Brimley, in a break from his usual kindly avuncular role) attempted cover-up fails, Wheeler goes on the warpath, which leads our S&S tandem, abetted by a nifty laser rifle, to take on the bad guys in the inevitable climactic blood bath. Basically a poor man's *The Border, American Justice* is rife with implausibilities but manages to supply considerable suspense, along with some surprisingly sadistic set pieces. There's also a horse named Brain Damage afoot and a fellow trooper named Hobie Landreth, in honor of the obscure former New York Mets catcher of the same name.

American Nightmare (1983) ◆◆
D: Don McBrearty. Lawrence Day, Lora Stanley, Lenore Zann. 85 minutes. (Interglobal)

An openly exploitative low-budget *Hardcore* reprise (complete with superior title, though minus the latter's campy flair) about a youth's descent into the urban sleaze maelstrom in search of his errant sister. Watchable, if less than spellbinding.

American Ninja (1985) ◆◆◇
D: Sam Firstenberg. Michael Dudikoff, Judie Aronson, Steve James, Guich Koock, Tadashi Yamashita, Don Stewart. 95 minutes. (MGM/UA)

Firstenberg's Philippines-filmed chopsocky opera pits Dudikoff as mysterious Ninja-trained GI Joe (no relation to Jack) Armstrong against evil Black Star Ninja Yamashita (of *Sword of Heaven*

obscurity—see index) and his sinister arms-dealing boss, the highly unpopular Señor Ortega (Stewart). In the course of this predictable but swiftly paced actioner, our laconic hero woos the base commander's daughter (JAPpily interpreted by Aronson), wins the grudging support of his fellow soldiers (including muscular sidekick James), and dispatches evildoers by the dozens. The end result: ninety-five minutes of fast, dumb formula fun.

American Ninja 2: The Confrontation (1987) ◆◆
D: Sam Firstenberg. Michael Dudikoff, Steve James, Gary Conway, Larry Poindexter. 90 minutes. (Media)

Once again abetted by James (reprising his role as army topkick Curtis Jackson), Dudikoff returns as titular martial arts ace Joe Armstrong, dispatched to an unnamed Carib isle where Marine embassy guards are disappearing at an alarming rate. Turns out there's a simple explanation: They're being kidnapped by villain Conway as part of his master plan to coerce a cancer-research genius into creating a race of black-suited bionic "super-Ninjas" to protect his lucrative island drug trade. Director Firstenberg supplies a number of violent stunts here, but the pic proceeds sans the visceral verve of either the original *American Ninja* or the same team's *Avenging Force* (see index). And co-scripter Conway's thesping has, sad to say, diminished greatly since his promising debut as the lead in *I Was a Teenage Frankenstein* (NA) three decades back.

Angel (1984) ♦♦
D: Robert Vincent O'Neil. Cliff Gorman, Donna Wilkes, Susan Tyrrell, Rory Calhoun. 94 minutes. (HBO)

"High-school honor student by day, hooker by night!" promised the original ad posters, but only the occasional dose of sleaze separates this popular exploitation flick from a "socially conscious" made-for-TV soaper. Not as flamboyantly stupid as *Avenging Angel* nor as limp as the series' closer (thus far), *Angel III*.

Angel III: The Final Chapter (1988) ♦
D: Tom DeSimone. Maud Adams, Mitzi Kapture, Mark Blankfield, Richard Roundtree, Dick Miller. 99 minutes. (New World)

Mitzi Kapture takes over the role of an overage Angel, now a combo undercover-agent/free-lance photog in NYC who returns to the El Lay streets to retrieve her abducted younger sister. Tom DeSimone's soulless sequel, a lame exercise in pure brand-X B-movie "product," will hopefully prompt our golden-hearted hooker to hang up her spiked heels for good.

Angels Die Hard (1970) ♦♦
D: Richard Compton. Tom Baker, William Smith, R. G. Armstrong. 86 minutes. (New World)

You'd have to be a die-hard celluloid biker buff to enjoy this apathetic exercise in ennui on wheels, though action fave Big Bill Smith *is* along for the ride and gets to deliver the deathless advice, "It's always better to wait before you thump a man's head." *Angels* is *so* slow, dull, and directionless that it comes close to capturing a true *verité* feel, which may appeal to more patient viewers. And it will doubtless be your only chance to hear the popular soundtrack ditty "Today the Man Who Kills the Ants Came By."

The Annihilators (1985) ♦♦
D: Charles E. Sellier, Jr. Christopher Stone, Andy Wood, Lawrence Hilton-Jacobs, Gerrit Graham, Paul Koslo, Dennis Redfield. 84 minutes. (New World)

The title tough guys are a quartet of macho 'Nam vets (including Hilton-Jacobs, formerly of *Welcome Back, Kotter* fame) who regroup in Atlanta to rid a seedy nabe of the vicious street scum who offed their buddy (Redfield). The hoods here are an especially mean lot: They torture paraplegics, rape and murder innocent women, beat up on bag ladies, and even kick a defenseless teddy bear down the street (!). Since the police, as always, are "handcuffed by the courts," our heroes waste little time in training fed-up area residents in the fine art of fighting back—at which point the red dye copiously flows. While *The Annihilators* leaves no urban-action cliché unturned, its gradual buildup and professional thesping at least place it a notch above countless others of its concrete-western ilk, and insatiable genre fans aren't likely to be bored.

Armed Response (1986) ♦♦
D: Fred Olen Ray. David Carradine, Lee Van Cleef, Lois Hamilton, Mako, Brent Huff, Michael Berryman, Dick Miller. 86 minutes. (RCA/Columbia)

Bargain-basement auteur Fred Olen Ray, making the first of many appearances in this volume, steps up to the relative big time with this B-star-studded affair. The pic pits the macho Roth clan (ex-cop Van Cleef and his three two-fisted sons) against Japanese Yakuza heavies led by Mako ("a two-bit thug in a three-piece suit"), who'd earlier clashed with Carradine in the *Rambo* rip-off *P.O.W.: The Escape* (see index). Filmmaker Fred gets the flick off to a flying start with an energetic desert shoot-out over a purloined million-dollar statue belonging to the malevolent Mako; Van Cleef's Number Three Son Clay (Goss) expires in the exchange, prompting the remaining Roths to embark on the requisite revenge rampage. Conveniently enough, Number One Son Carradine is a 'Nam vet haunted by combat flashbacks, which provides a perfect excuse for still more gratuitous onscreen bloodletting. And when Number Two Son Huff is captured and tortured by Mako ("Have you ever had your bones scraped, Mr. Roth?"), Fred hurtles the film into updated Fu Manchu territory. Unfortunately,

Armed Response ultimately degenerates from the creatively brain-damaged to the merely stupid, as director Ray inexorably reverts to his old Z-movie ways.

Assassination (1987) ♦♦
D: Peter Hunt. Charles Bronson, Jill Ireland, Stephen Elliott, Jan Gan Boyd, Michael Ansara, Randy Brooks. 88 minutes. (Media)

Geriatric action star Bronson gives both himself and his overworked stunt double a well-deserved rest in this decently scripted but not very actionful political thriller. Chuck plays a Secret Service agent assigned to protect feisty but endangered First Lady Ireland (Bronson's real-life better half); much of the running time is consumed by Chuck and Jill's less-than-scintillating banter as they gradually evolve from combatants to kindred spirits.

Assault on Precinct 13 (1976) ♦♦♦◊
D: John Carpenter. Austin Stoker, Darwin Joston, Laurie Zimmer. 91 minutes. (Media)

Carpenter's urban contempo *Rio Bravo* reprise is a model of expert low-budget genre filmmaking. L.A. youth gangs unite to mount a relentless attack on the nearly abandoned title site, defended by cop Stoker and motley crew. The obscure Darwin Joston is particularly good as a cool con named Napoleon. Carpenter also composed the taut minimalist synthesizer score. Better than *Colors*, at a fraction of the cost, *Assault* ranks as one of the best B actioners ever made.

Avenging Angel (1985) ◆◇
D: Robert Vincent O'Neil. Betsy Russell, Rory Calhoun, Robert F. Lyons, Ossie Davis, Susan Tyrrell. 93 minutes. (New World)

When we last left our plucky heroine, she'd been rescued from "the life" by white knight Hugh Andrews (Lyons), a cop with a heart big enough to drive a SWAT truck through. Now, four years later, Angel (Russell, replacing Donna Wilkes) has given up prostitution to enter the legal profession (though some may not see that as much of a leap). But when Andrews is blown away by ruthless Mafia killers, Angel puts her career on hold, takes her purple halter-top and hotpants out of mothballs, and hits the streets with mayhem in mind. To aid her in her self-styled jihad, Angel recruits a wild crew of would-be lovable street zanies, starting with former sagebrush star Rory Calhoun as eccentric ex–stunt man Kit Carson. Also along for the slaughter are foul-mouthed lesbian street-matriarch Solly Mosler (Tyrrell); whimsical acid casualty Johnny Glitter; mute bag lady Shopping Cart Sally; and Pat and Mike, a pair of two-fisted transvestites (!). It's the scum of the earth versus the salt of same, and the scum don't stand a chance. As Angel remarks, "Some things never change, do they?"

Avenging Force (1986) ◆◆◆
D: Sam Firstenberg. Michael Dudikoff, Steve James, John P. Ryan, James Booth, Bill ("Superfoot") Wallace, Karl Johnson. 103 minutes. (Media)

The Cannon Group's *Avenging Force* reverses '80s action-movie trends by pitting good-guy liberals against evil right-wingers. The *American Ninja* team of Michael Dudikoff and Steve James (the latter cast as your typical black senatorial-candidate-cum-kung-fu-ace) battle sinister Pentangle fanatics who, under the sicko supervision of crazed corporate head John P. ("Hitler was right!") Ryan, blow up federal agents, waste hordes of innocent tourists in a Mardi Gras massacre, and even gun down little kids in their ongoing efforts to wipe "yellow-bellied liberals" off the face of the nation. The script, penned by costar Booth—who performed the same dual functions for Sho Kosugi's energetic *Pray for Death* (see index)—makes more noise than sense, but action auteur Firstenberg keeps things moving at a sufficiently swift pace to more than compensate for the frequent plot holes.

Bad Boys (1983) ◆◆◆
D: Rick Rosenthal. Sean Penn, Ally Sheedy, Esai Morales. 123 minutes. (HBO)

An effective update of the boys' reformatory flicks of yore: Penn and Morales are strong as natural adversaries who find themselves

AVENGING FORCE

MAY THE FORCE BE WITH YOU: Steve James (left) and Michael Dudikoff (right) face fascist forces in Sam Firstenberg's first-rate action romp, *Avenging Force*. Photo courtesy of The Cannon Film Group.

Steve James, B Star of Tomorrow!

Equipped with a muscular physique, extensive martial arts expertise, and an easygoing onscreen charm, Steve James has fast become an action actor to watch. Steve initially impressed via his pivotal role as Odell the bartender in John Sayles's 1984 sci-fi fable *The Brother From Another Planet*, then teamed up with Michael Dudikoff for director Sam Firstenberg's action trilogy *American Ninja*, *American Ninja 2*, and *Avenging Force*. He also played supporting parts in *The Delta Force*, *Hero and the Terror*, *Mask*, *P.O.W.: The Escape*, *To Live and Die in L.A.*, and William Friedkin's TV-movie adventure *C.A.T. Squad*. That the acrobatic actor isn't afraid to make mock of his macho image is evidenced by his cameo in Robert Townsend's indie industry satire *Hollywood Shuffle*, where he donned a tutu (!) for the film's comic kung-fu sequence; he reinforced his comedic abilities as the terminally out-of-sync Kung-Fu Joe in Keenen Ivory Wayans's "blaxploitation" send-up *I'm Gonna Git You Sucka!* Steve also enjoys the rare distinction of having grown up *on* Forty-second Street and cites sighting three of his movies—*American Ninja, Delta Force,* and *P.O.W.*—sharing the same Deuce marquee as one of his greatest thrills.

locked behind the same bars. We missed Frankie Darro and Billy Halop's presence, but *Bad Boys* is still tough, tense, violent, top-of-the-genre stuff.

Bad Girls' Dormitory (1986) ♦♦
D: Tim Kincaid. Carey Zuris, Teresa Farley, Rick Gianasi, Jennifer DeLora. 95 minutes. (Active)

This relentlessly sleazy low-budget chicklets-in-chains item may be bottom-of-the-trash-barrel Tim (*Mutant Hunt*) Kincaid's best effort to date. Granted that's not saying much, but *Bad Girls Dormitory* shapes up as a worthy distaff video companion to the above-cited *Bad Boys*.

Best Revenge (1983) ♦♦◇
D: John Trent. John Heard, Levon Helm, Alberta Watson. 92 minutes. (Lorimar)

Heard and Helm are small-time hash smugglers in over their heads in a fairly taut and nearly credible crime flick set mostly in Morocco.

Big Bad Mama II (1987) ♦◇
D: Jim Wynorski. Angie Dickinson, Robert Culp, Danielle Brisebois, Julie McCullough, Jeff Yagher, Bruce Glover. 85 minutes. (MGM/UA)

A tedious action "comedy" from Wynorski—whose previous credits include such equally derivative duds as *The Lost Empire, Chopping Mall,* and *Deathstalker II* (see index for all)—*Big Bad Mama II* finds an older but apparently no wiser Angie D doing a distracted reprise of her original role as Depression-victim-turned-outlaw Wilma McClatchie. The story, padded with pathetic stabs at slapstick humor, involves bank robber Angie's and daughters' (Brisebois, McCullough) vendetta against the Texas gubernatorial candidate (Glover) who'd earlier foreclosed on their land and caused Pa McClatchie's demise. Culp puts in sporadic appearances as journalist Daryl Pearson and performs what may well be his first important nude scene since *Bob & Carol & Ted & Alice* (RCA/Columbia). Unfortunately for all concerned, *Big Bad Mama II* arrives fully a decade after the *Bonnie and Clyde*–clone genre had twitched its last; this flick lacks the strength even to kick the corpse. In the FYI department: *Mama's Dirty Girls*, with Gloria Grahame as a mean mother, is available from TWE. *Daddy's Boys,* lensed on sets left over from *Big Bad Mama II*, is a sure bet to surface eventually, as is the original *Big Bad Mama*.

The Big Brawl (1980) ◆◆

D: Robert Clouse. Jackie Chan, José Ferrer, Kristine DeBell, Mako. 96 minutes. (Warner)

A slapstick kung-fu tale set in a hood-run 1930s Chicago (!), *The Big Brawl* begins brightly but soon turns tedious for all but the most fanatical Jackie Chan fans. The latter can also catch Jackie in *The Cannonball Run I* (Vestron) and *II* (Warner), *Dragon Fist, Fantasy Mission Force, Fearless Hyena I* and *II, Half a Loaf of Kung Fu, In Eagle Shadow Fist, New Fist of Fury, Shaolin Wooden Men, Snake & Crane Arts of Shaolin, Spiritual Kung Fu,* and *To Kill With Intrigue* (all via All Seasons); *Dragon Lord* and *My Lucky Stars* (New Star); plus *Ninja Thunderbolt* (TWE) and *The Young Tiger* (Video Gems).

The Big Doll House (1971) ◆◆◆

D: Jack Hill. Judy Brown, Roberta Collins, Pam Grier. 95 minutes. (Embassy)

Jack (*Switchblade Sisters*) Hill's Philippines-filmed fine-fettered-femmes flick set forth many of the conventions still rigidly adhered to by broads-behind-bars movies today. One of the genre's better offerings is further boosted by the popular Grier's pulchritudinous presence. Pam returns for more in Hill's sequel, *The Big Bird Cage* (Warner), another mostly successful mix of broad humor and random violence. Vonetta McGee takes over as the foxy force behind another Filipino prison breakout in the similarly themed *Big Bust Out* (Embassy).

The Big Push (1975) NR

D: Tay Garnett, Chuck D. Keen. Leon Ames, Claude Akins, Joseph Cotten, Tab Hunter. 98 minutes. (Video Gems)

Originally titled *Timber Tramps*, this old-fashioned Alaskan lumberjack adventure features a unique veteran cast and represents longtime director Garnett's filmic farewell.

Billy Jack (1971) ◆◆◇

D: Tom Laughlin. Tom Laughlin, Delores Taylor, Bert Freed, Kenneth Tobey. 115 minutes. (Warner)

Laughlin, auteuring under the nom du cinema T. C. Frank, reprises his kill-for-peace ex–Green Beret character from *Born Losers* (see index). This one's preachier, with less out-and-out sleaze, but stacks up as an authentic curiosity piece. As of this writing, the sequels, *The Trial of Billy Jack* and *Billy Jack Goes to Washington*, have yet to be released to the home-vid market.

Black Caesar (1973) ◆◆◇
D: Larry Cohen. Fred Williamson, Art Lund, D'Urville Martin. 95 minutes. (Orion)

Former gridiron star Fred ("The Hammer") Williamson is smooth in this okay replay of the old crime-lord's-rise-and-fall story. The pic could have used a few more of director/writer Cohen's patented perverse flourishes—though the funky bass guitar under the tearful Italo mandolin strains *is* a neat soundtrack touch. In addition to the other Fred flicks featured in this volume, Hammer hounds can also catch their hero in *Adios Amigo* (Vidmark), *Black Cobra* and *White Fire* (both TWE), *Blind Rage* (MGM/UA), *Boss* (Blacast), *Bucktown* (Orion), *Deadly Impact* (Vestron), *Deadly Intent* (Prism), *Death Journey* (Unicorn), *Fear in the City* (Mogul), *Hell's Heroes* (Network), *Joshua* (Magnum), *The Last Fight* (HBO), *Mean Johnny Barrows* (Unicorn), *Mr. Mean* (Magnum), *New Gladiators* (Media), *No Way Back* (Unicorn), *Take a Hard Ride* (CBS/Fox), and *Vigilante* (Vestron).

Naked women come under suspicion in ad for The Hammer's *No Way Back.* Photo courtesy of Unicorn Video.

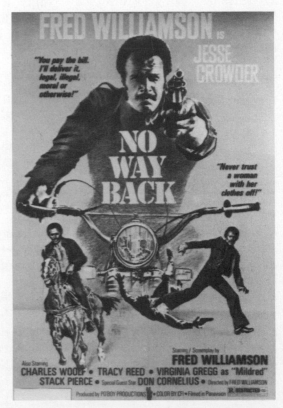

Black Eliminator (1977) ♦♦
D: Al Adamson. Jim Kelly, Aldo Ray, Terry Moore, Harold "Odd Job" Sakata. 87 minutes. (Unicorn)

Another Unicorn repackaging job (see *Black Sister's Revenge* in index), this was initially released as *Death Dimension* and is also available from the Canadian cassette company Lettuce Entertain You under the totally unrelated title *Icy Death*. This one's not bad for an Adamson effort and is further aided by a supporting cast rich in novelty value, if not talent. Fans of kung-fu ace Kelly's flying feet, furious fists, and Amazing Colossal Sideburns can also find their fave in *Black Belt Jones* and *Hot Potato* (both Warner), *Black Samurai* (Cinema Group), *The Kill Factor* (Academy), and *Tattoo Connection* (Embassy).

The Black Gestapo (1975) ♦♦◊
D: Lee Frost. Rod Perry, Charles P. Robinson, Phil Hoover. 88 minutes. (Unicorn)

An extremely brutal urban actioner about a quasi—Black Panther group battling back against white hoods and growing power mad in the process. A strong stomach helps here, particularly during the bathtub castration scene. Don't say you weren't warned! Rod Perry returns as *The Black Godfather* (Magnum).

Black Moon Rising (1986) ♦◊
D: Harley Cokliss. Tommy Lee Jones, Linda Hamilton, Robert Vaughn, Bubba Smith, Richard Jaeckel,

Keenan Wynn, Lee Ving. 100 minutes. (New World)

Despite a story by John (*Halloween*) Carpenter (who also co-scripted), *Black Moon Rising* is a thoroughly lead-footed, low-tech affair involving superthief Sam Quint's (Jones) efforts to rescue supercar Black Moon from an upscale "chop shop" operated by bad guy Vaughn. Linda (*The Terminator*) Hamilton is also along for the aimless ride as a distaff speed demon. The assembled thesps do what they can—Vaughn sneers with his customary aplomb, Bubba Smith mumbles convincingly as a government agent assigned to the case, and Jones manages to look more and more like Clint Eastwood the older he gets (a reward of aging to which your Phantom likewise looks forward). But Carpenter's script, totally bald on thrills, should have been left to collect additional dust in its author's dead-file drawer. Other recent vehicular adventures well worth avoiding include *Banzai Runner* and *Killing Cars* (both Vidmark), and *No Man's Land* (Orion).

Black Sister's Revenge (1987/ 1975) ♦♦◊
D: Jamaa Fanaka. Jerri Hayes, Ernest Williams II, Charles David Brooks III, Eddie Allen, Robert Slaughter, Malik Carter. 100 minutes. (Unicorn)

Unicorn pushed this vid as a new black action pic—an accompanying "still" depicts an entirely unrelated, obviously contempo fox brandishing a pistol and machine gun (!). But *Black Sister's Revenge* is actually a 1975 Jamaa (*Penitentiary*) Fanaka flick originally (and more appropriately) titled *Emma Mae*, a funky slice-of-lifer featuring a few mild and ephemeral exploitation elements. As such, the movie is not without its merits. Fanaka documents the social adjustment of heroine Emma Mae (Hayes), a naive but resourceful Deep South college girl who moves in with her more sophisticated and cynical cousins, a clan of California blacks. It's only when Em hooks up with local lowlife Jess (Williams) that the plot detours in some unlikely directions—as when Em, out of nowhere, decides to operate a car wash to raise bail for her errant beau; when that fails, she sticks up a nearby bank (!). Ridiculous retitling aside, *Black Sister's Revenge* is an uneven but compelling character study, rich in regional detail. Unicorn honchos should have trusted the film they had and not tried to con customers into thinking they were getting something less.

Blackbeard the Pirate (1952) ◆◆◆
D: Raoul Walsh. Robert Newton, Linda Darnell, William Bendix. 99 minutes. (RKO)

Our fave high-seas adventure, thanks to Newton's classic textbook lesson in the fine art of overacting. Newt proves it wasn't a fluke with his equally histrionic *Treasure Island* (Walt Disney) perf.

Bloodsport (1988) ◆◆◇
D: Newt Arnold. Jean-Claude Van Damme, Donald Gibb, Leah Ayres, Norman Burton, Forest Whitaker, Roy Chiso, Bolo Yeung. 92 minutes. (Warner)

Bloodsport stars Van Damme—a brash Belgian combo of Arnold Schwarzenegger and Bruce Lee—as real-life karate champ Frank Dux, the first Westerner to win the clandestine full-contact Kumite competition staged once every five years in a different exotic locale (in this case, Hong Kong). Between bouts, Jean-Claude finds time to befriend fellow competitor Ray Jackson (Gibb), romance reporter Janice (Ayres), antagonize sadistic defending champ Chong Li (Yeung), and consistently elude a pair of army investigators dispatched to return him to the special-service branch from which he's gone AWOL. While the plot—in large part a *Karate Kid* retread—is pretty predictable and the pic is further padded with several boring rock-video segments, *Bloodsport* comes alive where it counts—in the Kumite ring. Nearly half the flick, lensed largely within Hong Kong's exotic Walled City, consists of full-contact fight footage, expertly choreographed by Van Damme and far more compelling than the wraparound dramatics. You can also catch Jean-Claude in *Black Eagle* (Imperial), where, cast as a Russki heavy, he takes a thespic backseat to hard-hitting hero Sho Kosugi.

OUR COFFEE WITH JEAN-CLAUDE

"Coffee's not good for you! You should drink tea, my friend."

So Belgian martial-arts ace Jean-Claude Van Damme advised the Phantom during a clandestine visit in the midst of a *Bloodsport* promo blitz. The self-described Muscles From Brussels, who stands a modest five feet ten ("five eleven in my boots") and weighs in at roughly 175, also revealed that he's been competing in the martial-arts ring since age eleven.

"When I was young, I was very thin, so I trained in karate and weights and also did some ballet. That's why I'm so graceful. And why I catch not only the male but the female audience. Coffee is bad for the nerves, and the heart."

At age twenty-four, Jean-Claude chucked the Brussels gym he owned to take a shot at Hollywood. After working as a bouncer and trainer, he landed the role of a mean Russki karate champ in the no-budget indie *No Retreat, No Surrender* (see index). That led to a meatier part as the ever-mutating monster-suited title alien in the Arnold Schwarzenegger sci-fi actioner *Predator*.

"Well," Jean-Claude clarifies, "actually I only had *part* of the role. Do you remember the chameleon monster? *That* was me."

The muscular thesp still harbors fond memories of training with Arnold and Carl (*Action Jackson*) Weathers. "I really wanted to spar with them," he recalls almost wistfully, "but that never happened." As for Arn, J-C maintains, "He's a strong man mentally. He's the type of guy who if you're gonna have a fight with him, he's going to take a table and put it on your face."

Of course, injuries are a necessary evil of the action-movie game. "There were two broken jaws and one broken nose in *Bloodsport,*" admits Jean-Claude, who received some serious bruises himself, though they failed to dampen his seemingly limitless enthusiasm. "I'm so much in love with film—it's my life—that when I listened to the cameras rolling, I felt no pain. Are you sure you wouldn't rather have tea?"

While Jean-Claude cites Jon Voight, Robert De Niro, Bruce Lee, and the ever-influential Arn as his screen idols, he's nothing if not bent on making a name for himself.

"It's bigger than Arnold Schwarzenegger's," he points out between sips of tea. "It takes up more space on the screen."

VAN DAMME

CANNON INTERNATIONAL Presents JEAN CLAUDE VAN DAMME in a NEWT ARNOLD Film, "BLOODSPORT." DONALD GIBB, LEAH AYRES, NORMAN BURTON, and FOREST WHITAKER. Story by SHELDON LETTICH. Screenplay by SHELDON LETTICH and CHRISTOPHER COSBY & MEL FRIEDMAN. Produced by MARK DiSALLE. Directed by NEWT ARNOLD ©MCMLXXXVII CANNON FILMS, INC. and CANNON INTERNATIONAL.

"It's bigger than Arnold Schwarzenegger's."
Photo courtesy of The Cannon Film Group.

Bloody Mama (1970) ◆◆◇
D: Roger Corman. Shelley Winters, Pat Hingle, Robert De Niro. 90 minutes. (Vestron)

Shelley Winters *is* Ma Barker. Dern, Stroud, Walden, and a young Robert De Niro *are* her loyal sons. *Bloody Mama is* Roger Corman's satisfyingly sleazy salute to Middle American family values.

Bobbie Jo and the Outlaw (1976) ◆◆◇
D: Mark L. Lester. Lynda Carter, Marjoe Gortner, Jesse Vint. 89 minutes. (Vestron)

Future Wonder Woman Carter and former Holy Man Gortner join forces for a lively abrupt-and-senseless killing spree in this longtime drive-in fave. A clip from *Bobby-Jo* also appears in director Lester's *Class of 1984* (see index) in a modest self-homage.

Bonnie and Clyde (1967) ◆◆◆
D: Arthur Penn. Warren Beatty, Faye Dunaway, Estelle Parsons, Michael J. Pollard. 111 minutes. (Warner)

Penn's bloody paean to rural outlaws Dunaway and Beatty plays a bit self-consciously but remains arresting entertainment and was nothing if not instrumental in furthering the cause of slo-mo movie violence. Karen Black and Fabian teamed up for the low-budget *B&C* rip-off *Little Laura and Big John* (VidAmerica).

The Border (1982) ◆◆◆
D: Tony Richardson. Jack Nicholson, Valerie Perrine, Harvey Keitel, Warren Oates. 107 minutes. (MCA)

Nicholson is convincing as a guilt-stricken border patrolman who bucks the corrupt system in a solid, straightforward B flick with an A budget and cast. Other okay border-beat movies include *Borderline* (CBS/Fox), with Chuck Bronson as a brave ranger, and David Carradine in *On the Line* (Nelson).

Born American (1986) ◆◆◇
D: Renny Harlin. Mike Norris, Thalmus Rasulala, Steve Durham, David Coburn, Albert Salmi. 96 minutes. (Magnum)

Banned in the very Finland in which it was filmed, *Born American* stars Mike (Son of Chuck) Norris as Savoy Brown (not to be confused with the Brit blues band of the same name), one of three vacationing American party animals who, on a drunken lark, cross the border into Russki turf. There, after staging a few innocent pranks—they kill a local priest, incinerate a village, and knock off a dozen or so Russian soldiers— our boys are captured, tortured by a KGB sadist (a G. Gordon Liddy lookalike), and tossed into a correctional hellhole that makes the Gulag Archipelago resemble a Beverly Hills country club. Once inside, Mike not only gets to display some fancy kung-fu footwork but proves he's every bit the actor his old man is. The weirdest red-baiting pulp movie to surface since John Milius's madcap *Red Dawn* (see index), *Born American*—

lifting liberally and mindlessly from such diverse sources as *The Deer Hunter* (MCA) and *Mad Max Beyond Thunderdome* (see index)—achieves a brain-dead incoherence that borders on the downright surreal. Mike, meanwhile, returns for more mayhem in *Survival Game* (see index).

Born Innocent (1974) ◆◆◇
D: Donald Wrye. Linda Blair, Joanna Miles, Kim Hunter. 92 minutes. (WesternWorld)

Blair serves her first stretch in celluloid stir in a sanitized made-for-TV girls'-reformatory exposé that nonetheless earned its share of notoriety, principally for a girl-gang-rape vignette that put broomsticks on the movie-prop map. Not as compelling as Linda's later *Chained Heat* (see index).

Born Losers (1967) ◆◆◆
D: Tom Laughlin. Tom Laughlin, Elizabeth James, Jeremy Slate, Jane Russell. 112 minutes. (Vestron)

One of the best of the late-'60s/early-'70s low-budget biker flicks, director/star Laughlin introduced his high-kicking, high-hatted, high-handed Billy Jack character in a strikingly ugly look at Lowlife Americanus, further abetted by a good geekoid supporting cast.

Boxcar Bertha (1972) ◆◆◇
D: Martin Scorsese. Barbara Hershey, David Carradine, Barry Primus. 90 minutes. (Vestron)

AIP's roadshow *Bonnie and Clyde* clone gave auteur Scorsese the chance to helm his first Hollywood feature. Not among his more deathless efforts, but definitely worth a gander.

Breaker! Breaker! (1977) ◆◆
D: Don Hulette. Chuck Norris, George Murdock, Terry O'Connor. 86 minutes. (Embassy)

No, Chuck's not *that* kind of breaker; in fact, he doesn't moonwalk even once here. The title instead ties into CB lingo, and the flick finds Chuck adding a kung-fu twist to the then-popular truckers-amok genre.

Brotherhood of Death (1976) ◆◇
D: Bill Berry. Roy Jefferson, Mike Bass, Larry Jones. 85 minutes. (MPI)

Former Washington Redskins Jefferson, Bass, and Jones are three 'Nam vets who take on rampaging red-necks in a mediocre tale of southern inhospitality. It's a long wait—filled with our footballers' less-than-gripping thesping—till the climactic shoot-out.

Bruce Lee Fights Back from the Grave (1979) ◇
D: Doo Yong Lee, Bert Lenzi. Jun Chong, Deborah Chaplin, Anthony Bronson. 97 minutes. (Media)

Worst of the relentless rip-offs that desperately sought to cash in on the late Lee's name; a Lee poster flashed during the opening credits constitutes this atrociously dubbed kung-fu turkey's sole connection to Bruce.

Bulletproof (1988) ◆◆

D: Steve Carver. Gary Busey, Dar-lanne Fluegel, Henry Silva, L. Q. Jones, Thalmus Rasulala, William Smith. 92 minutes. (RCA/Columbia)

Associate-produced by the inde-fatigable Fred Olen Ray, who also receives co-story credit, *Bul-letproof* finds former rising star Busey a long way from his Buddy Holly days. The witless plot casts GB as a supercop coerced by the government into rescuing an equally super tank, the vaunted Thunderblast, from the clutches of your typical collection of inter-national terrorists encamped in the Mexican mountains (!). *Bul-letproof* may be short on gray mat-ter, but it does deliver the action goods as the flabby Busey stages the usual one-man *Rambo*esque raid on the Reds' hilly redoubt. Also on view are such familiar faces as top terrorist Silva, Jones as a captive Yank, and Big Bill Smith in a loose reprise of his *Red Dawn* Russki-officer role. If nothing else, their participation supports the venerable adage that old actors never die—they just work for Fred Olen Ray.

Bullies (1986) ◆◆◇

D: Paul Lynch. Stephen Hunter, Jon-athan Crombie, Janet Laine-Green, Dehl Berti, Olivia D'Abo. 96 minutes. (MCA)

Despite its tame title, *Bullies* is a no-nonsense stroll into second-rate *Straw Dogs* territory. The ur-ban Morris clan—teenage Matt, mom Jenny, and wimpy stepdad Clay—move to rural British Co-lumbia, where they suffer at the hands (or more accurately, at the fists) of the cruel Cullen clan—a loutish patriarch and his three sa-distic sons. When push comes to shove (to say nothing of beat, slash, torture, and rape), the Morrises fight back in a bloody climactic showdown. While thoroughly pre-dictable, *Bullies* is a solid pro job with a competent cast (we espe-cially enjoyed Berti in what used to be the Chief Dan George role of a wise old Native American neigh-bor) that supplies its fair share of gratuitous brutality and genuine suspense.

Bullitt (1968) ◆◆◆

D: Peter Yates. Steve McQueen, Jacqueline Bisset, Robert Vaughn. 113 minutes. (Warner)

Highlighted by an elaborate car chase through hilly 'Frisco, *Bul-litt* established many of the conventions—including the cyni-cal, single-minded antihero who bucks the bureaucracy to bag his prey—of the modern American *policier.*

The Bushido Blade (1979) ◆◆

D: Tom Kotani. Richard Boone, Toshiro Mifune, James Earl Jones, Sonny Chiba. 92 minutes. (HBO)

Boone meets martial-arts ace Chiba in a Samurai-saturated B-movie version (!) of Commodore

Perry's "opening" of Japan. Some fun, but more often meandering.

Caged Heat (1974) ◆◆◆

D: Jonathan Demme. Juanita Brown, Erica Gavin, Barbara Steele. 84 minutes. (Embassy)

Demme continued to pay his B-movie dues with this lively, semisatirical chicks-in-chains outing. Barbara Steele buffs will enjoy their femme fright fave's uptight turn as the wicked warden in a wheelchair.

Cannonball (1976) ◆◆◇

D: Paul Bartel. David Carradine, Bill McKinney, Veronica Hamel, Sylvester Stallone. 94 minutes. (Warner)

Essentially a retread of Bartel's earlier, wilder *Death Race 2000* (see index), sans the former flick's futuristic angle. Still a pretty fair vehicular violence romp.

Captain Kidd (1945) ◆◆◆ B&W

D: Rowland V. Lee. Charles Laughton, Randolph Scott, John Carradine, Gilbert Roland. 89 minutes. (Kartes, others)

A low-budget pirate adventure hoisted by Laughton's wonderfully sly and slimy titular portrayal, with a long-haired Scott serving as an ideal foil and Carradine sharp as one of Laughton's scurvy henchmen. Homoerotic subtexts abound. Laughton's fadeout exchange with several gallows hecklers is especially priceless.

Caribe (1988) ◆

D: Michael Kennedy. John Savage, Kara Glover, Stephen McHattie, Tommy Goff. 90 minutes. (Vestron)

The Phantom shudders to think what misbegotten deal went down to get this desiccated turkey committed to celluloid. Former rising star John (*The Deer Hunter*) Savage and ingenue Kara (*Salvador*) Glover topline as an endangered duo on the run from a gang of gun smugglers, headed by sadistic Stephen (*Call Me*) McHattie, in the pristine wilds of scenic Belize. After setting up the aforementioned chase, director Kennedy slows the action to an agonizing crawl. Mostly what we get is a leisurely Belizian travelogue. While the country in question (formerly British Honduras) looks like a nice enough place to visit, we'd much rather see it without a bad movie like *Caribe* blocking our view.

Castle of Fu Manchu (1968) ◆◇

D: Jess Franco. Christopher Lee, Richard Greene, Maria Perschy. 92 minutes. (American Videotape)

Chris Lee, as Sax Rohmer's Oriental archvillain, shows us what fiends are for in this campy Istanbul-set turkey. Greene, formerly of TV's *Robin Hood* fame, plays intrepid Scotland Yard op Nayland Smith, while Franco (mis)handles directorial chores. The Franco/Fu duo return in *Kiss and Kill* (Amvest).

Catch the Heat (1987) ◆◆
D: Joel Silberg. Tiana Alexandra, David Dukes, Rod Steiger, Brian Thompson, Jorge Martinez, John Hancock. 88 minutes. (Media)

Steiger's kung-fu debut (!) pits the portly former star against tiny Tiana Alexandra, a devastatingly fetching Amerasian martial-arts expert. Undercover agent Tiana, aided by male cohort Dukes, travels to Argentina, where she poses as a naive Chinese showgirl to infiltrate theatrical-agent-cum-drug-lord Steiger's inner org. Beyond offering a novel cast and a new wrinkle in drug-smuggling methods (in a Russ Meyeresque move, the smack is transported by unwitting femmes who think they've just had silicone implants!), *Catch the Heat* doesn't have a whole lot going for it. Unlike his relatively energetic patriarch psycho turn in *American Gothic* (see index), Rod just looks weary here, while Tiana, we're afraid, is better seen and not heard. A last-reel drug raid supplies an okay dose of action sorely missing from the flick's flabby middle.

Certain Fury (1985) ◆◆◆
D: Stephen Gyllenhaal. Irene Cara, Tatum O'Neal, Nicholas Campbell, George Murdock, Moses Gunn, and a "special appearance" by Peter Fonda. 88 minutes. (New World)

Certain Fury is a distaff urban update of *The Defiant Ones* (CBS/Fox), exploitation-style. Tracy (Cara), a well-to-do black doctor's daughter, meets Scarlet (O'Neal), an illiterate, lower-class white lass, during a typical courtroom shoot-out between a pair of shotgun-wielding femme defendants and a small army of cops. Wrongly implicated in the bloody incident (the body count's up to nine before five minutes of film's unspooled!), our heroines are forced to rely on each other to survive a series of fast-paced encounters with sewer rats, rapists, pornographers, dopers, and the ever-pursuing police. *Certain Fury* consistently delivers the sleazy goods, with high-energy bashings, slashings, and chases galore, all set to an adrenalizing rock score. Cara even briefly bares her modest upper-middle-class breasts in the pic's token gratuitous shower scene (though Tatum keeps her larger *lumpen* ones chastely concealed throughout). Add a memorable tag line—"One way or another, they'll blow you away!"—plus a "special appearance" by Peter Fonda, and who could ask for anything more?

Chained Heat (1983) ◆◆◆
D: Paul Nicolas. Linda Blair, Stella Stevens, Sybil Danning, Henry Silva, John Vernon, Tamara Dobson. 97 minutes. (Vestron)

In one of the best and sleaziest of the entire chicks-in-chains genre, Linda Blair once again learns the prison ropes the hard way. It's bolstered by a great B cast, including Danning and Silva, with Vernon as the warden who videotapes inmates in his office Jacuzzi while feeding them cocaine (!). Typical is Warden Vernon's impatient avuncular advice to a coke-injecting prisoner who's begging for a fix: "Oh, why can't you *snort* it like the rest of us?"

The Challenge (1982) ◆◆◇
D: John Frankenheimer. Scott Glenn, Toshiro Mifune, Donna Kai Benz. 112 minutes. (CBS/Fox)

Frankenheimer goes the martial-arts route with Glenn as a Yank involved in a search for sacred Japanese swords. You might want to keep your fast-forward control handy for the flick's myriad slow stretches.

Charley Varrick (1973) ◆◆◆
D: Don Siegel. Walter Matthau, Felicia Farr, Joe Don Baker. 111 minutes. (MCA)

Bank robber Matthau tries to elude sadistic mob hitman Baker (in one of his scurviest roles) in this tough modern noir directed by Clint Eastwood fave Siegel.

China Girl (1987) ◆◆◇
D: Abel Ferrara. James Russo, Sari Chang, Richard Panebianco, Russell Wong, Joey Chin, Judith Malina. 88 minutes. (Vestron)

Abel (*Ms. 45*) Ferrara's *China Girl* is a semiexploitation reworking of *West Side Story* (CBS/Fox), set to contempo blaster tunes and transplanted from Hell's Kitchen to the Little Italy/Chinatown border. The romance—or crush, anyway—that develops between teens Tony (Panebianco) and Tye (the appealing Chang) lacks the operatic, acrobatic passion that possessed the original Tony and Maria, but at least this pair gets to have sex once. More successful is Ferrara's depiction of the separate-but-equal collusion between elder Chinese and Italian crime lords, who seek to quell rebellious immigrant Su Shin (Chin) and his gang. Wong is especially effective as Tye's older brother, caught between his allegiance to China-town's criminal establishment and his wayward cousin Su. The pic ultimately and unwisely resorts to illogical plot twists and a forced tragic climax, but Ferrara managed to accomplish a lot on a low budget, and *China Girl* is well worth a look. Chinatown is also the focus of the 1986 gang-war movie *Tongs: An American Nightmare* (Academy), scripted by former TV journalist, Felipe Luciano.

The Chinese Connection (1972) ◆◆◇
D: Lo Wei. Bruce Lee, Miao Ker Hsio, James Tien. 107 minutes. (CBS/Fox)

A simple revenge plot, unfolding in exotic 1908 China, serves as an apt showcase for Lee's comic and kung-fu talents.

Chinese Godfather (1974) NR
Wu Chin, Chan Wei-Min, Pink Wu. 105 minutes. (Media)

A standard Hong Kong kung-fu yarn, but the video also contains the documentary short *The Final Days of Bruce Lee*, which is more compelling than the feature.

Chuck Norris—Karate Kommandos (1987) NR
Animated. 98 minutes. (Worldvision)

You've seen the movies—now catch the cartoon.

Circle of Iron (1978) ◆◆◇
D: Richard Moore. David Carradine, Jeff Cooper, Christopher Lee, Eli Wallach. 98 minutes. (Embassy)

Reportedly drawn from a Bruce Lee–penned story discovered after the latter's untimely demise, *Circle of Iron* is a relatively entertaining meta-martial-arts pic with an emphasis on the mystical. Philosophical kung-fu fans should enjoy. Warning: Carradine essays no fewer than *four* roles.

Class of 1984 (1982) ◆◆◆
D: Mark L. Lester. Perry King, Roddy McDowall, Merrie Lynn Ross, Timothy Van Patten, Michael Fox. 93 minutes. (Vestron)

Mark Lester's nearly peg-by-peg punk update of *The Blackboard Jungle* (NA) stars King in the Mr. Daddy-O role (originally essayed by Glenn Ford), McDowall as a cynical fellow teacher (who packs a gun in class!), Van Patten as a teen psycho with potential, and Michael Fox (so young in this one that he hadn't even grown his "J." yet) as a victimized student. While a fairly blatant rip-off, *Class* offers a decidedly different set of solutions for the teen troublemakers and rates overall as the sort of slick, sick trash entertainment sorely needed in our troubled world.

Cleopatra Jones (1973) ◆◆◆
D: Jack Starrett. Tamara Dobson, Bernie Casey, Shelley Winters. 89 minutes. (Warner)

Dobson attempted to unseat Pam Grier as then-reigning "blaxploitation" queen in busy B auteur Starrett's fun action entry. It was followed by *Cleopatra Jones and the Casino of Gold* (also Warner)—a title that preceded *Indiana Jones* (no relation) *and the Temple of Doom* by more than a decade. Former *Playboy* Playmate Jeanne Bell was the next to muscle in on the competition as the karate-chopping lead in Cirio H. Santiago's Philippines-lensed *TNT Jackson* (Charter), while chanteuse Lola Falana took a slinkier approach in the Vegas-shot *Lady Cocoa* (Unicorn).

Cobra (1986) ◆
D: George P. Cosmatos. Sylvester Stallone, Brigitte Nielsen, Reni Santoni, Brian Thompson, Andrew Robinson, Art Le Fleur. 87 minutes. (Warner)

Simian psychos, who perform mysterious displays that involve clanging axes over their heads, are knocking off random Angel City citizens, seemingly sans rhyme or reason. Local humans are helpless against them, so Cro-Magnon cop "Cobra" Cobretti (Stallone) and his equally primitive partner

Gonzalez (Santoni) are summoned to take matters firmly in paw. The pair protect endangered nature girl Nielsen and slaughter the villains in an outbreak of intense gorilla warfare. And that's about all Sly wrote: *Cobra* boasts what has to be one of the skinniest scripts to surface since the advent of talkies (or, in Sly's case, "grunties"). The rest of the flick is largely given over to multiple product plugs—including a Toys "R" You-Know-Who commercial that just happens to be playing when Cobra turns on his kitchen TV—while Cobra the character even goes so far as to advertise his own IQ, via a personalized license plate reading AWSOM 50. In yet another Sly move, the chief opposing ape-man (Thompson) not only bears a striking resemblance to BO rival Arnold Schwarzenegger but suffers from similar elocution problems. Sly and Bri's climactic confrontation—a heady debate re: American society's inefficacious judicial practices—cries out for subtitles, as do several earlier scenes involving Sly, a heavily accented Brigitte, and Santoni—who delivers most of *his* dialogue with a mouthful of junk food! Don't hold your breath for *Cobra 2*.

Cocaine Wars (1986) ◆◇
D: Hector Olivera. John Schneider, Kathryn Witt, Royal Dano, Federico Lupi, Rodolfo Ranni. 83 minutes. (Media)

This dim thriller manqué finds ex–*Duke of Hazzard* Schneider bidding to join the Stallone/Norris/Schwarzenegger One-Man Army ranks. Schneider plays Cliff, an undercover DEA cop who's posing as a dope pilot to get the goods on a South American coke kingpin. Along the way, he's attacked by crazed blow Nazis, tortured by corrupt police officials, and abetted—and of course, a-bedded—by fearless femme journalist Witt, before going one-on-one with "the World's Drug Armies." Unfortunately, all's *feh* in love *and* war in this pathetic rip-off.

The Cockfighter (1974) NR
D: Monte Hellman. Warren Oates, Millie Perkins, Harry Dean Stanton. 84 minutes. (Embassy)

An offbeat parable from Monte (*The Shooting*) Hellman, featuring a capable cast, including Hellman regular Oates as the titular killer-rooster trainer. Couchside sports fans are also referred to the obscure *Rooster: Spurs of Death!* (WesternWorld).

Code of Silence (1985) ◆◇
D: Andy Davis. Chuck Norris, Henry Silva, Molly Hagan, Bert Remsen, Joseph Guzaldo, Mike Genovese. 100 minutes. (HBO)

Chuck is maverick Windy City cop Hank Cusack, who—with the help of his police robot pal—wages a one-man war (or more accurately, a one-man, one-police-robot war) against Silva and his drug-dealing minions. Best line has Chuck informing a local hood, "When I want your opinion, I'll *beat* it out of you!" Not as good as *The French Connection*, which admittedly benefited from not having Chuck in its cast. But you have to give Chuck credit—otherwise he just may beat it out of you—for being the first of our contempo crop of screen action heroes to lay waste to Chicago, far ahead of cinematic competitors Arnold (*Raw Deal*) Schwarzenegger and Steven (*Above the Law*) Sea*gal*, who were forced to conduct what were little more than mop-up operations after Chuck's rampage.

Codename: Wild Geese (1986) ♦♦

D: Anthony M. Dawson (Antonio Margheriti). Lewis Collins, Lee Van Cleef, Mimsy Farmer, Ernest Borgnine, Klaus Kinski. 101 minutes. (New World)

The latest (and least) installment in a series that started with the quality 1978 A actioner *The Wild Geese* (CBS/Fox) and continued with the initially intriguing but ultimately dull *Wild Geese II* (HBO). *Codename: Wild Geese* features Collins in the original Richard Burton role, backed by Van Cleef, ex-ingenue Farmer, Klaus (father of Nastassia) Kinski, and the ever-popular Ernest (husband of Tova) Borgnine. Alas, bad dubbing (the East European Kinski is imaginatively looped by a Brit actor with a Sloan Ranger accent!) and lackluster direction by "Anthony M. Dawson" (real name:

Antonio Margheriti) seriously impede a predictable plot involving the Wild Geese mercenary band's assault on a Burmese opium warlord—a story line enlivened only by bursts of adequately choreographed battle scenes. On the plus side, Van Cleef acquits himself well as the mercenaries' grizzled pilot, while Borgnine, as the DEA honcho who commissions the raid, receives enough extreme close-ups to appease his legions of loyal fans.

Cold Steel (1987) ♦♦

D: Dorothy Ann Puzo. Brad Davis, Sharon Stone, Jonathan Banks, Jay Acovone, Eddie Egan, Adam Ant. 90 minutes. (RCA/Columbia)

After a pedestrian start, Dorothy Ann (daughter of Mario) Puzo's low-budget cops-and-killers thriller picks up steam and, over roughly the next hour, supplies its share of genuine suspense. Brad (*Midnight Express*) Davis is generally credible as an LAPD dick out to collar his father's slayer, while Banks (Dutch Schultz on *The Gangster Chronicles* teleseries) makes for a memorable villain as Iceman, a sadistic ex-cop who mainlines methedrine and speaks through an electronic larynx due to the gaping knife-scar in his throat. Rocker Ant is surprisingly effective as Iceman's slimey limey henchman, and Stone is both strong and sexy as the woman who walks into cop Davis's chaotic life. *Cold Steel* ultimately demolishes its own B-movie integrity via contrived plot complications, senseless character alterations, and a cheap, predictable climax. Which is too bad: with more sustained belief in itself, *Cold Steel* coulda been a contender.

Colors (1988) ◆◆◆

D: Dennis Hopper. Sean Penn, Robert Duvall, Maria Conchita Alonso, Randy Brooks, Grand Bush, Trinidad Silva. 127 minutes. (Orion)

Duval is a veteran cop with a conciliatory street style, while Penn is typecast as his hotheaded young partner in an action pic that purports to confront L.A.'s rampaging youth-gang problem but really settles for being a standard combat story. *Colors* sheds light less on the gangs than on the cops who patrol the ghettos where the turf and drug wars rage; the director-cinematographer team of Hopper and Haskell Wexler craft *Colors* so expertly that the flick is over before the viewer realizes how little's been revealed. A gratuitous, if crowd-pleasing, Sergio Leone–like shoot-out further blurs the issues, but the performances are first-rate, especially late *Hill Street Blues* regular Silva's as an ex-"gang-banger" who looks as if he's been around since Pachuco days. Look also for Jack (*Eraserhead*) Nance in an eyeblink cop cameo. The video restores seven minutes missing from the theatrical release, while the box bears the obnoxious banner "NOW WATCH IN THE SAFETY OF YOUR OWN HOME!"

Combat Shock (1986) ◆◆◇

D: Buddy Giovinazzo. Ricky Giovinazzo, Mitch Maglio, Asaph Livni, Nick Nasta, Michael Tierno. 85 minutes. (Prism)

Viet vet Frank Dunlan is *not* having a fun time of it. Not only is he jobless, about to be evicted, haunted by recurrent 'Nam nightmares, nagged by his blowsy bitter half ("You sure there's no shrapnel in your *skull?*"), and bugged by a mutant infant son right out of *Eraserhead* (see index), but he's just awakened to find the toilet's broken. All this before breakfast (stale Cocoa Puffs and sour milk!). Buddy Giovinazzo's *Combat Shock* is a relentlessly depressing, bleakly surreal, often dim and amateurish, but weirdly compelling day in Dunlan's (well played by Ricky Giovinazzo, who resembles a skid-row Henry Winkler) downtrodden life. For long stretches, nothing much happens: Frankie wanders a Staten Island hellscape that does nothing to boost that oft-benighted borough's image, encountering local hoods, junkies, and hookers while simultaneously enduring violent wartime flashbacks. The "action" doesn't heat up until the final reel, when *Combat Shock* takes a belated turn into *Taxi Driver* turf. A family affair all the way—the credits are crammed with Giovinazzos galore (star Ricky G also composed

Images the Phantom doubts he'll ever forget.
Photo courtesy of Troma, Inc.

the pic's loopy synthesizer score)—*Combat Shock* is definitely *not* corporate-culture schlock. The Phantom wasn't *entertained* exactly, but there are images in this fiercely idiosyncratic flick we doubt we'll ever forget.

Commando (1985) ◆
D: Mark L. Lester. Arnold Schwarzenegger, Rae Dawn Chong, Dan Hedaya, Vernon Wells, James Olson, Alyssa Milano, David Patrick Kelly. 90 minutes. (CBS/Fox)

In producer Joel Silver's combination comic-book-cum-video-game, Arnie unleashes his terminating powers at the expense of a gang of sadistic goons in the employ of a South American would-be dictator who wants our hero to off the present prez. These leering lowlifes commit the fatal error of snatching the muscle-bound ex-commando's young daughter (Milano). Arnie enlists the reluctant aid of foxy stewardess Chong and the chase is on, followed in swift order by whole reels of senseless slaughter (see sidebar). Unfor-

COMMANDO: A DAY IN THE DEATH

Unlike the Hollywood heroes of yore, who tended to concentrate on eliminating personalized villains who at least had speaking roles, today's action idols measure their kills in the dozens, scores, and even hundreds. At times it seems that the sole function of contempo screen foes—be they foreign terrorists and commies or homegrown gangsters and generic street scum—is to line up in vast quantities and wait to be wiped out by "heroes" wielding everything from laser-sighted machine guns to portable rocket launchers. We wonder why Sly and Arnie even bother working on their lavish lats, pumped-up pecs, and super 'ceps when, for our modern movie macho man, the only body that really counts is the body count.

The Phantom, surrendering to morbid curiosity (one of our favorite activities), freeze-framed his way through one such slaughterfest, *Commando,* to record Arnie's exact kill quota. To qualify as a Confirmed Kill, Arn's victim had to be hit directly by a lethal weapon or shown to be absolutely, positively kaput. Those merely belted, kicked, or karate-chopped and left in an ambiguous physical condition do not count here. We also list the primary weapons employed and the injuries sustained by our hero. Let's go to the videotape:

Time Log

1:36 Villains claim first victim.

4:00 First extreme close-up of Arnie's lats and 'ceps.

13:35 Arnie claims *his* first victim, machine-gunning an enemy messenger.

20:20 Arnie coughs up his first quip: "I like you, Solly, so I'm going to kill you last."

22:00 Arnie breaks bad guy's neck.

29:15 Arn rips out Rae Dawn Chong's seat.

35:00 Arn punches out several mall security guards and a phone booth.

37:25 Arn is hit by a car, lands on his head. No apparent damage.

41:00 Arn throws Solly from the cliff.

45:10 Arn is kicked in the head. No apparent damage.

46:30 Arn impales bad guy Bill Duke on furniture leg.

51:20 Arn karate-chops an airport sentry—fails to qualify as a confirmed kill.

54:00 Arn drives a bus through a gun-store window to facilitate some last-minute shopping.

57:05 Rae Dawn does her bit by destroying an innocent building and a police van with a four-barreled rocket launcher borrowed from Arn.

59:05 Arn busts another sentry upside the head. Kill unconfirmed.

60:30 Arn takes out two bad guys with a machine gun. Kills confirmed.

Intermission: The Phantom, taking a break, threatens his VCR with a sound thrashing. Appliance in question seems unimpressed.

67:00 Back to the couch as Arn dresses to kill in now-famous butch fashion montage.

69:45–

78:00 Arn gets serious, launches one-man assault, employing knives, machine guns, grenades, axes, and a pitchfork in claiming seventy-eight—count 'em yourself—*seventy-eight* additional victims over the next eight minutes.

79:00 Grenade blows up in Arn's face. No apparent damage.

80:00 Arn wounded below right shoulder—the same spot he gets shot in in almost every film

84:00 Arn receives severe beating before pummeling, electrocuting, and finally impaling his final foe.

Total Confirmed Kills: 92

Total Running Time: 90 minutes

tunately, all the essential ingredients that helped make *The Terminator* one of the best B movies of all time turn sour here. Arnie unwisely switches from a killer cyborg—a role he was built to play—to a run-of-the-mill superman who only *emotes* like a robot, which is akin to casting King Kong as James Bond. Through it all, no matter how many hapless mortals are thrown against him, Arnie comes off as a witless bully and the movie as a terminal bore.

Commando Squad (1987) ♦

D: Fred Olen Ray. William Smith, Kathy Shower, Brian Thompson, Sid Haig, Robert Quarry, Marie Windsor. 90 minutes. (TWE)

LAPD supercop Cat (ex-Playmate Shower), an unusually disingenuous heroine, slips into Mexico to rescue partner Thompson (the Schwarzenegger clone Stallone stomped in *Cobra*) from the clutches of drug magnate Smith. Aside from some creative casting—vets Sid (*Spider Baby*) Haig and Robert (*Count Yorga*) Quarry are aboard, while Marie (*Catwomen of the Moon*) Windsor cameos as an undercover weapons expert—*Commando Squad* plays like a weak *Extreme Prejudice* rip-off (see index), with none of the original's instinct for mindless fun. If one could accuse poverty-row auteur Ray of making a *serious* misstep, *Commando Squad* would be it.

The Concrete Jungle (1982) ♦♦◇

D: Tom DeSimone. Tracy Bregman, Peter Brown, Jill St. John. 99 minutes. (RCA/Columbia)

While it's not too big on originality, *The Concrete Jungle* delivers the expected thrills that chicks-in-chains devotees have come to know and love.

Cool Hand Luke (1967) ♦♦♦◇

D: Stuart Rosenberg. Paul Newman, George Kennedy, Strother Martin. 127 minutes. (Warner)

One of the last great *guys*-in-chains flicks, with rebel-without-a-pause Newman resisting oily warden Martin's (in the best role of his distinguished career) indefatigable efforts to break his will.

Crazy Mama (1975) ♦♦◇

D: Jonathan Demme. Cloris Leachman, Stuart Whitman, Ann Sothern. 82 minutes. (Embassy)

Another of Demme's popular pre-mainstream efforts, with Leachman enjoying a crime binge while our icon-minded auteur tours the '50s trash-culture 'scape.

The Crimson Pirate (1952) ♦♦♦

D: Robert Siodmak. Burt Lancaster, Eva Bartok, Nick Cravat, Christopher Lee. 104 minutes. (Warner)

A swift, tongue-in-cheek swashbuckler with Burt at his acrobatic best and Chris Lee in a supporting role.

Cruising (1980) NR
D: William Friedkin. Al Pacino, Paul Sorvino, Karen Allen. 106 minutes. (CBS/Fox)

Friedkin's *Cruising* stirred controversy during its initial release for exploiting/misrepresenting gay life-styles as undercover cop Pacino infiltrates NYC's rough-trade bars in search of a homophobic killer. Now you can watch in the safety of your own closet.

Cyclone (1987) ◆◇
D: Fred Olen Ray. Heather Thomas, Jeffrey Combs, Dar Robinson, Martin Landau, Martine Beswicke, Troy Donahue, Huntz Hall. 89 minutes. (RCA/Columbia)

Busy B auteur Ray again assembles an awesome cast: Landau, Quarry, former Hammer horror queen Martine Beswicke, Russ (*West Side Story, Satan's Sadists*) Tamblyn, Donahue, and last—but certainly not least—erstwhile Bowery Boy Huntz Hall. That Fred manages to waste such proven talent on an anemic tale about a sub-Bondian assault motorcycle (boasting the "firepower of an F-16") and its blond bimbo rider (Thomas) surely ranks as one of the great celluloid tragedies of our time. For Huntz Hall completists only.

Danger Zone (1987) ◆◆◇
D: Harry Vernon. Jason Williams, Robert Canada, Susanne Tara, Dana Dowell, Cynthia Gray, Daniel Friedman. 90 minutes. (Charter)

Biker-flick fans hard up for new product should get a bang out of *Danger Zone*, a hog-wild affair produced and co-scripted by Jason (*Flesh Gordon*) Williams, who also costars as an undercover narc who infiltrates a gang of coke-dealing Harley hounds headed by The Reaper (Canada, who rules with convincing menace). Six starstruck bimbettes on their way to a Vegas talent show suffer the misfortune of having their car break down near the bad guys' desert hideaway, and you can more or less fill in the blanks from there. While not startlingly original, *Danger Zone* is a taut, tense, and tough entry in the Six-Pack Cinema Sweepstakes.

Date Bait (1959) ◆◆ B&W
D: O'Dale Ireland. Gary Clarke, Marlo Ryan. 71 minutes. (Madhouse)

Gary Clarke—who played the Teen Werewolf in *How to Make a Monster* (NA) after original adolescent lycanthrope Michael Landon had moved on—refuses to let narrow-minded parents and meddling local hoods interfere with his teenage wedding plans. Originally shared a double bill with the slightly better *T-Bird Gang* (NA). Listen for the toe-tapping ditty "Purple Pleated Bermudas." For hard-core '50s JD fans. Auteur Ireland also directed *High School Caesar* (see index).

Day of the Cobra (1984) ◆◆◇
D: Enzo G. Castellari. Sybil Danning,

Franco Nero, Mario Maranzana. 95 minutes. (Media)

Danning plays femme fatale to Nero's disgraced sleuth in one of the B-screen queen's livelier Europe-lensed outings. Other Sybil D ventures not covered elsewhere in this volume include: *Cat in a Cage* (Genesis), *Nightkill* (Embassy), *Private Passions* (Prism), *The Salamander* (Charter), *Seven Magnificent Gladiators* (MGM/UA), and *They're Playing With Fire* (HBO).

The Dead Pool (1988) ◆◆◆

D: Buddy Van Horn. Clint Eastwood, Patricia Clarkson, Liam Neeson, Evan Kim. 91 minutes. (Warner)

Eastwood makes a smooth transition from mayor to slayer in *The Dead Pool*, his first Dirty Harry entry since 1983's *Sudden Impact* (Warner). The pic, light on elaborate car crashes and spectacular stunts, actually plays like a lively B movie (and we mean that in the most positive sense), even down to its choice of milieu—one near and dear to yours truly's heart: the horror/sleaze flick scene. When random celebs whose names appear on a morbid betting list start turning up dead, suspicion points to the list's owner, slice-and-dice director Peter Swann (Neeson), currently shooting a head-banger horror called *Hotel Satan*. (Clips from *Time After Time*, *Cujo*, and *It's Alive III* fill in as samples of Swann's fictional oeuvre.) While Clint seems a tad weary at times,

The Dead Pool itself is an energetic enough action outing. Unique highlights include the butchering of a contrary movie critic who'd panned Swann's sicko flicks (quips Clint's partner Evan Kim, "On a scale of one to ten, I'd give it an eight.") and a *Bullitt*-type chase parody that finds big Clint speeding from a foot-long remote-controlled model Corvette rigged with deadly explosives (!). Though slower on the draw than in days of yore, Clint still manages—with the aid of his trusty Magnum and a barely related subplot—to run up a decent body count.

Deadly Illusion (1987) ◆◆◇

D: Larry Cohen, William Tannen. Billy Dee Williams, Vanity, Morgan Fairchild, John Beck, Joe Cortese, Joe Spinell. 90 minutes. (RCA/Columbia)

Any flick that opens with a shootout on a gun-permit line (!) can't be all bad, and *Deadly Illusion* certainly isn't. While not one of maverick auteur Cohen's best efforts, *Deadly* is a cleverly plotted low-budget urban actioner, with Williams at once suave and earthy as the embattled Hamberger, an unlicensed private eye on the trail of fashion-model-turned-mogul Fairchild, who's actually fronting for an elite corporate drug syndicate. In addition to concocting a literate script, Cohen makes extensive if inexpensive use of such exotic Gotham locales as the Rockefeller Center ice-skating rink (great place for a chase) and even the Mets' dugout at Shea Stadium, site of the pic's climactic gun battle. The cut corners occasionally intrude on the action, but *Deadly Illusion* delivers enough entertainment to make it a worthwhile rental item. Joe (*Maniac*) Spinell puts in a neat cameo as a (what else?) maniac, and Vanity looks *great* in leather as Billy Dee's partner/main squeeze.

Deadly Prey (1987) ◆

D: David A. Prior. Troy Donahue, Cameron Mitchell, Ted Prior, Fritz Matthews, David Campbell, Dawn Abraham. 87 minutes. (Sony)

From David Winters's Action International Pictures comes *Deadly Prey*, yet another updated grade-Z *Most Dangerous Game* rehash. Mercenaries-in-training stalk and kill innocent prey abducted from the streets of nearby L.A. Villainous camp commander Colonel Hogan (Campbell) knows he's in for big trubs when his former ace 'Nam killing machine (wooden Stallone clone Prior) turns up as a proposed target and quickly turns the tables on the hunters. Former heartthrob Donahue cameos as the corrupt businessman funding the murderous mercenaries, while the ever-busy Mitchell puts in a lengthier stint as an ex-cop on the bad guys' trail. In the pic's most original scene, Prior hacks off a mercenary's arm and beats him to death with it (!). And as you

probably know, even *that* sequence was earlier executed in Ron Ormond's seminal *The Monster and the Stripper* (see index).

Death Before Dishonor (1987) ◆◆

D: Terry J. Leonard. Fred Dryer, Brian Keith, Joanna Pacula, Paul Winfield, Kasey Walker, Rockne Tarkington. 95 minutes. (New World)

This professionally rendered—it may well be the best 1943 war movie made in 1987—but thoroughly muscle-headed flick stars TV stalwart and former pigskin warrior Dryer as macho Marine Sergeant Jack ("Don't Get Us Mad!") Burns. When Jack's CO (Keith) is kidnapped by crazed terrorists in the mythical Middle Eastern nation of Jemali, Fred and a pair of equally gung-ho fellow grunts waste no time in swinging into action. There's plenty of the last-mentioned on view in this cynical flag-waver, and it's unwaveringly well staged. But the best moment unfolds between Keith and his driver, when the latter divulges, "My grandfather always said that the eyes are the mirror to the soul." Grunts Keith, "What's *that* supposed to mean?"

Death Wish (1974) ◆◆

D: Michael Winner. Charles Bronson, Vincent Gardenia, Hope Lange. 94 minutes. (Paramount)

This trend-setting trash epic inspired a wave of violent vigilante movies of which we've yet to witness the last. Architect Paul Kersey (Bronson) goes kill-crazy after his wife is slain and his daughter raped by a trio of Gotham goons (including a young Jeff Goldblum, playing against type). When the cops and courts prove predictably useless, CB takes matters into his own lethal hands, declaring a one-citizen war on NYC's street scum. Still foremost in the field it contrived, especially when compared with its own weak sequels.

Death Wish 2 (1982) ◆

D: Michael Winner. Charles Bronson, Jill Ireland, Vincent Gardenia. 89 minutes. (Warner)

Chuck takes his vigilante act to L.A. in the first of *Death Wish*'s belated follow-ups—and probably the most feeble, lacking both the marginal originality of the first and the over-the-top excesses of *3* and *4*.

Death Wish 3 (1985) ◆◇

D: Michael Winner. Charles Bronson, Martin Balsam, Deborah Raffin, Gavan O'Herlihy, Ed Lauter, Kirk Taylor. 94 minutes. (MGM/UA)

Seems that "the element" is at it again. A pack of wild street animals—a multiethnic mix of savage punks, bearded bikers, ghetto warriors, and leather-bar refugees who could coexist only in a hack screenwriter's addled imagination—bumps off an elderly pal of free-lance vigilante Paul ("Have Grenade Launcher, Will Travel") Kersey. And what do our impotent police do about it?

Why, they promptly bust Bronson (who wasn't doin' nothin'), then lovingly violate his civil rights! On top of *that* inhospitable display, they toss him in the hoosegow with gang leader O'Herlihy, who promises Chuck he'll "kill a little old lady just for you!" So once again Bronson is forced to chuck his "No More Mr. Vigilante" vow and dispense the only kind of justice these street scum understand—i.e., wholesale slaughter. *Death Wish 3* proceeds sans the relative subtleties of its predecessors, as our aged hero wastes little time in wasting the opposition and rallying the crime-infested nabe's besieged citizenry to his cause. "Look, Eli," exclaims one superannuated neighbor to her equally elderly spouse, "Mr. Kersey just shot some of the creeps!" And as the song puts it, he's only just begun.

Death Wish 4: The Crackdown (1987) ◆◇

D: J. Lee Thompson. Charles Bronson, Kay Lenz, John P. Ryan, Perry Lopez, Soon Teck-Oh, George Dickerson, Irwin Keyes. 100 minutes. (Media)

This time around, Chuck (with more than a little help from his stunt double J. P. Romano) tackles not one but three L.A. crack syndicates, including the bunch responsible for the demise of his latest disposable surrogate daughter, the offspring of girlfriend Lenz. With its brain-damaged dialogue and rampant illogic—flagrant enough to insult not only hard-core Bronson buffs' but even yours truly's intelligence—the flick plays like a kind of *Death Wish Meets Cocaine Fiends*. While there's abrupt and senseless violence galore, many of the action scenes are shoddily staged—particularly a climactic roller-rink slaughterfest. On the plus side, Chuck's more laconic than ever here, limiting his motivation to a lone line ("It's those damn drugs!") and behaving more indiscriminately than ever in his one-man crusade against helpless criminals. C'mon, CB, pick on someone your own age, why doncha!?

The Delta Force (1986) ◆◆◇
D: Menahem Golan. Chuck Norris, Lee Marvin, Robert Forster, George Kennedy, Shelley Winters, Joey Bishop, Hanna Schygulla, Bo Svenson. 125 minutes. (Media)

A revisionist exploitation-fantasy version of an actual Middle Eastern skyjacking incident, *Delta Force* supplies swift, tense cheap entertainment for its first eighty or so minutes. Terrorist Forster (excellent in a rare villainous role) and his Arab minions menace a planeload of celluloid has-beens— Kennedy, Martin Balsam, Susan Strasberg, Joey Bishop, Lainie Kazan and Shelley Winters (in a brief but patentedly hysterical cameo)—while the titular commando team, headed by Marvin and Norris, prepare for an eventual assault. The flick abruptly crashes,

however, when Chuck wrests control of the final two reels. With the aid of his trusty rocket-armed motorcycle, he doles out his trademark brand of bland justice and destroys not only scores of ragheaded extras but all traces of what slender credibility *Delta Force* has, to this point, possessed. The pic *is* far superior to the intended rip-off *Delta Force Commandos* (Vista), though, wherein Fred ("The Hammer") Williamson nearly single-handedly topples the entire Sandinista government (!) in a violent hostage-rescue mission.

The Destructors (1974) ◆◆◆
D: Robert Parrish. James Mason, Anthony Quinn, Michael Caine. 89 minutes. (Vestron)

A pretty obscure action item, considering the stellar thesps, with Mason cast against type as an international drug kingpin; Quinn is the agent out to nail him, while Caine steals the flick as a slick hitman. Not to be confused with the 1968 Richard Egan B flick (Magnum) of the same name.

Detroit 9000 (1973) ◆◆
D: Arthur Marks. Hari Rhodes, Alex Rocco, Vonetta McGee. 106 minutes. (HBO)

The titular city tries to live up to its Murder Capital of the World moniker in this crudely lensed, relentlessly violent cops-and-killers caper.

Dick Tracy, Detective (1945) NR B&W
D: William Berke. Morgan Conway,

Anne Jeffreys, Mike Mazurki. 62 minutes. (Sinister Cinema, others)

First of a quartet of '40s programmers based on Chet Gould's famous comic-strip shamus. Conway plays the master sleuth here and in *Dick Tracy Versus Cueball*; Tracy lookalike Ralph Byrd, who starred in the DT serials, takes over in *Dick Tracy's Dilemma* and *Dick Tracy Meets Gruesome* (with Boris Karloff as the villainous Mr. G), also available from Sinister Cinema and other public-domain specialists.

Die Hard (1988) ◆◆◆

D: John McTiernan. Bruce Willis, Alan Rickman, Alexander Gudonov, Bonnie Bedelia, Reginald Veljohnson, James Shigeta, Robert Davi. 132 minutes. (CBS/Fox)

While dubious '80s icon Bruce Willis's painful Mickey-Rourke-meets-Clint-Eastwood act represents a serious detriment, and producer Joel Silver's Beverly Hills brand of anarchy grows more irritating with each passing pic, *Die Hard* remains an action outing that amply delivers the pulse-pounding goods. The film further benefits from a band of memorable villains led by Rickman and some patented Irwin Allen–type disaster-movie moves as said bad guys, with a big assist from Bruce and some fatally meddlesome FBI fumblers, lay lavish waste to a forty-story L.A. office building. The Phantom found that lowering the volume during Bruce's soliloquies aided his enjoyment immensely.

Dillinger (1973) ◆◆◆

D: John Milius. Warren Oates, Ben Johnson, Cloris Leachman, Richard Dreyfuss, Harry Dean Stanton. 106 minutes. (Vestron)

Packed with vivid gunplay, this is the best and bloodiest of Hollywood's many Dillinger bios. Oates is especially convincing as the erstwhile Public Enemy Numero Uno, while Dreyfuss makes for an obnoxious Baby Face Nelson and Johnson and Leachman turn in solid work as G-man Melvin Purvis and the infamous Lady in Red, respectively. Stanton, as gang member Homer Van Meter, gets the best death scene here. The original 1945 William Castle-scripted *Dillinger*, which launched screen tough-guy Lawrence Tierney in the title role, is also available (CBS/Fox).

The Dirty Dozen (1967) ◆◆◇

D: Robert Aldrich. Lee Marvin, Telly Savalas, Charles Bronson, John Cassavetes, George Kennedy, Jim Brown. 151 minutes. (MGM/UA)

One of the sleaziest war flicks ever—a combat film for an anti-war age. Of the titular twelve, Telly steals the show as an out-of-control psycho. They're still cranking out variations on this one, including a couple of official (and lame) made-for-TV sequels.

Dirty Harry (1971) ◆◆◆

D: Don Siegel. Clint Eastwood, Harry

Guardino, Reni Santoni. 102 minutes. (Warner)

Clint transplants his Man With No Name character to modern-day 'Frisco, names him Dirty Harry, and starts a celluloid kick-ass-cop craze. The original—the series' best—finds him in lethal pursuit of psycho Andrew Robinson (who later played Liberace in the made-for-TV bio). Harry returns in *The Enforcer, Magnum Force,* and *Sudden Impact* (all also Warner), while Clint essayed similar tough-cop roles in *City Heat* (Warner), *Coogan's Bluff* (MCA), and *The Gauntlet* (Warner).

Dirty Mary Crazy Larry (1974) NR
D: John Hough. Peter Fonda, Susan George, Adam Roarke. 93 minutes. (CBS/Fox)

Nonstop chase action's the name of the game as wild drivers Fonda, Roarke, and George seek to elude lawmen after perpetrating an ill-advised heist. Believe it or not, this B romp ranked among the top BO grossers of 1974. The long-with-drawn video's a rarity, though.

The Dogs of War (1980) ◆◆◆
D: John Irvin. Christopher Walken, Tom Berenger, Colin Blakely. 102 minutes. (MGM/UA)

One of the best mainstream mercenary movies ever made, ranking right up there with the original *Wild Geese.* Walken is first-rate as the battered soldier of fortune hired to help overthrow an African dictatorship.

Dragnet (1954) ◆◆◇
D: Jack Webb. Jack Webb, Ben Alexander, Richard Boone, Stacy Harris. 71 minutes. (MCA)

LAPD officers Friday and Smith jump from TV to the big screen, in living color (make that living colorlessness), in a typically iconic tribute to the virtues of law and order. Makes a good warm-up for the Aykroyd/Hanks spoof.

Drums (1938) ◆◆◆
D: Zoltan Korda. Sabu, Raymond Massey, Roger Livesey. 99 minutes. (Embassy)

Sabu comes to the rescue of Brit troops endangered by power-crazed vizier Massey in ZK's Technicolor adventure classic. Not to be confused with 1976's singular *Drum* (Vestron), sequel to the popular antebellum sleaze soaper *Mandingo* (Paramount).

Dynasty: 3-D Martial Arts Movie NR
Bobby Ming. (Best Film & Video)

If you've a yen to see furious fists and flying feet comin' at you in 3-D, look no further than *Dynasty*, which comes complete with glasses. You may have to look *hard*, though, for this video rarity.

Electra Glide in Blue (1973) ◆◆◆◇
D: James William Guercio. Robert Blake, Billy "Green" Bush, Mitchell Ryan, Jeannine Riley, Elisha Cook, Jr., Royal Dano. 114 minutes. (MGM/UA)

Though less than a blockbuster during its initial release, Guercio's visually inventive karmic cop adventure has since acquired a cult rep that should only widen with its belated (1988) video release. Blake is a stunted Arizona cycle trooper who hankers to be a plainclothes dick, the better to tap his ratiocinative powers. A suicide-masked murder gives him his chance, but he learns the hard lesson that, in this life, ability often plays second fiddle to (in this case sexual) politics. Guercio's circular chain-of-pain plot is as effective as his ace directorial eye, even if said plot's cyclical imperative leads to what some view as a contrived climax. *Electra Glide in Blue* is a film that doesn't easily fade from memory—reason aplenty to place it among the celluloid elite.

The Emerald Forest (1985) ◆◆◆◇

D: John Boorman. Powers Boothe, Meg Foster, Charley Boorman. 113 minutes. (Embassy)

Boorman's adventure about a white youth (real-life son Charley) raised by South American Indians blends all the necessary ingredients—exoticism, cultural clashes, violence, and mysticism—that make for topflight cinematic escapism.

Enemy Territory (1987) ◆◆◇

D: Peter Manoogian. Gary Frank, Ray Parker, Jr., Stacey Dash, Jan-Michael Vincent, Frances Foster, Tony Todd. 89 minutes. (CBS/Fox)

A sort of ghetto *Rio Bravo* by way of *The Warriors*, *Enemy Territory*

features Frank as a struggling insurance agent sent by his sadistic boss to finalize a policy in an NYC housing project so perilous that "even the window-washers wear bulletproof vests." Frank inadvertently incurs the wrath of The Count (played by thesp Todd in a black Michael Berryman mode), leader of the violent Vampires street gang. Thereafter, Frank is forced to battle his way out of the building with the aid of phone company rep Ray (*Ghostbusters*) Parker, Jr., shapely concerned tenant Dash (in an ersatz Rae Dawn Chong role), and paranoid, wheelchair-bound Vietnam vet Vincent, who's converted his besieged apartment into an armed bunker. *Enemy Territory* is a thoroughly trashy, consistently tense urban thriller featuring able performances by Parker, Frank, and Frances Foster as Mrs. Briggs, a tough elderly policyholder who demonstrates she can also wield a pretty mean machine gun. The pic even rises above its formulaic antics on occasion with bits of sly wit and moments that are—well, almost *human*. We recommend it anyway.

Enter the Dragon (1973) ◆◆◇

D: Robert Clouse. Bruce Lee, John Saxon, Jim Kelly. 99 minutes. (Warner)

Action-film heavyweights Saxon, Kelly, and Lee gather for an elaborate martial-arts tournament in a popular chopsocky saga that—sadly—turned out to be Lee's last complete feature, though he continued to appear posthumously in any number of kung-fu rip-offs built around surviving footage.

Escape from Alcatraz (1979) ◆◆◆
D: Don Siegel. Clint Eastwood, Patrick McGoohan, Roberts Blossom. 112 minutes. (Paramount)

Clint toplines as a con bent on busting out of the seemingly escape-proof title facility in an essentially old-fashioned but suspenseful rehash of the once-popular male-jailbreak genre.

The Exterminator (1980) ◆◆
D: James Glickenhaus. Christopher George, Robert Ginty, Samantha Eggar. 101 minutes. (Embassy)

A 'Nam-vet variation on *Death Wish*, *The Exterminator* proved wildly successful at the B box office and launched both Ginty's and Glickenhaus's action-movie careers. Ginty returns, accompanied by his trusty flamethrower, in *Exterminator II* (MGM/UA).

Extreme Prejudice (1987) ◆◆◆
D: Walter Hill. Nick Nolte, Powers Boothe, Maria Conchita Alonso, Rip Torn, Clancy Brown, Michael Ironside. 104 minutes. (IVE)

Hill's *Extreme Prejudice* rates as a fun bad movie of the first rank. Based on a story co-concocted by John (*Red Dawn*) Milius, this manic updated pulp western moves at a frenetic pace, features mucho macho violence (capped by an extravagant *Wild Bunch*-style finale), and offers some of the choicest dumb dialogue on record (to say nothing of videotape). An ace cast, headed by Nolte and supported by the always-arresting Torn, brings the absurdist proceedings to admirably deadpan life. Well worth the price of an overnight rental.

Eye of the Tiger (1986) ◆◆◇
D: Richard Sarafian. Gary Busey, Yaphet Kotto, William Smith, Seymour Cassel, Bert Remsen, Kimberlin Ann Brown, Denise Galik. 90 minutes. (IVE)

In *Eye of the Tiger*, the flick that kicked off former legit thesp Busey's B-movie career, Gar stars as 'Nam vet and ex-con Buck Matthews, who returns to his corrupt southwestern town to tangle with a horde of uniformed Harley-hellions-cum-crack-manufacturers led by veteran heavy Smith (sporting a butch moustache and shaved head in his role as the World's Oldest Living Biker). When Buck rescues a potential rape victim, the bad guys retaliate by wrecking his house and killing his wife. With resourceful ex-army buddy Yaphet (*Alien*) Kotto on his side, Buck mounts a climactic assault on the bikers' desert redoubt, driving his customized cannon-equipped RV while Kotto drops grenades from his flame-red biplane as James Brown wails from his onboard blaster (!). Though laced with lame lines and countless lapses in logic, *Eye of the Tiger* careens along at a fairly brisk pace and offers a number of imaginatively sicko touches—as when Buck employs steel wire to decapitate several enemy bikers, and their cronies retaliate by digging up his late wife and depositing her coffin on his doorstep. What *will* they think of next? Stay tuned!

Fatal Beauty (1987) ◆
D: Tom Holland. Whoopi Goldberg, Sam Elliott, Ruben Blades, Harris Yulin, John P. Ryan, Brad Dourif. 104 minutes. (MGM/UA)

There's no disputing the fact that we're living in dangerous times. How dangerous are they? So dangerous that even a majority of our *comedians* are packing heat onscreen. Ever since Eddie Murphy raked it in as a funky, wisecracking, fast-drawing fuzz in *Beverly Hills Cop I* and *II* (Paramount), we've seen the likes of Joe Piscopo in *Dead Heat* (New World), Bruce Willis (*Die Hard*), and Billy Crystal (*Running Scared*) take up arms. This violent "high concept" reaches its nadir with *Fatal Beauty*, a sort of *Whoopi Got Her Gun* that not only arms the former monologist but awards her the personality of a Dirty Harry and the vocabulary of a Times Square pimp. (Can an Uzi-wielding Spalding Gray be far behind?) Beyond its killer-comic conceit, *Fatal Beauty* is an aggressively unwatchable affair that tries to hide its relentless cynicism behind a trendy "anti-drug" facade and that even lacks the guts to consummate black cop Whoopi and white bodyguard Elliott's onscreen affair. (Unless this, too, is another attempt at altruism, in the form of a "safe sex" message.) In sum, this is one of many '80s movies that future videophiles will be watching solely for its low-camp value. Whoopi, meanwhile, failed to make amends with her next venture, the ill-advised nonstop yakathon *The Telephone* (New World).

Fear City (1985) ◆◇
D: Abel Ferrara. Billy Dee Williams, Tom Berenger, Melanie Griffith, Jack Scalia, Rae Dawn Chong, Rossano Brazzi, Jan Murray. 93 minutes. (HBO)

On the spiked heels of *Ms. 45* (see index), Abel Ferrara's funky distaff *Death Wish*, comes the same director's debut Hollywood feature, *Fear City*. Pals Matty (Berenger) and Nicky (Scalia) manage the mob-owned Starlite Talent Agency, suppliers of fine, quality exotic dancers to nearby Times Square strip joints. When the New York Knifer—a moralistic maniac who records his punitive *pensées* in a diary entitled Fear City—starts slashing their foxy clients, ex-boxer Berenger assigns himself the task of bringing the blade-wielding wacko to swift street justice. Though blessed with a bigger budget, *Fear City* lacks the kinetic punch of Ferrara's previous outing, spinning its rather routine tale of retribution at a pace too languid to compensate for its thin characterizations and slender story line. For the record, top-billed Billy Dee Williams puts in only sporadic appearances here, though his personal hair stylist receives a well-deserved screen credit.

Fighting Back (1982) ◆◆◇
D: Lewis Teague. Tom Skerritt, Patti LuPone, Michael Sarrazin. 96 minutes. (Paramount)

Reliable character thesp Skerritt goes the *Death Wish* route in one of that urban paranoia pioneer's better imitations.

First Blood (1982) ◆◇
D: Ted Kotcheff. Sylvester Stallone, Brian Dennehy, Richard Crenna. 96 minutes. (HBO)

Of historic note as the film that introduced the most influential (if least coherent) macho icon of the Fightin' '80s, the one and only Rambo, a Billy Jack with machine guns and 'ceps.

Fists of Fury (1973) ◆◆◆
D: Lo Wei. Bruce Lee, Maria Yi, James Tien. 103 minutes. (CBS/Fox)

One of Bruce's authentic early Hong Kong–lensed kung-fu fests, with the accent on action. See also *Fists of Fury II* (Video Gems).

The Four Feathers (1939) ◆◆◆
D: Zoltan Korda. Ralph Richardson, John Clements, June Duprez. 115 minutes. (Embassy)

Another Korda adventure classic, with Richardson as the accused coward who must prove himself in the Sudan. Packed with sweeping battle scenes lensed in vivid Technicolor.

Foxtrap (1986) ◆
D: Fred Williamson. Fred Williamson, Chris Connelly, Arlene Golonka, Donna Owen, Beatrice Palme, Cleo Sebastian. 89 minutes. (Vestron)

Fred ("The Hammer") Williamson stars as free-lance enforcer Tom Fox ("He takes the jobs nobody wants . . . and gets the results nobody expects!"). We know Fox is a hardcase whose rep precedes when two teens attempting to steal his unattended car are scared off by the mere sight of his foreboding license plate, reading simply but eloquently, DA FOX (!). Nothing if not a one-man show, *Foxtrap*'s typo-plagued credits note that the flick is "directed, produced an [sic] from a story" by Fred. The nonaction kicks off in L.A., where Fred is hired by rich white sleazeball Connelly—we know he's a lowlife because he guzzles Colt 45 from a can while Fred delicately sips Drambuie from a glass—to find his "missing daughter." Fred next turns up in Cannes (see sidebar for the inside story), where between frequent sartorial changes—the pic's primarily an 89-minute showcase for Fred's admittedly extensive wardrobe—he hands out plugs for other, better films, from *Mishima* to *The Purple Rose of Cairo*. After a brief detour to Rome for another Drambuie, Fred heads back to L.A., where he unveils the last of his threads and dispatches a small army of malefactors without so much as wrinkling them (his threads, not the malefactors).

We recommend *Foxtrap* for diehard Fred fanatics and *GQ* subscribers only.

CANNES CONFIDENTIAL!: POWER BROKERING ON POVERTY ROW

Sawdust Memories by the Phantom of the Movies with the Phantomess

"Who let all these people in? Champagne costs money!"

Cannon Group exec, *American Ninja 2* champagne press conference, Cannes '87

CANNES 1987—It was a scene that surpassed even the gala Hollywood premieres of yore. The wide front steps of the elegant Palais du Festival were filled with black-tied gents and begowned gals. Kliegs splashed the sweeping stairway and its expectant occupants with blinding light. The palais's alfresco sound system trumpeted the strains of Richard Strauss's *Also Sprach Zarathustra,* popularized by Stanley Kubrick's *2001.* Tourists on extended May 8th Liberation Day Weekend jaunts and celebrity seekers—seemingly sprung from the pages of Nathanael West's *The Day of the Locust*—competed with hyper paparazzi for choice sight lines behind barricades guarded by white-gloved gendarmes.

The occasion? Damned if we knew. A festival awards ceremony, perhaps, or a star-packed screening of Paul Newman's *The Glass Menagerie,* or maybe another of the '87 film fest's many fortieth-anniversary celebrations. We couldn't get close enough to tell, and after a while, it didn't really matter. The above scene was pretty much a nightly occurrence—business as usual among the festival swells.

Contrasting with the stylized pomp and circumstances under way at the palais was the American Film Market Association action unfolding in the hotel suites, party rooms, and beach-front bistros where the *real* business of Cannes gets done. For years, the market has shared Cannes with the prestigious international film festival, even though it's traditionally received a fraction of the media attention routinely lavished upon the celeb-studded fest. But this is where the reel deals go down, largely among low-budget action/horror/sleaze movie moguls peddling foreign, theatrical, and video rights to product-hungry, bargain-minded exhibitors from around the globe.

During the day, said moguls rent Cannes's four downtown theaters—scattered along the narrow rue d'Antibes, one block north of the oceanfront La Croisette—using the combined twenty-two screens to air their wares for the benefit of checkbook-bearing buyers from such far-flung locales as Sweden, Zimbabwe, and Japan. From 9:30 A.M. to roughly 8 at night, the Star Cinema, Les Ambassades, and the Olympia 9 (which admittedly sounds more Canarsie than Cannes) host nonstop screenings (well over one hundred per day) of such genre outings as Arista's *Slaughterhouse Rock,* Troma's *Blood Hook,* Reel Movies's *Angel of Vengeance,* Manson International's *The Video Dead,* the PKG Group's *Escape From Miami* ("They Owned Miami. They Claimed Orlando!"), and their low-budget like. The ubiquitous Cannon Group, headed by embattled but colorful Israeli moguls Menahem Golan and Yoran Globus, had some forty-seven films on view, running the gamut from the critically acclaimed festival entry *Shy People,* with Jill Clayburgh and Barbara Hershey, to the actioner *American Ninja 2,* starring Michael Dudikoff and Steve James. They leased the Les Arcades three-plex for the market's duration, screening their offerings from early morning until after midnight.

In '87, several companies, apparently fearing negative advance notices, sought to discourage the press from viewing their products, preferring to expose them solely to buyers shopping for genre fare. This discriminatory policy occasionally applied to tonier efforts as well: Rex Reed, Alexander Walker of the *London Evening Standard,* and Victoria Mather of the same city's *Daily Telegraph* were shut out of a preview of the Kathleen Turner–starred *Julia and Julia.* (We've since learned why.)

The Phantom circumvented this problem by sporting a buyer's pass rather than press credentials. Even so, we were turned away from a *Zombie High* screening. (Unfortunately, we caught up with the flick back in the States—see index.) Similar mishaps occurred at several festival screenings, due in part to the confusing color-coded press badges issued by the infernal festival bureaucracy (by many of whose administrators English is considered a dead language). At the market, many puzzled buyers couldn't understand why they had to shell out nearly 900 francs (roughly $153) for the privilege of viewing potential purchases. One Oriental buyer was assured by festival bureaucrats that the very notion bordered on the absurd; they then informed him that he had to pay anyway.

Despite the press snafus and the occasionally overzealous efforts of the French security staffers, the screenings presented a veritable oasis of calm compared with the chaos surrounding the film-poster-festooned market hotel suites. Here, busy flacks handed out press-conference and screening invitations while trying to sort out buyers and journalists from the assorted freeloaders (who often included buyers and journalists) looking for everything from free champagne to a fleeting hit of transplanted Tinseltown glitz. Time was when low-budget moguls set up their booths in the "bunker" or basement of the Palais du Festival. That comparatively sedate setting has been largely abandoned in favor of the flashier suites lining the first- and second-floor corridors of the Carlton, Martinez, and Majestic Hotels.

Typical of the latter was minimogul David Winters's comfortable two-room suite in the Carlton's Salon Mistral. David is perhaps best remem-bered for dancing his way into the hearts of millions as the diminutive Jet "Ay-rab" in both the Broadway and the Hollywood versions of *West Side Story.* Now a tad over his terpsichorean weight, Winters—along with partners Peter Yuval and David A. Prior—heads the newly formed Action International Pictures. The three take turns planning, writing, producing, directing, and distributing low-budget (averaging under a million per pic) adventure titles like *Nightwars, Chase, Deadly Prey,* and *Mankillers,* the last-mentioned starring Edd (Kookie) Byrnes and bosomy Cannes perennial Edy Williams, who made her bones, as it were, in Russ Meyer epics like *Beyond the Valley of the Dolls.*

The Salon Mistral featured all the usual accoutrements of a market hotel suite—lurid film posters and promotional literature, a snack table, a fridge stocked with beer and soft drinks, and the ubiquitous VCR, TV, and demo tapes waiting to be screened for interested buyers. And for Action International's products, there appeared to be interest galore. While many moguls, like Cannon's Menahem Golan, judged Cannes '87 to be a comparatively down market, Winters experienced no such problems, claiming to have racked up $3 mil in sales during the mar-ket's first three days. "At first we thought [the buyers] were going to get tired of seeing the same names on every movie," he admitted, "but it's been just the opposite. I think it's comforting for them to know we oversee every aspect of production, from concept to delivery."

Winters, who cites the original AIP's (American-International Pictures) prolific Roger Corman as his B-film-making model, got into the directing end of the biz after watching directors botch his choreographic work—chores he performed on the Elvis Presley–Ann-Margret epic *Viva Las Vegas,* Alice Cooper's *Welcome to My Nightmare,* and the rock teleseries *Hullabaloo.* From there, he graduated to producing and distributing. He even lensed his *Last Horror Film,* featuring Joe (*Maniac*) Spinell and femme fright fave Caroline Munro, *at* the 1980 Cannes fest.

After making way for yet another team of buyers eager to view Winters's wares, we hastened through the Carlton's noisy corridors, past suites rented by the busy Troma Team (*Surf Nazis Must Die*), ADN Associates (*Raging Fury*), Starway International (*Survival Quest*), and other modest movie outfits, out into the ever-brilliant Riviera sunshine. At one o'clock, the festival crowd poured from the palais, many heading for the countless brasseries facing the marinas of La Croisette. The market movers and shakers likewise streamed from their hotels, drawn, lemminglike, to beach-front restaurants like the Macumba and Rado Plage, where a figurative and literal feeding frenzy was the order of the day.

The deal makers were escorted to their favorite table (the one they sat at the day before and will continue to occupy for the fest's duration), dividing their attention between the menu and the barebreasted sunbathers who, in casual Cannes, strolled topless through the restaurants on their way to the showers. Over salades niçoises, Campari, anise-flavored pastis, Sancerre wine, and full-course lunches, the wheelers and dealers, further addled by the intense noonday sun, engaged in business banter that grew increasingly surreal as the afternoon wore on. At the Rado Plage, the British owner of a London postproduction house discoursed on the subject of Hollywood excess. "They spent a quarter of a million on special effects—which reverted back to us—before turning our project down." He shook his bald head, chewed on the tip of his sunglasses, and wondered aloud where he might raise a mil to return to the States and shoot a low-budget movie to frame those flashy FX.

By three-thirty, most moguls had returned to their suites for some last-minute moving and shaking before nightfall and party time arrived. While high seriousness continued to prevail at the festival proper's nocturnal soirees, the market bashes emphasized noise, flash, gimmicks, gals, and hype of every conceivable stripe. Actually, there were *two* types of market affairs: those that aimed for a festivallike formality (e.g., Zupnik Enterprises' dinner for international distributors held at the ritzy L'Amandier de Mougins restaurant and favoring relatively restrained strolling magicians and gypsy violinists over the usual topless hula girls and dancing bears), and the wild and crazy blowouts staged by the likes of Fries Entertainment, New World International, and Shapiro Entertainment. (The Phantom was reminded of the seemingly universal Bogart line from *The Maltese Falcon*, "The cheaper the crook, the gaudier the patter.")

It's at bashes like the above that market movers are most likely to mingle with festival press reps out for action earthier than the fest events provide. New World's party, spotlighting video horror hostess Elvira (aka Cassandra Peterson)—she of the low-cut cleavage and mile-high bouffant—attracted some sixty photographers and five TV crews, as well as such tireless party animals as B-movie magnate Chuck Fries and action auteur James (*The Exterminator*) Glickenhaus.

The runaway smash of the '87 Cannes party circuit, however, had to be the Alaskan Gold Rush shindig staged at the Carlton Grand Ballroom and hosted by Shapiro Entertainment in honor of its family film, *The Legend of Grizzly Adams*—a bash whose budget may have exceeded that of the $3 million movie. (Shapiro's other credits include such legendary outings as *Goofballs, Berserker, Hangmen,* and *Zombie Nightmare.*)

The movie may be rated G, but the party proved a pure R. Mickey Gilley supplied the entertainment before being replaced by a local cover band, who rewarded the mostly oblivious throng with a spirited if off-key rendition of "Money for Nothing." Shapiro execs further emphasized the affair's frontier theme by serving antelope patties, keg beer, and white wine—just like the Klondike miners used to drink. Free coonskin caps for the lads, red garters for the ladies, and gratis rabbit's feet for all were distributed, while bare-breasted Indian maids competed for the crowd's attention with authentic can-can girls, a seminaked snake handler, and of course, the famed Shapiro dancing bear.

Business as usual at the Cannes market.

Cannes the Chatter
Wish I'd Said That: Cannes Quotes to Live By

"Buyer after buyer comes in and they want trash. And why do they want trash? Because these people are psychopaths. They only understand one thing: action."

Transcontinental's ISRAEL SHAKED
quoted in *Variety*, 5/27/87

"Too many people think that if you throw in half a can of ketchup and half a can of bikinis, a film will evolve. In fact, it takes a certain vision, sincerity, and something that will intrigue an audience. My inspiration is Roger Corman."

Troma Team prez LLOYD KAUFMAN
The Business 5/12/87

"It's a Karate Kid *story with no karate, but football instead."*

Arista president LOUIS GEORGE on his film *Hotshots*
Screen International, 5/15/87

"This is the prince of schpilkes. If you've got good news, say it. If not, cut your tongue out before the beep."

Harried agent's answering machine message
Cannes '87

"I've only got one tuchas; I can't put it in three locations!"

Harried mogul at the Majestic Hotel

"We made three million in our first three days."

DAVID WINTERS
Action International Pictures

But Can You Top *This* . . . ?

"OFG company chief Robert Little sold ninety percent of the world."

The Business, 5/11/87

Prizes

Most Generous Promotional Giveaways, Cannes '87

1. Disposable twenty-four-shot camera, Toho
2. Golf umbrella, Zupnik Enterprises
3. Outsize beach towel, Trans-World Entertainment
4. Mirrored sunglasses, Empire International
5. Coonskin cap, Shapiro Entertainment

Flimsiest Promotional Giveaway

Minuscule "Aroma du Troma" (the $mell of $uccess) perfume capsule, the Troma Team

Best Booth Placement
Stutz Company's documentary *Mother Theresa* next to Essex International's X-rated *Top Buns*

Foxy Brown (1974) ◆◆◇
D: Jack Hill. Pam Grier, Peter Brown, Terry Carter, Antonio Fargas, Sid Haig. 92 minutes. (Orion)

Prototypical Pam Grier movie covers all the "blaxploitation" bases as PG's efforts to bail out her low-life brother (Fargas) lead to her lawman lover Carter's demise. Pam poses as a hooker to get the goods on a gaggle of honky goons headed by former TV heartthrob Brown. Not one of Jack (*Spider Baby, Switchblade Sisters*) Hill's hotter efforts, but swift enough for hardcore Pam fans. Pam is also on view in *Coffy, Friday Foster,* and *Sheba, Baby* (all also from Orion), as well as in *Naked Warriors* (formerly *The Arena*) (MGM/UA).

French Connection (1971) ◆◆◆◇
D: William Friedkin. Gene Hackman, Roy Scheider, Fernando Rey. 104 minutes. (CBS/Fox)

Another groundbreaking genre movie that established the anti-hero cop as a contempo screen icon. Hackman gives a great gritty perf as narc Popeye Doyle, out to crack a Marseilles-based heroin ring. The car/el train race tops even *Bullitt*'s breakneck chase. *The French Connection II* (CBS/Fox), while a step down, is also well worth catching.

Fresh Kill (1987) ◆◇
D: Joseph Merhi. Flint Keller, Tricia Parks, Robert Zdar. 90 minutes. (City Lights)

An amateurish Hollywood-set sleaze opus, *Fresh Kill* is noteworthy mostly for an early appearance by up-and-coming screen heavy Robert (*Maniac Cop*) Zdar, the Richard (*Jaws*) Kiel of the '80s. You can also sight the menacing Mr. Z in the urban actioner *Dead End City* (AIP).

Gambling Samurai (1960) ◆◆◆
D: Senkichi Taniguchi. Toshiro Mifune, Michiyo Aratama, Kumi Mizuno. 93 minutes. (Video Action)

Samurai Toshiro chops up all who cross his wrathful path in a quality Japanese action encounter of a *Yojimbo* kind. Fans of the genre may also want to check out *Kojiro, One-Eyed Swordsman, Swords of Death, Sword of Fury I* and *II* (all via Video Action), plus *Sword of Doom* (Embassy).

Game of Death (1979) ◆◆◇
D: Robert Clouse. Bruce Lee, Gig Young, Dean Jagger, Colleen Camp, Hugh O'Brien, Chuck Norris. 102 minutes. (CBS/Fox)

The real Bruce Lee, who died during filming, shares screen time with an ersatz Bruce in a better-than-average belt-and-batter out-ing that features a name support-ing cast (including Chuck Norris) and a one-of-a-kind kung-fu match between the real Bruce and L.A. Lakers center Kareem Abdul-Jabbar (!). Posthumous Lee clips went on to costar with a live Fred Williamson in *Fist of Fear, Touch of Death* (Vestron).

The Getaway (1972) ◆◆◆

D: Sam Peckinpah. Steve McQueen, Ali McGraw, Ben Johnson. 123 min-utes. (Warner)

Another slick, twisty, violent, high-budget car-chase extrava-ganza, and a good one for fans of the genre, with an A cast (dis-counting the irritating Ali) and Peckinpah's patented hard edges. The garbage-truck scene is a lit-eral trash-movie highlight.

Getting Even (1986) ◆◆◆

D: Dwight Little. Edward Albert, Joe Don Baker, Audrey Landers, Caroline Williams, Ron Pilloud, Billy Streater. 90 minutes. (Vestron)

Originally titled *Hostage: Dallas*, *Getting Even* opens with a pitched battle between world superpowers Russia and Texas, as two-fisted biochemical whiz "Tag" Taggar—played with mucho macho pan-ache by Edward (*Butterflies Are Free*) Albert—leads his crack com-mando crew in a lightning raid on a secret Soviet chem-warfare plant. Amid whoops of "Don't mess with Texas!" and "Remember the Al-amo!" (where, if memory serves, Lone Star state patriots fought those selfsame Reds a century and a half back), our heroes make off with several canisters of nerve gas capable of melting the flesh right off your face. Back in Dallas, the animosity shifts from the pesky Russkis to homegrown arch-villain and rival chemical mogul King Kenderson (deftly overplayed by paunchy B-movie vet Baker). Seems King and his machine-gun-toting minions have copped the lethal canisters from Taggar's redoubt and are threatening to explode them over Dallas. Whether this represents high trag-edy doubtless depends on your regional loyalties. What *really* matters is that *Getting Even* is an enjoyably dumb, fast-paced throw-back to the pulp serials of yore, packed with kidnappings, torture tableaux, shoot-outs, and high-speed horse, car, and copter chases galore.

Ginger (1971) ◆◆

D: Don Schain. Cheri Caffaro, Cindy Barnett, Herb Kerr. 90 minutes. (Mon-terey)

Hard-core Cheri Caffaro fans will want to see the sleaze special that introduced the blond B-girl to drive-in-goers the nation over. Cheri reprises her tough-gal role in *The Abductors, Girls Are For Lov-ing* (both Monterey), *City in Fear* (formerly *A Place Called Today*) (Unicorn), and *Too Hot to Handle* (Warner).

The Glass House (1972) ◆◆◆
D: Tom Gries. Alan Alda, Clu Gulager, Vic Morrow, Billy Dee Williams. 89 minutes. (Showcase/WesternWorld)

For a made-for-TV movie starring Alda, this Truman Capote–scripted prison drama is a surprisingly gritty affair, with an especially strong turn by the late Vic Morrow as a behind-bars bully.

The Glove (1978) ◆◆◇
D: Ross Hagen. John Saxon, Rosey Grier, Joanna Cassidy. 93 minutes. (Media)

Not a Michael Jackson bio but a hilarious inept action oddity, misdirected by frequent onscreen villain Hagen, pitting a bounty hunter (Saxon) against an assailant (Grier) equipped with a steel riot glove. With cameos by Jack Carter, Joan Blondell, Keenan Wynn, and the ever-dependable Aldo Ray.

The Godfather (1972) ◆◆◆◇
D: Francis Ford Coppola. Marlon Brando, Al Pacino, Diane Keaton, Robert Duvall. 175 minutes.

The Godfather, Part II (1974) ◆◆◆
D: Francis Ford Coppola. Al Pacino, Robert De Niro, Diane Keaton, Robert Duvall. 201 minutes.

The Godfather: The Complete Epic, 1902–1959 (1981) ◆◆◆◇
D: Francis Ford Coppola. Marlon Brando, Al Pacino, Robert De Niro. 386 minutes. (Paramount)

If you catch only one Mafia movie in your lifetime, the Phantom ad-vises you make it Duke Mitchell's *The Executioner* (see index). If you have time for two, we'd suggest you catch part one of this Coppola classic. If you're looking for three, try *The Godfather, Part II* too. Or rent the reedited (by Coppola) TV version, combining parts one and two for the price of one.

Gone in 60 Seconds (1974) ◆◆
D: H. B. Halicki. H. B. Halicki, Marion Busia, George Cole. 97 minutes. (Media)

Cracker action star Halicki directs himself in this pioneering example of Demolition Derby Cinema that features a forty-minute car chase with ninety-three—count 'em—ninety-three wrecked autos. Not as good as HB's more mature *The Junkman* (TWE), which boasts of destroying fully 150 hapless vehicles!

Gordon's War (1973) ◆◆◇
D: Ossie Davis. Paul Winfield, Carl Lee, Tony King. 90 minutes. (CBS/Fox)

In this slicker-than-average "blaxploitation" flick, Winfield wages war against ghetto drug kingpins with the help of his 'Nam-vet buddies.

The Great Escape (1963) ◆◆◆◇
D: John Sturges. Steve McQueen, James Garner, Richard Attenborough. 173 minutes. (MGM/UA)

An expertly executed prisoner-of-war epic without a dull stretch in its elongated running time. Still the best of its genre.

The Grissom Gang (1971) ◆◆◆
D: Robert Aldrich. Kim Darby, Scott Wilson, Tony Musante. 128 minutes. (CBS/Fox)

More perversity from Aldrich, who mixes sardonic laughs and raw violence in retelling the well-known Brit kidnap story *No Orchids for Miss Blandish,* as mentally deficient hood Wilson falls for abducted deb Darby. Comic Joey Faye successfully plays against type as a gang member. Effective '30s feel also helps put this recommended rarity over.

Gymkata (1985) ◆◆◇
D: Robert Clouse. Kurt Thomas, Tetchie Agbayani, Richard Norton, Conan Lee, Buck Kartalian, Edward Bell. 90 minutes (MGM/UA)

Gymkata refers to an arcane combo of gymnastics and karate, of which young Jonathan Cabot (Olympian Thomas) is the world champ. Government agents pack him off to the primitive principality of Parmistan—the kind of back-lot mythical kingdom that proliferated in B pics past—to participate in The Game, sort of a freewheeling Splatter Olympics that few contestants have ever survived. If young Kurt wins, he stands to gain not only the hand of the beautiful Princess Rubali (fetching Agbayani) but the Khan's (wizened Mel Brooks lookalike Kartalian) permission to set up the first "Star Wars early warning system" in a Parmistani mountain range! So much for plot. The *real* action begins with Kurt's arrival in Parmistan (which, judging by the extras, has to be the Bad Teeth Capital of the World—and Kurt knocks out a few more before he's through). There he learns The Game's been rigged by the Khan's treacherous adviser Zamir (Norton). Kurt runs the course while alternately dodging and dispatching Zamir's evil minions and, in the movie's most memorable sequence, high-kicks his way through the Village of Crazies, a booby-trapped booby hatch populated by hooded, scythe-wielding lunatics. As an actor, Thomas makes for a great gymnast, but his lack of thespic talent never gets in the way of the action, and there's more than enough of the latter here to satisfy martial-arts addicts.

H-Bomb (1978) ◆◇
D: Krung Savrilai. Olivia Hussey, Chris Mitchum. 91 minutes. (Cinema Group)

If you've ever wondered what never happened to former teen "Juliet" Olivia Hussey, *H-Bomb*'s got the answer. Seems the one-time Zeffirelli ingenue made a bold career move by toplining in this Raymond Chow cheapie—costarring wooden blond hero Chris (Son of Robert) Mitchum—about evil nuke thieves. *H-Bomb* also offers awful dubbing and the catchy doomsday ditty "The End Is Near."

Hangmen (1987) ♦♦
D: J. Christian Ingvordsen. Richard R. Washburn, Jake LaMotta, Dog Thomas, Kosmo Vinyl, Keith Bogart. 88 minutes. (Academy)

One of the more entertainingly bad action flicks we've witnessed, *Hangmen* concerns CIA agent Richard R. Washburn's efforts to rescue his kidnapped teenage son from a cabal of evil renegade agents. To that end, our hero enlists the aid of (surprise!) his old 'Nam buddies, and the bloodbath begins. Director Ingvordsen and cinematographer Steven W. Kaman (they're also responsible for the null-skulled script) employ all manner of flashy techniques—the villains are lensed in extreme close-up and speak in echochambered voices; the good guys attack with balletic slo-mo stealth—in a bid to camouflage their dull characters and slim story. Still, *Hangmen* definitely has its high-camp high points: a gravelly cameo by LaMotta as an underground arms dealer; ten—count 'em—ten full-blown shoot-outs in only 88 minutes; and easily twice that many unintended laughs.

Hard Drivin' (1960) NR
D: Paul Helmick. Rory Calhoun, Alan Hale, Connie Hines. 92 minutes. (Magnum)

This is actually a 1960 racing antique originally called *Thunder in Carolina*, retitled and repackaged. As Bela would say, "Bevare!"

Hard Ticket to Hawaii (1987) ♦♦◊
D: Andy Sidaris. Ronn Moss, Dona Speir, Hope Marie Carlton, Harold Diamond, Rodrigo Obregon, Cynthia Brimhall. 96 minutes. (Lorimar)

In *Hard Ticket to Hawaii*, jiggle-action auteurs Andy and Arlene Sidaris (see sidebar) chronicle the glamorous, amorous adventures of hunky hero Rowdy Abilene, screen cousin to Travis Abilene of *Malibu Express* (MCA). This time around, Rowdy (Moss) and chopsocky sidekick Jade (Diamond) take a backseat to fighting femmes Speir and Carlton, a pair of bosomy blond ex-Playmates who tangle with your typical vicious drug ring on the sunny isle of Molokai, Hawaii. The result is a reasonably lively mix of exotic scenery, erotic escapades, sinister plot twists, violent shoot-outs, and mucho distaff skin that owes as much to Russ Meyer as it does to James Bond. The Sidarises also toss in Sumo wrestlers, transvestite spies, and—in an inspired subplot—an escaped giant snake "infected with deadly toxins from cancer-infested rats" (!). The pic's best moment plays off Rowdy's woeful lack of gun prowess: after running down a would-be skateboard assassin with his jeep, Rowdy completes the job by blasting the bad guy with a bazooka at point-blank range. Explains our hero, "It's the only gun I can hit a moving target with."

AN ANDY SIDARIS FILM

SNAKE'S ALIVE!: Ex-Playmates Hope Marie Carlton and Dona Speir have their hands full with a giant snake "infected with deadly toxins from cancer-infested rats" in Andy and Arlene Sidaris's T&E adventure *Hard Ticket to Hawaii*. Photo courtesy of Malibu Bay Films.

FILMMAKERS IN FOCUS:

Andy and Arlene Sidaris: King and Queen of T&E

Andy (writer/director) and better half Arlene (producer) Sidaris definitely make for an offbeat B-movie team. Both share backgrounds in network TV—Andy as an Emmy-winning director for ABC Sports and Arlene as a producer/writer (*The Hardy Boys/Nancy Drew Mysteries* (MCA) series, the made-for-TV *Obsessed with a Married Woman*)—as well as a part-time island home in Molokai, Hawaii, where, not surprisingly, most of their action flicks unfold. Though the Sidarises are well into their third decade of marriage (to each other), Andy initially established his Malibu Bay Films banner as a solo enterprise. His first venture in the T&E genre (the E stands for "explosions"), 1973's *Stacey* (aka *Stacey and Her Gangbusters,* available via Video Gems/Interglobal), starred Playmate Anne Randall as a sexy shamus out to break an extortion ring involved with a bogus religious cult.

Rugged B-movie vet William Smith toplined in Andy's second cinematic outing, *Seven* (IVE), released in 1979. *Seven* further codified the essential ingredients of a standard Sidaris adventure, with Smith leading a team of hunky guys and buxom gals against a Hawaiian crime org, in a flick that placed as much emphasis on sex, comedy, and a sort of Times Square variation on the *Playboy* philosophy as it did on violence.

Arlene's participation (as official producer and unofficial script doctor) began with 1985's *Malibu Express* (MCA), the movie that introduced the Abilene cousins (Travis and Rowdy) and friends and one that benefited from the one-shot presence of B-screen queen Sybil Danning. Andy and Arlene followed with *Hard Ticket* (1987), 1988's *Picasso Trigger* (see index), and *Savage Beach* (1989). In addition to the Abilene cousins (who never appear together)—Travis, played by Darby Hinton in *Malibu* and Steve Bond in *Picasso,* and *Ticket*'s Rowdy (Ronn Moss)—other series regulars include ex-Playmates Dona Speir and Hope Marie Carlton as a pair of shapely distaff lawpersons, and karate ace Harold Diamond as the Abilenes' partner Jade. And in the grand tradition of Alfred Hitchcock, auteur Andy Sidaris usually pencils in a klutzy cameo for himself to boot.

"The left side of the brain is intellectual, the right side instinctual," the short, portly director points out. "The left brain likes *The Last Emperor* (Nelson); the right brain likes my pictures. So before you see one of my movies, remember to leave your left brain at the door."

Hell's Angels on Wheels (1967) ◆◆◆
D: Richard Rush. Jack Nicholson, Adam Roarke, Sabrina Scharf. 95 minutes. (Interglobal)
One of your better biker epics—

superior, in fact, to its model, Corman's *Wild Angels* (see index)—with Jack Nicholson as a freelance rider named Poet whose rivalry with Angel leader Roarke leads to the hoped-for outbursts of abrupt-and-senseless violence.

Hell's Angels '69 (1969) ◆◆
D: Lee Madden. Jeremy Slate, Tom Stern, Conny Van Dyke, Sonny Barger. 97 minutes. (Media)

More of a standard heist caper than a biker movie. Brothers Jeremy Slate and Tom Stern pose as Angels in order to implicate the latter in a planned Vegas robbery. None too thrilling.

Hell Up in Harlem (1973) ◆◇
D: Larry Cohen. Fred Williamson, Julius W. Harris, Gloria Hendry. 96 minutes. (Orion)

A surprisingly weak sequel to Cohen's competent *Black Caesar* (see index), with Fred surviving an assassination attempt and plotting vengeance. For Fred W. and Larry Cohen completists only.

Hellhole (1985) ◆◇
D: Pierre de Moro. Judy Landers, Ray Sharkey, Mary Woronov, Marjoe Gortner, Edy Williams, Terry Moore. 95 minutes. (RCA/Columbia)

It's apparent from the outset that all is not well at Ashland's all-femme sanitarium: Dr. Dane (Marjoe) is in the basement mixing up his new chemical-lobotomy formula.   Lesbian-necrophiliac hospital head Dr. Fletcher (Woronov) keeps the Doc's hopelessly deranged "rejects" caged under the boiler room, the hellhole of the title. A greasy mad strangler named Silk (hammily portrayed by Sharkey) infiltrates the asylum by posing as a leering, gutter-mouthed aide. As Silk's intended prey, large-breasted amnesia victim Landers perceptively remarks, "This is crazy!" Crazy, yes; fun, no. Despite the pic's perverse premise (further abetted by sandbox cat-fights, a lesbian shower-room brawl, and mudbaths designed to "cure nymphomania"), *Hellhole* won't give Sam Fuller's *Shock Corridor* (see index) any sleepless nights. Burdened by Vincent Mongol's witless script, de Moro's disconnected direction and claustrophobic sets supplied by producers too cheap to spring for more than one or two token exteriors, *Hellhole* proceeds with all the verve of a terminal Thorazine zombie.

High School Caesar (1960) ◆◆◇ B&W
D: O'Dale Ireland. John Ashley, Gary Vinson, Judy Nugent. 75 minutes. (Rhino)

Neglected rich kid Ashley is a teen bully who cares more about his pompadour than about other people in this road-show *Rebel Without a Cause*. A fun entry in Rhino's Teenage Theater series, the pic packs enough punch-ups, drag races, and primitive rock 'n' roll into its brief running time to make it a worthwhile item for adolescents-amok buffs. Ashley went on to produce (and sometimes star in) countless bad Filipino flicks and later produced TV's *Werewolf* terror series. Guess you just can't keep a good greaser down.

Hollywood Vice Squad (1986) ◆◇
D: Penelope Spheeris. Leon Isaac Kennedy, Carrie Fisher, Trish Van Devere, Frank Gorshin, Ronny Cox, Joey Travolta, H. B. Haggerty. 108 minutes. (Cinema Group)

Borrowing its milieu from the *Angel* series, story elements from Paul Schrader's hysterical *Hardcore*, and its title from a well-known New Wave TV *policier*, *Hollywood Vice Squad* (a self-styled *Hell Street Blues*) follows four teams of LAPD undercover cops as they pursue pimps, prostitutes, porn mongers, and bookies in interlocking episodes based on "actual cases." Despite its undeniably creative casting, Spheeris's pic is an unwaveringly routine, shockingly tame hack job sorely lacking the normally down-and-dirty distaff director's patented lowlife punch. Ditto for Pen's terminally dumb punk-western dud *Dudes* (IVE). Rent *Suburbia* or *The Boys Next Door* (see index for both), and catch the *real*, unfettered Spheeris at work.

Hostage (1987) ◆◆
D: Hanro Mohr. Wings Hauser, Karen Black, Kevin McCarthy, Nancy Locke, Robert Whitehead, Billy Second. 94 minutes. (RCA/Columbia)

It's *Delta Force Revisited* as an African airliner carrying an international cast is skyjacked by the usual band of scurvy Arab cutthroats. Waiting in the wings is hero Hauser, who, financed by Colonel Shaw (McCarthy), assembles a singularly unappealing crew of slob commandos to spring his captive girlfriend (real-life wife Locke) and surrogate son Gerhard Hametner, who needs a kidney transplant but pronto. The plot proceeds predictably as Wings, in a move befitting his name, hangglides to the rescue of the downed plane and its ever-diminishing passenger list. Hauser, who impressed as *Vice Squad*'s psycho pimp a few years back (see index), proves a total stiff here. Far more riveting is passenger Black as softcore smut starlet Laura Lawrence ("I'm tired, tired, *tired* of being a stupid sex symbol!") and Whitehead as her gay agent, Harry. Joey Bishop and Shelley Winters, we're sorry to report, apparently missed this flight.

The Hot Box (1972) ◆◆◆
D: Joe Viola. Margaret Markov, Andrea Cagan, Ricky Richardson, Charles Dierkop. 89 minutes. (Embassy)

Co-written by Jonathan Demme during his Roger Corman apprenticeship, this action-filled entry sees a quartet of distaff Peace Corps nurses turn jungle revolutionaries after being abused by Marcos's goons. Never screened at Imelda's short-lived Manila Film Fest.

Hot Rod Girl (1956) ◆◆ B&W
D: Leslie Martinson. Lori Nelson,

Chuck Connors, John Smith, Frank Gorshin. 79 minutes. (Goodtimes)

Wholesome-looking Nelson helps cop Connors rid the world of reckless hot rodders. Not one of the era's more sizzling examples of JD junk, but the video lists for under ten bills and you can always tape over it later.

Hunter's Blood (1987) ♦♦
D: Robert C. Hughes. Sam Bottoms, Clu Gulager, Kim Delaney, Ken Swofford, Joey Travolta, Mayf Nutter. 102 minutes. (Embassy)

A belated *Deliverance* rip-off, *Hunter's Blood* generates some initial tension as a quintet of weekend sportsmen led by Clu (*Return of the Living Dead*) Gulager and Sam Bottoms wander deep into Arkansas woods ruled by inbred hillbilly poachers. The suspense subsides about four reels in, however, due to a poorly timed succession of serious lapses in basic B-movie logic. Top acting honors here go to the *talented* Travolta, Joey, who—while he never gets to squeal like a pig à la *Deliverance*'s Ned Beatty—does come through with an impressive prolonged crying jag. The violent climax is sprinkled with gratuitous gore FX that might please viewers who possess more patience than yours truly.

Hustler Squad (1976) NR
D: Cesar Gallardo. John Ericson, Karen Erickson, Lynda Sinclaire. 98 minutes. (United)

Another high-concept action flick, with hookers recruited to serve as guerrillas. As the original trailer put it, "It's a dirty war—they need all the help they can get!"

I, Mobster (1959) ♦♦◇ B&W
D: Roger Corman. Steve Cochran, Lita Milan, Robert Strauss. 80 minutes. (King Bee)

Screen tough guy Cochran—the mug who plugged Ma Jarrett in the back in *White Heat* (see index)—is at his hard-boiled best in this fast-paced B crime caper from Corman.

I Spit on Your Corpse (1976) NR
D: Al Adamson. Georgina Spelvin, Susan McIver, Kent Taylor. 88 minutes. (Super)

Porn starlet Georgina (*Devil in Miss Jones*) Spelvin's abortive crossover bid is not the upbeat, life-affirming ode its title implies, but a sleazy Al Adamson number about ruthless hitwomen who do in their victims while doing the deed.

I Spit on Your Grave (1978) ♦♦
D: Meir Zarchi. Camille Keaton, Eron Tabor, Richard Pace. 102 minutes. (VidAmerica)

Rape victim Keaton kills a quartet of attackers in sundry unpleasant ways in this illogical, ugly, vile, and highly popular exploitation staple, originally titled *Day of the Woman*. The similarly themed *I Want to Get Even* (Lorimar) and *Naked Vengeance* (Lightning) are also available, while director Zarchi strikes again with 1985's *Don't Mess with My Sister!* (Vid-America).

Indiana Jones and the Temple of Doom (1984) ◆◆◇
D: Steven Spielberg. Harrison Ford, Kate Capshaw, Ke Huy Quan. 118 minutes. (Paramount)

Finding this one shouldn't be too tough even at the most limited of video vending machines, but we feel compelled to include it for the record. Spielberg's over-blown, self-parasitic serial tribute is loud, cloying, and smug, but it does offer some terrific high-tech action tableaux, like the wild ride through the Indian mine. While we're at it, we should also mention *Raiders of the Lost Ark* (Paramount).

Instant Justice (1985) ◆◆
D: Christopher Bentley. Michael Paré, Tawny Kitaen, Charles Napier, Peter Crook, Eddie Avoth, Scott Del Amo. 101 minutes. (Warner)

Originally titled *Marine Issue, Instant Justice* gives us Michael (*Houston Knights*) Paré as Marine Corporal Scott Youngblood, a self-professed "flag-waver" stationed in Paris. When he learns his hooker sister has been murdered, our hero flees Gay Paree for the back alleys of Madrid. There he picks up a pair of allies—girly photog Crook and call girl Kitaen (usually one of the Phantom's faves but stuck here do-ing an irritating Rae Dawn Chong impersonation)—and an armful of guns. *Instant Justice* is far from the worst of its ilk, but it grows increasingly predictable as it inexorably approaches the inevitable showdown between our slick one-man army and your standard inept thugs.

Invasion U.S.A. (1985) ◆
D: Joseph Zito. Chuck Norris, Richard Lynch, Melissa Prophet, Alexander Zale, Alex Colon, Eddie Jones, Dehl Berti. 108 minutes (MGM/UA)

Americans have grown "soft," so Red hordes invade Miami (where were Crockett and Tubbs?) and have their heartless way with us. And don't miss it, brother: these Commies are *mean.* How mean are they? They're so mean, they crush a color TV set smack in the middle of a Merv Griffin–Phyllis Diller tête-à-tête! Then they blow up the Miami Beach 'burbs on Christmas Day! *Then* they try to explode a school bus full of kids singing "Row, Row, Row Your Boat" (the kids, not the Commies)! Finally, they make their biggest mistake of all—they wreck ex–CIA agent Matt Hunter's (Norris) Everglades shack and shoot his beloved old Indian pal John Eagle (Berti). So Chuck packs a pair of machine pistols, leaves his pet armadillo (!) behind, and hops aboard his airboat, hell-bent on going toe-to-toe with the Russkis. While never losing his cool (Chuck's performance here is nothing if not laid back—in fact, laid *out* might be closer to it), Chuck, throwing caution and logic to the winds, single-handedly saves both nation and day in a non-stop orgy of patriotic violence. At that, *Invasion U.S.A.* doesn't *end* so much as it runs out of ammo. Fear not, though: BO tallies have ensured that we'll never see an *Invasion U.S.A. II.*

MONDO MACHISMO OR, *BRAWN IN THE U.S.A.*

While relatively light on declared warfare, the Reagan years proved heavy in the military-posturing and muscle-flexing departments. Reflecting that atmosphere—presciently parodied in Buck Henry's 1980 political satire *The First Family* (Warner), wherein screen prez Bob Newhart promises to get America her "bigness" back—the period in question witnessed a host of Hollywood cartoon macho-men fighting a variety of real or imagined enemies. When not retroactively winning the war in Vietnam in revisionist revenge rampages like Sly Stallone's *Rambo: First Blood Part II* and Chuck Norris's *Missing In Action* series, they were taking on uppity Russkis (*Top Gun, Rambo III*), Arab terrorists (*Delta Force, Iron Eagle*), encroaching Cubans (*Invasion U.S.A.*), and sundry Central American troublemakers (*Commando, Cocaine Wars, Nightforce, Mission Kill*). Tinseltown's avengers were equally active on the domestic front, waging one-man wars against myriad homegrown heavies. The latter included big-time drug dealers (*Code of Silence*), Mafiosi (*Raw Deal*), and street scum of every conceivable—and often inconceivable—stripe (*The Annihilators, Death Wish 3*).

By mid-decade, patriotic potboilers—whether set stateside or abroad—were all the rage. And the pics' promo campaigns were anything but shy about laying their jingoistic cards on the table. *Vide:* the following flag-waving tag lines:

"Freedom is just a word . . . until you lose it."

Born American

"America wasn't ready . . . but *he* was!"

Invasion U.S.A.

BRADDOCK
MISSING IN ACTION II

CHUCK AMOK: Chuck Norris gave his sagging BO career a much-needed boost by dropping his chopsocky chores in favor of retro Ramboesque antics in flicks like *Braddock: Missing in Action III*.
Photo courtesy of The Cannon Film Group.

"One American against the world's drug armies!"

Cocaine Wars

"In America, if you push a man too far . . . he'll explode!"

American Justice

"He's America's most lethal weapon.
A living grenade waiting to explode.
Someone has just pulled the pin!"

Wanted Dead or Alive

The conservative hero cycle continued to prosper, but by 1987 a few film protagonists had begun venting their wrath at the expense of *right-wing* targets, ranging from organized racists (*Avenging Force*) to paramilitarists (*The Wild Pair*) to legalized outlaws in the CIA (*Above the Law* and the grippingly titled *Ninja in the Claws of the CIA*). Of course, mayhem—not political discourse—remained the action movie's real raison d'être. Whether the villains harbored right- or left-wing sympathies, it was a given that Our Hero couldn't count on handcuffed authorities for help. It was one man—make that one American (or one *adopted* American, like Austria's Arnold Schwarzenegger or Japan's Sho Kosugi)—against a world of evil.

Might Makes Money: Hollywood's Hierarchy of Heroes

Who that macho man happens to be plays a far more significant role than his political leanings in determining an action movie's BO and video success. At present, Hollywood's hierarchy of heroes is a multitiered affair operating within a fairly rigid caste system. On top stand Sly Stallone and Arnold Schwarzenegger, whose elaborate action vehicles—movies with megabuck budgets and B-movie souls—handily outdraw those of their brawny brethren. And when he chooses to work, the aging but still economically potent Clint Eastwood commands equally lucrative loyalty from *his* legions of action-film fans.

Tier number two is the sole possession of a couple of Chucks—Norris and Bronson—who continue to topline in a series of profitable if non-blockbuster B+ vehicles. Tier three shelters several heroes and heroines working in unabashed B flicks: ex-gridiron star and "blaxploitation" vet Fred ("The Hammer") Williamson (*The Messenger, Foxtrap*); reigning kung-fu/Ninja king Sho Kosugi (*Rage of Honor, Pray for Death*); secondary martial-arts ace Jackie Chan (*Police Force, The Protector*); laid-back Robert Ginty (*Mission Kill, Three Kinds of Heat*); Cannon's Michael Dudikoff/Steve James tandem (*American Ninja, Avenging Force*); and former little devil Linda Blair (*Red Heat, Savage Streets*), who long ago swapped her pea soup for an arsenal of high-tech peashooters and who's still holding her own in what's lately become an overwhelmingly male-dominated genre.

Newcomers and challengers include perennial second fiddle Carl Weathers, who scored fairly big in his first starring vehicle, *Action Jackson*; promising Eastwood clone Steven Seagal (*Above the Law*); and high-kicking karate ace Jean-Claude Van Damme (*Bloodsport*). Mel Gibson also took a critically and financially successful stab at outlandish action heroics in *Lethal Weapon*. In a misguided bid to revive his long-flagging career, Burt Reynolds also tried turning action icon in a succession of one-word box-office bombs that included *Stick, Heat*, and the ultraviolent but still boring *Malone*.

A number of novelty and one-shots also surfaced—among them Olympics heavyweight Kurt Thomas (*Gymkata*), karate champ Tonny Tulleners (*Scorpion*), and diminutive distaff kung-fu demon Tiana Alexandra (*Catch the Heat*)—never to be heard from again. Ancient Richard Farnsworth (*Space Rage*) and chunky Charles Durning, meanwhile, competed for World's Most Unlikely Kick-Ass Hero honors, with Durning winning on the dubious strength on his wheezing slo-mo acrobatics in the painful pulp effort *Stand Alone*.

Iron Eagle (1986) ◆

D: Sidney J. Furie. Louis Gossett, Jr., Jason Gedrick, Tim Thomerson, David Suchet, Caroline Lagerfelt, Larry G. Scott. 108 minutes. (CBS/Fox)

If nothing else, *Iron Eagle* boasts the hottest rock score of any war movie since *Apocalypse Now*. (The similarity definitely ends there.) Junior jet ace Doug's (Gedrick) dad (Thomerson) has been snatched by arrogant Ay-rabs, and it's up to Doug and mad-as-hell pilot Colonel Chappy Sinclair (Gossett) to spring him. So in a militaristic update of the old let's-put-on-a-show routine, Doug's teenage pals help him on his way by stealing vital computer data and secretly arming a souped-up F-16 in a lively let's-put-on-a-war montage set to Twisted Sister's "We Ain't Gonna Take It Anymore" (!). And our fly-boys really know how to get down before they go up too: Colonel Sinclair works out the covert flight plan while dancing to a James Brown ditty (the Godfather of Soul's first patriotic cameo since *Rocky IV*—see index). And young Doug even gives the 'Rabs what-for while "Gimme

Some Lovin' " roars from his airborne cassette deck! (The same song was used to score a similarly destructive scene in the pallid *policier Number One with a Bullet* (see index), proving once again the old Hollywood axiom that small minds think alike.) The climactic aerial scenes see Doug forcing Qadhafi-like Arab leader Suchet to eat rock 'n' roll justice. Forget the video—get the soundtrack LP. Beware also the *glasnost*-influenced but otherwise unimproved *Iron Eagle II* (IVE).

Jackie Chan's Police Force (1985) ◆◆◇
D: Jackie Chan. Jackie Chan, Brigette Lin, Maggie Cheung, Cho Yuen, Bill Tung, Kenneth Tong. 88 minutes. (Cinema Group)

One of the very few films to go directly from the prestigious (to say nothing of the pretentious) New York Film Festival, where it was a controversial 1987 entry, to Forty-second Street's Roxy Twin kung-fu video theater (!), *Jackie Chan's Police Force* represents our eponymous martial-arts hero's big-time crossover bid. While he's *not* the unique combo of "Bruce Lee and Buster Keaton" (!) that the fest program guide described him, Jackie the actor *does* come equipped with furious fists, flying feet, and an ample amount of disarming, self-mocking charm. Here he plays a Hong Kong cop assigned to protect a major drug lord's fetching government-witness mistress—a task that leads to romantic complications and considerable flak from JC's girlfriend. Jackie the director keeps the familiar plot careering along at a brisk clip, leavening the well-staged action with slapstick sight gags and satiric pokes at the local judicial system (mirroring Dirty Harry's similar stateside complaints) and exhibiting a fondness for fast cutting and frequent zoom-lensing. A modestly entertaining kung-fu comedy, *Police Force* is superior to most of Jackie's American efforts, and Chan fans are advised not to hold its oddball fest selection against it.

Jackson County Jail (1976) ◆◆◆
D: Michael Miller. Yvette Mimieux, Tommy Lee Jones, Robert Carradine. 84 minutes. (Warner)

Not the usual chicks-in-chains exercise but an almost-credible B flick about traveling L.A. exec Mimieux's disastrous encounter with southern "justice" and her subsequent bond with cracker con Jones as the duo decide to make a breathless run for it. Crossover exploitation at its best. Yvette also stars in the unofficial *JCL* remake *Outside Chance* (Charter).

Jailbird Rock (1988) ◆◆
D: Philip Schuman. Robin Antin, Ron Lacey, Rhonda Aldrich, Valerie Gene Richards, Jacqueline Houston, Robin Cleaver. 92 minutes. (TWE)

A sort of *Fame Goes to Reform School*, *Jailbird Rock* chronicles the trials, traumas, and triumphs of teen terpsichorean Jessie (the able-bodied Antin), who's sentenced to five years in distaff stir for shooting her abusive stepdad. There she's forced to contend with the usual lesbian overtures (treated quite casually here), indifferent authorities, and mean con queen Maxie. While the antics are thoroughly routine, *Jailbird Rock* runs through its catalog of *Chained Heat* and *Flashdance* clichés with admirable enthusiasm. Ingenue Antin is appealingly tough and vulnerable by turns, and the show-biz finale—wherein our unchained chicks dance in their scanties for the guv and other tuxedoed dignitaries (!)—makes for a riveting sequence. In fact, we would have awarded *Jailbird Rock* a higher rating, but its incredibly sloppy and distracting postsync job, which leaves the characters' lips and words worlds apart, forced us to subtract half a phan.

The Jesus Trip (1971) ◆◇
D: Russ Mayberry. Tippy Walker, Robert Porter, Billy "Green" Bush. 84 minutes. (Unicorn)

Fugitive Harley hounds are forced to kidnap a nun; romance blossoms between victim and decent-at-heart biker leader. *The Jesus Trip* tries for more than the average wheels-on-reels job but is just too dull for its own good, let alone yours. Another biker flick, *J.C.* (Charter), offers a hog-hound suffering from Christ delusions.

Johnny Firecloud (1977) ◆◆
D: William A. Castleman. Victor Mohica, Ralph Meeker, Frank DeKova, Sacheen Littlefeather. 90 minutes. (Prism)

Did you know? Before there was semi–Native American Avenger John Rambo, there was full-blooded Native American Avenger John Firecloud. Embodied by Victor Mohica, Johnny Firecloud, named after a desert atomic-test blast (!), avenges the murder of his grandfather (DeKova) by gore-killing Meeker and his goons in this low-budget, no-talent enterprise, costarring famous former Marlon Brando flame Sacheen Littlefeather. And *after* Messrs. Firecloud *and* Rambo, there came Native American Avenger Thunder Warrior (Mark Gregory), who's already been featured in no fewer than three installments, aptly titled *Thunder Warrior I, II,* and *III* (TWE).

Jungle Warriors (1984) ◆◆◆
D: Ernst R. von Theumer. Alex Cord, Sybil Danning, Nina Van Pallandt, Paul L. Smith, John Vernon, Marjoe Gortner, Woody Strode. 96 minutes. (Media)

Seven foxy fashion models with big American breasts crash-land in a South American jungle, where they run afoul of fat cocaine kingpin Cesar (Smith), his blond lesbian sis Angel (the one and only Sybil Danning), and various gun-toting minions. One of the gals is really a secret drug agent, out to get the goods on Cesar and a team of visiting Mafiosi, headed by B-movie vets Vernon and Cord. After a slow buildup, *Jungle Warriors* (*Jiggle Warriors* would have been closer to it) delivers its promised quota of slashings, bashings, and decapitations—and culminates in a lengthy shoot-out in which our beleaguered gals get to give as good as they've gotten. You might want to fast-forward through the early going—especially during ex-evangelist Gortner's scenes—but you won't want to miss a single shot of the flick's furious finale.

The Kansas City Massacre (1975) ◆◆◇
D: Dan Curtis. Dale Robertson, Bo Hopkins, Robert Walden. 99 minutes. (Vidmark)

Not up there with Milius's *Dillinger* (see index), but a surprisingly punchy made-for-TV sequel to *Melvin Purvis, G-Man* (HBO), with Robertson returning as Purvis in a fast-paced story packed with gunplay galore.

KGB: The Secret War (1986) ◆◆
D: Dwight Little. Michael Billington, Denise DuBarry, Michael Ansara, Walter Gotell, Sally Kellerman, Christopher Cary. 89 minutes. (Continental)

An intermittently effective B thriller, *KGB: The Secret War* (originally titled *Lethal* for its brief theatrical and ongoing cable-TV run) stars Brit thesp Billington as a Russian agent who—via various plot contrivances—becomes the target of vicious U.S.-based KGB agents led by veteran villain Gotell. The betrayed spy is recruited by CIA ops Ansara and Kellerman (in a forced tough-broad role) but still spends most of the flick running from the ruthless Russki assassins while trying to shield American main squeeze DuBarry from their deadly wrath. *KGB*'s chief flaw is its overreliance on seemingly endless exposition at the expense of action (though the final showdown is decently staged). Director Little did a better job with his breakneck contempo cliffhanger *Getting Even* (see index), which, though released earlier, was actually lensed *after* *KGB*.

Kill or Be Killed (1980) NR
D: Ivan Hall. James Ryan, Norman Combes, Charlotte Michelle. 90 minutes. (Media)

A chopsocky cheapie lensed in South Africa that introduced would-be action star Ryan, who lasted long enough to topline in a sequel *Kill and Kill Again* (Media), both popular items on Forty-second Street.

Killer Elephants (1975) NR
Sung Pa, Alan Yen, Nai Yen Ne. 83 minutes. (Unicorn)

When an avaricious land baron threatens his plantation and family, our hero recruits the rampaging title creatures to come to his aid in this exotic Thai action epic.

Killing Machine (1984) ◆◇
D: J. Anthony Loma. Jorge Rivero, Lee Van Cleef, Margaux Hemingway, Willie Aames, Richard Jaeckel, Hugo Stiglitz. 89 minutes. (ThrillerVideo)

Rivero, Van Cleef, Aames, Stiglitz, and Hemingway (as a French aerobics teacher!) head an international cast in this routine tale of an ex-hood-turned-trucker (Rivero) who swears vengeance on the French mobsters (led by a gallicized Van Cleef) who killed his wife, burned his truck, and ruined his tomatoes. Our story unfolds sans suspense or subtlety—corrupt cops are shown waving to rampaging gangsters; judges shake hands with crooked defendants— as Rivero, a demolitions expert, tracks down the villains one by one and blows 'em up real good. Sybil Danning looks busty but uncomfortable in her Elvira-like prologue turn.

King Solomon's Mines (1985) ◆◆◇
D: J. Lee Thompson. Richard Chamberlain, Sharon Stone, John Rhys-Davies, Herbert Lom, Ken Gampu. 101 minutes. (MGM/UA)

If you count 1959's *Watusi* (NA), a sequel of sorts starring George Montgomery (the former Mr. Dinah Shore) and built around footage left over from the lavish 1950 version (NA), this is the *fifth* go-round for H. Rider Haggard's venerable African treasure-hunt tale. Cannon's thoroughly *Raider*ized remake—easily the least solemn of the lot—unfolds in North Af-

rica, circa 1916. Ex–*Dr. Kildare* Chamberlain toplines as Allan Quatermain, a brave bwana recruited by bubbly blond Sharon Stone to rescue her archaeologist dad from Turkish bandit John Rhys-Davies and German officer Lom. On their way to the title site, our ever-endangered duo, joined at times by native ally Gampu, encounter peckish cannibals, aerial dogfights, runaway trains, quicksand, elephant stampedes, and giant spiders. While it's no *Raiders of the Lost Ark* in either the talent or the production-value department, *Mines* moves at a sufficiently breathless clip, maintains a modest, throwaway tone, and is at least superior to its limp sequel (lensed back-to-back with *Mines*), *Allan Quatermain and the Lost City of Gold* (MGM/UA).

Kinjite: Forbidden Subjects (1989) ◆◆◇
D: J. Lee Thompson. Charles Bronson, Juan Fernandez, Perry Lopez, Peggy Lipton, James Pax, Bill McKinney. 97 minutes. (Cannon)

Kinjite: Forbidden Subjects ranks as geriatric action star Bronson's *least* soporific suspenser in years. That's not to say that *Kinjite* is *good*—the flick is, in fact, an unholy mess. But it's a consistently *compelling* mess. Its converging plot lines follow prudish LAPD vice dick Chuck (in an unusually testy turn) as he overprotects his own teen daughter while trying to nail notorious jailbait pimp Fernandez. Equally repressed Japanese businessman Pax, meanwhile—and for reasons alternately too complex and too contrived to go into here—finds his fate inextricably bound with Bronson's. Until the formulaic final reel, *Kinjite* offers a fairly kinky, unpredictable mix of sleaze, suspense, and cross-cultural confusion, leavened with unintentional laughs galore (as when Chuck, in his big emotive moment, unleashes a garbled harangue at the expense of a crowd of understandably bewildered Japanese). In sum, *Kinjite* is well worth checking out.

Knights of the City (1986) ◆◆
D: Dominic Orlando. Leon Isaac Kennedy, Nicholas Campbell, Michael Ansara, Janine Turner, John Mengati, Jeff Moldovan. 88 minutes. (New World)

Our titular urban noblemen are your typical overage, multiethnic rock 'n' roll B-movie gang. Led by thirty-seven-year-old (!) Kennedy (who also scripted), the Knights steal cars and play guitars, breakdance, and bust heads with equal aplomb. As celluloid luck would have it, a seemingly ill-advised rumble with a rival outfit lands our heroes in jail, where they not only run into the Fat Boys (doing "Jailhouse Rap," natch) but meet a major-label mogul (all-purpose movie ethnic Ansara). Soon the Knights are vying with other nabe rockers to win a talent contest that will send them first-rungward up the ladder of success. Given that

the story line isn't exactly fresh (to say nothing of *chill*, let alone *def*), *Knights of the City* could have been a lot worse. The violence is surprisingly graphic, the rumbles and dances well choreographed, Smokey Robinson and Denny Terrio turn in the best emotive moments of their careers, and each scene finds the characters sporting a new set of colorful T-shirts. (KILL 'EM ALL reads the Phantom's fave.) Even *Knights'* end credits are livelier than most, listing three— count 'em—*three* dialogue coaches for Kennedy alone *and* a "production psychologist"(!). The jail sequence proves particularly prophetic since *Knights'* exec producer Michael Franzese later landed in that very locale after pleading guilty to sixty-five counts of racketeering.

The Lady in Red (1979) ◆◆◇
D: Lewis Teague. Pamela Sue Martin, Robert Conrad, Louise Fletcher. 90 minutes. (Vestron)

John Sayles scripted this revisionist road-show Dillinger (played by Conrad), which focuses more on his ultimately lethal paramour (Martin). Fairly entertaining, if more than a tad liberal with the facts.

The Last Dragon (1985) ◆◇
D: Michael Schultz. Taimak, Vanity, Chris Murney. 109 minutes. (CBS/Fox)

Veejay Vanity gets involved with gangsters, martial-arts ace Taimak, and nearly two hours of imbecilic intrigues. Vanity's admirers would be better off tuning in *Tanya's Island* (Simitar), a tacky campfest lensed during the Divine Ms. V's "D. D. Winters" days.

Lethal Obsession (1987) ◆◆
D: Peter Patzack. Peter Maffay, Tahnee Welch, Elliot Gould, Michael York, Massimo Ghini, Armin Mullter-Stahl. 100 minutes. (Vidmark)

An unusually downbeat "thriller" lensed in Germany, *Lethal Obsession* (rhymes with *Lethal Weapon*) stars rocker Maffay as a cop crippled in an explosion rigged by archvillain The Ace (Gould, no less, in what amounts to little more than a cameo)—a blast that also kills the father of Maffay's main squeeze, Welch (*Cocoon's* alluring alien). York turns in decent work as a free-lance hitman named Dr. Proper, and director Patzack manages to generate some suspense for the flick's final showdown. But *Lethal Obsession* is too relentlessly grim, poorly paced, and pointlessly padded with clichéd rock-vid visuals to rise above the level of the merely endurable.

Lethal Weapon (1987) ◆◆
D: Richard Donner. Mel Gibson, Danny Glover, Gary Busey, Mitchell Ryan, Tom Atkins, Darlene Love. 110 minutes. (Warner)

After "meeting cute," psychotic-white-cop/stable-black-cop tandem Gibson and Glover set out to nail a network of evil drug mercenaries headed by icy killer Busey (in albinoesque makeup). While *Lethal Weapon* unspools with suitably manic energy, it's ultimately an exercise in high-tech jive. A computerized blend of *Commando, Raw Deal, Mad Max, Miami Vice, To Live and Die in L.A., Rambo,* and *The Cosby Show* (!), the pic plays like a standard Schwarzenegger vehicle, with Gibson subbing for the mighty Arnie. And despite its endless array of gun battles, exploding cars, and Fu Manchu—style torture sequences, *Lethal Weapon* is a painfully predictable affair. (Producer Joel Silver even lifted the climactic kung-fu set-to from his earlier *Commando.*) As weary cop Glover at one point remarks, "Pretty thin stuff, huh?" The movie's boffo BO and vid-rental stats notwithstanding, the Phantom couldn't help but agree with Dan's candid assessment.

Lion of the Desert (1979) ◆◆◇
D: Moustapha Akkad. Anthony Quinn, Oliver Reed, Irene Papas, Rod Steiger, John Gielgud. 164 minutes. (Lorimar)

Quinn is the crafty Libyan guerrilla leader who thwarts attempted Italo invasions in 1911 and twenty years later. An old-fashioned, straightforward war movie that makes no bones about which side it's on.

Little Caesar (1930) ◆◆◆ B&W
D: Mervyn LeRoy. Edward G. Robinson, Douglas Fairbanks, Jr., Glenda Farrell. 80 minutes. (Fox Hills)

Edward G. sneers his way into the hearts of millions as Rico, a mug who makes it to the top of the racketeer heap. Still effective, though no match for Cagney's *Public Enemy* (see index).

The Lives of a Bengal Lancer (1935) ◆◆◆ B&W

D: Henry Hathaway. Gary Cooper, Richard Cromwell, Franchot Tone. 110 minutes. (MCA)

Coop, Cromwell, and Tone aid the Empire in rebuffing troublesome Afghans in a tale related with classic Hollywood sweep, courtesy of director Hathaway.

The Living Daylights (1987) ◆◆◇

D: John Glen. Timothy Dalton, Maryam d'Abo, Jeroen Krabbe, Joe Don Baker, John Rhys-Davies, Art Malik. 130 minutes. (CBS/Fox)

The first Bond entry to topline Dalton is an initially rousing retro adventure that doesn't pack enough punch to sustain its elongated running time. Dalton does a decent enough job as the new, relatively restrained, safe-sex Bond—though the patented Bondian sexism remains intact—caught up in an involved plot that finds him springing supposed KGB defector General Koskov (Krabbe, seen to more impressive effect as the Cajun thug in *No Mercy*—see index), battling a crazed arms dealer with military pretensions (B-movie vet Baker, in what should have been a more flamboyant role), and rather chastely romancing Russki cellist Maryam d'Abo. *The Living Daylights* incorporates the usual high-tech gimmickry and scenic globe-hopping and action sequences, including a high-energy kitchen duke-out employing ordinary household utensils (including the kitchen sink) in violently inventive ways. Sometime into the twentieth reel, however, *The Living Daylights* succeeded in boring the same out of us. MGM/UA, meanwhile, has remastered many of the original Bond movies for sell-through and rental release, including six Sean Connery editions (*Diamonds Are Forever, Dr. No, From Russia with Love, Goldfinger, Thunderball, You Only Live Twice*), six Roger Moores (*For Your Eyes Only, Live and Let Die, Man with the Golden Gun, Moonraker, Octopussy, The Spy Who Loved Me*), and George Lazenby's lone 007 turn, *On Her Majesty's Secret Service*. Connery's *Never Say Never Again* (Warner) and Moore's *A View to a Kill* (CBS/Fox) are also on cassette.

The Long Good Friday (1982) ◆◆◇

D: John Mackenzie. Bob Hoskins, Helen Mirren, Pierce Brosnan, Eddie Constantine. 109 minutes. (HBO)

An okay but overrated Brit gangster flick that's essentially a throwback to its Yank counterparts of yore. Hoskins, cast here as a sort of a limey Edward G. Robinson, is worth watching for his brutal mob-boss portrayal.

The Losers (1970) ◆◇

D: Jack Starrett. William Smith, Bernie Hamilton, Adam Roarke. 96 minutes. (Academy)

This bikers-go-to-war story predated the *Uncommon Valor/ Rambo/Missing In Action* Vietnam revisionist movies by more than a full decade, which makes it of some historical note, even if it doesn't offer much in the entertainment department.

The Lost Patrol (1934) ◆◆◆ **B&W**

D: John Ford. Victor McLaglen, Boris Karloff, Wallace Ford. 67 minutes. (Fox Hills)

Boris enjoys one of his best non-horror roles as a religious zealot suffering from sunstroke (a bad combo, to be sure) in this classic character study of a doomed Brit squad pinned down by desert snipers.

The Mack (1973) ◆◆◇

D: Michael Campus. Max Julien, Richard Pryor, Don Gordon, Carol Speed. 110 minutes. (Nelson)

A former Forty-second Street perennial, *The Mack* stars Julien as an ex-con-turned-pimp who, with a little help from his friend Pryor, rids the nabe of pushers. Pimp wars likewise rage in the recommended urban actioner *Candy Tangerine Man* (Unicorn).

Macon County Line (1974) ◆◆◇

D: Richard Compton. Max Baer, Jr., Alan Vint, Cheryl Waters, Jesse Vint. 89 minutes. (Embassy)

A tragic misunderstanding triggers sheriff Baer's vendetta against a trio of innocent Yankee youths in a fairly tense B flick that helped establish the "Wish I Wasn't in Dixie" genre. Followed by *Return to Macon County* (Vestron), with Don Johnson and Nick Nolte.

Malone (1987) ◆◆

D: Harley Cokliss. Burt Reynolds, Cliff Robertson, Cynthia Gibb, Scott Wilson, Lauren Hutton, Kenneth McMillan. 92 minutes. (Orion)

One of Burt's single-word titles—see *Stick* (MCA) and *Heat* (Paramount)—that bombed both with critics and at the box office, *Malone* is essentially a limp, contemporized *Shane* update. Burt's a retired CIA assassin who stumbles into rich right-winger Robertson's Pacific Northwest turf and tangles with the latter and his small, inept army of hired hoods. Wilson, in the Van Heflin role, plays a 'Nam-vet gas-station owner who refuses to sell his property to Robertson's goons; Gibb, as his daughter, serves as a distaff Brandon De-Wilde stand-in. The pic's most telling exchange unfolds 'twixt her and Burt. To wit:

> Burt: I'm getting too old for this.
> Cynthia: You're not so old.
> Burt: You have no idea.

Wounded in a shoot-out, Burt gets to spend about half the movie on his back before recovering in time to embark on the expected one-man rampage in the flick's predictably fiery finale. He largely limits his emoting to some occasional grunting and eye shifting here, but he has enough close-ups to satisfy fans of his famous hairpiece.

Man Who Would Be King (1975) ◆◆◆◇
D: John Huston. Sean Connery, Michael Caine, Christopher Plummer. 129 minutes. (CBS/Fox)

Connery and Caine make a fine thespic team as a pair of professional lowlifes who stumble onto a lost Himalayan civilization in Huston's sly, actionful adaptation of the Rudyard Kipling tale.

Manchurian Avenger (1985) ◆◆◇
D: Ed Warnick. Bobby Kim, Leila Hee, Bill ("Superfoot") Wallace, Michael Stuart, Jose Payo, Bob Coulson. 87 minutes. (HBO)

HANDS OF IRON, FEET OF STEEL. HE SMASHES BONES THAT NEVER HEAL—so reads the calling card of *Manchurian Avenger* Bobby Kim. And while it may not be as catchy as, say, HAVE GUN, WILL TRAVEL, you can't accuse Kim of violating any truth-in-advertising sanctions. In this chopsocky western, Bobby breaks enough bones to keep the staffs of *General Hospital* and *St. Elsewhere* busy for years. As laconic hero Joe, Kim helps a young couple battle the villainous Chang, a typical Oriental gang boss of an unnamed sagebrush town circa 1880. Aided by Mexican outlaw Diego (Stuart), Joe delivers high-kicking death blows to

a small army of six-gun goons, culminating in a feet-first showdown with Wallace's evil, multiethnic band of Old West martial artists, who, in full regalia, resemble a kung-fu version of the Village People. Kim himself has the distinction of being a dead ringer for Charles Bronson, albeit a compact (roughly five-foot-two) Oriental version. While Bobby may lack the latter's thespic abilities—he emotes as if he's been trained by Sly Stallone's vocal coach—he's got the pencil-line moustache down pat. And his movie's not half-bad either.

Massive Retaliation (1984) ◆◇
D: Thomas A. Cohen. Peter Donat, Karlene Crockett, Jason Gedrick. 90 minutes. (Vestron)

A strong title masks a wimpy parable about a wealthy doctor (Donat) who behaves poorly in his deluxe fallout shelter during a nuclear false alarm. Bob Goldthwait plays a local bad guy (!).

MasterBlaster (1987) ◆
D: Glenn R. Wilder. Jeff Moldovan, Donna Rosae, Joe Hess, Peter Lundblad, Robert Goodman, Richard St. George. 94 minutes. (Prism)

This Florida-lensed cheapie actually sports a potentially decent action-pic premise: A diverse group of macho guys and tough gals gather to compete in the Master Blaster Grand National Championship, a series of simulated war games played with harmless paint guns. The only problem is, there's a *real* killer among them who's taking the games a tad too literally. In the hack hands of producer William Grefe—the man responsible for such legendary losers as *Stanley* (VidAmerica) and *The Death Curse of Tartu* (Active)—the action quickly bogs down into a swamp of tired genre clichés.

The Mechanic (1972) ◆◆◇
D: Michael Winner. Charles Bronson, Jan-Michael Vincent, Jill Ireland, Keenan Wynn. 100 minutes. (MGM/UA)

A western twist on a martial-arts plot, with Vincent learning the tricks of the hit trade from master assassin Bronson in Chuck and director Winner's informal *Death Wish* tune-up.

The Messenger (1987) ◆◆
D: Fred Williamson. Fred Williamson, Sandy Cummings, Val Avery, Chris Connelly, Cameron Mitchell, Joe Spinell, Peter Brown, Michael Dante. 97 minutes. (Orion)

Yet another el cheapo *Death Wish* manqué, *The Messenger* features Fred ("The Hammer") Williamson as an ex-con "cocaine vigilante" out to eliminate the drug syndicate responsible for his wife's death. So far, so typical. Unfortunately, Williamson directs this hilariously inept "thriller" as if possessed by the soul of Ed Wood, Jr.: The editing, post-sync dubbing, marble-mouthed script, and maddeningly repetitious flatulent-synthesizer soundtrack are uniformly awful, as is Fred's increasingly flabby physique (lensed in self-loving close-up, no less, during the pic's lone sex scene). *The Messenger* also abounds in badly staged action sequences, utterly meaningless reaction shots, and thesps who act as if they'd never seen a script or each other before the cameras started rolling. For said cast, Fred rounded up the usual B-movie suspects—Connelly, Spinell, Dante, former pretty boy Brown, and (it goes virtually without saying) the ubiquitous Cameron Mitchell. This is infinitely funnier than Fred's merely boring *Foxtrap* (see index), but we can recommend it only for the most insatiable bad-movie addicts.

Messenger of Death (1988) ◆
D: J. Lee Thompson. Charles Bronson, Trish Van Devere, Laurence Luckinbill, John Ireland, Jeff Corey, Marilyn Hassett. 91 minutes. (Media)

Taking a break from his *Death Wish* duties, Chuck plays Denver-based journalist Garrett Smith, who doesn't run, fight, or fire a gun—thus giving his stunt double a well-deserved rest as well. *Messenger of Death* finds Chuck—investigating an opening-scene massacre in a remote sector of Colorado—caught between warring Mormon factions, led by antiquated character thesps Ireland and Corey (both sufficiently long in the tooth to make Chuck look merely middle-aged by comparison). Beyond its largely geriatric cast, *Messenger of Death*—based on Rex Burns's novel *Avenging Angel*—has an eerily old-fashioned feel, from its cliché-ridden dialogue to its '50s-schlock-style soundtrack. And Chuck, forced to rely on his natural emotive abilities, seems almost catatonic here. As for the flick's feeble stabs at cultural exoticism, suffice it to say that *Messenger of Death* isn't likely to do for the Mormons what *Witness* (Paramount) did for the Amish.

Missing in Action (1984) ♦
D: Joseph Zito. Chuck Norris, M. Emmett Walsh, Lenore Kasdorf. 101 minutes. (MGM/UA)

Chuck makes a major career move, abandoning his kung-fu Clint Eastwood persona to become a Rambo clone, an imitative tactic that succeeded in brightening his then-fading BO allure. Go figure.

Missing in Action 2: The Beginning (1985) ♦
D: Lance Hool. Chuck Norris, Soon Teck-Oh, Steven Williams, Bennett Ohta, Cosie Costa. 96 minutes. (MGM/UA)

A "prequel" to Chuck's *Missing in Action*, *MIA 2* chronicles Colonel Braddock's brutal stay in a Vietcong POW compound, where he and his fellow Americans suffer countless indignities at the hands of cruel camp commandant Colonel Yin (Soon Teck-Oh) before busting out and returning the favor in spades. The pic's most imaginative sequence sees Chuck strung upside down with a bag over his head. What's in the bag? A hungry rat! Chuck saves his neck and simultaneously registers his low opinion of VC cuisine by biting the hapless rodent's head off! Chuck returns, sans rat, for more of the same in 1988's *Braddock: Missing in Action III*. (Media).

Mission Kill (1985) ♦♦
D: David Winters. Robert Ginty, Cameron Mitchell, Olivia D'Abo, Henry Darrow, Sandy Baron, Merete Van Kamp. 97 minutes. (Media)

A poor man's *Under Fire* (Vestron), David Winters's *Mission Kill* stars laid-back B-movie hero Ginty as a demolitions expert caught up in a Central American revolution. After government-hired mercenaries off partner Cameron Mitchell, Ginty sides with the rebels; a subplot sees a grubby journalist (well played by Baron) set out to legendize the explosive gringo for his own self-aggrandizing purposes. While ultimately predictable, *Mission Kill*'s lively action sequences and impressive scope at least make it better than the pathetic quickies *Mankillers* (Sony) and *Deadly Prey* (see index) later produced under director Winters's Action International Pictures banner.

Ms. Don Juan (1973) NR

D: Roger Vadim. Brigitte Bardot, Maurice Ronet, Robert Hossein. 87 minutes. (Wizard)

Not to be confused with *Ms. 45*, this *Ms.* finds Brigitte taking orders from auteur Vadim in a tale of a ruthless femme fatale who lures unsuspecting men into her web of (what else?) sin. BB is also on view in *And God Created Woman* (Vestron), *The Bride Is Much Too Beautiful* (Captain Bijou), *Contempt* (Embassy), *Dear Brigitte* (CBS/Fox), *The Legend of Frenchie King* (Paragon), *Mademoiselle Striptease*, aka *Please, Mr. Balzac!* (Amvest), *The Ravishing Idiot* (Monterey), *Shalako* (Playhouse), *A Very Private Affair* (MGM/UA), and *The Women* (Unicorn).

Ms. 45 (1981) ◆◆◆

D: Abel Ferrara. Zoe Tamerlis, Steve Singer, Jack Thibeau. 84 minutes. (IVE)

The flick that put Abel (*China Girl*) Ferrara on the urban-action-cult-movie map, this distaff *Death Wish* with a difference stars Tamerlis as a rape victim who turns the tables (and the title weapon) on the city's male lowlife scum—and doesn't stop there. Not to be confused with *Ms. Stiletto* (Vestron), which is actually a period actioner about a fierce gypsy gal who swears revenge against the royalty who massacred her family. For a kung-fu variation on *Ms. 45*, see the former Forty-second Street stalwart *Alley Cat* (Vestron).

Murphy's Law (1986) ◆◆

D: J. Lee Thompson. Charles Bronson, Carrie Snodgress, Robert F. Lyons. 97 minutes. (Media)

Chuck takes time off from his busy vigilante chores to sneak in this unexciting actioner wherein he gets to play an actual cop; otherwise, it's bloody business as usual. Other Bronson action entries not covered elsewhere in this volume but available on video include the Alistair MacLean western *Breakheart Pass*, *Death Hunt* (both CBS/Fox), *Breakout*, *The Evil That Men Do*, *Hard Times*, *The Stone Killer* (all RCA/Columbia), *Capoblanco* (Media), *Chino*, *St. Ives* (both Warner), *Cold Sweat*, *Red Sun* (both Video Gems), *The Family* (MPI), *Honor Among Thieves* (Monterey), *Love and Bullets* (Key), Sam Fuller's *The Meanest Men in the West* (MCA), *Raid on Entebbe* (HBO), *Showdown at Boot Hill* (Republic), *Someone Behind the Door* (Showcase), *Mr. Majestyk*, *Telefon* and *Ten to Midnight* (all MGM/UA), and *Villa Rides!* (Kartes).

The Naked Cage (1986) ◆◆◆

D: Paul Nicholas. Shari Shattuck, Angel Tompkins, Lucinda Crosby, Christina Whitaker, Faith Minton, John Terlesky. 97 minutes. (Media)

Michelle (Shattuck) is a sweet, clean-cut blonde out for nothing more exciting than the occasional romp on her beloved mare, Misty. Unfortunately for Michelle, her lowlife ex-beau Willie (Terlesky) has gotten himself mixed up with escaped con Rita (Whitaker), a mean gutter scum queen who soon talks a coked-up Will into helping her pull a heist at the very bank where our hapless heroine works. By the time the smoke clears, Willie's wasted, while Michelle, wrongly implicated in the crime, winds up in a wild femme pen that makes the Snake Pit look like Sunnybrook Farm. Here Michelle encounters your typical ruthless blond lesbian warden (Tompkins), psychotic rapist screw Smiley (Benedict), and—worst of all—a vengeful, blade-wielding Rita. While not as hot as his *Chained Heat* (1983; see index), where he had the incomparable Linda Blair and Sybil Danning to work with, Paul Nicholas's *Naked Cage* ("Raw violence and hot rage explode behind bars!") supplies vicious catfights aplenty, gratuitous nudity galore, and more seething inmate unrest than you could shake a nightstick at. Toss in racial hostilities, brutal prison power struggles, and a lively climactic riot ("This used to be such a *nice* place," our crooked warden wistfully reminisces), and you have the best broads-behind-bars flick of 1986 (see sidebar).

BIMBOS BEHIND BARS

Even in the face of Hollywood's unending welter of macho-man movies, the venerable women's-prison picture also continues to hold its own. Though few recent entries capture the vile vitality of *Big Doll House* or *Chained Heat,* an effort like 1986's *The Naked Cage* can take its place among the best chicks-in-chains romps ever produced. In addition to inspiring a number of largely lame parodies, from Chuck Vincent's *Slammer Girls* to Fred Olen Ray's sci-fi variation, *Star Slammer,* the genre has provoked the ire of many mainstream critics who fail to realize that the flicks' overwhelmingly male audiences show up to root for the underdog inmates' inevitable reel-end revenge spree, not just to wallow in the sadistic treatment they receive along the way. The pics are a pulp recreation of class warfare, not of the battle between the sexes, and the oppressed always triumph in the end. Which probably goes a long way toward explaining the films' enviable durability.

Other available chicks-in-chains romps not listed as separate entries here include *Amazon Jail* and the intriguingly titled *American Beauty*

Hostages (formerly *Ebony, Ivory and Jade*) (both Cinema Group), *Caged Fury* (Vidmark), *Caged Women* (Vestron), *Chain Gang Women* (Academy), *Condemned to Hell* (TWE), *Escape from Cell Block Three* (Prism), *Escape from Women's Prison* (sharing a Cinema Group cassette with *Sweet Sugar*, starring the formidable Phyllis Elizabeth Davis), Edgar G. Ulmer's 1943 antique *Girls in Chains* (Sinister Cinema), *Girls Riot* (Academy), *House of Whipcord* (IVE), *The Muthers* (Cinema Group), Jess Franco's *99 Women* (Republic), Mai Zetterling's imported *Scrubbers* (HBO), *Terminal Island* (Cinema Group, with Tom Selleck in his screen debut), *Woman Hunt* (Charter), the Filipino-filmed *Women in Cages* (with Pam Grier sorely miscast as a sadistic prison guard) (Charter), *Women in Cell Block 7* (IVE), *Women in Fury* (Vestron), and *Women Unchained* (Video Gems).

The Naked Jungle (1954) ◆◆
D: Byron Haskin. Charlton Heston, Eleanor Parker. 95 minutes. (Paramount)

Heston is a virginal (!) ranch owner plagued by "impure" mail-order bride Parker *and* rampaging red-ant armies in this oddly neurotic South America–set adventure.

The Naked Prey (1966) ◆◆◆
D: Cornel Wilde. Cornel Wilde, Ken Gampu, Gert Van Den Bergh. 96 minutes. (Paramount)

Former matinee idol Wilde does a commendable job both directing and starring (virtually sans dialogue) as a white man pursued by a team of hostile African tribesmen in an almost film-long chase. Succeeds in generating suspense *and* in making its point.

Nightforce (1986) ◆
D: Lawrence D. Foldes. Linda Blair, James Van Patten, Richard Lynch, Chad McQueen, Cameron Mitchell, Claudia Udy. 87 minutes. (Vestron)

Hard to imagine that a flick combining the multiple talents of Linda Blair *and* Cameron Mitchell could be *all* bad, but Foldes's *Nightforce* manages to accomplish that difficult feat. Linda stars as a tough-minded co-ed who joins a foursome of fighting frat boys (!) out to rescue a senator's daughter (Udy) who's been snatched by the San Felipe Anarchist Army. The latter, led by a hefty jefe who resembles a cross between Fidel Castro and *Steel Helmet*'s Sergeant Zack, are a particularly scurvy lot of raping, murdering louts who keep their vulnerable blond victim chained naked (natch) in a bamboo cage. With the aid of flute-playing mercenary Lynch and his trained monkey, our collegiate combat unit springs into action for the pic's inevitable climactic slaughterfest. While Cameron acquits himself with customary aplomb in a brief cameo as the kidnappee's worried dad, Linda's sadly wasted in a just-one-of-the-guys role.

9 Deaths of the Ninja (1985) ◆◇
D: Sam Firstenberg. Sho Kosugi, Brent Huff, Emelia Lesniak, Regina Richardson, Shane Kosugi, Kane Kosugi. 93 minutes. (Media)

In this, his fourth and worst Ninja stint, Sho Kosugi returns as Spike Shinobi, fearless leader of an anti-terrorist team that also includes Lesniak and hunky Huff. Their mission: to free a busload of American hostages from the Filipino stronghold of crazed neo-Nazi heroin czar Alby the Cruel (the truly awful Blackie Dammett) and his colorful minions—lesbian guerrilla Colonel Honey Hump, mad terrorist Mohammed, and the markedly antisocial Dr. Woof. Except for an effective slo-mo rock-video credit sequence featuring Sho and a trio of leotarded Oriental dancing girls, *9 Deaths* has all the earmarks of an elaborate vanity production. Not only does Sho indulge in his usual Ninja nepotism by creating cameos for his kung-fu kids Kane and Shane, but even exec producer/tennis star Vijay Amritraj gets into the act as a DEA agent. There's nothing here that rivals the memorable scene in *Revenge of the Ninja* (MGM/UA), wherein six-year-old Kane Kosugi duked it out with a large-breasted blonde, though Sho's battle with a quartet of sunglassed dwarfs with bad teeth comes dangerously close.

Ninja in the Claws of the CIA (1986) NR
John Liu. 102 minutes. (Magnum)

One of our fave kung-fu titles of all time (starring John Liu, "successor to the immortal Bruce Lee legacy") is, unfortunately, extremely hard to find at most cassette outlets. We just hope we've done our part here by bringing that correctable fact to vid-store owners' attention. Other available Ninja titles include *Ninja: American Warrior* (Imperial), *Ninja Blacklist* (Best), *Ninja Champion* (TWE), *Ninja Connection* (Imperial), *Ninja Hunt* (TWE), *Ninja Hunter* (Ocean), *Ninja Massacre* (Video Gems), *Ninja Mission* (Media), *Ninja Squad* (TWE), *Ninja Turf* (RCA/Columbia), *Ninja Warriors* (IVE), and *Ninja Wars* (Prism), to cite a few.

Ninja III—The Domination (1984) ◆◆◆
D: Sam Firstenberg. Sho Kosugi, Lucinda Dickey, Jordan Bennett. 95 minutes. (MGM/UA)

One of Sho's best: Great plot has the spirit of a samurai psycho commandeer blond Dickey's body, transforming her into a mass-murder machine (!).

No Retreat, No Surrender (1986) ◆
D: Corey Yuen. Kurt McKinney, J. W. Fails, Kathie Sileno, Jean-Claude Van Damme, Kim Tai-Chong, Kent Lipham. 85 minutes. (New World)

No Retreat's original print ads made it look like a fourth-rate *Rocky IV* rip-off (itself a third-rate *Rocky* rip-off), but this home-movie-level loser has nothing so grandiose on its addled little mind. Instead, its story concerns the plight of teenage martial-arts hopeful McKinney, who runs away from his Seattle home after his karate-teacher/dad Tim Baker tears up his cherished Bruce Lee poster (!). With the help of his breakdancing buddy J. W. Fails, Kurt sets up his portable gym in an abandoned garage, where Bruce Lee's ghost (Kim Tai-Chong) treats him to a crash course in the latest full-contact karate techniques. This spirited training comes in handy during the pic's grand finale—the Full-Contact Karate Championship of the World, staged in what looks like a junior-high gym before a capacity crowd of dozens. Ruthless East Coast promoters (there must have been hundreds of dollars riding on this gala event) unleash a killer Russki (Van Damme, later of *Bloodsport* fame—see index), who wipes out the local pro talent but (natch) proves no match for the new, improved Jason. Now, what *we* want to know is who put up the dough for this amateur-night fiasco? The Seattle Chamber of Commerce? Ruthless East Coast promoters? The ghost of Bruce Lee? In any case, we're sure you can find better outlets for *your* video bucks. Believe it or not, a sequel, *No Retreat,*

No Surrender II, has since reared its empty head (Forum).

Nowhere to Hide (1987) ♦♦◊
D: Mario Azzopardi. Amy Madigan, Daniel Hugh Kelly, Robin Mac-Eachern, Michael Ironside, John Colicos, Maury Chaykin. 90 minutes. (Lorimar)

In *Nowhere to Hide*, a Canada-lensed quickie co-scripted by *Incredible Melting Man* star Alex Rebar (just thought you'd want to know), Madigan excels as a tough ex-Marine mom who is on the run—with her six-year-old son—from the vicious gunmen who've just killed her hubby (Kelly). Seems her spouse had uncovered a crooked defense contractor's plot to peddle shoddy machinery to the Marines—equipment that had already resulted in two fatal copter crashes. While predictable, *Nowhere to Hide* delivers some excitingly staged action, particularly when Amy teams up with laconic 'Nam vet/survivalist Ironside to take on a small army of bad guys. Character thesp Maury (*The Vindicator*) Chaykin, meanwhile, is appropriately malevolent in another of his patented fat villain roles.

Number One with a Bullet (1987) 0♦
D: Jack Smight. Robert Carradine, Billy Dee Williams, Valerie Bertinelli, Peter Graves, Doris Roberts, Bobby Di Cicco. 103 minutes. (MGM/UA)

The stupidest cop caper in recent memory, *Number One with a Bul-*

let offers nary a single *shtick* we haven't seen before (which, if nothing else, at least defies the law of averages). Carradine as the volatile Bersak and the ever-unflappable Williams as his sensible partner Hazeltine run through the entire catalog of cop-movie clichés. The lifeless fistfights, car chases, and shoot-outs are further slowed by a subplot involving Carradine's pursuit of Bertinelli's porcine charms. A junkie-torture scene that's played for laughs is base enough to come *this* close to offending even the Phantom. The flick's four scripters (including James Belushi) pull the slickest heist here by getting paid for their insulting efforts.

Omega Syndrome (1987) ◆◆
D: Joseph Manduke. Ken Wahl, George DiCenzo, Doug McClure, Ron Kuhlman. 90 minutes. (New World)

Ken (*The Soldier*) Wahl is a "wimp writer" who dares to take on the vicious neo-Nazi organization Omega (actually a dozen or so disorganized thugs hanging around an L.A. warehouse) after they kidnap his young daughter. The police—epitomized here by vet thesp McClure—are helpless at best, so our hero enlists the aid of grizzled arms dealer and former 'Nam buddy DiCenzo. *Omega Syndrome* had the potential to be a visceral thriller with (gasp) semi-serious overtones, but the suspense quickly fizzles under a choppy script and Manduke's peripatetic direction.

Once Upon a Time in America (1984) ◆◆◇
D: Sergio Leone. Robert De Niro, James Woods, Elizabeth McGovern, Treat Williams. 143 minutes. (Warner)

The video version represents the reedited 143-minute American release print—which accounts for the numerous plot lapses—of Leone's gangster epic.

One Down, Two to Go (1983) ◆◆◇
D: Fred Williamson. Fred Williamson, Jim Brown, Jim Kelly, Richard Roundtree. 84 minutes. (Media)

An all-star black action quartet takes on hoods who are trying to rig a major karate tournament. For fans of that fierce foursome.

Opposing Force (1986) ◆◆◇
D: Eric Karson. Tom Skerritt, Lisa Eichhorn, Anthony Zerbe, Richard Roundtree, Robert Wightman, John Considine. 99 minutes. (HBO)

Aging flier Skerritt and lone femme Eichhorn are among a group of military officers who volunteer to undergo a survival course in invasionary tactics in a remote Philippines jungle. What they *don't* know is that the maneuvers are actually part of a grueling POW endurance test. Nor do they realize that the officer in charge—sneering maniac Zerbe—has gone mentally AWOL. The result is a fairly realistically staged mini–civil war, Vietnam replayed with GIs on both sides, and a tense, at-times thoughtful thriller that doesn't stoop to cheap macho heroics but still delivers the action goods.

Over the Top (1987) ◆◆
D: Menahem Golan. Sylvester Stallone, Robert Loggia, David Mendenhall, Susan Blakely, Rick Zumwalt, Bruce Way. 94 minutes. (Warner)

A sort of *Rocky vs. Kramer, Over the Top* stars our man Sly as Lincoln Hawk, a trucker/arm-wrestler/errant dad who's sent to drive his estranged twelve-year-old son Mike (Mendenhall) cross-country to visit his ailing mom (Blakely). At first the kid, a military-academy prig, regards his primitive pop with less than loving affection. ("There's more to life than just muscles," Junior huffily opines.) But the boy soon changes his sour tune as Sly leads him on a merry descent down the evolutionary scale, introducing him to the joys of junk food, truck driving, and arm wrestling, while Giorgio Moroder's snappy synthesizer rhythms lend their musical support. It's at Vegas's international arm-wrestling gala that *Over the Top* reaches its high-concept peak, as Hawk matches blood, sweat, and 'ceps with a succession of macho throwbacks hulking enough to make Sly look like Danny De Vito, if not Dr. Ruth. The arm-wrestling scenes are lensed in *Raging Bull*–style slo-mo (!) while the soundtrack swells with anguished bellows not unlike those of bull elephants in musk. *Over the Top* represents a radical, risky departure from the typical Sly vehicle—a tale calculated to warm your heart and tug at your hamstrings (a strong stomach also helps)—and one that flopped miserably at the old BO (though Sly came out some 12 million of Cannon's dollars to the good).

Panther Squad (1985) ◆◇
D: Peter Knight. Sybil Danning, Jack Taylor, Karin Shubert, Robert Foster, Joan Virly, Shirley Knight. 77 minutes. (Lightning)

Panther Squad is a would-be Bondian adventure involving the Clean Space movement's strong-arm attempts to sabotage the New Organization of Nations' space program. Enter, on the NOON side, mercenary Danning, who should have known better: Ms. Danning wantonly endangers her hard-won standing as a quality B-movie icon not only by starring in but by *co-producing* this pathetic, spliced-together mess. *Panther Squad* is limp on every level, from its weak thesping and amateurishly staged "action" sequences to its lame script and stiff direction. Okay, we've had our say. Now come back, Syb—all is forgiven.

Papillon (1973) ◆◆◆
D: Franklin J. Schaffner. Steve McQueen, Dustin Hoffman, Victor Jory. 151 minutes. (CBS/Fox)

Steve and Dustin endure hardships, cruelties, and deprivations galore in a grueling prison bustout pic that's perfect for watching from the comfort of your couch.

The Patriot (1986) ◆◇
D: Frank Harris. Gregg Henry, Simone Griffeth, Michael J. Pollard, Jeff Conaway, Leslie Nielsen, Stack Pierce. 88 minutes. (Vestron)

When we first caught The Patriot during its unheralded theatrical run, we noted that, among its many deficiencies, this dull, disjointed actioner suffered from singularly inept editing. Only in The Patriot's long-unawaited video reincarnation did we learn that it was assembled with the dubious aid of a new computerized film-editing system called Editdroid, a process that George Lucas allegedly had something to do with. If The Patriot—which stars Gregg Henry (seen to far better effect as the psycho killer in Brian De Palma's Body Double—see index) as a naval officer hot on the trail of renegade nuke thieves—offers any indication, Editdroid may soon go the way of the Edsel. Ditto for the 'droids who produced, scripted, and directed this dim-witted mess.

Penitentiary (1979) ◆◆◆
D: Jamaa Fanaka. Leon Isaac Kennedy, Thommy Pollard, Hazel Spears, Chuck Mitchell. 99 minutes. (Unicorn)

Fanaka's bid to revive the flagging fellas-in-chains genre is a fast-paced, funny, funky mix of realism and exploitation focusing on framed con Kennedy's efforts to box his way out of stir. Fanaka's knowing script and almost verité direction combine to make this one of the best the genre's ever produced. Kennedy is convincing as Sugar Ray Leonard lookalike Too Sweet, as are Floyd Chatman as his elderly mentor Seldom Seen and Badja Djola as his bullying nemesis Half Dead. The pic's casually candid treatment of inmate homosexuality remains one of its strongest suits.

Penitentiary II (1982) ◆◇
D: Jamaa Fanaka. Leon Isaac Kennedy, Ernie Hudson, Peggy Blow, Mr. T. 103 minutes. (MGM/UA)

The formula doesn't work in Fanaka's first follow-up, despite the presence of the formidable Mr. T. Fanaka seems to be just coasting here, recycling Pen I without the latter's energy and invention.

Penitentiary III (1987) ◆◆
D: Jamaa Fanaka. Leon Isaac Kennedy, Anthony Geary, Steve Antin. 91 minutes. (Warner)

Kennedy's third stretch in stir restores some of the perverse, off-the-wall fun of the first film, but much of it seems willed rather than inspired and there aren't enough fresh twists to qualify the flick as essential viewing for non–Fanaka fanatics. Pro midget wrestler The Haiti Kid does impress, however, as a killer mutant dwarf (!) called The Midnight

Thud, who unexpectedly sheds his feral ways to serve as Too Sweet's latest boxing mentor.

Picasso Trigger (1988) ◆◆
D: Andy Sidaris. Steve Bond, Dona Speir, Hope Marie Carlton, Roberta Vasquez, John Aprea, Harold Diamond, Guich Koock. 98 minutes. (Warner)

Andy and Arlene Sidaris's *Picasso Trigger* continues the saga of crooked-shooting superstud Rowdy Abilene, last seen in the same team's *Hard Ticket to Hawaii* (see index). The original Rowdy, Ronn Moss, has been replaced by former soap star Steve (no relation to James) Bond, but two-fisted, large-breasted ex-Playmates Speir and Carlton reprise their earlier roles as undercover—or more precisely, *un*covered—agents Donna and Taryn, two gals who'll jump into the nearest Jacuzzi at the drop of a halter. (Fully seven ladies of the Playmate persuasion appear here in all.) The high-concept title refers both to an exotic breed of Hawaiian fish and to archvillian Aprea, who employs Picasso Trigger as his underworld nickname and who instigates an involved assassination spree that soon whips our sundry heroes and heroines into action. Despite its larger canvas, budget, and chests, *Picasso Trigger* fails to measure up to *Hard Ticket*'s standards, due largely to the self-mocking Moss's replacement by the self-serious

Bond and the glaring absence of *Ticket*'s giant killer snake—the one, you'll recall, who'd been "infected with deadly toxins from cancer-infested rats." On the plus side, *Picasso Trigger* still offers sufficient infusions of wanton sex, senseless violence, and sun-soaked sleaze to please fans of the Sidarises' ongoing action series.

P.O.W.: The Escape (1986) ◆◇
D: Gideon Amir. David Carradine, Charles Floyd, Steve James, Mako, Phil Brock. 90 minutes. (Media)

David (*Kung-Fu*) Carradine joins Hollywood's wooden-soldier (and actor) ranks as one-man army Colonel "Everybody Goes Home!" Cooper, who copters down into a secret VC camp to spring a group of POWs and simultaneously deliver a "loud message to Hanoi." Dave's bravery swiftly results in his own incarceration. Things look bleak until cruel Cong camp commandant Mako confesses that *he'd* like to cut out too—to Miami Beach, no less—so the two form an uneasy alliance as they lead the POWs on a wild, violent escape through VC territory. Along the way, Dave single-handedly slaughters the usual slew of Oriental extras (even dispatching a few via his patented kung-fu footwork) while wearing not only the requisite Rambo headband but an American flag over his shoulder! Afterward, Dave joins the rescued GIs in a spirited rendition of "Proud Mary," then informs them that

Jimi Hendrix was once a member of the 101st Airborne—"a Screaming Eagle all the way." Now, there's a line not even so prescient a sage as Ed Wood, Jr.'s, prophetic friend *Criswell* could have predicted!

Pray for Death (1985) ◆◆◆
D: Gordon Hessler. Sho Kosugi, James Booth, Donna Kei Benz, Michael Constantine, Robert Ito, Kane Kosugi, Shane Kosugi. 92 minutes. (IVE)

The kung-fu Kosugi clan makes amends for the lamentable *9 Deaths of the Ninja* (see index) with *Pray for Death*. This time, dad Sho portrays a Japanese businessman (and closet Ninja, natch) who, accompanied by screen wife Benz and real-life sons Kane and Shane, relocates to Houston in search of "success." At first, Sho is hesitant about the planned move. "American cities are so violent!" he protests. To which wife Donna Kei counters, "You've been watching too many movies" (like *this* one). Sure enough, faster than you can say "land of the free," Sho and family run afoul of a gang of vicious hoods led by Limehouse, interpreted with sadistic flair by Brit thesp Booth (once a supporting player in A pics like *Zulu*), who also penned the script. Limehouse and cronies are looking for a priceless necklace they think Sho has discovered in his newly purchased restaurant and will stop at the proverbial nothing to get their slimy hands on same. They prove that contention by killing Sho's wife and snatching son Shane. The cops, as always, are incapable of redressing these wrongs, so Sho dons his Ninja threads and heads out to "redefine revenge." *Pray for Death* may not be a great advertisement for life in these United States, but its predictable plot proceeds at a brisk clip, the action scenes (including a kiddie kung-fu set-to between young Kane and some preteen toughs) are excitingly mounted, and Booth makes for a memorable screen villain. In short, *Pray for Death* supplies a lively 92 minutes of chopsocky thrills.

Prime Cut (1972) ◆◆◆
D: Michael Ritchie. Lee Marvin, Gene Hackman, Angel Tompkins, Sissy Spacek. 88 minutes. (Key)

Marvin is a troubleshooter for an Irish Chicago mob being cheated by KC slaughterhouse-owner and all-around malefactor Hackman in a sleazy, irreverent A flick with a B-movie soul. Director Ritchie kicks the proceedings off to a fast, offbeat start, though he can't quite sustain the pic's idiosyncratic feel for the duration. Still well worth seeing, though, for the tough male leads, young Spacek as one of Hackman's white-slavery victims, bursts of bloody action, and Ritchie's skewed cinematic view.

The Principal (1987) ◆◆
D: Christopher Cain. James Belushi, Louis Gossett, Jr., Rae Dawn Chong, Michael Wright, J. J. Cohen, Esai Morales. 110 minutes. (RCA/Columbia)

That Jim Belushi sure is one whale of a brawlin', beer-swillin', hog-ridin' macho stud of an educator! When high school teach Jim screws up, sadistic school authorities appoint him head of the town's toughest facility, Brandell. There—despite indifference, rampant crime, and armed threats posed by teenage drug lord Wright—Jim takes it into his head to set these kids on the right track. On hand to help is Gossett, as head of Brandell's security. Hollywood to the core, *The Principal* compromises its own modest ambitions at every potentially exciting turn—from Belushi's ill-timed wisecracks to multiple product plugs to filler footage filmed solely for later insertion into the pic's inevitable rock-video promo. Stick with *Class of 1984* (see index) and *Massacre at Central High* (see index), or hope that *Blackboard Jungle* joins the video ranks.

The Protector (1985) ◆◇

D: James Glickenhaus. Jackie Chan, Danny Aiello, Bill ("Superfoot") Wallace, Harold Ko. 94 minutes. (Warner)

As Dirty Harry–type cop Billy Wong, Chan turns in a performance so wooden that watching for more than five minutes is to risk getting splinters. After an opening high-speed boat chase across the East River—a lavish display of derring-do that apparently put a major dent in the budget—the action quickly shifts to Hong Kong, where production costs are cheaper. (*The Protector*'s idea of high-tech FX is a lingering close-up on a helicopter control panel!) There, Billy and partner Aiello—undoubtedly seduced by the prospect of a (barely) working vacation—take on evil heroin czar Ko and henchman Wallace, who deals Chan a surprisingly savage, one-sided beating, which our hero survives with naught but a sore shoulder. Only in the admittedly vital area of gratuitous nudity does the pic offer an inventive twist: a quartet of distaff smack processors who work in the altogether so they can't sneak off with any of the merch (a riff reused in Whoopi's woeful *Fatal Beauty*).

Psych-Out (1968) ◆◆◆

D: Richard Rush. Susan Strasberg, Jack Nicholson, Dean Stockwell, Bruce Dern. 95 minutes. (HBO)

Rocker Nicholson helps deaf-mute Strasberg locate her zonked-out brother Stockwell in this pseudopsychedelic, acid-action howler. In one scene, future auteur Henry (*Sitting Ducks*) Jaglom threatens to unhand himself with a chainsaw (!) fully two decades before Bruce Campbell pulled the same stunt in Sam Raimi's *Evil Dead II* (see index).

Public Enemy (1931) ◆◆◆◆ B&W

D: William A. Wellman. James Cagney, Mae Clarke, Eddie Woods. 84 minutes. (Warner)

Still one of the best—and rawest—gangster films ever made, as tenement punk Cagney slaps, shoots, and sneers his way to the top. Only

Raoul Walsh's *White Heat* gave Cags as wonderful a role to work with.

Purgatory (1989) ◆◆
D: *Ami Artzi. Tanya Roberts, Julie Pop, Harold Orlandini, Rufus Swart. 92 minutes. (New Star)*

In Artzi's *Purgatory* ("The Women's Prison That's One Step From Hell!"), former *Charlie's Angel*/screen *Sheena* (RCA/Columbia) Tanya Roberts and newcomer Julie Pop topline as a pair of Peace Corps volunteers stationed in a mythical African nation. No sooner do the opening credits end than martial law is declared and all foreigners are advised to leave. Tanya takes the news in stride ("So much for the Peace Corps!") but proves less adaptable when she and Ms. Pop are tossed into the titular hoosegow on trumped-up drug charges. In fact, over the first 80 minutes or so, Tanya gives every indication of not being tough enough to hold her own in this demanding genre. Not only does she go to whining and weeping at the drop of a truncheon, but she proves exceedingly discreet in the gratuitous-nudity department, shows zero enthusiasm for her "work detail" chores as a loaned-out hooker at a local hotel, and even performs her token upchuck scene with a decided lack of conviction. Fortunately, Tanya finally snaps to in the actionful final reel of this otherwise utterly routine, low-energy *Midnight Express* manqué by leading the inevitable inmate breakout and violently settling the score with the prison's predictably sadistic authorities. While *Purgatory* may not constitute a major career move for Tanya, it's definitely a step up for the memorably monikered Skip Schoolnik, who'd earlier directed the hideous *Hide and Go Shriek* (see index) but who scores nothing less than an "executive producer" credit here.

Quiet Cool (1986) ◆
D: *Clay Borris. James Remar, Adam Coleman Howard, Daphne Ashbrook, Jared Martin, Nick Cassavetes. 80 minutes. (RCA/Columbia)*

Borris's *Quiet Cool* is a relentlessly predictable, dumber-than-average actioner set in the rural Northwest. (The title, in case you're wondering, refers to that "very special place inside yourself" wherein true courage dwells.) Remar, seen to far better advantage as the psycho in *48 Hours* (Paramount) and *The Cotton Club*'s (Embassy) Dutch Schultz, is totally wasted here as the laconic cop who teams with the teenage survivor (Howard) of a massacre perpetrated by marijuana Mafiosi led by Nick (Son of John) Cassavetes. *Quiet Cool* is just another stale spaghetti western cloaked in contempo garb.

Quiet Thunder (1987) ◆◇
D: *David Rice. Wayne Crawford, June Chadwick, Victor Steinbach, Ramolao Mahkene, Karl Johnson, Ken Gampu. 94 minutes. (IVE)*

Matinee idol manqué Wayne Crawford, who so unimpressed in 1986's *Jake Speed* (New World) (which he also wrote and co-produced), returns to the B screen in *Quiet Thunder*, a low-budget *African Queen*–type adventure that sees grizzled tour pilot Wayne and WASPy senator's wife June Chadwick on the run from a Russki-led team of African assassins. Unfortunately, Wayne and June are so downright disingenuous that we soon found ourselves rooting for the bad guys to put them out of their (and our) misery. While *Quiet Thunder* delivers a fair amount of action in its later reels and even manages to mix in a bit of muddled mysticism, arriving at that point requires more patience than the Phantom possesses. Particularly painful are those scenes wherein the would-be hard-boiled Wayne hits us with his world-weary soliloquies. We hate to be the one to tell you this, Wayne, but the camera just doesn't love you.

The Racketeer (1929) NR B&W
D: Howard Higgin. Carole Lombard, Robert Armstrong, Hedda Hopper. 68 minutes. (Cable, others)

An occasionally static but interesting and influential gangster flick pairing Lombard and Armstrong.

Rage of Honor (1987) ◆◇
D: Gordon Hessler. Sho Kosugi, Lewis Van Bergen, Robin Evans, Gerry Gibson, Chip Lucia, Richard Wiley. 92 minutes. (Media)

Rage of Honor is nothing if not a one-man Sho. In addition to personally designing all the "special weapons" on view, an out-of-control Kosugi shows Arnie, Sly, and Chuck what mass destruction's really all about as he single-handedly slays or maims a small army of Arizona drug dealers. Then, when a colleague is killed, Sho decides to get *serious*. With what seems like a single over-the-head leap, he lands in Argentina, where he wipes out a *large* army of South American drug dealers *and* half a native tribe that happens to get in his way. But it's not over yet—CIA choppers ostensibly sent to rescue Sho actually contain deadly Ninjas bent on eliminating our hero. Sho decimates 'em to a man (and a chopper), all the while delivering even the most innocuous dialogue with feral intensity. (He may be the only actor extant who can make "I cannot go on a date with you" sound like a death threat.) Tune in next time, when enemy forces hit him with a fifty-meg nuke warhead and Sho is momentarily dazed!

Raging Bull (1980) ◆◆◆◆ B&W
D: Martin Scorsese. Robert De Niro, Cathy Moriarty, Joe Pesci. 129 minutes. (MGM/UA)

In easily the best boxing movie of all time—including Robert Wise's excellent *The Set-Up* (see index)—the self-fattened De Niro is outstanding as simian slugger Jake LaMotta (himself a frequent cameo thesp in '80s B flicks). According to Steven Bach's book *Final Cut*, De Niro was also responsible for the script's final draft.

Rambo: First Blood Part II (1985) ♦

D: George P. Cosmatos. Sylvester Stallone, Richard Crenna, Charles Napier, Martin Kove. 93 minutes. (HBO)

"I believe that the mind is the best weapon," says Sly (an interpreter may be necessary), and who are we to argue? *Rambo III* (IVE) is also out there.

Raw Deal (1986) ♦♦

D: John Irvin. Arnold Schwarzenegger, Kathryn Harrold, Sam Wanamaker, Paul Shenar, Ed Lauter, Darren McGavin. 106 minutes. (HBO)

In *Raw Deal*, Schwarzenegger—cast as your typical Austrian-accented southern sheriff—is stuck not only with a demeaning job but with a dangerous domestic life. When he comes home after a hard day of collaring red-necks, his inebriated bitter half (Blanche Baker) tosses a chocolate cake at him. "You shouldn't drink und bake!" our hero sagely advises. *Raw Deal*'s real business begins when Arn, a former FBI agent, is summoned back to action by bureau honcho McGavin, who wants him to infiltrate the Chicago syndicate responsible for his son's murder. Over the next few reels, *Raw Deal* is a fairly punchy mobster yarn that sees Arn trade quips with veteran movie miscreants Wanamaker and Paul (*Scarface*) Shenar, mock-romance moll Harrold, and generally carry on with a certain cyborgian savoir-faire. The flick abruptly falls apart, however, when Arnie's mechanized monomania muscles in. Possibly due to an undetected circuitry malfunction, he obsessively repeats *shticks* from earlier outings—donning his leather-bar threads, replete with gun and grenade accessories, à la *Commando*; driving a truck, *Terminator*-style, through a local hood hangout, etc.—before losing *all* control, at which point he systematically wastes most of the cast. Thus depleted of supporting characters, *Raw Deal* has little choice but to end. *You*, on the other hand, have the choice of fast-forwarding through the flick's final reels or skipping this derivative exercise altogether.

Raw Force (1982) NR

D: Edward Murphy. Cameron Mitchell, Geoff Binney, Jillian Kessner. 90 minutes. (Media)

Suburban karate-club members from Burbank, led by Mitchell, journey to the Far East's Warrior Island, where they encounter kung-fu cannibals (!) with a taste for women. Just thought you'd want to know.

Rebel Rousers (1967) ◆◆◇
D: Martin B. Cohen. Cameron Mitchell, Jack Nicholson, Bruce Dern. 78 minutes. (Media, others)

A great cast—including Nicholson, Dern, Harry Dean Stanton, Diane Ladd, and the ubiquitous Cameron Mitchell—sleazes it up with improvisational gusto in one of the era's weirder biker debauches.

Rebel Without a Cause (1955) ◆◆◆◇
D: Nicholas Ray. James Dean, Natalie Wood, Sal Mineo, Dennis Hopper, Corey Allen, Nick Adams. 111 minutes. (Warner)

Dean, suffering from severe upper-middle-class adolescent angst, hooks up with equally needy soul-mates Wood and Mineo in Ray's still-terrific Technicolor tale of terminal teenage turmoil.

Red Heat (1988) ◆◆◆
D: Walter Hill. Arnold Schwarzenegger, James Belushi, Peter Boyle, Ed O'Ross. 106 minutes. (IVE)

Arn is cast as rock-bodied Russki cop Ivan "Iron Jaw" Danko in what ranks as the first official *glasnost* trash movie. After an opening duke-out set in a co-ed Russian steel-mill gym, wherein Arn performs his first major nearly nude scene since *The Terminator*, and a subsequent Moscow shoot-out, our pec-heavy hero hops a jet to Chicago to join jokey American cop Jim Belushi in a violent, high-energy search for Soviet émigré psycho killer/drug dealer Viktor Rosta (a neat, nasty turn by O'Ross). While ultimately predictable, *Red Heat* offers a number of fresh variations on the standard mismatched-cops clichés; Arn even shows a sensitive side here when he expresses concern re: the plight of the parakeet he left behind in Moscow. With its nonstop action, culminating in a vivid bus chase through the Windy City streets ("This is all too Russian for me!" Belushi moans), *Red Heat* rates as a reliable rental item for action buffs.

Red Heat (1985) ◆◆
D: Robert Collector. Linda Blair, Sylvia Kristel, Sue Kiel, William Ostrander, Albert Fortell, Elisabeth Volkmann. 105 minutes. (Vestron)

Not to be confused with the Schwarzenegger vehicle of the same title, this *Red Heat* stars chronic recidivist Blair as an American femme kidnapped by Commies while visiting her soldier fiancé (Ostrander) in Germany. By the second reel, poor Linda's in the can again—this time an East German joint dominated by sadistic queen con Kristel, of *Emmanuelle* infamy. From that pivotal point on, Linda's run through the usual gamut of indignities and perversions—rape, deprivation, physical abuse. When boyfriend Ostrander fails to rouse callous Western authorities to lift a bureaucratic finger on Linda's behalf, he takes matters into his own hands and, with the help of army pals and East German resistance fighters, stages a climactic commando raid. *Red Heat* does offer one creative moment amid the yawns when—in a witty *Exorcist* nod—Linda gets pea soup thrown in *her* face, courtesy of a hostile fellow inmate. Now you know how it feels, LB!

Remo Williams: The Adventure Begins . . . (1985) ♦♦◊

D: Guy Hamilton. Fred Ward, Joel Grey, Kate Mulgrew, Wilford Brimley, Charles Cioffi, J. A. Preston, Michael Pataki. 121 minutes. (HBO)

Essentially a lavish throwback to cliffhangers of yore—with some modern martial artistry, computer games, and military-industrial intrigues tossed in— *Remo Williams* charts the progress of a Fun City cop (ruggedly interpreted by the refreshingly unglamorous Ward) who's forcibly recruited into an intelligence department wing so secret that only three other people know about it (!). Grey effortlessly steals the show as Remo's wizened but invincible Korean karate-master mentor, who rails against junk food but is addicted to junk culture (especially soap operas) and given to insulting his reluctant protégé. (Remo is told he "moves like a pregnant yak," at one point; a "baboon with crub [sic] feet," at another.) Action set pieces include a punch-out atop the Statue of Lib-

erty; a raid on a cabal of crooked defense contractors' rural redoubt; and a chase through an army weapons-testing site. While *Remo*'s premise is slender, its villains lack flair, and some of the plot twists are less than novel, it's still a welcome change to see a celluloid superhero who relies on his fists, athletic ability, and smarts instead of on a high-tech arsenal. Not enough bijou-goers felt likewise, apparently, since Remo's adventures ended with *The Adventure Begins*.

Return of the Dragon (1973) ♦♦◊

D: Bruce Lee. Bruce Lee, Chuck Norris, Nora Miao. 91 minutes. (CBS/Fox)

Bruce journeys to Italy (!) to kick Mafia butt and squares off with Norris—making his film debut— in the Colosseum. Had to be that Roman weekend's hottest ticket.

Riot in Cell Block 11 (1954) ♦♦♦ B&W

D: Don Siegel. Neville Brand, Emile Meyer, Frank Faylen. 80 minutes. (Republic)

Brand, Meyer, Faylen, and Leo Gordon prove they're not just pretty faces in a hard-hitting account of a prison riot that's more realistic than most.

Rocky IV (1985) ♦

D: Sylvester Stallone. Sylvester Stallone, Talia Shire, Dolph Lundgren, Brigitte Nielsen, Carl Weathers, Burt Young. 91 minutes. (CBS/Fox)

You all know Rocky, of fistic fame
Now bashin' commies is his new
    game.
Ivan Drago's the name of the Russian
    contender
who's out to prove he's no pretender.
This Great Red Hope's a mountain of
    a man,
makes Schwarzenegger look like
    Peter Pan.
And when the monster commie
    creams Apollo Creed
Rocky vows to avenge that evil deed.
Rock goes into training, gets into
    shape
so he and Ive can go at it, ape to ape.
When the big bout unfolds in Moscow
    town
The home fans scream for Rocky to go
    down.
But Rock's so brave and devoid of fear
that even the Russians start to
    whistle and cheer.
Rock smacks that Russki upside the
    head
till our arrogant Commie's more dead
    than Red.
Now Rocky may seem stupid, but he's
    really Sly
'Cause on the box office he always
    keeps an eye.
So Rock socks it to us, blow by blow
He can't speak good English, but he
    rakes in the dough.
Now that we've suffered through
    Rocky one through four,
The Phantom's got a request for Mr.
    Balboa:
Time to hang 'em up, Sly,
We can't take it no mo-a!

Rolling Thunder (1977) ♦♦◇

D: John Flynn. William Devane,
Tommy Lee Jones, Linda Haynes,
James Best. 99 minutes. (Vestron)

A seminal 'Nam-vets-bring-the-war-back-home actioner, aided by a good cast, with Devane as the alienated returnee whose family's massacre gives him a reason to live.

Rolling Vengeance (1987) ♦♦◇

D: Steven H. Stern. Don Michael Paul, Lawrence Dane, Ned Beatty, Lisa Howard, Michael Kirby. 90 minutes. (Charter)

We don't know about you, but the Phantom had been waiting a long time for the definitive monster-truck movie, a pic that would put those macho Bigfoot and King Kong machines to more creative use than hauling giant prop six-packs around a dirt track on cable-TV monster-truck rallies. Well, we have seen the future of monster-truck movies, and its name is Rolling Vengeance. The flick kicks off to a slow start with several dull scenes detailing young trucker Paul's family life. But when said family gets totaled in a series of violent road "accidents" engineered by evil go-go bar owner Beatty (in greaseball hairstyle and black-leather threads) and his five dim-witted sons, Rolling Vengeance switches into high gear, turning into a Death Wish on wheels as Don squashes the opposition (and everything else in his sizable path) in lovingly lensed detail. Rolling Vengeance may be short on subtlety and logic, but it's long on authentic monster-truck thrills, and makes for a hot home-vid double bill with *MonsterMania!: Battle of the Monster Trucks* (Twin Towers).

Romancing the Stone (1984) ♦♦
D: Robert Zemeckis. Michael Douglas, Kathleen Turner, Danny De Vito. 105 minutes. (CBS/Fox)

We confess—the charm eludes us, though De Vito's funny at times. The sequel, *Jewel of the Nile* (CBS/Fox), offers some improvements, largely via Avner the Eccentric's comic contributions.

Rumble Fish (1983) ♦♦ B&W
D: Francis Ford Coppola. Mickey Rourke, Matt Dillon, Dennis Hopper. 94 minutes. (MCA)

Coppola's often visually startling youth-gang allegory, adapted from S. E. Hinton's novel, is extremely mannered as a drama and is further marred by a pretentious script. Turn the sound down, and you might enjoy it more.

Runaway Train (1985) ♦♦♦◇
D: Andrei Konchalovsky. Jon Voight, Eric Roberts, Rebecca DeMornay, John P. Ryan, Kyle T. Heffner, Kenneth McMillan, T. K. Carter. 112 minutes. (MGM/UA)

Based on a vintage screenplay by Akira (*Seven Samurai*) Kurosawa, *Runaway Train* is an exciting actioner with a high-budget body and a B-movie soul. Voight gives a rousing, primal performance as supercon Manny Manheim, who, accompanied by young Buck (Eric Roberts), busts out of Alaska's max-security Stonehaven Prison and unwisely boards the title train. Hot on the pair's frozen heels are Ryan, the meanest movie warden since Strother Martin in *Cool Hand Luke*, and a team of anxious railway employees tracking the train's chaotic path via an elaborate computer hookup. Minus the cusswords and computer motif, *Runaway Train* could pass for a classic '50s adventure flick—a jolting, emotionally intense thriller that should satisfy action fans of all stripes.

Satan's Sadists (1969) ♦♦◇
D: Al Adamson. Russ Tamblyn, Scott Brady, Kent Taylor. 86 minutes. (Super)

"Satan's Sadists are helling it like it is, baby!" asserts the trailer, and you won't want to miss a single hour of Adamson's vision of Harley hell or even so much as *one* of Tamblyn's bad teeth shown in extreme close-up and living color. Adamson failed to recapture the magic with his woeful distaff variation *Angels' Wild Women* (Super).

Savage Island (1985) 0 ♦
D: Edward Muller, Nicholas Beardsly. Linda Blair, Anthony Steffen, Christina Lai, Ajita Wilson, Leon Askin. 74 minutes. (Lightning)

Blair buffs beware: *Savage Island* is actually a badly butchered, back-date Spanish/Italian broads-behind-bars quickie (originally titled *Orinoco—Prison of Sex*) set in a South American slave-labor camp. Linda appears (fully clad—in *mink*, no less!) only in a clumsy prologue and epilogue that total

Former *Tom Thumb* Tamblyn kicks butt in Al Adamson's 1969 biker bashfest, *Satan's Sadists*.
Photo courtesy of Independent-International Pictures Corp.

nine—count 'em—*nine* onscreen minutes. On a positive note, *Savage Island* lasts only 74 minutes all told, with most of said screen time consumed by the usual quota of catfights, shower scenes, and harsh displays of authoritarian ill temper (e.g., "Eat it, or I'll rip your skin off!"). The Phantom suggests you save your video pesos for *genuine* Blair affairs, like the similar-sounding *Savage Streets*.

Savage Streets (1984) ◆◆◇
D: Danny Steinmann. Linda Blair, John Vernon, Robert Dryer, Johnny Venocur, Sal Landi, Linnea Quigley, Debra Blee. 93 minutes. (Vestron)

Speak of the devil! Vicious teen toughs push Linda too far, so she strikes back with a vengeance (and a crossbow!) in this violent, vulgar, relentlessly kinetic junk pic. While *Savage Streets* may be even dumber than the average Blair, it packs in plenty of quality gratuitous shower scenes, showing Linda B (in all her pudgy glory) lathering her big postadolescent breasts—plus locker-room catfights, disco brawls, and the oldest-looking high schoolers ever seen on celluloid, all set to a hot rock score. And it's all yours, overnight, for maybe 99 cents. What are you *waiting* for!? You can also spy Linda in *Silent Assassins* (Forum).

Scarface (1932) ◆◆◆ B&W
D: Howard Hawks. Paul Muni, George Raft, Ann Dvorak, Boris Karloff. 94 minutes. (MCA)

Muni plays a crazed Capone clone in one of the most blistering of the decade's pre-Code crime exposés.

Scarface (1983) ◆◆◆◆
D: Brian De Palma. Al Pacino, Steven Bauer, Michelle Pfeiffer, Robert Loggia, Harris Yulin, Mary Elizabeth Mastrantonio. 170 minutes. (MCA)

For the Phantom's moolah, De Palma's *Scarface* is the best crime movie ever made, and one of the best flicks of *any* kind. Pacino turns in his finest work as the Freedom Flotilla hustler who becomes an eager student of Yankee capitalism. Add vivid cinematography, exotic Miami locations, top supporting perfs, accurate dialogue, and sharp wit, and you have one of Hollywood's all-time sleaze winners. The final shoot-out tops the *Wild Bunch*'s.

The Scarlet Pimpernel (1934) ◆◆◆ B&W
D: Harold Young. Leslie Howard, Merle Oberon, Raymond Massey. 100 minutes. (Embassy)

Another lush, actionful adventure from Alexander Korda, with Howard cast as a sort of Brit Zorro leading a double life as a society wimp and a costumed crusader. The 1982 *Scarlet Pimpernel* remake, with Anthony Andrews in the title role, is also available (Vestron).

Scorchy (1976) NR
D: Howard Hikmet Avedis. Connie Stevens, William Smith, Cesare Danova. 100 minutes. (Vestron)

Wanna see Connie Stevens as a gun-toting supernarc wasting

pushers in Seattle while Big Bill Smith looks on? Here's your chance!

Scorpion (1987) ◆
D: William Riead. Tonny Tulleners, Robert Logan, Don Murray, Allen Williams, Kathryn Daley, John Anderson. 98 minutes. (RCA/Columbia)

While it's not the *worst* action flick we've ever witnessed, *Scorpion* may well be the *dullest*. Chopsocky champ Tulleners (make note of the name—you're not likely to hear it again), cast here as secret agent Scorpion (the guy whom "nobody takes the sting out of"), is so stiff, he makes Chuck Norris look like Pee-wee Herman. Action scenes are few and far between; the total body count runs to a stingy four (a figure Chuck can top just by cleaning his gun), a nonviolent approach dictated less, we suspect, by pacifistic than by budgetary considerations. *Scorpion* is not worth bending *your* budget even by 99 cents.

The Sea Hawk (1940) ◆◆◆
B&W/colorized D: Michael Curtiz. Errol Flynn, Brenda Marshall, Claude Rains. 109 minutes. (Key)

The apotheosis of Warner grandeur, with Flynn and a top supporting cast carrying on under Curtiz's expert direction. Also available in a (feh) colorized version.

Serpico (1973) ◆◆◆
D: Sidney Lumet. Al Pacino, John Randolph, Barbara Eda-Young. 130 minutes. (Paramount)

Lumet leads viewers through labyrinthine layers of police corruption, seen through the outraged eyes of honest cop Pacino, in a down-and-dirty adaptation of Peter Maas's nonfiction best seller.

Seven Miles from Alcatraz (1943) ◆◆◇ B&W
D: Edward Dmytryk. James Craig, Bonita Granville, Frank Jenks. 62 minutes. (RKO)

Seven Miles is a pretty funny propaganda piece showing how even craven escaped cons like Craig can do their bit for the war effort. The RKO cassette also contains a second feature, *Flight From Glory*, a moody, downbeat B about doomed fliers working for a third-rate South American air-freight outfit.

The Seven Samurai (1954) ◆◆◆◇ B&W
D: Akira Kurosawa. Toshiro Mifune, Takashi Shimura, Yoshio Inaba. 197 minutes. (Embassy, others)

Mifune leads a band of mercenaries hired to battle bandits plundering helpless farmers. One of the greatest action movies ever, plus it's deep (!).

Shaft (1971) ◆◆◆
D: Gordon Parks. Richard Roundtree, Moses Gunn, Charles Cioffi. 100 minutes. (MGM/UA)

Probably the most mainstream (and expensive) of the '70s' so-called blaxploitation flicks, with Roundtree as a tough shamus hired by a Harlem crime kingpin (Gunn) to rescue the latter's kidnapped daughter.

Shakedown (1988) ◆◆◆
D: James Glickenhaus. Peter Weller, Sam Elliott, Patricia Charbonneau, Blanche Baker, Antonio Fargas, Richard Brooks. 96 minutes. (MCA)

Peter (RoboCop) Weller is a public defender about to go yupscale until his would-be final client—crack dealer and accused cop-killer Brooks (in a skilled performance)—leads him into a web of police corruption. The situation likewise leads him into a hazardous alliance with shaggy maverick plainclothes cop Elliott, who spends much of his time in the balcony of Forty-second Street's now sadly defunct New Amsterdam theater. In fact, more than anything else, Shakedown is a kinetic tribute to Gotham's legendary Deuce, and director Glickenhaus makes extensive, inventive use of that notorious stretch of NYC real estate in crafting the pic's central action sequence. (He also works in plugs for his earlier The Soldier and The Exterminator—titles seen plastered across a Forty-second Street marquee!) Toss in strenuous stunts (including a frenetic Coney Island roller-coaster chase), copious gunplay, plus cameos by cult faves Paul Bartel (as a judge, no less!) and Shirley (Honeymoon Killers) Stoler, and you have a taut B sleazefest that ranks among the best.

Sharky's Machine (1981) ◆◆◆
D: Burt Reynolds. Burt Reynolds, Rachel Ward, Vittorio Gassman. 122 minutes. (Warner)

One of Burt's better policiers, packed with noise, violence, and action and featuring a fine, slimy perf by professional sleazeball extraordinaire Henry Silva, cast here as a coke-crazed assassin.

She Devils on Wheels (1968) ◆◆◇
D: Herschell Gordon Lewis. Betty Connell, Nancy Lee Noble, Cristie Wagner. 83 minutes. (WesternWorld)

H. G. (Blood Feast) Lewis turns his gory talents to the biker genre in a tawdry tale of chopper chicks—like Whitey (Pat Poston), "with the strength of a man and a voice to match"—on a lethal rampage. She Devils should at least silence those critics who think HG's afraid to stretch.

Shogun (1980) ◆◆◇
D: Jerry London. Richard Chamberlain, Toshiro Mifune, Yoko Shimada. 549 minutes. (Paramount)

This actionful sushi soaper, "the Television Event of 1980," is herein preserved for posterity through the magic of videotape. You want it, Paramount's got it—all 549 minutes.

Shogun Assassin (1980) ◆◆◆
D: Kenji Misumi and Robert Houston. Tomisaburo Wakayama, Masahiro Tomikawa. 82 minutes. (MCA)

Not a Shogun sequel but a bloody, fast-paced samurai swordfest chronicling the violent adventures of fourteenth-century Nipponese mercenary The Lone Wolf, originally filmed in 1974. The American release was redubbed by, among others, Marshall Efron and Sandra Bernhard.

Shoot to Kill (1988) ◆◆◇

D: Roger Spottiswoode. Sidney Poitier, Tom Berenger, Kirstie Alley, Clancy Brown, Richard Masur, Andrew Robinson. 109 minutes. (Touchstone)

Poitier ended a ten-year onscreen retirement to topline as a determined FBI agent out to eliminate a crafty psycho in this sporadically exciting, more often routine mismatched-partners pic. Sid's search for said psycho leads to a hazardous trek across the mountainous Northwest—a journey undertaken with the grudging assistance of guide Berenger, whose squeeze, fellow outdoorsperson Alley, has been kidnapped by the killer. Missed opportunities and pointless filler footage abound, detracting from what should have been a shorter, tauter caper. Still worth a look, though, and definitely better than Sid's second comeback bid, *Little Nikita* (RCA/Columbia).

Slaughter in San Francisco (1981) ◆

D: William Lowe. Don Wong, Sylvia Channing, Chuck Norris. 87 minutes. (Embassy)

This one's just an outright ripoff—an el cheapo chopsocky opera starring Wong, with Norris, prominently featured in the promo, in a supporting role as a villain—lensed in '73 and released in '81 to cash in on Chuck's burgeoning celebrity. Some of the more authentic Chuck chopsocky fests not elsewhere covered: *An Eye for an Eye* (Embassy), *Firewalker*, *Force of One*, and *The Octagon* (Media), *Forced Vengeance* (MGM/UA), *Good Guys Wear Black* and *Lone Wolf McQuade* (both Vestron), and *Silent Rage* (RCA/Columbia).

Sno-Line (1985) ◆◆◇

D: Douglas F. O'Neons. Vince Edwards, June Wilkinson, Paul Smith, Phil Foster, Louis Guss, Carey Clark. 89 minutes. (Lightning)

Any flick that resurrects superbuxom Brit blonde June Wilkinson—erstwhile starlet of such vintage exploitation fare as *Macumba Love, Career Girl, Twist All Night* (all NA), and *The Playgirls and the Bellboy* (see index)—can't be *all* bad. June, still busting out all over, is in fine form as the main squeeze of power-mad slimeball Edwards, a Gotham wise guy currently running gambling and cocaine rackets (hence the title) in Texas. The plot concerns a quartet of amateurs who rip Vince off and spend the rest of the pic attempting to elude his lethal clutches. While far from spectacular, *Sno-Line* offers enough action and suspense to qualify as a B flick worth catching.

The Soldier (1982) ◆◆

D: James Glickenhaus. Ken Wahl, Klaus Kinski, William Prince. 90 minutes. (Embassy)

The title mercenary (Wahl) rescues the United States from a

Russki threat in a predictable but popular potboiler helmed by action ace Glickenhaus, who'd earlier made his B-movie bones with the surprise sleaze hit *The Exterminator* (see index).

Soul Vengeance (1975) ♦♦♦
D: Jamaa Fanaka. Marlo Monte, Reatha Grey, Stan Kamber. 90 minutes. (Mercury/Xenon)

Originally titled *Welcome Home, Brother Charles,* Jamaa (*Penitentiary*) Fanaka's film debut defies description but demands the awed attention of serious Fanaka fans and action addicts who like their fare laced with the surreal and the bizarre. The infamous phallic strangulation scene alone must be seen to be disbelieved!

Southern Comfort (1981) ♦♦◊
D: Walter Hill. Keith Carradine, Powers Boothe, Fred Ward. 105 minutes. (Embassy)

Ragin' Cajuns wage guerrilla warfare against green Yankee National Guardsmen in a remote bayou. Not very credible and *2000 Maniacs* (see index) did it better, but good performances and pacing make Hill's Louisiana-set mini-'Nam replay work on a visceral level.

Special Delivery (1976) ♦♦◊
D: Paul Wendkos. Bo Svenson, Cybill Shepherd, Michael Gwynne. 89 minutes. (Vestron)

A reasonably clever comic crime caper, with B regular Svenson—during his brief mainstream semi-star period—as a bank robber involved with a flakey Cybill Shepherd.

The Spook Who Sat by the Door (1973) NR
D: Ivan Dixon. Lawrence Cook, Paula Lawrence, Janet League. 102 minutes. (Video City/Blacast)

A subversive if sometimes inept tale, based on the novel of the same name, about a token black CIA trainee who uses his expertise to organize an urban guerrilla (or "gorilla," as the Video City box has it!) movement. With music by Herbie Hancock. Video City also has the ambitious, O. C. Smith–scored "blaxploitation" rarity *The Bus Is Coming.*

Stand Alone (1985) ♦♦
D: Alan Beattie. Charles Durning, Pam Grier, James Keach, Bert Remsen, Barbara Sammeth, Luis Contreras. 90 minutes. (New World)

Bye-bye, Sly—say hi! to the screen's most improbable Rambo to date, as chunky Durning dons combat fatigues, digs out his trusty M-16, and shows the neighborhood drug scum who's boss! That's what unfolds in *Stand Alone*, as WWII vet Durning avenges the murder of an old army buddy by single-handedly confronting a contingent of vicious pushers responsible for the misdeed. While Charles may be a tad over his fighting weight, he *is* a dozen years younger than Bronson and demonstrates his military mettle in this empty-headed urban-action quickie. Former "blaxploitation" fave Grier is also along for the ride.

Steele Justice (1987) ♦♦
D: Robert Boris. Martin Kove, Sela Ward, Ronny Cox, Bernie Casey, Joseph Campanella, Soon Teck-Oh. 96 minutes. (Kartes)

Busy character thesp Kove requisitions the Rambo headband here as yet another vengeful Viet vet—"You don't recruit John Steele. You unleash him!"—who wages a one-man jihad against L.A.'s notorious Vietnamese mafia. This strictly routine affair is elevated solely by Soon Teck-Oh's perf (he's fast becoming a Vietnamese Philip Ahn) as oily villain General Kwan, who'd earlier tangled with Steele back in 'Nam, and by a flashback in which Steele narrowly escapes death via a rat with a grenade strapped to its back (!)—perhaps a vengeful relative of the rodent that had its head bitten off by Chuck Norris in *Missing In Action II* (see index).

Straight Time (1978) ♦♦♦
D: Ulu Grosbard. Dustin Hoffman, Theresa Russell, Gary Busey, Harry Dean Stanton. 114 minutes. (Warner)

Dusty gets tough as a paroled con who tries to adjust to a civilian world that has no use for him in an effective blend of social commentary and sleaze, featuring strong supporting turns by Stanton and Busey as a pair of criminal cohorts. The flick's jewel-robbery scene conveys the erotic excitement of a finely timed heist better than any film in recent memory.

Straw Dogs (1971) ♦♦♦
D: Sam Peckinpah. Dustin Hoffman, Susan George, David Warner. 118 minutes. (CBS/Fox)

A wimpy Dustin is forced to go primitive to protect his turf and slutty mate George from a band of barbaric locals in a harsh transplanted Western lensed with Peckinpah's patented hard-edged irony and violence. A cut below SP's best, but certainly a vid-rental must.

The Street Fighter (1975) ♦♦♦
D: S. Ozawa. Sonny Chiba, Gerald Yamada, Shirley Nakajima. 75 minutes. (CBS/Fox)

Chiba chops his way into the hearts of millions in a gritty, gory, nonstop martial-arts orgy that was rated X for violence during its theatrical release. In one scene, we even get an X-ray view of a skull being splintered by one of Sonny's harder blows! Unfortunately, we *don't* see it in the video version. Seems CBS/Fox did some heavy chopping of its own, removing more than 10 minutes, including most of the innovative violence; thus, our rating applies to the original film only. Sonny supporters can also catch their hero in the following slugfests: *Assassin* (CBS/Fox), *The Bodyguard* (Media),

Dragon Princess (IUD), *Karate Warriors* (IUD), *Killing Machine* (Prism), *Return of the Streetfighter* (Fox Hills), *Roaring Fire* (HBO), *Shogun's Ninja* (Media), and *The Streetfighter's Last Revenge* (Wizard), as well as in the sci-fi doomsday flick *Virus* (Media).

Street Love (1985) ♦♦◇
D: Rose-Marie Turko. Jennifer Mayo, David Dean, Jackie Berryman, Debbie Dion, Rico L. Richardson. 85 minutes. (Vestron)

Produced, written, and directed by Rose-Marie Turko and partially funded by an American Film Institute grant (a credit that, during the pic's original release, was wisely held to film's end to forestall a widespread grindhouse audience walkout), *Street Love* (aka *Scarred*) chronicles the daily degradations of sixteen-year-old runaway Ruby Starr (Mayo). To support herself and her two-year-old son, Ruby turns $20 tricks, dodges bust-happy cops, suffers the unwanted attentions of cowboy pimp Easy (Dean) and, in a funny, on-target sequence, even attempts an ill-advised stint in a porn pic called *Sex Wars*. The film balances these male-engineered indignities with the sidewalk solidarity shared by Ruby and her street sisters. (The feminist message is less subtly conveyed via strategically placed background graffiti reading WOMEN RULE NOW and CASTRATION SQUAD!) The best scene involves a row of preening pimps trading bitchy gossip and shop-talk at a hairstyling salon—a neat twist on the old house-wives-at-the-beauty-parlor routine. Though it ultimately depresses more than it enlightens or entertains, *Street Love* remains a spiked-heel step up from *Angel* (see index).

Streetfight (1975) NR
D: Ralph Bakshi. Voices of Philip Michael Thomas, Scatman Crothers, Charles Gordone, Barry White. 89 minutes. (Academy)

Bakshi's controversial ghetto-set animated feature is considered borderline racist by some (*Coonskin* was the pic's original title), gritty and brilliant by others. It's hard to tell from the vid version, though, since it's been heavily reedited and rescored. Beware!

Streets of Fire (1984) ♦♦
D: Walter Hill. Michael Paré, Diane Lane, Rick Moranis, Amy Madigan, Willem Dafoe. 93 minutes. (MCA)

The Phantom found the normally reliable Hill's rock-vid action fable—featuring a stable of then-rising young stars—artificial and ultimately dull, but it's not without its rabid fans. If you're one of them, then this vid's for you.

Streetwalkin' (1985) ♦
D: Joan Freeman. Melissa Leo, Dale Midkiff, Leon Robinson, Julie Newmar, Annie Golden, Antonio Fargas. 87 minutes. (Vestron)

Streetwalkin' pits innocent runaway-turned-hooker Cookie (Leo) against her psycho pimp Duke (Midkiff), who in turn incurs the wrath of rival procurer Jason (Robinson). The result: a monumental waste of shoe leather and a slack, static exercise in synthetic sleaze. Even the screen return of '60s sex object Julie Newmar—who's managed to preserve both her statuesque physique and her thespic ineptitude—as a vet trollop named Queen Bee fails to enliven the comatose proceedings. *Streetwalkin'* received kinder treatment than most of its exploitation ilk from several mainstream critics, largely because it was produced and directed by a "respectable" husband-wife team (Robert Alden and Joan Freeman, respectively) with tony credentials (PBS shows and "serious" documentaries). But don't be misled—*Streetwalkin'* is sleaze all the way, and boring sleaze at that.

Stripped to Kill (1987) ◆◇

D: *Katt Ruben Shea. Kay Lenz, Greg Evigan, Norman Fell, Tracy Crowder, Athena Worthy, Pia Kamaka. 88 minutes. (MGM/UA)*

In the grand tradition of Ed Wood, Jr.'s, *Orgy of the Dead*, this largely limp "thriller" features a slender story line sandwiched between a numbing number of strip acts staged at a sleazy L.A. club owned by a weary-looking Fell. When one of Fell's femmes falls fatal victim to an unidentified fiend, undercover cop Lenz gets into the (strip) act, while her oft-antagonistic male partner (played, in a bold image change, by *B.J. and the Bear's* Evigan, who tries here to make like a mix of Mel Gibson and Mickey Rourke) poses as a patron. *Stripped to Kill* tentatively ventures into potentially interesting territory when Lenz begins to *like* working in the lowlife limelight—a twist that in turn intensifies her love-hate relationship with Evigan. The script isn't up to dealing with such relative complexities, while the few action scenes are ineptly staged and the suspense wavers between minimal and nil.

Stunts (1977) ◆◆◇

D: *Mark Lester. Robert Forster, Fiona Lewis, Joanna Cassidy. 89 minutes. (HBO)*

A behind-the-scenes action flick with a good hook—stunt man Forster investigates his stunt-man brother's film-set death—fine thesping by lead Forster, and plenty of spectacular stunts.

Sudden Death (1985) ◆◆

D: *Sig Shore. Denise Coward, Frank Runyeon, Jamie Tirelli. 95 minutes. (Vestron)*

Another distaff *Death Wish*, with rape victim Denise proving she's no Coward by gunning for unsuspecting street scum. Not as good as *Ms. 45* (see index), but it has its share of unintentional laughs, plus a memorable disco theme song.

Sunset Strip (1985) ♦

D: William Webb. Tom Eppler, John Mayall, Cheri Cameron Newell. 87 minutes. (Vestron)

Brit blues vet John Mayall's screen debut as a mob-harassed Sunset Strip club owner supplies the sole (and soul) note of interest in this amateurish nonactioner, a kind of To Live and Yawn in L.A. While John acquits himself decently, his role is terminated early on, courtesy of a bullet in the brain. Center stage is thus left to his wrongly accused pal, the hunky but colorless Eppler, who spends most of the movie zooming through the streets of Angel City astride his trusty cycle, eluding the police and pursuing the real killers. Sunset Strip runs out of gas long before Tom's hog does.

Superfly (1972) ♦♦♦

D: Gordon Parks, Jr. Ron O'Neal, Carl Lee, Sheila Frazier. 93 minutes. (Warner)

One of the best "blaxploitation" films, with O'Neal first-rate as a midlevel uptown coke dealer whose crimes pale beside those perpetrated by local police and politicians. The pic has a knowing, accurate POV, though not an especially popular one with many mainstream critics of the day, and it represents B vet O'Neal's finest

movie moment. The inferior sequel, Superfly TNT, remains unavailable as we go to press.

Survival Game (1987) ♦◇

D: Herb Freed. Mike Norris, Deborah Goodrich, Seymour Cassel, John Sharp, Arlene Golonka, Rick Grasi. 94 minutes. (Media)

Mike (Son of Chuck) Norris follows his genuinely bizarre Born American with this weak, predictable action entry. Employed at the War in Peace Survival Camp, Mike gets involved with the blond daughter (Goodrich) of Tim Leary—like psychedelic pioneer Dr. Dave Forest (Cassel). Dr. Dave's just been released from a seventeen-year slammer stretch for manufacturing his homemade hallucinogen Forest Fire, and his former partners want the $2 million in cash he allegedly stashed before his bust. Survival Game supplies few surprises as Mike rides to the rescue, and the flick's Sixties vs. Eighties observations are superficial at best. In fact, the best thing here is a welcome reprise of the Count V's "Psychotic Reaction," heard in its entirety over Mike's jeep radio.

Sweet Revenge (1987) ♦

D: Mark Sobel. Nancy Allen, Ted Shackelford, Martin Landau, Sal Landi, Michelle Little, Gina Gershon. 79 minutes. (Media)

In case you were wondering what Nancy Allen was doing shortly before being rescued by *RoboCop*, the answer is that she was wasting her time in turkeys like *Sweet Revenge*. Director Sobel gives us two bad movies for the price of one here: a straightforward schlock-fest about a white-slavery ring that claims top newscaster Nancy as one of its victims, and a merry *Indiana Jones* clone whenever would-be madcap adventurer Shackelford enters the picture (which is far too often to suit *us*). Caught in the middle is the hapless Landau, stuck in another thank-less villain role as the head slaver. At least the flick is a short—if not especially sweet—79 minutes; subtract the slo-mo violence sequences, and it's probably not much more than an hour—time that would be infinitely better spent rewatching the first half of *RoboCop* (see index).

Sweet Sweetback's Baadasssss Song (1971) ◆◆◆
D: Melvin Van Peebles. Melvin Van Peebles, Rhetta Hughes, John Amos. 97 minutes. (Magnum)

An odd, often effective one-man mix of earnestness, rebellion, and exploitation as writer/director/composer Van Peebles traces the rise of a professional stud (Van Peebles) who runs afoul of (and away from) racist cops. Sweet-back's bizarre "duel" with a butch distaff biker stacks up as one of the flick's many highlights. A promised sequel never arrived.

Switchblade Sisters (1975) ◆◆◆
D: Jack Hill. Robbie Lee, Joanne Nail, Monica Gayle, Kitty Bruce, Asher Brauner, Michael Miller. 91 minutes. (Monterey)

Jack (*Spider Baby*) Hill's seminal *Switchblade Sisters* rates as a high-energy exercise in Trash with your proverbial capital T. Hill lets us know what's on his mind in the film's very first shot: a still life of two back-alley trash cans (!). (We later learn, via an onscreen tabloid headline, that the entire flick un-folds during a "12-Week Garbage Strike.") Our story involves fac-tional struggles unfolding within the ranks of the dread Silver Debs—sister gang to the equally menacing male aggregate the Sil-ver Daggers—as sexy teen leader Lee sees her exalted position chal-lenged by sexy teen newcomer Joanne Nail. Director Hill takes a kitchen-sink approach to this ex-ploitation classic, tossing in punch-ups, catfights, shoot-outs, switchblade duels, rampaging tanks (!), and gratuitous nudity ga-lore. Hill even includes a feminist message of sorts when the debs break from their male counter-parts to form their own all-girl guerrilla unit, the Jezebels. Kitty (daughter of Lenny) Bruce, mean-while, turns in memorable sup-porting work as Donut, a plump, passive deb who, in the course of our drama, is forced to give the best squealing-pig imitation seen onscreen since Ned Beatty's legendary porcine perf in *Deliverance*. *Switchblade Sisters* makes for ideal midnight video viewing.

Sword of Heaven (1985) ◆◆◇
D: Byron Meyers. Tadashi Yamashita, Mel Novak, Gerry Gibson, Joe Randazzo, Mika, Bill ('Superfoot') Wallace. 87 minutes. (TWE)

Sword of Heaven stars Tadashi Yamashita (yes, *the* Tadashi Yamashita) as a Japanese cop on loan to the LAPD. In the course of events, TY happens upon the title weapon, a glowing assegai that, according to the pic's original tag line, "fell from the heavens to create a hell on earth" some four hundred years back. Our hero proceeds to wield it against a band of mercenaries in the employ of a homicide (and homicidal) cop who moonlights as the overseer of a widespread murder-extortion ring. *Sword*'s first half is actually pretty entertaining, in its own idiosyncratically stupid way. There's a greasy, undersize pimp named Cain apparently written into the script (it took fully *four* talents all told to word-process *Sword*'s senseless scenario) to showcase the invisible thespian talents of one Joe Randazzo. (The pic's producer happens to be one Joseph P. Randazzo.) Joe's emotive highlight arrives when he pushes a wheelchair-bound nun off a cliff for the high crime of getting in his way! Yamashita's no slouch in the bad-acting department either, especially when, sans explanation,

he plays a bar scene in undercover drag (shades of Ed Wood, Jr.!). TY barely speaks English, and his reading of the Mark Twain–lifted line, "Reports of my death have been greatly exaggerated," ranks among B-moviedom's more memorable moments. While *Sword* runs out of this sort of brain-damaged inspiration long before it runs out of tape, it's still worth a look for those in the mood for kung-fu camp.

Tai-Pan (1986) ◆
D: Daryl Duke. Bryan Brown, Joan Chen, John Stanton, Tim Cuinee, Bill Leadbitter, Russell Wong. 127 minutes. (Vestron)

The Phantom must confess to experiencing mucho disappointment watching this one. Recalling the critical pans that greeted *Tai-Pan* during its brief, inglorious theatrical run, we'd hoped the flick would measure up as a bad movie of epic proportions. Instead, while often incoherent and thoroughly inept, *Tai-Pan*—set in 1840 Canton—is a lumpy, leaden bore that plays like a botched condensation of a hack TV miniseries. More a seagoing soap opera than a swashbuckling adventure yarn, *Tai-Pan* also features a groan-provoking performance by Chen as Scottish trader Bryan (*F/X*) Brown's longtime concubine Mei-Mei, who emotes in a pidgin English uniquely her own. Mei-Mei might find *Tai-Pan* the man "terrifical good," but we judge the flick fantastical bad.

Tenement (1985) ◆

D: Roberta Findlay. Joe Lynn, Martha DeLaCruz, Enrique Sandino, Corinne Chateau, Larry Lara, Karen Russell. 94 minutes. (IVE)

Former porn hack Roberta (*The Oracle*) Findlay tackles the burning social issues of the day in *Tenement*. A sort of *Last Tenement on the Left*, with elements of *Assault on Precinct 13* and *Night of the Living Dead* tossed in, the simpleminded story sees a multiethnic gang of overage junkies and general lowlifes evicted from the title site after a nosy tenant sics the cops on them. As *Dirty Harry* and *Death Wish* watchers can safely predict, our slack judicial system soon sets the animals free to prey upon their former home's helpless inhabitants. Findlay's utterly inauthentic pic contains a couple of truly repulsive sexual mutilation scenes among its more traditional antics (knifings, eye gougings, electrocutions, and the like) and only decent perfs from the unknown cast lift this loser a notch above the totally worthless. *Enemy Territory* (see index) tells essentially the same story with far greater talent and flair.

Terminal Entry (1987) ◆

D: John Kinkade. Edward Albert, Yaphet Kotto, Paul Smith, Heidi Helmer, Patrick Labyorteaux, Kavi Raz. 95 minutes. (Celebrity)

A potentially perverse premise—obnoxious teen hackers break into a terrorist computer network and, thinking they're playing an involved game, order the saboteurs to carry out their planned cataclysmic acts (!)—is utterly destroyed by a mindlessly amoral, terminally stupid script cohatched by Mark (*Sweet Revenge*) Sobel. It might have been fun to watch government operatives forced to waste these asinine brats; instead, *Terminal Entry* actually tries to cast them in an ultimately heroic light. Antiterrorist commandos Albert, Kotto, and Smith (in a rare good-guy role), meanwhile, carry on with merry machismo even as half the nation explodes!

Terror Squad (1987) ◆◆◆

D: Peter Maris. Chuck Connors, Bill Calvert, Jill Sanders, Kavi Raz, Ken Foree, Joseph Nasser. 90 minutes. (Forum)

"Terrorists in Indiana?" a high school teacher exclaims. "I've never heard such a ridiculous thing in my life!" He obviously hasn't seen Maris's *Terror Squad*, the first pic in recorded film history to recount a Libyan invasion of Kokomo, Indiana (!). After failing to blow up the local nuke power plant, a quartet of Qadhafi fanatics blast their way through the bustling Kokomo streets in an orgy of nonstop destruction. (For a low-budget flick, *Terror Squad* boasts an impressive array of exploding cars and toppling water towers.) In pursuit of the villains is police chief Connors, clad in a vintage Brooklyn Dodger jacket. (Chuck played one game for the Bums back in 1949.) The Libyans eventually hole up with several teenage hostages in a high school detention hall for a Chuck-Norris-meets-John-Hughes denouement. While *Terror Squad* owes much to both *Red Dawn* and *Invasion U.S.A.*, it's actually far superior to either: a trashy but tense, relentlessly kinetic treat for hardcore action fans, and a film that should put Kokomo on the B-movie map.

Thief (1981) ◆◆◆
D: Michael Mann. James Caan, Tuesday Weld, James Belushi, Willie Nelson, Robert Prosky. 126 minutes. (MGM/UA)

Michael Mann, later of *Miami Vice* fame, brings urgency to an elderly plot about burglar Caan's bid for a last big score. A showcase for Caan as the Zen ex-con; Prosky is appropriately repulsive in the lead villain role.

Thou Shalt Not Kill . . . Except (1987) ◆◇
D: Josh Becker. Brian Schulz, John Manfredi, Robert Rickman, Tim Quill, Sam Raimi, Cheryl Hanson. 94 minutes. (Prism)

A dismal throwback to the Manson rip-off quickies (e.g., *The Love Thrill Murders*—see index) of the early '70s, *Thou Shalt Not Kill . . . Except*, set in 1969, pits a quartet of macho GIs against a cult of bloodthirsty "hippies." The latter are led by low-budget auteur Sam (*Evil Dead*) Raimi (who should stick to directing) in a story coconceived by thesp Bruce (*Evil Dead II*) Campbell (who should stick to acting). Director Becker tries to enliven this dated, incoherent mess with clever film school camera tricks and a gory last-reel slaughterfest, but he fails to keep *Kill* from sinking into the abyss of its own amateurishness.

Three Kinds of Heat (1987) ◆◇
D: Leslie Stevens. Robert Ginty, Victoria Barrett, Shakti, Sylvester McCoy, Barry Foster, Jeannie Brown. 87 minutes. (Warner)

The embattled Cannon Group fires another blank with *Three Kinds of Heat* (formerly *Fireworks*). The pic teams a laid-back Ginty, busty blonde Barrett, and tall kung-fu femme Shakti (by far the flick's most memorable performer)—as a State Department agent, Fun City fuzz, and Hong Kong cop, respectively—on the desultory trail of the evil Anglo-Oriental organization the Black Lion. Most of the London-lensed "adventure" is supposed to unfold in New York, where the slow-paced caper climaxes in a fireworks factory blast. Best line belongs to the formidable Shakti, who, eyeing a bad guy with five bullets in his chest, deadpans, "It was not his day."

Three the Hard Way (1974) ◆◆◇
D: Gordon Parks, Jr. Jim Brown, Fred Williamson, Jim Kelly, Jay Robinson, Sheila Frazier. 93 minutes. (Mercury/ Xenon)

Another "all-star" martial-arts epic, with Jim, Fred, and the other Jim joining forces to stop madman Robinson's racist scheme to eliminate the black population by pumping a secret anti-Negro serum (!) into the water supply. A Forty-second Street perennial recently reintroduced to the video ranks by the black film specialists at Mercury/Xenon.

3:15—The Moment of Truth (1986) ◆◇
D: Larry Gross. Deborah Foreman, Adam Baldwin, Ed Lauter, Danny De La Paz. 86 minutes. (Media)

A high school gang-war cheapie that fails to generate either tension or sufficient sleaze, though Foreman fans might want to take a peek.

Thunder Road (1958) ◆◆◆
D: Arthur Ripley. Robert Mitchum, Gene Barry, Jacques Auchubon, Keely Smith, James Mitchum, Trevor Bardette. 92 minutes. (MGM/UA)

At the height of his bigtime mainstream-movie stardom, thesp Robert Mitchum took time out to topline in the low-budget 1958 B flick *Thunder Road*—an evocative, fast-paced moonshine movie that went on to become an enduring drive-in mainstay and cult fave. Our story, which Mitchum also concocted (he likewise penned the pic's "Whippoorwill" theme song), involves bootleg driver Bob's efforts to stop powerful villain Auchubon from muscling in on his turf and to keep younger brother—played by Bob's real-life *son* (!) Jim Mitchum—from following in his criminal footsteps (or in this case, tire tracks). Bob handles the role with his customary cool, while Barry is solid as Mitchum's tough-but-fair revenue agent nemesis and zombielike chanteuse Keely Smith supplies some laid-back love interest and also croons a tune or two. Beyond its kinetically choreographed high-speed car chases, *Thunder Road* offers low-key insights into the moonshiners' furtive but unashamed life-style. Kudos to MGM/UA honchos for springing this offbeat winner from their vaults.

Top Gun (1986) ◆
D: Tony Scott. Tom Cruise, Kelly McGillis, Val Kilmer, Anthony Edwards, Tom Skerritt, Michael Ironside, John Stockwell. 110 minutes. (Paramount)

This overrated flag-waver proceeds with all the passion, action, and suspense of a '50s air force training film as it follows sky ace Pete Mitchell (Cruise) and pilot pals from the Indian Ocean to Miramar, California (aka Fightertown, U.S.A.). You'll snooze as Cruise woos blond instructor McGillis ("I'd really like to hear about that MIG sometime," she croons seductively), clowns with copilot Edwards, and exchanges fiery glances with rival ace Ice (Kilmer). While it successfully avoids offering any real insights into the pilots' lives and psyches, *Top Gun* lacks the aggressive cartoon inanity of an *Iron Eagle*. A shamelessly contrived "international incident" gives Tom a chance to strut his aerial stuff at film's end, but even the high-tech sky stunts failed to thrill yours truly. *Star Wars* did it better; so did *Wings*. Sorry, Mr. Superblockbuster, but you get no votes here.

Top of the Heap (1972) NR
D: Christopher St. John. Christopher St. John, Paula Kelly, Patrick McVey. 91 minutes. (Unicorn)

In an ambitious "blaxploitation" effort, auteur St. John (late of Shaft) also toplines as a black cop whose disaffection with the system leads him into lawlessness.

Trained to Kill (1975) NR
D: Daniel J. Vance. Stephen Sandor, Rockne Tarkington, Richard X. Slattery. 91 minutes. (Paragon)

A popular cheapie in the raging 'Nam-vet genre, with Sandor as an ex-GI who goes up against the sadistic gang riding roughshod over his home town.

The Trip (1967) ◆◆◆
D: Roger Corman. Peter Fonda, Susan Strasberg, Bruce Dern, Dennis Hopper. 85 minutes. (Vestron)

Aging hippie Dern lays his trip on commercial director Fonda, who roams through forest sets left over

from Corman's Poe movies and takes time out to dig an orange's aura. Heavy. The laundromat scene's the topper here.

Tuff Turf (1985) ◆◇
D: Fritz Kiersch. James Spader, Kim Richards, Paul Mones, Robert Downey, Jr. 113 minutes. (New World)

Newcomer Spader takes on local Tuffs (that's the name of the gang) in a mediocre, overlong update of a '50s rumble movie. Best for Spader enthusiasts.

Under the Gun (1988) ◆◆◇
D: James Sbardellati. Sam Jones, Vanessa Williams, John Russell, Michael Halsey, Nick Cassavetes, Steven Williams. 90 minutes. (Magnum)

Under the Gun—dethroned Miss America Vanessa Williams's eagerly awaited (?) Thespian debut—gets off to a raging start with an armored-car robbery and high-energy shootout. The action shifts to L.A., where St. Louis cop Sam Jones investigates his younger brother's (Cassavetes) murder. The culprits are vet actor John (*The Lawman*) Russell and his unusually violent band of professional killers, the type of guys who never use a simple gun when a rocket launcher will do. Unfortunately, after a hot first half crammed with nonstop action, the pic begins a gradual descent into terminal stupidity soon after Vanessa's arrival on the scene (sorry, V.W.). In fairness to Vanessa, her ersatz Rae Dawn Chong–type role as Jones's forcibly recruited partner is nothing if not a thankless one, and it's not her fault that the script abruptly adopts a glib *Commando*-clone tone that sabotages the rest of the flick. *Under the Gun* still rates a look for hardcore action fans and inveterate Vanessa-watchers.

Underworld, U.S.A. (1961) ◆◆◆ B&W
D: Sam Fuller. Cliff Robertson, Dolores Dorn, Beatrice Kay. 99 minutes. (RCA/Columbia)

Robertson infiltrates the syndicate to avenge his father's murder in a tough, violent, and wonderfully lurid Fuller sleazefest. One of Sam's best, with a top supporting cast of veteran screen villains, including Robert Emhardt, Richard Rust, and Paul Dubov.

Unholy Rollers (1972) ◆◆◆
D: Vernon Zimmerman. Claudia Jennings, Louis Quinn, Betty Ann Rees. 88 minutes. (HBO)

A funky, funny lowlife odyssey, as late, great Playmate-turned-action-starlet Claudia Jennings overcomes all obstacles, from vicious rivals to domestic woes, in her relentless pursuit of roller-derby glory. Inspirational, and one of Claudia's best showcases as a distaff Rocky of the rink. Couchside Claudia lovers can also catch the curvaceous heroine in the swamp-set *Gator Bait* (Paramount), *The Great Texas Dynamite Chase*, the red-neck romp *Moonshine County Express* (both Warner), Stephanie Rothman's B-film feminist comedy *Group*

Marriage (Cinema Group), the sober-minded Viet-vet drama *Jud* (Prism), the horrific *Sisters of Death* (United), *The Stepmother* (Academy), and the energetic *Truck-Stop Women* (Vestron), with CJ in top form as a two-fisted business bimbo running a roadside cathouse.

The Untouchables (1987) ◆◆◇
D: Brian De Palma. Kevin Costner, Robert De Niro, Sean Connery, Andy Garcia, Charles Martin Smith, Richard Bradford. 119 minutes. (Paramount)

Talk about your low concepts! After fashioning a brilliant, electric update of Howard Hawks's *Scarface* (based on the life and crimes of Al Capone), De Palma designs a distorted remake of an old TV series dealing with Capone and his straight-arrow nemesis Eliot Ness. While *The Untouchables* is undeniably well crafted—even visually stunning at times (though we could've done without the elaborate, *oy*-provoking Odessa Steps sequence, already sent up quite nicely in Woody Allen's *Love and Death* (CBS/Fox) and bordering on *self*-parody here)—and while Connery gives a fine performance as the veteran Chicago cop who wises up Ness (Costner in a bland role), the exercise is ultimately as pointless and mechanical as *Scarface* was on-target and intense. De Niro's celebrated turn as Capone amounts to little more than a cameo and can't hold a tommygun to Rod Steiger's flamboyant interpretation of the crime czar in 1959's *Al Capone* (see index).

Vanishing Point (1971) ◆◆
D: Richard C. Sarafian. Barry Newman, Cleavon Little, Dean Jagger. 99 minutes. (CBS/Fox)

For some reason, this largely lame exercise about a speed freak (Newman) racing his car to oblivion while blind soul deejay Little cheers him on won a cult rep after its initial release. Plays pretty poorly today, though.

Vendetta (1986) ◆◆
D: Bruce Logan. Karen Chase, Lisa Clarson, Sandy Martin, Marshall Teague, Linda Lightfoot. 88 minutes. (Vestron)

Vendetta involves a bushido-trained Hollywood stunt woman named Laurie (Chase) who deliberately gets herself busted, the better to avenge the jailhouse murder of her innocent younger sibling (Michelle Newkirk). *Vendetta* starts slowly but heats up once our heroine confronts evil con Butler (an effectively repulsive perf by Martin) and her hard-boiled gal gang, whom she proceeds to knock off one by one. "Achieving honorable justice," Laurie explains to her skeptical boyfriend during a conjugal visit at a nearby sleazy motel, "that's bushido!" Highlights include the Screamin' Sirens' heartfelt rendition of "Love Slave," a spirited Prince impersonation performed in reverse drag (!) by an ample-bosomed jailbird, and some deft emotive work turned in by a largely unknown cast.

Verne Miller (1987) ◆◆◇
D: Rod Hewitt. Scott Glenn, Barbara Stock, Thomas G. Waites, Ed O'Ross, Andrew Robinson. 95 minutes. (Nelson)

Previously neglected Prohibition hitman Verne Miller (Glenn) finally gets a movie made about him, and it's not a bad one at that (even if it *did* play at a total of *one* theater—in Birmingham, Alabama!). Glenn is a bit too laid-back as the syphilitic gangster who worked for Capone and engineered the infamous Kansas City Massacre, and the flick as a whole could have used more juice, but there's enough historic mayhem here to interest gangster-movie fans. Burgeoning screen villain Ed (*The Hidden*, *Red Heat*) O'Ross impresses as Capone's (Waites) snarling top lieutenant. You can also see Scott in *Man on Fire* (Vestron).

Vice Squad (1982) ◆◆
D: Gary A. Sherman. Wings Hauser, Season Hubley, Gary Swanson. 97 minutes. (Embassy)

A bad movie lifted by Hauser's incredibly vile performance as a psycho pimp on a film-long abrupt-and-senseless slaughter spree. Fast-forward to Wings's scenes, and you won't be disappointed.

Walking the Edge (1985) ◆◇

D: Norbert Meisel. Robert Forster, Nancy Kwan, Joe Spinell, A. Martinez, Aarika Wells, Wayne Woodson. 94 minutes. (Lightning)

Dependable thesp Forster gives a sharp, textured performance well above and beyond the B-movie call in this routine action cheapie. As ex-ballplayer-turned-cabbie Jason Walk, Bob gets embroiled with vengeance-seeking Kwan and a gang of L.A. lowlifes led by Joe (*Maniac*) Spinell. *Walking the Edge* is a tepid potboiler in a would-be *Taxi Driver Meets Death Wish* vein, guaranteed to keep you a safe distance from the edge of your seat. Recommended for hard-core Forster fans only.

The Wanderers (1979) ◆◆◇

D: Philip Kaufman. Ken Wahl, John Friedrich, Karen Allen, Olympia Dukakis. 117 minutes. (Warner)

Richard Price's novel about a Bronx teen gang comes to effective Hollywood life. Only major drawback, also in the book, is the frequent, overly facile switches in tone.

Wanted: Dead or Alive (1986) ◆◆◇

D: Gary Sherman. Rutger Hauer, Gene Simmons, Mel Harris, Robert Guillaume. 104 minutes. (New World)

Wanted: Dead or Alive toplines celluloid supervillain Rutger (*Nighthawks, The Hitcher*) Hauer, in a rare contempo hero role, as the bounty-hunting, harmonica-tooting great-grandson of Josh Randall from the original *Wanted: Dead or Alive* teleseries. (How's *that* for high concept?) Hauer's hot on the trail of sneering terrorist Simmons (the Kiss crooner's finest B-pic perf to date), whose initial act of abrupt and senseless violence entails blowing up 138 *Rambo* fans (!) at an L.A. bijou. *Wanted: Dead or Alive* is a violent, tongue-in-cheek action outing that chronicles Rut's desperate race against time *and* a double-dealing pack of slimy CIA types who are using him as bait. Despite its occasionally meandering pace, *Wanted* is well worth an overnight rental.

WarCat (1987) ◆◆◆

D: Ted V. Mikels. Jannina Poynter, David O'Hara, Macka Foley, Carl Erwin, Joe Wilkerson, Jason Hole. 78 minutes. (TWE)

Bikers, psychos, and survivalists clash in the contempo American wasteland in *WarCat*, latest existential statement from T. V. (*Astro Zombies*) Mikels and a flick so obscure that it *world premiered* in Fort Smith, Arkansas (!), under its original title *Angel of Vengeance*. (The pic also surfaced briefly sporting the same moniker and a longer running time on the Midwest Video label.) Desert cycle sickos the Thrill Killers make the fatal mistake of tangling with a sadistic gang of hard-core survivalists led by Major Hargraves (O'Hara). Visiting "writer," the undeniably hot Jannina Poynter, is kidnapped—by a survivalist sex maniac named Manny—while singing "Blowin' in the Wind" (off key) over a solo campfire. The mad militarists lock her in the flimsiest jail cell seen onscreen since Barry Mahon's *Violent Women* and threaten her unmercifully ("Think about the snake pit!").

The Major decides to give Jannina a fighting chance, and once again it's *Most Dangerous Game* time; within hours, our buxom heroine transforms from a helpless scribe into a veritable Rambimbo, wasting the bad guys with consummate ease. Meanwhile, a virtually unrelated subplot follows the ex-

The odds are even in Matt (ex Mrs. Jayne Mansfield) Cimber's black biker odyssey, *The Black Six*. Photo courtesy of Unicorn Video.

ploits of a pair of "random killers," on hand primarily to pump up the pic's body count. *WarCat* lets down a bit in the final reel, but this is still a flick that demands to be seen.

The Warriors (1979) ◆◆◇
D: Walter Hill. Michael Beck, James Remar, Thomas Waites. 94 minutes. (Paramount)

Hill's stylized gang-war epic sparked riots during its initial release. You may find yourself slashing your couch cover with a switchblade as you watch the embattled title aggregate "bop" their way from the Bronx to Brooklyn.

White Hot (1989) ◆◇
D: Robby Benson. Robby Benson, Tawny Kitaen, Danny Aiello, Kevin Gray. 95 minutes. (Academy)

Multi-untalented Robby Benson directs and stars in this hitherto unreleased update of 1937's *Cocaine Fiends* (see index). *White Hot* stretches credulity right from reel one. First, you have to buy professional wimp RB as a cash-strapped yuppie who agrees to take over an imperiled dealer's coke-and-crack trade. Next, you're asked to accept the visually tantalizing Kitaen—who's been trapped in an ongoing career slide since her promising *Perils of Gwendoline* gig back in '85—as Rob's at-first concerned, eventually crack-addicted squeeze. And that's to say nothing of a plot that's got more holes than Al Pacino

had at the end of *Scarface*. Nile Rodgers's snappy soundtrack contributions, Judy Tenuta cameo, and Aiello's expansive turn as an angry Mafioso occasionally enliven the proceedings, and *White Hot* supplies a fair measure of stupid fun in its early going. But 90+ minutes of Robby B, in all his many thespic phases, ultimately add up to a video OD.

White Line Fever (1975) ◆◆◆
D: Jonathan Kaplan. Jan-Michael Vincent, Kay Lenz, Slim Pickens, L. Q. Jones. 89 minutes. (RCA/Columbia)

One of the earliest and best trucker-vengeance movies, with young Vincent as the angry Diesel driver who takes on the forces of corruption.

The Wild Angels (1966) ◆◆
D: Roger Corman. Peter Fonda, Bruce Dern, Nancy Sinatra. 93 minutes. (Embassy)

Corman kick-starts the biker-movie trend, although this relatively lavish trash epic manages to be a lot less compelling than many of its cheaper imitations.

Wild in the Streets (1968) ◆◆
D: Barry Shear. Christopher Jones, Shelley Winters, Diane Varsi, Richard Pryor. 97 minutes. (HBO)

An overrated youth fable from the deep thinkers at AIP, *Wild in the Streets* stars Chris Jones as a rock idol who's elected president and subsequently consigns over-thirty-fivers to LSD camps (!).

Baby-boomers who found it funny twenty years ago may not be laughing now.

The Wild One (1953) ♦♦◊ B&W
D: Laslo Benedek. Marlon Brando, Mary Murphy, Lee Marvin. 79 minutes. (RCA/Columbia)

The original '50s rebel movie, with a profoundly inarticulate Brando leading a gang of overage bikers through a small-town blitz. Campy and iconic, but not as exciting as it should have been. Beyond those cycle pics already covered here, we further refer biker buffs to the following: *Angels Hard as They Come* (Embassy), co-written by Jonathan Demme during his Roger Corman apprenticeship; Matt Cimber's *The Black Six* (Unicorn), with former gridiron greats Gene Washington, Mercury Morris, and Mean Joe Greene; the femme-oriented *Bury Me an Angel*, starring Dixie Peabody and directed by Barbara Peeters; the hog-hounds-versus-hippies variation *The Peace Killers* (both New World); *The Dirt Gang* (MPI); *A Great Ride* (IVE); *The Hellcats*; *Wild Rebels* (both Academy); 1987's *Hellriders* (TWE), starring Adam (*Batman*) West and Tina Louise; Dean Stockwell, during an arid stretch between *The Boy with Green Hair* and *Blue Velvet*, in *The Loners*; Big Bill Smith in *Run, Angel, Run* (both VidAmerica); Roger Corman's *Naked Angels* (Continental); *Nomad Riders* (Vestron); *Outlaw Riders* (WesternWorld), with Rafael Campos; George Kennedy and Karen Black in *Savage Dawn* (Media); *Sinner's Blood* (Saturn); the atrociously post-synced clinker *Warlords from Hell* (Warner); and the inimitable Casey Kasem in *Wild Wheels* (Video Gems).

The Wild Pair (1987) ♦◊
D: Beau Bridges. Beau Bridges, Bubba Smith, Lloyd Bridges, Gary Lockwood, Raymond St. Jacques, Danny De La Paz. 88 minutes. (Media)

A low-budget *Lethal Weapon* clone, *The Wild Pair* stars streetwise cop Smith and "wimpy white" FBI agent Bridges (who also directed) as mandatory partners who gradually develop an intense if platonic relationship while investigating an urban drug ring. The unlikely plot eventually involves them with a paramilitary organization of right-wing loonies led by Beau's dad, Lloyd Bridges. It's Bubba who supplies the lion's share of the violence, executing your standard last-reel one-man slaughter mission after the bad guys kill his girlfriend, kidnap partner Beau, and worst of all, waste his cat. For the first hour, *The Wild Pair* is an okay sleazeactioner, but its clichéd windup drains the flick of both credibility and interest. Punishment gluttons are also referred to *Bubba 'til It Hurts*, a killer-workout tape available via All Sports Books & Video. Bridges returns as director and star of the more ambitious but failed thriller *Seven Hours To Judgment* (Media).

The Wild Ride (1958) ◆◆ B&W

D: *Harvey Berman. Jack Nicholson, Georgianna Carter, Robert Bean. 59 minutes. (Video Yesteryear)*

Nicholson's first starring vehicle casts him as a speed-crazed hot rodder who drives afoul of the law in an okay JD sneerfest. Not as good as Dick Bakalyan's *Hot Car Girl* (NA), but we've got to make do with what we've got.

Women's Prison Massacre (1985) ◆◆

D: *Gilbert Roussel. Laura Gemser, Loraine De Selle, Françoise Perrot. 89 minutes. (Vestron)*

It's business as usual: Sadistic matrons merrily torture their scantily clad charges, while the distaff warden beams her approval. Jail "birds" duke it out in an endless prison power struggle. And, of course, innumerable showers are taken by the facility's shapelier inmates. This relative tranquillity is rudely interrupted, however, when four *male* escaped cons, led by the deranged "Crazy Boy" Henderson, take the entire prison hostage. It's only then that this determinedly lurid flick *really* gets rolling. *Women's Prison Massacre* exhibits all the expected virtues (stiff, stupid dubbed-in dialogue) and flaws (slapdash direction, the usual chainsaw method of film editing) of your typical Euro-trash-movie import. We're never even sure whether the story's set in America or Italy. (The characters sport Anglo names but are seen thumbing through Italian newspapers!) But why get bogged down in minor details? The important thing is that director Roussel doesn't forget to dish out a sufficient number of action scenes or see that justice is eventually and violently served.

Yellow Hair and the Fortress of Gold (1985) ◆◆

D: *Matt Cimber. Laurene Landon, Ken Roberson, John Ghaffari, Luis Lorenzo, Claudio Gravi, Aldo Sambre. 102 minutes. (Lightning)*

Despite its title, Cimber's Spanish import *Yellow Hair and the Fortress of Gold* isn't a direct *Raiders* rip-off but a genial (if generally airheaded) send-up of the sagebrush serials of yore. *Yellow Hair* makes its intentions clear right from reel one. The flick opens with a brief black-and-white sequence showing kids scrambling for seats at an unidentified bijou. The pic's central characters are then introduced, to the kids' accompanying cheers and jeers. *Yellow Hair* goes on from there to run through the entire catalog of cliffhanger clichés, as two-fisted half-breed heroine Yellow Hair (Landon) and her affable cowpoke partner, the Pecos Kid (Roberson), contend with Mexican soldiers, cutthroat comancheros, and wily Aztecs in an attempt to lay hands on the title treasure. At its best, *Yellow Hair* approximates the livelier Bud

Spencer/Terence Hill spaghetti-western spoofs (*They Call Me Trinity*, et al—see index) popular in the early '70s. Unfortunately, the energetic action scenes are separated by stretches as arid as the desert in which most of the movie takes place. A bit more bite and wit might have put *Yellow Hair* over the top.

Yojimbo (1961) ◆◆◆◇ B&W
D: Akira Kurosawa. Toshiro Mifune, Eijiro Tono, Seizaburo Kawazu. 110 minutes. (Embassy)

Itinerant samurai Mifune works for two conflicting factions in a violent, funny killfest that ranks right up there with *Seven Samurai*. Embassy/Nelson also carries the equally adept sequel, *Sanjuro*, while Ocean Video handles the popular sightless samurai hero *Zatoichi*.

Zebra Force (1977) ◆◆◇
D: Joe Tornatore. Mike Lane, Richard X. Slattery, Rockne Tarkington. 89 minutes. (Media)

Viet vets rip off the Mafia and mucho mayhem ensues in this cheap but lively and relentlessly violent pulp actioner piloted by Joe Tornatore, who gave us the deathless *Grotesque* (see index) a decade later. See also Tornatore's late-arriving (1987) sequel, *Codename: Zebra* (TWE).

Zero Boys (1986) ◆
D: Nico Mastorikis. Kelli Maroney, Daniel Hirsch, Tom Shell, Nicole Rio, Jared Moses, Joe Phelan. 89 minutes. (Lightning)

The title refers to a trio of young survival-game aces who, accompanied by their assorted squeezes (including the always welcome Maroney), stop off at a seemingly abandoned woodland home and find themselves trapped by a certified psycho who's not playing games. Unfortunately, more than half the flick unspools before we arrive at this point, and it's not worth wading through reels of dull, dim-witted filler footage to cut to a chase that, as it happens, is not all that exciting itself. Nice opening credit sequence, though—easily the *Zero Boys'* high point.

THE FRIGHT STUFF:
TERROR ON TAPE

"Welcome to prime time, bitch!"

Freddy Krueger
A Nightmare on Elm Street 3

Attack of the Killer Cassettes!

No genre has benefited more from the '80s video boom than the horror film. A 1988 *Variety* study showed domestic fright-flick production at an all-time high, swelling from 36 movies in 1977 to 105 in 1987. Not only does video feed interest in existing fear films—many of which turn up on cassette within weeks of their theatrical release—but it creates a demand for still *more* horror product—much of it slated solely for home viewing, a demand that enterprising low-budget indie outfits have rushed in to meet. Busy regional B-production units at United Home Video (which started the direct-to-home-vid horror trend with the Tulsa-set *Blood Cult* in '85 and continued with *Revenge, Forever Evil,* and *The Ripper,* with Tom Savini), San Francisco's City Lights (*The Newlydeads, Epitaph*), Prism (with Flash Features' Denver-lensed *Mind Killer* and *NightVision*), and Urban Classics (the Connecticut-based *Galactic Gigolo* and *Psychos in Love*) all cater almost exclusively to the genre-video market, although with only occasionally worthy results in terms of quality, so far. The current glut of terror titles will hopefully serve to sharpen competition

A Nightmare 3 ON ELM STREET
DREAM WARRIORS

"Welcome to prime time, bitch!"
Photo courtesy of New Line Cinema.

and weed out the amateur-night losers from the legit low-budget sleepers, as well as spur economy-minded outfits like the above to improve the quality of their output.

While many modestly budgeted movies proceed directly from the editing room (some look as if they skipped even that step), others undergo far more tortuous journeys through today's Brave New World of theatrical/video distribution. A case in point is Larry Cohen's genre gem *A Return to Salem's Lot*, sequel (if largely in name only) to the made-for-TV miniseries *Salem's Lot*, based on the Stephen King novel. The Phantom happened to catch *Return* at a 1987 Cannes market screening and fully expected that the film—boasting decent production values and a veteran cast headed by Cohen stalwart Michael Moriarty—would eventually "open wide" in this country. Instead, nothing further was heard from the movie for months until it snuck in for a one-week stand in Providence, Rhode Island (!), where much of the flick had been filmed. That extremely token appearance qualified the Warner Home Video version—which took several additional months to surface—to come equipped with a "Direct from Theatrical

Release" banner on the preview-cassette cover. In point of fact, though, almost no one had ever *heard* of the film. Fortunately, via positive video reviews, ample pay-cable TV exposure, auteur Cohen's established rep, and vid-renter word of mouth, *Return to Salem's Lot* has won at least the modest success it long deserved.

Rather than dwell on the oft-incomprehensible business end, we'll move along to those horror videos that, whatever their individual histories, now share vid-store shelf space. What with the literally thousands of terror titles currently available at cassette outlets, supermarket racks, video vending machines, and mail-order specialty firms, we've tried our best to grant equal coverage to those newer releases, creature classics, and interesting obscurities that we feel merit your attention.

But first a word about what constitutes a horror film. Hardly a day goes by that doesn't find some stranger sidling up to yours truly and saying, "Yo, you're the Phantom of the Movies, right? Maybe *you* can tell me: Exactly where does Science Fiction end and Horror begin? Or putting it another way, vice versa?"

Our by-now standard answer holds that, beyond such obvious elements as an outer-space or futuristic setting or the presence of visiting ETs, sci-fi films hang whatever horror content they may contain on a scientific hook (e.g., the many atomic mutants that ran amok in 1950s B flicks). Horror films may contain secondary sci-fi elements, but their main purpose is to frighten, rather than simply to astonish or amaze. In a few cases, though, it comes down to a judgment call. For example, we've included George A. Romero's *Night of the Living Dead* in our Horror chapter because the flick is much more an extended nightmare designed to shock than a sci-fi pic dealing with the dangers of wayward radiation—a detail employed simply as a perfunctory explanation for the Living Dead's sudden resurrection. Ditto for *Dead*'s sundry sequels and spin-offs. A *Living Dead* clone like the Italo *City of the Walking Dead*, on the other hand, is listed in our SF chapter because it lavishes more attention on the radiation angle, though its chief raison d'être is the loving depiction of gory wholesale slaughter. The point is, we've got a rationale for every organizational decision we've made (and if you don't believe us, we can make one up).

And if you think *that's* scary, wait till you feast your eyes on the following. . . .

The Abominable Dr. Phibes (1971) ◆◆◆
D: Robert Fuest. Vincent Price, Joseph Cotten, Terry-Thomas. 94 minutes. (Vestron)

AIP's deadpan send-up of Hammer's classy horror flicks features a witty script, gaudy art deco sets, a flamboyantly florid perf from fright pro Vincent Price, plus the memorable tag line, "Love means never having to say you're ugly." Price/Phibes strikes anew in *Dr. Phibes Rises Again* (Vestron).

Alice, Sweet Alice (1977) ◆◆◆◇
D: Alfred Sole. Louisa Horton, Tom Signorelli, Brooke Shields, Paula Sheppard, Linda Miller, Lillian Roth. 108 minutes. (Goodtimes)

Originally (and more aptly) titled *Holy Terror, Alice* is a wonderfully perverse low-budget *Bad Seed*–type tale, ably directed by Alfred Sole. Ten-year-old Brooke Shields barely makes it past the first reel before being strangled on her first communion day. Is her hostile older sister Alice (Sheppard) the culprit? Is the latter also responsible for the brutal slayings that follow in Brooke's wake? It will cost you less than a sawbuck to find out: The best Catholic-themed *verité* chiller ever lensed in New Jersey is in public domain due to a technical screw-up. The Goodtimes edition, though recorded at LP (middle) speed, boasts pretty fair transfer quality and represents the full 108-minute print. The cover art's better than usual, too.

Alligator (1980) ◆◆◇
D: Lewis Teague. Robert Forster, Robin Riker, Henry Silva. 92 minutes. (Lightning)

John Sayles supplies the in-joke-laden script, Robert Forster the low-key heroics, and Henry Silva (as a Great White Hunter stalking urban sewers!) the sardonic comic relief in a generally fun—if occasionally self-conscious—fright film about a giant alligator amok.

Alone in the Dark (1982) ◆◆◆◇
D: Jack Sholder. Donald Pleasence, Jack Palance, Martin Landau, Dwight Schultz, Deborah Hedwall, Erland van Lidth. 92 minutes. (RCA/Columbia)

Wacko war vet Jack ("I'm here because I enjoy the social life") Palance and paranoid preacher Landau lead a quartet of crazies who run amok in Jersey during a blackout caused by a faulty nuclear power plant. Imperiled psychiatric aide Dwight (*The A-Team*) Schultz tries to protect his endangered family from the psychos' wrath, while nutty head doc Pleasence insists that his errant charges—whom he dubs voyagers—are merely "confused." Sholder's sharp satiric splatter pic pokes fun at Laingian shrinks, suburban life, punk rock, American media-addiction, and voyeurism in general, and it features a brilliant opening nightmare sequence. The title applies as aptly to vicarious thrill-seeking bijou and home-vid viewers as it does to the onscreen victims' situation. An almost seamless B movie that's funny, scary, and equipped with a bright central metaphor. What more can we ask?

American Gothic (1988) ♦♦◇
D: John Hough. Rod Steiger, Yvonne DeCarlo, Sara Torgov, Michael J. Pollard, Fiona Hutchison, Mark Lindsay Chapman. 90 minutes. (Vidmark)

After a slow start that finds three yuppie couples landing their fuel-depleted plane on a scary uncharted isle *miles* from Seattle, *American Gothic* revs into high gear once our castaways encounter loony locals Ma and Pa, their two psycho sons, and their equally demented daughter. You know what direction the flick is headed as soon as one of Ma and Pa's infantile middle-aged offspring asks a bewildered yup, "Wanna ride our swing?" Its pedestrian Ed Gein–inspired plot aside, *American Gothic* comes through with an impressive array of truly sicko surprises, involving wholesale slaughter, necrophilia, and other activities seemingly at odds with traditional family values. Rod Steiger and Yvonne (*The Munsters*) DeCarlo are consistently entertaining in what may be the most humiliating roles of their already checkered careers, while Pollard giggles and drools convincingly as one of their dim-witted sons.

An American Werewolf in London (1981) ♦♦♦
D: John Landis. David Naughton, Jenny Agutter, Griffin Dunne. 97 minutes. (MCA)

Landis's lycanthrope lampoon is one of those rare creature comedies that succeed in supplying honest laughs without sacrificing the chills. Rick Baker's makeup FX netted him an Oscar.

The Amityville Horror (1979) ♦♦
D: Stuart Rosenberg. James Brolin, Margot Kidder, Rod Steiger. 117 minutes. (Warner)

Familiar, overblown, but marginally watchable schlock based on Jay Anson's best seller, wherein poltergeists frighten new inhabitants of the title site. The pic "inspired" two woefully weak sequels, *Amityville II: The Possession* (Embassy) and *Amityville 3-D* (Vestron).

And Now the Screaming Starts! (1973) ♦♦◇
D: Roy Ward Baker. Peter Cushing, Herbert Lom, Stephanie Beacham. 87 minutes. (Nostalgia Merchant)

The presence of horror vets Cushing and Lom help make this Amicus production a passable entry in the venerable haunted-house/severed-hand-amok genres.

Andy Warhol's Dracula (1974) ♦♦♦◇
D: Paul Morrisey. Udo Keir, Joe Dallesandro, Vittorio DeSica. 106 minutes. (Video Gems)

Morrisey fashioned the best fang farce to date in a period pic detailing anemic vampire Keir's futile search for "wirgin" blood in a houseful of single women. Dallesandro is a Brooklyn-accented Marxist gardener (in Europe, no less), while directors Roman Polanski and Vittorio DeSica cameo as a hostile villager and the gals' windbag dad, respectively. *Andy Warhol's Frankenstein* (Video Gems), originally screened in 3-D, is a far less successful spoof that relies more on gore than on wit.

Anguish (1988) ◆◆

D: Bigas Luna. Zelda Rubinstein, Michael Lerner, Talia Paul. 92 minutes. (Key)

Luna's metaphorical, metaphysical, perhaps even meta–brain-damaged *Anguish* is less a straight-ahead horror pic than a meditation on the movie medium itself. Four-foot *Poltergeist* psychic Rubinstein plays the supportive mom of eye-gouging oedipal wreck John (Lerner), an optometric aide whose hobby is slicing out—and collecting—human eyeballs. After following John on his ocular rounds, director Luna cuts to the audience *watching* the above proceedings on screen. John himself then ducks into a *different* theater, where the silent version of *The Lost World* is unspooling; also present is the same audience we saw in theater one, a few of whom John surreptitiously relieves of their eyes. Meanwhile, a second, "real" maniac turns up in theater one, responds to the onscreen Zelda, and runs around shooting patrons. (Is this *heavy* or what?) While thematically akin both to Lamberto Bava's *Demons* (whose febrile feel it shares) and to Peter Bogdanovich's *Targets* (see index),

Anguish dares to venture onto some relatively virgin turf, and auteur Luna definitely deserves an A for ambition. Unfortunately, *Anguish* is not nearly as much dark fun as it should have been, so we'll give BL a C for execution. In our view, *Anguish* is not worth keeping an eye out for; you may feel differently.

The Ape (1940) ◆◇

D: William Nigh. Boris Karloff, Maris Wrixon, Henry Hall. 62 minutes. (Kartes)

One of Monogram's lesser monster movies—with Boris as a mad medic in an ape suit—but essential for Boris buffs.

The Ape Man (1943) ◆◆◇ B&W

D: William Beaudine. Bela Lugosi, Louise Currie, Wallace Ford. 64 minutes. (Cable)

If little else, *The Ape Man* is at least an improvement over *The Ape*, with Bela delivering some creative line readings as a simian-regressed scientist who shares a cage with yet another guy in an ape suit. Their complex love-hate relationship forms the flick's thematic crux.

Appointment with Fear (1985) ◆

D: Alan Smithee (Ranzi Thomas). Michelle Little, Michael Wylie, Kerry Remsen, Douglas Rowe, Garrick Dowhen, Danny Dayton. 92 minutes. (IVE)

Helmed by the legendary Alan Smithee (the Hollywood pseudonym traditionally used by disgruntled directors), *Appointment* with *Fear* generates some initial suspense, if only on the strength of its own staggering incoherence— it really *is* impossible to guess where the pic will go next. All that's certain is that Kowalski (Rowe), your basic beat-out detective, is lukewarm on the trail of a mysterious psycho who's just murdered his wife and is now out to get his infant son. The kid is rescued by blond space cadette Remsen, whose best friend, winsome teen wench Little, keeps a philosophical pet bum (!) named Norman (former Steve Allen regular Dayton) in the back of her pickup truck. After that, it's anybody's guess—though we *do* learn that the killer's really the wandering spirit of the Egyptian God of Nature (!). In sum, not one of Smithee's smoother efforts.

April Fool's Day (1986) ◆
D: Fred Walton. Jay Baker, Deborah Foreman, Griffin O'Neal, Deborah Goodrich, Clayton Rohner, Ken Olandt. 90 minutes. (Paramount)

April Fool's Day is a decidedly low-concept "thriller" shrewdly calculated to alienate every conceivable segment of its target audience. Equally bereft of laughs, suspense, and gore, this perfectly pointless pic pits a pack of isolated preppies against an unidentified fiend who may or may not be doing them in. The flick's funniest line is delivered deadpan during one of the "scary" sequences: "But Muffy hasn't been in an institution for three years; she's been at Vassar!" Anyone who rents this rotten horror-day turkey will indeed find that the joke's on them.

HOLIDAY HORRORS

The holiday terror trend began in earnest with the lucrative *Halloween* trilogy of the late '70s. While not a holiday per se, Friday the 13th proved an even more popular date on the gore-movie calendar. No fewer than eight fear flicks and a syndicated TV series—along with a trio of near-misses, Mickey Rose's *Thursday the 12th* (aka *Student Bodies*) (Paramount) and Julie Corman's *Saturday the 14th* (Embassy) and *Saturday the 14th Strikes Back* (MGM/UA)—have celebrated that day, with no foreseeable end in sight. 1986 witnessed the release of yet another postholiday horror, *Night After Halloween* (Magnum), while the Halloween-set *Trick or Treats* (Vestron) arrived back in 1982.

It was the (mis)appropriation of the yuletide season for splatter purposes that aroused the greatest public outcry, however. *Black Christmas* (Warner), *Bloodbeat* (TWE), *Christmas Evil* (see index), *Home for the Holidays* (Vidmark), and *Don't Open till Christmas* (Vestron) ("Twas the night before Christmas/and all through the house/Not a creature was stirring ... they were all DEAD!") had been sufficiently obscure to sneak through sans fanfare or furor. But the saturated release of 1984's *Silent Night, Deadly Night*—replete with print ads and trailers showing a homicidal St. Nick-and-Cut wielding a bloodied assortment of instruments sharp and blunt—inspired widespread parental protests that led to the flick's hasty withdrawal from circulation. A USA Home Video (who'd already purchased the home-vid rights) press release blamed "elements of the (original) advertising campaign" that "depicted Santa Claus as a murderous marauder (*sic*)" for engendering the negative publicity. "It's NOT Santa Claus," the release went on to explain, "but a demented young man who dresses up in a Santa outfit and creates a nightmare of horror." (Hey, only the most curmudgeonly of anticelluloid Scrooges could find fault with *that*.) The flick pulled in sufficient numbers of unoffended patrons to warrant an even worse sequel, *Silent Night, Deadly Night Part II* (IVE), that recycled "the good parts" from *SN, DN I.*

It didn't do much for USA, though, since that vid label folded soon after. Rights to *Silent Night* were quickly picked up by IVE.

Schlockmeister Emmett Alston took a stab at holiday horror fun, meanwhile, via his 1980 *New Year's Evil* (Cannon), starring the Fonz's former TV squeeze Roz Kelly as a rock deejay stalked by a crazed killer offering a sure and permanent cure for January 1 hangovers. *Bloody New Year* (Academy) and *Ghost Keeper* (New World) also unfolded on that date, while *Home, Sweet Home* (Media) turned the carving knife against a family of Thanksgiving Day celebrants. Other cinematic slashers commemorated such traditional (and generally horrific) occasions as *Prom Night, Mother's Day* (see index for both), *Graduation Day* (RCA/Columbia), Valentine's Day (Paramount's *My Bloody Valentine*), and *Hell Night* (Video Treasures).

A few major holidays continue to be ignored by gore auteurs. While there have been any number of murderous mutant tree movies (*Day of the Triffids, Navy vs. the Night Monsters, From Hell It Came,* for example), none have been linked to an Arbor Day theme.

Perhaps the oddest of all the holiday horrors produced to date was 1983's *Groundhogs From Hell!* That admittedly obscure Groundhog Day thriller saw Punxatawney Phil and various furry friends—mutated by a toxic-waste spill from a nearby nuclear power plant—grow to giant proportions, devour dozens of visiting media reps, and otherwise terrorize the countryside. Phil and crew, you may recall, are ultimately destroyed by several unemployed Living Dead extras recruited from

George Romero's film complex in neighboring Pittsburgh, as mankind learns yet another costly lesson re: the dangers of careless atomic tinkering.

Missed that one? Well, April Fool to you too!

The Asphyx (1972) ◆◆◆

D: Peter Newbrook. Robert Stephens, Robert Powell, Jane Lapotaire. 98 minutes. (Interglobal)

The title refers to the spirit that approaches the body at the moment of death; photographer Stephens captures one in the hope it will make him immortal in this fairly novel period horror pic. Also out as *Spirit of the Dead* (Media).

Asylum (1972) ◆◆◆

D: Roy Ward Baker. Barbara Parkins, Richard Todd, Peter Cushing. 100 minutes. (Prism)

The title facility serves as the frame for four Robert (*Psycho*) Bloch–penned scare tales in this tight anthology from Amicus. Later rereleased as *House of Crazies*; the video version represents the longer, original print.

Atom Age Vampire (1961) ◆◆ B&W

D: Anton Giulio Majano. Alberto Lupo, Susan Loret, Sergio Fantoni. 87 minutes. (Loonic, others)

More of a restoring-the-disfigured-face exercise than a vampire outing, this badly dubbed import does boast some impressive atmospherics and rates as a worthwhile bet for patient Italo-horror lovers.

The Attic (1979) ◆◆◇

D: George Edwards. Ray Milland, Carrie Snodgress, Rosemary Murphy. 92 minutes. (Unicorn)

An occasionally funny, in its own grim way, familial fright flick pitting resentful spinster Snodgress against her unpleasant dad (interpreted with *elaborate* unpleasantness by Milland). Caught in the middle is Carrie's surrogate kid, Dickie the Chimp (!). Played with utter sincerity but a strange idea of entertainment, to put it mildly.

The Baby (1973) ◆◆

D: Ted Post. Ruth Roman, Anjanette Comer, Marianna Hill. 85 minutes. (WesternWorld)

More nuclear-family nuttiness: Man-hating Roman keeps her adult son in an infantile state, to the horror of social worker Comer. Poorly done but fairly compelling.

Backwoods (1987) ◆

D: Dean Crow. Christina Noonan, Brad Armacost, Dick Kreusser, Jack O'Hara, Leslie Denise, Gary Lott. 89 minutes. (Cinema Group)

See him drool!
See him bare his bad teeth!
See him bite the heads off live chickens!

Those are but three of the talents exhibited by one William (O'Hara), the feral psycho star of Crow's primitive *Backwoods*, formerly (and more appropriately) titled *Geek*. Our story, such as it is, involves a vacationing couple (Noonan, Armacost) who ignore a friendly forest ranger's (Lott) advice and camp in a dangerous neck of the woods. There they encounter cracker Kreusser and his subhuman son, the aforementioned William, who terrorizes all and sundry. That's about it plotwise, in this relentlessly stupid and consummately boring "thriller." You'd do well to let *Backwoods* rot on your local vidstore's back shelves.

Bad Dreams (1988) ◆◇
D: Andrew Fleming. Jennifer Rubin, Bruce Abbott, Richard Lynch, Dean Cameron, Harris Yulin, Susan Barnes. 84 minutes. (CBS/Fox)

Produced by the normally reliable Gale Ann (*Terminator*, *Aliens*) Hurd as the first effort of her low-budget No Frills company, *Bad Dreams* is a blatant rip-off of the *Nightmare on Elm Street* series in general and *Nightmare 3* specifically. The flick features vet villain Lynch as Harris, a sort of psychedelic Freddy who engineers a Jonestown-style mass suicide, of which Cynthia (Rubin) is the sole survivor. Upon awakening from a thirteen-year coma, our heroine is assigned to a therapy group that consists of "borderline personalities" and is run by Bruce (*Reanimator*) Abbott. Said group members begin dying in various violent ways, leading Cynthia to believe that their deaths are the handiwork of the presumably late Harris, whose scarred, leering visage haunts her every hallucination. On the plus side, Lynch (who suffered actual offscreen facial burns prior to filming) is pretty vivid in his limited role, and a few choice '60s tunes (like the Chambers Brothers' "Time Has Come Today") play on the soundtrack. Otherwise, *Bad Dreams* is as bald on thrills as it is on frills.

The Bad Seed (1956) ◆◆◆ **B&W**
D: Mervyn LeRoy. Patty McCormack, Nancy Kelly, Henry Jones. 129 minutes. (Warner)

Little blond brat Patty is literally a born psychopath in this extravagantly febrile adaptation of Maxwell Anderson's Broadway play. She might have been happier if Norman Bates had adopted her. We'd advise you to steer clear of Krishna Shah's obnoxious male variation on the theme, *Deadly Rivals* (Cinema Group), as well as the atrocious *Girly* (Prism).

Baron Blood (1972) ◆◆
D: Mario Bava. Joseph Cotten, Elke Sommer, Massimo Girotti. 90 minutes. (HBO)

The video represents a toned-down version of this atmospheric Bava bloodbath, featuring Cotten as a revivified sixteenth-century warlock determined to torture his castle's current inhabitants. Also out as *The Torture Chamber of Baron Blood.*

Basket Case (1982) ◆◆◆
D: Frank Henenlotter. Kevin VanHentenryck, Terri Susan Smith, Beverly Bonner. 89 minutes. (Media)

Henenlotter's 1982 cult creature comedy *Basket Case*—a cheap, sick, and thoroughly entertaining oddity—limns the (literally) side-splitting tale of a boy, his basket, and the dwarfed, deformed, and exceedingly hostile Siamese twin (dubbed Belial) who resides therein. As our story opens, young Duane Bradley (VanHentenryck) arrives in Fun City from Glen Falls, inseparable basket in tow, intent upon doing in the rogue surgeons who forcibly divorced him from his diminutive twin a decade or so earlier. An innocent in the wilds of darkest Times Square, Duane signs on at the seedy Broslin, the worst-run hotel this side of *Fawlty Towers.* Once ensconced, Duane and his benighted brother leave the discomfort of their temporary home only long enough to eliminate the medical ne'er-do-wells, a trio of truly repulsive docs (one's a veterinarian!) that only a malpractice lawyer could love. Sibling rivalry surfaces when Duane secretly dates a buxom receptionist (Smith) who knows not of Duane's bitter half, creating further schisms between the Bradley boys. While hampered by an invisible budget and rushed

shooting, *Basket Case* is bolstered by several surprisingly strong performances, most notably VanHentenryck as Duane and Bonner as a sympathetic hooker. *Basket Case* stacks up as one of the most compelling blackly comic scare pics of recent vintage and an ideal late-night video treat.

Beaks: the Movie (1987) ◆
D: Rene Cardona, Jr. Christopher Atkins, Michelle Johnson, Sonia Infante, Salvador Pineda, Carol Connery, Gabriel Tinti. 91 minutes. (IVE)

The video version of this inane *Birds* rip-off, originally titled *Birds of Prey,* was relabeled *Beaks: the Movie* to make the flick sound like a parody. Well, it's not. Mexican schlockmeister Cardona's script means every inane, badly dubbed word it babbles. When man's ecological blunders prompt our fine-feathered foes to strike back—engineering plane crashes, pecking at pedestrians, and generally causing high-flying havoc around the globe—bland blond newspersons Atkins and Johnson investigate the ornithological mayhem to generally soporific effect.

Beast from Haunted Cave (1959) ◆◆◇ B&W
D: Monte Hellman. Michael Forest, Sheila Carol, Frank Wolff. 65 minutes. (Sinister Cinema)

An atmospheric cheapie from cost-conscious AIP's even lower-budgeted Filmgroup wing, concerning crooks who get their comeuppance at the paws of the title thing (itself imaginatively designed by future thesp Chris Robinson). Hellman later directed the cult westerns *Ride in the Whirlwind* and *The Shooting* (see index).

The Beast Must Die (1974) ◆◆
D: *Paul Annett. Calvin Lockhart, Peter Cushing, Anton Diffring. 93 minutes. (Prism)*

A fairly clumsy Amicus werewolf outing, equipped with a gimmick that allowed audiences to Name That Lurking Lycanthrope, with top work being turned in by the ever-reliable Cushing.

Bedlam (1946) ◆◆◆ **B&W**
D: *Mark Robson. Boris Karloff, Anna Lee, Ian Wolfe. 79 minutes. (Fox Hills)*

Producer Val Lewton's look at the notorious Brit insane asylum, inspired by a series of Hogarth sketches that serve here as brief onscreen entr'actes, doesn't pretend to be a horror movie and even plays a bit tame as a belated exposé. But Boris has a great role as Bedlam's alternately toadying and bullying warden, while Robert Clarke, in his pre—*Hideous Sun Demon* daze, turns in a bizarre cameo as an inmate. Karloff's confrontations with feisty femme Lee—a sworn enemy · who's wrongfully entrusted to Boris's creepy "care"—are also vividly rendered. Not very frightening, but eccentrically entertaining.

Before I Hang (1940) ◆◆◆
D: *Nick Grinde. Boris Karloff, Evelyn Keyes, Bruce Bennett. 71 minutes. (RCA/Columbia)*

Boris reprises his patented kindly mad-scientist role as he seeks to perfect an antiaging serum, with dire side effects, in an intriguing, if ultimately compromised, chiller.

The Being (1983) ◆
D: *Jackie Kong. Martin Landau, Ruth Buzzi, Jose Ferrer. 82 minutes. (HBO)*

This awful junk about a toxic-waste mutant amok in Idaho at least boasts a once-in-a-lifetime cast: besides Buzzi, Landau, and Ferrer, Dorothy Malone, C&W satirist Kinky Friedman, and Murray ("The Unknown Comic") Langston are also along for the bumpy ride, navigated by Jackie (*Blood Diner*) Kong, who's asleep at the wheel more often than not.

The Believers (1987) ◆◆◇
D: *John Schlesinger. Martin Sheen, Helen Shaver, Robert Loggia, Harley Cross, Elizabeth Wilson, Harris Yulin, Richard Masur. 114 minutes. (HBO)*

John (*Marathon Man*) Schlesinger's high-budget horror flick opens with a hot Mr. Coffee Massacre sequence, then settles into a less inspired groove as widower/ police shrink Sheen, aided by squeeze Shaver and cop Loggia, seeks to save his young son (Cross) from the creepy clutches of a kid-sacrificing Brujeria (witchcraft) cult led by Harris (*Scarface*) Yulin. *The Believers* is a polished, professionally crafted pic, but its heralded gore FX have been done before and in far ghastlier fashion by the likes of Lamberto (*Demons*) Bava and Dario (*Inferno*) Argento, while the voodoo hook was employed to more visceral effect in Alan Parker's superior suspenser *Angel Heart* (see index). With its lack of sustained tension and emphasis on child mutilation, *The Believers* is ultimately more depressing than chilling.

A Bell from Hell (1973) ◆◆

D: Claudio Guerin Hill. Viveca Lindfors, Alfred Mayo. 80 minutes. (Unicorn)

After completing this offbeat Spanish horror thriller about a mental patient's plot to do in various family members, director Hill jumped or fell to his death from the movie's bell-tower set, adding a further bizarre note to the Gothic goings-on. Unfortunately, the Unicorn edition is missing some of the original footage; our rating applies to the video only.

Ben (1972) ◆◇

D: Phil Karlson. Joseph Campanella, Lee Harcourt Montgomery, Arthur O'Connell. 95 minutes. (Prism)

A fairly unwatchable *Willard* sequel, if you ask us, but rat rooters flocked from the woodworks to see it. And there *is* that touching title tune sung by young Michael Jackson.

Berserk! (1967) ◆◆

D: Jim O'Connolly. Joan Crawford, Ty Hardin, Diana Dors. 95 minutes. (RCA/Columbia)

Joan owns a small Brit circus beset by a series of gruesome killings. The unique cast includes limey Jayne Mansfield clone Dors, current right-wing activist Hardin, and Hammer horror vet Michael Gough. Not as good as *Circus of Horrors* (see index).

Berserker (1987) ◆

D: Jef Richard. Joseph Alan Johnson, Valerie Sheldon, Greg Dawson, Rodney Montague, John Goff, Buck Flower. 85 minutes. (Prism)

According to this low-budget regional horror, "berserkers" were psycho Viking shock troops who wore bear snouts, cannibalized their enemies, and generally behaved in a manner so unsocial that their own superiors kept them locked in cages between battles. Several centuries later, in the woods of northern Wisconsin, one such titular terror is still alive and sick and scouring the area in search of errant campers dumb enough to wander onto his turf. Enter a half-dozen dumb-enough teen campers, and you can fill in the blanks from there. Unlike Prism's earlier *Blood Hook* (see index), a regional fright flick that infused an equally unpromising premise with genuine wit and invention, *Berserker* proceeds utterly sans surprises, supplying nothing in the way of suspense, scares, or humor.

Beyond the Door (1975) ◆◇
D: *Ovidio Assonitis. Richard Johnson, Juliet Mills, Elizabeth Turner. 97 minutes. (Media)*

Those ever-imitative Italians kick off their series of *Exorcist* clones with this 'Frisco-set clinker. The trailer for the flick is quite entertaining, though.

Beyond the Door II (1979) ◆◆◇
D: *Mario Bava. Daria Nicolodi, John Steiner, David Colin, Jr. 90 minutes. (Media)*

Bearing no relation to *Beyond the Door* (thank God), this is actually a superior (though far from great) demonic-possession pic aided by Bava's always creepy direction. This was Mario's final fright-film fling. Son Lamberto (*Demons*) Bava co-directed and co-scripted.

The Birds (1963) ◆◆◆◇
D: *Alfred Hitchcock. Rod Taylor, Tippi Hedren, Jessica Tandy. 120 minutes. (MCA)*

Hitch launches a high-flying horror classic that finds man's fine-feathered friends turning into formidable foes. The film has lost none of its original impact, though the big screen remains the best place to see it. For info on other Hitchcock titles, see our Video Shopping List.

The Black Cat (1934) ◆◆◆◇ B&W
D: *Edgar G. Ulmer. Bela Lugosi, Boris Karloff, David Manners. 65 minutes. (MCA)*

Boris and Bela's first scream-screen teaming is a suitably bizarre bout pitting good guy Bela against devil-worshipper Boris. Surreal sets, Ulmer's atmospheric direction, and Karloff's New Wave hairstyle also help make this a memorable fright gem. The MCA video pairs *The Black Cat* with a second Boris-Bela duet, *The Raven* (see index).

The Black Room (1935) ◆◆◇ B&W
D: *Roy William Neill. Boris Karloff, Marian Marsh, Robert Allen. 67 minutes. (Goodtimes)*

Two Karloffs for the price of one! Boris plays twins—one good, the other evil—who labor under an ancient curse in this generally effective Gothic tale. Not to be confused with 1983's *Black Room* (Vestron), a psychosexual vampire yarn that's pretty strange in its own right.

Black Sabbath (1963) ◆◆◆
D: *Mario Bava. Boris Karloff, Mark Damon, Suzy Anderson. 99 minutes. (HBO)*

Boris hosts this atmospheric Italo terror trilogy and stars, under Bava's direction, in the film's final episode ("The Wurdulak").

The Black Sleep (1956) ◆◆◆ B&W
D: *Reginald LeBorg. Basil Rathbone, Akim Tamiroff, Herbert Rudley. 81 minutes. (Channel 13)*

A fun, sleazy chiller, set in nineteenth-century scientist Rathbone's back-lot castle, with a wonderful cast that—in addition to the headliners—boasts Lugosi (in his final, nonspeaking role), Chaney, Carradine, and the immortal Tor Johnson.

Black Sunday (1960) ◆◆◆ B&W
D: Mario Bava. Barbara Steele, John Richardson, Ivo Garrani. 83 minutes. (Sinister Cinema)

The pic that put graveyard beauty Barbara Steele—cast here as a reincarnated witch—on the horror-movie map also represents one of Gothic guru Bava's most atmospheric excursions. Sinister Cinema carries the *British* version of the film, with different thesps dubbing the voices and with the original Italo music track intact.

Blackenstein (1973) ◆◆
D: William A. Levey. John Hart, Ivory Stone, Liz Renay. 87 minutes. (Media)

A fairly awful race-reversal Frankenstein revamp, though the square-Afro'd Monster's encounter with beehive-wigged Liz (*Desperate Living*) Renay is *almost* worth the price of a rental.

Blacula (1972) ◆◆◇
D: William Crain. William Marshall, Denise Nicholas, Vonetta McGee. 92 minutes. (HBO)

Veteran Shakespearean thesp Marshall is excellent as a culture-shocked eighteenth-century African vampire loose in contempo L.A. Though the pic takes an eventual turn toward the predictable, it's a better-than-average blood-sucker romp. The sequel, *Scream, Blacula, Scream,* is also available (Orion).

Blood and Black Lace (1964) ◆◆◆
D: Mario Bava. Cameron Mitchell, Eva Bartok, Mary Arden. 90 minutes. (Media)

The slay's the thing in this inventively perverse Bava bloodbath, as a masked maniac murders models in Mitchell's employ.

Blood Beast Terror (1969) ◆◆
D: Vernon Sewell. Peter Cushing, Robert Flemyng, Wanda Ventham. 81 minutes. (Monterey)

Entomologist Cushing turns daughter Ventham into an outsize Deathshead Moth with vampiric tendencies. Must have seemed like a good idea at the time.

Blood Couple (1973) NR
D: Bill Gunn. Duane Jones, Marlene Clark, Bill Gunn. 83 minutes (Video Gems)

The video retitling of *Ganja and Hess,* a black vampire outing starring the late Duane Jones of *Night of the Living Dead* fame. Slow moving but earnest and not without its advocates.

Blood Cult (1985) ◆◇
D: Christopher Lewis. Chuck Ellis, Julie Andelman, Jim Vance. 92 minutes. (United)

Of interest chiefly for being the first direct-to-video fright feature, this flimsy occult "thriller" is otherwise a pretty tedious affair.

Blood Diner (1987) ◆◆
D: Jackie Kong. Rick Burks, Carl Crew, Roger Dauer, LaNette La France, Lisa Guggenheim, Drew Godderis. 90 minutes. (Lightning)

At heart (to say nothing of entrails), Jackie (no relation to King) Kong's *Blood Diner* is a sometimes sloppy, overtly slapstick reprise of blood-and-guts pioneer H. G. Lewis's trend-setting *Blood Feast* (see below). Our story entails the efforts of two bumbling brothers who, guided by the living brain of their mad Uncle Anwar, reconstruct the "Lumerian goddess" Sheetar using the body parts of "immoral girls" while dishing out the leftovers to their patrons at a local "health-food" eatery. The assorted skin dinners, vomit tableaux, and nude aerobics massacres serve as mere appetizers to a climactic all-out rock 'n' roll gore orgy staged at the notorious Club Dread. It's here that Kong and crew undoubtedly blew most of the pic's paltry budget— and possibly lunch as well.

Blood Feast (1963) ◆◆
D: Herschell Gordon Lewis. Thomas Wood, Connie Mason, Mal Arnold. 70 minutes. (Rhino)

The movie that invented the gore genre, from the fertile mind of H. G. Lewis, who seems to have become the major model for today's breed of low-budget blood 'n' guts auteurs. Lewis's cynical mutilation tableaux are relieved by this Florida-lensed lunch-loser's consummate bad acting, particularly from ex-Playmate Mason.

Blood Frenzy (1987) ◆
D: Hal Freeman. Wendy MacDonald, Lisa Loring, Tony Montero, John Clark, Hank Garrett, Lisa Savage. 90 minutes. (Hollywood Family Entertainment)

From the boldly misnomered Hollywood Family Entertainment comes *Blood Frenzy*. The pic's minimalist plot involves a svelte distaff shrink who drives a half-dozen mental patients—all the usual stereotypes, from your free-loving blond bimbo to your bonkers 'Nam vet, are represented—deep into the California desert to stage an intensive group-encounter session and simultaneously enable the pic's producers to save on sets. Good idea, huh? Well, maybe not. As it turns out, all that therapy goes right down the proverbial porcelain facility when an unidentified psycho starts slicing the loonies' throats while a jack-in-the-box rendition of "Pop Goes the Weasel" plinks on the soundtrack. It was all too heady for the Phantom's previously uncomplaining VCR, which sliced our screener tape in half about two-thirds of the way through.

Blood Hook (1987) ◆◆◇
D: James Mallon. Mark Jacobs, Lisa Todd, Patrick Danz, Sara Hauser, Christopher Whiting, Bill Lowrie. 93 minutes. (Prism)

"This ain't no Japanese monster movie," insists a character in *Blood Hook*, and we have to agree with him there. Fact is, *Blood Hook* is less a horror flick than a deadpan comedy of (mostly bad) manners. The pic follows a band of five young folks and a typically crass family of Ugly American vacationers ("Katharine Hepburn never put up with what *I* have to," ditzy Mom moans re: slob Dad) into the turbulent waters of Muskie, Wisconsin. (*Blood Hook* was lensed in Hayward, Wisconsin.) There an unknown maniac has been baiting the title implement for human prey. There are a number of inspired encounters between the innocent interlopers and several local eccentrics, including a paranoid 'Nam vet who's convinced the murders are part of a larger conspiracy. Todd is especially deft as the psychobabbling main squeeze of Jacobs, the unlikely hero who finally succeeds—via an inventive musical hook—in unmasking the killer. Fairly light on gore save for one victim-gutting scene, *Blood Hook* is fun most of the way, running out of creative gas only during its protracted last-reel punch line.

Blood Legacy (1971) ◆◇
D: Carl Monson. John Carradine, Faith Domergue, John Russell. 77 minutes. (Video Gems)

A veteran B cast—which also includes Jeff Morrow, Merry Anders, and Dick Davalos—is the chief attraction in this otherwise dull night-in-a-haunted-house exercise. Also out is *Legacy of Blood* (United American).

Blood Link (1983) ◆◆◇
D: Alberto De Martino. Michael Moriarty, Penelope Milford, Cameron Mitchell. 98 minutes. (Embassy)

A nightmare-plagued doc (Moriarty) discovers he has an evil twin brother in this interesting, overlooked, though uneven sleeper highlighted by Mike's ever-unpredictable work and by Mitchell in one of his more memorable later roles. Should have been even better, but certainly rates as a low-risk rental.

Blood of the Vampire (1958) ◆◆
D: Henry Cass. Donald Wolfit, Barbara Shelley, Vincent Ball. 87 minutes. (MPI)

A mostly mediocre sub-Hammer Brit mad-scientist outing, included here for '50s fright fanatics—who should beware the tape's inferior visual quality.

The Blood on Satan's Claw (1970) ◆◆◆
D: Piers Haggard. Patrick Wymark, Linda Hayden, Barry Andrews. 93 minutes. (Cannon)

Devil-worshipping kids in seventeenth-century England cause havoc for locals in a stylish Brit horror flick with a strong period flavor.

Blood Rage (1987/1984) ◇
D: John W. Grissmer. Louise Lasser, Mark Soper, Marianne Kanter, Julie

Gordon, Jane Bentzen, William Fuller. 83 minutes. (Prism)

Mary Hartman goes gore (!) in this pathetic slice-and-dicer, released regionally (and to cable TV) as *Nightmare at Shadow Woods*. It features a hapless Louise Lasser as the mother of a psycho slashing his merry way through friends, neighbors and strangers alike at a Jacksonville, Florida, apartment complex. (Hence another of this loser's high-concept working titles, *Complex*.) Sans sense, suspense, humor (though the pic's creators occasionally grope for same), or even the simplest motivation (beyond making a quick cassette buck), *Blood Rage* is a gory bore from reel one to its overdue end-credit crawl.

The Blood-Spattered Bride (1974) ◆◆◇
D: Vincente Aranda. Maribel Martin, Alexandra Bastedo, Simon Andreu. 84 minutes. (MPI)

One of several pics based on Sheridan Le Fanu's *Carmilla*, this Spain-lensed modern version is boosted by director Aranda's visual flair.

Blood Voyage (1977) ◆◆◇
D: Frank Mitchell. Jonathan Lippe, Laurie Rose, Mara Modair. 80 minutes. (Monterey)

A cheesy but surprisingly suspenseful seagoing psycho story wherein charter crewman Lippe tries to find out who's slaughtering his passengers one by one.

Bloodbath at the House of Death (1985) ◆◆◇
D: Ray Cameron. Vincent Price, Kenny Everett, Pamela Stephenson, Gareth Hunt, Don Warrington, John Fortune. 92 minutes. (Media)

Our story finds a team of inept scientists investigating the former site of a gory massacre. Trying to scare them away is an equally incompetent coven of dotty devil-worshippers headed by a testy Vincent Price (who delivers a fine high-camp performance). Unfortunately, while this British horror spoof—costarring comic Kenny Everett—features more flashes of wit than most of its Yank counterparts, flashes they remain. The hit-and-miss script too often sacrifices satire for cheap jokes that have become almost as clichéd as the scare-movie conventions they seek to mock. There are some high points, though—a killer teddy bear (!) and a bright sendup of *Alien*'s upset stomach scene. *Bloodbath* is worth a look for those who don't mind their laughs mixed with the occasional groan.

Bloodsuckers (1970) ◆◆
D: Robert Hartford-Davis. Patrick Macnee, Peter Cushing, Edward Woodward. 90 minutes. (Media)

A dull, shoddily assembled yarn involving Oxford dons and a Greek vampire cabal that's best for followers of the three leading thesps.

Bloodsucking Freaks (1978) ◆◇

D: Joel M. Reed. Seamus O'Brien, Louie DeJesus, Niles McMaster. 89 minutes. (Vestron)

Originally released as *The Incredible Torture Show* back in 1978, Reed's Gotham-lensed gore-and-guffaw fest stars O'Brien as Sardu, a sicko magician in a *Wizard of Gore* vein who seeks to shock all and sundry with his shoddy mutilation FX. Pretty gratuitous if you ask us, but it has its fervid admirers. Director Reed returned with *Night of the Zombies* (Prism).

Bloody Birthday (1980/1986) ◆◆

D: Ed Hunt. Susan Strasberg, Jose Ferrer, Lori Lethin, Billy Jacoby, Elizabeth Hoy, Joe Penny, Michael Dudikoff. 84 minutes. (Prism)

Despite its splatter-type title, *Bloody Birthday* is actually an entry in the ever-popular "killer kids" genre, involving three California ten-year-olds—two boys and a girl—who embark on a local slaughter spree. The script employs a dumb astrological explanation for the tykes' shared homicidal tendencies, but the sight of the seemingly innocent trio using bats, arrows, and Magnums (!) to terminate irritating teachers, neighbors, and family members does generate some perverse cheap chills. The attitude of the town's unflappable adults, meanwhile, is best summed up by a guest at a gala barbecue, who observes, "Sure is wonderful to see everyone enjoying themselves in spite of what's been going on!" Unfortunately, *Bloody Birthday* fails to sustain this level of lunacy, though the juve actors—along with such veteran thesps as Strasberg, Ferrer, Penny, and Michael (*American Ninja*) Dudikoff—do their best to keep things moving.

Bloody Pit of Horror (1966) ◆◆◇

D: Max Hunter (Massimo Pupillo). Mickey Hargitay, Walter Brandt, Louise Barrett, and The Cover Girls. 86 minutes. (Sinister Cinema)

Former Mr. Jayne Mansfield Mickey Hargitay stars as The Crimson Executioner, a musclebound torturer Iron-Maidened back in 1648 (in an opening that blatantly rips off Mario Bava's *Black Sunday*). He reawakens to impale and slaughter anew when a bunch of badly dubbed models and photographers invade his castle to snap cover photos for a lurid line of horror paperbacks. As an actor, Mickey doesn't really get to stretch here, though at least one of his victims winds up on the rack. Best exchange takes place between a catty brunette model and her bleached-blonde counterpart, to wit:

Blonde: I'm not just a dumb blonde, y'know.
Brunette: Who says you're a blonde?

For a work based on "the writings of Marquis de Sade," *Bloody Pit* is

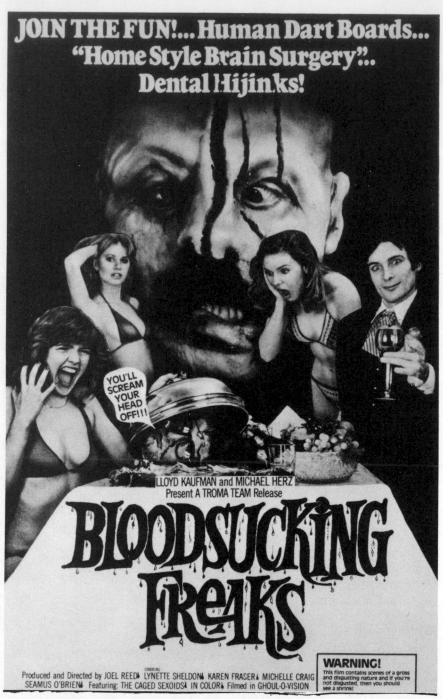

Joel Reed's Ghoul-O-Vision gore gala *Bloodsucking Freaks* has become a homevid horror staple.
Photo courtesy of Troma, Inc.

woefully lacking in discipline, but it shapes up as suitable fare for horrible-horror buffs.

Bloody Wednesday (1987) ◆◆◆
D: Mark G. Gilhuis. Raymond Elmendorf, Pamela Baker, Navarre Perry, Teresa Mae Allen, Jeff O'Haco, John Landrtroop. 89 minutes. (Prism)

Bloody Wednesday is one truly *strange* movie. The twisted script—by former more-or-less mainstream '50s scenarist Philip (*Johnny Guitar, Studs Lonigan*) Yordan (who now specializes in crafting bizarre B titles)—tells of chronic screw-up Harry (Elmendorf), who, after losing his job, holes up in an empty L.A. hotel owned by a client of his concerned older brother (Perry). Here, Harry unravels at an accelerated pace, enjoying the warped, pulpy fantasy life of a man who's seen too many B movies. (Hey, we can definitely relate to *that!*) He converses at length with his pet teddy bear (voice supplied by celebrity midget Billy Curtis, of *Terror of Tiny Town* fame), befriends a bonkers imaginary bellhop, and crosses paths with a violent street hood (ace stunt man O'Haco), who turns out to be all too real. *Bloody Wednesday* may not be up there with such paranoia epics as Polanski's *The Tenant* or Kubrick's *The Shining*, but it displays more sheer weirdness than most exploitation flicks of recent vintage. Only the pic's cheap, if inevitable, slaughter climax detracts from its sustained dementia.

The Body Snatcher (1945) ◆◆◆ B&W
D: Robert Wise. Boris Karloff, Bela Lugosi, Henry Daniell. 77 minutes. (RKO)

The Val Lewton version of the notorious Burke-and-Hare corpse-stealing team, based on a Robert Louis Stevenson story, finds desperate doc Daniell trafficking with vile grave-robber Boris. Bela is also aboard to lend his sinister support in this worthy Robert Wise–directed chiller.

The Boogeyman (1980) ◆◆◇
D: Ulli Lommel. John Carradine, Suzanna Love, Ron James. 86 minutes. (Magnum)

Teutonic auteur Lommel takes an arty approach to telling this tale of a lethal broken mirror that violently avenges the murders it has witnessed. Watch out for flying glass, and avoid the insipid sequel *Boogeyman II* (VCII).

Born of Fire (1987) ◆◆
D: Jamil Dehlavi. Peter Firth, Suzan Crowley, Stefan Kalipha, Oh-Tee, Nabil Shaban. 84 minutes. (Vidmark)

Brit flautist Firth travels to Turkey in search of the mysterious Master Musician (played by chrome-domed Oh-Tee) who'd tutored his father and precipitated the latter's premature death. A local holy man informs our hero that the very earth will be consumed by flame unless he can wage a successful battle of wills ("Your flute will guide you") with MM. *Born of Fire* unfolds at the decelerated pace and with the gauzy surrealism of a filmic fever dream. Skulls, serpents, a deformed dwarf, a giant baboon head, slo-mo birth and death scenes, and other hallucinatory tableaux like maybe you don't really want to witness abound in this *El Topo*esque exercise. The whole affair's apparently rooted in Muslim myths about man's struggle to achieve dominance over the elements. A working knowledge of the Koran might come in handy here.

Bowery at Midnight (1942) ◆◆◇ B&W
D: Wallace Fox. Bela Lugosi, Dave O'Brien, Tom Neal. 63 minutes. (Sinister Cinema)

Bela is a madman who keeps zombies in the basement of his Bowery mission. Pretty shoddy filmmaking, but the great, evocative title, the downbeat atmosphere, and the fine cult cast that includes—besides the immortal Bela—Dave (*Reefer Madness*) O'Brien and Tom (*Detour*) Neal make *Bowery* worth watching.

Brain Damage (1988) ◆◆◆◇
D: Frank Henenlotter. Rick Herbst, Gordon MacDonald, Jennifer Lowry, Theo Barnes, Lucille Saint-Peter. 89 minutes. (Paramount)

Like *Remote Control* and *Return to Salem's Lot* (see index), *Brain Damage* is another pointed example of a barely released genre gem

receiving new life via video. Here, indie auteur Henenlotter—the brains behind 1982's perverse cult fave *Basket Case*—scores again with this literally "mindblowing" tale about a boy and his parasite. The latter, a deceptively cute minimonster named Aylmer, supplies human host Herbst with hallucinogenic "juice" in exchange for live human brains—a deal that results in a rash of emptyheaded bodies turning up in downtown Gotham (more than usual, we mean). Less an antidrug film (as it's been characterized by some) than a meditation on addictions of *all* kinds and the subsequent surrender of personal autonomy they invariably entail, *Brain Damage* succeeds equally on the blackhumor, the visceral-shock, and even the—dare we say it?—*cerebral* level. A somewhat unsatisfying ending prompted us to subtract half a phan, but this bizarre, visually hypnotic, oft-brilliant, and thoroughly sick flick remains an absolute must for offbeathorror buffs.

The Bride (1985) ◆◆◆
D: Franc Roddam. Sting, Jennifer Beals, Clancy Brown, David Rappaport, Geraldine Page, Quentin Crisp. 118 minutes. (RCA/Columbia)

The Bride answers the fifty-yearold fright-film question, What would have happened if, in the original *Bride of Frankenstein*, the rejected Monster *hadn't* given in to his rage and blown up the lab but instead had gone off to "find himself" and granted his intended mate time to do likewise? In Roddam's revisionist version of the Frankenstein legend, the Monster (inventively interpreted by Brown) hits the road, hooks up with an enterprising dwarf named Rinaldo (Rappaport), and achieves a measure of show-biz success as part of a comedy high-wire act in a Budapest circus. A parallel story line charts the Bride's (*Flashdance*'s Beals, shown briefly sans leotards here) Pygmalionesque progress under the tutelage of her creator Baron Frankenstein (played by a largely zingless Sting), who wants to mold her into the perfect woman (i.e., "the equal of any man"). The stage is thus set for any number of other, equally relevant queries. Can the Monster redeem himself in the eyes of his beloved? Can the Bride—an independent, sophisticated creature (at least when she's not tearing her food apart or snarling at the castle cat)—escape the baron's increasingly possessive clutches? Though the flick goes on for about a reel too long, *The Bride* addresses these issues in a genuinely entertaining and imaginative way. Watch it with someone you love.

Bride of Frankenstein (1935) ◆◆◆◆ B&W

D: James Whale. Boris Karloff, Elsa Lanchester, Ernest Thesiger, Colin Clive. 75 minutes. (MCA)

Still ranks as one of horrordom's towering achievements, from Whale's atmospheric direction to Thesiger's perverse Dr. Pretorius turn to Elsa's electric hairdo and Boris's alternately poignant and pushy monster. Not to be missed.

Bride of the Gorilla (1951) ◆◆ B&W

D: Curt Siodmak. Raymond Burr, Barbara Payton, Lon Chaney, Jr. 76 minutes. (Sinister Cinema)

Lumbering Raymond Burr fears he's turning into a gorilla (big diff!), turning off lovely Payton; local cop Chaney investigates in the best back-lot jungle horror flick of 1951.

The Brood (1979) ◆◆◆

D: David Cronenberg. Oliver Reed, Samantha Eggar, Art Hindle. 92 minutes. (Embassy)

An often brilliant metashocker from David Cronenberg that sees Eggar's hostilities come to vengeful life as a killer crew of mallet-wielding munchkins! (Woody Allen employed a similar conceit for a very funny throwaway gag in *Stardust Memories*.) Cronenberg's bleak vision may be light on science, but it shapes up as a genuinely creepy, downright disturbing home-vid experience and represents DC at his megaphobic best.

Brotherhood of Satan (1971) ◆◆◆

D: Bernard McEveety. Strother Martin, L. Q. Jones, Ahna Capri. 92 minutes. (RCA/Columbia)

An earnest, eerie, imaginative indie—produced by character thesps Alvy (*Green Acres*) Moore and L. Q. Jones—about a satanic coven that covets the children of a small southern town. Alvy also turns up in *The Witchmaker* (Media).

Brutal Sorcery (1984) ◆◆◆
Lai Hon Chi, Lily Chan, Kwan Hoi Shan. 90 minutes. (Ocean)

A singularly surreal Hong Kong outing, liberally laced with both whimsy and horror, complete with children reincarnated (sort of) as chickens. The adventurous fright viewer will definitely want to take a gander.

Brute Man (1946) ◆◆◇ B&W
D: Jean Yarbrough. Rondo Hatton, Tom Neal, Jane Adams. 60 minutes. (Sony)

Real-life acromegaly sufferer Hatton (sensitively described as the man who needed no makeup) stars as the title killer in the only one of his horror vehicles currently available on video.

A Bucket of Blood (1959) ◆◆◆ B&W
D: Roger Corman. Dick Miller, Barboura Morris, Anthony Carbone. 66 minutes. (Sinister Cinema/J&J)

Miller shines as beatnik manqué Walter Paisley, who stumbles upon a grisly way to become an instant artistic success. Corman's cult quickie, scripted by Charles (*Little Shop of Horrors*) Griffith, plays like a '50s "sick joke" *House of Wax* variation. Highly recommended.

Buried Alive (1981) ◆◇
D: Joe D'Amato. Kieran Canter, Cinzia Monreale, Franca Stoppa. 90 minutes. (Thriller)

Of all the el disgusto Italo gore orgies flooding the home-vid market, this terminally tasteless tale of a sentimental, cannibalistic necrophiliac may be *the* sickest. Rent at your own risk!

The Cabinet of Dr. Caligari (1919) ◆◆◆ B&W
D: Robert Wiene. Conrad Veidt, Werner Krauss. 52 minutes. (Video Yesteryear)

The surreal journey of the mad Dr. Caligari and his somnambulist slave Cesare through a distorted dreamscape of expressionist sets fully retains its dark, disorienting power, thanks to Robert Wiene's masterful direction.

Caltiki, the Immortal Monster (1959) NR B&W
D: Riccardo Freda. John Merivale, Didi Sullivan, Gerard Herter. 76 minutes. (J&J)

This Mexican-set *Blob* variation has garnered its share of frightfilm fans. Mario Bava served as cinematographer.

Cameron's Closet (1988) ◆◆◇
D: Armand Mastroianni. Scott Curtis, Cotter Smith, Mel Harris, Tab Hunter, Chuck McCann. 85 minutes. (Sony)

Young Curtis is a telekinetic kid

who's unwittingly conjured an ancient demon. Worse, that decidedly unfriendly visitor—described as *"the* most evil" in the entire hierarchy of Hell's ne'er-do-wells—has taken up unwelcome residence in the titular locale, a transmigration that bodes ill for several of the unwary adults complicating Cameron's life, beginning with his widowed mom's abusive, musclebound boyfriend. Sympathetic distaff shrink Harris and kindly cop Smith soon arrive on the scene in a bid to help Cameron quash the sinister spirit, a struggle that consumes most of the pic's remaining running time. While *Cameron's Closet* opens strong, with a sequence that sees Cameron's dad (essayed, in a bit of inspired casting, by former heartthrob Tab Hunter) literally lose his head, the pic's overly complicated narrative structure fails to mask its basically flimsy, derivative story line. Earnest perfs by the leads, an odd cameo by erstwhile slapstick comic Chuck McCann as an eminent scientist (!), and a couple of genuine shocks that registered high on the Phantom's coronary palp-o-meter make *Cameron's Closet* a watchable if less than essential cassette.

Cannibal Holocaust (1985) 0 ◆
D: *Ruggero Deodato. R. Bolla, Francesca Ciardi, Perry Pirkanen, Pio Di Savola, Salvatore Basile. 95 minutes. (Video City)*
Unless close-ups of slaughtered animals, rotting corpses, amputa-tions, castrations, and sundry other, more arcane forms of self- and other-mutilation are your movie meat, you'd be advised to steer clear of this Italo turkey, along with such cannibalistic companions as *Emerald Jungle* (Cinema Group), *Make Them Die Slowly* (IVE), *Jungle Holocaust,* and *Slaves of the Cannibal God* (both Video City).

Captain Kronos: Vampire Hunter (1974) ◆◆◆
D: *Brian Clemens. Horst Janson, John Carson, Caroline Munro, Shane Briant, John Cater, Lois Dane. 91 minutes. (Paramount)*

In a bid to vary its vampire formula from the by-then predictable Chris Lee *Dracula* series, Hammer came up with *Captain Kronos: Vampire Hunter,* released in England simply as *Kronos.* Instead of focusing on your standard older, somber Van Helsing character (expertly but overfamiliarly embodied by Peter Cushing), Hammer cast newcomer Janson as a dashing young swordsman with long blond locks and a wit as sharp as his ever-ready rapier. Accompanying the handsome bloodsucker-basher is John Carson as Captain K's hunchbacked assistant, who tends to Kronos's arsenal of antivampire weaponry. Femme fright fave Munro is also on pulchritudinous view. Director Clemens blends horror, swashbuckler, comedy, and—to add further spice—

Soul Survivor: Candace Hilligoss strikes soulful pose in Herk Harvey's 1962 cult classic, *Carnival of Souls.*
Photo courtesy of Candace Hilligoss.

spaghetti western genres in what ranks as one of the brightest entries from Hammer's later period.

Carnival of Souls (1962) ♦♦♦♦ B&W
D: Herk Harvey. Candace Hilligoss, Sidney Berger, Frances Feist, Stan Levitt, Art Ellison, Herk Harvey. 81 minutes. (Sinister Cinema)

This legendary indie classic may represent the ultimate triumph of talent and care over budget. The film works both as a straight-ahead horror outing in an understated but genuinely eerie Val Lewton vein *and* as a dramatization of a mental breakdown, as alienated Mary Henry (Hilligoss), after surviving a car crash, finds herself drifting farther and farther from reality. Director Harvey (who doubles as one of the cadaverous phantoms pursuing our ever-endangered heroine) contrasts the determinedly mundane world of Mary's daily life (spent in such unotherworldly locales as Lawrence, Kansas, and Salt Lake City) with the haunting nocturnal images of a pier-front pavilion, where the title specters perform a nightly danse macabre. While *Carnival of Souls'* cult rep has grown steadily via its regional TV screenings over the decades, few viewers have seen it in its entirety and sans disruptive commercials. Several public-domain specialists carry *Carnival*, but as of this writing, only Sinister Cinema has the complete original print. *Carnival of Souls* is must viewing, not only for horror addicts but for film fans of every stripe.

WHAT NEVER HAPPENED TO . . .
Candace Hilligoss

Candace Hilligoss captured the imagination of many a fright-film fan via her haunting portrayal of anomic organist Mary Henry in the 1962 cult classic *Carnival of Souls*. As a car-accident survivor pursued by the silent, chalk-white title souls (forerunners of the Living Dead), Candace—with her detached demeanor, high cheekbones, and wide, wounded eyes—was an arresting study in spooky yet elegant alienation. Most of *Carnival*'s cast and crew hailed from the Lawrence area (before it was nuked into oblivion in *The Day After*), where director Herk Harvey and screenwriter John Clifford operated a successful industrial-film studio. Candace herself was recruited by actor/acting coach Sidney Berger (who plays Mary's leering greaseball neighbor, John Linden, in the film) in New York City, where she'd been studying under Method proponent Lee Strasberg. Berger persuaded her to take the lead role in the low-budget ($30,000) chiller, and the rest is horror-movie history.

Unfortunately, so was Candace. Her triumphant *Carnival* performance went largely unnoticed at the time, as the pic fell into the hands of distributors sufficiently inept to ensure its theatrical obscurity. She appeared in just one more movie—the redoubtable Del (*Horror of Party Beach*) Tenney's *Curse of the Living Corpse* (1964) (Prism), a Connecticut-lensed, no-budget quickie that also marked Roy Scheider's inauspicious screen debut. Candace eventually retired from the Thespian ranks and married a doctor. At last report she was alive and well and living in Beverly Hills, where she recently penned an epic novel titled *Dakota Ashes*.

Carrie (1976) ◆◆◇
D: *Brian De Palma. Sissy Spacek, William Katt, Piper Laurie, Amy Irving, John Travolta. 98 minutes. (MGM/UA)*

De Palma's adaptation of Stephen King's story about a telekinetic teen is an overrated affair that's still worth catching for Spacek's shyly spooky perf and the flick's frenzied finale.

The Carrier (1988) ♦♦◇

D: Nathan White. Gregory Fortescue, Stevie Lee, Steven Dixon, N. Paul Stevenson. 95 minutes. (Magnum)

The Carrier, a sort of *Blue Velvet Meets Masque of the Red Death*, depicts a mysterious flesh-melting disease sweeping through the isolated hamlet of Sleepy Rock, circa 1962. The plague is being unwittingly spread by the title character (Fortescue), a local pariah who appears to have contracted it from "the black thing"—a mysterious Bigfoot-like creature who may or may not be an hallucination. The predominantly Christian populace promptly panics, eventually splitting into rival factions and waging an all-out gore war (!). *The Carrier's* originality lies less in its bizarre plot, though, than in its pervasive aura of paranoia, its abundant religious imagery, and its almost Dark Ages sense of dread. White's Michigan-lensed indie is sometimes crude and occasionally downright ludicrous—though the sight of crazed fundamentalists, wrapped in protective plastic trash bags (!), cheerfully chopping each another to bits *is* a rather novel and compelling one—but it is rarely less than genuinely disturbing. Adventurous viewers could do worse than watch this one-of-a-kind weirdo.

Castle of Blood (1964) ♦♦♦ B&W

D: Antonio Margheriti. Barbara Steele, George Riviere, Montgomery Glenn. 85 minutes. (Sinister Cinema)

A night-in-a-haunted-house flick lensed with earnestly creepy flair and featuring the sepulchrally seductive Steele in the lead. Based on Poe's "Berenice," it's a good bet for Italo Gothic horror fans.

Castle of the Living Dead (1964) ♦♦◇ B&W

D: Luciano Ricci. Christopher Lee, Gala Germani, Donald Sutherland. 90 minutes. (Sinister Cinema)

Chris Lee torments a troupe of entertainers trapped in his titular abode in a decent Italo fearfest that also marked another of Sutherland's early celluloid appearances.

Cat's Eye (1985) ♦♦◇

D: Lewis Teague. Drew Barrymore, James Woods, Alan King, Kenneth McMillan, Robert Hays, Candy Clark. 93 minutes. (Key)

While he lifts freely from everything from EC Comics to *Gremlins*, the ubiquitous Stephen King strings together a generally entertaining trilogy framed by the peripatetic journey of a versatile feline thesp. The pacing is swift, the stories generate sufficient suspense, and the tone remains refreshingly throwaway throughout. Even the multiple in-jokes (e.g., cameos by King's killer car Christine and murderous mutt Cujo) are more self-mocking than self-aggrandizing. *Cat's Eye's* no *Creepshow* (see index), but it stacks up as an adequate time-filler.

Cauldron of Blood (1967) ◆◆
D: Santos Alcocer. Boris Karloff, Viveca Lindfors, Jean-Pierre Aumont. 95 minutes. (Republic)

Boris, in one of his last roles, plays a blind sculptor with a psychopathic wife in this Spanish import (also available from Vidcrest under the title *Blind Man's Bluff*). Mr. K concluded his creature-feature career with a quartet of Mexican turkeys—*Alien Terror*, *Cult of the Dead*, *Dance of Death*, and *Torture Zone*—available from MPI. Sinister Cinema carries the same foursome—with the original Mexican credits intact—under the alternate titles *Sinister Invasion*, *The Snake People*, *House of Evil*, and *The Fear Chamber*, respectively.

Chamber of Horrors (1940) NR B&W
D: Norman Lee. Leslie Banks, Lilli Palmer, Gina Malo. 80 minutes. (Sinister Cinema)

Not the 1966 gimmick flick with its infamous Fear Flasher and Horror Horn, but a 1940 Brit scare pic based on an Edgar Wallace story and offering Leslie (*Most Dangerous Game*) Banks as a rampaging psycho.

The Changeling (1979) ◆◆◇
D: Peter Medak. George C. Scott, Trish Van Devere, Melvyn Douglas. 113 minutes. (Vestron)

A juvenile ghost haunts George C. Scott in a well-crafted if overlong mainstream poltergeist outing.

The Child (1977) ◆◆
D: Robert Voskanian. Laurel Barnett, Rosalie Cole. 90 minutes. (Best)

The tormented title tyke befriends local graveyard zombies who eliminate her abusers in a regional horror that was later rereleased under the more rock 'n' roll title *Kill and Go Hide*.

Child's Play (1988) ◆◆◇
D: Tom Holland. Catherine Hicks, Chris Sarandon, Alex Vincent, Brad Dourif, Dinah Manoff, Tommy Swerdlow. 87 minutes. (MGM/UA)

In the terror-toy tradition of *Trilogy of Terror* and Stuart Gordon's *Dolls* (see index)—not to mention Chester N. Turner's immortal *Black Devil Doll From Hell*—comes Tom (*Fright Night*) Holland's killer-doll chiller *Child's Play*. Sort of a *Garbage Pail Kids Go Psycho*, the pic's slender premise sees dying madman Brad (*Wise Blood*) Dourif transfer his evil soul into a singularly homely but seemingly benign "Good Guy" doll. The toy in question winds up in the possession of Chicago tyke Vincent, who unwittingly aids the demonic doll in a vengeful plot to waste Windy City cop Sarandon. The result is a watchable, occasionally fun, but thoroughly contrived outing. While director Holland knows how to craft a decent scare scene—as when the doll assaults hero Sarandon during a high-speed car chase—and even names a character in honor of legendary Ed Wood, Jr., regular Criswell (!), *Child's Play* is neither as funny nor as terrifying as SCTV's memorable send-up "Slinky: Toy from Hell!"

Children Shouldn't Play with Dead Things (1972) ◆◇
D: Bob Clark. Alan Ormsby, Anya Ormsby, Jane Daly. 86 minutes. (MPI)

Bob (*Deathdream*) Clark's low-budget bid to get in on the Living Dead action stacks up as a fairly amateurish exercise that's nonetheless collected its share of fans.

Chillers (1988) ◆◆◇
D: Daniel Boyd. Jesse Emery, Marjorie Fitzsimmons, Laurie Pennington, Jim Wolfe, David Wohl. 90 minutes. (Raedon)

One of the better direct-to-home-vid regional horror efforts around, Boyd's West Virginia—lensed fright flick finds five stranded travelers swapping personal nightmare narratives to help pass the time. A pretty creaky premise, we'll admit, but *Chillers* manages to exhibit more imagination than many a fear film costing several times its modest budget. The best episode involves a youth who discovers he can bring back the dead just by wishing it, only to learn that the dead in question are less than grateful for his intervention. Hampered by uneven acting and at-times uncertain execution, *Chillers* may not appeal to fans of slicker Hollywood horror fare, but it rates as a low vid-rental risk for viewers who don't mind more idiosyncratic approaches. Also from

Raedon: *Hollywood's New Blood*, *L.A. Heat*, *Midnight News*, *Shotgun*, and *Slashdance*.

Christine (1983) ◆◆◇
D: John Carpenter. Keith Gordon, John Stockwell, Alexandra Paul, Harry Dean Stanton. 116 minutes. (RCA/Columbia)

Stephen King's violent if ultimately predictable vehicle remains a notch above most of the killer-car competition. King's killer-kid epics, *Children of the Corn* (Embassy) and *Firestarter* (MCA), his killer-canine romp *Cujo* (Warner), and his killer-machine misfire *Maximum Overdrive* (Lorimar) are also available.

Christmas Evil (1980/1987) ◆◆
D: Lewis Jackson. Brandon Maggart, Jeffrey DeMunn, Dianne Hull, Scott McKay, Joe Jamrog, Peter Friedman. 95 minutes. (Saturn)

In typical slasher style, 1980's *You Better Watch Out*—rereleased as *Christmas Evil* (not to be confused with 1975's *Christmas Evil*, itself retitled *Black Christmas*) and also available on tape as *Terror in Toyland* (Academy)—begins with a flashback, wherein impressionable young Harry sees Mommy and Santa having (rather mild) sex. We pick up our story thirty-three years later: Harry's (Maggart) now an unhinged, Xmas-obsessed Jolly Dream toy-factory worker who keeps secret tabs on the neighborhood kids and logs his findings in a ledger labeled "Bad Boys and

Girls." (He's especially miffed at a kid whose Christmas wish is a "lifetime subscription to *Penthouse*"!) After several slow, desultory reels, Harry dons his Santa suit and embarks on his self-appointed rounds, delivering stolen toys to needy kids and gory death to unsympathetic adults. Actually, there are only two murder scenes all told (and a meager body count of four), along a few jokes that work (including a running Geraldo Rivera riff), lots of filler that doesn't, and an *ET*-esque ending that hints at a sequel that will never arrive. *Christmas Evil* ranks a full notch above *Silent Night, Deadly Night I* and *II*, but it fails to qualify as essential seasonal viewing.

Circus of Horrors (1960) ◆◆◆
D: Sidney Hayers. Anton Diffring, Erika Remberg, Yvonne Monlaur, Donald Pleasence. 89 minutes. (HBO)

A superior, genuinely sadistic, and often haunting Hammer horror, with Anton Diffring as a homicidal plastic surgeon disguised as a circus owner. Pleasence impresses as the circus's soon-to-be-late original proprietor, as does the contrapuntal theme song "Look For a Star." John Moxey's *Circus of Fear* (Saturn), starring the redoubtable Christopher Lee, is likewise worth a look.

The Company of Wolves (1985) ◆◆
D: Neil Jordan. Angela Lansbury, David Warner, Graham Crowden,
Brian Glover, Sarah Patterson, Stephen Rea. 95 minutes. (Vestron)

A series of visually striking but otherwise vapid variations on the venerable Little-Red-Riding-Hood-Meets-the-Wolf Man myth, *The Company of Wolves* plays like a classy Hammer period horror piece gone pretentious. While Lansbury is effective as the archetypal eccentric Granny and Patterson is appropriately fetching as Little Red (herein redubbed Rosaleen), this Freudian fright mosaic left yours truly longing for Maria Ouspenskaya and Lon Chaney, Jr. Guess class is just wasted on some Phantoms.

The Corpse Vanishes (1942) ◆◆◆ B&W
D: Wallace Fox. Bela Lugosi, Luana Walters, Tris Coffin. 64 minutes. (Sinister Cinema)

One of Bela's better Monogram romps, wherein he kills and body-lifts brides-to-be and receives able thespic support from dwarf Angelo Rossitto. Perverse, fast-paced fun.

Corridors of Blood (1958) ◆◆◇ B&W
D: Robert Day. Boris Karloff, Betta St. John, Christopher Lee. 86 minutes. (MPI)

Boris is a compassionate surgeon seeking to perfect a workable anesthetic who gets embroiled with grave robber Resurrection Joe (sleazily enacted by Lee) in this downbeat but generally entertaining horror that went unreleased theatrically till 1963.

Count Dracula (1971) ◆◆◇
D: Jess Franco. Christopher Lee, Herbert Lom, Klaus Kinski. 98 minutes. (Republic)

Jess does Dracula in a more explicit rendition benefiting from Lee's smooth turn as the toothy one and Kinski's crazed Renfield.

Count Yorga, Vampire (1970) ◆◆◆
D: Bob Kelljan. Robert Quarry, Roger Perry, Donna Anders. 91 minutes. (HBO)

Quarry makes for a convincing bloodsucker in a clever Southern California–set vampire variation that successfully blends horror and wit.

Crawlspace (1986) ◆
D: David Schmoeller. Klaus Kinski, Talia Balsam, Barbara Whinnery, Sally Brown, Carol Francis, Kenneth Robert Shippy. 77 minutes. (Lightning)

Lensed at Empire Pictures' then–newly acquired Italian studio complex, *Crawlspace* retains the claustrophobic one-set-wonder look that characterized most of this now-defunct third-rate company's stateside pics. Kinski stars as a kinky ex-Nazi mad scientist-landlord who rents his apartments to sweet young things whom he later terminates in various gory ways—at least until feisty Balsam shows up to expose his perverted habits. A typically derivative Empire outing, *Crawlspace* manages

to be simultaneously sick *and* tired, turning 77 minutes into a video eternity.

Craze (1973) NR
D: Freddie Francis. Jack Palance, Diana Dors, Trevor Howard. 90 minutes. (Paragon)

Jack Palance fans won't want to miss their idol's febrile portrayal of an addled antique dealer with a fondness for human sacrifice. Also out as *The Demon Master* (VCR).

Creepers (1985) ◆◇
D: Dario Argento. Donald Pleasence, Jennifer Connelly, Daria Nicolodi, Dalila Di Lazzaro, Patrick Bachau. 82 minutes. (Media)

What a revolting development! Seems some maniac's decapitating gals at a posh private school in the alpine climes of "Swiss Transylvania," and entomologist Dr. McGregor (Pleasence) can establish time of death only by studying the maggots infesting the victims' decomposed domes! Into this icky situation comes lovely young student Jennifer Corvino (Connelly), who happens to "enjoy" an instant and loving rapport with insects of all kinds (*feh!*). When her roommate turns up dead and headless, Jen recruits her buggy buddies to help Doc McGregor solve the sickening case. Alas, aside from a few striking nightmare images (as when Jen topples into a slimy vat of human remains), Italo shock director Dario (*Unsane, Deep Red*) Argento's *Creepers* (originally titled *Phenomena*) is a boring and poorly told (and, in fairness to DA, reedited) exercise in gratuitous nausea and Grand Guignol gore, padded with stretches of static filler. Even Pleasence is uncharacteristically subdued here; in fact, acting honors easily go to Pleasence's simian servant, Inga the Chimp, who displays a great deal of natural talent. Not to be confused with the 1948 B chiller *The Creeper* (King Bee) or the British *The Creepers* (Genesis).

The Creeping Flesh (1972) ◆◆◆
D: *Freddie Francis. Peter Cushing, Christopher Lee, Lorna Heilbron. 89 minutes. (RCA/Columbia)*

Cushing is an Edwardian scientist out to rid the world of evil. Major obstacles include sinister rival Lee, an escaped maniac, Peter's own demented slut of a daughter, *plus* a prehistoric demon waiting to come to vengeful life. Frightful, multitiered fun.

Creepshow (1982) ◆◆◆
D: *George Romero. Hal Holbrook, Adrienne Barbeau, Ed Harris, E. G. Marshall, Fritz Weaver. 120 minutes. (Warner)*

Romero and Stephen King neatly capture the spirit (and flesh) of the beloved, verboten EC Horror Comics of yore in this lively anthology of ghoulishly funny fear tales. Marshall gives the performance of his career as a rich, roach-obsessed, Howard Hughes–like recluse. Romero adapted three more stories from King's smoking word processor for the generally derivative sequel but declined to direct.

Creepshow 2 (1987) ◆◆◇
D: *Michael Gornick. Lois Chiles, George Kennedy, Dorothy Lamour, Tom Savini, Domenick John, Frank S. Salsedo. 92 minutes. (New World)*

Creepshow 2 employs essentially the same framework as the original. A comics-crazed kid receives the latest issue of Creepshow Comics, personally delivered by The Creep (horror-makeup maven Savini) and delves straightway into three sinister stories involving a killer statue, a killer oil slick, and your ever-reliable killer corpse. The tales proper are imaginatively bridged by brief animation sequences, and King puts in his customary cameo as a thick-witted trucker in the final (and funniest) episode, "The Hitchhiker." While it lacks *Creepshow's* freshness and star power (though Chiles, Lamour, and the redoubtable Kennedy *are* on hand), *Creepshow 2* is a suitably sick crowd-pleaser in its own right, worth the price of an overnight rental.

Crucible of Terror (1971) ◆◆
D: *Ted Hooker. Mike Raven, Mary Maude, James Bolan. 91 minutes. (Goodtimes, others)*

Sort of a straightfaced, supernatural Brit *Bucket of Blood* (see index) variation that's longer on talk than terror.

Cry of the Banshee (1970) ◆◆◇
D: Gordon Hessler. Vincent Price, Elisabeth Bergner, Essy Person, Hugh Griffith. 87 minutes. (HBO)

A good bet for Vincent Price buffs. Here the flamboyant thesp essays an obsessed sixteenth-century witch-hunter hounded by demonic forces.

The Curse (1987) ◆◆
D: David Keith. Wil Wheaton, Claude Akins, Malcolm Danare, Cooper Huckabee, John Schneider, Kathleen Jordan Gregory. 90 minutes. (Media)

The Curse (formerly The Farm), loosely based on H. P. Lovecraft's The Colour Out of Space, stars professional red-neck Akins as beleaguered, Bible-quoting Tennessee farmer Nathan Crane, whose domestic life is rife with strife, much of it of his own making. He self-righteously bullies his new wife (Gregory) and adopted son (Wheaton), who's in turn tormented by Claude's cloddish natural offspring (Danare). One night your basic glowing sphere from outer space lands in the backyard, perpetrating even ghastlier havoc in the Crane household, whose members begin mutating into your equally basic antisocial zombies. While The Curse has its moments, the pic is marred by slow pacing, circuitous storytelling, and its ultimate degeneration into yet another road-show Living Dead rehash whose clichéd grossout scenes eviscerate rather than heighten the initial suspense. Director Keith impresses far more as

an actor, particularly in his psycho role in White of the Eye, though not in the pathetic Indiana Jones clone The Further Adventures of Tennessee Buck (Media).

The Curse of Frankenstein (1957) ◆◆◆
D: Terence Fisher. Peter Cushing, Christopher Lee, Hazel Court. 83 minutes. (Warner)

Cushing is the infamous Baron and Lee his misbegotten creation in the film that launched Hammer's long-lived horror-movie line. Not as good as Horror of Dracula, but entertaining enough.

The Curse of the Cat People (1944) ◆◆◆ B&W
D: Robert Wise & Gunther V. Fritsch. Simone Simon, Kent Smith, Jane Randolph, Elizabeth Russell, Ann Carter. 70 minutes. (RKO)

It's seven years after Cat People's conclusion. Oliver and Ann (Smith and Randolph reprising their original roles) have married and moved to the 'burbs (Tarrytown), but all is not well in the Reed household. Daughter Amy frequently retreats into a fantasy world, where she encounters her spiritual mother, Irena (Simon). The title is a downright cheat— Curse isn't really a horror film at all—but this is still an extremely haunting, often moving little pic pitting Amy's melancholy hallucinations against the overinsistent clarity and relentless reality of her suburban surroundings. Another neat job by producer Lewton, scripter Bodeen, and the RKO crew.

Curse of the Demon (1958) ◆◆◆◆ B&W
D: Jacques Tourneur. Dana Andrews, Peggy Cummins, Niall MacGinnis. 96 minutes. (Goodtimes)

Val Lewton protégé Tourneur helms an absolutely brilliant horror tale (originally titled *Night of the Demon*), pitting rational psychologist Andrews against sinister mystic MacGinnis. Despite the demon's sporadic appearances—a decision director Tourneur had openly protested (though, truth to tell, said creature cameos work quite well)—*Curse of the Demon* ranks right up there with any of Val Lewton's '40s fright classics. The Goodtimes video, licensed from RCA/Columbia, is recorded at LP (middle) speed but at least admits it on the video box (the cover art is fairly hideous, though), and the transfer quality is pretty good—plus you get the complete 96-minute print, all for under $10.

The Curse of the Werewolf (1961) ◆◆◆
D: Terence Fisher. Oliver Reed, Clifford Evans, Yvonne Romain. 91 minutes. (MCA)

One of the best of the early Hammers, with Reed as a Spanish lycanthrope on the loose. Romain also impresses as his hapless mom.

Dance of the Damned (1988) ◆◆◆
D: Katt Shea Ruben. Starr Andreeff, Cyril O'Reilly. 83 minutes. (Virgin Vision)

Not a prequel to Ed Wood, Jr.'s, *Orgy of the Dead*, Katt Shea (*Stripped to Kill*) Ruben's *Dance of the Damned* is, rather, a strange and quite eloquent romantic encounter between a self-destructive vampire and a suicidal stripper (!). This extremely odd couple—Jodi (Andreeff) and The Vampire (O'Reilly)—spend a single intense evening together exploring nothing less than the nature of the human (and vampiric) conditions. Essentially a two-character screenplay featuring strong work by both leads, *Dance of the Damned* manages to convey a sense of fear and dread despite its minimal blood and body count. Withal, *Dance* is a stylish and consistently involving flick, a legit low-budget sleeper for those in the market for thoughtful fright fare.

Dark Night of the Scarecrow (1981) NR
D: Frank DeFelitta. Charles Durning, Robert F. Lyons, Lane Smith. 100 minutes. (Key)

A popular made-for-TV terror item describing the dire fates that await a mob of small-town vigilantes who kill their resident village idiot.

Dark of the Night (1985) ◆◆◇
D: Gaylene Preston. Heather Bolton, David Letch, Margaret Umbers, Suzanne Lee, Gary Stalker. 88 minutes. (Lightning)

In the killer-car tradition of *Christine* (see index), *The Car* (NA), and other violent vehicles comes the haunted Jaguar of this New Zealand–lensed chiller. *Dark of the Night*, directed and co-scripted by Preston, ultimately emerges as something of a feminist fright film as the story interweaves new owner Bolton's terror-fraught auto troubles with her more mundane trials as a big-city single gal. (At one point, our plucky heroine is even seen defending herself with a Venus de Milo statuette!) While *Dark of the Night* frequently succeeds in creating a suitably unsettling ambience, it runs out of gas just when it should be revving into high gear—during the climactic scare scenes; here, helmer Preston's shock absorbers work a tad *too* well, resulting in a decidedly low-octane ending.

Dark Power (1987) ◆◇
D: Phil Smoot. Lash LaRue, Anna Lane Tatum, Cynthia Bailey, Mary Dalton, Paul Holman, Cynthia Farbman. 95 minutes. (Midwest)

LaRue's comeback venture was one of those indie projects that the Phantom had assumed existed only in optimistic press releases planted in *Variety*. We never heard of it opening theatrically, not even in Fort Smith, Arkansas, so you can imagine our surprise when the pic quietly surfaced on the obscure, San Juan–based (!) Midwest Video label. We wish we could report that the former B-western star's belated screen return is an unqualified success—especially in light of the erstwhile King of the Bullwhip's checkered career (bouts with alcohol, marijuana busts, financial difficulties, myriad marriages and divorces, and periods of alleged mental instability, to cite but a few)—but we're afraid it's merely unqualified. In fact, this stillborn story of four off-campus co-eds who rent a North Carolina house also occupied by a quartet of evil Toltec Indian spirits—"Toltec sorcerers are bad dudes!" one of the cuties is forced to conclude—starts off poorly before tumbling into the video abyss of the downright unwatchable. At least LaRue, cast as an heroic elderly ranger, acquits himself as well as might be expected, and the image of Lash taking his trademark bullwhip to the fright-masked Toltec demons is certainly one the Phantom won't soon forget. But *Dark Power* is for hardcore curiosity seekers only.

Daughter of Dr. Jekyll (1957) ◆◆◇ B&W
D: Edgar G. Ulmer. Gloria Talbott, John Agar, Arthur Shields. 67 minutes. (Key)

A typically tame but generally compelling '50s fright feature, highlighted by short-lived but effective scream-screen queen Talbott's title perf and the always-galvanizing Agar. Director Ulmer provides the atmospheric touches.

Daughter of Horror (1955) ◆◆◇
D: John Parker. Adrienne Barrett,

Bruno VeSota, Angelo Rossitto. 60 minutes. (Sinister Cinema)

Easily the best silent (or non-dialogue, anyway) movie of 1955, Exploitation Productions' florid Freudvoidian descent into the mad mind of a distaff maniac must be seen to be believed. Lensed in murky black and white by William C. Thompson—the selfsame cinematographer who had the dubious privilege of working for Dwain Esper *and* Ed Wood, Jr., in one lifetime—*Daughter of Horror* (originally titled *Dementia*) tracks our unhinged heroine through flashbacks in which she kills her drunken dad (who's already slain her bimbo mom), paranoid fantasies of relentless pursuit, and a rough night at the Club Pronto (informal successor to *Cocaine Fiends'* Dead Rat Cafe and forerunner of *Blue Velvet*'s Slow Club). *Daughter of Horror* also features the sci-fi vocal stylings of Marni Nixon, "New Concepts in Modern Sound" courtesy of Shorty Rogers and his Giants, and Angelo Rossitto as a dwarf. While the pic is best remembered as part of the midnight horror show the Blob invaded in *The Blob*, this one deserves to be seen in its idiosyncratic entirety.

Daughters of Darkness (1971) ◆◆◆
D: Harry Kumel. Delphine Seyrig, Daniele Ouimet, John Karlen. 87 minutes. (Cinema Group)

A lyrical, erotic vampire thriller highlighted by Seyrig's sweetly sinister interpretation of ancient but well-preserved bloodsucker Elizabeth Bathory, who intrudes her evil self on a susceptible honeymooning couple at an isolated hotel in modern-day Belgium. The violence is fairly restrained—save for a brilliantly executed razor-induced death scene—while the sexual messages are more explicit. Also out as *Children of the Night* on the defunct but still-visible AIR label.

Dawn of the Dead (1979) ◆◆◆◇
D: George Romero. David Emge, Ken Foree, Scott Reiniger, Gaylen Ross, Tom Savini. 126 minutes. (HBO)

Romero's *Living Dead* sequel rates as a horror-movie masterpiece, the *Gone With the Wind* of gore, replete with living-color flesh feasts and elongated running time. In the midst of the mall-set *Dawn*'s abundant carnage, Romero also manages to get off some sardonic zingers re: America's rampant brainwashed cult of consumerism. An ideal blend of black comedy and chunk-blowing horror.

Dawn of the Mummy (1981) ◆◆
D: Frank Agrama. Brenda King, Barry Sattels, George Peck. 93 minutes. (HBO)

What begins as a bad '50s-style mummy movie ultimately mutates into an equally bad contempo gorefest. The last-reel mummy holocaust sequence is pretty impressive, though.

Day of the Dead (1985) ◆◆
D: George Romero. Lori Cardille, Terry Alexander, Joseph Pilato, Jarlath Conroy, Richard Liberty, John Amplas. 102 minutes. (Video Treasures)

In *Day of the Dead*, Romero's celebrated zombies find themselves all messed up with no place to go, doomed to stagger on empty sans the shock value of *Night* or *Dawn's* retch-ed excesses. *Day* centers on a dozen or so soldiers and scientists who hole up in an underground bunker in a bid to find out what makes the cannibalistic corpses "tick." Much infighting and stale, obscenity-laced dialogue ensue between the disharmonious factions while the mindless zombies marshal their forces on the terra firma above, preparing for the inevitable assault on the outnumbered human survivors. *Day of the Dead* is not entirely bereft of redeeming moments, such as the scene that sees wacky scientist Dr. Logan (Liberty) attempt to "civilize" a captive zombie (whom he dubs Bub) via standard behavioral techniques. When the student ghoul grows unruly, petulantly upsetting a lab bench, the doc douses the lights and testily admonishes, "You can just sit there in the dark and think about what you've done" (!). *Day* also manages to generate some genuine last-reel suspense (full of Tom Savini's usual expertly revolting FX), but here it's a case of too much, too late.

Dead and Buried (1981) ◆◆◇
D: Gary A. Sherman. James Farentino, Jack Albertson, Melody Anderson. 95 minutes. (Vestron)

Dan (*Dark Star*) O'Bannon's agreeably perverse script pits small-town sheriff Farentino against local undertaker Albertson and a number of homicidal cadavers who refuse to stay dead in this uneven but generally entertaining sickie.

Dead Men Walk (1943) ◆◆◇ B&W
D: Sam Newfield. George Zucco, Mary Carlisle, Dwight Frye. 67 minutes. (Sinister Cinema)

It's Mondo Zucco time as George gets to portray twin brothers—one's good, the other's a vampire. Frye is a crazed assistant. The movie's typical but fun.

Dead of Night (1945) ◆◆◆◇ B&W
D: Alberto Cavalcanti, Robert Hamer, Charles Crichton, Basil Dearden. Mervyn Johns, Michael Redgrave, Googie Withers. 102 min. (HBO)

One of the best: An anthology of chilling tales (the "comic relief" golf sequence excepted), framed by an authentically disturbing wraparound. Redgrave's psycho ventriloquist and his demented dummy—a story hook also used to decent effect in the later Brit thriller *The Devil Doll* (MPI) before being mangled by the moronic *Magic* (Embassy)—are enough to give the hardiest horror fan sleepless nights.

The Dead Zone (1983) ♦♦◊
D: David Cronenberg. Christopher Walken, Brooke Adams, Martin Sheen. 104 min. (Paramount).

A fair filmic rendering of Stephen King's novel—about an accident victim (Walken) who develops sudden psychic powers—that ultimately promises more than it delivers. Pretty tame for a Cronenberg flick, but worth a look.

Deadly Blessing (1981) ♦♦
D: Wes Craven. Ernest Borgnine, Maren Jensen, Lois Nettleton, Michael Berryman. 102 minutes. (Embassy)

Ernest Borgnine is perfectly cast as the nutzoid leader of a Hittite sect out to harass nonbelievers in Wes Craven's middling, ultimately muddled chiller.

Deadly Sanctuary (1968) ♦♦
D: Jess Franco. Jack Palance, Klaus Kinski, Romina Power, Akim Tamiroff. 92 minutes. (Monterey)

Palance gives what easily rates as the most flamboyantly awful perf of his over-the-top career as a crazed Marquis de Sade in Jess Franco's sex 'n' gore Marat/Sade variation. Masochistic Francophiles will want to tune in.

Deadtime Stories (1987) ♦◊
D: Steven Mackler. Scott Valentine, Melissa Leo, Kathy Fleig, Matt Mitler, Mike Mesmer. 90 minutes. (Cinema Group)

A tripartite fright farce starring Valentine, of Family Ties fame, and Leo, of Streetwalkin' obscu-rity, Deadtime Stories aspires to be a low-level Creepshow. A sleepless tyke's relentless demands for bedtime stories from his babysitting Uncle Mike (who understandably would rather watch the Miss Nude Bayonne finals on the tube) supplies the wraparound for a trio of twisted monster-movie modernizations of traditional fairy tales. There are a few scattered laughs here—particularly in Uncle Mike's lascivious lycanthropic revamping of "Little Red Riding Hood"—as well as a couple of effective gross-out gore scenes. Unfortunately, the filmmakers lack the steady satirical hand needed to keep the flick from slipping into lengthy stretches of amateur-night insipidity.

Dear, Dead Delilah (1972) ♦♦
D: John Farris. Agnes Moorehead, Will Geer, Michael Ansara. 97 minutes. (Embassy)

A late-arriving, lighter-toned Straitjacket/Hush, Hush, Sweet Charlotte rip-off, with Moorehead as a "dying" southern dowager whose hidden loot sparks a series of ax murders. Some nice touches, but ultimately less than arresting.

Deathdream (1972) ♦♦♦
D: Bob Clark. John Marley, Richard Backus, Lynn Carlin. 90 min. (MPI).

Bob Clark—later of Porky (CBS/Fox) infamy—directed this brilliantly sick allegory about a Vietnam fatality who returns home unexpectedly and alive—sort of.

Ernest Hemingway's "Soldier's Home" meets *Night of the Living Dead*. Recommended.

Deep Red: The Hatchet Murders (1975) ♦♦♦

D: Dario Argento. David Hemmings, Daria Nicolodi, Gabriele Lavia. 100 minutes. (HBO)

Hemmings finds himself drawn into a hunt for a hatchet psycho; Argento's expertly rendered bloody set pieces are the film's raison d'être. Unfortunately for Dario disciples, the video represents an edited, less gruesome version of the original.

Dementia 13 (1963) ♦♦◇

D: Francis Ford Coppola. William Campbell, Luana Anders, Patrick Magee. 81 min. (Cable, others)

Notable more for being Coppola's first "legit" flick (after the softcore sex comedies *Playgirls and the Bellboy* and *Tonight For Sure*—see index) than for being a memorable frightfest in its own right, *Dementia 13* is not without its atmospheric moments, especially the justly famous opening rowboat-murder scene.

Demon of Paradise (1987) ♦

D: Cirio H. Santiago. Kathryn Witt, William Steis, Laura Banks, Frederick Bailey. 84 minutes. (Warner)

Demon of Paradise is one throwback to the rubber-suit monster movies of the '50s that definitely *deserves* to be thrown back. The titular terror—your typical "carnivorous lizard man of the Triassic Age," according to scientist Witt—surfaces in Hawaii to torment local fishermen, smugglers, and tourists alike, while Witt and skeptical lawman Steis struggle to defeat the beast. Resort owner Banks and PR flack Bailey (the latter scripted this "Hawaiian Oy" exercise) seek to exploit the demon's legend for personal gain. The ultimate loser is the unwary renter who plunks down two bucks for this subaqueous dud.

The Demons (197?) ♦♦♦

D: Chang Cheh. Kong Sen, Luk Fung. 95 minutes. (Ocean)

Actually titled *Nine Demons*, this is another surreal Hong Kong horror mixing ghosts, sorcerers, kung-fu displays, and a memorable journey through hell. Recommended for fans of Chinese-style chills.

Demons (1985) ♦♦

D: Lamberto Bava. Natasha Hovey, Urbano Barberini, Paolo Cozzo, Fiore Argento, Carl Zinni, Bobby Rhodes. 89 minutes. (New World)

Produced by shockmeister Dario Argento and directed by Lamberto (Son of Mario) Bava, *Demons* attempts to exploit every fear-film fan's fondest paranoid fantasy. Random pedestrians are given free theater passes to attend a horror-pic premiere. The fright-flick-within-a-fright-flick is a *Living Dead*–type gorefest about a group of kids who violate the tomb of Nostradamus and mutate into sharp-clawed, pus-oozing, canni-balistic zombies. Before we're halfway through the first reel, the unwitting movie patrons also start turning into—you guessed it—sharp-clawed, pus-oozing, canni-balistic zombies. Imbued with the wit of a George Romero or a Larry Cohen, *Demons* might have emerged as a splendid blend of blood and black humor, sort of a splatter version of *The Purple Rose of Cairo*. In Bava's heavy hands, *Demons* degenerates into a mondo disgusto FX exercise. Hard-core gorehounds will probably enjoy it, though.

Demons 2 (1988) ◆◇
D: Lamberto Bava. David Knight, Nancy Brilli, Coralina Cataldi Tassoni, Bobby Rhodes, Asia Argento, Virginia Bryant. 88 minutes. (Imperial)

Lamberto, Dario (as co-writer), and the boys are back with more of the same with *Demons 2*. This time the antisocial title characters emerge not from a theater but from a TV screen, where the same movie-within-a-movie we saw in *Demons* happens to be playing. The sprung zombies chomp their way through an apartment com-plex while a mixed cast of Yanks and Italians desperately battles back. *Demons 2* sports few sur-prises but does feature some pretty good gore FX, which is, after all, the name of the game here and about the only reason you'd want to rent this vid.

Demons of the Mind (1972) NR
D: Peter Sykes. Paul Jones, Gillian Hills, Robert Hardy, Patrick Magee, Mi-chael Hordern, Shane Briant. 89 min-utes. (HBO)

Hardy is The Baron, a domineering nineteenth-century British lord whose repressed desires are acted out by his son in a series of grisly murders in a Hammer horror fea-turing Paul (*Privilege*) Jones, a for-mer Manfred Mann lead singer. Also available as *Blood Evil* (Acad-emy) and *Nightmare of Terror*.

Demonwarp (1988) ◆
D: Emmet Alston. George Kennedy, David Michael O'Neill, Pamela Gil-bert, Billy Jacoby, Colleen McDer-mott, Michelle Bauer. 91 minutes. (Vidmark)

Demonwarp is a largely unwatch-able exercise in lame dialogue, dumb plotting, and inadept acting. Most of its seemingly endless run-ning time finds a fright-masked Bigfoot chasing an overweight George Kennedy and the usual crew of lobotomoid teens through the woods. After an hour or so of this not-so-hot pursuit, the pic drops its Bigfoot plot for a last-reel lurch into *Living Dead/Evil Aliens* territory (!) when our teen protagonists stumble upon a de-monic ET and his zombie slaves in a spaceship stashed in a nearby cave. The only pluses here are Ken-nedy and the terminally topless Michelle (*Hollywood Chainsaw Hookers*) Bauer, whose presence briefly boost the proceedings to the lofty level of the mediocre. Otherwise, we say to hell with *Demonwarp*.

Deranged (1987) ◆◆
D: *Chuck Vincent. Jane Hamilton, Paul Siederman, Jennifer Delora, Jill Cumer, James Gillis, Gary Goldman. 85 minutes. (Republic)*

A sort of road-company *Repulsion* by way of Robert Altman's *Images*, longtime porn auteur Vincent's *Deranged* details the mental disintegration of one Joyce, whose breakdown is further hastened when she's forced to snuff a ski-masked burglar in self-defense. After that, her apartment—where most of this claustrophobic low-budget thriller unfolds—is invaded by relatives and friends real and imagined, whom Joyce routinely greets with scissors, razors, kitchen knives, and other handy household items. Vincent does a decent job with the derivative material, and Jane Hamilton—formerly Veronica Hart, who, though apparently out of the smut biz, manages to shed her clothes on three separate occasions here—delivers a deft perf as our unhinged heroine. Ultimately, though, *Deranged* is more pointlessly grim than scary.

Destroyer (1988) ◆◇
D: *Robert Kirk. Deborah Foreman, Clayton Rohner, Anthony Perkins, Lyle Alzado. 93 minutes. (Virgin Vision)*

Destroyer opens with an admittedly neat sequence, as condemned killer Alzado watches a witless TV game show while being strapped into an electric chair (!). A power outage and (offscreen) prison riot soon ensue, enabling Lyle to survive the ordeal and slaughter anew. Unfortunately, the above is all part of a nightmare experienced by movie stunt woman Foreman, who wakes into an even worse nightmare—i.e., the rest of this cheap rip-off pic. Deb's part of a film crew headed by director Perkins (who should know better) using the now-abandoned prison as the set of a chicks-in-chains romp. Next, in what amounts to a step-by-step steal from the already unoriginal *Return to Horror High* (where an abandoned school subs for *Destroyer*'s prison—see index), the brain-fried Alzado shows up to knock off the film folk one by one. While former footballer Wild Lyle looks like he might have a future as a pro B-movie geek, the rest of the perfs are less than charismatic, and the flick itself a cynical bore.

The Devil (1985) ◆◆◇
D: *Chang Jen Chieh. Chow Shao Tung, Wang Pao Yu, Ou Ti. 90 minutes. (Video City)*

A truly strange fright flick from Hong Kong about poltergeists, demonic curses, and worm eating, among other arcane matters. Pretty gross going at times, but worth a look for Hong Kong horror buffs, or for those looking for a second feature to flesh out a home-vid screening of Herb Robins's similarly-themed *The Worm Eaters* (WesternWorld).

The Devil Bat (1941) ◆◆◇ B&W
D: Jean Yarbrough. Bela Lugosi, Suzanne Kaaren, Dave O'Brien. 69 minutes. (Sinister Cinema, others)

One of Lugosi's livelier Monogram outings finds him training the title creatures to carry out his vengeful schemes. Nearly every public-domain vid company carries this one, many under the title *Killer Bats.*

Devil Bat's Daughter (1946) ◆◆◇ B&W
D: Frank Wisbar. Rosemary La Planche, John James, Molly Lamont. 66 minutes. (Sony)

Belated sequel to Bela's *Devil Bat* is far from a classic but does offer more atmospheric touches than most PRC quickies. Bela, alas, didn't hang around for this one, though auteur Wisbar went on to direct the effective *Strangler of the Swamp* (see index) that same year.

The Devil-Doll (1936) ◆◆◇ B&W
D: Tod Browning. Lionel Barrymore, Maureen O'Sullivan, Frank Lawton. 79 minutes. (MGM/UA)

Another strange tale from Tod (*Freaks*) Browning. Lionel Barrymore, who plays much of the movie in drag, is an escaped con who invents living killer dolls to do his deadly bidding. It doesn't always work, but it *is* different.

The Devil's Nightmare (1971) ◆◆◇
D: Jean Brismee. Erika Blanc, Jean Servais, Daniel Emilfork. 90 minutes. (Monterey)

Blanc is a sexy succubus who subjects a group of stranded tourists to ritualistic killings keyed to a Seven Deadly Sins theme in a Euro-import that's short on sense but long on horror. Geeky Fellini regular Emilfork cameos as the Devil himself. It's also available as *The Devil Walks at Midnight* (Saturn) and in uncut form in the hard-to-find Applause Video version, where it's out as *Succubus.* Giving the Devil his video due, His Satanic Majesty and/or followers also appear in *Daughters of Satan* (Wood Knapp), another of Tom Selleck's early acting gigs; *The Demon* (VidAmerica); *Demon Queen* (Mogul); *Demon Witch Child* (Simitar); *Demoniac; Devil's Gift* (both Vestron); *Devil Times Five* (Video Treasures); *The Devil's Hand* (Sinister Cinema); *The Devil's Possessed* (All Seasons); Chris Lee and Peter Cushing in *The Devil's Undead* (Monterey); the extravagantly awful *Natas: The Reflection; The Other Hell* (a nice place to visit, if we didn't already live there); *Satan's Blade; Satan's School for Girls* (all Prism); *Satan's Black Wedding* (WesternWorld); *Satan's Supper* (Academy); *Satan's Touch* (Regal); and *Satanwar* (United), to cite a few.

The Devil's Partner (1958) ◆◆◇ B&W
D: Charles R. Rondeau. Ed Nelson,

Edgar Buchanan, Jean Allison, Richard Crane, Spencer Carlisle, Byron Foulger. 75 minutes. (Sinister Cinema)

A not-bad independent cheapie that's been gaining clout in 1950s fright-film cult circles, *The Devil's Partner* (co-scripted by former Bowery Boy Stanley Clements) stars AIP regular and future *Peyton Place* mainstay Nelson in a dual role as ancient conjurer Pete Jensen and young Nick Richards, Jensen's mysterious "nephew," whose arrival in desolate Furnace Flats, New Mexico, sparks an outbreak of local tragedies. Buchanan gives his patented folksy perf as the town doctor; Carlisle is the puzzled sheriff ("Doesn't make sense—a hunk of beef killing Dr. Marx!"), while Jean Allison and Richard (*Rocky Jones*) Crane are a couple whose lives are disrupted by the seemingly helpful Richards.

The Devil's Rain (1975) ◆◆
D: Robert Fuest. Ernest Borgnine, Ida Lupino, William Shatner. 85 minutes. (United)

Ernie B and his coven of satanists menace a B-star-studded cast in a pic that also witnesses John Travolta's screen debut. (Now *that's* scary!)

The Devils (1971) ◆◆◆
D: Ken Russell. Oliver Reed, Vanessa Redgrave, Dudley Sutton. 103 minutes. (Warner)

More antireligious hysteria from Ken Russell, centering on seventeenth-century French witch trials and loosely based on Huxley's *The Devils of Loudon.* Actually one of Ken's more coherent and compelling exercises.

Die! Die! My Darling! (1965) ◆◆◇
D: Silvio Narizzano. Tallulah Bankhead, Stephanie Powers, Donald Sutherland. 97 minutes. (RCA/Columbia)

Tallulah joins the then-popular parade of moviedom's mad matrons, started by Robert Aldrich's *Whatever Happened to Baby Jane?* (see index), in a performance whose strength is not restraint. Sutherland is her geeky Igor-like hunchbacked butler/henchman; Powers plays their victim.

The Doctor and the Devils (1985) ◆◆
D: Freddie Francis. Timothy Dalton, Jonathan Pryce, Twiggy, Stephen Rea, Julian Sands, Phyllis Logan. 93 minutes. (Key)

Based on an original screenplay by Dylan Thomas and directed with relative restraint by Hammer horror vet Freddie (*Evil of Frankenstein*) Francis, *The Doctor and the Devils* draws its inspiration from the real-life exploits of infamous nineteenth-century grave robbers Burke and Hare (herein renamed Fallon and Broom), who weren't above resorting to murder to meet their cadaver quota. Jonathan (*Brazil*) Pryce and Stephen Rea turn in credible work as the unsavory stiff-lifters; Dalton is properly self-righteous as Dr. Rock, who buys the bodies for "progressive" medical purposes; and a sur-prisingly buxom Twiggy emotes effectively as blond pub tart Jenny Bailey. Unfortunately, the script needs work (sorry, DT, wherever you are), and the flick grows less compelling with each passing reel. Although a polished, professional production, *The Doctor and the Devils* is itself a bit of a stiff.

Dr. Butcher, M.D. (1981) ◆

D: Francesco Martino. Ian McCulloch, Alexandra Cole, Donald O'Brien. 81 minutes. (Thriller)

A legendary gory mess and long-time Forty-second Street main-stay, *Dr. Butcher, M.D.* (as in "Medical Deviate"!) began life as an Italian island–set bloodbath called *Queen of the Cannibals.* American distrib Aquarius added unrelated opening footage from an unfinished opus titled *Tales That Tear Your Heart Out.* The result-ing package is sufficiently dis-gusto to prompt ThrillerVideo horror hostess Elvira to cancel her usual cassette appearance here. Proceed at your own risk.

Doctor Death, Seeker of Souls (1973) ◆◇

D: Eddie Saeta. John Considine, Barry Coe, Cheryl Miller, Moe Howard. 73 minutes. (Prism)

Stooge Moe Howard's comic cameo supplies the sole reason for seeing this otherwise soulless quickie about ancient soul-stealer Considine.

Dr. Heckyl and Mr. Hype (1980) ◆◆◇

D: Charles B. Griffith. Oliver Reed, Sunny Johnson, Jackie Coogan, Mel Welles. 99 minutes. (Paragon)

A fairly funny fright farce from for-mer Corman collaborator Charles B. (*Little Shop of Horrors, Bucket of Blood*) Griffith, starring Reed as an ugly doc whose abortive suicide attempt transforms him into a handsome psycho (!). Creative casting—vets Jackie Coogan, Co-rinne Calvert, and *Little Shop* alumnus Welles—adds to the fun.

Dr. Jekyll and Mr. Hyde (1941) ◆◆◆ B&W

D: Victor Fleming. Spencer Tracy, In-grid Bergman, Lana Turner. 113 min-utes. (MGM/UA)

Lavish MGM "classics" treatment of Stevenson's study of good versus evil is a solid show, but the accent's on Dr. J's emotional turmoil rather than on the pure horror aspects. Kirk Douglas does double duty in the 1973 *Dr. Jekyll and Mr. Hyde* remake (Sony), as does Jack Pal-ance in *Strange Case of Dr. Jekyll and Mr. Hyde* (Thriller). Variations include Hammer's clever *Dr. Jekyll and Sister Hyde* (HBO) and the "blaxploitation" edition, *Dr. Black, Mr. Hyde* (United). John Barrymore's 1920 silent *Dr. Jekyll and Mr. Hyde* is also out (via Video Yesteryear), but Reuben Mamoulian's 1932 version, with Fredric March, remains unavail-able as we go to press.

Dr. Tarr's Torture Dungeon (1972) ◆◆
D: John L. Monteczuma. Claudio Brook, Ellen Sherman, Martin La Salle. 88 minutes. (Magnum)

In sort of a Mexican horror variation on *Marat/Sade*, lethal loonies take over an asylum. Based on a story by Edgar Allan Poe. Slow going, though nicely lensed.

Dr. Terror's House of Horrors (1965) ◆◆◆
D: Freddie Francis. Peter Cushing, Christopher Lee, Donald Sutherland. 98 minutes. (Republic)

Pete and Chris are at it again, this time in a fun fright anthology helmed by reliable Hammer vet Francis. Cushing is the fortune-teller who frames the five tales.

Dolls (1987) ◆◆◇
D: Stuart Gordon. Carrie Lorraine, Ian Patrick Williams, Carolyn Purdy-Gordon, Guy Rolfe, Hilary Mason, Stephen Lee. 77 minutes. (Vestron)

Director Stuart (*Reanimator, From Beyond*) Gordon's third effort for Empire involves a sensitive little girl named Judy (Lorraine), part of a group of otherwise largely obnoxious travelers stranded at your standard old dark manse, this one inhabited by a pair of elderly doll-makers (Rolfe, Mason). The dolls come to aggressive life and begin eliminating those guests who deserve that fate, while befriending the empathetic Judy. Gordon does what he can with the mostly mediocre material. *Dolls*, in its defense, includes the best

killer-teddy-bear sequence we've seen since *Bloodbath at the House of Death* (see index). But those looking for another *Reanimator* won't find it here.

Don't Be Afraid of the Dark (1974) ◆◆◇
D: John Newland. Kim Darby, Jim Hutton, Barbara Anderson. 74 minutes. (IVE)

Darby is bedeviled by sneaky humanoid gremlins—a riff later recycled in Stephen King's *Cat's Eye*—in a pretty good made-for-TV terror effort that's easily stolen by the lilliputian predators.

Don't Look Now (1973) ◆◆◆
D: Nicolas Roeg. Donald Sutherland, Julie Christie, Hilary Mason. 110 minutes. (Paramount)

Not every frame works, but Roeg's adaptation of a Daphne du Maurier story about a couple (Sutherland, Christie) who take an ill-advised Venetian vacation to recover from their daughter's drowning death is one of the eeriest and most downright disturbing films ever made.

Doom Asylum (1988) ◆◇
D: Richard Friedman. Patty Mullen, Ruth Collins, Kristin Davis, William Hay, Kenny L. Price, Harrison White. 78 minutes. (Academy)

Doom Asylum involves a living-dead patrimony lawyer (!) who terrorizes several unwary post-teens who gather at an abandoned mental hospital. He then terminates them one by one with the help of his trusty autopsy tools. Richard (*Scared Stiff*) Friedman makes the mistake of interrupting his mostly feeble fright farce with far superior Tod Slaughter clips, any one of which is instantly more involving than *Doom Asylum*. In fact, the Phantom clocked an average of one genuine laugh per reel; at that rate, *Doom Asylum* would have to run another twenty-four hours or so to deliver enough chuckles to qualify it as a moderately funny creature feature.

Dracula (1931) ◆◆◆◇ B&W

D: *Tod Browning. Bela Lugosi, David Manners, Helen Chandler, Dwight Frye, Edward Van Sloane. 75 minutes. (MCA)*

What can we add? Still perverse and powerful after all these years, with a groundbreaking performance by Bela as Bram Stoker's thirsty Count and manic work by Frye as his insect-starved slave. Jack Palance and Frank Langella turn in decent perfs in remakes *Dracula* (ThrillerVideo) and *Dracula* (MCA), but they'll never cause Bela to lose any (daytime) sleep.

Driller Killer (1979) ◆◇

D: *Abel Ferrara. Carolyn Marz, Jimmy Laine. 90 minutes. (Magnum)*

Pretty useless slasher trash, of interest mostly to Abel Ferrara fans. This was the director's only feature before *Ms. 45* launched him on his more or less successful genre-film career.

Drums of Jeopardy (1931) ◆◆ B&W

D: *George B. Seitz. Warner Oland, June Collyer, Mischa Auer. 75 minutes. (Sinister Cinema)*

A strange though not especially good marginal horror item with future Charlie Chan Oland as mad doc Boris Karlov (!), whose pursuit of a lethal Indian necklace takes him to NYC.

The Dunwich Horror (1970) ◆◆

D: *Daniel Haller. Dean Stockwell, Sandra Dee, Ed Begley. 87 minutes. (Embassy)*

This mediocre movie version of a classic H. P. Lovecraft tale pales beside Stuart Gordon's later exercises in Lovecraftian lunacy, *Reanimator* and *From Beyond* (see index), but should be of interest to Lovecraft lovers.

Eaten Alive (1976) ◆◆◇

D: *Tobe Hooper. Neville Brand, Mel Ferrer, Carolyn Jones, Stuart Whitman. 96 minutes. (Prism)*

Brand enjoys a thespic field day as a crazed cracker who leads unsuspecting strangers to his croc-stocked swamp. Hooper's low-budget horror is no *Texas Chainsaw Massacre* (see index), but it's better than a lot of his later, more lavish Hollywood work.

The Entity (1983) ◆◆◆

D: *Sidney J. Furie. Barbara Hershey, Ron Silver, Jacqueline Brooks. 119 minutes. (CBS/Fox)*

Hershey is raped repeatedly by the titular demon and is also forced to contend with nonbelievers who think she's out of her mind in this offbeat chiller. Barbara's since found less grueling work under Woody Allen's direction.

Equinox (1967/1971) ◆◆◆
D: Jack Woods. Edward Connell, Barbara Hewitt, Fritz Leiber, Jack Woods. 80 minutes. (Wizard)

Amateur acting and a nonexistent budget can't kill the hallucinatory thrills provided by David Allen's stop-motion animation and the solid story line that informs this enduring cult fright fave. The devil appears as a forest ranger (!) played by director Jack Woods. Also out as *The Beast* (Lightning).

Eraserhead (1978) ◆◆◆ B&W
D: David Lynch. Jack Nance, Charlotte Stewart, Allen Joseph. 90 minutes. (RCA/Columbia)

The legendary film that put director David Lynch on the cult-movie map is a one-of-a-kind affair that plays like a nightmare experienced by a nuclear-holocaust survivor. Consistently creepy and often brilliant. DL later misfired with his ill-advised adaptation of Frank Herbert's *Dune* (MCA)—further butchered for a network TV airing, prompting Lynch to demand an "Alan Smithee" credit. But he regained control with his bleakly magical *Elephant Man* (Paramount) and his transcendent *Blue Velvet* (see index).

Escapes (1986) ◆
D: David Steensland. Vincent Price, *Jerry Grisham, Lee Canfield, John Mitchum, Gary Reade. 72 minutes. (Prism)*

From the fertile minds at Sacramento's Visual Perceptions Productions comes *Escapes*, a six-part anthology introduced by your host Vincent Price (who's onscreen for a total of maybe a minute and a half). The high-concept wraparound sees teen Matt Wilson receive an unordered video delivered by postman Price and—guess what?—it's *Escapes*, the very cassette we're watching! The kid proceeds to pop the vid into his VCR and watches a half-dozen null-skulled would-be *Twilight Zone*–type tales, followed by a blatant *Dead of Night* lift wherein the episodes' various fictional characters—along with your host Vincent Price—materialize in the flesh to terrorize our teen hero. *Escapes'* all-around ineptitude entertains for the first few minutes but quickly sinks from the so-dumb-it's-fun to the so-dumb-you're-numb level. Only the four-minute end-credit crawl, thanking the folks of Fiddletown, California, for doing their part to bring *Escapes* about, provides some last-ditch entertainment. The tripartite anthology *Screamtime* (Vestron) employs a similar frame.

Eternal Evil (1987) ◆◆◇
D: George Mihalka. Winston Rekert, Karen Black, John Novak, Andrew Bednarski, Patty Talbot, Lois Maxwell. 86 minutes. (Lightning)

This Canadian scare tale sports a fairly novel premise. Rekert is a depressed commercial director who dabbles in astral projection (beats watching hockey), a pastime apparently linked to the sudden, violent deaths of several associates. Complicating the case are a pair of ancient souls trapped in dying bodies and currently shopping for suitable replacements. *Eternal Evil* fails to exploit its plot to the max and makes the mistake of overtelegraphing several key story developments, but it does feature some neat, free-floating aerial photography in the astral-projection sequences. Black, fresh from her soft-core porn-starlet turn in *Hostage*, proffers another of her patented wacko performances here as the free-spirited lesbian dancer/astral-projection expert (you know the type) who starts our misguided protagonist on the flight path better not taken.

The Evil (1978) ◆◆

D: *Gus Trikonis. Richard Crenna, Joanna Pettet, Andrew Prine. 90 minutes. (Embassy)*

Crenna is a doctor who encounters hostile forces in a haunted house. Routine, save for Victor Buono's colorful climatic cameo. (!).

The Evil Dead (1983) ◆◆◇

D: *Sam Raimi. Bruce Campbell, Ellen Sandweiss, Betsy Baker. 90 minutes. (HBO)*

Sam Raimi's gory cult fave is longer on shocks and innovative camera work than on story and performances. Dull stretches serve to blunt the horror, but this one remains a must for serious fright-film scholars.

Evil Dead II: Dead by Dawn (1987) ◆◆◆◇

D: *Sam Raimi. Bruce Campbell, Sarah Berry, Dan Hicks, Kassie Wesley, Theodore Raimi, Denise Bixler. 84 minutes. (Vestron)*

Raimi's energetically brain-damaged sequel to his 1983 cult fave *The Evil Dead* may be the most maniacal and wildly hallucinogenic of horrordom's popular '80s spate of anything-for-a-gasp comic-nightmare movies. Raimi's hyperactive POV camera remains in constant frenzied motion throughout, even though most of the flick unfolds in a single claustrophobic cabin setting. As in the original, there's no real story here—just a simple situation. Five characters battle a succession of grotesque evil spirits (and each other) in a series of gross encounters of the absurd kind. One especially memorable tableau sees Campbell—reprising his role as Ash, the lone survivor of *The Evil Dead*—at war with his own left hand, now possessed by the title demons. When said hand begins *laughing* at its owner (!), Ash responds by plunging a knife into it and shouting triumphantly, "Who's laughing *now!?*" A won-

WHO'S LAUGHING NOW?: Bruce Campbell enjoys last laugh at the expense of his living–dead adversaries in climactic scene from Sam Raimi's surreal scarefest, *Evil Dead II.*
Photo courtesy of Vestron Video.

derfully neurotic moment, we'd warrant, and one that's already achieved classic status. Raimi's live-action cartoon style, exploding-id imagery, and outrageous FX make *Evil Dead II: Dead by Dawn* essential viewing for horror buffs.

The Evil Mind (1935) ◆◆◆ B&W
D: Maurice Elvey. Claude Rains, Fay Wray, Jane Baxter. 70 minutes. (Cable, others)

Claude's a phony clairvoyant whose predictions start coming true in an excellent, complex thriller (originally titled *The Clairvoyant*) marred only by a somewhat bland epilogue.

The Exorcist (1973) ◆◆◆
D: William Friedkin. Ellen Burstyn, Linda Blair, Jason Miller. 120 minutes. (Warner)

Still crazy after all these years. The framing story grows tedious at times, but Linda's demonic freakout scenes, with vocal help from Mercedes McCambridge, remain as fresh and revolutionary today as they seemed in '73, despite dozens of pale imitations (including *Exorcist II*).

Exorcist II: The Heretic (1977) ◆◇
D: John Boorman. Linda Blair, Richard Burton, Louise Fletcher. 110 minutes. (Warner)

Linda's older but not much wiser; worse, she's still got a bit of the devil in her, much to priest Bur-

ton's dismay, in Boorman's ill-received sequel.

Eyes of Fire (1986) ◆◆◇
D: Avery Crouse. Dennis Lipscomb, Guy Boyd, Rebecca Stanley, Fran Ryan, Rob Paulsen, Karlene Crockett. 86 minutes. (Vestron)

Set on the "American frontier" circa 1750, Crouse's *Eyes of Fire* follows the exodus of some rather eccentric pioneers, led by Lipscomb and Boyd, into a "promised land" that quickly turns into a valley of death. To Crouse's credit, *Eyes* admirably forgoes gore in favor of a quieter, Val Lewton–like approach, and his hallucinatory horror tale definitely has its black magic moments—naked ghosts come and go, living faces form on haunted trees, and blood flows freely from the earth. *Eyes* also succeeds in conveying the tenuous nature of frontier survival as our frightened pioneers try desperately to fight the elusive forest phantoms—the restless souls of innocent murder victims—that are destroying them one by one. Though flawed by a sluggish script and painfully slack pacing, *Eyes of Fire* actually plays better on video, where a quick fast-forward finger will propel impatient viewers past the pic's many somnolent stretches.

Eyes Without a Face (1960) ◆◆◆ B&W
D: Georges Franju. Pierre Brasseur, Alida Valli, Edith Scob. 88 minutes. (Interama)

French filmmaker / cinephile Franju accords stately treatment to a pulp plot involving surgeon Brasseur, who performs graphic skin-graft operations on his daughter's disfigured face in a flick rich in shock and entertainment value. The Anglicized edition, *The Horror Chamber of Dr. Faustus*, is available from Sinister Cinema, while Franju's infamous slaughter-house shockumentary, *Blood of the Beasts*, has been issued by Video Yesteryear.

Fade to Black (1980) ◆◆◇
D: Vernon Zimmerman. Dennis Christopher, Linda Kerridge, Tim Thomerson. 100 minutes. (Media)

This slasher tale is enlivened by countless in-references to genre-movie lore—plus clips from *Public Enemy*, *Creature from the Black Lagoon*, *Kiss of Death*, and *Night of the Living Dead*—as maladjusted movie maniac Christopher adopts the personas of famous thriller-film characters when carrying out his killings. Unfortunately, auteur Zimmerman ultimately runs out of inspiration before *Fade to Black* runs out of reels.

Fall of the House of Usher (1960) ◆◆◆
D: Roger Corman. Vincent Price, Mark Damon, Myrna Fahey. 79 minutes. (Warner)

Floyd Crosby's lush color cinematography and Daniel Haller's set designs lend this well-dressed low-budget Corman/Poe collaboration (the first of many) a classy, Hammer-like look. The 1949 B&W British version of Poe's claustrophobic tale, titled *The Fall of the House of Usher*, is likewise available, via Sinister Cinema.

Flesh and the Fiends (1960) ◆◆◆ B&W
D: John Gilling. Peter Cushing, Donald Pleasence, George Rose. 88 minutes. (Sinister Cinema)

A vivid, atmospheric retelling of the Burke and Hare story, with Cushing a standout as the ambitious surgeon who strikes a fatal bargain with the grave robbers in question.

Flowers in the Attic (1987) 0 ◆
D: Jeffrey Bloom. Victoria Tennant, Louise Fletcher, Kristy Swanson, Jeb Stuart Adams, Ben Granger, Lindsay Parker. 90 minutes. (New World)

Unless watching four bland blond kids languish in the title site, as circles spread under their pale eyes and cobwebs gather over yours, is your idea of entertainment, we'd advise you to avoid this lame TV-movie-type loser like your proverbial plague. Tin-eared dialogue, a total lack of action and suspense, plus cardboard performances by the kids (including *Deadly Friend*'s Swanson), by Tennant as their deceitful mom, and by Fletcher (who goes from Ratched to wretched here) as The Grandmother combine to make *Flowers* one of moviedom's all-time worst. Not even a director named Jeffrey *Bloom* could keep this horticultural horror from wilting on the celluloid vine. Still, we have to admit we admired *Flowers'* big climactic shock line, to wit: "Eat the cookie!"

The Fog (1980) ◆◆◇

D: John Carpenter. Adrienne Barbeau, Jamie Lee Curtis, Hal Holbrook. 91 minutes. (Embassy)

Not peak Carpenter, but a serviceable scarefest involving spectral seagoing lepers who move through coastal mists to massacre unsuspecting citizens.

Frankenstein: Restored Version (1931) ◆◆◆◇ B&W

D: James Whale. Colin Clive, Mae Clarke, Boris Karloff, Dwight Frye. 71 minutes. (MCA)

Considered incredibly shocking in its day, Whale's adaptation of Mary Shelley's novel remains a genuinely creepy experience. MCA's video includes brief snippets of footage excised from the original theatrical release.

Frankenstein Meets the Wolf Man (1943) ◆◆◆ B&W

D: Roy William Neill. Lon Chaney, Jr., Ilona Massey, Patric Knowles, Bela Lugosi, Lionel Atwill, Maria Ouspenskaya. 72 minutes. (MCA)

Universal's *Frankenstein Meets the Wolf Man* marked the first time two celebrity monsters shared the same marquee and screen. The sequel picks up where both the original *Wolf Man* (see index) and *Ghost of Frankenstein*

(NA) left off. Lycanthrope Larry Talbot (Chaney) is reawakened by a pair of grave robbers, finds his way to the dread Frankenstein castle, and stumbles across the Monster encased in ice. Actually, it's Bela Lugosi—in his only appearance as Frankenstein's creation (he rejected the original role back in 1931)—who does most of the stumbling. As initially scripted, the monster is blind. That detail was omitted in the final cut, however, which leaves Bela looking like he's perpetually drunk and searching desperately for the nearest men's room! That and other flaws prevent the flick from rising to classic status, but there's enough Universal back-lot charm, skilled thesping, and cheap thrills to keep it consistently entertaining.

The Freakmaker (1973) ◆◆

D: Jack Cardiff. Donald Pleasence, Tom Baker, Julie Ege, Michael Dunn. 92 minutes. (Vidcrest)

Donald Pleasence is characteristically vivid here as a mad doctor creating people/plant hybrids. The pic, released theatrically as *Mutations*, stirred some minor controversy for its employment of several actual "freaks." See also *Dr. Frankenstein's Castle of Freaks* (Magnum), with professional Euro-geek "Boris Lugosi" as a throwback named Ook.

Freaks (1932) ◆◆◆◇ B&W

D: Tod Browning. Wallace Ford, Leila Hyams, Olga Baclanova, Henry Vic-

tor, Harry Earles, Daisy Earles, Violet and Daisy Hilton, Angelo Rossitto, Johnny Eck, Prince Randian, Zip, and Pip. 66 minutes. (MGM/UA)

While yet a feckless youth, your (now thoroughly fecked) Phantom caught *Freaks* at Jamaica, Queens's, old Alden Theater on a weird killer bill with H. G. Lewis's *Blood Feast*. The video version, transferred from a far better print than the one we saw way back when, loses none of the flick's original shock value. The simple plot—beautiful trapeze bimbo Olga Baclanova, aided by callous strongman Henry Victor, woos, weds, and slowly poisons love-sick midget Harry Earles, the better to lay claim to his lucrative estate— is a perfectly serviceable excuse to draw the viewer into "freak" society, with its attendant bonds, codes, and rituals. Director Browning took a costly risk in recruiting actual circus freaks to play essentially themselves: "Human Torso" Prince Randian, legless Johnny Eck, dwarf Angelo Rossitto (still active in show biz and last seen as Master in *Mad Max Beyond Thunderdome*), Siamese twins Violet and Daisy Hilton (later of *Chained for Life* fame), "pinheads" Zip and Pip (who come off as quite charming here), and other anatomical oddities. Highlights include the notorious wedding banquet sequence, the freaks' sylvan frolic, and, of course, the fierce finale. The video also includes a choppy "happy" ending missing from

Browning's original release print. When mainstream exhibitors refused to book *Freaks*, MGM sold the rights to road-show sleazemeister Dwain (*Maniac*) Esper, who showed it in urban grindhouses and rural bijous under the title *Nature's Mistakes*. It was still playing into the '50s as *Loves of Freaks*.

Freeway Maniac (1989) ◆
D: Paul Winters. Loren Winters, James Courtney, Shepard Sanders, Donald Hotton, Jeff Morris, Robert Bruce. 90 minutes. (Media)

This celluloid challenge to human endurance—it took yours truly fully four separate couchside sessions to get through this mess— has nothing to do with wholesale highway slaughter (or, for that matter, much of anything else). Though promoted as a straightahead horror item, *Freeway Maniac* is actually yet another lame attempt at genre parody. A standard brand-X madman breaks out of a local asylum to embark on a trail of meaningless murders that eventually leads him to the site of an in-progress, desert-set, no-budget sci-fi flick. Unfortunately, the film not only fails both as horror and as humor but is relentlessly colorless, crammed with bland thesps delivering dull-witted dialogue. Discredit goes to auteur Paul Winters, who produced, directed, and co-wrote with Gahan Wilson. If the latter is *the* Gahan Wilson, the talented cartoonist, we can only advise him to get back to the drawing board posthaste. Just plain *Freeway* (Nelson) is another title that's well worth avoiding.

Friday the 13th, Part VI: Jason Lives (1986) ♦
D: Tom McLoughlin. Thom Mathews, Jennifer Cooke, David Kagen, Kerry Noonan, Renee Jones, Ron Palillo. 87 minutes. (Paramount)

Director Sean S. Cunningham and Paramount unleashed *Friday the 13th* back in 1980—essentially as a cheap rural rip-off of John Carpenter's wildly successful *Halloween*, detailing the murderous adventures of madman Michael Myers (aka The Shape). When *Friday* and *its* mindless slasher hero, Jason Voorhees, proved equally boffo at the old BO, Paramount spewed out *Friday the 13th Parts 2* and *3*. Hope arose when studio honchos tagged the lame series' fourth entry *Friday the 13th: The Final Chapter*. But no such luck—a year later (1985) there followed *Part V: A New Beginning*, which, naturally enough, led to this: *Friday the 13th, Part VI: Jason Lives*. Here, ex-mental patient Tommy Jarvis (Mathews), who supposedly slew the unstoppable Jason Voorhees in *Friday the 13th Part V: A New Beginning*, drops by the Forest Green (née Crystal Lake) cemetery to make sure the hockey-masked maniac is really dead and buried. Buried he is—but dead? No way. Why? Because it's Friday the 13th, a date on which the machete-wielding "maggot-head" (as Jarvis later refers to JV) gets to rise from his grave and slaughter anew. This time around, writer-director McLoughlin tries to breathe life into the lethally repetitive proceedings by alternating the hardcore gore with low-comedy *shticks*. Thus, Jason is sighted near Karloff's General Store; corporate creeps on a survivalist spree eat slapstick death; a juvenile camper is glimpsed sleeping with a copy of Sartre's *No Exit* resting on his chest. Beyond the generally obnoxious stabs at wit, *Jason Lives* offers nothing new; the splatter is all that matters. Final score: Jason 16, victims 0, viewers ditto.

Friday the 13th Part VII—The New Blood (1988) ♦◇
D: John Carl Buechler. Lar Park Lincoln, Kevin Blair, Terry Kiser, Kane Hodder. 90 minutes. (Paramount)

In *Part VII—The New Blood*, our unsinkable psycho is once again unwittingly revived, this time by a telekinetic teen named Tina (Lincoln). Seems that Tina's dad drowned at Crystal Lake years before, and she blames herself for that mishap. Accompanied by her devious shrink (Kiser), Tina returns to the scene of the crime—ever the preferred mode of therapy in cheap horror flicks—to confront her demons and, it goes sans saying, the ever-present Jason. A surprise birthday party at the cabin next door supplies the revivified killer with his requisite victims. The final body count (excluding the "prologue," which recycles clips from the previous six pics) runs to fifteen, down from *Part V*'s twenty-plus but almost even with *VI*'s sixteen. Of the above, Jason's trusty slamming-the-occupied-sleeping-bag-against-the-tree trick proves the most crowd-pleasing here.

Fright Night (1985) ◆◆◇
D: Tom Holland. Chris Sarandon, William Ragsdale, Roddy McDowall, Amanda Bearse, Stephen Geoffreys, Jonathan Stark. 105 minutes. (RCA/Columbia)

Tom Holland's *Fright Night* starts out looking like another dumb assembly-line teen-horror comedy, as young Charlie Brewster (Ragsdale) tries to convince girlfriend Amy (Bearse) and creepy pal Evil Ed (Geoffreys, doing an irritating junior Jack Nicholson imitation) that his suave new next-door neighbor (Sarandon) is really a vampire. The pace picks up considerably, however, once these typical screen-teen nonentities are usurped by polished pros Sarandon and McDowall (aptly tacky as hack-actor-cum-horror-show-host Peter Vincent). The kids recruit a reluctant Roddy to submit Sarandon to the "vampire test"— an exam Chris fails with flying colors (ranging from plasma-scarlet to blood-red). From that point on, *Fright Night* wisely leaves the low comedy behind and shifts into high fear gear. Sarandon's vampiric transformations rank among the best, while a femme bloodsucker who appears near film's end sports the champ vamp choppers of all time, stalactitic fangs gleaming from a crimson kisser that takes up half her face! The jolts are a long time coming but definitely worth the wait.

Frightmare II (1976) ◆◆◆
D: Peter Walker. Rupert Davies, Sheila Keith. 90 minutes. (Prism)

Originally titled simply *Frightmare* but redubbed in its video incarnation to distinguish it from another, lesser *Frightmare* (Vestron) about a living-dead horror thesp on the loose, *Frightmare II* is a bizarre, effective Brit terror tale. Keith is excellent as a matronly modern-day cannibal who can't kick her lethal habit, much to beleaguered hubby Davies's dismay.

Frogs (1972) ◆◆
D: George McCowan. Ray Milland, Sam Elliott, Joan Van Ark. 91 minutes. (Warner)

Wildlife destroyer Milland, in one of his patented petulant-patriarch parts, pays the price for his polluting ways when the title creatures exact their revenge. Nearly the whole cast croaks.

The Funhouse (1981) ◆◆◇
D: Tobe Hooper. Cooper Huckabee, Elizabeth Berridge, Miles Chapin. 96 minutes. (MCA)

Hooper's horror tale involving four teens trapped overnight in the title site has its fair share of genuine frights.

The Fury (1978) ◆◆◆
D: Brian De Palma. Kirk Douglas, Amy Irving, John Cassavetes. 117 minutes. (CBS/Fox)

De Palma plays with the fear genre and an extravagant budget in this overlong but generally fun story of psychokinetic destruction. Cassavetes blows up *real* good.

Garden of the Dead (1972) ◆◇
D: John Hayes. Duncan McLeod, Lee Frost, John Dennis. 70 minutes. (Video BanCorp.)

This fairly atrocious *Living Dead* rip-off (aka *Tombs of the Undead*) does boast the distinction of being one of the very few Brit movies about chloroform-sniffing convicts-turned-zombies.

The Gate (1987) ◆◆◇
D: Tibor Takacs. Stephen Dorff, Louis Tripp, Christa Denton, Kelly Rowan, Jennifer Irwin, Scot Denton. 92 minutes. (Vestron)

Takacs's fantasy focuses on two kids (Dorff, Tripp) who dig a hole in their backyard that leads directly to a satanic lair. ("We accidentally summoned demons who used to rule the universe," one youth blandly explains.) With the aid of an older sister (Denton) and an arcane heavy-metal LP, our half-pint heroes confront sundry forces of darkness over the course of a single harrowing—if low-budget—night. *The Gate*, which shares some thematic similarities with DEG's *Trick or Treat* (see index), was something of a surprise hit during its theatrical release and is not without its pluses. The on-screen tykes are likable for a change, the dialogue rings true (one kid's cry, "Suck my nose till my head caves in!" ranks as one of moviedom's more imaginative taunts), and the story unfolds with genuine suspense. The demons—more of your clichéd *Gremlins*-esque minimonsters—are disappointing, though, and the murky night photography pointlessly oppressive.

Gates of Hell (1983) ◆◇
D: Lucio Fulci. Christopher George, Daniela Doria, Robert Sampson. 90 minutes. (Paragon)

Not to be confused with Kinugasa's 1954 Japanese classic *Gate of Hell* (Embassy), this is a fairly fulsome Fulci gorefest recommended solely for fans of over-the-top Italo carnage.

Geek Maggot Bingo (1983) NR
D: Nick Zedd. John Zacherle, Richard Hell. 70 minutes. (Monday/Wednesday/Friday Video Club)

The surreal underground horror that put Nick Zedd on the cult-movie-manqué map can now be seen in the safety of your living room, as can Nick's equally anti-social debut flick, the legendary *They Eat Scum* (also from M/W/F), though that one doesn't feature a cameo by beloved TV horror host Zacherle.

The Ghost (1963) ◆◆◆

D: Riccardo Freda. Barbara Steele, Peter Baldwin, Leonard Elliott. 90 minutes. (Sinister Cinema)

Another effectively atmospheric example of early '60s spaghetti Gothic that rates as a must for Barbara Steele buffs.

Ghost Stories: Graveyard Thriller (1986) 0◆

D: Lynn Silver. With No One You'd Want to Know From. 60 minutes. (Vestron)

The Phantom has often fantasized about producing a feature film consisting entirely of expository title cards accompanied by a lush, booming music track. Well, the folks at Alamance Productions come close to duplicating that dubious idea with Ghost Stories: Graveyard Thriller. This hourlong anthology actually consists of single (bad) actors narrating "terror" tales while standing amid an el cheapo cemetery set. That's right, that's it—you never see any of the tales themselves, just the narrators! Ghost Stories outminimalizes anything Ed Wood, Jr., or SCTV's Monster Horror Chiller Theater ever conceived. In fact, it's the closest to radio that video is ever likely to get. Ghost Stories earns an A for low-concept originality and a Z for entertainment value.

Ghost Story (1981) ◆◆

D: John Irvin. Fred Astaire, Melvyn Douglas, John Houseman. 110 minutes. (MCA)

Peter Straub's best-selling hairraiser about four old-timers who share a dark secret makes for pretty slow going, though fans of the veteran cast might want to catch it.

Ghost Town (1988) ◆◇

D: Richard Governor. Franc Luz, Catherine Hickland, Jimmy F. Skaggs. 85 minutes. (New World)

A last gasp from Charles Band's thankfully disbanded Empire Pictures, Ghost Town finds modernday deputy Luz (earlier seen as a lawman in the mutant-roachfest The Nest) stranded in a desert ghost town that turns out to be more literal than most. In fact, the abandoned burg is populated solely by poltergeists trapped there by the evil spirit of outlaw Jimmy F. Skaggs, who's also kidnapped the flick's flesh-and-blood heroine (Hickland). On the plus side, Ghost Town—directed by Richard Governor—exhibits more atmosphere, sincerity, and visual style than the typical imitative Empire product and also sports some pretty fair ghost-and-ghoul makeup FX. But the pic is dully paced, poorly plotted, and peopled (to say nothing of ghosted) by a decidedly uncharismatic cast.

The Ghoul (1933) ◆◆◇ B&W

D: T. Hayes Hunter. Boris Karloff, Cedric

Hardwicke, Ernest Thesiger. 68 minutes. (Sinister Cinema)

Boris plays an avenging corpse out to eliminate the thieves who broke into his tomb in this atmospheric but often painfully slow Brit chiller. Sinister Cinema's tape is transferred from a rediscovered complete print, sans the Czech subtitles that appear on previous video versions.

The Ghoul (1975) ◆◆◇

D: Freddie Francis. Peter Cushing, John Hurt, Veronica Carlson. 88 minutes. (Media)

Cushing keeps the mysterious title character locked in his home in a solid 1920s-set Freddie Francis frightfest that eschews gore in favor of subtler, more traditional chills—at least until the hairy climax.

Ghoulies (1985) ◆

D: Luca Bercovici. Peter Liapis, Lisa Pelikan, Michael Des Barres, Jack Nance, Mariska Hargitay, Keith Joe Dick. 84 minutes. (Vestron)

The original ads featured a snarling, razor-toothed puppet popping over the rim of a porcelain facility. An episode from *The Toilet Zone*? No, it's a scene from *Ghoulies*, Empire Pictures's typically witless *Gremlins* rip-off. Ghoulies are vicious, salivating little devils (several bear a passing resemblance to Ben Gay's green-skinned nemesis Peter Pain) conjured by amateur occultist Jonathan Graves (Liapis) in the basement of the creaky old manse he recently inherited. After a slow buildup, the film offers a few moments of fun when the title creatures bite the faces off a half-dozen airheaded L.A. party animals. Throughout the proceedings, only an elderly caretaker played by Jack (*Eraserhead*) Nance seems to know what's going on. He may also be the only one who cares. And yes, Virginia, there is a *Ghoulies II* (Vestron).

God Told Me To (1976) ◆◆◆◇

D: Larry Cohen. Tony LoBianco, Sandy Dennis, Deborah Raffin. 91 minutes. (Charter)

The strangest of Cohen's oft-bizarre outings and one of the weirdest genre flicks of all time, *God Told Me To* (originally *Demon*) involves cop LoBianco, whose obsessive investigation into a series of random, seemingly religious-themed killings brings him face-to-face with a far odder plot. Essential viewing. Robert (*Alligator*) Forster, incidentally, was originally cast in the Lo-Bianco role but withdrew after conflicts with director Cohen.

The Godsend (1979) NR

D: Gabrielle Beaumont. Cyd Hayman, Malcolm Stoddard, Angela Pleasence. 93 minutes. (Vestron)

A family discovers that an adopted daughter is actually a murderous demon out to erase them one by one.

Goremet Zombie Chef From Hell (1987) ◆◆

D: Don Swan. Theo Dupuay, Kelley Kunicki, C. W. Casey, Alan Marx, Michael O'Neill, Jeff Pillars. 90 minutes. (Camp)

This extremely cheap direct-to-video amateur-night outing sports poor gore FX but manages to milk its own tackiness, filler footage, and repetitive minimalist music track for more laughs than we'd expected. The premise of this low-camp cannibal comedy is none too original: Goza (Dupuay), a fourteenth - century heretic cursed with immortality and a craving for human flesh, now runs a beachfront deli specializing in you-know-what. *Goremet* is not as professional as, say, *Blood Diner*, but at least it's less obnoxious than most of, say, Troma's unhip stabs at tastelessness. We should warn you, though, that the Phantom watched this vid while in the glow of an unusually benevolent mood (a check had just arrived), which may partially account for his relative generosity here. Other Camp offerings include *Demon Hunter, Las Vegas Serial Killer*, and *Video Violence I* and *II*.

The Gorgon (1964) ◆◆◇

D: Terence Fisher. Peter Cushing, Christopher Lee, Barbara Shelley. 83 minutes. (Goodtimes)

Shelley is an innocent possessed by the snake-tressed spirit of the title creature; the peerless Pete and Chris shine as a battling brain surgeon and an investigator, respectively, in this stylish Hammer outing that nonetheless falls a bit short of the monstrous mark.

Gothic (1987) ◆◆

D: Ken Russell. Gabriel Byrne, Julian Sands, Natasha Richardson, Miriam Cyr, Timothy Spall. 90 minutes. (Vestron)

Ken (*The Devils*) Russell's filmic fever dream traces a dark and stormy night in the laudanum-laced lives of a quintet of literary crazies—Lord Byron (Byrne), Percy and Mary Shelley (Sands, Richardson), Mary's half-sister Claire (Cyr), and Byron's unstable physician Dr. Polidori (Spall). In 1816, at Byron's sumptuous Swiss summer retreat, Villa Diodati, this rather self-indulgent lot set their febrile imaginations to conjuring demons who represented their deepest fears. The eventual result of this histrionic encounter was the birth (cesarean all the way, if you accept Russell's account) of Mary Shelley's immortal novel *Frankenstein*. A high-concept notion, we'll agree, but one that sounds like a lot more fun than it plays. Beyond a few perceptive scenes luridly dramatizing the sources of Mary's angst, *Gothic* is pretty much a one-note affair crowded with Russell's repetitive ruminations on religion, sex, and decay. There are some striking raging-id images and suitably sick sight gags on view but nothing to challenge *The Evil Dead 2* or Russell's own *Lair of the White Worm* (see index).

Graveyard Shift (1987) ◆◆◇

D: Gerard Ciccoritti. Silvio Oliviero, Helen Papas, Cliff Stoker, Dorin Ferber, Dan Rose, Don Jones. 88 minutes. (Virgin Vision)

Unlike his previous *Psycho Girls*, Ciccoritti's *Graveyard Shift* features a pretty neat central conceit. Lensed almost solely at night, the pic chronicles the bloody adventures of a vampire cabbie (!), limned by John Lurie–lookalike Oliviero, whose female converts are upping the body count all over town. Our toothy antihero ultimately enters into an eerie affair with an embittered music-video director (Papas) who's already dying of cancer. It's the latter character who embodies what the Phantom feels are two of this generally stylish flick's major turnoffs: an overreliance on rock-video visuals (wet streets, flashing neon, extensive use of slo-mo, et al.) and a tone unusually bleak and downbeat for a modern horror film. (Ciccoritti cites his own fright-movie model when he names one character Mario Bava after the Italian Gothic-horror auteur.) The often inferior FX constitute another drawback. Still, with its offbeat eroticism, stately style, and occasionally lyrical script, *Graveyard Shift* definitely has its points—

beyond those set in the assorted vampires' mouths. Ciccoritti's bloodsucker strikes again in *Graveyard Shift II* (Virgin Vision).

Gremlins (1984) ◆◆◇

D: Joe Dante. Zach Galligan, Phoebe Cates, Hoyt Axton, Dick Miller, Scott Brady, Jackie Joseph, Keye Luke. 109 minutes. (Warner)

Director Dante crafts a gala creature comedy that's as schizoid as its title thingies—a flick that alternately trashes and wallows in Mall-American pop culture. While there are inspired moments and a memorable supporting cast of B-movie vets, Dante and producer Steven Spielberg ultimately want to have their cake, eat it, and regurgitate onto the audience too.

Grotesque (1987) ◆◆◇

D: Joseph Tornatore. Linda Blair, Tab Hunter, Donna Wilkes, Brad Wilson, Guy Stockwell, Charles Dierkop, Robert Zdar. 80 minutes. (Media)

It would take the Phantom several pages to do justice to this aptly titled terror turkey, which is either a high-concept put-on (doubtful) or truly one of the most flamboyantly awful movies ever made (probable). The irrepressible Linda Blair (who also receives a co-producing credit) toplines as a Los Angeleno who takes her depressed friend Donna (*Angel*) Wilkes for a "quiet weekend" at her folks' secluded woodland redoubt. That planned idyll soon goes awry when a bunch of psycho punkers

—hulking Robert (*Maniac Cop*) Zdar among them—slaughter Linda B's family, including her semiretired horror-movie makeup expert dad, and severely provoke her previously unseen adopted mutant brother (!). Enter LB's avenging plastic-surgeon uncle (screen legend Tab Hunter) for the final reels, where *Grotesque* truly lives up to its name. Even though Tab and Linda don't play any scenes together and Linda threatens to take her customary onscreen shower but somehow never gets around to it, *Grotesque* still shapes up as a must for masochistic bad-movie buffs (and that includes yours truly).

Halloween (1978) ◆◆◆
D: John Carpenter. Donald Pleasence, Jamie Lee Curtis, P. J. Soles. 90 minutes. (Media)

Thin in the story department and the unfortunate inspiration for scores of inferior klutzy slasher clones, Carpenter's *Halloween* does deliver its intended shocks and deserves its status as a terror trail-blazer.

Halloween II (1981) ◆◇
D: Rick Rosenthal. Jamie Lee Curtis, Donald Pleasence, Charles Cyphers. 92 minutes. (MCA)

Carpenter co-scripted this pedestrian sequel, which boasts higher blood and body counts but offers less suspense than the original.

Halloween III: Season of the Witch (1982) ◆◆◇
D: Tommy Lee Wallace. Tom Atkins, Dan O'Herlihy, Stacey Nelkin. 98 minutes. (MCA)

While it bears no relation to the earlier *Halloween*s, *III*'s off-the-wall plot—detailing psycho toy-manufacturer O'Herlihy's scheme to massacre America's kiddie population—at least takes the series in a new direction (to understate the case).

Halloween IV: The Return of Michael Myers (1988) ◆◇
D: Dwight H. Little. Ellie Cornell, Danielle Harris, Donald Pleasence, George Wilbur. 88 minutes. (CBS/Fox)

After rotting on his laurels for nearly a decade, Halloween-masked misanthrope Michael Myers—aka The Shape—resurfaces in the aptly titled *Halloween IV: The Return of Michael Myers.* Our story picks up ten years after the original *Halloween* (*IV*'s producers ignore the earlier sequels, not that we blame them) with Mad Mike an invalid inhabitant of a midwestern psycho ward. When medical authorities unwisely decide to transfer the dormant dementoid from his hospital bed, Mike predictably breaks loose, and all hell swiftly follows in his wake. So does a desperate Donald Pleasence, reprising his role as semiunhinged shrink Dr. Loomis. Both wind up in Mike's hometown of Haddonfield, Illinois, where our homicidal hero steadily reduces the local population (though, in a cheap move, many of the slayings occur offscreen). The original *Halloween* worked because director John Carpenter knew how to deliver the gory goods *and* sustain a mood of relentless suspense. Despite Donald Pleasence's hyperactive presence, *Halloween IV* is a slack hack job utterly empty of even minimal scares or surprises.

The Hand (1981) ♦♦
D: Oliver Stone. Michael Caine, Andrea Marcovicci, Annie McEnroe. 104 minutes. (Warner)

Caine is a former cartoonist whose own severed hand seeks violent revenge. A none-too-gripping tale of ontological angst from Oliver (*Platoon, Wall Street*) Stone, who'd earlier made his directorial debut with the cheesier chiller *Seizure* (Prism). Stone cameos as a bum.

Hands of the Ripper (1971) ♦♦♦
D: Peter Sasdy. Eric Porter, Angharad Rees, Keith Bell. 82 minutes. (Vid-America)

A solid Hammer horror about a shrink's encounters with Jack the Ripper's daughter, thoughtfully directed by helmer Sasdy and containing footage cut from the original American theatrical release.

Hard-Rock Zombies (1986) 0 ♦
D: Krishna Shah. E. J. Curcio, Geno Andrews, Sam Mann, Mick McMains, Lisa Toothman. 94 minutes. (Vestron)

From the inept pen and lens of Krishna Shah comes *Hard-Rock Zombies*, a painfully brainless, utterly excruciating exercise in amateurish ennui. Essentially a feature-length head-banger video, *Hard-Rock Zombies* pits a colorless heavy-metal band against a town full of red-necks and satanists—the latter led by none other than *der Führer* himself (!). There may be worse ways to spend 94 minutes, but we wouldn't want to think of them.

The Haunted Strangler (1958) ♦♦♦ B&W
D: Robert Day. Boris Karloff, Elizabeth Allan, Anthony Dawson. 80 minutes. (MPI)

Boris is in fine form in this atmospheric story of a Victorian novelist who unconsciously reenacts the violent crimes of the dead killer whose exploits he's been researching. The plot eventually takes a twist that prefigures *Angel Heart* (see index).

The Haunting (1963) ♦♦♦ B&W
D: Robert Wise. Julie Harris, Claire Bloom, Russ Tamblyn. 113 minutes. (MGM/UA)

Though not quite the masterpiece it's cracked up to be, the film version of Shirley Jackson's *Haunting of Hill House* is an at-times disturbing haunted-house mood piece, definitely worth catching.

The Haunting of Julia (1976) NR
D: Richard Loncraine. Mia Farrow, Keir Dullea, Tom Conti. 96 minutes. (Magnum)

Originally titled *Full Circle*, this Canadian chiller casts the former *Rosemary's Baby* star as a guilt-stricken woman plagued by a juvenile poltergeist in a Peter Straub–based story that's won its fair share of admirers.

He Knows You're Alone (1980) ♦♦
D: Armand Mastroianni. Caitlin O'Heaney, Don Scardino, Tom Hanks. 94 minutes. (MGM/UA)

A slasher stalks brides-to-be in a predictable outing that recycles a hook seen to better effect in *The Corpse Vanishes* (see index).

Hellbound: Hellraiser II (1988) ♦♦♦◇
D: Tony Randel. Clare Higgins, Ashley Laurence, Kenneth Cranham, Imogen Boorman, William Hope, Doug Bradley. 93/98 minutes. (New World)

Hellbound represents one of those rare cases wherein a scare sequel actually surpasses the original. Directed by Tony Rand*el* (not to be confused with professional prig Tony Rand*all*) from a story by Barker (who also co-produced), *Hellbound* offers an ever-escalating procession of nightmare set pieces that succeed in being both darkly comic and genuinely chilling. Returning from *Hellraiser* is Ashley Laurence as Kirsty, whose kinky Uncle Frank and his box from hell had caused the death of Kirsty's kindly dad. As *Hellbound* opens, we find Kirsty stashed in a rather Gothic asylum, "recovering" from her recent traumas. Head shrink Dr. Chan-

nard (Cranham) is himself a dabbler in the occult; he encourages Kirsty's autistic but gifted fellow inmate Tiffany (Boorman) to unlock the dread secrets of that self-same infernal box. Also back from hell are Kirsty's wicked stepmother Julia (Higgins, reprising her original role) and the infamous Cenobites, led once again by punkoid pincushion Pinhead. The real treat for fright fans here is not *Hellbound*'s fragmented narrative but its impressive array of shock tableaux. (As Pinhead at one point proclaims, "Your suffering will be legendary—even in hell!") Highlights include imaginatively grotesque sets, horrific FX that out-nightmare *Elm Street*, and one of the sickest heavy-petting scenes the Phantom's ever seen onscreen. *Hellbound* may be a mite strong for fainter-hearted viewers, but hard-core horror buffs won't want to miss it. The video is available in both the rated and the gorier unrated version.

Hello Mary Lou: Prom Night II (1987) ♦♦
D: Bruce Pittman. Michael Ironside, Wendy Lyon, Justin Louis, Lisa Schrage, Richard Monette. 96 minutes. (Virgin Vision)

A belated sequel to 1981's *Prom Night* (see index)—itself a fairly shameless *Carrie* clone—*Hello Mary Lou* opens in 1957. Wild and crazy senior-class slut Mary Lou Malone—the kind of gal who scrawls her name and phone number in lipstick across the confessional wall—is somehow elected prom queen. Her moment of triumph is seriously marred, however, when her jealous boyfriend Bill sets her prom gown ablaze—and Mary Lou too. Cut to thirty years later. Bill (Ironside) is now the Hamilton High principal; his ex-rival, high school stud Bud Cooper (Monette), is the local priest. Mary Lou's vengeful spirit returns to possess the hitherto wholesome Vickie (Lyon), who begins talking "like she's in an Elvis Presley movie" and (natch) knocking off the student body in the usual variety of grisly ways. Quoth the class clown, "It's Linda Blairsville!" Alas, we don't have Linda to look at this time around, though we do witness your standard revolving-head tricks, telekinetic wipeouts, nude shower scenes, and exorcism attempts. There are a few more imaginative moments—Vickie gets sucked into a blackboard in one memorable scene and later shares a somewhat obscene interlude with an animated rocking horse—but nothing that hasn't already been topped by *Nightmare on Elm Street 3* and *Evil Dead II* (see index).

Hellraiser (1987) ♦♦♦

D: Clive Barker. Andrew Robinson, Clare Higgins, Ashley Laurence, Sean Chapman, Oliver Smith, Robert Hines. 95 minutes. (New World)

A surreal, claustrophobic gruefest, Clive Barker's *Hellraiser* depicts a Brit degenerate named Frank (Chapman) whose addiction to an arcane beelzebubian puzzle box capable of supplying unimaginable pleasure and pain ultimately results in his violent demise. When Frank's brother Larry (Robinson) buys the house wherein Frank's splattered remains lie undetected, a few drops of Larry's blood bring his sinister sibling to gradual slime-creature life. After that, it's up to Larry's unhappy wife and Frank's former lover (Higgins) to lure fresh victims to the house to complete Frank's physical restoration. Hot on Frank's trail, meanwhile, are the box's original owners—four demonic Cenobites who resemble refugees from a CBGB hard-core matinee. Though better known for his fright fiction, director/scripter Barker demonstrates in his directorial debut that he also knows how to deliver perverse *visual* chills as well.

Hide and Go Shriek (1988) ◊

D: Skip Schoolnik. George Thomas, Donna Baltron, Ria Pavia, Bunky Jones, Scott Kubay. 86 minutes. (New Star)

Four post–high school couples play a nocturnal game of hide and seek in a closed furniture store, where an unknown maniac stalks and slaughters them right before they have sex. It's amazing how little even *accidental* originality creeps its way into this feature-length catalog of decade-old slasher clichés. We awarded *Hide and Go Shriek* its half-phan solely on the strength of the director's name. Now, *that's* original. In R and unrated versions.

The Hills Have Eyes (1977) ◆◆◆

D: Wes Craven. Dee Wallace, James Whitmore, Michael Berryman. 89 minutes. (Magnum)

Desert mutants seek to ruin innocent campers' vacation in the best of Craven's early low-budget epics and the movie that introduced Michael Berryman, the '80s answer to Rondo Hatton. Director Craven's sharp sense of suspense and his willingness to go "too far" help overcome a slender story line and an uneven cast. The sequel, *The Hills Have Eyes Part II* (HBO), doesn't hack it.

The Hitcher (1986) ◆◆◇

D: Robert Harmon. Rutger Hauer, C. Thomas Howell, Jennifer Jason Leigh, Jeffrey DeMunn, John Jackson. 98 minutes. (HBO)

We'll say this much for *The Hitcher*: it may use up a lot of octane, but it doesn't waste any time. No sooner does naif Howell pick up highway menace Hauer than *The Hitcher* revs into high homicidal gear. Hauer flashes his famous sneer as icy superpsycho John Ryder, an archetypal Everyfiend who—sans identity or motive—embroils Howell in a harrowing desert intrigue that finds our young hero hounded not only by the nutjob but by a veritable army of enraged red-neck cops who think *he's* the killer. Howell is so rattled by this revolting development that, before the movie's halfway through, he barfs twice and tries to kill himself! Sympathetic waitress Leigh does her best to help our persecuted protagonist, but the paranoiac plot twists—and the body count—continue to mount. While it succeeds in generating some genuine shocks, *The Hitcher* is so determined to out-terminate *The Terminator* (even setting what may be a new celluloid cop-killing record) that it ultimately lapses into wild self-parody—or is that, as some *Hitcher* fans claim, its sly intent all along? Rent this sicko fable and judge for yourself.

Hollywood Chainsaw Hookers (1988) ◆◆◆

D: Fred Olen Ray. Gunnar Hansen, Linnea Quigley, Jay Richardson, Dawn Wildsmith, Michelle Bauer, Dennis Mooney. 90 minutes. (Camp)

Hollywood Chainsaw Hookers ("They Charge an Arm and a Leg!") is that rarity of rarities, a trash flick that actually achieves the low aspirations set forth by its title. What we're trying to say here is that Fred Olen Ray's famed indefatigability finally pays off with a *good* campy, stupid T&A gore comedy. Even though Ray resorts to the hoary narrative device of relating his tale from yet another mock hard-boiled private eye's POV (well played by Richardson), we *do* get the promised gang of chainsaw-toting tarts who kill for the love of their crazed Egyptian cult leader (rather woodenly interpreted by former "Leatherface" Hansen). In fact, there's more comedy than gore in this postmodern ode to splatter pioneer H. G. (*Blood Feast*) Lewis, much of it supplied by the ever-lovely Linnea Quigley, who not only solidifies her niche as a gutter-flick Goldie Hawn but even dances topless during a lengthy club scene. We also liked

Photo courtesy of Camp
Motion Pictures and Video.

the hooker who covers her treasured Elvis poster with plastic to protect it from her victim's flying innards. In sum, if you like the title, you'll doubtless dig the movie as well.

Hollywood Strangler Meets the Skid Row Slasher (1973) ◆◆◇

D: Wolfgang Schmidt (Ray Dennis Steckler). Chuck Alford, Carolyn Brandt, Pierre Agostino. 72 minutes. (Active)

It's love at first fright in Steckler's (working here under the nom du camera Wolfgang Schmidt) poverty-row production, filmed in conjunction with "Cine Paris" Films. For Wolfgang, a weekend well spent. Also available, in an 88-minute version, from Regal under the title *Model Killer.*

Horrible Dr. Hichcock (1962) ◆◆◆

D: Robert Hampton (Riccardo Freda). Robert Flemyng, Barbara Steele, Teresa Fitzgerald. 76 minutes. (Republic)

Barbara Steele buffs won't want to miss their fave fright femme, cast here as the understandably anxious bride of the insane titular surgeon. Sinister Cinema has a longer version titled *Terror of Dr. Hichcock.*

Horror Express (1973) ◆◆◆◇

D: Gene Martin. Peter Cushing, Christopher Lee, Telly Savalas. 90 minutes. (Goodtimes, others)

Just about every public domain vid-outfit stocks this immensely entertaining chiller about a brain-sucking alien loose aboard the Trans-Siberian Express, circa

1906. Pete and Chris excel as rival scientists, while Telly cameos as an overbearing Cossack in a pic rich in characterizations and period flavor (if not in budget) and offering everything from trepanning close-ups to mad monks to brain-drained zombies. Not to be missed.

Horror Hospital (1973) ◆◆◇

D: Anthony Balch. Michael Gough, Robin Askwith, Vanessa Shaw. 90 minutes. (MPI)

A not bad tongue-in-cheek Brit affair about a bonkers brain surgeon, Gough, who runs the titular facility. *Hospital of Terror* (Embassy), formerly *Nurse Sherri*, is also available.

Horror Hotel (1960) ◆◆◆ B&W

D: John Moxey. Christopher Lee, Dennis Lotis, Betta St. John. 76 minutes. (Sinister Cinema)

Set in New England but lensed in Britain, this moody scarefest about a reincarnated Salem witch who lures sacrificial victims to the title establishment has garnered a sizable (and well-deserved) cult following over the years.

Horror of Dracula (1958) ◆◆◆◇

D: Terence Fisher. Peter Cushing, Christopher Lee, Michael Gough. 82 minutes. (Warner)

One of Hammer's classiest productions, with Chris Lee perfectly cast as the caped Count and Cushing shaping up as an equally ideal Van Helsing. Widely condemned in its day for its high violence quotient. Great fun.

The Horror of Frankenstein (1970) ◆◆◇
D: Jimmy Sangster. Ralph Bates, Veronica Carlson, David Prowse. 93 minutes. (HBO)

Bates is an openly evil Dr. Frankenstein and Prowse is his outsize creation in this throwaway comic variation on a well-worn Hammer theme. Slightly better than Hammer's earlier loser, *Evil of Frankenstein* (MCA).

House (1986) ◆◇
D: Steve Miner. William Katt, George Wendt, Richard Moll, Kay Lenz, Mary Stavin, Michael Ensign. 92 minutes. (New World)

House is built on a particularly shaky premise. Divorced, blocked and hounded by his young son's apparent drowning death, Stephen King–type fright writer William (*Greatest American Hero*) Katt moves into his late nutty aunt's haunted house to work on his Vietnam memoirs. The house is haunted not only by the usual FX creations but by intrusive neighbor George (*Cheers*) Wendt (who himself played a Stephen King clone in *Dreamscape*). *House* opens as a straightforward—if mostly ineffectual—chiller, cluttered with grim 'Nam flashbacks featuring Richard (*Night Court*) Moll as a Ramboesque GI. With Wendt's arrival, *House* careens into broad comedy, then further collapses into a failed EC Comics–style windup. *House* boasts adequate FX, competent tech work, and a more than capable cast, but it is missing one essential component: a script.

House II: The Second Story (1987) ◆◆◇
D: Ethan Wiley. Arye Gross, Jonathan Stark, Royal Dano, Bill Maher, John Ratzenberger, Lar Park Lincoln, Gregory Walcott. 85 minutes. (New World)

Ethan Wiley's *House II: The Second Story* stacks up as a fairly entertaining fright farce, a definite step up from its more predictable predecessor. Gross stars as the title site's young inheritor, who—via plot contrivances too loose-screwed to go into here—decides to dig up his late, great great-grandfather, the better to lay hands on a bejeweled skull rumored to have been buried with him. Only catch is, Gramps creaks out of his coffin alive and relatively well, considering his 170 years. Vet thesp Dano does an excellent job here as the exhumed old-timer, a former Wild Westerner who leads Gross and his party-animal pal Stark on a wild chase through the house's seemingly endless supply of alternative universes, including a literal ghost town and a prehistoric jungle. In a deft cameo, John (*Cheers*) Ratzenberger turns up as a free-lance "electrician and adventurer." The flick maintains a refreshingly throwaway attitude toward its largely senseless but lively material, emerging as a sort of EC Comics Meets Pee-wee's Playhouse.

House of Exorcism (1975) ◆◆
D: Mario Bava. Telly Savalas, Elke Sommer, Sylvia Koscina, Robert Alda. 93 minutes. (Amvest, others)

An incomprehensible mess that consists of Mario Bava's *Lisa and the Devil* plus added footage fashioned to rip off *The Exorcist*, partially redeemed by Bava's deft directorial touches. Also known as *Devil in the House of Exorcism.* (MPI)

The House of Seven Corpses (1973) ◆◆◇
D: Paul Harrison. John Ireland, Faith Domergue, John Carradine. 90 minutes. (Video Gems)

Like *Frankenstein 1970* (NA), this pic involves a film crew, enacted by a veteran B cast, stalked by a real-life zombie during a dangerous location shoot. Good, cheap fun.

House of the Black Death (1965) ◆◇
B&W
D: Harold Daniels. Lon Chaney, Jr., John Carradine, Andrea King. 80 minutes. (Dixie/Loonic)

A boring brew of vengeful warlocks and satanic rituals, directed by Harold (*Terror in the Haunted House*) Daniels and recommended only for hard-core Carradine and Chaney fanatics.

House of Wax (1953) ◆◆◆
D: Andre de Toth. Vincent Price, Carolyn Jones, Phyllis Kirk. 88 minutes. (Warner)

VP hams it up with his usual élan as the scarred sculptor who turns his enemies into wax dummies.

Charles Bronson is his brain-damaged assistant. Originally lensed in 3-D, this pic plays funnier without it as all sorts of objects—for no apparent reason—hurl themselves at the camera with *Poltergeist*ian frenzy.

House on Haunted Hill (1958) ◆◆◇
B&W
D: William Castle. Vincent Price, Carol Ohmart, Richard Long. 75 minutes. (Key)

Castle lets Price run out of control as the host of a killer party. Uneven, but commands a loyal contingent of fans. Castle's popular chiller *The Bat*, also with Price, is available via Video Dimensions.

The House on Skull Mountain (1974) ◆◆
D: Ron Honthaner. Victor French, Janee Michelle, Mike Evans. 89 minutes. (CBS/Fox)

The Jeffersons' Evans made his movie debut in this mostly dull black horror film (discounting token cauc French) about modern-day voodoo mischief unfolding at the title abode.

The House That Dripped Blood (1971) ◆◆◇
D: Peter Duffell. Denholm Elliott, John Bennett, Peter Cushing, Christopher Lee. 101 minutes. (Prism)

Robert (*Psycho*) Bloch scripted this sometimes entertaining fright anthology that wavers between black comedy and straight-ahead horror. Cushing and Lee carry on with their usual aplomb.

The House Where Evil Dwells (1982) ◆◆◇

D: Kevin Connor. Edward Albert, Susan George, Doug McClure. 88 minutes. (MGM/UA)

Japanese ghosts terrorize Yank family who move into haunted Kyoto digs. Some inspired bad-movie moments, such as McClure's memorable exit and the infamous face-in-the-soup scene.

The Howling (1981) ◆◆◆

D: Joe Dante. Dee Wallace, Patrick Macnee, John Carradine. 90 minutes. (Embassy)

Dante's mostly on-target lycanthrope update, crammed with vet-thesp cameos, deals with werewolf troubles at a California therapy center. Steer clear of Howling II: Your Sister Is a Werewolf (HBO), a total misfire. The series picks up with Howling III (see below), prior to plummeting again with the (typically) unrelated turkey Howling IV (IVE).

Howling III (1987) ◆◆◆

D: Philippe Mora. Barry Otto, Imogen Annesley, Ralph Cotterill, Leigh Biolos, Dasha Blahova, Max Fairchild. 94 minutes. (Vista)

Annesley stars as a fetchingly feral wolfwench named Jerboa—one of an endangered species of "human marsupials"—who runs away from her backward Aussie tribe to try her luck in the big city (Sydney). There she meets handsome assistant director Donnie Martin (Biolos), who lands her a victim role in the horror pic Shape Shifters: Part 8. Jerboa eventually hooks up with her equally hirsute Soviet counterpart, defecting ballerina Blahova, and both cross paths with investigative scientist Otto and partner Cotterill. Mora's deadpan spoof of self-serious celluloid lycanthrope lore is a consis-

FILMMAKERS IN FOCUS:
Philippe Mora

Australian auteur Philippe Mora saw Howling III as a chance to erase the memory of the ill-received Howling II—a flick he directed but over which he had little artistic control—and "make the Howling movie I wanted to make—an affectionate tribute to horror movies." To that end, Mora scripted, directed, and co-produced his film and populated it with top Aussie actors; he cast Dasha Blahova (an actual Czech defector) as the defecting Russian werewolf ballerina. The result—one of 1987's brightest and funniest fright flicks.

A painter and movie scholar (he was one of the founders of Australia's influential Cinema Papers magazine) as well as a filmmaker, Philippe first attracted notice via his mad documentary/montage *Brother, Can You Spare a Dime?* (United) back in 1974. He piloted the outback western *Mad Dog Morgan* (HBO), starring Dennis Hopper, before embarking on his fear-film debut, 1980's *The Beast Within* (MGM/UA), which featured the world's "first bubbling bladder faces FX," soon to be popularized by John Landis's *An American Werewolf in London* and royally spoofed in *Howling III.*

Although *Howling III* is strong on humor and shocks, it's deliberately light on blood and gore. "I wanted the PG-13 rating," Mora asserts. "I want kids to be able to see the film. I don't mind blood and gore," he adds, "but you need a good dramatic reason for it."

As for his personal fright faves, Philippe places the original *Frankenstein, Bride of Frankenstein, Psycho, Rosemary's Baby,* Stuart Gordon's *Reanimator,* and Tod Browning's *Freaks* at the top of his list.

An ardent comic-book buff as well as film fan (his first movie project was scripting a never-lensed epic titled *The Phantom vs. the Fourth Reich,* based on the King Features' character), Philippe has also helmed *The Return of Captain Invincible* (Magnum), which pits alcoholic superhero Alan Arkin against megalomaniacal villain Christopher Lee; *Death of a Soldier* (Key), a fact-based story about a psychopathic GI stationed in Australia during World War II; and *A Breed Apart* (HBO), an adventure tale involving a naturalist's efforts to protect an endangered species of eagle.

The upcoming *Communion,* based on Whitney Schreiber's best-selling nonfiction account of his experiences with aliens and UFOs, represents Philippe Mora's most ambitious project to date. "This one," Mora promises, "will be totally serious."

tently twisty affair with some neat original set pieces, including a grisly ballet rehearsal and a movie wrap party invaded by a trio of werewolf nuns (!). Performances are uniformly fine, with Frank (*Mad Max Beyond Thunderdome*) Thring contributing an especially funny bit as a low-budget Hitchcock clone. The last two reels could do with some trimming and some of the makeup FX are pretty cheesy, but this one's a vast improvement over *Howling II* and well worth a rental.

The Human Monster (1939) ◆◆ B&W
D: *Walter Summers. Bela Lugosi, Hugh Williams, Greta Gynt. 73 minutes. (United, others)*

Based on an Edgar Wallace novel, this Britain-lensed Lugosi flick is more bleak than scary as Bela operates a home for the blind and operates *on* its sightless inhabitants.

The Hunchback of Notre Dame (1923) ◆◆◆ B&W

D: Wallace Worsley. Lon Chaney, Patsy Ruth Miller, Ernest Torrence. 99 minutes. (Cable)

Chaney plays the title role with a forty-eight-pound weight on his back. Well done throughout, but viewers unused to silent films may need a bit of patience.

The Hunchback of Notre Dame (1939) ◆◆◆ B&W

D: William Dieterle. Charles Laughton, Maureen O'Hara, Edmond O'Brien. 117 minutes. (RKO)

Still the definitive version of Hugo's novel, with Laughton not only poignant and menacing but *credible* as the ill-fated Quasimodo. Painstakingly detailed sets and crisp black-and-white cinematography likewise aid in making *Hunchback* a still-precious nugget from RKO's Golden Age.

The Hunger (1983) ◆◆◆

D: Tony Scott. David Bowie, Catherine Deneuve, Susan Sarandon. 100 minutes. (MGM/UA)

Bowie and Deneuve play decadent Fun Cityites who seek eternal life by draining the blood of others. Geriodontist Sarandon becomes Bowie's unwitting replacement in Scott's generally effective MTV-styled vampire variation.

Hush . . . Hush, Sweet Charlotte (1965) ◆◆◇

D: Robert Aldrich. Bette Davis, Olivia de Havilland, Joseph Cotten. 133 minutes. (Key)

Bette returned after her *Baby Jane* triumph as an aging, bonkers southern belle in a thriller that's decent but overlong and no match for the earlier flick.

I Dismember Mama (1974) NR

D: Paul Leder. Zooey Hall, Greg Mullavey. 88 minutes. (Simitar)

An undeniably great title for a cheap account of an oedipal wreck out to rid the world of sluts. Not to be confused with *Please Don't Eat My Mother* (NA).

I Eat Your Skin (1964) ◆ B&W

D: Del Tenney. William Joyce, Heather Hewitt, Walter Coy. 82 minutes. (Dixie)

Jerry Gross released this moldy Tenney terror turkey, originally titled *Voodoo Bloodbath*, on an infamous bijou double bill with the gory Mansonoid massacre movie *I Drink Your Blood* (Flamingo) back in 1971. Beware.

I Walked with a Zombie (1943) ◆◆◆◇

D: Jacques Tourneur. Frances Dee, Tom Conway, James Ellison, Edith Barrett, Christine Gordon, Sir Lancelot, Darby Jones. 69 minutes. (RKO)

The extremely fetching Frances Dee is Betsy, a Canadian nurse assigned to care for Jessica, the comatose wife of plantation owner Conway, on the gloomy Caribbean isle of San Sebastian, where the locals "cry when a child is born and make merry at burials." Is Jessica really a zombie, the victim of a voodoo curse? You'll enjoy finding out in this typically low-key but immensely disturbing Val Lewton chiller. You have to look closely to catch RKO's in-joke addition to the standard credit-sequence disclaimer: "Any similarity to actual persons, living, dead or *possessed* [!], is purely coincidental." Novelist/film critic James Agee recognized Lewton's genius early on and helped establish the latter's cult status long before the word was routinely applied to film-makers working the B-movie beat (see sidebar).

I Was a Teenage Zombie (1987) ◆◇
D: *John Elias Michalakias. Steve Mc-Coy, Michael Ruben, Cassie Madden, George Seminara, Cindy Keiter, Peter Bush. 92 minutes. (Charter)*

You know a flick has low aspirations when it goes out of its way to pay homage to the Troma Team, makers of such quality film fare as

FILMMAKERS IN FOCUS:
Val Lewton

RKO producer Val Lewton's 1940's fright-film series ranked as a sort of *Masterpiece Theater* of horror movies. At a time when Hollywood's reigning horror studio, Universal, was relying on slickly crafted but increasingly formulaic recyclings of their once-classic creatures (e.g., *Frankenstein Meets the Wolf Man*) and poverty-row outfits like Monogram and PRC were cranking out creaky quickies, Lewton navigated the genre in a new direction. Lewton rejected mad scientists and fright-masked monsters in favor of literate evocations of the silent and unseen, often tapping his own nightmares for inspiration.

An experienced fiction writer and former editorial assistant to David O. Selznick, the thirty-eight-year-old Russian-born (real name: Vladimir Leventon) producer signed on to oversee RKO's newly formed horror unit in 1942. Lewton was to have complete creative control as long as he agreed to work from the studio's sensationalistic, test-marketed titles (*Curse of the Cat People, I Walked With a Zombie*, et al.), to bring in his B films for less than $150,000 per, and to limit their length to 75 minutes. Assembling a creative team—directors Robert Wise, Mark Robson and Jacques Tourneur, scripter DeWitt Bodeen—that shared his vision, Lewton produced a series of moody cult classics that, despite their deliberately misleading monikers, rethought and revitalized the then-moribund horror genre.

Lewton left RKO in 1946 for a series of higher-paying but unsuccessful producing gigs at Paramount, Universal, and MGM. When he returned to RKO, he discovered that his power had been wrested by former protégés Wise, Robson, and Tourneur, who offered Lewton only a story editor position, then fired him from that. Lewton succumbed to a fatal heart attack in 1951, at the age of forty-six.

With the exception of 1943's *Ghost Ship* (unseen since its initial release due to an unresolved plagiarism suit), Lewton and crew's entire eerie oeuvre is now available on video.

Toxic Avenger, Splatter University (see index) and *Class of Nuke 'Em High* (Media). But that's just what Michalakias's *I Was a Teenage Zombie* does in naming an on-screen nuclear power plant spokesman after Troma prez Lloyd Kauffman. In all honesty, this highly derivative made-for-midnight (or vidnight) mix of '50s and '80s fright clichés is at least the equal of your average Troma effort, which is about as wild as we can get in terms of an endorsement. The pic—about a gang of typically overage high schoolers doing battle with an irradiated zombie drug dealer who won't take "just say no" for an answer—does offer scattered laughs (as when a paranoid doper excitedly relates, "I played a Duran Duran record backward, and you know what I heard? *Nothing!*"), along with a better-than-average face-ripping scene and a fairly hot rock soundtrack. Hard-core *Toxic Avenger* fans will probably like it; all others would be better off saving their bucks for the soundtrack LP.

Igor and the Lunatics (1985) 0 ♦
D: *Billy Parolini. Joseph Eero, Joe*
Niola, T. J. Michaels. 79 minutes. (Lightning)

Igor and the Lunatics has all the earmarks of a student film project (kindergarten students at that)—random footage full of minimalist filler, insipid dialogue, failed stabs at gore, and atrocious acting performed by a cast of unknowns destined to retain that status. The "plot"—set forth via a prolonged, anticinematic voice-over—involves a band of crazed '60s cultists who return to wreak revenge on the small town that turned them in some fifteen years earlier. The nonaction is set to a tone-deaf synthesizer soundtrack calculated to generate extreme irritation rather than "suspence" (as the typo-riddled credits refer to it). *Igor* represents exactly the kind of worthless rip-off a more competitive B-video market will hopefully eliminate in the future.

Impulse (1984) ♦♦♦
D: *Graham Baker. Tim Matheson, Meg Tilly, Hume Cronyn. 95 minutes. (Vestron)*

Toxic waste in the local milk supply makes hitherto normal townsfolk misbehave on a grand scale—like killing local kids—in a pic that doesn't fully exploit its promising premise but provides enough honestly perverse tableaux to qualify as worthwhile offbeat fright fare.

In the Shadow of Kilimanjaro (1986) ◆◆
D: Raju Patel. Timothy Bottoms, John Rhys-Davies, Irene Miracle, Michele Carey, Leonard Trolley, Calvin Jung. 97 minutes. (IVE)

In the tradition of such '50s animals-amok epics as *The Naked Jungle* (see index) and *Elephant Walk* (NA), *In the Shadow of Kilimanjaro* pits 90,000 killer baboons (!), driven mad by a drought, against a handful of natives and foreigners—the latter led by wildlife ranger Ringtree (blandly embodied by Bottoms), his yuppie wife Lee (Miracle), and mining contractor Tucker (Rhys-Davies). Since tensions among the various capable but uncharismatic cast members fail to catch fire, it's up to the peckish pongids to provide the pic with intermittent moments of excitement. Here, the Clint Rowe Animals (with "baboon voices created by Percy Edwards") definitely come through, attacking our isolated homo-saps and devouring them with gory efficiency. *In the Shadow of Kilimanjaro* purports to be based on a "true story" but supplies no evidence to verify that claim.

Inferno (1978/1985) ◆◆
D: Dario Argento. Leigh McCloskey, Irene Miracle, Sacha Pitoeff, Daria Nicolodi, Alida Valli, Veronica Lazar. 83 minutes. (Key)

Italo terror auteur Argento's *Inferno* follows in the earlier-lensed *Suspiria's* (see index) decidedly bloody footsteps in furthering the slim saga of the Three Mothers (alternately referred to as the Three Sisters), a mythical trio of distaff demons who orchestrate the world's evils from three separate, far-flung redoubts, including a stately old Fun City hotel. When curious young resident Miracle (prior to her close encounter with 90,000 killer baboons) of the last-mentioned establishment stumbles upon this sinister secret, all hell breaks loose. (And we mean that literally! So does Dario.) As usual, Argento is at his best when translating the surreal, time-suspended quality of nightmare to the screen, lensing his hallucinatory tableaux in vivid colors, particularly lurid purples and (natch) deep reds. There are a few knockout gross-out scenes on view, but Dario's lethargic storytelling, listless thesps, screeching soundtrack (courtesy of Keith Emerson), and deliberate (to put it charitably) pacing conspire to turn *Inferno* into a celluloid endurance test. Dario devotees should be warned that the video version omits a full 24 minutes from the screen print.

Inquisition (1976) ◆◆
D: Jacinto Molina (Paul Naschy). Paul Naschy, Daniela Giordano, Juan Luis Galiardo. 90 minutes. (Video City)

Euro-horror heavyweight Naschy (Jacinto Molina) directs himself in a slowly paced paean to pain and torture, as Spanish Inquisitors return from the grave to bedevil new victims. Pretty sick stuff, recommended solely for the hard-core gore set.

The Invisible Ghost (1941) ◆◆ B&W
D: Joseph H. Lewis. Bela Lugosi, Polly Ann Young, Clarence Muse. 64 minutes. (Video Yesteryear, others)

A pretty creaky Monogram quickie, with Lugosi spending most of his screen time staring out windows. Not as good as The Corpse Vanishes (see index); for Bela diehards only.

The Invisible Man (1933) ◆◆◆ B&W
D: James Whale. Claude Rains, Gloria Stuart, Una O'Connor. 71 minutes. (MCA)

More of a comedy/fantasy than a horror film, H. G. Wells's story is still fairly perverse, with a good perf by Rains as the scientist who loses his visibility and mind, in that order.

Isle of the Dead (1945) ◆◆◆ B&W
D: Mark Robson. Boris Karloff, Jason Robards, Ellen Drew, Marc Cramer. 72 minutes. (Fox Hills)

Boris is back for another atmospheric go-round with Lewton and company, this time cast as a Balkan army officer stranded, with an assortment of unlikely strangers, on a plague-endangered island. As usual, the horror is hinted at rather than openly revealed, but the fog-enshrouded ambience here provides genuine visual chills.

It's Alive (1974) ◆◆◆
D: Larry Cohen. John P. Ryan, Sharon Farrell, Andrew Duggan. 91 minutes. (Warner)

Cohen's breakthrough mutant-baby movie blames faulty fertility pharmaceuticals for causing normal couple Ryan and Farrell to procreate the title creature. Cohen again employs a fright format to deal with serious issues while still delivering the sicko goods in this recommended chiller. He continues the theme in the also-worthwhile sequels, 1978's It Lives Again (Warner) and It's Alive III: Island of the Alive.

It's Alive III: Island of the Alive (1988) ◆◆◆
D: Larry Cohen. Michael Moriarty, Karen Black, Laurene Landon, Gerrit Graham, Art Lund, MacDonald Carey. 95 minutes. (Warner)

Part the third of Cohen's killer-baby trilogy stars Moriarty as the concerned dad of one of five mutant infants who've been exiled to the title isle to protect them from a hostile world (and vice versa). After Moriarty exercises his visitation rights, the geekoid kids—who, at age six, are already reproducing!—follow him back to Florida, where they stage the flick's requisite gore rampage. While It's Alive III lacks the tight focus of its predecessors, it contains enough of auteur Cohen's patented perversity to make it a must for fright fans in general and for monster-baby-movie buffs in particular. Our only serious complaint is Moriarty's totally out-of-control performance: Mike chews so much scenery here that it's a wonder we weren't left with a blank screen by the end of reel one.

Jack the Ripper (1976) ♦♦
D: Jess Franco. Klaus Kinski, Josephine Chaplin, Lina Romay. 82 minutes. (Vestron)

A slow, gory Ripper revamp with the sinister Kinski appropriately crazed as Jack. For Kinski cultists and Francophiles. The earlier Ripper variation, the lyrically titled *He Kills Night After Night After Night*, is likewise on tape (Monterey).

Jack's Back (1988) ♦♦◊
D: Rowdy Herrington. James Spader, Cynthia Gibb, Rod Loomis, Rex Ryon, Chris Mulkey. 97 minutes. (Paramount)

Though it sounds like the most craven of clones, Herrington's *Jack's Back*—about a modern Ripper amok in L.A.—bears scant resemblance to Nicholas Meyer's *Time After Time* (see index) wherein the *real* Ripper time-tripped to modern 'Frisco, with H. G. Wells in pursuit. In fact, *Jack's Back* begins just as the current spate of Ripper-like hooker murders is about to *end*. The plot twists in an entirely different direction, into contempo thriller rather than gory Gothic horror

turf. And for a time, *Jack's Back* manages to generate considerable tension and surprise, as Spader scours both the streets of L.A. and his own subconscious for clues to the killer's (a) whereabouts and (b) ID. While the flick gradually grows too convoluted for its own good and fails to approach Meyer's 1979 variation, *Jack's Back* is very much worth a look. And director Rowdy Herrington ranks only behind *Young Einstein*'s Yahoo Serious and *Hide and Go Shriek*'s Skip Schoolnik in the Phantom's Most Memorable Auteur Names Sweepstakes.

Jaws the Revenge (1987) ♦◊
D: Joseph Sargent. Lance Guest, Lorraine Gray, Michael Caine, Mario Van Peebles, Karen Young. 87 minutes. (MCA)

The Phantom might as well 'fess up out front that he's never been a big killer-fish fan. He was bored by the original *Jaws* (MCA), and even the Black Lagoon's classic Creature pretty much leaves him cold. After skipping *Jaws 2* and *3-D* (both MCA), we came to grips with our aquaphobia by renting *Jaws the Revenge*—which, if nothing else, did make us better appreciate the original. This one, number four, plays like a made-for-TV hack job as a shark with brains and a motive (!) stalks *Jaws* survivor Gray and the rest of the Brody Bunch all the way to the Bahamas' warm waters, where wise sharks normally fear to tread, and the subaqueous slaughter begins anew. The only novel ingredient here is Mario Van Peebles's atrocious turn as a dreadlocked Jamaican scientist. Michael Caine literally drops in (he's a charter pilot) long enough to pick up a check. As of this writing, the Phantom harbors no plans to go back in the celluloid waters again. Oh yeah, according to the MCA box copy, *Jaws the Revenge* contains "new footage not seen in U.S. Theaters!" Lucky us.

Juggernaut (1936) NR B&W
D: Henry Edwards. Boris Karloff, Mona Goya. 64 minutes. (Video Yesteryear)

Boris is broke scientist Dr. Sartorius, who agrees to commit a murder in exchange for additional research funds. A pretty tame Brit mystery distinguished by Mr. K's dominating presence.

Junior (1986) ♦♦
D: Jim Henley. Linda Singer, Suzanne DeLaurentis, Jeremy Ratchford. 80 minutes. (Prism)

Though pitched as a chainsaw-psycho pic, *Junior* is far more concerned with the peripatetic adventures of KC and Jo (Singer, DeLaurentis), a pair of tough but winning bimbettes who, after gaining their prison release, rip off a pimp, steal his convertible, and tool off to Parts Unknown. Our feisty femmes ultimately (if unwisely) settle in a red-neck burg where they're forced to contend with hostile locals, including a sleazy sheriff and the thick-witted title geek (played by Ratchford). *Junior* traffics more in lovingly lensed soft-core jiggle action (our heroines never wear dresses when bikinis will do) than in hard-core gore, while Junior himself is strictly a second-rate sicko—he can take it but he can't dish it out—who spends much of his screen time consulting with his mute mom (portrayed, in a touch worthy of Ed Wood, Jr., by an ill-shaven *actor* in drag!). In short, slasher fans will rate *Junior* a total bust, but bust-and-bikini buffs may find it worth an overnight.

Keep My Grave Open (1979) ♦♦
D: S. F. Brownrigg. Gene Ross, Camilla Carr. 90 minutes. (Unicorn)

Regional auteur Brownrigg, earlier of the asylum-set chop-'em-up *Don't Look in the Basement* (MPI), at least succeeds in the atmosphere department with this low-budget psycho-killer pic starring Gene Ross of *Poor White Trash II* (see index) obscurity.

Kill, Baby, Kill (1966) ♦♦♦
D: Mario Bava. Erica Blanc, Fabienne Dali. 90 minutes. (Sinister Cinema)

This Euro-obscurity is actually one of Bava's best—an intensely atmospheric film about the vengeful ghost of a murdered little girl who returns to torture her assassins. Crammed with spectacular horror imagery, *Kill* prefigures Fellini's similarly themed sequence in *Spirits of the Dead* (NA).

Killer Party (1986) ◆◇
D: William Fruet. Martin Hewitt, Ralph Seymour, Elaine Wilkes, Paul Bartel, Sherry Willis-Burch, Alicia Fleer. 91 minutes. (Key)

Killer Party kicks off to a semi-promising start—a film-within-a-rock-video-within-a-film motif—but quickly drifts into yawnsville once our *real* story gets under way. Said stale tale, equally light on laughs and scares, involves lethal campus hazing high jinks that transpire during the titular bash, held on April Fool's Day. (Now, *that's* original!) While the production values here may be a notch above the slasher norm, this is still one party you'll want to leave early.

Killing Kind (1973) ◆◆◇
D: Curtis Harrington. John Savage, Ruth Roman, Cindy Williams, Ann Sothern. 95 minutes. (Paragon)

Curtis (*Night Tide*) Harrington crafts a relatively restrained psycho tale that further benefits from a name cast.

Killing of Satan (1975) ◆◆◇
D: Efron C. Pino. Ramon Revilla, Elizabeth Oroposa, George Estregan. 95 minutes. (Paragon)

A cheap but genuinely weird Catholic-influenced Filipino fear film, highlighted by a trip to hell, that's recommended for more adventurous horror viewers.

King Kong (1933) ◆◆◆◇ **B&W/Color**
D: Merian C. Cooper, Ernest B. Shoedsack. Fay Wray, Robert Armstrong, Bruce Cabot. 100 minutes. (RKO)

From Willis O'Brien's FX work to the feral charisma of cover-boy Kong, this mythic monster movie remains king of the Hollywood horror hill. Wray's leather lungs have lost none of their resonance; Armstrong, as fast-talking huckster Carl Denham, chews the scenery as thoroughly as Kong chews his crew; Cabot dashes nobly to the rescue, time and again; Noble Johnson turns in the greatest of his patented native-chieftain roles; and Kong accomplishes the seemingly impossible, threatening to reduce Fun City property values via a one-ape rampage. We subtracted half a phan for some less-than-necessary padding in the pic's early going (sorry, KK), but this one's still a monstrous must for any serious fright fan's permanent home-vid collection. Beware the blasphemous colorized version from Ted Turner's Turner/MGM/UA Video.

King Kong Lives (1986) ◆◆◇
D: John Guillermin. Linda Hamilton, Brian Kerwin, John Ashton, Peter Michael Goetz, Frank Maraden, Alan Sader. 105 minutes. (Lorimar)

The belated sequel to the DEG Group's useless *King Kong* (Paramount) remake of a decade ago, *King Kong Lives* posits that a comatose Kong survived his World Trade Center plummet in 1976 but needs giant-gorilla blood transfusions before his body can accept the outsize artificial heart designed by Atlanta University doc Hamilton. Meanwhile, back on Kong Island, a cut-rate Indiana Jones (Kerwin) captures Lady Kong and peddles her to Linda, who uses her blood for the operation. To make a slow story fast, the King awakes and springs his mate, and together they flee Atlanta for an idyllic romp in rural Honeymoon Ridge (!). Any comparisons with the original 1933 *King Kong* would leave *King Kong Lives* barely breathing, but our celebrity apes—alternately formidable and poignant—supply some fun, far outshining Kerwin/Hamilton's parallel romance, and the King kicks enough homo-sap butt to keep fans glued to their seats.

King of the Zombies (1941) ◆◆◇ **B&W**
D: *Jean Yarbrough. John Archer, Mantan Moreland, Dick Purcell, Joan Woodbury. 67 minutes. (Sinister Cinema)*

Black comedian Moreland carries the day in this otherwise wooden back-lot chiller. The pic's offhand but relentless racism (which extends to Irishman Purcell as well) is truly appalling, though Mantan manages to transcend. Like many '30s and '40s B movies, this one is more interesting as sociology than as horror. Sinister Cinema stocks the uncut edition.

The Kiss (1988) ◆◆
D: *Pen Densham. Joanna Pacula, Meredith Salenger, Nicholas Kil-bertus, Mimi Kuzyk, Jan Rubes. 105 minutes. (RCA/Columbia)*

Tough times for troubled teen Amy Halloran (appealingly portrayed by Salenger)—her mom's been mashed by a runaway RV, her best friend's been mauled by a mall escalator, and her dad's been scratched by a ferocious feline from hell. And that's only the beginning of the hapless Halloran clan's calamities when Amy's voodoo vampire-queen Aunt Felice (Pacula) decides to pay a deadly visit. Densham's Albany-set, Canada-lensed horror flick delivers its fair share of decent scares in the early going before careering headlong into dangerously stupid terrain that finds Aunt Felice—aided by FX maven Chris Walas—performing increasingly elaborate terror tricks in her venomous quest to steal young Amy's innocent soul. If little else, *The Kiss* tries hard, and its earnest plunge into over-the-top hysteria supplies enough flamboyantly bad entertainment to make it worth a rental for those in the right frame of mindlessness.

Kung-Fu Zombie (1981) ◆◆◇
D: *Hwa I. Hung. Billy Chong, Chan Lau, Chiang Tao. 92 minutes. (Ocean)*

Not as good as its title—then again, how *could* it be?—this off-the-wall mix of martial arts, monsters, and low slapstick comedy will be appreciated by fans of kung-fu surrealism, who should also try the same vid-outfit's superior ghost-and-voodoo scarefests *Brutal Sorcery* and *The Demons* (see index), as well as Saturn's *Dragon Against Vampire*, and Ocean's *Kung Fu from Beyond the Grave*, and truly bizarre *Kung-Fu Vampire Busters*.

Lady Frankenstein (1971) ◆◆

D: Mel Welles. Sarah Bay, Joseph Cotten, Mickey Hargitay. 84 minutes. (Embassy)

Bay is the scientist daughter of Baron F. (Cotten), who carries on dad's demented experiments. A fully clothed Mickey Hargitay investigates. Directed by Mel Welles, of *Little Shop of Horrors* fame.

Lady in White (1988) ◆◆◆

D: Frank LaLoggia. Lukas Haas, Len Cariou, Alex Rocco, Katherine Helmond, Jason Presson, Renata Vanni. 112 minutes. (Virgin Vision)

A strange mélange of the good, the bad, and the self-indulgent, LaLoggia's *Lady in White* ranges from trite to pretentious to downright brilliant. This ambitious one-man project (LaLoggia wrote, produced, directed, and composed the music), a ghost story with a psycho subplot, relates nine-year-old Haas's encounter with the wandering spirit of a little girl murdered a decade earlier by a still-rampaging serial killer. *The Lady in White* is at its best when LaLoggia applies a Val Lewton–like approach to his intricate fright material, powerfully conveying, via evocative writing and inspired imagery, a feeling of pervasive menace roiling just beneath the surface of Haas's small-town life—a life outwardly normal but for death's frequent, irrational intrusions. Unfortunately, LaLoggia often undermines his own surest instincts with ill-advised stabs at low humor, strained whimsy, and—worst of all—commercial-minded Hollywood hackery. While this allegorical chiller is simultaneously frustrating and unforgettable, it remains a must for genre fans and a good bet for anyone in the market for something potent and different. LaLoggia's earlier fright entry, *Fear No Evil* (Embassy), is also worth a look.

Lair of the White Worm (1988) ◆◆◆◇

D: Ken Russell. Amanda Donohue, Hugh Grant, Catherine Oxenberg, Sammi Davis, Peter Capaldi, Stratford Johns. 93 minutes. (Vestron)

Terminally febrile Brit filmmaker Russell fully atones for his largely groan-provoking *Gothic* with a wild parody that sends up the complete catalog of monster-movie clichés old and new in an outing that's actually enhanced by Russell's usual loony overlay of demented erotic-religious imagery. Our story, loosely (if not downright promiscuously) based on Bram (*Dracula*) Stoker's final novel, concerns a quartet of young English locals who stumble upon the title site *and* a venomous, vampiric snake-woman, the aristocratic Lady Sylvia. Of our fearless foursome, Davis especially impresses as the pic's petite but feisty blond heroine, while Donohue contributes a fine, sexy turn as the serpentine seductress Sylvia. Director Russell keeps a firm grip on the improbable ins and absurdist outs of his mock-serious story line. Deadpan visual and verbal puns abound, and the flick is further abetted by generous doses of gratuitous nudity and cheap but gaudy gore FX. This lusty fright lampoon supplies more than enough perverse, high-camp horror-pic fun to rate as essential video viewing.

The Last Horror Film (1982) ♦♦
D: David Winters. Joe Spinell, Caroline Munro, David Winters. 87 minutes. (Media)

Joe (*Maniac*) Spinell stalks horror-screen queen Munro at Cannes . . . and you are *there!*

Last House on the Left (1972) 0 ♦
D: Wes Craven. David Hess, Lucy Grantham, Fred Lincoln. 83/91 minutes. (Vestron)

Never one of the Phantom's faves, this generally repulsive and thoroughly amateurish cult item has gained nothing in the way of charm in its video incarnation, despite the unrated cassette's "Newly Discovered Scenes of Terror!" Still, it made millions and the careers of producer Sean Cunningham and director Craven. Also available in an R version.

The Last Wave (1977) ♦♦◇
D: Peter Weir. Richard Chamberlain, David Gulpilil, Olivia Hamnett. 104 minutes. (Warner)

An interesting if ultimately unsatisfying chiller about an Aussie lawyer (Chamberlain) who becomes involved with Aboriginal magic, courtesy of his accused-killer client Gulpilil.

The Legacy (1979) NR
D: Richard Marquand. Katharine Ross, Sam Elliott, Roger Daltrey. 100 minutes. (MCA)

A modern *Old Dark House* (NA) variation, with a group of strangers—The Who's Daltrey among them—stranded in a London mansion, where occult murders unfold.

The Legend of Hell House (1973) ♦♦◇
D: John Hough. Roddy McDowall, Pamela Franklin, Clive Revill. 94 minutes. (CBS/Fox)

Richard Matheson's script hoists this decent if unspectacular pre-*Poltergeist* tale of flying furniture and similar telekinetic terrors witnessed by a team of parapsychologists. The electronic score represents another plus, though Randy Newman's "Short People" would have made for a more appropriate closer.

Legend of the Seven Golden Vampires (1974) ♦♦♦
D: Roy Ward Baker. Peter Cushing, David Chiang, Julie Ege. 89 minutes. (Sinister Cinema)

Vampire tracker Van Helsing (Cushing) treks to nineteenth-century China, where he takes on Dracula with the help of a kung-fu crew (!). Pretty unique. Also exists in a shorter, less entertaining version titled *Seven Brothers Meet Dracula.* (AIR) Bevare!

Legend of the Werewolf (1975) ◆◆
D: Freddie Francis. Peter Cushing, Ron Moody, Hugh Griffith. 87 minutes. (Interglobal)

France-set lycanthropic effort offers little in the way of new ideas or situations, but hard-core Cushing fans might find it worth checking out. *Legend of the Wolfwoman* (United), meanwhile, offers equal time for the distaff lupine set (also out as *She Wolf* [Magnum]), while fans of hirsute hog-hound horrors can check out the not-so-self-explanatory *Werewolves on Wheels* (Unicorn).

The Leopard Man (1943) ◆◆◆ B&W
D: Jacques Tourneur. Dennis O'Keefe, Margo, Jean Brooks. 66 minutes. (Fox Hills)

Val Lewton returns to his trusty feline fright theme: A series of brutal Southwest slayings may or may not be the handiwork of an escaped circus leopard. The blood-under-the-door sequence, considered shocking in its day, still packs a punch in this nearly seamless, streamlined creature feature.

Let's Scare Jessica to Death (1971) ◆◆◆
D: John Hancock. Zohra Lampert, Kevin O'Connor, Barton Heyman. 89 minutes. (Paramount)

The title is admirably upfront re: what this non-gory but thoroughly sadistic thriller's about as conspirators conjure all manner of terrors to loosen unstable Lampert's cerebral screws.

The Lost Boys (1987) ◆◆
D: Joel Schumacher. Jason Patric, Corey Haim, Dianne Wiest, Barnard Hughes, Ed Herrmann, Kiefer Sutherland, Jami Gertz. 92 minutes. (Warner)

Another desperate entry in the Teen-Monsters-Amok genre, *The Lost Boys* finds widow Lucy (well limned by Wiest) and adolescent sons Mike and Sam (Patric and Haim) relocating to eccentric Grandpa's (Hughes) redoubt in sinister Santa Carla, California. Lured by the lovely young Gertz, Mike soon falls under the spell of the title crowd, a motley crew of MTV vampires led by Sutherland. It's up to savvy younger sibling Sam to save misled Mike from a fate worse than death—i.e., *un*death. Not half as much fun as Tom Holland's *Fright Night* (see index), from which it liberally borrows, *The Lost Boys* quickly degenerates into the usual half-baked Hollywood blend of glitzy rock-vid visuals, souped-up sit-com dialogue (including a raft of "old hippie" jokes), regurgitated junk-culture riffs, and elaborate but empty FX—all set to your standard ear-pounding soundtrack. In short, lotsa flash, few surprises, and even less true wit.

The Love Butcher (1975/1982) ◆◆◆
D: Mikel Angel, Don Jones. Erik Stern, Kay Neer, Robin Sherwood. 84 minutes. (Monterey)

Stern *is* Caleb, geeky gardener at a 'burb complex. He's also Caleb's self-described "male Adonis" twin brother Lester, a local stud of legendary proportions. Trouble is, only one of them is still alive. This clever, blackly comic schizo thriller, which sat on the shelf for seven years before receiving limited theatrical play in '82, has a lot to say re: male attitudes toward the opposite sex, as Lester systematically seduces and slays the women who've blithely rejected his hapless bitter half Caleb. To reveal more would be to risk ruining a genuinely entertaining, thoroughly sick sleeper.

Love Me Deadly (1972) ◆◇
D: Jacques La Certe. Mary Wilcox, Lyle Waggoner, Christopher Stone. 95 minutes. (Video Gems)

And speaking of sick—this exercise in *incestuous* necrophilia (!), while less splatterific, can take its rightful place beside *Buried Alive* (see index) in the all-time Mondo Pervo Sweepstakes. As morbid as they come.

Love Thrill Murders (1971) ◆◇
D: Bob Roberts. Troy Donahue, Renay Granville, Francine Middleton. 89 minutes. (Vestron)

Troy Donahue, already some distance from his *Summer Place/ Parrish* Warner Bros. days, plays a Mansonoid killer in a fairly hideous trashfest originally released as *Sweet Savior*. For Donahue diehards only.

The Mad Monster (1942) ◆◆ B&W
D: Sam Newfield. Johnny Downs, George Zucco, Glenn Strange. 72 minutes. (Sinister Cinema)

This PRC production is so impoverished that its paucity of production values actually enhances its bleak mood; in fact, it's downright depressing, despite the campy antics of mad doc Zucco and his moronic monster Strange.

Madhouse Mansion (1974) ◆◆
D: Stephen Weeks. Marianne Faithfull, Leigh Lawson, Anthony Bate. 86 minutes. (Cinema Group)

An obscure ghost story (*Ghost Story* was, in fact, its original title), about three Brit college boys stranded in a haunted house, circa 1928. Decently done but fairly slow going.

The Man Who Lived Again (1936) ◆◆◆ B&W
D: Robert Stevenson. Boris Karloff, John Loder, Anna Lee. 61 minutes. (Sinister Cinema)

A superior Boris vehicle, lensed in England, with Karloff as a surgeon who switches patients' personalities and brains—hence the original Brit title, *The Man Who Changed His Mind*.

Maniac (1962) NR B&W
D: Michael Carreras. Kerwin Mathews, Nadia Gray, Donald Houston. 87 minutes. (RCA/Columbia)

A well-regarded *Psycho* clone, with Mathews as an artist who arouses the ire of his French girlfriend's demented ex. Only hardcore gorehounds, on the other hand, would want to sit through Joe Spinell's 1982 sicko melodrama of the same title (Media).

Maniac Cop (1988) ◆◆◆
D: William Lustig. Tom Atkins, Bruce Campbell, Lurene Landon, Richard Roundtree, William Smith, Sheree North, Robert Zdar. 88 minutes. (TWE)

Prolific B-movie maverick Larry Cohen, who wrote and produced *Maniac Cop* (Lustig handled directorial chores), once again displays his patented flair for taking a simple but solid premise and cleverly exploiting every story hook with wit and style. The plot peg here finds the mysterious title character—a psycho killer-cop played by the hulking Zdar (previously seen as the psycho cop-*killer* in *The Night Stalker*—see index)—rapidly reducing Gotham's population via his nocturnal slaughter sprees, while frightened citizens respond by shooting innocent cops on sight (!) (an angle that could have been explored more fully here). Cohen also pens *human*-sounding dialogue and boasts a great cast of B-movie veterans to deliver it. Tom (*Night of the Creeps*) Atkins as the detective assigned to the case, Bruce (*Evil Dead II*) Campbell as the honest flatfoot wrongly accused of the crimes, Richard

Shaft) Roundtree and Big Bill Smith as police officials, and Laurene (*Yellow Hair*) Landon and Sheree North as distaff officers. While occasionally weakened by its low budget, some slapdash filmmaking, and an open-ended climax, *Maniac Cop*, like its massive villain, stands at least a head taller than most of its recent genre competition. Not to be confused with the mediocre actioner *Crazed Cop* (Unicorn).

The Manster (1962) ◆◆◆ B&W
D: George D. Breakston, Kenneth Crone. Peter Dyneley, Jane Hylton, Satoshi Nakamura. 72 minutes. (J&J)

One of our fave obscurities: an Occidental journalist in Japan discovers a second head growing from his shoulder! Turns out it's no brighter than the one that's already there. Shot on location but in English. A must.

Mark of the Devil (1971) ◆◆
D: Michael Armstrong. Herbert Lom, Udo Kier, Olivera Vuco. 96 minutes. (Vestron)

A case of a great ad campaign —including free barf-bags!— camouflaging a shoddy movie about a misogynistic murderer who slaughters women he thinks are witches. The related-in-name-only *Mark of the Devil II* is also available (Video Dimensions).

Mark of the Vampire (1935) ◆◆◇ B&W
D: Tod Browning. Bela Lugosi, Lionel Barrymore, Lionel Atwill. 61 minutes. (MGM/UA)

Tod (*Freaks*) Browning does a nice atmospheric job with this *London After Midnight* (NA) remake that further benefits from fine perfs delivered by a couple of Lionels (Atwill and Barrymore). Unfortunately, it's all an elaborate hoax, as *Mark* contorts itself to the point of breaking to avoid being an actual horror film. Red-herring Bela's few lines at flick's end are eerily prophetic.

Martin (1978) ◆◆◆
D: George Romero. John Amplas, Lincoln Maazel, Christine Forrest, Tom Savini. 96 minutes. (HBO)

Romero devises a new twist on traditional vampire lore: John Amplas is an otherwise sympathetic adolescent who happens to be addicted to human blood, and is willing to kill for it. An impressive, offbeat approach to modern horror.

The Masque of the Red Death (1964) ◆◆◆
D: Roger Corman. Vincent Price, Hazel Court, Jane Asher, David Weston, Patrick Magee, Skip Martin. 88 minutes. (Lightning)

The best of Corman's Edgar Allan Poe adaptations, *Masque of the Red Death* is probably Rog's greatest directorial effort *ever*, actually reaching into Ingmar Bergman territory—especially in those eerily poignant tableaux showing a crimson-cloaked Death marching wearily but inevitably through ravaged, fog-shrouded woods.

Price essays the decadent, sadistic devil-worshipping Prince Prospero, who gathers his fellow nobles at his castle for what proves to be a final round of degenerate revels as the Plague steals ever nearer. While there are touches of humor here—as when Prospero, busy tormenting the local peasants, sighs, "I have to do everything myself!"—*Masque* is a generally somber affair reeking of doomed amorality. Aiding immeasurably are the contributions of set designer Daniel Haller, who works miracles on a modest budget here, and cinematographer Nicolas Roeg, who soon went on to outclass Corman by directing such stylishly bizarre cult faves as *Performance* and *Don't Look Now* (see index). Despite its occasionally slow stretches, *Masque* is a movie that's not to be missed.

Midnight (1983) NR
D: John Russo. Lawrence Tierney, Melanie Verlin, John Amplas. 88 minutes. (Vidmark)

Fright novelist and Romero associate Russo directs a low-budget, paranoia-provoking story of a hapless teen who escapes from her abusive father (Tierney), only to encounter far worse.

Mill of the Stone Women (1960) ◆◆◇
D: Giorgio Ferroni. Pierre Brice, Wolfgang Preiss, Dany Carrel. 95 minutes. (Paragon)

An exceedingly slow, arty Gothic horror about a mad doc who drains blood from local femmes and transfuses it into his ailing daughter. Strong on atmosphere and composition, if not on suspense.

The Monster Club (1981) ♦♦◇
D: Roy Ward Baker. Vincent Price, John Carradine, Donald Pleasence. 97 minutes. (IVE)

Journalist Carradine journeys to a Transylvanian disco (!), where he pumps vampire/author Price for three macabre tales of varying quality. Worth watching for the cast alone.

The Monster from the Ocean Floor (1954) ♦◇ B&W
D: Wyott Ordung. Stuart Wade, Anne Kimball, Jonathan Haze. 64 minutes. (Vidmark)

Roger Corman's movie debut (as producer) is a mostly dull seagoing cheapie about a rarely seen cyclopean marine monster. Rog also acts in the pic, doubtless to save on casting costs; so does scripter/director Wyott Ordung (as a none-too-convincing Mexican), who made a more lasting celluloid contribution by scripting the immortal *Robot Monster* (see index) the previous year.

Monster Hunter (1982) ♦♦
D: Peter Newton. Edmond Purdom, George Eastman, Annie Belle. 90 minutes. (Lightning)

An Italo *Halloween* clone, with Purdom as a priest in pursuit of a superhuman psycho. Pretty grisly.

Monster in the Closet (1987) ♦♦♦
D: Bob Dahlin. Donald Grant, Denise

DuBarry, Henry Gibson, Claude Akins, Stella Stevens, Howard Duff, Paul Dooley, John Carradine, Jesse White, Paul Walker. 85 minutes. (Lorimar)*

Dahlin's *Monster in the Closet* amiably spoofs the entire array of ripe '50s creature-feature clichés while retaining much of the same charm that informed those low-budget fright faves of yore. A once-in-a-lifetime lineup of B-movie greats—in parts ranging from eye-blink cameos (Stevens, Dooley, Carradine, White) to more substantial roles (Gibson as an Einsteinian scientist, Duff as a priest, Akins as a bullheaded small-town sheriff)—contributes mightily to the fun. Grant and DuBarry likewise score as the eager young reporter and prim biology teacher, respectively, out to foil the mysterious title monster (one of your better man-in-a-gray-rubber-suit creations), while young Paul Walker gives a winning performance as a mechanical prodigy dubbed The Professor. Withal, a small-scale but entertaining and affectionate send-up.

The Monster Maker (1944) ♦♦◇ B&W
D: Sam Newfield. J. Carrol Naish, Ralph Morgan, Wanda McKay. 62 minutes. (Cable)

An authentically creepy flick that finds mad scientist Naish afflicting victim Morgan with disfiguring acromegaly (the disease that horror star Rondo Hatton suffered from). Pretty sick for its time.

Lloyd Kaufman and Michael Herz present A Troma Team Release

MONSTER
IN THE CLOSET

CLOSET ENCOUNTERS: Closet creature wants a word with pre-teen genius The Professor (Paul Walker) in a typically gripping scene from Bob Dahlin's affectionate '50s fright-film send-up, *Monster in the Closet*.
Photo courtesy of Troma, Inc.

The Monster of Piedras Blancas (1957) ◆◆◇ B&W

D: Irvin Berwick. Les Tremayne, Forrest Lewis, Don Sullivan. 71 minutes. (Video Dimensions)

Relatively gruesome for its day, this one has the title monster—an uglier version of the *Creature From the Black Lagoon*—terrorizing inhabitants of a remote lighthouse. Perennial Z-movie teen hero Sullivan is on hand to save the day. Surprisingly atmospheric, *Monster* has also developed an avid video following.

The Monster Squad (1987) ◆◆

D: Fred Dekker. Andre Gower, Robby Kiger, Stephen Macht, Duncan Regehr, Tom Noonan, Brent Chalem. 82 minutes. (Vestron)

A sort of updated *Our Gang Meets the Monsters, Monster Squad* is the brainchild of Fred (*Night of the Creeps*) Dekker and prototypical "hot young screenwriter" Shane (*Lethal Weapon*) Black. The plot pits the title pack of Mall-American kids against an all-star creature quintet composed of Dracula, the Wolfman, the Mummy, the Gill-Man, and Frankenstein's Monster (played by tall Tom Noonan, who earlier impressed as the psycho geek in *Manhunter*). While brimming with spectacular effects work (courtesy of busy monster-maker Stan Winston and FX ace Richard Edlund), *Monster Squad* offers few riffs we haven't seen before. Maybe we've overdosed on Hollywoodoid twelve-year-olds with unchecked Type-A personalities, but the Phantom soon found himself rooting for the monsters.

The Most Dangerous Game (1932) ◆◆◆ B&W

D: Ernest B. Shoedsack, Irving Pichel. Joel McCrea, Fay Wray, Robert Armstrong, Leslie Banks. 63 minutes. (Kartes/Cable)

The best of countless credited and uncredited versions of Richard Connell's tale of a mad hunter and his human prey. Lensed simultaneously with *King Kong* (see index), with many of the same thesps.

Motel Hell (1980) ◆◆◇

D: Kevin Connor. Rory Calhoun, Paul Linke, Nancy Parsons. 102 minutes. (MGM/UA)

Calhoun hits the comeback trail as meatman Farmer Vincent in a gory horror spoof that alternates between true wit and broad antics and should have been a lot leaner. Listen for Rory's famous last words.

Mother's Day (1980) ◆◆

D: Charles Kaufman. Tiana Pierce, Nancy Hendrickson, Deborah Luce. 98 minutes. (Video Treasures)

Another horror-cult fave in a *Texas Chainsaw Massacre* vein, as abused ex-coeds strike back at two nitwit psycho siblings and their demented mom. Warren Leight's satirical script affords some fun before falling back on oedipal-genre clichés.

Mountaintop Motel Massacre (1986) ◊
D: Jim McCullough, Sr. Bill Thurman, Anna Chappell, Will Mitchell, Virginia Loridans, Major Brock, James Bradford. 95 minutes. (New World)

Brought to you by the celluloid father-and-son team of Jim Mc-Cullough, Sr. (producer/director) and Jr. (scripter/co-producer), *Mountaintop Motel Massacre* stars former Larry Buchanan regular Thurman (best remembered as the cackling cracker mad scientist in LB's atrocious *It's Alive!*—[Loonic]) as Reverend McWilley, one of several deserving victims of the singularly unscary Evelyn (Chappell), a dumpy middle-aged maniac. Despite the pic's ungrammatical (though memorable) tag line ("Please do not disturb Evelyn. She *already* is."), Ev ranks among the most *un*menacing psychos in slasher-film history. Evelyn and the title site's assortment of snakes, rats, and roaches keep the doomed cast of mostly amateur actors awake over the dreary course of one dark and stormy night, but we doubt this soporific one-set wonder will do the same for you. The chief vacancy here, we're afraid, resides between the McCulloughs' ears.

The Mummy (1932) ◆◆◆ B&W
D: Karl Freund. Boris Karloff, Zita Johann, David Manners. 72 minutes. (MCA)

Boris (billed as "Karloff the Uncanny") steals the horror show here via his solemn portrayal of ancient Egyptian high priest Im-Ho-Tep, who returns to violent life following a 3,700-year snooze. Freund imbues the eerie proceedings with a darkly hallucinatory quality, while young archaeologist Bramwell Fletcher delivers the best onscreen nervous breakdown we've ever seen.

The Mummy (1959) ◆◆◊
D: Terence Fisher. Peter Cushing, Christopher Lee, Yvonne Furneaux. 88 minutes. (Warner)

While essentially a back-lot hack job, Hammer's remake is such a thoroughly *professional* pulp project that it's fun to watch anyway. Cushing is typically crisp as the tomb-desecrating archaeologist, though Lee doesn't get to do much with his limited Mummy role.

Munchies (1987) ◆
D: Bettina Hirsch. Harvey Korman, Charles Stratton, Nadine Van Der Velde, Alix Elias, Charlie Phillips, Hardy Rawls. 85 minutes. (MGM/UA)

A would-be creature comedy in a well-worn *Gremlins/Critters/Ghoulies* groove, this depressingly witless exercise involves several jive-talking Peruvian puppet monsters (you know the type) who return to life in Texas. There they harass junk-food/toxic-waste mogul Korman, who manages to rise above the pic's Crayola-scrawled script and point-the-Panaflex-and-pray direction. The rest of the cast, save for a 30-second bit by Paul

Bartel, proves as lame as the material. In short, *Munchies* is permanently out to lunch.

My Best Friend Is a Vampire (1988) ◆◇
D: Jimmy Huston. Robert Sean Leonard, Cheryl Pollak, David Warner, Rene Auberjonois, Evan Mirand, Fannie Flagg. 90 minutes. (HBO)

Yet another assembly-line teen horror-comedy hybrid in the less-than-grand tradition of *Vamp*, *I Was a Teenage Zombie*, et al., etc., ad nauseam and/or infinitum, the Houston-lensed *My Best Friend Is a Vampire* casts Leonard as a high-schooler who, in short order, is nipped by a seductive femme bloodsucker, instructed in the vampire life-style by undead guide Auberjonois and relentlessly pursued by a rabid vampire-hunter, played by an understandably uninspired Warner. While *Vampire* is less obnoxious than many of its teen-terror antecedents and manages to work in a few genuine laughs, the film is synthetic to the core, existing solely to lure a few bucks from unwary vidstore browsers.

My Demon Lover (1987) ◆◆
D: Charles Loventhal. Scott Valentine, Michelle Little, Arnold Johnson, Robert Trebor, Alan Fudge, Gina Gallego. 86 minutes. (RCA/Columbia)

Self-confessed "schlub" Denny (winningly played by the petite Little) falls in love with amiable lowlife Kaz (*Family Ties'* Valentine), only to discover that, due to an arcane Romanian curse, the mere thought of sex is enough to transform him into a literal demon. To its credit, *Demon* eschews the trite teen antics of a *Once Bitten* or *Teen Wolf*—the central characters are well into their twenties here—and adopts an advisably throwaway approach to its slender material. A talented cast—including Arnold (*Putney Swope*) Johnson—keep the proceedings from turning totally dull, and some of the makeup FX are fairly imaginative. But a lack of consistent comic invention reduces *My Demon Lover* to the watchable at best.

Mystery of the Wax Museum (1933) ◆◆◆◇
D: Michael Curtiz. Lionel Atwill, Fay Wray, Glenda Farrell. 77 minutes. (MGM/UA)

The inspiration for the later *3-D House of Wax* (see index), this early Technicolor outing boasts great sets, swift pacing, pre-Code candor, and a vivid performance by Atwill as the mad sculptor. A Golden Age fright film worthy of the name, with Fay supplying the screams and Glenda the wisecracks.

Nail Gun Massacre (1985) NR
D: Terry Loftin. Rocky Patterson, Ron Queen, Michelle Meyer. 90 minutes. (Magnum)

"It's Cheaper Than a Chainsaw!" They mean the movie, not the nail gun.

Near Dark (1987) ◆◆◆
D: Kathryn Bigelow. Adrian Pasdar, Jenny Wright, Lance Henriksen, Bill

Paxton, Jenette Goldstein, Tim Thomerson. 95 minutes. (HBO)

A vampire revamp of *Bonnie and Clyde*, Bigelow's *Near Dark* is a high-concept combo of the rural outlaw and vampire genres starring *Aliens* alumni Henriksen and Goldstein as the leaders of a gang of fanged red-necks who leave their victims' throats a similar hue. Accompanied by new inductee Caleb (Pasdar), an innocent Oklahoma ranch boy recruited by cute blond bloodsucker May (Wright), they steal cars, run up an impressive nightly body count, and keep one step ahead of both the law and the light. *Near Dark* features great trashy locations (from seedy motels to funky roadside dives), stylish direction, and enough blood to paint a small town red. The flick's only serious flaws are its often arbitrary alterations of established screen vampire lore and co-scripter Eric (*The Hitcher*) Red's bad habit of ripping off *The Terminator* for his endings. Those objections aside, *Near Dark* stands as a tense, sadistic, genuinely scary, and downright degenerate entertainment, one whose rep has deservedly grown during its video afterlife. A vast improvement over Bigelow's pretentious would-be cult debut feature, *The Loveless* (Media).

The Newlydeads (1988) ◆◇
D: Joseph Merhi. Jim Williams, Jean Levine, Jay Richardson, Roxanna Michaels, Scott Kaske, Captain Mike. 90 minutes. (City Lights)

A direct-to-home-vid horror quickie from the prolific folks at City Lights (who churn out highly avoidable hack action cheapies—like *Murder Rap, Heat Street, L.A. Crack Down I* and *II*, and the electrifying *Dance or Die*—literally by the dozens), *The Newlydeads* gets off to a decent start with transvestite Kaske driving solo to a honeymoon motel while "Spooky" plays on the car radio. A sexual misunderstanding prompts paunchy motel owner Williams to murder the innocent TV, who returns fifteen years later to haunt said owner on *his* wedding night by gore-killing his guests. One of the latter (Levine) happens to be an amateur psychic who's hip to what's happening. Alas, it's all downhill from there, as director Merhi relies on low comic relief and repetitious slaughter scenes to pad his increasingly plotless pic to feature length. Some of the same cast members return for City Lights' *Epitaph*, but we'd suggest you exercise better judgment.

Night of Bloody Horror (1969) ◆◇
D: Joy N. Houck. Gerald McRaney, Gaye Yellen, Evelyn Hendricks. 81 minutes. (Paragon)

A cheap, Catholic-themed *Psycho* rip-off, lensed in "ViolentVision" (!), that does include one classically sick confessional scene. With Gerald McRaney, later of *Simon & Simon* fame.

Night of 1000 Cats (1971) ◆◆◇
D: Rene Cardona. Anjanette Comer,

Hugo Stiglitz, Zulma Faiad. 83 minutes. (Paragon)

À la T. V. Mikels's *The Corpse Grinders* (see index), humans are ground into hamburger and fed to the title felines (who appear to number closer to fifty than the advertised thousand) in this unintentionally rib-tickling Mexican horror from the auteur who brought us *Night of the Bloody Apes* (see index). Also out as *Blood Feast* (not to be confused with H. G. Lewis's pioneering splatterfest) on the Academy label.

Night of the Demons (1988) ◆◇
D: Kevin S. Tenney. William Gallo, Hal Havins, Linnea Quigley, Mimi Kinkade, Cathy Podewell. 89 minutes. (Republic)

Night of the Demons, formerly titled *Halloween Party*, is yet another stereotypical-teens-turn-into-demons-in-a-haunted-house adventure. At the urging of "weird" cohort Angela (Kinkade), several overage high school party-animals—including your standard bimbos, punks, and one Fonz imitator (Gallo)—decide to stage a Halloween bash at a local haunted manse (actually a rather obvious miniature). The party proceeds with mindless, if rather mild, abandon until one of the teens takes lyrical note of "the noise, the stink, and the chill" (which, if little else, would have made for a more memorable title than the generic *Night of the Demons*). One by one, our revelers transform into drooling demons and start knocking each other off. Director Tenney, who fared far better with his earlier *Witchboard* (see index), does what he can to keep *Demons* moving but is done in by an unimaginative script riddled with obnoxious brain-dead dialogue. Aside from some decent though predictable FX and a neat animated opening-credits sequence, *Night of the Demons'* sole saving grace is the always-welcome presence of dependable B-screen scream queen Linnea (*Return of the Living Dead, Hollywood Chainsaw Hookers*) Quigley, who makes a memorable rearview entrance here and sticks around long enough to perform one of her patented topless scenes before transmogrifying into a screeching devil-creature further burdened by poor orthodontal work.

Night of the Howling Beast (1975) ◆◆
D: M. I. Bonns. Paul Naschy, Grace Mills, Gil Vidal. 95 minutes. (Super)

Naschy (Jacinto Molina) scripts and stars in this Spanish horror that opens with a striking moment of cross-cultural confusion—an establishing shot of London accompanied by a rousing bagpipe rendition of "Scotland the Brave" (!). Otherwise, it's a fairly desperate Naschy lycanthrope adventure that also works in a ludicrous Yeti plot. Still, Naschy is not without his fans; the latter can also catch their Catalan fright fave in *Beyond the Living Dead* (Unicorn), *The Craving* (Vestron), *Crimson* (TWE), *Dr. Jekyll and the*

Werewolf (Sinister Cinema), *Dracula's Great Love* (MPI), *Fury of the Wolfman* (Unicorn), *The Hanging Woman* and *Horror Rises from the Tomb* (both WesternWorld), *The Mummy's Revenge* (Unicorn), *Rue Morgue Massacres* (All Seasons), and *Werewolf vs. the Vampire Women* (Hollywood Select).

Night of the Living Dead (1968) ◆◆◆◇
B&W/colorized
D: George Romero. Duane Jones, Judith O'Dea, Russell Streiner, Karl Hard-

YOU'VE SEEN THE MOVIE, NOW COLLECT THE CARDS!: Another example of Living Dead staying power—a collector's card set from Imagine, Inc. Here, zombie Bill Hinzman (a sickly green in the colorized video) exhibits the form that made him famous in George A. Romero's original *Night of the Living Dead.*
Photo courtesy of Imagine, Inc.

man, Keith Wayne. 96 minutes. *(United, others)*

When Romero unleashed *Night of the Living Dead* on an unsuspecting public back in 1968, the pic represented a radical, truly shocking departure from the usual run of formulaic fear flicks. *Night* chucked all romantic and most pseudoscientific fright-film conventions and went straight for the jugular (to say nothing of the entrails), conveying a sense of visceral terror through its unrelieved atmosphere of frantic despair as much as through its relentless army of marching ghouls. Like a legit nightmare, *Night of the Living Dead* simply *starts*, sans rhyme or reason, and never lets up as the cannibalistic title zombies launch their blind but tireless assault against the living. Embattled Sanity, represented by beleaguered hero Jones, takes fragile shelter in a ramshackle house, while lethal (and seemingly limitless) Irrationality rages without. *Night's* popularity led not only to two Romero sequels, *Dawn of the Dead* and *Day of the Dead* (see index), but to countless imitations, lensed here and abroad (most notably in Italy, where directors like Fulci and Lenzi have forged careers ripping off the *Dead*), and the separate, lighter-veined *Return of the Living Dead* series (see sidebar).

The Night Stalker (1987) ◆◆◇
D: Max Kleven. Charles Napier, Michelle Reese, Katherine Kelly Lang,

Gary Crosby, Robert Zdar, Robert Viharo. 91 minutes. (Lightning)

Not to be confused with the Darren (*Kolchak*) McGavin TV terror movie (and subsequent series) of the same name, this *Night Stalker* stars ex–Russ Meyer stalwart Napier (sort of a B-movie Brian Dennehy) as hard-drinking cop J. J. Stryker. Stryker and his fellow fuzz are out to nail a semisupernatural psycho (the humongous Zdar), who's been ritualistically

---

FILMMAKERS IN FOCUS:

George A. Romero: Legacy of the Living Dead

George A. Romero and former partner John Russo, who remain close friends, own separate but equal rights to the "Living Dead" title and concept. Each is legally free to run with the idea in any direction he desires. Which led the Phantom, during a meeting with the legendary fright auteur, to wonder aloud whether another *Living Dead* installment might be lurking in Romero's future.

"I can't say I'll never do one," the director replied. "I've been playing with an idea that's a spoof. It would be pretty hard, though, after the O'Bannon film."

Dan O'Bannon's fright parody *Return of the Living Dead* was loosely based on Russo's novel of the same name; the film itself sparked a sequel, *Return of the Living Dead II*, which likewise played Romero/Russo's zombies for laughs.

"I liked O'Bannon's film okay," Romero contended. "*I* wouldn't have done that—it was a little too rock 'n' roll for me—but I thought it was sort of fun and could see why people would get off on it."

A straightforward remake looms as another possibility.

"We've talked about it," Romero revealed. "It's not something I'd want to direct, but maybe Tom Savini would."

Savini, responsible for the *Dead* series's innovative makeup FX, is one of several people who've built entire careers based on their initial involvement with *Night*. In addition to fashioning special makeup effects for myriad other films, Savini has also branched out into acting (*The Ripper, Creepshow II*) and directing. Late *Living Dead* star Duane Jones, meanwhile, went on to topline in such horror outings as *Blood Couple* (aka *Ganja and Hess*) and *Vampires* (NA). Even Bill Hinzman, who portrayed the first ghoul seen in *Night*'s opening cemetery scene, is due to direct and star in a film (*Revenge of the Living Zombies*) based on that ephemeral if memorable character's return!

"It's almost become a genre of its own," Romero shudders.

PD or Not PD?

We wondered how so famous and relatively recent a film, available on countless different video labels, became public domain.

"It's *not*, actually," Romero explained. "What happened was, when Walter Reade put the film out, they changed the title. They titled it *Night of the Living Dead*. Our title was *Night of the Flesh Eaters*. They didn't include the copyright on the titles when they did the new overprints. Our print of *Night of the Flesh Eaters* has a copyright. It's a technicality we argued for fifteen years. In 1983, we won a copyright in federal court, and now we're fighting for retro control. The company, Image 10, has no money and never made a lot of money off the movie. It's very hard to fight off the pirates unless you've got the bucks. So it's not legitimately public domain. And that's the name of that tune."

Horrors of Another Color

We also asked for George's thoughts re: the colorized cassette issued by Hal Roach.

"I'm not militant about colorization," Romero insisted. "But then again, I didn't make *It's a Wonderful Life* or *Maltese Falcon*. I think it's far more brutal to cut a film for syndicated television. As for *Night*'s colorization, I just think it's silly. I don't like to watch it in color. I think it looks awful, and it flat kills the gag in the beginning. The whole gag is, there's this guy walking across the cemetery for like two minutes and we think it's just a human. But now that he's *green*, we don't think he's human."

---

killing the prostie pals of Stryker's squeeze, ex-hooker Rene (Reese). *The Night Stalker*'s strengths include a tart-tongued script, swiftly paced direction, and Napier's compelling perf as the skid-row Dirty Harry. On the down side, the killer is poorly introduced and explained—a crucial flaw that detracts from the flick's overall suspense.

Night Tide (1961) ◆◆◆ B&W
D: Curtis Harrington. Dennis Hopper, Linda Lawson, Gavin Muir, Luanda Anders, Ben Roseman. 84 minutes. (Film Forum)

Openly inspired by Val Lewton's

Cat People (see index), Harrington's *Night Tide* is a generally effective seaside chiller—a *Catfish People*, if you will. Like Lewton's films, *Night Tide* is less an all-out horror flick than an eerie mood piece, heightened by black-and-white cinematography that captures the otherworldly quality of Venice, California's, seedy piers and amusement parlors. Hopper gives a layered perf as lonely young sailor Johnny Drake, entranced by the mysterious but undeniably alluring Mora (Lawson), who works as a midway mermaid. But there may be a stronger link than mere sideshow whimsy binding Mora to the denizens of the deep. While not all the thesps are up to Hopper's level in this low-budget indie, and Harrington's obsession with ambience sometimes slows the action to a crawl, *Night Tide*, a West Coast cousin to *Carnival of Souls* (see index)—though a notch below that cult classic—is well worth checking out. Roger Corman character actor Bruno (*Daughter of Horror*) VeSota contributes a walk-on, and we'd swear that's Ed Wood, Jr.'s, rubber octopus from *Bride of the Monster* we see wrestling with Hopper during one of *Night Tide*'s nautical nightmare sequences.

Night Train to Terror (1985) ◆◆
D: *John Carr, Jay Schlossberg-Cohen, Phillip Marshak, Tom McGowan, Greg Tallas. John Phillip Law, Cameron Mitchell, Marc Lawrence, Charles Moll, Meredith Haze, Ferdy Mayne. 93 minutes. (Prism)*

Human vivisection! Nazi massacres! Exploding eyeballs! Full-frontal lobotomies! Suicide cults! Kung-fu set-to's! Breakdancing! Cameron Mitchell! If one movie would seem to have it all, it would be the Philip Yordan–scripted *Night Train to Terror*. As the pic opens, a bad California preppie rock band breakdances through the title train crooning the pic's unforgettable theme song, "Everybody's Got Somethin' to Do," while God and Satan discuss situational ethics in the compartment next door. The flick quickly derails, however, when Satan decides to illustrate his points by narrating a trio of tales—unrelated sequences, actually—from three earlier Yordan epics: *Death Wish Club* (see index), *The Nightmare Never Ends* (Simitar), and an unfinished, untitled project featuring John Phillip Law. The result, as one might imagine, is an unholy—if often weirdly entertaining—mess. (That the pic's wraparound participants felt less than proud of their contributions is evidenced by the end credits, where the thesp essaying Satan is billed as "Lu Cifer," while the actor playing God (Mayne) is listed as "Himself" [!]. The movie's most memorable moment depicts a zombielike doctor, his forehead bisected by a fresh lobotomy scar, wandering a hospital corridor, wielding a scalpel, and muttering, "I've gotta get to Surgery!"

The Night Visitor (1970) NR
D: Laslo Benedek. Max von Sydow, Liv Ullmann, Trevor Howard. 106 minutes. (United)

This Sweden-lensed exercise stars von Sydow as a suspected psycho.

Night Warning (1982) ◆◆◆
D: William Asher. Susan Tyrrell, Jimmy McNichol, Bo Svenson. 96 minutes. (HBO)

A must for Susan Tyrrell fans (and we know you're out there, we can hear you shrieking), cast here as Jimmy McNichol's nutzoid killer aunt in Asher's effective chiller.

Nightmare Castle (1966) ◆◆◇
D: Mario Caiano. Barbara Steele, Paul Mueller, Helga Line. 90 minutes. (Sinister Cinema)

This Italo horror has truly eerie photography and the sepulchral beauty of Barbara Steele, who plays dual roles here.

Nightmare in Blood (1976) NR
D: John Stanley. Jerry Walter, Kathleen Quinlan, Kerwin Mathews. 89 minutes. (Video City)

A low-budget flick from the West Coast's Creature Features horror host and critic Stanley about a vampire stalking a monster-movie-fan convention.

Nightmare in Wax (1969) ◆◆◇
D: Bud Townsend. Cameron Mitchell, Anne Helm, Scott Brady. 95 minutes. (United)

Mitchell brings mucho intensity to his role as a mad movie-makeup man who coats actors in wax. An agreeably lurid *House of Wax Meets How to Make a Monster*.

A Nightmare on Elm Street (1984) ◆◆◇
D: Wes Craven. John Saxon, Ronee Blakley, Heather Langenkamp, Amanda Wyss, Nick Corri, Johnny Depp. 92 minutes. (Media)

Craven delivers the chills via several scary set pieces while introducing the shockingly popular dream-demon Freddy Krueger to a horror-hungry audience. Unfortunately, Craven here is far less adept at crafting credible dialogue or coaxing convincing perfs from many of his cast members—deficiencies that keep *Nightmare* from being a truly topflight terror flick, let alone a classic.

A Nightmare on Elm Street 2: Freddy's Revenge (1985) ◆◆
D: Jack Sholder. Mark Patton, Kim Myers, Robert Rusler, Clu Gulager, Hope Lange, Robert Englund. 84 minutes. (Media)

Our friendly neighborhood maniac, Freddy Krueger (Englund), returns to wreak more murder and mayhem in the 'burbs. In this, the first *Elm Street* sequel, Fred infiltrates the somnolent psyche of young Jesse (Patton), an unsuspecting teen whose family has unwisely moved into a house last occupied by one of Freddy's previous victims. When Jesse complains of recurring nightmares, Dad (Gulager) suspects his son's on drugs, while Mom (Lange) fears he needs psychiatric counsel. Only girlfriend Lisa (youthful Meryl Streep clone Myers) believes that Jesse's body and soul are being commandeered by the dread, not-quite-dead Fred. While *Nightmare 2*, under Jack (*Alone in the Dark*) Sholder's direction, contains its fair share of shock yoks, particularly in the early going, the chill factor—the original *Nightmare*'s strength—is virtually nil.

A Nightmare on Elm Street 3: Dream Warriors (1987) ◆◆◆

D: Chuck Russell. Heather Langenkamp, Craig Wasson, Robert Englund, Patricia Arquette, John Saxon, Dick Cavett, Zsa Zsa Gabor. 96 minutes. (Media)

Nightmare on Elm Street 3 finds "the last of the Elm Street children" undergoing group therapy for their Freddy Krueger–inspired sleep disorders. Working with them are bemused shrink Dr. Goldman (Wasson) and Nancy Thompson, the distaff survivor from *Nightmare 1*, played by eternally wide-eyed Heather Langenkamp, who herein returns as a psychiatric intern (which is akin to casting Brooke Shields as Madame Curie). The onscreen docs are consistently depicted as a

generally dim lot. They make light of the Freddy legend even as their patients die one by one in sleep-related mishaps perpetrated by our indefatigable fiend. In fact, few of *Nightmare 3*'s non-dream sequences possess much in the way of logic, serving simply as a convenient frame for the flick's real raison d'être. Happily, the numerous nightmare set pieces are well worth the price of a rental (they even prompted several serious palps in the Phantom's horror-hardened heart) as FK adopts such unlikely guises as a sexy blond nurse, a TV set, and talk-show host Dick Cavett (!). (Unfortunately, the camera cuts away before Freddy/Dick gets to shred guest Zsa Zsa Gabor.) *Nightmare 3* remains the sickest, funniest, and most outlandishly surreal of the Freddy series.

A Nightmare on Elm Street 4: The Dream Master (1988) ◆◆

D: Renny Harlin. Robert Englund, Andras Jones, Tuesday Knight, Brooke Theiss, Danny Hassel, Toy Newkirk. 93 minutes. (Media)

Despite its expanded budget and elaborate FX work, *Nightmare 4* lets Fred coast his way through the flick's sundry slaughter scenes as he slays three survivors from *3*, along with several new recruits, in a variety of increasingly predictable ways. Only an imaginative bijou-set sequence—wherein Fred

Photo by: Gary Farr

NEW LINE CINEMA
© MCMLXXXVIII NEW LINE CINEMA CORP.

Freddy Krueger: A bogeyman for all seasons.
Photo courtesy of New Line Cinema.

invades a *Reefer Madness* screening (!)—approaches the wacky inspiration that informed much of *3*. *Nightmare 4* also suffers from a self-congratulatory air. (The first three flicks have raked in over $100 mil.) Reigning B-movie ingenue Quigley is tragically wasted as a Soul from Freddy's Chest (though ex-Playmate and Andy Sidaris starlet Hope Marie Carlton fares better in her mute but elo-

Sequel and Ye Shall Find

The horror field has lately witnessed an accelerated form of fear-film franchising: More than a quarter of the recent terror cassettes covered here are connected with ongoing celluloid series. Paramount's *Friday the 13th* octet (at last count) has proven the most durable, as the low-budget adventures of unsinkable hockey-masked maniac Jason Voorhees continue to turn a steady profit, and long-buried Michael Myers likewise revived to a rousing response in 1988's *Halloween IV*.

No series, though, has approached the phenomenal success of New Line's *Nightmare on Elm Street*. The most recent installment, *Nightmare on Elm Street 4: The Dream Master,* while one of the weaker entries creatively, crossed over into big-time BO bucks, outgrossing many a major-studio blockbuster during the Summer of '88.

In addition to prompting rival producers to crank out seemingly nonstop sequels to what were originally intended as one-shots (ranging from the pretty fair *Fright Night* to the generally abysmal *Gremlins-*steal *Ghoulies*), *Nightmare* has inspired all manner of dream-related rip-offs bearing such imitative titles as *Bad Dreams* (see index), *Deadly Dreams* (Virgin Vision), *Dream Demon* (NA), *Dreamaniac* (Lightning), *Twisted Nightmare* (TWE), and *Nightmare at Shadow Woods* (later altered to *Blood Rage*—see index). And Freddy Krueger himself has since branched out into television (via the syndicated series *Freddy's Nightmares*), rock video, LPs, CDs, and a recorded phone-message line.

The secret of Freddy's success is the ability of the disfigured, razor-nailed dream demon (the "bastard son of a hundred maniacs," we're informed in the series's strongest entry, *Nightmare 3*) to exploit our fear of the destructive desires roiling within our own submerged ids. He's impossible to eradicate because he doesn't really exist; impossible to escape because he resides literally inside our own subconscious minds and can't operate without our unwitting cooperation. Also, like the classic Universal Dracula (Bela Lugosi) and Frankenstein Monster (Boris Karloff) of yore, Freddy is inseparably associated with a single thesp (Robert Englund) and has seen his repertoire expand—à la Arnie Schwarzenegger, he now dispatches his victims with vicious force *and* snappy one-liners—with each successive film. While his dangerously high profile threatens to lead to a fatal case of overexposure, for the present at least Freddy Krueger is truly a bogeyman for all seasons.

quent Waterbed Bunny bit). Withal, and despite isolated FX highlights, *A Nightmare on Elm Street 4* is pretty old hat—and we're not talking about Freddy's famous flea-bitten fedora.

NightVision (1987) ◆◇
D: Michael Krueger. Stacy Carson, Shirley Ross, Tony Carpenter, Ellie Martins, Tom Henry, Glenn Reed. 102 minutes. (Prism)

The Phantom harbored moderately high hopes for *NightVision*, crafted by the same direct-to-home-vid team who'd earlier given us the derivative but not-bad *Mind Killer*. But where the latter told its seriocomic nerd-monster tale with energy and occasional wit, the Denver-lensed *NightVision* takes forever to cut to the proverbial chase. Carson plays a naive would-be writer who journeys to the big bad city in search of "inspiration." Instead, he gets involved with a distaff vid-store clerk (Ross), a greasy street thief (Carpenter), and a satanic videotape. The fright factor is nearly nil here as director Michael (no relation to Freddy) Krueger spends more time taking us through Carson's dull period of big-city adjustment than advancing the plot's potentially horrific aspects. And the "haunted video" story line, already employed in *Escapes*, *The Video Dead*, and the far superior *Remote Control* (see index), is growing pretty stale. Surely fright auteurs can find fresher appliances to pick on.

Nosferatu (1922) ◆◆◆ B&W
D: F. W. Murnau. Max Schreck, Alexander Granach, Greta Schroeder. 105 minutes. (Video Yesteryear)

Murnau's silent Dracula may be the most hideous Count in movie history, and his imagery eerier than any of the later versions. Video Yesteryear offers the complete print, with English subtitles, correct projection speed, and the original organ score. Grim but memorable going.

The Oblong Box (1969) ◆◆◆
D: Gordon Hessler. Vincent Price, Christopher Lee, Alastair Williamson. 91 minutes. (HBO)

Price has a bonkers brother—victim of an African voodoo curse—stashed in the attic, who escapes to create mayhem in a well-mounted period piece loosely based on a Poe story.

The Offspring (1987) ◆◆◇
D: Jeff Burr. Vincent Price, Clu Gulager, Cameron Mitchell, Rosalind Cash, Terry Kiser, Susan Tyrrell. 96 minutes. (IVE)

The Offspring (formerly *From a Whisper to a Scream*) is a slow-moving fear anthology that muffs more opportunities than it exploits. The feeble though well-acted wraparound features a restrained Tyrrell as a reporter who quizzes Oldfield, Tennessee, librarian Price re: the town's sinister rep. Vinny obligingly reels off four fright vignettes centering on such wholesome small-town activities as necrophilia, glass eating, and torture of every insidious stripe. Of course, any flick dealing with such eternal topics would have a hard time being *completely* lame, and *The Offspring* occasionally succeeds in creating an honestly creepy atmosphere. Best here are the first story, with Gulager as a milquetoast necrophiliac who—in one of the pic's sicker twists—sires a living-dead mutant, and the Lovecraft's Traveling Circus episode, wherein pigging out on razor blades leads to a gory case of indigestion. Also of interest to B-movie buffs is *The Offspring*'s stellar supporting cast: ex-Hammer stalwart Martine Beswicke, the ubiquitous Cameron Mitchell, and Angelo Rossitto (typecast, once again, as a dwarf).

The Omen (1976) ◆◆◇
D: Richard Donner. Gregory Peck, Lee Remick, Billie Whitelaw. 111 minutes. (CBS/Fox)

An okay mainstream horror hit with beleaguered parents Peck and Remick trying to cope with a brat from hell. Better than the boring sequels, *Damien—The Omen II* and *The Final Conflict* (also CBS/Fox).

Open House (1987) ◆◆
D: Jag Mundhra. Joseph Bottoms, Adrienne Barbeau, Rudy Ramos, *Mary Stavin, Scott Thompson Baker, Robert Miano. 95 minutes. (Prism)*

Someone is slicing and dicing L.A. real estate agents and their wealthy clients. Radio shrink Bottoms thinks a deranged repeat caller is the culprit and has a more than passing interest in the case, since his wife (Barbeau in a Joan Collins–like sexpot role) happens to be just such a realtor. The result is a watchable but rarely gripping scare tale that features a few fairly sicko slay scenes. If *Open House* had been set in NYC, with landlords as the victims, we probably would have liked it a whole lot more.

The Oracle (1985) ◆
D: Roberta Findlay. Caroline Capers Powers, Roger Neil, Victoria Dryden, Pam LaTesta, Chris Maria DeKoron. 94 minutes. (IVE)

Vet X-rated director Findlay tries her hand at horror and comes up empty with *The Oracle*. The story involves one woman's (Powers) would-be harrowing encounter with a Ouija board and, subsequently, an evil spirit—a hook later employed to slicker if still imperfect effect in *Witchboard* (see index). *The Oracle* earns a lone phan for its entertainingly inept attempt to fashion a *Poltergeist*ian freak-out scene sans FX; Findlay's desperately tilting camera and ingenue Powers's writhing floorwork fail to cloak the pic's invisible budget but are pretty funny. The other 90 or so minutes of this dreary cheapie are merely unwatchable.

The Outing (1987) ◆
D: Tom Daley. Deborah Winters, James Huston, Andra St. Ivanyi, Scott Bankston, Mark Mitchell, Andre Chimene. 85 minutes. (IVE)

Formerly and more logically titled *The Lamp*, *The Outing* involves an Iraqi *jinn*, or evil genie, accidentally unleashed from an ancient lamp located in a Texas museum. Eight airheaded teenagers decide to stay overnight at that same electronically sealed museum: bad move. You can guess what happens next: bad movie. Among this otherwise by-rote horror turkey's few points of interest are an opera-singing security guard (something we *hadn't* seen before) and ex-ingenue Winters's screen return (she's married to director Daley) as a blond teacher.

Pandemonium (1982) ◆◇
D: Alfred Sole. Tom Smothers, Carol Kane, Paul (Pee-wee Herman) Reubens, Judge Reinhold, Tab Hunter, Eve Arden. 82 minutes. (MGM/UA)

It's hard to imagine a comic team composed of Tom Smothers (as a displaced Mountie) and Paul (Pee-wee Herman) Reubens (as his addled deputy) failing to generate laughs, but they achieve that negative goal here—thanks largely to *Pandemonium*'s pallid script. Cameos by veteran talents Tab Hunter, Donald O'Connor, Eve Arden, and Pat Ast (all of whom are

advised to leave this loser off their résumés) don't help much either, though the luckless thesps try their best. Ditto for director Sole, who helmed the infinitely wittier *and* genuinely disturbing *Alice, Sweet Alice* (see index) a few years earlier.

Paperhouse (1989) ◆◆◆
D: Bernard Rose. Glenn Headley, Charlotte Burke, Elliott Spiers, Ben Cross. 93 minutes. (Vestron)

When eleven-year-old Brit schoolgirl Anna (Burke) sketches a crude house on her note pad, she seems at first to be engaging in harmless play. That outwardly innocent artistic activity soon takes a scarier turn, however, when Anna begins visiting that selfsame haunt in a series of vivid nightmares that find her communing with the isolated abode's lone, unlikely inhabitant—a sickly adolescent named Marc (Spiers). Events grow downright *eerie* when Anna learns that Marc is not a figment of her nocturnal imagination but an actual patient of Anna's own physician, a boy she's never met in her waking life. While Rose's *Paperhouse* hinges on potentially life-threatening nightmares, in terror-territory terms the pic is situated a safe distance from Elm Street. Rock-vid vet Rose forgoes gore and standard haunted-house hallucinations in favor of a Val Lewton–like approach to his semisupernatural story line, adapted from Catherine Storr's novel *Marianne*

Dreams. The result is a largely successful mix of mystery, poignancy, and dread, weakened only by the presence of too many unexplained, unexplored plot threads, such as Anna's ambiguous relationship with her mostly absentee Dad (Cross). *Paperhouse* may disappoint fright fans in the market for straight-ahead horror, but it's well worth a look for those with a taste for a quieter brand of fear fare.

Phantasm (1979) ◆◆◆
D: Don Coscarelli. Michael Baldwin, Bill Thornbury, Reggie Bannister, Kathy Lester, Angus Scrimm. 90 minutes. (Nelson)

On the surface, Coscarelli's *Phantasm* seems like just another simpleminded scare pic. If viewed as the understandably lurid nightmare of an otherwise ordinary adolescent boy—Mike (Baldwin)—trying to adjust to the loss of his parents, his older brother, and his own vanishing childhood, parts of this pic weave a powerful primal spell. And Scrimm impresses as a memorable celluloid demon, The Tall Man.

Phantasm II (1988) ◆◆◇
D: Don Coscarelli. James LeGros, Reggie Bannister, Angus Scrimm, Paula Irvine, Samantha Phillips, Kenneth Tigar. 90 minutes. (MCA)

In Coscarelli's belated sequel— the appropriately if unimaginatively monikered *Phantasm II*—Mike (LeGros), now nineteen, is being released from a mental institution where he's passed the last seven years being treated for his horrific "hallucinations." No sooner does Mike set foot in "reality" than The Tall Man (reprised by spectral thesp Scrimm) is at it again, robbing graveyards of their cadaverous contents and unleashing his new, improved flying silver spheres—replete with brain-draining drills (!)—whenever the urge arises (which, as you might imagine, is certainly often enough). Mike enlists the aid of fellow *Phantasm* survivor Bannister, and together they fight this formidable (dis)embodiment of their deepest fears with a *Rambo*esque arsenal of chainsaws, flamethrowers, and four-barreled shotguns (!). Like its model, *Phantasm II*, while working on a lower plane, operates less on a logical than on a filmic fever-dream level.

The Phantom of the Opera (1925) ◆◆◆
B&W/color
D: Rupert Julian. Lon Chaney, Mary Philbin, Norman Kerry. 79 minutes. (Video Yesteryear)

Chaney's melodramatic film version of the Gaston Leroux novel is undeniably well done but may be slow going for contempo video viewers. Video Yesteryear's version includes the original music score, which helps, as does the superior print quality.

Phantom of the Opera (1943) ◆◆◇
D: Arthur Lubin. Claude Rains, Nelson

Eddy, Susanna Foster. 93 minutes. (MCA)

Too much opera, not enough Phantom—by *this* Phantom's lights, at least—though the chandelier scene and Claude's disastrous encounter with a crass music publisher impress, as do the film's lavish production values and striking Technicolor.

Phantom of the Paradise (1974) ◆◆◆◇
D: Brian De Palma. William Finley, Paul Williams, Jessica Harper, Gerrit Graham, George Memmoli. 92 minutes. (Key)

De Palma's twisty takeoff is a *Phantom of the Opera Meets Faust*, set against a decadent backstage rock world. Finley plays naive composer Winslow Leach, who suffers unceasingly at the hands of diabolical impresario Williams (whose presence represents the flick's only serious drawback) while trying to help ingenue Harper gain singing stardom. *Phantom* is a bright, savvy satire on the rock industry that also delivers its fair share of chills. Special kudos go to Graham as effeminate rock 'n' roll animal Beef, the key figure in the wittiest *Psycho* shower scene send-up ever lensed. And Sissy Spacek designed the sets!

Pharaoh's Curse (1957) ◆◆ B&W
D: Lee Sholem. Mark Dana, Ziva Rodann, Diane Brewster. 66 minutes. (J&J)

This derivative, low-budget *Mummy* retread has little going

for it beyond Rodann's seductive presence. For some of us, that's more than enough.

The Picture of Dorian Gray (1945) ◆◆◆ B&W/color
D: Albert Lewin. Hurd Hatfield, George Sanders, Donna Reed. 111 minutes. (MGM/UA)

Lewin's stately original remains the best of several adaptations. Those truly wild about Oscar's story can also obtain the 1971 remake, with Helmut Berger as Wilde's young/old antihero (Republic), the 1974 made-for-TV version (Thriller Video) starring Shane Briant, and 1982's *Sins of Dorian Gray* (Playhouse), with Anthony Perkins and Joseph Bottoms.

Pigs (1973) ◆◇
D: Marc Lawrence. Marc Lawrence, Jesse Vint, Katherine Ross. 90 minutes. (Simitar)

Vet pockmarked character actor Lawrence directs and toplines as a loyal dad who feeds his daft daughter's slay victims to the title swine in an uninspired oink orgy also available as *Daddy's Deadly Darling* (Paragon). Despite her prominent placement on the cassette box, by the way, this Katherine Ross is not *the* Katharine Ross of *The Graduate* and *Butch and Sundance* celebrity, but another Katherine Ross entirely. *Pigs* does make an ideal companion to *Evilspeak* (CBS/Fox), wherein nerd Clint Howard conjures up a herd of killer swine.

Piranha (1978) ◆◆◇
D: Joe Dante. Bradford Dillman, Heather Menzies, Kevin McCarthy. 90 minutes. (Warner)

Director Dante and scripter John Sayles send up fishy fright films from *The Creature of the Black Lagoon* to *Jaws* in a generally fun if formulaic pic buoyed by B-flick faves Dick Miller and Barbara Steele.

Piranha II: The Spawning (1982) ◆◇
D: James Cameron. Tricia O'Neil, Steve Marachuk, Lance Henriksen. 88 minutes. (Embassy)

The only interesting aspect of this dull cheapie—which has nothing to do with the original—is director James (*The Terminator, Aliens*) Cameron's unimpressive participation. For devoted genre auteurists only.

The Pit and the Pendulum (1961) ◆◆◇
D: Roger Corman. Vincent Price, Barbara Steele, John Kerr. 80 minutes. (Warner)

As usual, this Corman production has precious little connection to Poe's story, beyond the admittedly vital presence of the titular torture devices. But it's fun enough in its own right and represents Price and Steele's only screen pairing.

Poltergeist (1982) ◆◆◆◇
D: Tobe Hooper. JoBeth Williams, Craig T. Nelson, Heather O'Rourke, Zelda Rubinstein. 115 minutes. (MGM/UA)

After a cloyingly cute opening

reel, this Spielberg production gets down to serious business with one of the most visually spectacular spook-outs in celluloid history. While the flick's undeniably more effective on the big screen, video at least adds a certain *verité* to the evil spirits' initial entry via our Typical American Family's TV. And pint-sized psychic Rubinstein gets less lost in the smaller surroundings.

Poltergeist II: The Other Side (1986) ◆◆◇
D: Brian Gibson. Craig T. Nelson, Jo-Beth Williams, Will Sampson, Geraldine Fitzgerald, Julian Beck, Oliver Roberts, Heather O'Rourke, Zelda Rubinstein. 90 minutes. (MGM/UA)

This much-maligned first sequel to the Spielberg/Hooper horror hit follows the fleeing Freeling Family (Nelson, Williams, Roberts, O'Rourke) as they kiss their haunted hacienda good-bye and light out for hopefully greener pastures. Unfortunately for them, they're tailed by the evil spirit of the demented Reverend Kane (the late Julian Beck in a suitably sinister, serpentine turn), former leader of a nineteenth-century Jonestown-type cult, and the restless ghosts of his fellow cultists. "Magic munchkin" Rubinstein also shows up, accompanied by a free-lance Native American shaman (the late Will Sampson), to help the embattled Freelings win their latest spooky duke-out. While *Poltergeist II* can't hold a bell, book, or candle to its predecessor, there are enough grisly surprises to keep the ghostly goings-on from getting dull. A scene wherein young Robbie Freeling is nearly strangled to death by his own braces (!) adds a fresh dimension to the realm of orthodontal terror, and the floating chainsaw's good for a cheap chill. *Poltergeist II* also coughs up 1986's best credit line—Vomit Creature played by Noble Craig (even if his barf *is* worse than his bite).

Poltergeist III (1988) ◆

D: Gary Sherman. Tom Skerritt, Nancy Allen, Heather O'Rourke, Zelda Rubinstein, Richard Fire, Nathan Davis. 97 minutes. (MGM/UA)

A slack, lifeless affair, *Poltergeist III* makes the merely passable *Poltergeist II* look like—well, *Poltergeist.* This ghostly go-round finds the persistent Preacher Kane (Davis replacing the late Julian Beck) shadowing Carol Ann (the late O'Rourke, who died, at age twelve, shortly after the film's completion) to a Chicago condo managed by her uncle, Skerritt, and aunt, Nancy (*RoboCop*) Allen. Once ensconced therein, he spends most of the movie chasing them and the diminutive but indomitable Rubinstein through various condo mirrors and cheapjack fright sets. Nearly an hour passes before he even deigns to claim his first and only victim. Not even the weak FX work offers much relief from the hack script

and from Sherman's stilted direction (which, in its defense, at least yields a handful of unintentional yuks). But Richard Fire, as the pic's token obnoxious shrink, sums it up best when he shouts, "Enough! *Stop* this stupid sideshow!"

Poor White Trash II (1976) NR

D: S. F. Brownrigg. Gene Ross, Ann Stafford, Norma Moore. 90 minutes. (Magnum)

How's this for high concept? *Poor White Trash II* is not only *not* a sequel to *Poor White Trash,* but there was no *Poor White Trash* (Cinema Group)—*that* was a title later slapped on a tame '57 swamp drama originally released as *Bayou.* Number *II* is a marginal horror movie originally titled *Scum of the Earth,* not to be confused with the H. G. Lewis exploitation flick that still retains that title (NA).

The Premature Burial (1962) ◆◆◇

D: Roger Corman. Ray Milland, Hazel Court, Richard Ney. 81 minutes. (Vestron)

Milland has a phobia about being buried alive, which leads to the film's highlight—a nightmare sequence that finds our protagonist in precisely that predicament. The rest of the flick is pretty forgettable—until, of course, Ray *does* get buried alive, in the movie's other memorable scene.

Prince of Darkness (1987) ◆◆◇

D: John Carpenter. Donald Pleasence, Lisa Blount, Jameson Parker,

Victor Wong, Dennis Dun, Peter Jason. 100 minutes. (MCA)

Carpenter's *Prince of Darkness* pits a team of physicists (Parker, Blount, Wong, and Dun among them) against an agitated vat of vile living liquid brewing in the basement of an abandoned downtown L.A. church. Priest Pleasence determines that the churning green gunk, protected over the centuries by the secret Brotherhood of Sleep sect, is actually none other than the son of Satan struggling to be reborn. And that's Carpenter's cue to crowd the screen with a dizzying series of gore slaughters, demonic possessions, rampaging maggots and insects galore, shared nightmares, dark transmissions from the future, and other fun fright stuff. While *Prince of Darkness* gets off to a slow start and goes overboard on the bogus scientific/religious explanations re: the characters' nightmarish plight, Carpenter succeeds in delivering enough suspense and visceral shocks to satisfy most horror fans. Carpenter also composed the pic's minimalist score, while Alice Cooper contributes a thankfully silent cameo as a "street schizo." The movie's ultimate message, relayed midway through via a possessed computer, hails from the devil himself: "You will not be saved by the Holy Ghost. You will not be saved by the god Plutonium. In fact, *you will not be saved!*"

Prison (1988) ◆◆◆

D: Renny Harlin. Lane Smith, Viggo Mortensen, Chelsea Field, Lincoln Kilpatrick, Andre De Shields, Ivan Kane. 102 minutes. (New World)

The vengeful spirit of a convict that Creedmore Prison warden Smith railroaded into the chair a couple decades ago is back for blood, and he's not particularly choosy about whose he spills. Even liberal prison board rep Field can do little to improve the supernatural situation; as might be imagined, however, Harlin's *Prison* ("Horror Has a New Home!") is less an impassioned plea for penal reform than a straight-ahead slaughterfest. Surprisingly, the pic actually works better as a traditional men's-prison movie than it does as a horror outing. The characters are deftly sketched—especially Kilpatrick as a lifer who knows the warden's deep, dark secret, and Kane as Lasagna, a would-be Sly Stallone clone—the script is tight and knowledgeable, and the inmate intrigues are kept fairly credible. *Prison*'s plot is developed gradually enough to allow the fright elements to serve more as an extra twist than as the flick's sole raison d'être. And while the FX are pretty routine, the decaying Creedmore set aids immeasurably in augmenting the movie's genuinely claustrophobic feel. Withal, *Prison* is well worth a look.

Prom Night (1980) ◆◆◆

D: Paul Lynch. Leslie Nielsen, Jamie Lee Curtis, Casey Stevens. 91 minutes. (MCA)

Slightly better than your average teen-slaughter flick, though fans of that tired genre may find it light on gore.

Prophecy (1979) ◆◇

D: John Frankenheimer. Talia Shire, Robert Foxworth, Armand Assante. 103 minutes. (Paramount)

Some memorably ridiculous creatures populate this pretentious terror turkey about Man's inhumanity to Nature. Not Frankenheimer's best.

Psycho (1960) ◆◆◆◆ B&W

D: Alfred Hitchcock. Anthony Perkins, Janet Leigh, John Gavin, Martin Balsam. 109 minutes. (MCA)

What can we add about a film that's had entire books devoted to it and that virtually founded one of horrordom's most durable genres? Only that if you haven't seen it already, avail yourself of the video at once. One final thought: If Anthony Perkins had played the Vincent Price role, the Fly might still be alive today. For info on other Hitch vids, see our Video Shopping List.

Psycho II (1983) ◆◆◇

D: Richard Franklin. Anthony Perkins, Vera Miles, Meg Tilly, Robert Loggia. 113 minutes. (MCA)

Franklin's belated sequel doesn't approach the original but turned out better than might have been expected, thanks largely to Perkins's on-target reprise of his Norman Bates role. Psycho III, which Perkins also directed, is even better.

Psycho III (1986) ◆◆◆

D: Anthony Perkins. Anthony Perkins, Diana Scarwid, Jeff Fahey, Roberta Maxwell, Hugh Gillin, Lee Garlington. 93 minutes. (MCA)

Norman Bates is alive and sick and again running the Bates Motel. Into our loony's lonely life comes convent runaway Maureen Coyle (Scarwid), who (unfortunately for her) puts Norm in mind of former thwarted flame Marian Crane (Janet Leigh in Hitchcock's original). While snoopy journalist Maxwell dogs his twisted trail, Norman digs Mom's knife and wig out of the mothballs and reverts to his old nasty habits. All things considered, scripter Charles Pogue and auteur Perkins do a decent job with Psycho III (except when Tony the director lets Tony the thesp overact, stuttering and twitching as if there were no tomorrow—or at least no Psycho IV). There's a neat ironic twist on the original shower scene, a number of choice lines (as when Norman understates, "I feel a little sick!"), and even a tender moment or two between needy nutcases Norman and Maureen. Psycho III also depends less on wild contrivance than Psycho II did to keep its plot lurching forward, and the flick delivers its fair share of shocks.

Psycho Girls (1987) ◇
D: Gerard Ciccoritti. John Haslett Cuff, Darlene Mignacco, Rose Graham, Agi Gallus, Silvio Oliviero, Pier Giorgia DiCicco, Fernne Kane. 87 minutes. (MGM/UA)

Suffering from a severe case of amateuritis, this unwatchable mess shifts from earnest stabs at suspense to desperate pokes at parody and fails miserably on both levels. The main maniac here (Mignacco)—who, we're told, is "beyond insanity"—conducts a ritualistic psychodrama before a literally captive audience of shrinks and other perceived tormentors. With the aid of a duo of fellow dementoids, she eliminates her foes one by one, chanting poorly synched Freudvoidian incantations into the bargain. *Psycho Girls* covers just about all bad-movie bases. We give it half a phan for the title, zilch for the rest.

Psycho Sisters (1972) NR
D: Reginald LeBorg. Susan Strasberg, Faith Domergue, Sydney Chaplin. 80 minutes. (Prism)

Strasberg and former Howard Hughes paramour Domergue are the title characters, whose case of sibling rivalry reaches the lethal level.

Psychomania (1971) ◆◆◇
D: Don Sharp. George Sanders, Beryl Reid, Nicky Henson. 93 minutes. (Goodtimes)

A living dead Brit biker gang (!) rides amok in this intermittently entertaining combination of two fave genres. Sanders conveys boredom convincingly as a butler/occultist. Not to be confused with 1964's *Psychomania* (Sinister Cinema), an off-the-wall *Peeping Tom* (see index) lift that's not without its own tacky virtues.

Psychopath (1973) ◆◆◇
D: Larry Brown. Tom Basham, Henry Olek, Gretchen Kanne. 85 minutes. (Fox Hills)

A sort of *Mr. Rogers Goes Nutzoid!*, with Basham as an unhinged TV kiddie-show host on a one-man campaign to eliminate abusive parents (!). Pretty strange and compelling. From the people who brought you *The Pink Angels* (see index).

Psychos in Love (1986) ◆◇
D: Gorman Bechard. Carmine Copobianco, Debi Thibeault, Frank Stewart, Cecilia Wilde, Donna Davidge. 89 minutes. (Wizard)

This is yet another case of a great title and a promising premise masking a home-movie-level loser—this time from the Waterbury, Connecticut–based folks who brought you *Galactic Gigolo* (Urban Classics). Here, girl psycho and boy psycho "meet cute" in a bar, find they share the same homicidal hobby, and ultimately decide to go into partnership. A couple of gags work, but this is one of those oppressively cheap, completely unmagical amateur-night specials wherein three extras constitute a crowd scene. Why waste your video mad-money on an ultra-minimalist rip-off like *Psychos in Love* when there are so many *worthy* bad movies to be had?

The Pyx (1973) ◆◆◇
D: Harvey Hart. Karen Black, Christopher Plummer, Donald Pilon. 111 minutes. (Prism)

This earnest, well-produced Canadian chiller stars Black as a spiritual hooker and Plummer as a perplexed cop. The pic is relentlessly depressing, however—a mood in no way relieved by Karen crooning her own musical compositions on the soundtrack. FYI: Did you know that fully 48 percent of the world's most depressing films come from Canada? And if you don't believe us, you can look it up.

Race with the Devil (1975) ◆◆◆
D: Jack Starrett. Peter Fonda, Warren Oates, Lara Parker, Loretta Swit, R. G. Armstrong. 88 minutes. (Key)

Devil worshippers give high-speed chase to the hapless RV-driving vacationers (Fonda, Oates, Parker, Swit) who witnessed a ritualistic killing, in a generally exciting merger of the chase and chiller genres. An upscale entry from auteur Starrett, who also cameos as a suspicious pump jockey.

The Raven/The Black Cat (1935) ◆◆◆◇
B&W
D: Lew Landers. Bela Lugosi, Boris Karloff, Irene Ware. 62 minutes. (MCA)

This Universal classic also bears no connection to Poe, beyond mad plastic surgeon Bela's avowed interest in that author. He's even more interested in his home torture equipment and in bedeviling escaped con Boris. One of the B&B Boys' best, double-billed here with *The Black Cat.* Vintage fright fans can't go wrong with *this* cassette.

The Raven (1963) ◆◆◇
D: Roger Corman. Vincent Price, Boris Karloff, Peter Lorre, Jack Nicholson. 86 minutes. (Warner)

This Corman production has *absolutely* nothing to do with the Poe poem. Instead, Price, Karloff, and Lorre play a feature-length game of "dueling sorcerers," which is at least as much fun as the Poe poem anyway.

Rawhead Rex (1986) ◆◆
D: George Pavlou. David Dukes, Kelly Piper, Niall Tobin, Ronan Wilmot, Niall O'Brien, Heinrich Von Schellendorf. 89 minutes. (Vestron)

Famed fright writer Clive Barker has more or less disowned this celluloid version of his novella of the same name, and we more or less can't blame him. The flick plays like just another B monster movie, sans the visceral verve and sinister surreality of Barker's original tale. Our story, shifted to rural Ireland from pastoral England, involves a gardener who inadvertently unearths the title fiend, a nine-foot-tall, face-eating demon who proceeds to devour much of the local populace while simultaneously enlisting an evil church deacon to serve as his earthly minion. Yank tourist Dukes strives to end Rawhead's reign of gustatory terror and is not above wildly overacting to achieve that goal. Though Barker penned the script, Pavlou's pedestrian direction, the uncharismatic performances, and the unconvincing FX (beginning with Rex himself, played by the formidable Von Schellendorf) conspire to drag *Rawhead*, released directly to home-vid, down to the level of the merely endurable.

Razorback (1985) ♦♦
D: Russell Mulcahy. Gregory Harrison, Janet Morris, Bill Kerr, Chris Haywood, David Argue. 95 minutes. (Warner)

"*Tusks*" would have been a more fitting title for director Russell (*Highlander*) Mulcahy's imitative exercise in porcine paranoia, a *Jaws* clone transplanted to the landlocked Australian outback. Scripter Everett (*Link*) De Roche's predictable plot finds American newscaster Beth Winters (Morris) attempting to expose an illicit kangaroo-meat racket at an Aussie pet-food plant. Of greater concern to the locals, however, is a marauding razorback—"five times larger" (if not necessarily smarter) than your average boar—who quickly claims Beth as one of its hapless victims. Out for revenge are Beth's hubby Carl (*Trapper John, M.D.*'s Harrison) and crusty razorback hunter Jake Cullen (Kerr), who ex-

plains, "Razorbacks have only two states of being: dangerous and dead." *Razorback*'s at its best when exploring the outback's authentically eerie alienoid landscapes (credit Dean Semler's cinematography here) and colorfully primitive inhabitants. But while *Razorback*'s a polished, professional affair, it is, in the end, more bore than boar.

The Red House (1947) ♦♦◇ B&W
D: Delmer Daves. Edward G. Robinson, Lon McCallister, Judith Anderson. 100 minutes. (Congress, others)

Released during America's postwar horror-movie drought, this terror-tinged suspenser/soaper—starring Edward G. Robinson as a haunted farmer who knows the title site's dread secret—seems pretty tame today, though it still commands its share of fans.

Redneck Zombies (1988) ♦◇
D: Pericles Lewnes. Lisa De Haven, W. E. Benson, William W. Decker, James Housely, Tyrone Taylor, P. Floyd Piranha. 83 minutes. (TWE)

Seems the Troma Team is getting a tad formulaic. In *Toxic Avenger* and *Class of Nuke 'Em High* (see index), toxic waste turned Jersey youths into rampaging mutants; now an errant barrel of same (helpfully labeled "toxic waste") performs the same dubious service for a crew of dim-witted crackers, who celebrate their newfound radioactive state by eating a group of equally dim-witted campers.

Many of the cast members employ psuedonyms here—e.g., Sooy, Zoofoot, and our fave, P. Floyd Piranha—no doubt in a bid to retain their amateur status. (They needn't have worried.) There are a few crude laughs and still cruder el revolto FX in *Redneck Zombies,* but gore pioneer H. G. Lewis— not known as a perfectionist himself—did it a lot funnier in *2000 Maniacs* (see index) a quarter-century back.

The Reincarnation of Peter Proud (1975) NR

D: J. Lee Thompson. Michael Sarrazin, Margot Kidder, Jennifer O'Neill. 105 minutes. (Vestron)

Sarrazin is dismayed to learn that his body's the host for a murder victim's ghost.

Repulsion (1965) ◆◆◆◇ B&W

D: Roman Polanski. Catherine Deneuve, Ian Hendry, John Fraser. 105 minutes. (Video Dimensions)

Paranoia, claustrophobia, abrupt and senseless violence, and other of Polanski's treasured themes are expertly woven in this harrowing 105 minutes in the life and crimes of dissatisfied razor murderess Deneuve.

Rest in Pieces (1987) ◆◇

D: Joseph Braunstein. Scott Thompson Baker, Lorin Jean Vail, Dorothy Malone, Jack Taylor, Patty Shepard, David Rose. 90 minutes. (IVE)

Rest in Pieces sports one of your hoarier horror premises: In order to collect her inheritance, blond heroine Vail, niece of wealthy, demented suicide Malone, must journey (accompanied by ne'er-do-well hubby Baker) to her late aunt's estate. There she not only suffers nightmarish visions of her vengeful auntie but encounters eight initially well-mannered maniacs (an Irish priest and Malone's former shrink among them) who are living on the grounds. *Rest in Pieces* is essentially half-hour anthology material bloated to feature length. With the nutjobs outnumbering the potential victims, the script strains to reach an acceptable gore quotient by bringing in a guest string quartet (!) for the psychos to slaughter and dismember.

Return (1985) ◆◆

D: Andrew Silver. Karlene Crockett, John Walcutt, Anne Lloyd Francis, Frederic Forrest. 82 minutes. (Academy)

Young Crockett seeks to unlock a dark family secret, and the spirit of her late grandfather—currently residing in the back brain of amiable young gardener Walcutt— holds the key. *Return,* based on a Donald Harrington novel, squanders a decent idea via weak if earnest execution. Fifties femme fave Francis, her famous beauty mark intact, appears as a helpful parapsychologist, while Forrest— minus the prodigious gut he grew for 1986's *Where Are the Children?*—plays Karlene's father.

The Return of the Living Dead (1985)
♦♦♦

D: Dan O'Bannon. Clu Gulager, James Karen, Don Calfa, Thom Mathews, Beverly Randolph, Linnea Quigley. 90 minutes. (HBO)

If farcical flesh-eaters are your junk-movie meat, you won't be disappointed with O'Bannon's satiric splatcom. The plot posits that George Romero's *Night of the Living Dead* was based on a true incident involving army-owned corpses inadvertently revived by a certain toxic chemical. Said dead were subsequently sealed in airtight drums and erroneously delivered to the Uneeda Medical Supply Company in Louisville, Kentucky. Needless to say, it's not long before they're on their unsteady feet again, joined by the similarly reanimated residents of a nearby graveyard. *Return* works as a fairly faithful form parody of *Night* and sequels as Uneeda owners Burt (Gulager) and Frank (Karen), along with a pack of seemingly already brain-dead punks, are put through their paces by the cerebrum-starved ghouls. Unlike Romero's, these corpses can talk, and they spend much of their time chanting for "Brains!" and "More brains!" Top thespic honors, meanwhile, are easily copped by genre ingenue Linnea Quigley (see sidebar).

LINNEA QUIGLEY: B-SCREEN QUEEN

Assault of the Party Nerds. Treasure of the Moon Goddess. Creepozoids. Sorority Babes at the Slimeball Bowl-O-Rama. Hollywood Chainsaw Hookers.

The list of rising (and often writhing) B-screen scream queen Linnea Quigley's credits is as long as it is impressive. Though barely known beyond the B-movie ghetto, the lithe blond starlet has been brightening low-budget movies since her appearance in the shoestring shocker *Don't Go Near the Park* (NA) back in 1981. It was Linnea's pivotal role as the seminaked punkette Trash in 1985's raucous send-up *Return of the Living Dead,* however, that first attracted critical attention. In fact, Linnea may well hold the record for Longest Gratuitous Graveyard Nude Scene in a Rock 'n' Roll Gore Comedy.

While low-budget vet Linnea took the nudity in stride, she was less than thrilled about the filmmakers' plans re: the rest of her appearance.

"[Director] Dan O'Bannon was trying to convince me to shave my eyebrows, dye my hair pink, and shave my head!" Linnea confides. "I wouldn't have been able to work for two or three months!"

In the end, they settled for a series of red wigs, even though the compromise upped the budget by nearly a thousand bucks. Aside from that cosmetic conflict, Linnea recalls, "It was fun to do that role."

Adaptability and versatility are often necessities in the low-budget film biz. The Iowa-born actress—who's also an accomplished singer-songwriter-guitarist, ex of the distaff L.A. punk band Skirts—has learned how to wield a wicked chain saw, via her starring role in Fred Olen Ray's *Hollywood Chainsaw Hookers,* how to pull off a unique disappearing act in *Night of the Demons,* and how to survive a faulty prop during her bit as a Soul on Freddy's Chest in *A Nightmare on Elm Street 4.*

"It was funny"—Linnea laughs, safely after the fact—"because we almost got killed on the set doing it." Linnea and three other thesps were strapped into an outsize mock-up of dream demon Freddy Krueger's chest. "They slimed us all up with KY jelly," Linnea remembers. "We were supposed to break out of the chest. When we all leaned forward, the thing fell and landed on the cement," nearly maiming the performers and creaming the camera crew. "We had to do it again. This time they anchored it better."

Even Linnea's own extracurricular "moon dancing"—a self-styled ritual she routinely practices in the privacy of her California backyard in celebration of each new full moon (!)—came in handy for her titular role in *Treasure of the Moon Goddess,* where the script called for her character to perform a very similar dance. That's just one of the reasons why Linnea Quigley is in no great hurry to abandon the B-movie biz.

"You have more say on a low-budget film," the actress, who cites *Benji the Hunted* as her own personal film fave, points out. "You don't have a million people telling you what to do."

Return of the Living Dead Part II (1988)

D: Ken Wiederhorn. James Karen, Thom Mathews, Michael Kenworthy, Marsha Dietlein, Philip Bruns, Suzanne Snyder. 89 minutes. (Lorimar)

In the heavy hands of director/scripter Ken (*Meatballs Part II*) Weiderhorn, *Return of the Living Dead II* merely mimics the surface machinations of *Part I,* minus that flick's satiric thrusts, offering almost nothing in the way of fresh variations. Here, the Dead simply get up and give 89-minute chase to a handful of dull potential victims. Even James Karen and Thom Mathews, returnees from *Return I,* seem content to mug their way through the broad sitcom-level proceedings. A few scattered laughs survive (most supplied by Bruns as the town quack), and the initial graveyard exodus of the re-vivified cadavers is effectively revolting, but the Fried Zombies finale can't hold a crypt candle to *Part I*'s climactic nuking of Louisville, Kentucky.

The Return of the Vampire (1943) ♦♦◊ B&W
D: Lew Landers. Bela Lugosi, Frieda Inescort, Nina Foch. 69 minutes. (Goodtimes)

This often aimless Bela vehicle—slightly better produced than his Monogram and PRC efforts—has our hero wandering wartime London with his werewolf minion Matt Willis. There's a pretty good face-melting fade-out, though, and Goodtimes's price (under $10) is certainly right.

Return to Horror High (1987) ♦♦
D: Bill Froehlich. Vince Edwards, Bernard Hughes, Scott Jacoby, Lori Lethin, Philip McKeon, Alex Rocco. 95 minutes. (New World)

For videophiles like yours truly who've endured hundreds, or thousands, or even hundreds of thousands of bad fright flicks, *Return to Horror High* offers a welcome scenario: A low-budget movie crew settles in at the title site, former scene of several still-unsolved splatter murders, to make an exploitation pic on the subject. Natch, the unknown psycho begins slashing anew, this time slicing up Hollywood hacks in place of high school students. Utilizing an elaborate film-within-a-film-within-a-nightmare-within-a-film framework,

Return yields its fair share of shock yoks, at least in its early reels, and features deft bits by B vets Edwards and Rocco, as a sadistic biology teacher and a sleazy producer, respectively. Unlike broad spoofs such as *Pandemonium* (see index), *Return* suffers from comic *under*kill, dragging painfully to its overdue conclusion. Final grade: C+.

A Return to Salem's Lot (1987) ♦♦♦
D: Larry Cohen. Michael Moriarty, Samuel Fuller, Andrew Duggan, Ricky Addison Reed, June Havoc, Evelyn Keyes. 101 minutes. (Warner)

A *very* loose semisequel to Stephen King's TV movie *Salem's Lot* (see index), Cohen's *Return* to same is a lively fang-in-cheek tale detailing anthropologist Moriarty's visit to the title locale, where he's inherited a ramshackle farmhouse from a late, distant relation. At first he feels the scenery change might benefit his troubled young son (Reed). But that's *before* he gets acquainted with the native populace—vampires and their undead minions all. Director/scripter Cohen has fun playing with traditional vampire lore—we learn, for example, that most of the local bloodsuckers enjoy considerable financial security since, as town patriarch Duggan explains, real estate accrues in value and vampires live long enough (i.e., forever) to capitalize on that trend—and peppers his cast with such veteran thesps as Havoc and Keyes.

It's septuagenarian cult director Sam Fuller who steals the show, though, as a manic vampire-hunter who arrives in Salem's Lot with wholesale slaughter in mind. Barely released theatrically beyond a token Providence, Rhode Island, run, *Return to Salem's Lot* represents a genuine treat for Cohen cultists and general fright-film fans alike.

Revenge (1986) ◇
D: Christopher Lewis. Patrick Wayne, John Carradine, Bennie Lee McGowan, Josef Hanet, Stephanie Kropke, Fred Graves. 100 minutes. (United)

A sequel of sorts to 1985's *Blood Cult* (see index)—widely (if not highly) regarded as the first direct-to-video fright feature—*Revenge* pairs wooden Patrick (Son of Duke) Wayne and a hammy Carradine in a dog-eared tale of canine cultism (!) set in modern-day Oklahoma. The pic has a few inspired lines: "Man's best friend is now his worst enemy," a victim of the cultists (who kill for the love of the dog god Caninus) warns. "They wag their tails and tear out our hearts!" But the rest is an excruciatingly padded exercise in extraneous footage, blatant product tie-ins, and flamboyantly flubbed takes that the vid-makers didn't bother to reshoot. Want more demonic dogs? Try *Devil Dog: Hound of Hell* (Vestron), *Dogs of Hell*, formerly *Rotweiler* (Media),

Monster Dog (TWE), starring a re-dubbed (!) Alice Cooper, and *The Pack* (Vestron).

Revenge in the House of Usher (1982) ◆◆◇
D: Jess Franco. Howard Vernon, Dan Villers, Jean Tolzac. 90 minutes. (TWE)

Franco's *House of Usher* retread boasts the Euro-director's trademark atmospherics and leisurely pace, plus a major bonus for Francophiles: a half-hour B&W flashback consisting of footage from the otherwise unobtainable *Awful Dr. Orloff* (aka *Miss Muerte*). Franco regular Vernon gives a typically over-the-top Usher/Orloff interpretation in the new color scenes. Those in search of more historic Jesus, meanwhile, can also locate the following Franco films: *Attack of the Robots* (Sinister Cinema); *Bloody Moon* and *Man Hunter* (TWE); *The Invisible Dead, Oasis of the Zombies, Zombie Lake,* and *Erotikill* (Lightning), with the last also available in an overtly eroticized edition titled *The Loves of Irina* (Media/Private Screenings); *Revenge of the Dead* (Wizard); the flavorful *Sangre en Mis Zapatos (Blood in My Shoes)*, available from East Texas Distributing; sadly unavailable is the Franco spy farce *Two Female Spies in Flowered Panties*, where the translation may be loose but the panties are anything but. Clips from several of the above also appear in the creature-compilation tape *Zombiethon* (see index).

Revenge of the Stepford Wives (1980) ◆◆◆

D: Robert Fuest. Sharon Gless, Don Johnson, Julie Kavner. 95 minutes. (Embassy)

We actually enjoyed this made-for-TV sequel better than the original theatrical feature, Johnson's presence notwithstanding. Kavner is especially good as a motor-mouthed victim of the Stepford conspiracy.

Revolt of the Zombies (1936) ◆◇ B&W

D: Victor Halperin. Dean Jagger, Dorothy Stone, Roy D'Arcy. 65 minutes. (Loonic, others)

The Halperin Brothers here try to duplicate the success of their atmospheric White Zombie (see index), but this time they don't have Bela on hand to help them. The result is a fairly creaky antique of interest mostly to zombie-film historians.

The Ripper (1985) NR

D: Christopher Lewis. Tom Savini, Tom Schreier, Wade Tower. 104 minutes. (United)

Makeup ace Savini steps in front of the camera to star in this made-for-video cheapie. You may want to step aside.

Rocktober Blood (1986) ◆

D: Beverly Sebastian. Ben Sebastian, Tray Loren. 87 minutes. (Vestron)

Ferd and Beverly Sebastian, of Sebastian International Pictures obscurity, present Rocktober Blood, a heavy-metal horror pic costarring Ben Sebastian. With a plot thinner than Keith Richards, Rocktober Blood concerns a singing psycho (Loren) who rises from his grave to knock off deserving members of his former band and entourage during their Blood '84 tour. (Quoth he, "I'm gonna show you what rock 'n' roll gore is all about!") Of interest only to zealous members of the Parents' Music Resource Center.

Rosemary's Baby (1968) ◆◆◆◇

D: Roman Polanski. Mia Farrow, John Cassavetes, Ruth Gordon, Sidney Blackmer. 137 minutes. (Paramount)

William Castle and Roman Polanski, a match made in Hollywood hell, join forces to create this overlong but compelling horror biggie. Gordon makes for one of the screen's more eccentric menaces.

Ruby (1977) ◆◆◇

D: Curtis Harrington. Piper Laurie, Stuart Whitman, Roger Davis. 85 minutes. (United)

A possessed distaff deaf-mute goes violently mental at a horror-movie drive-in in a pic that benefits from Curtis (Night Tide) Harrington's directorial touches. With Piper (Carrie) Laurie and Stuart (Demonoid) Whitman. Fans of bijou-oriented bloodbaths are also referred to Drive-In Massacre (Magnum) and Movie House Massacre (Active).

Salem's Lot: The Movie (1979) ◆◆◇

D: Tobe Hooper. James Mason, David

Soul, Bonnie Bedelia. 111 minutes. (Warner)

The European theatrical release, reedited from the two-part made-for-TV adaptation of Stephen King's novel, contains violence cut from the tube print.

Satan's Cheerleaders (1977) ◆◆
D: Greydon Clark. John Ireland, Yvonne DeCarlo, Jack Kruschen. 92 minutes. (United)

A typically witless jiggle chiller, *Satan's Cheerleaders* offers a veteran cast and enough unintended laughs to qualify it as decent six-pack-video fare. John Carradine cameos as an irascible hobo, while peripatetic auteur/actor Clark went on to dabble in "blaxploitation" pics, like *The Bad Bunch* and *Black Shampoo* (both United), before making a major career move with the femme-oriented actioner *Angel's Brigade* (Vestron), where GC directed such thespic heavyweights as Jack Palance, Peter Lawford, Jim Backus, and Arthur Godfrey (!). Clark's latest contribution is the unforgettable mutant killer-cat movie *Uninvited* (see index).

SATURDAY NIGHT SHOCKERS, Vol. I 150 minutes (Rhino):
Pairs *The Creeping Terror* with *Chained for Life* (see index).

SATURDAY NIGHT SHOCKERS, Vol. 2 150 minutes. (Rhino):

Man Beast (1955) ◆◆ B&W
D: Jerry Warren. Rock Madison, Vir-

ginia Maynor, George Skaff. 72 minutes.

The Human Gorilla (1948) ◆◆◇ B&W
D: Budd Boetticher. Richard Carlson, Lucille Bremer, Douglas Fowley. 62 minutes.

This Rhino double feature offers *Man Beast*, a campy cut-rate Yeti adventure starring the immortal Rock Madison, plus *The Human Gorilla*, billed here as a Tor Johnson movie; actually, it's a retitling of a 1948 noir originally known as *Behind Locked Doors*, in which Tor appears briefly (albeit memorably) as an insane ex-boxer and which ranks as a not-bad B flick in its own right, with Fowley particularly effective as a sadistic attendant. The video also includes several trailers. *The Human Gorilla* is also out as a solo tape via Video Dimensions.

SATURDAY NIGHT SHOCKERS, Vol. 3 B&W 150 minutes. (Rhino):

Murder in the Red Barn (1935) NR B&W
D: George King. Tod Slaughter. 70 minutes.

Face at the Window (1939) NR B&W
D: George King. Tod Slaughter, Marjorie Taylor, John Warwick. 65 minutes.

Volume 3 offers two Tod Slaughter (sort of a Brit blend of Boris Karloff, Bela Lugosi, and Rondo Hatton) films, *Murder in the Red Barn* (1935) and *Face at the Window,* (1939), along with several trailers.

Sinister Cinema carries the same films on separate cassettes, plus several additional Tod titles, including *Crimes at the Dark House* (1940), 1937's *Crimes of Stephen Hawke* (with Slaughter as the Spinebreaker), 1936's *Demon Barber of Fleet Street* (with Tod as butcherous barber Sweeney Todd), 1948's *Greed of William Hart* (Tod's a body-snatcher), *Never Too Late to Mend* (1937, with Slaughter as a sadistic warden), *Sexton Blake and the Hooded Terror* (Tod's the latter in this 1938 thriller), and *Ticket of the Leave Man* (1939, with Tod cast as the mad killer The Tiger).

SATURDAY NIGHT SHOCKERS, Vol. 4
145 minutes. (Rhino):

Mates *Mesa of Lost Women* with *Monster of Piedras Blancas* (see index).

Scanners (1981) ◆◆◆
D: David Cronenberg. Jennifer O'Neill, Stephen Lack, Patrick McGoohan. 104 minutes. (Embassy)

Cronenberg's tale of telekinetic killers virtually invented the popular exploding-heads approach to horror. Vital viewing.

Scared Stiff (1987) ◆◆
D: Richard Friedman. Andrew Stevens, Nicole Fortier, Mary Page Keller, Josh Segal, David Ramsey, Jackie David. 85 minutes. (Republic)

Another entry in the popular soul-possession/haunted-house genres, Friedman's *Scared Stiff* finds shaky ex-mental patient/rock singer Keller and young son Segal moving into a renovated southern manse once inhabited by a psycho slave-trader. His ghost in turn moves into the body of Keller's beau, Stevens, causing the latter to run amok as the slaver's sinister spirit takes root. *Scared Stiff* is low in budget, mediocre in the FX department, and paced way too slow. The pic partially compensates via some suitably surreal and surprisingly effective nightmare imagery.

Scared to Death (1947) ◆◇
D: Christy Cabanne. Bela Lugosi, George Zucco, Nat Pendleton. 65 minutes. (Video Yesteryear, others)

Bela's only appearance in a color movie supplies viewers with the only reason to sit through this clunky "thriller" produced to showcase a cheap color-film process that looks a lot like today's computer-colorized flicks. George Zucco and Angelo Rossitto fans may also want to tune in.

Scars of Dracula (1971) ◆◆◆
D: Roy Ward Baker. Christopher Lee, Dennis Waterman, Jenny Hanley. 94 minutes. (HBO)

A fun Hammer *Dracula* sequel, with Chris sinking his fangs into the part with his customary vigor, highlighted by a memorable death scene.

Scream (1981/1985) 0 ♦
D: Byron Quisenberry. Pepper Martin, Hank Worden, Alvy Moore, John Ethan Wayne, Julie Marine, Gregg Palmer, Woody Strode. 86 minutes. (Vestron)

Quisenberry's *Scream*—formerly *The Outing* (not to be confused with 1987's *The Outing*, formerly *The Lamp*)—is a numbingly inept, badly butchered nonmovie originally released in '85 with a print carrying a 1981 copyright. The slender (not to say downright emaciated) premise involves several unsuspecting vacationers who visit a remote Old West ghost town, where they're bumped off far too slowly (and *off*screen at that). The flick is so flat and lifeless that we wonder whether Quisenberry and crew even had their Panaflexes pointed in the right direction. *Scream* not only squanders 86 minutes' worth of perfectly good film stock but wastes the rusty talents of such beloved B vets as Hank Worden, Woody Strode, Alvy (*Green Acres*) Moore, and Gregg Palmer (best remembered for his moving portrayal of Tabonga, the ambulatory tree, in 1957's arboreal horror *From Hell It Came* [NA]). Avoid at all costs.

Scream and Scream Again (1970) ♦♦
D: Gordon Hessler. Vincent Price, Christopher Lee, Peter Cushing. 95 minutes. (Vestron)

Though ultimately sabotaged by its convoluted plot, *Scream and Scream Again* features a solid cast and some strong initial shocks as mad surgeon Price raids living patients for body parts to create a race of superbeings.

Scream, Baby, Scream (1969) ♦♦
D: Robert J. Emery. Ross Harris, Eugenie Wingate, Chris Martell. 83 minutes. (Regal)

A wacko artist mutilates models so he can paint the grotesque results, in a mostly awful, amateurish effort that does offer its share of bizarre moments. Also available as *Nightmare House* on the Camp Video label.

Scream Bloody Murder (1973) ♦◇
D: Marc B. Ray. Fred Holbert, Leigh Mitchell, Robert Knox. 90 minutes. (VCI/United)

As the box so eloquently explains, "Michael was a strange little boy. His steel claw which replaced the hand he mangled while murdering his father is a weapon to punish his mother." Young Mike also suffers from hallucinations that provoke him to off strangers as well as loved ones in yet another troubling low-budget report from the Embattled American Family front.

Screaming Skull (1958) ♦♦ B&W
D: Alex Nicol. Alex Nichol, Peggy Webber, John Hudson. 68 minutes. (Sinister Cinema)

A cheap possession pic (as the trailer puts it, "See the revisualization of a woman scorned!"), recommended mostly for hardcore '50s fright fans.

Season of the Witch (1972) ◆◆

D: George Romero. Jan White, Joedda McClain, Virginia Greenwald. 89 minutes. (Vista)

Romero's (thus far) only feminist fright film (originally titled *Jack's Wife*) wavers between the good (some fine Freudian dream sequences), the bad, and the boring. A must for Romero rooters, though.

The Sender (1982) ◆◆◆

D: Roger Christian. Kathryn Harrold, Zeljko Ivanek, Shirley Knight. 92 minutes. (Paramount)

One of your better paranormal thrillers, with Ivanek cast as an unwitting psychic whose telepathic transmissions are received by concerned shrink Harrold.

Some clever story hooks and vivid nightmare imagery help move *The Sender* satisfyingly along, despite occasional lapses in logic.

The Serpent and the Rainbow (1988) ◆◆◇

D: Wes Craven. Bill Pullman, Cathy Tyson, Zakes Mokae, Paul Winfield, Brent Jennings, Michael Gough. 98 minutes. (MCA)

Craven's *The Serpent and the Rainbow*—"inspired" by Wade Davis's nonfiction book of the same title—charts the adventures of an anthropologist (Pullman) dispatched to Haiti by the Biocorp pharmaceutical company to retrieve some potent authentic "zombie powder" to market as an anesthetic. While tracking down a

FILMMAKERS IN FOCUS:
Wes Craven: From Elm Street to Haiti

Wes Craven, whose previous excursions into celluloid terror include *Last House on the Left, The Hills Have Eyes, Deadly Blessing,* and the influential *Nightmare on Elm Street,* was immediately drawn to the bizarre material detailed in Wade Davis's nonfiction investigation of Haitian voodoo lore, *The Serpent and the Rainbow.* "I didn't even see a script," he admits. "I read the book and committed to doing the film on the spot."

That commitment led Craven and crew to Haiti—a country devastated by corruption, abject poverty, and political chaos—where they became the first American unit ever to lens a feature film there. Filming lasted nearly a month, during which time two crew members began suffering from hallucinations sufficiently intense to prompt the director to send them stateside to recover.

"It was a combination of climate, unsanitary conditions, and exposure to the staged voodoo rituals," Craven opines.

It was also in Haiti that Craven encountered his first real-life zombie, a teenage girl who mirrored the lifelessness of his film zombie-character Christophe (Conrad Roberts). She had been poisoned, buried, and revived but had suffered permanent brain damage. "Only her eyes betrayed any sign of active life," the director recalls.

That *The Serpent and the Rainbow* ultimately veers from fact into scenes of hallucinatory horror became a source of conflict for Craven. "I was supposed to scare the pants off people and at the same time remain faithful to the book." For the latter reason, Craven rejected a suggested "army of zombies" ending but agreed to emphasize the more horrific aspects of voodoo beliefs for the film's terror-filled finale. As it stands, the director views *The Serpent and the Rainbow* as a film in an *Altered States/Exorcist* vein—a blend of fact, possibility, and flights of dark imagination.

local zombie, our hero runs afoul of one of Port au Prince's Meanest—secret police chief Peytreaud (menacingly interpreted by Mokae), who doubles as an evil voodoo sorcerer. Bill recruits distaff doc Tyson and benign voodoo priest Winfield to help him defeat his powerful new enemy. A blend of *The Believers*, *Nightmare on Elm Street*, and *Macumba Love*, *The Serpent and the Rainbow* (voodoo symbols for Earth and Heaven, respectively) beats around the graveyard bush for nearly an hour before deciding it's a fright flick. Once it does, Craven delivers a number of effectively horrific tableaux, especially when Peytreaud launches a full-scale voodoo "mind invasion." We get a creepy live-burial scene, several elastic limbs à la Freddy, rotting corpses galore, and a dinner party ruined by a live zombie hand in the soup (a common faux pas at Phantom feasts). Though there are some insights along the way—plus a detailed look at the art of zombie-powder preparation—viewers looking for a lucid exegesis of the role voodoo may have played in the Duvalier-dominated Haitian political system will probably be disappointed. But fright-film fans should find enough choice Cravenesque chills here to make a rental worthwhile.

The Seventh Sign (1988) ◆◇
D: Carl Schultz. Demi Moore, Michael Biehn, Jurgen Prochnow, Manny Jacobs, Akosua Busia, Arnold Johnson. 97 minutes. (RCA/Columbia)

A torpid exercise in yuppie egocentricity masquerading as a supernatural thriller, *The Seventh Sign* stars Moore as a pregnant West Coast yup who fears she's about to give birth to a baby with no soul. (Who said they could have it all?) What's worse, this event will signal the end of the world as we know it, since all the other signs of impending apocalypse—hailstorms, solar eclipses, blood moons, et al.—have already manifested themselves. *The Seventh Sign* relays its muddled mélange of New Testament prophecies, moral messages, and modern horror clichés with such unrelenting languor that, by that time, you'll be *ready* to sign off. The overloaded, inorganic script—even writers Clifford and Ellen Green use pseudonyms here—is unaided by a foundering cast dully directed by Schultz. If *The Seventh Sign* offers any indication, the world will end with neither a bang nor a whimper but a protracted yawn.

The Seventh Victim (1943) ♦♦◇ B&W
D: Mark Robson. Kim Hunter, Tom Conway, Jean Brooks. 70 minutes. (RKO)

Producer Val Lewton works with a suitably sinister theme—satanism in Greenwich Village—and gets the film off to an ominous, atmospheric start as schoolgirl Hunter's search for her errant weird sister leads her into a web of genteel evil. Trouble is, Val plays it a bit *too* subtle here as the movie meanders through its middle reels and

fails to deliver much of a payoff. Conway virtually reprises his fatuous *Cat People* shrink role here.

Shadows Run Black (1981) NR
D: Howard Heard. William J. Kulzer, Elizabeth Trosper, Kevin Costner. 89 minutes. (Lightning)

This otherwise forgettable slasher flick is included here solely for the benefit of hard-core Kevin Costner fans who may want to see what he was up to prior to making his mainstream-movie bones.

The She-Beast (1966) ♦♦
D: Michael Reeves. Barbara Steele, John Karlsen, Mel Welles. 74 minutes. (Sinister Cinema)

Steele embarks on a new rampage, this time as a tourist possessed by an eighteenth-century witch. Late director Reeves, who later gained fame for his work on *The Sorcerers* (NA) and *The Conqueror Worm* (HBO), made his debut with this low-budget outing. Recommended mostly for hard-core Barbara buffs.

She Freak (1967) ♦♦♦
D: Byron Mabe. Claire Brennen, Lee Raymond, Lynn Courtney, Bill McKinney, Claude Smith, Ben Moore. 87 minutes. (Magnum)

As an uncredited *Freaks* (see index) remake, *She Freak* is admittedly pretty weak. But as a slice of southwestern lowlife, Mabe's carnal carny parable, produced and well written by frequent H. G. Lewis cohort David F. Friedman, is

PREBOOK:
APRIL 14, 1988

NATIONAL RELEASE:
APRIL 28, 1988

It begins with the most evil cry, deep from
the twisted shadows of the night. Then, it's
laughter like some insane dog ringing in your
ears, it comes with the flaming jaws of
hungry horror. Oh yes, it hungers . . . for you!
Run! Run! But there is no escape for you who
will see the terrible true story of a man
caught in the icy fingers of

SHOCK! SHOCK! SHOCK!
A NEW LOW IN SLASHER FILMS!

STARRING **BRAD ISAAC** • **CYNDY McCROSSEN**
ALSO STARRING **ALLEN RICKMAN** • **BRIAN FUORRY** •
• **KELLY ROSS** MUSIC BY **BRUCE GORDON**
WRITTEN & DIRECTED BY **TODD RUTT**
AND **ARN McCONNELL**

B&W / RNVD 2933 / APPROX. 60 MINUTES
1987 / VHS ONLY

SUGGESTED RETAIL: **$29.95**

Yields lots of shock yoks from a low budget.
Photo courtesy of Arn McConnell and Rhino Video.

fairly riveting fare, a John Waters–type parody played almost straight. Brennen is especially memorable as desperate blond bimbo Jade Cochran, whose idea of upward mobility is to quit her greasy-spoon waitressing job to work a concession stand at a sleazoid traveling carnival. There, she's torn between her animal lust for stud ride-operator Raymond and the class yearnings that tilt her in the direction of relative high-roller McKinney, who owns the carny sideshow. The unbelievably inept *Freaks*-inspired climax shifts the flick from authentic sleaze to utter camp and plays as if

Friedman and company had simply run out of film and money (entirely possible). Still, we found *She Freak* a compelling, at times even poignant home-viewing experience.

The Shining (1980) ◆◆◇
D: Stanley Kubrick. Jack Nicholson, Shelley Duvall, Scatman Crothers. 144 minutes. (Warner)

The Phantom has to 'fess up here that he was among that camp bored rather than spellbound by Kubrick's elongated adaptation of the Stephen King novel. Others report they were anything but.

Shock! Shock! Shock! (1988) ◆◆◆ B&W
D: Todd Rutt, Arn McConnell. Brad Isaac, Cyndy McCrossen, Allen Rickman, Brad Fuorry, Kelly Ross, Sonny Greenberg. 60 minutes. (Rhino)

Rhino's catalog describes this no-budget, black-and-white, Brooklyn-lensed effort as "a new low in slasher films!" but *Shock! Shock! Shock!* is a good deal more than that. The pic isn't a so-bad-it's-good number; it's actually an oft-clever send-up, in a vintage Firesign Theater vein, of Z-movie clichés past and present. Filmmakers Rutt and McConnell spoof everything from *Friday the 13th* to *Zontar, the Thing from Venus*, as well as incorporating affectionate nods to such cherished obscurities as *Plan 9 from Outer Space, Spider Baby, Daughter of Horror*, TV's *Mr. Wizard*, and even Hong Kong's *Infra-Man*. Die-hard junk-culture buffs may glean the most from *Shock! Shock! Shock!*, but the flick furnishes sufficient fun in its own off-the-wall right to entertain casual viewers as well, and it's encouraging to see a fledgling film unit go for wit over cheap gore. We also dug Bruce Gordon's ultra-cheap surf guitar score; it sounded almost like music to our ears.

The Shout (1979) ◆◆◆
D: Jerzy Skolimowski. Alan Bates, Susannah York, John Hurt. 87 minutes. (RCA/Columbia)

An offbeat, metaphorical fright film about a mysterious nomad (Bates) who can kill by unleashing the title sound. Based on a novel by Robert Graves. Worth a look, if not a listen.

Silent Madness (1985) ◆
D: Simon Nuchtern. Belinda Montgomery, Viveca Lindfors, Solly Marx, David Greenan, Sydney Lassick. 93 minutes. (Media)

Silent Madness opens as a sort of *Schlock Corridor*, with shots of assorted lunatics wandering the halls of Manhattan's Cresthaven Mental Hospital. But the flick quickly segues into a psycho/slasher mode when dedicated shrink Dr. Joan Gilmore (Montgomery) discovers that Cresthaven's bumbling bureaucrats have inadvertently released the nutjob responsible for the infamous Barrington College Sorority Massacre of some two decades earlier. When the top docs attempt a craven cover-up, Dr. Joan heads to said Barrington, where she witnesses a renewed spate of splatter killings as, one by one, the college's comely co-eds succumb to a variety of instruments both sharp and blunt. *Silent Madness* is yet another predictable celluloid cut-and-waste job, with one novelty angle—it was shot in 3-D. You won't know that on video, but it's no great loss. The only potentially effective use of the process arrives when the maniac hurls a hatchet directly at the camera; unfortunately, he misses.

Silent Night, Bloody Night (1973) ◆◆◇

D: Ted Gershuny. Patrick O'Neal, Mary Woronov, John Carradine, Walter Abel, Tally Brown, Ondine, Candy Darling. 88 minutes. (Paragon)

An incoherent horror (reportedly the result of a troubled production) about an unidentified killer and a small town run by authorities who are actually former asylum inmates. The strange cast of screen veterans and Andy Warhol regulars (who populate a sepia-toned flashback) make the flick of interest to offbeat-movie buffs.

Silver Bullet (1985) ◆

D: Daniel Attias. Gary Busey, Corey Haim, Megan Follows, Everett McGill, Terry O'Quinn, Robin Groves. 95 minutes. (Paramount)

The Phantom's guess is that the film and publishing industries are suffering from some sort of localized *Brewster's Millions* syndrome: They feel they have to transfer a sizable portion of their fortune to Stephen King by a certain date or risk losing it *all*. That's the only earthly explanation we can fathom for the appearance of *Silver Bullet*. Based on King's *Cycle of the Werewolf, Silver Bullet* refers not only to the traditional ammo of choice among seasoned werewolf-hunters but to eleven-year-old Marty Caslow's (Haim) streamlined, motorized wheelchair. For most of the flick, Marty alone knows that the maniac responsible for significantly reducing the population of the small town of Tarker's Mills is actually a real live wolfman. Can the plucky, crippled lad convince his hostile older sister Jane (Follows) and bourbon-swilling uncle Red (unsteadily interpreted by Busey) before the werewolf catches up with him? Well, what do *you* think? With *Cujo* and *Cat's Eye* (see index) already under his belt, maybe Steve will run out of animals before Hollywood runs out of loot.

Sisters (1973) ◆◆◆

D: Brian De Palma. Margot Kidder, Jennifer Salt, Charles Durning. 92 minutes. (Warner)

De Palma achieves a deft balance between the sinister and the satiric in his story of distaff Siamese twins (Kidder) brain-twisted by an evil surgeon.

Sisters of Satan (1975) ◆◆◇

D: Juan Monteczuma. Tina Romero, Susana Kamini, Claudio Brook. 94 minutes. (Academy)

A Mexican attempt to cash in on the *Exorcist* craze, this gets pretty strange in its own right (and rites), with lesbian interludes, gratuitous nudity, arcane Inquisition rituals, and lots of exploding nuns.

Slaughter High (1987) ◆
D: George Dugdale, Mark Ezra, Peter Litten. Caroline Munro, Simon Scuddamore, Carmine Iannoccone, Donna Yeager, Gary Martin, Sally Cross. 89 minutes. (Vestron)

Originally titled *April Fool's Day* (not to be confused with the 1986 Paramount turkey of the same name), *Slaughter High* claims to be brought to you by "the makers of *Friday the 13th*" (a boast at once dubious and unfounded; only soundtrack composer Henry Manfredini had any connection to the original *Friday*). The pic's connect-the-dots plot finds a handful of student hoaxsters—among them longtime femme fright fave Munro, cast here as your typical middle-aged high school senior—playing a cruel trick on class nerd Marty (Scuddamore). The prank soon turns ugly, as does Marty himself when he winds up being doused with nitric acid. Five years later, the perpetrators show up for an April Fool's Day "class reunion" at the now-abandoned high. Also in attendance is a vengeful, jester-masked Marty. Since you can guess the rest, we'll move right along to the final stat sheet: three impalings, two electrocutions, one drowning, one hanging, one axing, one crushed-by-tractor, one needle-in-the-eye, and one explod-

ing stomach. Only hard-core Caroline Munro buffs will want to learn more. In R and unrated versions.

Slaughter Hotel (1971) ◆◇
D: Fernando Di Leo. Klaus Kinski, Rosalba Neri, John Ely. 100 minutes. (MPI)

Professional crazy Kinski gets to play the good guy in this hospital-set slaughter spree, costarring Rosalba Neri (aka Sarah Bay, of *Lady Frankenstein* fame). The flick is best remembered for its offensive ad campaign, which emphasized *Slaughter*'s coincidental parallel to the Richard Speck nurse murders. Also out as *Asylum Erotica*. The Belfast-set *Naked Massacre* (Vidcrest) represents a more deliberate exploitation of the Speck case.

Slaughterhouse (1988) ◆
D: Rick Roessler. Sherry Bendorf, Don Barrett, William Houck, Joe Barton, Jane Higginson, Jeff Grossi. 88 minutes. (Charter)

Slaughterhouse opens with a hog-slaughter montage set to a "funny" burlesque-type music track. It would seem a daunting task to maintain this level of creativity for 88 minutes, but scripter/director Roessler manages to pull off this negative trick with talentlessness to spare. A tired plot in a belated *Texas Chainsaw Massacre* vein finds local authorities about to foreclose on the inoperative title site, formerly run by one

Lester Bacon and his son Buddy (Barton). Said son, a fat moronic psycho who communicates via porcine snorts, employs his trusty meat cleaver to eliminate both the foreclosers and a band of typically witless teens using the slaughterhouse for a horror-video shoot (possibly the same group that lensed *this* turkey). Vidstore display ads for *Slaughterhouse* pushed Buddy as the next Freddy Krueger, but this gory bore isn't likely to give *Elm Street*'s dream demon any sleepless nights.

Slaughterhouse Rock (1987) ◆◇

D: Dimitri Logothetis. Nicholas Celozzi, Tom Reilly, Donna Denton, Toni Basil, Hope Marie Carlton, Steven Brian Smith. 90 minutes. (Sony)

Seems California college boy Celozzi (whose dad co-exec-produced) is plagued by bad dreams recreating the crimes of a cannibalistic cavalry commandant who terrorized Alcatraz isle long before the latter became a famous penal colony. At a teacher's urging, Nick and friends journey—in the dead of a dark and stormy night, natch!—to the abandoned prison, the better to exorcise the evil spirit's influence. There, said spirit commandeers the body of Nick's brother (Reilly), who promptly embarks on a psycho slaughter spree. Attempting to intervene is the ghost of a dead rock starlet (Basil), whose satanic tinkering released the evil spirit in the first place. *Slaughterhouse Rock* director/scripter Logothetis displays some visual flair, but the convoluted plot is clearly beyond his narrative grasp. Devo devotees are also likely to be disappointed with that band's prominently advertised but actually minimal soundtrack contributions.

Slime City (1988) ◆◇

D: Gregory Lamberson. Robert C. Sabin, Mary Hunter, T. J. Merrick, Dick Biel. 85 minutes. (Camp)

With plot elements that parallel everything from *The Tenant* to *Street Trash*, *Slime City* limns the sorry tale of young art student Alex, who moves into an NYC tenement wherein residents ply him with addictive wine. Turns out the elixir was the handiwork of a late satanist who wants to use Alex's body as his portal back to the present. Alex soon transforms into a homicidal slime fiend, presenting a clear and present danger to virginal girlfriend Lori, best friend Jerry, and assorted neighborhood lowlifes—including a hooker who, in the flick's funniest scene, informs our hero, "I'm only doing this till I graduate," while unwrapping his Invisible Man–type facial bandages to bare the slime beneath. Aside from a few bon mots like the above and generally decent performances, *Slime City* is an amateurish, derivative affair that fails to achieve its own decidedly low aspirations.

Slugs: The Movie (1988) ◆

D: J. P. Simon. Michael Garfield, Kim Terry, Philip Machale, Alicia Moro, Santiago Alvarez, Kris Mann. 90 minutes. (New World)

Yet another celluloid slime epic, this time about mutant slugs on the prowl, *Slugs* offers nothing for the old memory bank that wouldn't be marked "For Immediate Withdrawal." In fact, this extremely tired exercise in regurgitative filmmaking leaves no fright-flick cliché unturned—the climax even unfolds on Halloween (now *that's* original!)—and in several scenes, the pic is badly dubbed to boot. Unless you're dying to see naked teenagers slimed and devoured by the ravenous title creatures (and director Simon—who'd earlier helmed the truly repulsive sado-gore orgy *Pieces* [Vestron]— even manages to make *that* sequence dull), we'd suggest you let *Slugs* crawl off without you.

Snow Creature (1954) ◆◆ **B&W**

D: W. Lee Wilder. Paul Langton, Leslie Denison, Teru Shimada. 70 minutes. (Amvest)

The Wilder Boys (director W. Lee, scripter Myles) fashion the first official Yeti movie. Not as funny as *Man Beast* (see index) but okay for followers of cheap '50s fright fare.

Sole Survivor (1984) ◆◆◇

D: Thom Eberhardt. Anita Skinner, Kurt Johnson, Caren Larkey. 85 minutes. (Vestron)

The title of Thom (*Night of the Comet*) Eberhardt's debut feature, lensed in 1982 but unreleased till '84 (and then just barely), refers to commercial producer Skinner, the only survivor of a major plane crash predicted by psychic actress Larkey. Anita may have survived, but she's clearly not home free— not while a succession of walking cadavers follows her around. If *Sole Survivor* sounds like a rip-off of Herk Harvey's cult classic *Carnival of Souls* (see index), that's probably because it is. But while Eberhardt doesn't come close to matching *Carnival*'s haunting quality, *Sole Survivor* has its fair share of new twists and chills: The image of Anita, still buckled into her airline seat, sitting alone and alive amidst sprawling plane wreckage and human carnage is a powerful one. *Sole* may pale beside *Souls* but is worth seeing for its own minor merits and as a prelude to *Night of the Comet* (see index), where Eberhardt realizes more fully his considerable fright-pic potential.

Son of Dracula (1943) ◆◆◆ **B&W**

D: Robert Siodmak. Lon Chaney, Jr., Robert Paige, Louise Allbritton, Evelyn Ankers. 78 minutes. (MCA)

Actually, Lon plays *dad* Drac (under the imaginative alias Count Alucard) on a visit to the American South in an atmospheric Universal sequel.

Son of Frankenstein (1939) ◆◆◆◇ **B&W**

D: Rowland V. Lee. Basil Rathbone,

Boris Karloff, Bela Lugosi, Lionel Atwill, Josephine Hutchinson. 99 minutes. (MCA)

The third installment of Universal's classic Frankenstein series casts Rathbone in the tense title role, Lugosi as the broken-necked Ygor, Karloff in his final fling as the Monster, and Atwill as the one-armed police inspector covertly investigating a rash of murders that coincide with Herr Frankenstein Jr.'s ill-advised return to his father's infamous castle. All four principals turn in unforgettable work here, especially Basil as the increasingly agitated scientist whose plans to correct his dad's costly procedural errors are continuously complicated by the rest of the cast. Add Lee's atmospheric direction, Jack Otterson's majestically macabre, thoroughly intimidating sets and a deft script laced with unobtrusive dark humor and you have one of the legit giants of the fright-film industry.

Son of Ingagi (1940) NR B&W

D: Spencer Williams, Jr. Zack Williams, Laura Bowman, Spencer Williams, Jr. 65 minutes. (J&J)

A newly rediscovered all-black monster movie, starring black-film pioneer (before and behind the camera; he directed and wrote the story here) Williams, later of *Amos and Andy*'s Andy Brown fame. J&J's tape is transferred from an original 16mm print.

Son of Kong (1933) ◆◆◇ B&W

D: Ernest B. Shoedsack. Robert Armstrong, Helen Mack, Victor Wong. 70 minutes. (Fox Hills)

Carl Denham flees his creditors, returns to the South Pacific, and encounters the title offspring (who's more ET than KK) in a surprisingly cheesy sequel for its time, padded with footage from the first feature. Still fun going, though.

Sorority House Massacre (1986) ◆◇

D: Carol Frank. Angela O'Neill, Wendy Martel, Pamela Ross, Nicole Rio, John C. Russell. 74 minutes. (Warner)

Does this sound familiar? Moody sorority sister Beth (O'Neill) is troubled by what seem to be clairvoyant dreams depicting a past family massacre. When she claims to see blood dripping from the ceiling, her campus cohorts express concern:

"What's the matter with Beth?"
"Her aunt died."
"That was *weeks* ago."
"Gee, Terry, get *sensitive!*"

Soon the maniac of her dreams shows up in the flesh, with knife at the ready and mayhem in mind. While less gleefully mean-spirited than many of its ilk—e.g., 1988's *Slumber Party Massacre II* (Embassy)—*Sorority House Massacre* is a strictly by rote slice-and-dicer, replete with standard pulsing-heartbeat soundtrack, bass synthesizer stings, and killer's-POV camerawork. Only the pic's thankfully abbreviated running time earns it an extra half-phan.

Spasms (1983) ◆

D: William Fruet. Oliver Reed, Peter Fonda, Kerrie Keane, Al Waxman, Miguel Fernandes, Marilyn Lightstone. 92 minutes. (HBO)

Spasms (formerly *Death Bite*) opens with a hot voodoo number performed by an agitated cult of Micronesian snake-worshippers who are, in turn, violently dispatched by the mysterious super-serpent they revere. After this lively set piece, *Spasms* slows to a serpentine crawl. Reed is a wealthy hunter in telepathic touch with this selfsame "serpent god from hell," who, we're told, re-appears once every seven years. Seems that Reed narrowly escaped the snake monster's clutches six years earlier, and the thing has been after him ever since, much like Captain Hook and the killer croc. Except for the compulsory contempo doses of grue, gore, and gratuitous nudity, *Spasms* is essentially an old-fashioned monster movie, and a dull one at that. Rereleased in 1986.

Spider Baby, or the Maddest Story Ever Told (1964) ◆◆◆ B&W

D: Jack Hill. Lon Chaney, Jr., Carol Ohmart, Sid Haig, Quinn Redekker, Mantan Moreland. 80 minutes. (Loonic)

Certainly one of the *weirdest* sto-ries ever committed to celluloid, sort of like a William Castle vision on psychedelic drugs. Chaney, in one of his better, later roles, plays the chauffeur/cook/guardian of a family of regressive cannibals (who include chrome-domed Haig as a drooling imbecile) whose already bizarre life-style is sent spinning out of control by the arrival of a group of distant, untainted rela-tions and their lawyer, there to clear up certain inheritance mat-ters. Moreland, in his final screen appearance, cameos as a postman who becomes the crazed clan's first victim. Truly unique, and aided by a quality tape transfer courtesy of the archivists at Loonic Video.

Spirit of the Beehive (1973) ◆◆◇

D: Victor Erice. Fernando Fernan Gomez, Teresa Gimpera, Ana Torrent. 95 minutes. (Interama)

Not a horror film but a film in-spired by a horror film. When young Gimpera witnesses a screening of *Frankenstein* in her rural Spanish village in 1943, she becomes obsessed with the image of the lonely Monster and leads her older sister on a search for same. Auteur Erice's lyrical exploration of childhood fears and longings gets off to a fine start but proceeds at way too leisurely a pace to en-gage your typically Philistine Phantom. You may have a better time with it, though, as Erice's craft is never in doubt.

Splatter University (1984) ♦♦
D: Richard Haines. Francine Forbes, Cathy Lacommare, Dick Biel. 82 minutes. (Vestron)

A null-skulled Troma outing that has a few funny moments, most of them derived from the brain-dead college students' utter lack of interest in anything beyond sex and six-packs. Available in both Rated and unrated versions.

Spookies (1984/1988) ♦◇
D: Eugenie Joseph, Thomas Doran, Brendan Faulkner, Frank M. Farel. Felix Ward, Dan Scott, Alec Nemser, Maria Pechukas. 84 minutes. (Sony)

Spookies is actually two movies spliced into one decidedly incoherent hybrid: a 1984 outing originally tagged Twisted Souls, which was extensively reedited and to which new framing scenes and a misleading Gremlins/Ghoulies−type title were added. The result, as might be expected, is one unholy monster-movie mess. Of the two pics, Twisted Souls—though burdened by uninteresting characters in a tired situation (trapped, by a possessed Ouija board, in your stereotypical Old Dark House)— at least contributes its share of decent cheap scares, memorable monsters, and imaginative makeup FX. The newer inserts wallow in even hoarier horror-flick clichés centered on a German-accented sorcerer, his deformed geek of a henchman (who, for reasons unexplained, thinks he's a cat!), and a bride kept eternally young via the sorcerer's evil handiwork—all further diminished by woeful low-comedy relief.

Squirm (1976) ♦♦◇
D: Jeff Lieberman. Don Scardino, Patricia Pearcy, Jean Sullivan. 90 minutes. (Vestron)

As monster worm movies go, Squirm is one of the better ones. A rainy night in Georgia precipitates the rise of outsize sandworms from the mud.

Strait Jacket (1964) ♦♦◇ B&W
D: William Castle. Joan Crawford, Leif Erickson, Diane Baker. 89 minutes. (RCA/Columbia)

Castle strikes again with this suitably lurid ax-murder tale hinged on former psycho Crawford's current guilt or innocence. George Kennedy is one of the cast members who gets it in the neck.

The Strangler (1964) ♦♦◇ B&W
D: Burt Topper. Victor Buono, David McLean, Ellen Corby. 89 minutes. (Key)

Buono, late of Baby Jane, is quite impressive in his own star vehicle as an oedipal wreck who vents his wrath at the expense of the local (Boston) female population. Vic's even more violent in the Vienna-set Mad Butcher (Magnum).

Strangler of the Swamp (1946) ♦♦♦ B&W
D: Frank Wisbar. Rosemary LaPlanche, Charles Middleton, Blake Edwards. 60 minutes. (Sony)

A moody mise-en-scène adds much to this swamp-set story of retribution directed by German auteur Wisbar and based on an earlier Teutonic film of his creation. Slow pacing and PRC's no-budget production values hinder the pic's progress, but *Strangler* remains well worth seeing. That's *the* Blake Edwards, by the way, cast as the love interest.

Street Trash (1987) NR

D: Jim Muro. Bill Chepil, Mike Lackey, Vic Noto, Mark Sferrazza, R. L. Ryan, Nicole Potter, Tony Darrow. 91 minutes. (Lightning)

Not the impassioned plea re: the plight of the homeless its sensitive title implies, *Street Trash* is actually a determinedly tasteless splatcom set mostly in a Brooklyn collision yard. Deranged 'Nam vet Noto reigns as the leader of a pack of degenerate bums who torment young runaways Lackey and Sferrazza. Also making the errant youngsters' lives difficult is obese collision-yard-owner Ryan. A batch of poisoned vino (imaginatively labeled Tenafly Viper) causes the nabe wino population to start melting real good. Not much in the plot department, but novice auteur Muro, working from producer Roy (*Document of the Dead*) Frumkes's script, displays a sure visual and visceral sense. The cast's emotive abilities range from deft to nonexistent. Best are Darrow as a bullying Mafioso and James Corinz as an argumentative doorman, a team that supplies *Street Trash* with its funniest moments, which culminate in a brilliant coda. In sum, hard-core gore fans should lap it up; all others will more than likely want to keep their distance.

The Supernaturals (1985) ◆◆◆

D: Armand Mastroianni. Maxwell Caulfield, Nichelle Nichols, Talia Balsam, Bobby DiCicco, LeVar Burton, Bradford Bancroft. 86 minutes. (Embassy)

A sort of *Southern Comfort Meets 2000 Maniacs, The Supernaturals* tracks an army platoon on dangerous maneuvers in a Dixie landscape haunted by Confederate zombies. The premise may fall short in the originality department, but we found *The Supernaturals* a highly watchable, even compelling horror sleeper. Credit the tense script that actually incorporates real character development (what will they think of next!?) and the solid pro cast that includes Maxwell (*The Boys Next Door*) Caulfield, Balsam, Burton, and a chunky but still winning Nichols (*Star Trek*'s Lt. Uhuru) as the squad's no-nonsense topkick.

Superstition (1985) ◆◇

D: James W. Roberson. James Houghton, Albert Salmi, Lynn Carlin, Larry Pennell, Maylo McCaslin, Stacy Keach, Sr. 84 minutes. (Lightning)

A late-arriving *Amityville* rip-off, *Superstition* (formerly *The Witch*) concerns new dire doings at the old dark church-owned House on Mill Road, site of dozens of grisly murders perpetrated by fiends unknown and dating back some three hundred years. Young minister-hero Houghton inspires little confidence (for one thing, he's a dead ringer for wide-eyed movie reviewer Jeffrey Lyons) as he attempts to unravel the mystery. The rest of the cast members, among them B vets Salmi and Pennell, hang around waiting to see who'll be bumped off next and in what imaginative manner— drowned, decapitated, clawed, buzz-sawed, cut in half, or cooked in a microwave (the undeniable highpoint of this otherwise half-baked horror). Unfortunately, by the time Houghton solves the case, there's no one left to save!

Suspiria (1977) ◆◆◆
D: Dario Argento. Jessica Harper, Stefania Casini, Joan Bennett, Alida Valli, Udo Kier. 92 minutes. (Magnum)

The much-sought-after Argento masterwork finally made it to video in 1989 courtesy of Magnum Entertainment. A prequel of sorts to *Inferno* and *Tenebrae* (aka *Unsane;* see index), *Suspiria* stars Harper as a Yank ballet student who inadvertently dances into a witches' den. Vet actresses Bennett and Valli add to the fun, while Argento and his rock group Goblin supply the sinister score. Dario Argento's *Bird with the Crystal Plumage* is also available (United).

Swingers Massacre (1976) ◆◆◇
D: Ronald V. Garcia. Eastman Price, Jan Mitchell, Gary Kent, Marsha Jordan, Ushi Digart, Rene Bond. 90 minutes. (Standard)

A nerdy middle-aged lawyer (Price), suffering from intense, self-inflicted Swingin' '70s peer pressure, persuades his lovely, loyal wife (Mitchell) to join him in an ill-advised swapping adventure. Ill-advised for our hero at least, since the experience proves to be nothing if not humiliating: While he fails to function among the seasoned swingers, *she* gets it on with abandon, sampling every intimidating stud in the house. EP can't get no satisfaction on any level—his better half neither repents nor turns into a slut nor loses her affection for him, all of which further enrages our frustrated protagonist. The logical solution? Why, kill the studs one by one with a variety of phallic instruments! Less a soft-core sex-and-gore orgy (though there's grat nudity here and there) than an offbeat parable, *Swingers Massacre*—penned by distaff scripter Elene Arthur— shapes up as a crude but compelling chronicle that contains more than its expected share of ironic twists and raw truths. Also from Standard: *Attack of the Killer Cave Babes, Blood Hunter, Droid,* and *Midnight Intruder.*

Tales from the Crypt (1972) ◆◆◆
D: Freddie Francis. Peter Cushing,

Ralph Richardson, Joan Collins. 92 minutes. (Prism)

While it doesn't capture the flavor of EC Comics (on which it's based) as vividly as *Creepshow* does, *Tales* supplies an entertaining quintet of seriocomic scare vignettes brought to life by a cast of veteran Brit terror troopers.

Tales of Terror (1962) ◆◆◆

D: Roger Corman. Vincent Price, Peter Lorre, Basil Rathbone, Debra Paget. 90 minutes. (Warner)

One of Corman's classier productions, abetted by Richard Matheson's skilled (if loose) adaptation of several Poe tales and further boosted by Price-Lorre's memorably bizarre teaming.

The Tell-Tale Heart (1963) ◆◆◇ B&W

D: Ernest Morris. Laurence Payne, Adrienne Corri, Dermot Walsh. 81 minutes. (Loonic)

Poe's prose monologue is padded into an only partially successful Brit feature film that's nonetheless collected a following.

The Terror (1963) ◆◆

D: Roger Corman. Boris Karloff, Jack Nicholson, Sandra Knight. 81 minutes. (Goodtimes, others)

Lensed in three days with sets and thesps left over from Corman's *The Raven, The Terror* may be a triumph of impromptu filmmaking, but it's not much of a movie, though Karloff and Nicholson fans will want to take a look. This is another unprotected flick that's out on virtually every PD-oriented label.

Terror at Red Wolf Inn (1972) ◆◆◆

D: Bud Townsend. Linda Gillin, Arthur Space, John Neilson, Mary Jackson, Donald Macready. 90 minutes. (Academy)

Alternately titled *Terror House* and *Red Wolf Inn*, 1972's *Terror at Red Wolf Inn* is an authentically sick yet relatively subtle sleeper that functions both as a fun fright flick and as an effective visual dietary aid. Our story involves a family of folksy suspected cannibals—an elderly couple (Space, Jackson) and their unhinged grandson (Neilson)—who lure unsuspecting gals to the isolated title locale via a "free vacation" mail scam. Our heroine, a lonely but ebullient co-ed named Regina (winningly played by Gillin), gradually catches on to her attentive hosts' unorthodox eating habits when the other guests begin vanishing one by one. Despite a food-stamp budget, *Terror* is rich in sly wit and suspense. The filmmakers fashion their story with rare care, particularly during an elaborately choreographed banquet scene that plays like a *Tom Jones Meets Cannibals in the Streets*. *Terror at Red Wolf Inn* makes for a zesty—if tasteless—trash-movie morsel.

Terror Creatures From the Grave (1965) NR

D: Ralph Zucker (Massimo Pupillo). Barbara Steele, Riccardo Garrone, Walter Brandi. 85 minutes. (Sinister Cinema)

Plague victims return from the dead in an Italo chiller noteworthy primarily for Steele's ever-compelling presence.

Terror in the Crypt (1963) NR

D: Camillo Mastrocinque. Christopher Lee, Adriana Ambesi, Pier Ana Quaglia. 90 minutes. (Baker)

This slow-moving tale of exorcism, vaguely drawn from Sheridan Le Fanu's *Carmilla*, finds Chris in fine form.

Terror in the Haunted House (1958) ◆◆ B&W

D: Harold Daniels. Cathy O'Donnell, Gerald Mohr, William Ching. 90 minutes. (Rhino)

Shot in Psychorama, a process that involves subliminal imagery, *Terror* is an otherwise tame affair about O'Donnell's distant memory of a murder she witnessed as a child. With a VCR, you can freeze-frame the subliminal images (e.g., "Kill! Kill! Kill!"), which is at least a novel way to pass a slow night. Purists should be warned, however, that Rhino's tape contains *new* subliminal messages in place of the originals, missing from the transfer print. Director Daniels also helmed the similar gimmick flick *A Date with Death* (NA), starring gutter icon Liz Renay.

Terror in the Wax Museum (1973) ◆◆

D: Georg Fenady. Ray Milland, Broderick Crawford, Elsa Lanchester. 88 minutes. (Vestron)

Milland goes the Vincent Price route as the owner of the title establishment. Not as good as *House of Wax* (see index), but it features a cast of such intrepid old-timers as Louis Hayward, Patric Knowles, Maurice Evans, and, of course, John Carradine.

Terror Train (1980) ◆◆

D: Roger Spottiswoode. Ben Johnson, Jamie Lee Curtis, Hart Bochner, Vanity. 97 minutes. (Key)

A deranged disenchanted frat-rat wreaks havoc aboard the title train in this predictable but watchable vehicular chiller. Johnson and Curtis are also aboard, which helps.

The Texas Chainsaw Massacre (1974) ◆◆◆

D: Tobe Hooper. Marilyn Burns, Ed Neal, Gunnar Hansen. 84 minutes. (Video Treasures)

For a time there, it was hard to escape Hooper's semisatiric exercise in celluloid Gein-ocology, so ubiquitous had this midnight movie become. Not as gory as originally advertised, but still crazy after all these years and a must for fright-flick buffs and casual viewers alike. Ed ("My family's always been in meat") Neal's performance alone makes a rental worthwhile.

The Texas Chainsaw Massacre 2 (1986) ◆◇
D: Tobe Hooper. Dennis Hopper, Caroline Williams, Bill Johnson, Jim Siedow, Bill Moseley, Lou Perry. 101 minutes. (Media)

For all its well-intended pokes at American (or Texan, anyhow) violence, an amoral free-enterprise system run amok, and other worthy targets, Hooper's *Texas Chainsaw Massacre 2* isn't nearly as funny—or scary—as his original model. Dennis (Rebel Without a Pause) Hopper, as "Lefty" Enright, a hard-nosed Texas Ranger equipped with holstered chainsaws (!), seems but a pale shadow of his former shell, exhibiting little of the manic energy he would later display in *Blue Velvet* and *River's Edge* (see index). The plot finds Hopper hot on the trail of the sicko Sawyer clan—played in splatstick Three Stooges style by original chainsaw maniac Siedow, with Johnson and Moseley replacing Gunnar Hansen and Ed Neal— who butchered his wheelchair-bound brother Franklin twelve years earlier. A distaff rock deejay (Williams) leads Hop to the loonies' labyrinthine lair, where most of this virtually one-set wonder unfolds. (In fact, the Sawyers' ghoulishly appointed subterranean slaughterhouse is one of *TCM II*'s few major pluses.) Hardcore gore connoisseurs should be pleased with Tom Savini's reliably revolting FX work, and a few stray laughs (including a brief opening *Texas Chainsaw Massacre* rap song) manage to survive. Otherwise, *TCM II* didn't give us much of a buzz.

Theatre of Blood (1973) ◆◆◆
D: Douglas Hickox. Vincent Price, Diana Rigg, Jack Hawkins, Robert Morley. 105 minutes. (MGM/UA)

Vincent Price is typecast as an incurable Shakespearean ham who strikes back at his sundry critics. It takes considerable filler to pad the pic's lone idea to feature length, but there are enough payoffs to make watching worthwhile. The Grand Guignol–set *Theatre of Death* (VCI), with Chris Lee, is likewise worth an attentive look.

They Came from Within (1975) ◆◆◆
D: David Cronenberg. Paul Hampton, Joe Silver, Lynn Lowry, Barbara Steele. 87 minutes. (Vestron)

Cronenberg's debut film introduces his visceral concerns as hungry, aphrodisiacal parasites make their way through a Montreal apartment building and its inhabitants. Gross but compelling.

13 Ghosts (1960) ◆◆◇ B&W/color
D: William Castle. Donald Woods, Rosemary DeCamp, Margaret Hamilton. 85 minutes. (Goodtimes)

Another fun, dumb romp from

"Master of Movie Horror" William Castle. Tragically, much of the Illusion-O process that allowed theater audiences (with a little help from their Ghost Viewers) to see the advertised spirits has been lost in the tape transfer.

To the Devil—A Daughter (1976) NR
D: Peter Sykes. Christopher Lee, Richard Widmark, Nastassia Kinski. 93 minutes. (Cinema Group)
Lee's on the loose again, this time as an ex-priest-turned-satanist in hot pursuit of Kinski, whom he thinks is ripe for a demonic rite. Widmark is a fright novelist out to foil Chris's scheme.

The Tomb (1986) ◆◆◇
D: Fred Olen Ray. Cameron Mitchell, John Carradine, Sybil Danning, Susan Stokey, Michelle Bauer, Kitten Natividad. 90 minutes. (TWE)
One of Ray's more entertaining efforts, *The Tomb* features Fred's usual flair for creative casting: Mitchell, Carradine, and Danning all strut their thespic stuff in this suitably ludicrous tale of the undying evil Egyptian princess Nefrites wreaking havoc in the modern world. With veteran Russ Meyer vixen Natividad as a stripper and Gertie the Rat as "himself." Sample inspirational dialogue:

Nefrites: Where is the Eye of Horus?
Cameron: Where is the Golden Scarab?
Nefrites: I asked you first.

Tomb of Ligeia (1964) ◆◆◆
D: Roger Corman. Vincent Price, Elizabeth Shepherd, Richard Johnson. 82 minutes. (HBO)
One of Corman's better Poe adaptations finds Price haunted by the image of his late wife, causing complications in his new marriage.

Tombs of the Blind Dead (1971) ◆◆◇
D: Armando De Ossorio. Oscar Burner, Lone Fleming, Helen Harp. 86 minutes. (Vidcrest)
Vengeful Knights of Templar return as eyeless zombies in a moody, gory Spanish prequel to *Horror of the Zombies* (Super). Also out as *Night of the Seagulls* (Sony) and *Return of the Evil Dead* (Genesis).

The Toolbox Murders (1978) ◆◇
D: Dennis Donnelly. Cameron Mitchell, Pamelyn Ferdin, Wesley Eure. 93 minutes. (United)
Mitchell stretches as a homicidal landlord who perpetrates gore killings with his imaginative assortment of trusty power tools. Whether that whets your appetite or dampens your enthusiasm is up to you to decide. Cameron, meanwhile, also headlines in the Lone Star State duo *Texas Detour* (Prism) and *Texas Lightning* (Media).

The Torture Chamber of Dr. Sadism (1967) ◆◆◇
D: Harald Reinl. Christopher Lee,

Lex Barker, Karin Dor. 120 minutes. (Magnum)

Great title for a pretty good film, taken from Poe's *Pit and the Pendulum*, with Lee subjecting Barker and Dor to all manner of painful indignities. Surreal imagery abounds. Also out as *Blood Demon* and in a truncated version titled *Castle of the Walking Dead* (Interglobal).

Torture Garden (1967) ◆◆◆
D: Freddie Francis. Jack Palance, Burgess Meredith, Beverly Adams, Peter Cushing. 92 minutes. (RCA/Columbia)

Meredith is the mysterious Dr. Diabolo, a sideshow barker who treats spectators to terrifying forecasts of their uniformly awful futures. Fun going, with Palance particularly sharp as a crazed Poe fanatic.

Tourist Trap (1979) ◆◇
D: David Schmoeller. Chuck Connors, Jon Van Ness, Tanya Roberts. 94 minutes. (Media)

Those rabid to see Chuck (*The Rifleman*) Connors join the psycho ranks won't want to miss this exercise in Grand Guignol manqué, yet another *House of Wax* variation. All others will.

Tower of London (1962) ◆◆◇ B&W
D: Roger Corman. Vincent Price, Michael Pate, Joan Freeman. 79 minutes. (Wood Knapp)

Price slices the ham as Richard III in Corman's cardboard remake of Rowland V. Lee's 1939 opus of the same name. VP's fans will find it fun going, though.

The Town That Dreaded Sundown (1976) ◆◆
D: Charles B. Pierce. Ben Johnson, Andrew Prine, Dawn Wells. 90 minutes. (Warner)

Indie auteur Pierce, the man behind the *Boggy Creek* yawners, bases this mediocre chiller on the actual exploits of a hooded Texas killer.

Toxic Zombies (1980) ◆◆
D: Charles McCrann. Judy Brown, John Amplas, Claude Scales. 85 minutes. (Raedon)

A fairly awful regional horror (lensed in Pennsylvania) about cannibalistic paraquat zombies (you know the type) on the prowl, hoisted a bit by Brown's compelling perf as an imperiled blond teen. Originally released as *Bloodeaters*, then rereleased theatrically in 1985 under its present video title.

Transylvania 6-5000 (1985) ◆
D: Rudy DeLuca. Jeff Goldblum, Joseph Bologna, Ed Begley, Jr., Carol Kane, John Byner, Geena Davis. 94 minutes. (New World)

Unlike Carl Reiner/Steve Martin's brilliant horror-movie send-up *The Man With Two Brains* (see index), *Transylvania 6-5000*—starring Jeff (*The Fly*) Goldblum and Ed Begley, Jr., as a pair of sleaze journalists searching for tawdry terror material in a modern, image-conscious Transylvania—operates as a sort of *Two Men With No Brains*. You *know* an alleged comedy is in trouble when its wittiest components are its title and a few *deliberately* unfunny riffs, herein provided by Michael Richards as a Transylvanian butler-cum-would-be-slapstick-comic. "Is good, eh? Is funny?" he keeps asking. The Phantom's reply? Negative on both counts.

Trick or Treat (1986) ◆◆◇
D: Charles Martin Smith. Marc Price, Tony Fields, Gene Simmons, Lisa Orgoline, Doug Savant, Ozzy Osbourne. 97 minutes. (Lorimar)

Trick or Treat borrows liberally from both *Carrie* and *Nightmare on Elm Street*, yet manages to emerge as a well-crafted, fairly funny homage to heavy-metal hostility. Price toplines as high school scapegoat Eddie Weinbauer, who unwittingly conjures the disfigured ghost of his late rock idol Sammi ("Rock's chosen warriors will rule the apocalypse!") Curr to help rid him of his sundry tormentors. But it seems that Sammi (hammily interpreted by Fields) has more serious mischief of his own in mind. Director Smith—who played the nerd Terry in *American Graffiti* and appears here (in a clever cameo) as the equally nerdy teacher Mr. Wimley—gives us a far darker vision of adolescent life in this lively but nongory allegory. Real-life rockers Simmons and Osbourne

also turn up in brief bits, as a local deejay and an antirock evangelist (!), respectively.

Trilogy of Terror (1975) ◆◆◇
D: Dan Curtis. Karen Black, Robert Burton, John Karlen. 78 minutes. (MPI)

Black gives her lungs a killer workout in this well-wrought (if occasionally *over*wrought) trio of terror tales originally produced for TV. Best here is episode three, wherein KB is pursued by a hostile African devil doll, a theme later explored in the immortal direct-to-vid feature *Black Devil Doll from Hell* (Hollywood Home Theater), to say nothing of *Dolls*, *Child's Play*, and the legendary *Attack of the Beast Creatures* (see index).

Twice Dead (1988) ◆◇
D: Bert Dragin. Tom Breznahan, Jill Whitlow, Jonathan Chapin, Christopher Bugard, Sam Melville, Brooke Bundy. 85 minutes. (Nelson)

How's *this* for logic? A Normal American Family (dad Melville, mom Bundy, teen son Breznahan, and curvaceous daughter Whitlow) move into the dilapidated mansion they've just inherited from a late uncle. Trouble is, the château in question already has three strikes against it: One, it's a dump; two, it's haunted by the intrusive spirit of an earlier, quite demented owner; three, it's situated smack in the center of a dangerous nabe ruled by a gang of degenerate street punks. Oh yeah, and there's no electricity. Instead of giving up the ghost, our hardy if naive NAF decide to suck it up and tough it out. Then, when the previously mentioned punks beat up son Scott, attempt to rape daughter Jill, and outright murder family cat Meow, Mom and Dad split town for two weeks to attend to other business, leaving the kids to fend for themselves. Said kids, meanwhile, try to scare the bad guys away by staging a homemade FX orgy (!). When that ingenious ploy fails, it's up to our resident ghost to set matters right. That's just a sampling of the rampant stupidity on view in Bert (*Summer Camp Nightmare*) Dragin's brain-damaged JD-horror hybrid. On the plus side, *Twice Dead* does feature an impressive, literally shocking sex-electrocution scene and contributes a worthy addition to the Phantom's ever-growing Famous Last Words file: "Think I'll check out the basement." But screen dad Sam Melville sums it up best when he returns at film's end to comment, "Thank God they're all dead!"

Twice-Told Tales (1962) ◆◆

D: *Sidney Salkow. Vincent Price, Sebastian Cabot, Mari Blanchard. 120 minutes. (MGM/UA)*

Poe is passed over in favor of Hawthorne, and Roger Corman for Salkow, resulting in a middling anthology that's longer on talk than on terror.

Twins of Evil (1972) ◆◆◇

D: *John Hough. Peter Cushing, Madeleine Collinson, Mary Collinson, Dennis Price. 85 minutes. (Vid-America)*

Matching *Playboy* Playmates Mary and Madeleine Collinson play "Which One's the Vampire?" in a slick if predictable Hammer period piece. The video, transferred from the original Brit print, contains restored footage not seen in the American theatrical release.

2000 Maniacs (1964) ◆◆◆

D: *Herschell Gordon Lewis. Connie Mason, Thomas Wood, Jeffrey Allen, Ben Moore. 75 minutes. (Rhino)*

Lensed in scenic St. Cloud, Florida, *2000 Maniacs* is probably the closest goremeister Lewis ever came to crafting a crossover movie—or, for that matter, to *crafting* a movie. This splatter update of *Brigadoon* (though *Brigadoom* might be more accurate) succeeds in being genuinely sardonic, slickly paced, memorably scored (by HG himself, with major assists from the Pleasant Valley Boys) and even downright entertaining. Our story sees a sextet of vacationing Yankees wander into a long-defunct Confederate town that reappears for vengeance purposes every hundred years. The unlucky tourists—headed by Lewis mainstay Wood and ex-Playmate Mason—are treated to an elaborate, film-length display of southern inhospitality, climaxing in a series of blackly funny splatter set pieces. Though Lewis's assembled thesps are less than agile—with the exception of Allen as the phantom town's relentlessly affable mayor—this is easily HG's best effort, and even those disinclined to Lewis in particular, or gore in general, may well find this one as much fun as we did. Other Lewis horrors not covered separately in this volume include *The Gore-Gore Girls* (Midnight), with Henny Youngman(!), and *Something Weird* (Video Dimensions).

The Uncanny (1977) NR
D: Denis Heroux. Peter Cushing, Samantha Eggar, Ray Milland, Donald Pleasence. 85 minutes. (Media)

Felines of the world unite against their human oppressors in a trilogy of tales linked to killer cats and lifted by a top vet cast. Cat lovers should lap it up. We also refer the latter to *Because of the Cats* (Prism), *Night of 1000 Cats*, and *Uninvited* (see index).

The Undying Monster (1942) ◆◆◇ B&W
D: John Brahm. James Ellison, John Howard, Heather Angel. 60 minutes. (Sinister Cinema)

Coastal residents try to ascertain the identity of the werewolf who's been terrorizing the countryside. Director Brahm adds enough atmospheric touches to qualify this unsung B chiller as an hour well spent.

The Unholy (1988) ◆◇
D: Camilo Vila. Ben Cross, Hal Holbrook, Ned Beatty, William Russ, Trevor Howard, Jill Carroll. 100 minutes. (Vestron)

The Phantom harbored moderately high hopes for Vestron's *The Unholy*, largely due to vet screenwriter Philip (*Bloody Wednesday*) Yordan's co-scripter credit. Unfortunately, aside from an admittedly wacky climactic exorcism sequence, little of Yordan's patented weirdness is in evidence here. Instead, *The Unholy* plays like a belated, claustrophobic *Exorcist* clone, with New Orleans priest Cross (at least the name fits) battling a determined demon named Desidarius (though it's the movie's relentless offscreen wind machine that seems to do most of the damage). *The Unholy* also manages to waste such venerable thesps as Beatty, Holbrook, and the late Trevor Howard, seen here (in his film finale) as the blind survivor of a previous close encounter of the satanic kind. There are a few deft daft touches, as when Cross starts receiving crank calls from hell (!), but not enough to raise the flick's temp much above a low boil.

Unsane (1982) ◆◆◇
D: Dario Argento. Anthony Franciosa, Christian Borromeo, John Saxon, Daria Nicolodi, Mirella D'Angelo, Veronica Lario. 91 minutes. (Fox Hills)

Unsane finds Italo horror auteur Dario Argento up to his old sicko tricks in a mystery psycho pic that stresses suspense over all-out gore. Franciosa plays writer Peter Neal, currently in Rome to plug his latest thriller, *Tenebrae* (also the film's original title). Immediately upon his arrival, an unknown maniac begins aping the murders described in Neal's novel and sending fiendish fan notes to the author himself. Argento, aided by his flair for inventive visual touches, wrings considerable suspense from his story line, though the slayings themselves are repetitious, with the mostly distaff victims inevitably shown fleeing a merely unpleasant situation into a downright lethal one. Poor dubbing occasionally detracts, but *Unsane* shapes up as must viewing for Argento addicts and adequate fare for less committed fear fans.

The Unseen (1981) ◆◆◇
D: Peter Foleg. Barbara Bach, Sidney Lassick, Leila Goldoni, Stephen Furst. 89 minutes. (VidAmerica)

Ex—*Animal House* nerd-boy Furst is the cellar-dwelling, brain-damaged spawn of siblings Lassick and Goldoni's incestuous union. Barbara (Mrs. Ringo Starr) Bach unwisely investigates the unhealthy situation in this suitably sick geekfest.

Vamp (1986) ◆◇
D: Richard Wenk. Chris Makepeace, Sandy Baron, Robert Rusler, Dedee Pfeiffer, Gedde Watanabe, Grace Jones. 94 minutes. (New World)

Vamp is a largely laughless revamp of the superior *Fright Night*, with elements of Martin Scorsese's *After Hours* tossed in. The slender story line takes a trio of frat rats (Makepeace, Rusler, and Watanabe) to a seedy strip joint in search of an ecdysiast willing to peel at a campus bash. Said dive is actually a front for a gaggle of vampires, led by the insatiable Katrina (Jones) and sleazoid emcee Baron. Grace Jones fans (and we know you're out there, we can hear you posturing) should be advised that the Amazin' Amazon receives a scant 10 minutes or so of screentime here (a shabby way to treat such a major nontalent, if you ask us). She does perform one semistrip number—in whiteface, no less (where she bears a strong resemblance to Mary Woronov). Though a smattering of low-level laughs, chills, and mild surprises dot this claustrophobic creature comedy, there aren't enough to make a vid-viewing essential. Grace, meanwhile, also pops up in the 1982 B thriller *Deadly Vengeance* (Active).

Vampire at Midnight (1987) ◆◆◇
D: Gregory McClatchy. Jason Williams, Gustav Vintas, Lesley Milne, Esther Alise, Jeanie Moore, Robert Random. 93 minutes. (Key)

Jason (*Flesh Gordon, Danger Zone*) Williams toplines as an L.A. cop in hot pursuit of a bloodsucking serial killer. The psycho in question—a chic, wealthy New

Age hypnotherapist who's also equipped with a traditional Transylvanian accent—may or may not be a literal vampire but has no trouble claiming an ever-climbing number of mostly distaff victims. While occasionally slow of pace, *Vampire at Midnight* represents an admirable attempt to fashion an earnest fright film that's at once visually stylish and narratively straightforward. The flick features solid performances by Williams (who co-produced, as he did his previous vehicle, *Danger Zone*) as our laid-back hero, Roseanna Arquette–lookalike Milne as the pianist caught between cop and vampire, and Vintas as their toothy tormentor. With a bit more juice, *Vampire at Midnight* could've been a genuine sleeper; as it stands, the pic still rates as a minor but highly watchable horror outing and one of the better flicks in a recent spate of vampire entries that also include Chris Coppola's *Dracula's Widow* (HBO), Troma's *I Married a Vampire* (Prism), Louise Fletcher as *Mama Dracula* (TWE), and Nicholas Cage in *Vampire's Kiss* (HBO).

The Vampire Bat (1933) ◆◆◇ B&W
D: Frank Strayer. Lionel Atwill, Melvyn Douglas, Fay Wray, Dwight Frye. 71 minutes. (Goodtimes)

Atwill gives his emotive all as a demented doc who steadily diminishes an unwary local populace. Frye and premier screamer Wray also lend their talents.

Vampire Hookers (1979) ◆◆◇
D: Cirio H. Santiago. John Carradine, Bruce Fairbairn, Trey Wilson. 82 minutes. (Cinema Group)

Carradine, as cultured vampire Richmond Reed (Richmond Reed Carradine was the late thesp's real-life handle), steals the show in this amiable sleaze-horror farce, reciting Shakespeare, advancing his theory that the Bard was also a bloodsucker, and delivering punchlines with deadpan aplomb.

The Vampire Lovers (1971) ◆◆◆
D: Roy Ward Baker. Ingrid Pitt, Pippa Steele, Peter Cushing. 88 minutes. (Embassy)

Lesbian vampire Pitt drains Cushing's daughter in this slick, sexy Hammer redo of Sheridan Le Fanu's *Carmilla*. Followed by *Lust for a Vampire* (HBO).

Vampyr (1932) ◆◆◆ B&W
D: Carl Dreyer. Julian West, Sybille Schmitz, Harriet Gerard. 66 minutes. (Video Yesteryear)

Dreyer's loose *Carmilla* variation is stronger on style than on story, but the images *are* often striking and well worth a look. In German, with English subtitles.

The Velvet Vampire (1971) ◆◆◇
D: Stephanie Rothman. Michael Blodgett, Celeste Yarnall, Sherry Miles. 82 minutes. (Embassy)

Distaff director Rothman takes a mod approach to Carmilla in a fairly entertaining low-budget affair starring *Beyond the Valley of the Dolls* alumnus Blodgett.

Venom (1982) ◆◆
D: Piers Haggard. Klaus Kinski, Oliver Reed, Nicol Williamson, Sterling Hayden. 92 minutes. (Vestron)

Producers apparently felt that a stellar cast and a contempo terrorist/hostage plot weren't enough to lure today's jaded bijougoers, so they threw in a giant poisonous snake to boot. Reed suffered similar serpentine indignities in *Spasms* (see index), but this one's a bit more fun.

Video Dead (1987) ◆◆
D: Robert Scott. Roxanna Augesen, Rocky Duvall, Vickie Bastel, Sam David McClelland, Michael St. Michaels, and Jennifer Miro as "The Woman." 91 minutes. (Embassy)

Despite a great, perhaps even prophetic title, Scott's *Video Dead* represents yet another largely uninspired *Living Dead* rerun. Here the hostile deaders emerge from a haunted TV set to reduce the population of a 'Frisco burb. Among this otherwise derivative affair's few highlights are some effectively disgusto gore FX and dumb dialogue delivered by our addled teen hero Duvall (who's in unwitting possession of the killer TV) and his equally dim-witted co-ed sister (who's majoring in aerobics, with a minor in music videos!)—though his "Oh man, oh God!" cry isn't half as profound as Ryan O'Neal's "Oh God, oh man, oh God, oh man, oh God, oh man!" chant in Norman Mailer's *Tough Guys Don't Dance* (Media). If you want a clever killer-video movie, we'd suggest you stick with *Remote Control* (see index).

The Virgin Witch (1972) ◆◆◇
D: Roy Austin. Anne Michelle, Vicky Michelle, Neil Hallet. 88 minutes. (Prism)

Two innocent sisters (real-life siblings Anne and Vicky Michelle) journey to wicked London, where they become embroiled in a satanic sex cult. For further inquiries into virgin *terror*tory, we refer you to Jess Franco's *Virgin Among the Living Dead* (Lightning), *The Virgin of Nuremberg*, formerly *Horror Castle* (Twin Tower) with Christopher Lee, and the immortal (if ear-splitting) *Tower of Screaming Virgins* (Video Dimensions).

Warlock Moon (1973) ◆◆
D: Bill Herbert. Laurie Walters, Joe Spano. 89 minutes. (Unicorn)

An amateurish but sporadically interesting indie dealing with cannibalistic warlocks who take up residence at an abandoned health spa. Has its fans.

What Ever Happened to Baby Jane? (1962) ◆◆◆◇ B&W
D: Robert Aldrich. Bette Davis, Joan Crawford, Victor Buono. 132 minutes. (Warner)

A grand Gothic bitchfest pitting deranged ex–child star Davis against crippled sister Crawford, handled with care, flair, and perversity to spare by Aldrich. Still foremost in the middle-aged-madwomen genre it created.

When a Stranger Calls (1979) ◆◆◇
D: Fred Walton. Carol Kane, Charles Durning, Colleen Dewhurst. 97 minutes. (RCA/Columbia)
The pic gets pretty predictable—a psycho caller threatens to kill an ex-babysitter's kids—but Carol Kane convincingly conveys high anxiety of the hysterical kind.

White Zombie/The Phantom's Cult Classic Collection, Vol. 1 (1932) NR B&W
D: Victor Halperin. Bela Lugosi, Madge Bellamy, Robert Frazer. 66 minutes. (Video Resources)

A bizarre, moody chiller, sometimes slow of pace but packed with surreal imagery (the zombie-operated sugar mill, for one) and aided by Bela Lugosi's acting *and* uncredited directorial aid. Available with the *Phantom Creeps* (see index) final chapter and an intro hosted by yours truly. (Hey, if we can't plug ourselves, who *can* we plug?)

The Wicker Man (1973) ◆◆◆◇
D: Robin Hardy. Edward Woodward, Christopher Lee, Britt Ekland, Diane

A FELLA NAMED BELA: Bela rules as living-dead master "Murder" Legendre in poster montage from the eerie 1932 indie, *White Zombie*.

Edward (*The Equalizer*) Woodward looks either for a hand or a light in a scene from the excellent Anthony Schaffer-scripted thriller, *The Wicker Man*. Photo courtesy of Magnum Entertainment.

Cilento, Ingrid Pitt. 95 minutes. (Magnum)

An excellent offbeat chiller, starring a pre-*Equalizer* Woodward as a police sergeant out of his element (to say the least) among modern Druids living in a remote region of northern Scotland and led by the suavely ominous Lee. Scripted by Anthony (*Sleuth*) Shaffer.

Wild Beasts (1985) ◇
D: Franco E. Prosperi. John Aldrich, Lorraine DeSelle. 92 minutes. (Lightning)

Angel-dusted rats and zoo animals (!) launch a feral, drug-crazed assault against mankind! Can you prove that it *couldn't* happen?

Willard (1971) ◆◆
D: Daniel Mann. Bruce Davison, Elsa Lanchester, Ernest Borgnine. 95 minutes. (Prism)

This ratty revenge tale—wherein oppressed office clerk Davison turns the tables on his tormenters with the help of his pet rodents—did boffo business at the old BO. Go figure.

Witchboard (1987) ◆◆◇
D: Kevin S. Tenney. Tawny Kitaen, Todd Allen, Stephen Nichols, Kathleen Wilhoite, Burke Byrnes, Rose Marie. 98 minutes. (New Star)

Tenney's *Witchboard* starts out fairly strong: Amateur occultist Nichols contacts the spirit of a seemingly benign ten-year-old boy who's promptly (and understandably) smitten by Nichols's ex, Tawny (*Perils of Gwendoline*) Kitaen (who also contributes the pic's key gratuitous shower scene), currently involved with Nichols's best buddy (Allen). A series of violent deaths, coupled with Tawny's increasingly erratic behavior, lead our heroes to suspect that the ethereal kid is more of a deadly Dennis the Menace than a Caspar the Friendly Ghost. *Witchboard*'s pluses include an earnest if not always original script, decent acting—including Wilhoite as a punk psychic and a cameo by Rose Marie—and some suspense. But the flick grows increasingly contrived, and the last reel is strictly Cliché City.

Witches' Brew (1980) NR

D: Herbert L. Strock. Teri Garr, Richard Benjamin, Lana Turner. 99 minutes. (Embassy)

Garr turns to witchcraft to further academic hubby Benjamin's career. Any resemblance to the earlier *Burn, Witch, Burn* (NA) (itself based on Fritz Leiber's *Conjure Wife*) is both irreverent and intentional.

Witchfire (1985) ◆◇

D: Vincent J. Privitera. Shelley Winters, Frances De Sapio, Corrine Chateau, Gary Swanson, David Mendenhall. 92 minutes. (Lightning)

Shelley Winters swallows acres of scenery (which may account for her current figure) in an out-of-control perf as Lydia, a mental patient who leads two fellow distaff inmates on a break from a Texas asylum. They eventually return to Shel's childhood home, where they trap arrogant hunter Swanson, who turns up in search of his runaway son (Mendenhall, who later suffered Sly Stallone's paternal affections in the father-son armwrestling saga *Over the Top*—see index), and subjects him to a series of witchcraft rituals. *Witchfire* is best remembered, though, for incurring the ire of the National Alliance for the Mentally Ill via its sensitive tag line, "Not since *Cuckoo's Nest* has insanity been so much fun!" But the *best* line is uttered by Shel herself (who also served as the pic's producer): "I may be insane, but I'm not stupid." She couldn't prove it by *Witchfire*.

Wizard of Gore (1970) ◆◆◇

D: Herschell Gordon Lewis. Ray Sager, Judy Cler, Wayne Ratay. 96 minutes. (Rhino)

More heady high-concept gore from H. G. Lewis, with mad Montag the Magician displaying his skill at sawing women in half, among other sneaky tricks. Illusion or reality? Viewer, *you* decide!

The Wolf Man (1941) ◆◆◆◇ B&W

D: George Waggner. Lon Chaney, Jr., Claude Rains, Evelyn Ankers, Bela Lugosi, Maria Ouspenskaya. 70 minutes. (MCA)

Tightly scripted by Curt Siodmak and directed by Waggner, *The Wolf Man* can take its rightful, frightful place beside such other Universal gems as *Dracula* and *Frankenstein* (see index). Lon Chaney, Jr., stars as the ill-fated Larry Talbot, doomed to wail the full-moon blues after being bitten by a lycanthropic gypsy (a neat cameo by Bela). Not even the formidable Ouspenskaya can save Lon from wandering the nocturnal woods of his father's (Rains) estate in search of fresh victims. *The Wolf Man* accentuates human tragedy over lupine horror in its exploration of its traditional Good vs. Evil theme. We subtracted half a phan for Lon's rather meager body count (he bags only Bela and an anonymous gravedigger).

The Wraith (1986) ◇
D: Mike Marvin. Charlie Sheen, Nick Cassavetes, Randy Quaid, Sherilyn Fenn, Griffin O'Neal, Clint Howard. 92 minutes. (Lightning)

Marvin's *The Wraith* boasts a (hopefully) once-in-a-lifetime cast that consists almost entirely of close relatives of famous stars. Top-billed Charlie Sheen wisely puts in only sporadic appearances as Jake Kesey, the new kid in a town (scenic Brooks, Arizona) menaced by a pack of youthful psychos. The gang is led by "Pack" Walsh, played by Nick (Son of John) Cassavetes and includes Griffin (Son of Ryan) O'Neal and Clint (Brother of Ron) Howard, seen here sporting a sizable paunch and an *Eraserhead* hairdo. The boys steal and race cars, operate a secret chop shop, and generally ride roughshod over the locals. The flick switches gears when a souped-up supernatural killer car—a mysterious black Turbo with a helmeted, armor-suited unidentified driver—roars into the picture to avenge a character the gang snuffed in a poorly integrated flashback scene. *The Wraith*'s shaky story line is further sabotaged by auteur Marvin's purple dialogue and feeble stabs at wit. (His previous script credits, *Hot Dog* and *Six Pack*, would look more at home on a deli wall than on a resume.) Only the Turbo escapes unscathed.

Zombie (1980) ◆◇
D: Lucio Fulci. Tisa Farrow, Ian McCulloch, Richard Johnson. 93 minutes. (Lightning)

Typically fulsome fright flick from Italo gruemaster Fulci, with the accent placed firmly on gore galore.

Zombie High (1987) ◆
D: Ron Link. Virginia Madsen, Richard Cox, Kay Kuter, James Wilder, Sherilynn Fenn, Paul Feig. 91 minutes. (Cinema Group)

Our story unfolds at preppy Ettinger Academy—a sort of Stepford High where newly arrived misfits are covertly brain-changed into model students, while 100+-year-old faculty members keep from aging by shooting up the kids' excess cerebral fluids. Not *the* most promising premise, perhaps, but serviceable enough in the right hands to work as a fun fright satire, á la Fred Dekker's campus creature comedy *Night of the Creeps* (see index). Alas, said premise fell into the wrong hands here. In fact, *Zombie High* may well be the first movie actually to be made *by* zombies, *for* zombies. Except for heroine Madsen's earnest performance, the energy level is so woefully low that the Phantom felt tempted to check the pic's pulse. Director Link tries to juice up the final reels with some snappy wipes, dissolves, and similar film-school tricks, but it's a case of much too little, way too late.

Zombie Nightmare (1986) ◇

D: *Jack Bravman. Adam West, Jon Mikl Thor, Tia Carrere, Frank Dietz, Maruschka, Linda Singer. 89 minutes. (New World)*

Heavy-metal has-been John Mikl Thor, brains behind the head-banger band Thor, toplines here as Tony Washington, a long-haired, muscle-bound hit-and-run fatality who's revivified to wreak re-venge by "old" (she looks like she's maybe pushing 28) local 'burb voodoo queen Molly Mekembe (the mono-monikered Maruschka, in one of the most aggressively awful performances seen in many a full moon). Tony, or an unreasonable facsimile thereof in a mail-order zombie mask, slays the "savage suburban teens" who ran him down while cop Adam (*Batman*) West, in an ill-advised cameo, scratches his head and wonders what gives. Motorhead, Girls School, Fist, Death Mask, and of course, Thor lend their talents to the soundtrack. Avoid this Thor loser at all costs, along with JMT's similar-sounding *Rock 'n' Roll Nightmare* (Academy).

Zombies of Mora Tau (1957) ◆◆ B&W

D: *Edward L. Cahn. Gregg Palmer, Joel Ashley, Autumn Russell. 70 minutes. (RCA/Columbia)*

A tame, cheap, but occasionally atmospheric '50s fright flick about underwater zombies guarding a sunken treasure. Palmer, fresh from his walking-tree turn in *From Hell It Came* (NA), tries to get to the bottom of things.

MARTIANS, MUTANTS & MIND-MELDS FROM HELL!
SCIENCE FICTION & FANTASY

"Humans are such _easy_ prey!"

Dr. Pretorius
From Beyond

Genre auteur George A. Romero, in a conversation with your name-dropping Phantom, once described the film biz as a "parasitic medium." Though George wasn't the first to say so and doubtless won't be the last, the Phantom immediately filed that phrase away for eventual use here, for nowhere has that maxim held truer than in the contempo sci-fi field.

In fact, for a film area that's traditionally sought to explore the far parameters of the celluloid imagination, Hollywood's recent sci-fi output has exhibited precious little in the way of originality. The

268

majority of late-'80s SF flicks have consisted of relentless clones and rip-offs of three recent seminal films: *The Road Warrior* (e.g., *City Limits, Solarbabies, Radioactive Dreams,* and a whole host of Italo imitators), *The Terminator* (*The Vindicator, Eliminators, Programmed to Kill*), and *Aliens* (*Alien Predators, Creature, Predator,* and, in underwater variations, *Leviathan* and *Deep Star Six*).

While quality varies greatly from clone to clone, the stubborn persistence with which this troika's been sacked *is* fairly brain-boggling. Especially when you consider that *The Terminator* drew its inspiration from Harlan Ellison's 1964 *Outer Limits* episode, "Demon with the Glass Hand," while *Aliens* is a sequel to *Alien,* which itself (however unconsciously) replicated the plot of the 1958 B movie *It! The Terror from Beyond Space. The Road Warrior,* the most original of the three, is also a sequel to, though an improvement over, *Mad Max.*

When not aping the above trio, some sci-fi flicks were still reaching back to imitate the earlier *E.T.: The Extraterrestrial*—vide *The Brother from Another Planet, Explorers,* and the immortal *Mac and Me* (Orion). The last-mentioned had the further dubious distinction of being the first McDonald's movie (replete with "guest appearance" by Ronald McDonald!), essentially a feature-length commercial that took product plugs and tie-ins to a dangerous new plateau.

Fortunately, *all* is not derivative on the SF front. We did uncover a number of superior new genre gems, like the imaginative Australian effort *Death Warmed Up,* the clever direct-to-video *Remote Control,* and David Cronenberg's new, improved *The Fly.* We've also incorporated a wide range of older video-available sci-fi fare—from Fritz Lang's original *Metropolis* to Ridley Scott's SF noir *Blade Runner*—that should help fans over the hump of an intensely parasitic era.

We follow our sci-fi listings with a separate section devoted to fantasy films. While all fiction (as well as a good many purportedly nonfiction) films can, on a literal level, be classified as fantasy, we've reserved that designation for your various film fables (*The Man Who Could Work Miracles*), adult-oriented animation (*Lord of the Rings*), sorcery epics (*The Magic Sword*) and sword-and-sandal pics from Steve Reeves's *Hercules* to Brigitte Nielsen's *Red Sonja.* We've also incorporated a few generally unclassifiable efforts, old and new—like Joseph Losey's *The Boy with Green Hair* and Sondra Locke's homeless *Ratboy*—that seemed to have no place else to go.

Science Fiction

The Adventures of Buckaroo Banzai Across the Eighth Dimension (1984)
◆◆◆◇

D: W. D. Richter. Peter Weller, John Lithgow, Ellen Barkin, Jeff Goldblum, Christopher Lloyd, Clancy Brown. 103 minutes. (Vestron)

Buckaroo Banzai features a title hero (Weller) who lives out the American Everyboy's wildest dreams. Not only is he a neurosurgeon, a martial artist, an "astounding jet car" driver, and a rock star, but he's even got his own comic book chronicling his ongoing exploits! Throw in blond love interest Penny Priddy (Barkin) and a gang of loyal sidemen ("those hard-rocking scientists, the Hong Kong Cavaliers"), and you've got a hero who makes Flash Gordon look like a chartered accountant. (The Phantom was about to say investment banker, but they're considered pretty exciting these days, no?) An updated, high-tech spoof of the surreal sci-fi serials and pulp novels of the 30s, with touches of Robert Altman, MTV, and superhero comics tossed in, Buckaroo Banzai takes a fistful of berserko ideas and runs with them—in all directions at once. Lithgow gives a truly demented performance as Mussoliniesque mad scientist Dr. Emilio Lizardo, a loony in league with Eighth Dimension aliens. The FX are suitably flashy, the tempo swift, and Earl Mac Rauch's twisty script never lapses into the predictable or mundane. This imaginative study in sustained weirdness, largely misunderstood and/or overlooked during its initial release, definitely deserves your video attention.

After the Fall of New York (1985) ◆
D: Martin Dolman (Sergio Martino). Michael Sopkiw, Valentine Monnier, Edmund Purdom. 95 minutes. (Vestron)

If there's one thing the Phantom hates more than another, it's these cheapo Italo Road Warrior Meets Escape from New York rip-offs. After the Fall of New York stars one (let's hope there's only one of him) Michael Sopkiw as the ersatz Mel Gibson, a postnuke knucklehead named Parsifal. (Other characters carry such colorful monikers as Big Ape and Bronx.) Like most of its breed, After the Fall is not of the so-dumb-it's-fun but the so-dumb-it's-numbing school of trash moviemaking. And while it may be true that New York City is rapidly turning into a bad horror-chiller double bill (Planet of the Yups and The Homeless from Hell), do we need these camera-toting Italians to give it an even worse name than the unprintable one it already deserves? Other Italo titles to steer clear of include 1990: Bronx Warriors, *Endgame, Escape from the Bronx* (which, despite its title, is *not* about the hazards of hailing a cab on Mosholu Parkway), *The Sisterhood,* and *2020: Texas Gladiators* (all from Media); *Equalizer 2000* (MGM/UA); *Land of Doom, Rats,* and *Warriors of the Apocalypse* (all Lightning); *Rush* (IVE); *Exterminators in the Year 3000, Warriors of the Lost World,* and *Warriors of the Wasteland* (all HBO); and *Bronx Executioner* and *Urban Warriors* (Cannon). And that's the *last* we want to hear from you!

Alien (1979) ◆◆◆◇
D: Ridley Scott. Sigourney Weaver, Tom Skerritt, Harry Dean Stanton, Yaphet Kotto, John Hurt. 117 minutes. (CBS/Fox)

The plot may have been lifted from the elusive '50s B-movie *It! The Terror from Beyond Space* (NA), but Ridley Scott adds impressive sci-fi frills—from the spaceship set to the slimy FX and the ever-mutating monster (designed by H. R. Giger)—and knows how to deliver the chills. Hurt's postprandial encounter of the gross kind ranks as one of the scream screen's truly legendary scenes.

Alien Dead (1980) ◆
D: Fred Olen Ray. Buster Crabbe, Linda Lewis. 82 minutes. (Academy)

A fairly awful amateur-night special, lensed in Florida, noteworthy solely for being Ray's first movie and Crabbe's last. A footnote to life's inexorable cycle. Alien com-

pletists, meanwhile, can continue their research with *Alien Contamination, Alien Massacre* (both Regal), *Alien Factor, Alien from L.A.* (both Media), *Alien Prey* (Cinema Group), *Alien Warrior* (Vestron), *Alien Women* (Prism), the made-for-TV *The Aliens Are Coming* (Goodtimes), and *Invasion Earth: The Aliens Are Here* (New World).

Alien Nation (1988) ◆◆◇
D: Graham Baker. James Caan, Mandy Patinkin, Terence Stamp, Kevyn Major, Leslie Bevis, Peter Jason. 96 minutes. (CBS/Fox)

Baker's *Alien Nation* posits that a slave saucer carrying a quartermil genetically engineered ET workers landed near L.A. in 1988. The humanlike aliens, labeled Newcomers, were quickly integrated into that selfsame city, where presumably they wouldn't stand out so much. Three years later, bigoted human cop Caan sees his partner slain by a lowlife "slag" (as the aliens are pejoratively referred to), then volunteers to accept the first Newcomer LAPD detective (Pantinkin) as his new sidekick, the better to zero in on the killer ETs' whereabouts. Essentially a retread of Jack Sholder's superior *The Hidden* (see index), *Alien Nation*—produced by Gale Ann (*Aliens*) Hurd—stacks up as a fairly standard mismatched-cops caper with an alien overlay, though Rockne O'Bannon's script supplies enough inventive riffs to keep *Alien Nation* afloat, at least in the early going. We learn, among other things, that Newcomers own two hearts, get high on sour milk (in the most disgusto sour-milk scene seen since Buddy Giovinazzo's *Combat Shock*—see index), play their own weird sports, dissolve in salt water, and—in an Ellis Island replay—bear stupid Anglo names (e.g., Sam Francisco, Rudyard Kipling) handed out by contemptuous immigration authorities. Despite the flick's inexorable slide into increasingly contrived and predictable *shticks*, the above bits—along with thesps Caan and Pantinkin's lively work—make *Alien Nation* worth a rental.

Alien Predators (1986) ◇

D: *Deran Sarafian. Dennis Christopher, Martin Hewitt, Lynn-Holly Johnson, Luis Prendes, J. O. Bosso. 92 minutes. (Video Treasures)*

Besides being another blatant, dumb, and nearly actionless *Alien* rip-off, this *Close Encounters of the Nerd Kind* can't even make up its dim little mind whether it wants to be a straight-ahead sci-fi chiller or a cutesy spoof of same. The lazy script (by director Sarafian) takes a glib tone when depicting the asinine interplay among a trio of loose-screwed Los Angelenos—former teen heartthrobs Dennis (*Breaking Away*) Christopher, Martin (*Endless Love*) Hewitt, and Lynn-Holly (*Ice Castles*) Johnson—in an alien-microbe-imperiled Spain but attempts a more earnest approach

when chronicling a frantic scientist's (Prendes) efforts to combat the alien plague. The predictable result is that the flick fails miserably in both areas.

Aliens (1986) ◆◆◆◇

D: *James Cameron. Sigourney Weaver, Michael Biehn, Carrie Henn, Paul Reiser, Lance Henriksen, Jenette Goldstein. 138 minutes. (CBS/Fox)*

Aliens is one sequel that actually surpasses the original (Ridley Scott's *Alien*), at least in terms of sheer spectacle. In the capable hands of the *Terminator* team of director Cameron and producer Gale Ann Hurd, with a sizable assist from FX ace Stan Winston, *Aliens* hurtles headlong into a high-tech nightmare that delivers as many shocks per minute as any sci-fright film in recent memory. Weaver again proves tough as nails (and we don't mean the kind you polish), though she also reveals a softer, maternal side here when she adopts young space-colony alien-massacre survivor Henn. Michael (*The Terminator*) Biehn contributes a crisp stint as a resourceful, determinedly nonsexist Marine corporal, as do Reiser as an evil space yuppie and Henriksen as the crew's token android. On the down side, *Aliens* features too much macho cliché-swapping and generally dumb-grunt dialogue among the gun-happy space Marines (though we did appreciate Goldstein's turn as tough-gal Private Vasquez; she's as close to a female Stallone as *we'd* ever want to see). And yes—Sig does get to don T-shirt and panties, in not one but two scenes, though they're not nearly as brief as the scanties she wore during the original *Alien*'s climax. Equally important, *Aliens'* changing-sex-roles and motherhood-is-powerful subtexts are sufficiently superficial so as not to

ALIENS SAY THE DARNEDEST THINGS!

"All you of earth are idiots!"

 Eros the alien, *Plan 9 from Outer Space*

"There are some aspects of the life of an earth savage that are exciting and rewarding. Things that are missed by the brains on my planet."

 Gor, *The Brain from Planet Arous*

"All the knowledge that has been handed down is stored now in their complicated brain cells. So, if we eat their brains, that knowledge will help us adapt!"

 Hungry alien, *Destroy All Planets*

"You see, you see! You're stupid! Stupid!"

 Eros, *Plan 9 from Outer Space*

"They gave me convulsive shock treatment, which accounted for the lack of intelligence I experienced."

 Alien genius Jerry Lewis, *Slapstick of Another Kind*

"You want to do mankind a real service? Tell funnier jokes!"

 Alien critic to Woody Allen, *Stardust Memories*

"Klaatu barada nikto!"

 Alien to robot companion, *The Day the Earth Stood Still*

. . . And So Do Earthlings

One-eyed alien to sub commander: "It should interest you to know that I have visited hundreds of other worlds and of all of them your earth seems most suitable."

Sub commander to one-eyed alien: "Swell!"

 Atomic Submarine

"They're here already!"

Invasion of the Body Snatchers

"Saucers seen over Hollywood!"

Plan 9 from Outer Space

"What do we say to them?"
"Welcome to California!"

War of the Worlds

"You have no pulse. There are two possibilities: I'm drunk, or you're dead."

Doctor to alien, *Stranger from Venus*

"Marines have no qualms about killing Martians!"

General, *Invaders from Mars*

"Do you think they'll come back?"

Earth vs. the Flying Saucers

"Only God knows for sure."

Creeping Terror

"If they do, we'll be ready for them!"

Kronos

"Keep watching the skies!"

The Thing

get in the way of the nonstop action.

Alphaville (1965) ◆◆◆ B&W
D: Jean-Luc Godard. Eddie Constantine, Anna Karina, Akim Tamiroff. 100 minutes. (Sinister Cinema, others)
Jean-Luc looks into the future and sees a pulp-noir world dominated by alienating machinery in an off-beat effort that ranges from funny and perceptive to slow and pretentious.

Altered States (1980) ◆◆◆
D: Ken Russell. William Hurt, Blair Brown, Bob Balaban. 102 minutes. (Warner)
More Ken Russell than Paddy Chayefsky (who penned the orig-

inal novel), strong hallucinatory imagery (Russell's traditional forte) and top performances elevate this tale of scientist Hurt, whose isolation-tank tinkering causes him to regress to a primitive killer-simian state.

The Amazing Transparent Man (1960) ◆◆ B&W

D: Edgar G. Ulmer. Douglas Kennedy, Marguerite Chapman, James Griffith. 60 minutes. (J&J)

An impoverished quickie about an invisible bank-robber, recommended mostly for '50s genre-movie lovers who, if they're like yours truly, can watch this junk endlessly. Not one of Detour auteur Ulmer's better efforts, though.

America 3000 (1986) ◆◆

D: Dave Engelbach. Chuck Wagner, Laurene Landon. 94 minutes. (MGM/UA)

A hit-and-ms. postnuke-movie parody depicting an Earth run by butt-kicking femmes, led by Landon.

Android (1982) ◆◆◆

D: Aaron Lipstadt. Klaus Kinski, Don Opper, Brie Howard. 80 minutes. (Media)

A playful sci-fi flick about a Pinocchio-like, pop-culture-influenced android (Opper, who also co-scripted), the human object of his affections (Howard), and his cruel creator (Kinski). The instrumental theme, "Sergio Leone," is also a winner.

The Andromeda Strain (1971) ◆◆◆

D: Robert Wise. James Olson, David Wayne, Arthur Hill. 130 minutes. (MCA)

A tense if overlong thriller chronicling scientists' painstaking efforts to prevent an alien microbe from (dare we say it?) destroying the world. For hard-core SF fans.

The Angry Red Planet (1960) ◆◆◆

D: Ib Melchoir. Gerald Mohr, Nora Hayden, Les Tremayne. 84 minutes. (HBO)

Your standard astronauts-march-through-Mars plot is greatly enlivened by lurid color photography and an array of imaginative creatures. Beware the Bat-Rat-Spider!

At the Earth's Core (1976) ◆◆◇

D: Kevin Connor. Doug McClure, Peter Cushing, Caroline Munro. 90 minutes. (Warner)

Connor's adaptation of the Edgar Rice Burroughs tale finds Victorians Cushing and McClure encountering prehistoric creatures at the title site. Strong cast and FX make this one fun.

The Atomic Man (1956) ◆◆ B&W

D: Ken Hughes. Gene Nelson, Faith Domergue, Peter Arne. 78 minutes. (Sinister Cinema)

Radiation propels Nelson several seconds into the future, putting everyone else on a sort of tape delay. Not much is done with this interesting premise, but Domergue is always fun to watch.

The Atomic Submarine (1959) ◆◆◇ B&W

D: Spencer Bennett. Arthur Franz, Dick Foran, Brett Halsey, Bob Steele, Joi Lansing. 72 minutes. (Monterey)

Producer Alex Gordon stocks his low-budget but admirably earnest alien encounter with many of his fave old-time thesps, making *Atomic Sub* a must for nostalgia buffs.

Attack of the Giant Leeches (1959) ◆◆ B&W

D: Bernard Kowalski. Ken Clark, Yvette Vickers, Bruno VeSota. 62 minutes. (Sinister Cinema)

Scripted by actor Leo Gordon, this is one of AIP's less-inspired cheapies, with the title monsters terrorizing Florida swamp trash. Worth watching for Vickers's provocative turn as fatman VeSota's slutty, two-timing wife.

Attack of the Swamp Creature (1975) ◆

D: Don Barton. Frank Crowell, Nancy Lien, Marshall Graver. 96 minutes. (Thriller)

This Florida-lensed atrocity (alternatively titled *Zaat* and *The Blood Waters of Dr. Z*) is pretty amusing in small—make that microscopic—doses as a scientist transforms himself into a walking catfish, eyes his newfound face in the mirror, and muses, "Nothing at all like a catfish—but it's beautiful!" That's the best part; there—we saved you the price of a rental and the agony of 95½ additional minutes.

The Bamboo Saucer (1968) ◆◆

D: Frank Telford. Dan Duryea, John Ericson, Lois Nettleton. 103 minutes. (Republic)

American and Russian scientific teams, led by Duryea and Nettleton respectively, race each other and Chinese forces to find the title vehicle. Some funny moments.

Barbarella (1968) ◆◆◆

D: Roger Vadim. Jane Fonda, David Hemmings, John Phillip Law, Anita Von Pallenberg, Milo O'Shea. 98 minutes. (Paramount)

From Jane's opening antigravitational striptease to her chaste tryst with blind angel Law to former Keith Richards squeeze Pallenberg's eye-patched dominatrix, Roger Vadim's adaptation of the famed French comic—set in a psychedelic forty-first century—supplies a plethora of visual and verbal fun. In fact, this may be Ms. F's sexiest turn (outside of her workout tapes), though Jane can be feisty when the situation calls, as when she commands Anita, "Decrucify the Angel, or I'll melt your face!"

Battle Beneath the Earth (1968) ◆◆

D: Montgomery Tully. Kerwin Mathews, Viviane Ventura, Robert Ayres. 112 minutes. (MGM/UA)

Decent dumb fun for a while as Kerwin (*Octaman*) Mathews and Brit cohorts try to thwart the Red Chinese from tunneling through the earth with their super laser drill (!), but this one pales pretty quickly.

Battle Beyond the Stars (1980) ◆◆◇
D: Jimmy T. Murakami. George Peppard, John Saxon, Robert Vaughn. 104 minutes. (Vestron)

John Sayles's in-reference script plus a top cast of B-movie vets lift this postmodern, Roger Corman–produced space western above most of its low-budget ilk, even if it *does* steal shamelessly from *Star Wars* and *The Magnificent Seven* alike.

Battle for the Planet of the Apes (1973) ◆◆
D: J. Lee Thompson. Roddy McDowall, Natalie Trundy, Lew Ayres. 92 minutes. (Playhouse)

The fifth and final *Apes* entry is pretty bald on new ideas as humanoid mutants seek to topple the ruling chimp elite. Fans of the series will want to catch it, though.

Battlestar: Galactica (1979) NR
D: Richard A. Colla. Lorne Greene, Richard Hatch, Dirk Benedict. 125 minutes. (Goodtimes)

Feature film fashioned from the pilot episodes of the short-lived TV series about doomed-planet survivors' peripatetic trip to Earth. No *Star Trek*, but has its followers.

Beneath the Planet of the Apes ◆◆◇
(1970)
D: Ted Post. James Franciscus, Kim Hunter, Maurice Evans. 95 minutes. (Playhouse)

This shrill but effectively wacko *Planet of the Apes* sequel involves H-bomb-worshipping mutants.

Repeat after us: "Glory be to the Bomb/And to the holy Fallout . . ."

Beyond the Time Barrier (1960) ◆◆◇
B&W
D: Edgar G. Ulmer. Robert Clarke, Darlene Tompkins, Vladimir Sokoloff. 75 minutes. (Sinister Cinema)

Ulmer's cheap but entertaining sci-fi quickie, which he directed back-to-back with *The Amazing Transparent Man*, stars Robert *(Hideous Sun Demon)* Clarke as a time-traveling pilot.

The Big Zapper (1973) NR
D: Lindsay Shonteff. Linda Marlowe, Gary Hope, Sean Hewitt. 94 minutes. (Video City)

A cartoonlike Brit shamus spoof with sci-fi overtones—featuring Marlowe as a hard-boiled blonde—that's won its share of fans.

The Black Hole (1979) ◆◆◇
D: Gary Nelson. Maximilian Schell, Anthony Perkins, Robert Forster. 97 minutes. (Walt Disney)

A hot cast—in addition to the above principals, Yvette Mimieux and Ernest Borgnine are also aboard—and elaborate FX help buoy a dull story about a madman's search for the title aperture.

Blade Runner (1982) ◆◆◆
D: Ridley Scott. Harrison Ford, Rutger Hauer, Daryl Hannah. 118 minutes. (Nelson)

Scott's stylish sci-fi noir, based on Philip K. Dick's *Do Androids Dream of Electric Sheep?*, casts Ford as a futuristic dick up against killer "replicants" led by Hauer.

Underrated during its initial release, *Blade Runner* has since acquired critical respect and a sizable, deserved following.

The Blob (1958) ◆◆◆

D: Irwin Yeaworth, Jr. Steven McQueen, Aneta Corseaut, Olin Howlin, Earl Rowe, Vince Barbi. 91 minutes. (Video Warehouse)

"Steven" McQueen (in his thespic debut) and a gang of geeky teens take on an amorphous mass of killer Jell-O from outer space. From its Mexi-flavored theme song "Beware of the Blob" (composed by a mysteriously uncredited Burt Bacharach) to its vintage array of flashy land yachts, *The Blob* shapes up as *the* quintessential iconic late-'50s monster movie. The gaudy color, lightly self-mocking tone, and truly memorable title creature likewise add to the fun. The scene wherein the Blob invades the local bijou's Midnight Spook Show (the feature is Bruno VeSota's obscure experimental fright flick *Daughter of Horror*) provides a special treat for B-movie buffs. Though some of the pic's expository portions move almost as slowly as the Blob itself and the original has since been topped by Chuck Russell's updated FXplicit remake (see below), *The Blob* remains a must for the uninitiated and a musty delight for the rest. 1972's *Son of Blob*— aka *Beware! The Blob* and directed by Larry (J.R.) Hagman—(Video Gems) is better off forgotten.

The Blob (1988) ◆◆◆◇

D: Chuck Russell. Kevin Dillon, Shawnee Smith, Donovan Leitch, Jeffrey DeMunn, Candy Clark, Joe Seneca. 98 minutes. (RCA/Columbia)

Even dedicated Blobophiles will agree that, as fright flicks go, the 1958 *Blob* was more quintessential than classic, the celluloid equivalent of a sci-fi novelty record like "The Purple People Eater" (itself the basis for a weak 1988 SF comedy). Visceral chills did not rank high among *The Blob's* quirky virtues. Not so the new— and actually improved—edition. While sticking—quite literally at times—to the original story line, Chuck Russell's remake injects the shock-movie juice its model largely lacked. *This* Blob, from its initial onscreen appearance to its last-reel rampage, benefits mightily from high-tech FX and disgusto gore galore. Like David Cronenberg's fresh *Fly* revamp, *The Blob* never wallows in synthetic nostalgia but accurately updates its source material. The pic views our current, waning decade as a replay of the '50s, stripped of the latter's innocence (though ignorance and stupidity run more rampant than ever, with typically aggressive '80s abandon). Where reassuring authority figures supplied the solution in the first *Blob*, they constitute part—in fact, nearly all—of the problem here. The main characters are likewise reinvented. Dillon, as a local cycle

rebel, adds an outlaw note to the original McQueen role. And heroine Smith, while every bit as fetching as Aneta Corseaut, is far more active as the high school cheerleader who displays mucho grit and valor under fire (or more accurately, slime). *The Blob* is witty, scary, fast-paced fun.

Bloodsuckers from Outer Space (1984) ◆◆◇

D: Glenn Coburn. Thom Meyer, Laura Ellis, Pat Paulsen, Billie Keller, Robert Braden. 79 minutes. (Lorimar)

Seems that formerly fine, upstanding Texas farm folk are transforming into brainwashed bloodsuckers, and only free-lance photog Meyer and main squeeze Ellis can save mankind. Question is: Should they bother? Coburn's crude but frequently funny creature comedy poses this and other probing queries while taking broad satiric aim at ornery rednecks, lazy lawmen, spaced-out scientists, and mad military brass. Some of the performances here are rough-edged at best (guest star Paulsen literally phones in his cameo as our imperiled nation's distracted Chief Exec), but Coburn's casual, low-key approach keeps his free-form flick from self-destructing.

Blue Monkey (1987) ◆

D: William Fruet. Steve Railsback, Gwynyth Walsh, Susan Anspach, John Vernon, Joe Flaherty, Robin Duke. 98 minutes. (RCA/Columbia)

A Thorazine-paced throwback to the insect-fear flicks of the '50s, *Blue Monkey* features Railsback (late of the equally retro *Lifeforce*—this hapless thesp's stuck in a B-movie time warp!) as a heroic cop caught in a quarantined hospital menaced by your basic giant slime bug. The latter begins life as a single parasite in an elderly plant-bite victim; when mischievous junior patients inadvertently feed the freed creature a genetic growth serum (!), it prospers and threatens to multiply. The rest of the film attempts to recreate a claustrophobic *Them!*-like ambience but sinks into a slime pit of desperate stereotypes and clichés. We *do* learn that alcohol makes humans immune to the creature's germs (we'll drink to that), and you may well find yourself reaching for the hard stuff should you rent this useless yawnfest.

A Boy and His Dog (1975) ◆◆◆

D: L. Q. Jones. Don Johnson, Susanne Benton, Jason Robards. 89 minutes. (Media)

Don Johnson stars as an opportunistic postnuke survivor who discovers an underground totalitarian community that recreates vintage Topeka (!) in Jones's deadpan adaptation of Harlan Ellison's blackly comic fable. The flick once enjoyed a brief Forty-second Street reissue under the livelier title *Psycho Boy and His Killer Dog* (!).

The Brain (1962) ◆◆◇ B&W

D: Freddie Francis. Peter Van Eyck, Anne Heywood, Bernard Lee. 85 minutes. (Sinister Cinema)

Hammer horror vet Francis helms a decent *Donovan's Brain* (see index) remake, with Van Eyck as the scientist controlled by the power-crazed title organ.

The Brain (1988) ◆◇

D: Edward Hunt. Tom Breznahan, Cyndy Preston, David Gale, George Buza, Brett Pearson. 94 minutes. (IVE)

The Brain is yet another sci-fi cheapie employing a clichéd terror-by-television hook: A popular pop-psychology show, the extravagantly misnomered *Independent Thinking*, turns out to be a devious front for a dumber-than-average-looking alien brain bent on converting unsuspecting Earthlings to its cause. Standing in the way-out gray matter's way is a "bright" high schooler—though you have to accept the script's word for it, since thesp Breznahan (late of *Twice Dead*) is less than adept at projecting intelligence—who's on to the underhanded extraterrestrial's subversive scheme. Director Hunt wavers between a straightforward and tongue-in-cheek (or in this case, tongue-in-frontal-lobes) approach to his largely unoriginal material. While technically competent, *The Brain* pales beside *Videodrome, Remote Control,* and John Carpenter's *They Live* (see index), to cite but three

movies that have served the same basic premise with far more imagination.

Brainstorm (1983) ◆◆◇

D: Douglas Trumbull. Christopher Walken, Natalie Wood, Louise Fletcher. 106 minutes. (MGM/UA)

Scientists Walken and Fletcher design a headset capable of tapping into the sensations felt by other people. A pretty horrifying idea all right, but not much is done with it here. Fast-forward to the FX scenes, which are truly topnotch.

Brainwaves (1982) ◆◆

D: Ulli Lommel. Keir Dullea, Suzanna Love, Tony Curtis. 83 minutes. (Embassy)

Injured Love receives murder victim's brain and is forced to flee the latter's killer in a pic that slows down after a promising start. A similar premise informed *Blood Song* (Coast-to-Coast Video), with Frankie Avalon as a flute-playing ax murderer telepathically connected to an innocent blood donor. Frankie's not in this one, but Tony Curtis is—as a mad doctor, no less.

The Brother from Another Planet (1984) ◆◆◆

D: John Sayles. Joe Morton, Dee Dee Bridgewater, Ren Woods, Steve James, Maggie Renzi, John Sayles. 104 minutes. (Key)

The prolific Sayles's socially conscious sci-fi comedy could easily have drifted into a series of "E.T. Goes to the Ghetto" riffs. But

Sayles's generally crisp scripting and Morton's winning performance as the speechless title alien make this a witty, low-key exercise for sci-fi fans and mainstream moviegoers alike. Look for action fave James as Odell the Bartender and auteur Sayles in a cameo as an outer-space bounty hunter.

Bug (1975) ◆◇
D: Jeannot Szwarc. Bradford Dillman, Joanna Miles, Richard Gilliland. 100 minutes. (Paramount)

If there's one thing the Phantom hates more than killer-fish flicks, it's killer-bug movies (*Them!* and *The Fly*—both versions—excepted). Notable mostly for being producer William Castle's final filmic fling.

Cherry 2000 (1987) ◆◇
D: Steve De Jarnatt. Melanie Griffith, David Andrews, Ben Johnson, Tim Thomerson, Harry Carey, Jr., Pamela Gridley, Michael C. Gwynne. 99 minutes. (Orion)

Director De Jarnatt pegs his futuristic farce to an updated version of a time-honored Tinseltown formula: Boy (Andrews) meets android, boy loses android, boy hires tough distaff "tracker" (Griffith) to lead him into a perilous wasteland in search of a suitable robotic replacement. Unfortunately, once *Cherry 2000* abandons its already less-than-inspired sitcom premise, the pic swiftly skids into tired, tongue-in-cheek *Road Warrior* manqué territory, much like the similarly derivative dud *World Gone Wild* (see index). De Jarnatt's predictable mix of routine action and lazy satire wastes such vet thesps as Johnson and Carey, though Thomerson makes the most of his role as the laid-back, L.A.-style, psychobabbling sadist who seeks to impede our hero's—and heroine's—progress, and Gridley impresses as the cheerful blond android, sort of a transistorized stewardess. Otherwise, we're compelled to report that this long-shelved *Cherry* isn't very fresh.

The Children (1980) ◆◆◇
D: Max Kalmanowicz. Martin Shakar, Gale Garnett, Gil Rogers, Jesse Abrams, Tracy Griswold, Joy Glacum. 93 minutes. (Vestron)

This one's got to be *the* sickest entry in the short-lived let's-kill-the-kids craze. A nuke-plant leak transforms local schoolchildren into parent-disintegrating mutants with black fingernails and a lethal touch. The only way to croak 'em, as sheriff Rogers keeps shouting, is to "cut off their hands! Cut off their hands!" *The Children* may not hold out much hope for the nuclear family's future, but it plays pretty funny, especially after a few brews. Heroine Garnett is best remembered for her rendition of the upbeat ditty "We'll Sing in the Sunshine," but the Ramones' "Beat on the Brat" would have made for more appropriate background music here.

Chopping Mall (1986) ◆◇

D: Jim Wynorski. Kelli Maroney, Tony O'Dell, John Terlesky, Barbara Crampton, Dick Miller, Paul Bartel, Mary Woronov, Mel Welles, Gerrit Graham. 77 minutes. (Lightning)

Despite an admittedly great title, *Chopping Mall* (formerly *Killbots* and *Shopping Maul*) is an uninspired blend of *Dawn of the Dead, The Terminator,* and any number of dumb slasher flicks. Three heavily armed Protector 101 security robots run amok in a closed shopping mall after their master computer is struck by lightning, plunging a group of partying employees into an all-night orgy of gratuitous bloodletting. Unfortunately, *Chopping Mall* sticks strictly to formula, neglecting numerous satiric opportunities in favor of mechanical stalk-and-kill set pieces. Almost as predictable are the countless "in" references to B pics past: Bartel and Woronov briefly reprise their Bland Couple roles from *Eating Raoul;* Gerrit (*Phantom of the Paradise*) Graham and Mel (*Little Shop of Horrors*) Welles contribute micro cameos; and Miller appears once again as Walter Paisley, the bumbling beatnik from Roger Corman's cult fave *A Bucket of Blood* (see index)—a joke that may have worked in the first dozen or so flicks that used it but that plays pretty stale here. One positive note: *Chopping Mall* runs only 77 minutes, a good reel shorter than it might have.

C.H.U.D. (1984) ◆◆◆

D: Douglas Cheek. John Heard, Daniel Stern, Kim Greist. 88 minutes. (Media)

That's Cannibalistic Humanoid Underground Dwellers to you, pal, and a pretty fair semisatiric urban horror exercise in a *Homeless from Hell* vein.

City Limits (1985) ◆◆

D: Aaron Lipstadt. John Stockwell, Darrell Larson, Kim Cattrall, James Earl Jones, Robby Benson, Rae Dawn Chong. 85 minutes. (Vestron)

This "strikingly visual vision of the future" (according to the box copy), a kind of *Road Warrior Meets West Side Story,* stars Stockwell, Larson and the busy Rae Dawn Chong as gang leaders in the postplague world of 2003, forced to do battle with a rival outfit (headed by Danny De La Paz) and a team of sinister bureaucrats out to reclaim the youths' ravaged city. A weak, porous script robs the pic of its potential suspense, but the solid cast keeps things reasonably lively. Jones makes the most of his scant screen time, while the redoubtable Benson supplies unintentional comic relief as the bad bureaucrats' wimpy boss. A bit more care from its creators—the same crew that brought us the far superior *Android* (see index)—might have made *City Limits* a winner.

City of the Walking Dead (1983) ◆◆

D: Umberto Lenzi. Hugo Stiglitz, Mel

Ferrer, Laura Trotter. 90 minutes. (Cinema Group)

Workers return from a damaged nuke plant as disfigured, flesh-eating zombies! A wildly incoherent Italo *Dawn of the Dead* rip-off, but it does have a cheapjack nightmare quality, plus blood and gore galore.

A Clockwork Orange (1971) ♦♦◇

D: *Stanley Kubrick. Malcolm McDowell, Patrick Magee, Adrienne Corri. 137 minutes. (Warner)*

Kubrick's none-too-subtle dystopian satire, based on Anthony Burgess's even-less-subtle novel, has never been one of the Phantom's faves, but it *is* slick, violent, and undeniably popular in many quarters.

The Clonus Horror (1978) ♦♦♦

D: *Robert Fiveson. Tim Donnelly, Dick Sargent, Peter Graves, Paulette Breen, Keenan Wynn, Lurene Tuttle. 90 minutes. (Lightning)*

The Clonus Horror deals with a political/corporate clone plot that gradually unravels due to a stray can of Milwaukee beer (!). Beyond that, we can say no more without subtracting from this sci-fi sleeper's considerable suspense. (Even Lightning's video cover copy gives too much away, so don't read it.) Suffice it to say that *The Clonus Horror* is an excellent, intense chiller that demonstrates how a solid story line, a tight script, taut direction (by Fiveson), and good performances (from

Donnelly in the lead to vet thesps Graves, Sargent, Wynn, and Tuttle in key cameos) can overcome a low budget.

Close Encounters of the Third Kind: The Special Edition (1977/1980) ♦♦♦

D: *Steven Spielberg. Richard Dreyfuss, François Truffaut, Teri Garr. 135 minutes. (RCA/Columbia)*

One megabudgeted Spielbergian tale of benign aliens that's truly suspenseful rather than *just* sticky and sweet. Definitely recommended.

Cocoon (1985) ♦♦◇

D: *Ron Howard. Don Ameche, Wilford Brimley, Hume Cronyn, Jessica Tandy, Brian Dennehy, Steve Guttenberg, Gwen Verdon, Maureen Stapleton, Jack Gilford, Tahnee Welch. 117 minutes. (CBS/Fox)*

Howard's relentlessly crowd-pleasing sci-fi fable features bright performances by its three superannuated stars—Cronyn, Brimley, and especially Ameche (looking terrif at seventy-six in a gaudy assortment of Florida leisure suits)—an impressive flying saucer that spits lightning bolts, and even a brief clip from Laurel and Hardy's *Flying Deuces*. On the downside, the aliens—who resemble WASPy fugitives from some cosmic health club (their leader, Dennehy, even wears a USA jogging jacket!)—are bland at best; there are frequent descents into blatant sentimentality (the Phantom's heartstrings are still sore from the violent tugging they received); and Guttenberg, for our money, is a welcome subtraction from *any* flick. Though *Cocoon* is basically a *Splash* rehash, its top-notch cast—and some variously hard, sad, and bracing truths about Man's losing battle with Time—should keep your finger fairly far removed from your fast-forward control. Avoid the crass, hack sequel *Cocoon II: The Return* (CBS/Fox).

Colossus: The Forbin Project (1970) ◆◆◆

D: *Joseph Sargent. Eric Braeden, Susan Clark, William Schallert. 100 minutes. (MCA)*

Computers of the world unite to overthrow their human masters in one of your better technology-amok thrillers. Colossus the computer makes for a memorably arrogant villain.

Conquest of the Planet of the Apes (1972) ◆◆◇

D: *J. Lee Thompson. Roddy McDowall, Don Murray, Ricardo Montalban. 87 minutes. (Playhouse)*

Part four of the series details the origins of the apes' revolt as McDowall leads enslaved fellow simians against evil homo-sap overseers headed by Murray. Sometimes has a made-for-TV feel, but provides enough action to make it worth a look.

Cosmic Monsters (1958) ◆◆ B&W

D: *Gilbert Gunn. Forrest Tucker, Gaby Andre, Martin Benson. 75 minutes. (Media)*

One of two Tucker sci-fi flicks filmed back-to-back in Britain. This one's basically another boring bugs-amok movie. Not as good as *The Crawling Eye.*

The Crawling Eye (1958) ◆◆◆ B&W

D: *Quentin Lawrence. Forrest Tucker, Janet Munro, Laurence Payne. 85 minutes. (Fox Hills)*

The second and better of Forrest's Brit pics envisions an invasion of outsize alien eyeballs (!) who emerge from a radioactive cloud to terminate alpine Earthlings. Pretty unique.

The Crazies (1973) ◆◆

D: *George A. Romero. Lane Carroll, W. G. McMillan, Harold Wayne Jones. 103 minutes. (Vista)*

A generally failed bid to repeat *Night of the Living Dead*'s success, *The Crazies* (aka *Code Name: Trixie*) sports a similar story line—this time involving bacteria-infected citizens turning into cannibalistic zombies. There are some effective gore moments, but *The Crazies* pales beside *Night* or *Dawn of the Dead* (see index).

Creation of the Humanoids (1962) ◆◆◆◆

D: *Wesley E. Barry. Don Megowan, Erica Elliott, Don Doolittle, Dudley Manlove. 78 minutes. (Raedon)*

Part ontological meditation, part contempo civil-rights parable, this 1962 postnuke epic pits the

Klan-like Order of Flesh and Blood, led by one Craigus (Megowan), against a horde of well-meaning, chromedomed automatons (called clickers by their bigoted human overseers). When Craigus learns that his own sister is "in rapport" with a clicker named Pax, he vows to home-wreck that happy relationship. At one point, Pax breaks out in a fit of mechanical laughter. "It's the humor circuit," he explains; "it's much harder to control than the pain." Barry's low-key direction, Ted Rich's garish pop-art sets, and Jay (*The Killer Shrews*) Simms's genuinely witty script—to say nothing of Dr. Louis M. Zabner's "special eye effects"— should leave vid-viewers with a wry smile too.

Creature (1985) ◆◇
D: William Malone. Klaus Kinski, Wendy Schaal, Stan Ivar, Lyman Ward, Annette McCarthy, Diane Salinger. 97 minutes. (Media)

Stop us if you've heard this one: A rescue crew of seven finds itself trapped in space with a hungry ET. One by one, the astronauts are gorily transformed into alien Alpo. Frantic survivors—the toughest a laser-gun-wielding woman—try every conceivable means to destroy the gluttonous space ghoul, all to no avail. . . . Malone's *Creature* (originally *Titan Find*) isn't the worst *Alien* clone to come down the sci-fi pike over the past decade (*Alien Predators* thus far has that negative distinction),

but it's every bit as pointless as its similarly counterfeit counterparts. The requisite shock effects (including the ever-reliable exploding-head trick) are competently crafted; Kinski provides a measure of hammy élan as a horny German astronaut; and firm-breasted blond crewmember Salinger handles the pic's gratuitous nudity chores with adequate aplomb. Otherwise, you've *seen* it all before too.

Creature from the Black Lagoon (1954) ◆◆◆ B&W
D: Jack Arnold. Richard Carlson, Julie Adams, Richard Denning. 79 minutes. (Goodtimes)

One of the '50s' most popular sci-fi fables, featuring the femme-starved Gill-Man (played by pro swimmer Ricou Browning) and his lethal misadventures among mankind. Inspired two sequels, *Revenge of the Creature* and *The Creature Walks Among Us* (both NA), plus a Dave Edmunds rock song.

Crime Zone (1989) ◆◆
D: Liano Llosa. Peter Nelson, Sherilyn Fenn, David Carradine. 92 minutes. (MGM/UA)

"God Is Dead. Hell Still Exists."— So goes the cheery tag line for Llosa's *Crime Zone*, a high-tech, low-budget *Bonnie and Clyde* clone set in a futuristic "post-plague" America. Bone (Nelson) and Helen (Fenn) are young "sub-grades" doomed by a rigid caste system to spend their lives hanging out in a sleazy Dead End Zone bar (which only goes to show that some people are *never* satisfied). Their futures briefly brighten when slick villain Jason (Carradine, who also associate-produced) offers them a way out that leads instead to a life of violent crime. If little else, the Roger Corman–produced *Crime Zone* deserves credit for reaching back to rip off *Bonnie and Clyde* rather than *Road Warrior*. Other pluses include blond Sherilyn (*Two Moon Junction*) Fenn's feisty turn as the gun-toting ex-hooker Helen; a bouncy synthesizer score that's at violent attitudinal odds with the flick's grim dystopian visuals; and a handful of imaginative *1984*-type variations, like the Justice Superdome (where televised executions take place) and the Gardens of Hibernation (rejuvenation centers for the rich). Unfortunately, *Crime Zone* doesn't work in enough inventive touches to transcend its predictable intrigues and relentlessly murky lighting, offering little of the fun found in, say, Arnie Schwarzenegger's *The Running Man*.

Critters (1986) ◆◆
D: *Stephen Herek. Dee Wallace Stone, M. Emmet Walsh, Billy "Green" Bush, Scott Grimes, Don Opper, Terrence Mann. 86 minutes. (RCA/ Columbia)*

Stop us if you've heard *this* one: In a kind of reverse *Wizard of Oz* od-yssey, a gang of fugitive furballs called Krites—cutesy creatures with falsetto voices, voracious appetites, and razor-sharp teeth—beam down from outer space into the spacious Kansas backyard of a Typical American Family. Chaos reigns as our embattled TAF tries to fend off the little buggers' relentless assaults, while a pair of taciturn extraterrestrial bounty hunters turn up to track down the insatiable invaders. *Critters* is a pastiche of shameless lifts not only from *Gremlins*, *The Terminator*, and *The Brother from Another Planet*, but from such already secondhand sci-fi fare as *Empire's Ghoulies* and *TerrorVision*. To his credit, director/co-scripter Herek manages to shake these artificial ingredients with sufficient energy to bring the proceedings to the level of the watchable and occasionally beyond.

Critters 2: The Main Course (1988) ◆◇
D: *Mick Garris. Scott Grimes, Liane Curtis, Don Opper, Terrence Mann, Herta Ware, Eddie Deezen. 87 minutes. (RCA/Columbia)*

Critters 2, an intensely unnecessary sequel, finds a batch of alien hatchlings left over from the first flick resurfacing (on Easter Sunday, no less) in the hick burg of Grover's Bend. There are a few fairly decent setup scenes in the opening reels, including one wherein an early victim is eaten alive by the title hand puppets while wearing a full Easter Bunny suit (!). Unfortunately, it's precisely at the point when the Krites come alive in force that the film goes into its prolonged death throes, with particularly noxious work turned in by Ware (doing an awful Ruth Gordon impersonation) and B-movie low-comic relief specialist Deezen (identified here simply as The Geek).

The Cyclops (1957) ◆◆ B&W
D: Bert I. Gordon. James Craig, Gloria Talbott, Lon Chaney, Jr., Tom Drake. 75 minutes. (IVE)

Mr. BIG (Gordon) strikes again, this time with an enormous one-eyed atomic mutant amok in a back lot in Mexico. Not as good as the same auteur's *Amazing Colossal Man* (NA), but a must for Gloria Talbott fans. Not to be confused with the superior Technicolor sci-fi exercise *Dr. Cyclops* (1940), available via MCA.

Daleks—Invasion Earth 2150 A.D. (1966) NR
D: Gordon Flemyng. Peter Cushing, Bernard Cribbins, Jill Curzon. (HBO)

Cushing reprises his TV role as the civilized Dr. Who, who herein aids human survivors in their guerrilla war against the diabolical alien Daleks. The sequel to 1965's *Dr. Who and the Daleks*. (Goodtimes)

Damnation Alley (1977) ◆◆
D: Jack Smight. George Peppard, Jan-Michael Vincent, Dominique Sanda. 95 minutes. (Key)

A pretty bad adaptation of Roger Zelazny's postnuke novel about five survivors who traverse the American wasteland in an armored van. Has a few chilling FX, though.

Dark Star (1974) ◆◆◆◆
D: John Carpenter. Brian Narelle, Dan O'Bannon, Cal Kuniholm, Dre Pahich. 95 minutes. (Video Dimensions, others)

In addition to its other virtues, John (*Halloween*) Carpenter's *Dark Star* (which began life as a USC student project) has to be the best-*looking* $60,000 feature ever lensed. This witty, often brilliant sci-fi satire starts as a *2001* takeoff but swiftly soars into totally original terrain. Dark Star is a scoutship whose 20-year mission is to search out and destroy unstable planets approaching a nova state. Aboard are four cabin-fevered crewmembers (Pahich, Narelle, Kuniholm, and O'Bannon, who also co-scripted), the ship's late commander (stashed in a cryonics tank, where his brain is occasionally activated), a vicious alien "pet" (actually an animated beach-ball [!] with clawed feet and a voracious appetite), a nagging computer, and a prim, voice-equipped Franklin Pangborn–type thermonuclear device that's just itching to explode. The space jockeys' chief enemy, however, is relentless, overwhelming, utterly stultifying *boredom*; anyone who's ever worked too long in the same office will instantly relate to the crew's comically desperate attempts to relieve same. *Dark Star* remains Carpenter's most profound film.

Day of the Animals (1977) NR
D: William Girdler. Christopher George, Leslie Nielsen, Lynda Day George. 97 minutes. (Media)

Ecological erosion of the ozone layer causes ordinary creatures to freak out, polishing off a veteran B cast in the process.

The Day of the Triffids (1963) ◆◆◆
D: Steve Sekely. Howard Keel, Nicole Maurey, Janette Scott. 95 minutes. (Media)

Carnivorous plants from outer space cause an outbreak of mass blindness as they stalk their human prey. Keel and friends frantically work to reverse the situation. Probably the classiest of all killer-plant movies.

The Day the Earth Caught Fire (1962) ◆◆◆ B&W
D: Val Guest. Edward Judd, Janet Munro, Leo McKern. 100 minutes. (HBO)

A bleak Brit doomsday vision that emphasizes human reactions to an impending catastrophe triggered by nuclear recklessness. Engrossing, with a memorable fade-out.

The Day the Earth Stood Still (1951) ◆◆◆◇ B&W
D: Robert Wise. Michael Rennie, Patricia Neal, Sam Jaffe. 92 minutes. (CBS/Fox)

Still stands tall as one of celluloid sci-fidom's early greats. Rennie is an interplanetary peacenik out to warn foolhardy Earthlings re: their nuclear follies. His eight-foot robot, Gort, is on hand to supply the muscle. One of the McCarthy Era's few liberal-minded SF movies.

The Day Time Ended (1979) ◆◆◇
D: Bud Cardos. Jim Davis, Dorothy Malone. 79 minutes. (Media)

Time plays tricks on screen vets Davis and Malone in this oft-incoherent yet strangely compelling effort that features David Allen's deft stop-motion animation FX.

Dead-End Drive-In (1986) ◆◆
D: Brian Trenchard-Smith. Ned Manning, Natalie McCurry, Peter Whitford, Wilbur Wilde, Brett Climo, Ollie Hall. 92 minutes. (New World)

Considering the violent crime, food shortages, and rampant unemployment plaguing an Australia of the near future, young Jimmy (Manning) would seem to be having a pretty good time of it. In *Dead-End Drive-In*, we find him tooling along in his brother's refurbished red-and-white '56 Chevy convertible, girlfriend McCurry at his side, their destination the neon-lit Star Drive-In, where they have no intention of watching the movie. Things start to coast downhill, though, when someone steals Jimmy's wheels while our hero's otherwise engaged. They worsen considerably when he's informed by the theater manager (Whitford) that, not unlike the Roach Motel, no one *leaves* the Star Drive-In—it's been designated as a detention camp for jobless youths. While most of the inmates—decked out in de rigueur *Road Warrior* regalia—accept their fates (which *do* include free brew, junk food, and kung-fu movies), Jimmy will stop at the proverbial nothing to escape, and his relentless attempts to drive out of the drive-in consume most of the pic's running time. While the premise is solid enough, director Trenchard-Smith makes too little use of it, leaving *Dead-End Drive-In* an uneven mix of muddled social fable and tame action fare.

Deadly Friend (1986) ◆

D: Wes Craven. Matthew Laborteaux, Kristy Swanson, Michael Sharrett, Anne Twomey, Anne Ramsey, Richard Marcus. 91 minutes. (Warner)

Craven's *Deadly Friend* kicks off as another Teen-Genius-and-His-Pet-Robot comedy before switching gears and genres and taking a belated Bionic *Bad Seed* twist. When young Paul's (LaBorteaux) terminally cute automated pal BB (replete with Donald Duck voice) is terminated by shotgun-wielding Anne (*Throw Momma from the Train*) Ramsey, and Samantha (Swanson), the abused girl-next-door, is done in by her sadistic dad, Paul gets the bright idea to implant the robot's microchip brain into Sam's lifeless cerebrum. Not exactly High Concept City, but as a simple, serviceable horror-

movie hook, *Deadly Friend*'s Girl-with-the-Remote-Controlled-Brain premise might have worked. Alas, the pic turns up brain-dead long before Samantha does. For gorehounds, Craven does work in one compulsory exploding-head scene, lots of creepy brain-surgery close-ups, and even a few lifts from his far superior *Nightmare on Elm Street* (see index).

Death Race 2000 (1975) ◆◆◇

D: Paul Bartel. David Carradine, Simone Griffeth, Sylvester Stallone. 80 minutes. (Warner)

Bartel's promising premise—futuristic car wars, where death-dealing drivers try to rack up pedestrians in a kind of human demolition derby—plays a bit broadly for the Phantom's taste but boasts its fair share of loyal devotees. One of Sly's more intelligible roles casts him as tough-guy driver Machine Joe Viterbo.

Death Warmed Up (1985) ◆◆◆

D: David Blyth. Gary Day, Michael Hurst, Margaret Umbers, David Letch, Bruno Lawrence. 83 minutes. (Vestron)

A longtime Forty-second Street fave, *Death Warmed Up* is an admirably perverse, New Wave–style, New Zealand–lensed zombie outing in a *Reanimator* vein. Day is the loose-screwed Dr. Archer ("Trust me!") Howell, head living-dead doc at the isolated Trans-Cranial Applications hosp. Onto his island redoubt come two young couples led by Hurst, whom the bonkers brain surgeon had hypnotized into killing his own parents some seven years before. A prolonged bloody showdown—replete with eye-arresting subterranean motorcycle chases—ensues between the youths and Howell's undead minions (Bruno [*The Quiet Earth*] Lawrence among them). *Death Warmed Up* rates as a fun, tongue-in-cheek treat.

Deathsport (1978) ◆◆◇

D: Allan Arkush, Henry Suso. David Carradine, Claudia Jennings, Richard Lynch. 83 minutes. (Warner)

More futuristic vehicular violence from our friends at AIP. This one's set in the postapocalyptic year 3000, with Carradine and welcome addition Jennings battling bikers and mutants.

Deep Star Six (1989) ◆◆

D: Sean S. Cunningham. Greg Evigan, Miguel Ferrer, Nancy Everhard, Taurean Blaque, Cindy Pickett, Nia Peeples. 98 minutes. (IVE)

Deep Star Six concerns a co-ed submarine crew who pick the wrong place—a legendary sea monster's den—to install a subaqueous nuke-missile platform. While admirably earnest, reasonably well-crafted, and relatively restrained for a Cunningham opus—there's only one all-out gore scene—the flick nonetheless emerges as a generally dull and totally predictable underwater *Alien*

clone. What's worse, easily six reels unspool before we even get our first glimpse of the crew-starved creature (who isn't worth the wait), and he's forced to eat fast to finish off the cast within the movie's remaining minutes. Among our assembled thesps, *RoboCop*'s Ferrer earns kudos for his twitchy turn as a neurotic crewmember, while newcomer Peeples impresses as a sexy distaff scientist (who, unfortunately, winds up as fish food). As for hero Greg (*B.J. and the Bear*) Evigan, he demonstrates once again that breaking up with his former chimp partner ranks as the worst career move he could have made.

Def-Con 4 (1985) ◆◇

D: Paul Donovan. Lenore Zann, Maury Chaykin, Tim Choate, Kevin King, Kate Lynch, John Walsch. 85 minutes. (New World)

Set "the day after tomorrow," *Def-Con 4* opens with a (presumably unconscious) lift from 1967's *Doomsday Machine* (see index): The crewmembers of a nuke-equipped satellite anchored in deep space watch on their instrument panel as The Final War erupts on a distant Earth. Our astronauts return to a radiation-ravaged America overrun by plot elements from a dozen other, better postapocalyptic pulp pics: *The Road Warrior, The Terminator, Wargames*—the list is almost as endless as this movie. Sole survivor Commander Howe (wimpily enacted by Choate) encounters cannibalistic mutants (called terminals), half-crazed survivalists, and paramilitary punks, led by teenage army brat Gideon (King), who operate a brutal slave-labor camp. The flick quickly degenerates into a dull, repetitive cat-and-mouse game between Gideon and Howe, as once again the world ends not with a bang but with a yawn.

Demon Seed (1977) ◆◆◇
D: Donald Cammell. Julie Christie, Fritz Weaver, Gerrit Graham. 97 minutes. (MGM/UA)

A horny, power-crazed HAL clone (voice courtesy of Robert Vaughn) has the hots for Christie in this cautionary tale re: the dangers of computer rape. Some may deem it claustrophobic and overly febrile, but we found it pretty compelling. Director Cammell went on to helm the hallucinatory 1988 thriller White of the Eye (see index).

Destination Moon (1950) ◆◆◆
D: Irving Pichel. John Archer, Warner Anderson, Tom Powers. 91 minutes. (Nostalgia Merchant)

A fun '50s sci-fi effort, produced by George Pal and co-scripted by Robert Heinlein, that attempts to lend an air of scientific accuracy to its tale of man's first lunar landing.

Diabolical Dr. Z (1965) ◆◆◇
D: Jess Franco. Howard Vernon, Mabel Karr, Estella Blain. 83 minutes. (Sinister Cinema)

Howard is a mad doc who enlists his equally unbalanced daughter in an elaborate revenge scheme in Franco's atmospheric sequel to The Awful Dr. Orloff (NA).

Dr. X (1932) ◆◆◇
D: Michael Curtiz. Lionel Atwill, Fay Wray, Lee Tracy, Preston Foster. 77 minutes. (MGM/UA)

A weird, uneven mix of effective horror, creaky haunted-house doings, and tiresome comic "relief" supplied by nominal hero Tracy (essentially reprising his wisecracking-reporter role from Broadway's Front Page), Dr. X is highlighted by elaborate lab sets, Curtiz's direction, and an early two-strip Technicolor process. A graphic demonstration of the wonders of "synthetic flesh" supplies an undeniably memorable moment, as does young Foster's turn as a demented precursor to Reanimator's Herbert West. Premier screamer Wray gives her lungs a full airing as the daughter of head doc Atwill.

Donovan's Brain (1953) ◆◆◆ B&W
D: Felix Feist. Lew Ayres, Gene Evans, Nancy Davis. 85 minutes. (MGM/UA)

Curt Siodmak's cerebral story, lensed later both as The Brain (see index) and, with a Nostradamus twist, as W. Lee Wilder's unforgettable Man Without a Body (NA), finds scientist Ayres controlled by a dead power-broker's brain, while the future First Lady plays the dame in the case. Well done and influential.

Dreamscape (1984) ◆◆◆

D: Joseph Ruben. Dennis Quaid, Max von Sydow, Eddie Albert, Kate Capshaw, Christopher Plummer. 99 minutes. (HBO)

Though marred by occasionally glib treatment, *Dreamscape* posits a fascinating premise. Psychic Quaid enters guilt-plagued president Albert's recurrent postnuke nightmare to save him from paranormal assassin David Patrick Kelly. The flick's surreal centerpiece is an extended nightmare sequence that sees contempo FX techniques applied with uncommon skill and imagination.

Earth vs. the Flying Saucers (1956) ◆◆◆ B&W

D: Fred F. Sears. Hugh Marlowe, Joan Taylor, Donald Curtis. 82 minutes. (RCA/Columbia)

One of the best of the '50s invasion flicks, replete with the saucer-zapping of Washington, D.C., alien brainwashing, and faceless robot hordes on the march, with standout FX work by Ray Harryhausen.

Eliminators (1986) ◆◇

D: Peter Manoogian. Andrew Prine, Roy Dotrice, Denise Crosby, Patrick Reynolds, Conan Lee. 95 minutes. (Playhouse)

Eliminators' somnolent story line involves a "mandroid" (Reynolds), a mercenary (Prine), a scientist (Crosby) and a Ninja (the imag-inatively monikered Conan Lee) who, accompanied by their faithful, requisite cute robot, Spot, brave the low-budget perils of a South American jungle to foil a megalomaniacal madman from— dare we say it?—ruling the world. In all fairness, *Eliminators* represents a half-step up from Empire Pictures' usual dull, offensive, derivative dreck; this one's content to be merely dull and derivative. Prine, as the Michael Douglas/*Romancing the Stone* clone, even manages to give an animated performance not at all in keeping with Empire's Living Dead school of Thespianism. Still, *Eliminators* isn't as exciting as, say, watching a wax candle melt for 95 minutes.

Enemy Mine (1985) ◆◆◆

D: Wolfgang Petersen. Dennis Quaid, Louis Gossett, Jr., Brion James, Richard Marcus, Carolyn McCormick, Bumper Robinson. 108 minutes. (CBS/Fox)

Despite its occasional static stretches, lapses in logic, and descents into dumb dialogue, Petersen's gala space opera is an entertaining exercise in high-tech sci-fi pulp. Gossett gives a winning performance as the hermaphroditic Drac Jeriba, an alien fighter pilot downed on a barren asteroid who's forced to cooperate with his similarly stranded human counterpart, Willis Davidge (credibly played by Quaid). After a period of mutual hostility, the pair forge a survival bond that gradually grows into a genuine friendship. *Enemy Mine* essentially unfolds as a well-crafted B movie (its reputed $33 million budget sure doesn't show onscreen, cosmic FX work by the busy Industrial Light and Magic crew notwithstanding). The alien sets and skyscapes are imaginatively rendered, though, and a run-in with a gang of interplanetary slave-traders (who look more like fugitives from a vintage Roger Corman biker flick) supplies solid if unspectacular action.

Escape from New York (1981) ◆◆◆
D: John Carpenter. Kurt Russell, Lee Van Cleef, Ernest Borgnine, Donald Pleasence. 99 minutes. (Nelson)

A lively Carpenter caper that expertly exploits worldwide Applephobia: the NYC of 1997 is one sprawling alfresco penal colony! Lowlifes therein have kidnapped the prez, and it's surly antihero Russell's job to spring him or die. The ever-popular Borgnine is especially good here as an indomitable Gotham cabbie.

Escape from Safehaven (1989) ◇
D: Brian Thomas Jones, Mames McCalmont. Rick Gianasi, John Wittenbauer, Roy MacArthur, William Beckwith, Sammi Gavich. 85 minutes. (Sony)

Yet another no-budget *indoor* (!) *Road Warrior* rip-off, *Escape From Safehaven* chronicles the trials and tribulations of the troubled Colt clan, forced to cope with hordes of rapacious scavengers running amok amid the ruins of a postnuke NYC. Tired of this grueling life-style, the stressed-out Colts take shelter at the security-minded Safehaven 186. Trouble is, conditions are even *worse* on the inside, where Preacher (MacArthur), a leather-jacketed Lance Henriksen–lookalike, and his punkoid goons have turned the complex into a virtual prison. To the rescue of the captive Colts and their fellow inmates comes Mad Max manqué Pierce, stoically interpreted by Gianasi, a thesp wooden enough to make Miles O'Keefe look like Laurence Olivier—or at least Mel Gibson. From there on, it's strictly business as usual as Pierce and his fellow Safehaven freedom fighters run up the body count at the bad guys' expense. *Escape From Safehaven*'s tin-eared script, somnolent perfs, and grating fuzzguitar soundtrack make this derivative dud well worth avoiding.

Escape from the Planet of the Apes (1971) ◆◆◆
D: Don Taylor. Roddy McDowall, Kim Hunter, Ricardo Montalban. 98 minutes. (Playhouse)

Entertaining third entry in the *Apes* series propels brainy chimps Cornelius (McDowall) and Zira (Hunter) back to a preapocalyptic twentieth century for a series of fur-raising encounters with bigoted humans.

Escapement (aka *Electronic Monster*) (1957) ◆◆◆ B&W
D: Montgomery Tully. Rod Cameron, Mary Murphy, Peter Illing. 72 minutes. (Sinister Cinema)

Illing invents an infernal device "capable of drugging a man's brain with strange sounds and weird pictures." Cameron is the rugged insurance investigator assigned to the case; Murphy's the gal who wanders "into a web of terror, and is trapped." Well worth catching for the weird pictures alone, to say nothing of the strange sounds.

Evil Spawn (1987) ◆◆◇
D: Kenneth J. Hall. Bobbie Bresee, Drew Godderis, John Terrence, Donna Shock, Jerry Fox, John Carradine. 90 minutes. (Camp)

Hall's *Evil Spawn*, from Fred Olen Ray's American Independent Pictures, starts slowly as yet another alien-microbes amok retread but picks up sharply when it shifts to Hollywood, where it mutates into a fun, cheapo reprise of Roger Corman's *Wasp Woman*. Faded B-movie queen Lynn Roman (Bresee, whose own checkered career began with her cover appearance on *Famous Monsters of Filmland*'s first issue 30+ years ago) discovers that injecting the microbes reverses the aging process—enough, she hopes, to win her the lead in *Savage Goddess*. Unfortunately, the serum also turns her into a murderous bug-lady. Bresee's charismatically eccentric performance actually lurches this low-budget quickie into ersatz John Waters territory. Add mucho brain-damaged dialogue, lots of in-jokes for B buffs, flubbed lines, gratuitous nudity galore, and the ubiquitous Carradine in his usual generic mad-scientist cameo, and you've got a tacky but wacky flick that's poor in production values but rich in cheap laughs.

Evils of the Night (1985) 0 ◆
D: Mardi Rustam. Neville Brand, Aldo Ray, Tina Louise, John Carradine, Julie Newmar, Karrie Emerson. 85 minutes. (Lightning)

The redoubtable Rustam Brothers, Mardi and Mohammed, who brought us the hilariously awful *Psychic Killer* (see index) back in '75, come a cropper with this excruciatingly inept exercise. Five wholesome California airheads— Brian & Connie & Ron & Heather & Nancy (consider the possibilities!)—are enjoying a camping trip full of gratuitous nudity and unfettered sylvan frolics when they run afoul of a gaggle of silver-suited aliens conducting unspeakable experiments at a local hospital. Nominal stars Newmar, Louise, and Carradine receive but a few minutes of meaningless screen time, while B-movie vets Brand and Ray mug it up unmercifully as a pair of psycho garage attendants in the aliens' employ. Not as entertaining as your average blank cassette.

Explorers (1985) ♦
D: Joe Dante. Ethan Hawke, River Phoenix, Jason Presson, Amanda Peterson, Dick Miller, Robert Picardo. 109 minutes. (Paramount)

Joe (*Gremlins*) Dante's juvenile space fantasy embraces the Spielbergian formula of bringing white magic to Mall America ("the adventure begins in your own backyard"), that vast suburban expanse previously little noted for its mystery and wonder. Unlike *E.T.* and *Poltergeist*, which at least delivered what they promised, all *Explorers* delivers is one—count it—*one* lame joke. The setup consumes 80 interminable minutes; the punchline lasts another 20 and takes Spielberg's (and other film-buffs-turned-movie-moguls') pop-cultural tunnel vision to its outer limits: The three earth kids discover *not* the secrets of the universe but a hyper, popeyed alien who mimics American TV. To paraphrase Pogo, "We Have Met the Aliens, and They Are Us."

Fahrenheit 451 (1966) ♦♦♦
D: François Truffaut. Julie Christie, Oskar Werner, Anton Diffring. 111 minutes. (MCA)

Truffaut's screen adaptation of Ray Bradbury's vision of a totalitarian dystopia where books are banned and literacy is a crime is slow going at times but ultimately rewarding.

The Fantastic Planet (1973) ♦♦◇
D: Rene Laloux. 72 minutes. (Video Yesteryear, others)

This popular animated French sci-fi fantasy depicts a world where humans, called OMS, are pets of the 40-foot humanoid DRAAGs who rule the title site (there's even a DRAAG queen). Sometimes sluggish, but enough imagination shines through to make this a watchable item.

Fantastic Voyage (1966) ♦♦♦
D: Richard Fleischer. Stephen Boyd, Raquel Welch, Edmond O'Brien, Donald Pleasence. 100 minutes. (CBS/Fox)

A wonderfully ludicrous premise—shrunken scientists in a minisub journey through a human body—campy cast, and deft execution, along with wonderful FX, make this a highly entertaining pic, far superior to Joe Dante's more recent rip-off, *Innerspace* (see index).

Fiend Without a Face (1958) ♦♦♦ B&W
D: Arthur Crabtree. Marshall Thompson, Kim Parker, Terence Kilburn. 74 minutes. (Republic)

One of the '50s' better alien brain-sucker quickies, with earnest B hero Thompson out to foil the floating, cerebrum-starved intruders. Not as hot as the same year's *Brain From Planet Arous* (see index), but close enough for the Phantom's money.

The Final Countdown (1980) ♦♦◇
D: Don Taylor. Kirk Douglas, Katharine Ross, Martin Sheen. 103 minutes. (Vestron)

While this time-warp flick often plays like a bloated *Twilight Zone* episode, good performances and a '50s-style earnestness transform a potentially feeble fable about a nuke carrier whirled back to Pearl Harbor into fairly diverting SF fare.

The Final Programme (1973) ◆◆◇
D: Robert Fuest. Jon Finch, Jenny Runacre, Sterling Hayden. 85 minutes. (HBO)

The video version of this often cryptic satiric sci-fi saga based on Michael Moorcock's novel is at least an improvement over the shorter theatrical edition, released as *The Last Days of Man on Earth* back in 1973.

First Man into Space (1959) ◆◆◇ B&W
D: Robert Day. Marshall Thompson, Marla Landi, Robert Ayres. 78 minutes. (Rhino)

Fair '50s cheapie bears a story line similar to the superior *Creeping Unknown* (aka *The Quatermass Experiment*), to say nothing of *Night of the Blood Beast* (NA), as an irradiated pilot returns to earth only to mutate into your basic marauding monster.

Flash Gordon (1980) ◆◆◇
D: Mike Hodges. Sam J. Jones, Melody Anderson, Max von Sydow. 111 minutes. (MCA)

Lighthearted revamp of the comic strip/cliffhanger wisely declines to play its purloined material straight, and the results are fairly entertaining.

Flight to Mars (1951) ◆◆◇
D: Lesley Selander. Cameron Mitchell, Marguerite Chapman, Arthur Franz. 72 minutes. (Nostalgia Merchant)

The young Mitchell and Franz head the title journey, which leads to an encounter with a subterranean Martian race.

The Fly (1958) ◆◆◆
D: Kurt Neumann. Vincent Price, David Hedison, Patricia Owens. 94 minutes. (Key)

Actually, no match for the Cronenberg remake (see below) but still superior '50s sci-fi in its own right, with that unforgettable transformation scene that even Cronenberg didn't try to top. As scientist Hedison remarks, "It would almost be funny, if life weren't so sacred!"

The Fly (1986) ◆◆◆◇
D: David Cronenberg. Jeff Goldblum, Geena Davis, John Getz, Joy Boushel, Les Carlson. 100 minutes. (CBS/Fox)

The creative force behind such visceral chillers as *Videodrome*, *Scanners*, and the self-descriptive *They Came from Within* (see index), David Cronenberg lets it all hang out in (and *out of*) *The Fly*, his regurgitative remake of Kurt Neumann's comparatively genteel 1958 original. While liberally changing characters and locales, DC manages to stick to the first *Fly*'s essence. Goldblum is unexpectedly excellent as benignly awkward scientist Seth Brundle, who drunkenly spills the secret of his teleportation machine to journalist Davis. It's also after downing too much champagne that Seth decides to take his premature and ultimately disastrous teleportation trip. (Moral: If you drink, don't teleport.) What transpires after that is well worth seeing for yourself. Suffice it to say that Cronenberg succeeds in fashioning a *Fly* that's by turns funny, poignant, repulsive, and intense. As in his previous pics, DC plunges us into some pretty primal territory here, exploiting deep-seated fears of illness, aging, and other bodily treacheries: Seth's gradual transformation is like unto Shakespeare's famed seven stages of man, reduced to maybe two or three stages and not limited to man. We've gotta hand it to him (Cronenberg, not Shakespeare)—it's not every filmmaker who can work out his rawest phobias onscreen and entertain the rest of us in the process.

The Fly II (1989) ♦♦
D: Chris Walas. Eric Stoltz, Daphne Zuniga, Lee Richardson, Harley Cross, John Getz. 104 minutes. (CBS/Fox)

The sequel to David Cronenberg's masterful remake focuses on young Martin Brundle (Stoltz), the son of *Fly I*, a BAGS (Brundle's Accelerated Growth Syndrome) victim who, at age 5, is not only full-grown but a genius to boot. Sequestered at a secret lab overseen by corporate creep Bartok (Richardson), Brundle, Jr., soon takes up where his deceased dad left off, tinkering with the latter's still-unperfected matter-transmitting telepod device. What Brundle Jr. *doesn't* know is that it's only a matter of time before his dormant fly genes start kicking in, signaling his inevitable descent into a mutant insectoid state. While auteur Cronenberg operated on a metaphorical level while still delivering the disgusto fright-film goods, FX ace Walas, making his directorial debut, executes a competently crafted but utterly routine and painfully padded hack job. *The Fly II* flaps its expository wings for nearly an hour before transmogrifying into a standard monster movie, when Stoltz—by now in full Fly regalia and equipped with a Godzillaesque roar (!)—finally embarks on the expected slaughter spree. Aside from some admittedly vivid gore and makeup FX, the *Fly II*'s buzz is definitely worse than its sting.

The Flying Saucer (1949) ♦♦◊ B&W
D: Mikel Conrad. Mikel Conrad, Pat Garrison, Denver Pyle. 69/120 minutes. (United)

This vanity production made by and starring matinee idol manqué Mikel (*Untamed Women*) Conrad is noteworthy mostly for being the

"FROM BEYOND"

"Humans are such easy prey."
Photo courtesy of Vestron Video.

first flick to exploit the late-40s UFO craze. The video version includes new animated wraparound sequences, plus several SF coming-attractions trailers, which add to the cassette's overall entertainment value.

Forbidden Planet (1956) ◆◆◆◇
D: Fred McLeod Wilcox. Walter Pidgeon, Anne Francis, Leslie Nielsen. 98 minutes. (MGM/UA)

This Freudian sci-fi epic, loosely based on the Bard's *The Tempest*, fully deserves its vaunted rep. Tormented scientist Morbeus (Pidgeon) and his rampaging Id, nature girl Francis, and the unforgettable Robby the Robot head a compelling cast of characters. The *2001* of the '50s.

4D Man (1959) ◆◆◆
D: Irwin S. Yeaworth, Jr. Robert Lansing, Lee Meriwether, James Congdon. 85 minutes. (New World)

Solid low-budget sci-fi about scientist Lansing, whose matter-transposing experiments enable him to walk through walls. In promos for the original film, producer Jack H. Harris offered a million bucks to moviegoers who could prove they could duplicate Lansing's feat. Many broken bones undoubtedly ensued.

From Beyond (1986) ◆◆◆
D: Stuart Gordon. Jeffrey Combs, Barbara Crampton, Ted Sorel, Ken Foree, Carolyn Purdy-Gordon, Bunny Summers. 85 minutes. (Vestron)

From Beyond, director/co-scripter

(with Dennis Paoli) Gordon's second H. P. Lovecraft–based outing, toplines *Reanimator* alumnus Combs as Dr. Crawford Tillinghast, victim of perverted pineal gland experiments perpetrated by mad medico Dr. Pretorius (Sorel). Crampton again costars, this time as the svelte blond shrink who—along with cop Foree (late of *Dawn of the Dead*)—battles slimy, ill-tempered fourth-dimension demons conjured by Pretorius's sinister Resonator. While it lacks some of *Reanimator*'s sheer shock value, *From Beyond* packs plenty of punch in its own right, mixing elements of the original *Alien*, *The Tingler*, and even *The Brainiac* with typically twisted Lovecraftian lunacy and the director's own wild style.

From the Earth to the Moon (1958) ◆◆
D: Byron Haskin. Joseph Cotten, George Sanders, Debra Paget. 100 minutes. (United)

Snoozy screen version of Jules Verne's novel of lunar travel is recommended mostly for '50s-sci-fi addicts.

Future Kill (1985) ◆◆
D: Ronald W. Moore. Edwin Neal, Marilyn Burns, Gabriel Folse, Alice Vilareal, Wade Reese, Barton Faulks. 83 minutes. (Vestron)

It's frat boys vs. antinuke punks (self-dubbed "mutants") in this el cheapo *Road Warrior Meets Animal House by Way of The Terminator* trashfest. Six pledges invade the mutants' turf to kidnap their leader but instead run afoul of the psychotic Splatter (*Texas Chainsaw Massacre* standout Neal, who also co-produced), an armored radiation victim replete with a set of Freddy Krueger–like steel claws. Our clean-cut heroes have to scrap their way out, and the results are so off-the-wall awful that they verge on the compelling. Ed Neal fans will be disappointed that their idol is virtually unrecognizable here in his metal mask and electronically altered voice.

Futureworld (1976) ◆◆◆
D: Richard T. Heffron. Peter Fonda, Blythe Danner, Yul Brynner. 107 minutes. (Warner)

Solid *Westworld* sequel casts Fonda and Danner as journalists investigating what went "worng" at android amusement park, only to uncover an insidious robot plot. Brynner briefly reprises his cyborg gunslinger role.

Galaxy of Terror (1981) ◆◆
D: B. D. Clark. Erin Moran, Edward Albert, Ray Walston. 85 minutes. (Nelson)

A blatant Roger Corman *Alien* rip-off; with elements from *Journey to the 7th Planet* (NA) tossed in, *Galaxy* at least sports an interesting cast, including Erin (*Happy Days*) Moran, Edward (*Getting Even*) Albert, and Sid (*Spider Baby*) Haig, and enough blood and guts to entertain gorehounds. Followed by Corman's ultra-cheap *Forbidden*

World (Nelson), which recycles sets and scenes from *Galaxy* and *Battle Beyond the Stars* (see index).

The Gamma People (1956) ◆◆◇ B&W
D: John Gilling. Paul Douglas, Eva Bartok, Leslie Phillips. 79 minutes. (Goodtimes)

The offbeat tone and cast manage to make this poverty-row polemic about Commie brainwashers and their zombie-making machinery a fairly engrossing item. The lumbering, middle-aged Douglas makes for an unusual sci-fi hero.

Gas-s-s-s (1970) NR
D: Roger Corman. Cindy Williams, Ben Vereen, Talia Shire (Coppola), Bud Cort. 79 minutes. (Lightning)

Roger Corman reportedly swore off directing after agonizing—à la Coppola (Francis Ford, not Talia)—over this muddled "message" movie's final reels; it was later recut without RC's input. A lot of people like it anyway. You may find yourself one of them.

Glen and Randa (1971) ◆◆◆
D: Jim McBride. Steven Curry, Shelley Plimpton, Garry Goodrow. 94 minutes. (United)

An unsung indie sci-fi fable about postnuke nomads, this early effort by Jim (*The Big Easy*) McBride is a perverse, mostly effective mix of earnestness and satire. High points include the nomads' decelerated rendition of the Stones' "Time Is on My Side" (learned from a phonograph in need of new batteries) and Goodrow's turn as the Magician, the last "civilized" man. Occasional descents into pretentiousness constitute the flick's only major flaw.

Godzilla 1985 (1985) ◆◆◇
D: Kohji Hashimoto, R. J. Kizer. Raymond Burr, Keiju Kobayashi, Yosuke Natsuhi, Ten Tanaka, Yasuko Sa-

waguchi, Shin Takuma. 91 minutes. (New World)

"Godzilla!" exclaims Prime Minister Mitamura (Kobayashi). "I was hoping I'd never hear that name again!" Fat chance. After a decade-long absence, Godzilla returns to his old tricks in *Godzilla 1985*. Not only does our decidedly

Giant flying turtle *Gamera* gave Godzilla some stiff competition.
Photo courtesy of Celebrity Home Entertainment, Inc.

unjolly green giant sink ships, squash cities, and snack on nuclear reactors, he even finds time to create an international incident by pulling a Rambo and crunching a Russki sub! (Pipes a gung-ho American officer, "Put a uniform on him and sign him up!") Godzilla has more than political mayhem in mind, however—he's a "living nuclear weapon" out to punish all of mankind for its heedless atomic adventurism. Doing their best to halt the fire-breathing behemoth's progress are scientist Hayashida (Natsuki), journalist Goro (Tanaka), and screaming ingenue Naoko (Sawaguchi). Russia and the U.S. push to nuke the outsize nuisance, but the Nipponese will have none of it. Instead, Hayashida and crew, reasoning that Godzilla's reptilian cerebrum is almost identical in size and IQ to your average bird's, hatch a scheme to lure the rampaging saurian out of Tokyo via high-tech bird calls!

(As one military man opines, "It sounds possible!") While it may be thin in the plot department, *Godzilla 1985* has all the requisite elements of a vintage Godzilla flick: ridiculous dubbing, inane dialogue, cheap but fun FX, and the inevitable "cast of thousands"— most of whom spend their time repeatedly fleeing Tokyo. It even includes American inserts featuring a fatter, grayer, bearded Raymond Burr, reprising his original role as intrepid reporter Steve Martin (not *that* Steve Martin). Here, Ray's largely reduced to tsking from afar as Godzilla levels Tokyo, but it's good to see him up and about again after his sedentary *Ironside* stint. Throw in a score performed by the Tokyo Symphony Orchestra and lots of clean, old-fashioned mindless destruction, and it all adds up to the best Godzilla movie in two decades. For other Godzilla vids, see sidebar.

In Godzilla We Trust

IN THE BEGINNING, Godzilla was a straightforward *monster*, all business and considerably more than a yard wide. 1954's *Godzilla, King of the Monsters* (Vestron) represented Japan's Toho Films' attempt to emulate such popular American primal-beast-awakened-by-the-Bomb pics as the previous year's *Beast from 20,000 Fathoms* (NA). Like Beast before him, Godzilla (called Gojira in the Japanese release) was an avenging phoenix who rose form the ashes of careless atomic testing to exact his pound of flesh—or its equivalent in miniature cities—from an errant mankind. Though inserts featuring a pre–*Perry Mason* Raymond Burr as an intrepid reporter—added for the American release—cheapened the movie a mite, *Godzilla* still emerged as a serious sci-fi entry, and its star behaved accordingly. *That* Godzilla was an all-brawn, no-brain ("the size of a pea," we're told in the film), fire-breathing behemoth bent on nothing less than our destruction. The same held true for his second film, *Gigantis, the Fire Monster* (NA). His name may have been changed to protect the guilty, but Godzilla's dinosaurian dignity survived intact.

Godzilla's worldwide success soon prompted Toho to unleash an increasingly cartoonlike profusion of spin-off monster stars, like *Rodan* (Video Treasures), an outsize pterodactyl; *Mothra* (RCA/Columbia), a mammoth moth; and *Ghidrah* (Interglobal), a violent, volant three-headed dragon from Mars. When Godzilla himself returned after a four-year layoff in 1963's *King Kong vs. Godzilla* (Goodtimes), he was far less the no-nonsense nuclear nightmare of yore than a Nipponese right-cross between John Wayne and Muhammed Ali. For starters, this softer, cheaper-looking Godzilla resorted to using left hooks and leg kicks when tangling with his American opponent. The whole misguided affair reeked of studio compromise. Though Kong was clearly portrayed as the villain of the piece, Toho execs, not wishing to alienate their growing U.S. market, actually lensed two separate endings, with Kong besting Godzilla in the American version and Godzilla saving face in the native release!

Toho next took a cue from the Universal all-star fright line-ups of the '40s—when the likes of Boris Karloff, Lon Chaney, Jr., and John Carradine would team up in films like *House of Frankenstein* (NA)—and began pairing Godzilla with other rising contract creatures from the studio's star stable. Hence, 1964's *Godzilla vs. the Thing* (Paramount) found our hero and Mothra locked in fierce internecine conflict, while 1967's *Godzilla vs. the Sea Monster* (Interglobal) saw those former foes hiss and make up and join forces to defeat Ebirah, a "giant shrimp" (if that's not a contradiction in terms). In *Godzilla vs. Monster Zero* (NA), our hero shared screen time not only with the title nemesis but with a revived Rodan. Toho's all-star trend reached its absurdist apotheosis in *Destroy All Monsters* (1968, NA), wherein heavyweights Godzilla, Mothra, and Rodan were backed up by lesser lights like Baragon, Manda, and Varan ("the Unbelievable") to save earth from the rapacious Ghidrah.

By this time, Godzilla and his creature cohorts more closely resembled pop versions of the benign grotesques of Shinto mythology than the angry atomic monsters of the more recent past. They were even operating out of their own modest Olympus, Monster Island, where they remained at the service of our ever-imperiled planet. The unthinkable had come to pass: Godzilla had become a full-fledged hero!

And that wasn't the end of it. By the '70s, Godzilla had developed an entire repertoire of cutesy anthropomorphic traits. He expressed elation by playfully clapping his paws and anger by uttering untranslated oaths in his native tongue (Dinosaurian, we presume), and in *Son of Godzilla* (Interglobal) he even instructed his (relatively) diminutive offspring Minya in such tricks of the trade as blowing perfect smoke rings with his radioactive breath! Like the Dead End Kids—who started out as the earnest young eponymous stars of Sidney Kingsley's serious social drama *Dead End* and wound up as overage Bowery buffoons in a series of cheap slapstick farces—Godzilla had been reduced to a pathetic screen clown. It was all too much for Godzilla purists, who deserted their formerly favored pea-brained fiend en masse.

At the height of his popularity, Godzilla had enjoyed international-idol status. There were Godzilla toys, comic books, record albums. Rival studios desperately countered with their own creature celebs, such as Daiei Films' *Gamera* (a giant flying turtle) and Nikkatsu's *Gappa* (a large, amorphous, well—*thing*). Japanese tykes wore Godzilla masks and quaffed soft drinks dispensed by sidewalk vending machines made in the image and likeness of the great Godzilla. But the ill-exploited star's disastrous career moves finally forced him into early retirement and an outsize porch rocker at the Old Monsters' Home until his reemergence in New World's *Godzilla 1985*.

If you're looking for a complete set of Godzilla-related Asian monster movies to add to your home-vid library, we'd advise you check out the following:

Dagora, the Space Monster (Video Yesteryear)
Gamera (Celebrity)
Gamera vs. Barugon (Celebrity)
Gamera vs. Gaos (Celebrity)
Gamera vs. Guiron (Celebrity)
Gamera vs. Zigra (Celebrity)
Godzilla on Monster Island (Moore)
Godzilla vs. Megalon (Goodtimes)
Gorath (Video Gems)
Terror of Mecha Godzilla (Paramount)
Varan, the Unbelievable (United)
Yog (Sinister Cinema)

Gorgo (1961) ◆◆◇
D: Eugene Lourie. Bill Travers, William Sylvester, Vincent Winter. 78 minutes. (United)

A story of maternal affection among the dinosaur set. A young, newly captured sea monster destroys half of London during a tantrum before Mom shows up to reclaim him. Beasts will be beasts.

The H-Man (1958) ◆◆◆
D: Inoshiro Honda. Kenji Sahara, Yumi Shirakawa, Akihiko Hirata. 79 minutes. (RCA/Columbia)

Japanese monster-movie maven Honda helms a weird sci-fi noir involving a peripatetic pool of toxic liquid bent on dissolving Tokyo residents. Lensed in color, with strong FX. Other worthwhile Japanese sci-fi efforts that don't rely on Godzilla and gang include Honda's Yeti adventure *Half Human (Media)*, sci-fier *The Human Vapor* (Prism), and Hajaime Sato's compellingly bizarre *Body Snatcher from Hell* (VCR).

Hands of Steel (1986) ◆
D: Martin Dolman (Sergio Martino). John Saxon, Daniel Greene, Janet Agren, George Eastman, Amy Werba, Claudio Cassinelli. 94 minutes. (Vestron)

A skewed *Terminator* steal helmed by "Martin Dolman" (aka Sergio Martino), *Hands of Steel* stars hunky Greene as Paco, a muscleman turned cyborg by evil industrialist Saxon. The setting is a pollution-plagued America of 1997, and it's Paco's assignment to assassinate an elderly ecology leader who's standing in Saxon's sinister way. After failing in this task, Paco lights out for Page, Arizona (nice place to visit, we'd guess), driving through forbidden Acid Rain Zones before winding up at a desert motel run by token blonde Agren. The rest of our story concerns the confused bionic beefcake model's efforts to elude Saxon's laser-armed minions and the FBI. The only noteworthy scene here is an extended arm-wrestling match, and even *it's* inferior to Jeff Goldblum's similar bout in *The Fly.*

Hell Comes to Frogtown (1988) ◆◆◇
D: Donald G. Jackson. Rowdy Roddy Piper, Sandahl Bergman, Rory Calhoun, William Smith. 90 minutes. (New World)

Noted genre auteur Jackson, of *Demon Lover* (see index) and *Rollerblade* (see index) fame, furthers his already vastly distinguished directorial career with the imaginatively titled *Hell Comes to Frogtown.* Hell is *Sam* Hell (wrestler Piper, in what remains perhaps his finest thespic turn), a potent male selected by the distaff powers-that-be (headed by femme fave Bergman) to help repopulate a barren postapocalyptic America. But first he must rescue a gaggle of gals held captive at the title site: a dangerous redoubt ruled by one King Toady and his race of mutant frog-people (!). Aiding Rowdy

Roddy in his quest is ex-action stalwart Calhoun; opposing him is ubiquitous B-movie bad guy Big Bill Smith. To reveal more re: this flawed but undeniably demented exercise in pulp surrealism would (a) ruin your enjoyment and (b) steer the Phantom toward the nearest straitjacket. Better you should rent *Hell Comes to Frogtown* yourself and watch, jaw slack and mouth agape, Mr. Jackson's puerile but fertile mind at work.

The Hidden (1987) ◆◆◆

D: *Jack Sholder. Michael Nouri, Kyle MacLachlan, Ed O'Ross, Clu Gulager, Claudia Christian, William Boyett. 100 minutes. (Media)*

Sholder's *The Hidden* recycles elements from such varied sources as *Lethal Weapon, The Terminator, Night of the Creeps, Creature with the Atom Brain*, and even comicdom's "J'onn J'onzz, Martian Crimefighter," yet it manages to emerge as an entertaining sci-fi actioner with an eccentric tone all its own. Our story involves ace LAPD dick Nouri, spacy "FBI agent" (*Blue Velvet*) MacLachlan, and their mutual search for a series of random maniacs partial to loud music and fast Ferraris and who enjoy stealing and killing to get their hands on same. (Sounds about like your typical Hollywood personality profile to us.) As it quickly turns out, the assorted psychos—who include a fat guy with gastritis, a *zoftig* stripper, and a dog (!)—are merely serving as the human hosts for your basic amoral alien slime-creature

Filmmakers in Focus:

Jack Sholder: Sholder to the Reel

The man behind *The Hidden* is Jack Sholder, behind whose calm, vaguely academic exterior lurks a happily perverse imagination. Jack began his genre-movie career directing and co-scripting the 1982 cult fave *Alone in the Dark* and returned three years later with *Nightmare on Elm Street 2*. This after a lengthy stint as a writer/director/editor for PBS, where his credits included the documentary *King: From Montgomery to Memphis*, the teleseries *3-2-1 Contact* (for which he won an Emmy for his editing work), and *The Garden Party*, an adaptation of Katherine Mansfield's short story of the same name.

So what steered him onto the path of truth and frighteousness?

"I needed the money," Jack recalls. "I'd been free-lancing as a trailer-cutter for New Line Cinema, editing coming attractions for things like *Slaves of the Cannibal God* with Ursula Andress. New Line, previously a distribution company, was starting to move into production. They wanted an inexpensive horror film and asked me if I wanted to do one."

The answer was yes, and the result was *Alone in the Dark,* a clever, nearly seamless scare satire exploring the parameters of sanity. The pic, which also boasted an excellent cast of genre vets—including Donald Pleasence as a loony shrink and Jack Palance and Martin Landau as a pair of more overt maniacs—was unfortunately lost in the slice-and-dice shuffle but has since garnered a sizable video audience. The bigger-budgeted *Nightmare 2* (see index) was followed by *The Hidden,* Jack's most ambitious project to date. The director sees it as both an action-packed, sci-fi-tinged "buddy picture" and an inquiry into "what it means to be human. To the bad alien, Earth is an amusement park." And the flick itself—winner of the 1987 International Critics Award for Best Film at the Sitges International Festival of Film Fantastique—is an alternately wry and violent roller-coaster ride through same.

who uses them till their bodies give out, then moves on to his next victim, relay race–style. Lending texture to this lively film-long chase—which features a prolonged cop massacre to rival *The Terminator, The Hitcher,* and *Ninja 3: The Domination*—is the gradual bond that develops between human cop Nouri and his cosmic counterpart MacLachlan (though they never get as seriously involved as a couple as *Lethal Weapon*'s Mel Gibson and Danny Glover). Both leads turn in top work, as does Christian as the possessed go-go gal. A suspenseful, relentlessly kinetic affair, *The Hidden* is a welcome addition to any genre fan's video library.

Human Experiments (1980) ◆◇
D: Gregory Goodell. Jackie Coogan, Aldo Ray, Ellen Travolta. 82 minutes. (VidAmerica)

As in so many modern cheapies, nostalgic casting is the chief lure in this otherwise-grueling challenge to the human attention span.

Humanoids from the Deep (1980) ◆◆
D: Barbara Peeters. Doug McClure, Ann Turkel, Vic Morrow. 81 minutes. (Warner)

A lively, if predictable, killer-fish story chronicling the title creatures' carnal rampage, with a beachful of bikini'd bimbos at their sex-mad mercy. Almost as good as *Horror of Party Beach* (see index). Hard-core humanoid enthusiasts, meanwhile, might also want to check out *Humanoid Defender* (MCA) and *Humanoid Woman* (Celebrity).

I Married a Monster from Outer Space (1958) ◆◆◆◇ B&W
D: Gene Fowler, Jr. Tom Tryon, Gloria Talbott, Ken Lynch. 78 minutes. (Paramount)

A homophobic horror tale about aliens who commandeer men's bodies and turn them from their wives. Best-selling novelist Tom (*The Other*) Tryon stars as the distracted honeymooner who wantonly neglects spouse Talbott. Slapsy Maxie Rosenbloom is a suspicious barkeep at the roadhouse where our ET boys hang out. Compelling all the way.

Iceman (1984) ◆◆◆◇
D: Fred Schepisi. Timothy Hutton, John Lone, Lindsay Crouse, Josef Sommer, David Straithairn. 101 minutes. (MCA)

Iceman is an excellent, original, often moving story about a revivified 40,000-year-old Eskimo at the mercy of a modern American scientific team. John (*The Last Emperor*) Lone is tops as the titular Neanderthal whose attempts to make sense of his puzzling predicament prompt him to undertake a private religious quest. The film is further abetted by a haunting music score (including Lone and sympathetic scientist Hutton's unique a cappella rendition of Neil Young's "Heart of Gold") and Aussie auteur Schepisi's sure-handed

direction. *Iceman* is a wintry winner, best viewed on sultry summer nights.

Idaho Transfer (1971) ◆◆◆
D: Peter Fonda. Kelley Bonham, Keith Carradine, Kevin Hearst, Caroline Hildebrand, Joe Newman. 90 minutes. (MPI)

Virtually unseen since its completion in 1971, Peter Fonda's third directorial effort (following *Easy Rider* and *The Hired Hand*—see index) has finally surfaced on video, courtesy of MPI. A minimalist ecological allegory, *Idaho Transfer* stacks up as a sturdy offbeat item offering a novel sci-fi story line and deft, if economy-minded, execution. The title refers to a secret time machine that transports a group of youthful volunteers (including Keith Carradine, the only experienced thesp among an otherwise nonprofessional but credible cast) 56 years into a resource-depleted future. The precise nature of the planet's corroded condition is hinted at rather than explicitly explained, until the ironic punchline drives the movie's message home. While occasionally *too* taciturn and understated, *Idaho Transfer* is well worth checking out. The vid version arrives complete with a new intro, wherein auteur Fonda gives a brief account of the film's aims and troubled history.

The Illustrated Man (1969) ◆◆◇
D: Jack Smight. Rod Steiger, Claire

Bloom, Robert Drivas. 103 minutes. (Warner)

An okay distillation of several Ray Bradbury stories, with a fairly self-controlled Rod as a mysterious stranger whose myriad tattoos tell bizarre tales.

The Incredible Melting Man (1978) ◆◇
D: William Sachs. Alex Rebar, Burr De-Benning, Myron Healey. 85 minutes. (Vestron)

A fairly poor throwback to the cheap fright fare of the '50s—with era icon Myron (*The Unearthly*) Healey as a general—that may please those nostalgic for that decade's trashier entertainment. Rick Baker does a good job with the decompositional makeup FX.

The Incredible Shrinking Man (1957) ◆◆◇ B&W
D: Jack Arnold. Grant Williams, Randy Stuart, April Kent. 81 minutes. (MCA)

One of the best sci-fi fables ever, Arnold's tale (scripted by Richard Matheson) of the titular atomic mutant's (Williams) gradual descent into being and nothingness retains its irony and power. Williams turns in an ace job, particularly during his four-foot phase, when he rejects his unwanted celebrity, runs away from his "normal" wife and home, and takes up with a female midget (!). Grant's troubles *really* begin when his once-manageable cat attacks him, and they escalate when he's forced to battle a "giant" spider over a moldy morsel of rat-trap cheese. A cogent comment on the plight of the "little man" in today's technocratic world. Not to be missed.

The Indestructible Man (1956) ◆◆ B&W
D: Jack Pollexfen. Lon Chaney, Jr., Marian Carr, Casey Adams. 70 minutes. (Goodtimes)

Chaney is an electrically revived killer who embarks on a low-budget, high-voltage vengeance spree in a simpleminded '50s quickie that's fun mostly for fans of the era's poverty-row fright flicks.

Infra-Man (1976) ◆◆◆◇
D: Hua-Shan. Li Hsiu-hsien, Wang Hsieh, Terry Liu. 89 minutes. (Prism)

A totally surreal, off-the-wall juvenile superhero saga from Hong Kong featuring a wide assortment of demons, monsters, and kung-fu set-to's. Plays like a vintage American serial on hallucinogenic drugs. Unique and highly recommended.

Innerspace (1987) ◆◆◇
D: Joe Dante. Dennis Quaid, Martin Short, Meg Ryan, Kevin McCarthy, Fiona Lewis, Vernon Wells. 120 minutes. (Warner)

Joe (*The Howling, Gremlins*) Dante is an auteur with a fondness for vet thesps. For *Innerspace*, he rounds up such '50s fright-film refugees as Kevin (*Invasion of the Body Snatchers*) McCarthy, Dick Miller, Ken Tobey and, in his slyest move, William Schallert, from *The Incredible Shrinking Man.*

Dante also gets primo perfs from his leads, especially Short as a chronic hypochondriac whose body is unwittingly invaded by a miniature probe pod manned by pilot Quaid. At its center, *Innerspace* is a combination comic reworking of *Fantastic Voyage* (minus, alas, the ever-formidable Raquel Welch) and a literally visceral version of *Dreamscape*. But, while unwaveringly slick and sometimes funny—"Congratulations," a tiny Quaid tells host Short, "you've just digested the bad guy!"—the pic ultimately fails to measure up to either of its semi-predecessors. Predictable high-tech intrigues, rampant in-jokes (Dante dubs an onscreen punk club The Inferno), megacute Steven Spielberg *shticks*—like the teetotaling Short's mandatory drunk scene—and a pervasive self-congratulatory air undermine *Innerspace*'s genuinely original aspects.

Invaders from Mars (1953) ◆◆◆

D: William Cameron Menzies. Arthur Franz, Jimmy Hunt, Helena Carter. 78 minutes. (Nostalgia Merchant)

Menzies perfectly captures the febrile, paranoid, pulp-culture-drenched nightmare of a typical McCarthy Era tyke as parents and local authority figures become homicidal pawns of the encroaching Martian Menace. Nostalgia Merchant's tape also includes a few sci-fi trailers from the era.

Invaders from Mars (1986) ◆◆

D: Tobe Hooper. Karen Black, Hunter Carson, Timothy Bottoms, Laraine Newman, James Karen, Louise Fletcher. 100 minutes. (Media)

While clinging closely to the original story line, director Hooper and scripters Dan O'Bannon and Don Jakoby attempt to recast William Cameron Menzies's modest 1953 miniclassic *Invaders from Mars* as a deadpan sci-fi comedy. As in the original, young David Gardner (Carson) sees a saucer land in the sandpits just beyond his backyard; authority figures (parents Bottoms and Newman, local police, phone-company reps, et al.) are transmogrified into Martian allies via mind-controlling electrodes implanted in their necks; David enlists an adult ally (here, school nurse and real-life mom Black) to help him warn the world *before it's too late*! There are scattered high points—dictatorial teacher Fletcher, the Martians' most enthusiastic recruit, turns in a rousing perf, particularly when snacking on live frogs (!), while James Karen eschews the frogs but chews the scenery as the gung-ho General Wilson ("Marines have no qualms about killing Martians!"). But the original's genuine juvenile nightmare quality and primal paranoia give way to studied smirkery here, and *Invaders* plods along sans the crazed energy and menace of its model.

Invasion of the Bee Girls (1973) ◆◆◇
D: Denis Sanders. William Smith, Victoria Vetri, Cliff Osmond, Anitra Ford. 85 minutes. (Embassy)

Insectoid women in housewife guise sap guys of their precious bodily fluids and lives alike as part of an insidious alien plot. Big Bill Smith investigates. It's as good as it sounds, due to Nicholas (*Seven Percent Solution*) Meyer's witty script, which sends up the Swingin' '70s. A fine companion piece for *Swingers' Massacre* (see index).

Invasion of the Body Snatchers (1956) ◆◆◆◆ B&W
D: Don Siegel. Kevin McCarthy, Dana Wynter, Carolyn Jones. 80 minutes. (Republic)

The ultimate McCarthyesque Commie-Menace-as-sci-fi-movie can also be seen as an anticonformity exercise *and* comes equipped with a more existential Self vs. Other subtext as pods from outer space replicate our friends and neighbors, recasting them as bland, brainwashed slaves. Hero Kevin McCarthy's desperate cry of "They're here already!" will echo forever in celluloid history.

Invasion of the Body Snatchers (1978) ◆◆◇
D: Philip Kaufman. Donald Sutherland, Brooke Adams, Leonard Nimoy. 115 minutes. (MGM/UA)

Kaufman's thoughtful remake retains Don Siegel's basic story line while satirizing '70s trends, but in the Phantom's view, it remains redundant when compared with the original. Still worth a look for the fresh twists it brings to its model's classic plot.

The Invisible Ray (1936) ◆◆◆ B&W
D: Lambert Hillyer. Boris Karloff, Bela Lugosi, Frances Drake. 81 minutes. (MCA)

This early sci-fi effort reteams Boris and Bela, fresh from their *Raven/Black Cat* successes, with Boris as a scientist whose radium experiments give him a lethal touch and disintegrating mind. We would've preferred Bela in the demented-doc role, but this is still a strong, if downbeat, Universal outing.

The Island of Dr. Moreau (1977) ◆◆◇
D: Don Taylor. Burt Lancaster, Michael York, Barbara Carrera. 98 minutes. (Warner)

Another case of a decently assembled remake simply failing to match the original. Burt Lancaster is a powerful screen icon, but he can't go one on one with Charles Laughton's low self-monitoring, over-the-top interpretation of H. G. Wells's crazed title scientist. Unfortunately, as of this writing, the 1933 *Island of Lost Souls* has yet to join the video ranks.

Island of the Burning Doomed (1967) NR
D: Terence Fisher. Peter Cushing, Christopher Lee, Patrick Allen. 94 minutes. (New Star)

Lee and Cushing head a crisp (and crisped) Brit cast plagued by a heat wave engineered by mischievous aliens. At least the freeze-framed opening credits are pretty cool. Also known as *Night of the Big Heat*.

It Came from Beneath the Sea (1955) ◆◆◇ B&W
D: Robert Gordon. Kenneth Tobey, Faith Domergue, Donald Curtis. 80 minutes. (Goodtimes)

Careless atomic testing—earlier responsible for an angry Arctic dinosaur (*Beast From 20,000 Fathoms*) and giant ants (*Them!*)— here spawns an outsize octopus that lowers its titanic tentacles (the budget allowed for only five!) onto the panic-stricken streets of San Francisco. Predictable, natch, but good fun, further bolstered by Ray Harryhausen's FX and Domergue's subtly slutty perf.

It Came from Outer Space (1953) ◆◆◇ B&W
D: Jack Arnold. Richard Carlson, Barbara Rush, Charles Drake. 81 minutes. (Goodtimes)

Originally lensed in 3-D, Arnold's alien-visitation tale relies more on atmosphere and mood than on cheap chills to weave its cinematic spell. As a result, the film alternates between the genuinely haunting and the overly tame.

Journey to the Center of the Earth (1959) ◆◆◇
D: Henry Levin. James Mason, Arlene Dahl, Pat Boone. 132 minutes. (Playhouse)

A fairly lavish, well-crafted screen version of Jules Verne's tale, but way too long and wholesome for yours truly's taste. Boone, along for the trip, represents another major minus.

Journey to the Center of Time (1967) ◆◆◇
D: David L. Hewitt. Scott Brady, Gigi Perreau, Anthony Eisley, Poupee Gamin. 82 minutes. (Academy)

Scott, Gigi, and Tony time-trip 5,000 years into the future, where they encounter unforgettable chrome-domed, large-breasted alien Gamin (her only known film appearance, sadly enough) in what may be poverty-row auteur Hewitt's best effort.

Journey to the Far Side of the Sun (1969) ◆◆◆
D: Robert Parrish. Roy Thinnes, Lynn Loring, Herbert Lom. 99 minutes. (MCA)

Space explorers hie to the title site, where they discover a hitherto hidden planet in a well-done SF outing with a memorable twist ending.

Kamikaze '89 (1983) ◆◆◆
D: Wolf Gremm. Rainer Werner Fassbinder, Gunther Kaufmann, Boy Gobert. 106 minutes. (MGM/UA)

Gremm's engrossing futuristic noir stars late director Fassbinder as a cop out to foil a terrorist plot at a totalitarian "entertainment" combine.

Killer Klowns from Outer Space (1988) ◆◆

D: Stephen Chiodo. Grant Cramer, Suzanne Snyder, John Allen Nelson, Royal Dano, John Vernon, Michael Siegel. 88 minutes. (Media)

If little else, the Chiodo Brothers' colorfully labeled quickie at least deserves credit in the truth-in-advertising department. The pic does indeed detail a killer-klown invasion, replete with red-nosed, Bozo-like aliens and a circus-tent UFO. Actually, *Killer Klowns* boasts a *few* other pluses. The clown-makeup FX are first rate, while the sets and theme song also impress. Unfortunately, the Klowns are largely sabotaged by a weak script and performances that range from bland—Suzanne (*Prettykill*) Snyder—to downright embarrassing (normally reliable vets Dano and Vernon). Still, *Klowns* has its fair share of successful sight gags, is funnier than *Who Framed Roger Rabbit?*, and makes a suitable warm-up for Pee-wee Herman's superior *Big Top Pee-wee* (see index). Other colorfully titled sci-fi oddities deserving of further investigation: *Invasion of the Girl Snatchers* (United), *Revenge of the Teenage Vixens from Outer Space* (Cinema Group), and the alluring *Captive Planet: A Nightmare of Living Hell* (Mogul).

Killers from Space (1954) ◆◆◇ B&W

D: W. Lee Wilder. Peter Graves, Barbara Bestar, James Seay. 71 minutes. (Sinister Cinema, others)

Popeyed ETs kidnap scientist Graves and try to scare him with insect and wildlife stock footage. Pretty persuasive sci-fi from the man who brought us *Man Without a Body* (NA) and *Phantom from Space* (see index).

The Kirlian Witness (1978) ◆◆◇

D: Jonathan Sarno. Nancy Snyder, Joel Colodner, Ted Leplat. 88 minutes. (Magnum)

A telepathic plant is the sole witness to a murder; a telepathic-plant person gets to the root of the matter. Slow at times, but often suspenseful and easily the best sci-fi flick to emerge from the '70s brief-lived Plants-Are-People-Too craze.

Kronos (1957) ◆◆◆ B&W

D: Kurt Neumann. Jeff Morrow, Barbara Lawrence, John Emery. 78 minutes. (Nostalgia Merchant)

Despite its dependence on stock footage, cheap FX, and other cost-cutting measures, this earnest account of an energy-sucking mechanical colossus from outer space, assembled by *Fly* guy Neumann, is a prime example of fun '50s B-movie-making.

The Land That Time Forgot (1975) ◆◆◇

D: Kevin Connor. Doug McClure, Susan Penhaligon, John McEnery. 90 minutes. (Vestron)

Based on an Edgar Rice Burroughs tale, *Land* describes WWI sub crews—one German, one American—who surface on a prehistoric island overrun by dinosaurs. See also the sequel *People That Time Forgot* (Embassy). Connor also directed the Burroughs-derived *At the Earth's Core* (Warner) and *Island at the Top of the World* (Walt Disney).

Laserblast (1978) ◆◆
D: Michael Raye. Kim Milford, Cheryl Smith, Roddy McDowall. 90 minutes. (Media)

Abused youth Milford finds a super laser-gun left by some careless lizardlike stop-motion aliens (the handiwork of FX ace David Allen) and proceeds to eliminate his neighborhood enemies. Every alienated teen's dream come true! Not as good as *Lightblast*, though.

The Last Starfighter (1984) ◆◆
D: Nick Castle. Lance Guest, Robert Preston, Dan O'Herlihy. 100 minutes. (MCA)

The Last Starfighter boasts superior production values and performances, but this *Star Wars* variation is altogether too cute for the Phantom's constitution. You may feel differently.

The Last Woman on Earth (1960) ◆◇
D: Roger Corman. Antony Carbone, Betsy Jones-Moreland, Edward Wain. 71 minutes. (Sinister Cinema)

Carbone and screenwriter Robert Townsend (under the name Edward Wain) scrap over Betsy Jones-Moreland, which would make sense even if she *weren't* the last woman on earth. As for the alleged Armageddon that precedes this duke-out, well, we have to take Rog's word for it. Lensed back-to-back with *Creature from the Haunted Sea* in Puerto Rico.

Lifeforce (1985) ◆◆
D: Tobe Hooper. Steve Railsback, Peter Firth, Mathilda May, Frank Finlay, Patrick Stewart, Michael Gothard. 100 minutes. (Vestron)

Despite its ample budget, elaborate FX, and London Symphony Orchestra soundtrack, Hooper's *Lifeforce* is a laughably inept throwback to the '50s' cheesiest sci-fi cheapies. The pic begins on a promising note when a captive alien, imaginatively dubbed Space Girl (the genuinely alluring May in the most authentic Vampira imitation the Phantom's ever been privileged to witness) walks around naked, showing off her big extraterrestrial breasts and turning unsuspecting citizens into mad, dessicated ghouls. Astronaut Tom Carlson (Railsback) and Brit investigator Colonel Colin Kane (Firth) search for the elusive, energy-draining alien while, in a scene reminiscent of 1968's far superior *Five Million Years to Earth* (NA), London's crazed space-vampire victims run amok in a cannibalistic frenzy. *Lifeforce*'s ludicrous, clinker-ridden dialogue, solemnly delivered by a straight-faced, mostly British cast, will have you howling from reel one. We wouldn't mind seeing more of Mathilda, though.

The Lift (1985) ◆◆◆

D: Dick Maas. Huub Stapel, Willeka van Ammelrooy, Josine Van Dalsum, Hans Veerman, Ab Abspoel, Frederik de Groot. 90 minutes. (Media)

A 1985 Dutch import written and directed by Maas, *The Lift* is a sardonic sci-fi thriller about a killer elevator and the stubborn young repairman (Stapel) who's determined to defeat it. *The Lift* has a lot going for it—a laconically effective performance by Stapel, well-sketched supporting characters, deadpan humor mixed with moments of genuine suspense, and the most suspicious view of our machine-run world seen since Chaplin's *Modern Times*. Weak science and occasionally slack pacing prevent *The Lift* from reaching the top fright-flick floor, but this video is very definitely worth a look. Maas followed with the *Phantom of the Canals*-type thriller *Amsterdamned* (Vestron).

Light Years (1987) ◆◆

D: Rene Laloux. The voices of Glenn Close, Christopher Plummer, Jennifer Grey, John Shea, Earl Hyman, Terrence Mann. 83 minutes. (Vidmark)

French animator Laloux, of *Fantastic Planet* (see index) fame, fashions another whimsical sci-fi feature, "presented" and "adapted" by Isaac Asimov. The slight story line concerns a New Agey society threatened by an army of Darth Vader—like androids, and the efforts of young hero Sylvain to re-verse the deadly invasion. Laloux's parable warns of the dangers of unchecked technology, as the robot hordes turn out to be the creation of a synthetic brain that's grown independent from—and more powerful than—its creators. Aiding Sylvain in his mission are a breed of Boschian mutant outcasts, the tragic results of ill-advised genetic engineering experiments. The Phantom frankly 'fesses up to the fact that he's not a big fan of most animated sci-fi, and to him *Light Years* looked like it was lensed in Snooze-o-Rama and Slumberscope. But if you enjoy the genre in general, and *Fantastic Planet* in particular, you'll probably deem *Light Years* worthwhile vid-viewing as well and may want to check out the animated *Warriors of the Wind* (New World).

Lightblast (1984) ◆◆◇

D: Enzo Q. Castellari. Erik Estrada, Mike Pritchard. 89 minutes. (Lightning)

A sinister scientist is terrorizing San Francisco with his flesh-disintegrating mobile laser cannon. Estrada rides to the rescue. *Lightblast* didn't do much to further EE's comeback bid, but it's pretty entertaining sci-fi pulp, with lots of hot face-melting close-ups. Better than *Laserblast* (see index).

Link (1986) 0 ◆

D: Richard Franklin. Terence Stamp, Elisabeth Shue, Steven Pinner, Richard Garnett. 103 minutes. (HBO)

Avowed Hitchcock clone Franklin's misguided chimp-monster movie is an insult to simian and homo-sap home viewers alike. First he cites pongid authority Jane Goodall's research in a bid to make this monkey business sound more credible; then he casts an orangutan in the leading psycho-chimp role (!). Even beyond its bid to drag chimps down to our level, *Link* is a turgid mess whose own low-camp detours fail to provide enough unintended laughs to save it.

Liquid Sky (1983) ◆◆◆

D: Slava Tsukerman. Anne Carlisle, Paula E. Sheppard, Otto Von Wernherr. 112 minutes. (Media)

Pint-size aliens invade NYC's East Village, where they live off the orgasms (!) of narcissistic downtown poseurs in this original if sometimes smarmy and generally overlong sci-fi satire from Russian emigré Tsukerman. Better than *Batteries Not Included* (MCA) also about an East Village invasion. Star Carlisle later wrote the novelization, while lilliputian lesbian Paula E. Sheppard is the selfsame Paula Sheppard who played the unforgettable *Bad Seed*–type role in Alfred Sole's *Alice, Sweet Alice* (see index).

The Lost World (1925) ◆◆◆ B&W

D: Harry Hoyt. Wallace Beery, Bessie Love, Lewis Stone. 60 minutes. (Video Yesteryear)

An abbreviated version of the silent dinosaur romp, based on Arthur Conan Doyle's story and stocked with impressive FX by Willis (*King Kong*) O'Brien. The better-known 1960 color and Cinemascope remake still isn't available on video.

Mad Max (1980) ◆◆◆

D: George Miller. Mel Gibson, Joanne Samuel, Hugh Keays-Byrne. 90 minutes. (Vestron)

The original Thunder From Down Under introduced Gibson as a futuristic maverick motorcycle cop out to rid an already ruined Australia of its myriad road vermin. The American release is dubbed by American voices (!). Not as good as the sequel, *Road Warrior*, but far superior to *its* follow-up, *Mad Max Beyond Thunderdome* (see below).

Mad Max Beyond Thunderdome (1985) ◆◆

D: George Miller, George Ogilvie. Mel Gibson, Tina Turner, Angelo Rossitto, Helen Buday, Rod Zuanic, Angry Anderson, Frank Thring. 106 minutes. (Warner)

There's a not-so-thin line between taking a tongue-in-cheek approach and resorting to broad self-parody. Miller's *Mad Max Beyond Thunderdome* sinks below said line right from reel one and wallows therein the rest of the way. In this, the third installment of Miller's postnuke saga, Max (Gibson), looking ragged and gray, straggles off the fast track that the wonderfully kinetic *Road Warrior* (see index) traveled so successfully and wanders into Bartertown, a post-holocaust hellhole presided over by one Auntie Entity (oy!), ear-splittingly interpreted by Tina Turner, who's embroiled in a power struggle with a dwarf/giant tandem named Master and Blaster (double oy!). After duking it out with the latter, Max heads desert-ward, where he's soon adopted by a juvenile *Lord of the Flies*–type tribe. Not only are these kids af-flicted with a collective (and infi-nitely irritating) case of echolalia, but they talk in a bastardized ver-sion of the pidgin English spoken in the postnuke novel *Riddley Walker*. (They're also given to screeching a garbled variation on the "What is the law?" chant from *Island of Lost Souls* [NA].) Much expensive, high-decibel milling ensues before the climactic battle arrives; alas, it too is but a pale shadow of *Road Warrior*'s stirring, thrill-a-microsecond finale. *Beyond Thunderdome*'s only truly pulse-quickening sequence in-volves a gladiatorial punch-up be-tween Max and the cretinous Blaster, staged in the titular Thun-derdome, a caged arena sur-rounded by bloodthirsty geeks. On another positive note, it did the Phantom's heart good to see aged Angelo Rossitto—Bela Lugosi's henchdwarf in any number of '40s Monogram cheapies—back on the screen as Master, the nominal brains behind Bartertown. The Phantom was unamused, how-ever, to see the little guy lowered into a pile of pig manure. But then, what can you expect from a coun-try where dwarf-tossing ranks as a major sport?

Man Facing Southeast (1986) ◆◆◆
D: Eliseo Subiela. Lorenzo Quinteros, Hugo Soto, Ines Vernengo, Cristina Scaramuzza, Tomas Voth, David Ed-ery. 105 minutes. (New World)

A low-key allegory in a *Brother from Another Planet* vein, Sub-iela's *Man Facing Southeast* in-volves the mysterious, Christ-like Rantes (Soto), who turns up at a Buenos Aires mental institution claiming he's from outer space. Depressed shrink Dr. Denis (Quin-teros) assigns himself to the young stranger's case and, like Rantes's fellow patients, becomes a bene-ficiary of his strange restorative powers. Also in the picture is the beautiful but equally enigmatic Beatriz (Vernengo), Rantes's only outside ally. Auteur Subiela, who also scripted this compelling para-ble, hedges his bets by hinting that Rantes really *is* a literal alien while ultimately skirting the is-sue. Still, *Man Facing Southeast* shapes up as a quietly ironic if downbeat exploration of identity, belief systems, and society's in-ability to cope with the Outsider.

Man from Atlantis (1977) NR
D: Lee H. Katzin. Patrick Duffy, Belinda Montgomery, Art Lund. 96 minutes. (Goodtimes)

Made-for-TV sci-fi with Duffy as a subaqueous alien trying to survive in the topside world. Later a short-lived teleseries.

The Man They Could Not Hang (1939) ◆◆◇ B&W
D: Nick Grinde. Boris Karloff, Lorna Gray, Robert Wilcox. 72 minutes. (Goodtimes)

Karloff is a dead doc brought back to life to wreak vengeance on the jurors who sentenced him to die. The clichés kick in after a bright start; okay for Boris buffs.

The Man Who Fell to Earth (1976) ◆◆◆
D: Nicolas Roeg. David Bowie, Rip Torn, Candy Clark, Buck Henry. 140 minutes. (RCA/Columbia)

Nicholas Roeg's long, chilly, but original combo of corporate satire and effective sci-fi stars Bowie as an alien who makes it big as an earthly mogul. Based on the novel by Walter Tevis. The video restores 20 minutes of footage missing from the theatrical release.

Martian Chronicles Parts 1–3 (1979) NR
D: Michael Anderson. Rock Hudson, Gayle Hunnicutt, Bernie Casey. 294 minutes. (IVE)

This made-for-TV trilogy, available in three separate video volumes, doesn't capture the scope or tension of Ray Bradbury's novel about a starship's encounter with telepathic Martians but is not without its avid supporters.

Master of the World (1961) ◆◆◆
D: William Witney. Vincent Price, Charles Bronson, Mary Webster. 104 minutes. (Warner)

Price is a militant nineteenth-century pacifist who roams the skies in his airborne sub, bombing battleships and other military targets in this fun AIP adaptation of Jules Verne's Robur the Conqueror.

Metropolis (1926) ◆◆◆ B&W
D: Fritz Lang. Brigitte Helm, Alfred Abel, Gustav Froehlich. 139 minutes. (Cable)

The original version of Lang's spectacular vision of a future machine age on the brink of an apocalyptic class war is in the public domain, available on several different labels, and runs a full two hours. The colorized 1984 Metropolis, recut and scored by Giorgio Moroder, totals 87 minutes and is out via Vestron.

Mind Killer (1987) ◆◆◇
D: Michael Krueger. Joe McDonald, Christopher Wade, Shirley Ross, Kevin Hart. 87 minutes. (Prism)

Hopeless loser/library worker Warren (McDonald) is the type of guy who watches a "Manly Art of Seduction" video while spilling his way through a TV dinner. Warren's life changes dramatically, however, when he happens upon an esoteric "self-help" tome that really works—but only at the inevitable horrendous price. Despite its derivative story line and paltry budget, Mind Killer is a highly watchable comic/horror tale in an oft-mined Faustian vein. Supporting characters—including Warren's nerdy pal Larry (Wade), comely coworker Sandy (Ross), and Romeo roommate Brad (Hart)—are surprisingly three-dimensional, and McDonald brings a note of realism and even pathos to his lead role. The pic has its limitations—chintzy FX and a paucity of visceral shocks among them—but unlike your usual direct-to-home-vid fast-forward specials, *Mind Killer* makes for fairly compelling viewing.

Monkey Shines: An Experiment in Fear (1988) ♦♦

D: George A. Romero. Jason Beghe, John Pankow, Kate McNeil, Joyce Van Patten, Christine Forrest, John Tucci. 117 minutes. (Orion)

In the less-than-grand tradition of *Link* and *In the Shadow of Kilimanjaro* (see index), featuring 90,000 killer baboons, comes *Monkey Shines: An Experiment in Fear*, yet another misbegotten bid to exploit our lower primate cousins. Our story concerns quadriplegic Allan Mann (Beghe) and his furry companion Ella (Boo), a talented capuchin monkey who serves as Allan's live-in helpmate. Unbeknownst to Allan, friendly neighborhood mad scientist Geoffrey Fisher (vividly rendered by Pankow) has surreptitiously injected the simian servant with human brain-juice serum that not only augments Ella's intelligence but makes her a ready receptor for Allan's darkest thoughts— thoughts Ella interprets as violent

commands. Not the most promising premise ever to scamper down the scare-pic pike, and not even as proven a frightmeister as George (*Night of the Living Dead*) Romero can yield real chills from this uninspired situation. At the same time, *Monkey Shines* does proffer sights previously unseen onscreen. It's the first flick, for instance, that tries to wring gut-wrenching suspense from a climactic showdown whose vital components are a motionless quadriplegic, an equally stationary voice-controlled computer, a half-dead scientist shot through with enough barbituates to "bring down King Kong," and a cute little hyperactive capuchin monkey running amok with a straight razor (!). We feel compelled to grant *Monkey Shines* high marks in the Unprecedented Imagery department but a failing grade in all others.

Mutant Hunt (1986) ♦◇

D: Tim Kincaid. Rick Gianasi, Mary Fahey, Ron Reynaldi, Bill Peterson, Stormy Spill. 77 minutes. (Wizard)

Seems that the diabolical Z (Peterson) has introduced the notorious drug "euphoron" into the fluid systems of several impressionable Delta 7 cyborgs, prompting the Devoesque 'droids to embark on a rampage of abrupt and senseless violence. Looks like a job for mucho-muscled macho mercenary Matt Riker (Gianasi). While

Matt and cronies perform their cyborg-stomping chores with at least a modicum of efficiency, the same can't be said for writer/director Kincaid, whose flat, static sci-fi cheapie unfolds mostly in claustrophobic, hastily redecorated lofts and deserted nocturnal NYC streets, where characters pose such brain-teasing queries as, "Who'd want to get a robot high?" The only relief is supplied by the memorably monikered Stormy Spill (!) as evil distaff scientist Domina, who emotes with a loud nasal voice and a thick Brooklyn accent. Other Kincaid duds worth avoiding include *Breeders*, *Necropolis*, and *Robot Holocaust* (all Vestron).

The Mysterians (1959) ♦♦♦
D: Inoshiro Honda. Kenji Sahara, Yumi Shirakawa, Momoko Kochi. 85 minutes. (United)

This wonderfully lurid, high-decibel invasion staged by the horny, manic Mysterians from Mysteroid (where else?) is arguably director Honda's liveliest Toho terrorfest.

Neon Maniacs (1986) ◊
D: Joseph Mangine. Allan Hayes, Leilani Sarelle, Donna Locke, Victor Elliot Brandt. 91 minutes. (Lightning)

Neon Maniacs poses the musical question: What would happen if there were twelve Halloween-costumed mutants living under the Golden Gate Bridge and taking orders from the dumbest-looking one-eyed alien in sci-fi history? If you answered: Why, they'd sneak out at night and slaughter every onscreen teen they could lay knives, scythes, and axes on—well, you'd be absolutely right. *Neon Maniacs* goes on to chronicle the efforts of a teen trio who try to convince typically thickheaded authority figures that the aliens are indeed among us, though why, how, and from where are questions that remain unaddressed. We *do* learn that the space slashers dissolve when you douse them with water, though—a revelation that leads to a high-energy showdown between the antisocial ETs and several squirt-gun-toting teens. This amateur-night special fails on every level; even the shoddy gore FX are lost in the murky night photography. The pic's heroine sums it up best when she asks her onscreen beau, "Is this ever gonna end?"

The Nest (1988) ♦♦
D: Terence H. Winkless. Robert Lansing, Lisa Langlois, Frac Luz, Terri Treas, Stephen Davies, Diana Bellamy. 88 minutes. (MGM/UA)

It's *Days of Slime and Roaches* time as seasoned celluloid exterminator Lansing—who's previously battled outsize ants in *Empire of the Ants* (see index) and radioactive crabs in the immortal *Island Claws* (Vestron)—contends here with a special breed of rampaging designer roaches genetically engineered to destroy their more common bug brethren, then conveniently die out. Well, needless to say, die out they don't; in fact, they downright flourish. As the shady mayor of the resort town of Northport, it's Bob's job to stop the bugs not only from discouraging the tourist trade but from devouring Northport's native population. While competently assembled, *The Nest* breaks little in the way of new bug-movie ground. There's a clever montage depicting a restaurant roach massacre, set to the strains of "La Cucaracha," and some suitably sickening makeup FX, but *The Nest* is not as good as, say, *Them!* (see index) or even Kafka's *Metamorphosis*. The flick does deserve credit for coming up with 1988's best (if most cryptic) tag line, though: "Why is the cheese *moving*?" The answer, alas, is not as intriguing as the question.

Never Too Young to Die (1986) ◆◇

D: Gil Bettman. John Stamos, Vanity, Gene Simmons, George Lazenby, John Anderson, Robert Englund. 92 minutes. (Charter)

The only plus in this broad *Road Warrior* rip-off set in contempo L.A. is Gene Simmons's flamboyant performance as a hermaphroditic terrorist (!) out to poison the La-La-Land water supply "for the next 10,000 years" (which, if nothing else, would at least prevent future production of desperate trash like this). Ex–James Bond one-shot Lazenby cameos as su-

peragent Drew Stargrove, while Robert (Freddy Krueger) Englund moonlights as Gene's evil computer-whiz partner. Sample dialogue:

Simmons: Is the concentration lethal?
Englund: I'd say *worse!*

We'd say so too.

Night Caller from Outer Space (1966) ◆◆◇ B&W

D: John Gilling. John Saxon, Maurice Denham, Patricia Haines. 84 minutes. (Sony)

John (*Nightmare on Elm Street*) Saxon, in an early genre role, investigates a randy alien who's kidnapping Earth gals to show the boys back home. Pretty compelling, and superior to the similarly themed *Mars Needs Women* (Sinister Cinema).

Night of the Comet (1984) ◆◆◆

D: Thom Eberhardt. Catherine Mary Stewart, Kelli Maroney, Robert Beltran, John Achorn, Mary Woronov, Geoffrey Lewis. 95 minutes. (CBS/Fox)

A kind of *The World, the Flesh and the Brain-Damaged,* Eberhardt's *Night of the Comet* imagines an earth seemingly stripped of all human life but for three San Berdoo deadheads—Valley Girl sisters Stewart and Maroney, and truck driver Beltran—who soon find themselves imperiled by mad scientists (led by the always-welcome Woronov), marauding punks, and the usual flesh-eating zombies (who are, unfortunately, gravely underutilized here). While it doesn't quite attain first cult-movie rank—*Comet* indulges in too many mood-ruining wisecracks and lensward winks—the flick does take a perverse idea and, if not exactly runs, at least jogs briskly with it.

Night of the Creeps (1986) ◆◆◆

D: Fred Dekker. Jason Lively, Jill Whitlow, Tom Atkins, Bruce Solomon, Dick Miller, Steve Marshall. 89 minutes. (HBO)

While lifting wittily and openly from flicks as diverse as *Animal House* and *Night of the Living Dead*, director Dekker fills this fast-paced, freewheeling fright farce with ax maniacs, frat-house zombies (replete with obligatory exploding heads), and even killer slugs from outer space. The result is a thoroughly crazed collage whose full-tilt overkill approach actually makes for great grisly fun. Besides topliners Lively and Whitlow as a pair of embattled collegiates, the cast includes Roger Corman vet Miller, Solomon (the lovesick cop from the tube's *Mary Hartman*), and Atkins as a hard-boiled lawman extraordinaire. ("The good news is, your dates are here," he informs a gaggle of sorority sisters. "The bad news is, they're dead.")

Nightfall (1988) ◆◆◇

D: Paul Mayersberg. David Birney, Sarah Douglas, Alexis Kanner, Andra

Millian, Starr Andreeff, Charles Hayward. 82 minutes. (MGM/UA)

A fairly compelling parable penned by prolific sci-fi scribe Isaac Asimov, *Nightfall* unfolds at an unspecified place and time—from the characters' tonsorial, sartorial, and New Agey life-styles, our guess would be Santa Cruz, circa 1973—on a planet illuminated by three suns that are gradually growing dark. Attempting to cope with the impending disaster are a burned-out scientist (Birney) and a blind religious zealot (Kanner) who's trying to exploit the drastic situation to augment his own power. *Nightfall* works reasonably well as a kind of sci-fi-pulp version of a grade-B Greek myth. The mostly unknown thesps lend intensity to what's essentially a film-long Science vs. Religion debate ("Nature" is likewise represented, in the person of sensuous "desert woman" Millian) and a talky one at that. *Nightfall* is a flick that actually plays *better* on video, where its low-budget lack of action and FX are a lot less conspicuous than they were on the big screen.

Nightflyers (1987) ◆◆

D: T. C. Blake (Robert Collector). Catherine Mary Stewart, Michael Des Barres, Lisa Blount, Michael Praed, John Standing, Glenn Withrow. 89 minutes. (IVE)

Nightflyers is an *Alien*-cum-*2001* clone about a scientific space crew tormented not by the usual malignant beings from beyond but by their ship's computer, guided by the evil soul of the captain's twisted mom. Stewart, seen to more dynamic effect as *Night of the Comet*'s (see index) valiant Valley Girl, handles the Sigourney Weaver heroics, while rock singer Des Barres adds a new wrinkle as the professional mind reader, or "empath," who alerts the crew to the maternal computer's malevolent scheme. Director Collector (using the pseudonym T. C. Blake) does a fair job with the well-worn material. The starship set is pretty impressive, in an *MTV* sort of way, as is the live laser vivisection scene. *Nightflyers* is light on gratuitous gore, proceeding instead with the earnest dignity of a vintage *Star Trek* episode. With more juice, the pic could've been a cosmic contender instead of a spacebound bore.

Nightmare at Noon (1987) ◆◇
D: Nico Mastorikis. Wings Hauser, Bo Hopkins, George Kennedy, Brion James, Kimberly Beck, Kimberly Ross. 96 minutes. (Republic)

As an entry in your popular Toxic-Chemicals-Turn-Normal-Townsfolk-into-Rampaging-Psychotics genre, *Nightmare at Noon* kicks off to a fairly high-spirited start. No sooner do vacationers Hauser, Beck, and ex-cop Hopkins pull into the isolated desert burg of Canyonland than the locals commence killing one another, much to befuddled sheriff Kennedy's dismay. *Nightmare*'s able B cast and

fast-paced violence sprees keep things lively for several reels, as our imperiled heroes trace the town's collective craziness to the evil handiwork of mad albino biochemist James. The flick just as suddenly mutates into a dull updated western, replete with visual homages to a *Fistful of Dollars* and *High Noon* (!). Maybe auteur Mastorikis, late of the lamentable action/horror hybrid *The Zero Boys*, had his brains fried by the desert sun and lost sight of his original story line. (He even neglects to include an explanation re: the purpose of our mad scientist's experiments.) We can only advise you not to waste your brain cells on this ultimately tedious tease.

1984 (1984) ◆◆◇
D: Michael Bradford. Richard Burton, John Hurt, Suzanna Hamilton. 115 minutes. (IVE)

An earnest if possibly overly grim adaptation of Orwell's dystopian nightmare that didn't knock 'em out at the box office. The 1956 version, with Edmond O'Brien, remains unavailable as we go to press.

Nomads (1986) ◆◇
D: John McTiernan. Pierce Brosnan, Lesley-Ann Down, Adam Ant, Hector Mercado, Anna-Maria Monticelli, Mary Woronov. 95 minutes. (Paramount)

Every once in a while, the Phantom sees a movie or video that acts as though it really doesn't *want* to be watched. *Nomads* is a case in point. This determinedly non-communicative (roughly a third of the dialogue's in French!) exercise in convoluted catatonia features Brosnan as a bearded Gallic anthropologist who runs afoul of a pack of evil Eskimo spirits posing as a Mansonesque band of overage L.A. street punks (!). Said punks are led by rocker Ant and junk-film fave Woronov in what are virtually nonspeaking roles. (Seems that *Nomads* doesn't want to be *heard* either.) The Phantom, respecting the pic's obvious desire for privacy, spent most of *Nomads'* running time gazing wistfully at his wristwatch (which, unlike *Nomads*, at least glows in the dark).

Not of This Earth (1988) ◆◇
D: Jim Wynorski. Traci Lords, Arthur Roberts, Lenny Juliano, Ace Mask, Kelli Maroney. 80 minutes. (MGM/UA)

Much B-movie ballyhoo accompanied the casting of former underage porn starlet Traci Lords as the distaff lead in Roger Corman's own low-budget remake of his fairly obscure 1957 cheapie *Not of This Earth* (NA). As it turns out, Traci's not what's wrong with this picture. While no match for the formidable Beverly Garland as the feisty nurse who uncovers an alien vampire's dastardly plot for world conquest, Traci acquits herself quite adequately here, as does Roberts as the unemotional ET who likes to zap his victims with his glowing radioactive eyes. What's wrong here is the flick's campy, soulless film-nerd script and direction—ingredients that utterly destroy what fragile charm the original pic possessed.

The Omega Man (1971) ◆◆◆
D: Boris Sagal. Charlton Heston, Anthony Zerbe, Rosalind Cash. 98 minutes. (Warner)

Second screen version of Richard Matheson's *I Am Legend* features Heston as a plague survivor battling contaminated hordes in L.A. The pic's pretty good, though. As far as macho heroes go, Chuck's no match for Vincent Price in *The Last Man on Earth* (NA).

Outland (1981) ◆◆◆
D: Peter Hyams. Sean Connery, Frances Sternhagen, Peter Boyle. 109 minutes. (Warner)

A bleak but effective *High Noon* redo, shifted from the Wild West to a grim mining settlement in space. Connery is especially good in the updated Gary Cooper role.

Phantom from Space (1953) ◆◆◇ B&W
D: W. Lee Wilder. Harry Landers, Rudolph Anders, Noreen Nash. 72 minutes. (Goodtimes)

Okay, so nothing really *happens*—an invisible alien runs around an observatory—but the ensemble cast's admirable, if thoroughly willed, enthusiasm got *this* Phantom totally caught up in the nonaction. Besides, the tape lists for under ten bucks and represents one of Billy Wilder's brothers' (scripter Myles and director W. Lee) least ridiculous efforts.

Phantom from 10,000 Leagues (1956) ◆◆ B&W
D: Dan Milner. Kent Taylor, Cathy Downs, Michael Whalen. 78 minutes. (Sinister Cinema)

A fairly boring low-budget SF tale about a mostly motionless monster, but it may bring back memories for '50s nostalgia fans. Not as good as *Phantom from Space* (see index).

The Phantom Planet (1961) NR B&W
D: William Marshall. Dean Fredericks, Coleen Gray, Anthony Dexter. (Sinister Cinema)

Dean Fredericks is an astronaut who undergoes cut-rate Gulliver-type experiences in space. With Anthony (*Valentino*) Dexter, Coleen (*Leech Woman*) Gray, and Francis X. Bushman as the alien honcho.

Phase IV (1974) ◆◆
D: Saul Bass. Nigel Davenport, Lynne Frederick, Michael Murphy. 83 minutes. (Paramount)

Small but smarter-than-average ants mount offensive against an isolated scientific team, with an eye toward eventual world conquest. The treatment is a tad arty for the subject matter, but fans of sober sci-fi might enjoy.

The Philadelphia Experiment (1984) ◆◆◇
D: Stewart Raffill. Michael Paré, Nancy Allen, Bobby DiCicco. 102 minutes. (HBO)

This convoluted time-warp tale alternates between the admirably complex and the merely illogical, but World War II sailors Paré and DiCicco's jaunt from 1943 to 1984 is ultimately worth the trip.

Planet of Blood (1966) ◆◆
D: Curtis Harrington. John Saxon, Basil Rathbone, Dennis Hopper. 81 minutes. (Star Classics)

Originally titled *Queen of Blood*, this was Val Lewton–inspired auteur Harrington's second genre teaming (after *Night Tide*—see index) with actor Hopper. Hopper is part of the space crew that brings an ET vampire aboard their ship. The recycled FX (lifted from a Russian sci-fi flick) look fine but fatally delay the start of what might otherwise have been an interesting story line. Star Classics' inferior transfer quality doesn't help matters either.

Planet of the Apes (1968) ◆◆◆
D: Franklin J. Schaffner. Charlton Heston, Kim Hunter, Roddy McDowall, Maurice Evans. 112 minutes. (Playhouse)

The debut adaptation—Rod Serling was among the scripters—of Pierre Boulle's vision of a simian dystopia, wherein apes achieve primate supremacy over humans, remains the series's best. The flick's final twist image has deservedly achieved classic status.

Planet of the Vampires (1965) ◆◆
D: Mario Bava. Barry Sullivan, Norma Bengell, Angel Aranda. 86 minutes. (HBO)

Gothic auteur Bava gets lost in space in this sometimes static story of mind-controlled astronauts stranded on the title planet but still manages to deliver the atmospheric goods.

Predator (1987) ◆◆◇

D: John McTiernan. Arnold Schwarzenegger, Carl Weathers, Elpidia Carrillo, Bill Duke, Sonny Landham, R. G. Armstrong. 107 minutes. (CBS/Fox)

In *Predator*, Arnie toplines as "Dutch," macho leader of a wild and crazy mercenary band who land in a Central American jungle to stage a hostage-rescue mission with the dubious aid of CIA op and fellow Nautilus mutant Weathers. A high-concept combo of the action and alien-amok genres, the pic finds our heroes completing their violent guerrilla assignment with the usual consummate ease, only to wind up on the other end of the chase, targets of an outsize, laser-equipped ET (time-shared by Kevin Peter Hall, also seen as the far wimpier Bigfoot in *Harry and the Hendersons* (MCA) and *Bloodsport*'s Jean-Claude Van Damme) on an earthly hunting vacation. The extremely predictable but reasonably suspenseful proceedings ultimately narrow down to a *mano-a-mano*, toe-to-toe showdown between Arnie and the alien. We wouldn't want to give away *Predator*'s foregone conclusion, but suffice it to say that Arnie leaves the title aggressor in no shape for a rematch.

Programmed to Kill (1987) ◆◇

D: Allan Holzman. Robert Ginty, Sandahl Bergman, James Booth, Alex Courtney, Peter Walker. 90 minutes. (Media)

In this former Forty-second Street mainstay, Robert (*The Exterminator*) Ginty is a CIA-employed mercenary who captures badly wounded femme terrorist Bergman. Unbeknownst to RG, however, government docs led by veteran villain Booth (in an incestuous touch, two of the other medicos are named after the pic's producers) implant micro circuitry into the brain-dead Bergman's frontal lobes, turning her into a "Barbie Rambo killing machine" (!). CIA ops train her to wipe out her former allies, but Bergman's got, if not a mind, at least a microchip of her own: She soon decides to direct her ample android anger against her creators. As distaff *Terminator* rip-offs go, *Programmed to Kill* (aka *The Retaliator*), with its decent production values and well-staged action scenes, could have been a halfway decent one. But the pic's painfully slow pacing left yours truly glued to his fast-forward control instead of the edge of his seat. For Bergman buffs, we suggest *Sandahl Bergman's Body*, available for rent or sale (just $39.95) via Ingram Video.

Project Moon Base (1953) ◆◆

D: Richard Talmadge. Hayden Rorke, Donna Martell, Ross Ford. 63 minutes. (Vidmark)

Another low-budget '50s sci-fi odyssey, originally lensed as a TV pilot, featuring more talk—not much of it very compelling—than action or FX. Worthwhile for pulp buffs and fans of Robert Heinlein, who penned the script.

Project X (1987) ◆◆◆
D: Jonathan Kaplan. Matthew Broderick, Helen Hunt, Bill Sadler, Johnny Ray McGhee, Jonathan Stark, Dick Miller, Willie, Karanja, Okko, Luke. 108 minutes. (CBS/Fox)

A fun if formulaic fantasy, Project X toplines Broderick as Jimmy Garrett, a grounded airman assigned to work with chimps at a Florida-based Air Force flight-simulation program. Our hero forms a close attachment to young Virgil (vividly essayed by simian thesp Willie), a literate chimp dumped from sign-language experiments conducted by psych student Hunt. When Jimmy learns of the sinister fates awaiting the chimps, he enlists Hunt's aid in staging a maverick rescue mission. The pongid performers and their offscreen trainers do a fine job here and, unlike Richard Franklin with his ludicrous Link (see index), Kaplan treats his subject matter with admirable respect. (He also pays homage to his own B-movie roots by casting Roger Corman vet Miller in a brief cameo and, in a neat nod toward the immortal Ed Wood, Jr., naming a minor character Dr. Criswell.)

The flick's negative take re: the Air Force's callous attitudes supplies a welcome change from knee-jerk flag-wavers like Top Gun (though Project X does have its own fleeting "Top Chimp" moments). A padded running time and a claustrophobic paucity of exterior scenes constitute the pic's only serious drawbacks.

Pulse (1988) ◆◆◆
D: Paul Golding. Cliff DeYoung, Roxanne Hart, Joey Lawrence, Matthew Lawrence, Charles Tyner, Myron Healey. 91 minutes. (RCA/Columbia)

Something of an earnest sci-fi revamp of Buster Keaton's anarchic Electric House, Golding's Pulse pits a modern suburban family—dad DeYoung, stepmom Hart, and son Lawrence—against their hitherto normal abode's suddenly subversive electrical wiring, a malfunction that's already destroyed the inhabitants of the house across the street. At first, only young Lawrence—with an assist from "paranoid" electrician Tyner (who resembles Freddy Krueger sans scar tissue)—is on to the arcane scheme. But when TVs, washer-dryers, and heating systems start openly revolting, our imperiled nuclear unit realizes what they're up against. Pulse doesn't do full justice to its genuinely unnerving premise—its occasionally slack pacing, made-for-TV feel, and general lack of juice keep the electric chaos too low-key at times—but the pic supplies enough honest chills to make it a genuine sci-fi sleeper. And it's refreshing to find filmmakers picking on appliances other than VCRs for a change.

Q: The Winged Serpent (1982) ◆◆◆
D: Larry Cohen. Michael Moriarty, David Carradine, Candy Clark, Richard Roundtree. 92 minutes. (MCA)

Moriarty is an antsy lowlife junkie who happens to know where the titular Aztec horror is nesting in NYC. And he wants a million tax-free bucks for the info. Q, meanwhile, munches on vulnerable Fun Cityites while detective Carradine tries to track the outsize bird in a typically witty monster romp from low-budget auteur Cohen.

Quatermass II (1957) ◆◆◆ B&W
D: Val Guest. Brian Donlevy, Michael Ripper, Bryan Forbes. 85 minutes. (Corinth)

Released stateside as Enemy from Space, the second installment in the Quatermass series finds the dogged Prof Q. (Donlevy) battling blob monsters, brainwashed zombies, and alien invaders in this low-budget celluloid roller-coaster ride. See also The Quatermass Experiment (aka The Creeping Unknown [Discount]). The excellent Five Million Years to Earth has yet to join the video ranks.

Quatermass Conclusion (1980) NR
D: Piers Haggard. John Mills, Simon MacCorkindale, Barbara Kellerman. 105 minutes. (HBO)

John Mills assumes the Quatermass mantle in a cost-efficient but interesting tale about a ray from outer space that paralyzes the Earth's young people (an MTV satellite beam?). Originally produced for British TV.

The Quiet Earth (1985) ◆◆
D: Geoff Murphy. Bruno Lawrence, Alison Routledge, Peter Smith. 91 minutes. (CBS/Fox)

Borrowing heavily from 1959's The World, The Flesh and the Devil (NA) (replete with racial angle), 1986's New Zealand import The Quiet Earth stars Lawrence as scientist Zac Hobson, who seems to be the planet's sole survivor of a massive energy experiment gone awry. He eventually hooks up with fetching Routledge and tough Maori Smith, leading to a number of all-too-predictable conflicts. The Quiet Earth offers some striking visuals, an intriguing explanation for the trio's tenuous predicament, and several successfully wrought scenes detailing Hobson's increasingly mad methods of coping with his awesome loneliness. But the buildup is painfully slow—Lawrence doesn't encounter the other cast members till we've largely lost interest—and the payoff too slight to put The Quiet Earth over.

Rabid (1977) ◆◆◆

D: David Cronenberg. Marilyn Chambers, Frank Moore, Joe Silver. 91 minutes. (Warner)

Ex-porn starlet Chambers is an accident victim whose real troubles begin when she enters a research hospital, where she's subjected to experimental surgery, develops the titular condition, and subsequently spreads it through Montreal. Much graphic sexual/medical madness ensues in a flick that's somewhat basic by DC's current standards but that still stacks up as good sick fun. Marilyn, accompanied by trusty lesbian sidekick Mary Woronov, returns for more movie mayhem in 1982's sci-fi actioner *Angel of H.E.A.T.* (Vestron).

Radioactive Dreams (1986) ◇

D: Albert Pyun. John Stockwell, Michael Dudikoff, Lisa Blount, Don Murray, George Kennedy, Norbert Weisser. 98 minutes. (Vestron)

A would-be darkly satiric exercise in *Road Warrior* noir (the characters sport such scrambled famous-shamus names as Dash Hammer and Spade Chandler), Pyun's *Radioactive Dreams* features Stockwell and Michael (*American Ninja*) Dudikoff (in a rare and ill-advised comic-relief role) as a pair of postnuke youths who careen their way through the primitive "man-eat-man" wasteland of tomorrow, where assorted "hippies," punks, and greasers wage a pointless power struggle for control of what's left of civilization (basically a run-down rock club). *Radioactive Dreams* is the worst pop-apocalypse pic to surface since the equally awful *Cafe Flesh* (NA) reared its empty head back in 1984. Not even the abbreviated presence of the usually riveting Kennedy helps here.

Re-Animator (1985) ◆◆◆◇

D: Stuart Gordon. Jeffrey Combs, Bruce Abbott, Barbara Crampton, Robert Sampson, David Gale, Carolyn Purdy-Gordon. 88 minutes. (Vestron)

The best sci-fright movie of 1985, *Re-Animator* focuses on some grisly fun and games going on at the Miskatonic, Massachusetts, Med School morgue, where precocious mad scientist Herbert West (Combs) is perfecting a secret serum to reanimate the dead. To this end, he recruits fellow med student Daniel Kane (Abbott) and a number of soon-to-be-lively cadavers. Director Gordon, basing his loony gorefest on a venerable H. P. Lovecraft tale, keeps the demented action moving at a brisk pace. To learn why a murdered, revivified, and then lobotomized (!) med school dean delivers his naked blond daughter (Crampton) to the decapitated but still living head of a lascivious brain surgeon—well, you'll just have to lay hands on the video yourself. Remember: You have nothing to lose but your lunch! Available in R and Unrated versions.

FILMMAKERS IN FOCUS:
Stuart Gordon

In a field where most auteurs fail to hit their weight, portly director Stuart Gordon batted a lusty 1.000 with his first two films. His H. P. Lovecraft–based horror movies, *Re-Animator* and *From Beyond*, successfully blend primal terror, offbeat erotica, and copious gore with generous doses of gleeful graveyard humor. Though relatively new to the fright-film biz, Gordon has been working with weird themes for over two decades. As founder of Chicago's Organic Theater, he directed such eccentric items as *Warp*, a sci-fi anthology that later enjoyed a brief Broadway run, and *Dope*, a freewheeling adaptation of the Sax (*Fu Manchu*) Rohmer novel of the same name. Cohorts Dennis Paoli, who co-scripted *Re-Animator* and *From Beyond*, and actress/wife Carolyn Purdy-Gordon, who appears in the above films, are likewise Organic Theater alumni. While Gordon freely admits to being squeamish ("I was under the seat long before the end of Cronenberg's *They Came from Within*," he confides), he feels his films furnish healthy, cathartic entertainment. He lists David (*The Fly*) Cronenberg, Ridley (*Alien*) Scott and Alfred Hitchcock among his personal fright-film faves and singles out Hitch's *Psycho* as "the scariest movie ever made."

Rejuvenator (1988) ◆◆◇
D: *Brian Thomas Jones. Vivian Lanko, John MacKay, Jessica Dublin, James Hogue, Katell Pleven, Marcus Powell. 85 minutes. (Sony)*

Not to be confused with the superior *Re-Animator*, *Rejuvenator*—or *Rejuvenatrix*, as the title sequence has it—involves a rich, geriatric actress (Dublin) who's funding a scientist (MacKay) working on a human brain-juice serum that reverses the aging process. Unfortunately, if not unexpectedly, there are serious side effects, as when our rejuvenated heroine (now played by Lanko) runs out of juice and transmogrifies into a screeching disfigured hag, replete with pulsating face—a condition that prompts her to remove and devour the gray matter of those hapless victims who cross her voracious path. While not exactly big in the originality department—the effectively campy bug-lady romp *Evil Spawn*

Stuart Gordon's energetic exercise in Lovecraftian lunacy gave Empire Pictures a shot in the arm. Here, *Re-Animator*'s unhinged Dr. Herbert West (Jeffrey Combs) prepares to inject a bit of black levity.
Photo courtesy of Vestron Video.

(see index) sports virtually the same plot—*Rejuvenator* succeeds as a straightforward (or at any rate deadpan) gorified recreation of a typical '50s sci-fi/horror cheapie, à la Roger Corman's *Wasp Woman* (see index), that supplies its fair share of grisly retro fun.

Remote Control (1988) ♦♦♦
D: *Jeff Leiberman. Kevin Dillon, Deborah Goodrich, Christopher Wynne, Frank Beddor, Jennifer Tilly, Bert Remsen. 88 minutes. (IVE)*
An *Invasion of the Body Snatchers* for the video generation, *Remote Control* is a witty, high-concept sci-fi satire. Dillon toplines as a

vid-store clerk who notices that a new arrival—ostensibly a campy '50s sci-fi flick titled *Remote Control* (itself an expert send-up of that vanished genre)—is having a bizarre effect on viewers, turning them into murderous brainwashed alien slaves! The chase is soon on as Kev, abetted by blond Goodrich and video-store owner Wynne, race against time to destroy the alien cassettes before they destroy us video-addicted Earthlings. The crisp performances, fast-paced direction, funny futuristic set and wardrobe designs, and a consistently clever script conspire to make *Remote Control* a genuine sci-fi sleeper. An anticlimactic ending is the only serious flaw in this otherwise highly recommended obscurity.

The Resurrection of Zachary Wheeler (1971) NR
D: Bob Wynn. Angie Dickinson, Bradford Dillman, James Daly. 100 minutes. (United)

This made-for-TV sci-fi about synthetic bodies, called somas, manufactured in Alamagordo, New Mexico, bears some similarity to the earlier *Seconds* (NA) and the later *Clonus Horror* (see index).

The Return of the Fly (1959) ◆◆◇ B&W
D: Edward L. Bernds. Vincent Price, Brett Halsey, David Frankham. 80 minutes. (Key)

Halsey plays the original Fly's son, who repeats Dad's teleportation tinkering with similarly disastrous results in an okay if not especially inspired sequel.

Return of the Jedi (1983) ◆◆◇
D: Richard Marquand. Mark Hamill, Harrison Ford, Carrie Fisher. 132 minutes. (CBS/Fox)

You probably don't need us to tell you about *this* one. A bit rich and wholesome for the Phantom's blood (type B, of course), but Lucas and crew know how to entertain even if their flicks don't always rate among *our* faves.

The Road Warrior (1981) ◆◆◆◆
D: George Miller. Mel Gibson, Bruce Spence, Vernon Wells, Virginia Hay. 94 minutes. (Warner)

Simply one of the greatest genre movies of all time, ranking right up there with *The Terminator*. A transplanted postnuke western that brilliantly blends all the best elements of that defunct genre, *Road Warrior* (originally *Mad Max 2*) has become one of the most-imitated flicks ever. All would-be action auteurs should study *Road Warrior*'s kinetic climax, where creative editing, not budget, makes the difference.

RoboCop (1987) ◆◆◆◆
D: Paul Verhoeven. Peter Weller, Nancy Allen, Ronny Cox, Kurtwood Smith, Miguel Ferrer, Robert DoQui. 103 minutes. (Orion)

The title sounds like a typical Empire Pictures quickie and the original print ads played like yet another cheap *Terminator* clone, but *RoboCop* is one of the most brilliantly subversive movies to surface since David Lynch's *Blue Velvet*. The flick amply delivers on both the action and the lampoon levels, weaving abrupt and senseless violence galore into Dutch director Paul (*The 4th Man*) Verhoeven's deadpan dissection of America's corporate lusts, trashy sitcom culture, and pandemic greed for power, speed, and general *bigness* —in cars, guns, and bank accounts. Peter (*Buckaroo Banzai*) Weller joins the ranks of such celebrated celluloid androids as Arnold Schwarzenegger and Clint Eastwood as the titular *RoboCop*, a Detroit flatfoot-turned-cyborg who comes equipped with a snappy machine-pistol, an acute identity crisis, a baby-food diet (!), and a gait that should be registered with Monty Python's Ministry of Silly Walks. Nancy Allen supplies solid backup as Robo's partner, while Kurtwood Smith makes for a memorably scurvy villain. Cox and Ferrer are appropriately slimy as a pair of competing corporate creeps. A must for action, SF, and satire fans alike.

Rocketship X-M—Special Edition (1950) ◆◆◆ B&W

D: Kurt Neumann. Lloyd Bridges, Osa Massen, Hugh O'Brian. 77 minutes. (Nostalgia Merchant)

Moon-bound voyagers take a wrong turn and land on Mars in this fun '50s sci-fi pioneer. The video version features new special effects added in 1976, plus trailers for classic SF films.

Rollerball (1975) ◆◆◇

D: Norman Jewison. James Caan, John Houseman, Maud Adams. 123 minutes. (MGM/UA)

This sci-fi fable about futuristic gladiators who play the lethal title sport has a good premise and performances but a tad too many dull stretches. Still worth a look, though, for the violently staged Rollerball matches.

R.O.T.O.R. (1988) ◆◇

D: Cullen Blaine. Richard Gesswein, Margaret Trigg, Jayne Smith, James Cole, Clark Moore, Carroll Brandon Baker. 90 minutes. (Imperial)

A largely lame Dallas-lensed, direct-to-home-vid RoboCop/Terminator spoof, R.O.T.O.R. chronicles the murderous misadventures of a malfunctioning android motorcycle cop loose on the Texas highways. Parodying movies that are not only great but witty in their own right is a risky business at best. When a team of amateurs attempts it—R.O.T.O.R.'s the type of home movie that finds the "star" (Gesswein) doubling as a producer and the production designer (Budd Lewis) also penning the script— the results are usually uniformly awful. To their modest credit, R.O.T.O.R.'s creators do manage to work in some moderately funny sci-fi dialogue and a handful of decent sight gags. But the flick mostly relies on cheap slapstick riffs and dumb Short Circuit—style robotic comic relief to keep the clumsy proceedings clanking along.

Runaway (1984) ◆◆

D: Michael Crichton. Tom Selleck, Cynthia Rhodes, Gene Simmons, Joey Cramer, Kirstie Alley, Stan Shaw, G. W. Bailey. 100 minutes. (RCA/Columbia)

Widower Jack Ramsey (Selleck) seems to have it all under control: He enjoys his job with the runaway-robot tracking squad, he has just been assigned a pretty new partner (Rhodes), he has a glitch-free rapport with his lovable young son (Cramer), and he has his every domestic need seen to by a pleasant android named Lois, a surrogate housewife/mother/maid. But trouble soon arrives when several formerly friendly mechanized menials inexplicably begin going berserk ("popping their chips") and savagely attacking their unsuspecting owners. This mechanical mayhem is traced to crazed computer genius Luther (Simmons), a criminal mastermind out to sell his impressive array of electronic superweapons to the highest bidder. A lowbrow, medium-budget exercise in hightech paranoia, *Runaway* plays like a glossy update of a vintage serial as Tom dons his "electro-magnetic suit" to destroy a rabid robot, dodges "heat-seeking" minimissiles fired from Luther's silver handgun and even dines at a robotic sushi bar (!). For all its flaws, *Runaway* fashions a number of improbable images at once endearing and enduring, as when a cute little automated "household helper" with a serious Clint Eastwood complex scoots around a suburban home slaying its owners with a .357 Magnum (!). Of such stuff are B-movie memories made.

The Running Man (1987) ◆◆◆

D: Paul Michael Glaser. Arnold Schwarzenegger, Maria Conchita Alonso, Richard Dawson, Yaphet Kotto, Jim Brown, Jesse Ventura, Erland van Lidth, Mick Fleetwood, Dweezil Zappa. 101 minutes. (Vestron)

"Get me the Justice Department—Entertainment Division!" So demands an angry Dawson, who, in a bit of high-concept typecasting, portrays the repulsive sleazoid host of futuristic police-state America's most popular TV show, the titular *Running Man*, a sort of *Beat the Clock Meets the Most Dangerous Game*. Schwarzenegger is the unlucky contestant, a framed ex-flyer who's forced to flee a lethal lineup of professional "stalkers" (Ventura, Brown, Professor Toru Tanaka, and an opera-singing van Lidth) in a bid to claim the game's grand prize: trial by jury (!). Based on a Richard Bachman (Stephen King) novel depicting the ultimate merger of government and show biz, and borrowing liberally from *Blade Runner*, *Rollerball*, and *The Tenth Victim*, *The Running Man* is an often sophomoric but generally fun dystopian slaughterfest. The flick succeeds in sending up game shows, pro wrestling, and official duplicity while still filling the screen with enough chainsaws, shoot-outs, and exploding heads to hold hard-core action fans' attention. Arn delivers his by-now formulaic one-liners more stiffly than ever and meets his thespic match in Alonso—for sustained unintelligibility, their exchanges rival Sly and Brigitte Nielsen's in *Cobra* (though Sly managed *without* an accent).

The Sea Serpent (1985) NR

D: Gregory Greens. Ray Milland, Timothy Bottoms, Jared Martin. 92 minutes. (Lightning)

Pretty stupid adventure about A-bomb tests rousing a puppetlike title creature from the ocean depths. First time we've heard that one . . . *today*. Ray Milland's last movie.

Shock Waves (1977) ◆◆
D: Ken Wiederhorn. Peter Cushing, Brooke Adams, John Carradine, Jay Maeder. 90 minutes. (Prism)

Mad scientist Cushing's subaqueous Nazi zombies terrorize stranded travelers (including Adams) in what may well be director Ken (*Meatballs II*) Wiederhorn's best film. Cushing and Carradine have nary a single scene together.

Silent Running (1971) ◆◆◇
D: Douglas Trumbull. Bruce Dern, Cliff Potts, Ron Rifkin. 90 minutes. (MCA)

Pretty much a one-man show as space-station survivor Dern, accompanied only by three diminutive androids, seeks to preserve Earth's last vegetation samples in this sometimes slow ecological thriller.

Slaughterhouse-Five (1972) ◆◆◆
D: George Roy Hill. Michael Sacks, Valerie Perrine, Ron Leibman. 104 minutes. (MCA)

Hill helms a fairly faithful and effective adaptation of Kurt Vonnegut's time-and-space-hopping novel detailing the surreal adventures of GI "Candide" Billy Pilgrim (Sacks).

Slave Girls from Beyond Infinity (1987) ◆
D: Ken Dixon. Elizabeth Cayton, Cindy Beal, Brinke Stevens, Don Scribner, Carl Horner. 73 minutes. (Urban Classics)

Originally coupled theatrically with *Creepozoids* (Urban Classics) in an abortive bid to resurrect the double features of yore, *Slave Girls from Beyond Infinity* represents another sad case of an inspired title masking a lame flick. A naked *Most Dangerous Game* rip-off (*Running Man* does it much better, even if Arnie Schwarzenegger isn't as easy on the eye as the distaff topliners here), *Slave Girls* concerns itself with a trio of scantily clad space bimbettes' efforts to escape mad human-hunter Zed, his trusty laser-beam crossbow, and a pair of clanky android underlings. While relatively rich in T&A cinematography, *Slave Girls* is woefully low on thespic talent (Scribner, as Zed, does a bad Rod Serling imitation throughout), production values, and plot ideas. Those in search of a lively sci-fi jiggle spoof will have to keep on looking.

Slithis (1978) ◆◆
D: Stephen Traxler. Alan Blanchard, Judy Motulsky, Dennis Lee Falt. 86 minutes. (Media)

An amateurish but oddly watchable throwback to the fright films of the '50s, *Slithis* tells of yet another toxic terror from the deep. Slightly better than *The Incredible Melting Man* (see index).

Solarbabies (1986) 0 ◆
D: Alan Johnson. Richard Jordan, Jami Gertz, Jason Patric, Lukas Haas, Charles Durning, James Le Gros. 94 minutes. (MGM/UA)

Solarbabies, (Mel) Brooksfilms' pathetic *Mad Max* rip-off, hurtles us into a grim, totalitarian forty-second century, a time so bleak it could almost pass for the 1980s. In many ways, it's a *lot* like the '80s: The teens at the prisonlike Orphanage 43 use words like "awesome!", cover local walls with graffiti, and even do beat-box imitations à la the Fat Boys. Working from a script that must have been scrawled in Crayola, *Solarbabies* follows a band of said teens who—accompanied by little Lukas Haas (who looks here like a Walter Keene painting come to frightening life) and his magical alien pal Bodhi (a phosphorescent beachball)—escape sadistic orphanage overseer Jordan and make tracks for the desert. There they encounter virtually every futuristic cliché under the celluloid sun, even wandering into an ersatz *Beyond Thunderdome* set, replete with Aussie-accented (!) low- lifes. *Solarbabies* may be lacking in originality, but it's rich in brain-dead dialogue, as when ingenue Gertz growls at an overly amorous punker, "Get out, you creature of filth!" Our sentiments exactly.

Soylent Green (1973) ◆◆◆
D: Richard Fleischer. Charlton Heston, Edward G. Robinson, Leigh Taylor-Young. 100 minutes. (MGM/UA)

A prescient look at a (near-)future Manhattan where homeless victims crowd the streets and are cannibalized by their betters. Pretty strong sci-fi with a memorable turn by Robinson in his final film.

Space Rage (1986) ◆◆◇
D: Conrad E. Palmisano. Michael Paré, Richard Farnsworth, John Laughlin, Lee Purcell, William Windom, Hank Worden. 78 minutes. (Lightning)

Michael (*Houston Knights*) Paré lands a perfect role here as brutal superthug Grange, leader of a violent breakout on the prison planet of New Botany Bay in this derivative but lively sci-fi action quickie. When Mad Max–like bounty hunter John (*Crimes of Passion*) Laughlin fails to eradicate a murderous band of rampaging "scapers," Richard (*The Grey Fox*) Farnsworth—who's a good decade+ older than Charles Bronson, even—dons his black-leather battle fatigues, grabs his trusty shotgun, and creaks into action. Despite its *Outland*ish story line, *Space Rage* furnishes pretty fair nonstop violence fare, and Paré really delivers as one of the B screen's meaner villains. Only the straightfaced use of the line "It's *too* quiet—I don't like it" compelled us to subtract half a phan from *Space Rage*'s rating.

Star Crash (1979) ◆◆◇
D: Luigi Cozzi (aka Lewis Coates). Marjoe Gortner, Caroline Munro,

Christopher Plummer, Joe Spinell. 92 minutes. (Charter)

An enjoyably stupid Italo *Star Wars* rip-off, *Star Crash* further benefits from a cult cast that includes Plummer, scream queen Munro, and leering heavy Joe (*Maniac*) Spinell. Gortner's in there, too, but that's why God gave us fast-forward controls.

Star Crystal (1985) ◆◇

D: Lance Lindsay. C. Jutson Campbell, Faye Bolt, John W. Smith, Taylor Kingsley, Marcia Linn. 92 minutes. (New World)

We have to give this low-budget loser credit: It's the only cheap sci-fi hustler we've seen that rips off *Alien* AND *E.T.* in the same film! For the first hour or so, *Star Crystal* is a direct *Alien* clone, as a mutating monster stows away aboard a small spacecraft and devours the crew one by one. Then our voracious thingie suddenly transmogrifies into a contrite *benevolent* being, apologizes to the two surviving crewmembers for its previous bad manners (!), and helps them guide their errant ship home. Now, *that's* high concept and a half!

Star Slammer (1988) ◆◆

D: Fred Olen Ray. Ross Hagen, Sandy Brooke, Susan Stokey, Dawn Wildsmith, Bobbie Bresee, Aldo Ray, John Carradine. 86 minutes. (Vidmark)

The indefatigable Ray's *Star Slammer* gets off to a pretty grim start, due to the usual bad acting and poorly executed "comic" relief.

Heroine Brooke is captured by villain Hagen and locked up in a floating hoosegow administered by a band of cosmic perverts and their android aides. The pic picks up a bit past the midway point with some semi-inspired low-camp antics (including a witty Uncle Don homage) and is further lifted by cameos by Z-movie queen Bresee, plus old reliables John Carradine (who delivers his usual three-line monologue) and Aldo Ray as the prison ship's resident torturer. Not as good as *The Tomb* (see index), which rises to the comic-book level to which Fred aspires with far greater frequency than *Star Slammer* does. Fred also goes the SF route in the even less successful *Biohazard* (Cinema Group) and *Deep Space* (TWE).

Star Trek—The Motion Picture (Special Longer Version) (1979) ◆◆

D: Robert Wise. William Shatner, Leonard Nimoy, DeForest Kelley. 143 minutes. (Paramount)

The cult sci-fi teleseries's long-delayed big-screen debut is an overlong, overpriced yawn, by the Phantom's lights, though no self-respecting Trekkie would want to miss it. The video restores additional footage cut from the original theatrical print.

Star Trek II: The Wrath of Khan (1982) ◆◆

D: Nicholas Meyer. William Shatner, Leonard Nimoy, DeForest Kelley. 113 minutes. (Paramount)

Evil Ricardo (Khan) Montalban and his alien beach-boy types bother the *Enterprise* crew in this series' second misfire. It's a reel or so shorter than *Star Trek I* at least.

Star Trek III: The Search for Spock (1984) ◆◆◇

D: Leonard Nimoy. William Shatner, DeForest Kelley, Christopher Lloyd. 105 minutes. (Paramount)

Klingon Lloyd and his cosmic minions menace our heroes as they scour the universe for missing friend Spock. While this one also plays like a bloated TV episode, at least it's a pretty *good* episode. The series really hits its stride with *Star Trek IV*, though.

Star Trek IV: The Voyage Home (1986) ◆◆◆

D: Leonard Nimoy. William Shatner, Leonard Nimoy, Catherine Hicks, DeForest Kelley, James Doohan, George Takei. 119 minutes. (Paramount)

While the Phantom's never been a major fan of *Star Trek*'s office-in-space-type adventures, we must confess to enjoying *Star Trek IV*. This time around, it's our heroes who are the eccentrics, as they beam down to San Francisco 1986 in search of a pair of humpbacked whales who hold the key to a future Earth's salvation (itself a novel, if rather arcane, plot hook). The pic provides its primary fun in detailing Kirk and company's efforts to cope with our contempo "primitive, paranoid" culture.

Spock, still recovering from brain damage sustained in *Star Trek III*, is cleverly passed off as a '60s acid casualty (!)—he "took too much LDS," Kirk explains en route to a local aquarium, where Spock plans a mind-melding session with an imprisoned whale—while the Russki-accented Chekhov (Walter Koenig) asks startled passersby for directions to a nearby naval base with "nuclear wessels." Director Nimoy employs a consistently light touch in steering the veteran *Enterprise* crewmembers through their time-warped mission. While a bit bald on suspense, *Star Trek IV* emerges as a satisfying blend of bright comedy and high-tech effects.

Star Wars (1977) ◆◆◆

D: George Lucas. Mark Hamill, Harrison Ford, Carrie Fisher, Alec Guinness, Peter Cushing. 121 minutes. (CBS/Fox)

Only those who've spent the last decade or so vacationing in a galaxy far away need us to tell them about this overhyped but fun space spectacular.

Starman (1984) ◆◆◇

D: John Carpenter. Jeff Bridges, Karen Allen, Charles Martin Smith. 115 minutes. (RCA/Columbia)

Carpenter's cosmic-visitation parable gives Bridges a chance to stretch as the spaced-out title character and ranks as a generally suspenseful, occasionally funny outing until the clichés get in the way.

Starship (1985) ◆
D: Roger Christian. John Tarrant, Donough Rees, Deep Roy, Ralph Cotterill, Cassandra Webb. 85 minutes. (Cinema Group)

A Brit import originally titled *Lorca and the Outlaws, Starship* is a juvenile mélange of *Star Wars, Outland,* and *The Terminator* that finds a band of space rebels led by bland, blond Lorca (Tarrant) and aided by Grid (Roy), a miniature, immensely irritating 'droid, fighting back against evil mercenary Cotterill and his robot army. While competently assembled (with exteriors lensed in Australia), this futuristic sci-fi entry is so unrelentingly flat and colorless that it kept yours truly poised on the brink of unconsciousness for nearly all of its 85 minutes.

Stranded (1988) ◆◇
D: Tex Fuller. Ione Skye, Joe Morton, Maureen O'Sullivan, Susan Barnes, Cameron Dye, Michael Greene. 80 minutes. (RCA/Columbia)

Stranded involves a family of pale, long-haired, basically benign humanoid ETs, in flight from an interplanetary assassin, who take refuge in the rural redoubt of O'Sullivan and her granddaughter Skye. The outer-space unit comes complete with its own unisex *Terminator*-type bodyguard ("It's got tits and a raygun!" a startled deputy exclaims), whose intimidating presence leads to a brief shoot-out with panicked locals, followed by a prolonged "hostage situation." Attempting to cope with both the fearful visitors and the outraged Earthlings is beleaguered black sheriff Morton (himself a former alien, 1984's *The Brother from Another Planet*), who also has to fend off town racists. While director Fuller manages to wring some tension from this Mexican (*Martian?*) standoff, *Stranded* is a largely static one-set wonder lensed entirely in murky, eye-defying night photography.

Strange Behavior (1981) ◆◆◇
D: Michael Laughlin. Michael Murphy, Louise Fletcher, Dan Shor. 98 minutes. (RCA/Columbia)

Although undeserving of its fleeting cult rep, this New Zealand–lensed, America-set sci-fi about brainwashed teens has enough going to make a rental worthwhile. Also out as *Dead Kids* on the Canadian IFS label.

Strange Invaders (1983) ◆◆
D: Michael Laughlin. Paul LeMat, Nancy Allen, Michael Lerner. 94 minutes. (Vestron)

Michael (*Strange Behavior*) Laughlin returns with this deliberate attempt to fashion a '50s-style sci-fi flick for the '80s. Despite an initially intriguing plot and a strong cast, the pic is a pretty smarmy affair.

Stranger from Venus (1954) NR B&W
D: Burt Balaban. Patricia Neal, Helmut Dantine, Derek Bond. 78 minutes. (Nostalgia Merchant)

Sort of a road-show *Day the Earth Stood Still* (it's even got Patricia Neal), this Brit sci-fi features Dantine as a not-so-friendly visitor from the title planet. The video also contains several classic SF trailers. The film is available from Amvest Video under its alternate title *Immediate Disaster*.

The Stuff (1985) ◆◆◆
D: Larry Cohen. Michael Moriarty, Andrea Marcovicci, Garrett Morris, Paul Sorvino, Scott Bloom, Danny Aiello. 93 minutes. (New World)

Cohen mainstay Moriarty stars in *The Stuff* as ex-FBI-agent-cum-industrial-spy "Moe" Rutherford. It's Rutherford's task to uncover the secret formula of The Stuff, the cocaine of junk-food desserts, a killer product that's turning the nation into an army of crazed addicts, or Stuffies. Along the way, Moe enlists the aid of publicity whiz Nicole (Marcovicci), deposed cookie king Chocolate Chip Charlie (Morris), right-wing paramilitary lunatic Colonel Spears (Sorvino), and Jason (Bloom), a kid who's seen his entire family succumb to The Stuff's seductive but lethal allure. The able topliners are complemented by cameos from Brooke Adams, Abe Vigoda, Clara ("Where's The Stuff?") Peller, Danny Aiello, and Patrick O'Neal. Cohen's blackly comic attack on America's cult of instant-grat consumerism springs a wealth of perverse surprises.

Superman IV: The Quest for Peace (1987) ◆◆◇
D: Sidney J. Furie. Christopher Reeve, Margot Kidder, Gene Hackman, Jon Cryer, Mariel Hemingway, Sam Wanamaker. 90 minutes. (Warner)

The gala 1978 *Superman* remake (Warner) applied a lavish, high-tech treatment to the Man of Steel legend and, if lacking the tacky charm of the original Superman serials and teleseries, managed to stick to the point. The equally expensive *Superman II* (Warner) substituted action and FX for plot, while *III* (Warner) opted for an unwise comedic approach, enlisting Richard Pryor to play opposite Chris Reeve's superhero. With *this* entry, the series officially enters its low-budget Godzilla phase. Most of the flick details Supe's running—to say nothing of soaring and swooping—battle with the formidable Nuclear Man (Mark Pillow), an evil Superman clone clad in heavy-metal mufti and created by returning criminal mastermind Lex Luthor (again played by Hackman, picking up an easy check). The pair go at it on the streets, in space, and even—in one bravura scene—in front of the Great Wall of China (!). The deadheaded plot (Reeve receives a story credit) involves Supe's efforts to rid Earth of atomic weapons, Luthor's attempts to stop him, and the *Daily Planet* staffers' bid to triumph over yellow-press baron Wanamaker and his *zoftig* daughter Hemingway. While the FX are pretty cheesy compared to the earlier three entries, *Superman IV* supplies enough B-flick fun to make a rental a safe investment for fans of the Man of Steel.

Superman and the Mole Men (1951) ◆◆◆ B&W

D: Lee Sholem. George Reeves, Phyllis Coates, Jeff Corey, Walter Reed, Billy Curtis. 58 minutes. (Warner)

George Reeves assumes the Man of Steel role in this surprisingly liberal plea for the rights of Mole Men the world over. Not much in the FX department—the mini-ETs (led by Curtis) wield a sophisticated cosmic weapon that looks suspiciously like an earthly vacuum cleaner (!)—but a winning low-budget fable that led to Reeves's long-running Supe teleseries.

Supersonic Saucer (1956) NR

D: S. G. Ferguson. Donald Gray, Marcia Monolescue, Fella Edmonds. 50 minutes. (Sinister Cinema)

An obscure Brit precursor to *E.T.*, wherein a pint-size alien visits a group of children. Of interest to comparison-minded sci-fi fans.

Survivor (1987) ◆

D: Michael Shackleton. Chip Mayer, Sue Kiel, Richard Moll, Richard Haines, John Carson, Rex Garner. 97 minutes. (Vestron)

At first, Shackleton's *Survivor* plays like a Yank rip-off of all those useless Italo *Road Warrior* clones that clog sci-fi vid shelves. But the pic proves a bit more ambitious than that; in fact, it even strains for the profound as ex-astronaut-turned-title-nomad Mayer wanders the postnuke wasteland wondering Where It All Went Wrong, among other deep ontological queries. Several reels later, after a stormy romance of sorts with distaff survivor Kiel, Chip arrives at a subterranean Russian power station that's been taken over by outsize, Ayn Randian bully Kragge (the ever-imposing Moll), who first tries to talk our hero to death, then opts for more direct means. *Survivor* sports some nice nuclear-desert sets, but its alternately sparse and downright motor-mouthed script and sluglike pacing bored this viewer right out of his video gourd.

Swamp Thing (1982) ◆

D: Wes Craven. Louis Jourdan, Adrienne Barbeau, Ray Wise. 91 minutes. (Embassy)

Wes Craven's campy comic-book adaptation recounts the mucky misadventures of the unlucky research scientist-turned-veg-monster Wise. *Swamp Thing* ranks as the director's personal fave, after *Serpent and the Rainbow,* among his sundry film projects. The Phantom found it fairly unwatchable.

The Tenth Victim (1965) ◆◆◆

D: Elio Petri. Marcello Mastroianni, Ursula Andress, Elsa Martinelli. 92 minutes. (Embassy)

A futuristic society channels its violent impulses into legalized death hunts in this deft Italo satire whose theme was later reprised in *The Running Man* (see index). Great costumes, too, especially the one worn by ace huntress Andress.

The Terminal Man (1974) ◆◆
D: Mike Hodges. George Segal, Joan Hackett, Richard A. Dysart. 107 minutes. (Warner)

Segal is a computer scientist wired for violence in this slow retelling of Michael Crichton's novel. Has its following, though.

The Terminator (1984) ◆◆◆◆
D: James Cameron. Arnold Schwarzenegger, Linda Hamilton, Michael Biehn, Paul Winfield, Lance Henriksen, Dick Miller. 108 minutes. (HBO)

Quite possibly *the* greatest B movie of all time, *The Terminator* is a relentlessly kinetic roller-coaster ride that neatly integrates nearly every necessary genre-pic ingredient—from high-tech gadgetry and special effects to visceral bursts of abrupt and senseless violence. Though it's been ripped off endlessly and from every conceivable angle, *The Terminator* has yet to be duplicated, not even by its own creators, director Cameron and producer Gale Anne Hurd (though they came fairly close with *Aliens*). Schwarzenegger, incidentally, reportedly nixed the bland hero assignment (played by the wider-ranged if narrower-shouldered Biehn) in favor of the killer cyborg role—a move that proves that not *all* of Arnie's brains are in his biceps.

Hamilton is excellent as the endangered Sarah Connor, in whose salvation the fate of mankind lies, as are Winfield and Henriksen as a pair of beleaguered police officials.

Terror Is a Man (1959) ◆◆◇ B&W
D: Gerry DeLeon. Francis Lederer, Richard Derr, Greta Thyssen. 89 minutes. (Sinister Cinema)

A pretty good low-budget *Island of Lost Souls* (NA) rehash, lensed in the Philippines, and complete with an onscreen warning signal that buzzes before the "gruesome" scenes. Available from Sinister Cinema under the title *Blood Creature*.

TerrorVision (1986) ◆◇
D: Ted Nicolaou. Gerrit Graham, Mary Woronov, Diane Franklin, Chad Allen, Bert Remsen. 84 minutes. (Lightning)

A ravenous, brainless alien is beamed via satellite dish into the gaudy suburban *chez* of the conspicuously consuming Putterman clan, whose numbers the monster proceeds to reduce with some conspicuous consumption of its own. The youngest Putterman, eight-year-old Sherman (Allen), is hip to the hungry ET's tricks but can't get his swinging parents (Woronov and Graham), grape-soft grandpa (Remsen), or punkette sis (Franklin) to believe him. In the hands of a master scare satirist like Larry Cohen, *TerrorVision* might have sustained its bright but slender premise. As it stands, scripter/director Nicolaou takes a half-hour idea and painfully pads it to feature length.

Them! (1954) ◆◆◆◇ B&W
D: Gordon Douglas. Edmund Gwenn, James Arness, Joan Weldon, James Whitmore. 94 minutes. (Warner)

Still the best giant-insect movie ever made, with dad-daughter scientists Gwenn and Weldon, assisted by lawmen Whitmore and Arness, tracking atom-spawned ants from the New Mexican desert to the L.A. sewer system. Fess (Davy Crockett) Parker has a neat bit as an incredulous pilot.

They Live (1988) ◆◆◆
D: John Carpenter. Roddy Piper, Keith David, Meg Foster, Buck Flower, Peter Jason, Raymond St. Jacques, John Goff. 95 minutes. (MCA)

John (Halloween) Carpenter's They Live boasts a brilliant premise in an updated Invasion of the Body Snatchers vein: Seems the American media's secretly being run by manipulative aliens from outer space. (Hey, it's as good an explanation as we've ever heard! You don't believe Robin Leach really comes from England, do you?) Itinerant construction worker Nada (Rowdy Roddy Piper) stumbles upon this cosmic conspiracy after donning a pair of truth-seeking sunglasses (!) that reveal the skeletal visages hidden behind the human masks worn by the ET powers-that-be—faces as ugly as the aliens' rapacious instincts.

The shades also detect subliminal 1984esque messages—e.g., "Obey," "Consume," "Submit"—posted on billboards and TV screens. These scenes play like a politicized version of the old 3-D hallucination The Mask (only instead of spying floating skulls, Roddy sees corporate heads). The aliens' mission is to keep the general populace "asleep, selfish, sedate" while they—a race of cosmic corporate raiders aided by greedy human collaborators—plunder the planet of its natural resources. Our enlightened hero connects with a band of earthly resistance fighters, and the battle is on in earnest. Alas, it's a battle that's frequently lost due to Carpenter's failure to exploit his cogent plot's possibilities as he constantly sabotages the flick's genuinely eerie atmosphere and flashes of pointed satire with dull stretches of flat filler footage and ill-advised stabs at broad mock-macho humor. Roddy's another major part of the problem here. The role demands a far more charismatic player, a seasoned Thespian of great strength and range like Arnold Schwarzenegger. Still, flawed as it is, They Live is well worth watching for its more imaginative components and timely message.

The Thing (1982) ◆◆◆
D: John Carpenter. Kurt Russell, Wilford Brimley, Richard Dysart. 108 minutes. (MCA)

Carpenter pulls out all the slime-creature stops in his gory remake. Pretty good on its own but not up to the original's quality.

The Thing (From Another World) (1951) ◆◆◆ B&W

D: Christian Nyby. Kenneth Tobey, Margaret Sheridan, James Arness. 87 minutes. (RKO)

This pioneering SF outing emphasizes suspense over FX, as Arctic scientists try to cope with the first of the screen's Cold-War-Era aliens, a decidedly unfriendly veg-creature played by Arness.

Things to Come (1936) ◆◆◇ B&W

D: William Cameron Menzies. Raymond Massey, Ralph Richardson, Cedric Hardwicke. 92/113 minutes. (Kartes, others)

Rather elitist vision of the future, as "benign" high-flying fascist Massey imposes order on a chaotic post-world-war world. Spectacular sets at least make this H. G. Wells adaptation (Wells wrote the script) a visual treat. Other early SF efforts now available on cassette include F.P.1. Doesn't Answer (Sinister Cinema) and Transatlantic Tunnel (Moore Video).

This Is Not a Test (1962) ◆◆◇ B&W

D: Frederic Gadette. Seamon Glass, Mary Morlas, Thayer Roberts. 80 minutes. (Sinister Cinema, others)

This truly bizarre desert-set cheapie stars Glass as a harried state trooper who tries to warn singularly uncooperative motorists of an impending atomic attack. Not exactly good, but definitely different.

This Island Earth (1955) ◆◆◆

D: Joseph Newman. Rex Reason, Jeff Morrow, Faith Domergue. 86 minutes. (MCA)

Level-headed Earth scientist (the aptly named Rex Reason) constructs a mysterious machine (the immortal Interociter) that puts him in touch with the endangered planet Metaluna. A trip to same soon ensues in this gaudy sci-fi gala. Morrow plays the brainy alien; fetching former Howard Hughes paramour Domergue is Reason's distaff partner. Recommended.

Threads (1985) ◆◆◆

D: Mick Jackson. Karen Meagher, Reece Dinsdale, Rita May. 110 minutes. (New World)

An uncompromisingly grim, unsentimental Brit shocker dealing with life after a nuclear war. Ranks with Testament (Paramount) and Peter Watkins's The War Game (Budget) as one of the most genuinely depressing postnuke parables ever lensed.

THX-1138 (1971) ◆◆◆

D: George Lucas. Robert Duvall, Donald Pleasence, Maggie McOmie. 88 minutes. (Warner)

Lucas began this slow-moving but striking (especially if you like white) dystopian vision as a USC student project. Duvall is fine as the rebellious drone who works to escape from totalitarian control; his race against the cash register supplies a clever climactic highlight.

Time After Time (1979) ◆◆◆

D: Nicholas Meyer. Malcolm McDowell, David Warner, Mary Steenburgen. 112 minutes. (Warner)

Jack the Ripper and H. G. Wells time-trip to modern-day San Francisco, where Jack resumes his ripping ways and H. G. tries to thwart him. A deft exercise all around.

The Time Machine (1960) ◆◆◆

D: George Pal. Rod Taylor, Yvette Mimieux, Alan Young. 103 minutes. (MGM/UA)

Pal's pulpy adaptation of H. G. Wells's seminal sci-fi tale is occasionally hokey but entertaining overall. With teenage Mimieux as "the shape of things to come." A dull 1978 made-for-TV remake is also available (United).

The Time Travelers (1964) ◆◆◇

D: Ib Melchior. Preston Foster, Philip Carey, Merry Anders. 82 minutes. (HBO)

Foster leads a time-travel crew into the postnuke future, where hostile mutants abound. *Famous Monsters* founder Forry Ackerman cameos as a scientist.

Timerider: The Adventures of Lyle Swan (1983) ◆◆◇

D: William Dear. Fred Ward, Peter Coyote, Belinda Bauer. 93 minutes. (Pacific Arts)

A not-bad B flick about cycle racer Ward, who's time-transported to the Wild West, where he woos Bauer and battles villain Coyote. Co-written and produced by ex-Monkee Michael Nesmith.

Tobor the Great (1954) ◆◆ B&W

D: Lee Sholem. Charles Drake, Karin Booth, Billy Chapin. 77 minutes. (Republic)

Pretty stupid kids-oriented story about a boy and his robot; the latter combats Commie spies. Recommended for nostalgia buffs only.

Trancers (1985) ◆◆◇

D: Charles Band. Tim Thomerson, Helen Hunt, Michael Stefani, Art La Fleur, Biff Manard. 76 minutes. (Vestron).

Trancers (released theatrically as *Future Cop*) tells the highly derivative tale of tough-guy "trooper" Jack Deth (Thomerson), a hard-boiled Dirty Harry–type who ceaselessly battles malevolent mystic Whistler (Stefani) and his lobotomoid minions, called trancers, in the ruins of a twenty-third century L.A. destroyed by "the Great Quake." When Whistler time-trips back to Angel City '85 to wipe out the ancestors of his future enemies—our Mr. Deth among them—Jack is quick to give pursuit. There he enlists the aid of innocent femme Leena (Hunt) in his bid to rid the world of this once and future menace. One or two interesting notions are introduced here—only those possessed of dependent personalities are susceptible to trancerhood, for example—but these are swiftly trampled in Empire's mad haste to follow in the *Terminator*'s giant footsteps. A definite step up from most Empire products, *Trancers* boasts its share of backers.

Transmutations (1987) ◆◆◇

D: *George Pavlou. Denholm Elliot, Steven Berkoff, Larry Lamb, Miranda Richardson, Nicola Cowper, Ingrid Pitt. 103 minutes. (Vestron)*

Another film project (see *Rawhead Rex*) that famed fright writer Clive Barker has largely disowned, *Transmutations* (formerly *Underworld*) features a *C.H.U.D.*-like plot that finds free-lance hero Lamb on the trail of a band of subterranean mutant junkies. The unfortunates in question, portrayed sympathetically, have been addicted to a heroinlike euphoriant (with drastic side effects) by the evil Dr. Savory (Elliot), who's in league with a cabal of local gangsters. The flick gets off to an extremely desultory start, unaided by leaden lead Lamb, who makes for a decidedly dull protagonist. *Transmutations* picks up a mite about midway through when the pic itself mutates into a decent—if weird—action outing. *Transmutations* is not the total dud Barker has branded it, but it's no *Hellbound* (see index) either. Look for former Hammer horror queen Pitt in a bit part as a madam.

Tron (1982) ◆◆◇

D: *Steven Lisberger. Jeff Bridges, Bruce Boxleitner, David Warner. 96 minutes. (Walt Disney)*

The Disney folks miscalculated here by placing hero Bridges *inside* a computer game—a premise that ultimately goes nowhere. The graphics are great, though, and fun to watch with the sound turned down.

20,000 Leagues Under the Sea (1954) ◆◆◆

D: *Richard Fleischer. Kirk Douglas, James Mason, Peter Lorre. 127 minutes. (Walt Disney)*

Disney accords gala treatment to Jules Verne's venerable tale in this FX-laden sci-fi spectacular pitting sailor Douglas against sinister submarine commander Captain Nemo (Mason).

Twilight Zone—The Movie (1983) ◆◆

D: *John Landis, Steven Spielberg, Joe Dante, George Miller. Vic Morrow, John Lithgow, Scatman Crothers, Kathleen Quinlan, Albert Brooks, Dan Aykroyd. 102 minutes. (Warner)*

Film-nerds-turned-moguls fulfill their childhood fantasies by redoing three episodes (and adding one original) from Rod Serling's cult teleseries. Not as good as the original; in fact, it's downright pointless.

Two Lost Worlds (1950) ◆◇ B&W

D: *Norman Dawn. James Arness, Laura Elliot, Bill Kennedy. 63 minutes. (Sony)*

Anyone who's ever spent a week

there knows how boring even *one* lost world can be; that goes double ditto for this stock-footage yawnfest. For hard-core '50s sci-fi fanatics and incurable James Arness addicts.

2001: A Space Odyssey (1968) ◆◆◆
D: *Stanley Kubrick. Keir Dullea, Gary Lockwood, William Sylvester. 141 minutes. (MGM/UA)*

The *Birth of a Nation* of SF films, *2001* offers revolutionary FX and a tight final episode with HAL the singing computer. But there *are* dull stretches.

2010 (1984) ◆◆◇
D: *Peter Hyams. Roy Scheider, John Lithgow, Helen Mirren. 116 minutes. (MGM/UA)*

Arthur C. Clarke's earnest script and Richard Edlund's spectacular FX are the highlights of this *2001* sequel, which starts out brightly before running out of rocket fuel.

The Ultimate Warrior (1975) ◆◆
D: *Robert Clouse. Yul Brynner, Max von Sydow, Joanna Miles, William Smith. 92 minutes. (Warner)*

Ecological catastrophes leave a twenty-first-century New York City in ruins; rival leaders Brynner and von Sydow compete to control what's left. Better than 1952's similarly themed *Captive Women* (NA), but not as good as John Carpenter's later *Escape from New York* (see index).

Uninvited (1988) ◆◆◇
D: *Greydon Clark. Alex Cord, George Kennedy, Clu Gulager, Toni Hudson,* *Eric Larson, Sharri Shattuck. 89 minutes. (New Star)*

Greydon (*Satan's Cheerleaders*) Clark's long, undistinguished directorial career reaches its entertaining nadir in this must-see mutant killer-cat movie. That's right, the menace here is a cute orange kitty, accidentally subjected to radioactive anabolic steroids or something in an ill-advised lab experiment conducted by Greydon himself in an equally ill-advised thespic cameo (which pales beside his offbeat perf as Acid, the LSD-eating biker in Al Adamson's *Satan's Sadists*). The cat in question stows away on a Fort Lauderdale luxury yacht inhabited by a trio of Wall Street crooks (vet B regulars Cord, Kennedy, and, in an especially awful role, Gulager) *and* a quintet of Spring Break party animals (don't ask). When not squabbling among themselves, our Cayman Islands–bound passengers spend their time trying (unsuccessfully) to fend off the relentless assaults of the terrifying tabby, who emits from its mouth a poisonous, rodentlike hand puppet. Not to be confused with the classic 1944 ghost story *The Uninvited* (NA), this *Uninvited* still shapes up as an essential experience for hard-core bad-movie buffs who think they've seen it all.

Unknown World (1951) ◆◆ B&W
D: *Terrell O. Morse. Bruce Kellogg, Marilyn Nash, Victor Killian. 73 minutes. (Prism)*

THE PHANTOM'S ULTIMATE VIDEO GUIDE

Liberally bent sci-fi quickie about a group of scientists who bore into the earth to find a safe haven from nuclear annihilation. Trouble is, after a funny start, the flick will bore *you* too.

Videodrome (1983) ◆◆◆
D: David Cronenberg. James Woods, Debbie Harry, Sonja Smits. 87 minutes. (MCA)

Cronenberg's perverse exercise in teleparanoia pits sleazy cable-station operator Woods against a mysterious S&M network that uses Blondie as bait. The demented story line and bizarre FX make this one a winner.

Village of the Damned (1960) ◆◆◆ B&W
D: Wolf Rilla. George Sanders, Barbara Shelley, John Phillips. 78 minutes. (MGM/UA)

A creepy, suspenseful sci-fi film based on John Wyndham's *The Midwich Cuckoos,* about a dozen pregnant British women who give birth to blond alien offspring. The rushed climax is *Village's* only major flaw. The sequel, *Children of the Damned,* remains unavailable as we go to press.

The Vindicator (1985) ◆◆◇
D: Jean-Claude Lord. Terri Austin, Richard Cox, David McIlwraith, Maury Chaykin, Pam Grier. 92 minutes. (Key)

Another blatant *Terminator* take-off that also incorporates compo-

nents from such vintage cheapies as *Frankenstein vs. the Space Monster* (see index) and *Colossus of New York,* (NA). Canada's *The Vindicator* (formerly *Frankenstein '88*) chronicles the misadventures of handsome researcher Carl Lehman (McIlwraith), who blows up in an accident at a shady ARC Industries lab. In a hook that prefigures *Robocop,* sinister scientist Randolph Whyte (Cox) implants Carl's brain and what remains of his face into an armored, computerized spacesuit that's programmed to kill. A dumb move on *his* part, since Carl promptly employs his new superpowers to track down and terminate the villains. Despite its '80s overlay (corporate conspiracy, gratuitous nudity, R-rated language, and explicit violence), *The Vindicator* is essentially old-fashioned, generally enjoyable sci-fi pulp. Highlights include Grier's macho perf as a professional psycho-hunter (appropriately named Hunter), a prolonged fistfight between a pregnant woman (Austin) and an overweight wimp (Chaykin), and deathless lines like, "I reprogrammed myself in the computer room—I don't have to kill anymore!" *The Vindicator* is dumb but compelling B-movie fun.

Voyage of the Rock Aliens (1985/1988) ◇
D: James Fargo. Pia Zadora, Ruth Gordon, Michael Berryman, Jermaine Jackson. 97 minutes. (Prism)

This has to rank among the major disappointments of the Phantom's young life. After a nearly three-year wait, *Voyage of the Rock Aliens*—skipping even a token theatrical release—finally turned up on video and, wouldn't you know it, it's not very good at all. In fact, it's downright awful. Yes, *Voyage* is a rare major showcase for the ever-unique Pia Zadora, and she *does* get to perform a promised outer-space duet with Jermaine Jackson. But *Voyage* is strictly gravity-bound from that point on. The pic's terminally unhip producers pathetically attempt to push every teen-market button. The result is a weightless, witless frat "comedy" in alien garb, as a lame intergalactic rock band—replete with your standard "cute" robot (named Rheena)—competes with a crew of earthly musicians who are just as dull. *Voyage* wastes both the late Ruth Gordon (as the local sheriff!) and Berryman (as a stereotypical chainsaw loony) in their sole screen teaming. Only Pia's tight short shorts earn this extraterrestrial turkey its half-phan.

Voyage to the Bottom of the Sea (1961) ◆◆◇

D: Irwin Allen. Walter Pidgeon, Peter Lorre, Barbara Eden, Frankie Avalon. 105 minutes. (Playhouse)

An atomic sub races to extinguish a burning Van Allen radiation belt before it's too late. Great cast and solid central story line make this more fun than most Irwin (Master of Disaster) Allen epics.

Voyage to the Prehistoric Planet (1965) NR

D: Peter Bogdanovich. Basil Rathbone, Faith Domergue. 92 minutes. (Sinister Cinema)

Roger Corman let the young Bogdanovich work on this cut-and-paste job, combining new inserts with Rathbone and Domergue with footage from the Russian space epic *Planeta Burg* (NA).

War of the Worlds (1953) ◆◆◆◇

D: Byron Haskin. Gene Barry, Ann Robinson, Les Tremayne, Carolyn Jones. 85 minutes. (Paramount)

H. G. Wells's story and producer George Pal's magnificent FX make this a spellbinding—if occasionally corny (in the religion and love-story tangents)—example of '50s sci-fi filmmaking at its best.

WarGames (1983) ◆◆◆

D: John Badham. Matthew Broderick, Ally Sheedy, Dabney Coleman. 114 minutes. (MGM/UA)

An intriguing SF thriller about a teen computer genius (Broderick) who unwittingly taps into the Pentagon's nuke-defense network. While the pic ultimately takes too many easy, crowd-pleasing turns, it still rates as entertaining fare and a far better bet than Marshall Brickman's similarly themed but insufferably smarmy *Manhattan Project*. (HBO)

Warning from Space (1956) NR B&W
D: Koji Shima. Toyomi Karita, Keizo Kawasaki. 85 minutes. (Sinister Cinema)
Straightforward sci-fi from Japan about benign aliens who venture earthward to deliver a dire message.

Warning Sign (1985) ◆◇
D: Hal Barwood. Sam Waterston, Kathleen Quinlan, Yaphet Kotto, Jeffrey De Munn, Richard Dysart, G. W. Bailey. 100 minutes. (CBS/Fox)
Big trubs at BioTek Agronomics: Seems the scientists clustered at this isolated Utah redoubt *haven't* been splicing wheat-germ genes at all but perfecting germ-warfare weaponry in direct and flagrant violation of international accords! When butterfingered Dr. Schmidt (*Police Academy*'s Bailey) drops a bacterial vial, the germs crash out and all hell breaks loose. *Warning Sign* promptly transmogrifies into a sort of *Night of the Living Technocrats* as the contaminated scientists mutate into homicidal loonies. While Major Connally (Kotto) tries to cover up the scandal, a worried sheriff (Waterston), aided by a boozy ex–BioTek worker (De Munn), attempts to spring his security-chief spouse Joan (Quinlan), who's trapped inside with the nutjobs. *Warning Sign*, though derivative of a dozen other movies, from *China Syndrome* to George Romero's *The Crazies*, is great dumb fun at first.

The initial pacing is swift, the acting a notch above the B-movie norm, the dialogue inspiredly stupid (e.g., "It's *rage*, Joannie," mouth-foaming scientist Dysart rants, "beautiful *rage!*"). Alas, what could have been a tight, brief thriller bloats to 100 minutes of mounting ennui.

Wasp Woman (1959) ◆◆◇ B&W
D: Roger Corman. Susan Cabot, Anthony Eisley, Michael Marks. 61 minutes. (Sinister Cinema)
Not about a rampaging distaff White Anglo Saxon Protestant but a typically iconic Corman cheapie about an ambitious cosmetic queen's addiction to a beauty cream that transforms her into the titular creature. Later remade, more or less, as *Evil Spawn* and *Rejuvenator* (see index).

Wavelength (1983) ◆◆◇
D: Mike Gray. Robert Carradine, Cherie Currie, Keenan Wynn. 87 minutes. (Embassy)
Pretty good B flick about a reclusive folk-rocker (Carradine) and a distaff drifter (fetching ex-Runaway Currie), who uncover undersize aliens being held subterranean captives by evil government officials. With script and direction by *China Syndrome*'s Gray and music by Tangerine Dream.

Westworld (1973) ◆◆◆
D: Michael Crichton. Yul Brynner, Richard Benjamin, James Brolin. 88 minutes. (MGM/UA)

Costumed androids run wild in a Huxleyesque amusement park—sort of a mechanized *Fantasy Island*. Brynner makes for a great robot gunslinger in a fun flick that puts its one gimmick to consistently creative use.

What Waits Below (1985) ◆◆◇
D: Don Sharp. Robert Powell, Lisa Blount, Timothy Bottoms. 88 minutes. (Lightning)

A longtime Forty-second Street perennial, this low-budget spelunking adventure finds a military/scientific team burrowing beneath the earth in search of a lost civilization of pale aliens in what's virtually a throwback to '50s sci-fi flicks. Not the worst, though.

When Worlds Collide (1951) ◆◆◇
D: Rudolph Maté. Barbara Rush, Richard Derr, John Hoyt. 81 minutes. (Paramount)

Producer George Pal's paranoid parable about Earth's imminent collision with a runaway planet is strengthened by imaginative FX that balance out a generally bland cast.

Where Time Began (1978) NR
D: Piquer Simon. Kenneth More, Pep Munne, Jack Taylor. 87 minutes. (Embassy)

A lower-bracketed *Journey to the Center of the Earth* retread recommended mostly for inveterate dinosaur devotees.

Wild Thing (1987) ◆◇
D: Max Reid. Rob Knepper, Kathleen Quinlan, Robert Davi, Maury Chaykin, Betty Buckley, Sean Hewitt. 92 minutes. (Paramount)

A sort of *Tarzan of the Tenements*, *Wild Thing* stars Knepper as an orphaned feral kid brought up by a brain-fried bag lady (Buckley) in a generic contempo ghetto known only as The Zone. The kid grows up to become a self-appointed protector of innocents like kindly social worker Quinlan and a scourge to the crooked cop (Chaykin) and local drug czar (Davi) who murdered his hippie parents some two decades earlier. In a misguided bid to transcend its formulaic trash-movie roots, *Wild Thing* strains for the lyrical, forcing Knepper to sound like a cross between Johnny Weismuller and a raving street paranoiac, and prompting Quinlan to inquire, "Who taught you to talk that way?" The culprit is John (*Brother from Another Planet*) Sayles, who probably knocked out this inane script during an especially febrile *Clan of the Cave Bear* coffee break. If nothing else, *Wild Thing* demonstrates that determinedly liberal-minded hackwork can be as deadly as any other kind.

Wired to Kill (1987) ◆
D: Franky Schaeffer. Devin Hoelscher, Emily Longstreth, Merritt Butrick, Frank Collison. 96 minutes. (Lightning)

Set in the postplague American wasteland of 1998, Schaeffer's *Wired to Kill* represents yet one more lame *Road Warrior* rip-off. A roving band of degenerate sub-morons led by a bespectacled, Shakespeare-spouting (!) Butrick causes all kinds of trouble for teenage mechanical genius Hoelscher, killing his grandmother, hospitalizing his mom, and breaking his legs. The police, as always, are powerless to help, so Devin and romantic interest Longstreth are forced to take the law into their own hands. Or more accurately, into the single claw of Devin's homemade remote-controlled robot, a low-tech but well-armed walking Tinker Toy dubbed Winston. Beyond its staggering unoriginality, *Wired to Kill* has about the lowest energy level of any pic in the Phantom's recent memory: The assembled thesps look bored to the point of catatonia; the "action" limps along at 33⅓; and even the oddly subdued soundtrack frequently lapses into lengthy stretches of sullen silence. Watching this won't get *you* wired. Other homegrown *Road Warrior* clones worth avoiding: *Dead Man Walking* (Republic), *Firefight* (TWE), *Killing Edge* (Video City), *Survival Zone* (Prism), *Wheels of Fire* and Cirio (*Demon of Paradise*) Santiago's latest loser *Future Hunters* (both Vestron).

Woman in the Moon (1929) NR Silent. B&W
D: Fritz Lang. Gerda Maurus, Fritz Rasp, Willy Fritsch. 156 minutes. (Video Yesteryear)

Lang followed up his mega-opus *Metropolis* (see index) with this futuristic look at interplanetary travel. Video Yesteryear stocks the complete 156-minute print. Of interest mainly to serious SF scholars and Fritz Lang lovers.

World Gone Wild (1988) ◆◇
D: Lee H. Katzin. Bruce Dern, Michael Paré, Catherine Mary Stewart, Adam Ant, Anthony James, Rick Podell. 95 minutes. (Media)

As third-rate *Road Warrior* rip-offs go—and we promise this is the last one you'll hear about *here*—Katzin's postapocalyptic *World Gone Wild*, set in 2087, opens more promisingly than most, with a desert massacre perpetrated by power-mad Ant and a legion of brainwashed lackeys clad in white choir robes (!). There are, in fact, just enough imaginative riffs here—e.g., the killer choirboys' bible is an "ancient" tome titled *The Wit and Wisdom of Charles Manson*—to keep the optimistic viewer hanging on in the hope that the flick will eventually take off. Instead, *World Gone Wild* settles for being simultaneously smug and stupid. When postnuke hipster Dern recruits a band of scuzzy mercenaries led by Paré to defend an embattled community from Ant's hordes, the pic takes a lazy, predictable turn into *Magnificent Seven*-manqué turf. Withal, *World Gone Wild* is lame enough to make the Phantom yearn for Dern's comparatively inspired *Incredible Two-Headed Transplant* days.

X—the Man with the X-Ray Eyes (1963)
♦♦♦
D: Roger Corman. Ray Milland, Diana Van Der Vlis, John Hoyt, Harold J. Stone, Don Rickles. 79 minutes. (Warner)

William Castle's *The Tingler* (1959) may have been the first official LSD movie, and Corman's *The Trip* (1967) the definitive acid-exploitation experience, but Rog's sci-fi foray *X—the Man with the X-Ray Eyes* proves more harrowingly hallucinogenic than either of the above. Milland stars as a scientist who devises a formula enabling him to see through solid matter. The transformation is fun enough during its early *Immoral Mr. Teas*–type phase, where Ray employs his newfound ocular powers to penetrate distaff wardrobes (!). But Ray soon starts seeing far more than he bargained for on his way to eventual madness and the film's unforgettable revival-meeting climax. *The Man with the X-Ray Eyes* (which also contains Don Rickles's, as a carny barker, only major horror-movie contribution) is packed with surreal imagery worthy of frequent video replays.

Xtro (1983) ♦♦◊
D: Harry Bromley Davenport. Philip Sayer, Bernice Stegers. 82 minutes. (HBO)

A flawed but fairly bizarre tale of an alien takeover perpetrated on an unsuspecting earthling (Sayer), who returns, after three years in space, in radically altered form.

Zardoz (1974) ♦♦♦
D: John Boorman. Sean Connery, Charlotte Rampling, Sara Kestelman. 105 minutes. (Key)

Boorman's visually expressive vision of a futuristic dystopia (called Vortex) stars Connery as Zed the Exterminator, a "primitive" exploited by a ruling class of sexless intellectuals. The myth-minded auteur (*Excalibur, Emerald Forest*) manages to make this ontological SF satire consistently compelling fare.

Zone Troopers (1985) ♦♦
D: Danny Belson. Timothy Van Patten, Tim Thomerson, Biff Manard, Art La Fleur. 86 minutes. (Lightning)

Zone Troopers offers a fresh twist on the *E.T.* trend by integrating an alien-landing motif into an otherwise conventional, cartoon-level World War II flick. While the pic exhibits more range than most Empire products, it too often drifts into stupidity and imitation. (The dialogue covers the complete catalog of combat clichés, lifted from the likes of Sam Fuller's *Steel Helmet* and Lewis Milestone's *A Walk in the Sun*.) Thomerson, Manard, La Fleur, and Van Patten (as the GI sci-fi fan who first befriends the aliens) emote effectively in roles that, thirty years ago, would have been handled by Gene Evans, Keenan Wynn, Cameron Mitchell, and Harvey Lembeck. *Zone Troopers* could have been a solid low-budget entry, but its modest virtues are continually sabotaged by its relentlessly parasitic imagination.

Fantasy

Amazing Grace and Chuck (1987) ♦
D: Mike Newell. Jamie Lee Curtis, Gregory Peck, Alex English, Joshua Zuehlke, William L. Petersen, Dennis Lipscomb. 116 minutes. (HBO)

Amazing Grace and *Up*chuck, if you ask *us*. This mutantoid antinuke parable describes a worldwide jock revolt (!) triggered by concerned Little Leaguer Chuck (Zuehlke) and Celtics superstar "Amazing Grace" Smith (played by real-life hoopster and part-time poet English). Now, we deplore the prospect of global annihilation as much as the next phantom (we'd be out of a job, just for starters), but this movie almost makes us change our mind. Not only does producer/scripter David Field (cable-TV titan Ted Turner receives an "executive consultant" credit) have a bad case of static in the attic, but his fog-noggined flick also wastes the talents of *Halloween* ingenue Curtis, who, as Amazing's business manager, doesn't get to scream even *once*. (A brief crying jag and a moan of "Oh, God" are the most she musters here.) Watching *Amazing Grace and Chuck* shortened the Phantom's life by 116 minutes; think twice before you let it do the same to yours.

Ator the Fighting Eagle (1983) ♦◇
D: David Hills. Miles O'Keeffe, Sabrina Siani. 98 minutes. (HBO)

O'Keeffe, the '80s answer to Gordon Mitchell, plays Thor's son Ator in a boring sword-and-sorcery romp that prompted the equally dull sequel *Blademaster* (Media). For hard-core Miles maniacs only.

Barbarian Queen (1984) ♦♦
D: Hector Olivera. Lana Clarkson, Dawn Dunlap, Susana Traverso, Victor Bo. 78 minutes. (Vestron)

An innocent tribe is wantonly raped, looted, plundered, and pillaged by your basic savage horde, whose marauding members get their comeuppance at the hands and broadswords of buxom heroine Amethea (Clarkson) and her heavy-breathing hench-femmes. While primitive in plot and performance, this violent T&A-accented throwback to the Italo muscleman movies of yore boasts a few B-pic pluses: wonderfully bad dubbing, lots of gory swordplay, great-looking gals with health-club bods, and a mercifully brief running time. It's no *Wild Women of Wongo* (see index), but then, what *is*? Available in R and unrated versions.

The Barbarians (1987) ◆◇

D: Ruggero Deodato. David Paul, Peter Paul, Richard Lynch, Eve La Rue, Virginia Bryant, Michael Berryman. 88 minutes. (Media)

Cannon's aggressively stupid *Hercules in the Valley of the Road Warriors*–type adventure begins brightly enough with a strenuous pitched battle between the evil Kadar's (Lynch) forces and the beleaguered, peace-seeking, nomadic Ragnicks. Two of the captured Ragnicks are twin boys who grow up (though none of the other characters seem to age) to become the Barbarian Brothers, played by real-life megabicepped twins David and Peter Paul. *The Barbarians* starts its rapid celluloid slide as soon as our boneheaded bodybuilders—who come equipped with Bronx accents (!)—enter the picture and set out on a peripatetic (and mostly pathetic) quest to reunite with the surviving Ragnicks. The pic's tongue-in-cheek tone fails to salvage the proceedings, though La Rue offers some visual relief as a curvaceous fugitive the boys meet on the road, and Berryman sticks around long enough to show off his shiny dome.

The Beastmaster (1982) NR

D: Don Coscarelli. Marc Singer, Tanya Roberts, Rip Torn. 118 minutes. (MGM/UA)

Coscarelli, of *Phantasm* fame, tackles the sword-and-sandal genre with hero Singer stalking evil sorceror Torn and courting slave bimbo Roberts.

Beauty and the Beast (1946) ◆◆◆◇ B&W

D: Jean Cocteau. Jean Marais, Josette Day, Marcel André. 92 minutes. (Embassy)

Cocteau's classic reinterpretation of this venerable fable, filled with unforgettable black-and-white imagery, rates as must viewing for fantasy-film fans.

Big Trouble in Little China (1986) ◆◆◆

D: John Carpenter. Kurt Russell, Kim Cattrall, Dennis Dun, Victor Wong, James Hong, Kate Burton. 99 minutes. (CBS/Fox)

Kurt (*Escape from New York*) Russell is trucker Jack Burton, an All-American jerk noir who witnesses the airport abduction of his Chinese pal Wang's (Dun) bride-to-be, the emerald-eyed Suzee Pai. The ensuing chase leads our heroes to a subterranean Chinatown crawling with ornery kung-fu demons (superfluously equipped with machine guns) and ruled by the ancient evil spirit Lo Pan (Hong), a cross between Fu Manchu and a Chinese Howard Hughes. Carpenter directs his stoned pulp adventure in high, throwaway style, sending up everything from chopsocky cheapies to high-tech extravaganzas like *Raiders of the Lost Ark*. The action is alternately violent and absurdist (and nothing if not nonstop), while the characters exchange more clichés than you could, well, shake a stick at. At times, *Big Trouble* plays more broadly than it ought (Russell's Duke Wayne impersonation grows stale pretty pronto) and revels too much in its own lay-it-on-thick *shtick*. But *Big Trouble* moves fast, aims to please, and hits more often than it misses.

Bill and Coo (1947) NR

D: Dean Riesner. Narrated by Ken Murray. Starring lots of trained birds. 61 minutes. (Video Yesteryear)

The only feature film starring—and probably fashioned for—our fine-feathered friends. The bird "zoo" contains a caged kitten (!). Pretty hallucinatory going. You want it, Video Yesteryear's got it.

Black Orpheus (1959) ◆◆◆◇

D: Marcel Camus. Breno Mello, Marpessa Dawn, Lea Garcia. 103 minutes. (Connoisseur)

Camus's Brazil-set retelling of the Orpheus-Eurydice legend offers an exciting score, stunning color photography, and the ever-alluring Dawn in her only starring role. After years of virtual unavailability—CBS/Fox discontinued the tape—*Black Orpheus* was reissued on the art-oriented Connoisseur label. Subtitled.

The Boy with Green Hair (1948) ◆◆

D: Joseph Losey. Dean Stockwell, Pat O'Brien, Robert Ryan, Barbara Hale, Regis Toomey, Walter Catlett. 82 minutes. (Nostalgia Merchant)

A cult film long before the term was coined, Losey's fable about an American war orphan (Stockwell) whose hair turns the titular hue seems pretty dated today. Awk-wardly related via Stockwell's flashback narration—third-billed Ryan receives scant screen time here as the boy's patient auditor—the film explains that Dean's green mop (the color of spring, hope, and renewal) is a symbol for a war-free future. Director Losey was obviously attracted to the story's antiwar message—he would incur the wrath of McCarthyites a few years thence and relocate to England—but *Boy* is not a smoothly told or especially pointed tale.

The Clan of the Cave Bear (1985) ◆

D: Michael Chapman. Daryl Hannah, Pamela Reed, James Remar, Thomas G. Waites, John Doolittle, Curtis Armstrong. 100 minutes. (CBS/Fox)

Hannah is a lost blond Cro-Mag cutie taken in by a wandering tribe of Neanderthal uglies in Chapman's largely unsubtle adaptation of Jean Auel's best seller. Not only is Daryl smarter and prettier than her adoptive tribespeople, but she's *muy más macho* too, employing her superior hunting skills to further the cause of cave-age feminism. John Sayles's grunt-heavy script and Chapman's dull direction sink this misbegotten deal in the first reel, and the flick's scattered unintentional laughs fail to supply sufficient bad entertainment to make a rental worthwhile.

Clash of the Titans (1981) ◆◆

D: Desmond Davis. Laurence Olivier, Harry Hamlin, Judi Bowker, Ursula Andress. 118 minutes. (MGM/UA)

The plot may be pure comic-book mythology, and there are no actual Greek-type Titans on view, but there are enough spectacular FX set pieces to make *Clash* a treat for fantasy fans, if an overblown bore for the rest.

Conan the Barbarian (1982) ◆◆
D: John Milius. Arnold Schwarzenegger, Sandahl Bergman, James Earl Jones, Max von Sydow. 129 min. (MCA).

The pic that put Mr. 'Ceps on the movie map: Arnie brings his anvil acting style and bloodied broadsword to the screen as the first celluloid incarnation of Robert E. Howard's pulp hero.

Conan the Destroyer (1984) ◆◇
D: Richard Fleischer. Arnold Schwarzenegger, Wilt Chamberlain, Grace Jones. 103 min. (MCA)

This inferior sequel finds Arnie overstaying his welcome in Conanland in a flick light on logic and heavy on FX.

The Cosmic Eye (1985) NR
D: Faith Hubley. Voices of Maureen Stapleton, Dizzy Gillespie, Sam Hubley. 76 minutes. (Walt Disney)

An animated fable about jazzmen from outer space (!), aimed at kids and incorporating earlier work from the John and Faith Hubley animation team.

Darby O'Gill and the Little People (1959) ◆◆◆
D: Robert Stevenson. Albert Sharpe, Janet Munro, Sean Connery. 93 minutes. (Walt Disney)

One of Disney's best efforts, this imaginative leprechaun romp features fine FX and an original, idiosyncratic approach to juvenile fantasy that will involve adults as well.

The Dark Crystal (1983) ◆◇
D: Jim Henson, Frank Oz. Jim Henson, Billie Whitelaw, Frank Oz. 93 minutes. (HBO)

Muppet masters Henson and Oz designed this puppet sci-fi fantasy. The Phantom found it dull and depressing, but younger viewers may be made of sterner stuff.

Deathstalker II: Duel of the Titans (1987) ◆
D: Jim Wynorski. John Terlesky, Monique Gabrielle, John La Zar, Toni Naples, Maria Socas, Queen Kong. 78 minutes. (Vestron)

Even those few who remember Cirio H. Santiago's original *Deathstalker* (Vestron) are likely to be disappointed by this cheapjack garbage, which tries to cover its lack of production values and talent with desperate stabs at campy humor and sub-Stooges slapstick *shticks*. Aside from a few fetching femmes (including *Penthouse* Pet/heroine Gabrielle) and La Zar (Z-Man in Russ Meyer's *Beyond the Valley of the Dolls*), this one has nothing to offer. Monique says it all when she exclaims, "When the legend's told, nobody's gonna believe we were this stupid!"

Dinosaurus! (1960) ◆◆◇
D: Irvin S. Yeaworth, Jr. Ward Ramsey, Paul Lukather, Kristina Hanson. 85 minutes. (New World)

A generally fun, if mindless, tale of a reawakened caveman (Martell) and his slapstick efforts to cope with the modern world. Sort of like *Iceman,* recast with Shemp Howard in the lead. The titular prehistoric creature and ex–burlesque comic Mousie Garner also put in appearances.

Dr. Strange (1978) NR
D: Phillip DeGuere. Peter Hooten, Jessica Walter, John Mills. 94 minutes. (MCA)

Marvel Comics fans should appreciate this made-for-TV movie devoted to superhero Dr. Strange and bolstered by John Mills's turn as a veteran sorcerer.

Dragonslayer (1981) ♦♦
D: Matthew Robbins. Peter MacNicol, Ralph Richardson, Caitlin Clarke. 110 minutes. (Paramount)

Elaborate FX and Richardson's unfortunately brief cameo as an addled elderly magician are the highlights of this ultimately tedious medieval youth-pic.

Duel of Champions (1961) ♦♦
D: Ferdinando Baldi. Alan Ladd, Franca Bettoja, Franco Fabrizi. 106 minutes. (Lightning)

Noteworthy chiefly for constituting Ladd's total contribution to the sword-and-sandal genre. The diminutive star doesn't take on the Steve Reeves role, though.

The Dungeonmaster (1985) ♦◊
D: Rosemarie Turko, John Buechler, Charles Band, David Allen, Steve Ford, Peter Manoogian, Ted Nicolaou. Jeffrey Byron, Richard Moll, Leslie Wing, Blackie Lawless, Danny Dick. 80 minutes. (Lightning)

According to the credits, it required the efforts of seven directors to assemble this exercise in supernatural ennui. *The Dungeonmaster* borrows its basics from Empire's earlier *Ghoulies.* In that one, the plot centered on a girl, a boy, and his ghoulies; here, it's a girl, a boy, and his computer. (Hey, if you can't steal from yourself, who *can* you steal from? Certainly not the TSR Inc. game "Dungeons and Dragons": *Dungeonmaster's* original print ads even carried a disclaimer to that effect.) Some of the FX here are briefly entertaining, but unless you're a hard-core video-game buff, *The Dungeonmaster* represents a prime example of why the now-vanished Empire Pictures earned its defunct status.

Excalibur (1981) ♦♦♦
D: John Boorman. Nicol Williamson, Nigel Terry, Helen Mirren. 141 minutes. (Warner)

Boorman does a good job of translating the Arthurian legends into a crowd-pleasing FX orgy, while creating an effective medieval atmosphere and retaining an often eccentric POV. Better than *Sword of the Valiant* (MGM/UA), where even the presence of Peter Cushing and Sean Connery can't counteract casting Miles O'Keeffe as Sir Gawain. *Merlin and the Sword* (Vestron) and the animated *Sword in the Stone* (Walt Disney) offer further Excalibur variations. Fantasy-film fans of a medieval bent may also want to try the lavish *Ladyhawke* (Warner) and David Bowie's *Labyrinth* (Nelson).

The Fabulous Baron Munchausen (1943) ◆◆◇

D: Josef von Baky. Hans Albers, Wilhelm Bendow, Brigitte Sornay. 110 minutes. (Video City)

An all-star epic based on the hyperbolic adventures of the titular Teutonic hero (played by Albers), *Baron* was lensed at Germany's UFA Studios (to celebrate the latter's twenty-fifth anniversary) in Agfacolor and then-experimental 35mm and took five years to film (1939–43) and still longer to reconstruct once the negative deteriorated. While the film boasts impressive sweep and imaginative FX, we found it of more cultural than entertainment value. But it's a must for couchside celluloid historians and an interesting companion piece to Terry Gilliam's controversial revamp *The Adventures of Baron Munchausen*. International Historic Films also carries a cassette version, titled simply *Munchausen* and running 122 minutes.

Fantasy Film Worlds of George Pal (1988) NR

D: Arnold Leibovit. Appearances by Ray Bradbury, Charlton Heston, Janet Leigh. 93 minutes. (LCA)

A compendium of clips from Pal's best films—including *The Time Machine, War of the Worlds,* and *When Worlds Collide*—plus interviews with Pal associates and the FX pioneer himself, along with detailed looks at the master at work.

Fire and Ice (1983) NR

D: Ralph Bakshi. Voices of Susan Tyrrell, Maggie Roswell, William Ostrander. 81 minutes. (RCA/Columbia)

An animated sword-and-sorcery epic from Ralph Bakshi, of interest mostly to the hard-core headbanger set.

The Giant of Metropolis (1962) NR

D: Umberto Scarpelli. Gordon Mitchell, Roldano Lupi, Bella Cortez. 82 minutes. (Sinister Cinema)

The use of science-fiction elements adds some novelty value to an otherwise routine Steve Reeves rip-off, with Gordon Mitchell as the muscle-bound hero.

The Giants of Thessaly (1960) NR

D: Riccardo Freda. Roland Carey, Ziva Rodann, Massimo Girotti. 86 minutes. (Sinister Cinema)

Jason and Orpheus search for the Golden Fleece and encounter all manner of strange creatures and odd obstacles, but the real treat here is B-movie diva Ziva Rodann's always compelling presence.

Goliath and the Barbarians (1960) NR

D: Carlo Campogalliani. Steve Reeves, Bruce Cabot, Giulia Rubini. 86 minutes. (MGM/UA)

Mighty Reeves, who first bared his superpecs in Ed Wood, Jr.'s, *Jailbait*, still has a lot of fans out there in Videoland, judging by the copious mail the Phantom's received from Steve's supporters. This is considered one of his better Italo efforts.

Greystoke: The Legend of Tarzan, Lord of the Apes (1984) ◆◆◆

D: Hugh Hudson. Christopher Lambert, Ralph Richardson, Ian Holm. 130 minutes. (Warner)

A superior *Tarzan* remake, with fine supporting performances turned in by actual chimps *and* their costumed human stand-ins. Richardson's not bad either as wildman Lambert's doddering English grandfather. A fun package. Fans of more traditional Tarzan fare can also find Edgar Rice Burroughs's celebrated apeman in the original Elmo Lincoln silents *Tarzan of the Apes* and *The Adventures of Tarzan* (Video Yesteryear), Johnny Weismuller as *Tarzan the Apeman* (MGM/UA), Buster Crabbe as *Tarzan the Fearless*, Glen Morris in *Tarzan's Revenge*, and Gordon Scott in *Tarzan and the Trappers* (all from Sinister Cinema), and John and Bo Derek's legendary *Tarzan, the Ape Man* (MGM/UA), with Miles O'Keeffe.

Gulliver's Travels (1939) NR

D: Dave Fleischer. Voices of Lanny Ross, Jessica Dragonette. 74 minutes. (Video Warehouse, others)

A condescending and simplistic musical cartoon version of the classic novel that loses most of Swift's savage satire but remains a visual treat for fans of animator Fleischer. The 1979 animated version, directed by Peter R. Hunt, is also available (United).

Hercules (1959) ◆◆

D: Pietro Francisci. Steve Reeves, Sylva Koscina, Fabrizio Mioni. 107 minutes. (VidAmerica)

The Italo flick that launched a thousand sword-and-sandal cheapies and sent hordes of acting hopefuls scampering to the nearest gym. Reeves's less-than-vaunted thespic rep gains in value on video, at least when compared to Lou Ferrigno's imitative efforts *Hercules* (MGM/UA) and *Hercules II* (NA). VidAmerica has the uncut versions of *Hercules* and *Hercules Unchained*. For insatiable Reeves addicts, Steve is also on rippling view in *Last Days of Pompeii* (Goodtimes), *Last Glory of Troy* (Sinister Cinema), *Morgan the Pirate* and *Thief of Bagdad* (both Embassy), and *Pirates of the Seven Seas* (Lightning).

Hercules in the Haunted World (1961) ◆◆◇

D: Mario Bava. Reg Park, Christopher Lee, Leonora Ruffo. 83 minutes. (Sinister Cinema, others)

Gothic horror director Bava lends some eerily surreal touches that help elevate this Herc sequel above most of its cardboard ilk. Followed by *Hercules and the Captive Women* and *Hercules Against the Moon Men*, both available from Sinister Cinema, which also carries the deathless *Loves of Her-*

cules, with Jayne Mansfield and hubby Mickey Hargitay, plus a number of other sword-and-sandal obscurities, including several *Samson* and *Ursus* titles. Movies Unlimited (see Videorama) also stocks a wide array of muscleman movies, from Unicorn's *Maciste in Hell* to Charter's *Terror of Rome Against the Son of Hercules*.

Highlander (1986) ◇
D: Russell Mulcahy. Christopher Lambert, Roxanne Hart, Sean Connery, Clancy Brown, Beatie Edney, Alan North. 111 minutes. (HBO)

One thing you can't accuse Russell (*Razorback*) Mulcahy's *Highlander* of is typecasting. This mindless heavy-metal sword-and-sorcery clinker stars French thesp Christopher (*Greystoke*) Lambert as Connor McLeod, a remarkably spry 568-year-old Scotsman posing as an American antique dealer. Connor understandably owns one of the oddest accents ever heard on screen. (As a member of New York's Finest pithily puts it, "You talk funny!") But it's no odder than the one sported by costar Connery, a Welshman cast here as Connor's Yoda-like Spanish-Egyptian (!) mentor, Ramirez. Seems that Chris and Sean are fellow Immortals—mysterious warriors destined to spend their lengthy, even interminable, lives decapitating others of their ilk. (Why? you ask. Well, Chris puts that very query to Sean as the latter instructs him in the tricks of their

arcane trade. "Who knows?" comes Sean's reasoned reply.) While *Highlander* lifts liberally from such varied sources as *The Terminator*, *Conan*, *The Empire Strikes Back*, *Rocky*, and *Chariots of Fire*, our fave is its touching *Elvira Madigan* steal: Sean and Chris's slo-mo sylvan romp is almost worth the price of an overnight rental.

Iron Warrior (1987) ◆
D: Al Bradley. Miles O'Keeffe, Savina Gersak, Tim Lane, Elizabeth Kaza. 84 minutes. (Media)

This sequel to 1983's sword-and-sorcery snoozefest *Ator, the Fighting Eagle* (not to be confused with "Ajax, the Foaming Cleanser") finds O'Keeffe reprising his role as the hunky Ator, he of the rippling pecs and wooden personality. Here he's pitted against the skull-masked title villain and evil sorceress Kaza (who resembles Phyllis Diller in a bright red frightwig), united in their determination to thwart Ator's attempts to restore shapely princess Gersak to the throne of Dragmoor. This deadly dull dud comes to fleeting life only during Ator's snappy repartee with the Princess. To wit:

Princess: These dark powers are taking over my kingdom.
Ator: So I noticed.

To say nothing of:

Princess: What if they kill you?
Ator: Then I'd be dead.

Precisely the condition of this celluloid stiff. Miles and Savina are reunited in *Lone Runner* (TWE), which is even worse than *Iron Warrior*.

Jason and the Argonauts (1963) ◆◆◆
D: Don Chaffey. Todd Armstrong, Gary Raymond, Nancy Kovack, Honor Blackman. 104 minutes. (RCA/Columbia)

Not a rock band but a popular Brit retelling of the search for the Golden Fleece, bolstered by Ray Harryhausen's FX and Bernard Hermann's score.

Johnny in the Valley of the Giants (1950) NR
(Sinister Cinema)

An obscure animated feature about a group of boys whose overnight camp-out leads to a frightening journey through the title locale.

The Jungle Book (1942) ◆◆◆
D: Zoltan Korda. Sabu, Joseph Calleia, Rosemary DeCamp. 105 minutes. (Embassy, others)

The one-and-only Sabu is in fine form as Kipling's feral boy, who enjoys smoother relations with monkeys and elephants than he does with the civilized humans he encounters.

King of Hearts (1966) ◆◆◇
D: Philippe De Broca. Alan Bates, Genevieve Bujold, Pierre Brasseur. 102 minutes. (CBS/Fox)

Scottish soldier Bates wanders into an abandoned French village appropriated by escaped mental patients. De Broca's World War I—set fable wavers between the satiric and the sentimental and has been seen at least twice by virtually everyone who came of age in the late '60s.

Knightriders (1981) ◆◆◆
D: George A. Romero. Ed Harris, Gary Lahti, Tom Savini, Amy Ingersoll. 145 minutes. (Media)

Modern-day motorcycle knights stage jousting tournaments and strive against all odds to uphold a chivalrous code in an adventure fable that represented a worthy foray into new celluloid territory for *Living Dead* director Romero.

Legend (1986) ◆
D: Ridley Scott. Tom Cruise, Mia Sara, Tim Curry, David Bennent, Alice Playten, Billy Barty. 89 minutes. (MCA)

Universal execs reportedly repeatedly delayed the theatrical release of Scott's *Legend* while frantic film editors hacked the two-hour opus down to its present 89 minutes. Even in its current truncated video state, *Legend* manages to pack in more boredom per frame than most flicks; one can only shudder to think what unspeakable fragments lie rotting on the cutting-room floor. Our story unfolds long ago (though not in a galaxy far away) in an enchanted forest where feathers, leaves, and what looks like lint are all the time swirling about. (*Legend* is also a leading contender for the *Robot Monster* Memorial Award for Most Extensive Use of a Bubble Machine.) As we open, Princess Lily (Sara), a sprightly waif, glides through the expensive scenery for a rendezvous with young Jack (Cruise), the local unicorn keeper. Meanwhile, back in hell, the subterranean Lord of Darkness (Curry) decides he's had enough of this insufferable sweetness and light and so dispatches hit-goblin Barty to off one of the "ugly, one-horned mules." Once this is accomplished, the surviving unicorn silently informs Jack (Mr. Ed's voice would have come in handy here) that he must do battle with the L of D himself in order to restore the world's balance of darkness and light. As *Legend* limps along, we're further treated to endless enchanted-forest footage, elaborate but wasted FX work, and irritating elves who supply slapstick low-comedy relief of a sort unseen onscreen since Fuzzy St. John's heyday. If Tinkerbell had a nightmare, it would probably look a lot like this.

The Lord of the Rings (1978) NR
D: Ralph Bakshi. Voices of Christopher Guard, William Squire, John Hurt. 133 minutes. (HBO)

The Phantom's never made a hobbit of reading or watching Tolkien's whimsical works, but JRR buffs, as well as Bakshi

backers, may want to add this animated epic to their home-vid libraries.

Lost Horizon (1937) ◆◆◆ B&W
D: Frank Capra. Ronald Colman, Jane Wyatt, John Howard, Sam Jaffe, Edward Everett Horton. 132 minutes. (RCA/Columbia)

While maybe not quite the flawless masterpiece many have proclaimed it, *Lost Horizon* certainly ranks as quality offbeat entertainment, with Jaffe especially impressive as the High Lama. Still photos serve as narrative bridges over those brief segments missing from the original print; the audio track is intact. This is the only Frank Capra movie that made it into this volume.

The Magic Sword (1962) ◆◆◆
D: Bert I. Gordon. Basil Rathbone, Gary Lockwood, Estelle Winwood, Anne Helm. 80 minutes. (Video Yesteryear, others)

One of Mr. BIG's better productions, with Lockwood as Saint George, aided by a top veteran cast, improved FX, and a wisely brief running time.

The Man Who Could Work Miracles (1937) ◆◆◆◇ B&W
D: Lothar Mendes. Roland Young, Ralph Richardson, Joan Gardner. 82 minutes. (Embassy)

Young is a mega-ordinary haberdashery worker who discovers he possesses special powers in this popular and memorably bizarre Brit adaptation of H. G. Wells's famous fantasy. With fright fave George Zucco as an unflappable butler, Ernest Thesiger as an idealistic loony, and a young George Sanders typecast as the god "Indifference," plus neat FX courtesy of Ned Mann.

Masters of the Universe (1987) ◆◇
D: Gary Goddard. Dolph Lundgren, Frank Langella, Meg Foster, Billy Barty, Courtenay Cox, James Tolkan. 106 minutes. (Warner)

Cannon's fantasy kidfest *Masters of the Universe* toplines Lundgren as blond beefcake superhero He-Man. Dolph and pals battle evil sorcerer Skeletor—hammily interpreted in dinner-theater Shakespearean style by Langella, made up to resemble Jack Palance on a bad day—for possession of a cosmic key crafted by the pint-size Gwildor (Billy Barty). The struggle soon shifts from outer space to our own "primitive, tasteless planet" (as Skeletor describes it) and rages for a cerebrum-numbing 106 minutes. Kids under eight may not be bored; all others beware. Dolph's workout tape, *Maximum Potential*, is also available (IVE).

One Million B.C. (1940) ◆◆◇ B&W
D: Hal Roach. Hal Roach, Jr., Victor Mature, Carole Landis, Lon Chaney, Jr. 80 minutes. (Fox Hills)

Oddly ahead of its time in its overall weirdness, *One Million B.C.* remains an interesting curio and the model for countless caveman epics to come. Poverty-row auteurs raided the FX footage with reckless abandon in countless cheapies. The Raquel Welch remake remains unavailable.

The Perils of Gwendoline (in the Land of the Yik Yak) (1985) ◆◆◇
D: Just Jaeckin. Tawny Kitaen, Brent Huff, Zabou, Bernadette Lafont, Jean Rougerie. 88 minutes. (Vestron)

Throughout the '40s and '50s, Australian-born cartoonist John Alexander Scott Coutts, working under the pencil-name John Willie, created a series of sly high-camp comics, with an emphasis on mock-bondage tableaux, chronicling the exotic, erotic adventures of his oft-endangered heroine Sweet Gwendoline. In the celluloid version, Gwen, flawlessly embodied by the alluring Kitaen, hires hunky adventurer Huff to help her locate her long-lost lepidopterist dad, last sighted in the forbidden land of Yik Yak. ("Nobody goes there," an opium-smoking local informs them, adding, with impeccable logic, "and nobody comes back.") Gwen and friends brave perilous jungles, poisonous winds, cannibals, and a subterranean tribe of warrior women (in Valkyrie helmets and black leather scanties, no less—and no *more*, either). *The Perils of Gwendoline* succeeds in capturing the spirit if not the letter of cartoonist Coutts's decidedly offbeat imagination: The tone is light, the sets fanciful, the performances appropriately deadpan. The elaborate "Ben-Her" scene alone, featuring a femme-drawn chariot race, is enough to compensate for the flick's sloppy script and occasionally poor pacing.

The Point (1971) NR
D: Fred Wolf. Narrated by Ringo Starr. 74 minutes. (Vestron)

An animated fable, originally aired on network TV (where it was narrated by Dustin Hoffman), about a boy whose pointed head leads to social ostracism, *The Point* has garnered a considerable cassette following.

Quest for Fire (1981) ◆◆◆◇
D: Jean-Jacques Annaud. Everett McGill, Rae Dawn Chong, Ron Perlman, Nameer El Kadi. 97 minutes. (CBS/Fox)

Probably the greatest caveman movie ever made. A trio of prehistoric tribesmen—sort of earnest Stone-Age Stooges—set off for parts unknown in search of the title element. Along the way, they encounter hungry cannibals, hostile apemen, giant mastodons (who are at least willing to negotiate), and Rae Dawn Chong (a welcome find during any alfresco excursion) as a stray member of a more advanced tribe. While we weren't too impressed with An-

thony Burgess's minimal linguistic contributions, the gestural thesping (Desmond Morris, of *The Naked Ape* fame, served as a consultant here) is first-rate, the action exciting, and the story at once funny, rousing, and poignant. Unfairly ignored during its initial theatrical release, *Quest's* cable-TV and video afterlife have since gained it the audience support it has long merited.

Ratboy (1986) ◇
D: Sondra Locke. Sondra Locke, Robert Townsend, Christopher Hewett, Larry Hankin, Gerrit Graham, Louie Anderson. 105 minutes. (Warner)

Clint Eastwood must like former costar Sondra Locke a *lot* to lend a helping hand to this embarrassing "cult" movie manqué. The plot finds hopeless schemer Locke (who also directed) running into the title anomaly, an unexplained hybrid between rat and boy who, in his ubiquitous shades, resembles Bob Dylan on a *terrible* day. With the help of her "comic" relief brothers, Sondra runs Ratboy through the L.A. wringer in a misguided bid for fame and fortune. We strongly advise you to bypass this witless fable, which fails equally in the satire, whimsy, suspense, and poignancy departments. The brain cells you save may be your own.

Red Sonja (1985) ◆
D: Richard Fleischer. Brigitte Nielsen, Arnold Schwarzenegger, Sandahl

Bergman, Paul Smith, Ernie Reyes, Jr., Ronald Lacey. 89 minutes. (CBS/Fox)

On the cybernetic heels of his *Terminator* triumph, Arnie unwisely returns to the grunt-and-groan (he grunts; we groan) wastelands of Conan country (though in Arn's defense, it should be noted that he manages to stay offscreen for more than half the movie). Called Calidor here, Arnie assists manhating heroine Sonja (woodenly embodied by Sly's ex, Nielsen) in her quest for the dread Talisman, a glowing green globe that ranks as the pre-medieval equivalent of the H-bomb. Arnie and Brigitte are joined en route by an obnoxious young prince (professional kung-fu kid Ernie Reyes, Jr.) and his portly manservant (Smith), thrown in for redundant comic relief. Though the fur and heads fly in a few scattered battle scenes, *Red Sonja* is clankier than Arnie's abundant armor.

Arn on Tape: The Early Daze

Arnold Schwarzenegger, Mr. Olympia (1982) NR 50 minutes (Master Vision). A documentary look at Arnie's comeback bid to capture the world title at the seventh annual body-building competition, wherein Arn goes one-on-one with several former Mr. Universes.

Hercules Goes Bananas (1970) ◆ D: Arthur A. Seidelman. Deborah Loomis, James Karen, Arnold Stang. 75 minutes. (Unicorn)
It's the battle of the Arnolds—Schwarzenegger vs. Stang—and nobody wins in this airheaded tale of Hercules traveling across time to become an American pro wrestler. Arn's major motion picture debut was originally released as *Hercules in New York*, and Our Hero emoted under the alias Arnold Strong (!). By any other name, it's no *Terminator*—or even *Conan*.

The Jayne Mansfield Story (1980) ◆◆ D: Dick Lowry. Loni Anderson, Kathleen Lloyd. 100 minutes. (IVE)
Arnie costars in the role he was born to play—Mickey Hargitay—in this made-for-TV bio of America's second-greatest '50s blond icon, interpreted by Loni Anderson. Not as good as the shockumentary *The Wild, Wild World of Jayne Mansfield* (see index).

Pumping Iron (1977) NR D: George Butler, Robert Fiore. Lou Ferrigno, Mike Katz. 85 minutes. (RCA/Columbia)
This well-received documentary centers on Arn's pursuit of yet another Mr. Olympia title and helped establish the Austrian muscleman's

screen presence. Arn clearly outshines costar Lou (*Hercules*) Ferrigno, who's thus far had but minor impact on the B-movie Beefcake Sweepstakes.

Shape Up with Arnold (1982) NR 85 minutes. (Video Associates).
Haven't you always wanted a bod like Arnie's? In this exercise tape, Arn shares the joy of 'ceps with home viewers via three complete workouts.

Stay Hungry (1976) NR D: Bob Rafelson. Jeff Bridges, Sally Field, Roger E. Mosely. 102 minutes. (CBS/Fox)
This fictional companion to *Pumping Iron* stars Arn as a (what else?) body-builder, Field as a groupie, and Bridges as a rich kid who drifts into their world.

7 Faces of Dr. Lao (1964) NR
D: George Pal. Tony Randall, Barbara Eden, Arthur O'Connell. 101 minutes. (MGM/UA)

Randall plays six roles—Felix Unger not among them—in Pal's parable about a strange circus that descends upon an Old West town.

The Seventh Voyage of Sinbad (1958) ◆◆◆◇
D: Nathan Juran. Kerwin Mathews, Kathryn Grant, Torin Thatcher. 87 minutes. (RCA/Columbia)

One of the most popular fantasy films ever made, this kiddie-matinee perennial is aided and abetted by the Harryhausen/Hermann FX/music team, plus good work by Thatcher as an evil magician. Followed by *Golden Voyage of Sinbad* (RCA/Columbia).

She (1925) NR B&W
D: Leander D. Cordova. Betty Blythe, Carlysle Blackwell, Mary Odette. 98 minutes. (Video Yesteryear)

The silent version of the H. Rider Haggard tale about an Eternal Woman is the only one currently available on video, unless you count Sandahl Bergman's 1985 cheapie (Vestron), which is yet another Italo *Road Warrior* rip-off hiding behind Haggard's venerable title.

Sinbad and the Eye of the Tiger (1977) ◆◆
D: Sam Wanamaker. Patrick Wayne, Jane Seymour, Taryn Power. 113 minutes. (RCA/Columbia)

Not up to the earlier Sinbad movies—an inflated running time and Patrick (Son of Duke) Wayne's wooden title turn are partly responsible—but Harryhausen addicts will want to tune in.

Sinbad the Sailor (1947) ◆◆◆

D: Richard Wallace. Douglas Fairbanks, Jr., Maureen O'Hara, Walter Slezak, Anthony Quinn. 117 minutes. (RKO)

A Technicolor treat, with Doug Fairbanks, Jr., dashing in the title role and backed by an ace supporting cast. You can also check out the 1952 Soviet epic *Magic Voyage of Sinbad* (Sinister Cinema), which promised "1001 Chills and Delights."

Something Wicked This Way Comes (1983) ◆◆◇

D: Jack Clayton. Jason Robards, Jonathan Pryce, Diane Ladd, Pam Grier. 94 minutes. (Walt Disney)

Self-conscious handling undermines this Bradbury fable about a sinister carnival that steals into a turn-of-the-century Middle-American town. Bradbury buffs will want to take a look.

Steel Dawn (1987) ◇

D: Lance Hool. Patrick Swayze, Lisa Niemi, Christopher Neame, Brion James, Anthony Zerbe, Brett Hool. 103 minutes. (Vestron)

Not to be confused with Dawn Steel, Columbia Pictures prez, *Steel Dawn* is yet another puny *Road Warrior* rip-off, marked by dull TV-movie-type scripting, acting, and pacing—the kind of cerebrum-numbing fare designed to lower viewers' resistance to the comparatively zesty commercials that supply said television "entertainments' " sole raison d'être. Aside from an okay opening scene that finds hero Swayze, as a futuristic Shane, putting several squealing subterranean desert mutants to the sword, *Steel Dawn*—a family affair produced by Lance and Conrad Hool, directed by Lance, and costarring young Brett Hool in the original Brandon DeWilde role—is a lethargy-inducing loser. A reluctant ally (James) of the desert warrior tells Swayze, "You don't make me puke." Wish we could say the same about *Steel Dawn*.

Steppenwolf (1974) ◆◆◇

D: Fred Haines. Max von Sydow, Dominique Sanda, Pierre Clementi. 105 minutes. (Vidmark)

Pretty ponderous for the most part and doesn't really capture the febrile flavor of Hesse's novel, but the Magic Theater sequence has its share of hot hallucinatory moments.

Sword and the Dragon (1956) ◆◆◇

D: Alexander Ptushko. Boris Andreyev, Andrei Abrikosov, Nathalie Medvedeva. 81 minutes. (United)

Those harboring fond, distant memories of this Soviet spectacular detailing Russia's mythical struggle against the invading Tugar hordes may be disappointed with the video. For starters, this wide-screen epic (which boasts no fewer than 106,000—count 'em—106,000 extras) loses much of its grandeur on the home screen. (Letterboxing might have helped here.) Worse, United has added a tacky, shot-on-video wraparound showing an American tyke reading the legend of eleventh-century Russki hero Ilya Mouremetz (Andreyev) in a local library! Still intact, though, are such surreal sights as the wind demon, the giant Tugar emissary, the three-headed title dragon, and the immense human pyramid formed by the Tugar warriors. Voice-over ace Paul Frees, of *Rocky and Bullwinkle* fame, does a strong job of dubbing the evil Tugar chieftain Khalin. Withal, we recommend *Sword and the Dragon* as a nostalgic treat for its patient fans and as a curiosity piece for adventurous viewers. All others should beware.

The Thief of Bagdad (1940) ◆◆◆
D: Michael Powell, Ludwig Berger, Tim Whelan. Sabu, Conrad Veidt, Rex Ingram, June Duprez. 106 minutes. (Embassy)

Sabu, with more than a little help from his genie (Ingram), goes one on one with wicked conjuror Veidt in what still ranks as one of the most spectacular fantasies ever lensed. Doug Fairbanks's silent version, filmed in black and white, is also on cassette (Video Yesteryear), while a more mature Sabu's on view in the 1956 sci-fi obscurity *Jungle Hell* (Sinister Cinema).

tom thumb (1958) NR
D: George Pal. Russ Tamblyn, June Thorburn, Peter Sellers, Terry-Thomas, Alan Young. 92 minutes. (MGM/UA)

Tamblyn, in his pre-*Satan's Sadists* days, plays the incredible shrunken boy in a popular Disney fantasy featuring cameos by Pal's Puppetoons.

Warrior Queen (1987) 0 ◆
D: Chuck Vincent. Sybil Danning, Donald Pleasence, Richard Hill, Josephine Jacqueline Jones, Tally Chanel. 69 minutes. (Vestron)

Warrior Queen unites the ever-formidable Danning and a cackling Pleasence (as a demented Roman ruler stationed in a cardboard mock-up of Pompeii). Unfortunately for the duo's fans, our nominal stars receive scant screen time here. Most of the movie's abbreviated running time concerns the romantic intrigues (padded with gratuitous soft-core nudity galore) of several dully cast slaves. Not even Vesuvius's climactic eruption—footage obviously spliced in from an early '60s Italo spectacular—saves this muscle-headed loser. The unrated version runs ten dull minutes longer.

The Wizard of Oz (1939) ◆◆◆ Color/B&W
D: Victor Fleming. Judy Garland, Ray Bolger, Bert Lahr, Jack Haley, Margaret Hamilton. 101 minutes. (MGM/UA)

MGM went all out to bring L. Frank Baum's fantasy novel to

screen life, resulting in one of the most popular and profitable movies ever made. The all-black remake, *The Wiz*, is also available (MCA).

Wizards (1977) NR
D: Ralph Bakshi. Voices of Bob Holt, Richard Romanus, Mark Hamill. 80 minutes. (CBS/Fox)

Bakshi's back with another animated heavy-metal fantasy detailing postapocalyptic warfare between rival wizards and their armies.

Young Sherlock Holmes (1985) ◆◆
D: Barry Levinson. Nicholas Rowe, Alan Cox, Sophie Ward. 109 minutes. (Paramount)

A clever premise involving an adolescent Sherlock's debut case is eventually crushed under the weight of producer Steven Spielberg's usual anvil coyness.

KILLER THRILLERS:
MYSTERY & SUSPENSE

"It's a sunny, woodsy day in Lumberton: Get those chainsaws out!"

Radio announcer
Blue Velvet

You'll probably find a higher percentage of A titles here than in any other chapter of this volume. The reason is simple enough: Over the past few years, "thrillers" have accounted for an increasingly sizable segment of Tinseltown's mainstream output. Many an upscale psycho—from Glenn Close's modern succubus in Adrian Lyne's crowd-pleasing *Fatal Attraction* to Aidan Quinn's lowlife killer in John Badham's almost equally popular *Stakeout*—has succeeded in escaping the B-movie basement to bedevil major stars like Michael Douglas and Richard Dreyfuss. Big-budget thrillers have been taking further cues from their B brethren by upping their gore quotient (e.g., *No Mercy*) and sleaze content (*52 Pickup*). All but missing from today's thriller ranks are the East-West spy films of the '60s and

'70s—international relations have largely become the province of cartoonlike action movies—and the domestic conspiracy film (*Parallax View, Winter Kills*) rampant during that same period. Exceptions exist—*No Way Out*, for example, though even that's based on a 1948 novel, *The Big Clock*, and the contrived McCarthy Era–set *House on Carroll Street*. But the majority of modern suspense outings deal either in endangered families (*Fatal Attraction*) or vulnerable law enforcers working within lavish *Miami Vice* noir settings (*Manhunter, Eight Million Ways to Die*).

Not that we've neglected the numerous worthy indie and B thrillers that *have* proliferated of late. There are many fit to extol, including some, like Donald Cammell's *White of the Eye* and Andy Anderson's *Positive I.D.*, that were virtually unknown prior to their video release. Like too many excellent contempo movies, they were victims of nearly invisible theatrical runs—a fate that also awaited such superior fare as *The Stepfather*, whose sparse but almost unanimously positive notices at least helped fuel home-vid interest. Other indie winners, like David Lynch's *Blue Velvet* and Joel and Ethan Coen's *Blood Simple*, were lucky enough to enjoy greater bijou exposure.

For our older titles, we again focus on the best and the most offbeat: we've uncovered a number of interesting noirs (e.g., *Plunder Road*) and antique obscurities (*The Bat Whispers, The Phantom of Crestwood*), rescued from oblivion by some of the video specialty firms that have arisen to cater to those needs ignored by major labels and neighborhood vidstores. Among them are many titles that have rarely, if ever, aired on TV, and some that haven't been seen *anywhere* since their initial theatrical release decades back.

Access Code (1984) ◆◇
D: *Mark Sobel. Martin Landau, Michael Durrell, Michael Ansara, Mac-Donald Carey, Marcia Mueller, Michael Napoli. 88 minutes. (Prism)*

When we first sat through Sobel's *Access Code*, we thought we were—well, *missing* something. Could it be that this paranoid political thriller about an international cartel of would-be Big Brothers was trying to conceal its convoluted plot even from the *audience*? Fortunately, further Phantom research revealed that this botched video does indeed have key scenes missing (possibly never filmed) and therefore makes virtually no sense on a narrative level. If the filmmaker couldn't figure out what *he* was doing, why should *we* pay for the dubious privilege of filling in *his* blanks?

Adventures of Sherlock Holmes (1939) NR B&W

D: Alfred Werker. Basil Rathbone, Nigel Bruce, Ida Lupino, George Zucco. 86 minutes. (Key)

The second entry in the popular Rathbone-Bruce series followed *The Hound of the Baskervilles* (Key), released earlier the same year. Key carries an additional dozen Sherlock titles: *Dressed to Kill, House of Fear, Pearl of Death, Pursuit to Algiers, Scarlet Claw, Sherlock Holmes and the Secret Weapon, Sherlock Holmes and the Voice of Terror, Sherlock Holmes Faces Death, Sherlock Holmes in Washington, Spider Woman, Terror by Night*, and *The Woman in Green.* Key also has the 1959 *Hound* remake, with Peter Cushing and Christopher Lee, while RCA/Columbia counters with 1965's *A Study in Terror*, with John Neville and Donald Houston as Sherlock and Doc.

Against All Odds (1984) ◆◆◇

D: Taylor Hackford. Jeff Bridges, Rachel Ward, James Woods, Richard Widmark. 128 minutes. (RCA/ Columbia)

A slick more or less remake of *Out of the Past*, with new noir faves Bridges and Woods at odds over Ward. Overlong but not bad, with good work, in a characteristically over-the-top vein, turned in by Woods.

Anatomy of a Murder (1959) ◆◆◇ B&W

D: Otto Preminger. James Stewart, Lee Remick, Ben Gazzara. 160 minutes. (RCA/Columbia)

Preminger's then-controversial courtroom thriller revolving around rape victim Remick, accused assailant Gazzara, and defense lawyer Stewart plays more tamely today but remains a winner for fans of the genre.

And Hope to Die (1972) ◆◆◆

D: René Clement. Robert Ryan, Jean-Louis Trintignant, Tisa Farrow, Aldo Ray. 95 minutes. (Unicorn)

A clever, if initially claustrophobic, Clement caper that comes complete with a coherent central metaphor. Jean-Louis is cast as a kidnapped crook playing cat-and-mouse games with captors Ryan, the ever-reliable Ray, and their confederates. Other available Clement cassettes include *Forbidden Games* (Embassy), *Joy House*, and *Rider on the Rain* (both Monterey), with Charles Bronson.

And Then There Were None (1945) NR B&W

D: Rene Clair. Barry Fitzgerald, Walter Huston, Judith Anderson. 97 minutes. (United)

Rene Clair's definitive adaptation of Agatha Christie's *Ten Little Indians* has become a much-sought-after cassette among mystery-movie buffs. The 1975 remake, *Ten Little Indians*, is also available (Charter).

The Anderson Tapes (1971) ◆◆◆
D: Sidney Lumet. Sean Connery, Dyan Cannon, Martin Balsam. 98 minutes. (RCA/Columbia)

A detailed caper-planning pic that manages to sustain real suspense via its bright mix of colorful characters, top thesps, and tight script.

Angel Heart (1987) ◆◆◆
D: Alan Parker. Mickey Rourke, Robert De Niro, Lisa Bonet, Charlotte Rampling, Brownie McGhee, Stocker Fountelieu. 120 minutes. (IVE)

Set in the '50s, *Angel Heart* follows shamus Harry Angel (Rourke) on a shaggy-dog search for missing mystery man Johnny Favorite, a task commissioned by the sinister Louis Cyphers (a bearded De Niro). Corpses keep piling up in Harry's wake as he journeys to the voodoo dens of New Orleans, where he also takes up with Bonet for a bloody sex scene that raised hell with the MPAA. (The video version restores several seconds of footage scissored from the theatrical release.) For most of the way, *Angel Heart* succeeds in serving up sufficient suspense to keep you chewing your fingernails instead of your popcorn. Unfortunately, it winds up being a tad too existential for its own good (and ours) and compounds this movie misdemeanor by perpetrating the filmic felony of employing a cheap, clichéd climax. Still, the buildup alone makes *Angel Heart* well

worth the price of an overnight rental. The R version is also available.

Apology (1986) ◆◆◇
D: Robert Bierman. Lesley Ann Warren, Peter Weller, George Loros, John Glover, Jimmy Ray Weeks, Harvey Fierstein. 98 minutes. (HBO)

"Conceptual artist" Warren sets up a phone service inviting anonymous callers to confess their perceived sins to her answering machine. (An actual phone service has since employed a similar concept.) Among the otherwise petty phoned-in admissions are the gleeful confessions of a serial killer who soon embroils Lesley Ann in his homicidal madness. In addition to its solid premise, *Apology* sports a well-written script (by playwright Mark Medoff) and a nononsense perf by Peter (*RoboCop*) Weller as the disapproving detective assigned to Warren's case. Drawbacks include a crew of largely unlikable characters connected to NYC's notoriously lupine downtown art scene and a couple of meandering subplots that allow Medoff to flex his creative muscles a mite but contribute little to the overall suspense. Since *Apology* was originally produced for HBO, we also get our de rigueur quota of gratuitous expletives undeleted and perfunctory sex scenes, incorporated to remind cable-TV subscribers that they're not watching sanitized network fare. In the end, though, *Apology* supplies sufficient tension to make it worthwhile for thriller fans and anyone itching to see Harvey (*Torch Song Trilogy*) Fierstein cast as a bum.

Apprentice to Murder (1988) ◆◆
D: R. L. Thomas. Donald Sutherland, Chad Lowe, Mia Sara, Knut Husebro, Rutyana Adler, Eddie Jones, Tiger Haynes. 94 minutes. (New World)

Set in 1927 rural Pennsylvania (though actually lensed in Norway), *Apprentice to Murder* stars Sutherland as Dr. John Reese, an alternately maligned and respected practitioner of Pow Wow medicine, an arcane combo of Christian fundamentalism, herbal medicine and "white" voodoo. The bizarre events leading Reese and his naive teenage assistant Billy (Lowe) to murder should have been tense, fascinating material. Unfortunately, in the hands of director Thomas—who *does* do a good job in the brooding-ambience and period-flavor departments—*Apprentice* only hints at the story's possibilities and largely wastes a strong performance from Sutherland, who'd sleptwalked through his previous abortive "thriller," *The Rosary Murders* (see index).

The Arousers (1970) ◆◆◇
D: Curtis Hanson. Tab Hunter, Nadyne Turney, Isabel Jewell, Roberta Collins, Sandy Kenyon. 90 minutes. (Embassy)

Hunter's failed comeback bid (released theatrically as *Sweet Kill*) casts him as a Venice, California, high school gym teacher who inadvertently kills a woman who tries to interest him in sex. This fuels our femme-fearing hero's already strong necrophiliac tendencies, and Tab embarks on an all-out misogynistic murder-and-sex spree. Pretty thin in the suspense department—though the same can't be said for Tab, who looks fairly flabby for a thirty-nine-year-old phys ed teacher—but of interest to Tab-watchers who wondered what their idol had been up to a decade before John Waters rescued him from oblivion via a key role in *Polyester*. *The Arousers'* kinky candor represents another plus—the pic would make a fine companion feature for the same era's *Carnal Knowledge* (Embassy)—which may account for its still-building home-vid aud.

The Asphalt Jungle (1950) ◆◆◆◆ B&W
D: John Huston. Sterling Hayden, Marilyn Monroe, Sam Jaffe. 112 minutes. (MGM/UA)

One of the best heist films ever made, expertly piloted by the late John Huston, with Sam (*Lost Horizon*) Jaffe especially memorable as the quietly lecherous brains behind the operation.

At Close Range (1986) ◆◆◆
D: James Foley. Sean Penn, Christopher Walken, Mary Stuart Masterson, Christopher Penn, Crispin Glover, Candy Clark, Kiefer Sutherland. 115 minutes. (Vestron)

A suspenseful descent into pure American Sleaze country, *At*

Close Range features Penn as an aimless Pennsylvania youth who hooks up with his lowlife dad (Walken), leader of a pack of thieving red-necks. The pic's pacing is sometimes slow but faithful to the rhythms of our seedy characters' dead-end lives—stretches of mundane time-killing punctuated by bursts of sudden violence. Based on a true story, *At Close Range* admirably delivers in the action and tension departments without resorting to *Rambo*esque revenge theatrics.

Atlantic City (1980) ◆◆◆◇
D: Louis Malle. Burt Lancaster, Susan Sarandon, Kate Reid. 104 minutes. (Paramount)

Malle's excellent, atmospheric aubade (scripted by John Guare) to the then-faded resort town finds Burt in top form as an amiable, aged small-time lowlife involved with smack dealers and waitress Sarandon. Burt on the mighty Atlantic: "That's nothing. You should have seen it thirty years ago."

Bad Day at Black Rock (1954) ◆◆◆
D: John Sturges. Spencer Tracy, Robert Ryan, Anne Francis, Ernest Borgnine, Lee Marvin. 81 minutes. (MGM/UA)

Tracy's a one-armed war vet who seeks to uncover a remote town's deep dark secret in a trim thriller with a top supporting cast (including Borgnine as a Cro-Mag bad guy), great Technicolor cinematography, and CinemaScope desert scapes. The last-mentioned are largely lost on video, alas; this is one of many films that should have been letterboxed for cassette release.

Badlands (1973) ◆◆◆
D: Terrence Malick. Martin Sheen, Sissy Spacek, Warren Oates. 95 minutes. (Warner)

Malick's moody, disturbingly deadpan reprise of Charles Starkweather's psycho rampage stars Sheen as an alienated serial killer and Spacek as his loyal teenage girlfriend. A truly scary experience from the since-underutilized Malick that ranks right up there with Arch Hall, Jr.'s, Starkweather variation, *The Sadist* (see index).

The Bat Whispers (1930) ◆◆◆ B&W
D: Roland West. Chester Morris, Una Merkel, Richard Tucker. 82 minutes. (Captain Bijou)

A superior early mystery chiller that's especially strong on atmosphere and features some impressively surreal camerawork, courtesy of director West, that's unusually fluid for an early talkie. Based on a play by Mary Roberts Rinehart and Avery Hopwood.

Bedroom Eyes (1986) ◆◆◇
D: William Fruet. Kenneth Gilman, Dayle Haddon, Barbara Law, Christine Cattall. 90 minutes. (Key)

A sort of low-budget *Rear Window*

by way of *Body Double*, the Toronto-lensed *Bedroom Eyes* involves a yuppie jogger (Gilman) whose newfound voyeuristic compulsion unwittingly lands him in big trubs with the law. This obscure indie scores with its initial suspense and well-integrated comic relief but lacks the juice needed to hoist it into the same class as its movie models. Too many unrealized opportunities, a lazy denouement, and a retro running riff linking mildly kinky sex with hard-core violence work to cancel an often clever script and the credible performances turned in by a mostly unknown cast.

The Bedroom Window (1987) ◆◆◆
D: Curtis Hanson. Steve Guttenberg, Elizabeth McGovern, Isabelle Huppert, Paul Shenar, Frederick Coffin, Carl Lumbly. 113 minutes. (Vestron)

Guttenberg is in bed with the boss's wife (Huppert) when he witnesses, via the titular aperture, a woman being brutally attacked on the street below. The latter escapes relatively unharmed, but other victims around the city (Washington, D.C.) do not fare as well. Will Steve risk his career by going to the cops, or will he investigate on his own? We think you know the answer. *Bedroom Window* makes almost unbearably tense use of its premise before increasingly implausible plot complications begin to strain credulity. The film breaks down into a pointless chase movie in the final reels, but arriving at

that juncture was a sufficiently rewarding experience for the Phantom to recommend this flawed thriller.

Behind the Rising Sun (1943) ◆◆◇ B&W
D: Edward Dmytryk. Tom Neal, Margo, Robert Ryan, J. Carrol Naish. 88 minutes. (RKO)

A B-movie account of the militarists' ascension to power in prewar Japan, *Behind the Rising Sun* stars Tom (*Detour*) Neal in his first ersatz Japanese role and remains a notch above *First Yank Into Tokyo*'s (see index) absurdist propaganda antics.

Best Seller (1987) ◆◆◇
D: John Flynn. James Woods, Brian Dennehy, Victoria Tennant, Paul Shenar. 95 minutes. (Orion)

Woods is a hyperactive hitman who wants blocked writer/cop Dennehy to collaborate on his story in order to wreak revenge on his former corporate employers, led by Paul (*Scarface*) Shenar. A hit-and-miss affair scripted by the prolific Larry Cohen, *Best Seller* wavers between the contrived and the inspired—a visit with Woods' utterly ordinary suburban parents stands out as a sharp example of the latter. Director Flynn also does a good job in choreographing the pic's climactic showdown. The victim of a haphazard theatrical release, *Best Seller* is worth a look both for Cohen fans and for thriller addicts in the market for a decent fast-paced B flick.

The Big Combo (1955) ◆◆◆ B&W
D: Joseph H. Lewis. Cornel Wilde, Jean Wallace, Brian Donlevy, Lee Van Cleef. 89 minutes. (Congress)

A tough, hard-bitten treat for noir fans, with Wilde toplined as a cop, aided by betrayed moll Wallace, on the trail of a vicious gangster. Highlighted by inventive visuals, courtesy of director Joseph H. (*Gun Crazy*) Lewis.

The Big Easy (1987) ◆◆◇
D: Jim McBride. Dennis Quaid, Ellen Barkin, Ned Beatty, Charles Ludlam, Ebbe Roe Smith, John Goodman. 110 minutes. (HBO)

One of a recent rash of New Orleans–set movies—*No Mercy, Down By Law, Angel Heart, The Unholy*—*The Big Easy* (an affectionate sobriquet for the city in question) is rich in passion, local color, and authentic music but woefully lacking in action. Quaid, equipped with wavering accent and sporadic lisp, plays Cajun cop Remy McSwain, while Ellen (*Buckaroo Banzai*) Barkin is the assistant DA who specializes in police corruption cases and undertakes a coitus-interruptus affair with D.Q. The central plot concerns an alleged drug war between a local Mafia Don (vet thesp Marc Lawrence) and his black rival, Big Daddy (soul man Solomon Burke), and unfolds chiefly via seemingly endless reams of expository dialogue. If director McBride had paid as much attention to said plot as he did to the Quaid-Barkin connec-

tion and the admittedly exotic Cajun-flavored sights and sounds, *The Big Easy* might have been a winner.

The Big Heat (1953) ◆◆◆ B&W
D: Fritz Lang. Glenn Ford, Gloria Grahame, Lee Marvin. 89 minutes. (RCA/Columbia)

More hard-boiled noir action, the Fritz Lang way, wherein a superior cast, direction, pacing, and style more than compensate for a basically familiar story line.

The Black Hand (1950) NR B&W
D: Richard Thorpe. Gene Kelly, J. Carrol Naish, Teresa Celli. 92 minutes. (Magnum)

One of the earliest Mafia movies, *The Black Hand* stars Kelly as a turn-of-the-century crime victim out to turn the tables on the mob.

Black Sunday (1977) ◆◆◇
D: John Frankenheimer. Robert Shaw, Bruce Dern, Marthe Keller. 143 minutes. (Paramount)

Not to be confused with Mario Bava's horrific Barbara Steele–starrer, this *Black Sunday* is a contrived but fairly tense thriller about terrorists who threaten to trash our cherished Super Bowl. (Where's Mean Joe Greene when we need him?) The flick loses it during the padded football finale, but Dern turns in one of his more memorably loony perfs.

Black Widow (1987) ◆◆
D: Bob Rafelson. Debra Winger,

Theresa Russell, Sami Frey, Dennis Hopper, Nicol Williamson, Mary Woronov, Diane Ladd. 103 minutes. (CBS/Fox)

Rafelson's *Black Widow* is *not* a distaff remake of *Tarantula* but a glitzy "thriller" with a feminist twist. The plot pits obsessed Justice Department agent Alexandra Barnes (Winger) against wily Catherine (Russell), a foxy femme fatale who gets her kicks and cash by marrying, then murdering, a string of middle-aged millionaires (including Dennis Hopper in an eye-blink cameo). *Black Widow* might have worked within a tougher, action/catfight format, with Winger and Russell really going at it *womano a womano,* or as a gritty suspenser in a *Body Heat* vein. Instead, *Black Widow,* in typical computerized Hollywood "high-concept" fashion, opts for the trendy at every turn and ends up as just another contempo exercise in convoluted artificiality. The actresses are aces, though; we especially enjoyed Mary (*Eating Raoul*) Woronov's two-minute bit as a diving instructor.

Blood Simple (1984) ◆◆◆
D: Joel Coen. John Getz, M. Emmet Walsh, Frances McDormand, Dan Hedaya, Samm-Art Williams. 97 minutes. (MCA)

Joel and Ethan Coen's *Blood Simple* is a clever, twisty film noir, set in present-day Texas, that packs more surprises per reel than most

of its '40s and '50s models. The acting's first-rate (Walsh is especially effective as noirdom's sleaziest sleuth), the atmosphere appropriately brooding, and what's more, you *haven't* seen it all before.

Blow Out (1981) ◆◆◇
D: Brian De Palma. John Travolta, Nancy Allen, John Lithgow. 108 minutes. (Warner)

At least director De Palma is out front about his bid to rip off *Blowup* (MGM/UA), and his audio-*verité* variation on Antonioni's artsy thriller supplies sufficient suspense and black humor in its own right.

Blue City (1986) ◆◆
D: Michelle Manning. Judd Nelson, Ally Sheedy, Paul Winfield, David Caruso, Scott Wilson, Anita Morris. 83 minutes. (Paramount)

Disappointingly enough, Manning's much-maligned exercise in nerd noir isn't nearly as bad as we'd heard or hoped. True, Nelson is epically awful as jerky rebel Turner, who shows up in the South Florida title town (the pic was lensed entirely in California) to avenge the murder of his ex-mayor dad. And Sheedy is equally inept as Judd's whiny love interest. But the rest of the cast is competent, the revenge plot (liberally adapted from the Ross MacDonald novel of the same name) serviceable, and the running time mercifully brief.

Blue Collar (1978) ◆◆◆

D: Paul Schrader. Richard Pryor, Harvey Keitel, Yaphet Kotto. 114 minutes (MCA)

Schrader finds an effective outlet for his filmic rage and hysteria via a taut tale about a trio of mad-as-hell working stiffs (Pryor, Kotto, and Keitel) who decide to take radical action against the union bosses who've been ripping them off.

Blue Velvet (1986) ◆◆◆◆

D: David Lynch. Kyle MacLachlan, Isabella Rossellini, Dennis Hopper, Laura Dern, Dean Stockwell, Hope Lange, Jack Nance, Brad Dourif. 120 min. (Lorimar)

We suspected we were in for a treat as soon as a blandly cheerful radio voice announced, "It's a sunny, woodsy day in Lumberton: Get those chainsaws out!" From its brilliantly grotesque life-and-death-cycle opening, Lynch's *Blue Velvet* is an imaginatively bizarre, consistently unpredictable, blackly funny sleaze nightmare combining traces of his earlier cult fave *Eraserhead* (see index) with an offbeat urban thriller plot. Not only does Lynch rebound from his overblown *Dune* dud, but Hopper fully atones for his living dead *Texas Chainsaw Massacre II* turn with a wild perf as a lowlife psycho/pervert extraordinaire. Just remember to keep repeating, "It's only real life . . . it's only real life. . . ."

Body Double (1984) ◆◆◆

D: Brian De Palma. Craig Wasson, Melanie Griffith, Gregg Henry. 109 minutes. (RCA/Columbia)

De Palma strikes again, this time with his overtly voyeuristic version of Hitch's *Rear Window* (see Video Shopping List), updated to an '80s porn milieu. A tense, sleazy, and funny winner.

Body Heat (1981) ◆◆◆◇

D: Lawrence Kasdan. William Hurt, Kathleen Turner, Richard Crenna. 113 minutes. (Warner)

Kasdan modernizes a classic '40s noir plot, with sultry Turner and dim lawyer/lover Hurt scheming to off her rich sleazoid businessman hubby (Crenna). Kasdan executes with high style and flair to spare, while Mickey Rourke puts in a memorable cameo as an amiable lowlife.

The Boston Strangler (1968) ◆◆◆

D: Richard Fleischer. Tony Curtis, Henry Fonda, George Kennedy. 116 minutes. (Key)

Curtis stretches in the title role while an all-star lineup of celluloid lawmen tighten the net around Beantown's celebrated, long-elusive psycho.

The Boys from Brazil (1978) ◆◆◆

D: Franklin Schaffner. Laurence Olivier, Gregory Peck, James Mason. 123 minutes. (CBS/Fox)

Good trashy pulp with mild-mannered but tenacious Nazi-hunter Olivier tracking down notorious fugitive Josef Mengele, played against type by Peck. Mengele returned in Jess Franco's 1986 Z-movie reprise *Angel of Death* (New World).

The Boys Next Door (1985) ◆◆◆
D: Penelope Spheeris. Maxwell Caulfield, Charlie Sheen, Hank Garrett, Patti D'Arbanville, Christopher McDonald. 88 minutes. (New World)
The boys in question, surly Roy (Caulfield, of *Grease II* infamy) and his passive partner Bo (Sheen), are a pair of incorrigible high school grads who take off for a wild L.A. weekend before starting dead-end jobs at a local factory. Our working-class antiheroes let it all hang out, guzzling beer, stealing gum, and kidnapping a classmate's pet poodle before graduating to the requisite abrupt-and-senseless slaughter spree. In the tradition of such venerable exploitation pics as *Reefer Madness* and *High School Confidential* (see index), Penelope Spheeris's *Boys* pretends at first to be a sober probe into Psychopathia Americanus. But have no fear: this occasionally dim but never dull flick is actually a thoroughly sleazy wild-youth rampage, long on random violence, high-speed car chases, and trashy rock songs but refreshingly low on redeeming social value.

Brighton Strangler *with* **Before Dawn (1945) NR B&W**
D: Max Nosseck. John Loder, June Du-
prez, Miles Mander. 67 minutes (128 total). (RKO)
Loder, as an actor unhinged during the London blitz, goes on a strangling rampage in this atmospheric '40s B. Available on a double bill with the Warner Oland mystery *Before Dawn*.

Bring Me the Head of Alfredo Garcia (1974) ◆◆◆◇
D: Sam Peckinpah. Warren Oates, Isela Vega, Gig Young. 112 minutes. (MGM/UA)
Said to be one of Peckinpah's most personal pics, *Bring Me the Head of Alfredo Garcia* works brilliantly both as a psycho adventure story and as a metaphor for Sam's headhunting Hollywood experiences. A latecomer to the video ranks but well worth the wait.

Bulldog Drummond (1929) NR B&W
D: F. Richard Jones. Ronald Colman, Joan Bennett, Montagu Love. 85 minutes. (Embassy)
Ronald Colman, easily the screen's most dapper Drummond—a retired Brit army officer turned free-lance adventurer—imbued Bulldog with charm, wit, and bite. Unfortunately, he didn't stick around for the rest of this nonetheless popular B series. The capable, if less compelling, John Howard assumed the role in the following, also available via Embassy: *Arrest Bulldog Drummond, Bulldog Drummond Comes Back, Bulldog Drummond in Africa, Bulldog Drummond's Peril, Bull-*

dog Drummond's Revenge, Bulldog Drummond's Secret Police. Sinister Cinema stocks two other Bulldog titles: *Bulldog Drummond Escapes*, with Ray Milland, and *Bulldog Jack*, wherein Ralph Richardson portrays Drummond's temporary stand-in.

Call Me (1988) ◆◆◇
D: Sollace Mitchell. Patricia Charbonneau, Boyd Gaines, Stephen McHattie, Sam Freed, Steve Buscemi, Patti D'Arbanville. 98 minutes. (Vestron)

Journalist Charbonneau's troubles start with an obscene phone call she erroneously believes is from sluglike boyfriend Freed. The call instead leads Pat to an ill-fated assignation at a nearby bar, where she witnesses a drug-related murder, thus setting the scene for all manner of gritty intrigues as PC soon finds herself hounded by handsome hood McHattie *and* the persistent phone freak, who may or may not be one and the same. While this modest, East Village–set thriller comes up short in the credibility department, the assembled thesps acquit themselves well—the sneering Buscemi is especially memorable as Switchblade, McHattie's retro psycho henchman—and the script features a number of neat conceits. Director Mitchell's handling of the disparate (occasionally desperate) plot elements is less than seamless, though, making *Call Me* a highly watchable but ultimately flawed stab at '80s noir.

Cape Fear (1962) ◆◆◆ B&W
D: J. Lee Thompson. Robert Mitchum, Gregory Peck, Polly Bergen. 106 minutes. (MCA)

Mitchum essays his sleaziest role since *Night of the Hunter* as an embittered ex-con stalking Peck, the lawyer who put him away, and his understandably frightened family. Good lurid fun, based on a John D. MacDonald novel.

Capricorn One (1978) NR
D: Peter Hyams. Elliott Gould, James Brolin, Hal Holbrook, O. J. Simpson. 123 minutes. (CBS/Fox)

Seventies paranoia applied to the space program, with Brolin and Simpson as expendable astronauts seeking to elude government assassins.

The Cat and the Canary (1977) NR
D: Radley Metzger. Honor Blackman, Michael Callan, Wendy Hiller, Olivia Hussey. 90 minutes. (RCA/Columbia)

The much-in-demand 1939 Bob Hope edition of this venerable comedy/mystery remains unavailable as we go to print, but both Metzger's remake, with the ever-fetching Hussey, and Paul Leni's 1927 silent version (Video Yesteryear) can be had.

The Centerfold Girls (1974) NR
D: John Peyser. Andrew Prine, Tiffany Bolling, Aldo Ray. 93 minutes. (Media)

Prine, fresh from his Mansonoid *Simon, King of the Witches* (Unicorn) triumph, returns as a psycho calendar-girl killer in a cheapie with a top has-been B cast, including Ray Danton, Francine York, and Mike Mazurki.

The Charlie Chan Collection NR B&W.
With Warner Oland/Sidney Toler. 60 to 71 minutes each. (Key)

Earl Derr Biggers's famous Chinese shamus makes his overdue vid debut (discounting the public-domain *Meeting at Midnight*, available from a number of mail-order sources) with seven titles alternately featuring Toler and Oland in the lead. Hopefully, CBS/Fox subsidiary Key will keep the Chans coming. The inscrutable seven: *Charlie Chan at the Opera, Charlie Chan in Paris,* and *Charlie Chan's Secret* (Oland); *Castle in the Desert, Charlie Chan at the Wax Museum, Charlie Chan in Rio,* and *Murder over New York* (Toler).

The Chase (1966) ◆◆◆
D: Arthur Penn. Marlon Brando, Jane Fonda, Robert Redford, Angie Dickinson, E. G. Marshall, Robert Duvall. 135 minutes. (RCA/Columbia)

A fun combo of pre-*Dallas* power-moving and -shaking as Texas sheriff Brando tries to save escaped con Redford from corrupt, vengeful townsfolk. Compelling pulp from Penn.

Chinatown (1974) ◆◆◆
D: Roman Polanski. Jack Nicholson, Faye Dunaway, John Huston. 131 minutes. (Paramount)

Polanski's moody noir, set in '30s L.A., presents Jack and Faye in peak perfs, plus Roman himself as the screen's most memorable pint-size hood since Elisha Cook, Jr.'s, *Maltese Falcon* turn.

City of Blood (1986) ◆◆
D: Darrell Roodt. Joe Stewardson, Ian Yule, Ken Gampu, Susan Cottier, John Carson, Greg Latter. 96 minutes. (Magnum)

When several mostly lowlife South African whites turn up murdered and bearing wounds seemingly inflicted by the same ten-thousand-year-old native weapon, troubled medical examiner Stewardson—a kind of Afrikaaner Quincy—decides to conduct his own investigation. A parallel plot line finds him hounded by government officials who want him to authorize the falsified death certificate of a slain black militant. Director Roodt tries to apply a semisupernatural *Last Wave*–type treatment to his contempo B thriller material but explores his themes too cautiously to register much impact. *City of Blood* at least might have worked on a simple suspense level were Roodt not so enamored of his camera—the pic contains nearly two reels' worth of "lyrical" travelogue footage that totally breaks any tension the director fitfully manages to generate. If he'd lavished as much attention on his story, *City of Blood* could have been a solid political chiller instead of an only sporadically interesting try.

City of Shadows (1987) ♦♦

D: David Mitchell. Paul Coulo, Tony Rosato, Paul Harding, Sonja Belliveau, John P. Ryan. 97 minutes. (New World)

A determinedly grim modern B noir that attempts to emulate such big-budget brethren as *Manhunter* and *To Live and Die in L.A.*, *City of Shadows* casts Coulo as a gritty undercover cop on the trail of a vicious kidnapper/child-murderer who happens to be his own brother. The Canada-lensed caper is competent enough but never catches fire and manages to depress even as it fails to enlighten or entertain. John P. (*It's Alive*) Ryan goes above and beyond the call of hysteria as the pressured police chief, while former *SCTV* regular Rosato is wasted in the colorless part of Coulo's partner.

Cloak & Dagger (1984) ♦♦♦

D: Richard Franklin. Henry Thomas, Dabney Coleman, Michael Murphy. 101 minutes. (MCA)

Young Thomas relies on his imaginary friend, ace secret agent Jack Flack (Coleman), to help him thwart a nefarious spy ring in this well-crafted, swiftly paced kids' fantasy thriller.

The Clown Murders (1975) ♦◇

D: Martyn Burke. Stephen Young, Susan Keller, John Candy. 94 minutes. (TWE)

A pre-*SCTV* Candy is among the unfortunate cast members in this promisingly titled but ultimately dull and senseless kidnap caper lensed in Canada and set on Halloween.

The Collector (1965) ♦♦♦

D: William Wyler. Terence Stamp, Samantha Eggar, Mona Washbourne. 117 minutes. (RCA/Columbia)

A suitably creepy if ultimately downbeat thriller, with Stamp strong (albeit in a role tailor-made for the late Rondo Hatton) as the repressed wimp who imprisons hapless Eggar.

Coma (1978) ♦♦◇

D: Michael Crichton. Genevieve Bujold, Michael Douglas, Richard Widmark, Rip Torn. 112 minutes. (MGM/UA)

Petite Bujold takes on male chauvinist hospital authorities in a bid to solve the mystery of comatose patients. Intermittently gripping mainstream medical sleaze.

The Conversation (1974) ♦♦♦◇

D: Francis Ford Coppola. Gene Hackman, Frederico Forrest, Teri Garr, John Cazale. 114 minutes. (Paramount)

An excellent Coppola thriller, with ace work turned in by Hackman (and the late Cazale as his assistant) as a wiretap creep who overhears more than he bargained for.

Cop (1988) ♦♦◇

D: James B. Harris. James Woods, Lesley Ann Warren, Charles Durning, Charles Haid, Randi Brooks. 110 minutes. (Paramount)

Hollywood's hyper hero Woods

adds another intensely twitchy role to his résumé as a manic cop (a "deeply disturbed person," according to his soon-to-be-ex wife) obsessed with tracking down yet another of moviedom's misogynistic serial killers. *Cop* wavers between the genuinely riveting and the gratuitously contrived, but Woods and Durning (as his more level-headed partner) carry the day with their thespic teamwork; they're almost enough to overcome the pic's elaborate but ultimately punchless plot. Warren has a tougher time trying to convince in the weakly written role of a "feminist" who's become the killer's latest target.

Cornered (1945) ◆◆◆ **B&W**
D: Edward Dmytryk. Dick Powell, Walter Slezak, Micheline Cheirel. 102 minutes. (RKO)

Dick Powell is hard-boiled to perfection in this postwar noir about an ex-flier seeking his wife's killers in colorful Buenos Aires.

The Crime of Dr. Crespi (1935) ◆◆◇ **B&W**
D: John H. Auer. Erich von Stroheim, Dwight Frye, Paul Guilfoyle. 63 minutes. (Captain Bijou)

Von Stroheim turns in a strenuous perf as an unhinged medico who plunges into serious malpractice territory in this grim B thriller loosely based on Poe's *Premature Burial*. Frye lends a helping hand.

Crimes of Passion (1984) ◆◆◆
D: Ken Russell. Anthony Perkins, Kathleen Turner, John Laughlin. 101 minutes. (RCA/Columbia)

Perkins plays a psycho street preacher and Turner is designer-by-day/hooker-by-night ("B movies have always been my inspiration") Blue in Ken Russell's bright headlong leap into Russ Meyer territory. This entertainingly absurdist psychosexual exploitation romp is available in two video versions, one restoring theatrically scissored sequences, including a scene wherein Turner helps a cop client enjoy a more intimate relationship with his nightstick.

Criss Cross (1949) ◆◆◆ **B&W**
D: Robert Siodmak. Burt Lancaster, Yvonne DeCarlo, Dan Duryea. 98 minutes. (MCA)

Good guy Burt and bad guy Dan are crooks in conflict, Yvonne's the willing dame caught in the middle in a flavorful caper flick brightened by a top cast that also includes the young Tony Curtis in his movie debut. With exotic music supplied by Esy Morales and His Rumba Orchestra, and a rare meaty role for professional creep Percy Helton, cast here as Burt's sympathetic barkeep confidant.

Dangerously Close (1986) ◆◆◇
D: Albert Pyun. John Stockwell, J. Eddie Peck, Carey Lowell, Bradford Bancroft, Thom Matthews, Madison Mason. 96 minutes. (Media)

This *I Was a Teenage Fascist*-type flick comes dangerously close to being a note-for-note lift from 1976's *Massacre at Central High* (see index), minus the latter's all-out violence and final ironic plot twist. On its own, *Dangerously Close* manages to generate some genuine tension for the first six or seven reels, as impressionable Vista Verde transfer student Peck finds himself initially seduced and ultimately repulsed by The Sentinels, a pack of preppy bullies who routinely terrorize their intimidated peers. The tension breaks down toward film's end, unfortunately, leading to a cheap climax and much frantic loose-end-tying. On the plus side are strong perfs by Stockwell as smooth Sentinel leader Randy McDevitt and Bancroft as Kruger, the pic's token punkster. Pyun's flashy direction, which failed to elevate his *Radioactive Dreams*, abets the action quite nicely here.

The Dark Mirror (1946) NR B&W

D: Robert Siodmak. Olivia de Havilland, Lew Ayres, Thomas Mitchell. 85 minutes. (Republic)

Olivia plays twin sisters—one good, the other evil—in a popular psychological suspenser.

The Day of the Jackal (1973) NR

D: Fred Zinnemann. Edward Fox, Cyril Cusack, Delphine Seyrig. 143 minutes. (MCA)

An elaborate, detailed thriller, based on Frederick Forsyth's novel, pitting cops against ace hitman Fox, who's bent on assassinating De Gaulle.

Dead of Winter (1987) ◆◆◆

D: Arthur Penn. Mary Steenburgen, Roddy McDowall, Jan Rubes, William Russ, Ken Pogue, Wayne Robson. 100 minutes. (CBS/Fox)

Mary Steenburgen stars in this nearly seamless, literal "chiller" (a loose reworking of the '40s B flick *My Name Is Julia Ross* [NA]) as an out-of-work actress whose successful audition lands her in a bizarre role indeed. She's taken by the seemingly meek Mr. Murray (McDowall) to the frozen upstate New York estate of wheelchair-bound shrink Dr. Lewis (Rubes), who explains that she's to fill in for a lookalike actress whose nervous breakdown has forced her to leave an in-progress film. Nothing is what it seems, natch, and Mary soon finds herself a prisoner of the sinister pair and a doomed pawn in an elaborate blackmail game. *Dead of Winter* is a consistently suspenseful affair offering solid perfs (particularly by Steenburgen) and some surprisingly sadistic scenes for a mainstream thriller. Penn lends further flair to the proceedings via striking wintry visuals that contribute greatly to the flick's frigid fright ambience. Ideal for midsummer viewing.

Deadly Embrace (1989) ◆◆◇

D: Ellen Cabot. Jan Michael Vincent, Jack Carter, Michelle Bauer, Linnea Quigley, Ty Randolph. 85 minutes. (Prism)

Co-produced by David DeCoteau, of *Slave Girls from Beyond Infin-*

ity infamy, *Deadly Embrace* finds ruthless tycoon Vincent looking to dump better-half Michelle Bauer (there's just no accounting for taste!) in favor of his blond bimbo secretary. On the advice of his lawyer (vet comic Jack Carter), JMV covertly tapes a torrid affair undertaken by neglected wife Michelle and young hired hand Ty Randolph. As a would-be thriller, *Deadly Embrace* is a cheap, static and generally tacky affair. As an exercise in sleazy erotica, it's one of the more compelling pics we've witnessed in many a moon. In addition to the delectable Ms. Bauer, B-screen queen Linnea Quigley— who last partnered with Michelle in the immortal *Hollywood Chainsaw Hookers* (see index)—is also on ample view, most notably in a strobe-lit striptease sequence that threatened to wear out the slo-mo and freeze-frame functions on the Phantom's VCR. Viewers in search of cinematic suspense can skip this failed attempt at minimalist noir, but Michelle maniacs and Linnea lovers will want to add *Deadly Embrace* to their permanent home-vid library posthaste.

Death Wish Club (1983) ◆◆◆
D: *John Carr. Meredith Haze, Rick Barnes, J. Martin Sellers, Ann Fairchild, William Charles, Paul Keefer. 93 minutes. (Regal)*

An unclassifiable parable from the pen of Phillip Yordan, our story is basically about a college boy (Barnes) smitten by a weird piano-playing strip-joint bimbo (Haze) who, after several admittedly traumatic plot twists that have nothing to do with switching genders, later decides she's really a man. The title, meanwhile, refers to the suicide club to which Meredith belongs; those segments were later fleshed out with additional postproduction FX and recycled for Yordan's equally zany anthology *Night Train to Terror* (see index). Yordan's imagination is fascinating to behold in this free-form mix of confused characters, sick sex, and broad humor that's so obtrusive that it—well, fits right in. Yordan even manages to fashion a happy ending for this off-the-wall tale. Recommended. Also available on the AIR Video label as *Carnival of Fools*.

Deep End (1970) NR
D: *Jerzy Skolimowski. John Moulder-Brown, Jane Asher, Diana Dors. 88 minutes. (Paramount)*

Adolescent Moulder-Brown develops a dangerous crush on co-worker Asher in Skolimowski's offbeat psychological thriller.

Defense Play (1988) ◆◇
D: *Monte Markham. David Oliver, Susan Ursitti, Monte Markham, Eric Gilliom, William Frankfather, Tom Rosqui. 93 minutes. (TWE)*

Defense Play sees a deep-cover Russki agent, posing as a Yank grad student, infiltrate a military science project, the better to sabotage an impending Star Wars launch at a nearby Air Force base. To the rescue comes young Oliver, son of prestigious AF colonel Markham (doubling as director), who stumbles on the scheme with a little help from his trusty computer and fetching distaff teen-genius friend Ursitti. A shockingly tame, virtually nonviolent "thriller," *Defense Play* plays like a low-budget *WarGames*, without the war and minus most of the games. Several chase scenes involving laser-equipped model-size (!) DART helicopters constitute what passes for action in this relentlessly comatose outing, which also treats viewers to endless spellbinding close-ups of flickering computer screens. Your best defense would be to pass this yawner by.

Deliverance (1972) ◆◆◆

D: John Boorman. Burt Reynolds, Jon Voight, Ned Beatty. 109 minutes. (Warner)

A genre-spawning flick, whose imitators remain legion to this day (see *Backwoods*, *Hunter's Blood*, et al.). Based on James Dickey's novel, *Deliverance* takes time to develop its characters, so the violence has more impact here than it does in most of its clones.

Detour (1945) ◆◆◆◇ B&W

D: Edgar G. Ulmer. Tom Neal, Ann Savage, Claudia Drake. 69 minutes. (Video Yesteryear, others)

Neal takes an iconic, paranoiac rear-projection cross-country ride with amoral destiny in Ulmer's ul-tracheap but utterly hypnotic noir, the prototype of modern flicks like *After Hours* and *Something Wild*. Almost every public-domain video outfit stocks this one, the best indoor road movie ever made.

The Devil Thumbs a Ride (1947) ◆◆◇ B&W

D: Felix Feist. Lawrence Tierney, Ted North, Nan Leslie. 62 minutes/with **Having a Wonderful Crime** *132 minutes (total). (RKO)*

Supreme screen hardcase Lawrence (*Dillinger*) Tierney is a ruthless thug who preys on the highways in a fun if overly motor-mouthed RKO second feature, billed with the lighter-toned comedy mystery *Having a Wonderful Crime.*

Diabolique (1955) ◆◆◆◇ B&W

D: Henri-Georges Clouzot. Simone Signoret, Vera Clouzot, Paul Meurisse. 107 minutes. (Foothill, others)

A cruel school headmaster is bumped off by his vengeful mistress *and* wife—but that's only the beginning of the complications in Clouzot's classic suspense tale.

Distortions (1987) ◆◆

D: Armand Mastroianni. Olivia Hussey, Steve Railsback, Piper Laurie, June Chadwick, Edward Albert, Rita Gam. 98 minutes. (Academy)

Mastroianni's *Distortions* is a competent but unexciting variation on the old *Gaslight* gimmick, with villainess Laurie trying to drive her seemingly shaky niece Hussey over the edge in order to collect on the insurance policy purchased by Olivia's recently murdered hubby (Albert). There are further twists in store for the patient viewer, who may be sufficiently engaged by the veteran cast—including Gam as Piper's pal and Railsback as Olivia's potential savior—to hang on that long.

D.O.A. (1949) ◆◆◇ B&W
D: Rudolph Mate. Edmond O'Brien, Pamela Britton, Luther Adler, Neville Brand. 83 minutes. (Sinister Cinema, others)

Though a generally sturdy noir, *D.O.A.* is higher in concept than in execution. The central conceit, of a dying man tracking down his unknown killer, is brilliant but the trackdown itself ultimately wears thin. Still well worth catching, though, and miles ahead of its lightweight remake. Most public-domain specialists stock it. Hal Roach Video also carries a pointless colorized edition.

D.O.A. (1988) ◆◇
D: Rocky Morton, Annabel Jankel. Dennis Quaid, Meg Ryan, Daniel Stern, Charlotte Rampling, Jane Kaczmarek, Christopher Neame. 98 minutes. (Touchstone)

This utterly soulless remake of the 1949 cult noir—directed by *Max Headroom* helmers Morton and Jankel—transfers the action to contempo academe, where we're supposed to buy Quaid as a once-brilliant, now burned-out novelist who, like Edmond O'Brien before him, has twenty-four hours to find his own killer. Trouble is, Quaid's character is so useless and unpleasant that you probably wouldn't mind offing him yourself. The studied black-and-white opening and closing, sandwiching a series of repetitive rock-vid tableaux, also do nothing to recapture or reinvent the original's dizzying qualities. The plot, when finally unraveled, turns out to have been serviceable enough, but by that time this irritating flick is just about over. This *D.O.A.* definitely lives up to its title.

Dog Day Afternoon (1975) ◆◆◆◇
D: Sidney Lumet. Al Pacino, John Cazale, Chris Sarandon, Charles Durning. 124 minutes. (Warner)

Pacino shines as an amateur bank-robber forced to take hostages when his ill-laid plan goes awry. Based on a true story, *Dog Day* delivers outstanding suspense, an authentic mise-en-scène (as the French say), top ensemble acting, and a generous helping of big-city sleaze.

Dog Eat Dog (1965) ◆◆◆ B&W
D: Gustav Gavrin. Jayne Mansfield, Cameron Mitchell, Dody Heath, Ivor Salter, Isa Miranda, Werner Peters. 87 minutes. (Sinister Cinema)

Released shortly after the film version of Jean Genet's *The Balcony* (NA) and sharing a similar world-as-whorehouse central metaphor, *Dog Eat Dog* offers the unforgettable combo of Mansfield (first glimpsed writhing orgasmically, to a rock 'n' roll beat, atop a bed of thousand-dollar bills) and Mitchell in a cheap but twisty tale of greed and betrayal detailing the above duo and co-crook Salter's film-long squabble over the proceeds of a million-dollar heist. When the trio hole up in a would-be deserted bordello on an obscure Greek isle, they encounter several other avaricious interlopers, including a nutty German pimp (chromedomed Peters), a sleazy night-club manager and his sneaky sister, and a crazed ex-madam who's returned home "to die." *Dog Eat Dog* is a cheesy but admirably perverse B movie full of odd exchanges, bizarre behavior, and profound nonsequiturs. A somewhat chunky, towel-clad Jayne supplies the pic's deepest philosophical sentiment, however, when she muses, "Right now I'd settle for a fresh lipstick and panties in Teaneck, New Jersey!"

Dream Lover (1986) ◆◇

D: *Alan J. Pakula. Kristy McNichol, Ben Masters, Paul Shenar, Justin Deas, John McMartin, Gayle Hunnicutt. 104 minutes. (MGM/UA)*

Rich girl McNichol kills an attacker, then suffers from nightmares replaying the traumatic event. She visits dream therapist Masters, who succeeds only in making KM an unconscious menace to all and sundry. Director Pakula totally mishandles his potentially potent material, making *Dream Lover* a consummate yawner instead of a sleeper.

Dressed to Kill (1980) ◆◆◆

D: *Brian De Palma. Michael Caine, Angie Dickinson, Nancy Allen. 105 minutes. (Warner)*

De Palma does Hitchcock again but adds his own layers of wit and sickness to the proceedings.

The Drifter (1988) ◆◇

D: *Larry Brand. Kim Delaney, Timothy Bottoms, Al Shannon, Miles O'Keeffe, Anna Gray Garduno, Loren Haines. 89 minutes. (MGM/UA)*

Something of a low-budget, femme-slanted *Fatal Attraction*, *The Drifter* stars daytime soap ingenue Delaney as an L.A.-bound fashion designer who indulges in an ill-advised roadside tryst with hunky, laconic, and vaguely ominous hitcher O'Keeffe (of *Ator* and Bo Derek's *Tarzan* infamy). Kim's problems begin when Miles later goes out of his way to intrude himself on Ms. Delaney's domestic life with creepy lawyer/boyfriend Bottoms. They seriously escalate when her best friend (Garduno) turns up mysteriously murdered. While derivative, *The Drifter* introduces enough dependable crowd-pleasing plot elements to have made for a decent B thriller. But the pic's slack direction, slow pacing, and lackluster cast soon sent yours truly drifting not toward the edge of his seat but off to dreamland.

Duel (1971) ◆◆◆
D: Steven Spielberg. Dennis Weaver. 90 minutes. (MCA)

A trim made-for-TV thriller with Weaver as a random motorist senselessly and relentlessly pursued by a killer truck. Spielberg's directorial debut remains one of his best and certainly least sentimental efforts.

Empire State (1988) ◆◆◇
D: Ron Peck. Ray McAnally, Cathryn Harrison, Martin Landau, Emily Bolton, Lee Drysdale, Elizabeth Hickling. 104 minutes. (Vidmark)

An ambitious contempo Brit B noir in something of a *Long Good Friday* vein, *Empire State* is too diffuse in its lowlife Grand Hotel—or in this case, Grand Disco—plotting to be truly effective. Most of the action covers a single night at the title site, a sprawling London rock club and the scene of a power struggle between rough-edged East End owner McAnally and his upwardly mobile former gutter-scum protégé Drysdale. Numerous subplots are woven—none too seamlessly—into the flick's central story line, one involving Landau as a tough-minded Yank investor who doubles as a closet gay (in fact, gay-related strains abound here, just as they did in the aforementioned *Long Good Friday*). As we say, an admirably ambitious attempt—especially for a film that wound up preeming in NYC on the bottom end of a Forty-second Street double bill with Fred Olen Ray's *Star Slammer*(!)—but not a candidate for our essential-viewing list.

Executive Action (1973) ◆
D: David Miller. Burt Lancaster, Robert Ryan, Will Geer. 91 minutes. (Warner)

Loosely inspired by Mark Lane's book *Rush to Judgment, Executive Action* casts Lancaster and Ryan as the leaders of a cabal of right-wing Texas businessmen who conspire to kill JFK. Veteran Roger Corman regular Miller is one of the hitmen. This stiff, static polemic failed to sway bijougoers to its POV; they stayed away in record numbers.

Experiment in Terror (1962) ◆◆◆ B&W
D: Blake Edwards. Glenn Ford, Lee Remick, Ross Martin, Stefanie Powers. 123 minutes. (RCA/Columbia)

This tense change-of-pace from strained-comedy master Edwards features Martin as an asthmatic psycho, plus a spectacular climax set at 'Frisco's Candlestick Park.

Eyes of Laura Mars (1978) ◆◆◇
D: Irvin Kershner. Faye Dunaway, Tommy Lee Jones, Brad Dourif, Raul Julia. 103 minutes. (Goodtimes)

A standard B slasher story (co-scripted by John Carpenter and produced by Jack H. [*The Blob*] Harris) gets a glitzy mainstream-thriller treatment as psychic fashion photog Faye becomes embroiled in the antics of an eye-gouging psycho. Contrived, though decently done.

Fail-Safe (1964) ◆◆◆◇ B&W
D: Sidney Lumet. Henry Fonda, Dan O'Herlihy, Walter Matthau. 111 minutes. (Goodtimes)

After *Rocket Attack, USA* (see index), *Fail-Safe*, lensed in stark black and white, stacks up as the most memorable of the era's straight-faced nuclear thrillers.

Fatal Attraction (1987) ◆◆
D: Adrian Lyne. Michael Douglas, Glenn Close, Anne Archer, Stuart Pankin, Fred Gwynne. 119 minutes. (Paramount)

This fierce affirmation of traditional family values—an '80s *Psycho Meets Sex Madness by way of Father Should Know Better*—features Douglas as a model post-yuppie family-guy/publishing lawyer-type whose ill-fated fling with predatory associate editor Close nearly causes him to lose it all. Basically a protracted soaper stocked with crowd-pleasing contrivances, *Fatal Attraction* boasts "steamy sex" (Mike and Glenn get it on everywhere, most definitely including the kitchen sink), "unbearable suspense" (as Mike's car, career, daughter, wife, and rabbit are threatened, not necessarily in that order), *and* a climactic explosion of adrenalizing violence, replete with yet another *Terminator* lift. We *are* looking forward to the inevitable sequel, though—*Fetal Attraction*, wherein Glenn's baby survives the final-reel ordeal and wreaks revenge on an older Mike and family some two decades hence. Viewers in search of an already existing variation can check out the Japanese *F.A.*, the "suicide version," wherein Glenn cuts her own throat and Mike's busted for her murder. All it takes is a trip to Tokyo.

Fear (1988) ◆◇
D: Robert A. Ferretti. Cliff DeYoung, Kay Lenz, Frank Stallone, Robert Factor, Scott Schwartz, Geri Betzler. 96 minutes. (Virgin Vision)

Sly's talented brother Frank (*Barfly*) Stallone costars in Ferretti's *Fear*, a combo jailbreak/psycho-rampage venture that also utilizes the talents of Cliff (*Rocky Horror Picture Show*) DeYoung and Kay (*Stripped to Kill*) Lenz. Though prominently featured on the video box ("Frank Stallone Is Unchained!"), Frank reportedly nixed the crazed 'Nam-vet role (taken instead by Factor) to avoid comparisons with Sly's Rambo persona. A sly move on Frank's part since, in addition to avoiding going one-on-one with his younger bro, he gets to exit this movie, courtesy of a shotgun blast, earlier than most of his less fortunate Thespian brethren here. Still, Frank's fans won't be disappointed: The lesser-known Stallone is in fine, aggressive form as belligerent prison bully Armitage, one of a quartet of desperate cons who bust loose to terrorize a vacationing family unit led by Cliff and Kay. While Frank holds his own, the same can't be said for director Ferretti, who lets *Fear* degenerate from a promising prison actioner to a predictable *Deliverance* rip-off that grows increasingly lame as the reels drag on. In good conscience, then, we can recommend this thriller manqué to Frank Stallone fanatics only. Even *they*, by the way, should avoid his lamentable sci-fi "comedy," the unwatchable *Pink Chiquitas* (Prism).

52 Pick-Up (1986) ◆◆◆
D: John Frankenheimer. Roy Scheider, Ann-Margret, John Glover, Vanity, Robert Trebor, Clarence Williams III. 111 minutes. (Media)

Frankenheimer's utterly implausible but consistently tense and downright sleazy adaptation of Elmore Leonard's novel stars Scheider as a successful L.A. businessman whose casual fling with a porn-scene floozy embroils him in a harrowing blackmail scheme. Scheider is strong as the beleaguered blackmailee—ditto Ann-Margret as his equally imperiled wife—but the real show here belongs to three of the weirdest, sickest (to say nothing of clumsiest) villains ever seen on screen, vividly brought to lowlife by Glover, Trebor, and Williams. Scheider's desperate cat-and-mouse maneuvers with this geeky trio will keep your eyes glued to the tube, no matter how hard your head may shake with disbelief.

Five Corners (1988) ◆◆
D: Tony Bill. Jodie Foster, Tim Robbins, Todd Graff, John Turturro, Elizabeth Berridge. 92 minutes. (Cannon)

Five Corners finds a potentially good psycho flick trapped inside a celluloid lemon. Maniac Turturro's interplay with victim Foster is truly menacing, but John Patrick Shanley's insultingly lame Bronx Graffiti Laverne-and-Shirley-type sitcom subplots strip the pic of all authenticity. Those looking for pictorial perversity on a *Blue Velvet/River's Edge* scale won't find it in *Five Corners*.

Flashpoint (1984) ◆◆
D: William Tannen. Kris Kristofferson, Treat Williams, Rip Torn. 94 minutes. (Goodtimes)

Kristofferson and Williams are Texas Rangers who uncover new clues to the Kennedy killing, again portrayed as an internally engineered conspiracy.

The Fourth Man (1979) ◆◆◇
D: Paul Verhoeven. Jeroen Krabbe, Renee Soutendijk, Thom Hoffman. 104 minutes. (Media)

In his devotion to specificity, Dutch director Verhoeven loses sight of the suspense in this interesting but ultimately disappointing thriller from the man who would later bring us the excellent *RoboCop*.

Frantic (1988) ◆◆◆◇

D: Roman Polanski. Harrison Ford, Emmanuelle Seigner, Betty Buckley, John Mahoney, Jimmie Ray Weeks, Yorgo Voyagis. 120 minutes. (Warner)

Polanski again proves a master of paranoia, perversity, and suspense as he runs tourist Ford through a nightmare Parisian sojourn. When better half Buckley vanishes from their hotel room, Ford heads out in a confused, labyrinthine pursuit that ultimately unites him with flaky distaff drug-runner Seigner and embroils both in a network of elaborate international intrigues. Polanski expertly charts Ford's escalating loss of control and unerringly conveys the latter's stranger-in-a-strange-land fear and desperation. Polanski also cowrote (with Gerard Brach) the excellent script and does an ace job in rendering his evocative Parisian locales.

F/X (1986) ◆◆◆◇

D: Robert Mandel. Bryan Brown, Brian Dennehy, Diane Venora, Jerry Orbach, Cliff DeYoung, Mason Adams. 106 minutes. (HBO)

F/X is a true Hollywood rarity: an ultra-"high concept" thriller that actually *works*. Aussie actor Brown toplines as Rollie Tyler, a special effects ace whose credits include *Vermin from Venus, Planet of the Female Mummies,* and *I Dismember Mama*. (If you identified the last as the only real-movie title of the bunch, give yourself ten points.) Tyler's approached by Justice Department agents De-Young and Adams to stage the phony gangland-style slaying of mobster-turned-stoolie DeFranco (Orbach). The assignment takes a number of violent twists, and Tyler must resort to his bag of FX tricks to bring down the bad guys and save his own nonsynthetic skin. *F/X* is essentially a slick, expensive B flick, with all the visceral virtues that designation implies. The script remains faithful to its intriguing (if implausible) plot, and the assembled thesps—especially Brown, Orbach, Venora, and Dennehy as a workaholic cop—all turn in A-1 perfs. For action fans of all stripes, and effects buffs in particular, *F/X* supplies nimble, fast-paced video fun.

Gaslight (1944) NR B&W

D: George Cukor. Charles Boyer, Ingrid Bergman, Joseph Cotten. 114 minutes. (MGM/UA)

This relentlessly imitated Victorian thriller (itself earlier lensed in a 1939 British version later retitled *Angel Street* [NA]) details Boyer's efforts to drive wife Bergman over the edge. Our fave variation, Lana Turner's LSD-oriented *The Big Cube*, remains tragically unavailable as we go to press.

The Girl (1986) ◆◆

D: Arne Mattson. Franco Nero, Bernice Stegers, Clare Powney, Frank Brennan, Christopher Lee. 104 minutes. (New World)

One of the very few films to cast both Franco Nero and Christopher Lee as Swedes (!), *The Girl* is a torpid, illogical, *Lolita*esque "thriller" that mixes high-camp moments with solemn exchanges, to generally watchable if ultimately soporific effect. Powney is the sinister blond teen who leads married attorney Nero astray; Lee turns up briefly as a detective at film's end.

The Girl Hunters (1963) ◆◆◆ B&W
D: Roy Rowland. Mickey Spillane, Lloyd Nolan, Shirley Eaton, Hy Gardner. 103 minutes. (Sinister Cinema)

Before acting in beer commercials, Mickey did Mike (Hammer), his own hard-boiled creation, in this faithful mystery shot in England. Armand Assante, in *I, the Jury* (CBS/Fox), and Kevin Dobson, in *Mickey Spillane's Mike Hammer: Margin for Murder* (Prism), can also be seen as Spillane's gritty sleuth. But the best Hammer adventure, Robert Aldrich's dizzying *Kiss Me Deadly*, with Ralph Meeker, has yet to be cornered on cassette.

Gorky Park (1983) ◆◆◇
D: Michael Apted. William Hurt, Lee Marvin, Joanne Pacula. 127 minutes. (Vestron)

An overlong but generally engrossing mystery-thriller, helped by Marvin's presence and an exotic Moscow setting.

Ground Zero (1987) ◆◆◆
D: Michael Pattinson, Bruce Myles. Colin Friels, Jack Thompson, Donald Pleasence, Natalie Bate, Simon Chilvers. 109 minutes.

This trim, exciting Aussie thriller stars Friels as a cameraman who, via seemingly innocent home movies left by his late dad, stumbles onto a Down Under A-bomb scandal dating back to the early '50s, when Brit-sponsored atomic tests claimed the lives of several army personnel and untold numbers of Aborigines. The film, a multiple winner at the 1987 Australian film awards (though barely released in the U.S.), does an excellent job of using a pulp-thriller format to advertise a legitimate issue. Fear-film fave Pleasence enjoys one of his better recent roles as an embittered but resourceful test survivor who decides to aid Friels in his quest for the truth. *Ground Zero* represents another instance where an overlooked film has been salvaged by video. Friels virtually reprises his character, this time as a psycho-hunting reporter, in *Grievous Bodily Harm* (Fries), a well-crafted but ultimately unsatisfying Aussie thriller.

Hard Choices (1986) ◆◆◇
D: Rick King. Gary McCleery, Margaret Klenck, John Sayles. 90 minutes. (Lorimar)

Liberal lawyer falls for sensitive teenage con, springs him from jail, and leads him to a career opportunity as a drug-smuggling pilot. Played relatively low-key and worth catching.

Harem (1987) 0 ♦
D: Arthur Joffe. Ben Kingsley, Nastassia Kinski, Dennis Goldson, Michel Robin, Zohra Segal, Juliette Simpson. 107 minutes. (Vestron)

This would-be romantic turkey, never released theatrically, must be seen to be disbelieved. A dessicated '80s update of a typical '40s Maria Montez movie (herein replaced by heroine Kinski, who's no match at all), *Harem* casts a hapless Ben (*Gandhi*) Kingsley as a cultured, love-starved oil sheikh who kidnaps New Yorker Nastassia to his desert redoubt. There, against all odds, true love begins to blossom 'twixt the twain. This relentlessly retro affair features some of the most breathtakingly brain-dead dialogue we've ever heard, though even *it* wasn't enough to keep the Phantom's mind from wandering to more exciting activities—like listening to the latest Barry Manilow album or taking out the garbage. In the end, we opted for the latter, but not before tossing our *Harem* tape into the waiting bin.

He Walked by Night (1948) ♦♦♦ B&W
D: Alfred L. Werker. Richard Basehart, Scott Brady, Roy Roberts. 79 minutes. (Kartes, others)

A superior noir, related in semi-documentary style, about a manhunt through the L.A. sewers, where a psycho killer's at bay. Co-directed by Anthony Mann (uncredited) and featuring an early appearance by Jack Webb.

Hero and the Terror (1988) ♦◇
D: William Tannen. Chuck Norris, Brynn Thayer, Steve James, Jack O'Halloran, Jeffrey Kramer, Ron O'Neal. 96 minutes. (Media)

Erstwhile one-man army Chuck chooses to eschew his old killer ways in the clumsily titled *Hero and the Terror* (based, promisingly enough, on a novel by ex-actor Michael Blodgett, best remembered as the decapitation victim in Russ Meyer's *Beyond the Valley of the Dolls*), racking up a body count of *one* in this somnolent "thriller." Granted, the lone body in question is an uncommonly big one—belonging to mindless misogynistic maniac Simon Moon, aka The Terror (played by the three-hundred-pound O'Halloran)—but it's a nearly 90-minute wait before Chuck and Jack finally go at it. The rest of the flick details Chuck's dull domestic life with pregnant screen squeeze Thayer, scenes designed to let our hero display his "sensitive" side (!). We certainly have no objection to Chuck's admirable efforts to stretch as a Thespian; only trouble is, if you take away the violence factor, there's not a whole lot of Chuck left. And what there is is neither a pretty nor an especially engrossing sight. On the plus side, B-flick faves Steve James, as Chuck's partner, and Ron (*Superfly*) O'Neal, as the mayor, drop by sporadically, and we do get a thorough tour of L.A.'s Wiltern Theater, within whose innards The Terror decides to hide out. But even that's not enough to save *Hero and the Terror* from being a deadly bore.

The Hidden Room (1949) NR B&W

D: Edward Dmytryk. Robert Newton, Sally Gray, Naunton Wayne. 98 minutes. (Sinister Cinema)

Jealous hubby Newton schemes to eliminate the rival threatening his marriage to Gray in this quality Brit suspenser.

The Hit (1985) NR

D: Stephen Frears. Terence Stamp, John Hurt, Laura Del Sol. 101 minutes. (Embassy)

Stamp's a stoolie hounded by hired guns in a shaggy-lowlife story that uses the genre to score satirical points.

The Hitch-Hiker (1953) ◆◆◆ B&W

D: Ida Lupino. Edmond O'Brien, Frank Lovejoy, William Talman. 71 minutes. (J&J)

Talman is truly menacing as a homicidal hitcher in Lupino's tense psycho noir, a forerunner to Robert Harmon's more flamboyant *The Hitcher* (see index).

Hitler—Dead or Alive (1943) ◆◆◇ B&W

D: Nick Grinde. Ward Bond, Dorothy Tree, Warren Hymer. 70 minutes. (Goodtimes)

WW2 pulp about three Yank gangsters who go gunning for Adolf (!) to collect on a million-dollar bounty. Ahead of its time in its aggressive disregard for even margi-

nal credibility. A worthy cassette comparison for RKO's *First Yank into Tokyo* (see index).

Honeymoon (1986) ◆◆

D: Patrick Jamain. Nathalie Baye, John Shea, Richard Berry, Marla Lukowsky, Peter Donat. 98 minutes. (Lorimar)

Parisian Nathalie (*Return of Martin Guerre*) Baye's boyfriend Berry is busted in Gotham; to stay there legally, Nathalie agrees to a bogus marriage to an invisible partner. When said partner (Shea, a dead ringer for jock Jim Palmer, especially when seen in his shorts) shows up in the flesh, Baye is forced to spend most of her screen time trying to elude his creepy, if not downright psychotic, clutches. *Honeymoon* attempts to be a "stylish" thriller, but here that translates into torpid pacing, repetitive exposition, and a gradual drift into deadening predictability. While there are some tense moments and the alluring Baye is moodily effective in her stranger-in-hell role, *Honeymoon* ultimately fails to deliver the psycho-thriller goods.

The Honeymoon Killers (1970) ◆◆◇ B&W

D: Leonard Kastle. Shirley Stoler, Tony LoBianco, Doris Roberts. 130 minutes. (Vestron)

Hefty Stoler prefigures equally homicidal heavyweight Priscilla (*Crazy Fat Ethel*) Alden as she and greaseball partner LoBianco fleece and kill lonely older women in this suitably grotesque cult noir purportedly based on an actual case. After a prominent part in Lina Wertmuller's *Seven Beauties* (RCA/Columbia) as a fat Nazi death-camp matron, Shirl has largely been reduced to cameo roles, like her prison-guard turn in *Shakedown.*

Hot Target (1985) ◆
D: Dennis Lewiston. Simone Griffeth, Steve Marachuk, Brian Marshall, Peter McCaulety, Elizabeth Hawthorne, Ray Henwood. 93 minutes. (Vestron)

An Australian B-movie *Body Heat* rip-off, *Hot Target* tells the less-than-sizzling tale of a Yank hustler (Marachuk) who seduces the bored American wife (Griffeth) of a Down Under tycoon (Marshall) for the usual sinister and larcenous purposes. Unlike its beguilingly sordid and suspenseful model, *Hot Target* is a tepid waste of time.

The House Across the Bay (1940) NR B&W
D: Archie Mayo. George Raft, Joan Bennett, Walter Pidgeon. 86 minutes. (Monterey)

A prewar noir starring Raft as an ex-con who swears vengeance against Pidgeon for running off with wife Bennett while he was in stir.

House of Games (1987) ◆◆◆◇
D: David Mamet. Lindsay Crouse, Joe Mantegna, Lilia Skala, Ricky Jay. 102 minutes. (HBO)

House of Games represents another prime example of how a great

script—in this case penned by prizewinning playwright David Mamet (who also directed)—should be (and rarely is) the foundation of any narrative film. Add sharp performances and a diabolically tricky plot that explores the very core of human nature, sans pretentiousness or comfortable moralizing, and you have a near classic. Crouse excels as the sheltered shrink who, despite having a book (*Driven: Obsession and Compulsion in Everyday Life*) on the best-seller list, feels frustrated about her inability to help her own patients in any concrete way. When a compulsive-gambler patient tells her that his twenty-five-grand debt to a local tough guy has marked him for death, she decides to do something about it. Soon she's entangled with professional con man Mike (Mantegna, in an Oscar-quality perf), who leads her through a maze of increasingly elaborate scams that force her to face the fact that she actually knows precious little re: basic homo-sap psychology—especially her own. (She proves a fast learner, though.) *House of Games* also has a lot to say about "crime" and class. Withal, Mamet has crafted a true thinking-phan's thriller, flawed only by a couple of credibility-stretching details and occasionally static direction.

House of the Rising Sun (1987) ◆
D: Greg Gold. Frank Annese, Jamie Barrett, Tawny Moyer, Deborah

Wakeham, James Daughton, John J. York. 86 minutes. (Prism)

One of a trio of music-vid-style, direct-to-cassette "thrillers" from the folks at MediaCom (*Hot Child in the City* and *Nights in White Satin* complete the turkey troika), *House of the Rising Sun* is a glitz-manqué reprise of the old story that finds a feisty femme reporter (Barrett) infiltrating a high-priced L.A. call-girl ring to get the goods on a vicious pimp (Annese). Along the highly predictable way, *House* manages to bring new meaning to the word *boring* (too dull to go into here). Not even soundtrack contributions from Tina Turner and Bryan Ferry can keep this cassette from sinking quickly in the West.

The House on Carroll Street (1988) ◆◆
D: Peter Yates. Kelly McGillis, Jeff Daniels, Mandy Patinkin. 100 minutes. (HBO)

A thoroughly contrived, synthetic "thriller" set in McCarthy Era Greenwich Village, with a blacklisted McGillis, in a weak turn, and corn-fed FBI agent Daniels encountering a plot, engineered by professional Red-baiter Patinkin, to smuggle ex-Nazis into the country. Even the period details ring false, though there *is* a well-executed tumble from the top of Grand Central Station near film's end.

The Housekeeper (1987) ◆◆◆
D: Ousama Rawi. Rita Tushingham, Ross Petty, Tom Kneebone, Shelly Peterson, Jessica Stern, Jackie Burroughs. 96 minutes. (Lorimar)

Tushingham toplines as Eunice, a recessive, phobic Brit haunted by her lifelong case of dyslexic illiteracy. Figuring that housekeeping is one occupation that won't betray her condition, she moves to the States (the low-budget pic was actually lensed in London and Toronto) and takes a live-in gig with a well-heeled doctor (Petty) and his family. We don't want to reveal much more of this flawed but tense thriller's plot; suffice it to say that *The Housekeeper* would have been even more at home working for *The Stepfather* (see index). Rita does an exceptional job as the loveless, telly-addicted loner, especially when she reminisces re: her late mother's abuse and her dad's intervention: "He didn't like her hurting me. He thought it was *his* job." Beyond its basic psycho story line, *The Housekeeper*—based on Ruth Rendell's novel *A Judgment in Stone*—is laced with grim class ironies, sometimes playing like a B-movie *Upstairs, Downstairs*, with a distaff Norman Bates as one of the Downstairs "help." This is one sleeper guaranteed to keep suspense fans awake.

In the Heat of the Night (1967) ◆◆◆◇
D: Norman Jewison. Sidney Poitier, Rod Steiger, Lee Grant, Warren Oates. 109 minutes. (MGM/UA)

Poitier intros his intrepid detective character Virgil Tibbs, who locks horns with racist sheriff

Steiger in a tense Deep South–set thriller. Poitier/Tibbs returns in *The Organization* and *They Call Me Mister Tibbs* (both via Key).

Into the Fire (1988) ♦♦
D: *Graeme Campbell. Susan Anspach, Lee Montgomery, Art Hindle, Olivia D'Abo. 83 minutes. (Vestron)*

Into the Fire (formerly *Legend of Wolf Lodge*) finds naive young musician Montgomery hiring on with a sicko couple (Anspach and Hindle) at a remote Northwest estate and winding up as a pivotal player in an involved murder plot that builds slowly to a twist-heavy climax. While competently crafted, this derivative Canadian B thriller—as Montgomery's on-screen squeeze D'Abo puts it, "It's not that original an idea!"—shapes up as okay filler at best.

Jagged Edge (1985) ♦♦◊
D: *Richard Marquand. Jeff Bridges, Glenn Close, Robert Loggia, Peter Coyote. 108 minutes. (RCA/Columbia)*

Jagged edges and gaping plot holes ultimately undo what begins as a taut mainstream thriller involving accused murderer Bridges and femme lawyer Close.

The Jericho Mile (1979) ♦♦♦
D: *Michael Mann. Peter Strauss, Roger E. Mosley, Brian Dennehy. 100 minutes. (Charter)*

A surprisingly tough behind-bars made-for-TV movie, with Strauss as a lifer training for an Olympics spot against a backdrop of racially motivated inmate unrest.

Kansas City Confidential (1952) ♦♦♦ B&W
D: *Phil Karlson. John Payne, Coleen Gray, Preston Foster. 98 minutes. (J&J, others)*

One of the Phantom's fave '50s noirs. For starters, title notwithstanding, almost the whole film unfolds in Mexico (!), KC apparently having failed to measure up as a suitable celluloid sin spot. Beyond that, this is a tense, twisty, well-acted affair populated by such fine character thesps as Neville Brande, Jack Elam, and Lee Van Cleef.

Key Largo (1948) ♦♦♦ B&W
D: *John Huston. Humphrey Bogart, Edward G. Robinson, Lauren Bacall, Lionel Barrymore. 101 minutes. (Blackhawk, CBS/Fox)*

A mouthy but masterful downbeat noir with Edward G. and hoods putting the squeeze on Bogie and Bacall at a storm-swept Florida Keys hotel.

The Killer Elite (1975) ♦♦◊
D: *Sam Peckinpah. James Caan, Robert Duvall, Arthur Hill. 122 minutes. (MGM/UA)*

Not one of Peckinpah's pearls but still a serviceable big-budget B movie that finds rival soldiers of fortune Duvall and Caan at violent odds. Would have benefited from a shorter running time and a bigger payoff. (Then again, so would most of us.)

The Killer Inside Me (1976) ◆◆◇

D: Burt Kennedy. Stacy Keach, Susan Tyrrell, Tisha Sterling, John Carradine. 99 minutes. (Warner)

Based on a book by cult noir novelist Jim Thompson, The Killer Inside Me features Keach at his psychotic best as a deputy sheriff suffering from homicidal impulses in Kennedy's occasionally cryptic adaptation. Keach fans might want to rent this with The Ninth Configuration (see index) for a "Spacy Stacy" demented double bill.

The Killers (1964) ◆◆

D: Don Siegel. Lee Marvin, John Cassavetes, Angie Dickinson, Ronald Reagan. 95 minutes. (MCA)

Pretty pale compared to the 1946 version (NA) of Hemingway's short story but of note for casting Reagan in a rare villainous screen role—his final one before segueing into politics.

Killing Hour (1982) NR

D: Armand Mastroianni. Perry King, Norman Parker, Kenneth McMillan. 90 minutes. (CBS/Fox)

Mastroianni's low-budget thriller focuses on a telepathic woman who draws sketches of slayings while they're in progress.

Killing Time (1987) ◆◆◇

D: Rick King. Beau Bridges, Kiefer Sutherland, Wayne Rogers, Joe Don Baker, Camelia Kath. 95 minutes. (New World)

Killing Time sets up a decent premise, dealing with several deceitful denizens of a small West Coast town and a couple of competing murder plots, but it fails to sustain either energy or suspense. B vet Baker turns in the best work here as the burg's soon-to-retire sheriff, while Bridges, in the lead, looks like he hasn't been taking his charisma shots.

King (1978) ◆◆◆

D: Abby Mann. Paul Winfield, Cicely Tyson, Howard E. Rollins, Jr. 254 minutes. (HBO)

This made-for-TV Martin Luther King bio is surprisingly candid about the FBI's suspected involvement in the civil rights leader's slaying.

Kiss Daddy Goodnight (1988) ◆◇

D: Peter Ily Huemer. Uma Thurman, Paul Dillon, Paul Richards, David Brisbin, Steve Buscemi. 89 minutes. (Academy)

A self-described "international cult noir," Kiss Daddy Goodnight, though not without its fair share of professional performances and visual flair, reeks of the sort of chic, lazy, unearned anomie that informs many of Manhattan's downtown trust-fund art scene's products. The peripatetic plot centers on Thurman, a seductive thief who uses her Lolita-like charms to rip off rich older men. An exception is neighbor Richards, a cultured father figure who wants Uma as a substitute for his own long-lost, incestuously desired daughter. While there are several potentially okay thriller elements here, suspense is clearly not director Huemer's forte. Arto Lindsay's legion of fans can catch their No-Wave fave in a riveting cabbie cameo. Not to be confused with Fabian's *Kiss Daddy Goodbye* (IVE), also available as *Revenge of the Zombie* (Premier).

Klute (1971) ◆◆◆
D: Alan J. Pakula. Jane Fonda, Donald Sutherland, Charles Cioffi, Roy Scheider. 114 minutes. (Warner)

Jane's a sensitive, neurotic hooker being stalked by a buttoned-down psycho; Don's the earnest rube sheriff who comes to the big city to save her in an effective thriller that's sleazier than most mainstream fare.

The Lady from Shanghai (1948) ◆◆◆ B&W
D: Orson Welles. Rita Hayworth, Orson Welles, Everett Sloane. 87 minutes. (RCA/Columbia)

Welles's visually dizzying pulp thriller packs enough perverse flourishes, including one character's all-consuming A-bomb paranoia, to camouflage the fact that the story isn't much.

Lady in a Cage (1964) ◆◆◆◇ B&W
D: Walter Grauman. Olivia de Havilland, James Caan, Ann Sothern, Rafael Campos, Jeff Corey. 93 minutes. (Paramount)

After *Kitten with a Whip* (NA), *Lady in a Cage* ranks as the great-

est A-level sleaze movie of 1964. Olivia's the crippled captive of neanderthal lowlifes led by Caan in his impressively simian screen debut. Quoth Lady O, "You're one of the many bits of offal produced by the welfare state. You're what so many of my tax dollars go to the care and feeding of!"

Lady in the Death House (1944) ◆◆◆ B&W
D: Steve Sekely. Jean Parker, Lionel Atwill, Marcia Mae Jones. 57 minutes. (Video Yesteryear)

A brief but quite dense B noir with a complex flashbacks-within-flashbacks structure. One of Atwill's last roles casts him as a determined criminologist concerned with the title damsel's plight. (In a neat touch, her own boyfriend is the state executioner!)

Lady of Burlesque (1943) NR B&W
D: William A. Wellman. Barbara Stanwyck, Michael O'Shea, Pinky Lee. 93 minutes. (Kartes, others)

Stanwyck stars in a comedy mystery based on a novel (the more provocatively titled *The G String Murders*) penned by acclaimed ecdysiast Gypsy Rose Lee (!).

Laura (1944) NR B&W
D: Otto Preminger. Gene Tierney, Dana Andrews, Clifton Webb, Vincent Price. 88 minutes. (CBS/Fox)

An overheated but immensely popular thriller with a career performance by Tierney as an ostensible victim and Andrews as the smitten detective on the scene. It's not the easiest tape to locate, though.

Lies (1983) ◆◆◆
D: Ken and Jim Wheat. Ann Dusenberry, Gail Strickland, Bruce Davison, Clu Gulager, Terence Knox, Bert Remsen, Dick Miller. 98 minutes. (Key)

The Wheats' stylish low-budget thriller bears a passing thematic resemblance to *Dead of Winter* (which it predates): An actress (Dusenberry) is hired, under false pretenses, to impersonate a mental patient traumatized by the murder of her parents. It's all part of an elaborate inheritance scam, a plot hoary at heart but enlivened here by enough fresh twists, suspenseful pacing, and earnest performances by a more-than-capable cast to make it a minor home-video winner. The elevator scene alone is worth the price of a rental; check it out and see what we mean.

The Lightship (1985) ◆◆◇
D: Jerzy Skolimowski. Robert Duvall, Klaus Maria Brandauer, Michael Lyndon. 87 minutes. (CBS/Fox)

Effete criminal Duvall (in an entertainingly idiosyncratic perf) and goons confront accused-coward captain Brandauer aboard the title vessel. Less than profound as a morality play but not bad as a '50s-style B thriller that happened to be filmed three decades later.

M (1931) ◆◆◆ B&W
D: Fritz Lang. Peter Lorre, Ellen Widmann, Inge Landgut. 99 minutes. (Embassy)

Lorre is at once pathetic and chilling in Lang's grim story of a child murderer whose reckless rampage arouses the ire of Berlin's underworld denizens.

Madigan (1968) ◆◆◆
D: Don Siegel. Richard Widmark, Henry Fonda, Inger Stevens, Harry Guardino. 101 minutes. (MCA)

Widmark turns in strong work as a weary NYC detective up against a cunning psycho in this gritty modern noir.

The Maltese Falcon (1941) ◆◆◆◇ B&W/colorized
D: John Huston. Humphrey Bogart, Mary Astor, Sidney Greenstreet, Peter Lorre. 101 minutes. (CBS/Fox)

Here's another one you may already be familiar with. Still, there are plenty of video outlets that *don't* stock this Bogie classic, which also features unforgettable turns by two of the screen's other great short guys, Peter Lorre and Elisha Cook, Jr. (And let's not dismiss fat man Sidney Greenstreet or thin lady Mary Astor.) Avoid the sickly looking colorized version. Other hard-boiled Bogie biggies out on cassette include *Angels with Dirty Faces* (CBS/Fox), *Casablanca* (MGM/UA), *The Big Sleep* (Blackhawk), and *Dead End* (Embassy), *The Enforcer* (Republic), *The Harder They Fall, Knock on Any Door*, and *Sirocco* (all RCA/Columbia), *The Petrified Forest* (CBS/Fox), *Sahara* (MGM/UA) and *The Treasure of the Sierra*

Madre (Corinth). *Falcon* author Dashiell Hammett gets his own movie—Wim Wenders's *Hammett* (Warner).

The Man with Bogart's Face (1980) NR
D: Robert Day. Robert Sacchi, Franco Nero, Michelle Phillips, Olivia Hussey, Misty Rowe. 106 minutes. (Key)

The once-in-a-lifetime cast alone makes this comedy noir worth watching. Besides the principals, Victor Buono, Sybil Danning, Yvonne DeCarlo, George Raft, Herbert Lom, and the incomparable Richard Bakalyan are also along for the satiric ride. Employing a related theme is the SF fantasy *Overdrawn at the Memory Bank* (New World), wherein Raul Julia finds himself trapped *inside* a

Casablanca video (!). The official TV-movie bio, *Bogie: The Last Hero*, with Kevin O'Connor as HB, is also available (IVE).

The Manchurian Candidate (1962/1987) ◆◆◆◆ B&W
D: John Frankenheimer. Frank Sinatra, Laurence Harvey, Janet Leigh, Angela Lansbury, James Gregory, Henry Silva. 127 minutes. (MGM/UA)

All but unseen (largely at star Sinatra's behest—see sidebar) for a quarter-century, Frankenheimer's blackly comic thriller seems even more surreal, perverse, and brilliantly sick when measured against most of today's slick but comparatively pale fare. Highlights include one of the screen's earliest all-out karate battles, be-

CONSPIRACIES ON CASSETTE

Aside from the postwar rash of Red Menace movies, the Conspiracy Film didn't flourish as a genre until the '60s, when a series of political assassinations claimed the lives of John F. Kennedy, Bobby Kennedy, Martin Luther King, Jr., and Malcolm X, among others. Official mendacity in waging and reporting the war in Vietnam, the misdeeds and subsequent cover-ups engineered by Tricky Dick and the Watergate Gang, and inside exposés like Phillip Agee's *The Company*, further fostered a pandemic distrust of government agencies that cut across traditional ideological lines. That distrust has become a staple of today's action and sci-fi thrillers, from right-wing gruntfests like *Rambo* to middle-of-the-road suspensers (*Suspect*) to standard B chillers (e.g., *Warning Sign, The Blob* remake).

One of the most popular and pioneeringly perverse of all conspiracy pics, John Frankenheimer's *Manchurian Candidate* was itself the victim of an elaborate plot. Based on Richard Condon's novel of the same

name, the film represented star Frank Sinatra's second appearance in a presidential-assassination pic. (He'd earlier played the cold-blooded hitman in 1954's *Suddenly*.) According to a *Variety* article, Sinatra personally enlisted JFK's aid in getting a green light for the project, originally rejected by United Artists honcho Arthur Krim. Krim, serving at the time as the Democratic party's finance chairman, bowed to Kennedy's wishes, and *The Manchurian Candidate* reached American screens in 1962. When it was later learned that Lee Harvey Oswald had seen *Suddenly* only days before the slaying, Sinatra yanked both it and *The Manchurian Candidate* (which he owned a piece of) from distribution.

Suddenly has since turned up on TV and in any number of public domain mail-order video company catalogs. After a quarter-century quarantine, Sinatra allowed *The Manchurian Candidate* to unspool at the 1987 New York Film Festival before its 1988 theatrical—and subsequent video—release.

The following represents a few of the Phantom's conspiracy-pic picks currently available on cassette (see index for reviews):

Executive Action (Warner)
Flashpoint (Goodtimes)
King (HBO)
The Parallax View (Paramount)
The Private Files of J. Edgar Hoover (Embassy)
Suddenly (Foothill, others)
Three Days of the Condor (Paramount)
Winter Kills (Nelson)

tween Sinatra (then a merely Middle-Aged Blue Eyes) and consummate movie villain Silva; a train scene wherein Frank and Leigh "meet weird," featuring one of the greatest nonsequitur exchanges ever scripted; and, of course, the central premise itself, which finds oedipal wreck and bogus "war hero" Harvey operating as an unwitting assassin for the International Commie Conspiracy. ("His brain hasn't just been *washed*," laughs jovial Pavlov Institute heavy Kheigh Deigh, "it's been *dry-cleaned*.") Gregory and Lansbury also contribute key turns as a McCarthyesque senator and his Machiavellian spouse, respectively, while Sinatra's final two words succinctly convey the film's ultimate message (and we couldn't agree with it more). The video version includes a 12-minute docu segment, in which Sinatra, Frankenheimer, and scripter George Axelrod discuss the making of the film while, in credibly enough, avoiding the central controversy. A disappointing epilogue, but the movie itself rates as a home-vid must.

Manhunter (1986) ◆◆◆◇
D: Michael Mann. William Petersen, Kim Greist, Dennis Farina, Brian Cox, Joan Allen, Stephen Lang, Tom Noonan. 120 minutes. (Lorimar)

Unlike many of the '80s spate of glossy, high-tech noirs (To Live and Die in L.A., 8 Million Ways to Die, et al.), Michael (Miami Vice) Mann's Manhunter doesn't substitute style for substance but brings visual flair to a complex story line (adapted from the Thomas Harris novel Red Dragon). Petersen is ex-FBI agent Will Graham, recovering from severe physical and psychic wounds inflicted by a now-incarcerated psycho (Cox). When Graham is wooed from his idyllic Captiva, Florida, home and family to help fed Farina decipher clues left by a new serial killer, the former agent is forced to confront both the madman and the latent psychoses simmering within himself. Manhunter thus provides viewers with two levels of tension and explores both without resorting either to sensationalism or to pretension. A chilly but memorable, brutal, and disturbing thriller.

Masquerade (1988) ◆◆◆
D: Bob Swaim. Rob Lowe, Meg Tilly, Kim Cattrall, Doug Savant, John Glover, Dana Delany. 91 minutes. (CBS/Fox)

Murder among the money-heavy Hamptons set serves as the premise for ex-expatriate auteur Bob (La Balance [CBS/Fox]) Swaim's twisty mystery. Poor little orphaned rich girl Tilly—a retro wuss of the first rank—is abused by evil stepdad John (52 Pickup) Glover, wooed by suspect sailor Lowe, and vainly pursued by hunky local cop Savant. Credit goes to Swaim and scripter Dick Wolf for taking what could have been deadly dull material and shaping it into a consistently suspenseful thriller that kept yours truly's hand a far distance from his fast-forward control for the full 91 minutes.

Massacre at Central High (1976) ◆◆◆◇
D: Renee Daalder. Andrew Stevens, Derrel Maury, Robert Carradine, Kimberly Beck. 87 minutes. (MPI)

This horror-tinged high school Death Wish has acquired a strong cult rep over the years, and for good reason. What begins as a predictable nerds-battle-bullies plot takes several unexpected twists. Not at all the slasher flick its title suggests; very definitely worth seeing. It's been ripped off at least twice, in Dangerously Close and Summer Camp Nightmare (see index), but the original is still the greatest.

Mean Streets (1973) ◆◆◆
D: Martin Scorsese. Harvey Keitel, Robert De Niro, Amy Robinson, Richard Romanus. 112 minutes. (Warner)

Scorsese's first major feature offers unforgettable perfs by Keitel and De Niro in an effective slice of Little Italian lowlife.

Medium Cool (1969) ◆◆◆
D: Haskell Wexler. Robert Forster, Verna Bloom, Peter Bonerz. 110 minutes. (Paramount)

Director Wexler incorporated footage from the 1968 Democratic convention—including shots of actual undercover agents posing as an accredited camera crew—into his gritty story about disillusioned TV cameraman Forster and his relationship with widow Bloom.

Mr. Arkadin (1955) ◆◆◆ B&W
D: Orson Welles. Orson Welles, Michael Redgrave, Akim Tamiroff. 99 minutes. (J&J, others)

Orson Welles directs and stars in (as the enigmatic title tycoon) a surreal pulp thriller that's won almost as many devotees as OW's better-known noir Touch of Evil (see index).

Mr. Moto's Last Warning (1939) ◆◆◆ B&W
D: Norman Foster. Peter Lorre, Ricardo Cortez, George Sanders, John Carradine. 71 minutes. (Kartes, others)

Lorre's in good form as the dapper Chinese detective, seen here trying to prevent saboteurs from destroying the French fleet.

Mr. Wong, Detective (1938) NR B&W
D: William Nigh. Boris Karloff, Grant Withers, Maxine Jennings. 68 minutes. (Sinister Cinema)

Boris is Hugh Wiley's typically inscrutable Oriental sleuth, who returns for more in Doomed to Die, The Fatal Hour, Mr. Wong in Chinatown, and The Mystery of Mr. Wong (all Sinister Cinema).

Murder at the Vanities (1934) ◆◆◆ B&W
D: Mitchell Leisen. Jack Oakie, Kitty Carlisle, Victor McLaglen, Toby Wing, Duke Ellington. 89 minutes. (MCA)

McLaglen is a tough shamus on the trail of a backstage murderer in a stranger-than-usual all-star mystery, highlighted by musical numbers like "Ebony Rhapsody" and the memorable "Sweet Marijuana."

Murder, My Sweet (1944) ◆◆◆ B&W
D: Edward Dmytryk. Dick Powell, Claire Trevor, Otto Kruger, Mike Mazurki. 94 minutes. (Nostalgia Merchant)

Powell makes a persuasive Marlowe in an atmospheric adaptation of Raymond Chandler's Farewell, My Lovely.

Murder One (1988) ◆◆◆
D: Graeme Campbell. Henry Thomas, James Wilder, Stephen Shellen, Errol Slue. 86 minutes. (Nelson)

Based on a true story, Campbell's Murder One stars an almost-grown Henry (E.T.) Thomas as a basically decent teen who unwisely tags along with his trashy escaped-con brothers (Wilder and Shellen), who embark on a series of mindless thrill killings that culminate in the massacre of an entire rural Georgia clan. (Several

Georgia theaters refused to book the film during its brief theatrical release.) While director Campbell doesn't shed much light on the murderers' motivation, thesps Wilder and Shellen turn in convincing work as the lowlife gunmen, as does Slue as a fellow escapee who wants no part of the slaughter but can't flee the killers' company. Thomas's character remains the murkiest of the quartet, functioning mostly as a passive witness to the brutal proceedings. Campbell directs his simple but suspenseful story in admirably clean, lean style, and *Murder One* stacks up as a solid sleazoid B thriller.

The Naked Kiss (1964) ◆◆◆ B&W

D: Sam Fuller. Constance Towers, Anthony Eisley, Virginia Grey, Patsy Kelly, Michael Dante, Edy Williams. 93 minutes. (American Entertainment Industries)

From its infamous opening scene, wherein a welching pimp receives a strenuous purse-whipping at the hands of a bald-headed hooker (!), to its unpredictable climax, *The Naked Kiss* represents maverick auteur Fuller at his most earnestly and artfully deranged. Our story takes the above-mentioned courtesan, Kelly (Towers), to the small town of Grantville in search of a fresh start. At first Kelly's future appears bright: She not only lands a job as a nurse working with handicapped kids, but she wins the affections of Grantville's wealthiest bachelor (Dante). Kelly's Middle-American Dream is violently shattered, however, when she discovers her rich, cultured beau is actually the burg's biggest sicko. We don't want to ruin the flick by spilling too many plot beans here; suffice it to say that Fuller keeps the twists coming throughout this mad morality melodrama. In addition to its other virtues, *The Naked Kiss* also marked the feature-film debut of the irrepressible Edy Williams, glimpsed briefly but memorably as a brunette (!) hooker named Hatrack ("There isn't a customer here who doesn't want to hang his fedora on her," madame Grey explains). For the record, Edy's first screen line is "Did I do something wrong?" AEI also carries Sam's brilliant asylum-set classic *Shock Corridor*.

The Narrow Margin (1952) ◆◆◆◇ B&W

D: Richard Fleischer. Charles McGraw, Marie Windsor, Jacqueline White. 70 minutes. (RKO)

A tough, seamless suspense story that's full of inventive twists and doesn't waste a second of celluloid as cop McGraw escorts gun-moll-turned-government-witness Windsor on a cross-country train ride. One of the best, and a veritable blueprint for effective B-movie-making.

The New Kids (1985) ◆◆

D: Sean S. Cunningham. Shannon Presby, Lori Loughlin, James Spader, Ed Jones, John Philbin, Eric Stoltz. 90 minutes. (RCA/Columbia)

For a Cunningham production (the man who brought us such

groundbreaking gore orgies as *Last House on the Left* and *Friday the 13th*), *The New Kids* is an oddly tame affair. Until its violent resolution, the flick plays like a throwback to the JD movies of the '50s—where the ad campaigns routinely packed more punch than the pics they sought to promote—than the splatter exercises that usually carry the Cunningham imprimatur: Recently orphaned teens Lorn and Abby MacWilliams (Presby and Loughlin) move to Homestead, Florida, to live with their Uncle Charlie (Jones), loudmouthed proprietor of the tacky Santa's Fun Land (a perfect theme park for sunny Florida!). Comely Abby quickly attracts the unwanted attention of a gang of redneck punks led by blond-haired psycho Dutra (Spader). The bad kids terrorize the new kids until Lorn sets them straight in a climactic amusement-park bloodbath. In the course of a genuinely perverse "happy" ending, Cunningham and Co. leave the door open for a possible sequel (*The New, Improved Kids?*), but apparently that necessity never arose.

Niagara (1953) NR B&W
D: Henry Hathaway. Joseph Cotten, Marilyn Monroe, Jean Peters. 89 minutes. (CBS/Fox)

Honeymooning couples get their marriages off to a murderous start in a trim suspense tale featuring evocative Niagara Falls location shooting.

The Night of the Hunter (1955) ♦♦♦◇ B&W
D: Charles Laughton. Robert Mitchum, Lillian Gish, Shelley Winters. 93 minutes. (MGM/UA)

A truly creepy thriller, with many a bizarre flourish fashioned by one-shot director Laughton. Mitchum is memorably menacing as a psychotic preacher determined to lay his tattooed hands on buried bank loot. Essential viewing.

The Night Porter (1974) ♦♦♦
D: Liliana Cavani. Dirk Bogarde, Charlotte Rampling, Philippe Leroy. 118 minutes. (Embassy)

The Night Porter limns the sicko tale of former Nazi Bogarde and Jewish death-camp prisoner Rampling, who meet years later and pick up more or less where they left off.

Nighthawks (1981) ♦♦♦
D: Bruce Malmuth. Sylvester Stallone, Rutger Hauer, Billy Dee Williams, Lindsay Wagner. 99 minutes. (MCA)

Sly actually turns in a fairly credible perf—complete with drag scene (!)—as an NYC cop out to nail ultra-slimy terrorist Hauer. Tense, vicious, and violent—what more can we ask?

The Ninth Configuration (1979) ♦♦♦
D: William Peter Blatty. Stacy Keach, Scott Wilson, Ed Flanders, Jason Miller, Neville Brand, George DiCenzo. 115 minutes. (New World)

Produced, directed, and scripted (from his own novel) by William Peter (*The Exorcist*) Blatty, this surreal exercise (originally titled

Twinkle, Twinkle, Killer Kane) stars Stacy Keach as Kane, a shrink ostensibly sent to separate the men from the *meshuggenahs* at a remote Gothic castle in the Pacific Northwest that's been converted into a sort of military playpen for real and/or imagined 'Nam mental casualties. Only problem is: Kane may be the looniest of the lot. *The Ninth Configuration* is a wildly uneven mix of free-form Freudian vaudeville—at its best, its nonsequitur exchanges play like a *One Flew Over the Cuckoo's Nest* (HBO) script-doctored by Bill Griffith's Zippy the Pinhead— broad satire lifted intact from some bad college play, remedial theological probings, and at its core, an intriguing tug-of-war between Keach and off-balance ex-astronaut Cutshaw (imaginatively interpreted by Wilson). With a tighter focus and shorter running time, *The Ninth Configuration* could have been a cult classic (There are many who already deem it so.) As it stands (unsteadily), Blatty's one-man movie offers enough black humor, offbeat dramaturgy, and celluloid surprises to make it well worth an attentive viewing.

No Mercy (1986) ◆◆◆◇
D: Richard Pearce. Richard Gere, Kim Basinger, Jeroen Krabbe, George Dzundza, William Atherton, Ray Sharkey. 105 minutes. (RCA/Columbia)

A truly tense and *intense policier, No Mercy* stars Gere as tough Chi-cago cop Eddie Jillette, who ventures into the seamy depths of New Orleans's Algiers district in search of his partner's killer. Said killer, one Losado, is creepily interpreted by Krabbe, who lists disembowelment with a serrated knife as his preferred method of murder and ranks right up there with *Manhunter's* Tom Noonan and *52 Pick-Up's* John Glover in the Alltime Screen Slimebag Sweepstakes. Basinger is effective as the Cajun blonde sought by both Krabbe and Gere. The pace is fast, the action is violent, the production bucks are as well spent as the flick itself leaves the viewer.

No Way Out (1987) ◆◆◆
D: Roger Donaldson. Kevin Costner, Gene Hackman, Sean Young, Will Patton, George Dzundza, Howard Duff. 118 minutes. (HBO)

For its first 116 minutes, Donaldson's revamp of 1948's *The Big Clock* (both are based on the same Kenneth Fearing novel) represents classic filmmaking at its suspenseful best. Costner does an excellent job as naval commander Farrell, whose increasingly serious tryst with Washington mistress Young leads him into a claustrophobic labyrinth of mounting danger that truly lives up to the film's title. Despite its absence of elaborate action and violence, *No Way Out* expertly augments the onscreen tension with each passing frame. Director Donaldson's use of computer technology—intrusive window-dressing in most contempo thrillers—constitutes an integral part of the suspense. The thesps are uniformly fine, from Hackman's desperate defense secretary to Patton's wired perf as Hackman's high-strung, power-crazed homosexual assistant. Unfortunately, *No Way Out* proves prophetic when it delivers an overly twisty, unsatisfying denouement that just about negates the excellence preceding it. Still, suspense fans searching for the modern version of a vintage thriller shouldn't pass this one by.

No Way to Treat a Lady (1967) ◆◆◆
D: Jack Smight. Rod Steiger, George Segal, Lee Remick. 108 minutes. (Paramount)

Steiger earns Phantom plaudits for his wild work as a misogynistic madman who adopts a multitude of accents and disguises. Segal is the neurotic cop on the crazy's devious trail.

Northern Pursuit (1943) ◆◆◆ B&W
D: Raoul Walsh. Errol Flynn, Julie Bishop, Helmut Dantine. 94 minutes. (Key)

A tensely rendered WWII adventure that finds Flynn in fine form as a stalwart Mountie determined to get his man, downed Nazi pilot Dantine. The latter, accompanied by several POW escapees, forces Flynn to lead him on a chilly odyssey across the frozen Canadian wasteland. The pic effectively

combines cliff-hanger heroics with more complex plotting and a full measure of patriotic fervor.

Obsession (1976) ◆◆◇
D: Brian De Palma. Cliff Robertson, Genevieve Bujold, John Lithgow. 98 minutes. (RCA/Columbia)

Brian does *Vertigo*, but with enough fresh variations to keep his revamp engrossing.

The Osterman Weekend (1983) ◆◆◇
D: Sam Peckinpah. Burt Lancaster, Rutger Hauer, John Hurt, Craig T. Nelson, Dennis Hopper. 102 minutes. (HBO)

Peckinpah's filmic farewell doesn't match up with *The Wild Bunch* or *Bring Me the Head of Alfredo Garcia*, but we weren't bored by it either.

Out of the Blue (1980) ◆◆◇
D: Dennis Hopper. Dennis Hopper, Linda Manz, Sharon Farrell. 94 minutes. (Media)

Punkette Manz, obstructed by her junkie mom (Farrell) and drunken ex-con/biker dad (Hopper), searches for the meaninglessness of life in Hopper's downbeat look at West Coast white-trash angst.

Out of the Past (1947) ◆◆◆ B&W
D: Jacques Tourneur. Robert Mitchum, Kirk Douglas, Jane Greer. 97 minutes. (Fox Hills)

Tourneur's moody noir finds respectable citizen Mitchum squeezed by former lowlife cronies Douglas and Greer. Later remade as *Against All Odds* (Columbia). This one's better.

Over the Edge (1979) ◆◆◆
D: Jonathan Kaplan. Matt Dillon, Michael Kramer, Pamela Ludwig. 95 minutes. (Warner)

Pretty much ignored during its brief initial release, Kaplan's look at anomic teen life in a sterile planned community can take its place beside *River's Edge* and *Suburbia* as an insightful thriller-tinged entry in this suburban-manqué subgenre.

The Parallax View (1974) ◆◆◆
D: Alan J. Pakula. Warren Beatty, Paula Prentiss, William Daniels. 102 minutes. (Paramount)

Beatty is a Bernstein/Woodward—type reporter who uncovers a sinister assassination agency in one of the most febrile conspiracy movies ever made. Pakula directed *All the President's Men* (Warner) two years later.

The Paris Express (1953) ◆◆◇
D: Harold French. Claude Rains, Michael Nightingale, Felix Aylmer, Herbert Lom. 83 minutes. (MPI)

Claude's a wimpy small-town Dutch accountant who absconds with boss Lom's embezzled funds and boards the title train, a trip that leads to intrigue and murder. Claude, brimming with smothered rage, transcends the pic's melodramatic plot machinations.

Party Line (1988) ◆◆
D: William Webb. Richard Hatch, Shawn Weatherly, Richard Roundtree, Leif Garrett, Greta Blackburn. 90 minutes. (Sony)

Party Line is yet another in a recent rash of phone-connected B thrillers (e.g., *Call Me* [see index] and *Lady Beware* [IVE]). The hook here has hung-up oedipal wreck Seth (former teen idol Garrett) and his equally sicko sis Angelina (the alluring Blackburn) using a phone-dating service—the titular Party Line—to lure gullible guys to their suburban lair, where razor-wielding Seth gives them the old ear-to-ear treatment. Attempting to put an end to the psycho siblings' sinister shenanigans are maverick LAPD cop Hatch and blond assistant DA Weatherly. B vet Richard (*Shaft*) Roundtree also puts in sporadic appearances as Hatch's beleaguered boss. While not the worst of its ilk, *Party Line* suffers from disconnected direction and a phoned-in script.

Peeping Tom (1960) ◆◆◆◇
D: Michael Powell. Carl Boehm, Moira Shearer, Anna Massey, Brenda Bruce, Maxine Audley, Martin Miller. 109 minutes. (Admit One)

Snuff movies were seen as pretty shocking back in 1960, and they still are three decades later. The unsavory theme seemed an especially unlikely one for the likes of distinguished Brit auteur Michael Powell, whose name had previ-

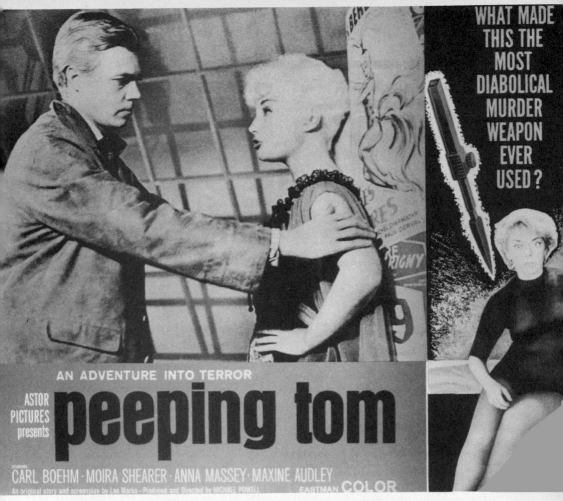

VISIONARY VIOLENCE: Michael Powell's perverse but brilliant meditation on homo-saps' voyeuristic instincts cost the heretofore esteemed British auteur nothing less than his celluloid career.

ously graced such classics as *The Thief of Bagdad, Stairway to Heaven* (both NA), and *The Red Shoes* (Paramount). The fact that *Peeping Tom* is less a thriller than a brilliant meditation on those voyeuristic impulses that make a film industry possible (even mandatory) in the first place was largely overlooked by critics at the time. Fortunately, through the efforts of influential cinephiles like Martin Scorsese (who lists it as his single strongest celluloid influence), *Peeping Tom* has since acquired the following it has always deserved. Boehm is alternately timid and creepy as the camera-obsessed film technician, part-time pornographer/full-time psycho determined to capture *verité* death on film, while Shearer is powerful as the blind neighbor who's onto his madness. Director Powell also works in sharp barbs aimed at commercial filmmaking and behavioral science, among other targets, in a daring exercise that ultimately cost him nothing less than his career. *Peeping Tom* is a film best viewed in the bijou void but unforgettable on video as well.

Perfect Strangers (1984) ◆◆◆
D: Larry Cohen. Anne Carlisle, Brad Rijn, John Woerhle. 90 minutes. (Embassy)

A killer seeks to eliminate the two-year-old witness to his crime, only to become romantically involved with the tot's mom—played by *Liquid Sky*'s Carlisle—in Cohen's suspenseful B precursor to the mainstream hit *Witness*.

Performance (1970) ◆◆◆
D: Nicolas Roeg, Donald Cammell. Mick Jagger, James Fox, Anita Pallenberg. 105 minutes. (Warner)

Reclusive rock star Jagger and cheap hood Fox play stoned mind games in this wittily perverse closet thriller co-directed by Roeg and Donald (*White of the Eye*) Cammell.

Phantom Fiend (1932) NR B&W
D: Maurice Elvy. Ivor Novello, Elizabeth Allen, Jack Hawkins. 58 minutes. (Rex Miller)

A rare, early sound version of *The Lodger* (NA), based on Jack the Ripper's exploits, with a young Hawkins making one of his first screen appearances.

Phantom Killer (1942) ◆◆ B&W
D: William Beaudine. Dick Purcell, Joan Woodbury, Mantan Moreland. 63 minutes. (United American Video)

A routine PRC mystery cheapie distinguished only by Moreland's bravura efforts to transcend racial stereotyping of the most demeaning and, in this case, convoluted sort.

Phantom of Chinatown (1940) NR B&W
D: Phil Rosen. Keye Luke, Grant Withers, Lotus Long. 62 minutes. (Sinister Cinema)

Noteworthy mainly for boasting the "novelty" (!) value of casting an actual Oriental actor (Luke) as famous shamus Mr. Wong. It happened only because projected lead Boris Karloff had been assigned to another pic.

The Phantom of Crestwood (1932) NR B&W
D: J. Walter Ruben. Ricardo Cortez, Karen Morley, Anita Louise. 77 minutes. (Rex Miller)

A reel rarity, both in terms of quality and availability—a low-budget early sound thriller that's *not* the standard static gabfest but a twisty, engrossing mystery filmed as the final chapter of a sixteen-part *radio* (!) serial.

Phantom of 42nd Street (1945) ◆◆ B&W
D: Sam Newfield. Dave O'Brien, Alan Mowbray, Frank Jenks. 61 minutes. (Sinister Cinema)

Frankly, this is a pretty dull PRC backstage murder mystery, with O'Brien supplying none of his sorely missed *Reefer Madness* histrionics. Understandably one of our all-time fave titles, though.

The Plumber (1980) ◆◆◇

D: Peter Weir. Judy Morris, Ivar Kants, Robert Coleby, Candy Raymond. 76 minutes. (Media)

Weir, of *Last Wave* fame, here concocts a minor, blackly comic closet thriller originally aired on Aussie TV. More of a *Last Leak*, the pic chronicles a series of mismatched cat-and-mouse games between pushy young plumber Kants and shaky academic Morris that end with an ultimately predictable twist. Not bad, but David Mamet's *House of Games* (see index) explores similar cons and class antagonisms with a far deeper sense of fear and loathing. So do *The Sadist* and *Lady in a Cage* (see index). Fans of Weir weirdness, meanwhile, can also locate the Down Under cult auteur's *The Cars That Ate Paris* (see index) and *Picnic at Hanging Rock* (Vestron), as well as Weir's later, more mainstream fare: *Gallipoli* (Paramount), *The Mosquito Coast* (Warner), *Witness* (Paramount), and *The Year of Living Dangerously* (MGM/UA).

Plunder Road (1958) ◆◆◆ B&W

D: Hubert Cornfield. Gene Raymond, Jeanne Cooper, Wayne Morris, Elisha Cook, Jr., Steven Ritch. 76 minutes. (Republic)

A realistic, no-nonsense heist caper, with a story by costar Ritch, *Plunder Road* shapes up as the *Detour* of the '50s as a band of humanized thieves pit old-fashioned guile against modern police technology. (As one character puts it, "Science is against you.") Enacted by a stellar B cast, *Plunder Road* was the best of the B's produced under 20th Century-Fox's brief-lived low-budget Regal Pictures wing. A must for fans of the era's unsung gems.

Point Blank (1967) ◆◆◆

D: John Boorman. Lee Marvin, Angie Dickinson, Keenan Wynn. 92 minutes. (MGM/UA)

Donald E. (*The Stepfather*) Westlake's novel serves as the basis for Boorman's dizzying noir, with Marvin ideal as a double-crossed hard guy gunning for vengeance.

The Pope of Greenwich Village (1984) ◆◆◆

D: Stuart Rosenberg. Mickey Rourke, Eric Roberts, Daryl Hannah, Geraldine Page. 121 minutes. (MGM/UA)

Rourke and Roberts are lowlifes who run afoul of crooked cops and Mafia hitmen in Rosenberg's rich adaptation of Vincent Patrick's Village-set novel.

Positive I.D. (1987) ◆◆◆◇

D: Andy Anderson. Stephanie Rascoe, John Davies, Steve Fromholz, Laura Lane, Gail Cronauer, Matthew Sacks. 96 minutes. (MCA)

From its triple-tiered title to its nearly flawless execution, Anderson's indie gem epitomizes that elusive "high concept" that Hollywood moguls relentlessly promise and rarely deliver. (That they virtually unanimously rejected Anderson's script before that first-time auteur decided to mortgage his home and shoot the movie himself goes a long way in explaining why.) In the film, Fort Worth housewife/rape victim Rascoe partially sheds her overburdened self by embarking on a double life. By day, she's a part-time realtor and depressive suburban mother, wed to wimpy hubby Davies; by night, a bimboized regular at a downtown lowlife bar. At first it appears that Stephanie seeks only temporary escape, but it turns out she has a far-better-laid plan in mind. Less a standard thriller than a complex but unpretentious meditation on the very nature of personal identity, Anderson's opus, slickly lensed on a low budget, rarely telegraphs its next move but cleverly toys with audience expectations on its way to a satisfying climax. Though shot at a fraction of the cost, one *Positive I.D.* is worth a dozen *Fatal Attractions*.

The President's Mystery (1936) NR B&W
D: Phil Rosen. Henry Wilcox, Betty Furness. 80 minutes. (Sinister Cinema)

Purportedly based on a story submitted by FDR (!) and partially scripted by novelist Nathanael West, this fanciful B thriller casts Wilcox as a society lawyer slum-

ming as a lowlife sleuth. Rich in curiosity value.

Pretty Poison (1968) ◆◆◆◇
D: Noel Black. Anthony Perkins, Tuesday Weld, Beverly Garland, John Randolph, Dick O'Neill. 89 minutes. (Ingram)

It took a while for this perverse high-concept thriller to join the video ranks, but it was definitely worth the wait. The title refers both to cheerleader Weld and the prismatic pollutants produced by the glass factory where pyromaniac outpatient Perkins works. When relatively harmless loony Tony hooks up with the genuinely unhinged Tuesday, *he's* the one who's in for a surprise as she gradually reveals her true psycho colors. We can say no more without telling too much, except to add that Tony, Tues, and ex–horror ingenue Garland all turn in top work in this low-key but twisty sleeper.

PrettyKill (1987) ◆
D: George Kaczender. David Birney, Season Hubley, Yaphet Kotto, Suzanne Snyder, Germain Houde, Susannah York. 105 minutes. (Lorimar)

A disjointed sleazola soap opera in would-be "thriller" guise, *PrettyKill* is noteworthy solely for Snyder's spirited turn as a schizoid hooker who carries a Raggedy Ann doll (!) and adopts the voice and persona of her misogynistic redneck psycho dad when offing her fellow street sisters. And "Mirror in My Mind" receives our enthusiastic nomination for Worst Theme Song of All Time (dis)honors. *PrettyKill* is almost worth catching for its monumentally stupid ending alone, so long as you remember to fast-forward through the rest.

Private Files of J. Edgar Hoover (1978) ◆◆◆

D: Larry Cohen. Broderick Crawford, Dan Dailey, Rip Torn, Michael Parks. 112 minutes. (HBO)

Cohen's deadpan bio focuses on the conflicts between the obsessive FBI head and such soon-to-be-late enemies as JFK, Bobby Kennedy, and Martin Luther King, Jr. Perverse political sleaze, and a good job all around.

Private Hell 36 (1954) NR B&W

D: Don Siegel. Steve Cochran, Ida Lupino, Howard Duff. 81 minutes. (Republic)

Cops Cochran and Duff relieve a dead mobster of eighty grand and stash it in a trailer park in a noir co-starring Ida Lupino, who also scripted, and co-produced.

Quicksand (1950) ◆◆◇ B&W

D: Irving Pichel. Mickey Rooney, Jeanne Cagney, Peter Lorre. 79 minutes. (United, others)

A pretty predictable, ultracautionary B pic about mechanic Rooney sinking ever deeper into a morass of crime and self-destruction as the result of a petty theft. The flick is worth watching for Lorre's sinister turn as a sleazy arcade owner.

The Racket (1951) ◆◆◆ B&W

D: John Cromwell. Robert Mitchum, Robert Ryan, Lizabeth Scott. 88 minutes. (Fox Hills)

Cop Mitchum and gangster Ryan clash loudly and often in this engrossing hard-boiled crime thriller.

Rage (1972) ◆◆◆

D: George C. Scott. George C. Scott, Martin Sheen, Richard Basehart. 100 minutes. (Warner)

When authorities institute a cover-up after his young son dies of radiation poisoning, contaminated rancher Scott embarks on a film-long vengeance spree. A decidedly exploitative and satisfying approach to a serious issue.

Railroaded (1947) ◆◆◇ B&W

D: Anthony Mann. John Ireland, Sheila Ryan, Hugh Beaumont. 71 minutes. (New World)

A sturdy second-feature *policier*, helmed by noir ace Mann, with Ireland strong as a sleazy killer who locks horns with cop Beaumont (in his pre–Ward Cleaver days).

Rififi (1954) ◆◆◆ B&W

D: Jules Dassin. Jean Servais, Carl Mohner, Magali Noel. 115 minutes. (Video Yesteryear, others)

Dassin's detailed dissection of a complex robbery remains a must for all serious crime-caper fans, though we found the aftermath more arresting than the heist itself.

River's Edge (1987) ◆◆◆◇

D: Tim Hunter. Keanu Reeves, Crispin Glover, Ione Skye Leitch, Daniel Roebuck, Dennis Hopper, Roxana Zal. 99 minutes. (Embassy)

Based partly on a true incident wherein a Milpitas, California, high schooler murdered his girlfriend and invited classmates to view the evidence over the course of several days, River's Edge is a funny/chilling chronicle of the teens' reactions (and nonreactions) to a similarly senseless killing perpetrated by the alienated, overweight Samson (Roebuck). Crispin (Back to the Future) Glover excels as Samson's speedfreak friend Layne, who desperately attempts to cover up the crime and protect his largely indifferent crony in a bid to give his own life—which is literally going nowhere fast—a hit of meaning. ("I feel like Chuck Norris!" he excitedly confides to a cohort.) Reeves is likewise strong as the confused but basically decent Matt who decides the slaying shouldn't go unpunished. A vivid account of kids brought up on a nonnutritional diet of prefab media visions, fast food, and cheap dreams. Hopper as a one-legged ex-biker and his faithful inflato doll Ellie, meanwhile, easily cop the Phantom's 1987 Celluloid Couple of the Year honors.

Road Games (1981) ◆◆◇

D: Richard Franklin. Stacy Keach, Jamie Lee Curtis, Marion Edward. 100 minutes. (Embassy)

A pretty solid latter-day road noir, with driver Keach and hitchhiker Curtis in pursuit of a killer. Better than Franklin's later loser, Link (see index).

The Rosary Murders (1987) ◆◇

D: Fred Walton. Donald Sutherland, Charles Durning, Belinda Bauer, Josef Sommer, James Murtaugh, John Danelle. 101 minutes. (Virgin Vision)

The only thing eternal about this Catholic-themed "thriller" is its running time. In a riff lifted from Hitchcock's I Confess, Detroit priest Sutherland knows the identity of the psycho who's been knocking off nuns and priests as part of an elaborate revenge scheme but is bound by the "seal of Confession" not to divulge same. The killings continue, while the pic—padded by an abortive "romantic" subplot involving reporter Bauer's crush on the celibate, sleepwalking Sutherland—plods along at a procession-al pace. The script, co-written by Elmore Leonard and based on William X. Kienzle's novel, harbors the necessary elements required for a decent B suspenser, but director Walton refuses to let the movie flow; thus, The Rosary Murders fails to take its place among such superior Catholic-killer classics as Alice, Sweet Alice (see index) and The Confessional (Prism).

The Sadist (1963) ◆◆◆ B&W

D: James Landis. Arch Hall, Jr., Helen Hovey, Don Russell, Marilyn Manning. 95 minutes. (Rhino)

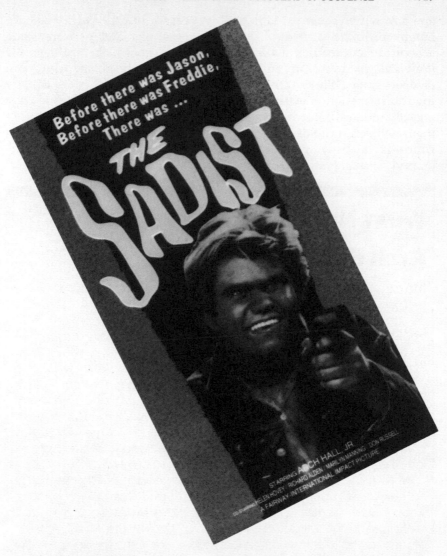

Before there was Jason,
Before there was Freddie,
There was ...

THE SADIST

STARRING ARCH HALL, JR.

CO-STARRING HELEN HOVEY · RICHARD ALDEN · MARILYN MANNING · DON RUSSELL
A FAIRWAY INTERNATIONAL IMPACT PICTURE

Arch Hall, Jr., unlikely star (his dad owned the movie company) of such legendary camp turkeys as *Eegah!*, *The Nasty Rabbit*, and *Wild Guitar* (see sidebar), actually once toplined in a *good* low-budget flick. Thanks to Rhino Video, said pic has been rescued from oblivion for all disbelieving eyes to behold. *The Sadist* (1963) finds Arch cast as a gun-toting maniac loosely based on real-life mass murderer Charles Starkweather (who also served as the violent inspiration for Terrence Malick's *Badlands* [see index] a decade later). Arch and dim-witted squeeze Manning herein terrorize a trio of lost schoolteachers derailed at a desert junkyard en route to an L.A. Dodgers game. While Arch's leering interpretation is occasionally ragged around the edges, the film itself—which unfolds in "real" time—is a truly tense, well-crafted sleazoid suspenser that successfully plays with audience expectations and delivers some genuine shocks. *The Sadist*, lensed in evocative black and white, can take its place with such equally perverse early '60s sickies as *Lady in a Cage* (see index) and *Kitten with a Whip* (NA). Well worth adding to your permanent home-vid library.

WHAT NEVER HAPPENED TO . . .

Arch Hall, Jr.

The pug-nosed, pompadoured star of such early '60s oddities as the teen caveman epic *Eegah!* (costarring Richard (*Jaws*) Kiel), *The Choppers* (a JD pic), and *Wild Guitar* (a rock 'n' roll odyssey wherein Arch Jr., backed by the Archers, showed off his musical talents via songs like "Twist Fever")—all from Rhino Video—achieved Z-movie infamy largely through the efforts of his dad, Arch Hall, Sr. The latter, who often employed the alias William Watters, was a legendary Jack-of-all-scams—said to be the inspiration for the comic novel and 1961 movie *The Last Time I Saw Archie*—who founded the low-budget Fairway International Pictures in 1960. After lensing a string of tame seminudies, in which he often took acting roles, Arch Sr. decided to concentrate on the drive-in youth audience by marketing youthful Arch Jr.

While Arch Jr. suffered from a discernible dearth of emotive ability, he possessed a certain amateurish charm and was lucky enough to star in flicks destined to attain camp status, even transcending his usual ineptitude in the miraculously effective shocker *The Sadist*. Arch Jr. atoned for that aberration with less facile perfs in the clumsy spy spoof *The Nasty Rabbit* and the virtually unseen western *Deadwood '76*.

According to an interview with onetime Arch intimate Ray Dennis Steckler in ReSearch Publications' *Incredibly Strange Films*, Arch drifted out of show biz and settled down in Colorado with his Vietnamese wife. The camp-cassette specialists at Rhino have ensured Arch a long video life by issuing *all* of Arch's oeuvre, save for the elusive *Deadwood '76*, on tape.

Salvador (1986) ◆◆◆
D: Oliver Stone. James Woods, James Belushi, Elpedia Carrillo. 123 minutes. (Vestron)

Stone offers a funkier *Under Fire* (Vestron), with Woods especially impressive as a hyper free-lance photog who runs afoul of the title country's dictator and goons.

Savage Attraction (1983) ◆◆◇
D: Frank Shields. Kerry Mach, Ralph Schicha. 93 minutes. (Embassy)

Aussie girl Mach marries psycho Neo-Nazi Schicha in a well-done, if not particularly pointed, tabloid-type pic based on a true story.

Scarlet Street (1945) ◆◆◆ B&W
D: Fritz Lang. Edward G. Robinson, Joan Bennett, Dan Duryea. 103 minutes. (Video Yesteryear, others)

Repressed Robinson is led astray by bad girl Bennett and sleazy cohort Duryea (in the kind of part only he could play to such oily perfection) in this smooth noir outing.

Séance on a Wet Afternoon (1964) ◆◆◇ B&W
D: Bryan Forbes. Kim Stanley, Richard Attenborough, Patrick Magee. 111 minutes. (VidAmerica)

Mad medium Stanley convinces wuss hubby Attenborough to carry out an ill-advised kidnapping. We know we're in the minority here, but we found this official "classic" more dreary and unpleasant than tense and suspenseful. Though *Séance* is well crafted and expertly acted, there is, in the end, less here than meets the eye.

Second Chance (1953) ◆◆◇
D: Rudolph Maté. Robert Mitchum, Linda Darnell, Jack Palance. 81 minutes. (Fox Hills)

The mob has a contract out on Darnell, who flees to Mexico, where Mitchum tries to protect her. Authentic locations and '50s flavor bolster a standard plot.

The Set-Up (1949) ◆◆◆◇ B&W
D: Robert Wise. Robert Ryan, Audrey Totter, George Tobias. 72 minutes. (Fox Hills)

After *Raging Bull*, this is the second-best boxing movie ever made, with Ryan as a fading fighter told to take a dive. The film unfolds in "real" time.

Seven Days in May (1963) ◆◆◆◇ B&W
D: John Frankenheimer. Burt Lancaster, Kirk Douglas, Fredric March, Ava Gardner, Edmond O'Brien. 118 minutes. (Paramount)

Not quite up there with *The Manchurian Candidate*, but an excellent entry in the early '60s rash of domestic political paranoia pics, this one dealing with an attempted right-wing U.S. military coup.

Seven Days to Noon (1950) ◆◆◆ B&W
D: John and Roy Boulting. Barry Jones, Olive Sloane, Andre Morell. 93 minutes. (J&J)

A tense antinuke thriller, with guilt-driven scientist Jones threatening to explode an A-bomb in London if atomic weapons aren't banned. More persuasive than *Amazing Grace and Chuck* (see index).

Shallow Grave (1987) ♦♦
D: *Richard Styles. Tony March, Linda Stahl, Tom Law, Carol Cadby, Just Kelly, Donna Baltron. 90 minutes. (Prism)*

In the early going, Styles's *Shallow Grave* shapes up as yet another dumb misogynistic sorority-sisters slashfest as four frolick-some co-eds set out in their red convertible for a perilous ride to Fort Lauderdale. But *Shallow Grave* is actually a return to the popular '70s *Macon County Line* genre: After one of the girls chances to witness a red-neck sheriff (March) murder his mistress, the pace picks up considerably and director Styles supplies a measure of style and suspense as our foursome seek to flee the sheriff's shotgun. The action is further buoyed by professional performances from an unknown cast, with the justly named Law especially convincing as the decent deputy caught between his homicidal boss and our endangered heroines. Unfortunately, Styles makes little use of his subplots, proffers an unsatisfying climax, and relies too much on repetition to put *Shallow Grave* over the top.

Shock (1946) NR B&W
D: *Alfred L. Werker. Vincent Price, Lynn Bari, Frank Latimore. 70 minutes. (Cable, others)*

Hawked as a horror flick during its initial release, *Shock* is a fairly tame thriller recommended primarily for voracious Vincent Price fans.

Shock Treatment (1964) NR B&W
D: *Denis Sanders. Roddy McDowall, Stuart Whitman, Carol Lynley, Lauren Bacall. 93 minutes. (Key)*

A fairly sleazy asylum-set movie, with a story line mirroring Sam Fuller's superior *Shock Corridor* (see index): Actor McDowall feigns insanity to infiltrate a sinister mental institution.

Shoot the Piano Player (1962) ♦♦♦ B&W
D: *François Truffaut. Charles Aznavour, Marie Dubois, Nicole Berger. 85 minutes. (Video Dimensions, National Cinema Service)*

Truffaut's alternately perverse and playful homage to American noir movies exhibits considerably more imagination than many of its models.

A Shriek in the Night (1933) NR B&W
D: *Albert Ray. Ginger Rogers, Lyle Talbot, Arthur Hoyt. 66 minutes. (Sinister Cinema, others)*

Shriek in the Night, Ginger and Lyle's second screen pairing, stacks up as one of the early '30s' better B-movie thrillers.

The Silent Partner (1979) ♦♦♦
D: *Daryl Duke. Elliott Gould, Christopher Plummer, Susannah York. 103 minutes. (Vestron)*

Bank teller Gould matches wits with sadistic robber Plummer in a sly, suspenseful sleeper lensed in Toronto. One of Plummer's best roles.

Sister, Sister (1988) ♦
D: Bill Condon. Eric Stoltz, Jennifer Jason Leigh, Judith Ivey, Dennis Lipscomb, Anne Pitoniak, Benjamin Moulton. 90 minutes. (New World)

Leigh and Ivey are southern sisters who run a bayou hotel and share a terrible secret. Stoltz is the handsome young stranger who threatens to disrupt their delicate balance and who may harbor a secret of his own. Then again, some secrets are better left untold, just as some movies are better left unwatched. This slow, narcissistic, and painfully pretentious thriller manqué is one of them.

Slamdance (1987) ♦♦◇
D: Wayne Wang. Tom Hulce, Mary Elizabeth Mastrantonio, Virginia Madsen, Harry Dean Stanton, Don Opper, Adam Ant. 99 minutes. (Key)

Slammed by most critics, Slamdance is a flawed but involving L.A.-set thriller starring Tom (Amadeus) Hulce as a free-lance cartoonist embroiled in the murder of an ex-flame, victim of a political-scandal cover-up. Hulce conducts his own often inept investigation while trying to reconciliate with ex-wife Mary Elizabeth (Scarface) Mastrantonio (in an unflattering role). Slamdance is burdened by padded footage, an overbearing overlay of El Lay glitz, and director Wayne (Chan Is Missing) Wang's fondness for clichéd rock-vid visuals, but there is a story underneath it all, and not a bad one at that. Opper easily cops top thespic honors as a neurotic, self-destructive hitman, though Stanton is uncharacteristically subdued as the LAPD dick assigned to the case.

Smooth Talk (1985) ♦♦◇
D: Joyce Chopra. Laura Dern, Treat Williams, Mary Kay Place, Levon Helm. 92 minutes. (Vestron)

Joyce Carol Oates's metaphorical coming-of-age tale loses a bit in the cinematic translation as yearning teen Dern is pursued by walking (and driving) phallic symbol Williams.

Someone to Watch Over Me (1987) ♦♦◇
D: Ridley Scott. Tom Berenger, Mimi Rogers, Lorraine Bracco, Jerry Orbach, John Rubinstein, Andreas Katsulas. 106 minutes. (RCA/Columbia)

Someone boasts a decidedly crowd-pleasing premise: Married working-class cop Berenger is assigned to bodyguard socialite murder-witness Rogers, who's being stalked by psycho killer Katsulas. A near-fatal attraction gradually develops between our cross-cultural leads—sort of a Joe Friday and Juliet—endangering Tom's home life with earthy wife Bracco. Scott, rebounding from his Legend superdud, directs the predictable proceedings with such controlled panache that you'll likely be reeled in anyway, only to be left to deal afterward with the video equivalent of postcoital depression.

Special Effects (1985) ◆◆◆
D: Larry Cohen. Eric Bogosian, Zoe Tamerlis, Brad Rijn, Kevin O'Connor, Bill Oland, Richard Greene. 103 minutes. (Embassy)

An ironic meditation on our American Mediacracy, *Special Effects* stars monologist Bogosian as Christopher Neville, a perverse, Michael Cimino–like director who's on the outs with Hollywood after blowing 30 mil on an unfinished film. The unpopular auteur attempts to repair his shattered outsize ego by starting work on a sinister *cinéma verité* project involving a real-life murder that he himself sets in motion. *Special Effects* takes an opposite approach to the conceptually similar *F/X* (see index) by incorporating no special effects at all—a strategy that's at once witty and, perhaps as important, money saving. In either case, an overnight rental will be money well spent.

Split Second (1953) ◆◆◇ B&W
D: Dick Powell. Stephen McNally, Alexis Smith, Jan Sterling, Richard Egan. 85 minutes. (RKO)

A bizarre noir, with McNally an escaped con holding hostages in an atomic test area. Features a great ending, followed by a deep-thought epilogue.

Stakeout (1987) ◆◆◇
D: John Badham. Richard Dreyfuss, Emilio Estevez, Madeleine Stowe, Aidan Quinn, Dan Lauria, Forest Whitaker. 115 minutes. (Touchstone)

Yet another entry in the popular mainstream action/comedy/thriller genre, *Stakeout* involves yet another unorthodox but dedicated cop (Dreyfuss) who becomes romantically embroiled with a woman (Stowe) he's assigned to observe from afar in case her ex-beau, an escaped killer (Quinn), should turn up at her doorstep. While predictable in plotting, *Stakeout*'s casual comic tone helps take the edge off some of its more credulity-stretching machinations. Dreyfuss is less obnoxious than usual as the smitten dick; Estevez is okay in what's essentially a glorified sidekick role; Quinn makes for an effective psycho; and Stowe is undeniably appealing as the woman in the case. *Stakeout* is a slick, polished time-killer without an authentic bone in its celluloid body.

The Stepfather (1987) ◆◆◆◇
D: Joseph Ruben. Terry O'Quinn, Shelley Hack, Jill Schoelen, Stephen Shellen, Charles Lanyer. 89 minutes. (Embassy)

Another cogent case of talent (particularly mystery writer Donald E. Westlake's tight, ingenious script) accomplishing what a megabudget in the hands of Hollywood hacks cannot, *The Stepfather* is a sardonic, unerringly suspenseful B thriller. O'Quinn is

"THE STEPFATHER"
from
New Century/Vista Film Co.

ALL-AMERICAN MANIAC: Terry O'Quinn as *The Stepfather.*
Photo courtesy of ITC Productions, Inc.

unforgettable as an All-American, middle-class maniac driven to violence first by his real, then by his adopted families' failure to live up to his scrambled Ward Cleaver standards. Hack and Schoelen are likewise effective as the lonely widow and suspicious daughter, respectively, whom O'Quinn embraces. In another neat touch, O'Quinn works as a suburban real estate agent ("selling the American Dream," he terms it), and the action unfolds against a backdrop of painfully mundane normality. A subplot involving a previous murder victim's justice-seeking brother is artfully integrated into the main story line. *The Stepfather* deserves to take its place among such similarly seamless suburban demimonde noirs as *Blue Velvet* and *River's Edge* (see index).

Stormy Monday (1988) ◆◆◆
D: Mike Figgis. Melanie Griffith, Tommy Lee Jones, Sting, Sean Bean. 93 minutes. (Paramount)

Stormy Monday is one shaggy modern noir whose oblique approach to plotting actually helps put the pic over. Fugitive lovers Griffith and Bean are caught between greedy Yank gangster Jones and stubborn Brit club-owner Sting. *Stormy Monday* bears some resemblance to *Empire State* (see index) but is a far more fully realized effort. Kudos go to the Krakow Jazz Ensemble for their musical and dramatic contributions.

The Stranger (1946) ◆◆◆ **B&W**
D: Orson Welles. Edward G. Robinson, Orson Welles, Loretta Young. 95 minutes. (Kartes, others)

Welles directs and stars as a Nazi war criminal passing as a prof at a remote New England college; Robinson's the investigator on his trail. Rich in inventive imagery and suspense.

The Stranger (1987) ◆◆◇
D: Adolfo Aristarain. Bonnie Bedelia, Peter Riegert, Barry Primus, Julio De Grazia, David Spielberg, Marcos Woinski. 93 minutes. (RCA/Columbia)

The Stranger stars Bedelia as a massacre witness suffering from amnesia. Riegert is her gambling-addicted shrink (an underutilized subplot), while Primus plays the hardworking California cop who's usually a step behind the action, and De Grazia, who resembles a reincarnated Akim Tamiroff, makes for an effective lead heavy. *The Stranger* has its slack stretches,

but it's a good-*looking* film, lensed in rich primary colors, and features one truly socko plot twist we've never seen before (and that's going some!). A not-bad B thriller.

The Stranger on the Third Floor (1940) ◆◆◆ **B&W**
D: Boris Ingster. Peter Lorre, John McGuire, Margaret Tallichet, Elisha Cook, Jr. 64 minutes. (Fox Hills)

A bizarre, febrile B flick, which features a fine *Caligari*esque hallucinatory sequence and an offbeat perf by Lorre as a reclusive immigrant.

Strangers Kiss (1984) ◆◆◇
D: Matthew Chapman. Peter Coyote, Victoria Tennant, Blaine Novak. 93 minutes. (HBO)

Coyote is an ersatz Stanley Kubrick making his first indie movie. Trouble ensues when he casts a mobster/backer's mistress as his star. An odd but interesting project that ranges from effective to pretentious.

Street Smart (1987) ◆◆
D: Jerry Schatzberg. Christopher Reeve, Kathy Baker, Mimi Rogers, Morgan Freeman, Jay Patterson, Andre Gregory. 97 minutes (Media)

If seeing Superman tortured by a Times Square pimp is your idea of entertainment (and it's definitely ours), you, like the Phantom, may have harbored high hopes for *Street Smart*. Christopher (Superman) Reeve stars as a yuppie wimp/journalist whose fabricated profile of a colorful pimp not only launches him into instant celebrityhood but circuitously embroils him in the murder trial of all-too-nonfictional mack Fast Black (convincingly played with modulated menace by Morgan Freeman). Unfortunately, David Freeman's trend-tossed script chooses to revel in the ridiculous, a mood to which Reeve gives his all. ("I'm a moron," he at one point confesses.) The pic is littered with strong perfs and vivid moments, but ultimately *Street Smart* is too studio stupid to mine its own potentially powerful story line.

Streets of Death (1987) ◆

D: *Jeff Hathcock. Tommy Kirk, Larry Thomas, Lawrence Scott, Susanne Smith, Simon DeSoto, Guy Ecker. 90 minutes. (Video Features/AEC)*

Two college film-school creeps posing as documentarians are actually making snuff movies on the side (for extra credit, maybe?). More or less to the rescue comes former kid-star Kirk, replete with too-tight sports jacket and seriously receding hairline. Tommy, whose career has been in terminal decline since his glory days at Disney (see *Mars Needs Women, It's Alive!* and *Mother Goose A Go-Go* in index), hits rock bottom in this pathetic shot-on-video "thriller" that looks as if it were designed for the late-night public-access circuit. For bad-video extremists and hard-core Kirk cultists only.

Suburbia (1984) ◆◆◆

D: *Penelope Spheeris. Chris Pederson, Bill Coyne, Jennifer Clay. 99 minutes. (Vestron)*

Teenage rejects live communally in an abandoned house in a trashy tract development, where they incur the wrath of belligerent locals. The situation may "suck big eggs, man" (as one of the punks is fond of putting it), but the flick itself is well worth seeing.

Suddenly (1954) ◆◆◆ B&W

D: *Lewis Allen. Frank Sinatra, Sterling Hayden, Nancy Gates. 77 minutes. (Video Resources, others)*

Frankie enjoys one of his finest roles as the icy assassin out to off the prez. With henchman Paul Frees (later the voice of *Rocky and Bullwinkle's* Boris Badenov), he holds a Typical American Family hostage and boldly debunks our cherished democratic ideals while calmly setting up his telescopic rifle.

Suicide Club (1988) ◇

D: *James Bruce. Mariel Hemingway, Robert Joy, Lenny Henry, Madeleine Potter, Michael O'Donoghue. 90 minutes. (Academy)*

Starring and co-produced by Mariel Hemingway, *Suicide Club*, loosely based on a Robert Louis Stevenson story, concerns a crew of poor jaded rich folks who have nothing better to do than knock themselves off. (More power to 'em, we say.) Mariel is the bored neurotic society babe who wanders into their web. The flick self-destructs by the end of reel one, but lingers on—aided no doubt by some unseen celluloid respirator/life-support system—for what seems a cinematic eternity. Do yourself a favor and let *Suicide Club* rot on local vid shelves; the 90 minutes you save may be your own.

Summer Camp Nightmare (1987) ◆◆◇
D: Bert L. Dragin. Chuck Connors, Charles Stratton, Adam Carl, Harold Pruett, Tom Fridley, Nancy Calabrese. 89 minutes. (Embassy)

Co-scripted by Penelope (*Suburbia, Dudes*) Spheeris and director Dragin from the novel *The Butterfly Revolution, Summer Camp Nightmare* is not the alfresco teen-slasher junk its title implies but sort of a sleazy, co-ed *Lord of the Flies* (Connoisseur) reprise set at the remote title site. When uptight new camp director ("warden" would be closer to it) Connors, who exhibits a passion for lepidoptery, discipline, and little else, clamps down on the kid campers' fun, egomaniacal teen Stratton leads his fellows in a "bloodless coup." The resultant partying soon takes a more sinister turn, as the increasingly fascistic Stratton's "revolutionary committee" members resort to rape and violence to control dissenting campers. While weakened by plot inconsistencies and a muddled POV, *Summer Camp Nightmare* is pretty exciting most of the way,

buoyed by strong perfs from the young cast. In short, one of your better '60s-style exploitation movies—a sort of *Wild in the Woods*—lensed in 1987.

Suspect (1987) ◆◆◇
D: Peter Yates. Cher, Dennis Quaid, Liam Neeson, John Mahoney, Joe Mantegna, Philip Bosco. 101 minutes. (RCA/Columbia)

Shapely dedicated lawyer Cher defends homeless mute Neeson with the (initially) unwanted help of handsome juror Quaid in a slick suspenser that starts out tight and ends up flabby. Cher and Dennis forget to have sex until the final fade-out, and even then it's still up in the air.

The Taking of Pelham One Two Three (1974) ◆◆◆
D: Joseph Sargent. Robert Shaw, Walter Matthau, Martin Balsam. 104 minutes. (CBS/Fox)

A desperate idea—a quartet of top criminals commandeer a Fun City subway train (as if anyone'd *want* it back!)—is saved here by cynical wit and director Sargent's sharp sense of suspense.

Target (1985) ◆◆◇
D: Arthur Penn. Gene Hackman, Matt Dillon, Gayle Hunnicutt, Josef Sommer, Victoria Fyodorova, Guy Boyd. 117 minutes. (CBS/Fox)

In Arthur (*Bonnie and Clyde*) Penn's *Target*, Hackman acts out the middle-aged American Every-dad's fondest fantasy: When wife Hunnicutt is kidnapped during a solo Parisian vacation, Gene shocks surly son Dillon by transforming from a dull Dallas businessman into an international superspy. (Seems that Gene is really an ex-CIA agent.) When he and his wide-eyed offspring hit Europe, Gene goes into action with a vengeance, leading said son through an involved maze of East-West intrigues past and present. *Target* is a contrived, often ridiculous, but fairly engrossing thriller, with Hackman in good form. Onscreen wife Hunnicutt lands one of the era's least inspiring femme roles here, spending most of her screen time bound, gagged, and trip-wired to a pile of explosives!

Targets (1968) ◆◆◆

D: Peter Bogdanovich. Boris Karloff, Tim O'Kelly, Nancy Hsueh, Peter Bogdanovich, James Brown, Sandy Baron. 91 minutes. (Paramount)

Bogdanovich's first complete feature—he'd previously worked on a couple of Roger Corman's cut-and-paste jobs—pits aged horror-film star Byron Orlok (Karloff, in his last good role) against an all-too-real monster, a colorless but lethal psycho sniper loose at a local drive-in. Bogdanovich's best film, along with the similarly bijou-related *Last Picture Show* (NA), deservedly became an instant cult fave with its pointed mix of sincerity and exploitation.

Taxi Driver (1976) ◆◆◆

D: Martin Scorsese. Robert De Niro, Jodie Foster, Cybill Shepherd, Albert Brooks, Harvey Keitel. 113 minutes. (RCA/Columbia)

One of those reel rarities that scored both with mainstream critics and with your hard-core lowlife scum set as scrambled 'Nam vet Travis Bickle (De Niro) sulks and kills. Celluloid sprinkled with angel dust.

The Tenant (1976) ◆◆◆◇

D: Roman Polanski. Roman Polanski, Isabelle Adjani, Melvyn Douglas, Shelley Winters, Jo Van Fleet, Bernard Fresson. 126 minutes. (Paramount)

Polanski's brilliantly perverse exercise in urban paranoia, adapted from Roland Topor's novel, deserves every bit of its vaunted cult rep. Polanski shines in three departments here—as co-scripter, director, and most of all, actor, in the lead role of a hapless office worker whose ill-advised move into a creepy Paris apartment house triggers his gradual breakdown. (Polanski recently resumed his Thespian career, playing Gregor Samsa in a Parisian mounting of Kafka's *Metamorphosis*.) You don't have to be a Parisian to identify with Polanski's claustrophobic plight, though living in Manhattan might help.

Terminal Choice (1985) ◆◇

D: Sheldon Larry. Joe Spano, Diane Venora, David McCallum, Robert Joy, Don Francks, Ellen Barkin. 97 minutes. (Vestron)

Released theatrically as *Death-bed*, this paranoid exercise in malpractice madness unfolds at the Dodson Clinic, where patients are expiring at an alarming rate via the malevolent influence of a killer computer operated by maniac unknown. When suspicion points to alcoholic doc Frank Holt (Spano), he and ex-squeeze Anna Lang (Venora)—the whiz who designed Dodson's deadly computer system—set out to find the true culprit while the corpses continue to mount. A middle-aged McCallum, who's added an extra chin since his *Man from U.N.C.L.E.* days but still sports his Ilya Kuryakin do, plays clinic head Dr. Dodson, while *Buckaroo Banzai* alumna Ellen Barkin (though Barfin' might've been an apter handle, since it's Ellen who's called upon to deliver the pic's major upchuck scene) turns up briefly as a wisecracking coroner. In addition to the requisite autopsy footage, *Terminal Choice* explores the many and varied medical atrocities a creative madman might commit with such everyday hospital equipment as poison IV's, death-dealing defibrillators, and malfunctioning pressure gauges. If not entertaining, *Terminal Choice* is at least educational.

They Live by Night (1949) NR B&W
D: *Nicholas Ray. Farley Granger, Cathy O'Donnell, Howard da Silva. 95 minutes. (Budget, others)*

Ray's offbeat noir stars Granger and O'Donnell as a young couple on the lam from the law. Remade by Robert Altman a quarter-century later as *Thieves like Us* (NA), the title of the original novel on which both films were based.

They Made Me a Criminal (1939) ◆◆◇ **B&W**
D: *Busby Berkeley. John Garfield, Ann Sheridan, Claude Rains, Dead End Kids. 92 minutes. (Video Yesteryear, others)*

Fugitive Garfield heads west, where he encounters the Dead End Kids (!). Busby Berkeley directs, but nobody dances.

The Thief (1952) ◆◆ **B&W**
D: *Russell Rouse. Ray Milland, Rita Gam, Martin Gabel. 85 minutes. (United)*

A gimmick spy movie, made without dialogue, with Milland as a nuclear physicist who passes secret documents to the Russkis. Worth a look for its novelty value, which wears thin pretty quickly.

The Thin Man (1934) NR B&W
D: *W. S. Van Dyke. William Powell, Myrna Loy, Maureen O'Sullivan, Cesar Romero. 93 minutes. (MGM/ UA)*

Powell and Loy portray Dashiell Hammett's sophisticated amateur sleuths Nick and Nora Charles in the first of that popular mystery/comedy series. The complete lineup is available as part of MGM/UA's sell-through Diamond Jubilee Collection: *After the Thin Man, Another Thin Man, Shadow of the Thin Man, Song of the Thin Man, The Thin Man Goes Home.*

The Third Man (1949) ◆◆◆ B&W
D: Carol Reed. Orson Welles, Joseph Cotten, Alida Valli. 104 minutes. (Republic, others)

Your Phantom feels this peripatetic manhunt set in postwar Vienna, while more than competent, has been wildly overrated. You may disagree.

The Thirteenth Guest (1932) NR ◆◆◇ B&W
D: Albert Ray. Ginger Rogers, Lyle Talbot, J. Farrell MacDonald. 69 minutes. (Sinister Cinema, others)

A creaky but entertaining haunted-house mystery, featuring Rogers and Talbot in their first screen pairing.

This Gun for Hire (1942) ◆◆◆ B&W
D: Frank Tuttle. Alan Ladd, Veronica Lake, Robert Preston. 80 minutes. (MCA)

Another topnotch noir, *This Gun* introduced Ladd as a short but hard-boiled hitman caught in a double cross. Lake looks great as the lady in the case.

This Man Must Die (1970) NR
D: Claude Chabrol. Michel Duchaussoy, Caroline Cellier, Jean Yanne. 112 minutes. (Key)

A popular thriller from "the French Hitchcock" about the writer/father (Duchaussoy) of a young hit-and-run victim and his labyrinthine quest for revenge. Other available Chabrol suspensers include *The Blood of Others* (Prism), *Bluebeard* (Charter), *The Twist* (IVE), and *Wedding in Blood* (RCA/Columbia).

Three Days of the Condor (1975) ◆◆◇
D: Sydney Pollack. Robert Redford, Max von Sydow, Faye Dunaway, Cliff Robertson. 117 minutes. (Paramount)

Robert Redford is a Company functionary who uncovers an internal plot that pits him against sinister CIA assassin Max von Sydow. Not too gripping.

T-Men (1947) ◆◆◆ B&W
D: Anthony Mann. Dennis O'Keefe, June Lockhart, Charles McGraw. 93 minutes. (King Bee)

Noir specialist Mann's ace direction makes this tough *Dragnet*-style semidocumentary Treasury Department adventure a lot more exciting than it might have been.

To Live and Die in L.A. (1985) ◆◆
D: William Friedkin. William L. Petersen, Willem Dafoe, John Pankow, Debra Feuer, John Turturro, Darlanne Fluegel, Dean Stockwell, Steve James. 114 minutes. (Vestron)

William (*The French Connection*) Friedkin's Angel City thriller has acquired something of a cult rep in certain high-tech sleaze-buff circles, but its alleged charm successfully eluded yours truly. The plot, a transplanted *French Con-*

nection rehash, concerns the extreme lengths to which two determined feds (Petersen, Pankow) go to crack a funny-money ring headed by sadistic artist-cum-counterfeiter Rick Masters (slimily interpreted by Dafoe). *To Live and Die in L.A.* does feature its fair share of kinetic car chases and high-energy shoot-outs set to an uptempo rock score. But take away the occasional raunch and explicit violence, and what you have is a painfully protracted *Miami Vice* episode relocated to L.A. Ditto for Hal Ashby's overblown *8 Million Ways to Die* (CBS/Fox).

Touch of Evil (1958) ◆◆◆◆ B&W
D: Orson Welles. Orson Welles, Charlton Heston, Janet Leigh, Marlene Dietrich. 108 minutes. (MCA)

Tijuana hoods hold police detective Heston's better half Leigh hostage while corrupt cop Welles tries to cover up his own multiple misdeeds. *Citizen Kane* (RKO) notwithstanding, Welles's nightmare noir, replete with crazed camera angles and a genuinely paranoiac aura, may be his best all-around movie. MCA carries the complete 108-minute version, not the shorter one seen during the film's initial theatrical release. A must.

Trouble in Mind (1985) ◆◇
D: Alan Rudolph. Kris Kristofferson, Keith Carradine, Genevieve Bujold, Lori Singer, Divine, Joe Morton. 111 minutes. (Charter)

More adolescent insights, pretentious patter, and pointless plot twists from the mind and lens of Robert Altman protégé Rudolph, who's gone way down since his debut feature, the immortal *Barn of the Naked Dead* (AIR) (also available as *Terror Circus* [Regal]), helmed under the alias Gerald Cormier. The basic story line—connecting the anomic lives of ex-cop/ex-con Kristofferson, petty thief/naif Carradine, his abandoned wife Singer, Kris's old flame Bujold, and effete gangster Divine as they intertwine in mythic Rain City—could have supplied solid entertainment, but Rudolph's self-conscious tone and heavy-handed irony kill it early on.

Try and Get Me! (1951) ◆◆◆ B&W
D: Cyril Endfield. Frank Lovejoy, Lloyd Bridges, Richard Carlson, Adele Jergens. 85 minutes. (Republic)

A bizarre noir that switches midway to a preachy social indictment, *Try and Get Me!* (aka *The Sound of Fury*) benefits mightily from scripter Jo Pagano's skillful adaptation of his own novel. Bridges stands out as a slick small-time hood who lures unemployed family man Lovejoy into an ill-advised kidnap caper. *Car 54*'s Joe E. Ross cameos as a menacing baggy-pants comic in a wonderfully febrile nightclub scene. For a McCarthy Era offering, *Try* paints a less-than-rosy picture of the realm. Recommended. Other '50s noirs now available from Republic: *City That Never Sleeps,*

Crashout, Cry Danger, and *Cry Vengeance.* Noir enthusiasts should also check out *The Chase* (United), *Dangerous Mission* (Fox Hills), *Killer Bait* (J&J), and *Man on the Eiffel Tower* (Video Gems).

Twilight's Last Gleaming (1977) ◆◆◇
D: Robert Aldrich. Burt Lancaster, Richard Widmark, Melvyn Douglas, Charles Durning, Paul Winfield. 146 minutes. (Key)

As in *Seven Days in May,* Burt again plays a mad military man, this time out to *end* nuclear proliferation by commandeering a nuke silo, in Robert Aldrich's farfetched but watchable pulp thriller. B-action fave Big Bill Smith is one of Burt's henchmen but doesn't make it past reel one.

Two-Moon Junction (1988) ◆◆◇
D: Zalman King. Sherilyn Fenn, Richard Tyson, Louise Fletcher, Burl Ives, Martin Hewitt, Millie Perkins. 104 minutes. (RCA/Columbia)

Actor/auteur King, the brains behind 1977's psychedelic psycho pic *Blue Sunshine* (Vestron), scripted and directed this steamy erotic thriller designed for the distaff market. Our story concerns a libidinous Alabama belle (Madonna lookalike Fenn) who tumbles for a traveling carny stud (hunky Tyson, *Three O'Clock High*'s teen-Terminator type), thereby endangering her impending marriage to rich frat boy Hewitt. The result is a sort of *Dirty Dancing* sans the dancing, or a *Last Tango in Tuscaloosa,* with Fenn living out femme fantasies with wildman Tyson, while her reproving grandmother (Fletcher) and the local sheriff (Ives) seek to discourage the trashy tryst. *Two-Moon Junction* is further bolstered by cameos by Herve Villechaize and Screamin' Jay Hawkins in their first—and thus far, only—screen teaming.

Uneasy Terms (1948) NR B&W
Michael Rennie, Moira Lister. 62 minutes. (Sinister Cinema)

A highly regarded Brit suspense tale with Rennie cast as a detective mixed up in blackmail and murder.

Variety (1985) ◆◆
D: Betty Gordon. Sandy McLeod, Will Patton, Richard Davidson. 101 minutes. (HBO)

Pretentious made-for-midnight "thriller" scripted by art hack Kathy Acker is worth watching for its primary set—NYC's legendary, ancient, but still operative (as a porn house) Variety PhotoPlays theater.

Vertigo (1958) ◆◆◆◇
D: Alfred Hitchcock. James Stewart, Kim Novak, Barbara Bel Geddes. 128 minutes. (MCA)

One of the suspense master's maddest plots, based on a novel by Pierre Boileau and Thomas Narcejac, finds fuzz Stewart falling for suspect Novak in a film that expands into a labyrinthine nightmare. After *Psycho,* this may be Hitch's best. See our Video

Shopping List for Alf's entire video lineup.

Vicious! (1988) ◆
D: Karl Zwicky. Tamblyn Lord, Craig Pearce, Tiffiny Dowe, Leather, Ralph Cotterill. 90 minutes. (Sony)

Directed by Zwicky from a script by Paul J. Hogan—not professional Outback promoter Paul (Croc Dundee) Hogan—this Aussie import limns the tedious tale of a pampered suburban teen (played by an irritating Lord) who gets embroiled with a trio of lowlife psychos. While Vicious! contains a fair amount of sadistic tableaux and abrupt-and-senseless violence sprees, the story defies even the most basic B-movie (let alone human) logic at every turn and transforms 90 minutes into a video eternity. One of the actresses is named Leather (how hip). Avoid this blunder from Down Under at all costs.

Video Murders (1987) ◆◆
D: Jim McCullough, Jr. Eric Brown, Virginia Lorridans, John Feritta, Frank Baggett, Lee Larrimore, Tracy Murrell. 90 minutes. (TWE)

From the father/son filmmaking team who brought us such celluloid swill as Mountaintop Motel Massacre (see index) and Charge of the Model T's (Nelson) comes Video Murders, a pointless but surprisingly professional and restrained B thriller about yet another misogynistic maniac on the loose. The story line is almost identical to Streets of Death's, only this time our psycho makes snuff videos (for his personal use only) and claims as his victims the hookers of Shreveport, Louisiana. The Phantom's Truth-in-Advertising Committee feels compelled to point out that, despite the pic's pluralized title, there's actually only one onscreen murder here; the bulk of the film—shot on 16mm and transferred to video—concerns serial killer Brown's Collector-like relationship with captive Lorridans, who, in the movie's most memorable moment, compliments him on his piano techniques while she's chained and hanging from the ceiling (!). Video Murders may be the McCulloughs' best effort, but it would take an awfully slow night to make it worth watching.

The Wages of Fear (1952) ◆◆◆ B&W
D: H. G. Clouzot. Yves Montand, Charles Vanel, Peter Van Eyck. 105 minutes. (Video Yesteryear, others)

An at-times unbearably tense look at the travails of a quartet of South America–based nitro truck drivers. Remade as Sorcerer (NA) in 1976.

Where Are the Children? (1986) ◆◇
D: Bruce Malmuth. Jill Clayburgh, Max Gail, Frederic Forrest, Barnard Hughes, Elizabeth Wilson, Harley Cross. 92 minutes. (RCA/Columbia)

A child-snatch/psycho opus, Where Are the Children? features

such once-vaunted stars as Clayburgh (former Late '30s Divorcee
On the Rocky Road to Liberation
specialist), Max (*Barney Miller*'s
Wojo) Gail, and former hot prospect Frederic (*The Rose, Hammett*) Forrest in the thankless
crazed-kidnapper role. Jill's never
had it worse: Not only must she, as
the snatched kids' mom (*and* a
prime suspect in the case), single-
handedly supply nearly all of the
pic's requisite histrionics, but
she's even spanked by a pervert in a
flashback sequence (!). As for Fred,
seen here sporting a gray beard and
an ungodly gut, he spends most of
the film talking like an addled
screenwriter's idea of a five-year-
old while simultaneously terrorizing Jill's hapless tots. *Where Are
the Children?* plays like a typical
made-for-TV "thriller"—with an
added dash of big-screen kink—
the type of film where the audience can figure out what's happening well in advance of the dim
onscreen characters.

White Heat (1949) ♦♦♦♦ B&W
*D: Raoul Walsh. James Cagney, Vir-
ginia Mayo, Edmond O'Brien, Steve
Cochran. 114 minutes. (CBS/Fox)*

Cagney's nothing short of brilliant
as migraine-plagued killer Cody
Jarrett in a crazed noir that also
portends the later celluloid-
psycho craze. An absolute must
for pop-psych pulp buffs and film
lovers of every stripe. Beware the
colorized version.

White of the Eye (1988) ♦♦♦
*D: Donald Cammell. Cathy Moriarty,
David Keith, Alan Rosenberg, Art
Evans, Marty Hayashi, William Schill-
ing. 111 minutes. (Paramount)*

Cammell, who co-directed the
1970 psychedelic cult fave *Performance* and helmed the later
computer-paranoia epic *Demon
Seed* (see index), returns with
White of the Eye, a flawed but bold,
bizarre, and truly sicko psycho-
killer thriller in a quasi–*Blue Velvet* vein. The action unfolds in
small-town Arizona, where Bronx
refugee Cathy (*Raging Bull*) Moriarty trades in her lowlife beau
Rosenberg for the possibly homicidal Keith. Auteur Cammell employs decidedly unconventional
methods, ranging from the hallucinogenic to the deliberately
mundane, in relating his often
terrifying tale. His creative camerawork and complex flashback
structure succeed more often than
not, while the principals turn in
solid work, with Art Evans a standout as a cagey Tucson detective.
Even occasional stretches of self-
indulgence and several less-than-
credible plot twists fail to strip
this surreal anti–ode to American
Romance of its intensity, power,
and primal rage.

Who'll Stop the Rain (1978) ♦♦♦
*D: Karel Reisz. Michael Moriarty, Nick
Nolte, Tuesday Weld. 126 minutes.
(MGM/UA)*

A pulpy action version of Robert
Stone's novel *Dog Soldiers* that

stumbles when it tries to wax pro-found but shines on a sleaze/suspense level. Richard Masur is especially repulsive as a sadistic hitman.

The Window (1949) ◆◆◆ B&W
D: Ted Tetzlaff. Bobby Driscoll, Barbara Hale, Arthur Kennedy. 73 minutes. (Fox Hills)

The original source for 1984's *Cloak and Dagger* (see index) stars Bobby Driscoll as a young boy who can't convince his incredulous parents (Hale, Kennedy) that he's actually witnessed a murder. A tight, effective '40s B.

Window in London (1939) NR B&W
D: Herbert Mason. Michael Redgrave, Paul Lukas, Sally Gray. 58 minutes. (Sinister Cinema)

An oft-praised Brit second feature about a man who witnesses a murder on a train passing by the titular aperture. Also available under its original title, *Lady in Distress* (Video Yesteryear).

Winter Kills (1979) ◆◆◆
D: William Richert. Jeff Bridges, John Huston, Anthony Perkins, Sterling Hayden. 97 minutes. (Embassy)

Bridges is a Bobby Kennedy stand-in who uncovers an involved plot behind his president-brother's assassination in another ace black comedy from novelist Richard Condon.

The Yakuza (1975) ◆◆◆
D: Sydney Pollack. Robert Mitchum, Takakura Ken, Brian Keith. 112 minutes. (Warner)

A modern noir set in Japan, where Yank Mitchum confronts the title organization—a sort of Nipponese Mafia that's since resurfaced in action pics like *Armed Response* (see index). We give it three phans for its slaughter sequences, though a single "pinky up" might be more appropriate here.

FUNNY BUSINESS
CURRENT, CULT, & CLASSIC
COMEDY CASSETTES

"So young! So bad! So what?"

Poster
Reform School Girls

It's oft been said that there's nothing in this world more subjective than humor, that one man's chuckle is another man's sob. Mel Brooks's 2,000-Year-Old Man may have summed it up best when he defined tragedy and comedy this way: "Tragedy is when *I* cut my finger and it bleeds and I have to go to Mount Sinai for a day and a half. Comedy is when *you* fall down a manhole and die—what do *I* care!"

Herein we cover comedy cassettes ranging from the sublime (*Lost in America, The Naked Gun*) to the sub*slime* (*Fat Guy Goes Nutzoid!, Ghost Fever*), from the big of budget (*Ishtar, Spaceballs*) to the paltry of purse (*Moron Movies, Ganjasaurus Rex*). Two things the Phantom *doesn't* do: windows and teen-oriented nerds-and-virgins

437

movies. Judging by the latter unlamented subgenre's steady decline, it appears we're not alone in our avowal.

We've also attempted to include as much complete video info on top vintage comedians (Chaplin, Keaton, W. C. Fields) and teams (Marx Brothers, The Three Stooges) as space allows. As is the case with other genres covered in this volume, a surprising number of comedy classics remain sadly unavailable on cassette. Fortunately, an even greater amount *are* out there, often at reasonable prices, if you know where to look—which is usually beyond your local vidstore.

Abbott and Costello Meet Frankenstein (1948) ◆◆◆ B&W

D: Charles T. Barton. Bud Abbott, Lou Costello, Bela Lugosi, Lon Chaney, Jr. 83 minutes. (MCA)

The boys encounter Bela, Lon, and even the voice of Invisible Man Vincent Price in what remains their best flick and one of Hollywood's premier horror spoofs. Other A&C features available on video include *Abbott and Costello in Hollywood* (MGM/UA), *Abbott and Costello Meet Captain Kidd* (United), *Abbott and Costello Meet Dr. Jekyll and Mr. Hyde* (MCA), *Abbott and Costello Meet the Killer, Boris Karloff* (Goodtimes), *Africa Screams* (Goodtimes, paired on the same cassette with *Jack and the Beanstalk* while United has a colorized *Africa Screams*), *Buck Privates, Hit the Ice,* and *Hold That Ghost* (all MCA). Also *Abbott and Costello Live, Vol. 1–3* (Blackhawk), *The Best of Abbott and Costello* (Warner), and *Hey Abbott!* (VidAmerica).

Adventures of the Little Rascals (1937–39) NR B&W

Spanky McFarland, Carl "Alfalfa" Switzer, Darla Hood. 100 minutes. (Republic)

Offers a half-dozen uncut Little Rascals shorts, as originally seen in '30s bijous, including "For Pete's Sake," "Glove Taps," and "Come the Brawn."

After Hours (1985) ◆◆◇

D: Martin Scorsese. Griffin Dunne, Rosanna Arquette, John Heard. 97 minutes. (Warner)

Scorsese's Hell-Down-in-SoHo comic nightmare ranges from inspired to desperate as he—like hopelessly lost hero Dunne—ultimately finds he has nowhere to go. Some brilliant paranoiac laughs brighten the film's first half, though.

Airplane! (1980) ◆◆◆◇

D: Jim Abrahams, David Zucker, Jerry Zucker. Peter Graves, Robert Hays, Julie Hagerty. 88 minutes. (Paramount)

This literalistic parody of air-disaster pics is the ultimate *MAD* magazine strip come to celluloid life and is thoroughly deserving of its vaunted comic rep. Not so the follow-up, *Airplane II: The Sequel* (Paramount), filmed without the ZAZ crew's participation. The trio returns with the rock 'n' roll spy-movie spoof *Top Secret!* (also Paramount) and their best effort to date, *The Naked Gun* (see index).

All of Me (1984) ◆◆◆
D: Carl Reiner. Steve Martin, Lily Tomlin, Victoria Tennant. 93 minutes. (HBO)

No *Glen or Glenda?* (see index), but a deft exercise in cross-sexual schizophrenia, with great physical comedy supplied by Martin as a man merged with the distaff spirit of eccentric dowager Tomlin.

All Over Town (1937) NR B&W
D: James W. Horne. Ole Olsen, Chic Johnson, James Finlayson. 62 minutes. (Kartes, J&J)

The then-popular comedy duo of Olsen and Johnson flee kidnappers and try to save a vaudeville theater from ruin in this typical romp, aided by Finlayson and Franklin Pangborn in supporting roles. O&J can also be seen in *Country Gentlemen* (Video Yesteryear).

. . . All the Marbles (1981) ◆◆◇
D: Robert Aldrich. Peter Falk, Laurene Landon, Vicki Frederick. 113 minutes. (MGM/UA)

Falk plays an amiably sleazy manager in a shaggy girl-wrestlers story that also provides a comic tour of truck-stop America.

Amazon Women on the Moon (1987) ◆◆◆
D: John Landis, Joe Dante, Robert K. Weiss, Peter Horton, Carl Gottlieb. Carrie Fisher, Griffin Dunne, Rosanna Arquette, Steve Guttenberg, Steve Forrest, Steve Allen, Sybil Danning, Ed Begley, Jr., Lou Jacobi. 85 minutes. (MCA)

Fashioned by five directors and featuring "Lots of Actors," *Amazon Women on the Moon* is a mostly on-target spoof of brain-damaged TV programming (pardon our redundancy), from Leonard Nimoy's *In Search of . . .* to late-night movie fests. Among the best bits are an *Invisible Man* takeoff, a generic '50s el cheapo sci-fi flick (the titular *Amazon Women on the Moon*), and the Dante-directed *Damaged Lives/Sex Madness* send-up *Reckless Youth*, starring Carrie Fisher and Paul Bartel. A "Funeral Roast" wherein Steve Allen, Henny Youngman, Slappy White, Rip Taylor, Jackie Vernon, and Charlie Callas skewer a deceased mere statistic before the latter's assembled mourners is another of the pic's amiably sick highlights. The once-in-a-lifetime cast includes Sybil Danning (as the Amazon Queen), Henry Silva, Robert Colbert, Mike Mazurki, Joey (John's talented brother) Travolta, William (*Blac-*

ula) Marshall (as the captain of a crew of bloodthirsty video pirates), and Russ Meyer as a shady vid-store clerk. A relatively low-budget labor of lunacy that lingered on the shelf for nearly a year before receiving a theatrical run, *Amazon Women on the Moon* has since been enjoying a deservedly healthy video afterlife.

American Graffiti (1973) ◆◆
D: George Lucas. Richard Dreyfuss, Ron Howard, Cindy Williams. 112 minutes. (MCA)

A generally overrated, mostly artificial homage to the California cruisers of the early '60s that rings especially false in Dreyfuss's scenes with the local overaged JDs. It does have a good rock soundtrack, though.

And Now for Something Completely Different (1972) ◆◆◆◇
D: Ian McNaughton. John Cleese, Graham Chapman, Terry Gilliam, Eric Idle, Terry Jones, Michael Palin. 89 minutes. (RCA/Columbia)

The Python gang recreate many of their greatest sketches, including "The Lumberjack Song" and "The Dead Parrot," in their feature film debut.

Andy Kaufman Sound Stage Show (1981) NR
Andy Kaufman. 60 minutes. (Lightning)

The late master of comic subversion holds forth in this filmed concert. Andy strikes again in *My Breakfast with Blassie* (Rhino).

Andy Warhol's Bad (1977) ◆◆◆
D: Jed Johnson. Carroll Baker, Perry King, Susan Tyrrell. 107 minutes. (Embassy)

Camp icon Carroll (*Harlow* [Paramount], *Baby Doll*) Baker is all business as a Queens housewife who uses her electrolysis biz as a cover for a free-lance assassination operation. A genuinely sick, frequently funny excursion into John Waters territory, further aided by authentic borough locales. Carroll cultists can also catch the mature Ms. B in the sleazy imports *Paranoia* and Jess Franco's *Venus in Furs* (both Republic), along with the 1984 farce *The Secret Diary of Sigmund Freud* (Key) and the otherwise useless Brit TV mystery *The Next Victim* (Thriller).

Animal Farm (1955) ◆◆◆
D: John Halas, Joy Batchelor. Narrated by Gordon Heath. 75 minutes. (Video Yesteryear, others)

Not quite as strong as Orwell's novel, but still a compelling animated satire debunking Soviet Communism in particular and human nature in general.

Armed and Dangerous (1986) ◆◇
D: Mark L. Lester. John Candy, Eugene Levy, Robert Loggia, Kenneth McMillan, Meg Ryan, Brion James. 88 minutes (RCA/Columbia)

It's depressing to watch the abundant comic talents of *SCTV* alumni Candy and Levy wasted in this weak attempt to apply the already moronic *Police Academy* formula to the security-guard biz. A few laughs ensue when Candy and Levy run afoul of their crooked union boss (Robert Loggia), but most of this lazy flick consists of careless setups sans punch lines.

Arnold (1973) ◆◆◇

D: Georg Fenady. Stella Stevens, Roddy McDowall, Elsa Lanchester. 96 minutes. (Lightning)

Gimmick guru William Castle's static but dependably bizarre affair is basically a series of weird-murder set pieces.

Arsenic and Old Lace (1944) ◆◆◆ B&W

D: Frank Capra. Cary Grant, Priscilla Lane, Raymond Massey, Peter Lorre. 118 minutes. (CBS/Fox)

Joseph Kesselring's cheerful black comedy about a pair of geriatric euthanasia enthusiasts and their strange family represents a change of pace for the usually sunny Capra. Still admirably sick for a slick '40s feature. This is the only other Capra movie to make it into this volume.

Assault of the Killer Bimbos (1988) ◆◆◇

D: Anita Rosenberg. Christina Whitaker, Elizabeth Kaitan, Tammara Souza, Nick Cassavetes, Arell Blanton, Griffin O'Neal. 85 minutes. (Urban Classics)

Assault of the Killer Bimbos could easily have been just another colorfully titled turkey—check out Creepozoids, Galactic Gigolo, and Slaves Girls from Beyond Infinity (see index—on second thought, don't bother)—bearing the low-budget Urban Classics label. In the capable hands of director Rosenberg, however, the pic emerges as a fairly funny, fast-paced chase comedy that earns Bimbos a hopefully permanent place on the B-movie map. Whitaker, Souza, and especially Kaitan (as Lulu, who at one point wails, "I'm never gonna make it as a go-go dancer; I'm too stupid!") are appealing (and often a-peeling) as the titular trio—two dancers and a waitress wrongly implicated in a topless-club owner's murder—while Cassavetes contributes a deft comic turn as an amiably brainless surfer named Wayne-O. We were tempted to subtract half a phan for the video's epilogue—a blatant pitch for a line of Bimbomania merchandise—but figured, what the heck, bimbos need all the help they can get. Besides, any flick that names a character Peaches Page, in honor of the buxom wrestling star of the 1951 exploitation obscurity Pin-Down Girls, will always get our vote.

Attack of the Killer Tomatoes (1979) ◆◇

D: John DeBello. George Wilson, Sharon Taylor, Jack Riley. 87 minutes. (Media)

Included as a warning, not a recommendation, since the title is hard to resist. The movie, we promise you, is low camp at its lowest. A belated sequel, Return of *the Killer Tomatoes*, is also available, via New World.

Avenging Disco Godfather (1977) ♦♦
D: Rudy Ray Moore. Rudy Ray Moore, Lady Reed, Carol Speed, Jimmy Lynch. 93 minutes. (Interglobal/Active)

Showcases the unique comedy stylings of Rudy Ray Moore, who used to cut risqué party records, á la Redd Foxx, back in the early '60s. Here he stars in his own kung-fu farce. For more of Rudy Ray, see Moore's best effort, *The Devil's Son-in-Law* (Interglobal), costarring fellow comics Wildman Steve and Leroy and Skillet, plus the "blaxploitation" parodies *Dolemite* and *Human Tornado* and the comedy concert pic *Rawer Than Raw*, aka *Rude* (all via Mercury/Xenon).

Back to School (1986) ♦♦♦
D: Alan Metter. Rodney Dangerfield, Keith Gordon, Sally Kellerman. 96 minutes. (HBO)

Rodney's best role to date casts him as a likable, extroverted fat-clothing king who enrolls in college in a misguided bid to get closer to son Gordon. Some of the bits fall flat, but Rodney gets on enough rolls to make this a must for Dangerfield devotees.

Back to the Beach (1987) ♦♦◇
D: Lyndall Hobbs. Frankie Avalon, Annette Funicello, Connie Stevens, Lori Loughlin, Tommy Hinckley, Demian Slade. 92 minutes. (Paramount)

This systematic dismantling of the Frankie/Annette beach-party mythos is a mixed but generally fun and subtly vicious affair. *Back to the Beach* finds "stressed-out car salesman" Frankie and zomboid Stepford-like housewife Annette returning to their sandy roots to chill out and, as it happens, "rescue" daughter Loughlin from her live-in arrangement with surfer boy Hinckley. Their fourteen-year-old son Bobby (Slade) serves as a deflating wise-ass stand-in for today's skeptical young viewer as he mocks the *derriere-garde* romantic machinations of his addled parents, "the world's corniest couple." The pic is peppered with numerous cameos—by *Gilligan's Island* castaways Bob Denver and Alan Hale, Jerry (The Beaver) Mathers and TV bro' Tony Dow, plus Don (*Get Smart*) Adams—but the best bits are turned in by reverb guitar ace Dick Dale ("Held over—25th year!") and Pee-wee Herman, who offers his unique interpretation of the Trashmen's "Surfin' Bird." Most memorable line belongs to an anonymous screen youngster who, upon hearing of Frankie's (aka the Big Kahuna) past surfing exploits, tells our hero, "That's really neat, 'specially since you *look* like an Italian loan shark!"

Back to the Future (1985) ♦♦♦◇
D: Robert Zemeckis. Michael J. Fox, Christopher Lloyd, Crispin Glover, Lea Thompson, Claudia Wells. 116 minutes. (MCA)

Back to the Future won yours truly over on the strength of its vintage-movie-nostalgia value alone. When young Marty McFly (Fox) rewinds to 1955, we see his hometown's two broken-down bijous—since converted into a porn house and a church, respectively—restored to their former glory. (One even advertises *Cattle Queen of Montana*, starring Ronald Reagan.) When Marty prepares to fast-forward to the present, his time machine (a souped-up DeLorean!) passes through the '50s bijou and emerges from the '80s church! Beyond its admirable bijou by-play, *Back to the Future* is a bright fantasy brimming with playful temporal conceits and clever pop-cultural comparisons between the '50s and the '80s. Director/co-scripter Zemeckis wisely relies on irony rather than sentimentality in charting the changes (and lack of same) those thirty years have wrought. Fox is properly bemused as the contempo teen who must bring his nerdy adolescent dad and flirty future mom together to ensure his eventual birth, while Lloyd turns in one of filmdom's flakiest mad scientist perfs. Easily the best megabudgeted, teen-targeted, crowd-pleasing, sci-fi fantasy flick we're likely to see.

Bagdad Cafe (1988) ◆◆◆
D: Percy Adlon. Marianne Säge-brecht, C.C.H. Pounder, Jack Pal-ance, Christine Kaufmann. 91 minutes. (Virgin Vision)

An offbeat but upbeat tale that finds abandoned Bavarian tourist Sägebrecht enlivening a deadbeat motel/café set in the Nevada desert. Palance offers a relatively restrained perf as an eccentric artist in this whimsical, mostly winning West German–produced indie.

Bananas (1971) ◆◆◆◇
D: Woody Allen. Woody Allen, Louise Lasser, Carlos Montalban. 82 minutes. (CBS/Fox)

One of the Woodman's wittiest finds him embroiled in a Central American revolution. Howard Cosell and Sly Stallone turn up in cameos, but *Bananas* is worth seeing anyway.

The Bank Dick (1940) ◆◆◆◇ B&W
D: Edward Cline. W. C. Fields, Cora Witherspoon, Una Merkel. 73 minutes. (MCA)

Fields is in top form in this free-wheeling tribute to the joys of insobriety, loosely adapted from his own script (written under the nom de plume Mahatma Kane Jeeves). Franklin Pangborn and Shemp Howard lend memorable comic support. Other available Fields fests include his best—*It's a Gift* (Kartes)—plus *International House* (MCA), *Mrs. Wiggs of the Cabbage Patch* (Goodtimes), *My Little Chickadee* (MCA), *Never Give a Sucker an Even Break* (MCA), the silents *Running Wild* (Paramount) and *Sally of the Sawdust* (Grapevine), *You Can't Cheat an Honest Man* (Kartes), and several compilation tapes: *Comedy Reel #2* (with W. C.'s "The Barber Shop," [Cable]), *A Flask of Fields* ("The Golf Specialist," "The Dentist," "The Fatal Glass of Beer," [Video Yesteryear]), *Fields for All* (J&J), and *W. C. Fields* (includes the short "Pool Sharks," plus Fields trailers [Captain Bijou]). The docu-compilation *W. C. Fields: On Stage, On Screen, On the Air* is also out (MPI).

Barfly (1987) ◆◆◆
D: Barbet Schroeder. Mickey Rourke, Faye Dunaway, Alice Krige, Jack Nance, J. C. Quinn, Frank Stallone. 99 minutes. (Warner)

Charles Bukowski's script, a deft distillation of several autobiographical short stories, takes the viewer through a few bar-hopping days (make that daze) in the life of CB's fictional alter ego, writer/drunk (not necessarily in that order) Henry Chinaski. This laid-back (occasionally passed-out) but consistently funny slice of lowlife is cleverly, unobtrusively framed by an identical opening and closing L.A. tavern travelogue, set to a jukebox rendition of Booker T.'s "Hip Hugg'er," that succinctly underscores the cyclical nature of Henry's barfly continuum. Personified by a simultaneously swaggering and staggering Rourke, HC drinks, writes, fights continuously with beefy barkeep Frank Stallone, drinks, has an *affair du liqueur*

with distaff lush Dunaway, is pursued by private dick Jack (*Eraserhead*) Nance, is wooed by slumming publisher Krige, and drinks. Rourke mutters many memorable Bukowski lines (though the actor's inflection unfortunately alters from scene to scene) and is himself summed up by a fellow wino who opines, "He hates help." Withal, *Barfly* makes for fluid video viewing—there's even a lively barroom catfight 'twixt Dunaway and Krige—preferably accompanied by a half-pint of cheap whiskey and a couple of brews. For a double shot of Bukowski, we'd recommend also renting Marco Ferrari's inferior but interesting *Tales of Ordinary Madness* (Vestron), featuring Ben Gazzara as a slightly older Chinaski/Bukowski incarnation. Barbet Schroeder's two-volume *verité* work *The Charles Bukowski Tapes* is also available on the Lagoon Video label, while Black Sparrow carries the appetizingly titled *Bukowski At Bellevue: Spring 1970*.

Batman: The Movie (1966) ◆◆◇
D: Leslie Martinson. Adam West, Burt Ward, Burgess Meredith, Cesar Romero, Lee Meriwether. 105 minutes. (Playhouse)

Produced at the height of the camp teleseries' popularity, *Batman* often plays like a patchwork TV movie. Some funny moments, though, and a must for fans of the show.

Beach Blanket Bingo (1965) ◆◆◇
D: William Asher. Frankie Avalon, Annette Funicello, Linda Evans. 96 minutes. (HBO)

Arguably the best of the Frankie and Annette sun 'n' fun fests—never yours truly's fave genre—this one works harder for laughs and benefits from the presence of a jeering Don Rickles and a prissy Paul Lynde. Other series entries include *Beach Party* (Warner), *Bikini Beach* (Embassy), *How to Stuff a Wild Bikini* (Warner), and *Muscle Beach Party* (HBO).

Beach House (1982) ◆◆◇
D: John Gallagher. Ileana Seidel, Richard Duggan, Kathy McNeil. 76 minutes. (HBO)

A sort of updated *Bowery Boys Meet Beach Blanket Bingo*, Gallagher's amiable low-budget surf-and-sand saga finds a gang of Brooklyn greasers sharing the title site with a gaggle of Philly WASPs. The least obnoxious teen-jiggle caper of the decade.

Beat the Devil (1954) ◆◆◇
D: John Huston. Humphrey Bogart, Jennifer Jones, Peter Lorre. 89 minutes. (RCA/Columbia)

Something of a flop in its time, this John Huston/Truman Capote collaboration is a laid-back (though not especially subtle) satire on human greed that's since enjoyed a long history as a revival-house—and now video—perennial.

Bedazzled (1967) ◆◆◆
D: Stanley Donen. Peter Cook, Dudley Moore, Eleanor Bron, Raquel Welch. 107 minutes. (CBS/Fox)

Moore is a London loser, Cook the Devil who offers a dubious helping hand, in this bright satire made back in the days when Dud was still funny.

Bedtime for Bonzo (1951) ◆◆◇ **B&W**
D: Frederick de Cordova. Ronald Reagan, Diana Lynn, Walter Slezak. 83 minutes. (MCA)

Ronald Reagan, later instrumental in refusing funds for chimp-language and learning experiments, here tries to communicate with the title primate. Pretty grotesque. Bonzo, sans Ronzo, starred in a sequel, *Bonzo Goes to College* (NA).

Beer (1985) ◆◆◇
D: Patrick Kelly. Loretta Swit, Rip Torn, Kenneth Mars. 82 minutes. (HBO)

A low-budget beer-campaign parody that was apparently tampered with, *Beer* doesn't deliver as consistently as it might have but has enough laughs to make for decent happy-hour vid-viewing.

Beetlejuice (1988) ◆◆◇
D: Tim Burton. Alec Baldwin, Geena Davis, Michael Keaton, Catherine O'Hara, Glen Shadix, Winona Ryder, Sylvia Sidney. 92 minutes. (Warner)

Maybe the Phantom's grown jaded, but he's reached the point where he can't accept elaborate FX as a substitute for wit. At the outset, *Beetlejuice* exhibits an admirable quantity of the latter as newlydeads Baldwin and Davis seek to evict their onetime Connecticut home's obnoxious new owners—a crew of insufferable downtown art yuppies (including our fave *SCTV* alumna, O'Hara). In one of the funniest sequences, our ghostly protagonists are assigned a caseworker (Sidney)—bureaucracy flourishes in the hereafter, too—but eventually hire bio-exorcist Betelgeuse, energetically interpreted by Keaton. Unfortunately, once that wild and crazy dead guy takes over, director Burton increasingly resorts to desperate, FX-dependent sight gags to carry the rest of the film. There are inventive moments here, plus cameos by *Nightmare on Elm Street 3*'s Dick Cavett and former singing star Robert Goulet, but we got more gory giggles out of *Re-Animator* and *Evil Dead II* (see index).

Best of the Big Laff Off (1983) NR
60 minutes. (Lorimar)

A compilation culled from comedy club concerts, hosted by David Steinberg and featuring Eddie Murphy, Sandra Bernhard, and Steve Mittleman, among others.

Best of the Festival of Claymation (1987) NR
60 minutes. (Pacific Arts)

Claymation comedy shorts from Will Vinton, Jimmy V. Picker, and other animators, originally shown theatrically.

Betrayal (1983) ◆◆◆◇
D: David Jones. Jeremy Irons, Ben Kingsley, Patricia Hodge. 95 minutes. (CBS/Fox)

Harold Pinter's perverse tale of a romantic triangle works backward from the end of the affair to its humble beginnings in Jones's successful celluloid adaptation of the play. Kingsley is especially strong as the not-so-innocent cuckold in the case.

Bingo Long Traveling All-Stars and Motor Kings (1976) ◆◆◆
D: John Badham. Billy Dee Williams, James Earl Jones, Richard Pryor. 111 minutes. (MCA)

Bingo Long packs lots of Negro League facts and lore into an entertaining if occasionally broad comedy about the misadventures of Billy Dee Williams's titular barnstorming baseball team.

The Blues Brothers (1980) ◆◆◆
D: John Landis. John Belushi, Dan Aykroyd, John Candy. 130 minutes. (MCA)

An overproduced but mostly fun account of honky bluesmen Belushi and Aykroyd's efforts to save a Chicago orphanage, with memorable musical cameos by Aretha Franklin and James Brown.

Blume in Love (1973) ◆◆◆
D: Paul Mazursky. George Segal, Susan Anspach, Kris Kristofferson. 117 minutes. (Warner).

Mazursky transcends his characters' middle-class concerns by piloting his pic into some pretty perverse, uncomfortable turf, like nerdy Segal's ill-advised visit with his ex (Anspach) and her new beau (Kristofferson).

Boy! What a Girl (1946) ◆◆◆ B&W

D: Arthur Leonard. Tim Moore, Duke Williams, Elwood Smith. 70 minutes. (Discount Video)

TV's Kingfish (Moore) goes the Divine route here, playing most of this black indie comedy in drag! Fine perfs, a funny plot, and a number of hot musical cameos make this one a winner.

Brazil (1985) ◆◆◆◇

D: Terry Gilliam. Jonathan Pryce, Robert De Niro, Michael Palin, Katherine Helmond, Kim Greist, Bob Hoskins. 131 minutes. (MCA)

Ex-Python Gilliam's suitably grotesque *1984* takeoff stars Pryce as Sam Lowry, a daydreaming clerk trapped in a future dystopia ruled by crazed bureaucrats and malfunctioning machines, both of which serve as frequent targets of mysterious terrorist attacks. Sam leads a life of relentless, usually arbitrary harassment—perpetrated by everyone from vengeful repairmen to his meddlesome mom—that's easily the equal of the average New Yorker's. While the central idea may not be the freshest, Gilliam's treatment (with assists from co-scripters Tom Stoppard and Charles McKeown)

is consistently witty and inventive. Bolstered by zany cameos from De Niro, Palin, Hoskins, and David Warner, and by Greist's solid turn as the elusive object of Sam's desire, *Brazil* plays like an extended $15-mil *Monty Python* skit. *Too* extended, in fact: *Brazil's* only flaw is that it goes on roughly a reel too long (the most expensive reel at that), descending into a violent FX orgy that adds little to the more inspired comedy preceding it. Still, *Brazil* offers a lively two hours of dark futuristic fun and comes highly recommended here.

Broadway Danny Rose (1984) ◆◆◆ B&W

D: Woody Allen. Woody Allen, Mia Farrow, Nick Apollo Forte. 86 minutes. (Vestron)

Allen's shaggy show-biz comedy introduces a great character in Broadway Danny, a loser agent who tries to steer lounge singer Forte to the top while romancing Mafia mistress Mia. Great fodder for the Italian-American Anti-Defamation League.

Car Wash (1976) ◆◆◇

D: Michael Schultz. George Carlin, Franklin Ajaye, Richard Pryor. 97 minutes. (MCA)

A sometimes broad, often on-target day in the life at a largely black-run car wash. Pryor has a neat bit as a flashy Reverend Ike–type preacher. The funky soundtrack is another plus.

Carry on Nurse (1958) ◆◆◇ **B&W**
*D: Gerald Thomas. Kenneth Connor,
Kenneth Williams, Charles Hawtrey.
86 minutes. (HBO)*

The flick that kicked off the popular Brit low-comedy series, based on a play by Patrick Cargill and Jack Beale and fun on a Benny Hill level. Other available series titles include: *Carry on Abroad* (RTS), *Carry on at Your Convenience* (Axon), *Carry on Behind* (Embassy), *Carry on Cleo, Carry on Cowboy, Carry on Cruising* (all HBO), *Carry on Doctor* (Paramount), *Carry on Emanuelle* (Paragon), *Carry on Screaming* (Sinister Cinema), *Carry on Up the Khyber* (Intra), and *Follow That Camel* (VidAmerica), costarring Phil Silvers. VidAmerica also carries three entries in Dirk Bogarde's popular Doctor series: *Doctor at Large, Doctor at Sea,* and *Doctor in Distress.*

The Cars That Ate Paris (1974) NR
*D: Peter Weir. Terry Camilleri, John
Meillon, Melissa Jaffa. 91 minutes.
(RCA/Columbia)*

That's not Paris, France, or even Paris, Texas, but Paris, Australia, where locals profit by arranging car accidents for strangers, then selling the scrap, in this early Peter Weir effort. Also known as *The Cars That Eat People.*

Casino Royale (1967) ◆◆◇
*D: John Huston, Ken Hughes, Robert
Parrish, Joe McGrath, Val Guest. Peter
Sellers, David Niven, Woody Allen, Ur-
sula Andress, Orson Welles. 130 min-
utes. (RCA/Columbia)*

A lavish budget, an all-star cast, and five—count 'em—five directors conspired to turn this Bondian spoof into more of a mess than a mirth marathon, but it still has its share of fun moments.

Catch a Rising Star: 10th Anniversary (1982) NR
60 minutes. (RCA/Columbia)

Interviews, monologues, and sketches by David Brenner, Billy Crystal, Andy Kaufman, Robin Williams, and others, marking the pioneering comedy club's debut decade.

The Comic (1969) ◆◆◇
*D: Carl Reiner. Dick Van Dyke, Mi-
chelle Lee, Mickey Rooney. 96 minutes. (RCA/Columbia)*

A bizarre mix of the on-target and the embarrassingly bad, as Reiner charts the rise and fall of a composite silent comedian embodied by Van Dyke. The silent films-within-the-film are a highlight.

Comic Relief (1986) NR
*Billy Crystal, Whoopi Goldberg, Dick
Gregory, Jerry Lewis, Robin Williams.
120 minutes. (Lorimar)*

The video version of the first all-star benefit for the homeless, filmed live, features over thirty comic performers.

Cracking Up (1983) ◆◆◇
*D: Jerry Lewis. Jerry Lewis, Herb Edel-
man, Foster Brooks, Milton Berle,
Sammy Davis, Jr., Zane Busby. 90 minutes. (Warner)*

Cracking Up (aka *Smorgasbord*) represents Jerry, if not at his best, then certainly at his most unfettered. The pic consists of a series of frequently surreal slapstick set pieces linked to chronic loser Warren Nefrin's (Jerry) sessions with beleaguered shrink Edelman. All the traditional Jerry trademarks are here: a big-band soundtrack; comic cameos by the likes of Milton Berle (as a nymphomaniac!) and Sammy Davis, Jr. (as "himself"); and the usual multiple product tie-ins. Jerry also plays shamelessly to the French (who awarded him a Legion of Honor medal some years back), from a "Title Song Sung by Marcel Marceau" credit to an extended French flashback that's easily the flick's weakest sequence. Some of the better conceptual sight gags are reminiscent of Ernie Kovacs's early video work, but *Cracking Up* is closer in spirit to *Never Give a Sucker an Even Break*, W. C. Fields's final and most wildly idiosyncratic outing. If you've ever wondered what Jerry would do with *total* creative freedom, *Cracking Up* supplies the answer.

Creature from the Haunted Sea (1961) ◆◆ B&W

D: Roger Corman. Antony Carbone, Betsy Jones-Moreland, Edward Wain. 72 minutes. (Video Home Library)

Quickie Corman comedy—lensed back-to-back with *Last Woman on Earth*—involving gangsters, Cubans, and sea creatures plays pretty broadly but boasts its share of loyal supporters. And underrated AIP regular Betsy Jones-Moreland is, in our book, always worth a look.

Crimewave (1985) ◆

D: Sam Raimi. Louise Lasser, Paul L. Smith, Brion James, Sheree J. Wilson, Bruce Campbell, Reed Birney. 83 minutes. (Charter)

This low-budget, Detroit-lensed collaboration between Sam (*The Evil Dead*) Raimi and co-scripters Joel and Ethan (*Blood Simple, Raising Arizona*) Coen offers some inventive sound and camera work but is otherwise an almost unbelievable embarrassment for all involved. In attempting to fashion a live-action cartoon (a task at which action director Hal Needham had earlier failed in his *Road Runner*–inspired western spoof *Villain* [NA]), the filmmakers regurgitate painfully witless movie and sitcom clichés, waste the talents of normally competent thesps Lasser, Smith, and Campbell (who also co-produced this fiasco), and sorely tested the limits of even the Phantom's patience.

"Crocodile" Dundee (1986) ◆◆◇

D: Peter Faiman. Paul Hogan, Linda Kozlowski. 98 minutes. (Paramount)

The Aussie sleeper that broke all kinds of BO records is a modest but uncompromised comedy that doesn't strain for laughs. Croc returns in the more labored but similarly lucrative *"Crocodile" Dundee II* (also Paramount).

Days of Thrills and Laughter (1961) ◆◆◆
B&W
Compiled by Robert Youngson. 93 minutes. (MPI)

A fast-moving compilation of clips from silent comedy shorts, featuring Fatty Arbuckle, the Keystone Kops, Chaplin, Sennett, and dozens more.

Dead Men Don't Wear Plaid (1982) ◆◆◇
B&W
D: Carl Reiner. Steve Martin, Rachel Ward, Reni Santoni. 91 minutes. (MCA)

Dead Men adopts a riff earlier used in *The Projectionist* (see index): Martin plays a private eye who interacts with characters from '30s and '40s noirs. Some laughs and imagination, but not really enough to sustain the film's feature length.

Deathrow Gameshow (1987) ◇
D: Mark Pirro. John McCafferty, Robin Blythe, Beano, Mark Lasky, Darwyn Carson, Debra Lamb. 78 minutes. (Media)

A painfully puerile skit idea padded to agonizing feature length, *Deathrow Gameshow* gives Troma's *Fat Guy Goes Nutzoid!* serious competition for Worst Comedy of 1987 (dis)honors. Unlike the latter, this one doesn't even boast an imaginative title (though, in all fairness, the same can't be said for *Deathrow* director Pirro's previous effort, *A Polish*

Vampire in Burbank [Simitar]). The Phantom tallied a total of one—count it—one laugh in 78 minutes of aggressive mirthlessness. For the record, the flick chronicles the would-be madcap misadventures of one Chuck Toedan (McCafferty), oft-imperiled host of a game show wherein deathrow inmates either win an eleventh-hour reprieve or die live on network TV. A similar premise is employed to far better—and funnier—effect in Arnold Schwarzenegger's *Running Man* (see index).

Desperate Living (1977) ◆◆◆◇
D: John Waters. Mink Stole, Edith Massey, Liz Renay, Mary Vivian Pearce. 90 minutes. (Cinema Group)

Late Waters, regular Edith. Massey enjoys her finest filmic hour here as the imposing Queen Carlotta of Mortville, a memorable patch of living hell located not far from Baltimore. It's in Mortville that hysterical housewife Mink Stole and her more sensible two-ton maid find themselves trapped after fleeing a murder rap. Despite Divine's conspicuous absence, *Desperate Living* ranks as one of Waters's sickest, truest, and funniest trash romps—must viewing for his fans and courageous curiosity-seekers alike. The immortal line "Will you ever be able to *love* my operation?" wins the Phantom's *Glen or Glenda?* Memorial Award for Distinguished Screenwriting.

Desperate Teenage Love Dolls (1985) ◇

D: David Markey. Jennifer Schwartz, Hilary Rubens, Steve McDonald, Tracy Lea. 60 minutes. (Hollywood Home Theater)

Ever see one of those awful made-for-public-access "comedies" that ruin otherwise perfectly good dead airtime on late-night cable TV? Well, this isn't up to even *those* subterranean standards. While we're sure final production costs soared into the high single-digit range, this utterly amateur, shot-on-splotchy-video special follows the "adventures" of a runaway-girls' band (the titular Love Dolls) searching for success on the streets, beaches, and boardwalks of sunny Santa Monica. A blend of '60s sloppiness and '80s idiocy, *Love Dolls* panhandled half a phan out of us solely on the strength of its inspired title, lively cartoon box-cover art, and the admittedly deathless line, "Gee, thanks for killing my mom!"

The Discreet Charm of the Bourgeoisie (1972) ◆◆◆◇

D: Luis Buñuel. Stephane Audran, Fernando Rey, Jean-Pierre Cassel. 100 minutes. (Corinth)

Approaching seventy himself here, Buñuel still enjoys thumbing his nose at middle-aged upper-middle-class hypocrites, by this time a generation his junior. The results are as savage as ever.

Dr. Minx (1975) ◆◆

D: Hikmet Avedis. Edy Williams, Randy Boone, William Smith. 94 minutes. (Continental)

The ever-irrepressible Edy is a rich doctor (!) in this unintentionally funny would-be erotic thriller. Big Bill Smith is her greedy ex-lover. For Edy addicts.

Dr. Strangelove, or: How I Learned to Stop Worrying and Love the Bomb (1964) ◆◆◆◆ B&W

D: Stanley Kubrick. Peter Sellers, Sterling Hayden, George C. Scott, Keenan Wynn. 102 minutes. (RCA/Columbia)

Kubrick and co-scripter Terry Southern's doomsday collaboration may be the best black comedy ever made. Repeated viewings are strongly advised.

Don's Party (1976) NR

D: Bruce Beresford. John Hargreaves, Pat Bishop, Graham Kennedy. 91 minutes. (VidAmerica)

A sardonic sleeper from Down Under, *Don's Party* covers a raucous night among young Aussie suburbanites who gather to watch the election results on TV.

Down Among the Z Men (1952) NR B&W

D: Maclean Rogers. Peter Sellers, Harry Secombe, Spike Milligan. 70 minutes. (Pacific Arts)

The cast of England's influential *Goon Show* take to the screen in their first feature-film fling. The

Goons returned four years later in the short *The Case of the Mukkinese Battle Horn* (Video Yesteryear).

Dragnet (1987) ◆◆◆

D: Tom Mankiewicz. Dan Aykroyd, Tom Hanks, Christopher Plummer, Alexandra Paul, Harry Morgan, Dabney Coleman. 106 minutes. (MCA)

Aykroyd deserved an Oscar nomination for his brilliant recreation of Jack Webb's warped straight-arrow LAPD-dick-cum-'50s-icon Joe Friday. As the original Friday's nephew/clone, Aykroyd actually imparts some genuine shading to Webb's wooden persona, gradually humanizing and socializing the character through close contact with carefree new partner, Pep Streebek (well limned by Hanks, though Bill Murray might have been an even better choice). The plot, while less than gripping, serves as an adequate frame for sundry clever bits, running riffs, and Aykroyd's earnest narration. The last-reel emphasis on unnecessary action drags the movie down some, and Coleman's lisping interpretation of a Hefner-like soft-core sex czar probably played funnier on the set than it does on-screen. But Dan and Tom—with a fine assist by Paul as "the virgin Connie Swail," the innocent object of Friday's chaste affections—are the show here, and their antics make *Dragnet* worthwhile.

Eat and Run (1986) ◆

D: Stan Hart. Ron Silver, R. L. Ryan,
Sharon Schlarth. 85 minutes. (New World)

If nothing else, *Eat and Run*—detailing a reign of gustatory terror perpetrated by an overweight alien fond of eating Italians—proves that there's more to making genre comedies than memorizing every line and frame of *Airplane!* On the plus side, veteran character thesp Silver does his best as a cop cold on the trail of the obese ET, wordlessly interpreted by hefty R. L. (*Toxic Avenger, Street Trash*) Ryan, who herein intensifies his bid to become the Tor Johnson of today. In toto, though, *Eat and Run* is enough to put anyone off their popcorn; the Phantom, long pasta point of caring, fast-forwarded through the final reels.

Eat the Peach (1986) ◆◆◇

D: Peter Ormrod. Stephen Brennan, Eamon Morrissey, Catherine Byrne. 95 minutes. (Key)

Irish dreamer Brennan is inspired by a vintage Elvis Presley movie to build his own backyard motorcycle pit in a taciturn Hibernian "dramedy" that's won its fair share of supporters. Not to be confused with the broad Brit cannibalistic class-war send-up *Eat the Rich* (RCA/Columbia).

Eating Raoul (1982) ◆◆◆

D: Paul Bartel. Mary Woronov, Paul Bartel, Robert Beltran. 83 minutes. (CBS/Fox)

Bartel strikes again, this time with a black comedy about a bland couple (Mr. and Mrs. Bland, in fact) who slay and rob local swingers to raise enough bread to open a restaurant. Burglar Beltran, as Raoul, complicates their plans in this hit-and-miss satire. The raw, straightforward *Swingers' Massacre* (see index) makes for an apt companion piece. Bartel returns, meanwhile, with *Not for Publication* (HBO).

Elvira, Mistress of the Dark (1988) ◆◆
D: James Signorelli. Elvira (Cassandra Peterson), W. Morgan Sheppard, Daniel Greene. 98 minutes. (New World)

Buxom video horror hostess Elvira's (monsterdom's answer to Mae West) movie debut opens with a clip from Roger Corman's seminal 1956 carrot-creature movie *It Conquered the World* (NA). An admittedly tough act to follow, and *Elvira*'s creators attempt that formidable feat more with desperate energy than with inspired wit. The flick's hoary premise finds Elvira inheriting your standard haunted house in the prudish province of Fallwell, Massachusetts, where our cheerfully trashy, Trademark-Registered horror hostess battles bluenosed town elders while evading evil uncle Sheppard, who's after the satanic "recipe" book that's likewise been bequeathed to our increasingly bemused heroine. Rallying to Elvira's side (to speak only of her side) are the town's oppressed teens and local hunk Greene, a lad innocent enough to ignore El's decidedly unsubtle advances. While Elvira does a decently indecent job of fleshing out her terror-TV persona and the movie maintains an essentially amiable, throwaway tone, most of the comedy here is cut as low as El's ubiquitous black dress. The script—which Elvira co-wrote under her real name Cassandra Peterson—relies mainly on retro sex jokes, most of them centering on El's Amazing Colossal Cleavage. There are a few genuine shock yoks scattered throughout the pic, but not enough to make *Mistress* a must for any but Elvira's most fervent admirers. The latter can also catch El in the sketch collection *Uncensored* (WesternWorld).

Everything You Always Wanted to Know About Sex (But Were Afraid to Ask) (1972) ◆◆◆
D: Woody Allen. Woody Allen, John Carradine, Louise Lasser, Burt Reynolds. 87 minutes. (CBS/Fox)

An uneven anthology from the Woodman; the Italo takeoff and mad medico John Carradine's runaway Brobdingnagian breast rate as the Phantom's faves here. Funnier than Alan Abel's *Is There Sex After Death?* (Magnum).

Fat Guy Goes Nutzoid (1986) ◇
D: John Golden. Tibor Feldman, Douglas Stone, Max Alexander, John Mackay, John Golden. 85 minutes. (Prism)

Troma devised its best title ever to mask one of its worst pickups, a 1984 "retard comedy" originally called *Zeisters*. Two nerds at a home for retarded adults lose the title character, an overweight moron who embarks on a series of singularly unfunny nonadventures emphasizing scatological "humor." Even this poor-taste premise would have been okay if *Fat Guy* had even a marginal satiric point to make—but it doesn't. In fact, only Leo Kottke's acoustic string score, which belongs on the soundtrack of a much better movie, emerges as unembarrassing here.

Female Trouble (1974) ◆◆◆◇
D: John Waters. Divine, David Lochary, Mink Stole, Edith Massey. 95 minutes. (Cinema Group)

Waters's 1974 Divine comedy toplines the tubby transvestite as troubled teen Dawn Davenport, who runs away from home after a traumatic Christmas squabble (over an absent pair of cha-cha heels!) with her exasperated parents. We follow Dawn through an unwise sexual encounter with a foul-mouthed slob (also, in a high-concept move, played by Divine, sans drag), an unhappy marriage to a hetero hairdresser, an abortive criminal career, and a brief, ill-fated fling as a media-fabricated "superstar." The result is a typically, often brilliantly sick sleaze opera that deftly mocks the media, effete Warholesque poseurs, trust-fund *artistes*, and sundry other seamy aspects of our contempo trash culture.

A Fish Called Wanda (1988) ◆◆◆
D: Charles Crichton. John Cleese, Jamie Lee Curtis, Kevin Kline, Michael Palin. 105 minutes. (CBS/Fox)

A semi-successful caper comedy that's boosted by ex-Pythonites Cleese and Palin, the latter as a stuttering cohort of crooked Yanks Curtis and Kline, who embroil barrister Cleese in their elaborate heist scheme. Worth seeing, though some *schticks* don't click. Python alumnus Eric Idle would have been preferable in the Kline role, in our humble op.

Flesh (1968) ◆◆◆
D: Paul Morrissey. Joe Dallesandro, Geraldine Smith, Patti D'Arbanville. 90 minutes.

Heat (1972) ◆◆◇
D: Paul Morrissey. Joe Dallesandro, Sylvia Miles, Pat Ast. 102 minutes.

Trash (1970) ◆◆◆
D: Paul Morrissey. Joe Dallesandro, Holly Woodlawn, Jane Forth. 110 minutes. (Paramount)

Morrissey's picaresque gutter trilogy follows charismatic junkie Dallesandro and friends on their zany underground rounds. Fairly sharp NYC-set social satires, if peripatetic at times, with *Trash* standing out as the best of the three.

Flesh Gordon (1972) ◆◆
D: Mike Light. Jason Williams, Suzanne Fields, John Hoyt. 82 minutes. (Video Dimensions)

This soft-core sex satire of *Flash Gordon* is pretty broad most of the way, but David Allen fashions several memorable monsters. Its flashes of wit and flesh have earned the flick a small but loyal following.

The Four Musketeers (1975) NR
D: Richard Lester. Michael York, Faye Dunaway, Richard Chamberlain. 108 minutes. (IVE)

Lester continues the irreverent misadventures of Dumas's heroic quartet in a popular sequel to his *Three Musketeers* (also IVE).

Frankenstein's Great Aunt Tillie (1985) ◆◇
D: Myron J. Gold. Donald Pleasence, Zsa Zsa Gabor, Aldo Ray, Yvonne Furneaux. 100 minutes. (Video City)

The title alone—to say nothing of the once-in-a-lifetime cast—demanded this Mexico-lensed fright farce's inclusion here. Too bad the flick itself is so unremittingly lame. The similarly aimed *Dr. Hackenstein* (Forum) and *Frankenstein General Hospital* (New Star) are likewise well worth avoiding.

Fritz the Cat (1972) ◆◆◇
D: Ralph Bakshi. 78 minutes. (Warner)

Bakshi's screen adaptation of the R. Crumb comix character loses a lot in the translation but is still worth a look for fans of either or both cartoonists. A sequel, *9 Lives of Fritz the Cat* (Warner), is also available.

Full Moon High (1981) ◆◆
D: Larry Cohen. Adam Arkin, Ed McMahon, Elizabeth Hartman, Kenneth Mars, Alan Arkin. 96 minutes. (HBO)

Sort of a low-budget *An American Werewolf in Transylvania, Full Moon High*—shot in '81 but unreleased till '86—represents a rare misfire for maverick auteur Cohen. *Full Moon* does have a few funny moments, though—many of them supplied by Ed McMahon (!) as teen lycanthrope Arkin's flag-waving dad—and provides more yoks than Milton Moses Ginsberg's promisingly titled but poorly executed political-scare satire *Werewolf of Washington* (Monterey).

Futz (1969) NR
D: Tom O'Horgan. The La Mama Repertory Troupe. 92 minutes. (IUD)

At long last, the minimalist film version of O'Horgan's off-Broadway parable, a sort of backwoods boy-meets-pig story, is available for the home-vid audience.

Ganjasaurus Rex (1987) ◆◇
D: Ursi Reynolds. Paul Bassis, Rosie Jones, Howard Phun, John Ivar, Rich Abernathy, Andy Barnett. 100 minutes. (Rhino)

We almost hate to slam an enterprise like *Ganjasaurus Rex*. With its amiable tone and obvious desire to entertain without resorting to the usual cheap gore tactics, this direct-to-video California-set marijuana comedy is likable without being particularly entertaining. The story involves a crop of Redwood-size *cannabis sativa* plants that attract the attention not only of local and federal drug authorities but of the title creature, a prehistoric monster who resembles an inflatable Godzilla doll and who survives by chomping on marijuana plants. Unfortunately, while scattered laughs crop up along the way, this sub–Cheech and Chong exercise is almost as short on true wit as it is on budget.

The General (1927) ◆◆◆ B&W
D: Buster Keaton. Buster Keaton, Marion Mack, Glen Cavender. 74 minutes. (Video Yesteryear)

In addition to being a talented director and brilliant mime, Keaton proved far ahead of his time as a master of conceptual comedy. *The General*, though perhaps his most famous feature film, and an expertly crafted one, is less perverse than his *Sherlock Jr.* or *The Three Ages* (both from Grapevine Video). Other available Keaton classics include *College*, *Steamboat Bill Jr.*, and the early talkie *Parlor, Bedroom and Bath*, all out via Video Yesteryear. Several BK features unavailable in this country can be ordered from Argentina's Henri Bouchard (see our Videorama listings), while domestic mail-order companies like Video Yesteryear, Grapevine, Foothill, and Cable offer various combos of Buster's best silent shorts.

Ghost Fever (1987) 0 ◆
D: Alan Smithee (Lee Madden). Sherman Helmsley, Luis Avalos, Myron Healey, Jennifer Rhodes, Pepper Martin, Joe Frazier. 86 minutes. (Charter)

Another example of the infamous Alan Smithee's more recent work, this subsitcom disaster is almost fascinatingly unfunny. Using a hoary haunted-house hook that was passé in the '30s, Smithee and a trio of so-called screenwriters put comics Sherman (*The Jeffersons*) Helmsley and Luis Avalos through some of the most painfully embarrassing paces ever seen on screen. The script is nearly totally bald on punch lines—even *bad* punch lines—and Smithee can't orchestrate the simplest professional pratfall. This incredibly cheap, cardboard production is badly postsynched, with the actors often left to improvise their lines. Helmsley has the worst time here, since he plays *two* humiliating roles—a detective tormented by a racist poltergeist, and the ghost of his ex-slave great-grandfather. B-movie vet Healey has a similarly degrading role as a white spirit. Only the hardiest of Z-movie masochists will want to taint their VCRs with this fiasco.

Ghostbusters (1984) ◆◆◆◇
D: Ivan Reitman. Bill Murray, Dan Aykroyd, Sigourney Weaver, Harold Ramis. 107 minutes. (RCA/Columbia)

An almost flawless blend of solid wit and lavish FX, this hip, satisfying comedy spent its huge budget well. Rick Moranis is especially funny as the nerdy-accountant-turned-virile-Keymaster. Ray Parker's soundtrack is another plus.

Ghosts on the Loose (1943) ◆◆◇ B&W
D: William Beaudine. Leo Gorcey, Bobby Jordan, Ava Gardner, Bela Lugosi. 65 minutes. (Goodtimes)

An otherwise typical havoc-wreaking East Side Kids haunted-house romp, directed by William ("One-Shot") Beaudine (so dubbed for his aversion to budget-consuming retakes), is lifted by young Gardner in one of her earliest screen appearances and the ever-galvanizing Lugosi (who also turns up in the ESKs' earlier *Spooks Run Wild* [Budget]). Public-domain specialists like Goodtimes, Amvest, Budget, and Congress all carry a number of other East Side Kids titles, while Kartes handles a pair of Gorcey and gang's postwar Bowery Boys pics, *Here Come the Marines* and *Mr. Hex.*

The Gig (1985) ◆◆◆◇
D: Frank Gilroy. Wayne Rogers, Cleavon Little, Andrew Duncan. 95 minutes. (Lorimar)

Gilroy's perceptive, accurate script takes a group of hitherto amateur middle-aged musicians through their first pro job at a second-rate Catskills resort in a topnotch comedy-drama that never strains for impact. Little is especially good as the lone professional hired to replace an ailing band member in this low-budget indie gem.

Gilda Live (1980) NR
D: Mike Nichols. Gilda Radner, Don Novello. 90 minutes. (Warner)

Radner reprises her best *Saturday Night Live* characters, from Lisa the Nerdette to overly candid newscaster Roseanna Rosanadanna, in Mike Nichols's filmization of her Broadway show. Father Guido Sarducci also lends comic support.

The Gods Must Be Crazy (1984) ◆◆◆
D: Jamie Uys. Marius Weyers, Sandra Prinsloo, Nxau. 109 minutes. (Playhouse)

Like the later *"Crocodile" Dundee*, albeit on a smaller scale, this South African import proved to be an unexpected hit with American audiences. Jamie Uys's comic culture-clash fable would have worked even better sans the slapstick interludes.

Going Berserk (1983) ◆◆◇
D: David Steinberg. John Candy, Joe Flaherty, Eugene Levy. 85 minutes. (MCA)

John Candy—with help from fellow *SCTV* alumni Flaherty and Levy—carries this freewheeling comedy through a bright first half and does what he can to salvage the sloppy second.

The Golden Age of Comedy (1960) ◆◆◆ B&W

Compiled by Robert Youngson. Laurel and Hardy, Ben Turpin, Keystone Kops. 78 minutes. (VidAmerica)

Another lively silent-comedy compilation from archivist Youngson, with especially choice clips from Laurel and Hardy's soundless oeuvre. See also *The Great Chase* (Embassy), likewise from Youngson.

The Gorilla (1939) ◆◆ B&W

D: Allen Dwan. Ritz Brothers, Bela Lugosi, Anita Louise, Lionel Atwill. 67 minutes. (Kartes)

Bela and the title primate scare the halfwits out of the Ritz Brothers, cast here as detectives, in a broad farce fit for Bela buffs and/or the trio's hard-core fans. The Ritzes are also on view in *Goldwyn Follies* (Embassy).

The Graduate (1967) ◆◆◆

D: Mike Nichols. Dustin Hoffman, Anne Bancroft, Katharine Ross. 105 minutes. (Embassy)

Nichols's social comedy about college-grad Hoffman's rude intro to the real world retains its satiric freshness, thanks largely to a witty script co-written by Buck Henry from Charles Webb's novel.

A Great Wall (1986) ◆◆◇

D: Peter Wang. Peter Wang, Sharon Iwai, Kelvin Han Yee. 100 minutes. (Pacific Arts)

While auteur/star Wang's culture-clash comedy too often sinks to a sitcom level, *A Great Wall* features its fair share of insights as a thoroughly Westernized Chinese-American family visits relatives in the People's Republic. The authentic location shooting also helps.

The Groove Tube (1972) ◆◆◇

D: Ken Shapiro. Chevy Chase, Buzzy Linhart, Richard Belzer. 75 minutes. (Media)

A scattershot blast at TV that hits often enough to deserve its enduring rep, *The Groove Tube* began life as an early video, graduated to the big screen, and returns now to its small-screen roots.

Grown-Ups (1985) NR

D: John Madden. Jean Stapleton, Martin Balsam, Charles Grodin. 106 minutes. (Lorimar)

The video version of Jules Feiffer's satiric dissection of a neurotic family, part of the On Stage Series.

Grunt! The Wrestling Movie (1986) ◆◇

D: Allan Holzman. Wally Greene, Steven Cepello, Dick Murdoch, John Tolos, Robert Glaudini. 91 minutes. (New World)

Director Holzman applies a *This Is Spinal Tap*–type mockumentary approach to the neanderthal world of pro wrestling, tracing the bone-crushing career of fictional mat maniac Mad Dog Joe De Curso, who disappears after accidentally decapitating a ring opponent, only to resurface as a masked hero fittingly dubbed The Mask. Despite Robert Glaudini's entertaining turn as a sleazy promoter, *Grunt!* promptly falls flat on its canvasback, delivering little in the way of either biting wit *or* gripping mat action. (The Phantom's witnessed livelier bouts in the orchestras of flea pits like the Deuce's Cine 42, where *Grunt!* originally enjoyed its less-than-gala Gotham premiere on a triple bill with *House* and *The Naked Cage.*) Unless you're a hard-core fan of Count Billy Varga, Greg "Magic" Schwartz, or Exotic Adrian Street—all of whom put in cameos here—you'd be well advised to stick with "real" wrestling, which is a lot funnier than either *Grunt!* or the equally worthless *Bad Guys* (IVE).

Hail to the Chief (1973) NR

D: Fred Levinson. Dan Resin, Richard B. Shull, Willard Waterman. 85 minutes. (Monterey)

Resin plays a paranoid prez who gives in to his power lusts in a Nixonian satire also known simply as *Hail.* Willard (*Great Gildersleeve*) Waterman also puts in an appearance. Other irreverent views of the notorious ex–chief exec include Emile de Antonio's docu-satire *Millhouse: A White Comedy* (MPI), the convent-set allegory *Nasty Habits* (Media), Robert Altman's adaptation of Philip Baker Hall's one-man stage show

Secret Honor (Vestron), and *The Way He Was* (United).

Hairspray (1988) ◆◆◆◇

D: John Waters. Ricki Lake, Divine, Jerry Stiller, Sonny Bono, Debbie Harry, Pia Zadora. 91 minutes. (RCA/ Columbia)

While Baltimore's erstwhile bijou bad boy John Waters eschews his customary gross-out tableaux in this, his debut crossover movie, *Hairspray* still succeeds as a lively, satiric, and—most vital of all—subversive send-up of the early '60s teen scene and the brain-damaged beehived "hairhoppers" who populated same. Lake—who looks like she really *could* have been Divine's daughter, had such a fate been biologically feasible—stars as Tracy Turnblad, a fat girl who dances her way into the hearts of thousands on the Corny Collins Show, a Baltimore B-TV version of *Bandstand.* Conflict ensues when Ricki's sudden popularity incurs the wrath of slender blond rival Amber Von Tussle (Colleen Fitzpatrick) and her scheming parents (Bono, Harry). Ricki not only triumphs but, with the aid of deejay Motormouth Maybell (memorably interpreted by R&B singer Ruth Brown), uses her celebrity to further the cause of integration. In addition to Waters's off-the-wall comedy, *Hairspray* offers an up-tempo array of choice period rock tunes. The late Divine is fine, as usual, in a dual role as Ricki's supportive mom *and* as racist male TV-station owner Arvin Hodgepile. Pia contributes a neat cameo as a raven-tressed beatnik chick (she even recites some of Allen Ginsberg's *Howl!*), and Waters himself turns up as a bonkers shrink. *Hairspray*, in sum, is bright, bouncy fun.

FILMMAKERS IN FOCUS:

John Waters: Baltimore's Bijou Bad Boy

In the course of his brilliantly sleazy celluloid career, outré auteur John Waters has reveled in mass murder, kinky sex, abnormal psychology, and deviant behavior of every stripe. With low-budget gutter epics like *Mondo Trasho* (1969), *Multiple Maniacs* (1970), *Pink Flamingos* (1972), *Female Trouble* (1974), *Desperate Living* (1977), and *Polyester* (1981)— populated by Waters's own informal repertory company, a sort of Ready-for-Slime-Time Players led by the late two-ton transvestite Divine—the Baltimore-based writer/director has raised (and razed) trash culture to an art form. What's more, Waters has freely confessed his sundry unhealthy obsessions, indiscretions, and "attitude problems" in his literary manifestos *Shock Value* and *Crackpot.*

All of which left veteran Waters-watchers unprepared for his 1988 crossover hit *Hairspray. Hairspray* is not only a relatively lavish affair, boasting both a sizable budget (roughly $2.5 mil) and a name cast, but it carries an intimidating PG rating.

"The audience *thinks* it's gonna be gross," Waters explains. "Like with the pimple-popping scene. Everybody starts screaming and flipping out—they're expecting it to splat onto the screen. But you don't even see it pop."

There *is* a rather horrible magnified *squish* accompanying said pimple's destruction on the Dolby soundtrack, though, plus a brief upchuck scene.

"PG puke," Waters dismisses the sequence. "It doesn't even fly through the air."

Hairspray may be bald in the scatological department, but the subversive elements survive intact. *Hairspray*, for example, contains what may be the movies' first slapstick civil-rights demonstration scene, and the film's intensely mindless teen intrigues, involving regulars on and aspirants to the *American Bandstand*–like Corny Collins Show, frames the flick's ultimately sincere pro-integration theme.

"It was a horrible era in a way," Waters reminisces, "right before everything changed. When people talk about the '60s, it's *not* that. It was just this weird time where people, *normal* people, looked very bizarre."

Which may be why the director felt his film didn't need disgusto riffs to heighten its integral weirdness. In any case, at this point in his career, Waters professes to be more concerned with grosses than gross-outs. Not that budgets, per se, are what make John Waters run.

"I don't have delusions of grandeur about getting huge budgets," he confides. "Although my ultimate fantasy is to make a movie where every *extra* is a star. During a street scene, people in the theater would be pointing, 'There's Lana Turner! Look, it's Joey Heatherton!' "

DIVINE COMEDY: Two-ton transvestite Divine (left) and screen hubby Jerry Stiller contemplate the fate of their "hair-hopping" daughter Ricki Lake in a scene from John Waters's early '60s-set satire, *Hairspray.*
Photo courtesy of New Line Cinema.

Since that prospect isn't too likely to be looming over the nearest horizon, Waters will settle for reaching that financial point "where I don't have to do every little chore myself—it's an odd job working those kinds of hours to get some stranger to laugh—where I could get the people I want to be in it and still make the movie *I* want to make."

We asked about *Hairspray*'s relatively star-studded cast. Was it tough landing Pia Zadora, *Hairspray*'s resident "beatnik chick"?

"No," Waters recalls. "She knew I really liked *Butterfly* a *lot.*" As for Jerry Stiller, "He wanted to make the movie because his kids told him to. With Sonny Bono, it was the busboys at his restaurant."

When asked to name a film that impressed him, Waters offers Katheryn Bigelow's *Near Dark.* "It was the only movie that made me want to quit being a filmmaker and be a vampire for real."

Which prompted the Phantom to wonder aloud whether Waters would ever consider doing a horror movie.

"I think they've *all* been horror movies." Waters laughs, "Except that *people* are the monsters."

Waters excludes *Hairspray* from the above appraisal. In fact, he admits to feeling more affection for his *Hairspray* characters than he does for the assorted merry miscreants and psychotics who frolicked through his earlier films. Maybe even to the point of eventually fashioning a sequel.

"If I ever do a *Hairspray* sequel," says Waters, applying a thoughtful index digit to his patented pencil-line moustache, "it would take place a few years later and be called *Headband.* Tracy Turnblad would move to San Francisco and become a terrorist."

Isn't he afraid, we wondered, that by thinking aloud someone might steal his ideas?

"No." John Waters laughs. "I'm never too worried about *that.*"

Half Shot at Sunrise (1930) ◆◆◇ **B&W**
D: Phil Sloane. Bert Wheeler, Robert Woolsey, Dorothy Lee. 78 minutes. (Video Yesteryear, others)

The popular vaudeville team of Wheeler and Woolsey are AWOL soldiers on a Parisian spree in this, their celluloid debut. Other W&W efforts out on cassette include *Cracked Nuts* (Rex Miller); *The Diplomaniacs* and *Dixiana* (both Foothill), *Hips Hips Hooray, Mummy's Boy, On Again —Off Again, The Rainmakers,* and *Silly Billies* (all Rex Miller); *Cockeyed Cavaliers,* and *Hold 'em Jail* (Video Dimensions); and *Hook, Line and Sinker* (Video Yesteryear).

The Happy Hooker (1975) NR
D: Nicholas Sgarro. Lynn Redgrave,

Jean-Pierre Aumont, Lovelady Powell, Tom Poston. 96 minutes. (Cannon)

Redgrave sluts it up as madam Xaviera Hollander, who raked it in with her titular best-seller during the '70s' short-lived "porno chic" craze. Joey Heatherton and former Hammer horror queen Martine Beswicke, respectively (if not respectably), take over the Divine Ms. X role in the sequels *The Happy Hooker Goes to Washington* and *The Happy Hooker Goes Hollywood* (also Cannon), while the X-rated Ms. X makes her own acting debut in *My Pleasure Is My Business* (MPI). Now what was the question?

Hardware Wars and Other Film Farces (1980) ◆◆◆
49 minutes. (Warner)

Four award-winning homemade movie send-ups—*Hardware Wars, Porklips Now, Closet Cases of the Nerd Kind,* and the always-welcome *Bambi Meets Godzilla*—conveniently assembled on one cassette.

Harold and Maude (1972) NR
D: Hal Ashby. Bud Cort, Ruth Gordon, Vivian Pickles. 90 minutes. (Paramount)

Romance blossoms between suicidal youth Cort and zany senior cit Gordon in a film that flopped as a mainstream release but became an instant and enduring cult comedy fave.

Head (1968) ◆◆◇
D: Bob Rafelson. The Monkees (Peter

Tork, Davy Jones, Mickey Dolenz, Michael Nesmith), Victor Mature, Annette Funicello, Teri Garr, Jack Nicholson, Vito Scotti. 86 minutes. (RCA/Columbia)*

The Monkees, deep into their ersatz Sgt. Pepper period (*you* remember), run amok on a movie set populated by a giant Victor Mature, a petite but large-breasted Annette Funicello, and—if you don't blink, sneeze, or yawn—a young Jack Nicholson. Nicholson also took credit for co-producing and co-writing *Head* (with director Rafelson), a free-form Hey-Hey-We're-Making-a-Movie romp that supplies more in the way of vanished pop-cultural artifacts than genuine laughs. A mock meditation on the old media-vs.-reality chestnut, this precociously postmodern relic-ahead-of-its-time and midnight-circuit staple finds the Not So Fab Four poking fun at war, cops, Coca-Cola, movies, and themselves. ("The money's in/ We're made of tin/We're here to give you more.") Highlights include psychedelic graphics, Nehru jackets, clips from Karloff/Lugosi's *The Raven*, and sprightly tunes delivered by diminutive Jones, the Dudley Moore of the group. If nothing else, *Head* offers a fascinating view of the '60s as they never were.

Heavy Traffic (1973) ◆◆
D: Ralph Bakshi. 77 minutes. (Warner)

Pretentiousness and an overreliance on specificity alternate with more cutting moments in a ghetto fantasy more remarkable for its animation/live-action mix than for its bite or insights.

Here Comes Mr. Jordan (1941) ◆◆◆ B&W

D: Alexander Hall. Robert Montgomery, Claude Rains, Evelyn Keyes. 93 minutes. (RCA/Columbia)

A fairly perverse fantasy about boxer Montgomery, who's reincarnated in a new body that leaves him hard pressed to pick up where he left off. Better than the Warren Beatty remake, Heaven Can Wait (Paramount).

His Girl Friday (1940) ◆◆◆◇ B&W

D: Howard Hawks. Cary Grant, Rosalind Russell, Ralph Bellamy. 92 minutes. (United, others)

Hawks's refreshingly cynical remake of Hecht and MacArthur's The Front Page (Cable) is funny, fast paced, and highlighted by great ensemble acting.

History of White People in America (1986) ◆◆◆

D: Harry Shearer. Martin Mull, Fred Willard, Mary Kay Place. 100 minutes. (MCA)

A quartet of episodes from Mull's cable-TV comedy series, a sort of Everyhonky's answer to Roots.

Hollywood Boulevard (1976) ◆◆◇

D: Joe Dante, Allan Arkush. Candice Rialson, Mary Woronov, Dick Miller, Paul Bartel. 83 minutes. (Warner)

Roger Corman–trained directors Dante and Arkush pay mock tribute to the Mentor They Love to Hate (and vice versa) with this hit-or-miss schlock-movie satire incorporating clips from, and recreations of actual Corman flicks. Devotees of Poverty-Row sendups helmed by then-unknown/now-famous directors should also check out John Landis's Schlock, available under the title Banana Monster (WesternWorld).

Hollywood Harry (1985) ◆◆◇

D: Robert Forster. Robert Forster, Shannon Wilcox, Katherine Forster, Joe Spinell, Pete Shrum, Redmond Gleason. 96 minutes. (Media)

Hollywood Harry recounts the misadventures of a down-and-out private dick (Forster, who also produced and directed), who spends his time scarfing cold pizza, guzzling Jim Beam, and quoting Arnold Toynbee(!). Harry's lowlife is suddenly and irrevocably altered, however, when his runaway teen niece (played by Bob's real-life daughter, Katherine) turns up at his doorstep. Hollywood Harry mixes overly broad bits and injokes with genuinely affecting, expertly scripted scenes delineating the mock-hard-boiled Harry and his hitherto neglected niece's growing rapport. Both Forsters turn in winning work, as does Spinell as Harry's equally inept partner.

Hollywood Shuffle (1987) ◆◆◆

D: Robert Townsend. Robert Townsend, Anne-Marie Johnson, Damon Wayans, Lisa Mende, Brad Sanders,

Franklin Ajaye. 80 minutes. (Virgin Vision)

Townsend's one-man movie—he produced, directed, starred, co-scripted, and raised the hundred grand it took to make this surprisingly slick-looking flick—is a consistently funny, sometimes brilliant look at the schizy life of struggling black actor Bobby Taylor (Townsend), who tries to keep his menial job at the Winky Dinky Dog fast-food joint while auditioning for a demeaning role as a stereotypical street hood in Tinseltown Pictures' *Jivetime Jimmy's Revenge*. Along the way, Townsend smoothly works in on-target exploitation-movie parodies ("Attack of the Killer Pimps," "Rambro"), sitcom send-ups ("There's a Bat in Our House!"), and celebrity film-critic satires ("Sneakin' into the Movies"). Townsend's pointed yet amiable pop parable also benefits from some fine ensemble work by the Hollywood Shuffle Players. Further proof that when it comes to making quality films, talent and hustle are worth more than mega-budgets.

Homebodies (1974) ◆◆◆
D: Larry Yust. Peter Brocco, Frances Fuller, Ken Tobey. 96 minutes. (Embassy)

A good, perverse Cincinnati-lensed black comedy about elderly tenants who kill to keep their homes. (And they do it without any help from Steven Spielberg or lovable extraterrestrials!) Sort of a geriatric version of *Massacre at Central High* (see index).

Honky Tonk Freeway (1981) NR
D: John Schlesinger. William Devane, Beverly D'Angelo, Beau Bridges. 107 minutes. (HBO)

Schlesinger's "Grand Highway" satire, operating under a bloated budget, proved a megabomb at the box office but has since won a modest home-vid following.

The Hospital (1971) ◆◆◆
D: Arthur Hiller. George C. Scott, Diana Rigg, Barnard Hughes. 103 minutes. (Key)

A sometimes smarmy, more often scary satire set in a title facility plagued by general incompetence and a specific killer. Scott is strong as the chief surgeon; Paddy Chayefsky contributed the equally unflinching script.

H.O.T.S. (1979) NR
D: Gerald Seth Sindell. Susan Kiger, Lisa London, Pamela Jean Bryant. 95 minutes. (Vestron)

This distaff *Animal House* is bereft of budget and brains but of interest to fans of lowlife screen-sleaze queen Cheri (*Ginger*) Chaffaro, who co-wrote this addled romp.

How I Won the War (1967) ◆◆◇
D: Richard Lester. Michael Crawford, Roy Kinnear, John Lennon. 111 minutes. (MGM/UA)

Lester's surreal antiwar film, featuring John Lennon as one of the unlucky Tommies, may play a bit heavy-handedly today—as, indeed, it did back in '67, when it first proved a midnight-circuit mainstay.

Howard the Duck (1986) ◆
D: Willard Huyck. Lea Thompson, Jeffrey Jones, Tim Robbins. 111 minutes. (MCA)

A few video revisionists now claim that George Lucas's bloated turkey isn't as bad as its rep, but don't believe them. From its original source—a puerile rip-off of underground comix—to its big-screen execution, *Howard* is the epitome of aggressive, high-decibel, mega-nerd Hollywood stupidity. Hardier couch sociologists may want to view it for its anti-phenomenon value, though.

I Love You, Alice B. Toklas (1968) ◆◆◆
D: Hy Averback. Peter Sellers, Jo Van Fleet, Leigh Taylor-Young. 93 minutes. (Warner)

Sellers gives one of his best American-movie perfs as a nerdy lawyer who goes the psychedelic route in a pic that yields more laughs than expected from its slender premise. Sellers fans can also find their fave in *After the Fox, Being There, The Pink Panther, Return of the Pink Panther, Revenge of the Pink Panther, A Shot in the Dark, Trail of the Pink Panther* (all CBS/Fox), *The Battle of the Sexes* (American Video Tape), *The Blockhouse* (Paragon), *The Bobo, The Fiendish Plot of Dr. Fu Manchu*

(both Warner), *Carlton Browne of the F.O.* (formerly *Man in a Cocked Hat*), *Heavens Above, I'm All Right Jack, The Ladykillers, Two-Way Stretch* (all HBO), *Casino Royale, Dr. Strangelove, Lolita, The Magic Christian, What's New Pussycat?* (see index), *The Great McGonegall* (Wizard), *The Mouse That Roared, Murder by Death, Only Two Can Play, There's a Girl in My Soup, The Wrong Box* (all RCA/Columbia), *The Pink Panther Strikes Again* (MGM/UA), *Prisoner of Zenda* (MCA), *Smallest Show on Earth* (Kartes), the Brit-comedy compilation *To See Such Fun* (Pacific Arts), *Up the Creek* (IVE), *Waltz of the Toreadors* (VidAmerica), *Woman Times Seven* (Embassy), *World of Henry Orient* (Key), and *Wrong Arm of the Law* (Monterey).

I Was a Teenage TV Terrorist (1985/1987) ◆◆
D: Stanford Singer. Julie Hanlon, Adam Nathan, John MacKay, Walt Willey, Saul Alpiner, Michael Druham. 86 minutes. (Vestron)

Originally titled *Amateur Hour* prior to its "Tromatization," Singer's 1985 tube satire is reminiscent in budget (low) and tone (irreverent) of such late-'60s comedies as Brian De Palma's *Hi, Mom!* (NA), Francis Ford Coppola's *You're a Big Boy Now* (Warner), and Robert Downey's *Putney Swope* (RCA/Columbia). Lead Nathan is properly surly but curiously lifeless as a seventeen-year-old entrusted to the grudging care of his estranged and less-than-loving dad (MacKay), VP at a cheesy cable-TV station. With his aspiring-actress girlfriend (Hanlon), Nathan plots to turn the tables on Pop and the outfit's right-wing owner by concocting a revenge scheme, which ultimately backfires. Despite scattered bright moments, *TV Terrorist* lacks the zaniness, urgency, light touch, and talent that distiguished its farcical forebears.

I Was a Zombie for the FBI (1982) ◆◆ B&W

D: Marius Penczner. James Raspberry, Larry Raspberry, John Gillick. 105 minutes. (Cinema Group)

A low-budget *Dragnet*-style '50s sci-fi spoof that's so deadpan, it threatens to disappear. Has its bright moments, but could have been better with more juice and tighter editing.

I'm Gonna Git You SUCKA (1988) ◆◆◇

D: Keenen Ivory Wayans. Keenen Ivory Wayans, Bernie Casey, Antonio Fargas, Isaac Hayes, Jan'et Dubois, Damon Wayans, Steve James. 90 minutes. (MGM/UA)

Wayans's "blaxploitation" parody boasts a powerful all-star lineup that includes Jim Brown and Isaac Hayes, who look convincingly aged and out of shape, as retired tough guys Hammer and Slammer; the always-welcome Fargas, deftly reprising his patented pimp roles; urban-action stalwart Casey; John Vernon as token honky heavy Mr. Big; and James as terminally out-of-sync chopsocky champ Kung-Fu Joe. Director Wayans doubles as *SUCKA*'s decidedly unmacho hero, a returning GI clerk-typist (!) who's continually rescued by his far fiercer mom (Dubois), while younger brother Daman Wayans scores as a Mr. Big henchman who suffers nonstop abuse at the hands of both the good guys and his own evil employers. Memorable moments include our over-the-hill gang's slapstick assault on the bad guys' HQ and one of the sickest "seduction" scenes the Phantom's ever seen onscreen. While it's no *Naked Gun* or even a *Hollywood Shuffle*—Wayans's sketchy script and occasionally ill-timed direction keep the flick from really taking off—*SUCKA* supplies enough laughs to make it a must for fans of back-date black actioners.

The Incredible Shrinking Woman (1981) ◆◆◆

D: Joel Schumacher. Lily Tomlin, Charles Grodin, Ned Beatty. 89 minutes. (MCA)

Though it didn't impress most mainstream critics, Lily Tomlin's distaff *Shrinking Man* update/parody scores its fair share of comedic points before running out of ideas in the final reels. FX ace Rick Baker cameos as Sidney the Gorilla.

The In-Laws (1979) ◆◆◆
D: Arthur Hiller. Peter Falk, Alan Arkin, Richard Libertini. 103 minutes. (Warner)

Falk is an extremely casual CIA agent who embroils timid dentist brother-in-law Arkin in a mad series of life-threatening adventures fueled by Andrew Bergman's roller-coaster script.

Ishtar (1987) ◆◆◇
D: Elaine May. Warren Beatty, Dustin Hoffman, Isabelle Adjani, Charles Grodin, Jack Weston, Carol Kane. 107 minutes. (RCA/Columbia)

May's infamous $51 million flop is not entirely without merit; the Phantom clocked well over a dozen honest laughs and/or chuckles in the flick's first half alone, and two more in the second. Warren and Dusty's portrayal of two pathetic overage aspiring tunesmiths (some of the song snatches, like "Dangerous Business" and "The Have-Not Blues," are inspiredly brain-damaged) work quite well in the early going; ditto for Grodin's bit as an exasperated CIA agent who can't quite penetrate the tunnel-visioned pair's thick craniums. On the downside, the stars' desert improv antics, which grind the flick to a total standstill, are embarrassing beyond belief. The fetching Adjani is likewise wasted as an Ishtarian freedom fighter in male drag (!). But what's truly astounding is that Ishtar looks less like a "modest" $20 mil project gone wild than a low-budget back-lot job. There are no special effects, elaborate battle scenes, casts of thousands, nor even a single panoramic aerial shot of the vast desert locations to which the Ishtar stars and crew journeyed at astronomical expense! At roughly $3 mil per laugh, Ishtar is an undeniably costly proposition. But as a $2 overnight video rental, it's not that bad a deal.

It's a Mad Mad Mad Mad World (1963) ◆◆◇
D: Stanley Kramer. Spencer Tracy, Edie Adams, Milton Berle. 154 minutes. (CBS/Fox)

Kramer's star-studded megacomedy about a frantic scramble for hidden loot too often sinks to sitcom highjinks but has belatedly engendered a fanatical following, including an entire fan club devoted to this one flick! Die-hard Mad World mavens will want to wait till the full 192-minute restored theatrical version hits the vid ranks.

It's in the Bag (1945) NR B&W
D: Richard Wallace. Jack Benny, Fred Allen, Binnie Barnes. 87 minutes. (Republic)

Feuding radio funnymen Benny and Allen take their hostilities to the screen in a popular comedy that also features Robert Benchley, Jerry Colonna, and William Bendix. Jack's back in 1930's The Medicine Man (Video Yesteryear), To Be or Not To Be (Vestron),

Transatlantic *Merry-Go-Round* (IVE), and *Without Reservations* (United).

It's Not Easy Being Me (1987) NR
D: Walter C. Miller. Rodney Danger-field, Sam Kinison, Robert Townsend. 59 minutes. (Orion)

Rodney bares his soul to the world and turns the mike over to several younger comics in a comedy concert that rates as a must for Dangerfield devotees.

Jabberwocky (1977) ◆◆◇
D: Terry Gilliam. Michael Palin, Deborah Fallender, Max Wall. 100 minutes. (RCA/Columbia)

Python animator Terry (*Brazil*) Gilliam sets his first solo feature in the perilous Middle Ages and casts fellow Python Palin as his questing hero.

Jane and the Lost City (1987) ◆◆◇
D: Terry Marcel. Kristen Hughes, Sam Jones, Maud Adams, Jasper Carrot, Robin Bailey, Graham Stark, Elsa O'Toole. 94 minutes. (New World)

A low-budget but often witty spin-off from the long-running *London Daily Mirror* comic strip *Jane, Jane and the Lost City* stars Hughes as the blond Brit heroine, who has the unfortunate (for her) habit of losing her dress in the most inappropriate situations. As our story opens, we find Jane and cohorts—the addled Colonel (Bailey), his intrepid valet (Stark), and hunky Jones as Great White Hunter "Jungle Jack" Buck, a vegetarian who's fond of quoting Hemingway—competing with a trio of inept Nazis in a race to locate the title town and its reputed treasures. The slender *Raiders of the Lost Ark Meets The Perils of Gwendoline* plot serves as an adequate excuse for a series of throwaway gags (as when the sight of a tomb filled with mummified corpses seated in ornate chairs prompts the Colonel to muse, "Reminds me of my club") that work more often than not. The sultry O'Toole is especially memorable as the British-reared Leopard Queen.

The Jerk (1979) ◆◆◆◇
D: Carl Reiner. Steve Martin, Bernadette Peters, Jackie Mason. 94 minutes. (MCA)

Sort of a head-comedy update of an old Jerry Lewis movie, with Martin as the adopted son of a southern black sharecropping family (!) who decides to strike out on his own. Not every riff works, but those that do are often brilliant.

The Jet Benny Show (1986) ◆◆◆
D: Roger D. Evans. Steve Norman, Polly MacIntyre, Kevin Dees, Ted Luedemann, Richard Sabel. 77 minutes. (United)

Imagine a vintage *Jack Benny Show* episode directed by John Waters right after he'd seen *Star Wars*, and you'll have some idea of what this offbeat video indie's all about. *The Jet Benny Show* opens with a quick, satiric flip around the American TV dial, circa 1959, settles briefly on a black-and-white recreation of a typical *Jack Benny Show* intro, then launches into a freewheeling sci-fi satire as Jack (Jet) crash-lands his Maxwell rocketship on a hostile planet dominated by the evil Lord Zane and his craven minions. Norman, who looks and sounds a *lot* like the young Benny, plays the late comic in a more openly effete style, while Dees supplies additional laughs as an android Rochester (with *Terminator*-like destructive powers) and MacIntyre is appropriately earnest as the embattled buxom heroine Jet's forced to rescue (against his better judgment). Not every riff works, the vid is technically crude at times, and the central conceit may be a tad arcane for some tastes, but the Phantom found the *Jet Benny Show* a surprisingly accomplished exercise in pop-cultural lunacy.

J-Men Forever! (1979) ◆◆◆ B&W
D: Richard Patterson. Philip Proctor, Peter Bergman. 75 minutes. (Lightning)

Taking a cue from Woody Allen's *What's Up Tiger Lily?*, Firesign Theater vets Proctor and Bergman reedit and redub scenes from vintage serials (especially Republic's *Fighting Devil Dogs*) and intercut with new footage to fashion a fresh story about a deejay from outer space. Funnier than *Dead Men Don't Wear Plaid*. Also from Firesign Theater: *Eat or Be Eaten, Firesign Theater's Hot Shorts* (both RCA/Columbia), and *Firesign Theater Presents Nick Danger* (Pacific Arts).

Joe (1970) ◆◆
D: John G. Avildsen. Peter Boyle, Dennis Patrick, K. Callan, Susan Sarandon. 107 minutes. (Cannon)

An odd mix of muddled messages and class insights from a pre-*Rocky* Avildsen, who'd earlier helmed the lowbrow cult comedy *Cry Uncle* (Prism), as crude hardhat Boyle and serpentine ad exec Patrick go gunning for unwary hippies.

The Kentucky Fried Movie (1977) ◆◆◆
D: John Landis. Donald Sutherland, Bill Bixby, Evan Kim, Tony Dow. 85 minutes. (Media)

John Landis and the ZAZ team (in their pre-*Airplane!* days) apply the *Groove Tube* approach to this bright anthology of movie parodies. Similar sketch-oriented celluloid satires include Peter Winograd's *Flicks* (Media) and Ira Miller's *Loose Shoes* (formerly *Coming Attractions*) on the Key label.

The King of Comedy (1983) ◆◆◆◆
D: Martin Scorsese. Robert De Niro, Jerry Lewis, Sandra Bernhard. 109 minutes. (RCA/Columbia)

Scorsese's sadly misunderstood media satire about would-be comic Rupert Pupkin (De Niro) hits nary a false note and features great performances by the three leads. It's depressing to note, however, that this was the *lowest*-grossing major-studio release of

1983. It's since found a loyal following on revival screens and home video.

L'Age d'Or (1930) ◆◆◆◇ B&W
D: Luis Buñuel and Salvador Dali. Max Ernst. 60 minutes. (Corinth)

Dali/Buñuel's surreal black comedy inspired no end of official ire during its initial release. While it's no longer shocking, it's still surprising, hypnotic, and most of all, funny.

The Last Detail (1973) ◆◆◆◇
D: Hal Ashby. Jack Nicholson, Randy Quaid, Otis Young. 103 minutes. (RCA/Columbia)

Charismatic perfs from young Quaid as a kleptomaniacal naif and Nicholson and Young as the MPs escorting him to a Virginia jail make this comedy/drama a gritty gem from beginning to end.

Last Night at the Alamo (1983) NR B&W
D: Eagle Pennell. Sonny Davis, Lou Perry, Tina Hubbard. 82 minutes. (Cinema Group)

Pennell chronicles a night in the life of local regulars saying their sad, if foul-mouthed, farewells to a doomed Texas tavern in this popular semi-*verité* indie comedy.

Life of Brian (1979) ◆◆◆◇
D: Terry Jones. Graham Chapman, Eric Idle, John Cleese. 94 minutes. (Warner)

The Pythons' inspired satire of political factionalism, set during Christ's lifetime, is one of their best, packed with brilliant invention.

Little Murders (1971) ◆◆◇
D: Alan Arkin. Elliott Gould, Marcia Rodd, Vincent Gardenia. 110 minutes. (Key)

Jules Feiffer's black comedy about beleaguered New Yorkers seems alternately dated and prophetic when reseen today.

The Little Shop of Horrors (1960) B&W ◆◆◆
D: Roger Corman. Jonathan Haze, Jackie Joseph, Mel Welles, Dick Miller, Jack Nicholson. 72 minutes. (Vestron, others)

A cinematic extension of the era's "sick joke" craze, Corman's original *Little Shop of Horrors*, the inspiration for the hit off-Broadway musical and the lavish celluloid remake, relates the heartwarming story of a boy and his carnivorous talking plant. As nerdy flower-shop menial Seymour, Haze makes like an ersatz Jerry Lewis. And while he's no Sammy Petrillo—the Lewis impersonator who starred in 1952's immortal *Bela Lugosi Meets a Brooklyn Gorilla* (see index)—Haze certainly gives it the old Corman try. Other highlights of this no-budget three-day wonder include young Nicholson's now-legendary stint as masochistic dental patient Wilbur Force; Corman regular Miller's bit as a floral gourmet; and Joseph's earnest interpretation of Audrey, the object of Seymour's bumbling affection. And let's not forget Audrey Jr., the peckish plant whose voice (supplied by *Shop* scripter Charles B. Griffith) and vocabulary grow apace with its appetite, prompting beleaguered florist Gravis Mushnick (Welles) to complain, "We not only got a talking plant, we got one that makes with smart cracks!" Vestron also has a colorized version of *Little Shop* available, for those who want the full impact of Dick Miller's yellow vest.

Little Shop of Horrors (1986) ◆◆◆
D: Frank Oz. Rick Moranis, Ellen Greene, Steve Martin, Vincent Gardenia, John Candy, Bill Murray. 88 minutes. (Warner)

The new *Little Shop*, based on the hit off-Broadway musical adaptation of Roger Corman's killer-plant parable, assembles an impressive lineup: Martin, Gardenia, Greene, Murray, and *SCTV* alumni Candy and Moranis (as Seymour). Of the above, Martin shines brightest in the revamped role of a sadistic dentist (pardon our redundancy) with a bent for black leather jackets and motorcycles, while Murray brings a deeper level of perversity to the Nicholson part. The Four Tops' Levi Stubbs is equally forceful as the voice of the demanding, man-eating plant (herein dubbed Audrey II); Ellen (Audrey I) Greene likewise possesses a great pair of lungs (to speak only of lungs).

While there are few real surprises here, *Little Shop*, fueled by a solid doo-wop score, moves along at a bouncy clip. And unlike George Lucas's overstuffed *Howard the Duck*, the pic wisely doesn't smother its slender material in an avalanche of megabuck FX.

Living on Tokyo Time (1986) ◆◆◆
D: Steven Okazaki. Minako Ohashi, Ken Nakagawa, Kate Connell, Judy Nihei, Mitzie Abe, Bill Bonham. 83 minutes. (Charter)

A refreshingly realistic, low-key, at times even taciturn indie comedy, *Living on Tokyo Time* relates the tale of a temporary marriage of convenience between green-card-seeking Japanese girl Kyoto (Ohashi) and Japanese-American "slug" Ken (Nakagawa). *Tokyo Time* admirably resists the temptation of turning the central situation into a cute love story. While Ken does tumble, in his lethargic way, Kyoto remains friendly, grateful, but resolutely unsmitten by the maintenance man/rock star manqué (whom she stolidly addresses as Mr. Ken) whose laid-back West Coast life-style is as alien to her as *any* American's, Asian or otherwise. *Tokyo Time* doesn't strain for scope, sweep, or profundity but consistently hits the targets it aims at and is far more entertaining and authentic than slicker, bigger-budgeted culture-clash comedies like *Something Wild* and *Desperately Seeking Susan*.

Local Hero (1983) ◆◆◇
D: Bill Forsyth. Peter Riegert, Burt Lancaster, Fulton MacKay. 111 minutes. (Warner)

While a mite coy for yours truly's taste, Forsyth's quirky comedies have acquired a sizable audience. Beyond *Local Hero*, a satire focusing on astrology and commerce, Bill's *Comfort and Joy* (MCA), *Gregory's Girl* (Embassy), *Housekeeping* (RCA/Columbia), and *That Sinking Feeling* (Embassy) are available.

Lolita (1962) ◆◆◆ B&W
D: Stanley Kubrick. James Mason, Sue Lyon, Peter Sellers, Shelley Winters. 150 minutes. (MGM/UA)

While it lacks some of Nabokov's elaborate trickery (which may be all to the good), Kubrick's version of middle-aged academic Humbert Humbert's (Mason) all-consuming lust for jailbait Lyon has garnered its fair share of celluloid supporters. For further research on the subject, see Elia Kazan's *Baby Doll* (Warner).

The Lonely Guy (1984) ◆◆◆
D: Arthur Hiller. Steve Martin, Charles Grodin, Judith Ivey. 91 minutes. (MCA)

Based on Bruce Jay Friedman's *Lonely Guy's Guide to Life, Lonely Guy* is peppered with brilliant bits and top work by Martin in the title role and Grodin as his pathetic pal.

Lost in America (1985) ◆◆◆◆
D: Albert Brooks. Albert Brooks, Julie Hagerty, Garry Marshall, Art Frankel, Michael Greene. 91 minutes. (Warner)

Brooks turns in his most brilliant work to date in this deadpan, dead-on odyssey of a yuppie couple who hit the open road in their spanking new Winnebago (!). "It's *Easy Rider*," Brooks exults, "with a nest egg!" Said nest egg—a tidy hundred grand in savings—is soon blown by wife Hagerty in a single orgasmic night of Vegas high-rolling. What follows is our plucky couple's increasingly "harrowing" descent into lower-middle-class life in Stafford, Arizona. Aces all the way, with a nice cameo by comedy producer Marshall as a bemused Vegas casino owner. If only Brooks had written, as well as acted in, *Broadcast News*, (CBS/Fox), it might have been as good as *Lost in America*.

Love at First Bite (1979) ◆◆◇
D: Stan Dragoti. George Hamilton, Susan St. James, Richard Benjamin. 96 minutes. (Warner)

Hamilton's comeback flick features the erstwhile MGM heart-throb manqué as an uprooted Dracula trying to adjust to life in the Big Apple. A notch below *Andy Warhol's Dracula*, but still pretty funny. And who woulda thought George had it in him?

Loves of a Blonde (1965) ◆◆◆ B&W
D: Milos Forman. Hana Brejchova, Josef Sebanek, Vladimir Pucholt. 88 minutes. (RCA/Columbia)

This perceptive, slice-of-life Czech comedy introduced audiences to auteur Forman's idiosyncratic *verité* style, replicated in his later *Closely Watched Trains* and *The Firemen's Ball* (also RCA/Columbia).

Luggage of the Gods! (1983) ◆◆
D: David Kendall. Mark Stolzenberg, Gabriel Barre, Gwen Ellison, Martin Haber, Rochelle Robins. 78 minutes. (Academy)

An extremely low-budget cargo-cult comedy lensed before the slicker *Gods Must Be Crazy*'s release, *Luggage* chronicles a lost tribe of fierce rabbit-hunters (!) and the cultural shocks they experience when an overhead plane deposits a load of Western junk artifacts on their uncharted turf. While amiable in spirit and sprinkled with several well-earned laughs, this is essentially a one-joke skit inflated to feature length. Stolzenberg and Barre turn in decent comic perfs, via mime and grunts (possibly learned from Sly Stallone's vocal coach), as Yuk and Tull, the tribal outcasts who uncover the title cache. Still, we can recommend this only for the hardiest of caveman-comedy connoisseurs.

Lunch Wagon (1980) ◆◆◇
D: Ernest Pintoff. Rosanne Katon, Pamela Jean Bryant, Chuck McCann. 88 minutes. (Media)

If you feel compelled to watch one low-budget jiggle comedy in your lifetime, we'd suggest this one, directed in lively throwaway fashion by former animator Pintoff. If you feel like a *second* helping, we'd recommend *Gas Pump Girls* (Vestron), which further benefits from having former Bowery Boy Huntz Hall in its cast.

Lust in the Dust (1985) ◆◆◇
D: Paul Bartel. Tab Hunter, Divine, Lainie Kazan, Geoffrey Lewis, Henry Silva, Cesar Romero, Woody Strode. 85 minutes. (New World)

Paul Bartel's *Lust in the Dust*, an amiably lewd lampoon of vintage American and '60s spaghetti westerns, concerns four avaricious souls (laconic gunslinger Hunter, fiery cantina-owner Kazan, long-suffering would-be chanteuse Divine, desperado Lewis) who converge on the dusty New Mexican town of Chili Verde in search of hidden gold. The sole clues to the loot's whereabouts are an unusual map (half of which is tattooed on Divine's ample hindquarters) and a cryptic limerick. At its liveliest, *Lust* itself plays like an extended celluloid limerick (*too* extended, unfortunately). While lacking the parodistic precision of a *Six-Gun Justice*, *SCTV*'s sagebrush serial send-up, *Lust* is not without its memorable moments, from its "Tarnished Tumbleweed" theme song to what might be the genre's first all-femme barroom brawl. (Lainie and Divine make for the most formidable distaff adversaries since Joan Crawford and Mercedes McCambridge went at it in *Johnny Guitar*.)

B-movie stalwarts Silva, Romero, and Strode add to the fun in supporting roles.

Mad Monster Party (1967) NR
D: Jules Bass. Boris Karloff, Phyllis Diller, Gale Garnett. 94 minutes. (Embassy)

Boris lends his vocal talents to this kids-oriented cartoon feature that's won an enthusiastic following among animation fans.

The Magic Christian (1970) ◆◆◆
D: Joseph McGrath. Peter Sellers, Ringo Starr, Raquel Welch, Christopher Lee. 88 minutes. (Republic)

Pretty much dismissed in its day, the film version of Terry Southern's novella is getting the attention it deserves on video. Great cast includes Roman Polanski and Pythonites Graham Chapman and John Cleese.

Malcolm (1986) ◆◆◇
D: Nadia Tass. Colin Friels, John Hargreaves, Lindy Davies, Chris Haywood. 86 minutes. (Vestron)

The titular hero (Friels) of this offbeat comic crime caper from Down Under is an unsocialized, somewhat slow-witted wretch who also happens to double as a casual mechanical genius. Into his oddball existence come two-fisted tough Hargreaves and main squeeze Davies, who find a practical application for Malcolm's hitherto untapped technical talents—i.e., robbing banks by remote control. Occasional drifts into pathos and strained whimsy detract from the straightforward comedy here, but *Malcolm* is worth seeing for its climactic heist sequence alone.

The Man with Two Brains (1983) ◆◆◆◆
D: Carl Reiner. Steve Martin, Kathleen Turner, David Warner, Merv Griffin. 90 minutes. (Warner)

One of the Phantom's all-time faves: A deft sci-fi movie spoof that also has some pointed things to say re: the stalemate between the sexes. Lensed in bright cartoon colors, with an inspired performance by Martin as the desperate scientist torn between cruel spouse Turner's tempting body and the disembodied distaff brain he *really* loves. Don't miss this brilliant variation on the classic *Brain That Wouldn't Die* (see index).

Melvin and Howard (1980) ◆◆◆
D: Jonathan Demme. Paul LeMat, Mary Steenburgen, Jason Robards. 95 minutes. (MCA)

An alternately perceptive and condescending story about amiable loser Melvin (LeMat) whom Howard Hughes (Robards) makes a beneficiary of his will. The famous opening scene, wherein Melvin picks up hitchhiker Howard, is a classic.

Microwave Massacre (1983) NR
D: Wayne Berwick. Jackie Vernon, Loren Schein, Al Troupe. 75 minutes. (Select-A-Tape)

The late Vernon's lone starring vehicle sees the deadpan comic play a henpecked hubby driven to hard-core violence by his nagging wife. Pretty unique.

Midnight Cowboy (1969) ◆◆◆◆
D: John Schlesinger. Dustin Hoffman, Jon Voight, Sylvia Miles. 113 minutes. (MGM/UA)

Schlesinger's brilliant, offbeat, seriocomic tale of transplanted Texan Voight and Deuce lowlife Hoffman has long been a revival-circuit staple. Schlesinger makes great evocative use of authentic Times Square locales, ideal for VCR freeze-framing for the nostalgia-minded.

Midnight Run (1988) ◆◆◆◇
D: Martin Brest. Robert De Niro, Charles Grodin, John Ashton, Yaphet Kotto, Dennis Farina, Joe Pantoliano. 125 minutes. (MCA)

De Niro, as a tough but humanized bounty hunter, and Grodin, as his alternately wimpy and wily prey, are both excellent in a light but witty action comedy that doesn't strain for cheap laughs. Yaphet Kotto, as an exasperated FBI guy, Dennis Farina as a Vegas Mafia biggie, and Robert Ashton as De Niro's bounty-hunting rival head an equally adept supporting cast.

A Midsummer Night's Sex Comedy (1982) ◆◆◆
D: Woody Allen. Woody Allen, Mary Steenburgen, Mia Farrow, Jose Ferrer. 88 minutes. (Warner)

Not peak Woody, but a pretty funny comedy of manners set in turn-of-the-century upstate New York, where several Manhattan professional types gather for a vacation weekend. Ferrer is especially good as an arrogant academic.

Million Dollar Mystery (1987) ◆◆
D: Richard Fleischer. Tom Bosley, Eddie Deezen, Penny Baker, Rich Hall, Rick Overton, Mona Lyden. 95 minutes. (HBO)

The then-ailing, now-defunct DEG Group's "gimmick comedy" (wherein a lucky bijou-goer had a chance to win a million bucks) set records for nonattendance during its initial theatrical release. While this low-budget *It's a Mad Mad Mad Mad World* clone isn't the *total* disaster many critics labeled it—there *are* scattered laughs strewn amidst the low-budget wreckage—the project proved considerably less than high concept and has no particular raison d'être.

Mr. Hulot's Holiday (1953) NR B&W
D: Jacques Tati. Jacques Tati, Nathalie Pascaud, Michelle Rolla. 86 minutes. (Embassy, others)

The most popular of Tati's films chronicling the misadventures of the ever-beleaguered Hulot relies on visual wit to score its satiric points. Video has sparked new interest in Tati's oeuvre. Embassy/Nelson also has *Jour de Fête, My Uncle* (Video Yesteryear), *Playtime,* and *Sylvia and the Phantom* (wherein Tati costars but doesn't direct).

Mr. Mike's Mondo Video (1979) NR

D: Michael O'Donoghue. Michael O'Donoghue, Teri Garr, Dan Aykroyd. 75 minutes. (Pacific Arts)

Saturday Night Live writer O'Donoghue fashioned this Mondo movie send-up for a late-night TV slot, but network execs ultimately nixed it. Now you can see it on *your* TV.

Mixed Blood (1985) ◆◆◆

D: Paul Morrissey. Marilia Pera, Richard Ulacia, Linda Kerridge. 98 minutes. (Media)

Morrissey demonstrates that urban action isn't his forte but offbeat culture-clash social comedy is. There's lots of the latter on view when naive young Brazilian drug-dealer Ulacia gets bemusedly involved with the downtown poseur set. Pera is a standout as his Faginesque mom.

Modern Romance (1981) ◆◆◆◇

D: Albert Brooks. Albert Brooks, Kathryn Harrold, Bruno Kirby, George Kennedy. 93 minutes. (RCA/Columbia)

Neurotic film editor Brooks whines his way through an on-again, off-again affair with Harrold. Clever bits include the el cheapo sci-fi-flick-within-a-movie that Brooks's character is editing and fun cameos by Kennedy and Brooks's offscreen brother Bob Einstein.

Modern Times (1936) ◆◆◆◇ B&W

D: Charlie Chaplin. Charlie Chaplin, Paulette Goddard, Henry Bergman, Chester Conklin. 87 minutes. (Playhouse)

Chaplin's satire may be anachronistically silent most of the way, but his technology-amok message was not only timely but prophetic. *And* very funny. Other Chaplin features available via Playhouse Video include: *City Lights*, *The Great Dictator*, *A King in New York*, *Limelight*, and *Monsieur Verdoux*. The Little Tramp's silent features and shorts are available in various combinations from Foothill, Grapevine, Video Yesteryear, and other mail-order video companies. See our Videorama listings.

Mondo Trasho (1969) ◆◆◆ B&W

D: John Waters. Divine, Mink Stole, Mary Vivian Pearce. 90 minutes. (Cinema Group)

Lensed in black and white, sans dialogue (but with an extensive, brilliantly edited music track that actively comments on the on-screen action), Waters's minimalist maiden feature chronicles a typically disastrous day in the life of troubled transvestite Divine. His/her woes begin when she/he accidentally runs down a blond bimbo whose unconscious body she's forced to tote with her through the remainder of the movie. Divine's travels take her to a thrift shop, a mental ward, a church (for a pivotal epiphany), and a quack surgeon's medical abattoir, among other offbeat locales. It's a tribute to Waters's talent that he manages to squeeze 90 watchable, even comically compelling minutes out of such sheer material. If you're curious to see what Waters was doing during his mock *Scorpio Rising* (see index) period, *Mondo Trasho* will more than fill you in.

Monty Python and the Holy Grail (1974) ◆◆◆◇

D: Terry Gilliam, Terry Jones. Graham Chapman, John Cleese, Terry Gilliam, Eric Idle, Terry Jones, Michael Palin. 89 minutes. (RCA/Columbia)

One of the Brit boys' best: a surreal retelling of the Arthurian legend, with John Cleese in particularly peak form as a hotheaded Sir Lancelot.

Monty Python Live at the Hollywood Bowl (1982) ◆◆◆

D: Terry Hughes. Graham Chapman, John Cleese, Terry Gilliam, Eric Idle, Terry Jones, Michael Palin. 78 minutes. (HBO)

The Python crew transcend the limits of live performance via a multimedia approach wherein they reprise many of their best sketches. The concert was originally shot on video, later transferred to film, then reconverted to cassette.

Monty Python's The Meaning of Life (1983) ◆◆◆

D: Terry Jones. Graham Chapman, John Cleese, Terry Gilliam, Eric Idle, Terry Jones, Michael Palin. 107 minutes. (MCA)

This Cartesian comedy from Britain's masters of mirth hits far more often than it misses. Highlights include a musical tour of the cosmos and the infamous restaurant pig-out scene.

Morgan! (1966) ◆◆◆ B&W

D: Karel Reisz. David Warner, Vanessa Redgrave, Robert Stephens. 97 minutes. (HBO)

A durable offbeat Brit comedy-drama—with Warner as an unhinged artist and Redgrave as the ex-wife he can't forget—that's enjoying a healthy video afterlife.

Moron Movies (1985) ◆◇

D: Len Cella. Len Cella. 60 minutes. (MPI)

This home-movie collection of some 150 minimalist sight gags and blackout sketches—bearing titles like "Why Jello Makes a Lousy Doorstop"—is literally a one-moron show: Len Cella is the pic's sole creator *and* performer. A kind of middle-aged Everyslob, Cella's specialty is building throwaway bits around common household items—refrigerators, bowling balls, plates of food—often to scatological, more occasionally to genuinely comic, effect. The wit and production values are sub–Uncle Floyd, about on a par with most public-access cable-TV comedy shows. *More Moron Movies* is also available from MPI.

Morons from Outer Space (1985) ◆◆
D: Mike Hodges. Griff Rhys Jones, Mel Smith, James B. Sikking, Dinsdale Landen, Joanne Pearce, Jimmy Nail. 87 minutes. (Cannon)

In the hands of the Pythons, the *SCTV* team, or the *Airplane!* crew, this Brit space oddity about a trio of cosmic cretins (where are the Three Stooges when we need them?), who astonish even dull-witted earthlings with their imbecilic antics, could have served as a sturdy frame for some sharp satiric barbs. Under the slack supervision of the U.K. comedy team of Smith (who plays the title morons' mostly absentee chaperone) and Rhys Jones (a bumbling TV news go-fer who winds up as the intergalactic airheads' promoter), *Morons* never leaves the launching pad. Nice title, though.

Movers and Shakers (1985) ◆◆◆
D: William Asher. Charles Grodin, Tyne Daly, Walter Matthau, Gilda Radner, Bill Macy. 80 minutes. (MGM/UA)

A limited but at-times brilliant Hollywood lampoon, scripted by Grodin, and starring Charles as a bemused screenwriter hired to make a meaningful movie out of a sensational but utterly useless property. Reportedly based on brain-damaged attempts to bring Gay Talese's overhyped *Thy Neighbor's Wife* to the screen. Deft characterizations abound, with Matthau, as a beleaguered studio exec, a particular standout here.

Multiple Maniacs (1970) ◆◆◆◇ B&W
D: John Waters. Divine, David Lochary, Mink Stole, Mary Vivian Pearce, Cookie Mueller, Edith Massey. 90 minutes. (Cinema Group)

Waters's first talkie, shot in black and white, is one of his wildest and most wonderfully hostile works. Divine and Lochary run a traveling freak show, Lady Divine's Cavalcade of Perversions, offering local lower-middle-class suckers such shocking sights as a junkie going cold turkey before their very eyes while a professional "puke-eater" does *his* thing in an adjacent ring. The show, though, is just a ruse for Divine to rob, abuse, and occasionally kill the assembled spectators. And that's only the start of the fun. Divine harangues beau Lochary for his mysterious role in the Sharon Tate killing, has a mystical anal/lesbian epiphany with Mink Stole in a local church, and finally embarks on an all-out mass-murder spree, wherein Waters spoofs the gamut of traditional monster-movie clichés. A brilliant display of pointed bad taste.

Munsters' Revenge (1981) NR
D: Don Weis. Fred Gwynne, Al Lewis, Yvonne DeCarlo, Sid Caesar. 96 minutes. (MCA)

Mad scientist Caesar designs android clones of the title clan and puts them to sinister use in this made-for-TV feature based on the popular sitcom.

My Dinner with Andre (1981) NR

D: Louis Malle. Andre Gregory, Wallace Shawn. 110 minutes. (Pacific Arts)

Andre and Wally's yakathon proved surprisingly popular during its theatrical release; now you can hear it all over again in the comfort of *your* dining room.

Myra Breckenridge (1970) NR

D: Michael Sarne. Mae West, John Huston, Raquel Welch, Rex Reed, John Carradine. 94 minutes. (CBS/Fox)

Sarne's campy adaptation of Gore Vidal's transsexual satire has almost as many fans as it does vehement detractors. While the video's been officially withdrawn, it's still visible on many vid-store shelves. Can *you* resist that cast?

The Naked Gun (1988) ◆◆◆◇

D: Jim Abrahams, David Zucker, Jerry Zucker. Leslie Nielsen, Priscilla Presley, Ricardo Montalban, George Kennedy, O. J. Simpson. 93 minutes. (Paramount)

From the Zucker/Abrahams/Zucker (or ZAZ) comedy crew—the funny folks who brought us *Airplane!, Top Secret!, Ruthless People,* and the short-lived teleseries *Police Squad!*—comes *The Naked Gun,* a feature-length *Police Squad!* outing. *The Naked Gun* finds the ZAZ team, who specialize in skewering screen clichés, in fine form, fashioning a freewheeling farce that flies even higher than *Airplane!* From the

Beirut-set prologue to the brilliant baseball-themed finale, *The Naked Gun* rarely misses any of its far-flung array of satiric targets. Nielsen, flawlessly reprising his deadpan LAPD dick Frank Drebin role, is ably assisted by a top tacky cast that includes Presley, Montalban, the ever-dependable Kennedy, Simpson (in a particularly painful part), and Reggie Jackson as a robotic right-fielder programmed to assassinate the Queen of England (!). A home-vid must.

National Lampoon's Vacation (1983) ◆◆◇

D: Harold Ramis. Chevy Chase, Beverly D'Angelo, Imogene Coca. 98 minutes. (Warner)

Chevy and brood's cross-country jaunt to WalleyWorld starts out swiftly before gradually running out of gas. There are enough laughs along the way—Randy Quaid's consummate slob provides quite a few of them—to make this worth a rental. Other NatLamp screen ventures include the seminal *Animal House* (MCA), the filmed revue *Class of '86* (Paramount), the lame *Class Reunion* (Vestron), and the holiday sequel *European Vacation* (Warner).

Neighbors (1981) ◆◆

D: John G. Avildsen. John Belushi, Dan Aykroyd, Cathy Moriarty. 95 minutes. (RCA/Columbia)

Though much of the dialogue is transcribed verbatim from

Thomas Berger's brilliant exercise in suburban paranoia, the film version falls flat. Aykroyd's all right, but Belushi is miscast in a role better suited to an Alan Arkin or a Jack Lemmon.

Network (1976) ◆◆◆

D: Sidney Lumet. William Holden, Faye Dunaway, Peter Finch. 116 minutes. (MGM/UA)

Paddy Chayefsky's scathing boobtube send-up overstates the case more than his previous *Hospital* but boasts more than its share of on-target moments.

Nice Girls Don't Explode (1987) ◆◆◇

D: Chuck Martinez. Barbara Harris, Michelle Meyrink, William O'Leary, Wallace Shawn, James Nardini, William Kuhlke. 92 minutes. (New World)

Nice Girls Don't Explode employs a bouncy score and sitcom tone to mask what's actually a nonviolent but truly neurotic story line. At first, the pic plays like a distaff version of *My Demon Lover*, by way of *Carrie* and *Firestarter*: Midwestern maiden April Flowers (Meyrink) starts telekinetic explosions whenever she's even mildly aroused. It's soon revealed, however, that April's seemingly scattered but ferociously possessive mom (Harris) has been *rigging* her daughter's fiery FX, with the help of lonely pyromaniac Shawn, in an effort to retard her development and keep her firmly in tow. Mom also engineers a number of odd sexual humiliations for April's would-be beau (O'Leary), a Ping-Pong whiz (!) who dreams of testing his skills in China. We can't say we exactly *enjoyed* watching Martinez's sitcom psychodrama, but we never hit the fast-forward control either. Special Phantom kudos, meanwhile, go to the flick's feline Fluffy, played by Orange Cat #5, and especially to his durable stunt double, Eric the Cat.

A Night at the Opera (1935) ◆◆◆◇ B&W

D: Sam Wood. Marx Brothers, Margaret Dumont, Sig Ruman. 87 minutes. (MGM/UA)

Arguably the boys' finest film, from the famous stateroom scene to the final operatic anarchy. More Marx mayhem available on cassette: *Animal Crackers* (MCA), *At the Circus* (MGM/UA), *The Big Store* (MGM/UA), *A Day at the Races* (MGM/UA), *Duck Soup* (MCA), *Go West* (MGM/UA), *Horsefeathers* (MCA), *Love Happy* (Republic), *Monkey Business* (MCA), *A Night in Casablanca* (IUD), and *Room Service* (Vid-America). Groucho goes solo in *Copacabana* (Republic), costarring Carmen Miranda. Marx mavens beware: The *Horsefeathers* vid was transferred from the shortened TV print, rather than the original.

Night Shift (1982) NR

D: Ron Howard. Michael Keaton, Henry Winkler, Shelley Long. 106 minutes. (Warner)

Keaton and Winkler operate a hooker service out of a city

morgue in a flick that wavers between black comedy and sitcom but that's not without its avid fans.

The Nutty Professor (1963) ◆◆◆◇
D: Jerry Lewis. Jerry Lewis, Stella Stevens, Del Moore. 108 minutes. (Paramount)

Discounting his performance in Scorsese's King of Comedy, this remains Jer's shining celluloid achievement (even if the French like it too much) as a scientific experiment turns Jerry into his smooth but evil other half—Dean Martin! A higher concept you'll never find. Other Lewis vehicles available on video include The Bellboy, Cinderfella, The Errand Boy, The Patsy (all IVE), The Big Mouth, Don't Raise the Bridge, Lower the River (both RCA/Columbia), Disorderly Orderly, The Family Jewels (both Paramount), Hardly Working (CBS/Fox), the painful Slapstick of Another Kind (Vestron), and the atrocious Which Way to the Front? (Warner). You can catch Jer with Dino in At War with the Army (Prism), The Caddy, and Hollywood or Bust (both Paramount); the pair also cameo in the Hope/Crosby comedy Road to Bali (Unicorn) and headline in the 1950 TV special Martin-Lewis TV Party (Budget). Jerry's concert tape, Jerry Lewis Live (IVE) is also available.

O Lucky Man! (1973) NR
D: Lindsay Anderson. Malcolm McDowell, Ralph Richardson, Rachel Roberts. 178 minutes. (2 cassettes) (Warner)

Anderson's epic comedy, an informal followup to If..., stars McDowell as a contempo Candide wending his way through corporate Britain. Malcolm returns in Anderson's 1982 continuation Britannia Hospital (HBO).

Ocean's Eleven (1960) ◆◆◆
D: Lewis Milestone. Frank Sinatra, Dean Martin, Sammy Davis, Jr., Peter Lawford, Angie Dickinson. 148 minutes. (Warner)

Still the best of the Rat Pack pics, if ultimately of more iconic interest than entertainment value. Still, this heist caper packs its fair share of irony and suspense, too, and dig Sammy's crazy beatnik number! The Rat Pack returns in Robin and the Seven Hoods (Warner).

Out Cold (1989) ◆◆◇
D: Malcolm Mowbray. John Lithgow, Teri Garr, Bruce McGill, Randy Quaid. 87 minutes. (HBO)

Essentially a sketch idea padded to feature length, Out Cold (formerly Stiffs) offers enough dark laughs to qualify the pic as a low-risk rental item. Quaid turns in the best work here, as a dim-witted dick hired by fed-up spouse Teri Garr to spy on her philandering butcher hubby McGill.

Parents (1989) ◆◆◇
D: Bob Balaban. Randy Quaid, Mary Beth Hurt, Bryan Madorsky, Sandy Dennis, Juno Mills-Cockell. 82 minutes. (Vestron)

An anti-ode to the once-hallowed '50s nuclear family unit, Balaban's *Parents* places young Michael Laemle (Madorsky) at the mercy of his ominous progenitors, ever-smiling Mom (Hurt) and overtly creepy Dad (Quaid), who spends his daylight hours perfecting defoliants at the local Toxico plant. The senior Laemles also share a secret passion that makes them unique among their suburban peers: consuming human flesh. While *Parents'* intentions are admirably sick, the flick is fatally burdened by slow pacing, padded footage, and Christopher Hawthorne's thin script. The lead thesps do what they can with the repetitious material—though Quaid's Nick Laemle character can't hold a carving knife to Terry O'Quinn's terrifying titular maniac in 1987's *The Stepfather* (see index)—and there are a number of blackly mirthful moments, lensed from Michael's understandably paranoiac POV. But nothing in *Parents* approaches the carefully choreographed cannibal dinner scene in the superior 1972 flesh-eating obscurity *Terror at Red Wolf Inn* (see index). It could be that *Parents'* plot is simply too bony to warrant feature-length treatment. The feeling here is that *Parents* would have played better as one of those hour-long educational after-school specials they show on daytime TV.

Pee-wee's Big Adventure (1985) ◆◆◆◇
D: Tim Burton. Paul Reubens, Elizabeth Daily, Mark Holton. 92 minutes. (Warner)

Paul Reubens devises a perfect plot—a cross-country quest for a stolen customized bike—for his Pee-wee persona and crafts his comic vehicle with nearly flawless precision. The pic also carries the single scariest moment, during the truck-driving sequence, of any film of 1985! See also the even weirder sequel *Big Top Pee-wee* (Paramount), which, though falling far short of *Big Adventure*, contains many a priceless pearl for Pee-wee hounds.

Pennies from Heaven (1981) ◆◆◇
D: Herbert Ross. Steve Martin, Bernadette Peters, Christopher Walken. 107 minutes. (MGM/UA)

A self-conscious seriocomic antimusical, set in the Depression '30s and based on Dennis Potter's BBC series of the same name, *Pennies* stars Martin as an itinerant sheet-music salesman making the low-life rounds. Walken, as a pimp, performs his (thus far) only onscreen striptease. The pic bombed with audiences expecting a typical Martin romp but has since found a cult niche on video.

The Pink Angels (1972) ◆◆
D: Lawrence Brown. John Alderman, Tom Basham, Henry Olek, Dan Haggerty, Michael Pataki. 88 minutes. (Prism)

A gay biker gang (!) called the Cupcakes encounters no end of trouble in the course of a dangerous run to a transvestite ball. Not exactly what you'd describe as an enlightened view of gay life-styles, but definitely a different, often grisly period curio. The same director and thesps fared better with their kiddie-host horror flick *Psychopath* (see index). Fans of *derriere-garde* gay-themed trash comedies might also want to look into 1969's equally inauthentic *Gay Deceivers* (Budget), wherein collegiates Kevin Coughlin and Larry Casey feign "going gay" to escape the draft.

Pink Flamingos (1972) ◆◆◇

D: *John Waters. Divine, David Lochary, Mary Vivian Pearce, Edith Massey, Mink Stole. 91 minutes. (Lightning)*

John Waters's most infamous film also ranks as the Phantom's least fave. Here, many of the gross-outs seem a tad too calculated and get in the way of Waters's deeper wit. Still, there are many hilarious moments as an upstart pervo couple (Lochary, Stole) attempt to wrest Filthiest Person in the World honors from Divine's tenacious grip. The incomparable Edith Massey gets her first major Waters role here as Divine's brain-damaged mother, the unforgettable Egg Lady, a cheerful unfortunate who spends her screen time in a crib, demanding, eating, and paying lyrical tribute to ova of every kind. *Pink Flamingos* also contains the first—possibly *only*—screen scene of authentic coprophagia, courtesy of Divine and a passing poodle.

Planes, Trains & Automobiles (1987) ◆◆◇

D: *John Hughes. Steve Martin, John Candy, Laila Robbins. 93 minutes. (Paramount)*

Martin and Candy carry the comedic day here with textured perfs that transcend a thin script chronicling an odd couple's disastrous odyssey from New York to Chicago in Hughes's "adult" film.

Play It Again, Sam (1972) ◆◆◆

D: *Herbert Ross. Woody Allen, Diane Keaton, Tony Roberts. 86 minutes. (Paramount)*

Woody summons Bogie's spirit to help him score with the opposite sex in the screen adaptation of Allen's popular Broadway play. A bit more one-note than many of Allen's later films, but still pretty funny.

Police Academy 1–6 (1984–1988) ◆

D: *Hugh Wilson (1), Jerry Paris (2, 3), Jim Drake (4), Alan Myerson (5), Peter Bonerz (6). Steve Guttenberg, Bubba Smith, Kim Cattrall. 84–97 minutes each. (Warner)*

It's one thing to steal slapstick ideas from classic comedies, but when you can't *execute* them, seems to us like it would be time to look for another line. Instead, these sub–Keystone Kops are among the biggest BO winners of recent years. Go figure.

Polyester (1981) ◆◆◆

D: *John Waters. Divine, Tab Hunter, Edith Massey, Stiv Bators, Cookie Mueller. 86 minutes. (HBO)*

Waters's most gala effort to that point, *Polyester* contains many brilliant bits but plays too often like a repetition of earlier riffs that were fresher the first time around. Still, Divine is just that as harried housewife/misunderstood mom Francine Fishpaw, who seeks relief from her stultifying life with her porn-merchant hubby in the arms of hunky Tod Tomorrow (Tab Hunter, in his first *low* camp role). Massey scores again, this time as a molasses-witted heiress and Francine's best friend. Unfortunately, the vid version doesn't come equipped with the all-important Odorama Scratch 'n' Sniff card, so the film's innovative olfactory element is lost to home viewers.

The President's Analyst (1967) ◆◆◆
D: Theodore J. Flicker. James Coburn, Godfrey Cambridge, Pat Harrington. 100 minutes. (Paramount)

Shrink Coburn's inside info on the prez embroils him in all kinds of comic intrigues. '60s pop paranoia at its best.

The Princess Bride (1987) ◆◆◇
D: Rob Reiner. Cary Elwes, Mandy Patinkin, Chris Sarandon. 98 minutes. (Nelson)

Reiner's storybook farce shapes up as pretty tame stuff next to *This Is Spinal Tap* (see index). What's worse, the video gives us a commercial *and* three trailers for other Nelson tapes before we even get to the feature. It's almost as bad as watching prime-time TV!

Prizzi's Honor (1985) ◆◆◆◇
D: John Huston. Jack Nicholson, Kathleen Turner, Robert Loggia. 130 minutes. (Vestron)

Not quite as sharp as Richard Condon's novel but still a fast and funny black farce about Mafia hit-persons Nicholson and Turner, who learn the hard way that love and business make a bad mix.

The Producers (1968) ◆◆◆
D: Mel Brooks. Mel Brooks, Gene Wilder, Kenneth Mars, Dick Shawn. 90 minutes. (Embassy)

Still Brooks's most original and perverse comedy, with top work turned in by Zero Mostel as a seedy producer, Wilder as his nerdy partner-in-slime, Mars as a sentimental Nazi playwright, and Shawn as an eccentric hipster.

The Projectionist (1971) ◆◆◆
D: Harry Hurwitz. Chuck McCann, Ina Balin, Rodney Dangerfield, Jara Kohout, Robert Staats. 85 minutes. (Vestron)

A more hit than miss exercise in cinematic whimsy detailing projectionist McCann's drab real life and rich reel life, where he assumes the guise of superhero Captain Flash and battles villain The Bat, played by Dangerfield (in his film debut), who doubles as Chuck's cranky bijou-manager boss. Several deft film parodies, plus trailers for imaginary movies like *The Terrible World of Tomorrow*, highlight this clever indie. Unfortunately, director Hurwitz has turned out an awesome array of unwatchable clinkers—*Nocturna* (Media), *Safari 3000* (MGM/UA), and *Rosebud Beach Hotel* (Vestron,) among others—since his bright start here.

The Purple Rose of Cairo (1985) ◆◆◆
D: Woody Allen. Mia Farrow, Jeff Daniels, Danny Aiello. 84 minutes. (Vestron)

Not 100 percent successful, but Allen's comic examination of the blurred lines between movies and reality makes for a tricky, ambitious, and rewarding experience.

Putney Swope (1969) ◆◆◆◇ B&W/color
D: Robert Downey. Arnold Johnson, Antonio Fargas, Allen Garfield. 84 minutes. (RCA/Columbia)

Subterranean satirist Downey's feature film debut chronicles the black takeover of a Mad Ave ad agency. Downey at his best, with a great cast of geeky secondary characters, including the legendary Stan Gottlieb. Other Downey flicks available on cassette include: *Greaser's Palace* (RCA/Columbia), the largely dismal *America* (Sony), and the teen-com misfire *Up the Academy* (Warner).

Raising Arizona (1987) ◆◆◆
D: Joel Coen. Nicolas Cage, Holly Hunter, Trey Wilson, John Goodman, William Forsythe, Tex Cobb. 94 minutes. (CBS/Fox)

Those *Blood Simple* boys, Joel (who directs) and Ethan (who co-scripts with Joel) Coen, take a hy-peractive Sam Raimi approach to their comedic plot and succeed in creating what plays like a feature-length live-action cartoon (and a funnier one than *Who Framed Roger Rabbit?*). Cage and Hunter turn in solid comic work as a reformed (more or less) thief and a retired cop, respectively, who desperately desire to complete their family unit by adopting a baby. When they're turned down, Cage learns that local furniture tycoon Nathan Arizona (Wilson) has kiddies to spare—quintuplets, in fact—so he decides to relieve him of one. While the Coens occasionally lapse into overly broad antics—especially when hog-riding bounty hunter Tex Cobb turns up—*Raising Arizona*, unlike the Coens/Raimi ill-advised collaboration *Crimewave* (see index), supplies fast-paced fun most of the way.

Real Life (1978) ◆◆◆
D: Albert Brooks. Albert Brooks, Charles Grodin, Frances Lee McCain. 99 minutes. (Paramount)

Brooks's first feature, inspired by PBS's *An American Family* series, may be his weakest, but this satire about intrusive electronic "journalists" still boasts many a priceless moment.

Reform School Girls (1986) ◆◆◇
D: Tom DeSimone. Linda Carol, Wendy O. Williams, Sybil Danning, Pat Ast, Charlotte McGinnis, Sherri Stoner. 94 minutes. (New World)

Reform School Girls—Tom (*Concrete Jungle*) DeSimone's send-up of every chicks-in-chains cliché ever committed to celluloid—stars Carol as the obligatory Young Innocent who runs afoul of the law and finds herself in the dread Pridemore Reformatory. There, she's forced to cope with ex-Plasmatic punkette Wendy O. ("I'm all the stud you need!") Williams as the world's oldest juvenile offender, former Warhol regular Ast (a sort of authentically distaff Divine) as the hilariously sadistic head matron, and the redoubtable Danning as the corrupt, religious-minded Warden Sutter, who likes to awaken her hapless charges in the dead of night by reading misogynistic Bible excerpts over the prison loudspeaker system (!). While *Reform School Girls* doesn't live up to its wonderful '50s-sleaze-style trailer—there are too many flat, redundant stretches where the script and energy level break down—the pic should score high with broads-behind-bars buffs while supplying enough tasteless yuks to entertain the uninitiated.

Repo Man (1984) ◆◆◆
D: Alex Cox. Emilio Estevez, Harry Dean Stanton, Vonetta McGee. 92 minutes. (MCA)

Cox's cult fave ranges from broad to brilliant as punk teen Estevez joins the ranks of a determined breed of car repossessors led by Stanton, who sums up his credo thus: "Ordinary people—I hate 'em!" Cox scores again with *Sid and Nancy* (see index) but fared less fortuitously with the self-conscious *Straight to Hell* (CBS/Fox) and *Walker* (MCA).

Richard Pryor—Live in Concert (1979) ◆◆◆◇
D: Jeff Margolis. Richard Pryor. 78 minutes. (Vestron)

The best of RP's filmed concerts includes his wino-and-junkie bit, among many other choice routines. Other Pryor concert pics on video: *Richard Pryor Here and Now* and *Richard Pryor Live on the Sunset Strip* (both RCA/Columbia) and *Richard Pryor: Live & Smokin'* (Vestron).

Ronnie Dearest—The Lost Episodes (1987) ◆◆◆ B&W/color.
60 minutes. (Congress)

Viewers of Manhattan Cable's long-running *Biograph Days, Biograph Nights* series, which features classic clips from vintage films and TV, are already familiar with Ira H. Gallen's elaborate video montages. In *Ronnie Dearest—The Lost Episodes*, Gallen traces the rise and rise of Ronald Reagan, from B-flick hero to television pitchman to U.S. prez, via a briskly edited compilation of movie, TV, and blooper clips. Gallen doesn't impose his views directly but lets the public material speak for itself, and it does so with wicked eloquence. The result is a simultaneously en-

RONNIE DEAREST
the lost episodes

a
video
montage
by
Ira H. Gallen

Photo courtesy of Video Resources.

tertaining and unsettling chronicle of an outlandish but true American Success Story, perhaps the (thus far) ultimate triumph of image over substance. (On the other hand, only in a democracy would Congress put this out.) See also *Rap Master Ronnie* (HBO) and *Rockin' Ronnie* (MPI). See sidebar for other celeb outtakes and blooper tapes.

Roxanne (1987) ♦♦♦
D: Fred Schepisi. Steve Martin, Daryl Hannah, Rick Rossovich. 107 minutes. (RCA/Columbia)

Martin is largely successful in his risky *Cyrano* update, transplanted to a Washington State firehouse. The only serious flaw was casting Hannah as an "intelligent" character.

Running Scared (1986) ♦◇
D: Peter Hyams. Billy Crystal, Gregory Hines, Steven Bauer, Darlanne

CELEB OUTTAKES & BLOOPER TAPES

Abbott and Costello Outtakes Series (1986) NR B&W 45 minutes. *(Video Resources)*
Less a blooper collection—though blunders are well represented—than a look at how the comedy team worked to hone their timing and delivery in lengthy outtakes culled from several feature films.

Bloopermania (1985) NR B&W/color 60 minutes. *(Goodtimes)*
A generic, all-purpose blooper collection available at sell-through prices from the budget-minded folks at Goodtimes.

Bloopers from Star Trek and Laugh-In (1983) NR B&W/color 26 minutes.
(Video Yesteryear)
A self-explanatory compilation of famous fluffs and outtakes taken
from two of the '60s' most popular prime-time teleseries.

Hollywood Bloopers (1985) NR B&W 85 minutes. *Video Dimensions)*
A fairly gala collection of classic star flubs, muffs, and bloopers. Eddie
Cantor, Humphrey Bogart, Bette Davis, Ronald Reagan, and Porky Pig
are but a few of the major celebs represented.

Presidential Blooper Reel (1984) NR B&W 55 minutes. *(Budget)*
Offers a plethora of Reagan outtakes, plus cameo blunders by Red
Skelton, Edward G. Robinson, James Arness, et al. Repeats many of the
clips found on other blooper videos.

Revenge of TV Bloopers (1986) NR B&W 45 minutes. *(Video Dimensions)*
Combines outtakes from *McHale's Navy, Laugh-In, Ben Casey,* and
other prime-time TV shows with antique commercials featuring Jack
Benny, the Marx Brothers, and the Three Stooges.

Soap Opera Scandals (1986) NR Color 45 minutes. *(Video Dimensions)*
Slip-ups, blown promos, and sundry other blunders from daytime
soaps.

Son of Video Yesterbloop (1986) NR B&W/color 54 minutes. *(Video Yesteryear)*
A mélange of classic B-movie goofs of '30s and '40s vintage, sports
mishaps, and a TV segment hosted by *Gunsmoke*'s James Arness.

Star Bloopers (1985) NR B&W 47 minutes. *(HBO)*
More assorted errors and outtakes from celebrities past.

Star Trek Bloopers (1983) NR Color 25 minutes. *(Video Dimensions)*
Uncensored outtakes and rare footage from the space series.

Super Bloopers #1 (1984) NR B&W/color 55 minutes. *(Video Dimensions)*
Reaches into the studio vaults for classic blunders by Boris Karloff,
Carole Lombard, Abbott and Costello, and William Powell, fleshed out
with a Rod Serling antidrug spot and assorted other videoddities.

Super Bloopers #2 (1985) NR B&W 53 minutes. *(Video Dimensions)*
Outtakes from *The Dick Van Dyke Show, The Twilight Zone,* and other

teleseries, plus news-show and commercial breakdowns and rarely seen celebrity public-service and ad spots.

TV Bloopers (1984) NR B&W/color 80 minutes. *(Video Dimensions)*
TV News' Hall of Shame and Soupy Sales segments highlight this lengthy video comedy of *verité* errors.

Video Yesterbloop (1982) NR B&W/color 76 minutes. *(Video Yesteryear)*
An admirably comprehensive blooper collection compiled from a wide range of sources: newsreels, antique TV shows, soap operas, plus Robin Williams runs amok in *Mork and Mindy,* and a *Price Is Right* contestant literally loses her shirt.

Warners Outtake Series (1986) NR B&W 45 minutes. *(Video Resources)*
Collected outtakes covering the years 1936–39 and including Cagney, Bogart, Davis, Flynn, and dozens of other notables.

Fleugel, Joe Pantoliano, Dan Hedaya. 106 minutes. (MGM/UA)

Hyams's relentlessly trivial action "comedy" represents a typical Hollywood waste of talents Crystal and Hines. The pair are cast here as a couple of wise-ass Windy City dicks torn between chucking it all for an early retirement to Key West and staying on to battle evildoers like local coke kingpin Gonzalez (Jimmy Smits). This substandard attempt to cash in on the *48 Hours/Beverly Hills Cop* trade is neither funny, exciting nor credible as our heroes spend their copious screen time simultaneously dodging lead and swapping leaden quips. A subplot involving Crystal's ex-wife (Fluegel) features some of the lamest dialogue ever uttered onscreen.

Rustlers' Rhapsody (1985) ◆◆
D: Hugh Wilson. Tom Berenger, Marilu Henner, G. W. Bailey. 89 minutes. (Paramount)

A belated spoof of the long-defunct B westerns of yore, *Rustlers' Rhapsody* fails to corral enough laughs to sustain its feature length.

Ruthless People (1986) ◆◆◆◇
D: Jim Abrahams, David Zucker, Jerry Zucker. Danny De Vito, Bette Midler, Judge Reinhold, Helen Slater, Anita Morris, Bill Pullman. 93 minutes. (Touchstone)

This clever, nearly seamless farce eschews cheap gags and stays true to its characters. Dale Launer's tight script is expertly abetted by the *Airplane!* crew's bouncy direction. De Vito is excellent as unscrupulous Spandex Miniskirt

King Sam Stone (there's not one "short" joke in the whole movie) who's thrilled that a pair of extremely amateur kidnappers (Reinhold, Slater) have snatched his loudmouthed, overweight wife (Midler). Morris and Pullman lend strong comic support as Sam's equally ruthless mistress and her dumb-as-they-come beau.

The Secret Cinema (1966) ◆◆◆◇ **B&W**
D: Paul Bartel. Amy Vane, Gordon Felio, Connie Ellison. 37 minutes. (Rhino)

Bartel's film debut is a wonderfully paranoiac featurette about a young woman (Vane) whose life is being secretly filmed, then screened at the title bijou for the general amusement of relatives, friends, and strangers alike. Bartel later remade the movie as a Steven Spielberg's *Amazing Stories* episode but lost the original's subversive quality somewhere along the way. Fortunately, thanks to the archivists at Rhino, you can catch the initial, superior edition on tape.

The Secret Policeman's Other Ball (1982) ◆◆◆
D: Julian Temple, Roger Graef. John Cleese, Graham Chapman, Michael Palin, Terry Jones. 101 minutes. (MGM/UA)

Pythons share the spotlight with rockers Eric Clapton, Jeff Beck, Peter Townsend, Phil Collins, and Sting in a concert film reedited from a pair of Amnesty International benefits. See also the follow-up, *The Secret Policeman's Private Parts* (Media).

Serial (1980) ◆◆◇
D: Bill Persky. Martin Mull, Tuesday Weld, Sally Kellerman. 95 minutes. (Paramount)

This fairly funny look at contempo faddism, based on Cyra McFadden's novel, could have used more bite but benefits from Mull's long-suffering turn as a normal person surrounded by New Age idiocy.

The Seven Percent Solution (1976) ◆◆◆
D: Herbert Ross. Nicol Williamson, Alan Arkin, Vanessa Redgrave, Robert Duvall. 113 minutes. (MCA)

Nicholas Meyer was wisely allowed to adapt his own novel to the screen. The result is an unpretentious, immensely entertaining fantasy pairing Sherlock Holmes (Williamson) and Sigmund Freud (Arkin) for a therapy session that segues into high comic adventure. Duvall is sharp as a deadpan Dr. Watson.

She Done Him Wrong (1933) ◆◆◆ **B&W**
D: Lowell Sherman. Mae West, Cary Grant, Gilbert Roland. 65 minutes. (MCA)

The original Divine Miss M adapts her cheerfully smutty Broadway hit *Diamond Lil* to the screen in what may be her purest movie vehicle. Mae maniacs can also find their frisky femme fave in *Sextette* (Media) and with W. C. in *My Little Chickadee* (MCA); otherwise, the wisecracking West remains grossly underrepresented on cassette.

She's Gotta Have It (1986) ◆◆◇ B&W/color

D: Spike Lee. Tracy Camilla Johns, Spike Lee, John Canada Terrell. 84 minutes. (Key)

Wildly overhyped debut comedy from "the black Woody Allen" (oy!) is a mixed affair, with amateurish stretches lifted by genuine and original insights. Question is: Will Woody one day be "the white Spike Lee"? Spike's controversial campus musical, School Daze, meanwhile, is also available via Key.

Sitting Ducks (1980) ◆◆◇

D: Henry Jaglom. Zack Norman, Michael Emil, Patrice Townsend. 90 minutes. (Media)

One of indefatigable indie auteur Jaglom's funnier efforts, with Norman and Emil well cast as a pair of impulsive crooks who decide to rip off the syndicate.

Skin Game (1971) NR

D: Paul Bogart. James Garner, Louis Gossett, Jr., Susan Clark. 102 minutes. (Warner)

A high-concept comedy, with conmen Garner and Gossett running a slavery scam in the pre–Civil War West.

Slammer Girls (1987) ◆

D: Chuck Vincent. Devon Jenkin, Jeff Eagle, Jane Hamilton, Ron Sullivan, Tally Brittany, Darcy Nychols, Captain Haggerty. 84 minutes. (Lightning)

Chuck Vincent sets his satiric sights on the chicks-in-chains genre but lenses a broad, out-of-focus farce that's not as funny as the flawed Reform School Girls (see index). Jenkin is the prototypical blond naif, framed for a crime she didn't commit, who leads us through the complete catalog of prison-pic clichés: guard and inmate brutality, Sapphic sex, gratuitous showers, official corruption, abortive escape attempts, riots, et al. The proceedings are in no way enhanced by a singularly unappealing cast, much of it recruited from porndom's ranks, from Hamilton (née Veronica Hart) as mean matron Crabapples to Sullivan (aka Henri Pachard) as the governor. A few funny bits—including Sullivan's pro–capital punishment campaign speech—manage to survive the otherwise anticomic carnage but not enough to elevate Slammer Girls above the generally dismal.

Sleeper (1973) ◆◆◆◇

D: Woody Allen. Woody Allen, Diane Keaton, John Beck. 88 minutes. (Playhouse)

One of Woody's best finds him awakening in a postapocalyptic future ("a man named Albert Schenker got hold of a nuclear device"), where he's pursued by totalitarian police. A deft blend of sharp social satire and imaginative sight gags, with strong comic support from Keaton as Allen's futuristic ally.

Some Like It Hot (1959) ◆◆◆◇ **B&W**
D: Billy Wilder. Jack Lemmon, Tony Curtis, Marilyn Monroe. 119 minutes. (MGM/UA)

Wilder's lively, perverse drag comedy pools the talents of Curtis, Lemon, Monroe, and Joe E. Brown for a Roaring Twenties romp fully deserving of its "classic" status.

Something Wild (1986) ◆◆◇
D: Jonathan Demme. Jeff Daniels, Melanie Griffith, Ray Liotta. (HBO)

Yet another wild-and-crazy-gal-leads-straight-guy-on-a-madcap-adventure entry. Demme's edition makes a bumpy transition from screwball comedy to gritty suspense, but first-half laughs and Liotta's lowlife perf make it worth a look.

Sons of the Desert (1934) ◆◆◆◇ **B&W**
D: William A. Seiter. Stan Laurel, Oliver Hardy, Charley Chase, Mae Busch. 69 minutes. (Nostalgia Merchant)

Quintessential Laurel and Hardy comedy sees Stan and Ollie sneak off to a lodge convention without the wives being any the wiser—or so they think. The national Laurel and Hardy fan club took its name from the title. Most of the duo's features, shorts, and selected silents are available on cassette. Their vintage Hal Roach features—*Blockheads, Bohemian Girl, Our Relations, Pardon Us, Swiss Miss,* and *Way Out West* are out on the Fox Hills label. MGM/UA has *Bonnie Scotland,* and a number of labels (e.g., Congress)

carry the public-domain *Flying Deuces* and L&H's last and weakest film, *Utopia.* CBS/Fox handles their later, inferior features *The Bullfighters* and *Great Guns,* while Video Dimensions carries *March of the Wooden Soldiers.* Most of their sound shorts have been issued by Fox Hills (*Laurel and Hardy Comedy Classics* series), while Grapevine Video has several volumes of their silent shorts available. Miscellaneous L&H videos include *Laurel and Hardy: Rare Home Movies* (Video Yesteryear), *Laurel and Hardy,* a compilation of TV appearances (Concord), *Laurel and Hardy on Parade* (Goodtimes), and *The Laurel and Hardy Scrapbook* (Discount Video). Hal Roach Video has issued colorized editions of *Way Out West* and the shorts *The Music Box* and *Helpmates. Movie Struck,* featuring an L&H cameo, is out via Amvest.

Sorority Babes in the Slimeball Bowl-O-Rama (1988) ◆◆◇
D: David DeCoteau. Linnea Quigley, Michelle Bauer, Andras Jones, Robin Rochelle, Brinke Stevens, Buck Flower. 78 minutes. (Urban Classics)

A tough title to live up to, we agree, but *Sorority Babes in the Slimeball Bowl-O-Rama* comes surprisingly close to achieving that formidable goal. Our story involves two shapely sorority pledges (Bauer, Stevens) who, accompanied by three klutzy nerdboys, are dispatched to the title site as part of their initiation rites. The plot takes a more sinister turn when an evil imp imprisoned in a bowling trophy (!) escapes and begins wreaking all manner of lethal havoc. While occasionally descending to the painfully stupid, *Sorority Babes* manages most of the time to sustain at least a middling level of inventive chaos and throwaway wit. Sleaze-screen queen Linnea Quigley shines as the pic's spunky punkette heroine, the Imp makes for a lively screen villain, and the low-budget affair is further abetted by authentic mall location-shooting. If you like the title, you'll probably enjoy the pic as well.

Spaceballs (1987) ◆◆◆
D: Mel Brooks. John Candy, Rick Moranis, Mel Brooks, Bill Pullman, Daphne Zuniga, Dick Van Patten, John Hurt. 96 minutes. (MGM/UA)

A clever if belated *Star Wars* spoof, *Spaceballs* finds Brooks in fine form, especially as alien elder Yogurt, a mix of Yoda, *SCTV*'s Sid Dithers, and Mel's own 2000-Year-Old Man. Also onboard are Moranis as Dark Helmet; Bill (*Ruthless People*) Pullman as macho space mercenary Lone Starr; Zuniga as Planet Druidia's Princess Vespa—frequent butt of "Druish Princess" jokes; the ever-excellent Candy as Barf the Mawg, half man, half dog ("I'm my own best friend"); and the wonderfully revolting mozzarella monster Pizza the Hut. Brooks largely eschews his usual scatological licks

in favor of riskier conceptual riffs. Yogurt is a wily merchandiser hawking *Spaceballs* lunchboxes and towels while praying for a sequel (*Spaceballs 2: The Search for More Money*); Dark Helmet literally stops the movie to preview the *Spaceballs* video; and the cosmic villains succeed in capturing not our heroes but their stunt doubles (including a short bearded guy in a Princess Vespa wig). Mel manages to pull off these self-referential gags with admirable low-key ease. Even the normally obnoxious Joan Rivers, who supplies the voice of Vespa's android chaperone, is relatively restrained here, which may well be Mel's greatest coup of all.

Spies like Us (1985) ◆◆◇
D: John Landis. Chevy Chase, Dan Aykroyd, Donna Dixon. 103 minutes. (Warner)

Most critics dumped on this one, but the Chase/Aykroyd team enlivens this fairly funny update of the Cold War comedies of old.

Splash (1984) ◆◆◇
D: Ron Howard. Tom Hanks, Daryl Hannah, John Candy, Eugene Levy. 109 minutes. (Walt Disney)

SCTV vets Candy and Levy help buoy this lightweight romantic comedy/fantasy about a boy (Hanks) and his mermaid (Hannah).

Stardust Memories (1980) ◆◆◆◇ B&W
D: Woody Allen. Woody Allen, Charlotte Rampling, Jessica Harper. 91 minutes. (Key)

A lot of critics didn't like this one either, feeling Allen had overstepped his satiric bounds in making mock of movie reviewers. But they're only one of many deserving targets—including self-serious auteurs—skewered here. The opening train scene, modeled after *8½*'s intro, is absolutely brilliant, and Allen's close encounter of the nerd kind with a gaggle of naggy aliens isn't half bad either.

Steve Martin: The Funnier Side of Eastern Canada (1974) NR
Steve Martin. 60 minutes. (IUD)

The vid version of Steve's debut TV-comedy special showcases many of the comic's vintage routines. The 1986 concert tape *Steve Martin Live!* (Vestron) gives us the more mature Martin.

Stoogemania (1985) ◆
D: Chuck Workman. Josh Mostel, Melanie Chartoff, Josh Miner, Sid Caesar, Thom Sharp, Mark Holton. 83 minutes. (Paramount)

Workman's would-be tribute to the Three Stooges takes a solid 10-minute skit idea and inflates it into a painfully padded 83-minute mess. Josh (son of Zero) Mostel stars as Howard F. Howard, a rotund Stooge nerd whose comedic cravings eventually land him on Stooge Row, where, in the pic's best sequence, hopeless Moe, Larry, and Curly addicts wander the streets endlessly repeating Stooge *shticks*. Caesar shows up briefly to perform his dog-eared German shrink bit at a Stooge re-hab center, while Holton manages a funnier turn as a terminal Curly clone. By comparison, the Stooges' posthumous contributions (mostly clips from their later shorts, after Shemp Howard had replaced the late Curly) only accentuate the ineptitude of Workman's slapstick set pieces. You'd be infinitely better off getting an original Stooges compilation.

Strange Brew (1983) ◆◆◇
D: Dave Thomas, Rick Moranis. Dave Thomas, Rick Moranis, Max von Sydow. 91 minutes. (MGM/UA)

Fans of *SCTV*'s "Great White North" will enjoy this comic odyssey that takes the beer-brained McKenzie Brothers to the lair of evil brewmeister von Sydow.

Stranger than Paradise (1984) ◆◆◆ B&W
D: Jim Jarmusch. John Lurie, Eszter Balint, Richard Edson. 90 minutes. (Key)

Jarmusch's low-key comic odyssey, lensed in evocative black and white, shapes up as a made-for-midnight movie that succeeds in achieving its modest goals. His more ambitious follow-up, *Down by Law* (Media), is also well worth a look.

The Student Nurses (1970) ◆◆
D: Stephanie Rothman. Elaine Giftos, Karen Carlson, Brioni Farrell. 89 minutes. (Charter)

First of Roger Corman's jiggle-comedy quintet dealing with the misadventures of the buxom title femmes is at least a notch above the '80s rash of teen-virgin gross-outs. See also (if you dare) *Candy Stripe Nurses* (Embassy), *Night Call Nurses, Private Duty Nurses,* and *Young Nurses* (all Charter). *The Stewardesses* (Video Dimensions) and *Swinging Stewardesses* (Budget) are likewise available.

Summer Rental (1985) ◆◆
D: Carl Reiner. John Candy, Richard Crenna, Rip Torn. 87 minutes. (Paramount)

Candy carries the day as a harried vacationer, partially compensating for the script's lack of solid comic material.

Surf Nazis Must Die (1987) ◆◇
D: Peter George. Barry Brenner, Gail Neely, Michael Sonye, Dawn Wildsmith, Tom Shell, Bobbie Bresee. 83 minutes. (Media)

With *Surf Nazis Must Die,* the tireless Troma Team continues its tradition of fashioning great sleaze titles and terrif trailers to mask mostly mediocre movies. George's *Surf Nazis Must Die,* a makeshift *Road Warrior* takeoff transferred to the sands of a quake-ravaged California, suffers from too many muffed scenes (retakes cost money) and a distinct lack of forward thrust in detailing the inter-tribal conflicts that arise between the title heavies, led by Adolf (Brenner) and Eva (Wildsmith), and their surfside rivals. On the plus side, the flick refreshingly breaks tradition by employing a hefty

middle-aged black woman, Leroy's Mama (nicely handled by Neely), as the heroine who marks the Surf Nazis for extinction. Obscure cult fave Bresee also turns in a neat comic stint as a Surf Nazi's unimpressed mom. "*Adolf!?*" she scoffs. "Is that what that snotty Ricky Johnson is calling himself now?" Unfortunately, *Surf Nazis* fails to sustain that lunacy level.

Swimming to Cambodia (1987) NR
D: Jonathan Demme. Spalding Gray. 87 minutes. (Lorimar)

Talking-head king Gray holds forth on his experiences on the set of *The Killing Fields* (Warner) and sundry other topics.

Take the Money and Run (1969) ◆◆◆
D: Woody Allen. Woody Allen, Janet Margolin, Marcel Hillaire, Jacqueline Hyde, Lonny Chapman. 85 minutes. (Key)

Allen's first feature, a mock documentary profile of career criminal manqué Fielding Mellish (Allen), remains one of his funniest, though it lacks some of the polish of a *Bananas* or a *Sleeper* (see index).

Takin' It All Off (1987) ◆
D: Ed Hansen. Kitten Natividad, Fred Hampton, Farley Maynard, John Alderman. 91 minutes. (Vestron)

It's let's-put-on-a-show-to-save-the-dance-studio time in this amiable but rather pathetic T&A comedy. The show in question is of the strip variety (natch), top-lining top-heavy ex–Russ Meyer vixen Natividad, whose highly compelling presence was the only reason your ever-optimistic Phantom was drawn to this tape in the first place. But not even the bouncy Kitten can salvage this oddly old-fashioned (not to say prehistoric) array of primitive performances, sex (especially gay) jokes, and for that matter, filmmaking craft (or lack of same). *Takin' It All Off* is for die-hard Natividad nuts only. The latter may also want to check out the prequel, *Takin' It Off* (Vestron).

Tampopo (1986) ◆◆◆

D: Juzo Itami. Ken Watanabe, Tsutomu Yamakazi, Nobuko Miyamoto, Koji Yakusho. 114 minutes. (Republic)

Itami's quirky comedy of gustatory manners is also a film buff's delight, incorporating deft parodies of everything from vintage American westerns, Clint Eastwood movies, and Nippon's own erotic epic *In the Realm of the Senses* (NA) as a laconic truck-drivin' macho man helps a struggling widow make a go of her ailing roadside noodle joint (!). An overly long running time and a few too many winks at the camera rank as this subtly subversive social satire's only serious flaws.

The 30 Foot Bride of Candy Rock (1959) ◆◆

D: Sidney Miller. Lou Costello, Dorothy Provine, Gale Gordon. 75 minutes. (RCA/Columbia)

A kind of *Abbott and Costello Meet the 50 Foot Woman*, minus Abbott and some 20 feet. Lou's lone solo vehicle rates as a must for his fans but a notch below even his weaker excursions with the irascible Abbott.

This Is Spinal Tap (1984) ◆◆◆◆

D: Rob Reiner. Christopher Guest, Michael McKean, Rob Reiner. 88 minutes. (Embassy)

Easily the funniest rock'n'll satire ever filmed, this mockumentary look at the fictitious title band never hits a false note. The Stonehenge production number is one of many highlights; band leaders Guest and McKean are excellent throughout. Director Reiner struggled mightily—even financing and filming a *Spinal Tap* demo reel—to get this offbeat gem produced but his efforts did not go unrewarded.

¡Three Amigos! (1986) ◆◆◇

D: John Landis. Steve Martin, Chevy Chase, Martin Short, Patrice Martinez, Alfonso Arau, Tony Plana. 105 minutes. (HBO)

Martin, Short, and Chase, as three ousted silent-movie cowboys on a misunderstood mission to an outlaw-plagued Mexican village, get a lot of sustained comic mileage out of what could have been a one-joke idea. Not every riff works, the ending's pretty weak, and the film runs on a reel too long, but there are enough laughs in this belated *Magnificent Seven* parody to justify the price of an overnight rental.

Three in the Attic (1968) ◆◆◇
D: Richard Wilson. Christopher Jones, Yvette Mimieux, Judy Pace. 92 minutes. (Embassy)

Jones is legendary campus stud Paxton Quigley, who finds himself the love slave of three vengeful co-eds in this fairly dumb but popular '60s romp. For a virtual replay of the same theme, see *Three in the Cellar* (HBO), formerly titled *Up in the Cellar* and actually superior to *Three in the Attic*.

Three O'Clock High (1987) ◆◆◇
D: Phil Joanou. Casey Siemaszko, Anne Ryan, Stacey Glick, Jonathan Wise, Richard Tyson, Jeffrey Tambor, John P. Ryan. 90 minutes. (Lorimar)

In *Three O'Clock High*, Hollywood whiz kid Joanou—sort of the Savage Steve Holland of 1987—fashions a teen *High (School) Noon Meets After Hours*, with *The Terminator* tossed in for good measure. The flick follows average nice kid Jerry Mitchell (Siemaszko, who resembles Richard Dreyfuss in his *American Graffiti* days), who inadvertently incurs the wrath of terrifying transfer student Buddy Revell (Tyson, who resembles John Cougar Mellencamp on steroids) and is due to meet him for a potentially disastrous duke-out at the title hour. *Three O'Clock High* boasts a tight structure, flashes of true wit, an intermittent vision of high school as hell, and, in its own exaggerated way, a stronger sense of *verité* than John Hughes's bubble-gum movies. Unfortunately, Joanou's film-school camera pyrotechnics—while falling short of the all-out manic intensity of Sam Raimi's *Evil Dead II* or the Coen Brothers' *Raising Arizona*—hinder more than help his story line, and the pic's morally dubious and unpointed resolution reflects '80s-think at its worst.

The Three Stooges Meet Hercules (1961) ◆◆◇ B&W
D: Edward Bernds. Moe Howard, Larry Fine, Joe DeRita. 89 minutes. (RCA/Columbia)

The Stooges' determinedly violent take on the human condition is more popular today than it's ever been. Unbelievably enough, as of this writing, the above and *Snow White and the Three Stooges* (Playhouse) are their only later features currently on cassette. Most of their seminal shorts—some with Curly Howard, others with Shemp Howard or Joe Besser as the third Stooge—are available via RCA/Columbia, as well as low-budget sell-through companies like Amvest, Congress, Goodtimes, and Trans-Atlantic. Other compilation cassettes include *The Making of the Stooges* (Lorimar), *Three Stooges Festival* (Kartes), and *Three Stooges Potpourri* (Budget). The single best source for Stooge arcana, though, is *Channel 13 Video* (see Videorama), which covers everything from the obscure '46 Stooge feature *Swing Parade of 1946* to the trio's TV guest shots. Couch potatoes can also take their lumps with the interactive *Three Stooges—The VCR Game* (RCA/Columbia).

Throw Momma from the Train (1987) ◆◆◇

D: Danny De Vito. Danny De Vito, Billy Crystal, Anne Ramsey. 89 minutes. (Orion)

The trouble with De Vito's oedipal *Strangers on a Train* wreck is that he doesn't take his sick material far *enough*. But he does yield enough laughs from his solid premise and comic persona to make *Momma* worth a look.

Time Bandits (1981) ◆◆◆

D: Terry Gilliam. Ralph Richardson, Sean Connery, John Cleese, Shelley Duvall. 117 minutes. (Paramount)

Gilliam recruits many of his Python mates for an idiosyncratic time-travel lark that lacks his later *Brazil*'s sharp focus but that manages to be fun most of the way. The Paramount video features the complete British version, six minutes longer than the American theatrical release.

Tin Men (1987) ◆◆◇

D: Barry Levinson. Richard Dreyfuss, Barbara Hershey, Danny De Vito. 112 minutes. (Touchstone)

Levinson lurches between genuine humor, pathos, and forced sitcom *shticks* in an interesting if uneven account of the fierce rivalry that develops between Baltimore siding salesmen Dreyfuss and De Vito.

The Toxic Avenger (1985) ◆◇

D: Michael Herz, Samuel Weil. Mitchell Cohen, Andree Maranda, Mark Torgi, Pat Ryan, Jr., Jennifer Baptist, Gary Schneider. 82 minutes. (Lightning)

Our story unfolds in Tromaville, New Jersey, Toxic Waste Capital of the World, where hopeless nerd Melvin (Torgi), janitor at a local health club favored by nubile nymphettes and muscle-headed jocks, winds up head-first in a nuclear-waste vat, victim of a practical joke engineered by local bully Bozo. It's Melvin who enjoys the last laugh, however, when he metamorphoses into the hideous but righteous title character and vows to rid Tromaville of its multifarious troublemakers. The Phantom's Rule of Thumb for Dumb Fun holds that if you're gonna dish out blind, cripple, crotch, dwarf, dope, and dead-dog jokes, then you better make sure they're *fresh* blind, cripple, crotch, dwarf, dope, and dead-dog jokes—an achievement apparently beyond the range of the Troma Team's assembled nontalents. Self-conscious stupidity is no substitute for authentically brain-damaged inspiration. And you can quote us. And that goes double for Troma's equally lame *Class of Nuke 'Em High*

(Media). Available in R and un-rated versions.

Treasure of the Moon Goddess (1988) ◆◇

D: Joseph Louis Agraz. Asher Brauner, Don Calfa, Linnea Quigley, Jo-Ann Ayres. 89 minutes. (Vidmark)

Treasure of the Moon Goddess pairs *Return of the Living Dead* alumni Calfa and Quigley as a low-rent agent and his singing client, respectively. Our story, awk-wardly related via flashbacks, finds the duo in a South American jungle, where Linnea's mistaken for the reincarnation of a mythical moon goddess. Madcap compli-cations involving adventurer Sam Kidd (Brauner, who also co-scripted), local heavies, the rumored title treasure, broad cap-tures, and narrow escapes ensue in short order. Essentially a throw-back to the back-lot B adventure-comedies of yore in the guise of a low-budget *Romancing the Stone/Indiana Jones* clone, *Moon God-dess* stacks up as an amiable but immensely feeble affair.

True Stories (1986) ◆◆

D: David Byrne. David Byrne, John Goodman, Annie McEnroe, Swoosie Kurtz, Pops Staples, Spalding Gray. 111 minutes. (Warner)

You've heard the album, you've read the book, you've caught the clips on MTV ... now see the movie. Uh-oh. This *ain't* no movie. Just a 96-minute rock video with head Talking Head Byrne tooling, strolling, and talk-ing his way—like some kind of Nuevo Wavo Will Rogers—through the eccentric lives of the common but secretly colorful folk of fictional Virgil, Texas. We hear some pretty fair tunes, but the air's a bit thick with condescension; sometimes it's kinder to be cruel. In sum, *True Stories* is the ulti-mate prepackaged multimedia poke at our prepackaged multi-media culture. We can't blame Byrne for striking while the irony's hot, but we'll stick with the soundtrack LP.

Tunnelvision (1976) NR

D: Brad Swirnoff. Phil Proctor, Howard Hesseman, Chevy Chase. 70 minutes. (MPI)

A shotgun satire aimed at TV, *Tun-nelvision* serves as an informal warm-up for soon-to-be Not Ready for Prime Time Players Chevy Chase, Laraine Newman, and the comedy duo of Franken and Davis.

UFOria (1981/1986) ◆◆◆◇

D: John Binder. Cindy Williams, Fred Ward, Harry Dean Stanton, Beverly Hope Atkinson, Harry Carey, Jr., Rob-ert Gray. 100 minutes. (MCA)

It took nearly five years for Binder's low-key comedy about California UFO nuts to reach the screen (Universal honchos, realiz-ing that they had a good pic on their hands, promptly panicked and shelved it back in '81), but it was well worth the wait. Cindy ("Shirley") Williams stars as Ar-lene, an intense if unconscious check-out girl with a fetish for UFOs and a burgeoning belief that one is about to land in a nearby desert. Into her lonely life rides Sheldon Bart (expertly played by Ward), a rhinestone cowboy manqué who hooks up with phony evangelist Brother Bud (Stanton). Arlene's saucermania soon attracts a following of fellow wackos, from free-lance futurists to New Age Jesus freaks, as well as Brother Bud's ever-avaricious attention. *UFOria* is basically a comic meditation on beliefs, the universal need to own a set of same, and the loony lengths to which said need can take people who don't have a hell of a lot of earthly options. As Brother Bud puts it, "Everybody ought to believe in somethin'. I believe I'll have another drink." To which the Phantom can only add a heartfelt, "Amen!"

Unfaithfully Yours (1948) ♦♦♦ B&W

D: Preston Sturges. Rex Harrison, Linda Darnell, Kurt Kreuger. 105 minutes. (CBS/Fox)

One of Preston Sturges's finest and funniest, with conductor Harrison entertaining all manner of mortal fantasies re: his allegedly unfaithful wife Darnell. Avoid the deadly Dudley Moore remake (also CBS/Fox). Other Sturges satires available on video include *Christmas in July, The Great McGinty, The Lady Eve,* and *Palm Beach Story* (all MCA); *Miracle of Morgan's Creek* (Paramount);

and the public-domain *The Sin of Harold Diddlebock* (Kartes, others).

Up in Smoke (1978) ♦♦◇

D: Lou Adler. Cheech Marin, Tommy Chong, Stacy Keach. 86 minutes. (Paramount)

The first and funniest of grassroots comics Cheech & Chong's marijuana misadventures. They return in *Cheech & Chong's Get Out of My Room* (MCA), *Cheech & Chong's Next Movie* (MCA), *Cheech & Chong's The Corsican Brothers* (Lightning), *Nice Dreams* (RCA/Columbia), *Still Smokin'* (Paramount), and *Things Are Tough All Over* (RCA/Columbia), while Cheech goes solo in *Born in East L.A.* (MCA).

War (1988) ♦

D: Michael Herz, Samuel Weil. Carolyn Beauchamp, Sean Bowen, Michael Ryder, Patrick Weathers, Jessica Dublin, Steven Crossley. 99 minutes. (Media)

Troma's assembled talents have once again managed to concoct a movie that's relentlessly, self-consciously offensive without being the least bit subversive. This brain-dead would-be war-pic parody pits a typical cross-section (typical for Troma, that is) of Carib plane-crash survivors against a motley army of all-purpose terrorists. To the usual plethora of lame ethnic, handicapped, sexist, and scatological gags, Troma adds a new wrinkle—the screen's first

AIDS jokes. If nothing else, *War* easily cops the Phantom's Rubber Crutch Award as the Unfunniest Comedy of 1988.

Watermelon Man (1970) ◆◆◆
D: Melvin Van Peebles. Godfrey Cambridge, Estelle Parsons, Howard Caine. 97 minutes. (RCA/Columbia)

Cambridge is a white suburbanite who turns black in Melvin Van Peebles's racial satire. Not as out there as the earnest *Black Like Me* (United) but pretty funny in its own right.

What's Up, Tiger Lily? (1966) ◆◆◆
D: Woody Allen, Sankichi Taniguchi. Tatsuya Mihashi, Woody Allen, China Lee. 80 minutes. (Amvest)

One of Woody's most inventive early projects: He took a bad Japanese spy movie and redubbed the soundtrack. Doesn't sustain for the entire running time but has more than enough laughs to make a rental essential. Other Allen comedies not previously covered here include the regressive *Hannah and Her Sisters* (HBO), the self-indulgent *Manhattan* (MGM/UA), and the overly nostalgic *Radio Days* (HBO). Woody also costars in the 1976 seriocomic Hollywood Blacklist pic *The Front* (RCA/Columbia) and wrote the original play-turned-film *Don't Drink the Water* (Embassy).

When Comedy Was King (1959) ◆◆◆ B&W
Compiled by Robert Youngson. 84 minutes. (VidAmerica)

Another topnotch comic compilation of choice clips featuring Buster Keaton, Charlie Chaplin, Laurel and Hardy, the Keystone Kops, and other silent faves.

When Women Had Tails (1970) NR
D: Pasquale Festa Campanile. Senta Berger, Frank Wolff, Guiliano Gemma. 110 minutes. (Western-World, others)

Caveman comedy connoisseurs and Senta Berger buffs alike should enjoy this neanderthal romp, co-scripted by Lina Wertmuller. The sequel, *When Women Lost Their Tails*, is also available via Western-World Video.

When's Your Birthday? (1937) NR B&W
D: Harry Beaumont. Joe E. Brown, Edgar Kennedy, Margaret Hamilton. 76 minutes. (J&J, others)

Brown is a third-rate boxer whose fortunes change when he consults an astrologer. J&J's video also contains several cartoons. Other Joe E. vehicles available on cassette: *Riding on Air* and *Fit for a King* (Discount).

Where's Poppa? (1970) ◆◆◆
D: Carl Reiner. George Segal, Ruth Gordon, Trish Van Devere. 82 minutes. (Key)

Reiner's raunchy comedy, scripted by Robert Klane from his novel, plays like an extended classic sick joke as lawyer/oedipal wreck Segal tries to cope with his senile mom Gordon and sundry courtroom insanities.

Wise Blood (1979) ◆◆◆◇
D: John Huston. Brad Dourif, Ned Beatty, Amy Wright. 106 minutes. (MCA)

Huston expertly captures the elusive, grotesque essence of Flannery O'Connor's black-comic novel about a self-made evangelist (Dourif) and his brain-damaged disciple. The flick flopped at the box office, but it's a one-of-a-kind winner that's not to be missed.

The Wit and Wisdom of Ronald Reagan (1987) NR
120 minutes. (Rhino)

A blank tape, what else?, courtesy of Rhino's resident wits.

The Witches of Eastwick (1987) ◆◆
D: George Miller. Jack Nicholson, Cher, Susan Sarandon, Michelle Pfeiffer, Veronica Cartwright, Richard Jenkins. 118 minutes. (Warner)

This muddled mess—John Updike's smarmy fable of bourgeois Connecticut carnality run through the Hollywood grinder—finds satanic satyr Darryl Van Horne (Nicholson) seducing a trio of frustrated upper-middle-class femmes (Cher, Sarandon, and Pfeiffer). A few laughs survive and the thesps give it their best, but the flick issues too many contradictory signals and is ultimately a soulless affair. While the pic's climactic Attack of the Fifty-Foot Jack Nicholson *is* impressive, it's hardly worth the nearly two-hour wait.

You'll Find Out (1940) ◆◆◇ **B&W**
D: David Butler. Kay Kyser, Boris Karloff, Bela Lugosi, Peter Lorre. 97 minutes. (Budget)

Boris, Bela, and Lorre encounter band leader Kay Kyser in a haunted house. Unfortunately, Kay and crew get more attention than our terror trio here.

Young Frankenstein (1974) ◆◆◆◇ **B&W**
D: Mel Brooks. Gene Wilder, Madeline Kahn, Cloris Leachman, Marty Feldman, Peter Boyle. 105 minutes. (Key)

One of Brooks's best and also one of the most thorough and successful fright-film-form parodies around, a send-up of Universal's chiller clichés. Other Mel movies out on cassette: *Blazing Saddles* and the featurette *The 2000-Year-Old Man* (Warner), *The Twelve Chairs* (Media), *High Anxiety, History of the World Part I, Silent Movie,* and *To Be or Not To Be* (CBS/Fox).

Zelig (1983) ◆◆◆◇ **B&W/color**
D: Woody Allen. Woody Allen, Mia Farrow, Garrett Brown. 79 minutes. (Warner)

Woody's conceptual comedy casts Allen as a human chameleon whose overwhelming desire to conform causes him to transform into those around him. A brilliant, risky conceit that Allen pulls off both verbally and visually.

Zotz! (1962) ◆◆ B&W
D: William Castle. Tom Poston, Julia Meade, Jim Backus, Cecil Kellaway. 87 minutes. (RCA/Columbia)

A fairly excruciating, though definitely bizarre, farce from the ever-unpredictable Castle, with Poston as an absent-minded academic who finds a magic coin and word (the eponymous *Zotz!*) that grants him supernatural powers. Castle cultists will want to tune in.

OFF-OFF HOLLYWOOD:
CAMP CLASSICS & ODDITIES FROM BEYOND BELIEF!

"Can you prove that it didn't happen?

Criswell
Plan 9 from Outer Space

Z-Movie Confidential, or the Bad, the Worse, and the (Downright) Ugly

If B stands for *bottom* of the bill, Z stands for bottom of the barrel. So why do Z movies retain their special appeal? Well, in many ways, they're closer to real life than the typical slick, expensive Hollywood product. After all, most lives are characterized not by glitter, high drama, and spectacular FX but by limited budgets, meandering plots, and lots of mental stock footage. Lacking the money and/or talent to create elaborate illusions, Z movies often succeed in achieving an unintended cheapjack verisimilitude—sometimes attaining the formidable goal of actually looking *smaller* than life!

It usually takes at least a few years for what might have initially been perceived as a merely bad or even extravagantly awful film to attain official camp-movie status (though video has often greatly accelerated that process). There are exceptions to this rule, however: not the cynically conceived, self-proclaimed "camp classics" that regularly find their way to midnight screenings and vid-store shelves, but the occasional earnestly created antigem, like Richard Horian's unique *Student Confidential*, whose idiosyncratic flaws fairly leap out at the disbelieving viewer.

In the main, however, we've channeled our energies into saluting those recognized camp antiquities that have surfaced on cassette (hordes more remain unavailable)—from the compellingly atrocious *Astro Zombies* to the (literal) last word in Z movies, the immortal *Zombie Island Massacre*. We've also ferreted out several hitherto

Tor makes his best Harpo Marx face for the camera in this typically tense moment from Ed Wood, Jr.'s, *Plan 9 from Outer Space*.

neglected anticlassics, like B. F. Grinter's *Blood Freak* and Duke Mitchell's *The Executioner.*

Along the way, we'll also encounter such *artistes* manqué as Donald (*Demon Lover*) Jackson and Jerry (*Frankenstein Island*) Warren—and, it goes virtually sans saying, *the* all-time Camp-Movie King, Ed (*Plan 9 from Outer Space*) Wood, Jr., as seen through the video eyes of yours truly and the vivid memory of film producer, historian, and former Ed cohort Alex Gordon.

Astro-Zombies (1968) ◆◆◆
D: T. V. Mikels. John Carradine, Wendell Corey, Tura Satana, Rafael Campos, Tom Pace. 94 minutes. (Wizard)

"See It and Die 1000 Deaths!"

So went the original tag line for T. V. Mikels's immortal *Astro-Zombies*, and truer words were rarely, if ever, spoken. The Phantom recalls catching this camp classic at the Lower East Side's Delancey Theater on a double bill with 1965's *The Undertaker and His Pals* (Flamingo Video) (on which T.V. served in a producing capacity). *Astro-Zombies* arrived as a serendipitous surprise, turning a rainy pre-video Sunday afternoon into an occasion of unexpected (if masochistic) joy. The flick details the efforts of demented Dr. DeMarco (the ubiquitous Carradine in a distracted performance) and his equally unbalanced hunchbacked assistant Francho (who conducts his own "experiments"—harassing a helpless gal strapped to a spare operating table—in his leisure time) to perfect the world's first "astro-man." The pic cross-cuts between the pair's woefully impoverished basement lab and a claustrophobic office occupied by a trio of CIA agents led by a mumbling Corey (in his last role). Meanwhile, at a nearby motel, Russ Meyer starlet Satana and a switchblade-wielding Campos, ruthless agents of an unidentified foreign power (presumably Tijuana), scheme to steal Carradine's scientific secrets. Produced and co-scripted by Wayne Rogers in his pre–*M*A*S*H* days, *Astro-Zombies* is low in budget and slow in pace, but rich in priceless dialogue. Vide the following exchange among the puzzled CIA men:

Agent #1: Knowledge from the minds of our top astrophysicists, aerospace medical scientists, neurosurgeons could be combined and projected into the receiving device of a quasi-man in interplanetary travel!

Agent #2: Quasi-man? You mean, a sort of a zombie?

Corey: What else would you call a man with a synthetic, electrically driven heart, a stainless-steel-mesh stomach, a plastic pancreas, cellulose liver—just to mention a few things for a starter [sic]?

Agent #2: Incredible.

Agent #1: Not for a minute. And Dr. DeMarco is working on a silicon treatment of the skin that would make it impervious to micro-meteorites!

To learn why the Astro-Zombie (an extra in a Halloween skull mask) can't function without holding a flashlight to his forehead (!)—well, you'll just have to see for yourself. *Astro-Zombies* is also out as *Space Vampires* in a mad-doctored edition that cuts the onscreen antics from an R to a PG. Beware!

FILMMAKERS IN FOCUS:
T. V. Mikels

Astro-Zombies auteur T. V. Mikels has earned a justifiable rep in indie-film circles as an authentic eccentric. For years he shared a twenty-three-room Glendale, California, castle with seven—count 'em—seven women. Mikels labored as a magician, accordionist, ventriloquist, stage actor, and stuntman before devoting his energies to the trash-movie field. His first modest moneymaker, 1965's *The Black Klansman* (Unicorn)—a film obviously inspired by the previous year's *Black Like Me* (Afro-Am)—recounted the unlikely adventures of a black man who infiltrates the Klan in order to unmask his daughter's murderer. With that exploitation oddity under his belt, there was no turning T.V. off. Mikels went on to direct *The Girl in Gold Boots, The Corpse Grinders, Blood Orgy of the She Devils, The Doll Squad* (a Tura Satana tour de farce later immortalized in song on Nile Rodgers's *B-Movie Matinee* LP), and the perennial Forty-second Street fave *10 Violent Women,* all, at last report, available via the WesternWorld Video label. T.V.'s most recent outings, the postnuke potboiler *Aftermath* (Prism) and the actioner *WarCat* (see index), formerly *Angel of Vengeance,* are likewise available on video. If you see only one T.V. epic in your lifetime, though, we suggest you make it *Astro-Zombies.*

The Atomic Brain (1964) ◆◆◆ B&W

D: Joseph Mascelli. Frank Gerstle, Erika Peters, Judy Bamber. 72 minutes. (Sinister Cinema)

One of the era's more obscure bad brain movies, this one (originally entitled *Monstrosity*) features Peters as a dowager who hires doc Gerstle to switch her gray matter into a young girl's body. One prospective subject gets a cat's brain. (!). Unique.

Attack of the Beast Creatures (1985) ◆◆◆

D: Michael Stanley. Robert Nolfi, Robert Lengye, Julia Rust. 82 minutes. (WesternWorld)

This hilarious obscurity pits a band of rowboat-wreck survivors against a horde of singularly unterrifying doll-people with stiff limbs and painted-on eyes. During the major titular assault, the creatures are literally *thrown* at the hapless (and hopelessly amateur) actors by offscreen crew members! "There must be hundreds of them!" one soon-to-be victim shrieks. (The *Phantom's* freeze-framed critter count ran to exactly eighteen.) Lensed in the sparse wilds of surburban Connecticut, where it actually almost could have happened (as the box puts it, "How Many Will Survive the Terror?"), and set in 1920, apparently the better to give the costume designer a chance to show off, *Attack of the Beast Creatures* stacks up as a camp classic of the first rank.

Attack of the 50 Ft. Woman (1958) ◆◆◆ B&W

D: Nathan Juran. Allison Hayes, William Hudson, Yvette Vickers. 66 minutes. (Key)

High camp at its highest: Wealthy Hayes zooms to the title height via an equally outsize male alien's touch, then uses her newfound status to torment her cheatin' hubby (Hudson) and the town tramp (Vickers). Great fun.

Beach Girls and the Monster (1965) ◆◆ B&W

D: Jon Hall. Jon Hall, Sue Casey, Walker Edmiston. 70 minutes. (Sinister Cinema)

Flabby has-been Hall directs, stars, and dons a sea-monster suit, the better to terrorize teen surfers, in this misbegotten, but marginally entertaining, turkey. Also known as *Monster from the Surf.*

The Betsy (1978) ◆◆◇

D: Daniel Petrie. Laurence Olivier, Robert Duvall, Katharine Ross. 125 minutes. (CBS/Fox)

This trashy adaptation of Harold Robbins's trashy novel about an international car czar (Olivier) is lifted/lowered largely by Larry's outrageous put-on performance.

Billy the Kid vs. Dracula (1966) ◆◆◇

D: William Beaudine. John Carradine, Melinda Plowman, Chuck Courtney, Virginia Christine, Bing Russell, Harry Carey, Jr. 74 minutes. (Embassy)

Infamous schlock auteur William ("One-Shot") Beaudine's filmic farewell is a no-budget back-lot western/horror hybrid originally released on a double bill with the same director's dumb but dull *Jesse James Meets Frankenstein's Daughter* (also Embassy). Carradine, looking authentically anemic and long in the fangs, portrays a cranky vampire who journeys west in search of fresh necks, particularly the one belonging to innocent blond ingenue Plowman. Attempting to keep the Count's teeth from Melinda's jugular is a "reformed" Billy the Kid, energetically enacted by stunt man Courtney. This entertaining cheapie features chintzy FX (the vampire-bat-on-a-string rivals *Plan 9*'s infamous flying saucer hubcaps), a veteran supporting cast, and more choice lines ("Oh, God! The vampire test!") than you can shake a stake at, as well as adding a few (mostly cost-efficient) twists to traditional vampire lore. A worthy addition to any B-movie buff's late-night video library.

Black Dragons (1942) ◆◆◇ B&W
D: William Nigh. Bela Lugosi, Joan Barclay, Clayton Moore. 62 minutes. (Sinister Cinema)

This enjoyably awful wartime atrocity casts Bela as a Teutonic plastic surgeon who rearranges the faces of Japanese spies until they look *just like us!* Incredible.

Blood Freak (1972) ◆◆◆◇
D: Steve Hawkes, Brad Grinter. Steve Hawkes, Dana Culliver, Randy Grin-ter, Jr., Tina Anderson, Heather Hughes. 86 minutes. (Regal)

The world's first (and thus far only) cautionary Christian antidrug gore movie (!), this *Jimmy Swaggart Meets Herschell Gordon Lewis* affair stars Steve Hawkes (who also co-produced this Florida-lensed amateur-night vanity job) *as* Herschell, a dim-witted, hog-ridin' Elvis manqué who meets a typical Scripture-quoting miniskirted gal named Angel. Angel's wild and crazy sister Ann—who, along with her geekoid friends, is "heavy into the drug scene"—soon leads Hersh down the path to perdition (which, we believe, is situated somewhere east of Tampa). To make a bizarre story short, our hero is addicted to some sort of superpot, gets a job at a local poultry ranch, eats a capon laced with experimental preservatives, and transmogrifies into a rampaging *turkey*-monster (!) who feeds off the blood of his fellow substance-abusers. The entire beyond-brain-damaged tale, meanwhile, is narrated by a Bible-quoting, sub-Criswellian sleaze-ball who delivers a disquisition re: the hazards of drug pollution while chain-smoking and eventually falling into an uncontrollable coughing fit! *Blood Freak* is either the craziest display of misguided sincerity or the most subversive deadpan put-on ever committed to celluloid. Or it may simply have landed from another distant but

VCR-equipped planet. In either or any case, *Blood Freak* is pretty scary stuff and earns our heartfelt recommendation here. It's also available on the Simitar label as the pluralized *Blood Freaks*, but with a shorter running time.

Blood of Dracula's Castle (1969) ♦♦
D: Al Adamson. John Carradine, Alex D'Arcy, Paula Raymond. 84 minutes. (Interglobal)

Former suave-foreigner specialist D'Arcy gives his only performance in years in this typically tacky, S&M-tinged Adamson cheapie stocked with such other Hollywood has-beens as Raymond, Adamson regular Robert (son of Richard) Dix and the ever-lurking Carradine. Adamson serves up more of the same in *Blood of Ghastly Horror*, part of VidAmerica's sell-through World's Worst Videos line, which also includes *Horror of the Blood Monsters*, *Horror of the Zombies*, and one of our fave titles, *House of Psychotic Women*, where guys who don't check out, don't check out.

Blue Demon vs. the Infernal Brains (1967) NR
D: Chano Urueta. Ana Martin, David Reynoso, Noe Murayama. 87 minutes. (Video Latino)

The brains behind *The Brainiac* helm another cerebral South-of-the-Border horror, this time pitting wrestler the Blue Demon against a mad medico who's sucking the intelligence out of doctors and athletes (!).

The Brain from Planet Arous (1958) ♦♦♦ B&W
D: Nathan Juran. John Agar, Joyce Meadows, Robert Fuller. 70 minutes. (Rhino)

One of the best bad brain movies of all time. Agar gets to stretch when a power-mad alien brain commandeers his body in a bid for earthly conquest. A good alien brain takes up residence in John's dog (!). Contains the thematic seeds for the newer, slicker *The Hidden* (see index).

The Brain That Wouldn't Die (1963) ♦♦♦ B&W
D: Joseph Green. Herb Evers, Virginia Leith, Adele Lamont. 71 minutes. (Warner)

Lensed in '59, this one lingered on the shelf long enough for lead Evers to change his name to Jason. He plays the ruthless brain surgeon who grafts his fiancée's severed head to a stripper's body while the Thing in the Closet (played by famed "Jewish Giant" Ed Carmel) watches and waits. Head to thing: "I'm just a head out here. What are you in there?" Unfortunately, the Warner cassette is drastically cut, severely shortening Evers's assistant's prolonged death scene and some choice views of the Thing in the Closet, among other important highlights.

Where guys who don't check out,
don't check out.
Photo courtesy of Independent-
International Pictures Corp.

The Brainiac (1961) ◆◆◆ B&W

D: Chano Urueta. Abel Salazar, Ariadne Welter, Mauricio Garces, Rosa Maria Gallardo. 75 minutes. (Hollywood Home Theater)

This Mexican monster-movie masterpiece stars Salazar as an Inquisition victim who, prior to being burned at the stake, vows vengeance the next time the Great Comet lights up the night sky, some three hundred years thence. True to his word, he materializes from a papier-mâché meteorite that bounces to Earth circa 1961. Our title fiend now boasts two distinct, if ill-explained personas: the suave, urbane Baron Batallas, and the bent-beaked, forked-tongued, cerebrum-sucking Brainiac. In addition to sporting what may well be the scream screen's first pulsating inflatable head (okay, so it's a cheap rubber mask hooked up to an air pump—there's more to life than special effects), the Brainiac can perform an impressive array of perverse party tricks: He can turn invisible at will, hypnotize via a pair of glowing eyes, and (his pièce de résistance) slurp the very brains out of his prey's skulls—*without* using a straw. All of which he proceeds to do, while simultaneously ducking a team of nosy scientists and dogged detectives, at a bloody bash staged for his killers' unwary descendants. And he *still* finds time for some indiscriminate between-slaughter snacking, munching on the brains of earlier victims kept in a colander stashed in his dining-room cabinet! *The Brainiac* stands inflatable-head-and-shoulders above most of his bad-fright-flick brethren, Mexican and Anglo alike. Inveterate Mexican-monster-movie fans, meanwhile, are referred to Sinister Cinema, which stocks such South-of-the-Border B faves as *Curse of the Aztec Mummy, The Living Head, Robot vs. the Aztec Mummy, The Vampire,* and *The Vampire's Coffin,* among others, while Rhino offers the redubbed send-up *Rock 'n' Roll Wrestling Women vs. the Aztec Ape.*

Butterfly (1981) ◆◆◆

D: Matt Cimber. Pia Zadora, Stacy Keach, Orson Welles. 105 minutes. (Vestron)

Pia Z models her panty collection while screen pa Keach pants approvingly in this agreeably complex sordid tale of white-trash incest. Welles is the disapproving judge. Stuart Whitman, Ed McMahon, and June (*Lassie*) Lockhart are along for the ride. You can also catch the Divine Miss Z in Cimber's *Fake Out* (HBO), *Feel the Motion* (Vidmark), *Pia Zadora's American Songbook* (CBS/Fox), and her most memorable movie, the Harold Robbins–based *Lonely Lady* (MCA), wherein Pia demonstrates her prowess by jogging and discussing Pushkin at the same time.

CatWomen of the Moon (1954) ◆◆◆
B&W
D: Arthur Hilton. Sonny Tufts, Marie Windsor, Victory Jory, Douglas Fowley. 64 minutes. (Nostalgia Merchant)

This legendary lunar loser, originally lensed in 3-D, lives up to its promise—specifically, that you'll "share man's greatest adventure as you rocket through space" to meet the "alluring, ferocious catwomen." As usual, Tufts makes the least of his screen time.

The Crawling Hand (1963) ◆◆◇ **B&W**
D: Herbert L. Strock. Peter Breck, Kent Taylor, Arline Judge. 89 minutes. (Video Gems)

Some dull stretches get in the way of the unintentional laughs here, but bad-movie buffs will want to hang on for the flick's imaginative climax, wherein our creature literally lends a hand to several starving cats.

Crazy Fat Ethel II (1987) ◆◆◆
D: Nick Philips. Priscilla Alden, Michael Flood, Jane Lambert, Robert Copple. 60 minutes. (Video City, Video Treasures)

In Nick Philips's seriously belated (by thirteen years!) sequel to his bizarre, no-budget psycho romp *Criminally Insane* (Western-World) obese actress Priscilla Alden reprises her gorging, gouging Crazy Fat Ethel character. *Crazy Fat Ethel II* shamelessly recycles the good parts from the 16mm *Criminally Insane*, within a new shot-on-video wraparound updating Ethel's stuff 'n' snuff—oriented life. The result is a technically shoddy but utterly compelling chronicle, perhaps the best bottom-of-the-trash-barrel slice-and-splice pastiche to surface since Ed Wood, Jr.'s, immortal cut-and-paste transvestite saga *Glen or Glenda?* (see index). With its almost frighteningly *verité* look and its alarmingly low level of alpha-wave activity, *Crazy Fat Ethel II* plays like a deranged homemade hybrid of the horror and documentary genres. The pic sees a long-institutionalized Ethel (sort of a Lizzie Borden on Thorazine) released to a halfway house—a move dictated by drastic state budget cuts—operated by elderly Hope Bartholomew (Lambert), whose oft-repeated motto is "Let's never give up hope." Our hefty heroine, older but no wiser nor any less compulsive when it comes to food (as it does here with numbing regularity), experiences numerous violent flashbacks from *Criminally Insane* while leisurely embarking on a new slaughter spree. As Hope puts it, "Ethel refused to take her medicine, and there was a terrible scene." Terrible scenes abound in this demented exercise, but there's no denying that Alden has star power to spare. Whether viewed wreaking vengeance on all who would stand between her and her food supply or simply glaring at an imagined enemy, Priscilla's largely negative charisma dominates every scene. Wise indeed would be the network TV exec who recognized *Crazy Fat Ethel*'s prime-time sitcom possibilities. (Well, maybe not.) Video City, whose *CFE II* is pricier than but superior to Video Treasures' sell-through edition, also stocks Priscilla's *Death Nurse*, wherein Alden essays bogus nurse Edith Mortley in another crazed shot-on-video exercise (also padded with *Criminally Insane* inserts) that's easily the equal of *CFE II*.

The Creeping Terror (1964) ♦♦♦ B&W
D: *Argyle Nelson. Vic Savage, Shannon O'Neill, William Thourlby, Louise Lawson, Robin James. 75 minutes. (United)*

Broadlooms from Hell! would have been a more fitting title for this celluloid scam about the misadventures of what appear to be a pair of animated alien rugs, which land near Lake Tahoe for the purpose of picnicking on unsuspecting Earthlings. Though the title creatures—leaf-covered carpets thrown over teams of crawling extras—perambulate at an agonizingly languid pace, they have no trouble vacuuming up victims at a fishing pier, a hootenanny, and a high school soirée. *The Creeping Terror* was shot on a reputed budget of $5,000 (little of which shows on screen) by director Argyle Nelson, who, under the nom de thesp Vic Savage, doubles as the movie's leading man (and strikes out in both roles). In the tradition of *Beast of Yucca Flats* (NA), an offscreen narrator paraphrases the unheard exchanges uttered by the onscreen actors. After an army sergeant sees his entire platoon devoured by one of the ravenous rugs, the solemn voice-over informs us, "The sergeant, a shaken man, returned babbling about what had happened." *The Creeping Terror* may not be *the* worst movie of all time, but it comes close enough to deserve your home-viewing attention.

Curse of the Alpha Stone (1985) ♦♦◊
D: *Stewart Malleson. Jim Scotlin, Sandy Carty, Lowell Simon. 90 minutes. (United)*

Curse of the Alpha Stone chronicles one young visionary's (Scotlin) quest to achieve better living through alchemy: Our hero first succeeds in turning metal into what looks like egg yolks. In its liquid form, however, this uncontrolled substance works as a powerful aphrodisiac, providing a perfect excuse for some soft-core "erotic" episodes. Though poor in every other department, *Curse* is rich in unintentional mirth, as when a shrink points to a straight-back chair and instructs his understandably confused patient to "lie down on the couch." (Guess the set designer never read the script—not that we blame him.) Or when a gay subject becomes so virulently "straight" that he runs out and abducts a female mannequin (!). Hard-core bad-movie buffs may want to sift through long stretches

AT LAST! THE TRUTH ABOUT DEMONS!

COPYRIGHT C 1976 WOLF LORE CINEMA LTD   ALL RIGHTS RESERVED

R RESTRICTED

IN COLOR

written, produced, and directed by
DONALD G. JACKSON/JERRY YOUNKINS

At last. Aka *Devil Master*.
Photo courtesy of Unicorn Video.

of dross to extract *Stone*'s gems of cinematic insipidity, but all others are advised to keep one finger firmly poised over the old fast-forward control.

Demonoid, Messenger of Death (1981) ◆◆

D: Alfred Zacharias. Samantha Eggar, Stuart Whitman, Roy Cameron Jenson. 85 minutes. (Media)

A hand from hell bedevils archaeologist Eggar and priest Whitman in this Mexico-lensed howler. Words to die by: "Cut off my hand, or I'll kill you!"

Devil Master (1977) ◆◆◆

D: Donald G. Jackson. Jerry Younkins, Ron Hively, Christmas Robbins, Gunnar Hansen, Val Mayerick. 91 minutes. (Regal)

Back in 1985, the Phantom caught a scary documentary titled *Demon Lover Diary*, all about the making of a Michigan-lensed, amateur-night fright fiasco called (coincidentally enough) *Demon Lover*. That *verité* chronicle ended with one of *Demon Lover*'s participants firing warning shots at the fleeing docu-filmmakers (!). While *Demon Lover Diary* remains sadly unavailable on video, *Demon Lover* itself is out in its entirety via the Regal label under the title *Devil Master*. (Unicorn also carries the movie, under its original title but in truncated form.) While it's nowhere near as frightening as the documentary, *The Devil Master* ranks right down there among

terrordom's most atrocious all-time turkeys. Nominal "star" Younkins—who, according to the documentary, co-financed this homemade horror with insurance money collected after he'd amputated a finger (in the film, he wears a lone leather glove to mask his mangled hand)—makes for a singularly loutish long-haired satanist, who commands the Devil himself to eliminate, in various gory ways, several traitorous former members of his sinister sect. In the grand tradition of Alfred Hitchcock and Ed Wood, Jr., director Jackson puts in a silent cameo as a cowardly patron at a local bar where Younkins trashes a bunch of nonbelieving red-necks via a spectacularly unconvincing kung-fu set-to—a sequence characterized by the same unsteady camerawork and awful acting that informs the rest of the film. *Texas Chainsaw Massacre*'s Gunnar (Leatherface) Hansen also turns up briefly as an academic who specializes in the occult.

Despite this seemingly inauspicious debut, auteur Jackson went on to forge a Hollywood B-movie career. Don's second effort, *Rollerblade* (New World)—not to be confused with *Blade Runner* or *Rollerball*—shapes up as a no-budget combo of *The Road Warrior* and *Skatetown, USA*, depicting a future America ruled by fascistic roller-skating head-bangers who are in turn opposed by peace-loving Holy Rollers, a band of

May the beast man win.
Photo courtesy of Independent-International Pictures Corp.

bimbos who wear nunlike headgear, babble mock-Shakespearean dialogue (yea, verily!), and worship a glowing Happy Face idol (!). *Rollerblade*'s lasting message lies in the oft-repeated phrase, "Skate or die!"

Don later stepped up to the relative big time with 1988's deranged postnuke fantasy *Hell Comes to Frogtown* (see index), wherein he directed such major screen talents as Rowdy Roddy Piper, Sandahl Bergman, Rory Calhoun, and Big Bill Smith. He also found time to helm the wrestling romp *I Like To Hurt People*, with Abdullah the Butcher and Andre the Giant (New World). Rent all four for an inspirational home-vid marathon you won't soon forget (*if* you survive!).

Devil Girl from Mars (1954) ◆◆◆ B&W
D: David MacDonald. Hazel Court, Patricia Laffen, Hugh McDermott. 78 minutes. (Sinister Cinema)

Future Hammer horror starlet Court essays the titular alien, who beams down to abduct suitable earthly breeders, in this Brit camp classic.

Devil's Mistress (1966) ◆◆
D: Wes Moreland. Arthur Resley, Joan Stapleton. 66 minutes. (Sinister Cinema)

An amateurish, lethargic, yet strangely compelling turkey about a quartet of outlaws who unwittingly and unwisely kidnap a satanic miss.

Dr. Terror's Gallery of Horrors (1967) ◆◆◇
D: David L. Hewitt. Lon Chaney, John Carradine, Rochelle Hudson, Roger Gentry. 84 minutes. (Ingram)

An unbelievably bad fright anthology teaming a trio of vet thesps with an otherwise amateur cast, many of whom also turn up in *Wizard of Mars* (see index). Not one of director Hewitt's better efforts. Also known simply as *Gallery of Horror* (Academy).

Dracula vs. Frankenstein (1971) ◆◇
D: Al Adamson. J. Carrol Naish, Lon Chaney, Jr., Zandor Vorkov, Russ Tamblyn, Jim Davis, Anthony Eisley. 91 minutes. (Super)

Another Al Adamson special, this pathetic pairing of horrordom's erstwhile greats is good for a few masochistic laughs, most of them supplied by the immortal Zandor Vorkov's portrayal of an echo-chambered Count; the wheelchair-bound Naish and the lumpy Chaney, Jr.—both in their final film roles (as a Dr. Frankenstein descendant and his bumbling minion, respectively)—make for pretty sad sights.

Dracula's Dog (1978) ◆◆
D: Albert Band. Jose Ferrer, Reggie Nalder, Michael Pataki. 90 minutes. (United)

This dog-eared *Dracula* variation has some amusing bits. Jose ("Is My Check in the Mail?") Ferrer slums as an undercover Transylvanian investigator on the trail of

Nalder's fanged fido. Directed by Albert (Father of Charles) Band. Also out as *Zoltan, Hound of Dracula* (HBO).

Empire of the Ants (1977) ◆◆

D: Bert I. Gordon. Joan Collins, Robert Lansing, Albert Salmi. 89 minutes. (Embassy)

Collins encounters outsize killer ants in one of Bert I. (Mr. BIG) Gordon's more extravagantly stupid efforts. Joan's genre credits also include *Dark Places* (Embassy), *The Devil Within Her* (Axon), *Fear in the Night* (HBO), *Fearless* (New World), *Quest for Love* (IUD), and *Terror Under the House* (Bargain).

Escape from Planet Earth (1967) ◆◆

D: Lee Sholem, Harry Hope. Grant Williams, Mala Powers, Bobby Van. 88 minutes. (Academy)

You might remember this comatose late-night loser as *Doomsday Machine*. A cosmic crew of Hollywood has-beens, including Grant (*Incredible Shrinking Man*) Williams and old-timer Henry Wilcoxon, find themselves lost in space after the Earth explodes in a nuclear holocaust, possibly attributable to Red China's tinkering. (Quoth space hipster Van, "You mean those chopstick jockeys came up with a planet-buster?!") Fun in small doses; in its entirety, a dependable insomniac's friend.

The Executioner (1979) ◆◆◆◆

D: Dominic Miceli (Duke Mitchell). Duke Mitchell, Lorenzo Dodo, Vic Caesar, John Strong. 84 minutes. (Video Gems)

Back in 1952, the imitation Martin and Lewis team of Duke Mitchell and Sammy Petrillo starred in the memorably monikered fright comedy *Bela Lugosi Meets a Brooklyn Gorilla* (Sinister Cinema). Jerry Lewis, one of the many who were unamused by the flick, threatened to sue Petrillo even deeper into oblivion should he mimic Jer again. Duke and Sammy eventually went their separate ways, with Duke pursuing a lounge-singer career and also turning up in an occasional film role (such as an overage juvenile delinquent in Hugo Haas's *Paradise Alley* [NA]), while Sammy still works East Coast clubs as a comic and starred in Doris Wishman's awful soft-core sex farce *Keyholes Are for Peeping* (Simitar) in 1974.

Nearly three decades after his *Brooklyn Gorilla* daze, Mitchell returned to write, direct, and star (under his real name, Dominic Miceli) as an emotional Mafia hitman in *The Executioner*, a hilariously inept *Godfather* clone featuring many of Duke's trademark tunes (including the Phantom's personal fave, the catchy "Rigatone, Mostacciolo, and Spaget," as well as the moving, philosophical ballad "One Hundred Years from Today"), clumsily staged action scenes, and monologues like they just don't make anymore (and, in fact, *never* did), such as Duke's tearful tribute to the Italian Woman ("She's the one they handed the organ grinder and monkey to when she got off the boat"). Duke's performance here is rivaled only by the undeservedly obscure Lorenzo Dodo as his dad, the Don. *The Executioner* is one video the serious bad-movie buff cannot afford to miss. And we bet you can't watch it just *once*.

First Yank into Tokyo (1945) ◆◆◆ B&W
D: Gordon Douglas. Tom Neal, Barbara Hale, Richard Loo. 83 minutes. (RKO)

Pretty amazing WWII propaganda pic has Yank officer Neal undergoing plastic surgery to infiltrate a Japanese prison camp. To quote a captive American nurse, "This idea has more BO than a Jap regiment!" Neal, who later served time for killing his real-life wife, played a similar role in RKO's somewhat more sober-minded *Behind the Rising Sun* (see index).

Five Minutes to Live (1961) ◆◆◇ B&W
D: Bill Karn. Johnny Cash, Donald Woods, Pamela Mason, Ron Howard. 80 minutes. (Video Dimensions)

Cash makes his movie debut as a mercenary psycho in a sleazy B thriller that the Phantom originally saw theatrically, in a slightly shorter version, under the more memorable title *Door-to-Door Maniac*. *Five Minutes to Live* is also the name of the song John croons to one of his potential victims. To further complicate matters, the tape is also out under the meaningless moniker *Last Blood* (Discount Video). Pretty unique, by any other name.

The Flesh Eaters (1964) ◆◆◇ B&W
D: Jack Curtis. Martin Kosleck, Rita Morley, Byron Sanders. 87 minutes. (Monterey)

A marine biologist and a beatnik are among the potential victims of a pack of mutant killer jellyfish. Watch for the high-tech disintegration scenes.

Flesh Feast (1970) ◆◆
D: B. F. Grinter. Veronica Lake, Phil Philbin, Heather Hughes. 72 minutes. (WesternWorld)

Forties sex siren Lake unwisely came out of retirement to co-produce and star (as a mad scientist) in this Florida-lensed abomination that takes its central ideas from *They Saved Hitler's Brain*. (Hey, why *not* steal from the best?) Director Grinter went on to helm the even more credulity-stretching *Blood Freak* (see index).

40-Acre Feud (1970) ◆◇
D: Ron Ormond. Ferlin Husky, Minnie Pearl, Loretta Lynn. 82 minutes. (Madhouse)

A fairly awful Ormond effort that might amuse Ferlin fans and *Las Vegas Hillbillys* (sic) (see index) lovers. Another of Ormond's redneck specials, 1971's *Girl from Tobacco Row*, is available on the Simitar label.

Frankenstein Island (1978) ◆◆◆
D: Jerry Warren. Robert Clarke, Steve Brodie, Cameron Mitchell, John Carradine, Katherine Victor. 88 minutes. (Monterey)

Jerry (*Teenage Zombies*) Warren strikes again! This time he accomplishes the seemingly impossible: crafting (and we use the word loosely, even recklessly) a perfectly awful '50s-style horror/sci-fi turkey in the advanced annum of 1978. Our story involves a quartet of foolhardy balloonists, led by Robert (*Hideous Sun Demon*) Clarke, who crash-land on your typical uncharted isle. Here they discover veteran B thesps Brodie and Mitchell, mad scientists the Van Helsings, a tribe of scantily clad bimbos—distaff descendants of an alien race—and a gang of zombies wearing black turtlenecks, ski caps, and white contact lenses, who worship a black-and-white photo of John Carradine (!). Carradine appears, à la *Wizard of Mars*, in a few outsize superimpositions, where he repeats the same cryptic lines ("The Power! The Power! The Power!"). And who but Jerry Warren would interrupt a "tense" exchange to cut to a "reaction shot" from a zombie? *Frankenstein Island* is authentically beyond belief and highly recommended.

Frankenstein Meets the Space Monster (1965) ◆◆◆ B&W
D: *Robert Gaffney. James Karen, Nancy Marshall, David Kerman, Marilyn Hanold, Lou Cutell. 78 minutes. (Prism)*

Quirky novelist/academic/movie-maven George Garrett scripted this low-camp lunacy as an affectionate lark. The pic's tone is earnest and unselfconscious (i.e., nonpostmodern) enough to camouflage Garrett's satiric intent; the result is a hilarious exercise in alien lechery as Martian "Princess" Hanold (a former *Ernie Kovacs Show* regular) leads the male survivors of her doomed planet on an earthly girl-raid. Cutell, as Hanold's effete, bald-headed right-hand eunuch, offers one of filmdom's most outrageous performances. James Karen, future Pathmark pitchman and *Return of the Living Dead* regular, is also onboard as a U.S. general. Filmed in Puerto Rico—hence the flick's working title *Mars Attacks Puerto Rico*.

Frankenstein's Daughter (1958) ◆◆◆ B&W
D: *Richard E. Cunha. John Ashley, Sally Todd, Donald Murphy. 85 minutes. (Media)*

Richard (*Missile to the Moon*) Cunha misdirects a distaff rip-off of *I Was a Teenage Frankenstein*, with Murphy in the Whit Bissell role; then again, *Teen Frankenstein* ripped off Mary Shelley.

The Gene Krupa Story (1960) ◆◆◇ B&W
D: *Don Weis. Sal Mineo, Susan Kohner, James Darren. 101 minutes. (RCA/Columbia)*

What purports to be a bio of the erstwhile percussion ace is really another '50s-style *Reefer Madness* update focusing on Gene's marijuana woes, including a notorious bust. As such, it's pretty compelling.

Giant from the Unknown (1958) ◆◆ B&W

D: Richard E. Cunha. Ed Kemmer, Buddy Baer, Sally Fraser. 69 minutes. (Media)

Baer is a long-dead conquistador who wakes up on the wrong side of the tomb in this stupider-than-average horror cheapie from director Cunha, who also gave us *Frankenstein's Daughter* and *Missile to the Moon* (see index).

The Giant Spider Invasion (1975) ◆◆◇

D: Bill Rebane. Steve Brodie, Barbara Hale, Leslie Parrish, Alan Hale, Bill Williams, Robert Easton. 82 minutes. (VCL)

An entertaining, Wisconsin-shot dud from Bill (*Incredible Melting Man*) Rebane, further enlivened by a veteran B cast, about a rash of outsize superimposed-spider sightings.

Hardcore (1979) ◆◆◆

D: Paul Schrader. George C. Scott, Peter Boyle, Season Hubley. 108 minutes. (RCA/Columbia)

Schrader applies the *Reefer Madness* treatment to the porn world in this hysterical (in both senses of the word) descent into the urban-smut maelstrom.

Her Life as a Man (1984) ◆◆◇

D: Robert Ellis Miller. Robyn Douglass, Robert Culp, Joan Collins. 100 minutes. (Lorimar)

A made-for-TV gender-bender tale, based on a real-life *Village Voice* confessional, about an enterprising gal who dons a male disguise to work as a sportswriter. Not as believable as *Death Wish Club*, let alone *Glen or Glenda?* (see index), but it has its mirthful moments. Now what we want to know is: *Is* it a comedy?

The Hideous Sun Demon (1959) ◆◆◆ B&W

D: Robert Clarke. Robert Clarke, Marilyn Manning, Nan Peterson. 74 minutes. (Nostalgia Merchant)

B-movie thesp Clarke decided he could make his own sci-fi movie. The result is this relentlessly clunky romp starring Bob himself as your basic nuclear-scientist-turned-atomic-mutant. Wade Williams's long-promised remake, *Hideous Sun Demon: The Special Edition*, will doubtless surface on home-vid soon.

Hillbillys in a Haunted House (1967) ◆◇

D: Jean Yarbrough. Ferlin Husky, Joi Lansing, Lon Chaney, Jr., John Carradine, Basil Rathbone. 88 minutes. (United)

More humiliation for Lon, Basil, and Long John as they team up for this cornpone rehash of a '30s-style haunted-house comedy. For more stillborn hillbilly hilarity, check out *Las Vegas Hillbillies* (United), wherein Ferlin Husky encounters Mamie Van Doren.

The Horror of Party Beach (1964) ◆◆◆ B&W

D: Del Tenney. John Scott, Alice Lyon, Allen Laurel. 72 minutes. (Prism)

Widely—and justly—hailed as one of terrordom's all-time turkeys, *Horror* involves a coastal invasion by a horde of hungry fish creatures created by a toxic-waste spill. The Del-Aires are on hand to swing "The Zombie Stomp" and other timely tunes. Unfortunately, the Prism video is riddled with senseless cuts; you may be better off taping this one off your TV—if you can wait that long (and we'll understand it if you can't).

The Human Duplicators (1965) ♦♦

D: Hugo Grimaldi. George Nader, Barbara Nichols, Hugh Beaumont, George Macready, Richard Kiel. 83 minutes. (IVE)

George (*Robot Monster*) Nader, Hugh (Ward Cleaver) Beaumont, and perennial dumb blonde Barbara Nichols join forces in this belated '50s-style howler about insidious aliens who replicate innocent humans for their own sinister purposes. George and Barbara supply many a memorable romantic moment. The ET leader, meanwhile, is none other than screen giant Richard (*Jaws*) Kiel—hence the Star Classics edition's creative retitling, *Jaws of the Alien* (!).

The Incredible Two-Headed Transplant (1971) ♦♦◇

D: Anthony M. Lanza. Bruce Dern, Pat Priest, Casey Kasem. 88 minutes. (Trans-Atlantic)

One of Dern's last important Z roles before he became a major Hollywood player. Here he's a mad scientist forced to think fast lest deejay Kasem figure out he's transplanted the head of a killer to the body of a moron. Spellbinding.

The Incredibly Strange Creatures Who Stopped Living and Became Mixed-Up Zombies (1964) ♦♦♦

D: Ray Dennis Steckler. Cash Flagg (Ray Dennis Steckler), Carolyn Brandt, Atlas King. 84 minutes. (Camp)

Video has rescued Steckler's legendary Las Vegas–lensed hallucination (billed as the "First Rock 'n' Roll Monster Movie") from the ranks of the World's Worst Movies, where it had been unfairly relegated, to the creative camp arena to which it more accurately belongs. Steckler's simple tale of a carefree loafer (played by Ray under his frequent nom de thesp Cash Flagg) who falls under the sinister spell of evil sideshow fortune-teller Estrella is rendered compelling by the amateur but likable and natural performances—particularly that of Atlas King as Ray's heavily accented Greek pal—authentically aimless action and dialogue, evocative amusement-park cinematography, tacky production numbers, and a wild extended nightmare sequence that serves as the flick's centerpiece. *The Incredibly Strange Creatures*, beyond boasting one of filmdom's longest titles, shapes up as a unique home-vid experience, with several scenes worthy of repeated replays.

FILMMAKERS IN FOCUS:

Ray Dennis Steckler

The creative force behind the enduring camp classic *The Incredibly Strange Creatures*, Ray Dennis Steckler got his cinematic start working on the camera crews of such unsung fare as 1962's *Drivers into Hell* and *The World's Greatest Sinner* (both NA), an obscure morality melodrama starring B-movie vet Timothy Carey (who also wrote, produced, and directed) as a megalomaniacal rock evangelist (singing tunes composed by the young Frank Zappa!). Ray next turned up onscreen, under his Cash Flagg pseudonym, in the unforgettable modern caveman opus *Eegah!* (Rhino), starring Richard (*Jaws*) Kiel in the title role. Steckler went on to produce, direct, and/or perform in such indie affairs as *The Maniacs Are Loose* (filmed in heart-stopping Hallucinogenic Hypnovision), *Teenage Psycho Meets Bloody Mary* and *The Lemon Grove Kids Meet the Monsters* (a Bowery Boys homage)—showstoppers all at Vegas's Skyline Drive-In but virtually unseen anywhere else. Ray later dabbled in R-rated outings like *The Velvet Trap* and *Sinthia, the Devil's Doll* under the aliases Sherwood Strickler and Sven Christian.

Thanks to video, it's now possible to sample more of Steckler's oddball oeuvre. Camp Video has issued not only *The Incredibly Strange Creatures* but the entertaining demented psychofest *Thrill Killers* (with Liz Renay) and Ray's hyperactive spy spoof *Rat Pfink and Boo Boo*, too. Later flicks, like the immortal *Hollywood Strangler Meets the Skid Row Slasher* (see index), *Body Fever,* and *The Chopper* (aka *Blood Shock,* and *Curse of the Evil Spirit*) are also available—on the Active, Nite Flite and Premiere labels, respectively—with direction credited to yet another of Ray's pseudonyms, Wolfgang Schmidt. Other Steckler titles will doubtless join the video ranks as more viewers become familiar with his off-the-wall endeavors.

Island Monster (1953) ◆ B&W
D: Roberto Montero. Boris Karloff, Renato Vicario. 87 minutes. (Hollywood Home Theater)

Boris Karloff must have been hard pressed for gainful employment when he agreed to appear, however marginally, in this 1953 Italo turkey. *Island Monster* isn't a horror movie (though it's most assuredly a horrible one) but a creaky narcs-and-smugglers nonactioner pitting dashing undercover cop Vicario against evil dope mogul Boris, who wisely spends most of his screen time hiding in heavily shadowed rooms. Mr. K didn't stick around for the dubbing; his voice is instead provided by a wonderfully inept would-be Boris impersonator (!). The scene wherein Boris attempts to terrorize the narc's kidnapped four-year-old daughter (herself dubbed by an adult actress in the throes of uncontrollable hysterics) is undeniably one of filmdom's more memorable moments. Unfortunately, 83 molasseslike minutes of this turgid inanity may be 80 more than the even fitfully sane viewer can bear.

Island of Desire (1952) NR
D: Stewart Heisler. Tab Hunter, Linda Darnell, Donald Gray. 91 minutes. (Fox Hills)

Tab's first starring role finds him competing with one-armed Gray for nurse Darnell's affections in this WWII–set soaper.

The Jazz Singer (1980) ◆◆
D: Richard Fleischer. Neil Diamond, Laurence Olivier, Lucie Arnaz. 116 minutes. (Paramount)

Diamond's aggressively awful Jolson update will make you pine for the silent-film era. Actually, it's fun in five- and ten-minute stretches, but more than that can result in severe brain-cell loss.

The Killer Shrews (1959) ◆◆◆◇ B&W
D: Ray Kellogg. James Best, Ingrid Goude, Ken Curtis, Gordon McLendon, Baruch Lumet. 70 minutes. (Sinister Cinema)

A one-of-a-kind monster cheapie, produced by right-wing radio magnate McLendon (who also costars as killer-shrew-maven Dr. Radford Bane), The Killer Shrews finds unlucky island inhabitants menaced by dogs wearing phony shrew fangs (!). Hero Best displays the fastest grin in the West as he tries to figure out how he got roped into this mess. Curtis, better remembered as Gunsmoke's Festus, is also along for the ride, as is the vastly underrated Goude. Replete with insulting retro racial stereotyping, bad acting, and a powerful climactic scene that sees our protagonists duckwalk to freedom while wearing empty trash barrels, The Killer Shrews is a camp-movie must. Its original cofeature, another McLendon Radio Pictures special, The Giant Gila Monster, is also available from Sinister Cinema; not as good/bad as the Shrews, but teen hero Don Sullivan does sing two unforgettable tunes.

Mad Doctor of Blood Island (1969) ◆◇
D: Eddie Romero. John Ashley, Eddie Romero, Angelique Pettyjohn. 110 minutes. (Magnum)

A John Ashley Filipino special, boasting a mindless script, pathetic production values, and a few topless gals in sarongs. (The Phantom always tries to find the good in everything.) See also the star-studded sequel, *Brain of Blood* (Magnum), with Kent Taylor and Grant (*Incredible Shrinking Man*) Williams (also out as simply *The Brain*, via Star Classics), and Ashley's equally arresting *Beast of the Yellow Night* (United). You can also find John in *Beyond Atlantis* and *The Twilight People* (both United).

Manos, the Hands of Fate (1966) ◆◆◆
D: Hal P. Warren. Tom Neyman, Diane Mahree, John Reynolds. 90 minutes. (Sinister Cinema)

Looking for *the* best worst movie of all time? *Manos* may well be it: a San Antonio–lensed satanist saga with one set, no talent, and a story line that's neither to be believed nor to be missed. Includes the memorable original ditties "The Way" and "Baby, Do a Thing with Me." Viva Torga!

Mesa of Lost Women (1953) ◆◆◆ B&W
D: Ron Ormond. Jackie Coogan, Richard Travis, Mary Hill. 78 minutes. (Sinister Cinema)

Undeservedly underrated classic dreck from Ormond, with Coogan (desperately disguised in bushy eyebrows and beard) playing a mad scientist developing a race of Mexican insect women. Must have seemed like a good idea at the time. The flamenco-guitar score later graced Ed Wood, Jr.'s, *Jailbait* (see index).

Milpitas Monster (1975) ◆◆
D: Robert L. Burrill. Doug Hagdahl, Scott A. Henderson, Scott Parker. Narrated by Paul Frees. 80 minutes. (United)

The citizens of Milpitas, California—site of the real-life teen murder that inspired *River's Edge* (see index)—decided to make a toxic-waste monster movie, with proceeds going to aid local high schools. The perfect second feature to team with *River's Edge* on your next Mondo Milpitas Homevideo Night.

Missile to the Moon (1959) ◆◆◇ B&W
D: Richard E. Cunha. Richard Travis, Cathy Downs, Tommy Cook. 78 minutes. (Media)

Cunha's uncredited remake of *Cat Women* of same lured '40s B star Travis out of (perhaps involuntary) retirement to topline as the lunar pilot. Z-movie teen tough Cook plays a JD stowaway. The moon spider reprises its original role. Recommended.

Mommie Dearest (1981) ◆◆◇
D: Frank Perry. Faye Dunaway, Diana Scarwid, Steve Forrest. 129 minutes. (Paramount)

High-camp highjinks based on Christina Crawford's literary indictment of her movie-star mom. As they say downtown, "a real hoot" from start to finish.

Monsignor (1982) ◆◆◇
D: Frank Perry. Christopher Reeve, Genevieve Bujold, Fernando Rey. 122 minutes. (CBS/Fox)

Mommie Dearest director Perry,

formerly of *David and Lisa* fame, applies similar camp treatment to this Catholic "thriller" about swinging superpriest Reeve.

Monster A Go-Go (1965) ◆◆◇ B&W

D: H. G. Lewis. Phil Morton, June Travis, Henry Hite. 70 minutes. (United)

Goremeister Lewis bought a stupid unfinished mutant-astronaut-amok flick, added bits of new even stupider footage, and slapped on the snappy moniker by which this slow (and slow-witted) but compelling mess is known today.

The Monster and the Stripper (1968) ◆◆◆

D: Ron Ormond. June Wilkinson, Titania. 86 minutes. (Simitar)

Originally released as *The Exotic Ones* and often erroneously described as a marijuana-monster movie, Ormond's New Orleans–set sleaze/horror hybrid stars buxom Brit Wilkinson in a crazed campfest that, among other firsts, finds a man beaten to death with his own arm *nearly two decades* before David Winters employed a similar stunt in *Deadly Prey* (see index). Sorry to be the one to break it to you, DW, but facts are facts, and we might as well face 'em.

Monster from Green Hell (1957) ◆◆◇ B&W

D: Kenneth Crane. Jim Davis, Robert E. Griffin, Barbara Turner. 71 minutes. (Media)

Davis leads a grueling safari through a back-lot jungle where dangers threaten from all corners of the stock footage. He's looking for giant radioactive wasps, the perilous results of a botched space probe. He finds 'em too, albeit briefly, in this enjoyably thick-witted trek.

The Mummy and the Curse of the Jackals (1967) ◆◆◆

D: Oliver Drake. Anthony Eisley, Martina Pons, John Carradine, Saul Goldsmith. 86 minutes. (Academy)

This riveting sub–Jerry Warren abomination can proudly take its place among the worst movies ever made. The film, in fact, was never actually completed, and the video version looks like it was assembled by stitching together every last bit of available footage (one explanation why entire scenes unfold in long shot!). Eisley turns into a "werejackal" when he awakens distaff mummy Pons (who experiences little difficulty in adjusting to her tacky new life-style as a downscale Vegas bimbo), thus invoking the title curse and prompting the murderous return of a male mummy (wordlessly interpreted by the underrated Goldsmith). Highlights include the mummy/werejackal "rampage" through the streets of Vegas, where onlookers openly grin at the "monsters'" antics and stare into the camera. Don't miss.

Murder by Television (1935) ◆◆ B&W

D: Clifford Sandforth. Bela Lugosi, June Collyer, Huntley Gordon. 60 minutes. (Video Resources, others)

This otherwise consummately boring grade-Z quickie offers Bela in a dual role and some curiously prophetic projections re: TV's future. Bela attributes the title homicide to the negative effects of "woice wibrations."

Nabonga (1944) ◆◆◆ B&W
D: Sam Newfield. Buster Crabbe, Julie London, Barton MacLane. 75 minutes. (Sinister Cinema, others)

A classic no-budget jungle tale, with Bwana Buster encountering teenage torch singer London in the back-lot bush; Samson the gorilla presents a serious obstacle to their burgeoning romance. Brimming with anthropological/cross-cultural insights.

New Orleans After Dark (1958) ◆◆◇ B&W
D: John Sledge. Stacy Harris, Louis Sirgo, Ellen Moore. 69 minutes. (Loonic)

A campy *Dragnet* clone—star Harris appeared in the 1954 *Dragnet* movie—set in the Big Easy that offers more than its share of unintentionally mirthful moments.

Night of the Bloody Apes (1968) ◆◆◆
D: Rene Cardona, Sr. Armando Silvestre, Jose Elias Moreno, Carlos Lopez Moctezuma, Norma Lazareno, Agustin Solares, Javier Rizo. 81 minutes. (MPI)

A classically awful wrestling/monster movie fashioned by the infamous father-and-son schlock team of Rene Cardona Sr. and Jr.—Mexico's answer to Arch Hall Sr.

and Jr., Jim McCullough Sr. and Jr., and the Weiss Family (we won't repeat the question)—*Night of the Bloody Apes* sports a deranged plot and great dubbed dialogue. (Doctor to detective: "Maybe you have been watching on your television too many pictures of terror!") A demented doc transplants the heart of a man in a gorilla suit into his dying son, who in turn transforms into a muscle-bound apeman with a taste for rape and murder. (Hence, the terror picture's admirably blunt Mexican title, *Horror y Sexo.*) The literally in-depth surgical and eye-gouging gore FX, all shown in extreme close-up, were apparently inserted by the flick's American distribs. Of the assembled thesps, Norma Lazareno, the lady wrestler in the case, makes the deepest impression, largely via her many and sundry gratuitous shower scenes. But why, we want to know, does the son still revert to a simian state after his ape heart is replaced by a woman's? That eternal conundrum aside, *Night of the Bloody Apes* rates as an anticlassic of the first rank.

Octaman (1971) ◆◆
D: Harry Essex. Kerwin Matthews, Pier Angeli, Jeff Morrow. 90 minutes. (Prism, others)

Former screen Sinbad Matthews stars in this absurdist Mexico-lensed monster movie about a lumbering humanoid octopus (!). As Kerwin rhetorically queries,

The one, the only.

"How can there exist a creature with the tentacles of an octopus that walks the earth like a man?"

The Oscar (1966) ◆◆◆
D: Russell Rouse. Stephen Boyd, Elke Sommer, Tony Bennett, Milton Berle. 119 minutes. (Embassy)

Bad actor Boyd claws to the top of the Hollywood heap, leaving a trail of stabbed backs and broken hearts in his wake. Great cameos, plus dialogue that would have turned Ed Wood a deep shade of envy-green.

Plan 9 from Outer Space (1956) ◆◆◆◆ B&W
D: Ed Wood, Jr. Bela Lugosi, Tor Johnson, Vampira, Gregory Walcott, Mona McKinnon, Lyle Talbot, Tom Keene. 78 minutes. (Nostalgia Merchant)

The movie that made Ed Wood, Jr., a household name—if, at first, only in the oddest of households. A trio of aliens—the dignified if short-tempered Eros (announcer Dudley Manlove, who later distinguished himself as one of *Creation of the Humanoids'* leading clickers), Tana (future TV writer Joanna Lee), and The Ruler (nonactor John Breckenridge, a weekend houseguest at Chez Wood, who resorts to reading from his script onscreen)—invade California and institute the titular scheme, which involves turning the massive Johnson, slinky Vampira, and aged Bela into (barely) living dead. Trouble was, Bela died in earnest two days into shooting and had to be replaced by Mrs. Wood, Jr.'s, chiropractor, who was something less than a Lugosi lookalike. Add amateur acting, cardboard sets, hubcaps serving as flying saucers, Ed's trademark confusion of day and night, and circular dialogue that can only be described as truly out of this world, and you have what's rightfully become *the* camp-classic king. Repeated viewings are not only recommended but essential.

Filmmakers in Focus:

Ed Wood, Jr.: The Man Behind the Plan

Legendary Z-pic auteur Edward Davis Wood, Jr., has been widely hailed as *the* worst filmmaker of all time. Ironically, video—the very medium that fueled the burgeoning Ed Wood cult movement—has since exposed *many* self-styled auteurs, from the distant past to the obscure present, who've enjoyed far weaker working relationships with the camera than Ed Wood could ever claim. That isn't to say that the Phantom includes himself among those zany revisionists who now credit Ed with having been possessed by genuine genius. Not even a jury of Ed's most loyal peers would convict him of so outrageous and trumped-up a charge. No, Ed *was* a *bad* filmmaker. But he was also a fascinating and immensely entertaining one: His oddball oeuvre, from the seminal *Glen or Glenda?* to the seedy *Sinister Urge*, contains among the most compellingly idiosyncratic visions ever committed to celluloid. Ed's movies may lack budgets, talent, and coherence, but bizarro flair and a consistent POV are qualities they boast in abundance. Ed's films bear as unmistakable an imprimatur as any of, say, Ingmar Bergman's or Alfred Hitchcock's (the similarities definitely end there).

Ed the man (and, occasionally, woman) was nothing if not a hard-core dreamer. Born in Poughkeepsie, New York, circa 1924, he received his informal film education while working as an usher at a local bijou, where he studied poverty-row chillers (many starring his idol Bela Lugosi), B westerns, and gutter noirs galore. After serving in the Pacific theater during WWII—Ed, already indulging in his notorious transvestite tendencies, would later boast of being the only U.S. Marine to participate in a Pacific landing while wearing a bra and panties under his uniform—where he was twice wounded, Ed headed west to try his luck in the film biz. He received his first professional screen credit via his involvement with the 1952 western *The Lawless Rider,* starring would-be Audie Murphy clone Johnny Carpenter, an obscure character thesp who longed to be a cowboy star as desperately as Ed desired to be a director.

Veteran film producer, scholar, and one-time Ed Wood associate Alex Gordon, also connected with the soon-to-be-troubled production, recalled the experience in a conversation with the Phantom: "When *The Lawless Rider* got going, John Carpenter hired Eddie Wood as assistant director/production manager. Eddie was supposed to make a budget breakdown." Movie novice Gordon was asked to assist Ed in this task. "I had only been out here a few months," the British-born filmmaker remembers, "and I knew nothing about productional breakdowns, so I didn't realize that Eddie didn't know it either. The picture turned out to be quite a disaster. Instead of costing $17,500, it went to $57,000 and ran into such tremendous difficulties that I needed a lawyer, which led me to Sam Arkoff."

That meeting also later led to Gordon's stint at Arkoff's as-yet-unborn American International Pictures, but at the time his association with Ed seemed an inauspicious entry into the movie biz. That didn't prevent

Gordon from entering into an informal partnership with the struggling would-be auteur.

"Ed was a young guy on the fringes. He'd been an actor and wanted to be a director and producer. At that time he was trying to peddle some scripts. I'd written a script called *The Atomic Monster* for Bela Lugosi, and I needed somebody to turn it into a professional screenplay." At least the price was right. "I bought him drinks," Gordon recalls, "and he turned *The Atomic Monster* into a screenplay."

While that enterprise failed to prove immediately fruitful, Gordon continued his association with Ed.

"I spent quite a lot of time with Eddie," he says today. "We wrote the scripts *Dr. Voodoo, The Vampire's Ghost, The Phantom Ghoul,* and a couple of others. We persuaded Bela Lugosi to do one (Lugosi would've done *any*thing), but we hadn't produced anything before. They didn't count *The Lawless Rider.*"

Alas, that project also came to naught. Still, while acknowledging Ed's obvious eccentricities, Gordon was loath to terminate their partnership.

"Admittedly he was a disturbed kind of a character," Alex Gordon alleges. "His drinking, his carousing, and so on really made him completely and utterly unreliable. But he was a very *likable* kind of a guy. He had a very nice sense of humor and was a very pleasant person to be around. He was a nice-looking guy too—the women all went for him in a big way. He was definitely not gay."

Glen or Glenda? (1953) ◆◆◆◇ **B&W** *D: Ed Wood, Jr. Bela Lugosi, Daniel Davis (Ed Wood, Jr.), Dolores Fuller, Lyle Talbot, Timothy Farrell, "Tommy" Haynes. 67 minutes. (Video Yesteryear, others)*
Ed's debut feature, financed by legendary sleaze mogul George (*Test Tube Babies*) Weiss, began life as a documentary but ended as a mélange of badly staged vignettes intercut with largely unrelated stock footage. Ed himself, under the nom de thesp Daniel Davis, essayed the title role(s) of he-guy/transvestite Glen/Glenda, whose fiancée (Ed's then-real-life wife Fuller) can't understand his burning desire to don her angora sweaters. As The Spirit, Bela sits on a threadbare throne and babbles stream-of-unconsciousness soliloquies not always related to the dramatic action. (To wit: "Man's constant groping of things unknown brings to light many startling things!") On hand to lend further obfuscation to the proceedings is narrator/screen shrink Farrell, who—as unrelated footage of cars endlessly rolling along an L.A. freeway unspools onscreen—explains, "The world is a strange place to live in. All those cars. All going somewhere. All carrying humans, which are carrying out their lives."

Beyond crafting one of Z-moviedom's most memorable nightmare sequences (supplemented by borrowed soft-core S&M stag-film clips), Ed distinguishes himself as a master of movie montage, if not of narrative filmmaking, since fully 18 of *Glen or Glenda?*'s 67 minutes are composed of stock footage. Also released under the alternate titles *I Changed My Sex* and *I Led Two Lives* and exhibited well into the '60s, *Glen or Glenda?* doubtless succeeded in confusing entire generations of grindhouse devotees.

Alex Gordon: "When Ed made *Glen or Glenda?*, it was a situation where he made the picture without any thought of Bela Lugosi. And he wanted to get somebody else to play the lead but couldn't because the money was so little. So finally he decided to play the role himself. He needed something else to make it salable because nobody wanted it. I suggested he just shoot a separate sequence for one day with Lugosi—give him a thousand bucks—and Lugosi did that without ever knowing what the rest of the picture was about."

As for Ed's own cross-dressing habits, Alex Gordon recalls, "I only once saw him in that outfit when he was going out with one of his friends, and I told him never to do it again in my presence. But he did enjoy doing it, apparently."

Jail Bait (1954) ◆◆◆ **B&W** *D: Ed Wood, Jr. Timothy Farrell, Lyle Talbot, Dolores Fuller, Clancy Malone, Herbert Rawlinson, Steve Reeves. 70 minutes. (Sinister Cinema, others)*
Originally called *The Hidden Face, Jail Bait* (the title refers to handguns, not underage girls) actually flirts with mediocrity, though it still boasts plenty of unsteady thesping (especially from lead Malone and his onscreen sister Dolores [Mrs. Ed] Fuller) and Ed's patented circular dialogue, which at one point prompts exasperated hood Farrell to bark, "What do I have to do? Repeat myself all night?!" Among its other distinctions, Ed's low-budget noir also features Steve Reeves's screen debut as LAPD dick Talbot's young partner, a plainclothes cop who likes to take off his shirt a lot. And let's not forget *Jail Bait*'s innovative score. After misplacing the original music track, Ed borrowed the score from friend Ron Ormond's Mexico—set monster movie *Mesa of Lost Women* (see index); thus, squad cars roar through the nocturnal L.A. streets to the adrenalizing accompaniment of soft flamenco guitars! Ormond also lent Ed footage from his own 1951 filmed minstrel show *Yessir, Mr. Bones!* (NA), seen here as the stage attraction currently playing at the theater hoods Farrell and Malone hold up. As an astute *Variety* reviewer remarked in 1954, little of *Jail Bait*'s reputed $21,000 budget shows onscreen.

Ed Wood, Jr. (right), inks historic pact to direct *Bride of the Monster* while Bela (standing) beams his approval.

Alex Gordon, on *Jail Bait*'s casting coups: "Helen Ainsworth, who was an agent who had a figure like Sidney Greenstreet, came to see us and said she had this young guy she was sure was going to be a big name someday but he needed to show something on film. It was Steve Reeves. We certainly never dreamed he'd go anywhere because he was kind of a nothing character.

"Clancy Malone, the guy who actually played the lead in the picture, was a guy who used to bring groceries to Eddie. He was a would-be actor, and we finally sort of paid him off by using him in that picture. But he never did anything else.

"Lyle Talbot, at that time, was also an alcoholic. He was on his fourth wife and always loaded. All these alcoholic actors were friends of Eddie's, and he would pay them back by giving them parts in his pictures. Talbot later straightened out and quit drinking."

Bride of the Monster (1955) ◆◆◆ **B&W** *D: Ed Wood, Jr. Bela Lugosi, Tor Johnson, Tony McCoy, Loretta King, Harvey B. Dunne, Paul Marcos. 69 minutes. (Sinister Cinema, others)*
Bela's only true starring role in an Ed Wood movie finds the Hungarian thesp at his hammiest as the mad Dr. Vornoff, a fugitive Russki physicist who's laboring, with the help of his mute, moronic minion Lobo (Johnson), to create a race of "superbeinks of unthinkable strength and size" in the basement lab of his secret redoubt—the fabled House on Lake Marsh Road. *Bride* was financed by an Arizona rancher who insisted that his scrawny, decidedly uncharismatic son play the hero; the rest of the cast is fleshed out by such Wood regulars as Don Nagel and Paul Marcos, cast as cops, Harvey B. Dunn as a Perry White–like newspaper editor, and former East Side Kid Billy Benedict in a bit role as a newsboy. *Bride* features some of Ed's most inspired touches: Bela turns into a "superman" by donning a pair of platform shoes, then does battle with an immobile prop octopus left over from 1948's *Wake of the Red Witch* (Republic). Ed's main triumph here, though, is making what looks, sounds, and plays like an authentic 1942 Monogram horror movie in 1955—and we bet he wasn't hardly even trying.

Alex Gordon: "Ed got involved with *Bride of the Monster*—that was our old *Atomic Monster* script—while I was out of town. Instead of the cast that we had lined up, which was a professional one—Richard Denning, Evelyn Ankers, and so on—he did it with all his cronies, who gave him a few bucks here and there and kept him in groceries. All the people in that film were either friends of his, hangers on, or friends of the man who backed it, a man named McCoy. I was very, very unhappy when I came back.

"Believe it or not, *Bride of the Monster* was sneak-previewed at the Paramount Theater on Hollywood Boulevard, with *End of the Affair* with Deborah Kerr (!). I found it absolutely unbelievable that the Paramount would agree to do that, but I guess they didn't know what the picture was."

But then, Ed Wood, Jr., always had a flair for pageantry.

"I remember when they had a sneak of *Plan 9*"—Alex Gordon shudders—"and he had all his so-called 'stars' there. Afterward, they gave him a standing ovation!"

As for said stars, Gordon remembers, "Most of his people were very strange. I enjoyed the professionals, like Lyle Talbot, Tom Keene, Tor Johnson—I got him into *Bride of the Monster* because I liked him in *Reap the Wild Wind*—but I didn't want to have anything to do with the weirdos."

Night of the Ghouls (1959) ◆◆◆◇ **B&W** *D: Ed Wood, Jr. Kenne Duncan, Duke Moore, Tor Johnson, Criswell, Valda Hansen, Paul Marcos, Don Nagel. 79 minutes. (Nostalgia Merchant)*
As is usually the case with Wood's work, it's not the plot but the bizarre execution that supplies *Ghouls*—a semisequel to *Bride of the Monster* (see index)—with its el cheapo charm. Here, the fun begins with the opening credits: In addition to "executive producer" Major Robert J. Foxworthy (U.S.M.C.R., Ret., he'll have you know), Ed lists no fewer than six "associate producers" (who must have kicked in at least five bucks apiece), many of whom enact bit parts in the film. The rest of the cast is composed of the usual suspects. The ever-flamboyant Criswell narrates from a customized coffin; ex–stunt man Duncan emotes as phony spiritualist Dr. Acula, a role originally designed with the late Bela Lugosi in mind; Moore is the intrepid detective investigating a series of mysterious murders at the doc's old dark lair; and Tor reprises his trademark role as the lumbering, dim-witted Lobo. Also along for the rocky ride are Marcos as comic-relief cop Kelton, sultry Hansen as the White Ghost, Vampira stand-in Jeannie Stevens as the Black Ghost, and Ed himself in a silent cameo as a corpse (!). While *Ghouls* lacks the crazed energy of *Plan 9*, it still delivers its share of Wood-en thrills. Most memorable is Dr. Acula's bogus séance, where floating trumpets (on visible strings) offer sour serenades; white-sheeted extras creak across the room; a "spirit guide" appears as a disembodied head wearing a pith helmet (!); and corpses rise from their caskets to proffer business advice to the living. (As one weary shade puts it, "The task of spanning

the everlasting'is so tiring!") In sum, *Night of the Ghouls,* also available via Lightning Video under the title *Revenge of the Dead,* supplies home viewers with 70 minutes of some of the best bad video extant.

Says Alex Gordon, "That was one of the pictures that was made while I was out of town."

The Violent Years (1956) ◆◆◆◇ **B&W** *D: Fritz Eichorn. Jean Moorehead, Timothy Farrell, Glenn Corbett, I. Stanford Jolley. 75 minutes. (Rhino, others)*
Ed wrote but didn't direct this wild tale about a quartet of crazy-for-kicks teen chicks who hold up gas stations, molest stray males, and generally ignore civilization's rules of decorum. The gals, hired by Commie lowlifes to trash the local high school, end up shooting it out with the fuzz, prompting one mortally wounded femme to utter the infamous Ed-scripted last words, "It ain't supposed to be . . . this way." The girls' philosophy is best summed up, however, by gang leader Moorehead's oft-repeated rhetorical query, "So *what*?" Judge Jolley's lengthy climactic ruling shows off Ed's writing talents as pointedly as anything found in the auteur's entire oeuvre.

The Sinister Urge (1961) ◆◆◆◇ **B&W** *D: Ed Wood, Jr. Kenne Duncan, Duke Moore, Dino Fantini, Harvey B. Dunne. 70 minutes. (Admit One, others)*
Cops Duncan and Moore pursue a "smut picture racket" hitman terrorizing the city. Ed obviously saw himself in the character of stag-moviemaker Johnny Ryde (Carl Anthony), a talented but unlucky auteur who coulda been a contender if he'd caught a few breaks. Cop Duncan takes a harder line: "Show me a crime," he maintains, "and I'll show you a picture that could've caused it." Top acting honors here go to Wood regular Dunne as concerned taxpayer Mr. Romaine. The stag-film-within-a-film (involving several blondes and a whip-wielding Mexican thesp in black leotards) and a lakeside drag scene supply other highlights.

Orgy of the Dead (1965) ◆◆◆ *D: A. C. Stephen (Stephen Apostoloff). Criswell, Fawn Silver, William Bates, Pat Barringer. 82 minutes. (Rhino)*
With this R-rated extravaganza shot in "Astravision and Sexicolor," screenwriter Ed locates the fine line separating Eros from Thanatos and promptly trips over it. Hapless writer Bob and main squeeze Shirley (Wood-enly interpreted by co-producer Bates and Barringer, respectively) stumble upon a remote graveyard where Criswell, as the Master of the Dead, presides over a "dance of the dead"—i.e., ten strip acts performed by an exotic succession of large-breasted L.A.

ecdysiasts. All the classic Ed Wood touches are here in abundance: Brain-dead dialogue (e.g., Bob to Shirley: "Your puritan upbringing may hold you back from my monsters, but it hasn't affected your art of kissing!"), constant confusion 'twixt day and night, and camerawork that harks back to the celluloid Stone Age (though pseudonymous director Stephen gets the credit/blame there). Special kudos go to choreographer Marc Desmond, particularly for his inventive work on Texas Starr's "Cat Dance."

Fugitive Girls (1971) ◆◆◆ *D: A. C. Stephen (Stephen Apostoloff). Jackie Abercrombie, Renee Bond, Talie Cochrane, Dona Desmond, Margie Lanier. "Special Appearance by Edw. D. Wood Jr." 90 minutes. (Nite Flite)*
While Ed doesn't direct this long-rumored, rarely seen obscurity—A. C. Stephen, returns to (mis)handle that chore—he did co-script and even appears onscreen as Pop, an elderly caretaker at a remote desert airstrip. Wood buffs should be warned, however, that this Ed is *not* the strapping young ingenue of *Glen or Glenda?* glory days but an older Wood who'd put on considerable weight and grizzle. Our hero acquits himself well in his brief but key role, though, gassing up the fugitive girls' getaway car before his not-so-furtive phone call to the local sheriff lands him a conk on the noggin, courtesy of one of the desperate babes (a fitting end to Ed's unique Thespian career). In large part an updated, R-rated reprise of Ed's 1956 JD classic *The Violent Years* (see index), *Fugitive Girls,* while not quintessential Wood, is an entertaining, offbeat cheapie, crammed with Ed's customary repetitive, logic-defying dialogue, and is a welcome addition to any dedicated sleaze-buff's home-video library.

Fugitive Girls turned out to be Ed's cinematic swan song, though he continued to keep active, mostly by penning numerous porn novels, like *T For Transvestite,* often under pseudonyms like Angora Peters. Unfortunately, the Ed Wood, Jr., Story lacks a happy ending. As Ed's alcoholism worsened and his desperation grew, he and his loyal wife Kathy hit the downscale trail. In 1978, with Ed at his ebb, they were evicted from their undersized Yucca Street apartment and moved in with Peter Coe, an actor who, like Ed's adopted father-figure Bela, hailed from Hungary and whose credits included some of Universal's '40s *Mummy* sequels. Less than two weeks later, Ed succumbed to a fatal heart attack while watching a TV football game in Coe's living room.
We'll let Alex Gordon supply the last words:

"He really wanted to make it," Gordon sums up Ed's checkered career. "He was very serious; he wasn't deliberately spoofing pictures. But he just didn't have much talent. Even if you'd given him a million dollars, I don't think he could have made a decent picture. I think poor old Eddie just didn't have it in him. But he was trying, in his weird way, with his weird stories, to do what he thought was the best that he could do."

The Phantom counts himself among the many who feel grateful that Ed Wood did what he could.

Playgirl Killer (1970) ◆◆◆
D: Erick Santamaria. William Kerwin, Jean Christopher, Neal Sedaka. 90 minutes. (New World)

Former H. G. Lewis mainstay Thomas (*Blood Feast, Scum of the Earth*) Wood (aka Thomas Sweet-wood), emoting under the alias William Kerwin, carries the day here as a temperamental artist who murders his distaff models when their involuntary movements disrupt his creative concentration (!). You may remember this camp classic as *Decoy for Terror*, its theatrical and TV title. Sedaka, collecting a check between comebacks, is also on hand to lend a lighter note to the turgid proceedings in this unofficial remake of Lewis's *Color Me Blood Red* (Rhino). Similar artist-model relationships are just as sensitively explored in the low-budget horrors *Headless Eyes* (Vestron) and *Sketches of a Strangler* (Fox Hills).

Prehistoric Women (1950) ◆◆◇
D: Greg Tallas. Allan Nixon, Laurette

Luez, Joan Shawlee. 74 minutes. (Rhino)

Engor (Nixon) and Tigri (Luez) share primitive love when not battling nine-foot jungle bully Gwadi in this alternately dull and entertainingly inept Stone Age romp related largely via voice-over. Not as good/bad as *Untamed Women*, let alone *Wild Women of Wongo* (see index), but worth a look for caveman camp completists.

Psychic Killer (1975) ◆◆◆
D: Ray Danton. Jim Hutton, Julie Adams, Nehemiah Persoff. 89 minutes. (Embassy)

Producer Mardi Rustam, who later gave us the insufferable *Evils of the Night* (see index), scores with this hilariously awful "thriller" about a telekinetic killer (Hutton). The unique cast also includes Rod Cameron, Neville Brand, Aldo Ray, and Della Reese, while ex-thesp Danton mishandles the directorial chores.

Queen of the Jungle (1935) ◆◆◆ B&W
D: Robert Hill. Mary Kornman, Reed Howes, Dickie Jones. 87 minutes. (Sinister Cinema)

This featurized version of the serial of the same name is one of the best of the back-lot jungle epics that Z-producers of the '30s and '40s were so fond of cranking out, with knee-jerk racism and sexism galore. Other choice bungled jungle yarns available from Sinister Cinema include *Savage Girl, Law of the Jungle, Lure of the Islands, Jungle Siren* (wherein Buster Crabbe encounters buxom Burly-Q queen Ann Corio!), *White Pongo,* and *Blonde Savage.*

R.P.M. (1970) ◆◇
D: Stanley Kramer. Anthony Quinn, Ann-Margret, Gary Lockwood. 92 minutes. (RCA/Columbia)

Sixties icons Stanley Kramer, Erich Segal, Ann-Margret, and Anthony Quinn pool their talents to create this campy look at campus revolt. The kind they don't hardly make anymore.

The Rats Are Coming! The Werewolves Are Here! (1972) ◆
D: Andy Milligan. Hope Stansbury, Jackie Skarvellis. 92 minutes. (Select-A-Tape)

Longtime Staten Island auteur Milligan has become synonymous with inferior entertainment of the shoddiest sort—and justly so. Any 10 minutes of this typical AM turkey will show you why. Milligan masochists are also referred to *The Body Beneath* (WesternWorld); *Carnage* (Media); *Bloodthirsty Butchers, Man with Two Heads,* and *Torture Dungeon* (all three from Midnight/Select-A-Tape); and *The Ghastly Ones* (Video Home Library) and *Legacy of Horror* (Vidcrest). Andy's livelier softcore sleaze fave, *Tricks of the Trade,* has yet to join the video ranks.

Red Dawn (1984) ◆◆◆
D: John Milius. Patrick Swayze, C. Thomas Howell, Charlie Sheen. 114 minutes. (MGM/UA)

The *Reefer Madness* of Red Menace movies, Milius's *Red Dawn* is a howler from start to finish as high school kids turn guerrilla killers to fight the high-tech invading Russki hordes. Camp aficionados and Commie-bashers alike should enjoy this one.

Repeated viewings of Robot Monster *have left your Phantom speechless. We therefore relinquish this space for a guest review from our own Guidance Ro-Woman, aka The Phantomess.*

Robot Monster (1953) ◆◆◆◇ B&W/3-D
D: Phil Tucker. George Nader, Gregory Moffett, Claudia Barrett, Selena Royle, John Mylong. 63 minutes. (Sony)

Notwithstanding the visual appeal of the hilarious Ro-Man monster padding about in a furry gorilla suit with a fishbowl for a helmet, it is impossible to view *Robot Monster* without being struck by its childlike, and therefore all the more poignant, homage to, and metaphor for, the post–World War II holocaust reality. The amiable and often befuddled Ro-Man shows us the blank face of the banality of evil as, receiving instructions from his outer-space Führer via a rickety TV awash in soap bubbles, he sets about his mission to destroy the last eight people left on earth. "Wouldn't it be nicer if we could live in peace with each other?" rhetorically asks the main resistance fighter (Mylong), who, not surprisingly, has a refugee's East European accent. But in this post-Armageddon world, annihilation seems inevitable. "For you humans"—read Jews, dissidents, or, within a Cold War context, wretched survivors—"there is no escape," parrots Ro-Man who, mindlessly reflecting the sadistic concerns of his Mengele-like master, holds out the cheery promise of a "painless death." "We must die," concurs the patriarch of the clan, which has already been barricaded behind barbed wire and whose furtive life resembles a stark Anne Frank–type existence. The story is told from a child's point of view within the framework of a nightmare. It is stripped down and movingly ludicrous in places, but it is an allegory nonetheless, a moral fable through which is distilled the sadness and horror of the contemporary world. The seriousness of filmmaker (and World War II veteran) Tucker's intent was borne out by his suicide attempt following the scathingly negative notices greeting the film's humble release. Luckily, Phil lived to create such other important works as *Dance Hall Racket* (see index), *Pachuco*, and *The Cape Canaveral Monsters* (both NA).

Back to you, Phantom.

—The Phantomess

You didn't even mention it's in 3-D!

Santa Claus Conquers the Martians (1964) ◆

D: Nicholas Webster. John Call, Pia Zadora, Leonard Hicks, Vincent Beck, Donna Conforti, Bill McCutcheon. 80 minutes. (Embassy)

A kind of *St. Nick a Go-Go Meets Sci-Fi Romper Room* (with music by early-TV immortal Milton Delugg), *Santa Claus Conquers the Martians* features an eight-year-old Pia Zadora as a Martian tyke. Lensed on Long Island on a budget that fell short of shoestring proportions, the pic opens on Mars, where a troubled alien leader-cum-concerned-father decides that the planet's passive, electronically educated kids need to get more fun out of life. To that end, he concocts a clever plot to kidnap Santa, with the help of several green-skinned minions and a tin-can robot named Torg. Following much clamorous intrigue, Santa, along with several junior Earthlings, arrives to shower joy, toys, and Christmas cheer on the Angry Red Planet's uptight inhabitants. In no time, the Martian kids (Pia Z prominent among them) swear off satellite-beamed Earth TV, willingly swallow their food pills, and no longer require a blast of "sleep spray" to nod off at night. Unless you're an insatiable Pia fanatic, after 80 minutes of this, you won't either.

Serpent Island (1954) ◆◇
D: Tom Gries. Sonny Tufts, Mary Munday, Tom Monroe, Dorothy Hayes, Don Blackman. 64 minutes. (Fox Hills)

Sonny's a San Pedro harbor bum hired by decidedly disingenuous starlet manqué Munday—a Scranton secretary looking for her great-grandfather's gold, rumored to be stashed somewhere near Haiti. Sonny, Mary, and hostile captain Monroe shove off for the title isle, battling stock-footage storms and each other. ("Where gold is concerned," Sonny says sagely, "everyone's a savage!") Stilted dramatic scenes are alternated with vintage voodoo footage, leading to a climactic snake fight that rivals Bela Lugosi's unforgettable bout with the rubber octopus in Ed Wood, Jr.'s, *Bride of the Monster* (see index). Recommended for hard-core Tufts buffs only.

Sextette (1978) ◆◆
D: Ken Hughes. Mae West, George Hamilton, Ringo Starr, Tony Curtis. 91 minutes. (Media)

It took half a century for West to adapt her once-bawdy play *Sex* to the screen. The result is this grotty affair, which finds an aged Mae fending off the affections of a half-dozen celluloid has-beens. Plus lots of songs.

Shack Out on 101 (1955) ◆◆◆ B&W
D: Edward Dein. Frank Lovejoy, Terry Moore, Lee Marvin, Keenan Wynn, Whit Bissell. 80 minutes. (Republic)

Lovejoy is an undercover agent posing as a nuclear scientist who hangs out at the title eatery. Among owner Wynn's employees are sexy waitress Moore, who's smitten by Lovejoy and describes him thusly: "He's a scientist! A nuclear *physicist*! BOOM! He's a big, big man!" Lurking in the kitchen is Marvin as a cook named Slob, who's really a Commie spy. None of them seems to get out of the restaurant. A prime example of McCarthyism on the march, on a budget only a producer could love.

She Demons (1959) ◆◆◇ B&W
D: Richard E. Cunha. Tod Andrews, Irish McCalla, Rudolph Anders. 80 minutes. (Media)

Tod (*From Hell It Came*) Andrews teams up with Irish (*Sheena*) McCalla to thwart mad Nazi scientist Rudolph (*Phantom from Space*) Anders and liberate the captive title skanks as director Cunha strikes (out) again.

Sincerely Yours (1955) NR
D: Gordon Douglas. Liberace, Joanne Dru, Dorothy Malone. 116 minutes. (Warner)

The late, great Liberace in his first and only Hollywood vehicle plays a hetero concert pianist who's slowly going blind. Accent on slowly. One of a kind.

The Slime People (1963) ♦♦♦ B&W
D: Robert Hutton. Robert Hutton, Les Tremayne, Susan Hart, Robert Burton. 76 minutes. (Video Gems)

Vet B thesp Hutton decided he could make a movie every bit as slick as W. Lee Wilder's *Man Without a Body* (in which he'd recently starred). The result was this low-budget tale, lensed largely in an L.A. warehouse, about subterranean atomic mutants. To further highlight his own comparative emotive aplomb, Hutton hired a klutzy cast (with the exception of ubiquitous '50s shock-movie trooper Tremayne) who fail to establish a working relationship with the camera. Highlights include a neat precredits visual intro to the title creatures and the following words to live by: "When I'm sitting here with you, I don't even *think* about slime people." Watch it with someone you love, and maybe you won't either.

Student Confidential (1987) ♦♦♦
D: Richard Horian. Produced by Richard Horian. Written by Richard Horian. Edited by Richard Horian. Music composed and performed by Richard Horian. Starring Richard Horian, Eric Douglas, Marlon Jackson, Susan Scott, Elizabeth Singer, Ronee Blakley. 95 minutes. (Media)

Richard Horian's one-man vanity prod, *Student Confidential*, may be the most enjoyably awful movie of 1987. The pic chronicles the solemn misadventures of Michael Drake, Millionaire Guidance Counselor (he quit big biz, we're told, to do something useful with his life) as he attempts to steer a quartet of troubled teens (Kirk's son Eric Douglas and Michael's brother Marlon Jackson among them) through the turbulent waters of adolescence. Complicating matters is Mike's unsympathetic bimbo of a wife (who considers our bearded hero something of a stiff) and his own efforts to make himself a more "feeling" person. *Director* Horian treats *thesp* Horian—a practitioner of the bulging-eyes and wild-grimace approach to acting—to any number of extreme close-ups, while *scripter* Horian contributes dialogue worthy of no less a genius than Ed Wood, Jr. We eagerly await RH's next one.

Sweet Country (1987) NR
D: Michael Cacoyannis. Jane Alexander, John Cullum, Carole Laure, Franco Nero, Joanna Pettet, Randy Quaid. 120 minutes. (Cinema Group)

Cacoyannis demonstrates that his atrocious atomic parable *The Day the Fish Came Out* (NA) was no fluke by returning twenty years later with this equally asinine account of a Latin American dictatorship. Quaid "stretches" as a sadistic Latino guard!

Teenage Zombies (1957) ♦♦ B&W
D: Jerry Warren. Don Sullivan, Katherine Victor, Steve Conte, Paul Pep-

per, Bri Murphy, Mitzi Albertson. 72 minutes. (Sinister Cinema)

The Phantom viewed Warren's *Teenage Zombies* back-to-back with the same schlockmeister's 1978 *Frankenstein Island* (see index) and was frankly amazed to discover that not only hadn't Warren learned anything in the intervening decades, he had actually forgotten the little he'd known! Hence, *Teenage Zombies* fails to mount a serious challenge to *Frankenstein Island* in the bad-movie department. That's not to say it's not a thoroughly rotten flick in its own right—it does, after all, feature Ivan the White-Eyed Russian Zombie, a guy in a gorilla suit, and a hot contempo story line describing a Commie plot to zombify the Free World via nerve-gas capsules. But *Teenage Zombies* never attains the nadir that *Frankenstein Island* sustains for nearly its entire running time. Z-movie masochists interested in investigating Warren's other no-budget wonders are referred to Sinister Cinema, which also carries Jer's *Attack of the Mayan Mummy, Creature of the Walking Dead,* and *Incredible Petrified World,* and to Loonic Video, which stocks *Curse of the Stone Hand* and *Invasion of the Animal People.*

Teenagers from Outer Space (1959) ◆◆◆ B&W
D: Tom Graeff. David Love, Dawn Anderson, Bryant Grant, Tom Lockyear, Harvey B. Dunne, Robert King Moody. 78 minutes. (Sinister Cinema)

Graeff's oft-debunked but rarely seen $20,000 space oddity actually sports a pretty decent plot that prefigures the likes of such contempo sci-fi hits as *The Terminator, The Hidden,* and *Brother from Another Planet.* When the powers-that-be on a distant planet select Earth as a breeding ground for beastly herds of fast-growing "gargons," sensitive alien teen Derek (Love) flees his flying saucer to warn unsuspecting Earthlings of the impending disaster. Derek is in turn pursued by Thor, a raygun-wielding extraterrestrial hitman in a *Terminator* mode. Derek finds Ed Wood, Jr., regular Dunne, tumbles for his fetching granddaughter (Anderson), and sets about saving the planet while Thor and a sample gargon pile up the body count. Auteur Graeff exhibits a knack for swift pacing but is sabotaged by his own hilariously awful dialogue and shaky thesps (who labor under the additional handicap of being poorly post-synced). Still, *Teenagers* will keep you both involved *and* in stitches—a rare combo that qualifies the pic as essential viewing for sci-fi, youth-and bad-movie buffs alike.

The Terror of Tiny Town (1938) ◆◆◆ B&W
D: Sam Newfield. Little Billy (Billy Curtis), Yvonne Moray, John Bambury, Billy Platt. 62 minutes. (Video Yesteryear, others)

Actually, the first and only all-midget singing western is played pretty straight by its diminutive cast; except for the outsize (i.e., normal) props, *Terror* comes across as a perfectly standard B oater of its era, replete with stunts, fistfights, chases, shoot-outs, and brutal killings. Hero Billy Curtis went on to make further crucial genre-movie contributions, essaying the lead mole-man role in *Superman and the Mole Men* (see index) and supplying the teddy bear's voice in the 1987 sleeper *Bloody Wednesday* (see index). Add two hot tunes, "The Wedding of Jack and Jill" (a duet performed by Curtis and ingenue Moray) and the ensemble song "Laugh Your Troubles Away," and you know you're getting your overnight rental's worth.

They Saved Hitler's Brain (1963) ♦♦ B&W

D: David Bradley. Walter Stocker, Audrey Claire, Carlos Rivas. 81 minutes. (United)

Two bad movies for the splice of one: a '63 Hitler cult epic *Madmen of Mandoras* (NA), plus a would-be Bondian wraparound filmed several years later. Only the most patient bad-movie fans will want to stick around for the flick's few memorable lowlights, though.

Times Square (1980) ♦♦

D: Alan Moyle. Tim Curry, Trini Alvarado, Herbert Berghof. 117 minutes. (HBO)

An at-times fascinatingly grotesque and extravagantly abysmal rock-runaway fable set in a glam-orized Times Square and sporting a decibel level guaranteed to shock your mind. (THE SCREEN-WRITER WAS REPORTEDLY INTO PRIMAL SCREAM THERAPY!) Pair this with the equally unbearable *Can't Stop the Music* (also HBO), the legendary Village People vehicle, for a video evening you won't soon forget.

Twisted Brain (1974) ♦♦◇

D: Larry Stouffer. Pat Cardi, Rosie Holotik, Austin Stoker. 85 minutes. (United)

Former child star Cardi is a misunderstood high school nerd/genius with a Jekyll/Hyde formula that enables him to wreak revenge on his tormentors. Several pro gridiron stars cameo as cops. You'll fall asleep humming the theme song.

The Unearthly (1957) ♦♦♦ B&W

D: Brooke L. Peters. John Carradine, Allison Hayes, Myron Healey, Tor Johnson. 73 minutes. (Rhino)

Carradine plays a crazed scientist who's a long way from perfecting your typical exotic glandular experiments. (Quoth the trailer, "What this gland does to this blond beauty when it's electrolated into her body is an experience in horror that's *almost* unbelievable!") Posing as a sanitarium shrink, Long John lures several potential victims to his isolated redoubt, including B-pic hero Healey and statuesque Allison (*50-Ft. Woman*) Hayes. It's Tor, though, in a rare speaking role, who sums it up best with his terse directive, "Time for go to bed!"

Untamed Women (1952) ◆◆◆◇ B&W
D: W. Merle Connell. Mikel Conrad, Doris Merrick, Richard Monahan. 70 minutes. (J&J)

Matinee idol manqué Mikel (*Flying Saucer*) Conrad tries again in this deservedly vaunted camp classic about four errant WWII fliers who wash up on your typical uncharted Pacific isle occupied by femme Druids and their apelike male enemies, the dread Hairy Men. Contains the immortal command, "Shoot anything with hair that moves!"

Vampire over London (1951) ◆◆ B&W
D: John Gilling. Bela Lugosi, Arthur Lucan, Kitty McShane. 72 minutes. (Sinister Cinema)

Directed by future Hammer helmer Gilling and released in Blighty as *Old Mother Riley Meets the Vampire*, this lowbrow farce (the last in a popular series) finds a confused Bela—in sort of an informal *Glen or Glenda?* warm-up—confronted by legendary Brit drag comic Lucan, in his Irish charwoman "Old Mother Riley" guise. Later rereleased stateside as *My Son, the Vampire*, and also briefly known as *King Robot*. A pretty painful spectacle, by any other name. See Sinister's *Old Mother Riley's Ghosts* for more of the same—minus Bela.

Village of the Giants (1965) ◆◆◆
D: Bert I. Gordon. Tommy Kirk, Ronny Howard, Beau Bridges, Joy Harmon, Johnny Crawford, Joseph Turkel. 82 minutes. (Embassy)

A loose-screwed revamp of H. G. Wells's "Food of the Gods," Gordon's stunningly stupid *Village of the Giants* tells the shocking tale of teen troublemakers who, led by young Bridges, eat a magic growth drug called Goo, sprout to Brobdingnagian proportions, and terrorize the hick town of Hainesville, California. They accomplish this mostly by playing their radios too loud and by not watching where they're dancing. The creative force behind such earlier outsize attractions as *The Cyclops* (see index), *Amazing Colossal Man* (NA), and *War of the Colossal Beast* (NA) (for which Bert inserts a clever plug in *Village*), Gordon reaches the heights of his Z-movie powers with this Goliaths a-Go-Go extravaganza. *Village* is one of those rare junk gems that has it all: One of filmdom's first major mud-wrestling scenes, music by Freddy Cannon and the Beau Brummels, go-go gals galore, a pair of giant dancing ducks (!), lots of hip dialogue (e.g., "Dig that nitty-gritty!"), and a thesp lineup that includes Johnny (*The Rifleman*) Crawford, Disney dropout Kirk, the still-active Toni Basil, and Howard as an eleven-year-old genius named Genius. Reserve *your* copy today.

Viva Knievel! (1977) NR

D: Gordon Douglas. Evel Knievel, Gene Kelly, Lauren Hutton. 104 minutes. (Warner)

If you see only one Evel Knievel movie in your lifetime, skip the George Hamilton biopic (*Evel Knievel* [MPI]) and pick this one, wherein Evel plays himself as a sort of stunt-cycle saint. Evel returns as himself in the documentary *Last of the Gladiators* (Twin Tower).

The Vulture (1967) ◆◆◇

D: Lawrence Huntington. Robert Hutton, Broderick Crawford, Akim Tamiroff. 92 minutes. (IVE)

A dumber-than-average ornithological romp starring an outsize vulture sporting Akim Tamiroff's head (!) that menaces B vets Crawford and Hutton. Released in B&W theatrically, but the vid's in living color.

Wild Women of Wongo (1958) ◆◆◆

D: James Wolcott. Ed Fury, Adrienne Barbeau, Jean Hawkshaw. 78 minutes. (Amvest)

Big trubs in Wongo: Seems that the wild women of same have lost their male counterparts in a sneak attack perpetrated by the local apemen. Their village, set on the sands of primordial Coral Gables, is deserted, so there's naught to do but hie to the neighboring land of Goona. As luck would have it, the Goona guys (who include future Steve Reeves clone Fury) are all hunks—vast improvements over the Wongo lunks. The rest, as they say, is prehistory. While *Wild Women of Wongo*—a classic 1958 nudist-camp-type romp *without* the nudity—may not be the worst flick ever made, it comes close enough to supply a real treat for devoted bad-movie buffs. The head Wongo woman's climactic battle with a plastic Crocodile God—which fully rivals Bela Lugosi's legendary duke-out with a rubber octopus in Ed Wood, Jr.'s, *Bride of the Monster*—is a scene you'll want to watch again and again.

Wizard of Mars (1964) ◆◆◇

D: David L. Hewitt. John Carradine, Roger Gentry, Vic McGee. 81 minutes. (Republic)

Another entertainingly bad sci-fi effort from David L. (*Journey to the Center of Time*) Hewitt, with Carradine especially memorable as the superimposed title figure. Also available via Genesis under the title *Horrors of the Red Planet*.

The Woman Inside (1981) NR

D: Joseph Van Winkle. Gloria Manon, Dane Clark, Joan Blondell. 94 minutes.

Granted it's no *Glen or Glenda?*, but this amateur-city transsexual soap opera is said to be about the closest anyone's come to replicating Ed's gender-bent epic.

The Yesterday Machine (1963) ◆◆◇ **B&W**

D: Russ Marker. Tim Holt, Robert Britton, Anne Pellegrino, Jack Herman, Bill Thurman. 85 minutes. (Video City)

RITA JENRETTE
Released by the TROMA TEAM
Zombie Island Massacre

Former congressional wife Rita Jenrette displays her multiple talents (not visible here) in the catatonic campfest, *Zombie Island Massacre*.
Photo courtesy of Troma, Inc.

Something of an informal companion piece to the same year's even more awful *They Saved Hitler's Brain* (see index), 1963's *The Yesterday Machine* is just one of countless previously unknown independent Z flicks surfacing today via the magic world of video. The film features a cameo by Tim (*Treasure of Sierra Madre*) Holt as a detective but centers on reporter Britton and local chanteuse (complete with blond beehive) Pellegrino's search for the latter's missing majorette sister. Turns out she's been kidnapped by a mad Nazi scientist (Herman) bent upon strapping her into his titular time device—a contraption that would have won the war for the Reich had he only been able to perfect it on sked. The pic's undeniable highlight is our nutty Nazi's lengthy lecture on the principles of time travel—a heavily accented monologue that halts *The Yesterday Machine's* already faltering forward thrust for a good 10 minutes. While we can recommend the flick for hard-core Mad Nazi Scientist Movie mavens and die-hard Tim Holt fans, *The Yesterday*

Machine fails in its challenge to top the immortal *Manos, Hands of Fate* (see index) in the celluloid Texas-bred-turkey sweepstakes.

Zombie Island Massacre (1985) ◆

D: John N. Carter. Rita Jenrette, David Broadnax, Tom Cantrell, Diane Clayre Holub, George Peters, Ian McMillian. 86 minutes. (Fox Hills)

Zombie Island Massacre, starring former congressional wife and *Playboy* model Rita Jenrette, gets off to an admittedly bright start: No sooner do the opening credits end than Rita's in the shower, soaping her big Washingtonian breasts while a reggae instrumental pounds on the soundtrack. Un-fortunately, it's all downhill from there. The plot concerns a Caribbean tour group stranded on a sinister isle populated by dancing voodoo girls and crazed killers unknown. After being promised "one of the most exciting and fun-filled evenings of your entire lives," our Ugly Americans (Rita, of course, excluded) are knocked off one and two at a time. Rita's big emotive moment arrives when—after her paunchy, loudmouthed boyfriend panics and literally loses his head—she's called on to sob for a full 30—count 'em—30 seconds, most of them in tight CU. Rita also performs the pic's "Di Reggae Picnic" theme. Guess what? She can't sing either.

THAT'S EXPLOITATION!
VINTAGE SLEAZE ON VIDEO

"See! The happy, normal laughter of physically adorable young girls give way to the hysterical outbursts of dope-maddened women!"

Pressbook
She Should'a Said No

Vintage sleaze and exploitation flicks may be an acquired tastelessness, but once acquired they can quickly prove habit-forming. Said flicks earned their sobriquet by exploiting taboo topics that major studios wouldn't touch, though they usually offered more in the way of tantalizing titles and hot poster art than in explicit celluloid content. The exploitation-film biz of the '30s through the early '60s constituted a cobwebbed corner of the larger movie industry that went ignored by all but those hardy few who frequented

551

the nation's sleaziest urban grindhouses and those backwoods bijous that hosted occasional "roadshow" pictures like the legendary Kroger Babb's shocking premarital sex exposé *Mom and Dad*, which came complete with requisite "birth of a baby" footage. (As earlier mentioned, your Phantom was fortunate enough to have just such a triple-feature grindhouse a mere ten-minute bus ride from his home, enabling him to get an early jump on the genre.)

The rediscovery of the 1938 antimarijuana chestnut *Reefer Madness* (originally titled *Tell Your Children*) circa 1970 by a generation that hitherto thought *it* had invented the controlled substance under scrutiny started the vintage-sleaze ball rolling. Soon other tawdry treasures, campily retitled *Sex Madness* (*They Must Be Told*) and *Cocaine Fiends* (*The Pace That Kills*), were giving *Reefer* a run for its money at campus screenings, midnight shows, and revival houses the nation 'round.

It wasn't until video's arrival that the sleaze-movie floodgates opened with a vengeance. Any enterprising indie vid whiz who could lay hands on a print of one of these predominantly public-domain titles could transfer it cheaply to tape. Those who did discovered a small but enthusiastic and burgeoning market for everything from creaky morality melodramas like *Sex Madness* and its ilk to the hilariously misinformative "sex education" cheapies of the '50s (*Mated, Test Tube Babies*) to the soft-core smut noirs (*Good Time with a Bad Girl, Motel Confidential*) and the ridiculous sun-drenched color nudist-camp romps of the early '60s (*Naked Complex, Daughter of the Sun*).

Our list offers a representative sampling of the sleaze of yore available on videotape. By the time this volume reaches a store near you, the sleaze-title roster will doubtless have expanded as more and more thought-to-be-lost prints turn up. Hope you'll excuse the sometimes spotty credits—in many cases, we were fortunate to track down these titles at all, and few of them can be found in previous film reference books. (The original credit sequences are often missing from the videos as well.) We've included no hard-core fare; in fact, in most cases the content is tamer than that found in most contempo mainstream Hollywood product. But the attitude, execution, and entertainment value are what count here, and the following films offer a unique peek through the keyhole of history at what was once considered the seamy side of life.

Artist's Studio Secrets (1964) NR B&W
78 minutes. (Video Dimensions)

An obscure soft-core sex film from 1964, involving fetishistic artist "Percy Green" and what transpires during the coarse course of his wild all-night "bohemian" bash.

Assassin of Youth (1937) ◆◆◇ B&W
D: Elmer Clifton. Luana Walters, Arthur Gardner, Dorothy Short. 67 minutes. (Sinister Cinema)

An early antimarijuana tract. Not as much fun as *Reefer Madness* (see index), though the final image, of joints falling seemingly from the heavens, is pretty memorable.

Assault of the Rebel Girls (1959) ◆◆◇ B&W
D: Barry Mahon. Errol Flynn, Beverly Aadland, John MacKay, Jackie Jackler. 66 minutes. (Fox Hills)

Shortly before his death, a dissipated Errol Flynn agreed to "present," narrate, and sporadically appear in this mud-stuck vehicle for his teenage flame, Beverly Aadland. *Cuban Rebel Girls* (retitled *Assault of the Rebel Girls* for its belated vid release) is an incredibly shoddy quickie featuring Flynn as himself (though currently on assignment as a roving Hearst reporter!) and Bev as a blond bimbo who joins Castro's guerrillas to be near her mercenary boyfriend (Mahon mainstay MacKay). Applying the same docu-schlock approach that informed *Rocket Attack, U.S.A.* (see index) (a far superior bad movie, by the way), Mahon uses stock and newsreel footage intercut with static "dramatic" scenes shot in murky black and white to craft this pro-Castro tract. (He wasn't doing Fidel any favors.) Flynn looks wan and embarrassed, while Bev enthusiastically mouths lines like, "I don't even know who these Batista

---

FILMMAKERS IN FOCUS:

Barry Mahon: A Mahon for All Sleazin'

Cuban Rebel Girls may have marked the ignoble end of Errol Flynn's formerly swashbuckling career, but it was the equally ignoble beginning for Flynn's former agent, budding schlockmeister Barry Mahon. After directing *Rebel Girls*, Mahon went on to lens over fifty films, mostly "nudies" and soft-core sleaze efforts with admittedly colorful titles—*The Beast That Killed Women* (your standard killer-gorilla-in-a-nudist-camp romp), *Hot Skin and Cold Cash* (both 1965), *Run Swinger Run!* (1967), *Prowl Girls, Some Like It Violent,* and the unforgettable *Forbidden Flesh: As Seen from a Hayloft in the Hills* (all 1968). But Barry wasn't afraid to stretch—in 1969, he even filmed an ambitious kiddie-targeted remake titled *The Wonder Land of Oz* (with a wistful reprise of "I Wish I Had a Brain"), a hippie exposé in a "Mondo" mode, *Weekend Rebellion* (1970), and what's arguably *the* greatest Iron Butterfly concert movie ever, *Musical Mutiny* (1970).

But it was Mahon's early efforts, released under the candidly yclept Exploit Films banner—*Cuban Rebel Girls, Violent Women* (1960), and *Rocket Attack, U.S.A.* (1961)—that earned him his permanent place in the Z-movie Hall of Infamy. Minimalist in the extreme, Barry's pics featured extended stationary camerawork, long takes of characters exchanging would-be expository—more often rambling—dialogue, static, ill-staged "action" scenes, lots of stock footage, and actresses who emoted like secretarial-school dropouts. His flicks depict a world of small rooms—*Rocket*'s stark Russki nightclub, *Violent Women*'s claustrophobic prison cell—and exteriors that look suspiciously like backyards. We've never seen Mahon's promising 1961 romantic epic *Pagan Island* (NA)—starring exotic Nani Maka and obscure ex-B-western hero Eddie Dew, scripted by Barry's better half, Clelle Mahon—but we *can* highly recommend *Assault of the Rebel Girls* (see review), *Violent Women* (Vidmark), *Rocket Attack, U.S.A.* (Sony), by far Barry's most memorable work, and his only late-'60s sleazefest to surface on video, 1967's Las Vegas–set *Good Time with a Bad Girl* (Video Dimensions).

and Castro guys are!" A prime example of artlessness imitating life, this campy curiosity piece is definitely worth the price of an overnight rental. Also out as *Attack of the Rebel Girls* (Discount).

The Bare Hunt (1963) NR B&W
69 minutes. (Video Dimensions)
Formerly titled *My Gun Is Jammed*, this low-comic "nudie" shadows low-down dirty shamus Max T. Unimportant through his erotic encounters with various seminaked starlets and models, including the infamous Boobsy Twins (!). You'll probably never see it on your local PBS.

Bedroom Fantasy/Love Moods (195?) NR
(Channel 13)
Two Lily St. Cyr featurettes, lensed in color, depicting the renowned sex goddess performing a pair of her infamous bubble-bath acts.

The Bloody Brood (1959) ◆◆◆ B&W
D: Julian Roffman. Peter Falk, Jack Betts, Barbara Lord. 80 minutes. (Movie Buff)

According to the original ads, "A Motion Picture That Peels Off the Dirty Sweaters Covering the Raw Emotions of Youth!" Peter Falk made his screen debut as a beatnik Raskolnikov who kills a delivery kid for kicks by feeding him a burger mixed with ground glass during a wild beat bacchanal; the victim's brother seeks revenge. Packed with all manner of Holy Profundities. Falk: "I don't *talk* my kicks. I *do* 'em." Recommended.

Burlesque in Harlem (194?) NR B&W
Pigmeat Markham. Approx. 60 minutes. (Channel 13)

An all-black burlesque film, with comic Markham leading the festivities, which also include strippers, dancing girls, and musical numbers. Other exotic Burlesque vids include *Best of Burlesque* (Active), *Great British Striptease* (IVE), *Here It Is—Burlesque!* (Vestron) (a burly-Q recreation with Ann Corio and Pinky Lee), and 1947's *Hollywood Revels* (Video Yesteryear).

Caligula (1980) NR
D: Tinto Brass. Malcolm McDowell, Peter O'Toole, Helen Mirren, John Gielgud. 156 minutes. (Vestron)

The World According to Gooch—as in *Penthouse* publisher Bob Guccione—thus far begins and ends with this histrionic sex-and-violence-bent account of Caligula's (McDowell) crazed Roman reign. Not without its novelty value, provided a quick fast-forward finger remains readily at hand. Available both in the original X edition and a softer R version.

Chained for Life (1950) ◆◆◇ B&W
D: Sam Newfield. Daisy and Violet Hilton, Allan Jenkins. 65 minutes. (Rhino)

Real-life Siamese Twins Daisy and Violet Hilton go on trial for a murder only one of them committed, posing a thorny ethical problem for the most sophisticated of judicial minds. Don't miss the Twins' musical duet, "Never Say You'll Never Fall in Love."

Cheesecake Files, Vols. 1 & 2 NR B&W/color
(Channel 13)

Classic "girlie" shorts, whose titles—"She Went Wild Out West," "How to Take a Bath"—tell all, though the girls themselves leave a lot to the imagination. Similar compilations in the Channel 13 series include *Jukebox Follies, Uncover Girls, Too Hot to Handle,* and *Hollywood Peepshow.*

Child Bride (1942) ◆◆◇ B&W
D: Harry Revier. Shirley Mills, Bob Bollinger, Warner Richmond. 60 minutes. (Hollywood Confidential/Marshall, Sinister Cinema, others)

An impassioned plea—directed by Revier, of *Lost City* notoriety—

fashioned to discourage Appalachian lechers from marrying barely pubescent girls. Only the Hollywood Confidential edition contains the infamous nude swimming scene. *Any* version will demand extreme patience on the viewer's part.

The Cocaine Fiends (1936) ◆◆◆ B&W
D: William A. O'Connor. Noel Madison, Lois January, Sheila Manners. 58 minutes. (Sinister Cinema, others)

Originally titled *The Pace That Kills* and based on a 1928 (NA) silent bearing the same name, this feature-length cocaine condemnation lacks the wacky energy of a *Reefer Madness* but depicts enough down and dirty doings at the notorious Dead Rat Cafe to make it a must for vintage-sleaze buffs. Hey, it wasn't condemned by the Legion of Decency for nothing—or was it?

Confessions of a Vice Baron (1942) ◆◆◆ B&W
Willy Castello. 70 minutes. (Sinister Cinema)

This "Real Life Dramas" presentation is actually a compilation of scenes culled from several '30s exploitation flicks—including *Cocaine Fiends, Mad Youth, Smashing the Vice Trust, Souls of Pawn, What Price Passion?*, and *Wages of Sin*—all conveniently featuring thesp Willy Castello, whose flashback narration (from Death Row!) supplies a flimsy frame for the tawdry goings-on.

Pretty unique, and a top video value for celluloid sleaze buffs.

Dance Hall Racket (1955) ◆◆◆ B&W
D: Phil Tucker. Lenny Bruce, Honey Bruce, Timothy Farrell, Sally Marr. 55 minutes. (Marshall Discount Video/ Hollywood Confidential)

A would-be shocking exposé produced by the infamous George (*Glen or Glenda?*) Weiss and directed by the one and only Phil (*Robot Monster*) Tucker, this 1955 exploitation oddity stars Lenny Bruce (who also scripted) as a switchblade-wielding bouncer (whose chief duty seems to be murdering unsatisfied customers!) at Scali's Dance Emporium, a waterfront clip joint operated by smooth-talking slimebag Umberto Scali (slickly embodied by unsung Ed Wood regular Farrell). Also in the cast are Lenny's then-wife, ecdysiast Honey Bruce, and mom, ex-vaudevillian Sally Marr. As an actor, Bruce makes like a psychotic Leo Gorcey ("Big deal—I killed a guy," he sneers. "That makes me a *criminal?*"), while his script is by turns functional, funny, and downright strange. (E.g., a mugging comic in a porkpie hat wanders in and out of the movie doing an anachronistic El Brendel imitation!) Highlights include fleeting nudity and Sally Marr's extremely gratuitous Charleston number. Don't miss this vital '50s sleaze item. You can also catch Lenny, in more characteristic modes, in the docu-salutes *Lenny Bruce* (Video Yesteryear) and *The Lenny Bruce Performance Film* (Vestron), which includes the famous animated "Thank You, Masked Man." Bob Fosse's *Lenny* bio, with Dustin Hoffman in the lead, is also available (Key).

Delinquent Daughters (1944) NR B&W
D: Albert Herman. June Carlson, Fifi D'Orsay, Teala Loring. 67 minutes. (Sinister Cinema)

Poverty-row sociologists at PRC examine the ill effects of World War II on unsupervised youth.

Delinquent Parents (1938) NR B&W
D: Albert Herman. Doris Weston. (Loonic)

An unwed mother's shady past catches up with her after she dumps her unwanted child. Another Loonic obscurity, originally released under another, still unknown title—possibly one of the turgid turkeys excerpted in *Confessions of a Vice Baron.*

Devil Monster (1946) ◆◆◇ B&W
D: S. Edward Graham, supervised by Adrian Weiss. Barry Norton, Blanche Mehaffey, J. Barton, Terry Grey, Jack Del Rio, Mary Carr. 60 minutes. (Sinister Cinema)

Another stock-footage special from the wonderful Weiss clan! A small crew of bad actors led by heartthrob Norton sets sail for the Pacific in search of a missing seaman. Along the way, they see lots and *lots* of stock footage, from octopus battles to bare-breasted Polynesian dancing girls—the latter providing this entertainingly pathetic outing with its chief raison d'être. Norton's gee-whiz voice-over moves our story forward, but never for very long before Adrian (Son of Louis, Brother of George) Weiss, who also edited, cues up the library music and trots out more travel footage, whence also appears the decidedly unterrifying title creature. At the sight of the latter, one brave sailor actually leaps into the stock-footage waters to do superimposed battle with the beast (!). Eat your heart out, Industrial Light & Magic!

The Devil on Wheels (1947) ◆◆◇ B&W
D: Crane Wilbur. Terry Moore, Darryl Hickman. 70 minutes. (Loonic)

A cautionary warning re: the New Hot-Rod Menace dealing with speed-crazy teens—like future Howard Hughes paramour Terry Moore and Dwayne (*Dobie Gillis*) Hickman's older bro Darryl—who have no respect for the rules of the road.

The Devil's Harvest (1942) ◆◆◇ B&W
D: Ray Test. Jane Doyle, Leo Anthony, George Graham. 60 minutes. (Hollywood Confidential/Marshall)

A belated entry in the Marijuana Menace sweepstakes, *Devil's Harvest* offers a hot first half—a superimposed Satan accompanies each reefer close-up—that cools off and drifts into standard melodramatics as undercover investigator

Doyle closes in on a band of vile pushers.

Double Agent 73 (1974) ◆
D: Doris Wishman. Chesty Morgan. 80 minutes. (American Video Tape)

Wishman's depressing soft-core spy "comedy," starring anatomical wonder Chesty Morgan, is recommended only for the hardiest rancid-sleaze fan. Ditto for Doris's *Amazing Transplant*, directed under the nom du cinema Louis Silverman and issued on the now-defunct Electric Video label. DW's *Nudes on the Moon, Blaze Starr Goes Nudist,* and *Another Day, Another Man* remain tragically unavailable as we go to press.

Ecstasy (1933) ◆◆◇ B&W
D: Gustav Machaty. Hedy Lamarr. 68 minutes. (Video Yesteryear)

The Czech flick that launched then-teenage Hedy Lamarr, on the strength of her notorious nude swim scene and generally sensuous presence. Otherwise, an arty, heavy-breathing take on life and lust.

Elysia (1933) NR B&W
D: Brian Foy. Constance Allen. 47 minutes. (Moore)

One of the earliest nudist talkies, *Elysia* can boast of few other distinctions. On the other hand, that should be enough.

Erotic Touch of Hot Skin (1964) NR B&W
D: Max Pecas. Fabienne Dali, Jean Valmont, Sophie Hardy. 77 minutes. (Video Dimensions)

This Euro-import deals with a frolicksome foursome trysting the nights away in southern France.

Faster, Pussycat! Kill! Kill! (1966) ◆◆◆◇ B&W
D: Russ Meyer. Tura Satana, Haji, Lori Williams, Stuart Lancaster, Susan Bernard, Mickey Foxx. 86 minutes. (RM)

Meyer's large-breasted desert noir finds three crazy-for-kicks go-go chicks, headed by the incomparable Tura Satana, embarking on a wild crime spree that includes murder, kidnapping, theft, and wanton exposure of seemingly limitless cleavage. Our top-heavy trio eventually tangles with a troika of mostly hapless males— including a lecherous old-timer and his moronic stud of a son—in a perverse cat-and-mouse game that leads to a violent denouement. Meyer's dense, double-entendre-laden script escalates the battle of the sexes to a grotesque war of attrition. While his later *Beyond the Valley of the Dolls* finishes a close second, *Faster, Pussycat! Kill! Kill!* shapes up as *the* definitive Meyer movie—in the Phantom's book, at least—an intensely crazed fable guaranteed to keep you on the edge of disbelief.

The Flaming Urge (1953) ◆◆◇ B&W
Harold Lloyd, Jr., Cathy Downs. 67 minutes. (Sinister Cinema)

Harold Lloyd, Jr., is a suspected arsonist in what may be the only exploitation flick on the subject of pyromania.

FILMMAKERS IN FOCUS:

Russ Meyer: Down Mammary Lane

Born in California in 1922, Russ Meyer learned his lensman's craft as an army photog during World War II. His directorial debut came in 1959 with the infamous nudie comedy *The Immoral Mr. Teas*. Meyer scored his initial cult success with a series of breast-obsessed mock morality melodramas—*Lorna, Common-Law Cabin, Mud Honey,* et al.— reaching his early creative zenith with *Faster, Pussycat!* Russ then turned his attention to lighter, more openly satirical films, lensed in vivid color, like *Vixen, Supervixens,* and the seminal *Cherry, Harry & Raquel.* Along the way, he introduced such buxom starlets as Lorna Maitland, Kitten Natividad, Ushi Digart, Haji, and the immortal Tura Satana.

Meyer gained his highest profile via his relatively gala, and generally brilliant, Hollywood trash satire *Beyond the Valley of the Dolls* (co-scripted by critic-heavyweight Roger Ebert). After bombing with his only major-studio-financed film, *The Seven Minutes,* in 1972, Meyer returned to crafting pictorial paeans to his two great loves in flicks like *Up!* and the raunchy *Our Town* send-up *Beneath the Valley of the Supervixens* (for which enterprise Ebert, under the alias R. Hyde, again lent his scripting talents). For the past several years, the maverick moviemaker has been assembling his titanic *The Breast of Russ Meyer,* a twelve-cassette video collection of highlights from his oeuvre, fleshed out with newly lensed *verité* accounts re: the making of same.

Beyond the extremely rare *Beyond the Valley of the Dolls* (CBS/Fox), *Fanny Hill* (Paragon), and *Faster, Pussycat! Kill! Kill!* (RM), a number of Meyer titles are available on Russ's very own video label, the RM Bosomania series: *Beneath the Valley of the Ultravixens, Cherry, Harry & Raquel, Common-Law Cabin, Finders Keepers, Lovers' Weepers, Good Morning . . . and Goodbye, The Immoral Mr. Teas, Lorna, Mondo Topless, Mud Honey, Supervixens, Up!,* and *Vixen.*

Gambling with Souls (1936) NR B&W
D: *Elmer Clifton. Martha Chapin, Wheeler Oakman. 68 minutes. (Video Dimensions)*

When an unwise gal runs up a heavy gambling debt, she pays it off the hard way rather than tell her sober-minded hubby.

Hallucination (1966) ◆◆◇ B&W/color.
D: Edward Mann. George Montgomery, Danny Stone, Tom Baker. 90 minutes. (Vidcrest)

Montgomery, the former Mr. Dinah Shore, makes like Tim Leary and leads his youthful followers into an unforgettable acid sequence lensed in living color. Originally released theatrically as *Hallucination Generation.*

High School Confidential! (1958) ◆◆◆◇ B&W

D: Jack Arnold. Russ Tamblyn, Jan Sterling, John Drew Barrymore, Mamie Van Doren. 85 minutes. (Republic)

Undercover narc Tamblyn poses as Van Doren's high-school-student nephew so he can "size up this townsville" and ferret out local dope pushers (who include band leader Ray Anthony and former child star Jackie Coogan). Hipster Barrymore offers a jive version of Columbus's discovery of America; Jerry Lee Lewis bangs his 88s. An Al Zugsmith trashfest of the first rank.

Hollywood Confidential (1950) ◆◆◇ B&W

D: Klaytan W. Kirby. Dorothy Abbott, Thad Swift, Phil Rhodes. 55 minutes. (Hollywood Confidential/Marshall)

Based on the shocking expose "A Virgin in Hollywood," *Hollywood Confidential* stars Abbott as a virginal reporter looking for the lowdown on the Tinseltown sin scene. She finds a cheesecake photo shoot, a bad John Barrymore impersonator, a lengthy lingerie show, and a surprise cameo by the African fertility mask that would later achieve lasting fame in Ed Wood, Jr.'s, *Glen or Glenda?.* As stimulating as it is educational.

I Accuse My Parents (1944) ◆◆◇ B&W
D: Sam Newfield. Mary Beth Hughes, John Miljan. (Loonic, others)

A decent high school kid (who looks about twenty-nine) stumbles onto the criminal path due to the neglect of his well-heeled (and well-oiled) parents. Ed Wood's distaff version, *The Violent Years* (see index), is far superior, but this one's pretty entertaining in its own right.

Ilsa, the Wicked Warden (1979) ◆◆◆
D: Jess Franco. Dyanne Thorne, Lina Romay, Tanya Busselier, Eric Falk, Jess Franco. 90 minutes. (American Video Tape)

Dyanne Thorne is the blond dominatrix you love to hate and hate to love in this hilariously offensive cult-sleaze effort from the prolific Jess Franco. Originally known as *Wanda, the Wicked Warden* but retitled to exploit the notoriety Thorne had gained as the hateful, horny, and peripatetic Ilsa in the earlier trilogy *Ilsa, She-Wolf of the S.S.; Ilsa, Harem Keeper of the Oil Sheiks* (both American) and *Ilsa, Tigress of Siberia* (Cinepix). *Tigress* is also available, in a cut version, from Embassy. Even non-fans of the Aryan sex symbol must admit she sports an impressive résumé.

Kipling's Women (1963) NR

D: Harry and Larry Smith. Margie Sutton, Lisa Gordon, Felix De Cola. 50 minutes. (Video Dimensions)

Former pinup queen Margie Sutton stars in a Brit color nudie based on Kipling's "The Ladies" (!), that just *might* turn up on your local PBS.

Lash of the Penitentes (1937) ◆◆◇ B&W

D: Harry Revier. 37 minutes. (Sinister Cinema, others)

The first flick—"photographed at the risk of the cameramen's lives"—to expose the bizarre rites of the titular religious fanatics, who espouse self- (and other-) flagellation, crucifixions, and, in this pic, fleeting nudity. More fun than 1988's treatment of the same subject, *The Penitent* (IVE). This 37-minute version is apparently all that remains of the original feature.

Mad Youth (1939) ◆◆◇ B&W

D: Willis Kent. Mary Ainslee, Betty Compson. 67 minutes. (Sinister Cinema)

One of the '30s' trashier treatises on the perennial concern of Girls Who Go Too Far. Has a pretty nifty baton-twirling sequence, though.

Maniac (1934) ◆◆◆◇ B&W

D: Dwain Esper. Bill Woods, Horace Carpenter, Ted Edwards, Phyllis Diller. 51 minutes. (Video Yesteryear, others)

Exploitation-pic pioneer Dwain Esper, under his Roadshow Attrac-

tions banner, contributed a number of tarnished treasures to the junk-movie archives: Dope exposés like 1937's *"Marihuana," the Weed with Roots in Hell* (Video Yesteryear) and jungle exploitationers like 1941's *Boru, the Ape Boy* (Discount), as well as such shocking shorts as *March of Crime* (1937), *The Facts of Life* (1944), *Narcotic* (1937), and the immortal *How to Undress for Your Husband* (also 1937, obviously a big year for Dwain). Some bad-movie buffs see Esper as the '30s' answer to Ed Wood, Jr. (we shudder to think of the question!) when it came to combining the bizarre with the inept. Dwain and Ed even shared the same poverty-row cinematographer, William C. Thompson, who owns the dubious distinction of lensing Esper's *Maniac* in 1934 and Woods's *Plan 9 from Outer Space* two decades later.

Maniac remains Dwain's most enduring contribution to our bad-cinema archives. Scripted by Esper's better (if not necessarily more competent) half Hildegarde, *Maniac* opens in the basement lab of one Dr. Meierschultz (Carpenter), a demented medico who dreams of raising the dead. His equally addled assistant Maxwell (Woods)—a hammy vaudevillian on the lam from his avaricious ex-wife—decides to knock off the doc and assume his identity (complete with specs-and-beard disguise). Immediately thereafter, Maxwell is visited by hellacious visions (actually borrowed clips from the silent version of *Dante's Inferno*) and quickly degenerates into the title fiend.

Maniac is rife with memorable sequences, including one wherein a psychotic patient (Edwards) transforms before your very eyes into the "orangutan murderer from Poe's *Murders in the Rue Morgue*" (!). Throw in femme fights, brief nudity, and a scene in which the mad Maxwell devours a cat's eye (go figure), and you have one of the strangest sustained hallucinations ever to flicker before a grindhouse audience's disbelieving eyes. As an arresting officer notes at film's end, "Man, you're crazy!"

Marihuana (1936) ◆◆◆ B&W
D: Dwain Esper. Harley Wood, Hugh McArthur, Pat Carlyle. 57 minutes. (Video Yesteryear, others)

Dwain strikes again! A down-and-dirty dealer takes innocent young girls to his beachfront digs for a wild all-night reefer party filled with illicit laughter, fleeting nudity (courtesy of the flick's rather fleshy femmes), and of course, high tragedy. A notch below *Reefer Madness*, but still a lot of fun.

Married Too Young (1962) ◆◆◇ B&W
D: George Moskov. Harold Lloyd, Jr., Trudy Marshall, Anthony Dexter. 76 minutes. (Budget)

A tame but relatively entertaining cautionary tract re: the dangers of teen wedlock. Young Harold Lloyd, Jr.'s, efforts to provide for spouse Marshall lead to a criminal alliance with nabe ne'er-do-well Anthony (*Valentino*) Dexter. Near tragedy and a protracted courtroom lecture, à la Ed Wood, Jr.'s, *The Violent Years*, ensues. In fact, Ed is alleged to have had a hand in the script.

Mated (195?) NR B&W
(Channel 13)

This hilarious sex-misinformation flick is a staged lecture, replete with "frank" slides and footage, that pushes "bust development" as a technique for bringing married couples closer together. Amazing.

Mom and Dad (1947) ◆◆◆ B&W
D: William Beaudine. Hardie Albright, Lois Austin. 97 minutes. (Video Dimensions)

Exploitation king Kroger Babb produced and William ("One-Shot") Beaudine directed this infamous road-show perennial—a "Vital Educational Production Appealing to All True Americans"—that opens with a "Star-Spangled Banner" sing-along (!) before telling the time-worn tale of a good gal (Austin) whose lone illicit fling leads to lifelong misery. *Mom and Dad* is best remembered, though, for its lengthy childbirth inserts, "shocking" enough to keep the pic on the road-show and grindhouse circuit for nearly two decades.

(There's even an onscreen intermission so that live "noted hygienist" Mr. Elliott Forbes could pitch the rubes a facts-of-life-type pamphlet.) Another important historical contribution from the enterprising archivists at Video Dimensions.

Morals for Women (1931) NR B&W
Bessie Love, Conway Tearle. (Loonic)
Aka *Big City Interlude, Morals for Women* involves your standard innocent Jane who's recruited into a call-girl service by your archetypal fast-talking lowlife Romeo.

Mystery of Womanhood/Painless Childbirth (194?) NR B&W
(Channel 13)
Two vintage road-show sex-ed films, originally screened for sex-segregated audiences, that feature real live-birth footage. For the hardy.

Naked Complex (1964) ◆◆◇
D: Roy Mart. Dolores Carlos, Roy Savage, Mary Margaret. 64 minutes. (Channel 13)
Classic early-'60s nudie sleaze about a woman-shy guy helped over the hump of his title condition by fun-and-sun-loving nudist gals (!). Filmed at Tampa, Florida's, famed Sunshine Beach Club, where it could have happened.

Naked Venus (1958) NR B&W
Patricia Conelle. 80 minutes. (Video Dimensions)
Nudist girl and clothed boy try to iron out their differences in this daring social-issue-oriented skinflick from those irrepressible French.

Naked Youth (1960) ◆◆◇ B&W
D: John F. Schreyer. Robert Hutton, Carol Ohmart, Steve Rowland. 80 minutes. (Rhino)
Ads for the film's original release (as *Wild Youth*) promised to show patrons an actual junkie in the act of shooting up! What it lacks in talent and tension, this entry in Rhino's Teenage Theater series makes up for in pure sleaze. An important addition to the understocked JD/exploitation video archives.

Nation Aflame! (1937) ◆◆ B&W
D: Victor Halperin. Noel Madison, Norma Trelvar, Lila Lee, Douglas Walton, Harry Holman, Snub Pollard. 70 minutes. (Sinister Cinema)
A combination exploitation flick and oblique attack on the Ku Klux Klan and similar secret organizations, *Nation Aflame!* follows the rise of five former real-estate frauds who cynically form the antiforeigner Avenging Angels league. Walton is ambitious sleazeball Frank Sands (née Sandino) who heads the group; Madison is his honest DA nemesis (though, oddly, *he's* the one wearing the symbolically evil pencil-line moustache here); Trelvar is the confused society girl caught 'twixt the twain. Pollard, sans trademark handlebar moustache, plays one of the villains while si-

multaneously supplying low-comedy relief (!). Created by the Halperin Brothers, of *White Zombie* fame, *Nation Aflame!* isn't much of a movie (the story is often propelled via the hoary newspaper-headline approach), but it should be of interest to pulp-history students.

Not Wanted (1949) ◆◇ B&W
D: Elmer Clifton. Sally Forrest, Keefe Brasselle, Leo Penn. 94 minutes. (Loonic)

There's more soap than sleaze in this marginal tearjerker, co-scripted by Ida Lupino, about an unwed mother's efforts to repay society for her "sins."

Paradisio (1962) ◆◇ B&W/color
D: Jacques Henri. Arthur Howard, Eva Waegner. 62 minutes. (New World)

Leslie Howard's black-sheep brother Arthur mugs outrageously in this Brit-lensed *Immoral Mr. Teas*–type affair about a lecherous but timid academic who finds a pair of magic specs that enable him to see gals naked, in color, *and* 3-D (a dimension the New World vid version loses). This painful exercise actually received mucho hoopla in its time, including a gala *Playboy* tie-in, as the first "nudie cutie" to go first class (i.e., it was lensed—cheaply—in several authentic Euro-locations). Recommended for dedicated exploitation historians only.

Party Girls (1929) NR B&W
D: Victor Halperin. Douglas Fairbanks, Jr. 67 minutes. (Sinister Cinema)

Jazz-age sleaze about flappers who go too far at a wild party. One of Fairbanks Jr.'s first film roles, as a 1929 yuppie type who tries to duck out on a gal in trouble. Helmed by Victor (*White Zombie*) Halperin.

The Payoff (1938) NR
(Loonic)

A lurid anti-alcohol short in a *Reefer Madness* vein, unearthed by Loonic.

Pin-Down Girls (1951) ◆◆◆ B&W
D: Robert C. Derteno. Timothy Farrell, Peaches Page, Clara Mortensen, Rita Martinez, Muriel Gardner, Don Ferrar. 65 minutes. (Sinister Cinema)

The great Timothy (*Glen or Glenda?*, *Jail Bait*) Farrell gives another of his patented sleazeball perfs as Scali, a mustachioed jack-of-all-rackets who runs a bookie operation, peddles pills, procures for a local cathouse, dopes horses, and—most central to our story—promotes up-and-coming lady wrestlers like bosomy blond bombshell Peaches Page. Produced by the ubiquitous George Weiss and lensed by William C. Thompson, *Pin-Down Girls* is structured around two prolonged stretches of actual mat footage, principally of then–World Champ Mortensen and Mexican Canvas Queen Martinez (who also put in brief thespic cameos), plus lots of jiggle-shots of Peaches doing her roadwork and her fellow distaff gym rats going through their bending and stretching paces. A simple plot eventually materializes when

Scali gets heat from a rival racketeer (imaginatively monikered Mr. Big!), testifies against him in the world's smallest courtroom (even tinier than the one viewed in Ed Wood, Jr.'s, *The Violent Years*), and eventually pays the ultimate gangland price. Director Robert C. (*Gun Girls*) Derteno lacks Ed Wood's flair, but Farrell, his hardworking femmes, and Ferrar as his diminutive minion Joe the Jockey make this sleazy cheesecake epic worth watching. The Sinister Cinema cassette also includes trailers for *Assassin of Youth* and the incredible *Dance Hall Racket*, wherein Farrell miraculously returns to life to reprise his Scali character.

Pleasure (1931) NR B&W
D: Otto Brower. Conway Tearle, Roscoe Karnes. (Loonic)

An obscure antidrinking disquisition detailing the ruinous effects of alcohol on young lives, rediscovered by Loonic's dedicated celluloid anthropologists.

Protect Your Daughters (1932) NR B&W
Doris Eaton, Betty Grable. (Sinister Cinema)

One of the more outrageous antivice tracts of the late Prohibition era, *Protect Your Daughters* reportedly proffers its share of high-camp fun.

The Psychic (1968) ◆
D: Herschell Gordon Lewis. Dick Genola, Robyn Guest. 90 minutes. (Camp)

The titular telepath possesses the power to "control men's minds and corrupt their women!" in a dull H. G. Lewis teaser alternatively known as *Copenhagen's Psychic Loves*. The pic's a bore, but the overexcited trailer for same is well worth repeated viewings.

Red Kimono (1925) NR B&W
D: Walter Lang. Tyrone Power, Sr., Priscilla Bonner. 100 minutes. (Video Yesteryear)

A cut above the usual sleazoid morality play, Lang's New Orleans–set tale of "the temptations and struggles of a modern Magdalen" was scripted by Adela Rogers St. John and Dorothy Arzner (who would later make her mark as one of Hollywood's first female directors). Silent with music score and correct projection speed.

Reefer Madness (1938) ◆◆◆◇ B&W
D: Louis Gasnier. Dave O'Brien, Dorothy Short, Warren McCollum. 67 minutes. (Sinister Cinema, others)

The film that put elderly exploitation movies on the contemporary camp map has probably enjoyed a wider audience than all its sleaze-bijou brethren combined. Gasnier's fast-paced anti-tea frolic, encouraged by ambitious DEA honcho Harry J. Anslinger (then embroiled in a fierce publicity war with rival image-obsessed FBI head J. Edgar Hoover), relates how a foursome of pot pushers infiltrate a local high school hangout, stage wild jitterbug, make-out, and marijuana parties, and ruin the young lives of what could have been the future leaders of our land. Highlights include busy B thesp Dave O'Brien's manic portrayal of a hard-core "addict," a sensational trial sequence, and the one-toke-over-the-line grass bashes themselves. Just about every public-domain sell-through outfit stocks *Reefer*, which is well worth adding to your permanent home-vid library.

Revenge of the Virgins (1961) ◆◆ B&W

D: Paul Perry, Jr. Charles Veltman, Jodean Russo, Stan Pritchard. 70 minutes. (Mike Lebell Video, others)

Ed Wood, Jr., regular Kenne Duncan narrates a dull grade-Z western, enlivened only by the occasional participation of your typical topless all-femme Indian tribe (!). Available from Lebell Video on a double bill with *Child Bride*.

Road to Ruin (1934) ◆◆◆ B&W

D: Melville Shyer, Mrs. Wallace Reid. Helen Foster, Nell O'Day, Glen Boles, Bobby Quirk, Paul Page, Richard Hemingway. 68 minutes. (Sinister Cinema)

"Eve, do you let boys *kiss* you?" That seemingly innocent query, posed by Eve's friend Ann (Foster), steers our heroine toward the titular destination in this remake of the 1928 (NA) silent of the same name. Both were produced (and this one "co-directed") by Mrs. Wallace Reid—the enterprising widow of matinee-idol-turned-morphine-fatality Wallace Reid—who kicked off her long-lived exploitation-flick career with 1923's evocatively titled *Human Wreckage* (NA). Actually, in *Road to Ruin* our gals get to have a pretty high time of it for several reels—smoking, drinking, partaking of strip crap-games and naked pool parties, and generally slutting it up to their hearts' content. When punishment time at last arrives, it does so with merciless alacrity, as Ann gets busted and branded a "sex delinquent," learns she's pregnant, has an abortion, and dies. Friend Eve escapes with naught but a curable social disease. Withal, one of the era's livelier wages-of-sin romps.

Room 43 (1958) NR B&W

Diana Dors, Eddie Constantine, Herbert Lom. 93 minutes. (Video Dimensions)

Also known as *The Girl in Room 43*, which refers to buxom star Dors, who's involved with a white-slavery ring.

Saturday Night Sleazies, Vols. 1–3 NR B&W/color

150 minutes each. (Rhino)

A sextet of authentic soft-core '60s sex flicks, all directed by Ed Wood collaborator A. C. (*Orgy of the Dead*) Stephen. Vol. 1 offers *Suburbia Confidential* (1966) and *College Girl Confidential* (1968), while vol. 2 features the lighter-hearted *Lady Godiva* (1969) and *The Bachelor's Dream* (1968), and vol. 3 pairs *Motel Confidential* (1967) with *Office Love-In* (1968). Sleaze lovers should be warned, though, that *Suburbia Confidential* is missing an entire reel.

Secret File: Hollywood (1962) ♦♦◇ B&W

D: Ralph Cushman. Robert Clarke, Francine York, Syd Mason, Maralou Gray, John Warburton, Bill White. 85 minutes. (Loonic)

It's Follow the Bouncing Boom time! Yes, this cheesy 1962 sleaze indie sets the all-time celluloid record for Most Visible Boom Mike Shots in a single film. It follows our hero, Robert (*Hideous Sun Demon*) Clarke—an ex-shamus (his license was revoked after his involvement in a "beatnik club" shoot-out, itself a scene that cops Most Bullfight Posters in a Single Set honors) now working for the titular scandal rag—everywhere he goes. Ed Wood, Jr., addicts, meanwhile, will immediately recognize snatches of the *Plan 9* theme on the audio track, while Bob and Ray buffs can detect the strains of the Hawaiian instrumental that intro'd the radio duo's "Wayside Doctor" playing incessantly during the gala Hollywood party scene. *Secret File: Hollywood* also anticipates the later spate of celeb lawsuits brought against its scandal-sheet model, *The National Enquirer*. In short, this vintage cheapie, while admittedly a tad on the static side, has something for everyone.

The Seventh Commandment (1958) ♦♦♦ B&W

D: Irvin Berwick. Jonathan Kidd, Lyn Stratten, Frank Arvidson, Wendy Berwick, Wayne Berwick, John Carpenter. 92 minutes. (Loonic)

Another bizarre noir gem rescued from oblivion via the wonderful world of video—in this case, courtesy of the offbeat folks at Loonic. Kidd, star of the even rarer should-be cult item *Wink of an Eye* (still not available on tape), is an adulted grad on a hot date with blond hussy Stratten. After they plow into an oncoming car, Kidd wanders away from the wreck and, suffering from total amnesia, hooks up with an impoverished traveling preacher. Seven years later, Kidd's a veritable Jimmy Swaggart, equipped not only with elocutive but with genuine healing powers! When Stratten, who did time for the accident, chances to see Kidd's picture in the paper, she cooks up a belated blackmail scheme, and it's here that the fun *really* begins. Among *The Seventh Commandment*'s sundry perverse charms is a sleazola wedding scene, second only to *Homicidal*'s. Look for obscure self-styled B-western hero and future Ed Wood, Jr., thesp John (*Night of the Ghouls*) Carpenter in a bit role. Young Wayne Berwick later grew up to direct *Microwave Massacre* (see index).

Sex (1920) NR B&W

D: Fred Niblo. Louise Glaum, William Conklin, Irving Cummings. 94 minutes. (Video Yesteryear)

Chronicles the fast and loose times of a Broadway starlet as she travels, according to a flash card, "The High-road of Surfeited Folly." The moral? "The standards of morality eternally demand that the naked soul of Sex be stripped of its falsehoods—which can only be atoned for through bitter tears." With music score.

Sex Madness (1934) ◆◆◆ B&W
53 minutes. (Video Yesteryear)

This relentlessly grim, hopelessly incompetent warning re: the ravages of VD (originally titled *They Must Be Told!*) and expertly spoofed by director Joe Dante in the comedy anthology *Amazon Women on the Moon*, tells the cautionary tale of an aspiring showgirl whose one-night stand leads to a lifetime of grief. Our heroine's case is further complicated when she innocently consults a vicious quack for treatment. Believing herself cured, she marries her small-town beau (who promptly goes blind) and gives birth to a blue-hued baby (who promptly expires). Watch for the prop window that accidentally slams shut in midscene (!). The type of flick that taught Ed Wood, Jr., most—if not all—he knew.

Shame (1961) ◆◆◆ B&W
D: Roger Corman. William Shatner, Frank Maxwell, Beverly Lunsford. 80 minutes. (Sinister Cinema)

A rare message-movie from Roger Corman! Originally titled *The In-truder* (and later reissued as *I Hate Your Guts!*), *Shame* stars Shatner as an itinerant hate-monger who stirs up racial unrest in a small southern town in an excellent—if unsung—civil rights drama pitched as an exploitation pic. Not to be confused with the 1988 femme-oriented Aussie action import *Shame* (Republic) or the Ingmar Bergman despair-fest of the same name (NA).

She Should'a Said No (1949) ◆◆◆ B&W
D: Sherman Scott. Lila Leeds, Alan Baxter, Michael Whelan, Lyle Talbot, Jack Elam, David Gorcey. 70 minutes. (Sinister Cinema)

Original ads for *She Should'a Said No* (aka *Wild Weed* and *The Devil's Weed*) promised patrons they'd witness how "the happy, normal laughter of physically adorable young girls gives way to the hysterical outbursts of dope-maddened women." (Hey, everybody's gotta grow up *sometime*!) Star Leeds—who had recently been released after serving six months on an infamous marijuana bust that also netted better-known thesp Robert Mitchum—apparently accepted the role as part of her postpenal penance and frequently delivered in-person antidrug lectures following road-show-circuit screenings. Produced by exploitation-pic pioneer Kroger (*Bob and Sally*) Babb under his Hallmark Roadshow Attractions banner, this already anachronistic *Reefer Madness Revisited* throwback is not without its high points, including the usual guided tour of marijuana's hopeless victims, plus a great hallucinatory piano-fantasy sequence (with "Chopsticks" performed by Rudolf Friml, Jr.) that puts *Reefer*'s keyboard scenes ("Faster! Play faster!") to shame. We likewise applaud Alicia Adams's choreographic contributions and the flick's special Theremin Effects. Besides Lila, Babb's "All-Star Hollywood Cast" includes Baxter as big-time pusher Markey, David (Brother of Leo) Gorcey as one of tea's tragic young victims, still-active heavy Elam in his youthful thug days, and perennial exploitation-pic authority figure Talbot as a cop.

Single Room Furnished (1968) NR

D: Matt Cimber. Jayne Mansfield, Dorothy Keller, Bruno VeSota (as "Mr. Duck"). With "Introductory Comments" by Walter Winchell. 93 minutes. (United)

Jayne's then-hubby Matt Cimber directed this grim story of a busty blonde's ill-advised *affaires de coeur* with a succession of unworthy men.

Street of Forgotten Women (1925) NR B&W

55 minutes. (Video Yesteryear)

A silent-screen exposé on the perils of prostitution, long thought (perhaps hoped) lost, but salvaged by the archivists at Sinister Cinema.

Striporama (195?) NR B&W

Sally Rand, Betty Rowland, Virginia Bell, Scarlet Knight, Helene Renee. 50 minutes. (Video Dimensions)

A collection of '50s burlesque acts featuring many of the top ecdysiasts of the day. See also Video Dim's *Teaserama* assortment.

Striptease College Girls (195?) NR B&W

(Channel 13)

A behind-the-scenes look at the simultaneously comic and curvy capers unfolding at Striptease College. Higher education is also the theme of *The Student Body*, paired with *Jailbait Babysitter* (Cinema Group).

Striptease Murder Case (195?) NR B&W

(Channel 13)

A naughty no-budget noir that, as the title indicates, provides an excuse for the camera to peek in on a few semiclad backstage strippers.

Striptease Terror (195?) NR B&W

(Channel 13)

Easily the weirdest of Channel 13's cheesecake quickies, with strippers performing for and/or with assorted demons, monsters, and apes.

Sweet Ecstasy (1962) B&W

D: Max Pecas. Elke Sommer, Pierre Brice, Vittoria Prada. 75 minutes. (Video Dimensions)

A soft-core Riviera romp with Aryan starlet Sommer, glimpsed briefly in the altogether, being courted by a pair of wealthy play-boys. For Elke's hard-core admirers.

Teenage Devil Dolls (1955) ♦♦ B&W
D: Bramlett L. Price. Barbara Marks, Robert A. Sherry, Robert Norman, Elaine Lindenbaum, Joel Climenhaga, B. L. Price, Sr. 70 minutes. (Rhino)

Bramlett L. Price's "semi-documentary" One-Way Ticket to Hell (retitled by Rhino for its Teenage Theater series) charts the decline of one Cassandra (Marks), an unstable eighteen-year-old who falls in with pot-smoking "bikers," graduates to H, and eventually gains admission to the title destination. The story is related via dull silent footage fueled (if that's the word, and it's probably not) by an equally monotonous Dragnet-style voice-over. The flick itself may be boring, but it does have an interesting history. Filmmaker Price was a UCLA grad student who submitted the $14,000 work as his thesis. The movie went on not only to cop first prize in the Screen Producers Guild Intercollegiate Awards competition (narrowly besting such fierce filmic rivals as This Is College Radio, The Living Room of the University, and Clay on Your Hands [a probing look at pottery]), but to secure widespread commercial release and (believe it or not) critical acclaim (!). The New York Times, for one, saw fit to extol its palmary portrayal of "how high schoolers go the 'route' from marijuana to morphine," while simultaneously expressing gratitude that the film (as perhaps befits a creation of the Silent Generation) was "fortunately without sound," especially during those scenes depicting the "convulsions and frothing at the mouth typical of narcotics withdrawal." The Paper of Record's reviewer felt more generous in '55 than your Phantom does today; we can recommend Teenage Devil Dolls only for the most dedicated of armchair celluloid sociologists.

Teenage Wolfpack (1958) NR B&W
D: Georg Tressler. Horst Buckholz (Henry Bookholt), Karen Baal, Christian Doermer. 90 minutes. (Madhouse)

An obscure West German JD flick, starring the young Horst Buckholz (then Henry Bookholt) as the surly leader of the title gang. A reel rarity from the folks at Madhouse.

Test Tube Babies (1953) NR B&W
D: W. Merle Connell. John Maitland, Monica Davis. 70 minutes. (Sinister Cinema, others)

This relevant George Weiss film poses the musical question: "How would you solve the problem of not being able to fulfill your marital obligations?" (Well, we're waiting!) Re-released in the Swingin' '60s, with new footage, as The Pill.

This Nude World (1932) NR B&W
55 minutes. (Video Dimensions)

This early Mondo Nudo exercise offers a campy glimpse at naturists around the world, from Germany and France to New York's Camp Olympia—including a rare look at the pioneering Great Birthday Suit Racing Association.

Three Nuts In Search of a Bolt (1964) ◆◇

D: Tommy Noonan. Mamie Van Doren, Ziva Rodann, Tommy Noonan. 80 minutes. (Simitar)

A groan-a-minute sex "comedy" buoyed by Mamie's unique presence and the always-welcome Ziva Rodann. "Comic" director/costar and former Pete Marshall partner Noonan would have been a worthy subtraction, though. See also *Promises! Promises!* (Simitar), wherein Jayne Mansfield goes the nudie farce route.

Tomorrow's Children (1934) ◆◆◇ B&W

D: Crane Wilbur. Sterling Holloway, Diana Douglas, Donald Douglas. 55 minutes. (Video Yesteryear, others)

A pro-mandatory-sterilization film; our lovely heroine is saved from the procedure only when it's learned she's an *adopted* member of her genetically tainted family of cripples, lushes, and perverts. Scary stuff from producer Brian Foy, the man who brought us *Elysia* (see index).

Tonight for Sure (1961) ◆◆

D: Francis Ford Coppola. Don Kenney, Virginia Gordon, Marli Renfro. 66 minutes. (Video Yesteryear)

Coppola's directorial debut limns a tale of two prudes who cruise California strip joints for evidence of distaff indecency. Guess what? They find it. FFC filmed this tame nudie while still at UCLA; dad Carmen Coppola supplied the musical score. A must for Coppola completists, as is *Bellboy and the Playgirls* (Ingram), a 1958 West Germany–lensed June Wilkinson frolic to which Coppola added a new color sequence (originally shot in 3-D to show June to her best advantage) for the flick's U.S. release.

Trapped by the Mormons (1922) NR B&W

D: H. B. Parkinson. E. Brent. 65 minutes. (Grapevine)

An early religious exploitation number, allegedly banned in the U.S.A. for decades, rediscovered by the silent-film buffs at Grapevine Video. An ideal companion piece for *Lash of the Penitentes* (see index).

Two Nights with Cleopatra (1954) NR

D: Mario Mattoli. Sophia Loren, Alberto Sordi, Ettore Manni. 77 minutes. (Video Dimensions)

Nineteen-year-old Sophia Loren plays the titular Egyptian princess in a slapstick comedy noteworthy mainly for Sophia's infamous starkers swim scene. Unreleased stateside till 1963.

Unashamed (1938) NR B&W

D: Allen Stuart. Rae Kidd, Emily Todd. 67 minutes. (Moore Video)

An early nudist-colony romp, which is reportedly low on eroticism but high on unintentional laughs.

The Unkissed Bride (1966) ◆◇
D: Jack H. Harris. Tommy Kirk, Anne Helm, Jacques Bergerac. 82 minutes. (New World)

Also—and more imaginatively—titled *Mother Goose a Go-Go* (!), this "sophisticated" sex farce stars former Disney towhead Kirk as a virginal groom. With Joe Pyne and Henny Youngman as "themselves." Pretty gruesome.

Virtue's Revolt (1924) NR B&W
Edith Thornton, Crawford Kent. 51 minutes. (Video Dimensions)

Silent howler about a small-town girl who braves the knaves, crooks, and lechers of show-biz hell, only to learn a grim and painful lesson.

What's Up Front (1964) NR
D: Arch Hall, Sr. Tommy Holden, Marilyn Manning. 90 minutes. (Rhino)

When he wasn't busy shaping his son's career, Arch Hall, Sr., cranked out soft-core farces like this breast-obsessed account of a door-to-door bra salesman, costarring Hall regular Manning, seen to more memorable effect as Arch Jr.'s dim-witted squeeze in *The Sadist* (see index).

Wild Women (1951) ◆◆◇ B&W
Lewis Wilson, Frances Dubay, Dana Wilson. 75 minutes. (Channel 13)

A tame, rather pathetic home movie about a backyard jungle trek through miles and miles of perilous stock footage, borrowed from dozens of known and unknown sources, leading to an encounter with the all-femme Bowanga tribe. The prop guy's arm is visible through much of one crucial scene. Pretty entertaining if you're in the right frame of mindlessness.

CINEMA VERITASTELESS:
SHOCKUMENTARIES, MONDO MOVIES, & PROPAGANDA PICS

"Every scene looks you straight in the eye—and spits!"

Africa, Blood and Guts

Shock It to Me!

For your further home-viewing enlightenment, we offer the following rundown of some of the more popular and/or curious "shockumentaries"—i.e., documentaries whose aim, in the main, is to titillate more than to enlighten, sort of the celluloid equivalents of "tabloid TV"—currently available on cassette. These range from such early "educational" fare as *Borneo* and *Beyond the Caribbean* (where bare native breasts often prove more prevalent than scholarly analyses of local cultures), through the more candidly exploitative "Mondo" movies of the '60s, a subgenre spawned by the influential *Mondo Cane* (or "Dog's World"), the flick that coined the "Mondo" term.

We've also included several speculative "documentary" specials catering to the conspiracy fads of the '70s and '80s: *Chariots of the Gods?, The Devil's Triangle,* and the belated Nostradamus-based shocku-cult fave *The Man Who Saw Tomorrow.* Several rare, bizarre propaganda efforts—from elaborate Leni Riefenstahl Nazi salutes like *Triumph of the Will* to the Klan-produced *Anarchy, USA*—are likewise listed for the edification of couchside historians.

In this chapter, you'll also find many of those "underground" films of the '50s through '70s that, while artistic in intent and sometimes in execution, dealt frankly with subject matter (e.g., transvestism in Shirley Clarke's *Portrait of Jason,* interracial love in John Cassavetes's intense quasi-fiction film debut *Shadows*) viewed as *verboten* by the mainstream media of the day. These often employed a *cinema verité* approach. Most of the propaganda and underground films, though rarely seen in local vidstores, can be ordered through several of the mail-order video specialists listed in our Videorama section.

As in the case of the more obscure exploitation oldies covered in the previous chapter, credits are spotty on some of the older, rarer titles and are often missing from the tapes themselves. We've refrained from rating most of the vintage shocku-videos given here, since subject matter and curiosity value often outweigh their overall quality, and what may be of intense interest to one viewer could well represent pure torture to the next. The most important thing to know is that the following shockumentaries—many of which had been feared lost forever prior to their video resurrections—are out there for those who want to watch them.

Africa, Blood and Guts (1966) NR
D: Gualtiero Jacopetti, Franco Prosperi. 90 minutes. (Vidcrest)

Formerly *Africa Addio,* this *Mondo Africa,* while incorporating some gruesome footage, is actually a fairly thoughtful comparative look at various African cultures.

After Mein Kampf (1940) NR B&W
43 minutes. (Video Yesteryear)

Famous British propaganda film uses cartoons, newsreel footage, dramatizations, and a minimum of subtlety and restraint to recreate Hitler's rise to power.

Anarchy, USA (1966) NR
78 minutes. (Video Yesteryear)

A truly amazing reactionary anti–civil rights "documentary" charting Commie attempts to establish a Soviet Negro Republic (!) right here in the U.S.A. A hate-mongering voice-over and obviously doctored footage fail to help this brain-damaged docu's credibility.

The Atomic Cafe (1982) ◆◆◆ Color/B&W
D: Kevin Rafferty, Pierce Rafferty, Jayne Loader. 92 minutes. (HBO)

An ace montage assembled from '40s and '50s news and propaganda clips offering utterly useless and latently lethal misinformation re: our New Atomic Age. Co-director Jayne Loader went on to pen the Hollywood trash-novel parody *Between Pictures*.

Atrocities of the Orient (1958) NR B&W
Fernando Roya, Linda Estrella. 78 minutes. (Video Dimensions)

A Filipino exploitation version of the Japanese invasion, liberally laced with actual atrocity footage, along with heavy doses of propaganda, resistance fighting, romance, and musical interludes (!). Unique.

Beyond the Caribbean (1932) NR B&W
(J&J)

A precocious Mondo movie in documentary disguise, this leering look at voodoo ceremonies, replete with staged native violence, ranks right up (or down, depending on your POV) there with the most blatant exploitation flicks.

Borneo (1937) NR B&W
D: Martin Johnson. Martin and Osa Johnson. Narrated by Lowell Thomas. 76 minutes. (Video Yesteryear)

Popular explorers Osa and Martin Johnson's final documentary fling takes them into the wilds of Borneo, where they encounter orangutans, flying snakes, and hostile headhunters. With a "comic" commentary by Lew Lehr, replete with racist jabs.

Bride of the Beast (1932) NR B&W
D: Martin Johnson. Martin and Osa Johnson. 57 minutes (Video Dimensions)

The Johnsons journey through the dark continent in search of wildlife, pausing long enough to offer racist observations re: the native populations.

The Brig (1964) ◆◆◆◇ B&W
D: Jonas Mekas. The Living Theater. 65 minutes. (Mystic Fire)

One of many long-neglected underground films rescued from oblivion by the folks at Mystic Fire Video, *The Brig* is Jonas Mekas's docu filming of the Living Theater's astounding (if exhausting) production of Kenneth Brown's play, a semi-*verité* exercise set in a Marine stockade. Mystic Fire also carries the Living Theater's *Para-*

dise Now and *Signals Through the Flames.*

Burroughs: The Movie (1985) NR
D: Howard Brookner. William S. Burroughs, Patti Smith, Allen Ginsberg, Terry Southern. 87 minutes. (Small Press)

A feature-length look at the renowned nihilistic novelist's surreal life, times, and works. Ideal viewing for the *Naked Lunch* bunch.

Cannibal Island (1956) NR B&W
60 minutes. (VCR)

A typically racist docu-look at "primitive" rites in modern Africa. Despite the pic's '56 copyright, the footage appears to be of 1930s vintage. For hard-core cassette curiosity-seekers only. Other newly issued African shock-docs include 1932's *Africa Speaks* (Video Yesteryear) and *Masters of the Congo Jungle* (Video Dimensions), narrated by Orson Welles.

The Commies Are Coming, The Commies Are Coming! (1953) ◆◆◆ B&W
Jack Webb, Jack Kelly, Jeanne Cooper. 60 minutes. (Rhino)

A pair of outrageous Red Menace docudramas, including the classic *Red Nightmare*, narrated by Commie-basher supreme Jack (*Dragnet*) Webb and starring future *Maverick* costar Kelly as Jerry, a Typical American Citizen. As Jack puts it, "Let's give Jerry a nightmare ... a real *Red* nightmare!"

The Connection (1961) ◆◆◇ B&W
D: Shirley Clarke. Warren Finnerty, Carl Lee, William Redfield. 105 minutes. (Mystic Fire)

Jack Gelber's then-radical *verité* beat play about a bunch of philosophical junkies sitting around talking dates pretty badly, but it still features strong performances (especially by the late Finnerty as whiny addict Leach) and considerable curiosity value.

Dances Sacred and Profane (1985) NR
D: Dan and Mark Jury. 80 minutes. (Mystic Fire)

Photog Charles Gatewood leads viewers on a Mondo tour that includes such mandatory sights as a Gotham S&M spot, an Indiana nudist club, and a look at California Hindu rites.

Dario Argento's World of Horror (1985) ◆◆◇
Dario Argento. 76 minutes. (Vidmark)

A behind-the-scenes look at the Italo terror master at work, *World of Horror* alternates generally interesting segments detailing Dario's screen techniques with sometimes repetitious interviews with the man himself. A must for Argento advocates, though.

DopeMania (1987) B&W/color
60 minutes. (Rhino)

A compilation of drug-related propaganda clips culled both from fictional exploitation flicks and from vintage "public service" spots. Rhino applies the same treatment to sexual propaganda in *Rhino's Guide to Safe Sex.*

Fabulous Fifties: Fads and Faces (1959) NR B&W/color
30 minutes. (Moore)

An iconic tribute to the Populuxe period, featuring rare TV, newsreel, and movie clips.

The Fabulous Sixties, Vols. 1–11 (1987) NR
Narrated by Peter Jennings. 60 minutes each. (MPI)

Want an eleven-volume overview of the decade in question, narrated by "expert" Peter Jennings? Well, MPI's got it waiting for *you!*

Fangoria's Weekend of Horrors (1986) NR
D: Tobe Hooper, Wes Craven. Robert Englund. 60 minutes. (Media)

The famed horror-and-gore mag—along with host Robert (Freddy) Englund—takes you inside the scary world of horror-film conventions. For *Fango's* salute to today's reigning makeup FX maven, check out Damon Santostefano's *Scream Greats, Vol. 1: Tom Savini, Master of Horror Effects.* Volume 2, *Satanism and Witchcraft* (both Paramount), focuses on real-life satanists and black-arts cultists.

Go! Go! Go! World (1966) NR
D: Anthony Dawson (Antonio Marghueriti), Renato Marui. 82 minutes. (Video Yesteryear)

One of the earliest *Mondo Cane* clones focuses on strip-teasers around the world, bikinis at Cannes, the "bloodsuckers" of Tobruk, dog-eating Hawaiians, and similar savory attractions.

Heaven (1987) ◆◆◆ B&W/color
D: Diane Keaton. 80 minutes. (Pacific Arts)

Though pretty much dismissed by most mainstream critics, Keaton's exploration of pop-cultural images of postlife paradise is a mostly clever, inventive, and often perverse compilation of choice film clips and interviews. On the down side, Keaton places too many out-and-out crackpots in front of the camera, which tends to dilute the film's integrity, and the entire epic goes on too long. But Keaton makes excellent use of clips culled from such variegated fare as *Metropolis, A Guy Named Joe,* and even *The Hypnotic Eye,* along with rare, scary Christian propaganda pieces, and her mock shockdoc, sort of a "Mondo Heaven," *does* address humankind's fundamental desire to believe in an afterlife. See also Errol Morris's pet-cemetery ode *Gates of Heaven* (RCA/Columbia); Morris also directs the chilling crime documentary *The Thin Blue Line* (HBO).

Hell's Angels Forever (1983) NR
D: Richard Chase, Kevin Keating, Leon Gast. With Bo Diddley, Jerry Garcia, Willie Nelson, and the Hell's Angels. 93 minutes. (Media)

An inside look at the way it was, is, and will be within the wonderful world of those free spirits on wheels, the Hell's Angels. There won't be a dry eye in the living room by the time this tape runs through your VCR.

The Hellstrom Chronicle (1971) ◆
D: Walon Green. Lawrence Pressman. 90 minutes. (RCA/Columbia)

Paranoid entymologist Professor Hellstrom (Pressman) babbles about an imminent insect takeover to provide an unintentionally hilarious frame for what's essentially your standard boring educational bug-related documentary. This actually opened wide in theaters across the country back in '71.

Hollywood Babylon (1971) ◇ B&W/color
D: Van Guylder. Jim Gentry, Myron Griffin, Ushi Digart. 90 minutes. (Neon)

This is a carelessly assembled compendium of antique film clips, stock footage, and newsreel items intercut with ludicrously staged soft-core "reenactments" of bygone Tinseltown sex scandals and held together by a wretchedly written voice-over. Even the brief presence of former Russ Meyer vixen Digart fails to elevate the proceedings. Stick with the book and boycott this unauthorized rip-off. Or try MPI's factoid *Hollywood Scandals and Tragedies* series.

Hollywood Ghost Stories (1986) ◆◆◆ B&W/color
D: James Forsher. Elke Sommer, William Peter Blatty, Susan Strasberg, Frank DeFelitta. 75 minutes. (Warner)

One of the Phantom's faves: a brain-damaged investigation into the title subject, hosted by the venerable John Carradine, wherein heavyweights like Elke Sommer describe spooky Tinseltown incidents, interspersed with some choice fright-flick clips. The pic also offers a classic example of high-concept Hollywoodthink when *Amityville Horror* producer Elliot Geisinger explains why that allegedly haunted house's original owners couldn't have been perpetrating a hoax: "What kind of gain could they possibly get from leaving the house and walking away from it? They didn't have a book contract when they left the house. Even if they *did* have a book contract, there was no guarantee the book would possibly be a bestseller. They did not have a movie contract. And if they *did* have a movie contract, there was no guarantee the movie would come out and be successful." Now *that's* scary!

Hollywood Uncensored (1987) ◆◆◇ B&W/color
D: James Forsher. Hosted by Douglas Fairbanks, Jr., Peter Fonda. With Mamie Van Doren, Martin Scorsese, Carroll Baker, Eli Wallach. 77 minutes. (IVE)

A spotty survey of Hollywood's ever-mutating censorship policies from the pre-Hays Era to the present, this compilation tape may be of more interest to buffs than to casual viewers. Highlights include brief clips from such candid early pre-Code fare as *Party Girl, Baby Face* (with a slutty Barbara Stanwyck), Dwain Esper's immortal *Love Life of a Gorilla* (aka *Forbidden Adventure*), and choice *verboten* moments from the original *King Kong*. Doug Fairbanks, Jr., and Peter Fonda make for adequate but hardly riveting hosts. In the interview segments, Scorsese scores best with his illustrated discussion of Michael Powell's perverse cult fave *Peeping Tom*, and Van Doren, seen here reminiscing re: such Albert Zugsmith sleazoid specials as *Girls Town* and *High School Confidential*, is always welcome on the Phantom's TV. Otherwise, selective fast-forwarding is advised.

Jabberwalk (1973) NR
110 minutes. (Video City)

A walk on the vile side through then-contempo America, focusing on everything from recreational torture dungeons to that old standby, female mud-wrestling, plus a particularly painful tattoo sequence. *Jabberwalk II*, offering more of the same, is likewise available from Video City.

Koyaanisqatsi: Life Out of Balance (1983) ◆◆◆
D: Godfrey Reggio. 87 minutes. (Pacific Arts)

Reggio's cinematic tone poem, set to Philip Glass's mesmerizing music, is a visually hypnotic meditation on modern civ, the *Gone With the Wind* of underground abstract film. We dozed through maybe half of it but still had a pretty good time. Not so with Reggio's pretentious follow-up, *Powasqatsi* (NA).

Lightning over Water (1980) NR
D: Wim Wenders. Nicholas Ray, Wim Wenders, Ronee Blakely. 91 minutes. (Pacific Arts)

Wenders's *verité* record of moviemaking mentor Ray's final days before the latter expired of cancer is pretty grim and parasitic going, by our lights, though it's not without impact.

The Man Who Saw Tomorrow (1981) NR
D: Robert Guenette. With Jeane Dixon. Narrated by Orson Welles. 88 minutes. (Warner)

This 1981 shockumentary dealing with sixteenth-century forecaster Nostradamus's far-flung predictions became an unexpectedly hot vid sales-and-rental item in early '88, due largely to its prediction of California's destruction in the spring of that year. (P.S.: It didn't happen). Fans of that celebrity seer should also check out *Nostradamus* (Bargain Video).

Mondo Cane (1963) ◆◆◇
D: Gualtiero Jacopetti. 105 minutes. (Vidcrest)

The Italo flick that kicked off the entire Mondo craze remains a must for shockumentary addicts, even if it did introduce the irritating ditty "More." *Mondo Cane II* (originally *Mondo Pazzo*) is also out via Vidcrest.

Mondo Magic (1972) NR
Text by Alberto Moravia. Narrated by Mark Mauro Smith. 90 minutes. (Magnum)

A semisleazoid, semiserious shockumentary focusing on bizarre religious and superstitious rites from obscure corners of the globe, with a narration written by famed Italo novelist Alberto Moravia.

Mondo New York (1988) ◆◆◆
D: Harvey Keith. Joey Arias, Luis Aviles, Charlie Barnett, Joe Coleman, Karen Finley, Dean Johnson, Shannah Laumeister, Phoebe Legere, Lydia Lunch, Ann Magnusson, John Sex. 83 minutes. (MPI)

Mondo New York is less a sleaze exposé of the Big Apple's wormier aspects than a performance film featuring a varied array of downtown comics, musicians, and "performance artists" lensed in their unnatural habitats: the theaters, clubs, basements, and streets of the Lower East Side. Acts include an on-target Charlie Barnett routine shot in Washington Square Park, a grating disco tune from the generally useless (if imaginatively coiffed) John Sex, an animated Karen Finley shriekfest, and a literally explosive monologue delivered by chic geek Joe Coleman. Director Keith and producer Stuart S. Shapiro also pay homage to the Mondo movies of yore by incorporating a voodoo ritual, a cockfight, an *Actual Junkie in the Act of Shooting Up!*, and a highly suspect "authentic Chinese slave auction" (!). Much depends on the viewer's taste, or lack of same, but for the Phantom *Mondo New York* supplies enough fun to make a rental worthwhile.

Mysteries from Beyond Earth (1976) NR
95 minutes. (United)

An all-purpose shockumentary that ranges from UFOs to the Bermuda Triangle to paranormal phenomena to cloning breakthroughs.

Nightmare in Red China (1955) NR B&W
67 minutes. (Video Dimensions)

A campy anti-Commie flick, enacted by an Indian cast, dramatizing the perils of the Red Menace in flagrantly propagandistic pseudo-documentary style.

Of the Dead (1979) NR
90 minutes. (MPI)

MPI withdrew its controversial *Faces of Death* shocku series (though the tapes are still available at many vid outlets), then issued this very similar compilation combining cremations, funeral lore, and surgical footage, and other morbid sights.

Photonos (1987) NR
60 minutes. (Video City)

What well-rounded home-vid library would be complete without at least one psychedelic laser-graphics tape? *Photonos* fills that vital gap.

Portrait of Jason (1967) ◆◆◇ B&W
D: Shirley Clarke. Jason Holiday. 105 minutes. (Mystic Fire)

A *verité* interview with black drag queen/professional hipster Holiday that manages to be fairly compelling despite Clarke's static camera and her subject's narcissistic stance.

The Quiet One (1948) NR B&W
D: Sidney Meyers. Donald Thompson, Sadie Stockton. 67 minutes. (Blacast)

One of the first American films to deal directly with the effects of racial prejudice, *The Quiet One* takes a semi-*verité* look at the life of an alienated black youth.

Richard Nixon—Checkers, Old Glory, Resignation (1952, 1957, 1974) NR B&W/color
45 minutes. (Video Yesteryear)

Sort of a *Tricky Dick's Greatest Hits* compilation, including the infamous Checkers Speech, a 1957 Flag Day oration, and his 1974 resignation speech.

Salesman (1969) ◆◆◆◇ B&W
D: Albert & David Maysles. 88 minutes. (HBO)

The Maysles follow four Bible salesmen on their oddball rounds in this alternately poignant, funny, and always winning documentary.

Salt of the Earth (1954) NR B&W
D: Herbert Biberman. Juan Chacon, Rosoura Revueltas, Will Geer. 94 minutes. (MPI)

A *verité*-style indie anomaly, lensed at the height of the McCarthy Era, that took a strong pro-labor stance in a story about a New Mexico zinc mine strike. Many of the principals, including director Biberman, had already been blacklisted when the film was made.

Scorpio Rising (1963) ◆◆◆
D: Kenneth Anger. 38 minutes. (Mystic Fire)

Underground auteur and *Hollywood Babylon* author Kenneth Anger's simultaneously scary and funny look, set to a contempo Top 40 rock score, at autoerotic bikers remains a milestone of subterranean semi-*verité* moviemaking. Mystic Fire also carries Anger's *Inauguration of the Pleasure Dome*, *Lucifer Rising*, and other offbeat works.

Sex and the Animals (1985) NR
93 minutes. (Video City)

A fun-filled full-length look at amusing animal mating habits around the world. Can you prove that it *doesn't* happen? Another unique Video City exclusive.

Shadows (1960) NR B&W
D: John Cassavetes. Hugh Hurd, Leila Goldoni, Rupert Crosse. 87 minutes. (Mystic Fire)

Cassavetes displays his trademark techniques—hand-held camera, improvisational acting, authentic locations, and overall *verité* ambience—in his debut feature, detailing an ill-fated Manhattan-set affair between a light-skinned black woman and her white beau.

Shocking Asia II (1986) NR
D: Emerson Fox. 105 minutes. (Video City)

For fans of plain old *Shocking Asia* (Magnum) comes this equally sadistic cinematic sequel. According to Video City, "They've saved the BEST, the GROSSEST, the WEIRDEST, the MOST DISGUSTING scenes for last!" Aren't we lucky?

Slave Trade in the World Today (1964) NR

D: Roberto Malenotti. With Robin Maugham, Eve Kenneth. 87 minutes. (Vidcrest)

A self-explanatory sleaze special that globe-hops from Asia to Africa to the Near East in its quest for bare-breasted women who don't require signed model releases. For an updated peek at similar sensuous sights, see *The Sensual Taboo* (Media).

Story of a Junkie (1985) NR

D: Lech Kowalski. John Spacely. 80 minutes. (Media)

A Troma-tized retitling of *Gringo*, Lech (*D.O.A.*) Kowalski's portrait of Anglo smack addict John Spacely and his junkie adventures in NYC's East Village.

Strangers in the City (1962) NR B&W

D: Rick Carrier. Robert Gentile, Camila Delgado, Rosita de Triana. 83 minutes. (Charter)

One of several *verité*-style indies filmed in Gotham in the early '60s, *Strangers*—dealing with the adjustment problems of a newly arrived Puerto Rican teen and his older sister—is one of the few to have surfaced on video.

Triumph of the Will (1934) NR B&W

D: Leni Riefenstahl. 110 minutes. (Video Yesteryear)

Riefenstahl's famous propaganda epic, the official record of the Sixth Nazi Party Congress at Nuremberg. No subtitles, but the pictures tell the chilling story. Video Yesteryear also carries several other Nazi propaganda films: Riefenstahl's *Olympia* (1938), *Day of Freedom* (1935), and *German Weekly Newsreel* (1941), as well as the anti-Nazi *Life of Adolph Hitler* (1961), *Secret Life of Adolph Hitler* (1958), *The Smashing of the Reich* (1962), and *Nazi War Crime Trials* (1945).

UFO: Top Secret (1979) NR

96 minutes. (United)

One of a rash of *Chariots of the Gods?*–inspired speculative looks at our possibly spacey origins. For further research, we steer you to *Aliens from Spaceship Earth* (Video Gems); *Force Beyond* (Media); *Attack from Outer Space, Mysteries of the Gods, Outer Space Connection*, and *UFOs: Are We Alone?* (all United); *Who's Out There?* (Video City); and, of course, the original *Chariots of the Gods?* (United).

USS VD: Ship of Shame (1942) NR B&W

40 minutes. (Video Yesteryear)

A notorious WWII service documentary outlining the horrors of venereal disease. Visual saltpeter for our boys overseas. Video Yes-

Junkie John Spacely confronts the camera in Lech Kowalski's picaresque shock-doc, *Story of a Junkie* (formerly *Gringo*).
Photo courtesy of Troma, Inc.

teryear also carries the 1969 Vietnam version *Where the Girls Are.*

Video Fireplace (1987) NR
60 minutes. (Videotakes)

What to do when you're tired of watching movies? Why not chill out with the legendary *Video Fireplace*? Is it as good as Relax Video's *Fireplace TV*? Shop and compare!

Wild Rapture (1950) NR B&W
68 minutes. (Video Dimensions)

Ubangi rituals, elephant hunts, and other jungle items are served up in this French-filmed doc-style.

Wild, Wild World of Jayne Mansfield (1968) ◆◆◆
D: Arthur Knight. 120 minutes. (United)

An appropriately sleazoid "salute" to the late B queen that includes on-site footage of the aftermath of Jayne's fatal car crash.

Witchcraft Through the Ages (1922) ◆◆◆ B&W
D: Benjamin Christensen. With Benjamin Christensen. 128 minutes. (New York Film Annex)

A surreal Medieval-set silent shockudrama, the horrific handiwork of Swede auteur Christensen, that "attempts to reconstruct those wretched aberrations of an age when satanism disturbed many souls." *Witchcraft*'s (originally titled *Haxan*) mix of nudity, sacrilegious imagery, and sheer weirdness caused it to be banned in many countries. The New York Film Annex has the complete uncensored versions. A unique experience.

World of Acid (1967) ◆◇
D: Edgar Beatty. 85 minutes. (VCI)

Not the brain-damaged, alarmist LSD exposé we'd naturally hoped for, but a dumb "oh, wow!" look at Haight-Ashbury and inhabitants during the Summer of '67.

You Can't Get There from Here: Ephemeral Films 1946–1960 (1987) ◆◆◆◇
B&W/color
Compiled by Rick Prelinger. Approx. 60 minutes. (Voyager Press Video)

A treasure-trove for pop-anthropology buffs, ace archivist Prelinger's *You Can't Get There from Here* is an alternately campy and chilling collection of vintage public-service and cultural propaganda shorts, many unseen since their original circulation. Among the highlights are the tense "A Date with Your Family"; the horror-tinged vehicular teen-suicide (or "teenicide") tract "Last Date"; "King Joe," an obnoxious "tribute" to the glories of being an American worker; and the pro-tranquilizer (!) ode "The Relaxed Wife." Uniting the nineteen excerpts is a postwar theme that could be summed up as "Better Living Through Conformity," but the anxiety and hostility bubbling beneath the surface of these chauvinistic shorts can't help but shine through. An earlier volume, titled *To New Horizons*, surveys the years 1931–45 with equal aplomb.

SERIAL MADNESS & SAGEBRUSH FAVES:
CLASSIC CLIFFHANGERS & CULT WESTERNS

"Shazam!"

Billy Batson
Adventures of Captain Marvel

Continued Next Week . . . or, Cliffhangers from Hell!

One of the biggest surprises the Phantom received after inaugurating his Mondo Video column in the *New York Daily News* back in 1986 was the incredible video demand for the Saturday Matinee serials of yore. At that time, few stores stocked *any* vintage serials. The Phantom gradually tracked down a number of mostly mail-order video specialty outfits that catered to the sizable cliff hanger crowd.
   Since then, a handful of serials have been accorded more

585

mainstream release, most notably via Warner (*Adventures of Superman, Atom Man vs. Superman*) and Republic (*Adventures of Captain Marvel, The Crimson Ghost*, et al.). But the serial market, while extensive, is a scattered one, resistant to a video-blitz approach. For that reason, the mail-order specialists listed in the back of this volume continue to serve as the chief and most reliable suppliers of classic cliffhangers.

Originally designed for a juvenile audience, the serials—a genre that more or less officially began in 1914 with Pearl White's *The Perils of Pauline*—were screened on a chapter-per-week basis, unspooling before the main features at Saturday matinees. Each chapter would invariably end with the hero or heroine in a grave situation—strapped into a car sent speeding off a cliff or, in Pearl White's case, fastened to the railroad tracks in the path of an oncoming train. Kids would have a full week to contemplate the worst until the next installment just as invariably rescued our imperiled protagonist from the last chapter's seemingly inescapable predicament.

With movie attendance booming in the early sound era and kids constituting a goodly percentage of the audience, the cliffhanger wings at indie studios like Mascot and First National, as well as such majors as Columbia, Republic, and Universal, kept the nation's bijous supplied with an unending stream of low-budget chapterplays, voraciously raiding popular comic strips (*Flash Gordon*), radio shows (*The Green Hornet*), and the pulps (*Drums of Fu Manchu*) for readily adaptable source material. Genres ranged from westerns (*Fighting with Kit Carson*) to sci-fi (*Buck Rogers*) to crime thrillers (*Holt of the Secret Service*) to jungle adventures (*Lost City of the Jungle*), with chapters numbering between ten and fifteen. Quality varied greatly, from Republic's impressive *Adventures of Captain Marvel* to the surreally tacky independent *The Lost City*, but most were lensed quickly and efficiently by cost-conscious auteurs who were rarely hesitant about using copious stock footage, library music, rear projection, and other money-saving methods whenever possible. Serial stars like Kane Richmond, Johnny Mack Brown, and Kay Aldridge usually split their time between cliffhangers and B features, though many, like Richmond, are remembered almost exclusively for their chapterplay work. Though cliffhanger villains were generally more colorful than their heroic counterparts, most wore elaborate disguises, and few of the actors who portrayed them enjoyed the audience recognition accorded the serial heroes. But the *real* cliffhanger heroes were those daring stunt men—many of whom, like Dave Sharpe and

Kenne Duncan, doubled as actors—who risked life and limb to supply the serials with their chief raison d'être: breakneck action.

The serials enjoyed their heyday between the early '30s and the early '50s, when they were usurped by even cheaper TV action programming. The last cliffhanger appeared in 1956, and beyond occasional theatrical and college screenings during the Batman craze of the mid-'60s, the genre went virtually ignored until its recent video revival.

Here we've spotlighted over one hundred chapterplays being offered by major labels and reliable vid-specialty firms. For further titles, we urge you to contact those relevant companies listed here and find out if they stock the title or titles you want. Westerns follow in a separate list.

Code Key to Vid Companies:

CB:	Captain Bijou
DV:	Discount Video
DX:	Dixie Entertainment
FH:	Foothill Video
RM:	Rex Miller
SC:	Sinister Cinema
2D:	Double D Video Ranch
VDim:	Video Dimensions
VY:	Video Yesteryear

Ace Drummond (1936) B&W

John King, Jean Rogers, Noah Beery Jr., Lon Chaney, Jr. 13 chapters. (CB/ DV/DX/FH/SC/VDim)

King, later one of B-westerndom's Three Mesquiteers, is the courageous title pilot who battles Mongolian mastervillain The Dragon over thirteen high-flying episodes.

The Adventures of Captain Marvel (1941) B&W

Frank Coughlan, Jr., Tom Tyler, Louise Currie, William Benedict, Reed Hadley, Kenne Duncan. 12 chapters. (Republic)

Considered by many serious serial scholars to be the finest cliffhanger ever filmed, *Captain Mar-*

vel opens in Thailand's taboo Valley of the Tombs, where an archaeological team can't wait to violate those sacred environs, the better to learn the "lost secret of the Scorpion Dynasty." Young Billy Batson (Coughlan) is the only expedition member to decline participation in the planned desecration. As a reward for his integrity, an ancient robed spirit named Shazam grants Billy the ability to change from his nerdy teenage self into the strapping Captain Marvel (Tyler) simply by uttering the secret word "Shazam!" Back in the States, Billy employs his newfound power to wage a twelve-episode battle against costumed supervillain The Scorpion, who's bent upon retrieving an alchemical icon called the golden scorpion. "Whoever controls this device," the Scorpion declaims (in a sonorous voice dubbed in by otherwise unseen actor Gerald Mohr), "will have power such as men have dreamed of since the beginning of time!" While admittedly not big in the logic department, *The Adventures of Captain Marvel*, with its relatively large budget, energetic stunts, swift pace and capable cast easily lives up to its advance billing.

Adventures of Red Ryder (1941) B&W
Don "Red" Barry. 12 chapters. (CB)

B-cowboy star Don "Red" Barry rides the serial range as his semi-namesake in a cliffhanger based on the popular comic strip.

Adventures of Rex and Rinty (1935) B&W
Kane Richmond, Norma Taylor, Smiley Burnette, Rin Tin Tin. 12 chapters. (CB/FH)

Chapterplay perennial Richmond shares starring honors with Hollywood's famous fido in this Wild West–set serial.

Adventures of Smilin' Jack (1943) B&W
Tom Brown. 13 chapters. (CB/FH/SC)

Brown, as the comic-strip air ace, foils Axis forces in typically outlandish, fast-paced fashion. As a Chinese sage puts it, "Do you not find this American's enthusiasm strangely contagious?"

Adventures of Superman (1948) B&W
Kirk Alyn, Noel Neill, Tommy Bond, Carol Forman, Pierre Watkin, Charles King. 15 chapters. (Warner)

A surreal combo of film, cartoon, (Supe's flights are rendered via obvious though expert animation), and radio, 1948's *The Adventures of Superman* toplines an unbilled Alyn as the comic-book Christ figure. Kirk is backed by tiny but feisty Neill as Lois Lane—she later reprised the role on the George Reeves–starred *Superman* teleseries—and Bond, who plays cub reporter Jimmy Olson in brash wiseacre style. The fifteen-chapter serial is strongest in its early installments, detailing (albeit with the aid of copious stock footage) the destruction of Krypton and young Supe's formative years with his adoptive parents, the kindly Kents. Especially moving is the scene wherein Ma Kent sends a now-grown Clark off to right the world's wrongs: "Here's a uniform I made for you out of the blankets you were wrapped in when we found you. It's a strange kind of cloth that resists both fire and acid. I hope it will protect you always." Our unflappable hero replies, "Well thank you, mother!" Equally riveting are the chapters introducing Clark to Metropolis and Superman to the world. Our story sinks a bit with the appearance of the notorious Spider Lady (Forman), who, abetted by her seemingly inexhaustible supply of devoted minions in fedoras and pencil-line moustaches, endlessly battles the Man of Steel for possession of the precious "reducer ray." The latter, by the way, is *not* a dietary device but a powerful weapon that, in the wrong hands, could well spell the end of civilization-as-we-know-it. There are enough plot twists, feats of derring-do, doses of campy dialogue ("How thoughtful of you," Lois chides Clark, "to be so considerate of yourself!"), and general cliffhanging here to keep Superman fans and serial buffs thoroughly engaged.

Adventures of Tarzan (1921) B&W
Elmo Lincoln, Louise Lorraine. 15 chapters. (Video Yesteryear)

Original Tarzan Lincoln tangles with Russian agents (one of whom employs a pin to tattoo a treasure map on poor Jane's back!) in this seminal silent serial, available from Video Yesteryear, with musical score and corrected projection speed.

Adventures of the Flying Cadets (1943) B&W
Johnny Downs, Bobby Jordan, Robert Armstrong, Jennifer Holt. 13 chapters. (CB/RM)

Downs and East Side Kid Jordan battle the Black Hangman in a World War II–themed aerial adventure benefiting from a bigger budget than most cliffhangers enjoyed.

Atom Man vs. Superman (1950) B&W
Kirk Alyn, Noel Neill, Lyle Talbot, Tommy Bond, Pierre Watkin, Don Harvey. 15 chapters. (Warner)

Alyn reprises his Man of Steel role to take on archvillain Lex Luthor (played by a chrome-domed Talbot) and his alter ego, the foreign-accented Atom Man, complete with glittering white frightmask. Like its forebear, the sequel alternates between live-action and animation (in Supe's more acrobatic aerial sequences), moves at a brisk if occasionally redundant clip, and brings back beloved *Daily Planet* personnel Lois Lane (Neill), Jimmy Olson (Bond), and Perry White (Watkin). Our fave episodes here deal with our hero's banishment to the Empty Doom, a nebulous netherworld where Superman exists only in superimposition and that prompts many of the serial's sharpest exchanges. To wit:

Atom Man: Before you depart for an eternity of aimless wandering into the Empty Doom, what have you to say?
Superman: I'll be back!

This time Warner has wisely included the opening credits preceding each chapter, rectifying an *Adventures of Superman* omission that had aroused the ire of many a hard-core cliffhanger buff.

Battling with Buffalo Bill (1932) B&W
Tom Tyler. 12 chapters. (FH)

Popular B-western and serial star (he toplined in seven of the latter) Tyler portrays the titular frontier legend in an early Universal serial.

Black Coin (1937) B&W
Ralph Graves. 15 chapters. (CB/DV/DX/FH/SC)

Federal agents led by Graves tangle with smugglers.

Blake of Scotland Yard (1937) B&W
Ralph Byrd, Joan Barclay, Herbert Rawlinson. 15 chapters. (CB/DV/DX/FH/SC)

Ralph (*Dick Tracy*) Byrd battles the sinister Scorpion and his menacing Death Ray. Also available in 70-minute featurized form (Video Yesteryear).

Buck Rogers (1939) B&W
Buster Crabbe, C. Montague Shaw, Constance Moore, Henry Brandon. 12 chapters. (FH)

Flash Gordon star Crabbe dons cosmic comic-strip hero Buck Rogers's superhero duds to combat villain Killer Kane (Warde) in a competent cliffhanger that lacks *Flash*'s intergalactic dash and panache. Also available in featurized form (Video Yesteryear). You can see Buster as Flash in the 1940 Flash Gordon sequel *Flash Gordon Conquers the Universe* (CB).

Burn 'Em Up Barnes (1934) B&W
Jack Mulhall, Frankie Darro. 12 chapters. (CB/DV/FH/SC)

B-flick regulars Mulhall and the diminutive Darro prevent gangsters from moving in on their trucking operation in a generally pedestrian serial from the soon-to-be-defunct Mascot Pictures.

Call of the Savage (1935) B&W
Noah Beery, Jr., Walter Miller, Dorothy Short. 12 chapters. (CB/FH)

Noah Beery, Jr., later a *Rockford Files* regular, *is* Jan of the Jungle in this bush adventure, highlighted by an elaborate and perilous "hidden city" set.

Clutching Hand (1936) B&W
Jack Mulhall, William Farnum, Marion Schilling, Yakima Canutt. 15 chapters. (CB/DV/DX/FH/VDim)

Mulhall is "scientific detective" Craig Kennedy, on the trail of a crazed alchemist known only as (what else?) The Clutching Hand, in a campy cliffhanger costarring former silent-screen action star Farnum and produced by exploitation patriarch Louis Weiss.

Crimson Ghost (1946) B&W
Charles Quigley, Linda Stirling, Clayton Moore, Kenne Duncan. 12 chapters. (Republic)

Handsome Quigley and lovely Stirling team up to stop the skull-masked miscreant the Crimson Ghost from perpetrating his planned atomic atrocities in this fast-moving chapterplay.

Custer's Last Stand (1936) B&W
Rex Lease, Lona Andre. 15 chapters. (CB/FH)

Kit Cardigan (Lease) is caught between vengeful Indians and the white outlaws who plundered their land.

Daredevils of Red Circle (1939) B&W
Charles Quigley, Bruce Bennett, Carole Landis, David Sharpe. 12 chapters. (Republic)

An aerial adventure highlighted by spectacular stunt work from the ever-agile Sharpe.

Darkest Africa (1936) B&W
Clyde Beatty, Manuel King, Elaine Shepard. 15 chapters. (Republic)

Republic Pictures' debut serial stars real-life animal trainer Beatty, accompanied by King (the World's Youngest Animal Trainer),

on a jungle journey filled with such surreal sights as "the flying Bat Men" and prehistoric reptiles, rendered with then-state-of-the-art FX.

Devil Horse (1932) B&W
Harry Carey, Noah Beery, Frankie Darro, Carli Russell. 12 chapters. (CB/DV/DX/FH)

Character thesp Carey takes on a more heroic role as a cowboy who adopts Darro, a feral youth who's been raised by the title equine (!) in this Mascot chapterplay.

Don Winslow of the Navy (1941) B&W
Don Terry, Walter Sande, Anne Nagel. 12 chapters. (CB/FH/VDim)

Title hero Terry tackles nefarious Nazi supervillain "the Scorpion" (see also the following year's *Don Winslow of the Coast Guard*) who's bent upon sabotaging the American war effort.

Fighting Devil Dogs (1938) B&W
Lee Powell, Herman Brix, Eleanor Stewart, Montagu Love. 12 chapters. (Republic)

Republic's *Fighting Devil Dogs* opens impressively, traveling from Shanghai to Manchuria to the States in the first episode alone. Sure, it's a *stock-footage* Shanghai and Manchuria (and even much of the States), but it demonstrates how *FFD*'s creators refused to let a meager budget crimp their expansive imaginations. That debut chapter also entails an unusually violent Marine massacre, as leatherneck lieutenants Powell and Brix (later Bruce Bennett) see their entire command wiped out by high-voltage missiles directed by The Lightning, your standard costumed supervillain. Our surviving officers team up with stateside scientists to unravel The Lightning's sinister secrets. As is the case with many vintage cliffhangers, the cut corners stand out in ever bolder relief as the chapters elapse. Still, *Fighting Devil Dogs* does deliver its fair share of action—much of it excitingly staged—and rarely pauses for excess expository filler.

Fighting Marines (1935) B&W
Grant Withers, Ann Rutherford, Adrian Morris. 12 chapters. (CB/FH/VDim/VY)

One of Mascot's last (and best) serials finds the title servicemen thwarted in their efforts to establish a Pacific base by contempo pirate the Tiger Shark and his trusty "radio gravity gun." With Adrian (brother of Chester) Morris.

Fighting with Kit Carson (1933) B&W
Johnny Mack Brown. 12 chapters. (CB/FH/VDim)

Durable sagebrush star Johnny Mack Brown clashes with the Mystery Riders, outlaws determined to snatch a government gold shipment.

Flaming Frontiers (1938) B&W
Johnny Mack Brown, Eleanor Hansen, Charles Middleton. 15 chapters. (CB/DV/DX/VY)

Mack is back to deal with marauding Cheyenne and greedy outlaws led by evil Bart Eaton (Middleton, of Ming the Merciless fame).

Galloping Ghost (1931) B&W
Red Grange. 12 chapters. (CB/FH/VDim)

Gridiron great Harold ("Red") Grange plays a framed footballer out to nail a gambling syndicate and clear his name in this early, slow-moving (at least off the football field) serial.

Gordon of Ghost City (1933) B&W
Buck Jones. 12 chapters. (CB)

Jones, one of the most rugged and authentic of Hollywood's western heroes, made his serial debut in this Universal cliffhanger.

Green Archer (1940) B&W
Victor Jory, Iris Meredith. 15 chapters. (CB/DV/DX/SC/VY)

The usually villainous Jory is the unlikely title hero in a frantic, campy cliffhanger crammed with devious devices, infernal gadgetry, and all manner of narrow escapes.

Green Hornet (1940) B&W
Gordon Jones, Wade Boteler, Keye Luke, Ann Nagel. 13 chapters. (FH/SC)

Jones, later Mike the Cop on Abbott and Costello's teleseries, is the costumed crime-buster ("His sting is death . . . as he stalks criminals no law can touch!"), while Luke plays Oriental cohort Kato, a popular serial recreation of the long-lived radio show.

Holt of the Secret Service (1941) B&W
Jack Holt. 15 chapters. (CB/SC)

Veteran action hero Holt, long in the tooth but still quick on the trigger, stars as a government agent on the trail of counterfeiters in this slapdash serial. Unfortunately, Jack's advanced age not only required frequent stunt-doubling but alienated kids who favored younger role models. The kids of 1941 can probably better relate to a more mature hero today, though.

Hurricane Express (1932) B&W
John Wayne. 12 chapters. (CB/DV/DX/FH/SC/VDim/VY)

Young John dukes it out with mysterious archvillain The Wrecker, who's determined to destroy the titular railroad in this early Mascot serial.

The Indians Are Coming (1930) B&W
Colonel Tim McCoy. 12 chapters. (FH)

McCoy toplines in the first all-talking chapterplay, simultaneously released in silent form for theaters unequipped for sound. Despite copious use of stock footage, this serial proved extremely popular and facilitated the genre's transition into the sound era.

Jungle Girl (1941) B&W
Frances Gifford, Tom Neal, Gerald Mohr. 15 chapters. (Republic)

The cliffhanger that introduced the formidable Nyoka (Gifford). Here our jungle heroine sets out to retrieve a hidden cache of diamonds before villain Mohr and native chieftain Shamba (Frank Lackteen) beat her to it.

Jungle Menace (1937) B&W
Frank Buck, Reginald Denny, Duncan Renaldo. 15 chapters. (CB/FH)

Stock footage holds sway in Columbia's debut serial, crafted to capitalize on real-life big-game hunter Frank Buck's then-current celebrity. Buck demonstrates why he was more at home in the jungle than on a soundstage.

Junior G-Men of the Air (1942) B&W
Bobby Jordan, Gabriel Dell. 12 chapters. (FH)

The Dead End Kids and the Little Tough Guys gang up on Axis agents in this patriotic sequel to the just plain *Junior G-Men* (CB/DV/DX/FH).

King of the Kongo (1929) B&W
Walter Miller, Jacqueline Logan, Boris Karloff. 10 chapters. (FH/VY)

The first serial from Mascot, released in both silent and minimal "talkie" editions, *King of the Kongo* chronicles the jungle intrigues of Secret Service ace Larry Trent (Miller), who clashes with ivory thief Karloff. Much of this antique chapterplay was lensed on location in Cambodia. Video Yesteryear has the silent version, with a music track added.

King of the Texas Rangers (1941) B&W
Slingin' Sammy Baugh. 12 chapters. (Republic)

Gridiron great Slingin' Sammy Baugh, following in the tradition of Red Grange, trades in his pigskin for six-shooters in his only serial vehicle.

Last Frontier (1932) B&W
Lon Chaney, Jr., Dorothy Gulliver, Francis X. Bushman, Yakima Canutt. 12 chapters. (CB/VY)

RKO's only cliffhanger—and it's pretty easy to see why, starting with casting Lon Chaney, Jr., as the dashing hero.

The Last of the Mohicans (1932) B&W
Harry Carey, Mischa Auer, Yakima Canutt. 12 chapters. (CB/DV/DX/VDim/VY)

Mascot version of James Fenimore Cooper's epic set against the backdrop of the French and Indian War.

Law of the Wild (1934) B&W
Rin Tin Tin, Jr. 12 chapters. (CB/FH)

Rin Tin Tin, Jr., successor to the original silent screen canine, stars in his own sound serial.

Lone Defender (1932) B&W
Rin Tin Tin, Walter Miller, June Marlowe. 12 chapters. (FH/VDim)

The original Rin Tin Tin, in one of his last major roles, saves a gold mine from the clutches of sundry evildoers, including the notorious Cactus Kid.

The Lost City (1935) B&W
Kane Richmond, William ("Stage") Boyd, Claudia Dell, George Hayes. 12 chapters. (Foothill)

Certainly one of the strangest of the early indie cliffhangers, *The Lost City* in question is the "ultramodern," gadget-stocked African redoubt of mad scientist Zoloch (Boyd), who's assisted by an odd assortment of characters, including captive genius Dr. Manus, musclebound minion Apollyn, diminutive hunchback Gorzo, and natives transformed into "black giant" zombies and given new names (like *Hugo* and *Pierre!*). Seems that Zoloch's massive electrical experiments are wreaking havoc the whole world over. To the rescue comes hero Richmond, who conspires with Dr. Manus and his rather stocky daughter (Dell) to foil the megalomaniac's plans. Hayes, in his pre-Gabby days, also gets involved. The characters spend most of their time running around in circles and generally losing track of each other; indeed, *The Lost City* is even more confusing than your typical suburban shopping mall. Words to ponder: "I'll have his mind under my control even if it means making him a white giant!" A classic.

Lost City of the Jungle (1946) B&W
Russell ("Lucky") Hayden, Jane Adams, Lionel Atwill, Keye Luke. 13 chapters. (CB/FH/VDim)

Former Hopalong Cassidy sidekick Hayden battles villain Atwill in a cost-conscious romp packed with priceless camp moments. At-will, who died during filming, is replaced by an obvious double.

Lost Jungle (1934) B&W

Clyde Beatty, Cecelia Parker. 12 chapters. (CB/DX/DV/FH/VDim/VY)

Self-described "World's Greatest Animal Trainer" Beatty uses everything from whips to hypnotism (!) to tame savage beasts running amok on an uncharted isle. Clyde returned for more of the same in 1937's *King of the Jungle-land* (CB).

Manhunt in the African Jungle (1943) B&W

Rod Cameron. 15 chapters. (Republic)

More World War II–related bush intrigues, this time with two-fisted Western stalwart Cameron handling the hero chores.

Masked Marvel (1944) B&W

William Forest, Tom Steele, Johnny Arthur. 12 chapters. (Republic)

One of Republic's most crowd-pleasing wartime cliffhangers—brought to you in "Twelve Spy-Smashing, Spine-Tingling, Episodes!"—pits the title hero (stunt man Steele) against evil Jap saboteur Sakima.

Miracle Rider (1935) B&W

Tom Mix, Jean Gale, Charles Middleton. 15 chapters (CB/DV/DX/FH/VY)

Time-tripping chapterplay opens in the early pioneer days before fast-forwarding to modern Texas Ranger Mix and his fight against a villain (Middleton) equipped with standard serial superweapons. Mix's last movie.

Mystery Mountain (1934) B&W

Ken Maynard, Tarzan the Wonder Horse. 12 chapters. (CB/DV/DX/FH/VY)

Railroad dick Maynard, astride Tarzan the Wonder Horse, foils masked villain The Rattler at every turn.

Mystery Squadron (1933) B&W

Bob Steele, Guinn "Big Boy" Williams, J. Carrol Naish. 12 episodes. (VY)

Airborne bad guy The Black Ace plagues a construction site until fearless stunt pilot Steele and his affable sidekick Williams take to the skies in a serial that emphasizes elaborate aerial stunts.

New Adventures of Tarzan (1935) B&W

Herman Brix, Ula Holt, Jiggs the monkey. 12 chapters. (CB/DV/DX/FH/VY)

Ex-Olympian Brix dons the sacred loincloth and, accompanied by his faithful primate companion N'kima (played by Jiggs), journeys to Guatemala (!) in quest of the Green Goddess. Most of this relatively lavish serial was lensed on location.

Nyoka and the Tigermen (1942) B&W

Kay Aldridge, Clayton Moore, Charles Middleton. 15 chapters. (CB)

Originally titled *Perils of Nyoka*, this sequel to *Jungle Girl* sees Aldridge replace Frances Gifford as the titular heroine, herein seeking a cancer cure and assisted by future Lone Ranger Moore.

Painted Stallion (1937) B&W
Ray Corrigan, Hoot Gibson, Duncan Renaldo, Yakima Canutt. 12 chapters. (CB/FH/VDim/VY)

An all-star B-western cast rides the cliffhanger range in a name-dropping adventure that manages to work Davy Crockett, Jim Bowie, Kit Carson, and other frontier legends into the action. The title steed is ridden by a mysterious Indian maid, informal predecessor of Russ Meyer's Soul, who uses her whistling arrows to warn our boys of impending peril.

Perils of Pauline (1934) B&W
Evelyn Knapp, Robert Allen, Pat O'Malley, Sonny Ray. 12 chapters. (CB/FH/VY)

Knapp assumes the title role in this elaborate globe-trotting continuation of the original 1914 silent *Perils* (itself available from Foothill Video). Quite impressive for its day and budget.

The Phantom Creeps (1939) B&W
Bela Lugosi, Robert Kent, Dorothy Arnold, Regis Toomey, Jack C. Smith. 12 chapters. (CB/SC)

Universal's 1939 high-camp cliffhanger features Bela as the extravagantly screw-loose Dr. Zorka, a monomaniacal madman who employs his eight-foot robot, ray gun, deadly mechanical spiders, and invisibility belt in a singleminded effort to conquer the world. "Working along lines contrary to mankind," Bela displays admirable determination in the face of constant defeat, engineered by army intelligence agents and his own fumbling lackey Monk (Smith). Part of the credit for *Phantom*'s considerable entertainment value goes to scripter Willis Cooper, who would later write for Arch Oboler's legendary *Lights Out!* radio series. An even larger part goes to the one and only Bela, whose unflappably evil style works even better the more ludicrous our story becomes.

The Phantom Empire (1935) B&W
Gene Autry, Dorothy Christy, Frankie Darro. 12 chapters. (CB/SC)

Many serials achieved a measure of slapdash surrealism, but Mascot's *Phantom Empire* is just downright *weird*. Autry stars as a contempo singing cowboy who runs the popular Radio Ranch (whence he broadcasts daily). When he's not busy with his entertainment chores, he descends into the nearby futuristic subterranean city of Murania. There, beautiful but cruel Queen Tika (Christy)—who prescribes "ten lashes of the scabula" for her minions' slightest offenses—hones her plans for world conquest, dispatches her mysterious Thunder Riders to execute her sinister wishes, and otherwise bedevils Gene and pals. A bizarre mélange of corny cowboy tunes, raygun shoot-outs, and robots on the march (later recycled in 1951's *Captain Video*—see index), *The Phantom Empire* is a must for both cliffhanger buffs and fans of demented moviemaking.

Phantom of the Air (1933) B&W
Tom Tyler. 12 chapters. (FH)

Aerial adventures with Tyler, later of *Captain Marvel* fame, with the accent on perilous sky stunts.

Phantom of the West (1931) B&W
Tom Tyler. 10 episodes. (CB/FH/VY)

Tom Tyler dons Phantom duds to discover the identity of his dad's killer in a hard-galloping chapterplay.

Phantom Rider (1936) B&W
Buck Jones. 15 chapters. (CB)

Sagebrush stalwart Jones takes the reigns in this actionful Universal oater.

Radio Patrol (1937) B&W
Grant Withers, Catherine Hughes. 12 chapters. (CB/FH/VDim)

A pretty standard cops-and-robbers caper, with Withers—as cop Pat O'Hara—seeking the crooks who've made off with a flexible-steel formula.

Raiders of Ghost City (1945) B&W
Dennis Moore. 13 episodes. (CB)

Former Range Buster Moore tackles the title outlaws in a well-paced Universal cliffhanger.

Red Barry (1938) B&W
Buster Crabbe. 13 chapters. (CB)

Former swim champ and then-current Flash Gordon Crabbe helped establish his western credentials in a serial based on the popular comic strip.

Return of Chandu (1934) B&W
Bela Lugosi, Maria Alba, Clara Kimball Young. 12 episodes. (CB/DV/DX/FH/VDim/VY)

Chandu (Bela) takes on the Black Magic Cult of Ubasti to prevent its followers from sacrificing the beautiful Princess Nadji and conquering the world. For more on this late-breaking story, order *your* copy today!

Riders of Death Valley (1941) B&W
Buck Jones, Dick Foran, Charles Bickford, Lon Chaney, Jr., Leo Carrillo, Noah Beery, Jr., Big Boy Williams. 15 chapters. (CB)

An all-star cowboy cast highlights Universal's self-described Million Dollar Serial. Better than most.

Robinson Crusoe of Clipper Island (1936) B&W
Ray Mala, Mamo Clark. 14 chapters. (DV/DX/VDim)

The only serial to feature a Polynesian actor in the lead: Mala is a secret agent out to smash an island spy ring.

Royal Mounted Rides Again (1943) B&W
Bill Kennedy, George Dolenz. 13 chapters. (CB)

One of many cliffhangers devoted to the exploits of the Men in Red. This one stars Kennedy as a two-fisted RMCP determined to get his man (even if it takes him thirteen episodes to do it).

Rustlers of Red Dog (1935) B&W
Johnny Mack Brown. 12 chapters. (CB)

Brown pursues the title miscreants in the first of his four Universal sagebrush serials.

Scarlet Horseman (1946) B&W
Paul Guilfoyle, Peter Cookson. 13 chapters. (CB/FH)

Character actor Guilfoyle enjoys a rare heroic role as a hooded avenger in this popular postwar serial.

Scouts to the Rescue (1939) B&W
Jackie Cooper. 12 chapters. (CB/FH)

Teenage Cooper leads his brave Boy Scout troop on a series of daring adventures.

Sea Raiders (1942) B&W
Dead End Kids. 12 chapters. (FH)

The Dead End Kids team with the Little Tough Guys to kick Axis butt in one of the earliest serials with a World War II theme.

The Secret Code (1942) B&W
Paul Kelly. 15 chapters. (FH)

Considered one of Columbia's best cliffhangers, *The Secret Code* stars Kelly as the patriotic Black Commando, working to prevent Axis spies from stealing a top-secret synthetic-rubber formula. At the end of each episode, our hero treated the kids to a brief lecture on the art of decoding secret messages.

Secret of Treasure Island (1938) B&W
Don Terry, Gwen Gaze. 15 chapters. (CB)

Terry, later of *Don Winslow* fame, contends with modern-day pirates, subterranean "mole men," and other unlikely perils in another of Columbia's better efforts.

Shadow of Chinatown (1936) B&W
Bela Lugosi, Herman Brix, Luana Walters. 15 chapters. (SC)

Bela menaces the title nabe while hero Brix does his best to halt the Hungarian evildoer in a recently rediscovered cliffhanger promising "Thrills and Chills and Shivering Shocks!" Sinister Cinema's tape was transferred from a mint 16mm print.

Shadow of the Eagle (1932) B&W
John Wayne, Yakima Canutt, Little Billy Curtis. 12 chapters. (CB/FH/VY)

Wayne forges his strong-silent-type image as cycle stunt rider Craig McCoy, determined to save a traveling carnival from destruction at the hands of mysterious villain The Eagle.

SOS Coast Guard (1937) B&W
Bela Lugosi, Ralph Byrd. 12 chapters. (CB/DV/DX/FH/VDim)

Bela, in flamboyant form as mad munitions expert Boroff, makes this Ralph Byrd serial worth a look.

Tailspin Tommy (1934) B&W
Maurice Murphy. 12 chapters. (CB/FH)

The first comic-strip character to be brought to the serial screen. Universal enlivened this high-flying chapterplay with spectacular aerial stunts and fashioned the equally popular sequel, *Tailspin Tommy in the Great Air Mystery* (CB/FH)

Tarzan the Tiger (1929) B&W
Frank Merrill. 15 chapters. (CB/FH)

Merrill essays the apeman role in one of the last of the silent serials, available with music and sound effects added.

Three Musketeers (1933) B&W
John Wayne, Lon Chaney, Jr., Francis X. Bushman. 12 chapters. (CB/DV/DX/ FH/VDim/VY)

The Duke is a desert D'Artagnan who teams with a trio of Foreign Legionnaires (from Brooklyn, no less!) to combat evil sheik El Shai-tain.

Tim Tyler's Luck (1937) B&W
Frankie Thomas. 12 chapters. (CB/FH)

Thomas toplines as the plucky young comic-strip hero on a jungle quest for an elephants' graveyard.

Valley of Vanishing Men (1942) B&W
Wild Bill Elliott. 15 chapters. (CB)

Elliott rides again in his final Columbia cliffhanger before moving on to B-western stardom at Republic.

Vanishing Legion (1931) B&W
Harry Carey. 12 chapters. (FH)

Veteran character actor Carey takes the hero's role in an early Mascot sagebrush serial.

Whispering Shadow (1933) B&W
Bela Lugosi, Henry B. Walthall, Viva Tattersall. 12 chapters. (CB/DV/DX/FH/ VDim/VY)

Bela adds life to this involved scramble over a fortune in jewels initiated by the disguised title menace, who employs his sinister "radio death ray" to eliminate all who stand in his avaricious way.

Winners of the West (1940) B&W
Dick Foran, Anne Nagel, James Craig. 13 chapters. (CB/FH/VY)

Dick Foran "blazes the rail trail of the iron horse" in a lively western serial costarring Craig as oily villain King Carter.

Young Eagles (1934) B&W
Jim Vance. 12 chapters. (CB/FH)

An obscure, amateurish, and often surreal serial from the short-lived indie company First Division, concerning a troop of heroic Boy Scouts.

Zombies of the Stratosphere (1952) B&W
Judd Holdren, Aline Town, Wilson Wood, Lane Bradford, Stanley Waxman, Leonard Nimoy. 12 chapters. (Republic)

Actually, they're not zombies as much as your standard glitter-suited men from Mars, led by authentically strange-looking ex-B-western star Bradford, on a mission to blow Earth off its axis, the better to commandeer our orbit for use by their own endangered planet. In venerable serial tradition, they hook up with some earthly lowlifes in fedoras to help them confiscate the atomic explosives they'll need to accomplish their Herculean task. Vehemently opposed to this blithe scheme is the bland Holdren as our crime-fighting Rocket Man (aka Commando Cody). Holdren's listless presence aside, *Zombies* makes for good clean campy fun, littered as it is with deathless dialogue, frantic action, myriad Cold War allusions, a robot recycled from 1940's *Mysterious Dr. Satan* (Republic), and a young Leonard Nimoy as one of the invading Martians. Two companion cliffhangers detailing the exploits of Commando Cody, "Sky Marshal of the Universe"—*King of the Rocket Men* (1949) and *Radar Men from the Moon* (1952)—represent other recommended Republic home-vid releases, as do the same outfit's sci-fi-tinged *Crimson Ghost* (1946), *Purple Monster Strikes* (1945), and *Spy Smasher* (1942).

Zorro Rides Again (1937) B&W
John Carroll, Helen Christian, Duncan Renaldo. 12 chapters. (CB/FH/VDim/VY)

Carroll dons the black duds as the justice-loving swordsman in the first of three Zorro cliffhanger titles. Set in modern-day California, this is an especially swift, action-oriented affair detailing the dashing Mr. Z's attempts to see that a much-needed rail line reaches completion.

Zorro's Black Whip (1944) B&W
George J. Lewis, Linda Stirling, Hal Taliaferro. 12 chapters. (CB/DV/DX/FH/VY)

Zorro is never even mentioned in this feminist cliffhanger chronicling the outlaw-fighting exploits of the mysterious Black Whip, who's actually none other than a feisty crime reporter (Stirling) in reverse drag!

Zorro's Fighting Legion (1939) B&W
Reed Hadley, Sheila Darcy. 12 chapters. (CB/DV/DX/FH/VDim)

Hadley plays the dashing Zorro, chasing Mexican bandits who've made off with a government gold-bullion shipment. *Son of Zorro* is also available (Republic).

The Last Roundup: Sagebrush Faves

As an active genre, the once-vaunted western is not only dead and gone but buried on the lone prairie. Every few years, an ambitious producer or studio will attempt to resurrect the genre, but so far with little success. 1985 witnessed two failed attempts—Clint Eastwood's

Pale Rider (Warner), a painstaking but ultimately derivative *Shane* retread, and the glitzy all-star dud *Silverado* (RCA/Columbia)—and 1988 found the utterly inauthentic "Brat Pack" western *The Young Guns* (Vestron), starring Emilio Estevez as Billy the Kid, meeting an only slightly better fate. All told, the Phantom can count the rest of the recent westerns on one spectral hand—three spoofs (*Lust in the Dust, Rustler's Rhapsody, Yellow Hair*—see index), a maverick kung-fu cowboy flick (*Manchurian Avenger*—see index), and the obscure belated sequel *The Return of Josey Wales* (Magnum), wherein Eastwood's hero is inherited by Michael Parks. That's it. Otherwise, such traditional sagebrush elements as intense male bonding, copious gunplay, and justice's ultimate triumph over evil have become integral parts of the action genre; updated westerns-in-disguise, from *Death Wish* to *Extreme Prejudice* to *The Road Warrior*, seem enough to satisfy contempo audiences.

For that reason, we'll keep this section short but sweet, with a select list of those classic and cult westerns currently available on video. For reliable sources for the still-beloved B westerns of yore, we refer you to our Videorama section.

Apache (1954) ♦♦◇
D: Robert Aldrich. Burt Lancaster, Jean Peters, John McIntire, Charles Bronson. 91 minutes. (Playhouse)

One of the few westerns of the period to unfold from a Native American POV, with Lancaster turning in acrobatic work in the title role.

B Westerns

The Phantom was frankly surprised by the huge write-in demand he's received for the hundreds of B westerns—second-feature staples from the early '30s through the mid-'50s—starring six-gun heroes like Rex Allen, William (Hopalong Cassidy) Boyd, Buster Crabbe, Buck Jones, Lash LaRue, Ken Maynard, Tom Mix, Tim McCoy, Charles (Durango Kid) Starrett, The Three Mesquiteers, and the young John Wayne, to cite a few of the more popular sagebrush icons. All of the above—and many more—*are* in the public domain and readily available on cassette, largely through mail-order specialty companies like Captain Bijou and Double D Video Ranch. See our Videorama section for a complete list of the best B-western sources.

Bad Company (1972) ◆◆◆
D: Robert Benton. Jeff Bridges, Barry Brown, Jim Davis. 94 minutes. (Paramount)

Bridges and Brown play a pair of young Civil War—era drifters in a popular seriocomic western lensed by helmer Benton in wry, low-key style.

The Ballad of Gregorio Cortez (1982) ◆◆◆
D: Robert M. Young. Edward James Olmos, James Gammon, Tom Bower. 99 minutes. (Embassy)

This dignified, PBS-style western tells the true story of a poor New Mexican rancher who shoots a sheriff in self-defense and becomes the target of the most massive manhunt in Wild West history.

The Belle Starr Story (1975) NR
D: Lina Wertmuller. Elsa Martinelli, Robert Wood, George Eastman. 90 minutes. (Video City)

Wertmuller's only western is a spaghetti salute to hard-riding outlawess Belle Starr, unforgettably interpreted by Martinelli. If you thought Cassidy was butch, wait'll you see Elsa.

Buck and the Preacher (1972) ◆◆◆
D: Sidney Poitier. Sidney Poitier, Harry Belafonte, Ruby Dee. 102 minutes. (RCA/Columbia)

One of the best of the latter-day black westerns, with the earnest Poitier and the shady Belafonte making for perfect foils.

Butch Cassidy and the Sundance Kid (1969) ◆◆◆
D: George Roy Hill. Paul Newman, Robert Redford, Katharine Ross. 112 minutes. (CBS/Fox)

One of the last westerns to emerge as a monster BO hit, *Butch and Sundance*, despite some overly cute moments, holds up well on video. The unsuccessful but not-bad prequel, *Butch and Sundance: The Early Days* (Playhouse), is also available.

Cat Ballou (1965) ◆◆◇
D: Elliot Silverstein. Jane Fonda, Lee Marvin, Dwayne Hickman. 97 minutes. (RCA/Columbia)

A cult comedy in its time, this sagebrush send-up has lost some of its lunatic luster, though Marvin remains memorable in his dual roles as a gunfighter and a drunk.

The Culpepper Cattle Company (1972) ◆◆◆
D: Dick Richards. Gary Grimes, Billy "Green" Bush, Bo Hopkins. 92 minutes. (Playhouse)

An admirable attempt to inject greater realism into the genre, *Culpepper* follows teen cowhand Grimes over the course of a gritty cattle drive.

Destry Rides Again (1939) ◆◆◆ B&W
D: George Marshall. James Stewart, Marlene Dietrich, Charles Winninger. 94 minutes. (MCA)

An enduring western satire, with Stewart as a reluctant town-tamer and Marlene as a raunchy saloon siren, based on Max Brand's novel.

A Fistful of Dollars (1964) ◆◆◆
D: Sergio Leone. Clint Eastwood, Gian Maria Volonté, Marianne Koch. 96 minutes. (MGM/UA)

Leone's initially ignored oater established a new genre, dubbed the spaghetti western, that took a fresh, downright fetishistic, icon-happy look at the mythologized West and created a new persona and career for Clint Eastwood as the laconic Man with No Name. All that's missing is Lee Van Cleef, who showed up in time for the sequels and dozens of his own Italo oaters. Sergio and Clint return in *For a Few Dollars More* (Key) and the grandiose *The Good, the Bad and the Ugly* (CBS/Fox). Other worthy Leone vehicles include *A Fistful of Dynamite* (MGM/UA) and *Once Upon a Time in the West* (Paramount).

The Great Northfield Minnesota Raid (1972) ◆◆◆
D: Philip Kaufman. Cliff Robertson, Robert Duvall, Luke Askew. 91 minutes. (MCA)

An offbeat recreation of the Jameses' and Youngers' ill-advised final caper, further hoisted by a top cast led by Robertson as a folksy Cole Younger and Duvall as a mean-spirited Jesse James.

Gunfight at the O.K. Corral (1957) ◆◆◇
D: John Sturges. Burt Lancaster, Kirk Douglas, Rhonda Fleming. 120 minutes. (Paramount)

An all-star recreation of the West's most infamous showdown that's longer on entertainment value than on fact.

The Gunfighter (1950) ◆◆◆◇ B&W
D: Henry King. Gregory Peck, Helen Westcott, Jean Parker, Karl Malden. 84 minutes. (Playhouse)

One of the best westerns ever made, with Peck appropriately trail-weary as the aging gunman whose rep, and a succession of glory-hungry challengers, won't let him quit.

Harlem Rides the Range (1939) ◆◆◇ B&W
D: Sam Newfield. Herb Jeffreys, Spencer Williams, Jr., Lucius Brooks. 60 minutes. (Afro-Am Publishing, Captain Bijou, others)

Despite its exotic (if not downright surreal) title, *Harlem Rides the Range*—one of several all-black westerns to surface in the late '30s—sticks close to standard B-oater conventions, with Jeffreys starring as the singing hero "Bronze Buckaroo" (!), Bob Blake, and F. E. Miller and Brooks supplying low-comedy relief. The flick was scripted by Spencer (Andy Brown) Williams, Jr., who also doubles onscreen as a troubled ranch-owner. If little else, black westerns at least helped balance the ethnic scales: Over a third of post–Civil War cowboys were, in fact, black—a stat almost totally ignored in the majority of mainstream Hollywood westerns. *Bronze Buckaroo,*

Harlem on the Prairie, and *Two-Gun Man from Harlem* are also available from Captain Bijou.

Heaven's Gate (1981) ◆◆◇
D: Michael Cimino. Kris Kristofferson, Isabelle Huppert, Christopher Walken. 149 minutes. (MGM/UA)

The movie that sank a studio (United Artists) is available only in its truncated (though still overlong) version. The narrative's a mess, but the action scenes are first rate, for those quick on the fast-forward trigger.

High Noon (1952) ◆◆◆ B&W
D: Fred Zinnemann. Gary Cooper, Grace Kelly, Lloyd Bridges. 85 minutes. (Republic)

Another quintessential tale that's been endlessly recycled since, with strong, silent sheriff Will Kane (Cooper) protecting an unworthy populace from a gang of vengeful killers. Like *The Set-Up* before it, *High Noon* unfolds in "real" time. High concept all the way. Not so the belated made-for-TV sequel, *High Noon, Part II: The Return of Will Kane* (IVE), where Lee Majors subs for Cooper.

High Plains Drifter (1973) ◆◆◆
D: Clint Eastwood. Clint Eastwood, Verna Bloom, Mitchell Ryan. 105 minutes. (MCA)

Clint goes all arty in this sagebrush fable about a mysterious stranger who inspires a townful of hypocrites to self-destruct. Still one of CE's better vehicles. Clint also twirls his six-guns in *Hang 'em High* (MGM/UA), *Joe Kidd* (MCA), and *The Outlaw Josey Wales* and *Pale Rider* (both Warner).

The Hired Hand (1971) ◆◆◆
D: Peter Fonda. Peter Fonda, Warren Oates, Verna Bloom. 93 minutes. (Kartes)

Fonda traded in his hog for a horse to star in and direct a laid-back oater about a retired outlaw's efforts to reconcile with his wife (Bloom); a gang led by ex–Second City satirist Severn Darden shows up to supply some last-reel action. Oates steals the pic as Fonda's partner. Fans of Fonda the filmmaker are also referred to Pete's picaresque *Wanda Nevada* (Wood Knapp).

Hombre (1967) ◆◆◆◇
D: Martin Ritt. Paul Newman, Fredric March, Diane Cilento. 111 minutes. (CBS/Fox)

A true western winner, with Newman as an alienated blue-eyed "breed" who protects a mixed crew of stranded stagecoach passengers from vile villain Richard Boone. Cameron Mitchell enjoys one of his more legit roles as a crooked sheriff.

I Will Fight No More Forever (1975) ◆◆◆◇
D: Richard T. Heffron. James Whitmore, Ned Romero, Sam Elliott. 100 minutes. (Congress, others)

Possibly the best Army vs. Indians saga ever lensed, *I Will Fight* is a fact-based account of how the Nez Perce tribe, under brilliant strategist Chief Joseph (Romero), waged an almost-successful campaign against superior cavalry forces.

Johnny Guitar (1954) ◆◆◆◇

D: Nicholas Ray. Joan Crawford, Sterling Hayden, Mercedes McCambridge, Scott Brady, John Carradine. 110 minutes. (Republic)

Ray's Freudian western about feuding femmes Crawford and McCambridge still seethes with hormonal fury. Scripter Philip Yordan went on to pen *Night Train to Terror, Death Wish Club,* and the bizarre *Bloody Wednesday* (see index) three decades later.

The Left-Handed Gun (1958) ◆◆◆ B&W

D: Arthur Penn. Paul Newman, Lita Milan, John Dehner. 102 minutes. (Warner)

Penn takes a deliberately offbeat, low-key approach to the Billy the Kid legend in an interesting flick that's also more factual than most.

Little Big Man (1970) ◆◆◆◇

D: Arthur Penn. Dustin Hoffman, Faye Dunaway, Chief Dan George. 147 minutes. (Key)

Penn strikes again: *Little Big Man* doesn't approximate the scope and depth of the Thomas Berger novel on which it's based, but this shaggy epic detailing Jack Crabb's (Hoffman) peripheral but ubiquitous involvement in the "win-

ning" of the West is still way above most Hollywood fare.

The Long Riders (1980) ◆◆◆

D: Walter Hill. David, Keith, and Robert Carradine, Randy and Dennis Quaid, Stacy and James Keach. 100 minutes. (MGM/UA)

One of the last good westerns, even without the gimmick of casting real-life siblings as outlaw brothers, *The Long Riders* covers much the same ground as *The Great Northfield Minnesota Raid* (see index), but from a sufficiently fresh angle to make it worthwhile viewing in its own right.

The Magnificent Seven (1960) ◆◆◆

D: John Sturges. Yul Brynner, Steve McQueen, Eli Wallach. 126 minutes. (MGM/UA)

The sagebrush version of *Seven Samurai* may pale beside Kurosawa's original, but it still supplies plenty of rousing western action. Followed by the far weaker sequels *Return of the Seven* and *Guns of the Magnificent Seven* (both MGM/UA).

A Man Called Horse (1970) NR

D: Elliot Silverstein. Richard Harris, Judith Anderson, Jean Gascon. 114 minutes. (CBS/Fox)

Upper-class Englishman Harris undergoes Sioux S&M rituals in a painful wilderness adventure that proved popular enough to spawn two sequels, *Return of a Man Called Horse* (CBS/Fox) and *Tri-*

umphs of a Man Called Horse (HBO).

The Man Who Shot Liberty Valance (1962) ◆◆◆ B&W
D: John Ford. James Stewart, John Wayne, Vera Miles, Lee Marvin. 122 minutes. (Paramount)

Ford chose to lense this major western in black and white—a bold move even in 1962—and succeeded in crafting what may well be the best of his later outings. Other Ford westerns available on video include: *Cheyenne Autumn* (Warner), *Fort Apache* (RKO), *My Darling Clementine* (Key), *Rio Grande* (Republic), *The Searchers* (Warner), *She Wore a Yellow Ribbon* (RKO), *Two Rode Together* (RCA/Columbia), and *Wagonmaster* (Fox Hills).

McCabe and Mrs. Miller (1971) ◆◆◆
D: Robert Altman. Warren Beatty, Julie Christie, Keith Carradine. 121 minutes. (Warner)

One of Altman's less pretentious efforts, *McCabe* manages to be trenchant, quirky, atmospheric, *and* loyal to traditional celluloid sagebrush conventions, with Beatty and Christie effective as an ambitious conman and mining-camp madam, respectively.

My Name Is Nobody (1974) ◆◆◆
D: Tonino Valerii. Henry Fonda, Terence Hill, Leo Gordon. 115 minutes. (Kartes)

Hill, who'd costarred with gruff comic sidekick Bud Spencer in a popular series of lighthearted spaghetti westerns—e.g., *They Call Me Trinity* and *Trinity Is Still My Name* (both Embassy) and *Boot Hill* (Simitar)—here plays a persistent admirer of aging gun legend Fonda in what's become a fave sagebrush fable.

One-Eyed Jacks (1961) ◆◆◆
D: Marlon Brando. Marlon Brando, Karl Malden, Pina Pellicer. 141 minutes. (Paramount)

Brando's once-controversial Method western, while occasionally lapsing into self-indulgence, holds up extremely well as outlaw Marlon matches wits with ex-crony-turned-lawman Malden.

The Outlaw (1943) ◆◆◆ B&W
D: Howard Hughes. Jane Russell, Jack Beutel, Walter Huston. 120 minutes. (Video Yesteryear, others)

Hughes's then-daring Billy the Kid (Beutel) revamp, which focuses more on Jane's hooters than on Jack's six-shooters, retains little of its shock value but remains a compelling character study.

Outlaw Women (1952) ◆◆◆
D: Ron Ormond, Sam Newfield. Marie Windsor, Jackie Coogan, Richard Robert. 76 minutes. (Monterey)

A sort of *Catfight at the O.K. Corral*, Ormond's odd indie oater unfolds in a femme-run town, complete with distaff sheriff. As he did in Ormond's companion feature, *Mesa of Lost Women* (see index), Jackie Coogan tries to hide his ID behind a beard and bushy eyebrows (!). Rousing cowboy camp.

The Plainsman (1937) ◆◆◇ B&W
D: Cecil B. DeMille. Gary Cooper, Jean Arthur, James Ellison, Gabby Hayes. 113 minutes. (MCA)

DeMille's mega-Hollywood tribute to the "winning of the West" boasts a top cast and still commands its fair share of fans—studio-bound exteriors and papier-mâché boulders notwithstanding.

The Professionals (1966) ◆◆◇
D: Richard Brooks. Burt Lancaster, Lee Marvin, Robert Ryan, Jack Palance, Claudia Cardinale, Woody Strode. 117 minutes. (RCA/Columbia)

Not one of yours truly's faves, but an undeniably popular adventure pitting mercenaries Lancaster, Marvin, Ryan, and Strode against Mexican bandit king Palance (his usual subdued self here) with captive beauty Cardinale as the prize.

Rebel Vixens (1976) ◆◆
D: Bob Cresse. Jonathan Bliss, Wes Bishop, Ushi Digart. 85 minutes. (Media/Private Screenings)

A weird mix of American spaghetti-western violence and soft-core sleaze from the busy regional filmmaking team of Bob Cresse and R. L. Frost, Rebel Vixens offers downbeat sex, uneven thesping, and a nearly naked appearance by former Russ Meyer vixen Digart in a tale about a band of Confederate renegades who commandeer a neutral town in hopes of robbing a Union payroll shipment. Not much as a movie, but holds a certain fascination for dedicated exploitation-pic buffs. Also out under its original title, The Scavengers, on the VCR label.

Ride the High Country (1962) ◆◆◆◆
D: Sam Peckinpah. Randolph Scott, Joel McCrea, Mariette Hartley, Ron Starr. 94 minutes. (MGM/UA)

Peckinpah's homage to the waning West, embodied by sagebrush greats Scott and McCrea, is an excellent mix of craggy grandeur and grit. Hartley makes an impressive bow as a mail-order bride slated for a fate worse than death, while unsung John Davis Chandler turns in another of his memorable creepy villain perfs. But what never happened to costar Ron Starr?

Rio Bravo (1959) ◆◆◆
D: Howard Hawks. John Wayne, Dean Martin, Walter Brennan, Ricky Nelson. 141 minutes. (Warner)

One of Wayne's best westerns, oft revamped in other genres (e.g. John Carpenter's Assault on Precinct 13), as Duke, Dino, Walter, and Rick seek to fend off an army of invading gunmen. Hawks's Duke-starred Red River is also available. (Blackhawk).

River of No Return (1954) ◆◆◆
D: Otto Preminger. Marilyn Monroe, Robert Mitchum, Rory Calhoun. 91 minutes. (Playhouse)

Preminger goes west with an offbeat odyssey detailing farmer Mitchum and saloon chanteuse Monroe's perilous journey up the title estuary.

Shane (1953) ◆◆◆
D: George Stevens. Alan Ladd, Jean Arthur, Van Heflin, Brandon de Wilde. 118 minutes. (Paramount)

An oft-imitated western giant, with diminutive Ladd as the laconic gunman who rides to the rescue of a crew of embattled nesters. Palance also impresses as a sadistic hired killer.

The Shooting (1967) ◆◆◆
D: Monte Hellman. Warren Oates, Millie Perkins, Jack Nicholson, Will Hutchins. 82 minutes. (Budget)

Hellman's quirky existential cult western stars Oates and Will (Sugarfoot) Hutchins as cowhands under the control of vengeful Perkins and slimy gunslinger Nicholson. Hellman also helmed the equally offbeat Ride in the Whirlwind (Cinema Group) and China 9, Liberty 37 (NA).

Stagecoach (1939) ◆◆◆ B&W
D: John Ford. John Wayne, Claire Trevor, Thomas Mitchell, John Carradine. 96 minutes. (Warner)

The western that gave the Duke his permanent place on the macho-man map rates as a topnotch John Ford job whether you're a Wayne fan or not. The staggeringly brain-dead TV-movie remake (Vidmark), cast with country music stars (!), plays almost like an Ed Wood, Jr., movie

and is worthwhile viewing for classic bad-cinema buffs.

There Was A Crooked Man (1970) ◆◆◆
D: Joseph L. Mankiewicz. Kirk Douglas, Henry Fonda, Hume Cronyn. 125 minutes. (Warner)

Delivers what you'd expect from a Mankiewicz pic: clever intrigues, sharp dialogue, and a cheerfully cynical POV, plus a deft turn by Kirk as a consummate conman.

3:10 to Yuma (1957) ◆◆◆ B&W
D: Delmer Daves. Glenn Ford, Van Heflin, Felicia Farr. 92 minutes. (Goodtimes)

Heflin, as a farmer assigned the unenviable task of guarding a notorious outlaw, and Ford, in the latter role, supply the dramatics in this tense High Noon variation.

True Grit (1969) ◆◆◇
D: Henry Hathaway. John Wayne, Kim Darby, Glen Campbell. 128 minutes. (Paramount)

Duke bronzes his screen legend with a larger-than-Cinemascope portrayal of crusty one-eyed lawman Rooster Cogburn and is given surprisingly solid support by Campbell as his reluctant partner.

Ulzana's Raid (1972) ◆◆◆◇
D: Robert Aldrich. Burt Lancaster, Bruce Davison, Jorge Luke. 103 minutes. (MCA)

Aldrich follows a cavalry detachment in pursuit of a small but lethal band of renegade Indian raiders in a realistically rendered western that ranks among the best.

Vera Cruz (1954) ◆◆◆
D: Robert Aldrich. Gary Cooper, Burt Lancaster, Denise Darcel. 94 minutes. (CBS/Fox)

An actionful account of mercenaries Cooper and Lancaster, who journey to the title city in a bid to overthrow Maximilian.

The Virginian (1929) ◆◆◆ B&W
D: Victor Fleming. Gary Cooper, Walter Huston, Richard Arlen, Mary Brian. 90 minutes. (Kartes)

Somewhat creaky but still compelling screen version of Owen Wister's novel, with Cooper scoring as a strong, silent icon up against sleazoid villain Huston.

The Wild Bunch (1969) ◆◆◆◇
D: Sam Peckinpah. William Holden, Ernest Borgnine, Robert Ryan, Edmond O'Brien. 143 minutes. (Warner)

Peckinpah's ultraviolent western classic is a must not only for oater addicts but for cinephiles of all

stripes. Sam's other sagebrush efforts now available on video include: Ballad of Cable Hogue (Warner), The Deadly Companions (New World), Major Dundee (RCA/Columbia), and Pat Garrett and Billy the Kid (MGM/UA).

Windwalker (1980) ◆◆◆
D: Keith Merrill. Trevor Howard, Nick Ramus, James Remar. 108 minutes. (CBS/Fox)

This tale of feuding twin Indian brothers, told from a Native American POV, with dialogue in Crow and Cheyenne (with English subtitles), is a noble and mostly successful attempt to take a different approach to western lore.

Zachariah (1971) NR
D: George Englund. John Rubinstein, Pat Quinn, Don Johnson, Country Joe and The Fish. 93 minutes. (Playhouse)

Firesign Theater members coscripted this rock 'n' roll cowboy parable that introduced Johnson but still managed to become a midnight-movie mainstay.

VIDEO A-GO-GO!
SOLID GOLD ROCK 'N' ROLL

"Wop bop a luba doo-wop bam boom!"

Little Richard
Chuck Berry: Hail! Hail! Rock 'n' Roll!

At the risk of slighting the massive rock-vid biz, we've focused mostly on older, harder-to-find titles here, covering the teen-music and mayhem movies of the '50s through the '70s. Our list is admittedly subjective, but we've tried to include as many relevant major and interesting minor rock-pics as space would allow. Further, there are several sources in our Videorama section that carry large quantities of music vids, ranging from rock (J. Rochet and Associates) to jazz (Facets) to big band swing (Captain Bijou) to opera (Kulture).

Since no rocker's been more ubiquitous onscreen or exerted a greater international youth-cult impact than the late Elvis Presley, we've devoted a subsection offering complete video info on all his feature cassettes as well as on those documentaries, compilations, and concert videos dealing with various aspects of The King's life and music.

Now, as Buckaroo Banzai so eloquently phrased it, "Let's rock 'n' roll!"

Absolute Beginners (1986) ◆◆◇
D: Julien Temple. Eddie O'Connell, Patsy Kensit, David Bowie, Ray Davies. 107 minutes. (HBO)

A lavish but rock-videoesque tribute to the rise of rock in Britain, circa 1958, based on Colin Mac-Innes's then-contempo novel. Not as good as Alan Freed's *Rock, Rock, Rock* (see index).

Acapulco A-Go-Go (197?) NR
Ana Martin, Fernando Lujan, Sonia Furio. 82 minutes. In Spanish. (Mex-cinema Video Corp.)

A tribute to the rise of rock in Mexico? Can you resist finding out for yourself?

Alice Cooper: The Nightmare (1975) NR
Alice Cooper. 67 minutes. (Warner)

The elderly rock star shakes and snakes it for the kids in a lively concert choreographed by ex-dancer David Winters, now head of Action International Pictures and hosted by Vincent Price. Personally, we preferred Coop's silent cameo in John Carpenter's *Prince of Darkness* (see index). Also

available: *Alice Cooper: The Nightmare Returns* (MCA).

Breaking Glass (1980) NR
D: Brian Gibson. Phil Daniels, Hazel O'Connor, Jon Finch. 93 minutes. (Paramount)

Hoary story line of a rocker's rise from Obscurity to Stardom, with a detour through Disillusionment, is adapted to the late-'70s London punk scene.

The Buddy Holly Story (1978) ◆◆◆
D: Steve Rash. Gary Busey, Charles Martin Smith, Maria Richwine. 113 minutes. (RCA/Columbia)

Unfortunately, Holly didn't live long enough to offer much of a life story, and his real contributions are already available on record. Still, the movie has a fairly authentic period feel, and Busey does an amazing job virtually *becoming* Buddy Holly.

Candy Mountain (1988) ◆◆◆
D: Rudy Wurlitzer. Kevin J. O'Connor, Tom Waits, Dr. John, Harris Yulin. 90 minutes. (Republic)

This wry account, scripted and directed by novelist Rudy Wurlitzer, of second-rate rocker Kevin J. O'Connor's quest for an elusive guitar-maker stacks up as a mostly winning anti-road ode. With additional cameos by David Johansen, Leon Redbone, and Joe Strummer.

Carnival Rock (1957) ◆◆ B&W
D: Roger Corman. Susan Cabot, Dick Miller, Brian Hutton. 75 minutes. (Rhino)

Some vintage rock numbers and Miller's always-welcome presence salvage an otherwise tepid excuse for a rock movie.

Chuck Berry: Hail! Hail! Rock 'n' Roll! (1987) ◆◆◆
D: Taylor Hackford. Chuck Berry, Keith Richards, Bo Diddley, Little Richard, Eric Clapton. 121 minutes. (MCA)

Though Chuck remains enigmatic, the music's great, Berry's backstage behavior's fascinating, and most of the guest commentary is compelling. What's missing is archival footage from Chuck's lengthy performing past. What's there is must viewing for anyone with the vaguest interest in American pop culture, Chuck Berry, or rock 'n' roll, which shouldn't leave out too many of us.

The Compleat Beatles (1982) ◆◆◆
D: Patrick Montgomery. Narrated by Malcolm McDowell. 119 minutes. (MGM/UA)

An at-times staid but generally absorbing docu-history of the beloved Moptops, including rare footage from their early Hamburg days. Moore Video, among others, carries the rare kinescopes *Around the Beatles, Beatles Live in London,* and *The Beatles' Tokyo Show,* along with the compilation tape *The Beatles Live.* A quartet of John Lennon tapes— *Interview with a Legend* (Lorimar), the docu-bio *Imagine* (RCA/Columbia), and *John Lennon* and *John Lennon Live in New York City* (both Sony)—are also available.

Crossover Dreams (1985) ◆◆◇
D: Leon Ichaso. Ruben Blades, Shawn Elliot, Tom Signorelli, Elizabeth Pena. 85 minutes. (HBO)

Okay, it's not a rock movie, but a Salsa story with the same plot about the ambitious musical genius who battles his way to the top only to topple from same. Blades gives a good account of himself, though, and the music's hot.

The Decline of Western Civilization (1981) ◆◆◆
D: Penelope Spheeris. Black Flag, Circle Jerks, Fear, Germs, X, others. 100 minutes. (Media)

A lively look at the L.A. punk scene circa 1981, with memorable performances by Fear and the late Darby Crash, among many other greats, near-greats, and nowhere-near-greats. Spheeris does an equally adept job covering the contemporary head-banger scene in *The Decline of Western Civilization II: The Metal Years* (RCA/

Columbia). For further journeys into punk-rock turf, try *Another State of Mind* (Videotakes), *Punk Rock Movie* (Sun), *Punk Special* (Sony), and *Urgh! A Music War* (CBS/Fox).

Dirty Dancing (1987) ♦♦

D: Emile Ardolino. Patrick Swayze, Jennifer Grey, Jerry Orbach. 105 minutes. (Vestron)

This simple, unexpectedly successful Catskills fairy tale—the *Flashdance* of its day—pushes all the right buttons, even inspiring a live touring musical review based on the movie (which may be a first) and a prime-time TV series. Did we mention the CD?

D.O.A.: A Right of Passage (1981) ♦♦

D: Lech Kowalski. Sex Pistols, Dead Boys, Generation X, Terry and the Idiots, X-Ray Specs, Sid Vicious, Nancy Spungen. 93 minutes. (Lightning)

Kowalski's *D.O.A.* pales beside Penelope Spheeris's superior *Decline of Western Civilization*, but this rockumentary look at London's prefab punks the Sex Pistols makes for a fitting companion to Alex Cox's fictional *Sid and Nancy* (see index).

Don't Look Back (1967) ♦♦♦ B&W

D: D. A. Pennebaker. Bob Dylan, Joan Baez, Donovan, Albert Grossman, Alan Price. 95 minutes. (Paramount)

Pennebaker's still-compelling *Portrait of the Artist as a Young Electric Folkie* captures an exciting time and preserves some of Bob's

finest perfs. Bob returns in 1987's *Hard to Handle* (CBS/Fox), with Tom Petty and the Heartbreakers, and the '88 fiction flick *Hearts of Fire* (Lorimar).

du-BEAT-e-o (1984) 0 ♦

D: Alan Sacks. Ray Sharkey, Joan Jett, Derf Scratch. 84 minutes. (Fox Hills)

Sharkey hits rock bottom as your typical greasy middle-aged Brooklyn-accented El Lay punk hipster in this made-for-midnight manqué mess. With the help of former Fear bassist Derf Scratch, Ray "edits" some useless Joan Jett footage while providing a running (make that limping) voice-over commentary re: the nonaction. Pretty amazing.

Eddie and the Cruisers (1983) ♦♦◇

D: Martin Davidson. Michael Paré, Tom Berenger, Ellen Barkin, John Stockwell. 110 minutes. (Embassy)

Paré makes like Bruce Springsteen in an overly compromised script that nonetheless has its moments. And while we agree that Bobby Freeman's original "Betty Lou Got a New Pair of Shoes" is a ditty of vast profundity, that's no excuse to beat it to death.

Fillmore (1972) ♦♦♦

D: Richard T. Heffron. Bill Graham, Grateful Dead, Santana, Jefferson Airplane, Quicksilver Messenger Service. 105 minutes. (All-Star Video)

The film that dares to take you backstage during 'Frisco's famed rock palace's final daze for a closeup look at rock-biz legend Bill Graham. The music makes it worth the trip.

Flashdance (1983) ◆◇
D: Adrian Lyne. Jennifer Beals, Michael Nouri, Lilia Skala. 95 minutes. (Paramount)

Beals fills her leotards to perfection, while a less heralded stand-in handles the more difficult terpsichorean chores. The *Dirty Dancing* of its day. What a feeling.

Forbidden Zone (1980) ◆◆◆ **B&W**
D: Richard Elfman. Herve Villechaize, Susan Tyrrell, Viva. 75 minutes. (Media)

A made-for-midnight musical freakshow featuring Villechaize and Tyrrell as the rulers of the Sixth Dimension. Original score by Oingo Boingo. Authentically demented.

Get Crazy (1983) ◆◆◇
D: Allan Arkush. Daniel Stern, Gail Edwards, Malcolm McDowell, Lou Reed, Fabian. 98 minutes. (Embassy)

A hit-and-miss rock parody whose ideas outshine the execution. Pales beside Rob Reiner's brilliant *This Is Spinal Tap* (see index).

Gimme Shelter (1970) ◆◆◇
D: David Maysles, Albert Maysles. Rolling Stones, Jefferson Airplane. 91 minutes. (RCA/Columbia)

Topnotch Stones concert footage is intercut with the widely hailed "end of an era" Altamont gig, where an onstage murder took place. Then again, any attempt to associate the real-life Hell's Angels with "good vibes" always represented a latently lethal case of wishful thinking.

The Girl Can't Help It (1956) ◆◆◇
D: Frank Tashlin. Jayne Mansfield, Tom Ewell, Edmond O'Brien, Julie London, Gene Vincent, Little Richard. 99 minutes. (Key)

A broad but undeniably iconic comedy, with Ewell as a boozy, has-been agent ordered by gangster O'Brien to transform buxom blond lust object Mansfield into a rock star. Uneven as entertainment, essential as pop history, featuring perfs by Little Richard, Gene Vincent, Fats Domino, and the Platters.

Go-Go Big Beat (1983) NR
70 minutes. (Rhino)

A '60s British Invasion video featuring in-concert clips of The Animals, Hollies, Merseybeats, Lulu, and others.

Go, Johnny, Go! (1959) ◆◆◇ **B&W**
D: Paul Landres. Alan Freed, Jimmy Clanton, Chuck Berry, Sandy Stewart. 75 minutes. (Video Treasures)

Clanton is amiably awful as a troubled teen transmuted into a rock star by Freed, but Chuck Berry, Jackie Wilson, the Cadillacs, and the Flamingos more than compensate for the flick's dramatic shortcomings.

Grease (1978) ◆◇
D: Randal Kleiser. John Travolta, Olivia Newton-John, Stockard Channing, Sid Caesar. 111 minutes. (Paramount)

A generally insufferable exercise in brain-dead nostalgia. *Grease 2* (also Paramount) at least had the advantage of being so bad it was occasionally funny, as well as a memorable musical ode to fallout shelters that left us humming the melody.

Hair (1979) ◆◇
D: Milos Forman. John Savage, Treat Williams, Beverly D'Angelo. 121 minutes. (MGM/UA)

Correctly perceived as the first major show-biz co-optation of the "counterculture," the Broadway smash made a belated movie debut and is now widely viewed as a more or less "authentic" artifact of its era! Which only goes to prove that the more things change, the less they alter.

A Hard Day's Night (1964) ◆◆◆ B&W
D: Richard Lester. John Lennon, Paul McCartney, Ringo Starr, George Harrison, Wilfred Brambell, Victor Spinetti. 88 minutes. (MPI)

Lester's classy Brit equivalent of a Sam Katzman youth-trend quickie plays too slight and cute today to earn the kudos it did back then. But it's still fun, catchy, and occasionally clever.

The Harder They Come (1973) ◆◆◆
D: Perry Henzell. Jimmy Cliff, Janet Barkley, Carl Bradshaw. 98 minutes. (HBO)

The sometimes-ragged filmmaking rarely gets in the way of this simple but idiosyncratic fable of failed reggae rocker Cliff, who becomes a local hero by acting out his spaghetti western fantasies. Music—by Toots and the Maytals, Cliff, et al.—is more than first-rate.

Help! (1965) ◆◆◇
D: Richard Lester. John Lennon, Paul McCartney, George Harrison, Ringo Starr, Victor Spinetti, Leo McKern, Eleanor Bron, Roy Kinnear. 90 minutes. (MPI)

The Fab Four's wild and crazy Bond spoof doesn't hold up as well as *A Hard Day's Night* (see index) but has enough hot tunes and mirthful moments to make it worth a viewing.

The Idolmaker (1980) ◆◆
D: Taylor Hackford. Ray Sharkey, Tovah Feldshuh, Peter Gallagher. 119 minutes. (MGM/UA)

Sharkey gets his big break playing a late-'50s rock-biz mover and shaker who launches the careers of fictional Fabian and Frankie Avalon counterparts. Better than *du-BEAT-e-o*, if not a whole lot more authentic.

Jailhouse Rock (1957) ◆◆◆ B&W
D: Richard Thorpe. Elvis Presley, Dean Jones, Judy Tyler. 96 minutes. (MGM/UA)

Probably Presley's best pure rock 'n' roll effort, this fun Elvis vehicle casts The King as a teen rebel who rises from convict to rock star. Elvis gets to act tough, sexy, and tender by turns, while wailing four of his better songs (composed by the top team of Leiber and Stoller, who wrote most of the Coasters' classic hits, among myriad other musical material), including "Treat Me Nice" and the title tune,

part of an impressive prison production number. *Jailhouse Rock* remains one of the few films to exploit Elvis properly, though several of his more dramatic turns— notably Don Siegel's *Flaming Star* (see index)—have stood the test of time. See sidebar for El's complete celluloid career.

Elvis Onscreen:

He Lost It at the Movies

Tall, hunky, handsome, topped by a patented mile-high pompadour (a shiny blue-black in Technicolor), with a swaying pelvis and a ready sneer, Elvis seemed nothing if not a screen natural. Yet he rarely landed roles that did justice to the bawdy, bluesy, black-leather image he'd so successfully created on vinyl. Even at the height of his recording and performing notoriety, Elvis failed to equal that rock-outlaw profile on film. And this at a time when the celluloid bad boy—pioneered by Marlon Brando and James Dean—was enjoying his Hollywood heyday.

Part of the blame can be assigned to El's own basic bad-boy/good-boy dichotomy. The Elvis who could visually and vocally seduce legions of adolescent girls and provide a tough role model for their male counterparts was offset by Elvis the loyal son, whose most urgent goal was to build a house for his mom. It was this softer side that El revealed in his first film, 1956's *Love Me Tender,* a routine western highlighted by Pres's earnest interpretation of the sentimental title tune.

El's next two vehicles—*Loving You* and *Jailhouse Rock* (both 1957)— came closest to capturing his bad-boy persona, showcasing him as a rock 'n' roll brawler. Elvis again got to mix it up pretty good, this time as a New Orleans rocker with underworld ties, in the following year's *King Creole,* a transplanted adaptation of Harold Robbins's *A Stone for Danny Fisher.* But in 1958, Uncle Sam stepped in to play a major role in erasing El's outlaw image by casting him as just another clean-cut, good-guy GI. Those widely circulated snaps immortalizing El's first military haircut represented nothing less than a symbolic, Samson-like castration that succeeded in shearing Elvis of his bad-boy image as well. The hair grew back; the image didn't.

Since El couldn't return to his pre-army teen roles—he was, after all, pushing twenty-six—the time seemed right to move him into heavier parts. Elvis seemed headed in that direction when he turned in a solid perf as Pacer, a conflicted half-breed Indian, in Don Siegel's *Flaming Star* (1960), followed by his portrayal of a moody country boy with literary ambitions in 1961's *Wild in the Country,* based on the J. R. Salamanca novel of the same name.

But instead of continuing in this vein, Elvis opted for a succession of mostly mindless musicals numbing in their vacuity and reliance on formula. Flick after flick found El sleepwalking through roles as a singing lifeguard or roustabout or bush pilot in Hawaii, Vegas, or Fort Lauderdale who wins, loses, and regains the affections of Donna Douglas, Shelley Fabares, Ann-Margret, pausing every ten minutes or so to belt out generally abysmal tunes like "Cotton Candy Land" and "Song of the Shrimp" (!). Elvis had gone beyond "good boy" to become the epitome of show-biz sterility.

The chief culprit here was El's agent/manager/father figure Colonel Tom Parker, who viewed his protégé as pure merchandise. From mid-1960 until 1968, Elvis made no TV or concert appearances. If you wanted to catch The King, you had to buy a movie ticket. And millions did, no matter how awful the films.

The venerable Tinseltown truism—adapt or die—finally caught up with Elvis in the late '60s. At a time when the Beatles were revolutionizing rock with "Sgt. Pepper," Elvis was wooing Nancy Sinatra with "There's Nothing Like a Song." The one-time King of Rock 'n' Roll couldn't have been more out of it. Or, suddenly, less bankable.

In a belated bid to escape this B-movie morass, El briefly tinkered with onscreen image changes, going the Clint Eastwood route as a laconic gunslinger in *Charro!* and portraying a ghetto-clinic doctor opposite aspiring nun Mary Tyler Moore in *Change of Habit*—flicks that failed to click even with El's hard-core fans. Adhering to past policy— the show-biz equivalent of strip-mining—the Colonel simply withdrew Elvis from this depleted vein and steered him back into TV specials and live concerts, sparking a musical comeback that lasted until El's fatal surrender to drugs and apathy.

The roster of rock stars who've failed to make a successful transition to the screen is a lengthy one: Paul Simon, Rick Springfield, and (thus far) Sting rank among the more recent. However undistinguished El's movie career may have been, his thirty-one-film output at least constitutes a tribute to his popularity and staying power.

There was one role El desperately wanted to play—that of the faded rock idol (eventually taken by Kris Kristofferson) in Barbra Streisand's remake of *A Star Is Born*. We don't know how Elvis might have fared, but it was surely a part for which he'd been well prepared.

ELVIDEO: THE KING ON CASSETTE

Blue Hawaii (1961) ◆◆ *D: Norman Taurog. Joan Blackman, Angela Lansbury, Roland Winters. 103 minutes. (Key)*
Lightweight island antics with El as an ex-GI-turned-travel-agent. Fourteen songs, some fairly awful. Said to be El's personal fave.

Change of Habit (1969) ◆◇ *D: William Graham. Mary Tyler Moore, Barbara McNair, Ed Asner. 97 minutes. (MCA)*
El goes through them changes, playing a ghetto clinic doctor opposite Moore's nun in what proved to be El's final filmic fling.

Charro! (1969) ◆◇ *D: Charles Marquis Warren. Ina Balin, Victor French. 98 minutes. (Playhouse)*
Elvis, limited to one song here, fails in his bid to play a Clint Eastwood—type hero in this dreary sagebrush mess.

Clambake (1967) ◆◇ *D: Arthur H. Nadel. Shelley Fabares, Bill Bixby, James Gregory. 100 minutes. (MGM/UA)*
This fairly dismal affair finds millionaire dropout Elvis charming Fabares.

Double Trouble (1966) ◆◇ *D: Norman Taurog. Annette Day, John Williams, Yvonne Romain. 91 minutes. (MGM/UA)*
Rock star El lands in London and the title jam in this predictable Presley outing. Along the way, Elvis offers his interpretation of "Old MacDonald."

Easy Come, Easy Go (1967) ◆◇ *D: John Rich. Dodie Marshal, Pat Priest, Pat Harrington. 96 minutes. (Paramount)*
Frogman Elvis dives for treasure, comes up with Marshal. Six songs.

Flaming Star (1960) ◆◆◆ *D: Don Siegel. Barbara Eden, Steve Forrest, Dolores Del Rio. 92 minutes. (Key)*
El shines as a conflicted half-breed Indian in this solid Don Siegel western. Light on music, but Pres contributes a strong perf.

Follow That Dream (1962) ◆◆◇ *D: Gordon Douglas. Arthur O'Connell, Anne Helm, Joanna Moore. 111 minutes. (MGM/UA)*
Elvis plays a Florida homesteader in a musical adaptation of Richard Powell's novel *Pioneer Go Home.*

Frankie and Johnny (1966) ◆◇ *D: Frederick de Cordova. Donna Douglas, Harry Morgan, Robert Strauss. 88 minutes. (MGM/UA)*
A pretty flat songfest, with El and Beverly Hillbilly Douglas in the title roles.

Fun in Acapulco (1963) ◆◆ *D: Richard Thorpe. Ursula Andress, Paul Lukas. 100 minutes. (Key)*
Singing lifeguard Elvis woos female matador (!) Andress South of the Border. Ten songs.

G.I. Blues (1960) ◆◆◇ *D: Norman Taurog. Juliet Prowse, James Douglas, Robert Ivers. 115 minutes. (Key)*
G.I. Elvis romances Prowse in a routine outing that marked the start of El's premature decline as a rock 'n' roll rebel.

Girls! Girls! Girls! (1962) ◆◆ *D: Norman Taurog. Stella Stevens, Laurel Goodwin. 106 minutes. (Key)*
El loses, regains Stella's affections in another island-set songfest featuring no fewer than fourteen tunes.

Harum Scarum (1965) ◆ *D: Gene Nelson. Mary Ann Mobley, Fran Jeffries, Michael Ansara. 85 minutes. (MGM/UA)*
El hits the pits in this dismal Middle East—set spy "comedy" that inspired the *Airplane!* crew's later spoof *Top Secret!* (see index). Ten songs.

It Happened at the World's Fair (1963) ◆◆ *D: Norman Taurog. Joan O'Brien, Gary Lockwood, Yvonne Craig. 105 minutes. (MGM/UA)*
Bush pilot El romances O'Brien in Seattle. Pretty bleak, with ten songs.

Kid Galahad (1962) ◆◆ *D: Phil Karlson. Lola Albright, Charles Bronson, Gig Young. 95 minutes. (MGM/UA)*
A remake of the old Warner Bros.' boxing classic, wherein Elvis rocks and rolls with the punches.

King Creole (1958) ◆◆◇ **B&W** *D: Michael Curtiz. Carolyn Jones, Dolores Hart, Walter Matthau. 116 minutes. (Key)*
This downbeat flick—the only Presley pic directed by Michael (*Casablanca*) Curtiz—features El as a New Orleans singer with underworld ties.

Love Me Tender (1956) ◆◆◇ **B&W** *D: Robert D. Webb. Richard Egan, Debra Paget, Neville Brand. 94 minutes. (Key)*
In his feature debut, Elvis plays Egan's kid brother in a standard Civil War western.

Loving You (1957) ◆◆◇ *D: Hal Kanter. Wendell Corey, Lizabeth Scott, Dolores Hart. 102 minutes. (Warner)*
Rock success swells El's head till he learns his lesson. A pretty fair Pres pic with several choice songs, including "Teddy Bear."

Paradise, Hawaiian Style (1964) ◆◇ *D: Michael Moore. Suzanna Leigh, James Shigeta, Donna Butterworth. 91 minutes. (Key)*
Charter pilot El flies Hawaii-ward to woo Leigh and warble eleven songs.

Roustabout (1964) ◆◆◇ *D: John Rich. Barbara Stanwyck, Leif Erickson. 101 minutes. (Key)*
El's got sawdust in his blood, a song in his heart, and Joan Freeman under his skin. He still finds time to emote with Stanwyck and sing eleven songs.

Speedway (1968) ◆◇ *D: Norman Taurog. Nancy Sinatra, Bill Bixby, Gale Gordon. 90 minutes. (MGM/UA)*
Stock-car racer El romances IRS agent Nancy Sinatra (!) while successfully avoiding the latter's latently lethal boots.

Tickle Me (1965) ◆◇ *D: Norman Taurog. Julie Adams, Jocelyn Lane. 90 minutes. (Key)*
EP's a rodeo rider at an all-femme ranch. Consider the possibilities! Nine songs.

Viva Las Vegas (1963) ◆◆◇ *D: George Sidney. Ann-Margret, William Demarest. 85 minutes. (MGM/UA)*
Grand Prix racer Pres romances Ann-Margret at the title locale, dances to David Winters's choreography, croons eight tunes.

Wild in the Country (1961) ◆◆◇ *D: Philip Dunne. Hope Lange, Tuesday Weld, Gary Lockwood. 112 minutes. (Key)*
Elvis again goes the dramatic route as a rural youth with a hankerin' to become a big-time writer.

At long last completing El's video oeuvre are: *Girl Happy, Kissin' Cousins, Live a Little, Love a Little, Spinout, Stay Away, Joe,* and *The Trouble with Girls,* recently issued by MGM/UA.

Documentaries, Compilations, and Concert Cassettes

Early Elvis (1983) B&W *56 minutes. (Video Yesteryear)*
Includes El's TV appearances on Steve Allen, Ed Sullivan, and the Dorsey Brothers' "Stage Show" series. Ten tunes and a comedy skit.

Elvis, Vol. 1–4 (1987) *30 minutes each. (New Image)*
An Elvis-oriented series examining various aspects of El's life, music, legacy, and fans.

Elvis . . . Aloha From Hawaii (1985) *75 minutes. (Media)*
El's 1973 Hawaiian concert special.

Elvis and Marilyn (1982) B&W *60 minutes. (Discount)*
Includes El's Ed Sullivan appearances.

Elvis '56 (1985) B&W *61 minutes. (Videotakes)*
Levon Helm narrates a docu-recreation of El's breakthrough year.

Elvis in the 50s (1984) B&W *60 minutes. (Discount)*
El's rare TV appearances.

Elvis Memories (1986) B&W/color *48 minutes. (Vestron)*
A docu-look at the King, with home-movie and concert clips, interviews, and salutes from Cybill Shepherd, Merle Haggard, Dick Clark, and others.

Elvis' 1968 Comeback Special (1985) *76 minutes. (Media)*
The famous TV special that led to El's concert comeback. Pres delivers many early hits, along with "Guitar Man," and gets down with his sidemen in an informal jam session.

Elvis on Tour (1986) *93 minutes. (MGM/UA)*
Elvis on and off-stage during a whirlwind 1972 concert tour.

Elvis—One Night with You (1985) *53 minutes. (Media)*
Unedited performance from his 1968 Christmas special finds El singing "Are You Lonesome Tonight," among other songs.

Elvis Presley's Graceland (1984) *60 minutes. (Congress)*
Priscilla Presley conducts a tour of the title site.

Elvis—That's The Way It Is (1970) *109 minutes. (MGM/UA)*
Behind-the-scenes look at Elvis's 1970 concert tour, featuring live performances of over 30 songs.

Elvis: The Echo Will Never Die (1986) B&W/color *50 minutes. (MPI)*
Friends, family members, and fellow celebs—including B. B. King, Ursula Andress, and Sammy Davis Jr.—share their thoughts re: Elvis's career.

King of Rock 'n' Roll Collection (1987) B&W/color *86 minutes. (Cinemacabre)*
Trailers from all of Elvis's movies, from *Love Me Tender* to *Charro!*, and three documentary features. An Elvis addict's dream.

Mondo Elvis (1985) B&W/color *60 minutes. (Rhino)*
A less flattering look at El's life, times, and fanatical followers.

Rock 'n' Roll Heaven (1984) B&W/color *60 minutes. MGM/UA*
A Don Kirschner compilation focusing on deceased rock stars, including Elvis, Buddy Holly, Eddie Cochran, Bill Haley, and John Lennon.

Singer Presents "Elvis" (the 1968 Comeback Special) Outtakes (1986) *54 minutes. (Video Yesteryear)*
Like it says.

Stage Show (1983) B&W *29 minutes. (Video Yesteryear)*
The complete episode of the Dorsey Brothers' 1955 show, with El's tunes and the original commercials intact.

This Is Elvis (1981) B&W/color *144 minutes. (Warner)*
A thorough look at El's life and times, featuring nearly forty songs and some 40 minutes of previously unseen footage.

Fictional features *about* the King include *Elvis* (Vestron), *Elvis and Me* (New World), and *Heartbreak Hotel* [Touchstone].

Test Your EQ (Elvis Quotient)

Match the awful tunes Elvis was compelled to sing with the movies in which they were performed.

1. "Edge of Reality"	a. *Girl Happy*
2. "Cotton Candy Land"	b. *Live a Little, Love a Little*
3. "Ito Eats"	c. *Speedway*
4. "Do the Clam"	d. *Blue Hawaii*
5. "Song of the Shrimp"	e. *Clambake*
6. "Your Groovy Self"	f. *Paradise, Hawaiian Style*
7. "Yoga Is As Yoga Does"	g. *Fun in Acapulco*
8. "No Room to Rhumba in a Sportscar"	h. *It Happened At the World's Fair*
9. "Queen Washine's Papaya"	i. *Easy Come, Easy Go*
10. "Who Needs Money?"	j. *Girls! Girls! Girls!*

Answers:
1. b
2. h
3. d
4. a
5. j
6. c
7. i
8. g
9. f
10. e

Janis (1975) ◆◆◆
D: Howard Alk, Seaton Findlay. Janis Joplin. 96 minutes. (MCA)

While not tremendously insightful in the psychobio department, *Janis* more than pulls its weight musically, making it a must for Joplin's still-flourishing fan ranks.

Joe Cocker: Mad Dogs and Englishmen (1971) ◆◆◇
D: Pierre Adidge. Joe Cocker, Rita Coolidge, Leon Russell. 118 minutes. (RCA/Columbia)

If you like the twitchy singer, you'll go for this rousing rockumentary. It also helps if you can tolerate erstwhile "Cosmic Master of Time and Space" Leon Russell.

Jubilee (1981) NR
D: Derek Jarman. Adam Ant, Toyah Wilcox, Jenny Runacre. 103 minutes. (Media)

A popular anarchic Brit fantasy depicting a punk takeover of Old Blighty that features music by Adam Ant, Eno, Jayne County, Souixsie and the Banshees, plus an appearance by Rocky Horror's Little Nell.

The Kids Are Alright (1979) NR
D: Jeff Stein. The Who, Steve Martin, Ringo Starr. 106 minutes. (HBO)

Who enthusiasts will enjoy this long look at the pioneering Brit rockers; others won't be tempted.

La Bamba (1987) ◆◆◇
D: Luis Valdez. Lou Diamond Phillips, Esai Morales, Joe Pantoliano. 103 minutes. (RCA/Columbia)

La Bamba's fetishistic devotion to '50s artifacts results in postcard sets iconized to the point of utter artificiality. Clumsy comic-book plot contrivances and wild anachronisms (did they really say "Right on!" and "Tell me about it!" in the '50s? Yeah? Well, far out!) further reduce credibility. The upside: the music.

The Last Waltz (1978) ◆◆◆◇
D: Martin Scorsese. The Band, Bob Dylan, Neil Diamond, Ringo Starr. 117 minutes. (MGM/UA)

Scorsese succeeded in raising the rockumentary to a new cinematic plateau with his preservation of The Band's farewell concert.

Let It Be (1970) ◆◆◆
D: Michael Lindsay-Hogg. John Lennon, Paul McCartney, George Harrison, Ringo Starr, Yoko Ono. 80 minutes. (CBS/Fox)

The Beatles bicker and play in an interesting rock-doc that illustrates many of the reasons behind the boys' encroaching breakup.

Let It Rock (1988) ◆◆
D: Roland Klick. Dennis Hopper, Terrance Robay, Ramona Sweeney, David Hess. 90 minutes. (Media)

Hopper, toplining as a sleazy rock 'n' roll promoter (pardon our redundancy), is the main point of interest in Klick's competently told but unexciting story about a gimmick rocker named White Star (also the pic's original handle), played by Robay.

Let's Spend the Night Together (1982) ◆◆◇
D: Hal Ashby. The Rolling Stones. 94 minutes. (Embassy)

A fairly pedestrian account of the Stones' 1981 tour that's enjoyable enough for their hard-core fans.

Lisztomania (1975) NR
D: Ken Russell. Roger Daltrey, Sarah Kestelman, Fiona Lewis, Ringo Starr. 106 minutes. (Warner)

Russell's determinedly bizarro Liszt bio may be beyond our Ken, but if you dig Daltrey and

Russell, you may have a better time with it.

Magical Mystery Tour (1968) ♦♦♦
D: The Beatles. John Lennon, Paul Mc-Cartney, George Harrison, Ringo Starr. 60 minutes. (MPI)

Essentially a 60-minute rock video illustrating the 1967 title LP, the group's follow-up to *Sgt. Pepper.* Songs include "I Am the Walrus" and "Fool on the Hill." MPI's video has been digitally remastered from the 35mm print and original LP recording sessions.

Monterey Pop (1969) ♦♦♦
D: Albert Maysles, D. A. Pennebaker, others. Otis Redding, The Animals, Jimi Hendrix, Janis Joplin, The Who. 72 minutes. (Sony)

Seven documentarians shared filmmaking chores on this trail-blazing concert pic, highlighted by legendary turns by Janis and Jimi. Jimi likewise rules in *Rainbow Bridge* (Rhino), along with *Jimi Hendrix* (Warner), *Jimi Hendrix: Johnny B. Goode, Jimi Hendrix Videogram,* and *Jimi Plays Berkeley* (all Sony).

One Trick Pony (1980) NR
D: Robert M. Young. Paul Simon, Blair Brown, Rip Torn. 100 minutes. (Warner)

Simon's rock lament is best left to the diminutive balladeer's boosters; Garfunkel fans, on the other hand, will be sorely disappointed.

Pink Floyd—The Wall (1982) NR
D: Alan Parker. Bob Geldof, Christine Hargreaves, Bob Hoskins. 95 minutes. (MGM/UA)

Pink Floyd's rather grim, pretentious rock video has been a staple on the midnight circuit for years. Now you can watch it without waiting on line.

Purple Rain (1984) ♦♦
D: Albert Magnoli. Prince, Apollonia Kotero, Morris Day, Jerome Benton. 111 minutes. (Warner)

Prince's feature-length self-homage offers a number of catchy songs, Apollonia's pulchritudinous presence, and funny perfs by Benton and Day. Now, if only Prince weren't in the way. Then again, *Purple* shines compared with the feeble follow-up fantasy *Under the Cherry Moon* (Warner).

Quadrophenia (1979) ♦♦
D: Franc Roddam. Phil Daniels, Mark Wingett, Leslie Ash, Sting. 115 minutes. (RCA/Columbia)

A highly praised Mods-vs.-Rockers duke-out set in mid-'60s Britain and inspired by the Who album of the same name, *Quadrophenia* works okay as pop sociology, but profound it ain't.

Ray Davies: Return to Waterloo (1985) NR
D: Ray Davies. Ken Colley, Valerie Holliman, Dominique Barnes. 61 minutes. (RCA/Columbia)

Davies and his Kinks have crafted some top concept LPs over the decades; the movie should please, or at least intrigue, Kink cultists.

Rock, Baby, Rock It (1957) ♦♦◇ B&W
D: Murray Sporup. Kay Wheeler, Johnny Carroll, Preacher Smith and The Deacons, Cell Block Seven, The Five Stars. 80 minutes. (Rhino)

A Dallas-lensed amateur-night special offering '50s rock fans their sole opportunity to catch such rockabilly and doo-wop originals as Preacher Smith and The Deacons, Rosco Gordon and The Red Tops, and the immortal Cell Block Seven. So *carpe diem*, dig?

Rock & Rule (1983) NR
D: Clive A. Smith. Voices of Catherine O'Hara, Don Francks, Paul Le Mat. 85 minutes. (MGM/UA)

The animation and rock score, with contributions from Lou Reed, Iggy Pop, and Debbie Harry, among others, bolster a frail, fabulistic story line.

Rock 'n' Roll High School (1979) ♦♦◇
D: Allan Arkush. P. J. Soles, Vincent Van Patten, Clint Howard, Mary Woronov, Paul Bartel, The Ramones. 93 minutes. (Warner)

The comedy is fairly lame, but The Ramones, in their first and only celluloid vehicle, along with B-movie cult couple Woronov and Bartel, make this one worth a look and listen.

Rock 'n' Roll Wrestling (1985) NR
"Exotic" Adrian Street, Randy "Macho Man" Savage, The Fabulous Ones. 60 minutes. (Rhino)

Savage, Kamala the Ugandan Giant, and other canvas cult figures twist and shout for your viewing and listening pleasure.

Rock, Pretty Baby (1956) ♦♦
D: Richard H. Bartlett. John Saxon, Sal Mineo, Luana Patten, Rod McKuen, Fay Wray. 88 minutes. (Kartes)

One of the '50s' more wholesome and less compelling youth movies, complete with a Henry Mancini (!) score, involving a high school band competition. The answer to the popular trivia query: What was Fay Wray and Rod McKuen's only screen teaming?

Rock, Rock, Rock! (1956) ♦♦◇ B&W
D: Will Price. Alan Freed, Tuesday Weld, Teddy Randazzo. 78 minutes. (Goodtimes)

A barely pubescent Weld schemes to buy a prom dress and win the affection of greasy heartthrob Randazzo. The music, supplied by Chuck Berry, Frankie Lymon, The Flamingos, and the vastly underrated Cirino and the Bowties, makes it all worthwhile.

Rock You Sinners (1957) NR B&W
D: Dennis Kavanaugh. Phillip Gilbert, Colin Craft, Adrienne Scott. 59 minutes. (Video Yesteryear)

A less-than-stellar assemblage of early Brit rockers hold forth in a black-and-white curio recommended for '50s rock-roots completists, who many also want to check out the Brit-based obscurity *Sweetbeat* (Vidcrest), featuring cameos by '50s doo-wop wizards

The 5 Satins and the MellowKings. Freddy and the Dreamers fans, meanwhile, can find their faves in their only screen vehicle, *Seaside Swingers* (Charter).

The Rose (1979) ◆◆◆
D: Mark Rydell. Bette Midler, Alan Bates, Frederic Forrest, Harry Dean Stanton. 134 minutes. (CBS/Fox)

Bette does Janis in a sometimes maudlin, more often engrossing bio of a manic-depressive rock goddess's triumphs and travails.

Shock Treatment (1981) NR
D: Jim Sharman. Jessica Harper, Cliff De Young, Richard O'Brien, Nell Campbell. 94 minutes. (CBS/Fox)

The all-time cult-movie king, *The Rocky Horror Picture Show*, continues to make money on the midnight circuit and remains legally unavailable on video (though the Japanese-subtitled laserdisc can be had). Sharman's *Rocky* revamp, which returns many of the same characters to the fore, is still out on cassette, if not always easy to find.

Sid and Nancy (1986) ◆◆◆
D: Alex Cox. Gary Oldman, Chloe Webb, Drew Schofield, David Hayman, Debby Bishop, Tony London. 111 minutes. (Embassy)

Alex (*Repo Man*) Cox's *Sid and Nancy* is basically a blatant exploitation film masquerading as a biopic, but how else to depict the pathetic, determinedly self-destructive lowlives of addled, prefab punk "star" Sid Vicious and his whining groupie girlfriend Nancy Spungen? Cox's camera acts as an inveterate voyeur, spying on the pair—expertly embodied by Oldman and Webb—as they conduct their chemical-laced courtship in London, tour the States with The Sex Pistols, and further degenerate into smack zombies in NYC, leading to their early, violent demises. Despite the duo's downbeat antics, the flick is rich in black irony and mordant wit. Sid himself can be seen in *Sex Pistols: Buried Alive* (Sony).

Smithereens (1982) ◆◆◇
D: Susan Seidelman. Susan Berman, Brad Rijn, Richard Hell. 90 minutes. (Media)

Seidelman's debut feature is an alternately pungent and self-conscious account of aggressive nonentity Berman's vague search for ill-defined New Wave fame in NYC's East Village.

Starstruck (1982) ◆
D: Gillian Armstrong. Jo Kennedy, Ross O'Donovan, Pat Evison. 95 minutes. (Embassy)

Some, like yours truly, find this Aussie rock musical—sort of a Down Under *Smithereens*—smarmy in the extreme; others like it a lot. A hit or the pits? Videophile, *you* decide!

Stop Making Sense (1984) ◆◆◆◇
D: Jonathan Demme. The Talking Heads. 99 minutes. (RCA/Columbia)

An excellent concert film, with Talking Heads head Byrne performing an acoustic solo act, then leading his troops through a lively second set. Demme's camera ever complements, never competes with, the music.

Sympathy for the Devil (1970) ◆◆◇
D: Jean-Luc Godard. The Rolling Stones. 110 minutes. (CBS/Fox)

Godard a-Go-Go! Jean-Luc looks to the Stones as revolutionary symbols (or, in Charlie Watts's case, cymbals) in a studied mockumentary that's too dull for its—and our—own good.

That Was Rock (1965/1988) ◆◆◆◇
B&W/color
D: Larry Peerce. Chuck Berry, James Brown, Ray Charles, Bo Diddley, The Rolling Stones, The Supremes. 90 minutes. (Media)

A reedited compilation film that comprises the best of two dynamite '60s concert films, The T.A.M.I. Show and The Big T.N.T. Show (both NA), with new linking footage featuring Chuck Berry. One of the best rock-docs around.

That'll Be the Day (1974) NR
D: Claude Whatham. Ringo Starr, David Essex, Keith Moon. 86 minutes. (HBO)

Loosely based on John Lennon's early life, this kitchen-sink drama traces a working-class Brit youth's entry into rock and roll, a story continued in the sequel Stardust (NA).

That's the Way of the World (1975) ◆◆◆
D: Sig Shore. Harvey Keitel, Bert Parks, Cynthia Bostick, Jimmy Boyd, Ed Nelson. 100 minutes. (USA)

Aka Shining Star, Sig (Sudden Death) Shore's inside-rock exposé is a crudely lensed but oddly compelling tale (scripted by columnist Robert Lipsyte) about a maverick engineer (Keitel) and his involvement with Mafia bigs and a "wholesome" singing trio who include ex–Miss America emcee Parks (as a child molester!) and ex-juve sitcom stalwart Boyd as Bert's junkie son. Soulsters Earth, Wind and Fire appear as another band under Keitel's audio wing; they also recorded the soundtrack LP, which is better known than the movie. The tape, on the defunct USA label, is an elusive item, however.

Tommy (1975) NR
D: Ken Russell. Roger Daltrey, Ann-Margret, Tina Turner, Oliver Reed. 111 minutes. (RCA/Columbia)

The Who's lavish rock opera is a taste we admittedly haven't acquired. If you have, well, here it is in all its psychedelic glory.

Two Hundred Motels (1971) ◆◆◆
D: Frank Zappa, Tony Palmer. Frank Zappa, Theodore Bikel, Ringo Starr, Keith Moon. 98 minutes. (MGM/UA)

Two Hundred Motels is a must for Zappa lovers, and a fairly funny paranoia-tinged shaggy-rock-band satire for the rest. Frank zaps couch potatoes anew with his

Baby Snakes, Does Humor Belong in Music?, The True Story of Two Hundred Motels, Uncle Meat, and *Video From Hell* (all MPI).

Wild Style (1983) NR

D: Charlie Ahearn. Lee Quinones, Sandra Fabara, Grand Master Flash. 82 minutes. (WesternWorld, Program Hunter's, Inc.)

Probably the best of the brief wave of breakin'/rappin' pics. Gluttons for the genre may also want to try *Beat Street* (Vestron), *Breakin', Breakin' 2, Rappin'* (all MGM/UA), The Fat Boys in *The Disorderlies, Krush Groove* (both Warner), and *Tougher Than Leather* (RCA/Columbia).

Woodstock (1970) ◆◆◇

D: Michael Wadleigh. Joe Cocker, Country Joe and the Fish, Jimi Hendrix. 184 minutes. (Warner) 2 cassettes.

Many fine moments to be sure, but this visual record of the "gathering of the tribes" comes too close to matching the original marathon's length to keep yours truly's spectral toes tapping.

X: The Unheard Music (1985) ◆◆◆

D: W. T. Morgan. John Doe, Exene Cervenka, Billy Zoom, D. J. Bonebrake. 87 minutes. (Key)

Well-done rock-doc detailing the genesis of L.A.'s preem punksters, X, shown offstage and in performance.

Yellow Submarine (1968) ◆◆◆

D: George Dunning. Voices of the Beatles. 85 minutes. (MGM/UA)

A faithful animated visualization of the Fab Fours' whimsical side, with plenty of great cuts from the *Sgt. Pepper* LP. Better than *Sgt. Pepper's Lonely Hearts Club Band* (MCA).

DON'T TOUCH THAT DIAL!
CULT TV & CATHODE FAVES

"Hiya, kids! Hiya, hiya!"

Froggy the Gremlin
Andy's Gang

Don't Touch That Dial!

In its infancy in the late '40s/early '50s, the television medium was just as often referred to as "video" as "TV." (Which probably explains why Al Hodge portrayed pioneering tube space hero Captain Video, rather than Captain Television.) Lately, a sizable industry has developed to cater to those committed couch potatoes interested less in contemporary TV offerings—or movies on video—than in reexperiencing the vintage telefare of their youth, dating as far back as the days when TV and video were synonymous designations. Beyond the efforts of major labels, like Paramount with its highly successful

630

Midnight fiddles while Andy
yearns.

Star Trek video reissues and Warner's repackaging of the long-running
George Reeves–starred *Adventures of Superman*, smaller outfits like
Video Yesteryear, Shokus, Video Resources, and Captain Bijou have
discovered that cassette markets exist for all manner of TV arcana,
from primitive variety shows to commercial collections to pilot
episodes from unsold series.

In our Cult TV section, we've tried to cover a representative range
of the more proven vintage television fare currently being offered.
This includes antique kid-vid shows (*Howdy Doody, Andy's Gang*),
prime-time series (*The Jack Benny Show, Bonanza*), quality specials
(from the likes of video's then-underrated Ernie Kovacs) enduring cult
faves (*The Prisoner*, the aforementioned *Star Trek*), and anything else
we feel fits within the parameters of the Phantom readership's
interests.

We've omitted ratings, along with directorial and guest-cast info,
since most of the entries arranged in this chapter represent TV *series*,
whose quality, behind-the-scenes personnel, and guest casts usually
varied from episode to episode. As with much of the material
contained in this volume, many of the videos listed here—and we're
touching only the proverbial tip of the metaphorical iceberg—are
available only from the vid specialists found in our Videorama
section. The nation's combined television archives contain literally

hundreds of thousands of hours of vintage tube entertainment—good, bad, and indifferent—from which video companies, big and small, will continue to draw. A daunting thought, that, if not a downright scary one.

Abbott and Costello Show (1950s) B&W
Bud Abbott, Lou Costello, Sidney Fields, Hillary Brooke, Joe Besser, Gordon Jones. 50 minutes. (Fox Hills)

A three-episode sampler from A&C's teleseries, funnier and purer than most of their movies and featuring a classic supporting cast.

Adventures of Robin Hood (1955) B&W
Richard Greene. (Video Resources)

Filmed in England, with Greene in the title role, this syndicated series became a big stateside hit as well.

Adventures of Sherlock Holmes (1984)
Jeremy Brett, David Burke. Six episodes. 52 minutes each. (Corinth, Paramount)

The 1984 British series, with Brett as Conan Doyle's famous shamus and Burke as Dr. Watson, offers Sherlock adaptations that are more faithful than most. Most episodes from the '50s black-and-white Brit series of the same title, starring Ronald Howard as Sherlock, are also available, via Discount Video.

Adventures of the Lone Ranger: Justice of the West/Count the Clues (1957) Color/colorized.
Clayton Moore, Jay Silverheels. 72 minutes each. (MGM/UA)

Two tapes, each featuring three episodes from the original teleseries, with definitive Masked Man Moore and Silverheels as his faithful Indian friend Tonto. *Justice of the West* is in color; *Count the Clues* is colorized.

Amos and Andy (1950s) B&W
Tim Moore, Spencer Williams, Jr., Alvin Childress, Ernestine Wade, Nick O'Demus. 52 minutes per two-episode cassette. (Captain Bijou)

The classic series, starring top comic Moore as the Kingfish and actor/director Williams as Andy Brown, has been released on video after being banned from the airwaves for its alleged racism. Actually, it's less racist than, say, *The Jeffersons* (and a lot funnier). The entire Amos and Andy brouhaha—beginning with its radio roots (which, perpetrated by whites Gosden and Correll, were undeniably racist)—is examined in depth in the interesting docuvideo *Amos and Andy: Anatomy of a Controversy* (Goodtimes) featuring Freeman Gosden, Charles

Correll, Jesse Jackson, Ernestine Wade, Redd Foxx, and others.

Andy Griffith Show (1960s) B&W/color
Andy Griffith, Don Knotts, Ronny Howard, Jim Nabors. 60 minutes each. (Premier Promotions/Andy Griffith Videos)

Fully sixty-two episodes, two per cassette and many in color, of this influential South-set sitcom are available, so you can renew your acquaintanceship with the Mayberry crew. In fact, you can even get them packaged according to your favorite star, including *The Best of Floyd* (!).

Andy's Gang (1950s) B&W
Andy Devine. 60 minutes per two-episode tape. (Video Resources)

Possibly the most bizarre kid show ever, Ferrin's long-running series starred Devine as your host. Each episode offers a dull segment from an ongoing India-set serial about a Sabu-like elephant boy; a musical duet between Midnight the Cat (violin, keyboards) and Squeaky the Mouse (accordion); and the baby-boom generation's intro to anarchy, the ever-irreverent Froggy Gremlin. Plus the same out-of-date stock-footage reaction shots of Andy's "audience." Video Resources plans to issue over thirty twin Andy's Gang vids in all and also has a color episode with Andy's predecessor and the show's original host, Smilin' Ed McConnell.

Ann Magnusson's Vandemonium Plus (1987)
Ann Magnusson, Meat Loaf. 43 minutes. (HBO)

NYC's much-vaunted downtown comedienne stars in a made-for-cable comedy special, a jaunt through American trash culture.

Atomic TV (1950s–60s) B&W/color
45 minutes. (Video Resources)

A compendium of Cathode Ray-diation clips, including the infamous "Duck and Cover" public-service cartoon, "A Is For Atom," and "The Future Is Now," a breathless salute to the home-tech advances of the era.

The Avengers (1965–66)
Patrick Macnee, Diana Rigg. 54 minutes per episode. (Video Dimensions, others)

Suave spies Steed (Macnee) and unflappable karate queen Mrs. Emma Peel (Rigg) get embroiled in all manner of international intrigues while keeping tongues firmly in stiff upper lips in this popular Brit import.

Battlestar: Galactica Series (1980–81)
Lorne Greene, Richard Hatch, Dirk Benedict. 47 minutes each. (MCA)

Episodes of this sci-fi series, starring Greene and detailing the plight of doomed-planet survivors, are being gradually issued by MCA.

Beauty and the Beast (1987–88)
Linda Hamilton, Ron Perlman. 52 minutes each. (Republic)

The urban adventures of contempo Beauty Linda (*The Terminator*) Hamilton and gentle mutant Beast Ron (*Quest for Fire*) Perlman became an instant cult hit and a rare case of an ongoing series also going to home video.

Jack Benny (1958) B&W
Jack Benny, Dennis Day, Audrey Meadows, Eddie Anderson. 25 minutes. (Video Yesteryear)

Jack and crew, with help from Audrey (Alice) Meadows, parody *The Honeymooners*, with Jack as Ralph and Day as Norton. Video Yesteryear also has several additional Benny programs available.

Best of Alfred Hitchcock Presents (1950s–60s) B&W
Alfred Hitchcock. 78 minutes per three-episode tape. (MCA)

One of the era's primo sources of video perversity. Episodes vary in quality, but Hitch's wraparounds remain fresh.

Best of Bonanza (1950s–60s)
Lorne Greene, Michael Landon, Dan Blocker, Pernell Roberts. 100 minutes per two-episode tape. (Republic)

The Cartwrights ride again in repackaged double episodes from the long-running sagebrush series.

Best of Candid Camera (1950s–70s) Color/B&W
D: Alan Funt. Alan Funt. 56 minutes each. (Vestron)

Clips from the original Funt series, bolstered by celebrity-guest appearances by the likes of Woody Allen and Loni Anderson.

Best of John Belushi (1985)
John Belushi. 60 minutes. (Warner)

Warner assembles a first-rate compilation of the late comic's most memorable *Saturday Night Live* performances, including his classic Joe Cocker takeoff. Companion videos *The Best of Dan Aykroyd* (Warner) and *The Best of Chevy Chase* (Lorimar) are also available.

Best of Mary Hartman, Mary Hartman (1977)
Louise Lasser, Dody Goodman, Greg Mullavey. 75 minutes each. (Embassy)

A sampling of select episodes from the cult soaper satire, though doubtless not enough to satisfy the offbeat telecomedy's dedicated fans.

Best of Spike Jones (1957) B&W
Spike Jones and the City Slickers. 53 minutes each. (Paramount)

Accentuates mirthful musical moments from the comic bandleader's 1957 teleseries. Former Stooge Joe Besser turns up in Vol. 2. A *Colgate Comedy Hour* episode featuring Spike is also available (Discount Video).

Best of the Benny Hill Show (1970s–80s)
Benny Hill. 95 to 120 minutes per volume. (HBO)

Collected episodes featuring comic Hill's videoized update of broad bawd in the venerable Brit music-hall tradition.

Best of the Golden Age of Television (1950s) B&W/color
60 minutes. (Video Resources)

A party-video approach to TV's Golden Age, replete with clips, bloopers, promos, and other fascinating ephemera from the tube's toddling days.

Best of Upstairs, Downstairs (1970s)
Jean Marsh, David Langton, Rachel Gurney, Simon Williams. 50 minutes each. (HBO)

HBO has been releasing chronologically arranged episodes from this popular *Masterpiece Theater* series paralleling the lives of a wealthy Edwardian family and their live-in servants. Now you can watch the show uninterrupted by PBS pledge drives! Ditto for the popular tele-adaptation of Evelyn Waugh's *Brideshead Revisited*, available in its entirety in a six-cassette set from Virgin Vision.

Best of Your Show of Shows Vols. 1 & 2 (1950s) B&W
Sid Caesar, Imogene Coca, Carl Reiner, Howard Morris. 60 minutes each. (Trans-Atlantic)

Caesar's pioneering telecomedy series featured a top repertory company (Coca, Reiner, Morris) and writers, including Neil Simon, Woody Allen, and Mel Brooks. The theatrical compilation, *10 from Your Show of Shows* (Media), is also on tape, as are several original *Caesar's Hour* episodes (Video Yesteryear)

Bob & Ray, Jane, Laraine & Gilda (1979)
Bob Elliott, Ray Goulding, Jane Curtin, Laraine Newman, Gilda Radner. 75 minutes. (Pacific Arts)

While it's true that the brilliant radio duo never look quite comfortable on camera, Bob & Ray, with help from the above *Saturday Night Live* trio, still come through with a consistently funny special spotlighting such unique B&R characters as the inseparable McBeeBee Twins, who attempt to double-date Jane and Gilda. Willie Nelson also cameos. B&R addicts can also view one of the pair's short-lived early TV series, *The Name's the Same* (Loonic).

Buck Rogers in the 25th Century (1979)
Gil Gerard, Pamela Hensley, Erin Gray, Henry Silva. Voice of Mel Blanc. 47 minutes per episode, plus 88-minute pilot. (MCA)

Fans of this short-lived series updating the adventures of comic-strip spaceman Buck Rogers can enjoy the show anew via MCA.

Captain Gallant of the Foreign Legion (1955) B&W
Buster Crabbe, Fuzzy Knight, Cuffy Crabbe. 60 minutes. (Video Resources)

Starring Crabbe and son Cuffy, *Captain Gallant* was basically a western transplanted to the sands of Morocco (where the first thirty-nine episodes were actually lensed).

Captain Midnight Vols. 1–3 (1955) B&W
Richard Webb, Sid Melton, Olan Soule. Approx. 60 minutes per two-episode tape. (Rhino)

Jet ace Webb, comic sidekick Ichabod Mudd (Melton), scientist Soule, and the Cap's trusty airborne steed The Silver Dart keep America safe for democracy in this '50s kid-fave. Original commercials included. Secret Squadron decoder not included.

Captain Video and His Video Rangers (1953) B&W
Al Hodge. (Video Resources)

What began as a local live NYC show went national in 1953 and both reflected and fueled the era's sci-fi cravings. A cheapjack but fascinating series.

Cisco Kid (1950s)
Duncan Renaldo, Leo Carrillo. 30 minutes each. (Goodtimes)

Oh Pancho! Oh Cisco! Those daring cathode caballeros ride again in the first color teleseries, one that still commands a loyal following.

Classic TV Commercials of the 50s and 60s Vols. 1–5 Color/B&W
Approx. 60 minutes each. (Video Resources)

For those who find nostalgia and/or anthropological value in the ads of old, Video Resources has five hours' worth of same, ranging from the tame to the truly bizarre.

The same outfit offers several specialized commercial compilations as well, like *The Official Captain Midnight Commercials* and numerous other vintage kids-oriented ad fare aimed at nostalgic baby boomers.

Combat (1962) B&W
Vic Morrow, Rick Jason. 50 minutes each. (Goodtimes)

Several episodes of this still-in-demand WWII-set series detailing the rigors of combat life are available from Goodtimes.

Commercial Mania (1950s–60s) Color/B&W
Approx. 60 minutes. (Rhino)

An irreverent roundup of vintage boob-tube ads, with the emphasis on the tasteless and bizarre. Goodtimes counters with *Celebrity Commercials* and *Those Crazy Ol' Commercials.*

Divorce Hearing (1958) B&W
Paul Popenoe. 27 minutes. (Video Yesteryear)

For a vicarious view of just plain folks at their worst, Video Yesteryear has an especially vile edition of this nasty precursor to *People's Court.*

Dr. Who (1983)
Tom Baker. 90 minutes per episode. (Playhouse)

CBS/Fox's Playhouse wing is bringing out the Baker–starred series three episodes at a time for the edification of fanatical *Dr. Who* cultists, who already subscribe to a nearly pro-quality *Dr. Who* tabloid, join *Dr. Who* fan clubs, and attend annual *Dr. Who* conventions.

Dragnet (1950s) B&W
Jack Webb, Ben Alexander. 26 minutes per episode. (Goodtimes, others)

Just the facts, ma'am: For those who miss Webb's wooden ways, choice installments of this iconic '50s cop show are available.

Fawlty Towers (1979)
John Cleese, Prunella Scales, Connie Booth. 90 minutes per three-episode tape. (Playhouse)

Playhouse has all twelve installments of Cleese's classic BBC comedy series, which may well rank as the best sitcom ever aired.

Flash Gordon (1950s) B&W
Steve Holland. 52 minutes per tape. (Captain Bijou, others)

Holland plays Flash in this low-budget but surreal early-TV incarnation of the durable comic-strip and serial hero.

Fu Manchu (1956) B&W
Glen Gordon. 52 minutes. (Budget)

Two episodes from the rare syndicated series, starring Gordon as Sax Rohmer's evil Oriental genius, including "The Master Plan," wherein Fu resurrects Hitler (!).

The Fugitive: The Final Judgement I & II (1964) B&W
David Janssen. 103 minutes. (Goodtimes)

One of the most widely hyped TV events of its era: the final two episodes of *The Fugitive*, wherein accused killer Dr. Richard Kimble (Janssen) at last unmasks the real culprit.

Green Hornet/Captain Midnight (1967) Color/B&W
Van Williams, Bruce Lee. 52 minutes. (Captain Bijou)

The pilot episode, lensed in color, of the short-lived cult-TV series, featuring Lee as Kato, the kung-fu chauffeur. Paired with a vintage *Captain Midnight* episode.

Groucho Marx (1950) B&W
Groucho Marx. (Captain Bijou)

The rare 1950 pilot show for *You Bet Your Life*, with all the original bloopers left intact.

Have Gun, Will Travel (1958) B&W
Richard Boone. (Captain Bijou)

Pushy hero Paladin (Boone) rides the range anew in the first two episodes from this popular series.

The Hitchhiker (1980s)
90 minutes per three-episode tape. (Lorimar)

The twisty made-for-cable mystery series is being gradually released by Lorimar.

The Honeymooners: The Lost Episodes (1950s) B&W
Jackie Gleason, Audrey Meadows, Art Carney, Jane Randolph. Approx. 50 minutes per two-episode tape. (MPI)

Probably the truest, certainly one of the funniest, American sitcoms ever produced. MPI has the complete Lost Episodes line. Missing are the thirty-nine shows still in syndication. You can also see Jackie G in *Cavalcade of Stars* (Video Yesteryear), *The Great Gleason* (MPI), and *Jackie Gleason American Scene* (Goodtimes).

Howdy Doody (1950s) B&W
Buffalo Bob Smith, Bob Keeshan. Approx. 50 minutes per two-episode tape. (Video Resources)

Video Resources carries several episodes and specials of the most influential—and outrageously manipulative—kiddie show in television history.

I Spy (1964–65)
Bill Cosby, Robert Culp. 120-minutes per two-episode tape. (Video Home Library)

Cos and Culp jive their way through international capers in selected episodes available at sell-through prices.

The Invaders (1967)
52 minutes per episode. (Goodtimes)

Goodtimes has the entire slate of episodes from this short-lived but popular sci-fi series aired during the *Star Trek* era.

Ernie Kovacs Show (1961) B&W
Ernie Kovacs. 29 minutes. (Video Yesteryear)

This is Kovacs's classic "Eugene" special in its entirety, complete with silent Dutch Masters commercials. Video Yesteryear also carries *Kovacs on the Corner*, an episode from Ern's 1952 Philly series, and *Take a Good Look*, Kovacs's '50s quiz show, while Discount Video has *The Best of Ernie Kovacs, Vols. 1–3.*—and Vestron issued *Ernie Kovacs: TV's Original Genius.* You can't go wrong with any of these compilations featuring the comic who understood the TV/video medium better than any of his peers. In fact, much of EK's material is *still* ahead of the times.

Kukla, Fran & Ollie (1948–52) B&W
Burr Tillstrom, Fran Allison, Hugh Downs. 26 minutes. (Video Resources)

One of TV's earliest efforts and quite likely the tube's first cult show, which attracted at least as many adults as it did kids. Tillstrom's puppets, Kukla the Clown and Ollie the Dragon, share the screen with host Allison.

Leave It to Beaver (1950s) B&W
Hugh Beaumont, Barbara Billingsley, Tony Dow, Jerry Mathers as "The Beaver." 30 minutes. (Goodtimes)

The All-American Family strikes again.

Lights Out! (1950s) B&W
Francis L. Sullivan, Otto Kruger. 55 minutes. (Goodtimes)

Two episodes from the short-lived Cathode version of Arch Oboler's long-running cult radio series, sort of an audio *Twilight Zone* precursor.

Lost in Space (1965) B&W
Guy Williams, June Lockhart, Jonathan Harris. 60 minutes. (Video Resources)

Two separate pilot episodes were filmed for this popular juvenile space opera; Video Resources has them both on one tape.

M*A*S*H: Goodbye, Farewell & Amen (1986)
Alan Alda, Harry Morgan, Wayne Rogers. 78 minutes. (CBS/Fox)

Not one of the Phantom's faves, but an undeniably popular sitcom. CBS/Fox has the famous farewell episode for those who can't let go.

Mastermind (1981)
Sam Waterston, George Innes, Julian Glover. 48 minutes per episode. (Playhouse)

Another popular if short-lived BBC series, starring Sam Waterston as a turn-of-the-century scientist/detective.

Max Headroom (1986)
60 minutes. (Lorimar)

TV's foremost Stuttering Head holds forth in an hour-long video culled from the best of Max's tube appearances. Directors Rocky Morton and Annabel Jankel went on to direct the dismal *D.O.A.* remake.

Mr. Bill Looks Back (1983)
30 minutes. (Pacific Arts)

Mr. Bill's Real Life Adventures (1986)
43 minutes. (Paramount)

The ongoing adventures of the masochistic kid-show clay figure

introduced on *Saturday Night Live.*

Mr. Ed (1961) B&W
Alan Young, Chill Wills. 30 minutes. (Goodtimes)

Goodtimes has a sample episode from this oddly popular sitcom featuring Young and Chill Wills as the voice of the title character, a talking horse. Good theme song, though.

The Monkees (1967–68)
Michael Nesmith, Davy Jones, Mickey Dolenz, Peter Tork. 50 minutes each. (RCA/Columbia)

The gleefully inauthentic adventures of the Not-So-Fab Four have gained in popularity over the decades; here they're packaged on a two-shows-per-tape basis.

Monty Python's Flying Circus (1970–73)
John Cleese, Graham Chapman, Eric Idle, Terry Gilliam, Terry Jones, Michael Palin. Approx. 60 minutes per two-episode tape. (Paramount)

You can't go wrong with any of Paramount's double-cassettes of the Brit satirists' classic teleseries.

The Night Stalker (1974)
D: John Lewellyn Moxey. Darren McGavin, Simon Oakland, Carol Lynley. 98 minutes. (MCA)

This instant cult telehorror hit, starring McGavin as a vet-newsman-turned-monster-hunter, later evolved into the equally popular *Kolchak* series.

The Nut House (1962) B&W
Dan Rowan, Dick Martin. 29 minutes. (Video Yesteryear)

A wild but unsold live-action comedy pilot—prefiguring *Laugh-In*, with Rowan and Martin hosting within a free-for-all format—from *Rocky & Bullwinkle* creator Jay Ward.

The Outer Limits (1963–64) B&W
52 minutes per episode. (MGM/UA)

Do Not Adjust Your Set! MGM/UA has been gradually issuing episodes from this seminal SF series, including Robert Culp in "Demon with the Glass Hand," inspiration for *The Terminator*.

Ozzie and Harriet (1953–66) B&W/color
Ozzie, Harriet, Ricky, and David Nelson. 26 minutes each. (Goodtimes)

Episodes from one of the tube's longest-running sitcoms (featuring what may have been TV's most self-conscious clan) are available from several sources, including Video Yesteryear, Shokus, and Goodtimes, for anyone itching to lip-sync along with Ricky or admire Ozzie's sweater collection.

Pee-wee's Playhouse (1987)
Pee-wee Herman. 25 minutes each. (Hi-Tops)

Hi-Tops is issuing Pee-wee's postmodern "kiddie" show, which, while lacking the control and precision of his feature films, can be addictive. A pair of cable specials, *The Pee-wee Herman Show* and *The Pee-wee Herman Story*, are also available, via HBO.

Playhouse 90: The Comedian (1957) B&W
D: John Frankenheimer. Mickey Rooney, Edmond O'Brien, Kim Hunter, Mel Torme. 83 minutes. (Video Yesteryear)

Rod Serling's incisive teleplay concerns vicious comic Rooney and burnt-out gag writer O'Brien in a dead-on behind-the-scenes psychodrama, the *King of Comedy* of its day.

Police Squad!/More Police Squad! (1982)
Created by Jim Abrahams, David Zucker, Jerry Zucker. Leslie Nielsen. 75/90 minutes. (Paramount)

The ZAZ *Airplane!* crew apply their *MAD* magazine–type technique to cop shows in this short-lived but oft-brilliant series, progenitor of the feature *The Naked Gun* (see index). All six episodes are available, three on each tape. Also in a police-parody vein is the four-episode *Hammered—The Best of Sledge* (New World).

A Prairie Home Companion: The Last Show (1987)
Garrison Keillor, Chet Atkins, Jean Redpath. 90 minutes. (Walt Disney)

New Age rage Keillor concluded his popular Lake Woebegon radio series with a farewell taped at St. Paul's World Theatre. Visually static, but essential for GK fanatics.

The Prisoner (1970s)
Patrick McGoohan. 52 minutes each. (MPI)

McGoohan is the confused captive of a mysterious totalitarian society in an existential teleseries that became an enduring cult fave. All the episodes are finally available via MPI.

Racket Squad (1950s) B&W
Reed Hadley. 26 minutes per episode. (Concord)

Hadley exposes all manner of wily criminals out to rip you off in an early, radio-spawned teleseries.

Ramar of the Jungle (1950s) B&W
Jon Hall, Ray Montgomery. 26 minutes per episode. (Video Resources)

A fun back-lot jungle series starring Hall as a Great White Doctor and Montgomery as his loyal assistant.

Really Weird Tales (1987)
John Candy, Joe Flaherty, Catherine O'Hara, Martin Short. 85 minutes. (HBO)

A bright spoof of *Twilight Zone*–type-TV terror anthologies from the *SCTV* crew, originally aired on HBO pay cable.

Rin Tin Tin (1955) Colorized.
Lee Aaker, Jim Brown, Joe Sawyer, Rand Brooks, Rin Tin Tin. 75 minutes. (Monterey)

Monterey strings together three—colorized, unfortunately—episodes of the vintage kid teleseries featuring Rinty, Rusty, Rip, and the gang.

Ripping Yarns (1986)
Michael Palin. 90 minutes per three-episode cassette. (CBS/Fox)

Ex-Python Palin goes solo in a series of bright send-ups of vintage Brit boys' adventure pulps. See also *More Ripping Yarns* and *Even More Ripping Yarns* (both also CBS/Fox).

Rocky Jones (1954) B&W
Richard Crane, Robert Lyden. 78 minutes per three-episode tape. (Video Yesteryear)

A televersion of the waning serial-genre, Rocky stars B-pic perennial Crane as a brave space explorer battling cosmic villains, stock-footage meteors, and the like.

Rootie Kazootie (1950) B&W
26 minutes. (Video Resources)

This bizarre early kid-vid show was thought to be long lost until archivist Ira Gallen found an episode in a Hell's Kitchen trash can! It's since been cleaned up, transferred to video, and paired with the rare *Howdy Doody for President* on one gloriously regressive cassette.

Roots, 6 Volumes (1977)
John Amos, Ben Vereen, Ed Asner, LeVar Burton. 540 minutes. (Warner)

The complete uncut version of Alex Haley's epic tracing of an American black family's heritage from its distant African ancestry forward.

The Rutles (1978)
Eric Idle, Michael Palin, Neal Innes, George Harrison. 70 minutes. (Pacific Arts)

Ex-Python Idle's Beatles send-up isn't quite up there with Cleese's *Fawlty Towers* or Palin's *Ripping Yarns*—or, for that matter, Rob Reiner's *This Is Spinal Tap* (see index)—but offers enough bright moments to make it worth a look and listen.

The Saint (1960s) B&W
Roger Moore. (IVE)

Moore, in his pre–James Bond days, stars as the TV incarnation of Leslie Charteris's suave sleuth.

Saturday Night Live (1975–79)
Dan Aykroyd, John Belushi, Chevy Chase, Jane Curtin, Garrett Morris, Laraine Newman, Gilda Radner. 53 to 67 minutes per tape. (Warner)

The live late-night show that revolutionized TV comedy is now available on cassette. Covers Lorne Michaels's reign only.

Secret Agent (1960s) B&W
Patrick McGoohan. 55 minutes per episode. (MPI)

A pre-*Prisoner* McGoohan essays the role of agent John Drake in a James Bond clone benefiting from literate scripts and Brit understatement.

Shmenges: The Last Polka (1985)
John Candy, Eugene Levy, Catherine O'Hara. 54 minutes. (Vestron)

The brilliant *SCTV* gang send up *The Last Waltz*, Lawrence Welk, second-rate ethnic musicians, and third-rate musical documentaries in this mock-doc farewell to Leutonian folk heroes Stan (Candy) and Yosh (Levy) Shmenge. The extended tuba solo is just one of many musical highlights. Originally aired on cable TV.

Space: 1999 (1970)
Martin Landau, Barbara Bain. 52 minutes. (IVE)

Though the original show proved short-lived, its rabid boosters are still among us. IVE is gradually releasing the entire series.

Space Patrol (1955) B&W
Ed Kemmer, Lyn Osborn, Ken Lynch. 78 minutes. (Media)

A hokey but fun no-budget '50s space opera, with Osborn as the ever-irrepressible Cadet Happy.

Star Trek (1966–68)
William Shatner, Leonard Nimoy, DeForest Kelley, Nichelle Nichols. 51 minutes per show. (Paramount)

TV's all-time sci-fi cult fave is also a highly visible video offering, easily located at most of your decent-sized cassette outlets. We include it here only to avoid incurring Trekkie (or "Trekker") wrath.

Tales from the Darkside (1980s)
78 minutes per tape. (IVE)

Despite its nonexistent production values, *Tales* proved surprisingly durable on the tube and continues to attract viewers in its video reincarnation.

Tales of Tomorrow (1953) B&W
120 minutes. (Fox Hills)

The folks at Fox Hills have two volumes of this largely forgotten supernatural series available. Vol. 1 features Lon Chaney, Jr., while Vol. 2 has both Boris Karloff and Paul Newman among its cast.

Tom Corbett, Space Cadet (1951) B&W
Frankie Thomas, Jack Grimes, Al Markhim. 30 minutes. (Media)

Another juvenile sci-fi entry in a *Space Patrol* mode, starring former '30s child star Thomas in the title role.

TV Turkeys (1987) B&W/color
60 minutes. (Rhino)

Some of the best of the worst of the tube's long line of turkeys, assembled by the camp aficionados at Rhino.

TV's Greatest Adventures of Superman (1951/1958) B&W/color
George Reeves, Noel Neill, Jack Larson. 52 minutes per tape. (Warner)

Warner has been gradually releasing episodes from the enormously popular George Reeves teleseries, pairing black-and-white shows from the first season (1951) with color installments from the final year (1958).

The Twilight Zone (1960) B&W
30 minutes per episode. (CBS/Fox)

Rod Serling's pioneering sci-fi/fantasy series remains the best supernatural-anthology show ever aired.

Wanted Dead or Alive (1959) B&W
Steve McQueen. (VidAmerica)

McQueen's Method cowboy, bounty hunter Josh Randall, distantly revived in the Rutger Hauer pic of the same name, menaces miscreants with his sawed-off Winchester.

Watch Mr. Wizard (1958) B&W
Mr. Wizard. (Video Yesteryear)

Suburban scientist Mr. Wizard amazes one and all with forceful demonstrations of elemental scientific principles.

Zorro (1950s) B&W
Guy Williams, Henry Garcia. 26 minutes per episode. (Walt Disney)

Williams enjoyed brief fame and glory as the titular swordsman in Disney's TV update of the old serial.

HAPPY TRAILERS TO YOU:
PREVIEW & TRAILER TAPES

"It is safe to say that the grandchildren of many of the people watching in this theater will not be born on Earth!"

Trailer
Plan 9 from Outer Space

Previews, trailers, coming attractions—call 'em what you will, they've been an integral part of the movie-going experience since the silent era. While the occasional trailer-and-clip compilation—e.g., *It Came from Hollywood* and *Terror in the Aisles*—has played theatrically, the trailer collection has largely been an invention of the video industry, where it's far cheaper to assemble public-domain or inexpensively licensed theme-trailer tapes for low-priced sale to sundry special-interest audiences.

Some find a solid hour or two of uninterrupted trailers fairly dull going; others, like yours truly, can't get enough of them, for their entertainment, nostalgia, and sociological value, plus they don't strain the old attention span. Where were we?

Oh yeah: Whatever your fave film area might be, there are trailer tapes available that cater to your interests. In addition to the trailer titles you're likely to discover at your local vidstore (usually a pretty limited selection), mail-order houses like the excellent SF Rush Video/ Trailers on Tape stock scores of trailer collections covering everything from vintage comedies and classics to obscure horror and exploitation quickies. Many of the aforementioned SF Rush's titles come equipped with second-channel audio narrations offering a verbal history of the onscreen trailers.

The Phantom herein samples (sans ratings) some dozen or so typical trailers/comp offerings in depth, within a more complete list of those trailer tapes and clip compilations available from some of Videoland's more remote sectors.

Academy Awards: Oscar's Best (1987) B&W/color
60 minutes. With second audio channel narration. (SF Rush)

Trailers for "Best Picture" Academy Award–winners from 1927 (*Wings*) to 1959 (*Ben Hur*). Others include *On the Waterfront, Lost Weekend,* and *The Greatest Show on Earth*. The ultimate trailer tape for classics fans from the quality-minded folks at SF Rush.

Adventure (1985) B&W/color
61 minutes. (SF Rush)

Previews of action and adventure films, from *King Solomon's Mines* to *Murder on the Orient Express*.

AIP: Fast and Furious (1985) B&W/color
59 minutes. (SF Rush)

American International Pictures previews from the '50s (*I Was a Teenage Frankenstein, Bucket of Blood*) through the '60s (*Muscle Beach Party, Masque of the Red Death*) and '70s (*Meteor, Return of Count Yorga*).

AIP, Vol. II: The Cool and the Crazy (1986) B&W/color
60 minutes. With second audio channel narration. (SF Rush)

More previews from the schlock pioneers at AIP: *Amazing Colossal Man, Cool and the Crazy, Pajama Party,* and *War of the Colossal Beast* (complete with color end titles), among many others.

Bad Girls in the Movies (1986) B&W/color
58 minutes. (Lightning)

A pretty uninspired collection of clips featuring distaff JDs and other antisocial femmes. None of the clips are credited—a move sure to frustrate dedicated sleaze-film buffs.

Baker's Dozen (1985) B&W/color
120 minutes. (J&J)

Among the thirteen 1930s shorts and cartoons in this eclectic collection are footage from the first live-TV broadcast (1939 World's Fair) and the first live-action Technicolor film.

Battle of the Bombs (1985) B&W/color
60 minutes. (Rhino)

Trailers and clips from some of the worst films ever made, many culled from Rhino's own feature-flick catalog, from Arch Hall's *Eegah!* to the cosmic crawling carpet classic *The Creeping Terror.*

Best of Sex and Violence (1981)
78 minutes. (Wizard)

The immortal Carradine hosts Ken Dixon's hit-and-miss schlock-fest, featuring trailers that run the gamut from gore to exploitation to soft-core porn.

Black and White Horror and Science Fiction Trailers, Vols. I & II (1987) B&W
67 minutes. (Cinemacabre)

The Phantom is admittedly partial to the black-and-white fright flicks of the '50s, when the trailers were often superior to the films they sought to promote. This Cinemacabre collection includes over forty in all, among them such greats as *The Black Sleep, Brain from Planet Arous, The Mole People,* and *I Married a Monster from Outer Space.* Vol. II, running 89 minutes, offers even more in terms of rarities—e.g., *Panther Girl of the Kongo, Four Skulls of Jonathan Drake, The Flesh Eaters, The Woman Eater,* and *The Hypnotic Eye.* For our moolah, a topnotch terror treat, further abetted by Cinemacabre's high-quality tape transfers.

Cinema Shrapnel (1987) B&W/color
Hosted by Bob Shaw. 60 minutes. (SF Rush)

Schlock scholar Shaw conducts a misguided tour through movie hypes, gimmicks, and hard sells, mixing trailers, promos, and fund-raising pitches.

Classic Horror Trailers, Vol. 1 (1987) B&W/color
60 minutes. (Sinister Cinema)

Mostly black-and-white horrors from the '50s, including such obscurities as *Giant from the Unknown* and *The Devil's Hand,* cult faves *I Bury the Living* and *Hypnotic Eye,* plus ten William Castle winners, including *The Tingler* and *Homicidal.*

Classic Horror Trailers, Vol. 2 (1987) B&W/color
60 minutes. (Sinister Cinema)

Emphasizes Roger Corman's Edgar Allan Poe adaptations (*House of Usher, Haunted Palace*), Brit horrors (*Blood of the Vampire, Burn Witch Burn*), and other '60s shockers.

Classic Horror Trailers, Vol. 3 (1987)
60 minutes. (Sinister Cinema)

Seventies frightfests like the *Abominable Dr. Phibes, Count Yorga, Blacula, The Wicker Man,* and *The Rocky Horror Picture Show* dominate the third of Sinister's terror-trailer trilogy.

Classic Movie Prevues Vols. 1–4 (1987)
B&W/color
60 minutes. (Discount Video)

Emphasizes mainstream movies from the '30s through the '60s, including *Grand Hotel, Samson and Delilah, Shane,* and *Sands of Iwo Jima.*

Classic Sci-Fi Trailers Vol. 1 (1987)
B&W/color
60 minutes. (Sinister Cinema)

Includes sci-fi previews from the '30s (*Things To Come*) to the early '60s (*Godzilla, Children of the Damned*), with the bulk being of '50s vintage (*When Worlds Collide, It! The Terror from Beyond Space*); classics and fun cheapies receive roughly equal representation here.

Classic Sci-Fi Trailers Vol. 2 (1987)
B&W/color
60 minutes. (Sinister Cinema)

The accent's on '50s B classics, quickies, and obscurities, including *Robot Monster, Invaders from Mars, The Incredible Shrinking Man,* and *The Brain That Wouldn't Die.*

Classic Sci-Fi Trailers Vol. 3 (1987)
B&W/color
60 minutes. (Sinister Cinema)

Another mixed bag of '50s and '60s SF previews: *This Island Earth, The Crawling Eye, The Brain Eaters* on through to *Barbarella, Planet of the Apes,* and *2001.*

Classic Sci-Fi Trailers Vol. 4 (1988)
B&W/color
60 minutes. (Sinister Cinema)

Sinister Cinema's fourth SF collection presents another lineup of trailers culled largely from the prolific '50s: *Creature with the Atom Brain, Invasion of the Body Snatchers, Kronos,* and *Rodan* among them.

Classic Serial Trailers Vols. 1–3 (1987)
B&W
60 minutes. (Sinister Cinema)

Frank Merriwell, The Iron Claw, and *Pirates of the High Seas* are represented, along with such better-known chapterplays as *King of the Rocketmen, Mysterious Dr. Satan,* and *The Crimson Ghost.*

Cliffhangers Vols. 1 and 2 (1987) B&W
56 minutes and 59 minutes, respectively. (Captain Bijou)

Vol. 1 offers serial trailers from *Captain America, Perils of Nyoka,* and *Congo Bill,* among others; Vol. 2 lists *Blackhawk, King of the Congo*, and *Winners of the West* among its coming attractions.

Color Horror and Science Fiction Trailers, Vols. 1 and 2 (1986)
83 minutes. (Cinemacabre)

An extensive, impressive array of sci-fi and terror trailers ranging from '50s faves like *Forbidden Planet* and *The Blob* to '60s fantasy films like *Jack the Giant Killer* and *The Magic Sword*. Vol. 2 runs 87 minutes, with more emphasis on the '60s.

Comedy Vol. 1 (1985) B&W/color
60 minutes. (SF Rush)

Trailers range from the '30s (*A Night at the Opera*) and '40s (*Abbott & Costello in Hollywood*) through the '70s (*Airplane!, Cold Turkey*).

Comedy Prevues (1986) B&W
60 minutes. (Discount Video)

The Marx Brothers, W. C. Fields, and Olson and Johnson are among the '30s and '40s comedians represented here.

Coming Again (1985) B&W/color
80 minutes. (J & J)

Trailers from '30's & '40's film classics like *Casablanca, Juarez, Mr. Skeffington*, and others, followed by three animated *Popeye* featurettes (*Aladdin, Ali Baba,* and *Sinbad*).

Coming at Last (1985) B&W
120 minutes. (J&J)

More trailers from classics (*Petrified Forest, Footlight Parade, Key Largo*), including a rare *Public Enemy* preview, plus the W. C. Fields shorts *The Barber Shop* and *The Pharmacist* and a Max Fleischer cartoonfest.

Coming Attractions #1—The Super Stars (1984) B&W/color
31 minutes. (Video Yesteryear)

A dozen trailers culled mostly from lavish vintage musicals: *Presenting Lily Mars, Funny Lady,* and the Al Jolson rarity *The Singing Kid*.

Coming Next Week (1985) B&W/color
100 minutes. (Nostalgia Merchant)

A fairly randomly assembled array of trailers, mixing genre fare like 1960's *The Time Machine* with more mainstream hits. Best trailer here is Ernie Kovac's *anti*-promo for the '57 service comedy *Operation Mad Ball*.

Coming Once More (1986) B&W/color
120 minutes. (J&J)

A mixed bag of vintage Bette Davis trailers, plus promos and previews from '70s films like *Tommy, Taxi Driver,* and *Close Encounters* and cartoons from animation's Golden Age.

Coming Soon (1984) B&W/color
55 minutes. (MCA)

Halloween screamer Jamie Lee Curtis hosts vintage Universal trailers, among them *Phantom of the Opera, Psycho, Dracula, Jaws,* and *The Twilight Zone*.

Coming Soon (1985)
120 minutes. (J&J)

Two hours of Universal horror trailers from the '30s through the '60s and several Ray Harryhausen films, plus a potpourri of promos and shorts, including choice Lugosi clips and "Today's Teens," wherein Boris Karloff narrates a horror story about '60s youth (!).

Cowboy Previews (1985) B&W
60 minutes. (Nostalgia Merchant)

Over thirty-five B-western trailers, including *King of the Bullwhip*, *Utah Wagon Train*, *Trail of Robin Hood*, and *Riders in the Sky.*

Cowboys of the Saturday Matinee (1984) B&W
75 minutes. (Lorimar)

James Coburn hosts a history of B westerns and their stars—including Gene Autry, Roy Rogers, and Tex Ritter—incorporating numerous clips and trailers.

Drama-Romance (1986) B&W/color
60 minutes. (SF Rush)

An eclectic collection bordering on the downright random, this catchall tape incorporates everything from *La Dolce Vita* and *Jezebel* to *Pride of the Yankees* and *Women in Cell Block 7.* Over forty previews in all.

Drive-In Madness (1988)
(Imagine Video)

Tim Ferrante's tribute to that most endangered of movie species, the drive-in, is a mostly successful mix of junk-flick clips, interviews with genre-film personalities, and fond evocations of those alfresco bijous of yore, narrated by James Karen. Highlights include trailers for such drive-in faves as *The Green Slime, Human Duplicators, House of Psychotic Women*, and Curtis Harrington's *Queen of Blood* ("She turns the Milky Way into a galaxy of gore!") and relevant insights supplied by the likes of George A. Romero, monster-makeup maven Tom Savini, professional minor cult figure Bobbie (*Evil Spawn*) Bresee, genre ingenue Linnea Quigley, producer Sam Sherman, and legendary *Famous Monsters of Filmland* founder Forrest J. Ackerman. Ferrante's feature-length compilation could use some overall tightening, but *Drive-In Madness* remains a must for hard-core horror and sleaze buffs.

Drive-In Sleaze (1985) B&W/color
55 minutes. (Video Dimensions)

One of the Phantom's fave trailer tapes. *Drive-In Sleaze: 1934–70* offers coming attractions (nineteen in all) from such exploitation obscurities as *Mundo Depravados* (ecdysiast Tempest Storm's gala thespic debut), soft-core-smut auteur Doris Wishman's *Another Day, Another Man* (backed by one of the greatest sleazoid

DRIVE-IN MADNESS! The Video

HOSTED BY...
James Karen
George A. Romero
Bobbie Bresee
Tom Savini
Linnea Quigley
Sam Sherman
Forrest Ackerman
John Russo
Russell Streiner

Popcorn

THE MOST FUN YOU'LL EVER HAVE IN THE BACKSEAT OF YOUR LIVING ROOM!

Drive-In Madness pays trailer tribute to passion pits past.
Photo courtesy of Imagine, Inc.

instrumental tracks— complete with sax, bongos, *and* fuzz guitar—we've ever heard) and nudie "romps" like *Garden of Eden* (with its unforgettable theme song, "Let's Go Sunnin' "). Some of the earlier trailers (e.g., *Marijuana*) have turned up on other compilation cassettes, but *Drive-In Sleaze* can boast of more reel rarities and exploitation exclusives than most.

Exploitation Classics (1988) B&W/color
60 minutes. (Sinister Cinema)

Vintage sleaze and shockers, from *Freaks* to *Pin-Down Girls* to *Myra Breckenridge*.

Fast and Sexy (1986) B&W
50 minutes. (Channel 13)

Not the collection of choice cheesy exploitation flicks it sounds like, *Fast and Sexy* instead offers nineteen mostly standard '50s noir previews, for films like *Miami Exposé* and *The Crooked Web*. Fans of same (and that includes yours truly) will enjoy it. There are a few gems for general sleaze buffs, too: *Teenage Crime Wave, The Burglar* (pairing Dan Duryea and Jayne Mansfield), an hysterical trailer for *The Night Holds Terror,* and a duo of Hugo Haas melodramas, *Bait* (with Cleo Moore and John Agar) and *One Girl's Confession,* wherein Cleo meets her male match in Glenn (*The Amazing Colossal Man*) Langan.

Filmgore (1984)
60 minutes. (Wizard)

Mostly worthless visual viscera from a string of Empire Pictures turkeys.

Film House Fever (1986) B&W/color
58 minutes. (Vestron)

A poor buff's *It Came from Hollywood,* Dominic Paris's *Film House Fever* features trailers and clips from an assortment of awful Z flicks, from *Dracula vs. Frankenstein* to vintage pre–melanoma scare nudist-colony clinkers to black-and-white soft-core sex melodramas like the immortal *Bad Girls Don't Cry.* The wraparound comedy bits are not the freshest (though co-host Steve Buscemi later won acclaim for his work as the gay punk-rocker in *Parting Glances*) and there are too many mindless gore sequences, mostly from such

overexposed H. G. Lewis atrocities as *Blood Feast* and *Wizard of Gore.* But hard-core sleaze aficionados will find enough forgotten (if ever known) Z-film footage here to make an overnight rental worthwhile.

A Fistful of Previews (1985)
43 minutes. (Imagine Video)

A violent ride along the spaghetti western trail, with previews from Sergio Leone's *The Good, The Bad and the Ugly* and lesser-known Italo frontier fare like *The Stranger Returns, Deaf Smith and Johnny Eyes,* and *God Forgives, I Don't.*

Golden Age Horror Classics Vols. 1 & 2 (1986) B&W
60 minutes. (Sinister Cinema)

A topnotch array of terror trailers from the '30s and '40s, including *King Kong, White Zombie,* Dwayne Esper's *Maniac,* and a trio of Val Lewton titles. A good supplement to Sinister's *Universal Horror Classics.*

Great B-Movie Previews (1987) B&W
58 minutes. (Captain Bijou)

Concentrates on second features of 1940s vintage, including trailers for Laurel and Hardy's *The Bullfighters,* Val Lewton's *Leopard Man,* and *The Falcon in Mexico.*

The Hitchcock Collection (1986) B&W/color
55 minutes. (SF Rush)

The thoughtful archivists at SF Rush have arranged this lineup of

Hitchcock classics in chronological order (from *Rebecca* to *Torn Curtain*) to enable viewers to get a better sense of the suspense master's celluloid evolution.

Hollywood Outtakes and Rare Footage (1983) B&W/color
84 minutes. (RCA/Columbia)

Bruce Goldstein's video version of the outtake compilations that used to unspool at NYC's now-defunct Thalia Uptown theater, *Hollywood Outtakes and Rare Footage* features classic star bloopers of the '30s and '40s, along with such random but fascinating sequences as the 1939 Academy Awards ceremonies (including Hattie McDaniels's acceptance speech), the premiere of *A Star Is Born* (complete with a glassy-eyed Judy Garland), and *Constance Bennett's Beauty Secrets* (filmed in gloriously ugly Cinecolor). Especially chilling is Joan (*Mommie Dearest*) Crawford's perfect-mom pitch for the Jimmy Fund. The eeriest segment shows Gig Young (who later killed his wife, then took his own life) interviewing James Dean re: the importance of highway safety. (Dean died in a car crash only months later.) Much of the public-domain footage here also surfaces in other comp cassettes, so check the box copy before you buy or rent.

Hollywood Party Tape (1986) B&W
90 minutes. (J&J)

Star commercials, promos, shorts, Ronald Reagan bloopers, the 1939 Academy Awards, *Constance Bennett's Beauty Secrets*, and Porky Pig are a few of the components of this parade of crazed images.

Hollywood's Greatest Trailers (1984) B&W/color
60 minutes. (Nostalgia Merchant)

The emphasis here is on Golden Age epics. Included are *Citizen Kane, Top Hat, Fort Apache*, and *It's a Wonderful Life.*

Horrible Horror (1986) B&W/color
110 minutes. (Goodtimes)

Former NYC horror host John Zacherle presents this nearly two-hour compilation tape offering trailers, clips, and outtakes from the likes of *The Alligator People, Robot Monster, 13 Ghosts*, and *Abbott and Costello Meet Frankenstein.* Spliced in are bits by Zach, loosely recreating his old Shock Theater *shticks*. While Zach's routines seem sometimes hurried and less than inspired here, and most of the clips can be found on various other compilation and trailer tapes, the transfer quality isn't bad and it's hard to argue with 110 minutes of choice inept fright fare, wrapped by a nostalgic reunion with Zach, priced at under ten bucks.

Horror/Sci-Fi I (1986) B&W/color
60 minutes. (SF Rush)

A variety of terror trailers, including *Mad Monster Party, They Came from Within, Man of a Thousand Faces*, and *Invasion of the Saucer Men.*

Horror/Sci-Fi II: Atomic Terrors (1987) B&W/color
59 minutes. (SF Rush)

Horrordom's answer to *The Atomic Cafe, Atomic Terrors* offers a horde of movie mutants from such cautionary creature features as *Attack of the Crab Monsters, The Alligator People, Five, Unknown Terror,* and *The Omega Man.*

Horror/Sci-Fi III: Classic Horrors (1987) B&W/color
59 minutes. (SF Rush)

No theme this time, but plenty of previews from reel rarities, like *The Killer Shrews, Frankenstein 1970, The Manster,* and such older fear faves as *Bride of Frankenstein* and *Frankenstein Meets the Wolfman.*

Horror/Sci-Fi IV: House of Hammer B&W/color
60 minutes. (SF Rush)

SF Rush's Hammer collection boasts high-quality 35mm transfers and a second audio channel narration while covering much the same ground as Sinister Cinema's Hammer horror tape.

Horror/Sci-Fi V: Horrible Honeys (1987) B&W/color
90 minutes. (SF Rush)

Narrated by Bob Shaw on a second audio channel, this thematic collection focuses on frightdom's most ferocious femmes: *Wasp Woman, She Freak, Teenage Gang Debs,* and the unforgettable *Wild Women of Wongo,* among many others.

Horror/Sci-Fi VI: Super Giants—The Big and the Bigger (1987) B&W/color
60 minutes. (SF Rush)

The screen's "biggest" stars— *King Kong, Godzilla, Gorgo, Rodan, Reptilicus,* and other outsize movie monsters—appear in all their glory in this preview parade.

House of Hammer Vols. 1–2 (1986) B&W/color
60 minutes. (Sinister Cinema)

A strong sampling of Hammer's horror and sci-fi outings from the '50s (*Horror of Dracula, The Mummy*) through the fertile '60s (*Five Million Years to Earth*) to the '70s (*Captain Kronos, Twins of Evil, Dracula AD 1972*).

It Came from Hollywood (1982) B&W/color
87 minutes. (Paramount)

A rich fan's *Film House Fever,* Dana Olson's *It Came From Hollywood* offers truly choice excerpts from scores of bad films, including *The Brain from Planet Arous* and Tinseltown's top walking-tree movie, *From Hell It Came.* The clips are generally unabetted by intrusive guest turns by such as Gilda Radner, Dan Aykroyd, and Cheech and Chong, who succeed only in getting in the way of the superior inferior found footage. John Candy, however, is properly respectful in his salute to Ed Wood, Jr. (which would nonetheless have benefited from a wider selection of

Wood works). The clips are priceless, though, and *It Came from Hollywood* should not be missed by any Z-movie fan worthy of the name.

John Wayne Previews Vol. 1 (1986) B&W/color
59 minutes. (Captain Bijou)

Covers a wide range of Wayne vehicles, from the '40s (*Sands of Iwo Jima*), through the '50s (*The Quiet Man*) and into the '60s (*The Alamo*).

Mad Ron's Prevues from Hell (1988) B&W/color
82 minutes. (Off the Wall Video)

A treat for hard-core gorehounds, Jim Monaco's *Mad Ron's Prevues from Hell* features over forty fright-film trailers, including such rare terror titles as *Bloody Pit of Horror*, *Flesh Feast*, *Bloodeaters* (aka *Toxic Zombies*), H. G. Lewis bloodbaths *2000 Maniacs* and *Color Me Blood Red*, and exploitation items like *Ilsa—She Wolf of the S.S.* and *Africa, Blood and Guts*. An agile fast-forward finger comes in handy, though, to propel you through the Off the Wall crew's wraparound segments and "comic" inserts with ventriloquist host Nick Pawlow and his living-dead dummy Happy, which reek of horror-film nerdism at its nadir. Still, the trailers alone are worth the price of admission here.

Midnight Movie Madness (1986) B&W/color
58 minutes. (SF Rush)

A recommended collection of cult films, including *Blood Feast*, *Bloody Pit of Horror*, *Freaks*, *Sex Madness*, *Plan 9*, and *The Rocky Horror Picture Show*, plus a few ringers (*Up the Sandbox*, *Citizen Kane*).

Miscellaneous Movie Trailers, Vol. 1 (1987) B&W/color
95 minutes. (Cinemacabre)

A potpourri of previews from classics (*Gone With the Wind*) to westerns (*Magnificent Seven*) to exploitation (H. G. Lewis's *Scum of the Earth*) and even sports (*The Super Fight*).

Mondo Lugosi (1986) B&W
60 minutes. (Rhino)

This compilation of Bela clips is low on actual scenes from his flicks but rich in vintage trailers—for *Dracula*, *The Invisible Ray*, and *Black Friday* (focusing on its much-ballyhooed hypnotism gimmick), among many others. Novelty cameos and interviews with the unique Hungarian horror master represent another plus. We see Bela bite Betty Boop, perform the "vampire bat trick" on *You Asked For It* (and plug several projects, including Ed Wood's proposed *Phantom Ghoul*, that were—alas—never to be), and undergo a relaxed Q&A with Britain's "Shipboard Reporter." It's in the last-mentioned that Bela has the final word. To wit: "I make a living!"

Monsters, Madmen and Machines (1984) B&W/color
57 minutes. (RKO)

Gil (*Buck Rogers*) Gerard hosts a so-so collection of sci-fi segments, spanning the decades from George Melies's *A Trip to the Moon* to *Star Wars* and sequels.

Monsters on the March (1983) B&W
25 minutes. (Video Yesteryear)

Fourteen trailers from black-and-white fright films, circa 1932 to 1960, Val Lewton's *Isle of the Dead* and *I Walked with a Zombie* among them. Good transfer quality.

Musicals 1 (1985) B&W/color
60 minutes. (SF Rush)

Nearly forty trailers from Hollywood musicals, culled mostly from the '50s on: *Singin' in the Rain, Funny Lady, The Boy Friend, Yellow Submarine, West Side Story.*

Musicals 2 (1986) B&W/color
60 minutes. (SF Rush)

A mixed bag of musical trailers, from *The Red Shoes* to *Coney Island* to *Rock Around the Clock* and a trio of Elvis epics.

1939—The Vintage Year (1986) B&W/color
60 minutes. (SF Rush)

SF Rush salutes 1939 with a sampling that includes previews from *Gone With the Wind, The Wizard of Oz, Gunga Din, Wuthering*

Heights, and twenty more trailers from that sterling annum.

100% Bonded (1987)
50 minutes. (SF Rush)

Trailers from all the Sean Connery—starred James Bond movies, from both the British and American versions.

Selling Movies on Television (1985) B&W/color
55 minutes. (Video Yesteryear)

This gala collection contains sixty-nine TV spots and promos for a wide array of feature films, from *The Great Dictator* to *Electra Glide in Blue.*

Serial Prevues, Vol. I (1986) B&W
60 minutes. (Foothill)

Not, as the title implies, a trailer collection (though several are inserted as filler), but sample episodes from *Adventures of Smilin' Jack, Gangbusters,* and *The Last Frontier.*

Six-Gun Previews (1986) B&W/color
57 minutes. (Captain Bijou)

Emphasizes vintage B westerns, including several obscurities. Among the titles are *Colorado Sundown* and *Texans Never Cry.*

Sleazemania Vols. 1–3 (1986–1988) B&W/color
60 minutes. (Rhino)

Three coming-attractions comps assembled by Rhino's Johnny Legend. Best is Vol. 1, offering elderly exploitation pics (*Marijuana—Assassin of Youth*), rare B&W soft-core sex outings (*The Smut Peddler, Strange Rampage*), and other assorted sordid screen highlights. The series takes a dip with Vol. 2 but picks up with Vol. 3. A shorter, lower-priced sampler, *Sleazemania: The Special Edition*, is also available.

Son of Monsters on the March (1985)
27 minutes. (Video Yesteryear)

Ten color horror and sci-fi trailers of more recent vintage: *This Island Earth, Planet of the Apes, The Fearless Vampire Killers*, and the all-time cult fave *The Rocky Horror Picture Show*.

The Tarzan and Alfred Hitchcock Collections (1985) B&W/color
83 minutes. (Cinemacabre)

Two collections on one tape. The Hitchcock section duplicates many trailers from SF Rush's Hitchcock compendium, but the more extensive Tarzan segment, ranging from *Tarzan the Apeman* to *Greystoke*, is a treat for apeman enthusiasts and Edgar Rice Burroughs buffs.

Teen Schlock Classics (1988) B&W/color
60 minutes. (Sinister Cinema)

Covers teen sleaze like *Unwed Mother* and *Speed Crazy* to more wholesome fare like *Gidget* and *How to Stuff a Wild Bikini.*

Teenage Confidential (1987) B&W/color
60 minutes. (Rhino)

This lively compilation of clips culled from Rhino's camp-cassette catalog is a must for vintage teen-sleaze buffs. Lurid trailers for such greasy '50s and early-'60s obscurities as *Curfew Breakers, Teenage Crime Wave*, and Ed Wood, Jr.'s, *The Violent Years* are balanced with '40s National Probation Association—produced items like *Boy in Court* and *The Birth of Juvenile Delinquency*, which warns of WWII-era teens who find "abnormal outlets for their wartime excitement." Also on view: a religious tract entitled *Satan Was a Teenager* (!), plus then-heart-throb/future camp Casanova Tab Hunter on the importance of maintaining mental health. We don't know if watching *Teenage Confidential* will help viewers achieve the last-mentioned goal, but it's a fun way to spend a fast-paced late-night hour.

Terror in the Aisles (1983) B&W/color
84 minutes. (MCA)

Jamie Lee Curtis, accompanied by mad doc specialist Donald Pleasence, hosts a briskly edited collage of clips from (mostly recent) action/chiller flicks, including *Vice Squad, The Omen, Halloween, Alone in the Dark, Nighthawks*, and *Rosemary's Baby*. A greater range of movies would have been appreciated, but this still makes for a bright 84 minutes.

Terror on Tape (1980) B&W/color
80 minutes. (Continental)

John (*The Addams Family*) Astin intros horror scenes from thirty classic chillers.

Today's Trailers Vols. 1–3 (1986)
120 minutes each. (J&J)

Vols. 1 and 2 feature sixty-five full-length theatrical trailers each; spanning 1977 through 1985; Vol. 3 contains forty-four trailers, plus a 30-minute promo on the making of *The Greatest Story Ever Told.*

Trasharama (1984) B&W/color
60 minutes. (Madhouse)

Trasharama relies less on soft-core sleaze trailers than semi-mainstream foreign features (peddled stateside as racy fare back in the Fab '50s) and dated burlesque shorts. Still, this camp compilation has its moments, including a trailer for the rare 1942 antimarijuana movie *The Devil's Harvest* and the promise of Pat Flannery (Miss Dublin 1954) doing her Famous Irish Strip (what—she puts her clothes *on?*). Recommended more for trailer-camp completists than for the casual viewer.

True Duke: A Tribute to John Wayne (1987) B&W/color
60 minutes. (SF Rush)

Covers the complete range of Wayne's macho movie career, from early B westerns to his final films, including a few of the Duke's little-known clinkers. A Duke devotee's delight.

Universal Horror Classics (1987) B&W/color
60 minutes. (Sinister Cinema)

An excellent, essential assortment of Universal's Golden Age horror and B films: *Dracula, Frankenstein, The Wolf Man, Night Monster, Phantom of the Opera, Abbott and Costello Meet Frankenstein,* and many more.

The Walt Disney and Musical Collections (1986) B&W/color
70 minutes. (Cinemacabre)

The Musical Collection portion provides ten rock-movie trailers, from *Rock, Rock, Rock* to *The Blues Brothers;* the Walt Disney segment features fifteen Disney previews—*Snow White, Song of the South, Mary Poppins,* and twelve more.

Zombiethon (1984)
60 minutes. (Lightning)

Another selection of less-than-gripping clips culled mostly from fairly recent Euro-zombie outings, including several from Jess Franco.

VIDEO SHOPPING LIST:
1,000 FILMS AT A GLANCE

The following represents 1,000—well, the actual figure runs closer to 1,073, but who's counting—of the movies re: which the Phantom's received the most write-in requests from *Daily News* readers. While many of these may be too rich for the Phantom's type-B blood, we respect *all* video persuasions here, even those wrongheaded enough to diverge from our own. Hence, several of our Video Shopping List groupings differ from those given in our main text, embracing such traditional mainstream categories as Foreign Classics, Drama, nonrock Musicals, and respected Silents. Accompanying each well-known title is the video label on which the film has been issued. As of this writing, all are available on cassette—though, like some of the more obscure genre entries already covered in this volume, you won't always find them in stock at your neighborhood vidstore. We advise you to check the video-specialty sources—e.g., Video Yesteryear and Movies Unlimited—in our Videorama section, where most of the following films are readily available, many at sell-through prices (under $30 each). We hope you find your own personal faves among them.

Adventure Classics

Adventures of Captain Fabian
(Republic)

Adventures of Don Juan
(MGM/UA)

African Queen
(CBS/Fox)

Against All Flags
(Kartes)

Airport
(MCA)

Airport 1975
(MCA)

Airport '77
(MCA)

The Ambushers
(RCA/Col)

Around the World in 80 Days
(Warner)

At Sword's Point
(Fox Hills)

Avalanche!
(Embassy)

Back from Eternity
(United)

Beau Geste
(MCA)

The Bedford Incident
(RCA/Columbia)

Black Arrow
(RCA/Columbia)

Buccaneer
(Kartes)

China Seas
(MGM/UA)

The Conqueror
(MCA)

Count of Monte Cristo
(Video Yesteryear)

Diamond Head
(RCA/Col)

Doc Savage: Man of Bronze!
(Warner)

55 Days at Peking
(United)

Fighting Kentuckian
(Republic)

Fire Down Below
(RCA/Col)

Five Came Back
(RKO)

Flame and the Arrow
(Warner)

Flight of the Phoenix
(Key)

Gunga Din
(RKO)

The Horsemen
(RCA/Col)

Hurricane (1937)
(Embassy)

Iron Mask
(Video Yesteryear)

Ivanhoe (1952)
(MGM/UA)

Jack London
(Kartes)

Kim
(MGM/UA)

Lord Jim
(RCA/Col)

Macao
(Nostalgia Merchant)

Man in the Iron Mask (1939)
(Nostalgia Merchant)

Man in the Iron Mask (1976)
(CBS/Fox)

Marie Galante
(J&J)

Mr. Lucky
(Nostalgia Merchant)

Mr. Robinson Crusoe (1932)
(MPI)

Moby Dick
(Corinth)

Mogambo
(MGM/UA)

The Mountain
(Paramount)

Murderers Row
(RCA/Col)

Pimpernel Smith
(Video Yesteryear)

Poseidon Adventure
(CBS/Fox)

Prisoner of Zenda (1952)
(MGM/UA)

Red Dust
(MGM/UA)

Sand Pebbles
(CBS/Fox)

Scarlet Pimpernel (1935)
(Embassy)

Snows of Kilimanjaro
(Goodtimes)

Son of Monte Cristo
(Video Yesteryear)

Son of Sinbad
(United)

South of Pago Pago
(IVE)

Story of Robin Hood
(Walt Disney)

Sword of Lancelot
(MCA)

Taras Bulba
(MGM/UA)

Three Muskeeters (1935)
(RKO)

Three Musketeers (1948)
(MGM/UA)

Towering Inferno
(CBS/Fox)

Treasure Island (1934)
(MGM/UA)

The Vikings
(MGM/UA)

Walking Tall 1–3
(Lightning)

Zulu
(Charter)

Zulu Dawn
(Video Treasures)

Drama

Abe Lincoln in Illinois
(RKO)

Abraham Lincoln
(Congress)

Adam Had Four Sons
(RCA/Col)

Advise and Consent
(Video Treasures)

Agony and the Ecstasy
(CBS/Fox)

Alexander the Great
(MGM/UA)

Alfie
(Paramount)

Algiers
(Kartes)

Alice Adams
(Blackhawk)

Alice Doesn't Live Here Anymore
(Warner)

All About Eve
(Key)

All Creatures Great and Small
(Playhouse)

All Mine to Give
(United)

All My Sons (1986)
(MCA)

All the King's Men
(RCA/Col)

All This and Heaven Too
(MGM/UA)

Allegheny Uprising
(RKO)

Amadeus
(HBO)

American Short Story Collection
(IVE)

Angels with Dirty Faces
(CBS/Fox)

Anna Christie
(MGM/UA)

Anna Karenina (1935)
(Budget)

Anna Karenina (1948)
(J&J)

Anne of Green Gables
(RKO)

Anthony Adverse
(MGM/UA)

Arch of Triumph
(Republic)

Arrowsmith
(Embassy)

Assassination of Trotsky
(Republic)

Autobiography of Miss Jane Pittman
(Prism)

Autumn Leaves
(RCA/Col)

Baby, the Rain Must Fall
(RCA/Col)

Back Street
(MCA)

Bad and the Beautiful
(MGM/UA)

Bang the Drum Slowly
(Paramount)

Barabbas
(RCA/Col)

Barbarian and the Geisha
(Key)

Barbary Coast
(Embassy)

Beggars in Ermine
(J&J)

Ben Hur
(MGM/UA)

Best Years of Our Lives
(Embassy)

The Bible
(CBS/Fox)

Billy Budd
(Corinth)

Black Narcissus
(VidAmerica)

Black Orchid
(Kartes)

Bleak House
(CBS/Fox)

Blonde Venus
(MCA)

Body and Soul
(Republic)

The Bostonians
(Vestron)

Botany Bay
(Kartes)

Boys in the Band
(CBS/Fox)

Brief Encounter
(Paramount)

Brother John
(RCA/Col)

Brothers Karamazov
(MGM/UA)

Bus Stop
(CBS/Fox)

Camille
(MGM/UA)

Captains Courageous
(MGM/UA)

The Cardinal
(Hal Roach)

The Carpetbaggers
(Paramount)

Cat on a Hot Tin Roof
(MGM/UA)

Catherine the Great
(Kartes)

The Chalk Garden
(MCA)

Champion
(Republic)

Chariots of Fire
(Warner)

Cincinnati Kid
(MGM/UA)

Citizen Kane
(RKO)

Cleopatra (1934)
(Goodtimes)

Cleopatra (1963)
(CBS/Fox)

The Corn Is Green
(MGM/UA)

Cornbread, Earl and Me
(HBO)

Country Girl
(Paramount)

Cyrano de Bergerac
(Republic)

Dark Victory
(MGM/UA)

Darling
(Embassy)

David and Lisa
(RCA/Col)

David Copperfield
(MGM/UA)

Day of the Locust
(Paramount)

Days of Heaven
(Paramount)

Days of Wine and Roses
(Warner)

Death in Venice
(Warner)

Death of a Salesman (1986)
(Warner)

Desire Under the Elms
(Kartes)

Devil and Daniel Webster
(Embassy)

Devil at 4 O'Clock
(RCA/Col)

The D.I.
(Warner)

Diary of Anne Frank
(CBS/Fox)

Dino
(Republic)

Dishonored Lady
(Cable)

Divorce of Lady X
(J&J)

Doctor Zhivago
(MGM/UA)

Dodsworth
(Embassy)

Dragon Seed
(MGM/UA)

Drums Along the Mohawk
(Key)

East of Eden
(Warner)

Education of Sonny Carson
(Fox Hills)

El Cid
(United)

Enchanted Cottage
(Fox Hills)

End of the Road
(Key)

Entertaining Mr. Sloane
(HBO)

Equus
(MGM/UA)

The Europeans
(Vestron)

Executioner's Song
(IVE)

Executive Suite
(MGM/UA)

A Face in the Crowd
(Warner)

Fall of the Roman Empire
(Lightning)

Fallen Idol
(Kartes)

Fallen Sparrow
(Fox Hills)

Far Pavillions
(HBO)

A Farewell to Arms
(Discount)

Farmer's Daughter
(CBS/Fox)

Fat City
(RCA/Col)

Fatso
(Playhouse)

Five Easy Pieces
(RCA/Col)

Force of Evil
(Republic)

Four Horsemen of the Apocalypse
(MGM/UA)

Friendly Persuasion
(CBS/Fox)

Front Page
(Kartes)

Gal Young 'Un
(Academy)

Georgia, Georgia
(Prism)

Giant
(Warner)

The Goddess
(RCA/Col)

Golden Boy
(RCA/Col)

Gone With the Wind
(MGM/UA)

Good Earth
(MGM/UA)

Goodbye, Mr. Chips
(MGM/UA)

Grand Hotel
(MGM/UA)

Grapes of Wrath
(Key)

Great Expectations (1946)
(Paramount)

Great Gatsby (1974)
(Paramount)

Great Imposter
(MCA)

Great Santini
(Warner)

Greek Tycoon
(MCA)

The Hairy Ape
(Amvest)

Hamlet (1948)
(Paramount)

Harlow
(Paramount)

The Heart Is a Lonely Hunter
(Warner)

Heartland
(HBO)

The Heiress
(MCA)

Hell to Eternity
(Key)

Henry V
(Paramount)

Hobson's Choice
(Embassy)

Hud
(Paramount)

The Hustler
(Paramount)

I Am a Camera
(IVE)

I Remember Mama
(RKO)

I Want to Live!
(MGM/UA)

Ice Palace
(Warner)

Idiot's Delight
(MGM/UA)

Imitation of Life (1958)
(MCA)

In Cold Blood
(RCA/Col)

The Informer
(VidAmerica)

Isadora
(MCA)

Jackie Robinson Story
(Goodtimes)

Jewel in the Crown
(Pacific Arts)

Jezebel
(MGM/UA)

Joan of Arc
(VidAmerica)

Johnny Belinda
(MGM/UA)

Judge Priest
(Video Yesteryear)

Julius Caesar
(Republic)

Justine
(Key)

Killing of Sister George
(CBS/Fox)

King Lear
(Corinth)

King of Kings (1961)
(MGM/UA)

Kiss of the Spider Woman
(Charter)

Kiss Tomorrow Goodbye
(Republic)

Kitty Foyle
(VidAmerica)

Lady Chatterley's Lover (1955)
(Budget)

Lady from Louisiana
(Republic)

Last Angry Man
(RCA/Col)

Last Command
(Republic)

Last Hurrah
(RCA/Col)

Last Mile
(Kartes)

Last of the Mohicans
(IVE)

Last Time I Saw Paris
(Goodtimes)

Last Tycoon
(Paramount)

Lawrence of Arabia
(RCA/Col)

Learning Tree
(Warner)

Leather Boys
(VidAmerica)

Left Hand of God
(Key)

The Letter
(MGM/UA)

Life and Death of Colonel Blimp
(VidAmerica)

Life of Emile Zola
(MGM/UA)

Liberation of L. B. Jones
(RCA/Col)

Lilies of the Field
(RCA/Col)

Lilith
(RCA/Col)

A Lion in Winter
(Nelson)

Little Foxes
(Embassy)

Little Minister
(RKO)

Little Orphan Annie (1932)
(Video Dimensions)

Little Women (1933)
(MGM/UA)

Little Women (1949)
(MGM/UA)

Lonely Are the Brave
(MCA)

Lonelyhearts
(MGM/UA)

Long Day's Journey into Night
(Republic)

Long Voyage Home
(Warner)

Lord Jim
(RCA/Col)

Lost Weekend
(MCA)

Louisiana Story
(Video Yesteryear)

Love in the Afternoon
(CBS/Fox)

Love Me or Leave Me
(MGM/UA)

The Lusty Men
(United)

Macbeth (1948)
(Republic)

Macbeth (1971)
(RCA/Col)

Madame Bovary
(MGM/UA)

Madame X
(MCA)

Magic Town
(Republic)

Magnificent Ambersons
(RKO)

Magnificent Obsession
(MCA)

A Man Called Adam
(Embassy)

A Man For All Seasons
(RCA/Col)

Man with the Golden Arm
(Congress)

Marjorie Morningstar
(Republic)

Marked Woman
(MGM/UA)

Marty
(MGM/UA)

Mary of Scotland
(Nostalgia Merchant)

Master Harold and the Boys
(Lorimar)

Mayerling
(Embassy)

Member of the Wedding
(RCA/Col)

The Men
(Republic)

The Message
(IVE)

Mildred Pierce
(Warner)

Mine Own Executioner
(Budget)

Miracle Worker
(MGM/UA)

Les Miserables (1935)
(Key)

Mishima
(Warner)

Miss Julie
(Embassy)

Miss Sadie Thompson
(RCA/Col)

Mr. Skeffington
(MGM/UA)

Mr. Smith Goes to Washington
(RCA/Col)

Mrs. Miniver
(MGM/UA)

Moliere
(RKO)

Molly Maguires
(Paramount)

Morocco
(Kartes)

Mutiny on the Bounty (1935)
(MGM/UA)

Mutiny on the Bounty (1962)
(MGM/UA)

Napoleon (1955)
(MPI)

Never Love a Stranger
(Republic)

Nicholas and Alexandra
(RCA/Col)

Nicholas Nickleby
(HBO)

Night of the Iguana
(MGM/UA)

A Night to Remember
(Paramount)

Ninotchka
(MGM/UA)

None But the Lonely Heart
(Fox Hills)

Now, Voyager
(MGM/UA)

Nurse Edith Cavell
(Kartes)

Odd Man Out
(Paramount)

Of Human Bondage
(Congress)

Of Mice and Men
(Prism)

Old Curiosity Shop
(Embassy)

The Old Maid
(MGM/UA)

On the Waterfront
(RCA/Col)

One Flew Over the Cuckoo's Nest
(HBO)

One Third of a Nation
(Captain Bijou)

Our Daily Bread
(Embassy)

Our Town
(Goodtimes)

Outpost in Morocco
(Goodtimes)

Paper Chase
(CBS/Fox)

The Passenger
(Warner)

Passion of Joan of Arc
(Video Yesteryear)

The Pawnbroker
(Republic)

Payday
(HBO)

A Place in the Sun
(Paramount)

Possessed
(MGM/UA)

Pride and Prejudice
(MGM/UA)

Priest of Love
(HBO)

Private Life of Don Juan
(Embassy)

Private Life of Henry VIII
(Embassy)

The Quiet Man
(Republic)

Quo Vadis
(MGM/UA)

Rachel and the Stranger
(Nostalgia Merchant)

Rachel, Rachel
(Warner)

Rain
(Cable)

Rain People
(Warner)

The Rainmaker
(Paramount)

Raintree County
(MGM/UA)

Raisin in the Sun
(RCA/Col)

Razor's Edge (1946)
(RCA/Col)

Rebecca
(Key)

Red Badge of Courage
(MGM/UA)

Reflections in a Golden Eye
(Warner)

The Reivers
(Key)

Requiem for a Heavyweight
(MGM/UA)

Resurrection
(MCA)

Return of the Secaucus Seven
(RCA/Col)

The River Niger
(Cinema Group)

The Robe
(CBS/Fox)

Roman Spring of Mrs. Stone
(Warner)

Romeo and Juliet (1968)
(Paramount)

Ruby Gentry
(CBS/Fox)

Ryan's Daughter
(MGM/UA)

Saint Jack
(Vestron)

Saint Joan
(Video Treasures)

Salome
(RCA/Col)

Samson and Delilah
(Paramount)

San Francisco
(MGM/UA)

Scarlet Letter
(Kartes)

September Affair
(Paramount)

The Servant
(HBO)

Seven Sinners
(Kartes)

Shakespeare Wallah
(Embassy)

The Shanghai Gesture
(Mystic Fire)

Ship of Fools
(RCA/Col)

Shoes of the Fisherman
(MGM/UA)

The Shooting Party
(HBO)

Shop Around the Corner
(MGM/UA)

Shop on Main Street
(RCA/Col)

Short Eyes
(Lightning)

Silver Chalice
(Warner)

Soldier in the Rain
(Key)

Soldier's Story
(RCA/Col)

Some Came Running
(MGM/UA)

Something for Everyone
(Key)

Something of Value
(MGM/UA)

Sometimes a Great Notion
(MCA)

A Song to Remember
(RCA/Col)

The Southerner
(Cable)

Spartacus
(HBO)

Spirit of St. Louis
(Warner)

Spirit of West Point
(New World)

Splendor in the Grass
(Warner)

The Sporting Club
(Charter)

Stars Look Down
(Budget)

State of the Union
(MCA)

State of Things
(Pacific Arts)

Stella Dallas
(Embassy)

Stopover Tokyo
(Key)

Strangers When We Meet
(RCA/Col)

Strategic Air Command
(Paramount)

Strawberry Statement
(MGM/UA)

Streamers
(Media)

Street Scene
(Kartes)

Streetcar Named Desire
(Warner)

The Stripper
(Key)

Studs Lonigan
(MGM/UA)

Suddenly, Last Summer
(RCA/Col)

Sundown
(Video Yesteryear)

Sundowners
(Warner)

Sunrise at Campobello
(Warner)

Sunset Boulevard
(Paramount)

Svengali
(Kartes)

Sweet Smell of Success
(MGM/UA)

The Swimmer
(RCA/Col)

Sybil
(CBS/Fox)

Sylvia Scarlet
(Fox Hills)

Tale of Two Cities
(MGM/UA)

Talk of the Town
(RCA/Col)

Tamarind Seed
(Embassy)

Taming of the Shrew
(RCA/Col)

A Taste of Honey
(American Video Tape)

Ten Commandments
(Paramount)

Tender Mercies
(HBO)

That Cold Day in the Park
(Republic)

That Hamilton Woman
(Embassy)

This Property Is Condemned
(Paramount)

The Time of Your Life
(Goodtimes)

A Time to Love and a Time to Die
(Kartes)

To Have and Have Not
(MGM/UA)

To Kill a Mockingbird
(MCA)

To Sir with Love
(RCA/Col)

Tomorrow
(IVE)

A Town Like Alice
(New World)

A Tree Grows in Brooklyn
(Playhouse)

Triangle Factory Fire Scandal
(IVE)

Trip to Bountiful
(Embassy)

Trojan Women
(IVE)

True West
(Academy)

Tunes of Glory
(Embassy)

12 Angry Men
(Corinth)

Ugly American
(MCA)

Victim
(Embassy)

Viva Zapata
(Key)

A Walk in the Spring Rain
(RCA/Col)

A Walk on the Wild Side
(RCA/Col)

War and Peace
(Connoisseur)

The Well
(United)

Whistle Down the Wind
(Embassy)

Who's Afraid of Virginia Woolf?
(Warner)

Winslow Boy
(HBO)

Winterset
(Congress)

The Women
(MGM/UA)

World of Suzie Wong
(Paramount)

Written on the Wind
(MCA)

Wuthering Heights
(Embassy)

The Yearling
(MGM/UA)

Young Man with a Horn
(Warner)

The Young Philadelphians
(Warner)

Zabriskie Point
(MGM/UA)

Foreign Films

Alexander Nevsky
(Video Yesteryear)

Amarcord
(Warner)

And the Ship Sails On
(RCA/Col)

Aparajito
(Foothill)

Ashes and Diamonds
(Embassy)

The Bad Sleep Well
(Sony)

Ballad of a Soldier
(Video Yesteryear)

Battle of Algiers
(Axon)

Bicycle Thief
(Discount)

Beau Pere
(Media/Cinematheque)

Berlin Alexanderplatz
(MGM/UA)

Big Deal on Madonna Street
(Connoisseur)

Black and White in Color
(Lorimar)

Black Magic
(Video Yesteryear)

Blood of a Poet
(Video Yesteryear)

Blood Wedding
(Media/Cinematheque)

The Blue Angel
(Cable)

Bob Le Flambeur
(Video Dimensions)

Boudou Saved from Drowning
(New York Film Annex)

Brink of Life
(Video Yesteryear)

Buffet Froid
(Interama)

Cabiria
(Video Yesteryear)

Caravaggio
(Embassy)

The Castle
(Cinema Group)

Cesar and Rosalie
(Axon)

La Chevre
(Euro-American)

Chloe in the Afternoon
(Media/Cinematheque)

Claire's Knee
(Media/Cinematheque)

Cries and Whispers
(Warner)

Danton
(RCA/Columbia)

Day for Night
(Warner)

Death in Venice
(Warner)

Devil's Playground
(Today)

Discreet Charm of the Bourgeoisie
(Corinth)

Diva
(MGM/UA)

Dodes 'Ka-Den
(Embassy)

Don Quixote (1935)
(Kartes)

Dona Herlinda and Her Son
(Cinevista)

Earth
(Video Yesteryear)

8½
(Vestron)

Eli, Eli
(Video Dimensions)

Elvira Madigan
(HBO)

Entre Nous
(MGM/UA)

Exterminating Angel
(Viewfinders)

Fanny and Alexander
(Embassy)

Father
(Video Yesteryear)

Fires on the Plain
(Embassy)

Fitzcarraldo
(Warner)

Floating Weeds
(Connoisseur)

Forbidden Games
(Embassy)

400 Blows
(Corinth)

Ghost of Yotsuya
(Video Action)

Going Places
(RCA/Col)

Golden Demon
(Embassy)

Grand Illusion
(Connoisseur)

Hail Mary
(Vestron)

Harp of Burma
(Foothill)

Hidden Fortress
(Media/Cinematheque)

High and Low
(MCA)

Hiroshima, Mon Amour
(Embassy)

I Vitelloni
(Corinth)

Ikiru
(Media)

Italian Straw Hat
(Video Yesteryear)

Jean de Florette
(Orion)

Judex
(Foothill)

Kameradschaft
(Embassy)

Kanal
(Embassy)

Knife in the Water
(Video Dimensions)

Kwaidan
(Video Yesteryear)

Land Without Bread
(Discount)

Last Metro
(Key)

Last Year at Marienbad
(Cable)

L'Atalante
(CVCCC)

L'Avventura
(Video Dimensions)

Life of Oharu
(Video Yesteryear)

Lola Montes
(Embassy)

Lost Honor of Katherine Blum
(Embassy)

Lower Depths
(CVCCC)

Maedchen in Uniform
(Foothill)

Magic Flute
(National Cinema Service)

The Magician
(Embassy)

A Man and a Woman
(Warner)

Manon of the Spring
(Orion)

Marius
(Applause)

Mayerling
(Video Yesteryear)

Mephisto
(HBO)

Mill on the Floss
(Kartes)

Miracle of Marcellino
(Henwood)

Miss Julie
(Embassy)

Mon Oncle d'Amerique
(Embassy)

Monsieur Vincent
(Foothill)

Montenegro
(HBO)

Moscow Does Not Believe in Tears
(RCA/Col)

My Life to Live
(Cable)

My Night at Maud's
(Media/Cinematheque)

Never on Sunday
(MGM/UA)

Night of the Shooting Stars
(MGM/UA)

A Nous La Liberte
(National Cinema Service)

Los Olvidados
(Budget)

Open City
(Foothill)

Orpheus
(Embassy)

The Overcoat
(National Cinema Service)

Paisan
(Cable)

Panique
(Budget)

Pather Panchali
(Foothill)

Pauline at the Beach
(Media/Cinematheque)

Pepe Le Moko
(Video Yesteryear)

Persona
(Video Yesteryear)

Ran
(CBS/Fox)

Rashomon
(Embassy)

Red Beard
(Embassy)

Return of Martin Guerre
(Embassy)

Rules of the Game
(Embassy)

Sansho the Bailiff
(National Cinema Service)

Seduced and Abandoned
(Foothill)

Serpent's Egg
(Vestron)

Seventh Seal
(Embassy)

Shop on Main Street
(RCA/Col)

Simon of the Desert
(Budget)

Smash Palace
(Vestron)

Smiles of a Summer Night
(Embassy)

State of Siege
(RCA/Col)

Stromboli
(United)

Stolen Kisses
(RCA/Col)

Sundays and Cybele
(Video Dimensions)

That Obscure Object of Desire
(Embassy)

Throne of Blood
(Media)

Through a Glass Darkly
(Embassy)

The Tin Drum
(Warner)

Two Women
(Embassy)

Ugetsu
(Embassy)

Umberto D
(Embassy)

Under the Roofs of Paris
(Applause)

Virgin Spring
(Embassy)

Viridiana
(Budget)

Wild Strawberries
(Connoisseur)

Winter Light
(Embassy)

Yesterday, Today and Tomorrow
(Showcase)

Zero for Conduct
(Festival)

Musicals

All That Jazz
(CBS/Fox)

An American in Paris
(MGM/UA)

Anchors Aweigh
(MGM/UA)

Angels Over Broadway
(RCA/Col)

Auntie Mame
(Warner)

Babes in Arms
(MGM/UA)

Band Wagon
(MGM/UA)

Barkleys of Broadway
(MGM/UA)

Bells Are Ringing
(MGM/UA)

Best Foot Forward
(MGM/UA)

Billy Rose's Jumbo
(MGM/UA)

Born Yesterday
(RCA/Col)

Breaking the Ice
(Discount)

Brigadoon
(MGM/UA)

Broadway Melody
(MGM/UA)

Broadway Melody of 1938
(MGM/UA)

Broadway Melody of 1940
(MGM/UA)

Broadway Through a Keyhole
(Captain Bijou)

Bugsy Malone
(Paramount)

Bye, Bye Birdie
(RCA/Col)

Cabaret
(CBS/Fox)

Cabin in the Sky
(MGM/UA)

Calamity Jane
(Warner)

Camelot
(Warner)

Can Can
(CBS/Fox)

Carefree
(Fox Hills)

A Chorus Line
(Embassy)

A Connecticut Yankee in
King Arthur's Court
(MCA)

Dance of Life
(Mike Lebell Video)

Dancing Lady
(MGM/UA)

Dancing Pirate
(Discount)

Dangerous When Wet
(MGM/UA)

A Date with Judy
(MGM/UA)

Deep in My Heart
(MGM/UA)

Doll Face
(Budget)

DuBarry Was a Lady
(MGM/UA)

Easter Parade
(MGM/UA)

Evergreen
(Foothill)

Fabulous Dorseys
(Republic)

Fanny
(Warner)

Fashions of 1934
(Video Dimensions)

Fiddler on the Roof
(MGM/UA)

Finian's Rainbow
(Warner)

Flower Drum Song
(MCA)

Flying Down to Rio
(Fox Hills)

Follow the Fleet
(Fox Hills)

For Me and My Gal
(MGM/UA)

French Way
(Video Dimensions)

Funny Face
(Paramount)

Funny Girl
(RCA/Col)

Funny Lady
(RCA/Col)

Gaiety
(Hal Roach)

Gay Divorcee
(Fox Hills)

Gentlemen Prefer Blondes
(CBS/Fox)

George White's Scandals
(Video Dimensions)

Gigi
(MGM/UA)

A Girl, a Guy, and a Gob
(RKO)

Girl Crazy
(MGM/UA)

Glenn Miller Story
(MCA)

Glorifying the American Girl
(Video Yesteryear)

Goldwyn Follies
(Embassy)

Good News
(MGM/UA)

Great Caruso
(MGM/UA)

Great Ziegfeld
(MGM/UA)

Guys and Dolls
(CBS/Fox)

Gypsy
(Warner)

Happy Go Lovely
(Foothill)

Harvey Girls
(MGM/UA)

Hello, Dolly!
(CBS/Fox)

High Society
(MGM/UA)

Higher and Higher
(Video Dimensions)

Hit the Deck
(MGM/UA)

Holiday Inn
(MCA)

If You Knew Susie
(Video Dimensions)

In the Good Old Summertime
(MGM/UA)

Invitation to Dance
(MGM/UA)

It's Always Fair Weather
(MGM/UA)

Jazz Singer (1927)
(CBS/Fox)

Jesus Christ Superstar
(MCA)

Jolson Story
(RCA/Col)

Jolson Sings Again
(RCA/Col)

King of Jazz
(MCA)

Kismet
(MGM/UA)

Kiss Me Kate
(MGM/UA)

Les Girls
(MGM/UA)

Let's Make Love
(CBS/Fox)

Let's Sing Again
(J&J)

Lili
(MGM/UA)

A Little Night Music
(Embassy)

Mahler
(HBO)

Make a Wish
(Discount)

Manhattan Merry-Go-Round
(Budget)

Maytime
(MGM/UA)

Meet Me in St. Louis
(MGM/UA)

Movie Struck
(Video Yesteryear)

Murder at the Vanities
(MCA)

Music Man
(Warner)

My Fair Lady
(CBS/Fox)

Naughty Marietta
(MGM/UA)

Neptune's Daughter
(MGM/UA)

Never Steal Anything Small
(MCA)

New Faces of 1952
(Video Artists International)

New Moon
(MGM/UA)

Oklahoma!
(CBS/Fox)

Oliver!
(RCA/Col)

On a Clear Day
(Paramount)

On the Town
(MGM/UA)

One from the Heart
(RCA/Col)

Pal Joey
(RCA/Col)

The Pirate
(MGM/UA)

Pirates of Penzance
(MCA)

Prince and the Showgirl
(Warner)

Private Buckaroo
(Discount)

Pygmalion
(Embassy)

Queen of the Stardust Ballroom
(Prism)

Red Shoes
(Paramount)

Roberta
(MGM/UA)

Roman Scandals
(Embassy)

Rosalie
(MGM/UA)

Rose Marie
(MGM/UA)

Royal Wedding
(MGM/UA)

Say Amen, Somebody
(Pacific Arts)

Scrooge
(CBS/Fox)

Second Chorus
(Video Resources)

Sensations of 1945
(Video Dimensions)

Seven Brides for Seven Brothers
(MGM/UA)

1776
(RCA/Col)

Shall We Dance?
(RKO)

Show Boat (1951)
(MGM/UA)

Silk Stockings
(MGM/UA)

Singin' in the Rain
(MGM/UA)

Sky's the Limit
(Hal Roach)

Smilin' Through
(MGM/UA)

Song of Norway
(Playhouse)

Sound of Music
(CBS/Fox)

South Pacific
(CBS/Fox)

Stagedoor Canteen
(Discount)

A Star Is Born
(Warner)

State Fair
(CBS/Fox)

Step Lively
(RKO)

Stormy Weather
(Key)

Story of Vernon and Irene Castle
(Fox Hills)

Strike Up the Band
(MGM/UA)

Summer Stock
(MGM/UA)

Sunday in the Park with George
(Warner)

Sweet Charity
(MCA)

Swing Time
(Fox Hills)

Take Me Out to the Ball Game
(MGM/UA)

Thank Your Lucky Stars
(MGM/UA)

That's Dancing
(MGM/UA)

That's Entertainment
(MGM/UA)

There's No Business Like Show Business
(CBS/Fox)

They Shall Have Music
(Embassy)

This Is the Army
(Goodtimes)

Thoroughly Modern Millie
(MCA)

Thousands Cheer
(MGM/UA)

Three Little Words
(MGM/UA)

Till the Clouds Roll By
(MGM/UA)

Toast of New Orleans
(MGM/UA)

Top Hat
(Fox Hills)

Unsinkable Molly Brown
(MGM/UA)

Vagabond Lover
(Discount)

West Side Story
(MGM/UA)

White Christmas
(MCA)

Whoopee!
(Embassy)

Words and Music
(MGM/UA)

Yankee Doodle Dandy
(MGM/UA)

Yolanda and the Thief
(MGM/UA)

You Were Never Lovelier
(RCA/Col)

You'll Never Get Rich
(RCA/Col)

Ziegfeld Follies
(MGM/UA)

Mystery/Suspense/Intrigue

Arabesque
(MCA)

The Beguiled
(MCA)

Black Veil for Lisa
(Republic)

Brainwash
(Media)

Charade
(MCA)

Crossfire
(Nostalgia Merchant)

Double Indemnity
(MCA)

A Double Life
(Republic)

Drowning Pool
(Warner)

Falcon and the Snowman
(Vestron)

Funeral in Berlin
(Paramount)

Gambit
(MCA)

Gilda
(RCA/Col)

Green Dolphin Street
(MGM/UA)

Groundstar Conspiracy
(MCA)

Gumshoe
(RCA/Col)

Harper
(Warner)

I Cover the Waterfront
(King Bee)

Ipcress File
(MCA)

Johnny Angel
(RKO)

Journey Into Fear
(Fox Hills)

The List of Adrian Messenger
(MCA)

Little Girl Who Lives Down the Lane
(Vestron)

Looking Glass War
(RCA/Col)

Mackintosh Man
(Warner)

Marathon Man
(Paramount)

Midnight Lace
(MCA)

Mirage
(Kartes)

Mr. Ace
(Sony)

Morituri
(Key)

Murder on the Orient Express
(Paramount)

My Forbidden Past
(Nostalgia Merchant)

Night Moves
(Warner)

Night Watch
(Fox Hills)

The Nightcomers
(Charter)

Odessa File
(RCA/Col)

Play Misty For Me
(MCA)

The Postman Always Rings Twice (1981)
(CBS/Fox)

Quiller Memorandum
(Key)

Rollercoaster
(MCA)

Secret Beyond the Door
(Republic)

Secret Ceremony
(Kartes)

Shoot
(Embassy)

Sleuth
(Media)

Smash-up
(Amvest)

Sorry, Wrong Number
(Paramount)

Strange Love of Martha Ivers
(Kartes)

Tattered Web
(Kartes)

They Won't Believe Me
(Fox Hills)

13 Rue Madeleine
(Key)

Thunderbolt & Lightfoot
(MGM/UA)

True Confessions
(MGM/UA)

Wait Until Dark
(Warner)

While the City Sleeps
(United)

Wilby Conspiracy
(MGM/UA)

The Alfred Hitchcock Collection

Blackmail
(Sinister Cinema)

Dial M For Murder
(Warner)

Easy Virtue
(Showcase)

Family Plot
(MCA)

The Farmer's Wife
(Sinister Cinema)

Foreign Correspondent
(Lightning)

Frenzy
(MCA)

I Confess
(Warner)

Jamaica Inn
(Sinister Cinema)

The Lady Vanishes
(Sinister Cinema)

Lifeboat
(Key)

The Lodger (1926)
(Video Yesteryear)

The Man Who Knew Too Much (1934)
(Sinister Cinema)

The Man Who Knew Too Much (1956)
(MCA)

The Manxman
(Video Yesteryear)

Marnie
(MCA)

Mr. & Mrs. Smith
(Media)

Murder
(Sinister Cinema)

North by Northwest
(MGM/UA)

Notorious
(CBS/Fox)

Number 17
(Sinister Cinema)

Paradine Case
(CBS/Fox)

Rear Window
(MCA)

Rebecca
(CBS/Fox)

Rich and Strange
(Sinister Cinema)

Sabotage
(Sinister Cinema)

Saboteur
(MCA)

Secret Agent
(Sinister Cinema)

Shadow of a Doubt
(MCA)

Skin Game
(Sinister Cinema)

Spellbound
(CBS/Fox)

Suspicion
(RKO)

The 39 Steps
(MPI)

To Catch a Thief
(Paramount)

Topaz
(MCA)

Torn Curtain
(MCA)

The Trouble with Harry
(MCA)

Under Capricorn
(VidAmerica)

The Wrong Man
(Warner)

Young and Innocent
(Sinister Cinema)

Silent Classics

The Americano/Mystery of the Leaning Fish
(CVCCC)

Arsenal
(Embassy)

Battleship Potemkin
(Discount)

Beau Brummel
(Budget)

The Bells
(Video Yesteryear)

Ben-Hur
(MGM/UA)

The Big Parade
(MGM/UA)

Birth of a Nation
(Video Resources)

Black Pirate
(Video Yesteryear)

Blind Husbands
(Video Yesteryear)

Blood and Sand
(Video Yesteryear)

Broken Blossoms
(CVCCC)

Cat and the Canary
(Budget)

Civilization
(Video Resources)

The Cobra
(Budget)

Dancing Mothers
(Discount)

Destiny
(J&J)

Diary of a Lost Girl
(Video Dimensions)

Docks of New York
(Paramount)

Dr. Mabuse, the Gambler
(Embassy)

Don Juan
(Discount)

Don Q., Son of Zorro
(Video Dimensions)

Down to the Sea in Ships
(Video Dimensions)

The Eagle
(Video Yesteryear)

Foolish Wives
(J&J)

The Golem
(Video Yesteryear)

History of Color in Silent Films
(Video Yesteryear)

Intolerance
(Video Resources)

Iron Mask
(Video Dimensions)

It
(Foothill)

Juve Contra Fantomas
(Embassy)

Kriemhilde's Revenge
(Video Dimensions)

Last Command
(Paramount)

Last Laugh
(Cable)

Man with the Movie Camera
(Embassy)

Mantrap
(Grapevine)

Mark of Zorro
(Video Dimensions)

Marriage Circle
(Discount)

Midnight Girl
(Video Yesteryear)

Napoleon
(MCA)

Orphans of the Storm
(Grapevine)

Pandora's Box
(Embassy)

Peck's Bad Boy
(Video Dimensions)

Phantom Chariot
(Danny Burk)

Pioneers of the French Cinema Vols. 1–2
(Embassy)

Queen Kelly
(Video Yesteryear)

Reaching for the Moon
(Discount)

Road to Yesterday
(Video Yesteryear)

Robin Hood
(Discount)

Shadows
(Video Dimensions)

Son of the Sheik
(Video Dimensions)

Sparrows
(Video Yesteryear)

Spies
(Video Dimensions)

Strike
(Video Yesteryear)

Student of Prague
(Embassy)

The Tempest
(Discount)

Thief of Bagdad
(Video Dimensions)

Tol'able David
(Video Dimensions)

Tumbleweeds
(Video Dimensions)

The Vanishing American
(Video Yesteryear)

Variety
(Video Yesteryear)

Way Down East
(Video Resources)

The Wedding March
(Paramount)

Wings
(Paramount)

Vintage Black Films 1932–1953

Beware
(Budget)

Big Timers
(Budget)

Black Artists Short Subjects Vols. 1–3
(Discount)

Black King
(Discount)

Blood of Jesus
(Channel 13)

Boardinghouse Blues
(Foothill)

Broken Strings
(Video Yesteryear)

Devil's Daughter
(Discount)

Dirty Gertie from Harlem USA
(Video Dimensions)

Double Deal
(Discount)

Drums O'Voodoo
(Sinister Cinema)

The Duke Is Tops
(Discount)

Emperor Jones
(Embassy)

Gang War (1940)
(Discount)

Girl from Chicago
(Discount)

Go Down Death
(Foothill)

God's Stepchildren
(Budget)

Harlem Swings Vols. 1–5
(Discount)

Hi-De-Ho
(United)

Jericho
(Foothill)

Jive Junction
(Video Yesteryear)

Jivin' in Bebop
(Video Yesteryear)

Joe Louis Story
(J&J)

Juke Joint
(Discount)

Junction 88
(Foothill)

Killer Diller
(Discount)

King Solomon's Mines (1937)
(Discount)

Look Out Sister
(Budget)

Lying Lips
(Discount)

Miracle in Harlem
(Captain Bijou)

Mistaken Identity
(Discount)

Mr. Adams' Bomb
(Loonic)

Moon Over Harlem
(Foothill)

Murder On Lenox Avenue
(Budget)

Murder with Music
(Discount)

Mystery in Swing
(Discount)

Native Son (1951)
(Captain Bijou)

Paradise in Harlem
(Video Yesteryear)

Purlie Victorious
(Mastervision)

Reet, Petite and Gone
(Video Yesteryear)

Sanders of the River
(Foothill)

Sepia Cinderella
(Discount)

Song of Freedom
(Kartes)

Spirit of Youth
(Discount)

Stars on Parade
(Video Yesteryear)

Sunday Sinners
(Discount)

Swing
(Budget)

Tall, Tan and Terrific
(Discount)

Ten Minutes to Live
(Budget)

War Dramas

Action in Arabia
(RKO)

Air Force
(Kartes)

All Quiet on the Western Front
(MCA)

Anzio
(RCA/Columbia)

Apocalypse Now
(Paramount)

The Assault
(MGM/UA)

Away All Boats
(MCA)

Back to Bataan
(RKO)

Bataan
(MGM/UA)

Battle Cry
(Warner)

Battle Force
(Cinema Group)

Battle Hell
(VidAmerica)

Battle of Algiers
(Axon)

Battle of Britain
(MGM/UA)

Battle of El Alamein
(Video Gems)

Battle of the Bulge
(Warner)

Blood on the Sun
(Goodtimes)

Blue Max
(CBS/Fox)

Bombardier
(RKO)

Boys in Company C
(RCA/Col)

Breakthrough
(Goodtimes)

Bridge of San Luis Rey
(New World)

Bridge on the River Kwai
(RCA/Columbia)

Bridge at Remagen
(Wood Knapp)

Bridges at Toko-Ri
(Paramount)

The Caine Mutiny
(RCA/Col)

Colditz Story
(HBO)

Commandos Strike at Dawn
(RCA/Col)

Cross of Iron
(Media)

Cry of Battle
(Kartes)

Dam Busters
(HBO)

Deer Hunter
(MCA)

Desert Fox
(CBS/Fox)

Dragonfly Squadron
(Sony)

The Eagle Has Landed
(CBS/Fox)

Enemy of Women
(Dixie)

Enola Gay
(Prism)

Fighting Seabees
(Republic)

Fire Over England
(Goodtimes)

Flat Top
(Republic)

Flying Leathernecks
(RKO)

Flying Tigers
(Republic)

Four in a Jeep
(Sony)

49th Parallel
(Vidmark)

From Here to Eternity
(RCA/Col)

Full Metal Jacket
(Warner)

Gung Ho
(Republic)

Guns of Navarone
(RCA/Col)

A Guy Named Joe
(MGM/UA)

Hell to Eternity
(Key)

Hellcats of the Navy
(RCA/Col)

Hitler
(Key)

Hitler: The Last Ten Days
(Paramount)

Hitler's Children
(Fox Hills)

Home of the Brave
(Republic)

Immortal Battalion
(Video Yesteryear)

Immortal Sergeant
(Key)

Johnny Got His Gun
(Media)

King Rat
(RCA/Col)

Longest Day
(CBS/Fox)

MacArthur
(MCA)

Master Race
(RKO)

Men in War
(Congress)

Midway
(MCA)

Mr. Winkle Goes to War
(RCA/Columbia)

Naked and the Dead
(United)

Never So Few
(MGM/UA)

Night of the Generals
(RCA/Columbia)

North Star
(Republic)

One of Our Aircraft Is Missing
(Republic)

One That Got Away
(IUD)

Only the Valiant
(Republic)

Patton
(CBS/Fox)

Platoon
(Vestron)

Pork Chop Hill
(MGM/UA)

PT 109
(Warner)

Pursuit of the Graf Spee
(IUD)

Raid on Rommel
(MCA)

Red Tent
(Paramount)

Sands of Iwo Jima
(Republic)

Soldier of Orange
(Media)

Stalag 17
(Paramount)

They Were Expendable
(MGM/UA)

30 Seconds over Tokyo
(MGM/UA)

To Hell and Back
(MCA)

Tobruk
(MCA)

Tora! Tora! Tora!
(CBS/Fox)

12 O'Clock High
(CBS/Fox)

Victory at Sea
(Embassy)

Visions of War
(Pacific Arts)

Von Ryan's Express
(CBS/Fox)

Wake Island
(MCA)

A Walk in the Sun
(Kartes)

War and Remembrance
(MPI)

The War Lover
(RCA/Col)

Where Eagles Dare
(MGM/UA)

Why We Fight
(Video City)

World at War
(HBO)

The Young Lions
(Key)

THE PHANTOM
OF THE MOVIES'
VIDEORAMA
YOUR COMPLETE HOME-VIDEO DIRECTORY

THE PHANTOM OF THE MOVIES' VIDEORAMA:
MAIL-ORDER & SPECIALTY VIDEO SUPPLIERS

Okay, we've given you a head start; now it's time for the more adventurous videastes among you to play video detective on your own. To supplement the thousands of titles already listed in this book, we've assembled over fifty of the top mail-order and specialty-tape suppliers who offer literally tens of thousands of more specific, exotic, and offbeat fare—from A classics to B westerns to Z movies and oldies of every stripe—than you're likely to find at your corner cassette store. We've listed each company's address and phone number (if any) and areas of expertise, along with the cassette formats available (VHS, Beta, 8mm), and we identify those that accept MasterCard, Visa, or other major credit cards. You'll also meet an independent supplier, archivist Ira H. Gallen of Video Resources.

A few rough guidelines to keep in mind. In general, money orders speed delivery; personal checks can take up to several weeks to process. Sending cash is acceptable but ill-advised. Most of the firms listed here ship via UPS or Priority Mail, and nearly all have catalogs or title and price lists for your advance perusal—many offered gratis, others with an SASE, some for a slight fee. Several also have mail-order rental systems for those who want to look but not keep.

The Phantom has spot-tested a majority of the nation's video suppliers by ordering tapes anonymously (i.e., under one of his other aliases). Those outfits that proved tardy or irresponsible or that delivered substandard tapes were deleted from our vid-company roster. Ditto for those discovered to carry (however unwittingly) illegal titles among their offerings. To the best of our knowledge, the suppliers listed below traffic in *legal* videos only, though naturally this is an area no lone Phantom can hope to monitor with 100 percent efficiency.

The same applies to a video's visual and/or audio quality. Quality varies from cassette to cassette within a supplier's inventory. The Phantom may have received an acceptable tape from the same supplier who sends you an unacceptable one. In that case, you should contact the supplier for a refund or a replacement tape. Some suppliers, like Jim Harmon and Rex Miller, specify in their catalogs those tapes that are of lesser quality; the collector can then decide whether or not he or she wants a film rarity of substandard quality.

Our listing of mail-order and specialty-video suppliers is followed by a list of the video labels—major, minor, and arcane alike—cited in our main text, complete with addresses and phone numbers to help you track down a specific tape you may otherwise have difficulty locating. Be aware that addresses and numbers are subject to change.

Other reliable video suppliers—of both the public-domain and licensed-video varieties—will undoubtedly surface between the time of this (last-minute) writing and publication. We suggest you keep track of our weekly "Mondo Video" column in the New York *Daily News* for word of the latest changes and updates.

In the meantime, happy video-hunting.

Mail-Order & Specialty-Video Suppliers

American Entertainment Industries, Inc.
(see Henwood Cinema and Video*)*

Baker Video,
Box 7068, South Dartmouth MA 02748. (617) 992-8916.

Specializes in public-domain nostalgia titles, horror/sci-fi, silents, cartoon collections, and B westerns. VHS/Beta. MC/Visa. Write for catalog.

Beta Library,
836224 Promenade Station, Richardson TX 75083. (214) 385-BETA.

As its name implies, this Texas-based mail-order outfit handles

Beta tapes only. Beta Library stocks a varied array of both mainstream and lesser-known titles, many of them otherwise difficult to locate in the Beta format. Write for catalog.

Eddie Brandt's Saturday Matinee,

6310 Colfax Avenue, North Hollywood CA 91606. (818) 506-4242. Eddie Brandt.

A full-service video supplier with a vast inventory, Eddie Brandt stocks new releases and mainstream titles as well as B westerns and serials, mysteries, older musicals, sci-fi, horror, and rarities of all kinds. Offers weekly mail-order rentals as well as sales. VHS/Beta. MC/Visa. Write for catalog.

Danny Burk,

2316 Mishawaka Avenue, South Bend IN 46615. No phone. Danny Burk.

Carries silent films only, over one hundred titles, including many rarities (e.g., Rudolph Valentino's *Cobra*). Write for title and price list.

BVM Video,

P.O. Box 448, Princeton WI 54968. No phone.

BVM is a complete video supplier but sidelines in "strange, sick, obscure, weird videos," many offered at discount prices. A monthly title update is available for a small fee. VHS/Beta. MC/Visa. Write for further info.

Cable Films,

P.O. Box 7171, Kansas City MO 64113. (913) 362-2804. Herbert Miller.

One of the nation's oldest and most respected video suppliers, founded in 1976, with over three hundred titles in stock, Cable specializes in public-domain film classics of the '30s and '40s. Also carries serials, foreign films, silents, westerns, and a limited sci-fi/horror selection. Visual quality is stressed; videos are transferred from 16mm, $3/4$" U-matic or 1" tape. VHS/Beta. Write for catalog.

Captain Bijou,

P.O. Box 87, Toney AL 35773. (205) 852-0198. Earl Blair.

A reliable, full-service supplier, Captain Bijou (a wing of Earl Blair Enterprises, Inc.) carries a wide assortment of new and older releases, along with an exhaustive array of B westerns and serials, budget videos, vintage B films (including the "Black Artists of the Silver Screen" collection), and documentaries—thousands of titles in all. Also sells posters, photos, and collectibles of all kinds. A well-produced *Captain Bijou Bulletin* is updated quarterly to list the latest videos and collectibles in stock. VHS/Beta. MC/Visa. Write for bulletin.

Cassette Express,

3123 Sylvania Avenue, Toledo OH 43613. (419) 472-7727 or 1-800-325-0449. John Day.

One of the nation's largest video outlets and a reliable discount mail-order firm covering the entire gamut of available cassettes. Stocks new releases along with bargain lines, low-priced B westerns and serials, and Twin Theater double-feature tapes. VHS/Beta. MC/Visa. Write for latest catalog.

Channel 13/Madhouse Video,

P.O. Box 15602, North Hollywood CA 91615. 1-800-TV-CALLS. Dave Stuckey, Mark Gilman, Jr.

"Your Window to the Weird," Channel 13/Madhouse can boast of the nation's most extensive selection of Three Stooges tapes (e.g., *Mondo Shemp* and the rare Stooge feature film *Swing Parade of 1946*), a varied all-Black B-movie catalog, many exclusive vintage exploitation titles, and diverse horror, sci-fi, and JD rarities. VHS/Beta II. MC/Visa. Write for catalog.

Cinemacabre,

P.O. Box 10005-D, Baltimore MD 21285-0005. No phone. George Stover.

Specializes in genre trailer tapes, primarily covering science fiction and horror, both color and black and white. Owner George Stover is himself a collector and takes special care in offering the best possible transfer quality. VHS/Beta. Write for catalog.

Circulo Cultural Del Cine,

Charcas 3858, 60 Piso "A," 1425 Buenos Aires, Argentina. Phone 71-3035. Enrique J. Bouchard.

CCDC has been supplying American customers with Super 8mm films since 1962 and has since branched out into video. At present, the mail-order outfit is offering several vintage Buster Keaton titles (e.g., *The Saphead*) unavailable elsewhere and plans to expand into other cinematic areas. Write for title list, payment, and shipping info.

CVCCC: Classic Video Cinema Collector's Club, Inc.,

6954 Pebble Park Circle, West Bloomfield MI 48033. (313) 737-0373. Lloyd Paul, Norman Rosenzwieg.

The long-established and highly regarded CVCCC is strongest in vintage classics, both American and foreign, and in silent films, including many exclusives. Pricier than some, but stresses top transfer quality and reliable service. VHS/Beta II. MC/Visa. Allow 4–8 weeks for delivery. A catalog is available.

Discount Video Tapes, Inc.,

P.O. Box 7122, Burbank CA 91510. (818) 843-3366. Woody Wise.

Offers what may be the largest selection of reasonably priced public-domain titles—including foreign films, westerns, serials, vintage B films, and TV shows—of any mail-order supplier. While DVT concentrates on sell-through, a mail-order rental system has also been established. VHS/Beta. MC/Visa. Write for catalog.

Dixie Entertainment Production, Inc.
215 Long Beach Boulevard, 2nd floor, Long Beach CA 90802. (213) 491-0332/491-1082.

Dixie carries a large, low-priced assortment of public-domain films, ranging from comedies to horror/sci-fi to B westerns and serials, including a number of scarce titles currently unavailable elsewhere. VHS/Beta. Write for catalog.

Double D Video Ranch,
4823 48 Avenue, Moline IL 61265. (309) 797-2893. Dennis L. Witt.

Strongest in its B-western line, Double D also handles an extensive number of serials and selected public-domain titles. Also stocks a variety of older A musicals. VHS/Beta. Write for catalog.

Ergo Media, Inc.,
P.O. Box 2037, Teaneck NJ 07666. (201) 692-0404.

Specializes in rare Yiddish movies of the '30s, with over 300 titles in stock, from *Yidl With His Fiddle* to *Overture to Glory*. Most films are of U.S. or Polish origin. Also carries the Orson Welles-narrated *Almonds and Raisins*, a 1983 documentary look at the Yiddish film industry. Write for title list and ordering details.

Evergreen Video Society,
213 West 35th Street, 2nd Floor, New York NY 10001-4024. *(212) 714-9860 or 1-800-225-7783 (outside New York, Hawaii, and Alaska). Steve Feltes.*

Evergreen specializes in American and foreign classic films, many from the Kino and Cinematheque catalogs, not found at most video stores. The company also stocks many discontinued titles and hard-to-get Beta tapes and will search for titles on customer's request. Offers videos for sale and mail-order rentals. A highly respected and recommended outfit that stresses visual quality, Evergreen currently carries over 1,800 titles. Catalog is updated via the informative *Evergreen Video* tabloid, which also features rarevid news. VHS/Beta/Laser. MC/Visa.

Facets Video,
1517 West Fullerton Avenue, Chicago IL 60614. 1-800-331-6197.

Billed as "The Nation's Greatest Collection of Foreign, Classic and Independent American Films on Video," Facets Video is the cassette wing of Facets, a Chicago-based nonprofit arts organization. Facets features over 5,000 titles— from *The Marriage of Figaro* to Russ Meyer's *Faster, Pussycat! Kill! Kill!*—available for sale (VHS/Beta) and mail-order rental (VHS only). Beta deliveries take longer than VHS. MC/Visa/American Express. A complete catalog is available for a fee.

Festival Films,
2841 Irving Avenue South, Minneapolis MN 55048. (612) 870-4744.

Festival specializes in vintage foreign and domestic rarities (e.g., *American Avant-Garde Shorts*, a collection of featurettes dating from 1906 to 1933, including Georges Melies's *Dream of a Rarebit Fiend* and *Ladislas Starevitch, Puppet Master*, a selection of Starevitch's puppet animation films). Write for catalog and complete ordering info.

Final Chapter,
P.O. Box 7062, Philadelphia PA 19149-0062. No phone.

Voted the "Best Cliffhanger/Serial Tape Supplier" of 1987 by the FIMGA (that's the Fridaynight Independent Movie Goers Association, 1050 Cedar Crest Drive, Crystal Lake, IL 60014), Final Chapter focuses on cliffhangers and B westerns, stressing prompt service and high quality. VHS/Beta. Write for title list.

Foothill Video, Inc.,
P.O. Box 547, Tujunga CA 91042. (818) 353-8591. Ed Reagan.

Foothill stocks a wide array of public-domain titles at low prices. The outfit is especially strong on foreign classics, serials, B westerns, Black B films, and vintage TV shows. A reliable supplier that often undersells outfits carrying the same tapes at far higher prices (and sometimes lower visual quality).

VHS/Beta. MC/Visa. Write for catalog.

Grapevine Video,
P.O. Box 46161, Phoenix AZ 85063. (602) 245-0210. J. B. Hardy.

Grapevine deals almost exclusively in silent features and shorts, including many hard-to-find titles, most of them modestly priced. Also carries a limited number of early talkies, mostly rare B-action films. Silent-movie buffs in particular will want to check Grapevine out. VHS/Beta. Write for catalog and complete ordering info.

Jim Harmon,
634 South Orchard Drive, Burbank CA 91506. (818) 843-5472. Jim Harmon.

Specializes in cliffhangers, including hard-to-find titles. Harmon openly rates the visual quality of his own products in his catalog and deals in public-domain titles only. Also offers a wide range of movie collectibles, from posters to stills to toys. VHS/Beta. Write for catalog and complete ordering info.

Henwood Cinema Video,
Box 376, Jamison PA 18929-0376. (215) 639-8806. Alan Henwood.

Affiliated with American Entertainment Industries, Inc. Henwood stocks an interesting, offbeat lineup of public-domain films, along with many older, rare B titles, offered at sell-through prices. VHS/Beta. MC/Visa. Write for title list.

Hollywood Home Theater,
1540 North Highland Avenue, Suite 110, Hollywood CA 90028. 1-800-621-0849 ext. 176 or (213) 466-0121.

A division of Budget Video, Hollywood Home Theater supplies both video stores and individual customers with mostly public-domain titles, including a complete line of "Black Cast Classic Films" and many foreign movies. VHS/Beta. Write or call for catalog.

Home Film Festival,
305 Linden Street, Scranton PA 18503. 1-800-258-FILM.

A mail-order sales-and-rental video club specializing in quality feature films, foreign and domestic, old and new. HFF is especially strong on foreign-film classics and documentaries. VHS/Beta. MC/Visa. Write or call for catalog.

International Historic Films, Inc.,
Box 29035, Chicago IL 60629. (312) 927-2900. Peter Bernotas.

As its name indicates, IHF specializes in licensed documentaries and fiction films of historical import. Its documentary lineup is one of the most extensive extant, encompassing many exclusives. VHS/Beta. MC/Visa. Write for catalog.

J&J Video,
157-15 14th Avenue, Whitestone NY 11357. No phone. Bill Brent.

Stocks an eclectic variety of public-domain foreign films, silents, vintage comedies, and '50s horror and sci-fi titles, including many rarities and exclusives, offered at low prices. Owner Bill Brent, a dedicated collector, strives for quality, transferring the majority of his tapes from 16mm and 35mm prints. VHS/Beta. Write for catalog.

Kartes Video Communications,
7225 Woodland Drive, Indianapolis IN 46268-0881. 1-800-582-2000.

A sell-through-oriented outfit, Kartes specializes in information videos—exercise and fitness, cooking, personal improvement, et al.—as well as releasing many licensed exclusives under its Video Film Classics banner. The latter include such popular features as *Lover, Come Back, The Black Orchid,* and *The Trap* (with Richard Widmark). VHS/Beta. Major credit cards. Write for catalog.

Mike LeBell's Video,
75 Fremont Place, Los Angeles CA 90005. (213) 938-3333. Mike LeBell.

Covers a wide range of public-domain B westerns, cliffhangers, horror, documentaries, sports, foreign films, animation, and classic TV. Includes many rarities. VHS/Beta. MC/Visa. Write for catalog.

Loonic Video,
2022 Taraval Street, Suite 6427, San Francisco CA 94116. (415) 526-8070. Lory Ringuette.

Offers an eclectic range of low-priced rare and unusual titles, some public domain, others licensed exclusives. Loonic is particularly strong on obscure B and horror/sci-fi films, campy flicks like *Secret File Hollywood,* vintage JD films, cartoon collections, and obscure old-time comedy shorts (Clark and McCullough, Leon Erroll, Andy Clyde, et al.). Also selected vintage TV shows. Loonic videos are mastered on ³/₄" tape from the best available prints and transferred to high-grade tape. VHS only. Write for catalog.

M&M Enterprises,
708 Springbrook, Allen TX 75002. (214) 727-2679. David Miller.

A prime source for B westerns and serials. Prices vary. VHS/Beta. A free catalog is available with an SASE.

Madhouse Video
(see Channel 13)

Marshall Discount Video Service,
3130 Edsel Drive, Box 328, Trenton MI 48183. (313) 671-5483. Dave Marshall.

Marshall has a huge inventory of new releases, both mainstream and genre, as well as a large selection of hard-to-find horror, SF,

and exploitation titles, including the rare *Hollywood Confidential* series, and many obscure domestic and Euro-genre films, some of which have been otherwise discontinued. VHS/Beta. MC/Visa. Write or call for catalog.

Rex Miller,
Route 1, Box 457-D, East Prairie MO 63845. (314) 649-5048. Rex Miller.

Rex Miller specializes in serials made from high-quality prints (which makes it pricier than some), plus B westerns and general titles, along with vintage TV shows. Many B films are available with two features on a tape at reduced rates. An extremely eclectic and unusual selection, with many rarities and exclusives. Also deals in movie memorabilia and collectibles of all kinds. A very entertaining catalog is available. VHS/Beta. MC/Visa. Some Beta orders are slightly higher.

Moore Video,
P.O. Box 5703, Richmond VA 23220. (804) 270-6836. Michael D. Moore, Colleen V. Cavanaugh.

Offers nearly 1,000 titles, most of them public domain and affordably priced. Moore covers an impressive range of categories, with a special emphasis on cult films. Also stocks many vintage TV titles, foreign films, music videos, and a large selection of martial-arts movies. VHS/Beta/8mm Video. A complete catalog, with periodic updates, is available for $5. Allow 4-6 weeks for delivery.

Movie Buff Video,
15 Vandam Street, New York NY 10013. (212) 645-3899.

The video adjunct of the Thalia SoHo, one of NYC's prime surviving revival houses, Movie Buff offers an interesting line of public-domain titles, including many vintage Black B films. VHS/Beta. Write for catalog and ordering info.

Movies Unlimited,
6736 Castor Avenue, Philadelphia PA 19149. (215) 722-8298 or 1-800-523-0823.

One of the nation's largest and most reliable video suppliers, Movies Unlimited prides itself on carrying the most complete cassette stock possible. VHS/Beta/Laser. MC/Visa. An exhaustive catalog is available. Call or write for price.

Mystic Fire Video,
24 Horatio Street #3C, New York NY 10014. (212) 645-2733 or 1-800-727-VIDEO.

Mystic Fire has virtually cornered the underground-indie market with its arcane array of licensed exclusives, including many Kenneth Anger titles, Shirley Clarke's *The Connection* and *A Portrait of Jason*, Jonas Mekas's *The Brig*, performed by Julian Beck's Living Theater, plus New Age videos, instructional tapes, and other un-

usual items. VHS/Beta. MC/Visa. Write for catalog and ordering info.

National Cinema Service,
P.O. Box 43, Ho-Ho-Kus NJ 07423. (201) 445-0776. Bill Flohr.

In the 16mm business since 1936, National Cinema Service has branched out into video, offering a large selection of primarily foreign-film classics both old and new, including many rarities, most equipped with English subtitles. VHS/Beta. Write for title list.

New York Film Annex,
163 Joralemon Street, Suite 1282, Brooklyn NY 11215. (718) 499-1621.

"International Titles For the Discriminating Collector" is the NYFA's official motto. The mail-order outfit offers over 400 films, including rare foreign fare, vintage avant-garde works, silent films, and documentaries, along with more common public-domain titles. VHS/Beta. A catalog can be had for $1.

Paragon Video,
P.O. Box 3478, San Mateo CA 94403. No phone.

Specializes in early TV game shows, comedies, and variety shows, many of the hard-to-find variety, plus a small selection of feature films. VHS/Beta. Write for title list.

Red Fox Enterprises,
P.O. Box 1, Elizabethville PA 17023; 110 West Main Street, Lykens PA

*17048. (717) 453-9876 or
1-800-233-7514.*

A full-service video supplier with an emphasis on both new and nostalgia-oriented mainstream titles. VHS/Beta/Laser. MC/Visa/American Express. Write for updated catalog.

J. Rochet & Associates,

Box 127, 114-41 Queens Boulevard, Forest Hills NY 11375. No phone.

J. Rochet stocks rare music videos ranging from rock to jazz to vintage swing, as well as music-oriented feature films (e.g., *Jubilee*, and *Corrupt* with Johnny Rotten), and a complete Elvis lineup. Allow up to six weeks for delivery. VHS/Beta. A *Music Video Collector* catalog is available.

RTS Video,

Box 1829, Novato CA 94948. (707) 778-8009. Ron Soeda.

A complete video supplier, offering a large selection of general and specialty titles, including hundreds of exclusives. Also publishes the newsletter *Video Gazette* and carries over 2,000 soundtrack recordings. Stocks many hard-to-find oldies as well as mainstream videos that have been discontinued, including many Beta cassettes. MC/Visa. Write for list.

Second Feature Video,

1427 85th Street, Brooklyn NY 11228. (718) 232-4978 (after 1 P.M.). Pamela Boccaccio.

Offers vintage features, both public domain and licensed, including a large selection of serials and B westerns. All films are recorded on high-grade tape. VHS only. Write for catalog.

Shokus Video,

Box 8434, Van Nuys CA 91409. (818) 704-0400. Stuart Shostak.

Deals in vintage TV only, with the emphasis on variety shows, including many rarities. Most of Shokus's tapes are assembled potpourri-style, with different shows sharing the same cassette. VHS/Beta. Write for catalog.

Sinister Cinema,

P.O. Box 777, Pacifica CA 94044. (415) 359-3292. Greg Luce.

One of the best suppliers of vintage horror, sci-fi, serials, and B movies extant, with low prices, generally good transfer quality, and a fantastic variety of obscure public-domain titles. Owner Luce is constantly expanding his title list and will provide customers with updates. VHS/Beta. An entertaining catalog is available; write for further info.

Urban Video Network,

P.O. Box 5207, East Orange NJ 07018. Derrick J. Browning.

Claims to have the "world's largest jazz and blues video catalogue," offering everything from Bessie

Smith to Robert Cray, Avant-Garde to Zydeco, the earliest "soundies" to the latest vids. Urban's head Derrick J. Browning is himself an avid collector. VHS/Beta. A complete catalog is available.

Video City Productions,
4266-A Broadway, Oakland CA 94611. (415) 428-0202.

A cross between an offbeat mail-order supplier and an indie B-video company, Video City sports one of the oddest cassette rosters around. Titles range from exclusive new horror, sci-fi, comedy, cult, and sleaze movies to shockumentaries to rare family films. Also incorporates Art House Video (original-language foreign films), the direct-to-home-vid Chop-'Em-Ups Video (e.g., *Crazy Fat Ethel II*), and Combat and World Aviation Video (with a wide selection of aviation tapes). Video City sells to distributors, stores, and individual customers. VHS/Beta. A catalog sells for $3.

Video Dimensions,
530 West 23rd Street, New York NY 10011. (212) 929-6135. Allan Greenfield.

Established in 1977, Video Dimensions offers an eclectic mix of bargain-price videos, including serials, B westerns, foreign fare, cartoon and short-comedy collec-

tions, nostalgic TV, and an interesting line of vintage exploitation films, many of them Video Dimensions exclusives. VHS/Beta. Write for catalog.

Video Placement International,
240 East 27th Street, New York NY 10016. (212) 696-9207. Stuart Young.

VPI specializes in silent video montages on all subjects—sports, cartoons, horror, commercials, et al.—that can be set to the music of your choice. Others come with musical tracks already provided. A few compilation films also come with complete soundtrack—narration, dialogue, and music. A unique outfit. VHS/Beta. Write for catalog.

Video Resources,
220 West 71st Street, New York NY 10023. (212) 724-7055. Ira H. Gallen.

Offers one of the most eclectic collections extant, ranging from D. W. Griffith silents to public-domain features to obscure TV commercials and even toy-oriented videos. Owner Gallen is himself an avid collector, archivist, film restorer, and montage ace who hosts a vintage-film TV show on NYC's Manhattan Cable Network (see sidebar). Video Resources insists on presenting the best possible video quality and caters to the serious collector as well as to the casual fan. VHS/Beta. An entertaining catalog, rich in media history, is available.

Who runs the video-specialty firms listed here? The Phantom dropped in on one such entrepreneurial videophile, Video Resources' head Ira H. Gallen, and filed the following report.

IRA H. GALLEN: A MAN FOR ALL MEDIA

Stepping into former film technician/current Video Resources honcho Ira H. Gallen's NYC Upper West Side HQ is akin to entering an alternative universe: a media addict's paradise. In one room, somewhat dwarfed by a six-foot projection TV screen, we see a Tiffany lamp from the set of *Serpico,* a barber's chair from *Johnny, We Hardly Knew Ye,* an "Indian Rubber Tire" sign from *Summer Wishes, Winter Dreams*—all mementos from his days as a production assistant, assistant director, and second-unit director on films like *Death Wish, Harry and Tonto,* and *Three Days of the Condor.* Said days ended, or were at least temporarily suspended, in 1980, when, around the time of his thirtieth birthday, Gallen decided to switch from film to the then-nascent video industry.

"Too much nepotism," Gallen explains his disenchantment with the movie biz. "And politics. But basically I wanted to run my own show, control my own art—and that's what I've been doing."

Gallen is quick to credit his grueling filmmaking experiences with preparing him for his present pressured sked. In addition to running his own video-specialty company, Gallen produces and hosts a popular Manhattan Cable TV series, *Biograph Days, Biograph Nights,* fashions elaborate video montages, and labors as a tireless tracer and restorer of lost films. "I couldn't have lasted six months in video," he confesses, "without those ten years in film."

Gallen's ongoing love affair with the movies—especially those crafted by D. W. Griffith (his personal hero), Abel Gance, and other silent-film pioneers—is amply evidenced by the many film cans vying for space with the thousands of $3/4$-inch, one-inch, and half-inch video-tapes lining the walls of his home lab, a compact but complete video-production facility. It's here that Gallen not only creates his elaborate movie-and-music montages that play in dance clubs from Gotham to Tokyo but performs his demanding dubbing, editing, film-to-video transfer, and all-important film-restoration chores. He has restored everything from rare Griffith originals to his current obsession, vintage TV commercials.

BIOGRAPH DAYS, BIOGRAPH NIGHTS

A
video montage
by
IRA H. GALLEN

Gallen has often obtained lost footage via unconventional, even accidental means. One of his greatest professional epiphanies occurred while he was scouting locations for *Death Wish* back in 1974. He was checking out an empty Hell's Kitchen warehouse when he spied a reel of unidentified film protruding from a trash can. It turned out to be an original episode of the long-lost early-'50s kiddie show, *Rootie Kazootie*. Gallen wasted no time in restoring the rare footage. After making copies for himself, he donated the repaired print to the Museum of Broadcasting and, years later, released the vid version via Video Resources.

The effervescent archivist and inveterate toy collector beckons us into yet another room to show us his original Rootie Kazootie doll, one of hundreds of vintage toys surrounding the desk that serves as the center of his combination home-video office and informal TV studio. Felix the Cat, Howdy Doody, Mr. Machine, Robert the Robot, and Betty Boop are but a few of the famous likenesses lining the bookshelves and walls. "I collect everything I destroyed as a kid," Gallen cheerfully explains. "Back then I couldn't have a toy two minutes without taking it apart to see how it worked."

Does he do that with his current collection? we wondered.

"No!" Gallen shouts with a shudder. "Too expensive!" He takes a moment to recover, then adds, "*These* I'm giving away, though." Gallen locates a jar filled with authentic Howdy Doody puzzle keychains of circa 1953 vintage. They're free with the purchase of any of the $19.95 Howdy Doody videotapes advertised in Gallen's vidcassette catalog, which includes everything from *Captain Midnight*'s original commercials to a pristine transfer of Griffith's *Birth of a Nation*. To Ira Gallen, film purist extraordinaire, visual quality is everything.

"I can't believe those outfits who record on slow speed," Gallen fumes. "Sure the prices are low, but what you're often getting is a two-hour movie on a thirty- to sixty-minute tape, which really destroys a film's visual integrity."

The enraged archivist is about to elaborate when his Kermit the Frog phone rings. His mood swiftly brightens as he listens to the voice on the other end. Gallen cups the mouthpiece and confides enthusiastically, "Sixty-five *Andy's Gang* episodes on mint 16mm!"

We quickly exit Ira's universe; it's clear the man's got work to do.

Video Yesteryear,
Box C, Sandy Hook CT 06482.
1-800-243-0987. In Connecticut,
Alaska, and Hawaii: (203) 426-2574.

One of the nation's oldest vintage-video suppliers (established in 1978), Video Yesteryear stocks over 1,000 titles, including many rarities and exclusives, covering the entire spectrum of pre-1970 cassettes—classics, camp, horror, documentaries, and TV. The company is especially expert in the area of silent films, restoring them to their original speed and eliminating the flickering that plagues many silents. Most come equipped with musical accompaniment, often the films' original scores. VHS/Beta/8mm. Major credit cards. An informative, in-depth catalog is available for a slight fee.

VIDEO DIRECTORY
MAJORS, MINORS, SELL-THROUGH, SPECIALISTS, AND INDEPENDENTS

(NOTE: ADDRESSES AND PHONE NUMBERS ARE SUBJECT TO CHANGE.)

ACADEMY HOME ENTERTAINMENT
SUBSIDIARY OF ARTEC, INC.
1 PINE HAVEN SHORE ROAD
P.O. BOX 788
SHELBURNE VT 05482
(802) 985-2060

ACTIVE HOME VIDEO
9300 W. PICO BLVD.
LOS ANGELES CA 90035
(213) 274-8233

AFRO-AM PUBLISHING CO., INC.
DIVISION OF AFRO-AM, INC.
819 SOUTH WABASH AVE.
ROOM 610
CHICAGO IL 60605
(312) 922-1147

A.I.P. HOME VIDEO, INC.
10726 MCCUNE AVE.
LOS ANGELES CA 90034
(800) 456-2471

ALL SEASONS ENTERTAINMENT
18121 NAPA STREET
NORTHRIDGE CA 91325
(818) 886-8972

AMERICAN VIDEO TAPE
(SEE POWERSPORTS/
AMERICAN VIDEO)

AMVEST VIDEO CORP.
P.O. BOX 1124
RAHWAY NJ 07065
(201) 396-3113

APPLAUSE PRODUCTIONS
85 LONGVIEW ROAD
PORT WASHINGTON NY 11050-3099
(516) 979-6670

AVIATION BK. CO.
1640 VICTORY BOULEVARD
GLENDALE CA 91201-2999
(818) 240-1771

AXON VIDEO CORP.
1900 BROADWAY
NEW YORK NY 10023
(212) 787-8228

BEST FILM & VIDEO CORP.
98 CUTTER MILL ROAD
GREAT NECK NY 11021
(516) 487-4515

BLACAST
199-19 LINDEN BOULEVARD
JAMAICA NY 11412
(718) 527-2417

BLACK SPARROW PRESS
24 TENTH STREET
SANTA ROSA CA 95401
(707) 579-4011

BLACKHAWK FILMS/VIDEO
P.O. BOX 3990
DAVENPORT IA 52802
(319) 323-8637

BUDGET VIDEO
1540 NORTH HIGHLAND AVENUE
NUMBER 108
LOS ANGELES CA 90028
(213) 466-0121

CAMP VIDEO CORP.
8841 WILBUR
SUITE 101
NORTHRIDGE CA 91324
(213) 935-8650

CANNON VIDEO
640 SOUTH SAN VICENTE BLVD.
LOS ANGELES CA 90048
(213) 658-2100

CBS/FOX VIDEO
1211 AVENUE OF THE AMERICAS
NEW YORK NY 10036
(212) 819-3200

CELEBRITY HOME ENTERTAINMENT
6320 CANOGA AVENUE
PENTHOUSE SUITE
P.O. BOX 4112
WOODLAND HILLS CA 91365-4112
(818) 715-1980

CHARTER ENTERTAINMENT
335 NORTH MAPLE DRIVE
BEVERLY HILLS CA 90210
(213) 285-6333

CITY LIGHTS HOME VIDEO
8981 SUNSET BOULEVARD
SUITE 310
WEST HOLLYWOOD CA 90069
(213) 859-9702

CONGRESS VIDEO GROUP
1776 BROADWAY
SUITE 1010
NEW YORK NY 10019
(212) 581-4962

CONNOISSEUR VIDEO
8455 BEVERLY BOULEVARD
LOS ANGELES CA 90048
(213) 653-8873

CORINTH FILMS AND VIDEO
34 GANSEVOORT STREET
NEW YORK NY 10014
(212) 463-0305

DISNEY HOME VIDEO
500 S. BUENA VISTA STREET
BURBANK CA 91521
(818) 560-1111

EMBASSY HOME ENTERTAINMENT
A NELSON ENTERTAINMENT COMPANY
335 NORTH MAPLE DRIVE
SUITE 350
BEVERLY HILLS CA 90210
(213) 285-6000

FILM FORUM
1000 EAST WILLIAM STREET
CARSON CITY NV 89701
(702) 559-5033

FLOWER FILMS & VIDEO
10341 SAN PABLO AVENUE
EL CERRITO CA 94530
(415) 525-0942

FORUM HOME VIDEO
575 FIFTH AVE
SUITE 24C
NEW YORK NY 10017
(212) 983-5799

FOX HILLS VIDEO
(SEE *MEDIA HOME ENTERTAINMENT*)

FRIES HOME VIDEO
6922 HOLLYWOOD BOULEVARD
LOS ANGELES CA 90028
(213) 466-2266

GENESIS HOME VIDEO
15820 ARMINTA STREET
VAN NUYS CA 91406
(818) 787-0660

GOODTIMES/KIDS KLASSICS
401 FIFTH AVENUE
NEW YORK NY 10016
(212) 889-0044

HBO VIDEO, INC.
1370 AVENUE OF THE AMERICAS
NEW YORK NY 10019
(212) 977-8990

HOLLYWOOD FAMILY ENTERTAINMENT
7959 DEERING AVENUE
CANOGA PARK CA 91304-5009
(818) 992-6800

IMAGE ENTERTAINMENT
6311 ROMAINE STREET
HOLLYWOOD CA 90038
(213) 468-8867

IMAGINE VIDEO, INC.
P.O. BOX 9674
PITTSBURGH PA 15226
NO PHONE

IMPERIAL ENTERTAINMENT
6430 SUNSET BOULEVARD
SUITE 1500
LOS ANGELES CA 90028
(213) 463-4003

INCREASE VIDEO/SILVER MINE VIDEO
6914 CANBY STREET
SUITE 110
RESEDA CA 91335
(818) 342-2880

INDEPENDENT UNITED DISTRIBUTORS
430 WEST 54TH STREET
NEW YORK NY 10019
(212) 489-8130

INGRAM VIDEO
347 REEDWOOD DRIVE
NASHVILLE TN 37217
(615) 361-5000

INTERAMA VIDEO CLASSICS
301 WEST 53RD STREET
SUITE 19E
NEW YORK NY 10019
(212) 977-4830

INTERGLOBAL HOME VIDEO
20 MERIDAN ROAD
EATONTOWN NJ 07724
(201) 389-8700

INTERNATIONAL VIDEO ENTERTAINMENT (IVE)
500 NORTH VENTU PARK ROAD
P.O. BOX 2520
NEWBURY PARK CA 91320
(805) 499-5827

J2 COMMUNICATIONS
10850 WILSHIRE BOULEVARD
SUITE 1000
LOS ANGELES CA 90024
(213) 474-5252

KARTES VIDEO COMMUNICATIONS, INC. (KVC)
7225 WOODLAND DRIVE
P.O. BOX 68881
INDIANAPOLIS IN 46268-0881
(317) 297-1888

KEY VIDEO
1211 AVENUE OF THE AMERICAS
2ND FLOOR
NEW YORK NY 10036
(212) 819-3200

KING BEE
(SEE *INTERNATIONAL VIDEO ENTERTAINMENT*)

KING OF VIDEO
3529 SOUTH VALLEY VIEW BOULEVARD
LAS VEGAS NV 89103
(702) 362-2520

KINO INTERNATIONAL
333 WEST 39TH STREET
SUITE 503
NEW YORK NY 10018
(212) 629-6880

KULTUR VIDEO
121 HIGHWAY 36
WEST LONG BRANCH NJ 07764
(201) 229-2343

LETTUCE ENTERTAIN YOU
111 ELIZABETH STREET
9TH FLOOR
TORONTO, ONTARIO M5G 1P7
NO PHONE

LEARNING CORP. OF AMERICA (LCA)
(SEE *NEW WORLD VIDEO*)

LIGHTNING VIDEO
(SEE *VESTRON/LIGHTNING VIDEO*)

LORIMAR HOME VIDEO
17942 COWAN AVENUE
IRVINE CA 92714
(714) 474-0355

MCA HOME VIDEO
70 UNIVERSAL CITY PLAZA
UNIVERSAL CITY CA 91608
(818) 777-4300

MGM/UA ENTERTAINMENT
10000 WASHINGTON BOULEVARD
CULVER CITY CA 90232-2728
(213) 280-6000
OR
1350 AVENUE OF AMERICAS
NEW YORK NY 10019
(212) 408-0500

MPI HOME VIDEO
15825 ROB ROY DRIVE
OAK FOREST IL 60452
(312) 687-7881

MAGNUM ENTERTAINMENT
9301 WILSHIRE BOULEVARD
SUITE 602
BEVERLY HILLS CA 90212
(213) 278-9981

MAJOR LEAGUE BASEBALL PRODUCTIONS
1212 AVENUE OF THE AMERICAS
NEW YORK NY 10036
(212) 921-8100

MASTER ARTS VIDEO
11549 AMIGO AVENUE
NORTHRIDGE CA 91326
(818) 368-9220

MASTERVISION
969 PARK AVENUE
NEW YORK NY 10028
(212) 879-0448

MAYSLES FILMS
250 WEST 54TH STREET
NEW YORK NY 10019
(212) 582-6050

MEDIA HOME ENTERTAINMENT
5730 BUCKINGHAM PARKWAY
CULVER CITY CA 90230
(213) 216-7900

MERCURY/XENON HOME VIDEO FILMS
309 SANTA MONICA BOULEVARD
SUITE 405
SANTA MONICA CA 90401
(213) 451-5510

MEXCINEMA VIDEO CORP.
7231 SANTA MONICA BOULEVARD
LOS ANGELES CA 90046
(213) 874-1114

MODERN SOUND PICTURES
1402 HOWARD STREET
OMAHA NE 68102
(402) 341-8476

MOGUL COMMUNICATIONS, INC.
1311 NORTH MANSFIELD AVENUE
HOLLYWOOD CA 90028
(213) 650-2122

MONARCH HOME VIDEO
1501 50TH STREET
SUITE 300
WEST DES MOINES IA 50265
(515) 224-1784

MONDAY/WEDNESDAY/FRIDAY VIDEO CLUB
73 EAST HOUSTON STREET
NEW YORK NY 10012
(212) 219-0765

MONOGRAM ENTERTAINMENT GROUP, INC.
5710 EAST SHEILA STREET
BUILDING T
CITY OF COMMERCE CA 90040
(213) 726-0452

MONTEREY HOME VIDEO
P.O. BOX 2648
MALIBU CA 90265
(213) 457-5595

MYSTIC FIRE VIDEO
24 HORATIO STREET
NUMBER 3C
NEW YORK NY 10014
(212) 645-2733

NATIONAL GEOGRAPHIC SOCIETY
17TH & M STREETS, NW
WASHINGTON DC 20036
(202) 857-7000

NELSON ENTERTAINMENT, INC.
335 NORTH MAPLE DRIVE
SUITE 350
BEVERLY HILLS, CA 90210
(213) 285-6000

NETWORK HOME ENTERTAINMENT
1140 S. ROBERTSON BOULEVARD
SUITE 4
LOS ANGELES CA 90035
(213) 938-4747

NEW STAR VIDEO
260 SOUTH BEVERLY DRIVE
BEVERLY HILLS CA 90212
(213) 205-0666

NEW WORLD VIDEO
1440 SOUTH SEPULVEDA BOULEVARD
LOS ANGELES CA 90025
(213) 444-8100

NOSTALGIA MERCHANT
(SEE *MEDIA HOME ENTERTAINMENT*)

OCEAN VIDEO, INC.
4605 LANKERSHIM BOULEVARD
NUMBER 601
NORTH HOLLYWOOD CA 91602
(818) 506-3216

ORION HOME VIDEO
540 MADISON AVENUE
NEW YORK NY 10022
(212) 888-4500

PBS VIDEO
DIVISION OF PUBLIC BROADCASTING
SERVICE
1320 BRADDOCK PLACE
ALEXANDRIA VA 22314-1698
(703) 739-5380

PACIFIC ARTS VIDEO
50 NORTH LA CIENEGA BOULEVARD
SUITE 210
BEVERLY HILLS CA 90211
(213) 657-2233

PARAGON
(SEE *KING OF VIDEO*)

PARAMOUNT HOME VIDEO
5555 MELROSE AVENUE
HOLLYWOOD, CA 90038
(213) 468-5000

PLAYHOUSE
(SEE CBS/FOX)

POWERSPORTS/AMERICAN VIDEO
157000 DICKENS STREET
ENCINO CA 90025
(818) 907-0590

PREMIER PROMOTIONS/ANDY GRIFFITH VIDEOS
P.O. BOX 19022
CHARLOTTE NC 28219
(704) 399-1111

PREMIERE HOME VIDEO
6824 MELROSE AVENUE
HOLLYWOOD CA 90038
(213) 934-8903

PRISM ENTERTAINMENT CORP.
1888 CENTURY PARK EAST
SUITE 1000
LOS ANGELES CA 90067
(213) 277-3270

RCA/COLUMBIA PICTURES HOME VIDEO
3500 WEST OLIVE AVENUE
BURBANK CA 91505
(818) 953-7900

RM (RUSS MEYER) FILMS
P.O. BOX 3748
HOLLYWOOD CA 90078
(213) 466-7791

RKO PICTURES HOME VIDEO
1900 AVE OF THE STARS
SUITE 1562
LOS ANGELES CA 90067
(213) 277-3133

REGAL VIDEO, INC.
5 BEEKMAN STREET
SUITE 828
NEW YORK NY 10038
(212) 732-3515

RELAX VIDEO
2901 BROADWAY
SUITE 128
NEW YORK NY 10025
(212) 222-4313

REPUBLIC PICTURES HOME VIDEO
12636 BEATRICE ST.
LOS ANGELES CA 90066-0930
(213) 306-4040

RHINO VIDEO
2225 COLORADO AVE
SANTA MONICA CA 90404
(213) 828-1980

ROACH, HAL, FILM CLASSICS, INC.
345 NORTH MAPLE DRIVE
BEVERLY HILLS CA 90210
(213) 281-2600

SATURN PRODUCTIONS, INC.
1697 BROADWAY
SUITE 1102
NEW YORK NY 10019
(212) 489-2460

SELECT-A-TAPE
3960 LAUREL CANYON BOULEVARD
NUMBER 275
STUDIO CITY CA 91604
NO PHONE

SF RUSH VIDEO/TRAILERS ON TAPE
1554 GROVE STREET
SAN FRANCISCO CA 94117
(415) 921-8273

SHOWCASE PRODUCTIONS, INC.
6910 HAYVENHURST AVENUE
SUITE 100
VAN NUYS CA 91406
(818) 785-7977

SIMITAR ENTERTAINMENT, INC.
3955 ANNAPOLIS LANE
PLYMOUTH MN 55447
(612) 559-6660

SONY VIDEO SOFTWARE (SYS)
1700 BROADWAY
16TH FLOOR
NEW YORK NY 10019
(212) 757-4990

STANDARD VIDEO
16838 1/2 SATICOY STREET
VAN NUYS CA 91406
(818) 989-4802

STAR CLASSICS
4301 GLENWOOD ROAD
BROOKLYN NY 11210
(718) 434-1100

TAMARELLE'S INTERNATIONAL FILMS
110 COHASSET STAGE ROAD
CHICO CA 95926
(916) 895-3429
(800) 356-3577

TAPEWORM VIDEO DISTRIBUTOR
12229 MONTAGUE STREET
ARLETA CA 91331
(818) 896-8899

TODAY HOME ENTERTAINMENT
9200 SUNSET BOULEVARD
LOS ANGELES CA 90069
(213) 278-6490

TOUCHSTONE HOME VIDEO
500 SOUTH BUENA VISTA STREET
BURBANK CA 91521
(818) 840-1875

TRANS WORLD ENTERTAINMENT (TWE)
3330 W. CAHUENGA BOULEVARD
SUITE 500
LOS ANGELES CA 90068
(213) 969-2800

TRANS-ATLANTIC VIDEO, INC.
607 MONTROSE
SOUTH PLAINFIELD NJ 07080
(201) 756-9800

TRI COAST VIDEO
134 WESTGATE PARKWAY
DOTHAN AL 36303
(205) 677-1111
(800) 832-8338

TRI-STAR HOME VIDEO
1875 CENTURY PARK EAST
LOS ANGELES CA 90067
(213) 201-2300

TURNER HOME ENTERTAINMENT CO.
1 CNN CENTER
P.O. BOX 105366
ATLANTA GA 30348
(404) 827-1264

TWIN TOWER ENTERPRISES, INC.
18720 OXNARD STREET
SUITE 101
TARZANA CA 91356
(818) 344-8424

UNICORN VIDEO
20822 DEARBORN STREET
CHATSWORTH CA 91311
(818) 407-1333

UNITED HOME VIDEO
4111 SOUTH DARLINGTON
SUITE 600
TULSA OK 74135
(918) 622-6460

URBAN CLASSICS VIDEO
7080 HOLLYWOOD BOULEVARD
HOLLYWOOD CA 90028
(213) 462-3070

VCII—FILM CLASSIC
7313 VARNA AVENUE
NORTH HOLLYWOOD CA 91605
(213) 764-0319

VCL COMMUNICATIONS
5730 BUCKINGHAM PARKWAY
CULVER CITY CA 90230
(213) 216-7900

VCR ENTERPRISES, INC.
115 ISSAQUENA AVENUE
CLARKSDALE MS 38614
NO PHONE

VESTRON/LIGHTNING VIDEO
1010 WASHINGTON BLVD
STAMFORD CT 06901
(203) 978-5400

VIDAMERICA
231 E. 55TH STREET
NEW YORK NY 10022
(212) 355-1600

VIDCREST
8561 COLE CREST DRIVE
LOS ANGELES CA 90046
(213) 654-4810

VIDEO ACTION
708 W. FIRST STREET
LOS ANGELES CA 90012
(213) 687-8262

VIDEO ARTISTS INTERNATIONAL, INC.
P.O. BOX 153
ANSONIA STATION
NEW YORK NY 10023
(212) 799-7798

VIDEO BANCORP.
20154 SATICOY BOULEVARD
SUITE A4
CANOGA PARK CA 91306-2650
(818) 407-8928

VIDEO CONNECTION
3123 SYLVANIA AVENUE
TOLEDO OH 43613
(419) 472-7727

VIDEO GEMS
731 NORTH LA BREA AVENUE
BOX 38188
LOS ANGELES CA 90038
(213) 938-2385

VIDEO HOME LIBRARY
244 WEST 42ND STREET
FIFTH FLOOR
NEW YORK NY 10036
(212) 921-8130

VIDEO LATINO
409 NORTH FIGUEROA STREET
WILMINGTON CA 90744
(213) 549-4490

VIDEO TREASURES
87 ESSEX STREET
BOX 380
HACKENSACK NJ 07601
(201) 489-7991

VIDEO WAREHOUSE, INC.
1201 CORLIES AVENUE
NEPTUNE NJ 07753
(201) 775-7100

VIDEOTAKES
187 PARKER AVENUE
MANASQUAN NJ 08736
(201) 528-5000

VIDEOVISA, INC.
1185 WEST OLYMPIC BOULEVARD
LOS ANGELES CA 90064
(213) 827-7222

VIDMARK ENTERTAINMENT
2901 OCEAN PARK BOULEVARD
SANTA MONICA CA 90405-2906
(213) 399-8877

VINTAGE VIDEO
P.O. BOX 86
RAHWAY NJ 07065
NO PHONE

VIRGIN VISION, INC.
6100 WILSHIRE BOULEVARD
16TH FLOOR
LOS ANGELES CA 90048
(213) 857-5252

VISTA HOME VIDEO
1370 AVENUE OF THE AMERICAS
NEW YORK NY 10019
(212) 582-0500

VOYAGER CO.
1351 PACIFIC COAST HIGHWAY
SANTA MONICA CA 90401

WARNER HOME VIDEO, INC.
4000 WARNER BOULEVARD
BURBANK CA 91522
(818) 954-6000

WESTERNWORLD VIDEO
10523 BURBANK BOULEVARD
NORTH HOLLYWOOD CA 91601
(818) 735-3000

WIZARD VIDEO
7080 HOLLYWOOD BOULEVARD
HOLLYWOOD CA 90028
(213) 462-3070

WOOD KNAPP VIDEO
5900 WILSHIRE BOULEVARD
LOS ANGELES CA 90036
(213) 938-2484

WORLDVISION HOME VIDEO, INC.
660 MADISON AVENUE
NEW YORK NY 10021
(212) 832-3838

INDEX

Those titles that receive separate reviews or entries are printed in upper case. Lowercased titles indicate those vids for which we supply video label info only. A separate list of films mentioned in the text but not yet legally available on cassette follows immediately thereafter. Last you'll find an index of featured articles that you may find of interest.

Videos

Cited Films Not Yet Legally Available on Video

Index of Featured Articles

B STARS OF TOMORROW!:

FILMMAKERS IN FOCUS:

VIDEOPHILES IN FOCUS:

WHAT NEVER HAPPENED TO . . . ?: